# STRANGERS TO THESE SHORES

## RACE AND ETHNIC RELATIONS IN THE UNITED STATES

ELEVENTH EDITION

## Vincent N. Parrillo

William Paterson University

**PEARSON**

Boston   Columbus   Indianapolis   New York   San Francisco   Upper Saddle River
Amsterdam   Cape Town   Dubai   London   Madrid   Milan   Munich   Paris   Montréal   Toronto
Delhi   Mexico City   São Paulo   Sydney   Hong Kong   Seoul   Singapore   Taipei   Tokyo

**Editor in Chief:** Dickson Musslewhite
**Publisher:** Charlyce Jones Owen
**Editorial Program Manager:** Beverly Fong
**Editorial Assistant:** Maureen Diana
**Director of Marketing:** Brandy Dawson
**Senior Marketing Manager:** Maureen Prado Roberts
**Marketing Assistant:** Karen Tanico
**Senior Managing Editor:** Ann Marie McCarthy
**Production Project Manager:** Fran Russello
**Manufacturing Manager:** Mary Fischer
**Operations Specialist:** Diane Pairano

**Art Director, Interior:** Anne Bonanno Nieglos
**Manager, Visual Research:** Martha Shethar
**Cover Art:** Design Pics/Alamy
**Media Director:** Brian Hyland
**Lead Media Project Manager:** Alison Lorber
**Full-Service Project Management:** George Jacob / Integra
**Composition:** Integra Software Services, Pvt. Ld.
**Printer/Binder:** Courier Companies, Inc.
**Cover Printer:** Lehigh Phoenix
**Text Font:** 10/13, Adobe Caslon Pro

Credits and acknowledgments borrowed from other sources and reproduced, with permission, in this textbook appear on pages 569–571.

**Library of Congress Cataloging-in-Publication Data**

Parrillo, Vincent N.
Strangers to these shores : race and ethnic relations in the United States / Vincent N. Parrillo,
William Paterson University. — Eleventh Edition.
    pages cm
  ISBN-13: 978-0-205-97040-7
  ISBN-10: 0-205-97040-0
1. United States—Race relations.  2. United States—Ethnic relations.  I. Title.
  E184.A1P33 2014
  305.800973—dc23

                                                              2013011273

10 9 8 7 6 5 4 3 2

Student Edition:
ISBN 10:      0-205-97040-0
ISBN 13: 978-0-205-97040-7

Instructor's Review Copy:
ISBN 10:      0-205-97041-9
ISBN 13: 978-0-205-97041-4

a la carte Edition:
ISBN 10:      0-205-99512-8
ISBN 13: 978-0-205-99512-7

**PEARSON**

*To my Italian-American father
and to my Irish/German-American mother*

# BRIEF CONTENTS

# CONTENTS

# 3 PREJUDICE AND DISCRIMINATION 53

# 4 INTERGROUP RELATIONS 83

**PART 3**
**VISIBLE MINORITIES**

**7 AMERICAN INDIANS** 187

**8 ASIAN AMERICANS** 231

# 9 MIDDLE EASTERN AND NORTH AFRICAN AMERICANS 275

**PART 4**
**OTHER MINORITIES**

# 12 RELIGIOUS MINORITIES 387

# FEATURES

# REALITY check

# the GENDER experience

# the MINORITY experience

# FOREWORD

Americans spend a lot of time thinking about race. Yet we often have a hard time talking about it. The subject is fraught, complicated, and deeply emotional. We worry that whatever we say may cause offense or perhaps betray a bias we know is inappropriate to express. Part of the problem is that the concept is hard to define. "Race," social scientists tell us, is more a social construction than a biological reality. As the sociologist Ruben Rumbaut likes to say, it is "a pigment of our imagination." Yet the fact that race is to a large degree imaginary does not mean it can simply be imagined away. It is real, because it has real effects on people's lives.

Ethnicity is even harder to grasp. People often feel they are part of ethnic groups. They sense that ethnic identity is a central part of who they are, something with deep roots that connects them to a long history. Yet a closer examination shows that the content of ethnic identities is constantly in flux and that ethnic boundaries change from time to time and place to place.

In order to have the conversation about race and ethnicity that Americans are so good at avoiding, perhaps the first step is in understanding where these categories come from and where they are going. For anyone ready to take that step, I cannot imagine a better starting place than this book. Simply put, Vincent Parrillo's *Strangers to These Shores* is the best textbook on race and ethnicity currently on the market, as well as one of the best introductions to the topic for the general reader.

The book stands out in a number of ways. First, it is wonderfully written. It avoids clichés and presents complex and controversial material in a style that is clear, fresh, and almost totally free of dogma and jargon. In a time of globalization, the book takes a truly global view of its subject. It recognizes that, while race and ethnicity play a distinct role in American life, they also shape the lives of people in countries around the world, and ethnic conflicts and ethnic identities spill over national borders. The book is also timely; by updating it with frequent new editions, Parrillo has kept abreast of the latest in social scientific research, and in this edition he has added the innovative "Students Speak" boxes, a feature that makes the book even more accessible. Furthermore, his book takes an expansive view of its subject. In the chapters on "new" ethnic groups, such as the one on Middle Eastern and North African Americans, and in examining the experience of other types of minority (and majority) groups such as Gays and Lesbians and women, the book broadens our view of who the "stranger" is. Parrillo shows how ideas that emerged from the struggles for racial and ethnic equality can come to shape the self understandings of very different sorts of social groups. Finally, one of the things I like best about *Strangers to These Shores* is its historical context. While racial and ethnic identities are often thought of as primordial and unchanging, Parrillo places racial and ethnic groups in their historically specific contexts. In these pages readers will see not only how racial and ethnic groups came to be, but also how they are changing, and how they will no doubt continue to change in the future.

This is a crucial insight at this historical moment. America is now more racially and culturally diverse than at any time in its history, thanks to the combination of immigration, the aging of the white population, and the increasing number of racially mixed families. And it is thinking differently about diversity. The election of an African American President may not have ushered in a "post-racial era," but it certainly signals that some things have changed, even while others remain the same. The re-election of President Obama in 2012 underlined even further the ways in which changing demography is transforming the society in ways that were unimaginable only a few decades ago. And as that election showed, elites who ignore these changes do so at their peril.

Every few years demographers make headlines by predicting that, at some point in the not-too-far distant future, "whites" will become a minority in the U.S. population. But what exactly does this ominous-sounding statistic mean? Sadly, it probably does not mean the end of racial inequality or of ethnic conflict. Nor does it imply the end of racism, which is, it seems, a stubbornly persistent fact of American life. It *may* mean, however, that racial and ethnic boundaries are becoming more complicated and possibly more porous.

Consider the impact of immigration. Since the resumption of mass immigration in the late 1960s, the United States has incorporated tens of millions of new immigrants, the large majority of whom are non-European. Being neither unambiguously "white" nor African American, most of these newcomers do not "fit" easily into traditional North American racial categories. Of course, the presence of Americans who are neither "black" nor "white" is nothing new. Native Americans, Latinos, and Asians have been part of the American story since its beginning. Yet their presence in such large numbers, plus the fact that those numbers are now growing much faster than the numbers of either whites or blacks, raises new questions about what sort of multicultural society the United States is becoming.

This impact is compounded by the aging of the baby boomers, as Richard Alba makes clear in his recent book *Blurring the Color Line*.[1] Alba argues that the retirement of this huge age group will open many positions to the more racially diverse generations that will follow them. That does not, of course, guarantee more opportunity for racial minorities. However, the fact that there are simply not going to be enough whites to fill all of the positions of wealth, power, and influence that whites currently hold opens the possibility, Alba argues, of "non-zero sum mobility" in which new groups can move ahead without their gains coming at the direct expense of others.

Of course, we must also ask if racial and ethnic categories even mean the same things in coming decades. With increased intermarriage and interracial adoption, racially diverse families are now challenging many of our assumptions and perhaps creating more flexibility in racial definitions. It is worth remembering that when President Barack Obama's parents wed in the early 1960s, their marriage was still illegal in many states. That fact, thankfully, is now hard for many Americans in their teens, 20s, and 30s to even imagine.

My point is not to embrace a Polly Anna-ish optimism about the future of diversity in American life. Recent anti-immigrant movements, the violence toward South Asian and Middle Eastern Americans in the wake of 9/11, the massive increase in the number of Americans—overwhelmingly dark-skinned young men—being incarcerated, as well as the continuing poverty and social exclusion of many in our urban ghettos all point to how far we still have to go when it comes to including the "stranger" among us. But I do think the last few decades have clearly taught us that the nature of diversity in American life is dynamic, unpredictable, and always fascinating for anyone ready to put aside their assumptions and look at our nation of strangers and former strangers with fresh eyes. I cannot think of a better way to begin that journey than with this book.

Philip Kasinitz
*The Graduate Center,*
*City University of New York*

---

[1] Richard D. Alba, *Blurring the Color Line: The New Chance for a More Integrated America* (Nathan I. Huggins Lectures). Cambridge: Harvard University Press, 2009.

# PREFACE

You will be reading and learning about one of the most interesting, ever-changing, and personally relevant subjects in your academic career, because the area of race and ethnic relations is an exciting, challenging, and dynamic field of study. It touches all of us, directly and indirectly in many ways, and on personal, regional, national, even global levels. Each generation thinks it lives through a unique situation, as shaped by the times or the "peculiarities" of a group's characteristics. In truth, each generation is part of a larger process that includes behavioral patterns inherited from past generations, who also thought their situation was unique.

Intergroup relations change continually, through alternating periods of quiet and turmoil, of entry of new groups of immigrants or refugees, and of problems sporadically arising between native-born racial or ethnic groups within the country. Often we can best understand these changes within the context of detectable, recurring patterns that are influenced by economic, political, psychological, and sociological factors. This is partly what C. Wright Mills meant when he spoke of the intricate connection between the patterns of individual lives and the larger historical context of society, a concept we discuss in Chapter 1.

To understand both the interpersonal dynamics and the larger context of changing intergroup relations—particularly the reality of historical repetitions of behavior—we must use social science theory, research, and analysis. Moreover, we can only truly appreciate a diverse society like the United States, as well as the broader applications of social science, by examining many groups, rather than focusing only on a few groups.

I am gratified by the continued widespread adoptions of *Strangers to These Shores* and the favorable response from colleagues and students throughout the United States, Canada, Europe, and Asia. Their helpful comments and suggestions have been incorporated into this 11th edition to make an even better book.

## THE ORGANIZATION OF THIS BOOK

The first four chapters present a conceptual and theoretical overview of the subject area, giving students a basis for examining the experiences of the different minority groups discussed in subsequent chapters. Major sociological perspectives (functionalist, conflict, and interactionist), as well as some middle-range theories, are applied throughout the book, though overall its treatment of topics remains eclectic. Instructors can either follow this approach or emphasize their own theoretical viewpoint, since the book's structure allows for varying applications.

Following a presentation of some introductory concepts in the first chapter—particularly that of the stranger as a social phenomenon and the concept of the Dillingham Flaw—the first group of chapters examines differences in culture, reality perceptions, social class, and power as reasons for intergroup conflict. They also look at the dominant group's varying expectations about how minorities should "fit" into its society. Chapters 1 and 2 include coverage of some middle-range conflict and interactionist theories. Chapter 3 explores the dimensions and interrelationships of prejudice and discrimination, and Chapter 4 covers the dominant–minority response patterns so common across different groups and time periods.

Chapters 5 through 14 offer the reader insights into the experiences of a wide array of minority groups. In-depth studies of the cultural orientations and degree of assimilation of each group are not possible, because the intent is to provide a broad comparative scope rather than extensive coverage of only a few groups. Not every racial and ethnic group is discussed, though nearly 60 groups are included to illustrate the diversity of U.S. society. For a more comprehensive examination of any subject or group discussed in this book, the reader should consult the sources listed in the chapter notes and the Internet activities.

Chapter 15 returns to holistic sociological concepts in discussing ethnic consciousness; ethnicity as a social process; current racial and ethnic issues, fears, and reactions; and the various indicators of U.S. diversity now and two generations from now.

## SPECIAL FEATURES IN THIS BOOK

As in the past, this edition of the book incorporates several features to enhance understanding of the topics.

- As the first text in its field to begin chapters with a sociohistorical perspective for the study of specific groups, and to close each chapter with a sociological analysis of the groups' experiences using the functionalist, conflict, and interactionist perspectives, we again do so in this edition.
- Sociological concepts of the stranger, the Dillingham Flaw, and the interrelationship of personal and societal issues (Mills) offer students insights into the study of race and ethnic relations.
- Furthermore, in examining intergroup relations among nearly 60 minority groups, this book remains the most comprehensive one in its sociological coverage of U.S. diversity.
- Use of tables, graphics, and text on social indicators provide clear insights into the socioeconomic status of contemporary minority groups.
- **The Ethnic Experience** boxed features give firsthand accounts by immigrants of their experiences.
- **The International Scene** boxes offer cross-cultural parallels and include critical-thinking questions.
- The **Reality Check** boxes provide applications to everyday life or geo-political profiles.
- The **Students Speak** boxes provide comments from recent readers of this book about some aspect in that chapter provoking their reaction, a feature new to this edition.
- **What's in a Name?"** boxes in Chapters 7, 10, and 11 explain changes over the years in accepted terms to identify American Indians, black, and Hispanic Americans.
- An extensive, up-to-date array of photo, map, and line-art illustrations give an appealing visual complement to the text material.
- Review questions and Internet activities appear at the end of each chapter, along with a list of key terms.
- At the end of the book, students will find all chapter research notes, a glossary, and an appendix giving immigration statistics for the period 1820–2012.

## HELPFUL FEATURES FOR STUDENTS

- Use of endnotes instead of parenthetical citations enhances readability as words and thoughts flow smoothly from one sentence or paragraph to the next.
- Learning objectives at the beginning of the chapter enable students to focus on themes and key topics.
- The closing Retrospect section in each chapter provides an opportunity for students to review and retain the main points covered.
- Key terms appear in bold type and are page-numbered in the summary list at the end of the chapter, and are explained in the end-of-book glossary.

- Discussion questions stimulate reflection and critical thinking.
- Internet activities offer opportunities for exploring other dimensions of the subject matter.
- The "Students Speak" boxes reveal how other readers reacted to parts of the book.
- The "Reality Check" boxes—many of them about student behavior—offer a recognizable example that relates to material in the chapter.
- The "International Scene" boxes help students develop a wider perspective.
- The "Ethnic" or "Gender Experience" boxes help to humanize the text content.
- Numerous photos, historical political cartoons, graphs, and maps enrich the text material by bringing appealing visual components to the pages.

## WHAT'S NEW IN THE ELEVENTH EDITION

First, and most important, this new edition continues our policy to provide a thorough updating to supply the most recent data and information throughout the book and the inclusion of the most current and relevant studies not only in sociology but in many other related fields as well. Of the nearly 1,200 reference citations in this edition, 38 percent are either new or updated since the previous edition. In the Notes section in the back of the book, these new references appear in blue for easy identification.

Second, this book—often imitated by competitors—has always been the content leader and the most comprehensive in the field and the leader in including new focus areas, and we continue that proud tradition. For example, in this edition you will find a new boxed feature, "Students Speak," appearing 49 times throughout the book and offering reactive comments from recent readers.

Third, another new boxed feature, "What's in a Name?" appears in Chapters 7, 10 and 11 to explain the accepted name changes over the years to identify American Indians, Latinos, and Black Americans.

Fourth, we've added learning objectives at the beginning of each chapter to serve as a guide to upcoming topics.

## CHANGES IN EACH CHAPTER

As always, each chapter in this new edition contains the latest data and research findings. In addition, here is a detailed list of additions and updates:

**CHAPTER 1**
- 2012 largest-ever national social distance study
- Students Speak: social distance, ethnocentrism, and the Dillingham Flaw

**CHAPTER 2**
- 2012–2013 racial and ethnic demographics in professional sports
- Students Speak: chain migration and parallel social institutions

**CHAPTER 3**
- Affirmative action and universities, updated
- Reality Check: college student TV watching
- Students Speak: prejudice, stereotyping, and racial profiling

**CHAPTER 4**
- 2011 hate crime statistics
- 2012 map of hate groups in the United States
- International Scene: 2012 minority youth riot in France
- Students Speak: middleman minorities, segregation, and hate groups

**CHAPTER 5**

- Matriarchal role of the Irish-American mother
- 2011 European ancestry table
- 2010 map, North and West European ancestry
- Students Speak: functionalist, conflict, and interactionist theories

**CHAPTER 6**

- 2010 map, South, Central, and East European ancestry
- Students Speak: "America fever," working conditions, and literacy bills

**CHAPTER 7**

- What's in a Name? from American Indian to Native American and back again
- 2011 social indicators of American Indian progress
- 2011 American Indian and white occupations, updated
- 2011 cities with largest American Indian populations
- 2010 class-action suit settlements with U.S. government
- 2011 water rights settlements
- Reality Check: American Indian politicians
- Students Speak: media images, being an Indian, and the Cleveland Indians mascot

**CHAPTER 8**

- 2011 Asian American occupational distribution by sex
- 2011 cities with largest Asian American populations
- 2011 social indicators of Asian American progress
- Higher percentage of married couples among Asian foreign-born
- 2011 Asian subgroup populations
- 2010, map Asian ancestry
- International Scene: Japanese Brazilians living in Japan today
- Students Speak: cultural similarities, Japanese camps, miscegenation laws

**CHAPTER 9**

- 2011 social indicators of Arab American progress, including subgroups
- New and expanded discussion on Iranian *Nowruz* and *Sizdah Behar* celebrations
- 2011 Middle Eastern and North African immigration
- 2010 map, Arab ancestry
- Students Speak: social isolation, visiting Turkey, and theoretical perspectives

**CHAPTER 10**

- What's in a Name? from Colored to Negro to African American
- 2010 black–white segregation changes
- 2011 social indicators of black progress
- Expanded discussion of color-blindness
- 2010 map, Detroit segregation
- 2010 map, black geographic distribution
- Critical race theory
- Re-election of President Obama and race relations
- Students Speak: being black, being labeled, or being African

**CHAPTER 11**

- Hispanic influence on the 2012 presidential election
- What's in a Name? Is Pope Francis a Latino?
- Catholicism and Pentecostalism among Latinos
- 2011 social indicators of Hispanic progress
- Table, Hispanic immigration through 2011

- Table, 2011 Hispanic subgroup populations
- 2011 occupational distribution
- 2011 married-couple families, by national origin
- 2011 leading Western countries for immigrants
- Students Speak: culture, speaking English, assimilating

**CHAPTER 12**
- Court ruling on Santerían animal sacrifice
- Students Speak: interreligious marriage, Amish, Hinduism

**CHAPTER 13**
- Why women are considered a minority group
- Intersectionality of race, ethnicity, and class with gender
- International Scene: gender discrimination in Japan
- 2011 data on educational attainment, occupational distribution
- Increase of women in the 113th Congress
- Students Speak: past rights, gender role socialization, income disparity

**CHAPTER 14**
- 2012 national study on LGBT self-identification
- Changing public opinion on same-sex marriage
- State law changes on same-sex marriages
- Supreme Court ruling on age discrimination
- 2012 total fertility rates in more developed countries
- Table on 65+ population in 2010 and 2050
- Students Speak: homosexuality, disabled veterans, minority elderly poor

**CHAPTER 15**
- New terminology for English language acquisition classes
- Recent Supreme Court ruling on bilingual education
- Table, leading suppliers of immigrants to United States through 2011
- Table,15 leading sources of immigrants in 2011
- Reality Check: immigrant contributions to the United States
- Students Speak:1.5 generation, transnationalism, Kwanzaa, telecommunications

## ACKNOWLEDGMENTS

Many people helped in the writing of this book. A number of students completed exceptional immigrant tape projects; excerpts of their projects appear in Chapters 5 through 14: Eunice Adjei, Bruce Bisciotti, Doris Brown, Michael Carosone, Hermione Cox, Milly Gottlieb, Daniel Kazan, Doreen LaGuardia, David Lenox, Sarah Martinez, Chairath Phaladiganon, Terrence Royful, Michelle Schwartz, Geri Squire, Luba Tkatchov, Leo Uebelein, and Yu-Jie Zeng. Dozens of my students from recent years kindly contributed comments about parts of the book in the Students Speak boxes, where their names appear. Their contributions bring a very human touch to the study of minority peoples. David Fogmeg, my graduate assistant, was most helpful in some of the data collection.

I would like to thank the following reviewers for their helpful suggestions for this edition: I also want to acknowledge my deep appreciation to colleagues who reviewed previous editions and offered useful comments.

I have also had the good fortune to work with a team at Pearson whose competence, cooperation, and dedication have made the production of this edition a most satisfying project. My special thanks go to Karen Hanson, former Publisher, for her many years of support and encouragement, and to Charlyce Jones-Owen, my new Publisher, for helping to get this revision underway, and for offering valuable input on the book's features and to George Jacob, Project Manager with Integra Software Services, for shepherding the book through its production phase. I also thank all the other members of the Pearson team for their collective efforts in developing, publishing, and distributing this book.

I am especially grateful to my friend and colleague, Phil Kasinitz, for writing the Forewords to this and the previous edition. My thanks also go to other friends and colleagues: Charles V. Willie for writing the Forewords to the eighth and ninth editions; Rubén Rumbaut, for those in the sixth and seventh editions; Peter I. Rose, for those in the fourth and fifth editions; and the late Stanford M. Lyman, for those in the second and third editions, as well as for his guidance in the development of the first edition.

Finally, I want to acknowledge my gratitude to Beth for her support, and to my children, Chrysti, Cara, Beverley, and Elizabeth, as well as my grandchildren for the joy they bring to my life.

Vincent N. Parrillo
*William Paterson University*
Wayne, New Jersey 07470
*E-mail: parrillov@wpunj.edu*

# SUPPLEMENTARY MATERIALS

## FOR INSTRUCTORS

- *Instructor's Manual/Test Bank* (ISBN: ). This combined manual/test bank contains chapter summaries, learning objectives, suggestions for class activities and media materials, and over 1,000 test questions (multiple choice, true/false, fill-in, short answer, and essay). The Instructor's Manual/Test Bank is available to adopters within the Instructor section of the MySocLab for *Strangers to These Shores,* Tenth Edition at www.pearsonhighered.com/irc.

- *MyTest* (ISBN:). This software allows instructors to create their own personalized exams, to edit any or all of the existing test questions, and to add new questions. Other special features of this program include random generation of test questions, creation of alternate versions of the same test, scrambling question sequence, and test preview before printing. For easy access, this software is available within the Instructor section of the MySocLab for *Strangers to These Shores,* Eleventh Edition, or at www.pearsonhighered.com/irc.

- *PowerPoint Presentations* (ISBN:). The PowerPoint presentations are informed by instructional and design theory. Lecture PowerPoint slides follow the chapter outline and the Clicker Response System allows you to get immediate feedback from your students regardless of class size. Additionally, all of the PowerPoints are uniquely designed to present concepts in a clear and succinct way. They are available to adopters within the Instructor section of the MySocLab for *Strangers to These Shores,* Eleventh Edition, or at www.pearsonhighered.com/irc.

## MYSOCLAB™

**MySocLab** is a state-of-the-art interactive and instructive solution for the Social Problems course, designed to be used as a supplement to a traditional lecture course, or to completely administer an online course. MySocLab provides access to a wealth of resources all geared to meet the individual teaching and learning needs of every instructor and every student.

Highlights of MySocLab include:

- MySocLab for *Strangers to these Shores* provides all the tools you need to engage every student before, during, and after class. An assignment calendar and gradebook allow you to assign specific activities with due dates and to measure your students' progress throughout the semester.

- The **Pearson Etext** lets students access their textbook anytime, anywhere, and anyway they want, including *listening online*. The eText for *Strangers to these Shores* features integrated videos, Social Explorer activities, additional readings and interactive self-quizzes.

- A **Personalized Study Plan** for each student, based on Bloom's Taxonomy, arranges activities from those that require less complex thinking—like remembering and understanding—to more complex critical thinking—like applying and analyzing. This layered approach promotes better critical thinking skills, helping students succeed in the course and beyond.

- **Sociology in Focus** (www.sociologyinfocus.com) is a blog by sociologists for students that highlights a sociological perspective on current events, pop culture, and everyday life. Updated weekly, Sociology in Focus is a terrific way to bring current examples into the classroom.

## NEW FEATURES OF MYSOCLAB

Three exciting new features of MySocLab are Social Explorer and MySocLibrary.

- **Social Explorer** activities connect with topics from the text, engaging students with data visualizations, comparisons of change over time, and data localized to their own communities.
- **MySocLibrary** available in the Pearson eText 200 classic and contemporary articles that enable students to explore the discipline more deeply. Multiple choice questions for each reading help students review what they've learned—and allow instructors to monitor their performance.

## MYSOCLAB AND *STRANGERS TO THESE SHORES,* ELEVENTH EDITION

Correlations to the many resources in MySocLab with topics within the each chapter are included within the text to connect resources and content and make the integration of MySocLab even more flexible and useful for making assignments and for engaging students by giving them the opportunity to explore important sociological concepts, and enhance their performance in this course.

# ABOUT THE AUTHOR

Born and raised in Paterson, New Jersey, Vincent N. Parrillo experienced multiculturalism early as the son of a second-generation Italian American father and Irish/German American mother. He grew up in an ethnically diverse neighborhood, developing friendships and teenage romances with second- and third-generation Dutch, German, Italian, and Polish Americans. As he grew older, he developed other friendships that frequently crossed racial and religious lines.

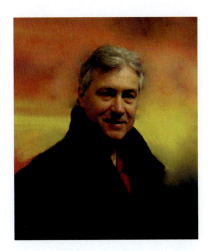

Professor Parrillo came to the field of sociology after first completing a bachelor's degree in business management and a master's degree in English. After teaching high school English and then serving as a college administrator, he took his first sociology course when he began doctoral studies at Rutgers University. Inspired by a discipline that scientifically investigates social issues, he changed his major and completed his degree in sociology.

Leaving his administrative post but staying at William Paterson University, Prof. Parrillo has since taught sociology for more than 35 years. He has lectured throughout the United States, Canada, Europe, and Asia, and often conducted diversity leadership programs for the military and large corporations. His keynote address at a bilingual educators' conference was published in *Vital Speeches of the Day,* which normally contains only speeches by national political leaders and heads of corporations and organizations.

Prof. Parrillo was a Fulbright Scholar in the Czech Republic and Scholar-in-Residence at both the University of Pisa and the University of Liege. Currently a Fulbright Senior Specialist, he has been a keynote speaker at international conferences in Belgium, Canada, Denmark, Germany, Italy, Korea, Poland, and Sweden. He has met with government leaders, nongovernment agency leaders, law enforcement officials, and educators in more than a dozen countries as a consultant on immigration policy, hate crimes, and multicultural education. He has done on-air interviews with *Radio Free Europe* and *Voice of America,* appeared on national Asian, Canadian, and European television programs, and often has been interviewed by numerous Asian, Canadian, and European reporters.

Prof. Parrillo's ventures into U.S. media include writing, narrating, and producing three PBS documentaries: *Ellis Island: Gateway to America; Smokestacks and Steeples: A Portrait of Paterson;* and *Gaetano Federici: The Sculptor Laureate of Paterson.* Contacted by reporters across the nation for his views on race and ethnic relations, he has been quoted in dozens of newspapers, including the *Chicago Sun-Times, Cincinnati Inquirer, Houston Chronicle, Hartford Courant, Omaha World-Herald, Orlando Sentinel,* and *Virginian Pilot.* He has also appeared on numerous U.S. radio and television programs.

Prof. Parrillo is also the author of *Understanding Race and Ethnic Relations,* Fourth Edition (Allyn & Bacon), *Contemporary Social Problems,* Sixth Edition (Allyn & Bacon), *Cities and Urban Life,* Sixth Edition (with John Macionis), *Diversity in America,* Fourth Edition, and *Rethinking Today's Minorities.* His articles and book reviews have appeared in journals such as *Sociological Forum, Social Forces, Journal of Comparative Family Studies, Journal of American Ethnic History, The Social Science Journal, Encyclopedia of American Immigration,* and the *Encyclopedia of Race, Ethnicity, and Society.* He was General Editor of the *Encyclopedia of Social Problems* for Sage Publications. Several of his books and articles have been translated into other languages, including Chinese, Czech, Danish, German, Italian, Japanese, Korean, Polish, Romanian, and Swedish.

An active participant in various capacities throughout the years in the American Sociological Association and Eastern Sociological Society, Prof. Parrillo has been listed in *Who's Who in International Education, Outstanding Educators of America, American Men and Women of Science,* and *Who's Who in the East.* Recipient in 2013 of the Faculty Achievement Award for Excellence in Scholarship from William Paterson University, he was Robin M. Williams, Jr. Distinguished Lecturer (2005–2006) and vice president (2008–2009) of the Eastern Sociological Society.

# The Study of Minorities

# 1

((· Listen to Chapter 1 on MySocLab

*Ever-increasing diversity in our communities, schools, and the workplace is the reality that all of us face. Such a mixture of peoples can produce cultural misunderstandings but to open-minded individuals it presents innumerable enrichment opportunities. This book is an effort to help you lessen the problems and enjoy the benefits of a pluralist society.*

## LEARNING OBJECTIVES | After reading this chapter you will be able to:

**1-1** Explain how the concept of the stranger helps us understand others.

**1-2** Identify the characteristics of a minority group.

**1-3** Distinguish the complex differences between a racial and ethnic group.

**1-4** Explain how ethnocentrism affects our acceptance of others.

**1-5** Explain the Dillingham Flaw and why it is important in studying diversity.

**1-6** Identify the connection between personal troubles and public issues.

**1-7** Examine the dynamics of intergroup relations.

**1-8** Evaluate what sociological perspectives tell us about minority groups.

Americans pride themselves as being part of a nation of immigrants. Many still call the United States a great melting pot where people of all races, religions, and nationalities come to be free and to improve their lives. Certainly, a great number of immigrants offer living testimony to that ideal; their enthusiasm for their adopted country is evident in countless interviews, some of which you will read in this book. As college students, regardless of how recently or long ago your family immigrated to the United States, most of you also provide evidence of the American Dream of freedom of choice, economic opportunity, and upward mobility.

Yet beneath the Fourth of July speeches, the nation's absorption of diverse peoples throughout the years, and the numerous success stories lies a disquieting truth. Native-born Americans have not always welcomed newcomers with open arms; indeed, they often have responded with overt acts of discrimination, ranging from avoidance to violence and murder. The dominant group's treatment of native-born blacks and Native Americans disturbingly illustrates the persistence of subjugation and entrenched inequality. Today, serious problems remain in attitudes toward, and treatment of, Native Americans on reservations; poor blacks in urban ghettos; large concentrations of Arab, Asian, Hispanic, and Muslim Americans struggling to gain acceptance. For some, the American Dream becomes a reality; for others, blocked opportunities create an American nightmare.

Interethnic tensions and hostilities within a nation's borders are a worldwide phenomenon dating from thousands of years ago to the present. In recent years, we have witnessed the horror of terrorist killings in Afghanistan, Egypt, Indonesia, Iraq, Mynamar, Pakistan, the Philippines, Spain, Turkey, and the United States. Religious factions in India and the Middle East still harbor such animosity toward one another that violence continues to erupt sporadically. A decade ago, more than 5.4 million died in the armed conflict in the Democratic Republic of the Congo and more than 300,000 in Darfur, a vast region in the west of Sudan. In the 1990s, Orthodox Christian Serbians killed an estimated 60,000 Bosnian Muslims in the name of "ethnic cleansing," and Serbians killed thousands of ethnic Albanians in Kosovo, prompting military action by NATO. Tribal warfare between the Hutu and Tutsi in Rwanda led to the massacre of hundreds of thousands. In the 1980s, a bloody war raged among the Hausa, Ibo, and Yoruba tribes of Nigeria, and Iraq killed hundreds of Kurds with poisonous gas. A few years earlier, appalling bloodbaths among Kampucheans (Cambodians), Chinese, Laotians, and Vietnamese horrified the world. Elsewhere, other minorities, such as West Indians in Britain, Algerians in France, Turks in Germany, Roma (Gypsies) in eastern Europe, and Palestinians in Israel, have encountered prejudice, discrimination, and physical attacks. Within any society, groupings of people by race, religion, tribe, culture, or lifestyle can generate prejudices, tensions, and sporadic outbursts of violence.

Individuals of the dominant group usually absolve themselves of blame for a minority group's low status and problems, attributing these instead to supposed flaws within the group itself (for example, slowness in learning the mainstream language or lack of a work ethic). Sociologists, however, note that interaction patterns among different groups transcend national boundaries, specific periods, or group idiosyncrasies. Opinions may vary as to the causes of these patterns of behavior, but a consensus does exist about their presence.

## The Stranger as a Social Phenomenon

1-1 Explain how the concept of the stranger helps us understand others.

To understand intergroup relations, we must recognize that differences among various peoples cause each group to view other groups as strangers. Among isolated peoples, the arrival of a stranger has always been a momentous occasion, often eliciting strong emotional responses. Reactions might range from warm hospitality to conciliatory or protective ceremonies to hostile acts. In an urbanized and mobile society, the stranger still evokes similar responses. From the Tiwi of northern Australia, who consistently killed

Because a health club attracts people who share similar interests in health, exercise, and weight control, new social interactions in that environment are likely, especially among those going regularly. Strangers feel comfortable in striking up casual conversations with one another and it is not uncommon for friendships, even romances, to develop.

intruders, to the nativists of any country or time, who continually strive to keep out "undesirable elements," the underlying premise is the same: The outsiders are not good enough to share the land and resources with the "chosen people" already there.

## SIMILARITY AND ATTRACTION

At least since Aristotle commented that we like "those like ourselves … of our own race or country or age or family, and generally those who are on our own level," social observers have been aware of the similarity–attraction relationship.[1] Numerous studies have explored the extent to which a person likes others because of similar attitudes, values, beliefs, social status, or physical appearance. Examining the development of attraction among people who are initially strangers to one another, an impressive number of these studies have found a positive relationship between the similarity of two people and their liking for each other. Most significantly, the findings show that people's perception of similarity between themselves is a more powerful determinant than actual similarity.[2] Cross-cultural studies also support this conclusion.[3] Thus, a significant amount of evidence exists showing greater human receptivity to strangers considered as more similar than to those who are viewed as different.

## SOCIAL DISTANCE

One excellent technique for evaluating how perceptions of similarity attract closer interaction patterns consists of ranking **social distance**, the degree of closeness or remoteness individuals prefer in interaction with members of other groups. In 1926, Emory Bogardus created a measurement device that has been used repeatedly since then.[4] In seven comparable studies spanning 85 years, researchers obtained responses from college students to identify what changes and continuities in attitudes about minorities occurred over the generations. To measure the level of social acceptance, the social distance studies offered respondents seven choices for each group.

1. Would accept marrying into my family (1 point)
2. Would accept as a personal friend in my social circle (2 points)
3. Would accept as a neighbor on my street (3 points)
4. Would work in the same office (4 points)

5. Would only have as speaking acquaintances (5 points)

6. Would only have as visitors to my country (6 points)

7. Would bar from entering my country (7 points)

In the twenty-first-century studies (Table 1.1), non-ethnic whites still remained in the top position as the most accepted, with many of the other top 10 slots filled by Canadians, British, Irish, French, and Germans, essentially continuing an 85-year pattern. Particularly striking, though, was the dramatic rise of African Americans. Now ranking fifth, they first broke the racial barrier by entering the top sector in 2001 and placing ahead of most other white ethnic groups in 2012. Other significant changes were the rise of Italians into the second position—ahead of the previously dominating English, Canadians, and French. Generally though, the distribution showed non-ethnic white Americans, Canadians, and northern and

**TABLE 1.1   Mean Social Distance Rankings in 2012 and Comparisons to 2001**

| RANK IN 2012 | GROUP | MEAN | (SD) | +/− VS. 2001 | RANK IN 2001 |
|---|---|---|---|---|---|
| 1. | Americans | 1.15 | (.57) | + .08 | 1 |
| 2. | Italians | 1.32 | (.80) | + .17 | 2 |
| 3. | Canadians | 1.35 | (.89) | + .15 | 3 |
| 4. | British | 1.36 | (.91) | + .13 | 4 |
| 5. | African Americans | 1.42 | (.78) | + .09 | 9 |
| 6. | Irish | 1.46 | (.94) | + .23 | 5 |
| 7. | French | 1.50 | (1.03) | + .22 | 6 |
| 8. | Germans | 1.51 | (1.01) | + .18 | 8 |
| 9. | Greeks | 1.52 | (1.01) | + .19 | 7 |
| 10. | Indians (American) | 1.57 | (.94) | + .17 | 12 |
| 11. | Africans | 1.61 | (.93) | + .18 | 13 |
| 12. | Dutch | 1.62 | (1.09) | + .27 | 10 |
| 13. | Polish | 1.64 | (1.08) | + .19 | 14 |
| 14. | Puerto Ricans | 1.64 | (1.09) | + .17 | 18 |
| 15. | Filipinos | 1.68 | (1.08) | +. 22 | 16 |
| 16. | Dominicans | 1.71 | (1.14) | + .20 | 21 |
| 17. | Chinese | 1.72 | (1.04) | + .25 | 17 |
| 18. | Other Hispanics/Latinos | 1.72 | (1.14) | + .27 | 15 |
| 19. | Russians | 1.73 | (1.17) | + .23 | 20 |
| 20. | Cubans | 1.74 | (1.20) | + .21 | 23 |
| 21. | Jews | 1.74 | (1.11) | + .36 | 11 |
| 22. | Jamaicans | 1.74 | (1.08) | + .25 | 19 |
| 23. | Japanese | 1.80 | (1.14) | + .28 | 22 |
| 24. | Mexicans | 1.80 | (1.29) | + .25 | 25 |
| 25. | Vietnamese | 1.85 | (1.11) | + .16 | 28 |
| 26. | Koreans | 1.87 | (1.24) | + .33 | 24 |
| 27. | Indians (India) | 1.89 | (1.22) | + .29 | 26 |
| 28. | Haitians | 1.91 | (1.27) | + .28 | 27 |
| 29. | Arabs | 2.16 | (1.55) | + .22 | 30 |
| 30. | Muslims | 2.23 | (1.52) | + .35 | 29 |
| **All Groups** | | **1.68** | **(.80)** | | |

*Source:* Vincent N. Parrillo and Christopher Donoghue, "The National Social Distance Study: Ten Years Later," *Sociological Forum* 28:3 (September 2013); and "Updating the Bogardus Social Distance Studies: A New National Study," *The Social Science Journal* 42 (2005): 257–71.

# REALITY check

## Cross-Racial College Friendships

Do college students actually have close friends in everyday life from outside their own racial or ethnic group? A recent study offers one insight into that question.

While measuring social distance among college students at a midsize state university in the northeastern United States, three researchers also examined friendship patterns between Blacks–Hispanics, Blacks–Whites, Hispanics–Blacks, Hispanics–Whites, Whites–Blacks, and Whites–Hispanics. Their sample consisted of 297 freshmen, 52 sophomores, 73 juniors, and 83 seniors, of whom 297 were white, 71 black, and 80 Hispanic. No significant differences in responses existed among grade levels, but variances did occur among groups.

For black students, 60 percent had white friends and 38 percent had Hispanic friends. About 37 percent of Hispanic students had black friends and 42 percent reported having white friends. Among white students, 42 percent had black friends and 36 percent had Hispanic friends.

In an academic setting with a diverse student body (about 12 percent each of blacks and Hispanics), 3 of 5 black students have at least one white friend, meaning 2 of 5 do not. In the other five friendship possibilities, on average, 2 of 5 students have a cross-racial friend but 3 of 5 do not. The good news is that cross-racial friendships have increased in recent years, but the bad news is that these generally do not exist yet for the majority of college students.

### CRITICAL THINKING QUESTION

What percentage of your friends is not part of your own racial or ethnic group? Why do you think it is that way?

Source: Adapted from Patricia Odell, Kathleen Korgen, and Gabe Wang, "Cross-Racial Friendships and Social Distance between Racial Groups on a College Campus," *Innovative Higher Education, 29* (2005): 291–305. Copyright © 2005 Springer. Used with permission.

---

western Europeans in the top third, with southern, central, and eastern Europeans in the middle third, and racial minorities in the bottom third. However, the researchers cautioned that the exact placement of a group in relation to those near it should not be given much importance because, due to the close scores, these rankings may be the result of sampling variability.

However, the upward movement of African Americans over many white ethnic groups is particularly noteworthy. First, it reveals their strong social acceptance level and may therefore reflect students' ease in racial interactions on their more diverse campuses. Making this strong level of social acceptance even more striking is the underrepresentation of blacks among respondents. In the 2012 study, only 6.9 percent of the sample was black, lower than in all previous national studies, yet African Americans attained the best-ever social distance ranking. Furthermore, Asians and Hispanics expressed greater social distances than did whites toward African Americans. These findings suggest that it is not the greater presence of people of color among respondents that explains the strong showing of blacks, but rather a much greater receptivity among white college students.

A slight increase in social distance occurred between 2001 and 2012, but that may be due to the passage of time. The 2001 study occurred just 2 months after the terrorist attacks, causing what the researchers called a "unity syndrome," the reactive coalescing of diverse respondents into a shared group identity of "Americans" united against a common enemy.[5] If so, then the 2012 data is perhaps an adjustment in attitudes a bit less tempered by the immediacy of that tragic and traumatic event. Generally speaking, college students of the twenty-first century are more receptive to outgroups than their twentieth-century counterparts, but their level of social acceptance of others still appears dependent on the similarity–attraction bond (see the Reality Check box).

**STUDENTS SPEAK** "All over the campus—in the student center, dining hall, and outside walking from class to class—mostly everywhere you look, a group of students of one ethnic group is sitting together separate from other ethnic groups that are sitting with their own as well. I don't think people do this intentionally because they dislike people of other ethnic groups. I just think it is something based on interests. People make friends with others who have the same interests and values, so they enjoy hanging out with each other."

**—German Decena**

*With women and/or people of color now constituting three-fourths of new workers entering the U.S. labor force, such diversity poses challenges to managers and employees alike. Cultural and gender differences usually affect social distances among workers, which in turn could impact on employee morale, motivation, and teamwork.*

*Perception and reality are often not the same thing, whether it is an observation about the characteristics of a minority group or an optical illusion like this one. Since light travels at different speeds in and out of such different optical mediums as air and water, it creates the impression that the straw in the water is in a different place than its true position.*

## PERCEPTIONS

By definition, the stranger is not only an outsider but also someone different and personally unknown. People perceive strangers primarily through **categoric knowing**—the classification of others on the basis of limited information obtained visually and perhaps verbally.[6] People make judgments and generalizations on the basis of scanty information, confusing an individual's characteristics with typical group-member characteristics. For instance, if a visiting Swede asks for tea rather than coffee, the host may conclude incorrectly that all Swedes dislike coffee.

Native-born Americans usually have viewed immigrants—first-generation Americans of different racial and ethnic groups—as a particular kind of stranger: one who intended to stay. A common reaction pattern is an initial curiosity about the presence of immigrants replaced by fear, suspicion, and distrust as their numbers increase. As a result, the strangers remain strangers as each group seeks its own kind for personal interaction.

The status of a stranger is consistent, whether we speak of the past, present, or future. German sociologist Georg Simmel (1858–1918) explained that strangers represent both *nearness*, because they are physically close, and *remoteness*, because they react differently to the immediate situation and have different values and ways of doing things.[7] The stranger is both inside and outside: physically present and participating but also mentally outside the situation with a mindset influenced by a different culture.

The natives perceive the stranger in an abstract, typified way and so the individual becomes the *totality*, or stereotype, of the entire group. In other words, because it is someone unknown or unfamiliar, someone not understood, they see the stranger only in generalized terms, as a representative member of a "different" group.

# the INTERNATIONAL scene

## Enhancing German Interaction with Americans

U.S. International, an organization that runs exchange programs, distributed a pamphlet, "An Information Guide for Germans on American Culture," to Germans working as interns in U.S. companies. The pamphlet was based on previous German interns' experiences and on their interviews with other colleagues; its intent was to provide insights into U.S. culture to ease German interactions with Americans. Here are some examples:

- Americans say "Hello" or "How are you?" when they see each other. "How are you?" is like "Hello." A long answer is not expected; just answer, "Thank you, fine. How are you?"
- Using deodorant is a must.
- American women usually shave their legs and under their arms. Women who don't like to do this should consider wearing clothes that cover these areas.

- Expect to be treated like all other Americans. You won't receive special treatment because you are a German. Try not to talk with other Germans in German if Americans are around; this could make them feel uncomfortable.
- Please consider the differences in verbal communication styles between Americans and Germans. The typical German speaking style sounds abrupt and rude to Americans. Keep this in mind when talking to Americans.
- Be polite. Use words like "please" and "thank you." It is better to use these too often than not enough. Also, be conscious of your voice and the expression on your face. Your voice should be friendly, and you should wear a smile. Don't be confused by the friendliness and easygoing, non-excitable nature of the people. They are deliberate,

think independently, and do things their own way. Americans are proud of their independence.
- Keep yourself out of any discussions at work about race, sex, religion, or politics. Be open-minded; don't make judgments based on past experiences in Germany.
- Be aware that there are a lot of different cultures in the United States. There also are many different churches, which mean a great deal to their members. Don't be quick to judge these cultures; this could hurt people's feelings.
- Do it the American way, and try to intermingle with the Americans. Think positive.

### CRITICAL THINKING QUESTION

What guidelines for overcoming ethnocentrism should Americans follow when traveling to or working in other countries?

---

In contrast, said Simmel, the stranger perceives the natives not in abstract but in specific, individual terms. Strangers are more objective about the natives because the strangers' geographic mobility enhances their mental mobility as well. The stranger—not caught up in taken-for-granted assumptions, habits, and traditions, and also not participating fully in society—has a certain mental detachment and so observes each situation more acutely.

## INTERACTIONS

Simmel approached the role of the stranger through an analysis of the formal structures of life. In contrast, Alfred Schutz—himself an immigrant from Austria to the United States—analyzed the stranger as lacking "intersubjective understanding."[8] By this, he meant that people from the same social world mutually "know" the language (including slang), customs, beliefs, symbols, and everyday behavior patterns that the stranger usually does not.

For the native then, every social situation is a coming together not only of roles and identities but also of shared realities—the intersubjective structure of consciousness. What is taken for granted by the native is problematic to the stranger. In a familiar world, people live through the day by responding to the daily routine without questions or reflection. To strangers, however, every situation is new and is therefore experienced as a crisis (see the accompanying International Scene box).

Strangers experience a "lack of historicity"—a lack of the shared memory of those with whom they live. Human beings who interact together over a period of time "grow old together"; strangers, however, are "young"; as newcomers they experience at least an approximation of the freshness of childhood. They are aware of things that go unnoticed by the natives, such as the natives' customs, social institutions, appearance, and lifestyle. Also existing within the natives' taken-for-granted world are social constructions of race and ethnicity that, to the stranger, are new realities. Race as a social construct can be illustrated by the case of Barack Obama. To many whites, he is a black man. With a longstanding, rigid, racial classification system in the United States of white or non-white, perhaps this perception is understandable. Obama, however, had a black Kenyan father and a white American mother, so he is actually biracial. This, however, led some blacks to question whether he was "black enough" to be their "authentic" representative when he sought his party's nomination for the presidency.[9] Within the racial divide, both blacks and whites are often strangers to each other, perceiving reality through different social constructs.

In time, however, strangers take on the natives' perspective; the strangers' consciousness decreases because the freshness of their perceptions is lost. At the same time, the natives' generalizations about the strangers become more concrete through social interaction. As Schutz said, "The vacant frames become occupied by vivid experiences." As acculturation takes place, the native begins to view the stranger more concretely, and the stranger becomes less questioning about daily activities. Use of the term *naturalized citizen* takes on a curious connotation when examined from this perspective because it implies that people are, in some way, odd or unnatural until they have acquired the characteristics of the natives.

As its title suggests, this book is about strangers—whether they be those who came—and still are coming—to the United States in search of a better life or those who are strangers in their native land because of their minority status. In our sociological examination of the experiences of these groups of people, we will be continually telling the story of how the stranger perceives the society and how society receives that stranger. The adjustment from stranger to neighbor is a movement along a familiar continuum, but this continuum is not frictionless, and assimilation is not inevitable. Rather, it is a process of varying social interactions among different groups of people.

Before we proceed further, let us clarify three terms used extensively in this book. **Migration** is the general term that refers to the movement of people into and out of a specified area, which could either be within a country or from one country to another. Examples are the migration of people from one continent to another or the migration of U.S. blacks from the South to the North. **Emigration** is a narrower term that refers to the movement of people *out of* a country to settle in another, while **immigration** refers to the movement of people *into* a new country to become permanent residents. So we could speak, for example, of the *emigration* of people from Peru and their *immigration* into the United States. To the sending country, they are emigrants and to the receiving country, they are immigrants.

## Minority Groups

1-2 Identify the characteristics of a minority group.

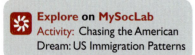

**Explore on MySocLab**
Activity: Chasing the American Dream: US Immigration Patterns

Sociologists use the term **minority group** not to designate a group's numerical representation but to indicate its relative power and status in a society. Although first used in World War I peace treaties to protect approximately 22 million of 110 million people in east central Europe, the term's most frequent use has been as a description of biological features or national traits because people do make distinctions among people according to race and national origin. In time, social scientists broadened the definition of *minority group* to encompass any physical or cultural trait, not just race or national origin, thereby

This joyful event in Florida—the Miami Japanese Cultural Festival—illustrates how certain characteristics help define a minority group. Easily identifiable by their facial features and distinctive clothing, these Japanese share their sense of peoplehood through a cultural celebration of their religion and through social interaction.

also including the aged, people with disabilities, members of various religions or sects, and groups with unconventional lifestyles.[10]

As researchers studied the social consequences of minority status, their emphasis became centered on prejudice, discrimination, and oppression. Others found this "victimological" tactic too limiting, instead preferring to analyze the similarities and differences among groups, as well as relationships between majority and minority groups.[11]

A third approach in defining minority groups rests on the relationships between groups in terms of each group's position in the social hierarchy.[12] This approach stresses a group's social power, which may vary from one country to another as, for example, does that of the Jews in Russia and in Israel. The emphasis on stratification instead of population size explains situations in which a relatively small group subjugates a larger number of people, such as the European colonization of African and Asian populations.

## MINORITY-GROUP CHARACTERISTICS

As social scientists refined their approaches to studying minority groups, a consensus evolved on the five characteristics shared by minorities worldwide:

1. The group receives unequal treatment from the larger society.
2. The group is easily identifiable because of distinguishing physical or cultural characteristics that are held in low esteem.
3. The group feels a sense of group identity, that each of them shares something in common with other members.
4. Membership in the minority group has **ascribed status**: One is born into it.
5. Group members practice **endogamy**: They tend to marry within their group, either by choice or by necessity, because of their social isolation.[13]

Although these five features provide helpful guidelines when discussing racial and ethnic minorities, the last two characteristics do not apply to such minority groups as the aged, disabled, gays, or women. One is not born old, and people with disabilities are not always born that way. Only a small percentage of gays are easily identifiable by physical characteristics. Same-sex marriages aside, most women do not marry their own kind, nor necessarily do the aged or people with disabilities.

What all minority groups do have in common is their subordinate status to a more powerful, although not necessarily, larger group. Women outnumber men in U.S. society, for example, but as we will discuss in Chapter 13, numerous social indicators reveal they have not yet achieved full equality with men.

Therefore, we will use the term **dominant group** when referring to a minority group's relationships with the rest of society. A complication is that a person may be a member of both dominant and minority groups in different categories. For example, a white Roman Catholic belongs to a prominent religious minority group but also is a member of the U.S. racially dominant group.

## Racial and Ethnic Groups

**1-3** Distinguish the complex differences between a racial and ethnic group.

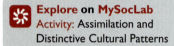

**Explore on MySocLab**
Activity: Assimilation and Distinctive Cultural Patterns

**Race** is a categorization in which people sharing visible biological characteristics regard themselves or are regarded by others as a single group on that basis. At first glance, race may seem an easy way to group people, but it is not. The 7 billion humans inhabiting this planet exhibit a wide range of physical differences in body build, hair texture, facial features, and skin color. Centuries of migration, conquest, intermarriage, and evolutionary physical adaptation to the environment have caused these varieties. Anthropologists have attempted racial categorizations ranging from three to more than a hundred. Some, such as Ashley Montagu, even argue that only one race exists—the human race.[14] Just as anthropologists apply different interpretations to biological groupings, so do most people. By examining these social interpretations, sociologists attempt to analyze and explain racial prejudice.

The social construction of race varies by culture and in history. The United States, for example, has long had a rigid racial classification ("White" and "non-White"), unlike Latin America, which acknowledges various gradations of race, reflecting that region's multiracial heritage. U.S. purists have even subscribed to the "one-drop theory," that someone with even a tiny portion of non-white ancestry should be classified as black. However, it is not only outsider classifications. Sometimes people will identify as, say, black or Native American, when their DNA reveals a higher percentage of a different race. Racial classifications thus are often arbitrary, with individuals or society placing undue emphasis on race. Indeed, some geneticists argue that race is a meaningless concept, that far more genetic variation exists within races than between them, and that many racial traits overlap without distinct boundaries.[15] Furthermore, with approximately 6 million people of mixed racial parentage living in the United States, many social scientists have called for the "deconstruction of race," arguing against the artificial boundaries that promote racial prejudice.[16]

**Racism** is the linking of biological conditions with alleged abilities and behavior to assert the superiority of one race. When people believe that one race is superior to another because of innate abilities or specific achievements, racist thinking prevails. The subordinate group experiences prejudice and discrimination, which the dominant group justifies by reference to such undesirable perceptions. In this book, we will discuss how not only blacks but also Native Americans, Asians, Hispanics, and even white southern Europeans have encountered hostility because of such social categorizations based simply on physical appearance.

Racism is a human invention, a good example of the social construction of reality. It slowly evolved out of efforts to sort humans into distinctive categories based on skin color and facial features. These developments included philosophers such as Immanuel Kant (1724–1804) offering biological distinctions of the "races of mankind" and nineteenth-century Social Darwinists seeing human society as a "survival of the fittest" in which the naturally superior will win out. Some physical anthropologists suggested that physically distinctive groups fell into a hierarchy, with white Europeans (like themselves) at the top and blacks at the bottom, as rationalized by their dark color, their supposedly primitive culture, and especially because Europeans then knew of blacks as slaves. It was in this pseudo-scientific context that racism emerged as an ideology. Although most modern scientists and social scientists have debunked the "scientific" claims of racism, as discussed in Chapters 6 and 10, racist ideologies still attract many followers.[17]

While *race* deals with visible physical characteristics, **ethnicity** goes beyond a simple racial similarity to encompass shared cultural traits and/or national origin. People may be of the same race but different in language and cultural practices, such as Africans, Haitians, and Jamaicans. Conversely, people may be of different races but members of the same ethnic group, such as Hispanics. The complexities of social groups by ethnicity do not stop there. People may be members of the same race and ethnic group, such as the Belgians, but speak different languages (Dutch, French, or German) and so also be members of different subcultural ethnic groups. Moreover, if we add the element of social class, we will find even more differences within these subcultural ethnic groups.

Religion is another determinant of ethnic group composition. Sometimes religion and national origin seem like dual attributes of ethnicity, such as Irish and Italian Catholics (although not all Irish or Italians are Catholic). Sometimes, too, what appear to be these dual attributes—Arab Muslims, for example—are not so; for example, the majority of Arabs in the United States are Christians, and 35 percent of the total Arab American population is Catholic.[18] Religion most commonly links with other elements of ethnicity—national origin, culture, and language—among immigrant groups. Even here, though, we should refrain from generalizing about all members of any national origin group (or any racial group) because of the extensive differences within such groups.

Some people have used incorrectly the word *race* as a social rather than as a biological concept. Thus, the British and Japanese have often been classified as races, as have Hindus, Aryans, Gypsies, Arabs, Basques, and Jews.[19] Many people—even sociologists, anthropologists, and psychologists—use *race* in a general sense that includes racial and ethnic groups, thereby giving the term both a biological and a social meaning. Since the 1960s, *ethnic group* has been used more frequently to include the three elements of race, religion, and national origin.[20] Such varied use of these terms results in endless confusion, for racial distinctions are socially defined categories based on physical distinctions.

Some groups, such as African Americans, cannot simply be defined on racial grounds, for their diversity as native-born Americans or African or Caribbean immigrants places them in ethnocultural groups as well. Similarly, Asians and Native Americans incorrectly get lumped together in broad racial categories despite their significant ethnic differences.

In this book, the word *race* refers to the common social distinctions made on the basis of physical appearance. The term *ethnic group* refers only to social groupings that are unique because of religious, linguistic, or cultural characteristics. We will use both terms in discussing groups whose racial and ethnic characteristics overlap.

## Ethnocentrism

Understanding the concept of the stranger is important to understanding **ethnocentrism**—a "view of things in which one's own group is the center of everything, and all others are scaled and rated with reference to it."[21] *Ethnocentrism* thus refers to people's tendency to identify with their own ethnic or national group as a means of fulfilling their needs for group belongingness and security. (The word derives from two Greek words: *ethnos* meaning "nation" and *kentron* meaning "center.") As a result of ethnocentrism, people usually view their own cultural values as somehow more real, and therefore superior to, those of other groups, and so they prefer their own way of

**1-4** Explain how ethnocentrism affects our acceptance of others.

**STUDENTS SPEAK** *"When I began reading the textbook and learning about ethnocentrism, one of my favorite movies came to mind: My Big Fat Greek Wedding. Gus is a sweet man who is living in a country that is not his 'home' and he relentlessly makes sure that everyone he reaches out to understands the significance and importance of the Greek culture and its influence on the world. Gus truly believes that Greek culture is the best culture, and has a hard time understanding the differences found in American culture. When I watch movies like this, I am reminded that families with strong traditions and beliefs stemming from their culture exist and I think it is interesting observing the differences."*
**—Courtney Hall**

doing things. Unfortunately for human relations, such ethnocentric thought often negatively affects attitudes toward, and emotions about, those perceived as different.

Fortunately, social scientists are making increasing numbers of people aware of a more enlightened and positive alternative to ethnocentrism. **Cultural relativism** evaluates beliefs and behavior in the context of that culture. The more widespread this perspective becomes known and applied, the more intergroup understanding and mutual acceptance grows.

Sociologists define an **ingroup** as a group to which individuals belong and feel loyal; thus, everyone—whether a member of a majority group or a minority group—is part of some ingroup. An **outgroup** consists of all people who are not members of one's ingroup. Studying majority groups as ingroups helps us understand their reactions to strangers of another race or culture entering their society. Conversely, considering minority groups as ingroups enables us to understand their efforts to maintain their ethnic identity and solidarity in the midst of the dominant culture.

From European social psychologists comes one of the more helpful explanations for ingroup favoritism. **Social identity theory** holds that ingroup members almost automatically think of their group as being better than outgroups because doing so enhances their own social status or social identity and thus raises the value of their personal identity or self-image.[22]

Ample evidence exists about people from past civilizations who regarded other cultures as inferior, incorrect, or immoral. This assumption that *we* are better than *they* generally results in outgroups becoming objects of ridicule, contempt, or hatred. Such attitudes may lead to stereotyping, prejudice, discrimination, and even violence. What actually occurs depends on many factors, including structural and economic conditions, to be discussed in subsequent chapters.

Despite its ethnocentric beliefs, the ingroup does not always view an outgroup as being inferior. An outgroup may become a positive **reference group**—that is, it may serve as an exemplary model—if members of the ingroup think it has a conspicuous advantage over them. A good example would be immigrants who try to shed their ethnic identity and Americanize themselves as quickly as possible. Ethnocentrism is an important factor in determining minority-group status in society, but because of many variations in intergroup relations, it alone cannot explain the causes of prejudice. For example, majority-group members may view minority groups with suspicion, but not all minority groups become the targets of prejudice and discrimination.

Some social-conflict theorists argue that ethnocentrism leads to negative consequences when the ingroup feels threatened by the outgroup competing with them for scarce resources. Then the ingroup reacts with increased solidarity and exhibits prejudice, discrimination, and hostility toward the outgroup.[23] The severity of this hostility depends on various economic and geographic considerations. One counterargument to this view is that ethnocentric attitudes—thinking that because others are different, they are thus a threat—initially *caused* the problem. The primary difficulty with this approach, however, is that it does not explain variations in the frequency, type, or intensity of intergroup conflict from one society to the next or between different immigrant groups and the ingroup.

## IN THE UNITED STATES

Often, an ethnocentric attitude is not deliberate but rather an outgrowth of growing up and living within a familiar environment. Even so, if recognized for the bias it is, ethnocentrism can be overcome. Consider, for example, that Americans have labeled their major league baseball championship games a *World Series,* although until recently not even Canadian teams were included in an otherwise exclusively U.S. professional sports program. *American* is another word we use—even in this book— to identify ourselves to the exclusion of people in other parts of North and South America. The Organization of American States (OAS), which consists of countries in both North and Latin America, should remind us that others are equally entitled to call themselves Americans.

At one point in this country's history, many state and national leaders identified their expansionist goals as *Manifest Destiny,* as if divine providence had ordained specific boundaries for the United States. Indeed, many members of the clergy throughout the years preached fiery sermons regarding God's special plans for this country, and all presidents have invoked the deity in their inaugural addresses for special assistance to this country.

## IN OTHER TIMES AND LANDS

Throughout history, people of many cultures have demonstrated an ethnocentric view of the world. For example, British Victorians, believing their way of life superior to all others, concluded they were obliged to carry the "white man's burden" of cultural and intellectual superiority in colonizing and "civilizing" the non-Western world. Yet 2,000 years earlier, the Romans had thought natives of Britain were an especially inferior people, as indicated in this excerpt from a letter written by the orator Cicero to his friend Atticus: "Do not obtain your slaves from Britain because they are so stupid and so utterly incapable of being taught that they are not fit to form a part of the household of Athens."

The Greeks, whose civilization predated the Roman Empire, considered all those around them—Persians, Egyptians, Macedonians, and others—distinctly inferior and called them barbarians. (*Barbarikos,* a Greek word, described those who did not speak Greek as making noises that sounded like "bar-bar.")

Religious chauvinism blended with ethnocentrism in the Middle Ages when the Crusaders, spurred on by their beliefs, considered it their duty to free the Holy Land from the control of the "infidels." They traveled a great distance by land and sea, taking with them horses, armor, and armaments, to wrest control from the native inhabitants because those "infidels" had the audacity to follow the teachings of Muhammad rather than Jesus. On their journey across Europe, the Crusaders slaughtered Jews (whom they falsely labeled "Christ-killers"), regardless of whether they were men, women, or children, all in the name of the Prince of Peace. The Crusaders saw both Muslims and Jews not only as inferior peoples but also as enemies. Here are a few more examples of ethnocentric thinking in past times:

> The Roman, Vitruvius, maintained that those who live in southern climates have the keener intelligence, due to the rarity of the atmosphere, whereas "northern nations, being enveloped in a dense atmosphere, and chilled by moisture from the obstructing air, have a sluggish intelligence." … Ibn Khaldun argued that the Arabians were the superior people, because their country, although in a warm zone, was surrounded by water, which exerted a cooling effect. Bodin, in the sixteenth century, found an astrological explanation for ethnic group differences. The planets, he thought, exerted their combined and best influence upon that section of the globe occupied by France, and the French, accordingly, were destined by nature to be the masters of the world. Needless to say, Ibn Khaldun was an Arab, and Bodin, a Frenchman.[24]

**STUDENTS SPEAK** "We have had a very recent example in our society of ethnocentrism: the World Cup. For one month, everyone was under the impression that the country that they, or even their ancestors, hailed from was the best, and they showed it in any way possible. Flags hung from doors, and many people wore the jerseys of their country's top players to show their pride. Emotions ran high, and with each eliminated country, there were thousands of broken hearts and shattered dreams. This is just one very recent example of how people can believe, subconsciously or even very openly, that the country that they hail from is the very best in the world."

**—Kelsey Dennehy**

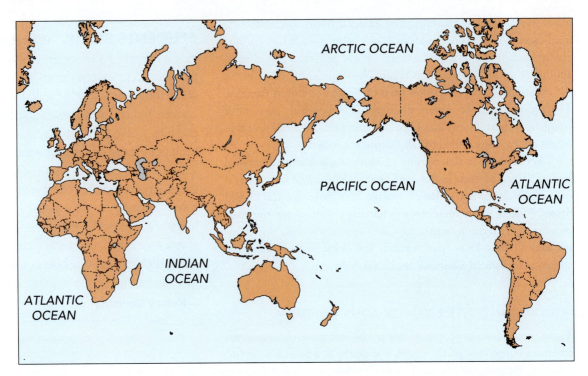

**FIGURE 1.1** Unlike most U.S. maps of the world showing the American continents on the left side, this map—a common one in many Asian countries—puts the Americas on the right. The effect is to place these countries (such as Japan) in the center and not the edge, thus emphasizing the Pacific Rim rather than the Atlantic. Such repositioning is a form of ethnocentrism, shaping perceptions of the rest of the world.

Anthropologists examining the cultures of other peoples have identified countless instances of ethnocentric attitudes. One frequent practice has been in geographic reference and mapmaking. For example, some commercially prepared Australian or Japanese world maps depicted that continent at the center in relation to the rest of the world (see Figure 1.1). Throughout world history, we can find many examples of such nationalistic ethnocentrism. European mapmakers drew world maps with Europe at the center and North Americans put their continent in the center. In Asia, the Chinese called their country the "Middle Kingdom," on the assumption their country was the center of the world.

But beyond providing a group-centered approach to living, ethnocentrism is of utmost significance in understanding motivation, attitudes, and behavior when members of racially or ethnically distinct groups interact, for it often helps explain misunderstandings, prejudice, and discrimination.

## EUROCENTRISM AND AFROCENTRISM

In recent years, many scholars and minority leaders have criticized the underrepresentation of non-European curriculum materials in the schools and colleges, calling this approach Eurocentric. **Eurocentrism** is a variation of ethnocentrism in which the content, emphasis, or both, in history, literature, and other humanities primarily, if not exclusively, concern Western culture. Critics argue that this focus, ranging from the ancient civilizations of Greece and Rome to the writings of Shakespeare, Dickens, and other English poets and authors, ignores the accomplishments and importance of other peoples.

One counterforce to Eurocentrism is **Afrocentrism**, a viewpoint that emphasizes African culture and its influence on Western civilization and the behavior of American blacks. In its moderate form, Afrocentrism is an effort to counterbalance Eurocentrism and the suppression of the African influence in American culture by teaching African

*This teacher stands among her students at the New Concept Development Center, a storefront school on Chicago's South Side. It offers an Afrocentric curriculum, with African themes infused in all subjects—English, history, math, science, and the arts. Advocates say such schools enhance educational achievement, motivation, and self-esteem .*

heritage as well.[25] In its bolder form, Afrocentrism becomes another variation of ethnocentrism. For example, a few years ago a New York professor of African American studies became embroiled in controversy when he asserted the superiority of African "sun people" over European "ice people." Others who argue that Western civilization merely reflects the black African influence on Egyptian civilization find critics who charge them with excessively distorting history.[26]

For most advocates of pluralism, however, ethnocentrism in any form produces erroneous views. What is needed is a balanced approach that is inclusive, not exclusive, of the cultures, civilizations, and contributions of all peoples, both in the school curriculum and in our thinking.

# Objectivity

When we are talking about people, usually those who differ from us, we commonly offer our own assumptions and opinions more readily than when we are discussing some other area, such as astronomy or biology. But if we are to undertake a sociological study of race and ethnicity, we must question our assumptions and opinions—everything we have always believed without question. How can we scientifically investigate a problem if we already have reached a conclusion?

Sociologists investigate many aspects of society and social behavior—including the study of minority groups, race, class, and gender—through the **scientific method**. This involves repeated objective observation, precise measurement, careful description, the formulation of theories based on the best possible explanations, and the gathering of additional information about the questions that followed from those theories. Although sociologists attempt to examine group relationships objectively, it is impossible to exclude their own subjectivity altogether. All human beings have **values**—socially shared conceptions of what is good, desirable, and proper or bad, undesirable, and improper. Because we are human, we cannot be completely objective as these values influence our orientations, actions, reactions, and interpretations. For example, selecting intergroup relations as an area of interest and concern, emphasizing the sociological perspective of this subject, and organizing the material in this book thematically all represent value judgments regarding priorities.

**Read on MySocLab**
Document: The Promises and Pitfalls of Going into the Field

Trying to be *objective* about race and ethnic relations presents a strong challenge. People tend to use selective perception, accepting only information that agrees with their values or interpreting data in a way that confirms their attitudes about other groups. Many variables in life influence people's subjectivity about minority relations. Some views may be based on personal or emotional considerations or even on false premises. Sometimes, however, reasonable and responsible people disagree on the matter in an unemotional way. Whatever the situation, the study of minority-group relations poses a challenge for objective examination.

The subject of race and ethnic relations is complex and touches our lives in many ways. As members of the groups we are studying, all readers of this book come to this subject with preconceived notions. Because many individuals have a strong tendency to tune out disagreeable information, you must make a continual effort to remain open-minded and receptive to new data.

# The Dillingham Flaw

1-5 Explain the Dillingham Flaw and why it is important in studying diversity.

Complaints about today's foreign-born presence in the United States often flow from the critics' mistaken belief that they are reaching their judgments objectively. In comparing today's supposedly non-assimilating newcomers to past immigrants, many detractors fall victim to a false logic known as the **Dillingham Flaw**.[27]

Senator William P. Dillingham chaired a congressional commission on immigration that conducted extensive hearings between 1907 and 1911 on the massive immigration then occurring. In issuing its 41-volume report, the commission erred in its interpretation of the data by using simplistic categories and unfair comparisons of past and present immigrants and by ignoring three important factors: (1) differences of technological evolution in the immigrants' countries of origin; (2) the longer interval during which past

**"Looking Backward"**

*"They desire to ban the newest arrivals at the bridge over which they and theirs arrived." Five wealthy men—from left to right, an Englishman, a German Jew, an Irishman, a German, and a Scandinavian—prevent the new immigrants from coming ashore and enjoying the same privileges they now enjoy. The shadows of the five wealthy men are representations of their social status before immigration. The Englishman's shadow is a stableman, the German Jew's is a notions peddler, and the others' are peasant farm workers. (This cartoon by Joseph Keppler appeared in* Puck *on January 11, 1893.)*

immigrants had time to acculturate; and (3) changed structural conditions in the United States wrought by industrialization and urbanization.[28]

The *Dillingham Flaw* thus refers to any inaccurate comparison based on simplistic categorizations and anachronistic judgments. It is thus faulty logic in making *incorrect assumptions about the past* and *applying stereotypes to the present to compare two groups.* The older group probably went through the same acculturation process over time. It's an apples-and-oranges approach, trying to compare two groups that are not comparable because of the time factor. To avoid the Dillingham Flaw, we must resist the temptation to use modern perceptions to explain a past that the people back then viewed differently.

Here is an illustration of this concept. Anyone who criticizes today's immigrants as being slower to Americanize, learn English, and become a cohesive part of U.S. society than did past immigrants is overlooking the reality of the past. Previous immigrant groups went through the same gradual acculturation process and encountered the same complaints. Ethnic groups held up as role models and as studies in contrast to today's immigrants were themselves once the objects of scorn and condemnation for the same reasons.

To understand what is happening today, we need to view the present in a larger context—from a sociohistorical perspective. That is, in part, the approach taken in this book. By understanding past patterns in intergroup relations, we will better comprehend what is occurring in our times, and we will avoid becoming judgmental perpetrators of the Dillingham Flaw.

**STUDENTS SPEAK** "My uncle's parents came here from Italy and worked super hard to become Americanized and make a great life for themselves and their family. My uncle is constantly making negative comparisons of present-day immigrants to the ones of the past. He believes that if people come to America, then they should be eager to learn the American way of living and pick up all of our customs and traditions, and he doesn't think that they do."
—**Joseph Cordato**

# Personal Troubles and Public Issues

Both ethnocentrism and subjectivity are commonplace in problems involving intergroup relations. In *The Sociological Imagination,* C. Wright Mills explained that an intricate connection exists between the patterns of individual lives and the larger historical context of society. Ordinary people do not realize this, however, and so view their personal troubles as private matters. Their awareness is limited to their "immediate relations with others" and "the social setting that is directly open to personal experience and to some extent [their] willful activity."[29] Personal troubles occur when individuals believe their values are threatened.

However, said Mills, what we experience in diverse social settings often results from structural changes and institutional contradictions. The individual's local environment merely reflects the public issues of the larger social structure of life. An issue is a public matter concerning segments of the public who believe that one of their cherished values is threatened.

To illustrate: If a handful of undocumented aliens are smuggled into the United States and placed in a sweatshop in virtual slavery, that is their personal trouble, and we look for a resolution of that particular problem. But if large-scale smuggling of undocumented aliens into the country occurs, resulting in an underground economy of illegal sweatshops in many locales (as indeed happens), we need "to consider the economic and political institutions of the society, not just the personal situation and character of a scatter of individuals."[30]

Similarly, if a few urban African American or Hispanic American youths drop out of school, the personal problems leading to their quitting and the means by which they secure economic stability in their lives become the focus of our attention. But if their dropout rate in most U.S. cities is consistently far greater than the national average (and it is), we must examine the economic, educational, and political issues that confront our urban

**1-6** Identify the connection between personal troubles and public issues.

institutions. These are larger issues, and we cannot resolve them by improving motivation, discipline, and opportunities for a few individuals.

Throughout this book, and particularly in the next chapter, we will examine this interplay of culture and social structure, ethnicity, and social class. What often passes for assumed group characteristics—or for individual character flaws or troubles—needs to be understood within the larger context of public issues involving the social structure and interaction patterns.

Mills also said, "All sociology worthy of the name is 'historical' sociology."[31] Agreeing with that point, I will place all groups we study within a sociohistorical perspective so that we can understand both historical and contemporary social structures that affect intergroup relations.

# The Dynamics of Intergroup Relations

1-7 Examine the dynamics of intergroup relations.

**Listen on MySocLab**
Audio: How Race Is Lived in America: Listen to Comments on Race

The study of intergroup relations is both fascinating and challenging because relationships continually change. The patterns of relating may change for many reasons: industrialization, urbanization, shifts in migration patterns, social movements, upward or downward economic trends, and so on. However, sometimes the changing relationships also reflect changing attitudes, as, for example, in the interaction between whites and Native Americans. Whites continually changed the emphasis: exploitation, extermination, isolation, segregation, paternalism, forced assimilation, and more recently, tolerance for pluralism and restoration of certain (but not all) Native American ways. Similarly, African Americans, Asian Americans, Jews, Catholics, and other minority groups all have had varying relations with the host society.

Some recent world events also illustrate changing dominant-group orientations toward minority groups. The large migrations of diverse peoples into Belgium, Denmark, France, Germany, Italy, the Netherlands, Sweden, and the United Kingdom triggered a backlash in each of those countries. Strict new laws enacted in most of these nations in the 1990s resulted in a marked increase in deportations. Violence also flared up, particularly in Germany and Italy, where neo-Nazi youths assaulted foreigners and firebombed their residences.

*The 2008–2010 recession put millions of Americans out of work and desperate to find new jobs, like these individuals waiting in line to enter a job fair at the Cleveland Convention Center in 2009. Functionalist theorists would analyze the reasons for this societal dysfunction and what adjustments may be necessary to restore equilibrium.*

Elsewhere, intergroup relations fluctuate, as between Hindus and Muslims in India, Muslims and Christians in Lebanon and Africa, Arabs and Jews in the Middle East, Sunni and Shiite Muslims in Iraq, and others. All go through varying periods of tumult and calm in their dealings with one another.

The field of race and ethnic relations has many theoreticians and investigators examining changing events and migration patterns. Each year, a vast outpouring of new research and information adds to our knowledge. New insights, new concepts, and new interpretations of old knowledge inundate the interested observer. What both the sociologist and the student must attempt to understand, therefore, is not a fixed and static phenomenon but a dynamic, ever-changing one about which we learn more all the time.

# Sociological Perspectives

Through scientific investigation, sociologists seek to determine the social forces that influence behavior as well as to identify recurring patterns that help them better understand that behavior. Using historical documents, reports, surveys, ethnographies, journalistic materials, and direct observation, they systematically gather empirical evidence about such intergroup relations. Sociologists then analyze these data to discover and describe the causes, functions, relationships, meanings, and consequences of intergroup harmony or tension. Not all sociologists agree when interpreting the data, however. Different theories, ideas, concepts, and even ideologies and prejudices may influence a sociologist's conclusions, too.

Disagreement among sociologists is no more unusual than in other areas of scientific investigation, such as physics debates about the creation of the universe, psychiatric debates on what constitutes a mental disorder, or genetic and social science debates on whether heredity or environment is more important in shaping behavior. Nonetheless, differing sociological theories play an important role in the focus of analysis and conclusions. In sociological investigation, three major perspectives shape the study of minorities: functionalist theory, conflict theory, and interactionist theory. The first two are **macrosocial theories** that focus on society itself, while the third one is a **microsocial theory** because it examines only one aspect within society. All three have a contribution to make, for each acts as a different lens that provides a distinct focus on the subject. In this book, each will serve as a basis for sociological analysis at the end of every chapter.

**1-8** Evaluate what sociological perspectives tell us about minority groups.

**Explore on MySocLab**
Activity: Applying Theory: Major Theoretical Approaches

**Watch on MySocLab**
Video: The Basics: Sociological Theory and Research

## FUNCTIONALIST THEORY

Proponents of **functionalist theory** emphasize that the various parts of society have functions, or positive effects, that promote solidarity and maintain the stability of the whole. Sometimes called *structural-functionalism*, it represents the core tradition of sociology, inspired by the writings of Auguste Comte (1798–1857), Herbert Spencer (1829–1905), and Émile Durkheim (1858–1917) in Europe, and developed further in the United States by Talcott Parsons (1902–1979) and Robert Merton (1910–2003).

Functionalists maintain that all the elements of a society should function together to maintain order and stability. Under ideal conditions, a society would be in a state of balance, with all its parts interacting harmoniously. Problems arise when parts of the social system become dysfunctional, upsetting the society's equilibrium. This system disorganization can occur for many reasons, but the most frequent cause is rapid social change. Changes in one part of the system necessitate compensatory adjustments elsewhere, but these usually do not occur fast enough, resulting in tension and conflict.

Some components of the social structure have **manifest functions** (obvious and intended results), but they often have **latent functions** (hidden and unexpected results).

For example, the obvious functions of the tourist visa program are to attract foreign visitors to build goodwill and to stimulate local economies at places they visit, thereby increasing the gross domestic product (GDP). One unintended result is thousands of visitors not returning after their visas expire and remaining here as illegal aliens.

Functionalists view dysfunctions as temporary maladjustments to an otherwise interdependent and relatively harmonious society. Because this perspective focuses on societal stability, the key issue in this analysis of social disorganization is whether to restore the equilibrium to its pre-disturbed state or to seek a new and different equilibrium. For example, how do we overcome the problem of undocumented aliens? Do we expel them to eliminate their exploitation, their alleged depression of regional wage scales, and their high costs to taxpayers in the form of health, education, and welfare benefits? Or do we grant them amnesty, help them enter the economic mainstream, and seal our borders against further undocumented entries? Whatever the solution—and these two suggestions do not exhaust the possibilities—functionalists emphasize that all problems regarding minorities can be resolved through adjustments to the social system that restore it to a state of equilibrium. Instead of major changes in the society, they prefer smaller corrections in the already functioning society.

Critics argue that because this theoretical viewpoint focuses on order and stability, it thus ignores the inequalities of gender, race, and social class that often generate tension and conflict. Those who see structural-functionalism as too conservative often favor the conflict perspective.

## CONFLICT THEORY

Proponents of **conflict theory**, influenced by Karl Marx's socioeconomic view of an elite exploiting the masses, see society as being continually engaged in a series of disagreements, tensions, and clashes as different groups compete for limited resources. They argue that the social structure fails to promote the society as a whole, as evidenced by existing social patterns benefiting some people while depriving others.

Rejecting the functionalist model of societal parts that usually work harmoniously, conflict theorists see disequilibrium and change as the norm. They examine the ongoing conflict between the dominant and subordinate groups in society—such as between whites and people of color, men and women, or native born and foreign born. Regardless of the category studied, say conflict analysts, the pattern is usually that of those with power seeking to protect their privileges and those lower on the socioeconomic level struggling to gain a greater share than they have.

Conflict theorists focus on the inequalities that generate racial and ethnic antagonisms between groups. To explain why discrimination persists, they ask this question: Who benefits? Those already in power—employers and holders of wealth and property—exploit the powerless, seeking additional profits at the expense of unassimilated minorities. Because lower wages allow higher profits, ethnic discrimination serves the interests of investors and owners by weakening workers' bargaining power.

By emphasizing economics, Marxist analysis offers penetrating insight into intergroup relations and contemporary racism and problems associated with it. Conflict theorists insist that racism has much to do with maintaining power and controlling resources. In fact, racism is an **ideology**—a set of generalized beliefs used to explain and justify the interests of those who hold them.

In this sense, **false consciousness**—holding attitudes that do not accurately reflect the objective facts of the situation—exists and it impels workers to adopt attitudes that run counter to their own real interests. If workers believe that the economic gains by workers of other groups would adversely affect their own living standards, they will not support actions to end discriminatory practices. If workers struggling to improve their situation believe other groups entrenched in better job positions are holding them back,

Conflict theorists examine inequality in society and how existing social patterns benefit some people while depriving others. That contrast is evident in this photo of homeless men living on the streets of New York City keeping warm by lying on top of a warm air vent, while the store window behind them displays warm coats they so badly need.

they will view their own gains as possible only at the expense of the better established groups. In both cases, the wealthy and powerful benefit by pitting exploited workers of different racial and ethnic groups against each other, causing each to have strong negative feelings about the other. This distorted view stirs up conflict and occasional outbursts of violence between groups, preventing workers from recognizing their common bond of joint oppression and uniting to overcome it.[32]

Critics contend that this theoretical viewpoint focuses too much on inequality and thus ignores the achieved unity of a society through the social cement of shared values and mutual interdependence among its members. Those who see conflict theory as too radical often favor the functionalist perspective. Still other critics reject both of these macrosocial theories as too broad and favor instead an entirely different approach, as explained in the next section.

## INTERACTIONIST THEORY

A third theoretical approach, **interactionist theory**, examines the microsocial world of personal interaction patterns in everyday life rather than the macrosocial aspects of social institutions and their harmony or conflict. **Symbolic interaction**—the shared symbols and definitions people use when communicating with one another—provides the focus for understanding how individuals create and interpret the life situations they experience. Symbols—our spoken language, expressions, body language, tone of voice, appearance, and images of television and other mass media—are what constitute our social worlds.[33] Through these symbols we communicate, create impressions, and develop understandings of the surrounding world. Symbolic interaction theories are useful in understanding race and ethnic relations because they assume that minority groups are responsive and creative rather than passive.[34]

Essential to this perspective is how people define their reality through a process called the **social construction of reality**.[35] Individuals create a background against which to understand their separate actions and interactions with others. Taken-for-granted routines emerge on the basis of shared expectations. Participants see this socially constructed world as legitimate by virtue of its "objective" existence. In other words, people create cultural products: material artifacts, social institutions, ideologies, and so on (*externalization*).

A November 2009 photo showing President Obama bowing to Japanese Emperor Akihito at the Imperial Palace in Tokyo led critics to complain about a U.S. president bowing to a foreign leader (he was not the first to do so). In Japanese culture though, this is an act of respect. Interactionists often study misunderstandings arising from cultural differences.

Over time, they lose awareness of having created their own social and cultural environment (*objectification*), and subsequently, they learn these supposedly objective facts of reality through the socialization process (*internalization*).

The interactionist perspective can be particularly helpful in understanding some of the false perceptions that occur in dominant–minority relations. As we will discuss shortly, racism is a good example of the social construction of reality. In addition to its focus on shared understandings among members of the same group, this viewpoint also provides insight into misunderstandings about different groups. One example is the oft-heard complaint that today's immigrants do not want to learn English or assimilate. Those who so believe offer as evidence the presence of foreign-language media programs or signs in stores and other public places, they cite overheard conversations in languages other than English and/or differences in dress, or they point to residential ethnic clusters where "non-American" customs and practices, along with language, seemingly prevent assimilation. Critics often link such complaints with a comparison to previous immigrants, typically European, who were not like this and who chose to assimilate rather than remain apart from the rest of society.

In reality, such people fail to realize that they simply are witnessing a new version of a common pattern among all immigrants who come to the United States. They create in their minds a reality about the newcomers' subculture as being permanent instead of temporary, whereas their positive role model of past immigrant groups assimilating was actually seen by other nativists back then as also not assimilating, for the same reasons cited today. Interactionists would thus examine this reality that people create, the meaning they attach to that subjective reality, and how it affects their interactions with one another.

Critics complain that this focus on everyday interactions neglects the important roles played by culture and social structure and the critical elements of class, gender, and race. Interactionists say they do not ignore the macro-elements of society but that, by definition, a society is a structure in which people interact, and why and how they do that needs investigation and explanation.

Perhaps it would be most helpful if you viewed all three theoretical perspectives as different camera lenses looking at the same reality. Whether a wide-angle lens (a macrosocial view) or a telephoto lens (a microsocial view), each has something to reveal, and together, they offer a more complete understanding of society. Table 1.2 summarizes the three sociological perspectives just discussed.

## Retrospect

Human beings follow certain patterns when responding to strangers. Their perceptions of newcomers reflect categoric knowing. If they perceive that the newcomers are similar, people are more receptive to their presence. What makes interaction with strangers difficult is the varying perceptions of each to the other, occasioned by a lack of shared

**Explore on MySocLab**
Activity: Demographic Changes: Fifty Years in Brooklyn

**TABLE 1.2** Sociological Perspectives

| Emphasis | FUNCTIONALIST<br>Macrosocial View | CONFLICT<br>Macrosocial View | INTERACTIONIST<br>Microsocial View |
|---|---|---|---|
| *View of Society* | Focus on a cooperative social system of interrelated parts that is relatively stable. | Focus on society as continually engaged in a series of disagreements, tensions, and clashes. | Focus on the microsocial world of personal interaction patterns in everyday life. |
| *Interaction Processes* | Societal elements function together to maintain order, stability, and equilibrium. | Conflict is inevitable since there is always a societal elite and an oppressed group. | Shared symbols and definitions provide the basis for interpreting life experiences. |
| *Interaction Results* | Societal dysfunctions result from temporary disorganization or maladjustment. | Disequilibrium and change are the norm because of societal inequalities. | An internalized social construction of reality makes it seem to be objective fact. |
| *Reason for Problems* | Rapid social change is the most frequent cause of loss of societal equilibrium. | False consciousness allows the ruling elite to maintain power and benefit from exploitation. | Shared expectations and understandings, or their absence, explain intergroup relations. |
| *How to Improve Society* | Necessary adjustments will restore the social system to equilibrium. | Group struggle against oppression is necessary to effect social change. | Better intercultural awareness will improve interaction patterns. |

understandings and perceptions of reality. Social distance is one means of determining the level of a group's social acceptance.

By definition, minority groups—regardless of their size—receive unequal treatment, possess identifying physical or cultural characteristics held in low esteem, are conscious of their shared ascribed status, and tend to practice endogamy. Racial groups are biologically similar groups, and ethnic groups are groups that share a learned cultural heritage. Intergroup relations are dynamic and continually changing.

Ethnocentrism—the tendency to identify with one's own group—is a universal human condition that contributes to potential problems in relating to outgroups. Examples of ethnocentric thinking and actions can be found in all countries throughout history. Eurocentrism and Afrocentrism are views emphasizing one culture or civilization over others.

The study of minorities presents a difficult challenge because our value orientations and life experiences can impair our objectivity. Even trained sociologists, being human, encounter difficulty in maintaining value neutrality. Indeed, some people argue that sociologists should take sides and not attempt a sterile approach to the subject. The Dillingham Flaw—using an inaccurate comparison based on simplistic categorizations and anachronistic judgments—seriously undermines the scientific worth of supposedly objective evaluations. Both ethnocentrism and subjectivity are commonplace in problems involving intergroup relations. Clearer understanding occurs by examining the larger context of how so-called personal troubles connect with public issues.

In the sociological investigation of minorities, three perspectives shape analysis. Functionalist theory stresses the orderly interdependence of a society and the adjustments needed to restore equilibrium when dysfunctions occur. Conflict theory emphasizes the tensions and conflicts that result from exploitation and competition for limited resources. Interactionist theory concentrates on everyday interaction patterns operating within a socially constructed perception of reality.

# On MySocLab

✓ Study and Review on MySocLab

## KEY TERMS

## DISCUSSION QUESTIONS

1. Can you offer any examples of social distance or ethno-centrism from your own experiences and/or observations with family, friends, or neighbors, on campus or at work?
2. How does the similarity–attraction concept help us to understand intergroup relations?
3. What is ethnocentrism? Why is it important in relations between dominant and minority groups?
4. Why is objective study of racial and ethnic minorities difficult?
5. What about the Dillingham Flaw? Have you ever heard comments from anyone about other minorities that would illustrate this flawed thinking?
6. How does a minority group differ from an ethnic group? How does a race differ from an ethnic group?
7. What are the main points of the functionalist, conflict, and interactionist theories?

## INTERNET ACTIVITIES

1. In the world community, through the United Nations, the rights and liberties that all should enjoy have been formalized in the Universal Declaration of Human Rights (http://www.un.org/rights/50/decla.htm). Read this important document. What similarities do you find in it with the Declaration of Independence and the U.S. Constitution? Can you identify specific violations of it in the situation of minorities in the United States?
2. To learn more about the social construction of race (page 10), go to "Confusion about Human Races" for a forum on the subject sponsored by the Social Science Research Council (http://raceandgenomics.ssrc.org/Lewontin). Share with classmates something you learned from this source.

# Culture and Social Structure

((( **Listen** to Chapter 2 on **MySocLab**

Ethnic celebrations, whether festivals or parades, typically provide a colorful display of native costumes, music, dance, and other traditions, as illustrated by these participants in the Philippines Independence Day parade on Madison Avenue in New York City. Such happy events reaffirm ethnic identity, bonding, and pride in one's heritage.

## LEARNING OBJECTIVES | After reading this chapter you will be able to:

**2-1** Explain how culture impacts on one's perceptions.

**2-2** Examine how culture changes and spreads.

**2-3** Explain how structural conditions affect intergroup relations.

**2-4** Explain how stratification also affects intergroup relations.

**2-5** Evaluate the role of social class in intergroup relations.

**2-6** Examine factors that underlie intergroup conflict.

**2-7** Explain how sociology helps us understand ethnic stratification.

**2-8** Understand the existence of a White culture.

25

Understanding what makes people receptive to some, but not all, strangers requires knowledge of how culture and social structure affect perceptions and response patterns. Culture provides the guidelines for people's interpretations of situations they encounter and for the responses they consider appropriate. **Social structure**—the organized patterns of behavior among the basic components of a social system—establishes relatively predictable social relationships among the different peoples in a society. The distinctions and interplay between culture and social structure are important to the assimilation process as well. For example, cultural orientations of both minority and dominant groups shape expectations about how a minority group should fit into the society.

This chapter first examines the various aspects of culture that affect dominant–minority relations. We then discuss the significance of social class within the social structure. Next, we'll look at cultural differentiation and structural differentiation as bases for conflict, followed by a discussion about white culture.

## The Concept of Culture

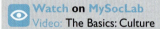

**2-1** Explain how culture impacts on one's perceptions.

**Watch on MySocLab**
Video: **The Basics: Culture**

Human beings create their own social worlds and evolve further within them. Adapting to the environment, to new knowledge, and to technology, we learn a way of life within our society. We invent and share rules and patterns of behavior that shape our lives and the way we experience the world about us. The shared products of society that we call *culture*, whether material or nonmaterial, make social life possible and give our lives meaning. **Material culture** consists of all physical objects created by members of a society and the meanings/significance attached to them (for example, cars, cell phones, DVDs, iPods, high-top sneakers, or clothing). **Nonmaterial culture** consists of abstract human creations and their meanings/significance in life (such as attitudes, beliefs, customs, ideas, languages, lifestyles, norms, social institutions, and values). **Culture**, then, consists of all of these elements shared by members of a society and transmitted to the next generation.

These cultural attributes provide a sense of peoplehood and common bonds through which members of a society can relate (see the Reality Check box). Most sociologists therefore emphasize the impact of culture in shaping behavior.[1] Through language and other forms of symbolic interaction, the members of a society learn the thought and behavior patterns that constitute their commonality as a people.[2] In this sense, culture is the social cement that binds a society together.

*A Knighthawk helicopter departs after bringing supplies to Indonesian victim of the 2005 tsunami that ravaged so many areas in Southeast Asia. Humanitarianism, one of the strong American core values, was readily evident in donations from millions of Americans, and in the relief efforts of U.S. nonprofit organizations and the military.*

# REALITY check

## Basic U.S. Values

Within the diverse U.S. society of racial, ethnic, and religious groups, each with their own distinctive set of values, are the common core of values that define American culture. Numerous social scientists have created lists of these value orientations. Although some small differences occur among them, a general consensus does exist as to which ones serve as the foundation of American beliefs, behaviors, social goal definitions, and life expectations.

Foremost among these are **freedom** and **independence**, the cherishing of personal rights in contrast to domination by others. Closely aligned to these two values are two others, **equality** and **self-reliance**; we relate to one another informally as equals and believe everyone should work, and that anyone who does not is lazy. Accordingly, we are **competition-oriented**, and place a high value on **achievement** and **success**, in terms of power, prestige, and wealth.

In subscribing to these values, Americans also adopt other cultural orientations to complement them. These include a reliance on **science** and **rationality**, that technology—whether existing or still to be developed—can help us master the environment, create ever-better lifestyles, and solve all problems. Perhaps not surprisingly, we also place importance on **efficiency**, **practicality**, and **openness**. Both in communication style and approach to problems, Americans tend to be direct, seeking the quickest means to inform others or resolve issues.

Although other societies may subscribe to many of these values as well, this particular combination of values—virtually present from the nation's founding—have had and continue to have enormous impact in shaping U.S. society.

Shared cultural norms encourage solidarity and orient the behavior of members of the ingroup. **Norms** are a culture's rules of conduct—internalized by the members—embodying the society's fundamental expectations. Through norms, ingroup members (majority or minority) know how to react toward the acts of outgroup members that surprise, shock, or annoy them or in any way go against their shared expectations. Anything contrary to this "normal" state is seen as negative or deviant. When minority-group members "act uppity" or "don't know their place," majority-group members often get upset and sometimes act out their anger. Violations of norms usually trigger strong reactions because they appear to threaten the social fabric of a community or society. Eventually, most minority groups adapt their distinctive cultural traits to those of the host society through a process called **acculturation**. Intragroup variations remain, though, because ethnic-group members use different reference groups as role models.

An important component of intragroup cultural variations, seldom a part of the acculturation process, is religion. Indeed, not only does religion have strong links to the immigrant experience in the United States, as well as to African American slavery and pacification efforts toward Native Americans, but it also has many other connections to prejudice and social conflict. As subsequent chapters detail, the Catholic and Jewish faiths of past European immigrants often provoked nativist Protestant reactions, some quite violent and vicious. Similarly, recent immigrants who are believers of such religions as Hinduism, Islam, Rastafarianism, or Santería often experience prejudice and conflict because of their faith, as have the Amish, Mormons, Quakers, and many others in the United States in past years. Religious conflict is a sad reality in many parts of the world—the Balkans, India, and the Middle East, to mention just a few.

Professional sports are another part of culture that provides an area for the study of prejudice and racism. Long excluded from major league sports, people of color now are prominent participants in baseball, basketball, boxing, football, and track (see Table 2.1).

**TABLE 2.1**  Racial and Ethnic Demographics in U.S. Professional Sports

| Players | NATIONAL BASKETBALL ASSOCIATION | | NATIONAL FOOTBALL LEAGUE | | MAJOR LEAGUE BASEBALL | |
|---|---|---|---|---|---|---|
| | 2001–2002 | 2011–2012 | 1999 | 2011 | 2002 | 2013 |
| White | 20% | 18% | 32% | 31% | 60% | 61% |
| Black | 78% | 78% | 67% | 67% | 10% | 8% |
| Latino | 1% | 3% | <1% | 1% | 28% | 28% |
| Asian | <1% | <1% | 0% | 2% | 2% | 2% |
| Other | 0% | <1% | <1% | 1% | 0% | <1% |
| **Head Coach or Manager** | 2001–2002 | 2011–2012 | 2001 | 2012 | 2002 | 2013 |
| White | 52% | 47% | 94% | 81% | 68% | 87% |
| Black | 48% | 47% | 6% | 16% | 26% | 10% |
| Latino | 0% | 3% | 0% | 0% | 6% | 3% |
| Asian | 0% | 3% | 0% | 3% | 0% | 0% |

*Source:* The Institute for Diversity and Ethics in Sport, *The Racial and Gender Report Card*, 2013.

Nevertheless, the vast majority of owners, managers, and head coaches in all sports are white.[3]

U.S. colleges continue to provide limited opportunities for people of color at the top management level. In 2012, white men held 92 of the 120 athletic director positions at Football Bowl Subdivision (FBS) schools (formerly Division I-A). Women athletic directors comprised 3.3 percent. The percentage of head coaches of color was a record 15.4 percent.[4] Lagging far behind professional sports regarding equal opportunities for the top jobs, college sports still need to do more to overcome embedded cultural biases.

## THE REALITY CONSTRUCT

Our perception of reality is related to our culture: Through our culture, we learn how to perceive the world about us. Cultural definitions help us interpret the sensory stimuli from our environment and tell us how to respond to them. In other words, culture helps us "make sense" of what we encounter. It is the screen through which we "see" and "understand" (Figure 2.1).

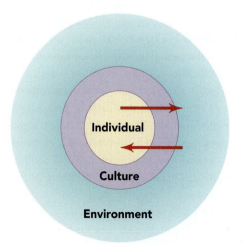

Each **Individual** observes the world through **Sense Perceptions**, which are evaluated in terms of **Culture** — values, attitudes, customs, and beliefs.

**FIGURE 2.1**  Cultural Reality

Fredi González, who is the manager of the Atlanta Braves, was born in Havana, Cuba, and grew up in Miami. With a steadily increasing number of Latino ballplayers (approximately 350) in Major League Baseball, he is one of only the few Latino managers for the 2013 season, but that number will likely increase in future years.

**LANGUAGE AND OTHER SYMBOLS.** Culture is learned behavior, acquired chiefly through verbal communication, or language. A word is nothing more than a symbol—something that stands for something else. Whether it is tangible (*chair*) or intangible (*honesty*), the word represents a mental concept that is based on empirical reality. Words reflect culture, however, and one word may have different meanings in different cultures. If you are *carrying the torch* in England, you are holding a flashlight, not yearning for a lost love; if you could use a *lift*, you want an elevator, not a ride or a boost to your spirits. Because words symbolically interpret the world to us, the **linguistic relativity** of language may connote both intended and unintended prejudicial meanings. For example, *black* is the symbol for darkness (in the sense of lightlessness) or evil, and *white* symbolizes cleanliness or goodness; and a society may subtly (or not so subtly) transfer these meanings to black and white people.

Walter Lippmann, a prominent political columnist, once remarked, "First we look, then we name, and only then do we see." He meant that until we learn the symbols of our world, we cannot understand the world. A popular pastime in the early 1950s, called "Droodles," illustrates Lippmann's point. The object was to interpret drawings such as those in Figure 2.2. Many people were unable to see the meaning of the drawings until it was explained. They looked but did not see until they knew the "names." Can you guess what these drawings depict before looking up this endnote?[5]

Interpreting symbols is not merely an amusing game; it is significant in real life. Human beings do not respond to stimuli but to their definitions of those stimuli as

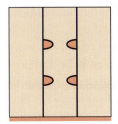 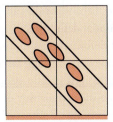 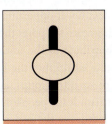 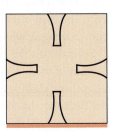

**FIGURE 2.2** "Droodles"

mediated by their culture.[6] The definition of beauty is one example. Beyond the realm of personal taste, definitions of beauty have cultural variations. For instance, in different times and places, societies have based their appraisal of a woman's beauty on her having scar markings, tattoos, or beauty marks or on how plump or thin she was.

Nonverbal communication—or body language—is highly important, too. Body movements, gestures, physical proximity, facial expressions (there are as many as 136 facial expressions, each of which conveys a distinct meaning),[7] and **paralinguistic signals** (sounds but not words, such as a sigh, a kiss-puckering sound, or the *m-m-m* sound of tasting something good) all convey information to the observer–listener. Body language is important in intergroup relations, too, whether in conversation, interaction, or perception. Body language may support or belie one's words; it may suggest friendliness, aloofness, or deference.

Although some forms of body language are fairly universal (for example, most facial expressions), many cultural variations exist in body language itself and in the interpretation of its meanings. Body movements such as posture, bearing, and gait vary from culture to culture. The degree of formality in a person's environment (both past and present) and other cultural factors influence such forms of nonverbal communication. Consider the different meanings one could attach to a student's unwillingness to look directly into the eyes of a teacher. In the United States, the teacher may assume that this behavior reflects embarrassment, guilt, shyness, inattention, or even disrespect. Yet if the student is Asian or Hispanic, such demeanor is a mark of respect. The symbol's definition, in this case the teacher's interpretation of what the student's body language means, determines the meaning the observer ascribes to it.

A person who is foreign to a culture must learn both its language and the rest of its symbol system, as the members born into that culture did through socialization. Certain gestures may be signs of friendliness in one culture but obscene or vengeful symbols in another. For example, in the United States, placing thumb and forefinger in a circle with the other fingers upraised indicates that everything is fine, but in Japan, this sign refers to money, and in Greece, it is an insulting anal expression.[8] Kisses, tears, dances, emblems, silence, open displays of emotions, and thousands of other symbols can and often do have divergent meanings in different cultures. Symbols, including language, help an ingroup construct a reality that may be unknown to or altogether different for an outgroup. Members of one group may then select, reject, ignore, or distort their sensory input regarding the other group because of cultural definitions.

**THE THOMAS THEOREM.** William I. Thomas once observed that if people define situations as real, those situations become real in their consequences.[9] His statement, known as the **Thomas theorem**, relates directly to the *Dillingham Flaw* discussed in the first chapter. Whereas Thomas emphasized how definitions lead to actions that produce consequences to conform to the original, ill-founded definition, the Dillingham Flaw suggests the misguided thought process that may result in that definition in the first place.

The Thomas theorem is thus further testimony to the truth of reality constructs: Human beings respond to their definitions of stimuli rather than to the stimuli themselves. People often associate images (for example, "terrorists" or "illegal aliens") with specific minority groups. They then behave according to the meaning they assign to the situation, and the consequences of their behavior could serve to reaffirm the meaning; the definition becomes a self-fulfilling prophecy. For example, when whites define blacks as inferior and then offer them fewer opportunities because of that alleged inferiority, blacks are disadvantaged, which in turn supports the initial definition.

Several variables contribute to the initial definition, but culture is one of the most important of these. Culture establishes the framework through which an individual perceives others, classifies them into groups, and assigns certain general characteristics to them. Because ethnocentrism leads people to consider their way of life as being the best and most natural, their culturally defined perceptions of others often lead to suspicion and differential treatment of other groups. In effect, each group constructs myths about other groups and supports those myths through ingroup solidarity and outgroup hostility. In such instances, people create a culturally determined world of reality, and their actions reinforce their beliefs. Social interaction or social change may counteract such situations, however, leading to their redefinition.

Social scientists have long known how cultural definitions can influence perception. For example, more than a half century ago, within a two-month period, Gregory Razran twice showed the same set of 30 pictures of unknown young women to the same group of 100 male college students and 50 noncollege men. Using a five-point scale, the subjects rated each woman's beauty, character, intelligence, ambition, and general likeability. At the first presentation, the pictures had no ethnic identification, but at the second presentation, they were labeled with Irish, Italian, Jewish, and old American (English) surnames. All women were rated equally on the first presentation, but when the names were given, the ratings changed. The "Jewish" women received higher ratings in ambition and intelligence. Both "Jewish" and "Italian" women suffered a large decline in general likeability and a slight decline in beauty and character evaluations.[10] This study is one of many illustrating how cultural definitions affect judgments about others.

Through **cultural transmission**, each generation transmits its culture to the next generation, which learns those cultural definitions at an early age. This fact is expressed dramatically in the Rodgers and Hammerstein musical *South Pacific*. The tragic subplot is the touching romance between Lieutenant Cable and the young Tonkinese woman Liat. Although Cable and Liat are deeply in love, Cable's friends remind him that the couple's life would not be the same in the United States. Their differences in race and culture would work against a happy marriage for them, as would his own acceptance in Philadelphia high society. Miserable because of the choice his cultural values force him to make, he sings "Carefully Taught," a poignant song about how prejudice is taught to children.

Within the cynical lyrics are statements about adults continually teaching children to fear and hate; that from year to year they are conditioning children to be afraid of those with differently shaped eyes or skin colors; and that they must teach children to hate all people that their family members hate. This shaping of children's attitudes must be done before it's "too late." Implied by that last point is that family members need to teach prejudice to children before they are of school age and begin to develop their own viewpoints through education and social interactions. As contained in the show, the song is a rebuke of this practice even as it explains the process.

These lyrics reinforce the reality construct discussed earlier and illustrated in Figure 2.1. From family, friends, school, mass media, and all other sources of informational input, we learn our values, attitudes, and beliefs. Some of our learning reflects the prejudices of others, which we may incorporate in our own attitudes and actions.

## Cultural Change

Culture continually changes. Discoveries, inventions, technological advances, innovations, and natural disasters alter the customs, values, attitudes, and beliefs of a society. This section focuses on two common processes of cultural change: cultural diffusion within a whole society and changes within a particular subculture of that society.

**2-2** Examine how culture changes and spreads.

### CULTURAL DIFFUSION

Even if the members of a dominant culture wish to keep their society untainted by contact with foreign elements, cultures are influenced inevitably by other cultures—a phenomenon termed **cultural diffusion**. Ideas, inventions, and practices spread from one culture

*An excellent example of culture diffusion and cultural change is mobile phone texting, which only began in the 1990s and was widely used in Europe before it became popular in the United States. Even today, 80 percent of Europeans send text messages compared to about 60 percent in North America, although that gap is rapidly closing.*

to another, but they may do so at different rates, depending on societal attitudes, conditions, and the distance between groups. Sometimes material culture objects get modified or reinterpreted, such as when some native Latin American tribes of the early twentieth century showed a unique fondness for automobile tires, using them to make sandals, for they neither owned nor drove cars.[11]

**BORROWED ELEMENTS.** U.S. anthropologist Ralph Linton calculated that any given culture contains about 90 percent borrowed elements. To demonstrate both the unrealized enormity and subtlety of cultural diffusion, he offered a classic portrait of the "100 percent American" male:

> Our solid American citizen awakens in a bed built on a pattern which originated in the Near East but which was modified in Northern Europe before it was transmitted to America. He throws back covers made from cotton, domesticated in India, or linen, domesticated in the Near East, or wool, from sheep, also domesticated in the Near East, or silk, the use of which was discovered in China. All of these materials have been spun or woven by processes invented in the Near East. He slips into his moccasins, invented by the Indians of the Eastern woodlands, and goes to the bathroom, whose fixtures are a mixture of European and American inventions, both of recent date. He takes off his pajamas, a garment invented in India, and washes with soap, invented by the ancient Gauls. He then shaves, a masochistic rite which seems to have been derived from either Sumer or ancient Egypt.
>
> Returning to the bedroom, he removes his clothes from a chair of southern European type and proceeds to dress. He puts on garments whose form originally derived from the skin clothing of the nomads of the Asiatic steppes, puts on shoes made from skins tanned by a process invented in ancient Egypt and cut to a pattern derived from the classical civilizations of the Mediterranean, and ties around his neck a strip of bright-colored cloth which is a vestigial survival of the shoulder shawls worn by the seventeenth-century Croatians. Before going out for breakfast, he glances through the window, made of glass invented in Egypt, and if it is raining puts on overshoes made of rubber discovered by the Central American Indians and takes an umbrella, invented in southeastern Asia. Upon his head, he puts a hat made of felt, a material invented in the Asiatic steppes.

On his way to breakfast, he stops to buy a paper, paying for it with coins, an ancient Lydian invention. At the restaurant, a whole new series of borrowed elements confronts him. His plate is made of a form of pottery invented in China. His knife is of steel, an alloy first made in southern India, his fork a medieval Italian invention, and his spoon a derivative of a Roman original. He begins breakfast with an orange, from the eastern Mediterranean, a cantaloupe from Persia, or perhaps a piece of African watermelon. With this he has coffee, an Abyssinian plant, with cream and sugar. Both the domestication of cows and the idea of milking them originated in the Near East, while sugar was first made in India. After his fruit and first coffee, he goes on to waffles, cakes made by a Scandinavian technique from wheat domesticated in Asia Minor. Over these, he pours maple syrup, invented by the Indians of the Eastern woodlands. As a side dish, he may have the egg of a species of bird domesticated in Indo-China, or thin strips of the flesh of an animal domesticated in Eastern Asia, which have been salted and smoked by a process developed in northern Europe.

When our friend has finished eating he settles back to smoke, an American Indian habit, consuming a plant domesticated in Brazil in either a pipe, derived from the Indians of Virginia, or a cigarette, derived from Mexico. If he is hardy enough, he may even attempt a cigar, transmitted to us from the Antilles by way of Spain. While smoking, he reads the news of the day, imprinted in characters invented by the ancient Semites upon a material invented in China by a process invented in Germany. As he absorbs the accounts of foreign troubles, he will, if he is a good conservative citizen, thank a Hebrew deity in an Indo-European language that he is 100 percent American.*

Typically, cultural diffusion is widespread in our pluralistic society. It can take many forms, including widened food preferences such as tacos or burritos or U.S. corporations using the Japanese management technique of employee participation in setting work goals. Whatever its form, cultural diffusion is an ongoing process that influences a society and sometimes even alters our views of other cultures.

**CULTURAL CONTACT.** Culture also can undergo change when people of different cultures come into contact with one another. Because people tend to take their own culture for granted, it operates at a subconscious level in forming their expectations. When assumptions are jolted through contact with an unfamiliar culture, people often experience **culture shock**, characterized by feelings of disorientation, anxiety, and a sense of being threatened.

Culture shock does not occur always. When people of two different cultures interact, many possible patterns can emerge. The two groups may peacefully coexist, with gradual cultural diffusion occurring. History offers some excellent examples of connections between migrations and innovations, wherein geographic conditions and native attitudes determined the extent to which a group resisted cultural innovations, despite invasions, settlements, or missionary work. The persistent pastoral lifestyle of Bedouin tribes and the long-sustained resistance to industrialization by Native Americans are two examples.

Some social scientists suggest that power alone determines the outcome, causing one group to become dominant and the other subservient.[12] If the native population becomes subordinate, the changes to its social organization can be devastating. No longer possessing the flexibility and autonomy it once enjoyed, it may suffer material deprivation and find its institutions undermined. If the migratory group finds itself in the subordinate position, it must adapt to its new environment to survive. Most commonly, this minority group draws from its familiar world as it attempts to cope with the prevailing conditions. Group

---

*Ralph Linton, *The Study of Man* (1936), pp. 326–27. Reprinted by permission of the author and Prentice Hall, Inc., Upper Saddle River, NJ.

members form a subculture with unique behavior and interests—neither completely those of the larger society nor fully those of their old culture. For example, both Catholicism and Judaism have undergone significant changes in form and expression since taking root in the United States. In other words, U.S. ethnic subcultures typically blend elements of their homeland culture and the dominant U.S. culture as group members adapt to their new environment.

## SUBCULTURES

Usually, immigrants follow a pattern of **chain migration**, settling in an area already containing family, friends, or compatriots who located there earlier. An ethnic community evolves, providing an emotional support system to these strangers in a strange land as they strive to forge a better life for themselves. Part of this process of cultural insulation among others like themselves is the re-creation in miniature of the world they left behind. Thus, **parallel social institutions**—their own clubs, organizations, newspapers, stores, churches, and schools duplicating those of the host society—appear, creating cohesiveness within the minority subculture, whether it is an immigrant or native-born grouping.

As **ethnic subcultures** among immigrants in the United States evolve in response to conditions within the host society, the immigrants sometimes develop a group consciousness unknown in their old countries. Many first-generation Americans possess a village orientation toward their homeland rather than a national identity. They may speak different dialects, feud with other regions, and have different values, but their common experience in the United States causes them to coalesce into a national grouping. One example is Italian Americans, who initially identified with their cities of origin: Calabria, Palermo, Naples, Genoa, Salerno, and so on. Within a generation, many came to view themselves as Italians, partly because the host society classified them as such.

Yet even as a newly arrived group forges its community and subculture, a process called **ethnogenesis** occurs.[13] Shaped partly by the core culture in selectively absorbing some elements and modifying others, the group also retains, modifies, or drops elements from its cultural heritage as it adapts to its new country. The result is a distinctive new ethnic group unlike others in the host country, dominant or minority, but also somewhat different from the people who still live in the group's homeland. Thus, first-generation German Americans, for example, differ from other ethnic groups and from native-born U.S. citizens, but they also possess cultural traits and values that distinguish them from nonmigrating Germans.

**CONVERGENT SUBCULTURES.** Some ethnic subcultures are **convergent subcultures**; that is, they tend toward assimilation with the dominant society. Although recognizable by residential clustering and adherence to the language, dress, and cultural norms of their native land, these ethnic groups nonetheless eventually assimilate. As the years pass—possibly across several generations—the distinctions between the dominant culture and the convergent subculture gradually lessen. Eventually, this form of subculture becomes completely integrated into the dominant culture.

Because the subculture is undergoing change, its members may experience problems of **marginality**—living under stress in two cultures simultaneously. The older generation may seek to preserve its traditions and heritage, whereas the younger generation may be

**STUDENTS SPEAK** "My parents came from Haiti and decided to settle in the same Florida area of family members and friends, similar to the reading in the book about chain migration. Growing up there, my experience with people of my subculture was wonderful. We looked out for and helped each other whenever someone had a problem. I did not experience any culture shock in that environment because the people there were all familiar faces."

**—Jean Colas**

**STUDENTS SPEAK** "If you ever drive around the southern part of Paterson, you will encounter Arabic markets, restaurants, cafes, barbers, and salons. Most of the people hanging outside during the summer at night are Middle Eastern men, sitting at tables, and drinking tea. I love this side of town! They have their own parallel social institutions (clubs, stores, organizations, etc.). They are basically replicating from where they originally migrated, just as the book says, by re-creating a miniature world of what they might have left behind."

**—Marleny Sanchez**

*Ethnic neighborhoods, such as this Pakistani one in Brooklyn, New York, are distinct in the visible sights and bustling activities of their first-generation residents. Outsiders often mistakenly assume such areas will remain as they are, but usually the people are part of a convergent subculture who eventually move out, replaced by a different group.*

impatient to achieve full acceptance within the dominant society. Because of the impetus toward assimilation, time obviously favors the younger generation. The Dutch, German, and Irish subcultures are examples of once-prevalent ethnic subcultures that are barely visible today; Italian, Polish, and Slovak subcultures have also begun to converge more fully. These nationality groups still exhibit ethnic pride in many ways, but, for the most part, they are no longer set apart by place of residence or subcultural behavior. Because of their multigenerational length of residence, these nationality groups are less likely to live in clustered housing arrangements or to display behavior patterns such as conflict, deviance, or endogamy to any greater degree than the rest of the majority group.

**PERSISTENT SUBCULTURES.** Not all subcultures assimilate. Some even do not desire to do so, and others, particularly non-white groups, face difficulties in assimilating. These unassimilated subcultures are known as **persistent subcultures**. Some adhere as much as possible to their own way of life, resisting absorption into the dominant culture. Religious groups such as the Amish, some Hutterites, and Hasidic Jews reject modernity and insist on maintaining their traditional ways of life; they may represent the purest form of a persistent subculture in U.S. society. Other ethnic groups adopt a few aspects of the dominant culture but adamantly preserve their own way of life; examples are most Native Americans who live on reservations and many *Hispanos* (Spanish Americans) in the Southwest. Chinatowns also support preservation of the Chinese way of life in many ways.

A minority group's insistence on the right to be different usually has not been well received among dominant-group members. This clash of wills sometimes leads to conflict; at the very least, it invites stereotyping and prejudice on both sides.

Just as convergent subcultures illustrate assimilation, persistent subcultures illustrate pluralism. We will examine these two forms of minority integration in Chapter 4.

## Structural Conditions

Relations between dominant and minority groups are influenced as much by structural conditions as by differences in culture. The nature of the social structure influences not only the distribution of power resources (economic, political, and social), but also

**2-3** Explain how structural conditions affect intergroup relations.

**Explore on MySocLab**
Activity: How Class Works

*Some neighborhoods—usually an ethnic enclave of a religious community, such as this Hasidic one in New York's Williamsburg section—contain the social institutions and homes of a persistent subculture. Unlike neighborhoods of convergent subcultures, these are more likely to retain their ethnic characteristics for multiple generations.*

the accessibility of those resources to groups who seek upward mobility. An expanding economy and an open social system create increased opportunities for minority-group members, thereby reducing the likelihood that tensions will arise. In contrast, a stagnant or contracting economy thwarts many efforts to improve status and antagonizes those who feel most threatened by another group's competition for scarce resources. Such a situation may serve as a breeding ground for conflicts *among minority groups* even more than between majority and minority groups. This could occur because both minority groups may view the other as an economic threat.

The state of the economy is only one important structural factor influencing the opportunities for upward mobility. Another is the degree of change between a minority group's old society and the new one. A person who leaves an agrarian society for an industrial one is poorly prepared to enter any but the lowest social stratum in a low-paying position. Opportunities for upward mobility may exist, however, if the new land's economy is growing rapidly. In this sense, the structural conditions in the United States from 1880 to 1920 were better for unskilled immigrants than are conditions today. Low-skill jobs are less plentiful today, and an unskilled worker's desire to support a family through hard work may not be matched by the opportunity to do so.

Meanwhile, technological advances have made the world smaller. Rapid transportation and communications (radio, television, telephone, computers, the Internet, fax machines, and e-mail) permit stronger ties to other parts of the world than in the past.[14] Accessibility to their homeland, friends, or relatives may make people less interested in becoming fully assimilated in a new land. Befriending strangers in the new country becomes less necessary. In addition, people's greater knowledge of the world, the rising social consciousness of a society, and the structural opportunities for mobility all help to create a more hospitable environment for minority-group members.

**2-4** Explain how stratification also affects intergroup relations.

**Read on MySocLab**
Document: Witnesses to Hunger

## Stratification

**Social stratification** is the hierarchical ranking of the members of society based on the unequal distribution of resources, power, and prestige. The word *resources* refers to such factors as income, property, and borrowing capacity. *Power* is the ability to influence or control others. *Prestige* relates to status and is either *ascribed* (based on age, sex, race, or family background) or *achieved* (based on individual accomplishments).

Stratification may reduce or worsen any strains or conflicts between groups, depending on how rigid and explicit or flexible and subtle are the class distinctions and discrimination based on race or ethnic group. The more rigid the stratification, the more likely is the emergence of racial, religious, or other ideologies justifying the existing arrangements—as happened with the rise of racism during slavery in the United States.

Stratification also affects how groups within the various strata of society view one another. Some people confuse structural differentiation with cultural differentiation. For example, they may believe that a group's low socioeconomic status is due to its values and attitudes rather than to such structural conditions as racism, economic stagnation, and high urban unemployment. Racial or ethnic stratification can be an important determinant of the potential for intergroup conflict. In the United States, both the possibility of upward mobility and the existence of obstacles blocking that possibility have long co-existed. When the disparity between the ideal of the American Dream and the reality of its achievement grows too great, the possibility of conflict increases.

# Social Class

**Social class** designates people's place in the stratification hierarchy, identifying those in each grouping who share similar levels of income and status, amounts of property and power, and types of lifestyle. The individual's race and religion also could factor into one's status. Although no clearly defined boundaries exist between class groupings in the United States, people have a tendency to cluster together according to certain socioeconomic similarities. The concept or image of social-class reality results from sociopsychological distinctions people make about one another, including where they live and what they own, as well as to interactions that occur because of those distinctions.

In the 1930s, W. Lloyd Warner headed a now-classic study of social-class differentiation in the United States.[15] Using the **reputational method**—asking people how they thought others compared to them—Warner found a well-formulated class system in place. In "Yankee City"—actually Newburyport, Massachusetts, a small town at that time with approximately 17,000 inhabitants—Warner identified six classes: upper-upper, lower-upper, upper-middle, lower-middle, upper-lower, and lower-lower.

Although Warner reached several faulty conclusions because he failed to take a sociohistorical approach,[16] some of his findings have validity for our focus. First, a significant relationship existed between an ethnic group's length of residence and class status; the more recent arrivals tended to be in the lower classes. In addition, an ethnic group tended to be less assimilated and less upwardly mobile if its population in the community was relatively large, if its homeland was close (such as in the case of immigrant French Canadians), if its members had a sojourner rather than a permanent-settler orientation, and if limited opportunities for advancement existed in the community.[17]

Social class becomes important in intergroup relations because it provides a basis for expectations and also serves as a point of reference in others' responses and in one's self-perception. As a result, social class helps to shape an individual's world of reality and influences group interactions. Attitudes and behavior formed within a social-class framework are not permanent, however; they can change if circumstances change.

## CLASS CONSCIOUSNESS

Just how important are the ethnic factors that Warner and others reported in shaping an awareness of social class? The significance of ethnic factors depends on numerous variables, including economic conditions, mobility patterns, and prevailing attitudes.

**2-5** Evaluate the role of social class in intergroup relations.

**Watch on MySocLab**
Video: The Basics: Social Class in the US

**Read on MySocLab**
Document: Census Poverty Data

**Explore on MySocLab**
Activity: Next Door to Greatness: Poverty in Cambridge, MA

Because ethnic minorities are disproportionately represented among the lower classes and because middle-class values dominate in the United States, it seems reasonable to conclude that at least some of the attitudes about a group may result from people's value judgments about social class. That is to say, the dominant group's criticism and stereotyping of the minority group probably rest in part on class distinctions. Such class-based views extend to racial groups as well. Researchers note that whites tend to categorize lower-class blacks by race, but categorize middle-class blacks by social class and react accordingly.[18]

Social-class status also plays an important role in determining a minority group's adjustment to, and acceptance by, society. For example, because the first waves of Cuban (1960s) and Vietnamese (1970s) refugees who arrived in the United States possessed the education and occupational experience of the middle class, they succeeded in overcoming early native concerns and did not encounter the same degree of negativism as did lower-class migrants from the same two countries in the 1980s. Whether generations ago or now, when unskilled and often illiterate peasants enter the lower-class positions in U.S. society, many U.S. citizens belittle, avoid, and discriminate against them because of their supposedly inferior ways. Frequently, these attitudes and actions reflect an awareness of class differences as well as cultural differences. Because the dominant group usually occupies a higher stratum in the social-class hierarchy, differences in social-class values and lifestyles—in addition to ethnic cultural differences—can be sources of friction.

## ETHNICITY AND SOCIAL CLASS

Differences in stratification among various groups cannot be explained by a single cause, even though some social scientists emphasize one factor over another. For example, in *The Ethnic Myth*, Stephen Steinberg stressed the importance of social structure and minimized cultural factors.[19] For him, the success of Jews in the United States resulted more from their occupational skills in the urbanized country than from their values. Conversely, Thomas Sowell wrote in *Ethnic America* that the compatibility of a group's cultural characteristics with those of the dominant culture determines the level of a group's economic success.[20] In reality, structural and cultural elements intertwine. Emphasizing only social structure ignores important cultural variables, such as values about education. Emphasizing only culture can lead to blaming people who do not succeed.

*In this ESL class, a Hispanic teacher helps many newcomers master English to ease their entry into the societal mainstream. Nationwide, there is a shortage of such classes in this important step in the acculturation process that helps reduce cultural differentiation and enhance opportunities for occupational mobility.*

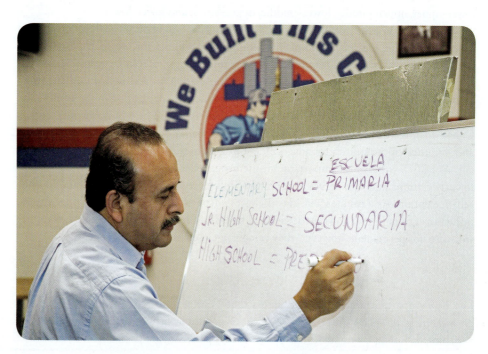

In a 1964 ground-breaking book, *Assimilation in American Life*, Milton Gordon first suggested that dominant–minority relations be examined within the larger context of the social structure.[21] Although he believed that all groups would eventually become assimilated, his central thesis about a pluralistic society was that four factors, or social categories, play a part in forming subsocieties within the nation: ethnicity (by which Gordon also meant race), social class, rural or urban residence, and regionalism.[22] These factors unite in various combinations to create a number of **ethclasses**—subsocieties resulting from the intersection of stratifications of race and ethnic group with stratifications of social class. Additional determinants are the rural or urban setting and the particular region of the country in which a group lives. Examples of ethclasses are lower-middle-class white Catholics in a northern city, lower-class black Baptists in the rural South, and upper-class white Jews in a western suburb.

Numerous studies support the concept that race and ethnicity, together with social class, are important in social structures and intergroup conflicts.[23] For example, only by recognizing the intersection of race and class as a key element can we understand the continued widespread existence of black poverty.[24] Not only do ethclass groupings exist, but people tend to interact within them for their intimate primary relationships. To the extent that this is true, multiple allegiances and conflicts are inevitable. Both cultural and structural pluralism currently exist, with numerous groups presently coexisting in separate subsocieties based on social class and cultural distinctions. Even people whose families have been in the United States for several generations are affiliated with, and participate in, subsocieties. Nonetheless, Gordon optimistically views assimilation as a linear process in which even **structural assimilation** (the large-scale entrance of minorities into mainstream social organization and institutions) eventually will occur.

## BLAMING THE POOR OR SOCIETY?

In 1932, E. Franklin Frazier formulated his conception of a disorganized and pathological lower-class culture. This thesis served as the inspiration for the controversy about the existence of a **culture of poverty** that emerged in the 1960s.[25] The writings of two men, Daniel P. Moynihan and Oscar Lewis, sparked an intense debate that continues to resonate today. In his 1965 government report, "The Negro Family: The Case for National Action," Moynihan used Frazier's observations as a springboard for arguing that a "tangle of pathology" so pervaded the black community that it perpetuated a cycle of poverty and deprivation that only outside (government) intervention could overcome.[26]

**FAMILY DISINTEGRATION.** Moynihan argued that family deterioration was a core cause of the problems of high unemployment, welfare dependency, illegitimacy, low achievement, juvenile delinquency, and adult crime:

> At the heart of the deterioration of the fabric of Negro society is the deterioration of the Negro family. It is the fundamental source of weakness of the Negro community at the present time.... The white family has achieved a high degree of stability and is maintaining that stability. By contrast, the family structure of the lower-class Negroes is highly unstable, and in many urban centers is approaching complete breakdown.[27]

Moynihan described black males as occupying an unstable place in the economy, which prevented them from functioning as strong fathers and husbands. This environment, he said, served as a breeding ground for a continuing vicious circle: The women often not only raised the children but also earned the family income. Consequently, the children grew up in a poorly supervised, unstable environment; they often performed poorly or dropped out of school; they could secure only low-paying jobs—and so the cycle began anew.[28] The Moynihan Report called for federal action to create, among other things, jobs for black, male heads of household in the inner city:

> At the center of the tangle of pathology is the weakness of the family structure. Once or twice removed, it will be found to be the principal source of most of the aberrant, inadequate, or anti-social behavior that did not establish but now serves to perpetuate the cycle of poverty and deprivation....
>
> What then is the problem? We feel that the answer is clear enough. Three centuries of injustice have brought about deep-seated structural distortions in the life of the Negro American. At this point, the present tangle of pathology is capable of perpetuating itself without assistance from the white world. The cycle can be broken only if these distortions are set right.[29]

In 1990, Moynihan reaffirmed his view that a link existed between specific cultural values and deteriorating conditions in lower-class black family life. Citing further social deterioration since the 1960s, he noted in particular the startling rise in out-of-wedlock births from 3 percent of white births and 24 percent of black births in 1963 to 16 percent and 63 percent, respectively, in 1987.[30] These distressing statistics led Moynihan to repeat a statement from his 1965 report:

> From the wild Irish slums of the nineteenth-century Eastern seaboard, to the riot-torn suburbs of Los Angeles, there is one unmistakable lesson in American history: A community that allows a large number of young men to grow up in broken families, dominated by women, never acquiring a stable relationship to male authority, never acquiring any set of rational expectations about the future—that community asks for and gets chaos. Crime, violence, unrest, disorder—most particularly, the furious, unrestrained lashing out at the whole social structure—that is not only to be expected; it is very near to inevitable.[31]

**PERPETUATION OF POVERTY.** Moynihan's position shares the same premises as Oscar Lewis's theory about a subculture of poverty, detailed in *The Children of Sanchez* (1961) and *La Vida* (1966):[32]

> The culture of poverty, however, is not only an adaptation to a set of objective conditions of the larger society. Once it comes into existence, it tends to perpetuate itself from generation to generation because of its effect on the children. By the time slum children are age six or seven, they have usually absorbed the basic values and attitudes of their subculture and are not psychologically geared to take full advantage of changing conditions or increased opportunities which may occur in their lifetime.[33]

Politically, Lewis was a leftist, and he did not blame the poor as some critics misinterpreted. Rather, he emphasized the institutionalized tenacity of their poverty, arguing that the system

*This single, homeless mother of four children works as an administrative assistant for a high-tech company in California, but the family lives in a church-supported shelter because of her limited income. Living in a homeless shelter not only can be stressful on both the children and mother, but also may lead to multi-generational poverty.*

damaged them.[34] Edward Banfield, a conservative, recast Lewis's position to assert that poverty continues because of subcultural patterns. Whereas Lewis held that the mechanics of capitalist production for profit caused poverty, Banfield found its cause in the folkways of its victims. Banfield argued that good jobs, good housing, tripled welfare payments, new schools, quality education, and armies of police officers would not stop the problem. He added,

> If, however, the lower classes were to disappear—if, say, their members were overnight to acquire the attitudes, motivations, and habits of the working class— the most serious and intractable problems of the city would all disappear.... The lower-class forms of all problems are at bottom a single problem: The existence of an outlook and style of life, which is radically present-oriented and which therefore attaches no value to work, sacrifice, self-improvement, or service to family, friends, or community.[35]

Another form of the "blame game" occurs during the political wrangling that goes on whenever welfare measures are considered. For example, in 1996, when Congress passed the welfare reform act, its official title was the Personal Responsibility and Work Opportunity Reconciliation Act of 1996, a not-too-subtle implication that the poor must change their ways if they want to escape poverty. The act's key provisions were a time limit on welfare payments and a requirement that welfare recipients, after two years, must work. No doubt some lazy people preferred living off a government handout to working, but that was only an extremely small percentage of the welfare recipients. Then, as now, the heavy majority of those living in poverty *do* work, but their limited education and job skills restrict them to low-paying, often unstable, work.[36]

**CRITICISM.** Although they were not saying the same thing, Moynihan, Lewis, and Banfield all came under heavy criticism during the 1960s and 1970s—the height of the civil rights movement—from commentators who felt they were blaming the victim. Critics argued that intergenerational poverty results from discrimination, structural conditions, or stratification rigidity. Fatalism, apathy, low aspiration, and other similar orientations found in lower-class culture are thus situational responses within each generation and not the result of cultural deficiencies transmitted from parents to children.

To William Ryan, blaming the victim results in misdirected social programs. If we rationalize away the socially acquired stigma of poverty as the expression of a subcultural trait, we ignore the continuing effect of current victimizing social forces. As a result, we focus on helping the "disorganized" black family instead of on overcoming racism or we strive to develop "better" attitudes and skills in low-income children rather than revamping the poor-quality schools they attend.[37]

Charles A. Valentine led an attack on the culture-of-poverty thesis and on Lewis himself. He argued that many of Lewis's "class distinctive traits" of the poor are either "externally imposed conditions" (unemployment, crowded and deteriorated housing, and lack of education) or "unavoidable matters of situational expediency" (hostility toward social institutions and low expectations and self-image).[38] Only by changing the total social structure and the resources available to the poor can we alter any subcultural traits of survival.

Yet Lewis also was saying this.[39] Michael Harrington, whose *The Other America* (1963) helped spark the federal government's War on Poverty program, defended Lewis. Harrington—like Lewis—said that society was to blame for the culture of poverty: "The real explanation of why the poor are where they are is that they made the mistake of being born to the wrong parents, in the wrong section of the country, in the wrong industry, or in the wrong racial or ethnic group."[40]

Like Lewis, Valentine, and Harrington, others argued that all people would desire the same things and cherish the same values if they were in an economic position to do so. Because they are not, they adopt an alternative set of values to survive.[41] Eliot Liebow, in a participant–observer study of lower-class black males, concluded that they try to achieve many of the goals of the larger society but fail for many of the same reasons their fathers did: discrimination, unpreparedness, lack of job skills, and self-doubt.[42] The similarities between generations are due not to cultural transmission but to the sons' independent experience of the same failures. What appears to be a self-sustaining cultural process is actually a secondary adaptation to an adult inability to overcome structural constraints, such as racism, for example.

The debate continues on whether the culture of poverty results from **economic determinism** (structural barriers and discrimination) or from **cultural determinism** (transmission of cultural inadequacies). Some scholars continue to advance arguments about power relations and racial subjugation as the primary culprits, while others insist that cultural values and beliefs primarily explain a group's self-perpetuating world of dependence.[43]

Whatever the cause, most people's attitudes toward welfare and the urban poor (who are predominantly racial and ethnic minorities) reflect a belief in one position or the other.

Is poverty the result of personal deficiencies? Does long-term poverty result in the development of negative values passed from one generation to the next? Are personal characteristics of the poor the result of long-term poverty, or are they simply adjustments to conditions of poverty? Such questions of blaming the poor and/or existing socioeconomic systems for the existence of poverty, particularly among minority groups, evoke different answers depending on one's perspective. How would we answer the larger question: Is inequality an inevitable part of society?

# Intergroup Conflict

**2-6** Examine factors that underlie intergroup conflict.

Is conflict inevitable when culturally distinct groups interact? Do structural conditions encourage or reduce the probability of conflict? In this section, we examine the major factors that may underlie such conflict: cultural differentiation and structural differentiation.

## CULTURAL DIFFERENTIATION

When similarities between the arriving minority group and the indigenous group exist, the relationship tends to be relatively harmonious and assimilation is likely to occur eventually.[44] Conversely, the greater and more visible the **cultural differentiation**, the greater

*Some of their cultural differences readily apparent by their clothing, Sikhs—like many other ethnic groups in the United States— also celebrate with an annual parade, one that these observers are watching in New York City. Sikh translates to "disciple" or "learner," the words themselves providing insight into some of this group's core cultural values.*

# REALITY check

## Cultural Differentiation, Contact Hypothesis, and College Friendships

Do cultural differences affect college student friendships? Apparently so, according to a longitudinal study that tracked more than 1,000 male and female UCLA students from just before they began their freshmen year through to their senior spring quarter of classes. As freshmen, the mix was 36 percent Asian, 32 percent white, 18 percent Latino, 6 percent black, 8 percent other, and changed only slightly by senior year.

Overall, students in all four racial/ethnic groups followed similar patterns throughout their college careers in their selection and maintenance of friends. Essentially, ingroup bias and intergroup anxiety were the determining factors. That is, students who held attitudes that were more favorable of their own group but felt more uneasy and less competent interacting with members of different groups had fewer outgroup friends and more ingroup friends.

Although these results are hardly surprising given the similarity–attraction bond discussed in Chapter 1, another finding further lends support to the **contact hypothesis** (having outgroup friends is strongly associated with lower intergroup prejudice). In this study, the researchers found two equally significant causal paths. Students who had more outgroup friendships did indeed register lower ingroup bias and outgroup anxiety, but by the end of their college days, those with more ingroup friends in college had greater negative attitudes about other ethnic or racial groups.

Peer socialization may explain these differing effects. Students are likely to change their attitudes and behaviors to be consistent with those of their ingroup. If that group is heterogeneous, a higher level of mutual respect and acceptance occurs and reduces ethnocentric bias. A homogeneous group, if isolated from different attitudes and ideas, finds its views continually reinforced by friends and judges more negatively those outsiders with whom they have had no primary group contact.

### CRITICAL THINKING QUESTIONS

Is your group of college friends any different racially and ethnically from those you had in high school? Are your views about other groups any different now than they were then?

Source: Adapted from Shana Levin, Colette van Laar, and Jim Sidanius, "The Effects of Ingroup and Outgroup Friendships on Ethnic Attitudes in College: A Longitudinal Study," *Group Processes & Intergroup Relations* 6 (2003): 76–92.

---

the likelihood that conflict will occur. When large numbers of German and Irish Catholics came to the United States in the mid-nineteenth century, Protestants grew uneasy. As priests and nuns arrived and Catholics built churches, convents, and schools, Protestants became alarmed at what they feared was a papal conspiracy to gain control of the country. Emotions ran high, resulting in civil unrest and violence.

Religion often has been a basis for cultural conflict in the United States as is demonstrated by the history of discriminatory treatment also suffered in this country by Mormons, Jews, and Quakers. Yet many other aspects of cultural visibility can serve as sources of strife as well. Cultural differences may range from clothing (Sikh turbans and Muslim hijabs, for example) to leisure activities (Hispanic cockfights, for example). Americans once condemned the Chinese as opium smokers, even though the British had introduced opium smoking into China, promoted it among the lower-class Chinese population, and even fought wars against the Chinese government to maintain the lucrative trade.

Cultural differentiation does not necessarily cause intergroup conflict though. A partial explanation of variances in relations between culturally distinct groups comes from interactionist theory, which holds that the extent of shared symbols and definitions between intercommunicating groups determines the nature of their interaction patterns. Although actual differences may support conflict, interactionists say the key to harmonious or disharmonious relations lies in the definitions or interpretations of those differences. Tolerance or intolerance—acceptance or rejection of others—depends on whether others are viewed as threatening or nonthreatening, assimilable or nonassimilable, worthy or unworthy (see the Reality Check box).

## STRUCTURAL DIFFERENTIATION

Because they offer macrosocial analyses of a society, both functionalist and conflict theorists provide bases for understanding how structural conditions (**structural differentiation**) affect intergroup relations. Functionalists seek explanations for the dysfunctions in the social system and the adjustments needed to correct them. Conflict theorists emphasize the conscious, purposeful actions of dominant groups to maintain systems of inequality.

Functionalists explain how sometimes economic and technological conditions facilitate minority integration. When the economy is healthy and jobs are plentiful, newcomers find it easier to become established and work their way up the socioeconomic ladder. In the United States today, however, technological progress has reduced the number of low-status, blue-collar jobs and increased the number of jobs requiring more highly skilled and educated workers. As a result, fewer jobs are available for unskilled, foreign, marginal, or unassimilated people.

Perhaps because jobs are an important source of economic security and status, **occupational mobility**—the ability of individuals to improve their job position—seems to be a key factor in affecting the level of prejudice. Numerous studies have shown that a fear of economic insecurity increases ethnic hostility. One study of U.S. workers found that a perceived threat to either their cultural norms or economic well-being led to more negative attitudes toward immigrants.[45] Other researchers found that worsening economic circumstances intensify prejudicial stereotypes and attitudes about immigration.[46] In addition, upwardly mobile people are generally more tolerant than nonmobile individuals. Loss of status and prestige appears to increase hostility toward outgroups, whereas upward gains enable people to feel more benevolent toward others.

American scholar Thomas F. Pettigrew and five European colleagues (2008) reported similar findings from extensive data collected from France, Germany, Great Britain, and the Netherlands. They found a direct correlation between intergroup prejudice and group relative deprivation (comparative income, education, and housing). Specifically, respondents from a lower socioeconomic background were more likely to express prejudicial attitudes toward immigration and various ethnic groups. However, they denied any discrimination against such outgroups, instead placing responsibility for their problems on the outgroups themselves, a classic example of blaming the victim.[47]

# Ethnic Stratification

If one group becomes dominant and another becomes subservient, obviously one group has more power than the other. Social-class status partly reflects this unequal distribution of power, which also may fall along racial or ethnic lines. **Ethnic stratification** is the structured inequality of different groups with different access to social rewards as a result of their status in the social hierarchy. Because most Americans associate ethnicity with anything different from the mainstream, they don't realize that ethnicity also exists at the top. Dominant-group ethnicity lies "hidden," however, because it passes as the taken-for-granted societal norm.[48]

Stratification is a normal component of all societies but typically falls along racial and ethnic lines in diverse societies. How does ethnic stratification continue in a democracy where supposedly all have an equal opportunity for upward mobility? Functionalists suggest that the ethnocentrism of those in the societal mainstream leads to discrimination against those in outgroups, as determined by their racial or cultural differences. Conflict analysts instead stress the subordination of minorities by the dominant group because that group benefits from such ethnic stratification. Two middle-range conflict theories offer helpful insights into this perspective. The power-differential theory helps explain the initial phases of domination and conflict, and the internal-colonialism theory examines the continuation of such subordination.

**2-7** Explain how sociology helps us understand ethnic stratification.

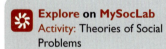

**Explore on MySocLab**
Activity: Theories of Social Problems

Multi-generational occupational patterning often occurs among working-class ethnic Americans, as son joins father in the same line of work to carry on the tradition. A good example is found among the miners in the Appalachian coal regions, where men from families of Slavic ancestry have worked in the mines for three or more generations.

## THE POWER-DIFFERENTIAL THEORY

Stanley Lieberson suggested a **power-differential theory**, in which intergroup relations depend on the relative power of the migrant group and the indigenous group.[49] Because the two groups usually do not share the same culture, each strives to maintain its own institutions. Which group becomes dominant and which becomes subordinate governs subsequent relations.

If the newcomers possess superior technology (particularly weapons) and a cohesive social organization, conflict may occur at an early stage, with a consequent native population decline due to warfare, disease, or disruption of sustenance activities. Finding their institutions undermined or co-opted, the local inhabitants eventually may participate in the institutions of the dominant group. In time, a group consciousness may arise, and sometimes, the indigenous group even succeeds in ousting the formerly dominant migrant group. When this happened in many former African colonies and in Southeast Asia, interethnic fighting among the many indigenous groups led to new forms of dominance and subordination within countries (as with the Hutu and Tutsi peoples in Burundi and Rwanda).

Lieberson maintained that neither conflict nor assimilation is an inevitable outcome of racial and ethnic contact. Instead, the particular relationship between the two groups involved determines which alternative will occur. Conflict between a dominant migrant group and a subordinate indigenous group can be immediate and violent. If the relationship is the reverse, and the indigenous group is dominant, conflict will be limited and sporadic, and the host society will exert a great deal of pressure on the subordinate migrant group to assimilate, acquiesce, or leave.

In addition, a dominant indigenous group can limit the numbers and groups entering to reduce the threat of demographic or institutional imbalance. Restrictive U.S. immigration laws against the Chinese in 1882 and against all but northern and western Europeans in 1921 and 1924 illustrate this process. Labor union hostility against African American and Asian workers, government efforts to expel foreigners (for example, Indians, Japanese, and Filipinos), and planned attempts to revolutionize the social order (Native American boarding schools and the Americanization movement) all illustrate the use of institutional power against minority groups.

Another sociologist, William J. Wilson, suggested that power relations between dominant and subordinate groups differ in paternalistic and competitive systems.[50] With **paternalism** (the system that once governed South Africa and the Old South of the United States), the dominant group exercises almost absolute control over the subordinate group and can direct virtually unlimited coercion to maintain societal order. In a competitive system (such as the United States today), some degree of power reciprocity exists, so the dominant group in society is somewhat vulnerable to political pressures and economic boycotts.

Rapid social change—industrialization, unionization, urbanization, migration, and political change—usually loosens the social structure, leading to new tensions as both groups seek new power resources. If the minority group increases its power resources, through protective laws and improved economic opportunities, it may foresee even greater improvement in its condition. This heightened awareness is likely to lead to conflict unless additional gains are forthcoming. For example, the civil rights movement of the mid-1960s brought about legislation ensuring minority rights and opportunities in jobs, housing, education, and other aspects of life, but this led to new tensions. The 1960s were marked by urban riots and arson, protest demonstrations and human barricades to stop construction of low-income housing sites, school-busing controversies, and challenges to labor discrimination.

## THE INTERNAL-COLONIALISM THEORY

In analyzing the black militancy of the late 1960s, Robert Blauner attempted to integrate the factors of caste and racism, ethnicity, culture, and economic exploitation.[51] His major point was that U.S. treatment of its black population resembled past European subjugation and exploitation of non-Western peoples in their own lands. Although he focused on black–white relations in the United States, he suggested that Mexican Americans also might fit his **internal-colonialism theory** and that Native Americans could be added as another suitable example.

Immigrant ghettoes, he argued, evolved through the voluntary clustering of immigrants wanting to live among their compatriots. Their residential buildings, retail stores, and other commercial enterprises may have been owned by outsiders at first, but that changed within a short period. Soon, as the acculturation and assimilation processes unfolded, ethnic group members moved out of the neighborhood. Any long-term concentration, such as San Francisco's Chinatown, was also a matter of choice, because the tourist trade generated profitable businesses for the ethnics, whose presence was augmented by new arrivals from their homeland.

In contrast, the black ghetto has been more permanent, both in the concentration of low-income people and in the outside control of its economic, educational, and political institutions. Unlike the Chinese and Japanese who successfully overcame racial prejudice and gained control over their own communities, blacks were unable to do so. The reason, Blauner said, was because African Americans suffered the destruction of their traditional culture and social organization first through slavery and then through continuing internal colonialism.[52] Several of these statements need to be modified. Chinatowns long persisted not because of any business advantage but because of racial discrimination. In proportion to the Chinatown population, only a few Chinese actually benefit from the tourist trade. Also, the Chinese and Japanese *always* had "control of their internal communities," although they differed greatly from each other in their structure and cohesiveness.

Blauner considered the exploitation phase that was temporary for other groups as more nearly permanent for blacks and possibly Chicanos. He believed that conflict and confrontation, as well as real or apparent chaos and disorder, will continue because this may be the only way an internally colonized group can deal with the dominant society.

**TABLE 2.2   Middle-Range Conflict Theories**

| The Power-Differential Theory |
| --- |
| 1. Neither conflict nor assimilation is inevitable. |
| 2. The relative power of indigenous and migrant groups determines events. |
| 3. If the migrant group is dominant, early conflict and colonization will occur. |
| 4. If the indigenous group is dominant, occasional labor and racial strife, legislative restrictions, and pressures to assimilate are common. |
| 5. In a paternalistic society, the dominant group has almost absolute power. |
| 6. A competitive society is vulnerable to political pressures and economic boycotts. |

| The Internal-Colonialism Theory |
| --- |
| 1. U.S. treatment of its black population resembles past European subjugation and exploitation of non-Western peoples. |
| 2. Black ghettos are more nearly permanent than immigrant ghettos. |
| 3. Black ghettos are controlled economically, politically, and administratively from the outside. |
| 4. Continual exploitation produces conflict and confrontation. |
| 5. Mexican Americans and Native Americans may also fit this model. |

This conflict orientation suggests that the multigenerational exploitation of certain groups creates a unique situation and a basis for the often violent conflict that sporadically flared up in our cities (Table 2.2).

## CHALLENGES TO THE STATUS QUO

Even if the stratification system allows for upward mobility, some members of the dominant group may believe that the lower-class racial and ethnic groups are challenging the social order as they strive for their share of the "good life." If the dominant group does not feel threatened, the change will be peaceful. If the minority group meets resistance but retains hope and a sense of belonging to the larger society, the struggle for more power will occur within the system (for example, by means of demonstrations, boycotts, voter-registration drives, or lobbying) rather than through violence. The late-nineteenth-century race-baiting riots on the West Coast against Chinese and Japanese workers and the 1919 Chicago race riots against blacks attempting to enter the meat-packing industry illustrate violent responses of a dominant group against a minority group over power resources. Similarly, the black–Korean violence in several urban neighborhoods during the late twentieth century, including during the 1992 Los Angeles riots, and the violence between U.S. blacks and Cubans in Miami in 1988, typify minority-against-minority clashes over limited resources.

Conflict theorists argue that class-based prejudice, oppression, and violence are predictable occurrences in a competitive capitalist system.[53] A connection exists between a group's economic position and the intensity of its conflict with the dominant society. The greater the deprivation in economic resources, social status, and social power, the likelier the weaker group is to resort to violent conflict to achieve gains in any of these three areas (see the International Scene box). As the social-class position of a group increases, intergroup conflict becomes less intense and less violent.

Conflict occurs not only because a lower-class group seeks an end to deprivation but also because the group next higher on the socioeconomic ladder feels threatened. Often, the working-class group displays the greatest hostility and prejudice of all established groups in the society toward the upward-striving minority group. Other factors may be at work as well, but status competition is a significant source of conflict, as we'll discuss in Chapters 5 to 12.

# the INTERNATIONAL scene

## Cultural Clashes in China

In July 2009, three days of ethnic violence broke out in the northwestern desert region of Xinjiang, a region that covers about one-sixth of China's land mass. The rioting broke out between the Han Chinese, the dominant ethnic group in the entire country, and the Uyghurs, a Turkic ethnic group that is predominantly Muslim. Although government censorship prevented full news coverage, at least 156 people (129 men and 27 women) were reported killed and more than 1,000 injured, making this the deadliest ethnic violence to strike China in decades.

The violence began when police in Urumqi, the area's largest city with a population of 2.3 million, attempted to break up a peaceful protest march by at least 1,000 Uyghurs. Although sparked by dissatisfaction of the government's handling of the death of two Uyghur workers 10 days earlier, the ensuing ethnic brawl was the culmination of decades of resentment by Uyghurs over government policies that they believe threaten their culture and livelihoods.

Essentially, the Uyghurs illustrate the internal colonialism model. Since the Communists took power in 1949,

the Han have held power in Xinjiang, even though they then only comprised 6 percent of the area's population, the rest of whom were mostly Uyghurs. However, government incentives have since encouraged a massive migration and the Han proportion reached 40 percent in 2000. This figure does not include the large number of Han migrant workers and military personnel stationed there with their families. The 10 million Uyghurs now constitute 45 percent of the region's total population.

The increased influx of Han in recent years, coupled with what the Uyghurs claim is "cultural imperialism," has heightened ethnic tensions. The besieged minority points to such government actions as the ordered demolition of parts of the old town of Kashgar, the phasing out of Uyghur-language instruction in the schools, and restrictions on their religious practices. Students and government workers, for example, are compelled to eat during the fasting period of Ramadan, and the pilgrimage (hajj) to Mecca—one of Islam's five pillars—only can be done through official government tours.

Uyghurs also complain that they are being squeezed out economically.

Frustrations and grievances about limited economic opportunities, job discrimination, and preferential treatment for the Han are some of the deeper causes of the unrest. In rebuttal, the Han Chinese say the Uyghurs, like other ethnic minorities in China, have such advantages as an exemption from China's strict policy of one child per family or pay a fine, as well as extra points added to their standardized test scores to determine university placement. Uyghurs counter that these advantages do little for their primary concerns about their group identity, culture, dignity, fair treatment, equality, and economic well-being.

### CRITICAL THINKING QUESTION

What other persistent subcultures have faced harsh repressive actions? Are there common reasons for these government-endorsed actions?

Sources: Adapted from Edward Wong, "New Protests Flare in Chinese City After Deadly Ethnic Clashes," *New York Times* (July 8, 2009), p. A4; "Death Toll in Xinjiang Riot Rises to 156," *China View*, at http://news.xinhuanet.com/english/2009-07/07/content_11663866.htm; and Wenran Jiang, "New Frontier, Same Old Problems for China," *The Globe and Mail* (January 9, 2010), at http://www.theglobeandmail.com/news/opinions/new-frontier-same-old-problems/article1208363.

Social-class antagonisms influence people's perceptions of racial and ethnic groups also. Some social scientists suggest parallels between Irish, Italian, Jewish, and Polish immigrants and southern blacks who migrated to northern cities (the Chinese, some of the Japanese, and others also could fit this model). All emigrated from poverty-stricken agrarian regions to urban industrial slums. Encountering prejudice and discrimination, they sought various routes to material success: stable but unskilled employment, ethnic politics and, for some, crime.[54] Other social scientists, however, argue that the black experience does not equate with that of European immigrants. They hold, as did the Kerner Commission investigating the urban riots of the late 1960s, that the dominant society's practice of internal colonialism toward blacks deprived them of the strong social organizations that other groups had. Moreover, today's labor market offers fewer unskilled jobs for blacks than it offered other immigrant groups in earlier times, thereby depriving poor urban blacks of a means to begin moving upward.[55]

Whether race or social class is the primary factor in assessing full integration of blacks in the United States is a still-continuing debate, particularly among black social scientists. We will devote more attention to this topic in Chapter 10.

## Is There a White Culture?

In the mid-1990s, interest in white studies rose significantly. White studies essentially focus on how whiteness has led to racial domination and hegemony, in which white American culture is simply called "American," thereby presuming that black, Native American, Asian, or Hispanic cultures are not "American" but instead racial and/or ethnic subcultures. The idea that a white culture also exists is difficult for many people to grasp, say the white studies advocates, much as a fish is unaware of water until out of it, because of its environmental universality.

The premise for a white culture existing independent of an "American" culture is that all racial groups have large social/cultural characteristics that change throughout time. These white values, attitudes, shared understandings, and behavior patterns—like many aspects of culture—are often unrealized by group members because they are part of a taken-for-granted world. Yet even though white culture may not be identifiable among its members, it is nonetheless real and easily recognizable by non-whites. For example, says Jeff Hitchcock in *Lifting the White Veil,* in black culture, one's feelings are given precedence over sensibilities. He explains that when a feeling comes on a person, black culture says it is appropriate to express it, but white culture…

> … works hard to keep the volume down, lest we all go crazy from the demands we place on each other's capacity for self-control. Experience in the culture helps. We learn how not to step on toes, hurt other people's "feelings," to not make a scene, and all the other little social rules and practices of a lifetime. We rein it in, and trade spontaneity…for an orderly demeanor and generally predictable and controlled everyday existence.[56]

Lacking an understanding of the existence of white culture, say its proponents, results in the dominant group misinterpreting alternative cultural experiences as racial or as the personal failings of someone of color. Recognizing its existence could be a first step toward building a truly multiracial society.

## Retrospect

Culture provides the normative definitions by which members of a society perceive and interpret the world around them. Language and other forms of symbolic interaction provide the means by which this accumulated knowledge is transmitted. Becoming acculturated requires learning both the language and the symbol system of the new society. Sometimes, though, situations become real in their consequences because people earlier defined them as real (the Thomas theorem). Unless it is isolated from the rest of the world, a society undergoes change through culture contact and the diffusion of ideas, inventions, and practices. Within large societies, subcultures usually exist. They may gradually be assimilated (convergent subcultures), or they may remain distinct (persistent subcultures).

Structural conditions also influence people's perceptions of the world—whether they live in an industrialized or agrarian society, a closed or open social system, a growing or

**2-8** Understand the existence of a White culture.

contracting economy, a friendly or unfriendly environment, and whether their homeland, friends, and relatives are accessible or remote. Distribution of power resources and compatibility with the existing social structure greatly influence majority–minority relations as well. Interactionists concentrate on perceptions of cultural differences as they affect intergroup relations. Functionalists and conflict theorists emphasize structural conditions.

The interplay between the variables of race, ethnic group, and social class is important for understanding how some problems and conflicts arise. A feature interpreted as an attribute of a race or ethnic group in fact may be a broader aspect of social class. Because many attitudes and values are situational responses to socioeconomic status, a change in status or opportunities will bring about a change in those attitudes and values. Investigative studies have not supported the culture-of-poverty hypothesis of family disintegration and a self-perpetuating poverty value orientation.

Stratification along racial and ethnic lines is common in a diverse society. Functionalists think ethnocentrism leads to discrimination to cause this. One middle-range conflict perspective focuses on the power differential. Whether the indigenous group or migrant group possesses superior power determines the nature of subsequent intergroup relations. Another factor is whether the social system is paternalistic or competitive. Considering black and Hispanic ghettos or Native American reservations as examples of internal colonialism offers a second conflict perspective.

The existence of a white culture, separate and distinct from American culture, is a debatable issue but one that offers intriguing talking points about intercultural interactions and understandings.

# On MySocLab

 **Study and Review on MySocLab**

## KEY TERMS

Acculturation, p. 27

Chain migration, p. 34

Contact hypothesis, p. 43

Convergent subcultures, p. 34

Cultural determinism, p. 42

Cultural differentiation, p. 42

Cultural diffusion, p. 31

Cultural transmission, p. 31

Culture, p. 26

Culture of poverty, p. 39

Culture shock, p. 33

Economic determinism, p. 42

Ethclasses, p. 39

Ethnic stratification, p. 44

Ethnic subcultures, p. 34

Ethnogenesis, p. 34

Internal-colonialism theory, p. 46

Linguistic relativity, p. 29

Marginality, p. 34

Material culture, p. 26

Nonmaterial culture, p. 26

Norms, p. 27

Occupational mobility, p. 44

Paralinguistic signals, p. 30

Parallel social institutions, p. 34

Paternalism, p. 46

Persistent subcultures, p. 35

Power-differential theory, p. 45

Reputational method, p. 37

Social class, p. 37

Social stratification, p. 36

Social structure, p. 26

Structural assimilation, p. 39

Structural differentiation, p. 44

Thomas theorem, p. 30

## DISCUSSION QUESTIONS

1. What is the relationship among culture, reality, and intergroup relations?
2. Do you belong to, or interact with, people from any subcultures? What have been your experiences with them?
3. Do any persistent subcultures live near your campus? Who are they? What do you know about them? What are the largest concentrations of convergent subcultures near your school? What makes them convergent and not persistent?
4. What is the relationship between ethnicity and social class?
5. What is meant by the *culture of poverty?* What criticisms exist about this thinking?
6. How do the functional and conflict perspectives approach the factors likely to contribute to intergroup conflict?

## INTERNET ACTIVITIES

1. Are we a melting pot? Most social scientists say this is a romantic myth that ignores the past and present realities of the United States. In "The Myth of the Melting Pot" (http://www.washingtonpost.com/wp-srv/national/longterm/meltingpot/melt0222.htm), the *Washington Post* offered an in-depth, six-part series (with graphs) that explored this issue. Take a look at any or all of these articles. Perhaps the most controversial is Part Three: Immigrants Shunning Idea of Assimilation. Do you agree with this claim? Why or why not? Feel free to comment on any part of any article as well.

2. To learn about the many ethnic subcultures in the United States, go to the Multiethnic America website (http://www.everyculture.com/multi) and choose from among the dozens of listed groups.

# Prejudice and Discrimination

# 3

 Listen to Chapter 3 on MySocLab

The burning cross—such as at this rally in Smackover, Arkansas—has long been synonymous with the Ku Klux Klan. Although the group claims it is a religious celebration of the truth and light of sacred doctrine, most observers view it as a symbolic tool of intimidation, as demonstrated by its uninvited appearance on the property of minorities.

## LEARNING OBJECTIVES | After reading this chapter you will be able to:

**3-1** Distinguish how psychology and sociology differ on the causes of prejudice.

**3-2** Describe how the media influence perceptions.

**3-3** Explain how prejudice can be reduced.

**3-4** Identify what levels of discrimination exist.

**3-5** Explain why affirmative action is so controversial.

**3-6** Analyze how current attitudes vary about racial profiling.

53

When strangers from different groups come into contact with one another, their interaction patterns may take many forms. So far, we have discussed the roles that ethnocentrism, social distance, culture, and social structure play in shaping perceptions of any outgroup. Prejudice and discrimination also emerge as major considerations in understanding intergroup relations. Why do they exist? Why do they persist? Why do certain groups become targets more frequently? How can we eliminate prejudicial attitudes and discriminatory actions?

# Prejudice

**3-1** Distinguish how psychology and sociology differ on the causes of prejudice.

**Explore on MySocLab**
Activity: Stereotypes of Crime and Justice

**Watch on MySocLab**
Video: The Basics: Deviance

**Explore on MySocLab**
Activity: How Race Is Lived in America: Officers Enlisted in the Military by Race

The word prejudice, derived from the Latin word *praejudicium*, originally meant "prejudgment." Thus, some scholars defined a prejudiced person as one who hastily reached a conclusion before examining the facts.[1] This definition proved inadequate, however, because social scientists discovered that prejudice often arose *after* groups came into contact and had at least some knowledge of one another. For that reason, most social scientists now consider prejudice as an attitude with an emotional bias.

Because feelings shape our attitudes, they reduce our receptivity to additional information that may alter those attitudes. This is especially true if prejudice is embedded in cultural norms and systematically instilled in members of society through socialization.[2] In fact, a deeply prejudiced person is almost totally immune to absorbing such additional information. Gordon Allport offered a classic example of such an individual in the following dialogue:

*Mr. X:* The trouble with the Jews is that they only take care of their own group.
*Mr. Y:* But the record of the Community Chest campaign shows that they gave more generously, in proportion to their numbers, to the general charities of the community, than did non-Jews.
*Mr. X:* That shows they are always trying to buy favor and intrude into Christian affairs. They think of nothing but money; that is why there are so many Jewish bankers.
*Mr. Y:* But a recent study shows that the percentage of Jews in the banking business is negligible, far smaller than the percentage of non-Jews.
*Mr. X:* That's just it; they don't go in for respectable business; they are only in the movie business or run night clubs.*

It is almost as if Mr. X were saying, "My mind is made up; don't confuse me with the facts." He does not refute the argument; rather, he ignores each bit of new and contradictory information and moves on to a new area in which he distorts other facts to support his prejudice against Jews.

Prejudicial attitudes may be either positive or negative. Sociologists primarily study the latter, however, because only negative attitudes can lead to turbulent social relations between dominant and minority groups. Therefore, a good working definition of **prejudice** is that it is an attitudinal system of negative beliefs, feelings, and action-orientations regarding a certain group or groups of people. The status of the strangers is an important factor in the development of such negative attitudes. Moreover, prejudicial attitudes exist among members of both dominant and minority groups. Thus, in relations between dominant and minority groups, the antipathy felt by one group for another is quite often reciprocated.

Psychological perspectives on prejudice—whether behaviorist, cognitive, or psychoanalytic—focus on the subjective states of mind of individuals. In these perspectives, a person's prejudicial attitudes may result from imitation or conditioning (behaviorist), perceived similarity–dissimilarity of beliefs (cognitive), or specific personality characteristics

---

*Gordon W. Allport, *The Nature of Prejudice*, 25th anniversary ed. (New York: Basic Books, 1979), pp. 13–14.

(psychoanalytic). In contrast, sociological perspectives focus on societal conditions as the social forces behind prejudicial attitudes and behind racial and ethnic relations. Individuals do not live in a vacuum; social reality affects their states of mind.

Both perspectives are necessary to understand prejudice. Besides needing a close study of habits, perceptions, motivation, and personality, we need an analysis of social settings, situational forces, demographic and ecological variables, and legal and economic trends.[3] Psychological and sociological perspectives thus complement each other in providing a fuller explanation of intergroup relations.

## THE PSYCHOLOGY OF PREJUDICE

The psychological approach to prejudice is to examine individual behavior. We can understand more about prejudice among individuals by focusing on four areas of study: levels of prejudice, self-justification, personality, and frustration.

**LEVELS OF PREJUDICE.** Prejudice exists on three levels: cognitive, emotional, and action orientation.[4] The **cognitive level of prejudice** encompasses a person's beliefs and perceptions of a group as threatening or nonthreatening, inferior or equal (for example, in terms of intellect, status, or biological composition), seclusive or intrusive, impulse gratifying, acquisitive, or possessing other positive or negative characteristics. Mr. X's cognitive beliefs are that Jews are intrusive and acquisitive. Other illustrations of cognitive beliefs are that the Irish are heavy drinkers and fighters, African Americans are rhythmic and lazy, and the Poles are thick-headed and unintelligent.

Generalizations shape both ethnocentric and prejudicial attitudes, but there is a difference. *Ethnocentrism* is a generalized rejection of all outgroups on the basis of an ingroup focus, whereas *prejudice* is a rejection of certain people solely on the basis of their membership in particular outgroups.

In many societies, members of the majority group may believe that a particular low-status minority group is dirty, immoral, violent, or law breaking. In the United States, the Irish, Italians, African Americans, Mexicans, Chinese, Puerto Ricans, and others have at one time or another been labeled with most, if not all, of these adjectives. In most European countries and in the United States, the group lowest on the socioeconomic ladder has often been depicted in caricature as also lowest on the evolutionary ladder. The Irish and African Americans in the United States and the peasants and various ethnic groups in Europe have all been depicted in the past as ape-like:

> The Victorian images of the Irish as "white Negro" and simian Celt, or a combination of the two, derived much of its force and inspiration from physiognomical beliefs…[but] every country in Europe had its equivalent of "white Negroes" and simianized men, whether or not they happened to be stereotypes of criminals, assassins, political radicals, revolutionaries, Slavs, gypsies, Jews, or peasants.[5]

The **emotional level of prejudice** encompasses the feelings that a minority group arouses in an individual. Although these feelings may be based on stereotypes from the cognitive level, they represent a more intense stage of personal involvement. The emotional attitudes may be negative or positive, such as fear/envy, distrust/trust, disgust/admiration, or contempt/empathy. These feelings, based on beliefs about the group, may be triggered by social interaction or by the possibility of interaction. For example, whites might react with fear or anger to the integration of their schools or neighborhoods, or Protestants might be jealous of the lifestyle of a highly successful Catholic business executive.

An **action-orientation level of prejudice** is the positive or negative predisposition to engage in discriminatory behavior. A person who harbors strong feelings about members of a certain racial or ethnic group may have a tendency to act for or against them—being aggressive or nonaggressive, offering assistance or withholding it. Such an individual also would be likely to want to exclude or include members of that group both in close, personal social relations and in peripheral social relations. For example, some people would want to exclude members of the disliked group from doing business with them or living in their neighborhood. Another manifestation of the action-orientation level of prejudice is the desire to change or maintain the status differential or inequality between the two groups. Note that an action orientation is a predisposition to act, not the action itself.

**SELF-JUSTIFICATION.** The practice of **self-justification** involves denigrating a person or group to justify maltreatment of them. In this situation, self-justification leads to prejudice and discrimination against members of another group.

Some philosophers argue that we are not so much rational creatures as we are rationalizing creatures. We require reassurance that the things we do and the lives we live are proper and that good reasons for our actions exist. If we can convince ourselves that another group is inferior, immoral, or dangerous, we may feel justified in discriminating against its members, enslaving them, or even killing them.

History is filled with examples of people who thought their maltreatment of others was just and necessary: As defenders of the "true faith," the Crusaders killed "Christ-killers" (Jews) and "infidels" (Muslims). Participants in the Spanish Inquisition imprisoned, tortured, and executed "heretics," "the disciples of the Devil." Similarly, the Puritans burned witches, whose refusal to confess "proved they were evil"; pioneers exploited or killed Native Americans who were "heathen savages"; and whites mistreated, enslaved, or killed African Americans, who were "an inferior species." U.S. Army officers in 1968 thought the villagers of My Lai were "probably" aiding the Viet Cong; so U.S. soldiers fighting in the Vietnam War felt justified in slaughtering more than 300 unarmed people there, including women, children, and the elderly. In recent years, suicide bombers and terrorists have killed innocent civilians, also justifying their actions through their religious fanaticism.

Another example of self-justification serving as a source of prejudice is the dominant group's assumption of an attitude of superiority over other groups. In this respect, establishing a prestige hierarchy—ranking the status of various ethnic groups—results in differential association. To enhance or maintain self-esteem, a person may avoid social

*Ku Klux Klan members, shown here demonstrating outside the New York State Supreme Court building, frequently use self-justification and assumptions of group superiority to explain their attitudes and actions. Displaying all three levels of prejudice, they focus today on Latinos more often than on the black, Catholic and Jewish group members who were once their main targets.*

contact with groups deemed inferior and associate only with those identified as being of high status. Through such behavior, self-justification may intensify the social distance between groups. As discussed in Chapter 1, *social distance* refers to the degree of social acceptance of ingroup members with members of various outgroups.

**PERSONALITY.** In a famous study, T. W. Adorno and his colleagues reported a correlation between individuals' early childhood experiences of harsh parental discipline and their development of an **authoritarian personality** as adults.[6] If parents assume an excessively domineering posture in their relations with a child, exercising stern measures and threatening to withdraw love if the child does not respond with weakness and submission, the child tends to be insecure and to nurture much latent hostility against the parents. When such children become adults, they may demonstrate **displaced aggression,** directing their hostility against a powerless group to compensate for their feelings of insecurity and fear. Highly prejudiced individuals tend to come from families that emphasize obedience.

The authors identified authoritarianism by the use of a measuring instrument called an F scale (the *F* stands for potential fascism). Other tests included the A-S (anti-Semitism) and E (ethnocentrism) scales, the latter measuring attitudes toward various minorities. One of their major findings was that people who scored high on authoritarianism also consistently showed a high degree of prejudice against all minority groups. These highly prejudiced people were characterized by rigidity of viewpoint, dislike for ambiguity, strict obedience to leaders, and intolerance of weakness in themselves and others.

No sooner did *The Authoritarian Personality* appear than controversy began. Critics challenged the methodology, questioned the assumptions that the F scale responses represented a belief system, and argued that social factors (for example, ideologies, stratification, mobility, intelligence, and education) relate far more to prejudice than one's personality. Others complained that the authors were interested only in measuring authoritarianism of the political right while ignoring such tendencies in those on the political left.

Although studies of authoritarian personality have helped us understand some aspects of prejudice, they have not provided a causal explanation. Most of the findings in this area show a correlation, but the findings do not prove, for example, that harsh discipline of children causes them to become prejudiced adults. Perhaps the strict parents were themselves prejudiced, and the child learned those attitudes from them.

For some people, prejudice indeed may be rooted in subconscious childhood tensions, but we simply do not know whether these tensions directly cause a high degree of prejudice in the adult or whether other powerful social forces are the determinants. Whatever the explanation, authoritarianism is a significant phenomenon worthy of continued investigation. Recent research, however, has stressed social and situational factors, rather than personality, as primary causes of prejudice and discrimination.[7]

Yet another dimension of the personality component is the role of self-esteem. Those with high self-esteem tend to evaluate an outgroup more positively than those with low self-esteem.[8] Also, individuals' awareness of potential discrimination against themselves can provide self-esteem protection, in contrast to the lower self-esteem experienced by those less aware of such external factors.[9] Thus, it would appear that the level of one's self-esteem affects attitudes both about oneself and others.

**FRUSTRATION.** One result of relative deprivation is frustration, when expectations remain unsatisfied. **Relative deprivation** is a lack of resources, or rewards, in one's standard of living in comparison with others in the society. A number of investigators have suggested that frustrations tend to increase aggression toward others.[10] Frustrated people may easily strike out against the perceived cause of their frustration. However, this reaction may not be possible because the true source of the frustration often is too nebulous to be identified or too powerful to act against. In such instances, the result may be displaced aggression, where the frustrated individual or group redirects anger against a more visible, vulnerable, and socially sanctioned target that is unable to strike back. Minorities meet these criteria and thus are frequently the recipients of displaced aggression by the dominant or another minority group.

Blaming others for something that is not their fault is known as **scapegoating.** The term comes from the ancient Hebrew custom of using a goat during the Day of Atonement as a symbol of the sins of the people. In an annual ceremony, a priest placed his hands on the head of a goat and listed the people's sins in a symbolic transference of guilt; he then chased the goat out of the community, thereby freeing the people of sin.[11] Since those times, the powerful group usually has punished the scapegoat group rather than allowing it to escape.

Throughout world history, minority groups often served as scapegoats, including the Christians in ancient Rome, the Huguenots in France, the Jews in Europe and Russia, and the Puritans and Quakers in England. Certain characteristics are necessary for a group to become a suitable scapegoat. The group must be (1) highly visible in physical appearance or observable customs and actions; (2) not strong enough to strike back; (3) situated within easy access of the dominant group and, ideally, concentrated in one area; (4) a past target of hostility for whom latent hostility still exists; and (5) the symbol of an unpopular concept.[12]

Some groups fit this typology better than others, but minority racial and ethnic groups have been a perennial choice. Irish, Italians, Catholics, Jews, Quakers, Mormons, Chinese, Japanese, blacks, Puerto Ricans, Mexicans, and Koreans have all been treated, at one time or another, as the scapegoat in the United States. Especially in times of economic hardship, societies tend to blame some group for the general conditions, which often leads to aggressive action against the group as an expression of frustration. For example, in the South between 1882 and 1930, whenever cotton prices declined the number of lynchings of blacks increased.[13]

A growing number of studies show that unanticipated failure to reach a desired goal is more unpleasant than an expected failure. Frustrations then will generate aggressive inclinations to the extent of how bad individuals feel about not getting what they wanted. Confronted with unexpected frustrating situations, highly prejudiced individuals are more likely to seek scapegoats than are unprejudiced individuals. Another intervening variable is that personal frustrations (marital failure, injury, or mental illness) make people more likely to seek scapegoats than do shared frustrations (dangers of flood or hurricane).[14]

Frustration–aggression theory, although helpful, is not completely satisfactory. It ignores the role of culture and the reality of actual social conflict and fails to show any causal relationship. Most of the responses measured in these studies were of people already biased. Why did one group rather than another become the object of the aggression? Moreover, frustration does not necessarily precede aggression, and aggression does not necessarily flow from frustration.

## THE SOCIOLOGY OF PREJUDICE

The sociological approach to prejudice is not to examine individual behavior, as psychologists do, but rather to examine behavior within a group setting. Sociologist Talcott Parsons provided one bridge between psychology and sociology by introducing social forces as a variable in frustration–aggression theory. He suggested that both the family and the occupational structure may produce anxieties and insecurities that create frustration.[15] According to this view, the growing-up process (gaining parental affection and approval, identifying with and imitating sexual role models, and competing with others in adulthood) sometimes involves severe emotional strain. The result is an adult personality with a large reservoir of repressed aggression that becomes *free-floating*—susceptible to redirection against convenient scapegoats. Similarly, the occupational system is a source of frustration: Its emphasis on competitiveness and individual achievement, its function of conferring status, its requirement that people inhibit their natural impulses at work, and its ties to the state of the economy can generate emotional anxieties. Parsons pessimistically concluded that minorities fulfill a functional "need" as targets for displaced aggression and therefore will remain targets.[16]

Perhaps most influential in staking out the sociological position on prejudice was Herbert Blumer, who suggested that prejudice always involves the "sense of group position" in society. Echoing other social scientists, about the three levels of prejudice we discussed earlier, Blumer argued that prejudice can include beliefs, feelings, and a predisposition to action, thus motivating behavior that derives from the social hierarchy.[17] By emphasizing historically established group positions and relationships, Blumer shifted the focus away from attitudes and personality compositions of individuals. As a social phenomenon, prejudice rises or falls according to issues that alter one group's position in relation to that of another group.

**SOCIALIZATION.** In the **socialization process,** individuals acquire the values, attitudes, beliefs, and perceptions of their culture or subculture, including religion, nationality, and social class. Generally, the child conforms to the parents' expectations in acquiring an understanding of the world and its people. Being impressionable and knowing of no alternative conceptions of the world, the child usually accepts these concepts without questioning. We thus learn the prejudices of our parents and others, which then become part of our values and beliefs. Even when based on false stereotypes, prejudices shape our perceptions of various peoples and influence our attitudes and actions toward particular groups. For example, if we develop negative attitudes about Jews because we are taught that they are shrewd, acquisitive, and clannish—all-too-familiar stereotypes—as adults, we may refrain from business or social relationships with them. We may not even realize the reason for such avoidance, so subtle has been the prejudice instilled within us.

People may learn certain prejudices because of their pervasiveness. The cultural screen that we develop and through which we view the surrounding world is not always accurate, but it does permit transmission of shared values and attitudes, which are reinforced by others. Prejudice, like cultural values, is taught and learned through the socialization process. The prevailing prejudicial attitudes and actions may be embedded deeply in custom or law (for example, the **Jim Crow laws** of the 1890s and early twentieth century

*No one is born prejudiced. Through the socialization process, children learn the values and attitudes of their parents, no matter whether those are positive or negative. Brought to this hate-laden demonstration and given a sign to hold, such continuing exposure may develop this boy into becoming part of the next generation's bigots and hate mongers.*

# the INTERNATIONAL scene

## Economic Competition in the Czech Republic

The 83,000 Vietnamese currently living in the Czech Republic are mostly first- and second-generation families, many of whom came in recent decades when the country experienced a booming economy. While times were good, the Vietnamese quietly prospered and the Czechs ignored their presence. A severe 2008–2009 economic downturn and high unemployment drove many Czechs to seek the low-paying work they once left to foreigners. Polls revealed that two-thirds of Czechs no longer wanted the Vietnamese in their country.

That attitude led to an outpouring of bitterness against minorities, particularly the Vietnamese. Verbal taunts, physical attacks, denial of access to discos and restaurants, and public expressions that the Vietnamese should "go home" became common. In 2009, the government initiated a voluntary policy for any unemployed foreign worker wanting to go home, offering free one-way air or rail fare and about $700 in cash. However, many workers, saddled with debt and ashamed to return home with so little money, decided to wait for the economy to improve.

Nevertheless, the numbers of Vietnamese Czechs is higher than ever before. Many are store owners, speak Czech fluently, and send their children to the public schools, where they typically are among the highest academic achievers. However, the backlash against the newer Vietnamese workers, whether employed or jobless, has threatened even the decades-old coexistence of the longer-residing Vietnamese and the host society. Until the economy improves, tensions likely will remain.

### CRITICAL THINKING QUESTION

What parallels do you see in dominant–minority relations in the Czech Republic and the United States?

Source: Based on the observations of Vincent N. Parrillo, a former Fulbright scholar in the Czech Republic and frequent visitor.

---

**STUDENTS SPEAK** "Living in the state of Alabama, I got to see a lot of prejudiced people. In fact, I went to a historically black school. Therefore, everyone would call me *Mexican* and say that all Hispanics are the same. Many didn't talk to me because they thought I didn't know good enough English because I was Hispanic. In the same way, I have family members who are prejudiced about African Americans, not realizing that we have many things in common."

**—Lourdes Fabian**

establishing segregated public facilities throughout the South, which subsequent generations accepted as proper and maintained in their own adult lives).

Although socialization explains how prejudicial attitudes may be transmitted from one generation to the next, it does not explain their origin or why they intensify or diminish throughout the years. These aspects of prejudice must be explained in another way.

**ECONOMIC COMPETITION.** People tend to be more hostile toward others when they feel that their security is threatened; thus, many social scientists conclude that economic competition and conflict breed prejudice. Certainly, considerable evidence shows that negative stereotyping, prejudice, and discrimination increase markedly whenever competition for available jobs increases (see the International Scene box).

An excellent illustration relates to the Chinese sojourners in the nineteenth-century United States. Prior to the 1870s, the transcontinental railroad was being built, and the Chinese filled many of the jobs made available by this project in the sparsely populated West. Although they were expelled from the region's gold mines and schools, and could not obtain justice in the courts, they managed to convey to some whites the image of being clean, hardworking, and law-abiding people. The completion of the railroad, the flood of former Civil War soldiers into the job market, and the economic depression of 1873 worsened their situation. The Chinese became more frequent victims of open discrimination and hostility. Their positive stereotype among some whites was widely displaced by a negative one: They were now "conniving," "crafty," "criminal," and "the yellow menace." Only after they retreated into Chinatowns and entered specialty occupations that minimized their competition with whites did the intense hostility abate.

One pioneer in the scientific study of prejudice, John Dollard, demonstrated how prejudice against the Germans, which had been virtually nonexistent in a small U.S. industrial town, arose when times got bad:

> Local Whites largely drawn from the surrounding farms manifested considerable direct aggression toward the newcomers. Scornful and derogatory opinions were expressed about the Germans, and the native Whites had a satisfying sense of superiority toward them….The chief element in the permission to be aggressive against the Germans was rivalry for jobs and status in the local woodenware plants. The native Whites felt definitely crowded for their jobs by the entering German groups and, in case of bad times, had a chance to blame the Germans who by their presence provided more competitors for the scarcer jobs. There seemed to be no traditional pattern of prejudice against Germans unless the skeletal suspicion of all out-groupers (always present) be invoked in this place.[18]

Both experimental studies and historical analyses have provided support for the economic-competition theory. In an oft-cited classic study, Muzafer Sherif directed several experiments showing how intergroup competition at a boys' camp led to conflict and escalating hostility.[19] On a much larger scale, throughout U.S. history, in times of high unemployment and thus intense job competition, nativist movements against minorities have flourished.[20] This pattern has held true regionally—against Asians on the West Coast, Italians in Louisiana, and French Canadians in New England—and nationally, with the anti-foreign movements always peaking during periods of depression. So it was with the Native American Party in the 1830s, the Know-Nothing Party in the 1850s, the American Protective Association in the 1890s, and the Ku Klux Klan after World War I.

In our times, one group's pressure of job competition on another group continues to be a factor in its becoming a target of prejudice. For example, one study conducted in the southern United States found that although both blacks and non-blacks perceived a potential economic threat from continued Latino immigration, blacks were more concerned about its effects on them than were whites.[21] It appears they may have some cause for concern. Studies show that many employers view Latinos as far more desirable employees than blacks, in part, because they see immigrants as more easily controllable.[22] In an urban labor market where limited low-skill jobs exist, such a situation can generate hostility between the two groups.

Once again though, a theory that offers some excellent insights into prejudice—in particular, that economic competition sparks increased hostility toward or between minorities—also has some serious shortcomings. Not all groups that have been objects of hostility (for example, Quakers and Mormons) have been economic competitors. Moreover, why is hostility against some groups greater than against others? Why do the negative feelings in some communities run against groups whose numbers are so small that they cannot possibly pose an economic threat? Evidently, values besides economic ones cause people to be antagonistic to a group considered an actual or potential threat.

**SOCIAL NORMS.** Many social scientists insist that a relationship exists between prejudice and a person's tendency to conform to societal expectations.[23] **Social norms**—the cultural guidelines—form the generally shared rules defining what is and is not proper behavior in one's culture. By learning and unknowingly accepting the prevailing prejudices, an individual is simply conforming to those norms.

This theory holds that a direct relationship exists between degree of conformity and degree of prejudice. If so, people's prejudices should decrease or increase significantly when

*Economic globalization has been particularly hard on U.S. workers, as manufacturing jobs go overseas where cheaper labor allows companies to lower their production costs. This results not only in rallies, such as this one by steelworkers in Michigan in 2009, but also in generating feelings of bitterness and prejudicial anti-foreign attitudes.*

they move into areas where the prejudicial norm is different. An abundance of research, both classical and current, offers evidence to support this view.

John Dollard's classic study, *Caste and Class in a Southern Town,* provided an in-depth look at the emotional adjustment of whites and blacks to rigid social norms in the 1930s.[24] Intimidation—sometimes even severe reprisals for going against social norms—ensured compliance. However, reprisals usually were unnecessary. The advantages whites and blacks gained in personal security and stability set in motion a vicious circle. They encouraged a way of life that reinforced the rationale of the social system in this community. Later, Thomas Pettigrew found that southerners in the 1950s became less prejudiced against blacks when they interacted with them in the army, where the social norms were less prejudicial.[25] Another researcher found that people moving into an anti-Semitic neighborhood in New York City became more anti-Semitic.[26]

In recent years, researchers have further documented how ingroup norms influence attitudes and behavior.[27] As individuals conform to the norms and prejudices of a desirable group, they begin to identify with this group and internalize its norms.[28] Further, in a majority-group controlled setting such as the workplace, members of a stigmatized minority group are likely to adopt a pragmatic strategy of stigmatizing a different minority group both to conform to the majority group's recognized prejudicial norms and to deflect prejudice from itself. In time, their repeated accommodation to these norms for self-preservation could lead to internalization or conversion of their own beliefs to prejudicial attitudes.[29]

Although the social-norms theory explains prevailing attitudes, it does not explain either their origins or the reasons new prejudices develop when other groups move into an area. In addition, the theory does not explain why prejudicial attitudes against a particular group rise and fall cyclically throughout the years.

Although many social scientists have attempted to identify the causes of prejudice, no single factor provides an adequate explanation. Prejudice is a complex phenomenon, and it is most likely the product of more than one causal agent (see Table 3.1). Sociologists today tend either to emphasize multiple-cause explanations or to stress social forces encountered in specific and similar situations—forces such as economic conditions, stratification, and hostility toward an outgroup.

**TABLE 3.1  Approaches to the Study of Prejudice**

| PSYCHOLOGICAL | | |
|---|---|---|
| **Approach** | **Concept** | **Example** |
| Self-Justification | We blame others to justify our mistreatment of them. | "They asked for it!" |
| Personality | Strict child rearing results in an intolerant adult. | "I can't stand people who aren't neat!" |
| Frustration | Unmet expectations lead to finding a scapegoat. | "She didn't deserve that promotion! I did!" |
| **SOCIOLOGICAL** | | |
| Socialization | We learn tolerance or intolerance from others. | "They're just not like us. They're lazy!" |
| Economic Competition | We become hostile when we think others are a threat. | "Immigrants take jobs away from Americans!" |
| Social Norms | We learn to conform to prevailing attitudes. | "Don't be seen talking to those people!" |

## STEREOTYPING

One common reaction to strangers is to categorize them broadly. Prejudice at the cognitive level often arises from false perceptions that are enhanced by cultural or racial stereotypes. A **stereotype** is an oversimplified generalization by which we attribute certain traits or characteristics to an entire group without regard to individual differences. Sometimes stereotypes are positive—for example, that African Americans are good athletes and that Asians are good mathematicians. Even here, however, they can create pressures and problems—for example, for African Americans who are not athletic or for Asians who are weak in math. Stereotypes may distort reality but they nevertheless are images one group may hold about another.[30]

Stereotypes easily can become embedded within everyday thinking and serve to enhance a group's self-esteem and social identity by favorably comparing oneself to outgroups. Even if an outgroup is economically successful, stereotyping it as clannish, mercenary, or unscrupulous enables other groups to affirm their own moral superiority.

Not only do stereotypes deny individuals the right to be judged and treated on the basis of their own personal merit, but also, by assigning a particular image to the entire group, it becomes a justification for discriminatory behavior. Negative stereotypes also serve as important reference points in people's evaluations of what they observe in everyday life. Here is an excellent illustration of how a prejudiced person arbitrarily uses stereotypes to interpret other people's motives and behavior:

> Prejudiced people see the world in ways that are consistent with their prejudice. If Mr. Bigot sees a well-dressed, white, Anglo-Saxon Protestant sitting on a park bench sunning himself at three o'clock on a Wednesday afternoon, he thinks nothing of it. If he sees a well-dressed black man doing the same thing, he is liable to leap to the conclusion that the person is unemployed—and he becomes infuriated, because he assumes that his hard-earned taxes are paying that shiftless good-for-nothing enough in welfare subsidies to keep him in good clothes. If Mr. Bigot passes Mr. Anglo's house and notices that a trash can is overturned and some garbage is strewn about, he is apt to conclude that a stray dog has been searching for food. If he passes Mr. Garcia's house and notices the same thing, he is inclined to become annoyed, and to assert that "those people live like pigs." Not only does prejudice influence his conclusions, his erroneous conclusions justify and intensify his negative feelings.[31]

Both dominant-group and minority-group members may hold stereotypes about each other. The activation of a stereotype in one's mind can validate negative thoughts

# the ETHNIC experience

## The Impact of the Media

As a reflector of society's values, the media have a tremendous impact on the shaping of our personal and group identities. Radio, television, films, newspapers, magazines, and comics can convey the rich textures of a pluralistic society or they can, directly or indirectly (by omission and distortion), alter our perception of other ethnic groups and reinforce our defensiveness and ambivalence about our own cultural backgrounds. As an Italian American, I've realized this myself when comparing the ethnic invisibility of 1950s television with modern shows that concentrate on Mafia hit men and multiple biographies of Mussolini. Having squirmed as I watched some of these portrayals, I can empathize with Arabs who resent being characterized as villainous sheikhs, Jews seen as mendacious moguls, or even the current vogue for matching a Russian accent with a kind of oafish villain. Although such stereotypes may

or may not serve political ends, they share the cartoonlike isolation of a few traits that ignore the humanity and variety of a group's members.

What is the impact of ethnic stereotypes on television and in film on how people feel about themselves and how they perceive other ethnic groups?

Although research in this area is limited, what is available suggests that TV's and film's portrayal of ethnics does have a deleterious effect on perceptions of self and others. In my own clinical work, I have found that minority children and adults often will internalize negative stereotypes about their own group. Other studies have shown that ethnic stereotypes on television and in the movies can contribute to prejudice against a particular group—especially when the person is not acquainted with any members of that group.

In studies of youngsters who commit hate acts—desecration of religious institutions and racial and anti-Semitic

incidents, for example—many apprehended youngsters reported they got the idea of performing vandalism from news coverage of similar acts (the copycat syndrome). They saw media coverage as conferring recognition and prestige, so was a means of temporarily raising their low self-esteem.

The combination of TV fiction and news with the rash of "truly tasteless" joke books, radio call-in shows that invite bigoted calls from listeners, and late-night TV hosts and comedians who denigrate ethnic groups has a considerable impact on people's perceptions. While the media cannot be blamed for creating the bigotry, their insensitive reporting and encouragement of inflammatory comments establish a societal norm that gives license to such attitudes and behavior.

Source: Joseph Giordano, "Identity Crisis: Stereotypes Stifle Self-Development." Used with permission, Center for Media Literacy, www.medialit.com

**STUDENTS SPEAK** *"When people ask me what my ethnicity is, I tell them that I am Mexican and Portuguese. A response I get a lot is, 'Oh, you don't look Mexican. You're light-skinned.' I respond by asking them what is a Mexican supposed to look like? Because of what they had heard and seen (through friends, media, etc.), they have a perception of what Mexicans are supposed to look like."*

**—Jennifer Fernandes**

about others.[32] Often, people are aware of the stereotypes others may have of them, and they may believe that more individuals hold that view than actually do. Stereotypes can affect both self-image and social interactions, creating social barriers to intergroup understanding and respect. Mass-media portrayals further reinforce stereotypes, giving such thinking a false aura of validity (see the Ethnic Experience box).

**ETHNOPHAULISMS.** An **ethnophaulism** is a derogatory word or expression used to describe a racial or ethnic group. This is the language of prejudice—the verbal picture of a negative stereotype that reflects the prejudice and bigotry of a society's past and present.

Ethnophaulisms fall into three types: (1) disparaging names (for example, chink, dago, polack, jungle bunny, honky, or Bruno, from the film of that title to disparage homosexuals); (2) alleged physical characteristics or foods (for example, darky, skirt, porker, potato eater, frog, spaghetti eater); and (3) alleged behaviors (for example, "jew him down" for trying to get something for a lower price, "luck of the Irish" suggesting undeserved good fortune, "to be in Dutch" meaning to be in trouble, or "welsh on a bet" for failure to honor a debt).[33] The context of words is important though. For example, the once derogatory expressions "Dutch treat" and "luck of the Irish" now have a neutral or positive concept.

Both majority and minority groups coin and use ethnophaulisms to degrade outgroups. The emotional power of such labels has the effect of reducing people to a less-than-human abstraction.[34] Such usage helps justify discrimination, inequality, and social privilege for the dominant group, and it helps the minority cope with social injustices caused by others. Them-versus-us name-calling is divisive, and the frequency of its usage reveals the degree of group prejudice in a society. In addition, people tend to express these negative terms more often as a function of the size, "foreignness," and appearance of groups.[35]

Sometimes members of a racial- or ethnic-minority group use an ethnophaulism directed against themselves in their conversations with one another. On occasion, they may use the term as a reprimand to one of their own kind for acting out the stereotype, but more often, they mean it as a humorous expression of friendship and endearment. However, when an outsider uses that same term, they resent it because of its prejudicial connotations.

The use of ethnophaulisms has behavioral consequences. For example, in an examination of archival research data spanning a 150-year period of U.S. history, Brian Mullen explored the effects of using ethnophaulisms in the representation of ethnic immigrant groups.[36] He found that the smaller, less familiar, and "more foreign" ethnic immigrant groups were typically portrayed in a simplistic and negative manner, with a corresponding tendency to exclude those groups from the host society. His study illustrates the "them" and "us" divisiveness, mentioned earlier, that results from the use of disparaging terms to refer to others.

**ETHNIC HUMOR.** Why do some people find ethnic jokes funny, whereas others find them distasteful? Studies show the response often reflects the listener's attitude toward the group being ridiculed. If you hold favorable or positive attitudes toward the group that is the butt of the joke, then you are less likely to find it funny than if you hold unfavorable or negative views. If you dislike a group about which a joke implies something negative, you will tend to appreciate the joke.[37]

A common minority practice is to use ethnic humor as a strategy for defining one's ethnicity positively. In telling ethnic jokes about one's own group, the speaker may be challenging stereotypes within the dominant culture. If an ethnic tells the joke to the ethnic ingroup, the phenomenon of laughing together through joke sharing is "an ethnicizing phenomenon" that develops a sense of "we-ness" in laughing with others. If an ethnic tells the joke to outsiders, it can serve as a means to undermine the stereotype by ridiculing it.[38] Ethnic humor thus can serve as a powerful force to facilitate a positive, empowered position for the ethnic individual within the dominant culture. Of course, we must realize that there also is the potential risk that the joke will confirm the stereotype, not undermine it.

## THE INFLUENCE OF TELEVISION

Virtually every U.S. household owns at least one television set, and families in the United States watch more than seven hours of TV daily, on average. Does all this viewing make us think or act differently? Does it change our attitudes or shape our feelings and reactions about minority groups? Or is it only entertainment with no appreciable effect on perceptions and behavior? Abundant research evidence indicates television programming distorts reality, promotes stereotypical role models, and significantly shapes and reinforces our attitudes about men, women, and minority groups.

**3-2** Describe how the media influence perceptions.

**PERPETUATION OF STEREOTYPES.** Twice in the late 1970s, the U.S. Commission on Civil Rights charged the television industry with perpetuating racial and sexual stereotypes in programming and news.[39] A generation later and a second decade into the twenty-first century, how much improvement do we see? In programs on some cable stations or small, independent stations, we now can find strong female, ethnic, or racial lead characters. However, in news, commercials, and programming, many problems remain.

Studies of regular viewers reveal a strong association of their exposure to local or national newscasts and their racial attitudes and perceptions. They were more likely to think African Americans were poor, intimidating, violent, and/or criminal. They also were more prone to hold racially prejudiced views (see the Reality Check box).[40]

Prime-time commercials still perpetuate traditional stereotypes of women and men.[41] "Distinct racial segregation" occurs in prime-time ads, with mostly whites appearing in ads for upscale, beauty, or home products (with the notable exceptions of such celebrities as Halle Berry and Beyoncé). People of color, in contrast, appeared in ads for low-cost, low-nutrition products (for example, fast food and soft drinks) and in athletic and sports equipment ads. Such depictions raise questions about the continuance of racial stereotypes, notably a somewhat one-dimensional view of people of color as key consumers of low-cost products.[42] The niche station, Black Entertainment Television (BET), is more likely to offer some positive black female representations compared to the network stations, but they too are often portrayed in commercials as sexually desirable and available, continuing the problematic stereotyped representations of gender.[43] Even most major, active characters in commercials aired during children's cartoon programming are male, thus perpetuating stereotyped sex-typed behaviors, despite their decrease in the real world.[44]

Reality television shows such as "COPS," "Deal or No Deal," The Contender," and "The Real World" are edited or directed for desired effects and thus present characters from various races that reinforce stereotypes.[45] Other minorities, such as Asian and Pacific Islander Americans, are underrepresented, stereotyped, and marginalized in prime-time

**"Mutual: Both Are Glad There Are Bars between 'Em!"**

*This visual stereotype of an apelike Irishman reinforced prevailing beliefs that the Irish were emotionally unstable and morally primitive. This cartoon appeared in Judge on November 7, 1891, and is typical of a worldwide tendency to depict minorities as apelike.*

*The reality show, "Desperate Housewives of New Jersey," furthers existing stereotypes about Italian-American families and women from northern New Jersey. The moments of over-the-top drama, obnoxious behavior, and material excesses convey images that bear little resemblance to most Italian Americans or New Jerseyans.*

# REALITY check

## College Student Television Viewing and Ethnic Stereotypes

Do U.S. college students who view television 15 or more hours a week hold primarily positive or negative stereotypes of African Americans, Asians, Caucasians, Latino/Hispanics, and Native Americans? Researchers surveyed 450 students, 58 percent of them male, to find out. The respondents were mostly white (79 percent), with Asians comprising 5 percent; African Americans, 4 percent; Latinos, 4 percent; Native Americans, 1 percent; and 7 percent other or non-identified.

On a 1-to-7 scale, the students—60 percent attending a university in the Northwest and 40 percent at a university in the Southwest—rated their personal perceptions of each group as closer to one or the other of two bi-polar adjectives from a list of 10 personality traits (e.g., "shy-outgoing, lazy-hard working, quiet-talkative").

Generally, college students who were heavy viewers held more negative stereotypes than light viewers, particularly against Asians and Native Americans. Caucasians benefited from the most positive typecasting (and least negative) in comparison to the other four groups. They were viewed as more dependable, stable, and less angry. Heavy viewers of educational television programming, however, rated Caucasians low in conscientiousness.

The type of programming watched affected the findings. Heavy viewers of entertainment, educational, and sports programs had more negative ethnic perceptions, while heavy viewers of information programs revealed more positively skewed perceptions. Within the categories, much variation occurred. Heavy viewers of entertainment programs saw Asians as less conscientious and African Americans as less agreeable. Heavy viewers of information programming rated Asians and Native Americans as less extroverted, and African Americans as more open. Few significant differences existed between heavy and light television viewers regarding stereotypical personality traits for Latino/Hispanics.

### CRITICAL THINKING QUESTION

How many hours of television do you watch each week? On reflection, do you detect any differing patterns in the portrayals of members of these five groups?

Source: Adapted from Moon J. Lee, et al., "Television Viewing and Ethnic Stereotypes: Do College Students Form Stereotypical Perceptions of Ethnic Groups as a Result of Heavy Television Consumption?" *Howard Journal of Communications* 20:1 (2009): 95–110.

---

programs.[46] Female characters mostly inhabit interpersonal roles involved with romance, family, and friends, while male characters are more likely to enact work-related roles. Interestingly, shows with women writers or creators are likely to feature both female and male characters in interpersonal roles, whereas programs employing all-male writers and creators are more likely to feature both female and male characters in work roles.[47]

**INFLUENCING OF ATTITUDES.** Television influences attitudes toward racial or ethnic groups by the status of the parts it assigns to their members, the kind of behavior they display within these parts, and even the type of products they promote. Television greatly influences children's attitudes in this area. Children watch television during prime time more than any other time of day. Yet prime time remains overwhelmingly white, with people of color appearing largely in secondary and guest roles. Whites account for 73 percent of the prime-time population, followed by African Americans (16 percent), Hispanics (6.5 percent), Asian/Pacific Islanders (3 percent), and Arab/Middle Easterners (0.4 percent). However, prime-time diversity dramatically increases as the evening progresses—with the 8:00 P.M. hour, the least racially diverse, and the 10:00 P.M. hour, the most racially diverse. Thus, children and youths are more likely to see a much more homogeneous prime-time world than are adults who watch television later in the evening.[48]

*All in the Family,* a popular comedy series in the 1970s and still in syndicated reruns, received an NAACP award for its contribution to race relations but divided critics on the question of whether it reduced or reinforced racial bigotry. Liberal viewers saw the program as satire, with son-in-law Mike effectively rebutting Archie's ignorance and bigotry or minority members besting Archie by the end of the program. In contrast, prejudiced viewers—particularly adolescents—were significantly more likely to admire Archie than Mike and to perceive Archie as the winner in the end. Thus, the program probably reinforced prejudice and discrimination as much as it combated it.

Similarly, ethnic humor in such televisions shows as *South Park*, *The Simpsons*, or *The Family Guy*, along with such films as *Borat* and *Bruno*, have the same dangerous potential. Although they can be viewed as humorous, exaggerated exposures of bigotry, they also can ring true to prejudiced individuals.[49]

## THE INFLUENCE OF ADVERTISING AND MUSIC

Social scientists are paying increasing attention to the impact of corporate advertising, rap music lyrics, and music videos on attitudes about men and women. Beyond the obviousness of marketing products and entertainment lie their powers of seduction, imagery, and conditioning of attitudes.

**ADVERTISING.** The average American watches three years' worth of television ads during the course of a lifetime. What effect do they have on our attitudes? In a content analysis of popular TV commercials designed for specific target audiences, researchers found the characters in them enjoyed more prominence and exercised more authority if they were white or if they were male. Images of romantic and domestic fulfillment also differed by race and gender, with women and whites disproportionately shown in family settings and in gender interactions. In general, the researchers found that these commercials tended to portray white men as powerful, white women as sex objects, African American men as aggressive, and African American women as inconsequential. They suggest that these commercial images help perpetuate subtle prejudice against African Americans by exaggerating cultural differences and denying positive emotions.[50]

Another study of prime-time television ads found blacks generally portrayed in a more diverse, equitable manner compared to whites, but Asians, Hispanics, and Native Americans were underrepresented and sometimes negatively depicted. Hispanics often were suggestively clad and shown engaging in alluring behaviors and sexual gazing, thus stressing physical appearance and sexuality over intelligence. Asians were most commonly young, passive adults at work in technology ads, thus promoting the stereotype of submissiveness and superior achievements as measures of their self-worth.[51]

Exploitation of women in ads is an ongoing reality, often showing sexed-up girls or women posing as adolescents. One recent shoe ad, for example, featured pop singer Christina Aguilera dressed as a schoolgirl with pigtails and a short skirt, her shirt unbuttoned, and licking a lollipop.[52] Women—and girls in particular—need to be mindful of the influential power of advertising. Women's bodies, frequently portrayed as headless torsos, have long been used to sell everything from toothbrushes to chain saws. In addition, endless glossy spreads in women's magazines feature beauty products, fashion, and diets to keep women focused on exterior "problems." Ads alone are not to blame for demonizing fat women or causing binge drinking, teenage pregnancy, and violence against women, but their cumulative effect fosters an inescapable, poisonous environment in which sexist stereotypes, cynicism and self-hatred, and the search for quick fixes flourish. Consumers may think they are unaffected, but advertisers successfully create a false consciousness and teach young women that they are appetizing only when "plucked, polished, and painted."[53]

**MUSIC.** One of the major criticisms of rap music is that it may affect attitudes and behavior regarding the use of violence, especially violence against women. Although some rap artists, such as Arrested Development and Queen Latifah, reflect a concern for humanity and offer inspiration and hope, others—such as Eminem, 2 Live Crew, Apache, N.W.A., and Scarface—routinely endorse violence, homophobia, and portray women as punching bags, strippers, or simply sperm receptacles. Such portrayals prompted the National Black Women's Political Caucus to seek legislation to control the access to rap music. In 2005, *Essence,* one of the leading magazines for black women, launched a one-year "Take Back the Music" campaign against anti-women lyrics in rap music. In 2007, after the firing of radio and TV personality Don Imus (now back on the air) for his racist remarks about the Rutgers University women's basketball team, some black leaders next went after rap music producers to curtail offensive lyrics.

Pop culture has enormous influence on how young men and women see themselves and each other in terms of sexuality and gender. Powerful sexual imagery in hundreds of music videos, produced mostly by men, objectifies and dehumanizes women by calling them derogatory names and frequently portraying them as existing solely for males' sexual satisfaction. Through these videos and lyrics, male rappers—both black and Chicano—assert their sexual prowess in having the most beautiful women, the most women, and the ability to take other men's women. Rap lyrics thus reinforce the concept of male dominance over women.[54]

## CAN PREJUDICE BE REDUCED?

Organized efforts to lessen or eliminate prejudice generally fall into one of three approaches: intergroup contact, education, and workplace diversity programs. No approach has been successful in all instances, probably because the inequalities that encourage prejudicial attitudes still exist.

**INTERACTION.** The intergroup **contact hypothesis** speaks to the importance of contact for improving intergroup relations. However, interaction between people of different racial and ethnic backgrounds does not necessarily lead to more positive attitudes. In fact, the situation may worsen if such contact is unwelcome, as happened frequently when schools and neighborhoods experienced an influx of people from a different group. Even so, interaction can reduce prejudice, depending on the frequency and duration of contacts; the relative status of the two parties and their backgrounds and common goals; and whether they meet in a political, religious, occupational, residential, or recreational situation.[55]

Successful outcomes, as predicted by the contact hypothesis, are more likely to happen through perspective taking. Because differences in perspective shape perceptions and reactions when contact occurs, the ability to assume temporarily the viewpoint of the other, and to understand it on its own terms, is a prerequisite for that interaction to conclude with a positive result.[56]

An important element, then, is the commonalities shared by the members of different groups in their joint efforts. If culturally different individuals are in a situation that is competitive, such as being rivals for a promotion, or forced, such as busing students to integrate a school, then increased hostility, not less, is a likely result. Only when the contact is positive does prejudice decrease. As minority group members experience upward mobility through better education and good-paying jobs, their entry into the middle class offers a good example of the contact hypothesis at work. The emerging cross-group friendships and work relationships typically lessen prejudices.

A good example of the significance of the type of contact emerges from the experiments in the **jigsaw classroom** of Elliot Aronson and Neal Osherow.[57] This research team observed that classroom competition for teacher recognition and approval often created a special hardship on minority children less fluent in English or less self-assured about participating in class. The researchers created interdependent learning groups of five or six children, each member charged with learning one portion of the day's lesson in a particular subject. The children learned the complete lesson from one another and then took a test on all the material. Because it creates interdependent groups, this technique

**3-3** Explain how prejudice can be reduced.

*Cooperative learning is now a common teaching technique in U.S. elementary schools. Research shows that a variation of the approach, the jigsaw method, is also an effective means of reducing the walls of prejudice and social distance, while simultaneously building self-esteem and motivation in minority youngsters.*

is *not* the same as the cooperative learning approach so common in U.S. schools. In fact, Australian researchers compared use of the two approaches among children in grades 4–6 and found that the jigsaw classroom produced significant improvements on measures of academic performance, liking of peers, and racial prejudice, in contrast to the effect of the cooperative approach that worsened preexisting intergroup tensions[58] (see the Ethnic Experience box).

**EDUCATION.** Most people have long cherished the hope that education would reduce prejudice. Evaluation research studies show that special programs aimed at promoting intergroup understanding do have a positive effect.[59] Still, these positive results are not necessarily universal among all students nor long-lasting among other students.

One reason for this failure is that people tend to use **selective perception;** that is, they absorb information that accords with their own beliefs and rationalize away information that does not. Another reason is the almost quantum leap from the classroom to real-life situations. Dealing with prejudice from a detached perspective in a classroom setting is one thing; dealing with it in everyday life is quite another because emotions, social pressures, and many other factors are involved.

Despite these limitations, courses in race and ethnic relations certainly have value because they raise the students' level of consciousness about intergroup dynamics. However, a significant reduction or elimination of prejudice is more likely to occur by changing the structural conditions of inequality that promote and maintain prejudicial attitudes. As long as the dominant group does not react with fear and institute a countermovement, the improvement of a minority's social position changes power relations and reduces negative stereotypes. Therefore, continued efforts at public enlightenment and extension of constitutional rights and equal opportunities to all Americans, regardless of race, religion, or national origin, appear to be the most promising means of attaining an unprejudiced society.

One measure of shifting group positions is the expanding inclusiveness of the mainstream U.S. ingroup; previously excluded minority groups, once victims of prejudice, are

# the ETHNIC experience

## Reducing Prejudice through the Jigsaw Classroom

The experience of a Mexican American child in one of our groups serves as a useful illustration. We will call him Carlos. Carlos was not very articulate in English, his second language. Because he often was ridiculed when he had spoken up in the past, throughout the years, he learned to keep quiet in class. He was one of those students…who had entered into an implicit contract of silence with his teacher: He opted for anonymity and she called on him only rarely.

While Carlos hated school and was learning very little in the traditional classroom, at least he was left alone. Accordingly, he was quite uncomfortable with the jigsaw system, which required him to talk to his groupmates. He had a great deal of trouble communicating his paragraph, stammering and hesitating. The other children reacted out of old habits, resorting to insults and teasing. "Aw, you don't know it," Susan accused. "You're dumb, you're stupid. You don't know what you are doing."

One of the researchers, assigned to observe the group process, intervened with a bit of advice when she overheard such comments: "Okay, you can tease him if you want to. It might be fun for you, but it's not going to help you learn about Eleanor Roosevelt's young adulthood. And let me remind you, the exam will take place in less than an hour." Note how this statement brings home the fact that the reinforcement contingencies have shifted considerably. Now Susan does not gain much from putting down Carlos. And she stands to lose a great deal, not just from the teacher singling her out for criticism but because she needs to know Carlos' information.

Gradually, but inexorably, it began to dawn on the students that the only chance they had to learn about Carlos' segment was by paying attention to what he had to say. If they ignored Carlos or continued to ridicule him, his segment would be unavailable to them, and the most they could hope for would be an 80 percent score on the exam—an unattractive prospect to most of the children. And with that realization, the kids began to become pretty good interviewers, learning to pay attention to Carlos, to draw him out, and to ask probing questions. Carlos, in turn, began to relax more and found it easier to explain out loud what was in his head. What the children came to learn about Carlos is even more important than the information about the lesson that they got from him. After a couple of days, they began to appreciate that Carlos was not nearly as dumb as they had thought he was. After a few weeks, they noticed talents in him they had not seen before. They began to like Carlos, and he began to enjoy school more and to think of his Anglo classmates as helpful friends and interested colleagues rather than as tormentors.

Source: Elliot Aronson and Neal Osherow, "Cooperation, Prosocial Behavior, and Academic Performance: Experiments in the Desegregated Classroom," *Applied Social Psychology Annual, 1* (1980): 174–175. Reprinted by permission.

gaining the social acceptance of structural assimilation. Since its founding, the United States has experienced a changing definition of *mainstream "American"*—from only those whose ancestry was English, to the British (English, Welsh, Scots, and Scots-Irish), to peoples from northern and western Europe, and now to all Europeans. People of color, however, have yet to gain unquestioned entry into this national cultural-identity group, and that entry is the challenge before us.[60]

## DIVERSITY TRAINING

A workplace environment that promotes positive intergroup interaction is more efficient, has higher morale, and retains experienced personnel. Conversely, a hostile work environment has lower productivity, disgruntled personnel, and a higher attrition rate. Moreover, if an organization develops a reputation for insensitivity to diversity, it will attract fewer qualified job applicants among women and people of color, and businesses will lose market share by attracting fewer clients from our increasingly diverse society for their goods and services.

*Most corporate managers recognize that an inclusive, hospitable work environment within their organization is essential to attract and keep qualified personnel. Diversity workshops to promote awareness and sensitivity are one approach; another is diversity councils to maintain a positive climate, such as this Nike Ethnic Diversity Council meeting.*

**3-4** Identify what levels of discrimination exist.

**Explore on MySocLab**
Activity: Race: Affirmative Action

**Explore on MySocLab**
Activity: Funding the Justice System

**Read on MySocLab**
Document: Race and Class in the American Justice System

With women and non-white males now constituting 75 percent of the people entering the U.S. labor force, and with 30 percent of the nation's enlisted military personnel identifying themselves as a minority, it has become critical for all organizations, even our armed forces, to take steps to prevent prejudice from creating dysfunctions within their daily operations.[61]

As someone who has conducted numerous diversity-training workshops for military leaders and corporate management (including health care), let me give you some insight into these programs. The best programs heighten awareness by providing informational insights into the diversity of cultural value orientations, as well as into the current and future demographics of employees and clients. Most valuable in broadening perceptions is the inclusion of interactive learning sessions such as role-playing demonstrations of the wrong and right handlings of situations and the creation of small groups to discuss and offer solutions to hypothetical but realistic problems. Although programs vary greatly in their length, structure, and content, the most effective ones are comprehensive, actively supported by management as part of the organization's general mission statement, and fully integrated into all aspects of the organization. The latter includes a diversity orientation session for new employees, occasional reinforcement sessions for continuing employees, and all levels of management working together to promote an inclusive, hospitable work climate. Such efforts can make a significant contribution in reducing prejudice in the workplace.

How effective are these programs? The majority of studies conclude that they are effective, but a key variable appears to be selection bias. That is, when participants attend by choice, the positive effects are stronger.[62] Critics, however, say most interventions are not grounded in theory and there is little evidence of program impact. They call for action research to study and improve diversity training to achieve greater prejudice reduction.[63]

## Discrimination

**Discrimination** is actual behavior, the practice of differential and unequal treatment of other groups of people, usually along racial, religious, or ethnic lines. The Latin word *discriminatus,* from which the English word is derived, means "to divide or distinguish," and its subsequent negative connotation has remained relatively unchanged through the centuries.

## LEVELS OF DISCRIMINATION

Actions, like attitudes, have different levels of intensity. As a result, discrimination may be analyzed at five levels. The first level is *verbal expression,* a statement of dislike or the use of a derogatory term. The next level is *avoidance,* in which the prejudiced person takes steps to avoid social interaction with a group. Actions of this type may include choice of residence, organizational membership, activities located in urban centers, and primary relationships in any social setting.

At the third level, *exclusion* from certain jobs, housing, education, or social organizations occurs. In the United States, the practice of **de jure** segregation was once widespread throughout the South. Not only were children specifically assigned to certain schools to maintain racial separation, but segregationist laws kept all public places (theaters, restaurants, restrooms, transportation, etc.) racially separated as well. This exclusion also can take the form of **de facto** segregation as residential patterns become embedded in social customs and institutions. Thus, the standard practice of building and maintaining neighborhood schools in racially segregated communities creates and preserves segregated schools.

The fourth level of discrimination is *physical abuse*—violent attacks on members of the disliked group. Unfortunately, this behavior—**ethnoviolence**—still occurs often in the United States. *Ethnoviolence* can apply to a range of actions—verbal harassment and threats, vandalism, graffiti, swastika painting, arson, cross burning, physical assault, and murder—committed against people targeted solely because of their race, religion, ethnic background, or sexual orientation.[64] Thousands of incidents of ethnoviolence against members of various minority groups occur each year throughout the nation on college campuses and in both suburban and urban areas.

The most extreme level of discrimination is *extermination:* the massacres, genocide, or pogroms conducted against a people. In modern times, such barbarous actions, from the monstrous actions of Stalin in the 1930s and the Nazis in the 1940s, continue to occur in modern times. Among the most recent examples are Bosnia, Rwanda, and the Darfur region of the Sudan.

### RELATIONSHIPS BETWEEN PREJUDICE AND DISCRIMINATION

Prejudice can lead to discrimination, or discrimination can lead to prejudice, or neither can lead to the other. No simplistic cause–effect relationship exists. Our attitudes and our overt behavior are closely related, but they are not identical. We may harbor hostile feelings toward certain groups without ever making them known through word or deed. Conversely, our overt behavior effectively may conceal our real attitudes.

Prejudiced people are more likely than others to practice discrimination and so discrimination quite often represents the overt expression of prejudice. It is wrong, however, to assume that discrimination is always the simple acting out of prejudice. It instead may be the result of a policy decision protecting the interests of the majority group, as happens when legal immigration is curtailed for economic reasons. It may be due to social conformity, as when people submit to outside pressures despite their personal views. Sometimes discriminatory behavior may precede prejudicial attitudes, as, for example, when organizations insist that all job applicants take aptitude or IQ tests based on middle-class experiences and then form negative judgments of lower-income people who do not score well.

Robert Merton created a model showing how relationships between prejudice and discrimination can vary (Figure 3.1). He illustrates that an unprejudiced person in fact

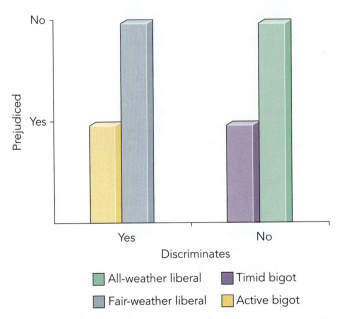

**FIGURE 3.1** Relationships between Prejudice and Discrimination

may discriminate and a prejudiced person might not do so. In his four categories, Merton classified people according to how they accept or reject the American Creed: "the right of equitable access to justice, freedom and opportunity, irrespective of race or religion, or ethnic origin."[65]

**THE UNPREJUDICED NONDISCRIMINATOR.** Unprejudiced nondiscriminators, or all-weather liberals, are not prejudiced and do not discriminate. Merton observed, though, that they often are not in direct contact or competition with minority group members. They talk chiefly to others who share their viewpoint, and so they deceive themselves into thinking that they represent the general consensus. Furthermore, because their "own spiritual house is in order," they feel no pangs of conscience pressing them to fight discrimination elsewhere. Despite Merton's cynicism about this group, in reality, many unprejudiced non-discriminators are activists and do what they can to reduce prejudice and discrimination in society.

**THE UNPREJUDICED DISCRIMINATOR.** Expediency is the byword for these "fair-weather liberals," for their actions often conflict with their personal beliefs. For example, they may be free of racial prejudice, but they will join clubs that exclude racially different people, they will vote for unfair measures if they would benefit materially from these, and they will support efforts to keep certain minorities out of their neighborhood for fear of its deterioration. These people frequently feel guilt and shame because they are acting against their beliefs.

**THE PREJUDICED NONDISCRIMINATOR.** Merton's term *timid bigots* best describes prejudiced nondiscriminators. They believe in many stereotypes about other groups and definitely feel hostility toward these groups. However, they keep silent in the presence of those who are more tolerant; they conform because they must. If there were no laws or pressures to avoid bias in certain actions, they would probably discriminate.

**THE PREJUDICED DISCRIMINATOR.** Prejudiced discriminators are active bigots. They experience no conflict between attitudes and behavior. Not only do they openly express their beliefs, practice discrimination, and defy the law if necessary, but they also consider such conduct virtuous.

The unprejudiced discriminator and the prejudiced nondiscriminator are the most sociologically interesting classifications because they demonstrate that social-situation variables often determine whether discriminatory behavior occurs. The pressure of group norms may force individuals to act in a manner inconsistent with their beliefs.

## SOCIAL AND INSTITUTIONAL DISCRIMINATION

Discriminatory practices occur frequently in the areas of employment and residence, although such actions often are concealed and denied by those who take them. Another dimension of discrimination, often unrealized, is **social discrimination**—the creation of a "social distance" between groups that we discussed in Chapter 1. Simply stated, in their close, primary relationships, people tend to associate with others of a similar ethnic background and socioeconomic level; thus, dominant-group members usually exclude minority-group members from close relations with them. Therefore, we can make a distinction between *active* and *passive* discrimination. In the first, one takes action against someone, while in the second, one's silent acquiescence to others' discriminatory actions is still a form of discrimination, just as theologians speak of sins of omission as well as sins of commission.

Discrimination is more than the biased actions of individuals, however. Far greater harm occurs from **institutional discrimination,** the unequal treatment of subordinate groups inherent in the ongoing operations of society's institutions.[66] Entrenched in customs, laws, and practices, these discriminatory patterns can exist in banking, criminal justice, employment, education, health care, housing, and many other areas in the private and public sectors. Critical to understanding this concept is the fact that practices are so widespread that individuals helping to perpetuate them may be completely unaware of their existence. Examples are:

1. Banks rejecting a disproportionate number of minority home mortgage applicants;
2. Sentencing inequities in the criminal justice system;
3. The concentration of minorities in low-paying jobs;
4. The former "separate but equal" educational structure in the South; and
5. Segregated housing.

Another form of institutional discrimination can be found in religious bigotry. Throughout U.S. history, religious minorities have fallen victim to systemic biased actions, as we will explore in Chapter 12. Whenever a dominant group feels that its self-interests—such as primacy and the preservation of cherished values—are threatened, reactionary and discriminatory measures usually result. Numerous studies have found that the dominant group will not hesitate to act discriminatorily if it thinks that this approach will effectively undercut the minority group as a social or economic competitor.[67] (See the International Scene box.)

## THE AFFIRMATIVE-ACTION CONTROVERSY

At what point do efforts to secure justice and equal opportunities in life for one group infringe on the rights of other groups? Is justice a utilitarian concept—the greatest happiness for the greatest number? Or is it a moral concept—a sense of good that all people share? Is the proper role of government to foster a climate in which people have equal opportunity to participate in a competitive system of occupations and rewards, or should government ensure equal results in any competition? These issues have engaged moral and political philosophers for centuries, and they go to the core of the affirmative-action controversy.

**3-5** Explain why affirmative action is so controversial.

*For centuries, demonstrations have been a means for people to express their views and put pressure on the decision makers to make a change. For example, in October 2012, supporters of affirmative action rallied outside the U.S. Supreme Court in Washington, DC, as the Court heard a case that challenged how universities make admission decisions. In June 2013, the Court sent the case back to a lower court to reconsider under stricter legal standards.*

**THE CONCEPTS OF JUSTICE, LIBERTY, AND EQUALITY.** More than 2,300 years ago, Plato wrote in the *Republic* that justice must be relative to the needs of the people who are served, not to the desires of those who serve them. For example, physicians must make patients' health their primary concern if they are to be just, and justice is essentially fairness that maximizes equal liberty for all.[68] To provide the greatest benefit to the least advantaged, society must eliminate social and economic inequalities by placing minority persons in offices and positions that are open to all under conditions of fair equality of opportunity. Social observers, whether from ancient or present times, have often envisioned the ideal society as well ordered and strongly pluralistic: Each component performs a functionally differentiated role in working harmony; society therefore must arrange its practices to make this so.

Americans, though, often have been more concerned with liberty than with equality, identifying liberty with the absence of government interference, a viewpoint strongly promoted by Tea Party political activists. When government becomes more powerful, bringing an area of activity under its control or regulation (like health care), to that extent equality (health insurance coverage for all) replaces liberty (freedom to reject coverage) as the dominant ideal and constitutional demand. In contrast, those who insist on constitutional rights for all are not demanding the removal of government restraints but instead are asking for positive government action to provide equal treatment for the less powerful.[69] Since the 1960s, responsibility for promoting individual rights has increasingly been placed on the federal government.

**AFFIRMATIVE ACTION BEGINS.** We can trace the origin of government affirmative-action policy to July 1941, when President Franklin D. Roosevelt issued Executive Order 8802, obligating defense contractors "not to discriminate against any worker because of race, creed, color, or national origin." Subsequent executive orders by virtually all presidents continued or expanded the government's efforts to curb discrimination in employment. President John F. Kennedy's Executive Order 10925 in 1961 was the first to use the term *affirmative action*; it stipulated that government contractors would "take affirmative action that applicants are employed, and that employees are treated during employment, without regard to their race, creed, color, or national origin."

The legal basis for affirmative action appears to rest on two points. Passage of the Thirteenth Amendment, which abolished slavery, also set the precedent for action against any vestiges of slavery manifest through racial discrimination.[70] Both supporters and opponents, however, point to Title VII, Section 703(j), of the 1964 Civil Rights Act as the keystone of their positions on affirmative action.

Title VII seems to address the need for fairness, openness, and color-blind equal opportunity. It specifically bans preference by race, ethnicity, gender, and religion in business and government. Opponents claim that this clear language outlawing preferences makes affirmative action unnecessary and illegal. Supporters contend that President Lyndon Johnson's Executive Order 11246 is linked to Title VII by mandating employer affirmative-action plans to correct existing deficiencies through specific goals and deadlines. This was, supporters say, a logical step from concern about equal rights to concern about actual equal opportunity.[71]

Addressing an expanded list of protected categories (Asians, blacks, Hispanics, Native Americans, women, the elderly, people with disabilities, and homosexuals), an array of state and federal policy guidelines began to regulate many aspects of business, education, and government practices. Legislation in 1972 amended the 1964 Civil Rights Act, giving the courts the power to enforce affirmative-action standards. Preference programs became the rule through reserved minority quotas in college and graduate school admissions and in job hiring and promotions, as well as through government set-aside work contracts for minority firms.[72]

**COURT CHALLENGES AND RULINGS.** The resentment of whites on "reverse discrimination" crystallized in the 1978 *Regents of the University of California v. Bakke* case, when the U.S. Supreme Court ruled that quotas were not permitted but race could be a factor in university admissions. In a separate opinion, Justice Harry A. Blackmun stated,

> In order to get beyond racism, we must first take account of race. There is no other way. And in order to treat some persons equally, we must treat them differently. We cannot—we dare not—let the Equal Protection Clause perpetuate racial superiority.[73]

For the next 11 years, the Supreme Court upheld the principle of affirmative action in a series of rulings. Since 1989, however, a more conservative Supreme Court has shown a growing reluctance to use "race-conscious remedies"—the practice of trying to overcome the effects of past discrimination by helping minorities. This has been true not only in affirmative-action cases involving jobs and contracts but in school desegregation and voting rights as well. The 1995 *Adarand Constructors v. Peña* decision scaled back the federal government's own affirmative-action program, mandating "strict scrutiny and evidence" of alleged past discrimination, not only a "general history of racial discrimination in the nation." In another 1995 decision, the Supreme Court declared that race could no longer be the "predominant factor" in drawing congressional districts—or, by implication, any jurisdiction for any government body, from school boards to state legislatures.

In 1995, the California Board of Regents banned affirmative action for graduate and undergraduate admissions. The following year, California voters overwhelmingly passed the California Civil Rights Initiative to dismantle state affirmative-action programs. Also in 1996, a sweeping ruling by the U.S. Circuit Court of Appeals in *Hopwood v. Texas* banned affirmative action in admissions, scholarships, and outreach programs. When Florida ended its affirmative-action program in 1999, three of the four largest states in the nation (New York excluded), and the three with the largest high school and college student populations, had rescinded affirmative action for the purpose of achieving racial and ethnic diversity. Soon, seven states had banned completely the use of racial preferences in admissions: Arizona, California, Florida, Michigan, Nebraska, New Hampshire, and Washington.

In 2003, a 5–4 Supreme Court decision preserved affirmative action in university admissions at the University of Michigan law school, while at the same time, striking down that university's undergraduate admissions program that used a point system based in part on race. Its endorsement of the role of racial diversity on campus in achieving a more equal society strengthened the solitary view of Justice Lewis Powell at the time of the *Bakke* decision that there was a "compelling state interest" in racial diversity. At the same time, the Court suggested a time limit on such programs, with Justice Sandra Day O'Connor writing in the majority opinion, "We expect that 25 years from now the use of racial preferences will no longer be necessary to further the interest approved today."[74] Since then, many public universities in other states, like Texas and Georgia, have used a race-neutral system. However, the University of Texas partially retained an affirmative-action element in its admissions policy, and a challenge to that policy by a rejected white female applicant went before the U.S. Supreme Court, which, in June 2013, threw out a Fifth Circuit Court of Appeals decision upholding the Texas admission plan and sent the case back for reconsideration under a more demanding standard. Possibly endangered, the Texas admissions program and similar ones may still continue without changes for the time being until the lower court acts. Another case—appealing the Sixth Circuit Court's ruling that Michigan's anti-affirmative action referendum was unconstitutional—is currently under review by the Supreme Court, and its decision will also affect the standing of a similar referendum passed in California.

The impact on minority enrollments at universities no longer using affirmative action has been mixed. Despite expanded efforts, University of California campuses have about half the percentage of black students as in 1995. In contrast, after an initial decline, the University of Washington, after an initial decline, has higher levels of black and Latino enrollment. The University of Florida also has higher Hispanic enrollment but black enrollment, after remaining comparable for a decade, has recently dropped by one-third.[75]

The Court's 5–4 ruling in 2009 in *Ricci v. DeStefano* in favor of 18 white (including one Hispanic) New Haven fire fighters brought another interpretation to the issue of affirmative action. In this case, the justices said promotion test results cannot be tossed out over fear of litigation because they favored whites.

**HAS AFFIRMATIVE ACTION WORKED?** Evidence about the success of affirmative-action programs is as mixed as public debate on the subject. Research on the impact of affirmative action offers evidence that it does increase employment, college enrollments, and minority contracts, with opportunities for white males decreasing only slightly. Women appear to have benefited the most, and no significant negative effect on productivity or performance occurred in organizations where such programs existed.[76]

Although some of the motivations behind the challenges to affirmative action may well be racist or sexist, the preservation of white privilege and conservative political ideology appear to be more significant underpinnings. Defenders of affirmative action argue that reverse discrimination is a myth fueled by white hysteria, and that the prevalence of racism and its negative impact on the life chances of people of color makes affirmative action still an important necessity.[77]

Still, some minority-group spokespersons, conservatives themselves, have spoken against affirmative action, arguing that it has had a destructive influence on their own communities. Thomas Sowell (black) and Linda Chavez (Latina) maintain that universities recruit talented minority students away from local colleges where they might do very well and into learning environments where the competition for grades is intense. Opponents also argue that affirmative action is "misplaced condescension" that has poisoned race relations and that the achievements of minorities become tainted by the possibility that they resulted from special favorable treatment rather than being earned on merit.[78]

**PUBLIC OPINION.** When asked in a 2009 NBC/*Wall Street Journal* nationwide poll about affirmative action, 63 percent said it was still needed and 28 percent said it should be ended. A 2009 AP-GfK national poll found 56 percent in favor of affirmative-action programs for racial and ethnic minorities and 63 percent approving such programs for women. In contrast, a 2009 Quinnipiac national poll found Americans evenly divided with 20 percent endorsing affirmative-action programs to overcome discrimination, another 27 percent in favor to increase diversity, but 47 percent saying we should not have such programs at all.[79] Interestingly, other studies also show a public acceptance of programs to increase diversity but opposition for ones "to overcome past discrimination." Follow-up questions reveal that respondents' thinking that "the past is the past" is not a denial of historic events, but they dismiss their connection to today's racial realities.[80]

Although divided on preferences based on race and gender (blacks less in opposition than whites), most Americans seem willing to support affirmative action based on economic class. Under such a provision, for example, the white son of a poor coal miner in West Virginia could be eligible for special help, but the daughter of an affluent African American stockbroker would not. Even as affirmative action withers in some states, it continues in others. Supporters of affirmative action argue "mend it, don't end it," whereas opponents urge that it be dismantled completely. The next few years undoubtedly will see a continuing battle and perhaps even significant changes in affirmative action as we know it.

### RACIAL PROFILING

Although racial profiling has a long history, only in recent years have the government and public given it so much attention. **Racial profiling** refers to action taken by law enforcement officials on the basis of race or ethnicity instead of an individual's behavior. Such thinking, for instance, has led authorities routinely to stop vehicles driven by blacks and Hispanics in the expectation of finding drugs in their possession. Their experiences led blacks to use the term "driving while black" or "DWB" to express their outrage about such discriminatory actions.[81]

Some argue that overall discrepancies in crime rates among racial groups justify such profiling in traffic enforcement activities to produce a greater number of arrests for non-traffic offenses (narcotics trafficking, for example). Critics contend that an emphasis on minority-group drug use naturally would result in more minority arrests. In fact, a Human

**3-6** Analyze how current attitudes vary about racial profiling.

*Although police officers have an obligation to stop motorists who commit traffic violations, members of the black community complain that often they get stopped for no other cause than "DWB," or driving while black. Although official guidelines against all forms of racial profiling exist, some studies show that it continues in numerous locales.*

Rights Watch report covering the last three decades revealed that, even though blacks and whites engage in drug offenses—possession and sales—at roughly comparable rates, blacks are the principal targets of the "war on drugs" and thus are three to six times more likely to be arrested. This occurs because, even though whites are just as likely to be pulled over in routine traffic actions as are minorities, blacks and Hispanics are far more likely to have their vehicles searched.[82]

In the 1990s, racial profiling received a great deal of attention through media exposés, special reports, commissions, and legislative initiatives. In 2001, the U.S. government took steps and acted to ban it in federal law enforcement, but the terrorist attacks later that year changed its view of racial profiling from an undesirable police activity to one of necessity for national security. As a result, airline security, customs officials, and police place Arab and Muslim Americans under special scrutiny, and immigration officials prosecute them for minor violations often ignored for resident aliens of other ethnic backgrounds. In national surveys, more than half of all Americans favor the racial profiling of Arab male airline passengers.[83]

The U.S. Department of Justice has guidelines rejecting racial profiling. It argues that such activity is immoral and perpetuates negative racial stereotypes that are "harmful to our diverse democracy, and materially impair our efforts to maintain a fair and just society." However, in that same statement, it included a broad and largely undefined exception when "national security" concerns come into play, thereby creating a dichotomy in racial profiling attitudes and actions.[84]

Pressure from the media, coupled with changes in police leadership, though, can reduce racial inequality in aggressive enforcement practices, as revealed in a study comparing different years of traffic stop data in Rhode Island.[85] However, the American Civil Liberties Union (ACLU) reports that racial minorities in Rhode Island are still disproportionately stopped in virtually every municipality and twice as likely as white drivers to be searched, even though they were *less* likely to be found with contraband.[86]

**STUDENTS SPEAK** "At 12:30 A.M. last week, I was pulled over, asked to step out of the car and put my hands on the car roof. The officer searched me for drugs and weapons, and then asked for my license and other information, still not telling me what I had done wrong. Fifteen minutes later, he comes back to the car, hands back my information, and says, 'Where are you headed, boy?' Just then, another officer pulls up, and once again I was asked to put my hands back on top of the car. After they converse amongst themselves, they both walk toward me and flash a bright light in my face. The first officer says, 'Well, the reason why I pulled you over was because your back driver's side tail light is beginning to dim, and it looks like it was almost going to go out. You are free to go. Have a nice day.' Now maybe I am a little bit clueless, but I'm pretty sure having a 'dimming' taillight isn't cause to pull someone out of a car and search him."

**—Larry Banks**

## Retrospect

The psychology of prejudice focuses on individuals' subjective states of mind, emphasizing the levels of prejudice held and the factors of self-justification, personality, frustration, and scapegoating. The sociology of prejudice examines the social forces in society behind prejudicial attitudes, such as socialization, economic competition, and social norms.

Stereotyping often reflects prejudice as a sense of group position. Once established, stereotypes are difficult to eradicate and often manifested in ethnophaulisms and ethnic humor. Television has a profound impact in shaping and reinforcing attitudes; unfortunately, it tends to perpetuate racial and sexual stereotypes instead of combating them.

Increased contact between groups and improved information do not reduce prejudice necessarily. The nature of the contact, particularly whether it is competitive or cooperative, is a key determinant. Information can develop heightened awareness as a means of improving relations, but external factors (economic conditions and social pressures) may override rational considerations.

The imagery in advertising, rap and hip hop music lyrics, and music videos can have a cumulative effect in shaping values about men and women. These images and words help perpetuate subtle prejudice and a false consciousness.

Diversity in the workplace, whether corporate or military, has prompted many organizations to create a more positive, inclusive environment through diversity training workshops. The most effective programs are comprehensive, actively supported by management, and fully integrated into all aspects of the organization.

Discriminatory behavior operates at five levels of intensity: verbal expression, avoidance, exclusion, physical abuse, and extermination. Discrimination is not necessarily the acting out of prejudice. Social pressures may oblige unprejudiced individuals to discriminate or may prevent prejudiced people from discriminating.

The debate on affirmative action involves these questions: Is it a democratic government's responsibility to provide a climate for equal opportunity or to ensure equal results? If the latter, at what point do efforts to secure equality for one group infringe on the rights of other groups? After several decades of implementation, affirmative-action programs face dismantling through court decisions, public initiatives, and legislative action.

Racial profiling remains a serious concern, given its mixed interpretation since the 2001 terrorist attacks.

# On MySocLab

 **Study and Review on MySocLab**

## KEY TERMS

Action-orientation level of prejudice, p. 55

Affirmative action, p. 76

Authoritarian personality, p. 57

Cognitive level of prejudice, p. 55

Contact hypothesis, p. 69

*De facto* segregation, p. 73

*De jure* segregation, p. 73

Discrimination, p. 72

Displaced aggression, p. 57

Emotional level of prejudice, p. 55

Ethnophaulism, p. 64

Ethnoviolence, p. 73

Institutional discrimination, p. 75

Jigsaw classroom, p. 69

Jim Crow laws, p. 59

Prejudice, p. 54

Racial profiling, p. 79

Relative deprivation, p. 57

Scapegoating, p. 58

Selective perception, p. 70

Self-justification, p. 56

Social discrimination, p. 75

Social norms, p. 61

Socialization process, p. 59

Stereotype, p. 63

## DISCUSSION QUESTIONS

1. This chapter offers various causes of prejudice. Have you ever seen or experienced any examples of any of these causes?
2. What are some of the possible causes of prejudice?
3. Did you ever see any of those "humorous" caveman TV commercials for GEICO insurance? How are they related to the material in Chapter 3?
4. What is the relationship between prejudice and discrimination?
5. Some whites and minority leaders complain about affirmative action as being unfair and attaching a stigma to minority achievement. Other whites and minority leaders say it is still necessary to create a level playing field. What do you think and why?
6. Is racial profiling always bad? Why or why not?

# INTERNET ACTIVITIES

1. "Ethnic Prejudice, Stereotypes, Discrimination, and the Free Market" (http://www.friesian.com/discrim.htm) is a provocative article about past hiring biases relating to Irish and Italian workers and modern times. This article suggests that anti-discrimination laws may have unintended negative consequences. What do you think?

2. If you're a teacher or planning to become one, you might want to visit http://www.jigsaw.org to learn some tips and strategies for implementing the jigsaw classroom.

3. Did you follow the Jena 6 story from a few years ago? Want to know the story? Go to http://www.youtube.com/watch?v=YuoiZnr4jLY. Much has happened since this posting, including the overturning of the conviction and prison sentence. Look for updates.

# Intergroup Relations

 **Listen** to Chapter 4 on **MySocLab**

# 4

WE AFFIRM OUR COMMON HUMANITY AS JEWS, MUSLIMS, AND CHRISTIANS

Not all demonstrations are acts of defiance and/or protest by minorities. Sometimes coalitions of majority and minority groups will stand together for a common cause. For example, this 2009 interfaith vigil was held at the Boston Common to ask for peace in Gaza and Israel by calling on Hamas and Israel to stop fighting in the Gaza Strip.

**LEARNING OBJECTIVES** | After reading this chapter you will be able to:

**4-1** Analyze common patterns of minority-group responses.

**4-2** Examine consequences of minority-group status.

**4-3** Analyze common patterns of dominant-group responses to minorities.

**4-4** Analyze various patterns of exploitation.

**4-5** Explain concern over potential dangers in minority-minority relations.

**4-6** Evaluate three models of possible minority integration in society.

S o far, we have looked at people's behavioral patterns in relating to strangers, the role of culture and social structure in shaping perceptions and interactions, and the complexity of prejudice and discrimination. In this chapter, we examine response patterns that dominant and minority groups follow in their dealings with each other.

The following pages suggest that these patterns occur in varying degrees for most groups regardless of race, ethnicity, or time period. They are not mutually exclusive categories, and groups do not necessarily follow all these patterns at one time. To some degree, though, each minority or dominant group in any society shares these pattern commonalities. Before we examine these general patterns, two cautionary notes are necessary. First, all groups are not alike, for each has its own unique beliefs, habits, and history. Second, variations *within* a group prevent any group from being a homogeneous entity.

## Minority-Group Responses

4-1 Analyze common patterns of minority-group responses.

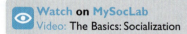
Watch on MySocLab
Video: **The Basics: Socialization**

Although personality characteristics play a large role in determining how individuals respond to unfavorable situations, behavioral patterns for almost any group are similar to those of other groups in comparable circumstances. External factors play an important role, but social interpretation also is a critical determinant, as I will discuss in the formation of ethnic- and racial-group identity. Also, the minority group's perception of its power resource—its ability to change established relationships with the dominant group in a significant way—significantly influences its response, which might include avoidance, deviance, defiance, acceptance, and/or negative self-image.[1]

### ETHNIC- AND RACIAL-GROUP IDENTITY

Any group unable to participate fully in the societal mainstream typically develops its own group identity. This is a normal pattern in ingroup–outgroup relationships. In the field of race and ethnic relations, group identity can serve as a basis for positive encounters, a source of comfort and strength, or entry into the mainstream. It also can be a foundation for prejudice and discrimination, negative self-image, a barrier to social acceptance, or a source of conflict.

*Ethnic-group identity* exists when individuals choose to emphasize cultural or national ties as the basis for their primary social interactions and sense of self. Leaving the taken-for-granted world of their homeland, immigrants—as strangers in a strange land—become more self-conscious of their group identity. Even as the acculturation process and ethnogenesis unfold, these group members retain some of the "cultural baggage" they brought with them and see themselves—as does the mainstream society—as possessing distinctiveness because of their ethnicity.

Many factors determine the duration of an ethnic-group identity. A cohesive ethnic community, continually revitalized by the steady influx of newcomers, will maintain a strong resilience. Ethnic-minority media can play a significant role in strengthening that sense of identity. Indeed, minority media even can affect the assimilation process, either by promoting it (as did the New York *Daily Forward* newspaper among Jewish immigrants in the late nineteenth and early twentieth centuries) or by delaying that process by stressing the retention of language, customs, and values.

Socialization into one's own ethnic group also promotes this identity. Part of the growing-up process for minorities often involves the existence of a dual identity: one in the larger society and another within the person's own group. This multiple reality affects one's roles, behavior, and sense of self, depending on the social setting.

Ethnic-group identity can be especially long-lasting on the basis of religion. Some good examples are persistent subcultures, such as the Amish, Hutterites, and Hasidic Jews mentioned in Chapter 2. Although a group identity usually remains among the adherents of any faith, its existence along other ethnic lines depends on racial and assimilation considerations. For example, Catholic immigrants in the nineteenth century and other Catholic and Jewish immigrants in the early twentieth century once stood apart not only for their religion but also for their other subcultural traits. Although traces of anti-Catholicism and anti-Semitism remain today in the United States, most members of these religious groups hold a mainstream-group identity alongside their religious-group identity, which was not the case a few generations ago. More recent arrivals—such as Buddhists, Hindus, Muslims, and Sikhs—not only are religiously distinct from the longstanding three main U.S. religions but also are culturally distinct in other ways and often racially distinct as well. Currently, their ethnic-group identities embody all these aspects (religion, race, culture), and only time will tell what evolution in group identity will occur among them.

For most white ethnics, everyday ethnicity eventually yields to assimilation throughout the generations, and ethnic-group identity fades. That change is possible because gradually the group identifies more and more with mainstream society and its own subcultural "marks" (clothing, language, customs, behavior, residential clustering) disappear, making the group less noticeable to the rest of society as its members become absorbed into the dominant white culture.

Because of the social definition of race, this metamorphosis is difficult for non-whites in a color-conscious society. Physical identification through skin color, facial features, and/or hair texture thus maintains differences between the mainstream racial group and others. With their race as an inescapable feature affecting their social acceptance and interaction patterns, non-white ethnics typically develop a *racial-group identity*. This ingroup bonding satisfies the human need for a sense of belonging while simultaneously serving as a basis for racial and cultural pride. Such an arrangement can foster a healthier, more positive self-identity than would otherwise develop among racial minorities relegated to secondary social status.

People of color—whether black, brown, yellow, or red—typically affirm their identity and heritage in a variety of ways. These include combating their stereotypes, teaching the younger generation about their racial history and achievements, adopting slogans (for example, "Black Is Beautiful") or special names (for example, "La Raza" [the race]), and using a dual identity (for example, African American, Mexican American, Korean American, Native American) as a positive designator of their dual reality. The more militant racial group members often use ethnophaulisms against their own whom they criticize for "thinking or acting white" and call them, depending on the racial group, "oreos," "coconuts," "bananas," or "apples"—that is, one color on the outside, but white on the inside.

Ethnic- or racial-group identity, then, can have positive and negative consequences. Examining it in both a social and historical context can lead to a more complete understanding of this social phenomenon, something we do in most of the following chapters.

## AVOIDANCE

One way of dealing with discriminatory practices is through **avoidance**, if this avenue is available. Throughout history, minority groups—from the ancient Hebrews to the Pilgrims to Sudanese Christians in recent years—have attempted to solve their problems by leaving them behind. One motive for migrating, then, is to avoid discrimination. If leaving is not possible, minorities may turn inward to their own group for social and economic activities. This approach insulates the minority group from antagonistic actions by the dominant group, but also it promotes charges of "clannishness" and "nonassimilation." Lacking adequate economic, legal, or political power, however, the minority group may find avoidance its only choice.

By clustering together in small subcommunities, minority peoples not only create a miniature version of their familiar world in the strange land but also establish a safe place in which they can live, relax, and interact with others like themselves, who understand their needs and interests. For some minority groups, seeking shelter from prejudice probably is a secondary motivation, following a primary desire to live among their own kind.

Asian immigrants, for example, have followed this pattern. When the Chinese first came to this country, they worked in many occupations in which workers were needed, frequently clustering together in neighborhoods close to their jobs. In the United States, prejudicial attitudes always had existed against the Chinese, but in the post–Civil War period, they became even more the targets of bitter hatred and discrimination for economic and other reasons. Evicted from their jobs as a result of race-baiting union strikes and limited in their choice of residence by restrictive housing covenants, many had no choice but to live in insular Chinatowns within the larger cities. They entered businesses that did not compete with those of whites (curio shops, laundries, restaurants, etc.) and followed their old-country tradition of settling disputes among themselves rather than appealing to government authorities for adjudication.

## DEVIANCE

When a group continually experiences rejection and discrimination, some of its members are unable to identify with the dominant society or accept its norms. People at the bottom of the socioeconomic ladder, particularly members of victimized racial and ethnic groups, may respond to the pressures of everyday life in ways they consider reasonable but that others view as **deviance**. This situation occurs in particular when laws serve to impose the moral standards of the dominant group on the behavior of other groups.

Many minority groups in the United States—Irish, Germans, Chinese, Italians, Polish, African Americans, Native Americans, and Hispanics—at one time or another, have been arrested and punished in disproportionate numbers for so-called crimes of personal disorganization. Among the offenses to the dominant group's morality have been public drunkenness, drug abuse, gambling, and sexual "misconduct." It is unclear whether this disproportion reflects the frequency of misconduct or a pattern of selective arrests. Moreover, some types of conduct are deviant only from the perspective of the majority group, such as cockfighting or female genital cutting, whereas other types, such as wife-beating, also may be considered deviant by the minority community.

*Of the various parallel social institutions within an ethnic community, social clubs have been popular among all immigrant groups for hundreds of years. Like this Belgian Club in Superior, Wisconsin, they provide a refuge from the everyday concerns of life by offering a friendly atmosphere through their interactive social activities and networking.*

Part of the problem with law enforcement is its subjective nature and the discretionary handling of violations. Many people criticize the U.S. criminal justice system for its failure to accord fair and equal treatment to the poor and to minority-group members as compared with people from the middle and upper classes.[2] Criticisms include the:

1. Tendency of police to arrest suspects from minority groups at substantially higher rates than those from the majority group in situations in which discretionary judgment is possible;
2. Overrepresentation of nonminority groups on juries;
3. Difficulty the poor encounter in affording bail;
4. Poor quality of free legal defense; and
5. Disparities in sentencing for members of dominant and minority groups.

Because social background constitutes one of the factors that the police and courts consider, individuals who belong to a racial or ethnic group with a negative stereotype find themselves at a severe disadvantage.

When some racial or ethnic group members commit a noticeable number of deviant offenses, such as delinquency, crime, drunkenness, or some public nuisance problem, the public often extends a negative stereotype to all members of that group even though it applies to only a few. Some common associations, for example, are Italians and gangsters, Irish and heavy drinking and fighting, Chinese and opium, African Americans and street crimes such as mugging and purse snatching, and Puerto Ricans and knife fighting. A number of factors—including values, behavior patterns, and structural conditions in both the native and adopted lands—help explain certain kinds of so-called deviance among different minority groups. The appropriate means of stopping that deviance is itself subject to debate between proponents of corrective versus preventive measures.

Deviant behavior among minority groups occurs not because of race or ethnicity, as prejudiced people think, but usually because of poverty and lack of opportunity. A classic study of juvenile delinquency in Chicago in the 1940s documented this pattern.[3] The highest rates of juvenile delinquency occurred in areas with poor housing, few job opportunities, and widespread prostitution, gambling, and drug use. The delinquency rate consistently was high during a 30-year period, even though five different ethnic groups moved in and out of those areas during that period. *Nationality was unimportant; the unchanged living conditions brought unchanged results, regardless of the group.* Subsequent studies still demonstrate a correlation between higher rates of juvenile or adult crime and income level and place of residence.[4]

Because many minority groups are represented heavily among low-income populations, studies emphasizing social-class variables often provide insight into the minority experience. The most common finding is that a lack of opportunities encourages delinquency among lower-class males.[5] Social aspirations may be similar at all levels of society, but opportunities are not. Belonging to a gang may give a youth a sense of power and help overcome feelings of inadequacy; hoodlumism becomes a conduit for expressing resentment against a society whose approved norms seem impossible to follow.[6] Notwithstanding the economic and environmental difficulties they face, the large majority of racial-group and ethnic-group members do not join gangs or engage in criminally deviant behavior. However, because some minority groups are represented disproportionately in such activities, the public image of the group as a whole suffers.

Some social factors, particularly parental attitudes about education, appear related to delinquency rates. Generally, parental emphasis on academic achievement and extensive involvement in their children's schooling lead to more educationally committed adolescents. The greater their commitment is, the lower the rates of delinquency are, and vice versa. Sometimes though, a high-quality school environment can offset a lack of parental involvement.[7]

In recent years on May 1st, tens of thousands march for immigrant rights in cities across the country, including New York, Chicago, Detroit, Milwaukee, and Los Angeles (shown here). Calling for the legalization of the undocumented, an end to raids and deportation, and maintaining family unity, their actions echo past minority attempts to gain fair treatment.

## DEFIANCE

If a minority group is sufficiently cohesive and conscious of its growing economic or political power, its members may act openly to challenge and eliminate discriminatory practices, through **defiance**. In previous years, some activists may have been pioneers with court challenges or other individual actions, but at this stage, the group takes a strong stand in defying the discrimination it is experiencing.

Sometimes the defiance is violent and seems spontaneous, although it usually grows out of long-standing conditions. One example is the Irish draft riot in New York in 1863 during the Civil War. When its volunteer armies proved insufficient, the Union used a military draft to secure needed troops. In those days, well-to-do males of draft age could avoid conscription legally by buying the military services of a substitute. Meanwhile, because the Irish were mostly poor and concentrated in urban areas, many of them had no recourse when drafted. Their defiance at what they considered an unfair practice blossomed into a riot in which blacks became the scapegoats, with lives lost and property destroyed or damaged. Similarly, the 1969 Stonewall riots (a series of violent demonstrations by the New York Greenwich Village homosexual community to a police raid on their club) and the 1992 Los Angeles riot (following the acquittal of white police officers videotaped beating Rodney King, a black man) both may have been spontaneous reactions, but only within the larger context of smoldering, deep-seated, long-standing resentments.

A militant action, such as the takeover of a symbolic site, is a moderately aggressive act of defiance. The late 1960s witnessed many building takeovers by African Americans and other disaffected, angry, alienated students on college campuses. In many instances, the purpose of the action was to call public attention to what the group considered administrative indifference toward or discrimination against their people. Similar actions occurred in this period to protest the war in Vietnam. A small group of Native Americans took this approach in the 1970s to protest their living conditions; at different times, they seized Alcatraz Island in California, the Bureau of Indian Affairs in Washington, DC, and the village of Wounded Knee in South Dakota. Media attention helped validate and spread the idea of using militant actions to promote a group's agenda.

Any peaceful action that challenges the status quo, though less aggressive, is defiant nonetheless; parades, marches, picket lines, mass meetings, boycotts, and demonstrations are examples. Another form of peaceful protest consists of civil disobedience: deliberately breaking discriminatory laws and then challenging their constitutionality or breaking a discriminatory tradition. The Civil Rights actions of the 1960s—sit-ins, lie-ins, and freedom rides—challenged decades-old Jim Crow laws that restricted access by blacks to public establishments in the South. Shop-ins at stores that catered to an exclusively white clientele represented deliberate efforts to break traditional store practices by attempting to make purchases.

## ACCEPTANCE

Many minority people, to the frequent consternation of their leaders and sympathizers, accept the situation in which they find themselves. Some do so stoically, justifying their decision by subtle rationalizations. Others are resentful but accept the situation for reasons of personal security or economic necessity. Still others accept it through false consciousness, a consequence of the dominant group's control over sources of information. Although **acceptance** maintains the superior position in society of the dominant group and the subordinate position of the minority group, it does diminish the open tensions and conflicts between the two groups.

In some instances, conforming to prevailing patterns of interaction between dominant and minority groups occurs subconsciously, the result of social conditioning. Just as socialization can instill prejudice, so too can it cause minority-group members to disregard or be unaware of alternative status possibilities. How much acceptance of lower status takes this form and how much is characterized by resentful submission and mental rejection is difficult to determine.

African Americans, Mexican Americans, and Native Americans have experienced a subordinate position in the United States for multiple generations. Until the 1960s, a combination of structural discrimination, racial stratification, powerlessness, and a sense of the futility of trying to change things caused many to submit to the situation imposed on them. Similarly, Japanese Americans had little choice when, following the bombing of Pearl Harbor and the subsequent rise in anti-Japanese sentiment, the U.S. government in 1942 dispossessed and imprisoned 110,000 of them in "temporary relocation centers."[8]

Acceptance as a minority response is less common in the United States than it once was. More aware of the alternative ways of living presented in the media, today's minorities are more hopeful about sharing in them. No longer do they passively accept the status quo, which denies them the quality of life and leisure pursuits others enjoy. Simultaneously, through court decisions, legislation, new social services, and other efforts, society has created a more favorable climate for improving the status of minority groups. Televised news features and behavioral science courses may have heightened the public's social awareness as well.

# Consequences of Minority-Group Status

Among the possible outcomes faced by minority groups that experience sustained inequality are: negative self-image, a vicious circle of continued discrimination, marginality, and status as middleman minorities.

**4-2** Examine consequences of minority-group status.

## NEGATIVE SELF-IMAGE

The apathy that militant leaders sometimes find among their own people may result from a **negative self-image**, a common consequence of prejudice and discrimination. **Labeling theory** helps us to understand this process. Using racial or ethnic stereotypes, the mainstream group may stigmatize a minority group and thereafter identify and treat its members as having those negative attributes. If the labeling process is pervasive and powerful enough, group members may come to accept the definition society forces on them and thus have lowered self-esteem.[9]

Continual treatment as an inferior encourages a loss of self-confidence. If everything about a person's position and experiences—jobs with low pay, substandard housing, the hostility of others, and the need for assistance from government agencies—works to destroy pride and hope, the person may become apathetic. To remain optimistic and determined in the face of constant negative experiences from all directions is extremely difficult.

The pervasiveness of dominant-group values and attitudes, which include negative stereotypes of the minority group, may cause the minority-group member to develop a negative self-image.[10] A person's self-image includes race, religion, and nationality; thus, individuals may feel embarrassed, even inferior, if they see that one or more of the attributes they possess are scorned within the society. In effect, minority-group members may begin to perceive themselves as negatively as the dominant group originally did.

Negative self-image, or self-hatred, manifests itself in many ways. People may try to "pass" as members of the dominant group and deny membership in a disparaged group. They may adopt the dominant group's prejudices and accept their devalued status. They may engage in ego defense by blaming others within the group for the low esteem in which society holds them:

> Some Jews refer to other Jews as "kikes"—blaming them exclusively for the anti-Semitism from which all alike suffer. Class distinctions within groups are often a result of trying to free oneself from responsibility for the handicap from which the group as a whole suffers. "Lace curtain" Irish look down on "shanty" Irish. Wealthy Spanish and Portuguese Jews have long regarded themselves as the top of the pyramid of Hebraic peoples. But Jews of German origin, having a rich culture, view themselves as the aristocrats, often looking down on Austrian, Hungarian, and Balkan Jews, and regarding Polish and Russian Jews at the very bottom.[11]

Negative self-image, then, can cause people to accept their fate passively. It also can encourage personal shame for possessing undesired qualities or dislike toward other members of one's group for possessing them. Minority-group members may attempt to overcome their negative self-image by changing their name or religion, having cosmetic surgery, or moving to a locale where the stereotype is less prevalent.

We must not assume, however, that negative self-image is a fairly general tendency among minority-group members. For example, members of tightly cohesive religious groups may draw emotional support from their faith and from one another. The insulation of living in an ethnic community, having strong ingroup loyalty, and/or having a determination to maintain a cultural heritage may prevent minority-group members from developing a negative self-image.

Studies show that people who are stigmatized can protect their self-esteem by attributing the negative feedback they receive to prejudice. Ethnic identity pride can serve as a buffer against the effects of dominant-group stigmatizing.[12] A positive group image enhances personal self-esteem, and high personal self-esteem enhances one's ability to cope more successfully with ethnic and racial discrimination.[13]

## THE VICIOUS-CIRCLE PHENOMENON

Sometimes the relationship between prejudice and discrimination is circular. Gunnar Myrdal referred to this pattern as **cumulative causation**—a **vicious-circle phenomenon** in which prejudice and discrimination perpetuate each other.[14] For example, a discriminatory action in filling jobs leads to a minority reaction, poverty, which in turn reinforces the dominant-group attitude that the minority group is inferior, leading to more discrimination, and so on.

In addition, the pattern of expectation and reaction may produce desirable or undesirable results. To illustrate, if the dominant group makes newcomers welcome, they in turn are likely to react in a positive manner, which reinforces their friendly reception. If the new group is ignored or made to feel unwelcome, the members may react negatively, which again reaffirms original attitudes and actions. As Gordon Allport says, "If we foresee evil in our fellow man, we tend to provoke it; if good, we elicit it."[15] In other words, negative expectations lead to negative reactions, broadening the social distance between the groups and causing the vicious circle to continue.

When Jews were denied access to many U.S. vacation resorts during the nineteenth century, their reactions served to reinforce their negative stereotype in the minds of some, reinforcing the discriminatory behavior. Some Jews demanded equal access, which the resort operators took as proof that Jews were "pushy." When Jews responded to this discriminatory policy by establishing and patronizing their own resorts in the Catskill Mountains, the majority group labeled them "clannish." Similarly, the Irish encountered severe job discrimination in the mid-nineteenth century; the resulting poverty forced many of them to live in urban slums, where they often had trouble with the law. Given this evidence of their "inferiority" and "undesirability," majority-group employers curtailed Irish job opportunities further. In the same way, discrimination by whites against blacks, based partly on the low standard of living endured by many of the latter, worsened even more the problems of poverty and fueled even more the antipathy of some whites toward blacks.

**MARGINALITY.** Minority-group members sometimes find themselves caught in a conflict between their own identity and values and the necessity to behave in a certain way to gain acceptance by the dominant group. This situation—**marginality**—usually arises when a member of a minority group is passing through a transitional period. In attempting to enter the mainstream of society, the *marginal* person internalizes the dominant group's cultural patterns without having gained full acceptance. Such individuals occupy an ill-defined position, no longer at ease within their own group but not yet fully a part of the *reference group*, the one by whose standards they evaluate themselves and their behavior.

Some sociologists have believed that marginality caused the individual a great deal of strain and difficulty.[16] The marginal person, whether an adult or a child, can suffer anxiety due to a conflict of values and loyalties. Adults leave the security of their cultural group and thereby risk being labeled renegades by their own people. They seek sustained social contacts with members of the dominant group, which may view them as outsiders. No longer comfortable with the old ways but nonetheless influenced by them and identified with them, marginal adults often experience feelings of frustration, hypersensitivity, and self-consciousness.

Children of immigrants likewise find themselves caught between two worlds. At home, their parents attempt to raise them in their social heritage, according to the established ways of the old country. Meanwhile, through school and other outside experiences, the children are exposed to the U.S. culture and

*Marginality can take its toll, particularly on immigrant teenagers caught between the world of their parents and that of their native-born schoolmates and yet not fully part of either. This excluded young man, sitting on the bench away from a group of five teens, personifies the social isolation that members of an outgroup often experience.*

want to be like other children in the society. Moreover, they may learn that the dominant group views their parents' ways as inferior and so they, too, are rejected socially because of their background. Consequently, many young people in transition develop emotional problems and are embarrassed to bring classmates home.

Not all sociologists share this view of marginality resulting from cultural conflict caused primarily by the clash of values within the individual. Instead, they believe that the reaction to marginal status depends largely on whether the individual receives reassurances of self-worth from the surrounding community. Thus, successfully defining the situation and adjusting to it are contingent on the individual's sense of security, solidarity, and support within the community.[17] What exists, they say, is a transitional phase involving stable individuals in a marginal culture rather than marginal persons in a dominant culture. Individuals in a marginal culture share their cultural duality with many others in primary-group relationships, in institutional activities, and in interacting with members of the dominant society without encountering any contradiction between their desires and actuality.[18]

Whether this phase of the assimilation process represents an emotionally stressful experience or a comfortably protected one, minority-group members nonetheless pass through a transitional period during which they are not fully a part of either world. An immigrant group may move into the mainstream of U.S. society within the lifetimes of the first-generation members, it may choose not to do so, or it may not be permitted to do so. Usually, marginality is a one- or two-generation phenomenon. After that, members of the minority group either have assimilated or have formed a distinctive subculture. Whichever route they take, they usually are no longer caught between two cultural worlds.

## MIDDLEMAN MINORITIES

Building on theories of marginality is the model of **middleman minorities**.[19] This model identifies certain minorities in middle-income positions, typically in trade and commerce, where they play the role of middleman between producer and consumer and between the elite and the masses.[20] Historically, minorities commonly were trading peoples whose history of persecution (Jews, Greeks, and Armenians) or sojourner orientation (Chinese, Japanese, and Koreans) obliged them to perform risky or marginal tasks that permitted easy liquidation of their assets when necessary.[21]

*German, Irish, Italian, and Jewish merchants and small businesses once served as middleman minorities to other ethnic groups. Today some Africans, Asians, and Hispanics repeat the pattern, such as these Asian Indians following a familiar ethnic group occupational pattern by operating a newsstand in midtown Manhattan.*

Middleman groups often serve as buffers and occasionally experience hostility and conflict from above and below. Jews in Nazi Germany and Asians in Uganda in the early 1970s, for instance, became scapegoats for the economic turmoil in those societies. Their susceptibility to such antagonism and their nonassimilation into the host society promoted high ingroup solidarity.

Systematic discrimination can prolong the duration of a group's middleman-minority status, as in the case of European Jews throughout the medieval period. Sometimes the entrepreneurial skills developed in trade and commerce provide middleman minorities with adaptive capabilities and competitive advantages, enabling them to achieve upward mobility and to assimilate more easily, such as with earlier Jewish, Lebanese, and Syrian immigrants and more recent Korean and Asian Indian immigrants. In other cases, a group may emerge as a middleman minority because of changing residential patterns. One example is Jewish store owners in city neighborhoods where they once served their own people. When their original neighbors moved away and they found themselves unable to follow them, these urban merchants then served new urban minority groups that were situated lower on the socioeconomic ladder.

**STUDENTS SPEAK** "I live in an urban area in Atlantic City. When I first moved into the area, I was expecting to see Italians at the local corner store, because Italian foods like pizza and lasagne were being sold. However, when I saw Muslims ran the store, I was surprised. Because Arabic Muslims were there, I was expecting Middle Eastern food to be sold, but that was not the case."

**—Hamirah Bunch**

# Dominant-Group Responses

Members of a dominant group may react to minority peoples with hostility, indifference, welcoming tolerance, or condescension. The more favorable responses usually occur when the minority is numerically small, not perceived as a threat, or both. As the minority group's population increases, threatening the natives' monopoly on jobs and other claims to privileged cultural resources, the dominant group's attitude likely is to become suspicious or fearful. If the fear becomes great enough, the dominant group may take action against the minority group.

Dominant groups often use religion in varying aggressive ways against minority groups. Besides religious persecution (a push factor in many migrations throughout world history), they often use missionaries to convert minorities. Dominant groups do not necessarily conduct these sometimes forced conversions with the intent of assimilating a minority group. For example, teaching Christianity to slaves enabled southern whites to create a false consciousness among the Africans in accepting their fate by working hard to please their masters. In the case of Native Americans, the federal government gave reservation land to several Protestant religions in an effort to convert the "heathens" and remake them in the white man's image, while maintaining their isolated, segregated confinement.

**4-3** Analyze common patterns of dominant-group responses to minorities.

**Read on MySocLab**
Document: **Overview of U.S. White Supremacist Groups**

## LEGISLATIVE CONTROLS

If the influx of racial and ethnic groups appears to the dominant group to be too great for a country to absorb, or if prejudicial fears prevail, the nation may enact measures to regulate and restrict their entry. Australia, Canada, and the United States—the three greatest receiving countries in international migration—once had discriminatory immigration laws that either excluded or curtailed the number of immigrants from countries other than those of northern and western Europe. Through similar patterns of policy change, Canada (in 1962), the United States (in 1965), and Australia (in 1973) began to permit entry from all parts of the world.

To maintain a paternalistic social system, the dominant group frequently restricts the subordinate group's educational and voting opportunities. This denial assures the dominant group of maintaining its system of control, whether over internal minorities, such as blacks in the Old South and various ethnic minorities in the former Soviet Union, or over colonized peoples, such as Africans and Asians once ruled by the Belgians, British, Dutch, French, Japanese, and Portuguese. Most colonial powers committed themselves to stability, trade, and tapping the natural resources of a country rather than developing its infrastructure and preparing it for self-governance. As a result, native populations under colonial rule largely experienced ceremonial leadership from figureheads installed and approved by the colonial authority (and who lacked real power in important matters), limited educational opportunities, and restricted political participation. Other means of denying political power have included disenfranchising voters through high property qualifications (British West Indies), high income qualifications (Trinidad), and poll taxes (United States), although none of these practices exist today in these areas. The most conspicuous recent example of rigid social control was in South Africa, where a legislated apartheid society denied blacks not only equal education and the ballot but also almost every other privilege as well.

## SEGREGATION

Through a policy of containment—avoiding social interaction with members of a minority group as much as possible and keeping them "in their place"—the dominant group effectively can create both spatial and social segregation.

**Spatial segregation** is the physical separation of a minority people from the rest of society. This most commonly occurs in residential patterns, but it also takes place in education, in the use of public facilities, and in occupations. The majority group may institutionalize this form of segregation by law (*de jure* segregation) or establish it informally through pervasive practices (*de facto* segregation).

Spatial segregation of minorities has a long history. Since the days of the preindustrial city with its heterogeneous populations, the dominant group has relegated minorities to special sections of the city, often the least desirable areas.[22] In Europe, this medieval ecological pattern resulted in minority groups being situated on the city outskirts nearest the encircling wall. Because this pattern remains in much of Europe today, Europeans, unlike people in the United States, consider it a sign of high prestige to live near the center of the city.[23]

The dominant group may use hidden or obvious means to achieve spatial segregation of a minority group. Examples of hidden actions include restrictive covenants, "gentlemen's agreements," and collusion between the community and real estate agents to steer "undesirable" minorities into certain neighborhoods.[24] Obvious actions include restrictive zoning, segregation laws, and intimidation. Since the 1954 *Brown v. Board of Education* desegregation ruling, U.S. courts continually have declared both methods of segregation unlawful.

An important dimension of spatial segregation is that the dominant group can achieve it through avoidance or residential mobility. Usually referred to as the invasion-succession ecological pattern, this common process has involved different religions and nationalities as well as different races. The most widely recognized example in the United States is previously all-white neighborhoods becoming black, but any study of old urban neighborhoods would reveal the same pattern, as successive waves of immigrants arrived throughout the years. Residents of a neighborhood initially may resist the influx of a minority group, but eventually, they abandon the area when their efforts are not successful. This pattern results in neighborhoods with a concentration of a new racial or ethnic group—a new segregated area.

**Social segregation** involves confining participation in social, service, political, and other types of activities to members of the ingroup and thereby excluding the outgroup from any involvement. Organizations may use screening procedures to keep out unwanted types and informal groups may act to preserve the composition of their membership.

Segregation, whether spatial or social, may be voluntary or involuntary. Minority-group members may choose to live by themselves rather than among the dominant group; this is an avoidance response, discussed previously. In contrast, minority-group members may have no choice about where they live because of economic or residential discrimination.

Whether by choice or against their will, minority groups form ethnic subcommunities, the existence of which in turn promotes and maintains the social distance between them and the rest of society. Not only do minority-group members physically congregate in one area and thus find themselves spatially segregated, but they also do not engage in any social interaction with others outside their own group.

Under the right conditions, frequent interaction reduces prejudice, but when interaction is limited severely, the acculturation process slows considerably. Meanwhile, values regarding what is normal or different are reinforced, paving the way for stereotyping, social comparisons, and prestige ranking.

**STUDENTS SPEAK** *"When my cousin and I were in high school, he would often talk about the segregation between the white and Hispanic students. His school wasn't actually segregated but the students did not interact with each other outside of their groups. He told me that in the school the white kids hung out together and the Hispanics hung out together. It was pretty rare to see the groups together, which was weird for me to hear since my school was much less diverse, about 95% white. But, we still hung out with the kids from other races and didn't see them as any different. I think the white students in my cousin's school didn't like the Hispanics that much because their town had, until recently, been highly populated with Italian and Irish families. It's like they took that away from them."*

**—Daniel Penett**

## EXPULSION

When other methods of dealing with a minority group fail—and sometimes not even as a last resort—an intolerant dominant group may persecute the minority group or eject it from the territory where it resides (**expulsion**). Henry VIII banished the Gypsies from England in the sixteenth century, Spanish rulers drove out the Moors in the early seventeenth century, and the British expelled the French Acadians from Nova Scotia in the mid-eighteenth century. More recent examples include Idi Amin, who decreed in 1972 that all Asians must leave Uganda; Muammar al-Qaddafi, who expelled Libya's ethnic Italian community in 1970; and Serbs who forced ethnic Albanians out of Kosovo in 1999.

The United States has its examples of mass expulsion. In colonial times, the Puritans forced Roger Williams and his followers out of Massachusetts for their nonconformity, and the group resettled in what became Rhode Island. The forcible removal of the Cherokee from rich Georgia land and the subsequent "Trail of Tears," during which 4,000 perished along the 1,000-mile forced march to Oklahoma Territory, is another illustration.

Mass expulsion is an effort to drive out a group that is seen as a social problem rather than attempting to resolve the problem cooperatively. This policy often arises after other methods, such as assimilation or extermination, have failed. Whether a dominant group chooses to remove a minority group by extermination or by expulsion depends in part on how sensitive the country is to world opinion, which in turn may be related to the country's economic dependence on other nations.

## XENOPHOBIA

If the dominant group's suspicions and fears of the minority group become serious enough, they may produce volatile, irrational feelings and actions. This overreaction is known as **xenophobia**—the undue fear of or contempt for strangers or foreigners. This almost hysterical response—reflected in print, speeches, sermons, legislation, and violent actions—begins with ethnocentric views. Ethnocentrism encourages the creation of negative stereotypes, which in turn invites prejudice and discrimination and can escalate through some catalyst into a highly emotional reaction (see the International Scene box).

# the INTERNATIONAL scene

## Segregation and Defiance in France

In late 2005, three weeks of riots and violent clashes broke out in Paris and spread to other French cities, eventually engulfing all fifteen of the country's largest urban areas. By the time the riots ended, the counts were one dead, approximately 2,900 arrested, and thousands of vehicles and numerous public buildings burned, including a Roman Catholic Church.

The spiraling events began with the accidental electrocution of two teenagers—one the son of West African immigrants and the other the son of Tunisian immigrants—who ran from police (conducting one of their frequent identity checks of minorities) and hid in a power substation. A third teenager, the son of Turkish Kurdish immigrants, was injured and hospitalized. The three victims thus represented the primary minority groups in France—Arab, black, and Muslim—and became the catalyst to ignite the pre-existing tensions.

In November 2007 and July 2009, other riots occurred, also sparked by the deaths of minority teens or young adults. In 2007, more than 70 cars and buildings (including a library, two schools, a police station, and several shops) were burned and 130 policemen injured. In 2009, 317 cars were burned and 13 police officers injured. In 2012, minority youth again rioted, this time in Amiens for two nights, with 17 police officers injured, and a primary school and sports center torched.

For decades, French government policy had concentrated immigrants and their families in well-defined districts of poorly maintained public housing projects on the edges of cities. Isolated from the city center, these de facto ethnic ghettos have little activity at night or on Sundays, and there is limited public transportation to the center. In addition, much higher unemployment for the foreign-born compared to the native-born—even worse among college graduates—contributed extensively to the mounting frustration and desperation.

Amid charges of job discrimination and police harassment, the common use by the media and general population of the expression "second generation of immigrants" (even for those born in France) suggested a cultural mindset that differentiated who was "really" French. (At age 18, immigrant children born in France may go through a bureaucratic application process to be citizens; their birth in France does not automatically give them citizenship as it does in the United States.)

Experts cite the racial and social discrimination against persons with dark skin or Arabic- and/or African-sounding names as a major cause of unhappiness in the riot-torn areas. Although such discrimination is illegal, children of immigrants claim that they frequently encounter economic segregation, problems getting a job or renting an apartment, or even getting into a nightclub, just because of their name or the color of their skin. Since the riots, little has changed, and thus the potential for still other violent outbreaks remains.

### CRITICAL THINKING QUESTIONS

How similar or dissimilar are the experiences of U.S. minorities today? Does the difference in French and U.S. citizenship laws have any impact on the acceptance and integration of minorities into society? If so, how?

---

Many examples of xenophobia exist in U.S. history. In 1798, the Federalists, fearful of "wild Irishmen" and "French radicals" and eager to eliminate what they saw as a foreign threat to the country's stability, passed the Alien and Sedition Acts to arrest, even deport, "undesirables." When a bomb exploded at an anarchist gathering at Chicago's Haymarket Square in 1886, many Americans thereafter linked foreigners with radicals. The Bolshevik Revolution in 1917 led to the Palmer raids, in which foreign-born U.S. residents were rounded up illegally and incarcerated for their alleged Communist Party affiliation; some even were deported. In 1942, 110,000 Japanese Americans, many of them second- and third-generation U.S. citizens, were interned in concentration camps as a result of irrational suspicions that they would prove less loyal during the ongoing World War II than German Americans and Italian Americans, although the United States was fighting all three countries. The U.S. English movement's current efforts to pass English official laws reflect a xenophobic fear that foreigners won't learn English.

Xenophobia is not limited to any one country. In 2008 in Johannesburg, marchers protested attacks against foreigners that killed about 50 people, seriously injured hundreds, and displaced about 15,000 African immigrants, mostly refugees from Zimbabwe, who poor South Africans blamed for taking their scarce job opportunities.

## ANNIHILATION

The Nazi extermination of more than 6 million Jews brought the term *genocide* into the English language, but the practice of **annihilation**—killing all the men, women, and children of a particular group—goes back to ancient times. In warfare among the ancient Assyrians, Babylonians, Egyptians, Hebrews, and others, the usual practice was for the victor to slay every member of an enemy civilization, partly to prevent their children from seeking revenge. For example, preserved in Deuteronomy are these words of Moses:

> Then Sihon came out against us, he and all his people, to fight at Jahaz. And the LORD our God delivered him before us; and we smote him, and his sons, and all his people. And we took all his cities at that time, and utterly destroyed the men, and the women, and the little ones, of every city, we left none to remain: Only the cattle we took for a prey unto ourselves, and the spoil of the cities which we took.
>
> Then we turned, and went up the way to Bashan: and Og the king of Bashan came out against us, he and all his people, to battle at Edrei....So the LORD our God delivered into our hands Og also, the king of Bashan, and all his people: and we smote him until none was left to him remaining. And we took all his cities at that time, there was not a city which we took not from them, threescore cities, all the region of Argob, the kingdom of Og in Bashan....And we utterly destroyed them, as we did unto Sihon king of Heshbon, utterly destroying the men, women, and children, of every city. But all the cattle, and the spoil of the cities, we took for a prey to ourselves.[25]

In modern times, various countries have used extermination as a means of solving a so-called race problem. The British, through extermination and close confinement of survivors, annihilated the entire aboriginal population of Tasmania between 1803 and 1876.[26] The Dutch considered South African San (Bushmen) less than human and attempted to obliterate them.[27] In the 1890s and again in 1915, the Turkish government systematically massacred hundreds of thousands of Armenians, events still solemnly remembered each year by Armenian Americans. One of the largest genocides in U.S. history occurred at Wounded Knee in 1890, when the U.S. Seventh Cavalry killed approximately 200 Native American men, women, and children. In the past 50 years, campaigns of genocide have occurred around the globe in such countries as Bangladesh, Bosnia, Burundi, Cambodia, Indonesia, Iraq, Kosovo, Nigeria, Rwanda, and Sudan.

Lynchings are not a form of annihilation because the intent is not to exterminate an entire group but to set an example through selective, drastic punishment (most frequently, hanging). Nonetheless, the victims usually are minority-group members. Although lynchings occurred throughout U.S. history, only since 1882 do we have reasonably reliable statistics on their frequency (Figure 4.1). Archived data at the *Chicago Tribune* and the Tuskegee Institute reveal that at least 5,000 lynchings have occurred since 1882. They happened in almost every state, with southern states (especially Mississippi, Georgia, and Texas) claiming the most victims. In fact, 90 percent of all lynchings during this period occurred in the southern states, with blacks accounting for 80 percent of the victims. The statistics, however, do not cover lynchings during the nation's first 100 years, including those in the western frontier, when many Mexican and Native Americans also met this fate.[28]

Annihilation sometimes occurred unintentionally, as when whites inadvertently spread Old World sicknesses to Native Americans in the United States and Canada, to Inuit (Eskimos), and to Polynesians. With no prior exposure to ailments such as measles, mumps, chicken pox, and smallpox, the native populations had little physiological resistance to them and thus succumbed to these contagious diseases in unusually high numbers. Other forms of annihilation, usually intentional, occur during times of mob violence, overzealous police actions, and the calculated actions of small private groups.[29]

## HATE GROUPS

Like most nations, the United States has had its share of hate groups and hate crimes. Most prominent among hate groups of the past were the Know-Nothings of the mid-nineteenth century and the Ku Klux Klan in the late nineteenth and early twentieth centuries. As you will read in subsequent chapters, bias crimes against Europeans, Native Americans, Asians, and numerous religious groups frequently occurred in the nineteenth

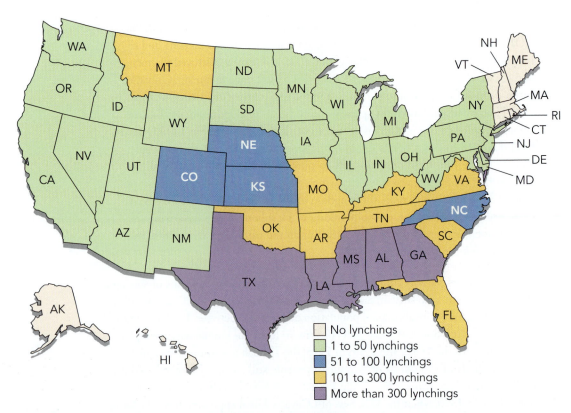

No lynchings
1 to 50 lynchings
51 to 100 lynchings
101 to 300 lynchings
More than 300 lynchings

**FIGURE 4.1  Lynchings in the United States Since 1882**

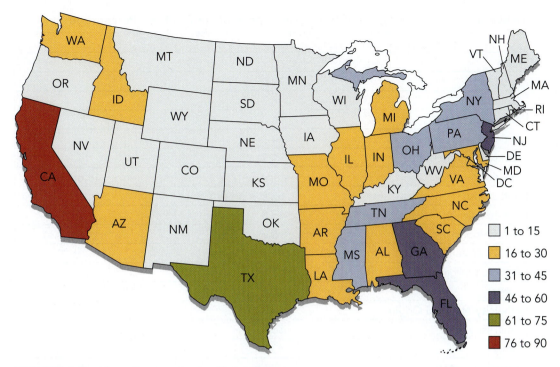

**FIGURE 4.2** Hate Groups in the United States

*Source:* Courtesy of Southern Poverty Law Center.

Legend:
- 1 to 15
- 16 to 30
- 31 to 45
- 46 to 60
- 61 to 75
- 76 to 90

and twentieth centuries. Deplorably, in the twenty-first century, this ugly pattern remains a brutal force in U.S. society.

The Intelligence Project of the Southern Poverty Law Center—the nation's preeminent monitor and analyst of American extremism—reported that the number of hate groups in the United States increased by 70 percent since 2000, driven in large measure by immigration and economic issues (Figure 4.2).[30] Of the 1,007 organized, active hate groups in 2012, the largest types were neo-Nazi organizations, the Ku Klux Klan, white nationalists, neo-Confederates, and black separatist groups, including the Nation of Islam. Although the Nation of Islam group is not involved in political violence, its tenets are based on racial hatred according to the Intelligence Project. Other hate groups are racist skinheads and Christian Identity groups, which identify whites as the Bible's chosen people and Jews as satanic.

Active hate groups are not confined to one geographic region. California contained the largest number of hate groups (82), followed by Texas (62), Florida (59), Georgia (53), New Jersey (51), New York (38), Mississippi and Ohio (36), Pennsylvania (35), Tennessee (33), Arizona and North Carolina (28), Alabama and Virginia (30), Illinois (27), Michigan (25), Arkansas (23). Louisiana, Missouri and South Carolina (21).

**STUDENTS SPEAK** *"Looking at all the hate groups that exist makes me sick to my stomach. All of these groups are so brainwashed and have the most ridiculous views about other races in our country. There is much more to life than being part of a hate group and having your life revolve around hate and anger. These people need to take a look at themselves and realize that they're a huge reason why there is so much anger in our country."*
—**Michael Sasso**

## HATE CRIMES

Hate crime offenses—only some of which are committed by members of organized hate groups—have declined; 6,216 hate crimes in 2011 claimed 7,697 victims. Racial bias motivated 47 percent of the incidents; religious bias, another 20 percent; sexual-orientation bias, 21 percent; ethnicity/national origin bias, 12 percent; and disability, less than 1 percent (Table 4.1). Crimes against persons accounted for 64 percent of hate crime offenses, while damage/destruction/vandalism of property constituted 36 percent.[31]

**TABLE 4.1** Bias Motivation of Hate-Crime Incidents in 2011, by Percentage

| | PERCENTAGE OF CATEGORY | PERCENTAGE OF TOTAL |
|---|---|---|
| **Race** | | 46.9 |
| Anti-black | 72.0 | |
| Anti-white | 16.7 | |
| Anti-Asian | 4.8 | |
| Anti-multiracial group | 4.7 | |
| Anti-Native American | 1.9 | |
| **Religion** | | 19.8 |
| Anti-Jewish | 62.2 | |
| Anti-Islamic | 13.3 | |
| Anti-Catholic | 5.2 | |
| Anti-Protestant | 3.7 | |
| Anti-multireligious group | 4.8 | |
| Other | 10.8 | |
| **Ethnicity/National Origin** | | 11.6 |
| Anti-Hispanic | 56.8 | |
| Other | 43.2 | |
| **Sexual Orientation** | | 20.8 |
| Anti-male homosexual | 57.8 | |
| Anti-female homosexual | 11.1 | |
| Anti-homosexual | 28.4 | |
| Anti-bisexual | 1.5 | |
| Anti-heterosexual | 1.1 | |
| **Disability** | | 0.9 |
| Anti-physical | 39.7 | |
| Anti-mental | 60.3 | |

Source: Adapted from the Federal Bureau of Investigation, *"Hate Crime Statistics: 2011."* Retrieved June 4, 2013 (http://www.fbi.gov/about-us/cjis/ucr/hate-crime/2011).

*Sadly, in the U.S. a hate crime occurs every hour on average. About one-third each are acts of intimidation, assaults against individuals, and vandalism or property damage. Two months earlier than this photo, in California's Orange County, teens assaulted this 18-year-old Muslim youth with bats and beer bottles, while shouting supremacist slogans.*

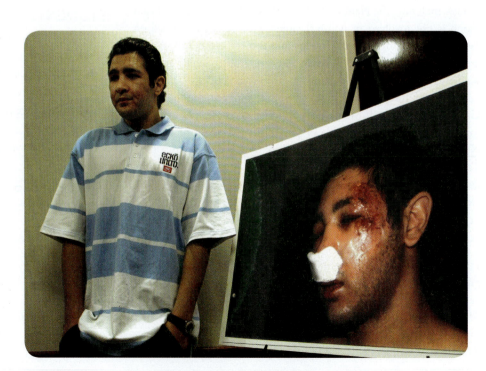

# REALITY check

## College Campuses and Hate Crimes

Many people assume that those who commit hate crimes typically are ignorant, poorly educated individuals with little to no respect for those unlike themselves. If that were true, then we would expect that bias incidents would be few and far between on college campuses. After all, these are learning environments of diversity, intellectual curiosity, offering courses promoting intergroup relations. Open-mindedness should be the norm and narrow-minded bigotry the rare exception. Colleges in many ways, however, are microcosms of the larger society, and the reality is that hatred exists on campuses too.

The Southern Poverty Law Center (SPLC), after a two-year study, found campuses across the country—from north to south, from east to west—struggling with the problem of bias incidents and hate crimes. In fact, the statistics are disturbing. The SPLC has reported that every single year, more than a half million college students are targets of bias-driven slurs or physical assaults.

Such a large number may be hard to put in perspective. Perhaps this statistic will make the problem clearer. Every day at least one hate crime occurs on a U.S. college campus. Some experts argue that this figure is too low because it only covers reported crimes, and that the actual number may be three to five hate crimes every day.

More common than hate crimes are bias incidents: name-calling, threatening e-mails and telephone calls, insulting signs and symbols, and other forms of verbal aggression or intimidation. Every minute, a U.S. college student somewhere sees or hears racist, sexist, homophobic, or otherwise biased words or images. The Prejudice Institute estimated that as many as one million college students are targets of ethnoviolence in any given year on the nation's college campuses.

### CRITICAL THINKING QUESTION

What can you do to make a difference in promoting mutual respect and tolerance at your college?

To combat hate crimes—commonly defined as any criminal offense against a person or property that is motivated in whole or part by the offender's bias against a race, religion, ethnic/national origin, group, or sexual orientation—states have passed laws mandating severe punishments for persons convicted of these crimes. Federal law (18 U.S.C. 245) also permits federal prosecution of a hate crime as a civil rights violation if the assailant intended to prevent the victim from exercising a "federally protected right" such as voting or attending school. Despite such sanctions, however, the numbers of hate groups and hate crimes continue to rise (see the Reality Check box).

# Exploitation

The **exploitation** of minority groups has been a common occurrence in virtually all countries. Sometimes the perpetrators of this abuse are members of the same group—the operators of Asian sweatshops in U.S. cities, for instance, and the *padroni* of earlier Italian American immigrant communities, both of whom often benefited at the expense of their own people. Most often, however, members of dominant groups exploit minority groups.

Middle-range conflict theories often are helpful in understanding specific forms of exploitation, such as the internal-colonialism theory discussed in Chapter 2. Another analytical explanation came to us from Edna Bonacich, who introduced the concept of a **split** or **dual labor market** as a means of understanding ethnic antagonism in the workplace.[32] This model refers to two fields of employment, the *primary labor market* where workers enjoy decent wages, pay payroll taxes, and receive health insurance and other benefits,

**4-4** Analyze various patterns of exploitation.

**Explore on MySocLab**
Activity: Dubai Labor

compared to the *secondary labor market*, in which minorities, mostly, work in unregulated low-paying jobs, usually on a cash basis with no payroll tax deductions, health insurance, or other benefits.

Part of the secondary labor market also is known as the **underground economy**, where employers pay workers in cash "under the table." Neither employers nor workers report these hidden services and earnings to the government. As a result, employers—such as those in lawn and landscaping services, home construction and remodeling, and in food service industries—do not pay into employee health or pension plans, Medicare, or Social Security, and those savings enable them to be more competitive in getting work and in maximizing profits. The workers—many of them immigrants familiar only with a cash economy in their homeland—do not pay any payroll or income taxes but also have no health insurance coverage and will not qualify for Social Security in their old age.

To understand how a split labor market works, we first must realize that, even though higher-price workers are quick to blame minorities for undercutting their wages, the reality is that the vulnerability of both groups to economic pressures enables businesses to control the situation.[33] Ethnic antagonism subsequently results from a combination of economic exploitation by employers and economic competition between two or more groups of laborers, which produces a wage differential for labor. Much ethnic antagonism thus is based not on ethnicity and race but on the conflict between higher-paid and lower-paid labor.

The lower-paid group—its wages nonetheless higher than its members can find back home—threatens the higher-paid labor group with possible displacement through such wage undercutting. When a labor market splits along ethnic lines, racial and ethnic stereotyping becomes a key factor in the labor conflict, and prejudice, ethnic antagonism, and racism become overt. Bonacich argues that the one characteristic shared by all societies in which ethnic antagonism is acute is an indigenous working class that earns higher wages than do immigrant workers.

This common characteristic fuels anti-immigration sentiments, intensified even more these days by the concern over the millions of undocumented immigrants in the country. The generations-old complaint that "they're taking jobs away from Americans" has at its core the fear of higher-priced American labor being displaced by cheaper immigrant labor.

*Unseen by tourists flocking to ground-level stores and restaurants in Manhattan's Chinatown district are cramped sweatshop factories, often on the upper floors. These sweatshops remain a place of rough working conditions and economic exploitation just as they were three generations ago. Today, other newcomers—many undocumented—work long hours for low pay.*

Employers seldom are passive observers of this clash between higher-priced and cheaper labor along racial and ethnic lines. They are the ones, after all, who control the lower wages offered to the minority workers. Moreover, employers often will actively manipulate the situation to keep the groups divided. For example, they could practice *majority paternalism* (promoting a racial hierarchy to cultivate majority-group loyalty) or *minority paternalism* (cultivating minority-group loyalty through jobs, home loans, or funds for community projects to encourage company unionism). A more militant approach would be a divide-and-rule strategy either by hiring minorities as strikebreakers or by encouraging state intervention to demobilize a possible coalition of workers.[34]

Today, employers are less likely to assign workers to inferior jobs on the basis of race and sex than to create nonstandard work arrangements with immigrants lacking U.S. citizenship. Employers can more easily persuade a group to work for a lower price if that group's initial standard of living—either in the United States or in the homeland left behind—is low; they can less easily tempt another group coming from a more favorable economic resource position. Although this labor market segmentation has increased substantially since the 1970s, recent studies also show that most workers who begin their careers in these secondary (bad) jobs eventually do move on to better jobs.[35]

## Minority-Minority Relations

Much research in the field of race and ethnic relations focuses on the interactions between the dominant group and minority groups, as did the preceding pages in this chapter. However, another important aspect of intergroup relations is the interactions that occur *between* minority groups. Sometimes, these can be positive, as in coalitions formed to fight for a cause at the local or national levels.

Most times, however, tensions and conflicts arise between minority groups who jockey for power, compete for jobs, see the other as gaining an "unfair" advantage, or become resentful of the other's presence in their neighborhood. In the chapters that follow, for example, you will read about how the dual labor market created conflicts between the Irish and Germans, Hungarians, Chinese, and Syrians. You also will read about tensions between Korean storeowners and the black communities they serve and about past minority-against-minority riots. These are but a few of many such instances of violent outbursts.

In the twenty-first century, relations among peoples of color remain a central concern. With Hispanics now the largest U.S. minority group and still growing rapidly, the African American community worries about the potential erosion of its political strength. Both groups live in close proximity to one another in urban areas; and, in many of these school districts, Hispanics are the majority. Also, often African Americans and Hispanics compete against one another for elected and appointed offices previously occupied by whites. Adding to the tension is the growing number of Hispanic immigrants, whom African Americans, particularly in the lower class, see as an economic threat.

Although it is true that accommodation and cooperation versus conflict between black and Hispanic Americans will depend on the local context, several factors clearly will affect black–brown relations in the years to come. Increasing numbers of Hispanic newcomers, legal and illegal, will not only generate further competition for resources and status, but also put into close proximity two groups with little direct knowledge or interaction with one another. Such limited awareness, plus the prevalence of cultural and language differences, will affect perceptions, attitudes, and behaviors on both sides. The resultant social distance sets the stage for friction, misunderstandings, and negative stereotyping. Intergroup relations thus will rest on whether consensus on or conflict over issues will prevail.[36]

4-5 Explain concern over potential dangers in minority-minority relations.

# Theories of Minority Integration

**4-6** Evaluate three models of possible minority integration in society.

**Explore on MySocLab**
Activity: Assimilation and Distinctive Cultural Patterns

**Explore on MySocLab**
Activity: Of Melting Pots and Mosaics: A Look at Maui

**Read on MySocLab**
Document: Beyond the Melting Pot Reconsidered

More than 80 million immigrants have come to the United States since its founding as a nation. Throughout the course of this extensive migration, three different theories emerged regarding how these ethnically different peoples either should or did fit into U.S. society. These theories are (1) assimilation or majority-conformity theory; (2) amalgamation or melting-pot theory; and (3) accommodation or pluralistic theory.

The type of interaction between minority peoples and those of the dominant culture has depended partly on which ideology then prevailed among both groups. People formulate attitudes and expectations based on the values they hold. If those values include a clear image of how an "American" should look, talk, and act, people who differ from that model will find their adjustment and acceptance by others more difficult. Conversely, if those values allow for diversity, a greater possibility exists that harmonious relationships will evolve.

## ASSIMILATION (MAJORITY-CONFORMITY) THEORY

Generally speaking, **assimilation (majority-conformity) theory** refers to the functioning within a society of racial or ethnic minority-group members who no longer possess any marked cultural, social, or personal differences from the people of the dominant group. Physical or racial differences may persist, but they do not serve as the basis for group prejudice or discrimination. In effect, these minority group members no longer appear to be strangers because they have abandoned their own cultural traditions and successfully blended into the dominant group. Assimilation thus may be described as $A + B + C = A$.[37]

**ANGLO-CONFORMITY.** Because most of the people in power in the United States during the eighteenth century were of English descent, English influence on the new nation's culture was enormous—in language, institutional forms, values, and attitudes. By the first quarter of the nineteenth century, a distinct national consciousness had emerged, and many U.S. citizens wanted to deemphasize their English origins and influences. However, when migration patterns changed the composition of the U.S. population in the 1880s, the "Yankees" re-established the Anglo-Saxon as the superior model.[38] Anglo-Saxonism remained dominant well into the twentieth century as the mold into which newcomers must fit.

To preserve their Anglo-Saxon heritage, people in the United States often attempted, sometimes with success, to curtail the large numbers of non–Anglo-Saxon immigrants. Social pressures demanded that new arrivals shed their native culture and attachments as quickly as possible and be remade into "Americans" along cherished Anglo-Saxon lines. The schools served as an important socializing agent in promoting the shedding of cultural differences.

Sometimes insistence on assimilation reached feverish heights, as evidenced by the **Americanization movement** during World War I. The arrival of a large number of "inferior" people in the preceding 30 years and the participation of the United States in a European conflict raised questions about those who were not "100 percent American." Government agencies at all levels, together with many private organizations, acted to encourage more immediate adoption by foreigners of U.S. practices: citizenship, reverence for U.S. institutions, and use of the English language.[39]

Other assimilation efforts have not been very successful—for example, with people whose ancestral history in an area predates the nation's expansion into that territory. Most Native American tribes throughout the United States as well as the *Hispanos* of the Southwest have resisted this cultural hegemony.

**TYPES OF ASSIMILATION.** Milton Gordon suggested assimilation has several phases.[40] One important phase is **cultural assimilation (acculturation)**—the change of cultural

This cartoon pictures Uncle Sam annoyed by groups that were seen as unassimilable. Both racial differences (blacks, Chinese, and Native Americans) and religious differences (Catholics and Mormons) were cause for being kicked out of the symbolic bed. This cartoon appeared in a San Francisco illustrated weekly, The Wasp, on February 8, 1879.

patterns to match those of the host society. **Marital assimilation**—large-scale intermarriage with members of the majority society—and **structural assimilation**—large-scale entrance into the cliques, clubs, and institutions of the host society on a primary-group level—best reveal the extent of acceptance of minority groups in the larger society.

Gordon believed that once structural assimilation occurred, all other types of assimilation—including the end of an ethnic identity and residual ethnic prejudice—would follow. Some researchers agree, offering evidence that migration generates similar consequences for successive generations, irrespective of ethnicity.[41] Other studies, however, suggest that cultural assimilation (English language usage and embeddedness in Anglo social contexts) is a necessary precondition to structural assimilation.[42]

Similar to the primary and secondary labor markets discussed previously, sociologists also divide structural assimilation into primary and secondary processes. **Secondary structural assimilation** typically involves the more impersonal public sphere of social interaction, such as intergroup mingling in civic, recreational, school, or work environments. **Primary structural assimilation** typically involves close, personal interactions between dominant- and minority-group members in small-group settings, such as parties, social clubs, and other interactive gatherings.

Assimilation as a belief, goal, or pattern helps explain many aspects of dominant–minority relations, particularly acceptance and adjustment. For approximately three-fourths of this nation's existence, members of the dominant society interpreted the assimilation of minorities to mean their absorption into the white Anglo-Saxon Protestant mold. For physically or culturally distinct groups (Asians, blacks, Catholics, Hispanics, Jews, Muslims, and Native Americans), this concept, at the time, raised a seemingly insurmountable barrier. Even for those physically and culturally fitting the Anglo-Saxon role model, assimilation is preceded by a transitional period in which the newcomer gradually blends in with dominant-group members. During that process, the individual may encounter others' impatience at the pace and also experience an identity crisis as well.

Because of the complexity of the assimilation process, peppered as it is by conflicting views on both sides on whether or not assimilation is even desirable, the dynamics of dominant–minority relations can vary from one group to another. Not all sociologists accept Gordon's view that the assimilation process is linear, that is, that all groups steadily move from a visible subculture to absorption into the dominant culture. Instead of this "one size fits all" approach, an alternative theory is that assimilation is segmented and so several outcomes are possible, depending on a group's vulnerability and resources.[43] This perspective is popular among social scientists today and is one that we will apply throughout this book.

## AMALGAMATION (MELTING-POT) THEORY

The democratic experiment in the United States fired many eighteenth-century imaginations in Europe. A new society had emerged, peopled by immigrants from different European nations and not traditionally bound by the customs and traditions of the past. Their bold initiatives generated a romantic notion of the United States as a melting pot. Conceptualized as the **amalgamation** or **melting-pot theory**, it holds that all the diverse peoples blend their biological and cultural differences (through intermarriage and creation of a unique culture) into an altogether new breed—the American. This concept may be expressed as $A + B + C = D$.[44]

**ADVOCATES.** J. Hector St. John de Crèvecoeur, a French settler in New York, first popularized the idea of a melting pot. Envisioning the United States as more than just a land of opportunity, Crèvecoeur in 1782 spoke of a new breed of humanity emerging from the new society. That he included only white Europeans partly explains the weakness of this approach to minority integration:

> What is an American? He is either a European, or the descendant of a European; hence that strange mixture of blood which you will find in no other country. I could point out to you a man whose grandfather was an Englishman, whose wife was Dutch, whose son married a French woman, and whose present four sons have now four wives of different nations. He is an American, who, leaving behind him all his ancient prejudices and manners, receives new ones from the new mode of life he has embraced, the new government he obeys and the new rank he holds.…Here individuals of all nations are melted into a new race of men, whose labors and posterity will one day cause great changes in the world.[45]

This idealistic concept found many advocates throughout the years. In 1893, Frederick Jackson Turner updated it with his frontier thesis, a notion that greatly influenced historical scholarship for half a century. Turner believed that the challenge of frontier life was the catalyst that fused immigrants into a composite new national stock within an evolving social order:

> Thus the Middle West was teaching the lesson of national cross-fertilization instead of national enmities, the possibility of a newer and richer civilization, not by preserving unmodified or isolated the old component elements, but by breaking down the line-fences, by merging the individual life in the common product—a new product, which held the promise of world brotherhood.[46]

In 1908, the play *The Melting-Pot* by English author Israel Zangwill enthusiastically etched a permanent symbol on the assimilationist ideal:

> There she lies, the great melting pot. Listen! Can't you hear the roaring and the bubbling? There gapes her mouth—the harbor where a thousand mammoth feeders come from the ends of the world to pour in their human freight. Ah, what a stirring and a seething—Celt and Latin, Slav and Teuton, Greek

and Syrian. America is God's Crucible, the great Melting Pot where all the races of Europe are melting and reforming!—Here you stand good folk, think I, when I see you at Ellis Island, here you stand, in your fifty groups, with your fifty languages and histories, and your fifty hatreds and rivalries. But you won't be long like that, brothers, for these are the fires of God you come to—these are the fires of God!…Germans and Frenchmen, Irishmen and English, Jews and Russians, into the Crucible with you all! God is making the American!…the real American has not yet arrived.…He will be the fusion of all races, perhaps the coming superman.…Ah, Vera, what is the glory of Rome and Jerusalem, where all races and nations come to worship and look back, compared with the glory of America, where all races and nations come to labor and look forward.[47]

Both the frontier thesis and the melting-pot concept have come under heavy criticism since. Although many still pay homage to the melting-pot concept, few social scientists accept this explanation of a minority integration that creates a new citizenry. Moreover, when U.S. citizens insist that others "blend in," they want ethnic groups to assimilate and have no desire that they themselves also should be "blended" with the foreign-born.

**DID WE MELT?** Throughout several generations, intermarriages frequently occur between people of different nationalities, less frequently between people of different religions, and still less frequently between people of different races. Thus, one could argue that a biological merging of previously distinct ethnic stocks, and to a smaller extent of different races, has taken place.[48] However, the melting-pot theory spoke not only of intermarriages among the different groups but also of a distinct new national culture evolving from elements of all other cultures. Here the theory has proved to be unrealistic. At its founding, the United States was dominated by an Anglo-Saxon population and thus by the English language and Anglo-Saxon institutional forms. Given the large numbers of non-British and non-Protestant arrivals, the definition of "Americanism" may have broadened, but Anglo-Protestant culture still defines the meaning of America more than any other.[49] Rather than various cultural patterns melting into a new U.S. culture, elements of minority cultures evolved into the Anglo-Saxon mold.

Only in the institution of religion did minority groups alter the national culture. From a mostly Protestant nation in its early history, the United States has become a land of four major faiths: Protestantism, Catholicism, Judaism, and Islam, with Hinduism and other non-Western religions increasing as well. As ethnic differences disappeared among older immigrant groups, religious groupings became the primary foci of identity and interaction throughout most of the twentieth century. Today, the high religious intermarriage rate (discussed in Chapter 12) is reshaping ethnic boundaries as, for some groups at least, assimilation blurs previous distinctions of cultural differentiation.[50]

In other areas, the entry of diverse minority groups into U.S. society has not produced new social structures or institutional forms in the larger society. Instead, subcultural social structures and institutions have evolved to meet group needs, and the dominant culture has benefited from the labors and certain cultural aspects of minority groups within the already existing dominant culture. For example, minority influences are found in word usage, place names, cuisine, architecture, art, recreational activities, and music.

Sociologist Henry Pratt Fairchild offered a physiological analogy to describe how the absorption of various cultural components or peoples produces assimilation and not amalgamation. An organism consumes food and is affected (nourished) by it somewhat; the food, though, is assimilated in the sense that it becomes an integral part of the organism, retaining none of its original characteristics. This is a one-way process. In a similar manner, U.S. culture has remained unchanged basically, though strengthened, despite the influx of many minority groups.[51]

Most social scientists view the melting-pot theory as a romantic myth. Its idealistic rhetoric continues to attract many followers, however. In reality, the melting meant **Anglo-conformity**—being remade according to the idealized Anglo-Saxon mold:

> But it would be a mistake to infer from this that the American's image of himself—and that means the ethnic group member's image of himself as he becomes American—is a composite or synthesis of the ethnic elements that have gone into the making of the American. It is nothing of the kind; the American's image of himself is still the Anglo-American ideal it was at the beginning of our independent existence. The "national type" as ideal has always been, and remains, pretty well fixed. It is the *Mayflower*, John Smith, Davy Crockett, George Washington, and Abraham Lincoln that define the American's self-image, and this is true whether the American in question is a descendant of the Pilgrims or the grandson of an immigrant from southeastern Europe.[52]

The rejection of the melting-pot theory by many people, coupled with an ethnic consciousness, spawned a third ideology: the accommodation (pluralistic) theory.

## ACCOMMODATION (PLURALISTIC) THEORY

The **accommodation (pluralistic) theory** recognizes the persistence of racial and ethnic diversity, as in Canada, where the government has adopted multiculturalism as official policy. Pluralist theorists argue that minorities can maintain their distinctive subcultures and simultaneously interact with relative equality in the larger society. In countries such as Switzerland and the United States, this combination of diversity and togetherness is possible to varying degrees because the people agree on certain basic values (see Table 2.1). At the same time, minorities may interact mostly among themselves, live within well-defined communities, have their own forms of organizations, work in similar occupations, and marry within their own group. Applying our descriptive equation, pluralism would be $A + B + C = A + B + C$.[53]

**EARLY ANALYSIS.** Horace Kallen generally is recognized as the first exponent of cultural pluralism. In 1915, he published "Democracy Versus the Melting Pot," in which he

*Most large U.S. cities offer ample evidence of the multiethnic society that now comprises the American population—in their school populations, in their diverse work forces, and in the faces and clothing of the shoppers. This New York City street corner furnishes additional confirmation: the side-by-side Korean, French, and Arab small businesses.*

rejected the assimilation and amalgamation theories.[54] Not only did each group tend to preserve its own language, institutions, and cultural heritage, he maintained, but democracy gave each group the right to do so. To be sure, minority groups learned the English language and participated in U.S. institutions, but what the United States really had become was a "cooperation of cultural diversities." Seeing Americanization movements as a threat to minority groups and the melting-pot notion as unrealistic, Kallen believed that cultural pluralism could be the basis for a great democratic commonwealth. A philosopher, not a sociologist, Kallen nonetheless directed sociological attention to a long-standing U.S. pattern.

**PLURALISTIC REALITY.** From its colonial beginnings, the United States has been a pluralistic country. Early settlements were small ethnic enclaves, each peopled by different nationalities or religious groups. New Amsterdam and Philadelphia were exceptions, as both were heavily pluralistic within their boundaries. Chain-migration patterns resulted in immigrants settling in clusters. Germans and Scandinavians in the Midwest, Poles in Chicago, Irish in New York and Boston, French in Louisiana, Chinese in California, Cubans in Miami, for example, illustrate how groups ease their adjustment to a new country by recreating in miniature the world they left behind. Current immigrant groups and remnants of past immigrant groups are testimony to the pluralism in U.S. society.

Cultural pluralism—two or more culturally distinct groups living in the same society in relative harmony—has been the more noticeable form of pluralism. **Structural pluralism**—the coexistence of racial and ethnic groups in subsocieties within social-class and regional boundaries—is less noticeable. Many minority groups lose their visibility when they acculturate. They, however, may identify with and take pride in their heritage and maintain primary relationships within their own racial/ethnic and social-class grouping. Despite this long-standing pluralistic reality, criticism of such self-segregating diversity remains a problem within U.S. society.

**DUAL REALITIES.** Although Americans give lip service to the concept of a melting pot, they typically expect foreigners to assimilate as quickly as possible. Mainstream Americans often tolerate pluralism only as a short-term phenomenon, believing that sustained pluralism is the enemy of assimilation, a threat to the cohesiveness of U.S. society.

Assimilation and pluralism are not mutually exclusive, however, nor are they necessarily enemies. In fact, they always have existed simultaneously among different groups, at different levels. Whether as persistent subcultures or as convergent ones gradually merging into the dominant culture throughout several generations, culturally distinct groups always have existed. And even when their numbers have been great, they never threatened the core culture, as we will see. Assimilation remains a powerful force affecting most minority groups, despite the assertions of anti-immigration fearmongers and radical multiculturalists. Although proponents of one position may decry the other, both pluralism and assimilation always have been dual realities within U.S. society.

Assimilation occurs in different ways and to different degrees, and it does not necessarily mean the elimination of all traces of ethnic origins. It can occur even as ethnic communities continue to exist in numerous cities and as many individuals continue to identify with their ethnic ancestry.

> [Assimilation] refers, above all, to long-term processes that have whittled away at the social foundations for ethnic distinctions. These processes have brought about a rough parity of opportunities to attain such socioeconomic goods as educational credentials and prestigious jobs, loosened the ties between ethnicity and specific economic niches, diminished cultural differences that serve to signal ethnic membership to others and to sustain ethnic solidarity, shifted

residence away from central-city ethnic neighborhoods to ethnically intermixed suburbs, and finally, fostered relatively easy social intermixing across ethnic lines, resulting ultimately in high rates of ethnic intermarriage and ethnically mixed ancestry.[55]

Perhaps the dual realities of assimilation and pluralism may be appreciated more fully by realizing that acculturation occurs more quickly than assimilation. A group's acculturation gives supporting testimony to assimilationist theory, yet its accompanying lack of complete assimilation provides evidence in support of pluralist—or ethnic retention—theory. The existence of this twofold dynamic is the natural order of minority communities.

# Retrospect

Ethnic- and racial-group identity is a normal pattern in ingroup–outgroup relationships. It can have positive and negative results depending on the social context in which it exists. A group identity based on immigrant status is normally of shorter duration than one based on religion or race. Minorities typically experience a dual identity, one in the larger society and another within their own group.

Minority-group responses to prejudice and discrimination include avoidance, deviance, defiance, and acceptance, depending in large measure on the group's perception of its power to change the status quo. After prolonged treatment as an inferior, a person may develop a negative self-image. Continued inequality intensifies through a vicious circle or cumulative causation.

Marginality is a social phenomenon that occurs during the transitional period of assimilation; it may be either a stressful or a sheltered experience, depending on the support system of the ethnic community. Some groups become middleman minorities because of their historical background or sojourner orientation. They may remain indefinitely in that intermediate place in the social hierarchy, a potential scapegoat for those above and below them, or they may achieve upward mobility and assimilation.

Dominant-group actions toward the minority group may take various forms, including favorable, indifferent, or hostile responses. When the reaction is negative, the group in power may place restraints on the minority group (for example, legislative controls and segregation). If the reaction becomes more emotional or even xenophobic, expulsion or annihilation may occur. Sensitivity to world opinion and economic dependence on other nations may restrain such actions. Another dominant response is exploitation, as illustrated by the internal-colonialism theory discussed in Chapter 2, or by the split-labor-market theory, in which differential wage levels can spark ethnic antagonism. An ethnic bourgeoisie may arise that is both exploitive and benevolent.

Three theories of minority integration have emerged since the nation's beginning. Assimilation, or majority-conformity, became a goal of many, both native-born and foreign-born; yet not all sought this goal or were able to achieve it. The romantic notion of amalgamation, or a melting pot, in which a new breed of people with a distinct culture would emerge, proved unrealistic. Finally, accommodation, or pluralism, arose as a school of thought recognizing the persistence of ethnic diversity in a society with a commonly shared core culture. Assimilation and pluralism are not mutually exclusive; both always have existed simultaneously, with assimilation exerting a constant, powerful force.

# On MySocLab

 **Study** and **Review** on **MySocLab**

## KEY TERMS

Acceptance, p. 89

Accommodation (pluralistic) theory, p. 108

Amalgamation (melting-pot) theory, p. 106

Americanization movement, p. 104

Anglo-conformity, p. 108

Annihilation, p. 97

Assimilation (majority-conformity) theory, p. 104

Avoidance, p. 85

Cultural assimilation (acculturation), p. 104

Cultural pluralism, p. 109

Cumulative causation, p. 90

Defiance, p. 88

Deviance, p. 86

Exploitation, p. 101

Expulsion, p. 95

Labeling theory, p. 89

Marginality, p. 91

Marital assimilation, p. 105

Middleman minorities, p. 92

Negative self-image, p. 89

Primary structural assimilation, p. 105

Secondary structural assimilation, p. 105

Social segregation, p. 94

Spatial segregation, p. 94

Split or dual labor market, p. 101

Structural assimilation, p. 105

Structural pluralism, p. 109

Underground economy, p. 102

Vicious-circle phenomenon, p. 90

Xenophobia, p. 95

## DISCUSSION QUESTIONS

1. What are some common minority-group responses to prejudice and discrimination?
2. What is marginality? Why may it be a stressful experience in some cases but not in others?
3. Have you yourself, or do you know anyone personally who has, experienced marginality, being caught between two worlds?
4. Can you give specific local examples of a middleman-minority enterprise where members of one minority group provide services to members of a different minority group?
5. What are middleman minorities? How do they affect acceptance?
6. What are some common majority-group responses to minorities?
7. Segregation: Can you give a specific example of residential (and thus school) segregation in any nearby communities?
8. Discuss the major theories of minority integration.

## INTERNET ACTIVITIES

1. Go to the Hate Groups Map at the Southern Poverty Law Center (http://www.splcenter.org/intel/map/hate.jsp). Take a look at what hate groups are in your state and nearby ones by moving your cursor to that state, left-clicking your mouse, and scrolling down. Were you surprised?
2. Read one of the articles in the Intelligence Report of the Southern Poverty Law Center, called "Number Hate Sites Increase Online" (http://www.splcenter.org/intel/intelreport/article.jsp?aid=455). What is your reaction?
3. "The Lynching Calendar" (http://www.autopsis.org/foot/lynch.html) gives the dates, places, and names of the more than 6,000 African Americans who died in racial violence in the United States.

# North and West European Americans

((•)) Listen to Chapter 5 on MySocLab

*Scots, one of the oldest U.S. ethnic groups, still celebrate their heritage with annual Highland festivals in Florida, Indiana, Michigan, North and South Carolina that draw thousands of people from all over. Through their traditional dances, bagpipe playing, food booths, and competitive Scottish athletic events, they reaffirm their ethnicity.*

## LEARNING OBJECTIVES | After reading this chapter you will be able to:

**5-1** Describe the sociohistorical context for studying North and West Europeans.

**5-2** Describe the immigrant experiences of the English, Dutch, and French.

**5-3** Describe the immigrant experiences of the Germans, Irish, and Scandinavians.

**5-4** Describe social realities for women in past centuries.

**5-5** Compare and contrast the assimilation paths followed by these immigrants.

**5-6** Evaluate insights gained through sociological analysis.

Although Native Americans lived on this continent in rich cultures for centuries before the Europeans arrived, this part of the book deliberately begins with the North and West Europeans (Figure 5.1). This group established the foundation for the dominant culture to which others have had to adjust. To understand fully the dynamics of intergroup relations involving Native Americans and all immigrants, past and present, we first must examine how the creation of a white Anglo-Saxon Protestant (WASP) society set the stage for conflict. As we will see, religion, nationality, and social class were causal factors for conflict even within this North and West European grouping. Even though a trickle of immigrants from almost all parts of the world arrived during the early history of the United States, the story of its colonial period and first 100 years as an independent nation is the experience of immigrants primarily from the British Isles, France, Holland, Germany, and Scandinavia and of their descendants.

## Sociohistorical Perspective

**5-1** Describe the sociohistorical context for studying North and West Europeans.

Like all immigrants, the first European colonists to reach the Americas were strangers to these shores, and they responded with wonder and excitement in their journals and reports about the vastness, resources, and promise of the New World. In those early years, all

**FIGURE 5.1** Northern and Western Europe

shared in the adventure of creating a new society. First the necessity to survive, then religious preference, and finally pro- or anti-British sentiments dominated relations among diverse peoples in the North American colonies. As life stabilized and a common culture evolved, other newcomers found themselves not only in strange surroundings but also they were perceived as strangers in a society in which WASP homogeneity was the norm. Thus, many Irish and Germans—with their cultural, religious, and social-class differences—experienced open hostility on their arrival.

Before we examine the connection between theory and the experiences of any group, we need to recognize the pitfall in considering ethnic groups within a limited historical framework: Immigration patterns vary among countries and peak at different times. The word *peak* provides a clue as to how we should view the experiences of each racial or ethnic group. Although most minority groups experience one especially intensive period of migration, which provides a logical time frame to emphasize, most countries have sent a continual flow of immigrants throughout the years. Consequently, the immigrants' experiences have varied with changing conditions, and each nationality usually has a first-generation American grouping at any given time.

Watch on MySocLab
Video: Sociology in Focus: Politics and Government

## THE COLONIAL PERIOD

Members of each ethnic group came to the New World for economic, political, or religious reasons, or sometimes for the adventure of beginning a new life in a new land. As strangers, most encountered yet another ethnic group—the Native Americans. Although limited social interaction between the European settlers and the natives occurred, their cultural differences frequently resulted in xenophobic reactions from both sides, as will be discussed in Chapter 7.

**CULTURAL DIVERSITY.** From the moment the first Europeans settled in what became the United States, cultural differences existed among them. The settlements were distinct culturally from one another in nationality or religion, such as the Puritans in Massachusetts and Congregationalists in Connecticut. Some settlements, even in their early stages, were a mixture of ethnic groups. To strengthen his Pennsylvania colony, the English Quaker William Penn recruited several hundred Dutch and many more German settlers. In fact, the "Pennsylvania Dutch" are actually of German descent; the word *Dutch* is a corruption of *Deutsch,* which means "German." The settlement of New Amsterdam in the colony of New Netherland also was a pluralistic community, reflecting Holland's positive attitude toward minorities and refugees within its European borders:

> In 1660, William Kieft, the Dutch governor of New Netherland, remarked to the French Jesuit Isaac Jogues [later canonized as a saint] that there were eighteen languages spoken at or near Fort Amsterdam at the tip of Manhattan Island....The first shipload of settlers sent out by the Dutch was made up largely of French-speaking Protestants. British, Germans, Finns, Jews, Swedes, Africans, Italians, Irish [quickly] followed, beginning a stream that has never yet stopped.[1]

**RELIGIOUS INTOLERANCE.** Religious differences caused social problems more frequently than did nationality differences during this period. Many people who first crossed the Atlantic as immigrants had been religious dissenters in their native land and were seeking a utopia in the new land—a place of religious harmony. Unfortunately, they brought with them their own religious prejudices. Although they themselves came seeking religious freedom, many were intolerant of others with different religious beliefs.

The expulsion of religious dissident Roger Williams from the Massachusetts colony led to the founding in 1639 of the Baptist Church in Rhode Island. For the rest of the seventeenth century, Baptists were the most persecuted sect in New England. Fines, beatings, and whippings of adherents were not uncommon, and not until 1708 could Baptists legally maintain a house of worship in Connecticut. In contrast, Baptists thrived in the more tolerant Middle Colonies, establishing in Philadelphia, by 1700, the strongest Baptist center in the colonies.

When the 1691 Massachusetts Charter extended "liberty of conscience" to all Christians, including Baptists, it specifically excluded "Papists" (Catholics). Dislike of Catholics was the one common ground on which all Protestants could agree.

The Presbyterians, Baptists, Quakers, German Reformed, and Lutherans along the "frontier" were intolerant of one another, but they shared a strong dislike of Anglicans. The Anglicans, strongest in Virginia but prevalent throughout the South, looked disdainfully on the New England Puritans. The New Englanders reciprocated and jealously guarded their communities against any inroads by Anglicans in their region.

Religious clashes in the eighteenth century were not uncommon. Prior to the American Revolution, clashes in the Chesapeake colonies between Anglicans and Baptists were frequent, the result of class antagonism between the planter elite on one side and poor whites on the other. Armed bands of planters and law officials forcibly broke up Baptist meetings, where preachers were condemning the planters' lifestyle of horse racing, gambling, whoring, and cockfighting.

Animosity between England-loyalist Anglicans and England-hating Scots-Irish Presbyterians was common. The latter group, living along the western frontier from Maine to Georgia, where they frequently fought the Native Americans, also often came into dispute with the pacifist Quakers and with German sectarian groups that advocated peaceful coexistence with the Native Americans.

Even though many colonists shared a common nationality, religious intolerance created wide cultural gulfs and social distance among the various denominations. As historian Gary B. Nash stated, "Any attempt to portray the colonies as unified and homogeneous would be misguided."[2]

## THE EARLY NATIONAL PERIOD

As a new nation, the United States was forged under the cultural, economic, and political dominance of Anglo-Americans. Their culture, however, was at first a diverse one of Puritans, Anglican Cavaliers, Quakers, and Scots-Irish Presbyterians. With a common language and history, though, they soon coalesced into what Lawrence H. Fuchs calls a "civic culture."[3] This common culture solidified by 1820, when the first great wave of non-Protestant immigrants began. The civic culture included strong beliefs in Protestantism, individual enterprise, and political democracy.

Because no single religion dominated the colonies, religious tolerance slowly evolved. When the Constitution was drafted in 1789, the nation's leading statesmen put aside their prejudices to institutionalize such tolerance, creating a bedrock principle of U.S. culture: the separation of church and state. Congregationalists in New England retained a privileged tax position for a few more decades though, until their diminishing political power no longer could sustain that contradiction. In addition, some states barred Catholics and Jews from running for elected office in the early years of the republic. But this institutionalized bias eventually yielded, though not without a struggle, to the democratic principle of freedom of religion that had emerged from the primeval diversity of the nation's beginnings.

**THE 1790 CENSUS.** Although WASPs were the dominant group in 1790, the nation's first census revealed a society that was both culturally and racially diverse. As Table 5.1 shows, one in every five people in the 13 states was a member of a racial minority (African American or Native American); this compares to the one in four (including Asians) found

**TABLE 5.1**  Total U.S. Population in 1790

| NATIONALITY | PERCENTAGE |
|---|---|
| English | 48.3 |
| African | 18.9 |
| German | 6.9 |
| Scots | 6.6 |
| Unassigned | 5.2 |
| Scots-Irish | 4.8 |
| Irish | 2.9 |
| Dutch | 2.7 |
| Native American | 1.8 |
| French and Swedish | 1.8 |

*Source:* U.S. Census Bureau.

in the 2010 census. The English constituted less than half the total population, and one in nine was not English (Dutch, French, German, and Swedish). If we include the Irish Catholics who clearly were not part of the WASP mainstream, we find that at least one in seven was an ethnic minority. Even among the WASPs, cultural differentiation existed. The Scots—nearly 7 percent of the total population—and the Welsh—a small population still large enough to warrant newspapers and books printed in Welsh—did not consider themselves "English."

Scots-Irish Presbyterians lived mainly on the western frontier, away from the more established English American towns and cities. The Dutch lived in mostly self-contained communities, primarily in New York and New Jersey. The Germans also clustered within their own urban or rural communities in a "German belt" that began in the Eastern Seaboard Middle Atlantic states and soon stretched westward into the Midwest.

**EARLY SIGNS OF NATIVIST REACTIONS.** Many new immigrants arrived during the immediate post-Revolution period, igniting a broad-based anti-foreign attitude. Both the Jeffersonian and the Federalist political factions feared that their opponents would benefit from the newcomers. The populist Jeffersonians were alarmed at the arrival of so many refugees, particularly French, from collapsing European aristocracies. Meanwhile, the Federalists, the conservatives of their day, feared that the ranks of anti-Federalists would grow because poor immigrants, particularly the Irish, had no commitment to preserving a strong central government.

Whatever their motives, the dominant English Americans' reactions toward the newly arriving northern and western European immigrants followed what was to become a familiar pattern in dominant–minority relations. Suspicious of those who differed from themselves, the members of the dominant culture felt threatened.

In a letter to John Adams in 1794, George Washington indicated his reservations about newcomers, especially when they settled in their own separate communities. His words anticipate what many others have uttered ever since:

My opinion, with respect to immigration, is that except of useful mechanics and some particular descriptions of men or professions, there is no need of encouragement, while the policy or advantage of its taking place in a body (I mean the settling of them in a body) may be much questioned; for, by so doing, they retain the language, habits and principles (good or bad) which they bring with them.[4]

**XENOPHOBIA.** Many Federalists, in fact, believed that the large foreign-born population was the root of all evil in the United States. In letters, speeches, and newspapers, they expressed fear that:

> ...immigrants would "contaminate the purity and simplicity of the American character." Noah Webster stated that for each "good" European who entered the country, "we receive three or four discontented...men...the convicts, fugitives of justice, hirelings of France, and disaffected offscourings of other nations."[5]
>
> One Federalist wrote, "Generally speaking, none but the most vile and worthless, none but the idle and discontented, the disorderly and the wicked, have inundated upon us from Europe."[6]

William Smith Shaw, the young nephew of President John Adams, wrote to the First Lady in 1798: "The grand cause of our present difficulties may be traced...to so many hordes of Foreigners immigrating [sic] to America....Let us no longer pray that America may become an asylum to all nations."[7]

These xenophobic remarks, and thousands of similar ones throughout this period, illustrate some of the dynamics of Anglo-conformity and assimilation. It really was not the presence of *all* foreigners that disturbed the Federalists but rather the increasing numbers of non-English foreigners. Wrapped in the dominant group's negative perceptions were concerns that those newcomers' cultures, religions, and political ideologies—indeed, their very essence as people—were so unlike themselves as to make their blending into the mainstream a virtual impossibility. Such ethnocentrism blinded these early nativists from any other consideration except that of an undermining of their culture and society, a reaction similar to nativist reactions still heard in the twenty-first century.

**LEGISLATIVE ACTION.** The Federalists attempted to limit all office holding to the native-born and to extend the period for naturalization from 5 to 14 years. Although they succeeded in having the longer period enacted, the states—faced with the problems of establishing a new nation—successfully fought office-holding restrictions.

In 1798, with a volatile situation in Europe and a distinct possibility of war with France, the Federalists passed a series of laws known collectively as the Alien and Sedition Acts, designed to discourage political activity by pro-French immigrants. One factor contributing to the successful passage of this notorious legislation was the widespread belief that a large foreign-born population threatened the stability of the United States. Significantly, the legislation passed because of sectional block voting, with New England almost unanimously in favor of the bills. Few foreigners resided in New England, and hence, little contact had occurred there; nonetheless, negative stereotyping flourished in that region. Jefferson's election to the presidency in 1800 ended this xenophobia and legislation.

## THE PRE–CIVIL WAR PERIOD

Not until 1820 did the national census include a person's country of origin as part of its data, and new regulations required shipmasters to submit passenger lists to customs officials. The 1820 census (which excluded Native Americans) listed approximately 9.6 million Americans, of whom 20 percent were blacks and most of the remainder white Protestants from northern and western Europe. Between 1820 and 1860, more than 5 million immigrants—more than half of the U.S. population of 1820 and more than the entire population of 1790—crossed the Atlantic and Pacific Oceans to disembark on U.S. shores.

In these 40 years preceding the Civil War, the first great wave of immigrants produced additional arrivals from England and Scandinavia. Ireland and Germany, however, supplied the greatest numbers. In fact, so large was Irish immigration that the Irish accounted for 44 percent of all immigration in the 1830s and 49 percent of all immigration in the 1840s. Consequently, they accounted for 7 percent of the total population by the end of the Civil War. The fact that so many of the newcomers were Catholic—a religion toward which many Protestant groups openly were hostile—made the rising tide of foreigners a major concern for nativists.

## STRUCTURAL CONDITIONS

Along the East Coast and in the newer cities west of the Appalachian Mountains, life was stable and established. Although regional variations existed as did differences in religion and social status, the prevailing cultural norms were relatively homogeneous.

Urban living conditions, particularly among the poor Irish immigrants, were substandard, even for those days. The poverty-stricken newcomers, forced to live in squalid slums, suffered high disease and mortality rates, and endured the condemnation of the dominant society for living as they did. Like so many others in succeeding generations, these critics did not realize that their own attitudes and actions may have helped to create the situation in the first place:

> Typical of overcrowded cellars was a house in Pike Street [in mid-nineteenth century New York City] which contained a cellar ten feet square and seven feet high, with one small window and an old-fashioned inclined cellar door; here lived two families consisting of ten persons of all ages. The occupants of these basements led miserable lives as troglodytes amid darkness, dampness, and poor ventilation. Rain water leaked through cracks in the walls and floors and frequently flooded the cellars; refuse filtered down from the upper stories and mingled with the seepage from outdoor privies.[8]

**XENOPHOBIA.** U.S. citizens saw the large influx of immigrants between 1820 and 1860 as a threat to their institutions and their social order. Not only were many of the newcomers Catholic, but they came from countries embroiled in political turmoil. Anxiety mounted due to the imagined radical threat as well as the Catholic threat.

RIOT AT HOBOKEN.

*In the mid-19th century, fights and riots between native-born Americans and Irish or German immigrants were an all-too-frequent occurrence in many locales. In this instance, local toughs—angered at the sight of German immigrants picnicking at the Cricket Ground in Hoboken, New Jersey—attacked them and a full-scale riot broke out.*

In the 1830s, anti-foreign associations, calling themselves "native" American organizations, arose in many cities. Mobs frequently burned Catholic convents, churches and homes, assaulted nuns, and indiscriminately killed Irish, Germans, and blacks that they encountered. These sporadic outbursts gradually coalesced into the powerful Know-Nothing movement of the 1850s. The Know-Nothings unleashed a vicious hate campaign, frequently accompanied by brutal violence, particularly in large cities, where many immigrants lived. Surprisingly successful, the Know-Nothings attracted those fearful of foreigners and escalated their worries into irrational thoughts and actions.

A Whig presidential candidate, General Winfield Scott, waged an anti-Catholic, anti-foreign campaign with Know-Nothing support but lost badly to Democrat Franklin Pierce in 1852. By 1854, the Know-Nothing Party was strong enough to elect 75 congressmen (out of 252) and many city, county, and state officials. In 1855, the party elected six governors, and many contemporaries believed this reactionary movement would capture the White House in the 1856 election.[9] A candidate familiar to the electorate, former President Millard Fillmore, sought to return to office on the Know-Nothing ticket. The conservative Whig party endorsed Fillmore, but a serious split within its ranks, with defections to Republican candidate John C. Frémont, enabled Democrat James Buchanan to win the three-way race. The bitter sectional rivalry of the Civil War period then effectively ended this ethnocentric-turned-xenophobic movement.

Not all voices were raised against the European expatriates. In defense of the newcomers, Harriet Martineau (often called the "mother of sociology") answered some of the criticisms:

> It would certainly be better that the immigrants should be well-clothed, educated, respectable people (except that, in that case, they would probably never arrive). But the blame of their bad condition rests elsewhere, while their arrival is, generally speaking, a pure benefit….Every American can acknowledge that few or no canals or railroads would be in existence now in the United States, but for the Irish labor by which they have been completed; and the best cultivation that is to be seen in the land is owing to the Dutch and Germans it contains.[10]

Ralph Waldo Emerson, an articulate literary figure of the times, also was a popular speaker on the lyceum lecture circuit. (In those days, many communities had a lyceum, or association, for lectures, discussions, and entertainment.) One of his journal entries in 1845 shows how he tried to combat the **nativist** movement in those lectures by stressing the "smelting-pot" concept:

> I hate the narrowness of the Native American Party. It is the dog in the manger. It is precisely…opposite to true wisdom….Well, as in the old burning of the Temple at Corinth, by the melting and intermixture of silver and gold and other metals, a new compound more precious than any, called Corinthian brass, was formed; so in this continent—asylum of all nations—the energy of Irish, Swedes, Poles, and Cossacks, and all the European tribes—of the Africans, and of the Polynesians, will construct a new race, a new religion, a new state, a new literature, which will be as vigorous as the new Europe which came out of the smelting-pot of the Dark Ages, or that which earlier emerged from Pelasgic and Etruscan barbarism.[11]

Currents and countercurrents occurred then, as now. Not all members of the same ethnic group encountered problems, nor did all native-born Americans react negatively to the newcomers. Yet patterns of harmony or conflict did exist, and they often depended on the degree of cultural and structural differentiation that existed in each region, as well as on economic prosperity or whatever competition the newcomers appeared to present.

# English Americans

Despite earlier explorations by other countries, the English were one of the first white ethnic groups to establish permanent settlements in the New World. The first two successful ones were Jamestown and Plimmoth (Plymouth) Plantation (the word *plantation* was first used in the North).

These two settlements were quite different culturally from one another and so they offer an excellent example of cultural diversity within the same nationality, as opposed to a simplistic concept of "the English." Jamestown was the seed from which the southern aristocracy and the slave-based agrarian economy of the South grew, and Plymouth was the forerunner of town meetings (participatory democracy), the abolition movement, and "Yankee ingenuity" (capitalistic enterprise). Many factors—including the different purposes of the settlements, religions, climates, and terrains—played a role in the unfolding of events and lifestyles.

The writings of William Bradford, the first governor of the Plymouth colony, provide evidence that the English were an ethnically conscious people. Nearly 400 years have passed since the time of the Pilgrims, but Bradford's words in the following sections regarding their experiences could apply to many other immigrant groups—past, present, and future.

5-2 Describe the immigrant experiences of the English, Dutch, and French.

**Explore on MySocLab**
Activity: The English in Big Sky Country

## THE DEPARTURE

Leaving one's native land for another country known only by reputation usually is an emotional experience. For many, it is a time of joy and sorrow and anticipation and anxiety. People know what they are leaving behind, but they are uncertain what they will find. The Pilgrims first fled England for Holland, which opened its doors to all refugees, and later they journeyed to the New World. In the following passage, Bradford speaks about the Pilgrims' journey to Holland, but the locale is only incidental to the expression of typical immigrant sensations:

> To be thus constrained to leave their native soil, their lands and livings, and all their friends, was a great sacrifice, and wondered at by many. But to go into a country unknown to them where they must learn a new language and get their livings they knew not how, seemed an almost desperate adventure, and a misery worse than death.[12]

## CULTURE SHOCK

Arrival at one's destination brings with it unfamiliar cultural contact, which jolts one's world of reality—that subconsciously accepted way of life—as the group encounters a different civilization. Bradford continues,

> Having reached the Netherlands, they saw many fine fortified cities, strongly walled, and guarded with troops of armed men; and they heard a strange and uncouth language, and beheld the different manners and customs of the people, with their strange fashions and attires—all so far differing from that of their plain country villages wherein they were bred and had lived so long, that it seemed they had come into a new world.[13]

**RESISTING ASSIMILATION.** Not all immigrants desire to become full, participating citizens in the country to which they move. Many, in fact, never become naturalized citizens. Although they are starting a new life, they do not necessarily intend to forsake their cultural heritage. More often, they seek to preserve that heritage as a familiar world in a strange land and to pass it on to their children. Often, the children become assimilated into the new ways despite their parents' efforts. The strict Pilgrims feared that their children would be assimilated into the more liberal Dutch culture and viewed such an outcome as an evil to be avoided:

> But still more lamentable, and of all sorrows most heavy to be borne, was that many of the children, influenced by these conditions, and the great licentiousness of the young people of the country, and the many temptations of the city, were led by evil example into dangerous courses, getting the reins off their necks and leaving their parents....So they saw their posterity would be in danger to degenerate and become corrupt.[14]

**ENGLISH INFLUENCE.** English immigrants' greatest impact on U.S. culture occurred during the colonial period. Settling in the 13 original colonies, they so established themselves that succeeding generations were culturally and politically dominant by the time of the American Revolution. In 1790, approximately 63 percent of the U.S. population could claim nationality or descent from the British Isles (see Table 5.1). This large majority of English-speaking citizens made an indelible imprint on U.S. culture in language, law, customs, and values. The wars of 1776 and 1812 notwithstanding, the descendants of English immigrants prided themselves on their heritage, as indicated in their contemporary writings. For example, in his *Sketchbook* (1819–1820), Washington Irving encouraged Americans to pattern themselves after the English nation rather than any other.

After 1825, when the British Parliament repealed its ban on the emigration of artisans, many English, Scottish, and Irish mill hands found work in U.S. textile factories, often at more than twice the salary they had been earning at home. Many British coal miners also came, but by the latter part of the nineteenth century, Slavic and Italian workers largely had replaced them. Those who remained in the coal industry tended to be supervisors and foremen. Some British farmers also immigrated to the United States, scattering throughout the Midwest. British immigrants of any occupation seldom concentrated in any one area, though, going instead wherever the job market led them.[15]

Conventional wisdom would suggest that English immigrants would adjust easily to U.S. society. After all, they spoke the same language, had the same cultural heritage as the dominant Anglo-Americans, and seldom experienced prejudice or discrimination as did other arriving groups.[16] Yet the British were not always comfortable in the new land. Perhaps because they had exaggerated expectations of similarity between the new country and the old, they did not expect to be strangers and thus were unprepared when they realized that they actually were strangers.

In examining the motivations of British immigrants returning to their homeland prior to 1865, historian Wilbur Shepperson found some common themes reflecting a failure of the new land to live up to their expectations:

> Rather than vigorous, they found America boring; rather than questioning and vital, republican communities were suspicious and moribund. Although they were often unemployed, Americans boasted of their economic opportunities; although they condemned politicians, they defended the political system; although they advocated freedom, they enforced conformity....
>
> Knowledge of the language allowed for rapid assimilation of English immigrants, but at the same time, it permitted them to compare critically American authors, newspapers, and theaters with those at home. Acquaintance with English government and legal traditions provided easy understanding of American law, but it sometimes provoked censure of political methods and frontier justice. Nearness to markets, cheap labor, and advanced technological methods in Britain often led immigrants of the entrepreneur class to despair of the New World's inefficient agricultural methods and unorthodox business

practices. British workers once associated with the trade union or Chartist movements found American labor groups lacking in organization, leadership, and purpose.[17]

In the post–Civil War period, an undercurrent of Anglophobia prevailed, and British immigrants discovered that they had to exercise self-restraint to be accepted among U.S. natives. An ethnic consciousness led many British to resent this necessity and to dislike the ways of the new country. Between 1881 and 1889, more than 370,000 British and Irish aliens left the United States to return to their native lands.[18]

In fact, in all things but money and quick promotion, British-Americans thought the United States a debased copy of their homeland. Many seemingly familiar customs and institutions had lost their British essence. "The Land of Slipshod," one immigrant in 1885 called the country, its language not English but a "silly idiotic jargon—a mere jumble of German idioms and popular solecisms, savored by a few Irish blunders," the enforcement of its basically English legal code "totally farcical," and its children half-educated, spoiled, and unruly.…Many returned home discontented with "the manners and habits of the people."

…Although as the years passed, the immigrants' personal ties came to be in America rather than in Britain, their fondness for and pride in the old country waxed. British travelers found them everywhere, "British in heart and memory… always with a touch of the exile, eager to see an English face and to hear an English voice!"[19]

With the passage of years, these English immigrants held onto a pride in and fondness for their old country, even as their personal ties became more and more American. Second-generation British Americans, however, had no such mixed feelings and easily identified the United States as their country.

The United Kingdom has been the source of a great many immigrants throughout the years; between 1820 and 2011, approximately 5.5 million of its people came to the United States. It ranks third in the list of nations that have supplied immigrants to the United States since 1820, and more than 13,000 new British immigrants still arrive

*With more than 13,000 new British immigrants arriving in the United States each year, and with many times that number claiming British ancestry, it is not surprising to find ethnic establishments that appeal to them. British pubs are found in many states, and the Six Pence Pub on Bull Street in the historic district of Savannah, Georgia, is one such place.*

# the INTERNATIONAL scene

## Britain's Approach Toward Ethnic Minorities

The British government's terminology and policies regarding immigrants—most of whom are people of color—have some interesting effects on dominant–minority relations.

Approximately 14 percent of Britain's population—some 7.8 million people—are non-white ethnic minorities, almost all of them present as a consequence of immigration. Called "new commonwealth peoples"—the euphemism for ex-colonials of color—they became naturalized citizens fairly easily. Nevertheless, nationality often carries biological connotations among native-born Britons—"British stock," as Prime Minister Margaret Thatcher once phrased it. Thus, many multi-generational Britons view the new minorities as not belonging—even the growing numbers of the second- and third-generation minority citizens who have lived only in the United Kingdom (U.K.).

To combat this mindset, the government—in its statistical and legal classifications and the publications of official bodies such as the Commission for Racial Equality—uses the term *ethnic minority* instead of *immigrant* to refer to immigrants and to their U.K.-born descendants. This nomenclature deliberately ignores the reality that most ethnic-minority-group members are immigrants. It serves in job monitoring and in the census to identify and rectify problems of inequality, not to settle arguments about the number or growth rate of immigrant subgroups per se.

Many experts view Britain's Race Relations Act of 1976 (RRA), amended in 2000, as a model for Europe in addressing discrimination. The law expanded the concept of discrimination to include indirect discrimination (for example, seemingly neutral rules that have an indefensibly discriminatory effect), and it created a new body, the Commission for Racial Equality (CRE), to undertake formal investigations under the law and to encourage equality of opportunity more broadly. The core of the law is its definition of racial discrimination, which is race neutral: "A person discriminates against another...if on racial grounds he treats that other less favourably than he treats or would treat other persons" (RRA, Part I, Section 1).

The law permits but does not require employers to offer racial minorities "access to facilities or services to meet the special needs of persons of that group in regard to their education, training or welfare, or any ancillary benefits" (RRA, Part VI, Section 35). This enables minorities to overcome seniority or test competence limitations through employer initiatives. The law emphasizes encouraging employers to seek minority inclusiveness rather than mandating preferential policies that would affect outcomes. The law does not set positive-action requirements in employment, mandate recordkeeping of minority employment statistics, or establish quota set-asides for government to do business with set percentages of minority-owned businesses—all of which exist in the United States.

The prevailing belief is that government cannot build good race relations by implementing laws or policies that create resentment. As a result, preferential treatment, quotas, and set-aside policies are not part of British anti-discrimination practice. Rather than imitating U.S. practice, Britain pursues its own model of equal opportunity policy.

### CRITICAL THINKING QUESTION

Why does the shorter history of non-white settlement in Britain free that country to attempt a less-prescriptive solution to racial inequality?

yearly.[20] Although today's immigrants settle in many states, Southern California, particularly Santa Monica, has become the permanent home of several hundred thousand first-generation British Americans, who maintain their pubs and traditions amidst the surfers and rollerbladers. (See the International Scene box for a discussion on how Britain handles its own immigrant minorities.)

English Americans today construct different versions of their English identity to others. They may accept or exaggerate (with word choice and pronounced accents) the stereotypical perception, or downplay or reject that interpretation, seeking instead to distance themselves from images of England and Englishness they consider as unrepresentative.[21]

# Dutch Americans

The two greatest periods of Dutch immigration were 1881 to 1930, with 1.6 million, and 1941 to 1970, with nearly 98,000 new arrivals. Since 1971, the level of immigration has been relatively low and now averages approximately 1,300 annually.[22] In any case, the most significant impact of Dutch influence on U.S. society occurred at a much earlier period.

Pearl Street in present-day New York City marks the limit of dry land in the days of New Amsterdam, where palisades had been erected against Native American raiders. In Dutch, these were called *de wal,* and thus the northern boundary gave its name to the Wall Street of today. Breukelen (later Brooklyn) became a town in 1646. Peter Stuyvesant's farm, or *bouwerij,* in Manhattan, where Stuyvesant lived after the English takeover in 1664 until his death in 1672, gave its name to the Bowery, a well-known street in New York.

Other Dutch settlements sprang up in the Bronx, on Staten Island, in New Jersey at Bergen (named after a town in Holland, and later known as Jersey City), at Ridgewood, at Hackensack, in the Raritan and Ramapo valleys, and in South Carolina at St. James Island. So widespread were the Dutch settlements and so strong was the Dutch imprint that Dutch remained a major language in this region for generations and numerous Dutch colonial homes still remain in much of the Northeast.

## STRUCTURAL CONDITIONS

During the colonial period, few Dutch were willing to exchange the security at home for the hardships of the New World. With their stable economy and harmonious society, they had few inducements or "push" factors to migrate in such great numbers as had other ethnic groups. Urban areas in Holland had heterogeneous populations because the Dutch had offered shelter to many refugees from other countries. When seeking to establish trading settlements in the New World, the Dutch therefore sought other minority-group members willing to journey to the New World. As a result, immigrant Dutch settlements became as heterogeneous as their counterparts in Holland.

The spirit of seventeenth-century Holland resulted in a cosmopolitan and tolerant atmosphere in New Amsterdam that outlasted Holland's rule. The somewhat more relaxed atmosphere of New Amsterdam contrasted with that of the English colonies, whose rigid "blue laws" limited behavior, particularly on Sundays. Sports were popular, too. The colonists loved boat and carriage races, and from Holland, they imported the indoor game of *kolf,* a cross between ice hockey and golf.

The English takeover of New Amsterdam in 1664 caused no hardship for the Dutch settlers. They enjoyed a basically favorable social environment during the colonial and post–Revolutionary War periods and thereafter. A relatively tolerant people in an intolerant age, similar in physical appearance and religious beliefs to other Americans, the Dutch generally were accepted, though sometimes they were the butt of gentle humor, as illustrated in the writings of Washington Irving about the Dutch in New York.

In 1846, a group of Dutch religious separatists settled in what became Holland, Michigan. Spurred by religious and economic motives, a new wave of immigrants from the Netherlands followed suit, settling mostly in Michigan, Iowa, Wisconsin, and Illinois because of favorable soil and climate conditions. The social bond proved to be religion rather than nationality, and sectarian schisms ensued, resulting in the Dutch Reformed Church, the Christian Reformed Church, and the Netherland Reformed Church. The first group's efforts to propagate the faith and achieve higher social standing rested partly on Hope College in Holland, Michigan. Its success encouraged the Christian Reformed Church, a more conservative group, to establish Calvin College in Grand Rapids to achieve similar objectives for its people.

## PLURALISM

For several reasons, Dutch culture and influence persisted for many generations despite Anglo-Saxon cultural dominance. The Dutch were self-sufficient and enjoyed high social standing in the new society. Their church, rather than mainstream secular ways, formed the basis of their social life; the more orthodox they were, the more they resisted assimilation. A steady migration into concentrated residential communities reinforced the old ways. Finally, a friendly atmosphere enabled the Dutch to coexist with other groups in a pluralistic society.

One good example of their subcultural vitality was Dutch language retention. Only in 1763 did the Dutch Reformed Church hold its first English-language service in New York City, and it took another 10 years before the Dutch introduced English into their schools.[23] This passage of more than 100 years after New York became an English colony before the institutional usage of English is truly astounding! In fact, extensive use of the Dutch language and resistance to using the English language continued in rural New York and New Jersey until late in the nineteenth century.

President Martin Van Buren illustrated another aspect of the Dutch persistent subculture—endogamy—during the colonial and federal periods when he proudly wrote in his autobiography that the entire Van Buren family had resisted intermarriage with non-Dutch for five generations.[24] Van Buren's comment could have applied to most of the Dutch families and other ethnics of his time. Fluent in Dutch, Van Buren was chided, rather unfairly, by critics such as John Randolph for his inability to "speak, or write, the English language correctly," a complaint often made today about newcomers.[25]

Although most of the Dutch immigrants came to the United States during the same period as did the southern, central, and eastern Europeans (1880–1920), they did not encounter ethnic antagonism and eventually assimilated. Their physical features, their religion, and their relatively urbanized background enabled them both to adapt to and gain approval from the dominant society more easily than other groups.

Today, approximately 4.4 million Americans claim Dutch ancestry and celebrate their heritage with annual festivals and celebrations.[26] U.S. Census Bureau data show that

*In states where large numbers of Dutch settled, one lasting influence of their presence to the contemporary observer is their architecture. Dutch colonial houses, dating from the 17th and 18th centuries, were often of brick or stone construction, with a gambrel roof (two slopes on each side), and many dormer windows on the upper floor.*

the Dutch Americans are found in every region but they are also still clustered in a few well-defined areas. Heavy concentrations of Dutch Americans live in central and western New York, eastern and western Pennsylvania, central and southern Michigan, central Florida, eastern Wisconsin, central Washington, western and central Iowa, northeastern and southwestern Ohio, and central and northeastern Illinois.

# French Americans

French Americans fall into three population segments: migrants from France, migrants from French Canada (who settled primarily in New England), and French Louisianans. Many of the latter, also known as Cajuns, were expelled from Acadia (primarily Nova Scotia) by the British in 1755; by 1790, approximately 4,000 of them had resettled in Louisiana, where their descendants now live. Each group's experience has been somewhat different, illustrating varying patterns in dominant–minority relations.

### MARGINALITY AND ASSIMILATION

In the seventeenth century, the Huguenots fled either to Holland or to colonial America to escape religious persecution. Their Protestantism, willingness to work hard, conversion to the Anglican Church, and rapid adoption of the English language eased the Huguenots' assimilation into colonial society. However, the transition was not altogether smooth, and members of the second generation apparently agonized about their marginal status much as those in other groups would later do:

> By 1706, sufficient time had elapsed…to give rise to a younger generation unsatisfied with the adherence to old French forms, a generation adverse to a language not in general use in the province, clamoring for the new and the popular…. The children of many of the refugees were even ashamed to bear French names. The idea of remaining foreigners in a land in which they were born and reared was alien to their thought.[27]

Encountering distrust and occasional violence from the dominant society, partly explained by the frequent hostilities between England and France, the Huguenots tried to Anglicize themselves as quickly as possible to avoid further unpleasantness. They changed their names and their customs, learned to speak English, and soon succeeded in assimilating completely into the host society. For them, assimilation and loss of ethnic identity were the desired goals. By 1750, the Huguenots were no longer a distinct subculture.

### FRANCOPHOBIA

While the French Revolution was still in its moderately liberal stage, the Jeffersonians were French sympathizers and the Federalists were vehemently anti-French. Then the infamous XYZ Affair arose, when French officials demanded bribes before permitting U.S. diplomats to secure desired conferences or agreements. This inflamed public opinion against the French and their sympathizers. The lives of French immigrants during those passionate times at best were uncomfortable and at worst were filled with trouble and turmoil. In the eyes of the Federalists, every French American was a potential enemy, not only because of fears they might join a French army to invade the United States, but because these political conservatives worried that the perceived loose morals and irreligion of the French might infect Americans:

> The fear and detestation in which American "Jacobins" were held were no less powerful than the abhorrence felt for the French revolutionists themselves.

"Medusa's Snakes are not more venomous," declared a Federalist, "than the wretches who are seeking to bend us to the views of France." "The open enemies of our country," declared the *Albany Centinel*, "have never taken half the pains to render our Government and our rulers infamous and contemptible in the eyes of the world, than those wretches who call themselves Americans, Patriots, and Republicans." This "Gallic faction" was believed to be in close communication with Paris, "the immense reservoir, and native spring of all immorality, corruption, wickedness, and methodized duplicity."[28]

By 1801, the Republicans effectively had ended the Federalists' political dominance in the United States. President Thomas Jefferson purchased the Louisiana Territory from France in 1803 and, with it, the French city of New Orleans, which retains much of its ethnic flavor to this day, including the famed Mardi Gras celebration.

## PLURALISM

Two vibrant, persistent French subcultures give testimony to the cultural pluralism that is a constant feature of U.S. society: the Louisiana French and the French Canadians.

**LOUISIANA FRENCH.** The French subculture in southern Louisiana suggests ethnic homogeneity to the outsider, but its communities include two subgroups: the Creoles and the Acadians (or Cajuns). Creoles are people of color—a blend of French and African American, Native American, Jamaican American, or other ethnic groups of color. Cajuns are a blend of French and German, Italian, Polish, or other white ethnic groups. Both groups practice endogamy, usually based around skin color, hair texture, and shared cultures.

For approximately 200 years, the Cajun subculture remained strong and resisted assimilation. A system of common values—perpetuated by language, family, kinship, and religious ties—served as social integrative forces. Cajun ethnic identity remained solid, thanks to tight-knit communities and suspicion of outsiders. After the oil industry came to the bayous in the 1930s, the Cajuns' socioeconomic position changed from agricultural to working class. This in turn led to an interesting form of suburbanization for approximately two-thirds of Cajuns, one in which their ethnicity remained strong but fluency in Cajun French among the young declined.

The emergence of television in the 1950s further accelerated the process of ethnogenesis. Cajun parents typically gave their children Anglicized names and encouraged them to go to college, thereby doubling their numbers in the 1960s at southern Louisiana universities. However, these upwardly mobile, college-educated Cajuns did not completely abandon their parents' subculture, and by the late 1960s, they again embraced their heritage. For the past two decades, community-based French immersion education programs have generated a growing youth population proficient in Louisiana French. Also facilitating this resurgence was the commercialization of Cajun ethnicity into the consumer economy as the state government began promoting Cajun-themed tourism. Cajun culture—food, music, and festivals—became a key element in developing Louisiana's $9 billion tourism industry, a source of ethnic pride and a reaffirmation of Cajun identity.[29]

Lafayette, a city of approximately 121,000 located 135 miles west of New Orleans, essentially is the Cajun capital. It is the principal city of an area known as Acadiana, comprising approximately one-third of the state and home to approximately 522,000 people. Here is where you'll find the heart of Cajun culture in food, music, dancing, a fondness for large, extended families, and where street signs say *rue*, not *street*.[30]

The 2011 American Community Survey identified only 104,658 claiming Cajun ancestry, a dramatic decline from more than 407,000 in the 1990 census. However, refined analyses showed the change resulted more from changes in the wording and interpretation of the survey form, including alternate choices of "French" (not Basque) and "French

Cajun women, displaying one form of extended family bonding, in Arnaudville, Louisiana. This shared craft activity helps maintain a cohesive subculture through the cultural transmission from one generation to the next of traditional designs, skills, and time-honored practices.

Canadian." The distinctiveness of Cajun culture may be fraying a bit, but this ethnic group remains a strong presence in Louisiana.[31] Today, Cajun music and cuisine remain resilient entities, as do nuclear-family cohesiveness and extended-family bonds.

**FRENCH CANADIANS.** Another persistent subculture exists among the Americans of French/French Canadian ancestry living in New England. The nearly 2 million people of French Canadian ancestry number approximately 51,000 in Vermont, 101,100 in Maine, 109,100 in New Hampshire, and 240,500 in Massachusetts.[32]

Although some French Canadians immigrated to the United States prior to the Civil War, the largest movement came afterwards. The Industrial Revolution brought rapid expansion to the New England factories, and the owners actively recruited labor in Quebec. In response, French Canadians became the largest immigrant group in most textile centers in New England. Their number in that region jumped from 103,500 in 1870 to 573,000 by 1900. Approximately 140,000 additional French Canadians by then lived in the Midwest, primarily in Illinois and Michigan.[33]

As in Louisiana, in French New England the family and the church serve as strong cohesive units for retaining language and culture. French parochial schools also have a unifying effect on the community. Ethnic French Canadians remain a distinct subgroup, and their loyalties to their institutions and to their original home, Quebec, suggest that they will retain their identity as a strong subculture in the foreseeable future. Moreover, their proximity to Quebec—with its French-language press, radio, and television stations, as well as its cultural influences—fosters a vibrant ethnicity.

## German Americans

Germany has supplied the greatest number of immigrants to the United States—more than 7.3 million since 1820. Today, 47.4 million people, about one of seven Americans, trace at least some of their forebears to Germany (Table 5.2). In several earlier periods, the large concentrations of German Americans raised nativist fears, but today's average citizen no longer thinks of them as a distinct ethnic group, even though more than 7,000 new German immigrants arrive annually.

**5-3** Describe the immigrant experiences of the Germans, Irish, and Scandinavians.

**TABLE 5.2** U.S. Population of European Ancestry in 1990 and 2011

| | 1990 | | 2011 | |
|---|---|---|---|---|
| | Number (in Millions) | Percentage | Number (in millions) | Percentage |
| German | 57.9 | 23.3 | 47.9 | 15.3 |
| Irish | 38.7 | 15.6 | 34.7 | 11.2 |
| English | 32.7 | 13.1 | 25.9 | 8.4 |
| Italian | 14.7 | 5.9 | 17.2 | 5.6 |
| Scottish and Scots-Irish | 11.0 | 4.5 | 8.7 | 2.8 |
| French and French Canadian | 10.3 | 4.1 | 10.8 | 3.5 |
| Polish | 9.4 | 3.8 | 9.6 | 3.1 |
| Scandinavian | 9.2 | 3.8 | 9.9 | 3.2 |
| Dutch | 6.2 | 2.5 | 4.6 | 1.5 |
| Russian | 2.9 | 1.2 | 3.0 | 1.0 |

*Note:* The most dramatic changes since the 1990 census were large declines in Americans of European ancestry except among Italians, Russians, and Scandinavians. The decline in percentages also is due to the large increase of Africans, Asians, and Hispanics in the total population.

Americans claiming German, Polish, Scandinavian, or Dutch ancestry are most concentrated in the northern Midwest. Those of Irish, English, Italian, French, or Russian descent are most concentrated in the Northeast. Scottish and Scots-Irish concentrations are scattered around the nation. Still, more than half of all Americans trace their bloodlines to northern and western Europe.

*Source:* Adapted from U.S. Census Bureau, *2011 American Community Survey.*

## EARLY REACTIONS

William Penn was so successful in recruiting German immigrants to his Pennsylvania colony that by the outbreak of the Revolutionary War, they numbered more than 100,000—a third of the colony's total population. England's deployment of Hessian (German) mercenary troops in this territory during the Revolutionary War may have been part of an unsuccessful effort to secure sympathetic German colonial assistance in such areas as provision of supplies and intelligence reports.

The German immigrants' experience provides a good example of how a distinct minority group sometimes incurs the hostility of the dominant culture. The Germans were different in language, customs, and religion (mostly Lutherans), as were other groups. But their high visibility in numbers and settlement patterns set them apart and the Anglo majority worried about them as a possible threat.

By 1750, the influx of German immigrants had become so great that a concerned Benjamin Franklin asked,

> Why should the Palatine Boors be suffered to swarm into our Settlements, and by herding together establish their Language and Manners to the Exclusion of ours? Why should Pennsylvania, founded by the English, become a Colony of Aliens, who will shortly be so numerous as to Germanize us instead of our Anglifying them, and will never adopt our Language and Customs, any more than they can acquire our complexion.[34]

These fears were expressed repeatedly in later years by other representatives of the dominant group about other immigrant groups. Indeed, Franklin's worries about the duality of language markedly resemble some contemporary concerns about the Spanish-speaking populace and bilingual education. Substitute "Spanish" for "German" in these next comments of Franklin and see the universality of nativist fears about immigration and language:

> The signs in our streets have inscriptions in both languages, and in some places only German. They begin of late to make all their bonds and other legal writings in their own language, which (though I think it ought not to be) are allowed good in our courts, where the German business so increases that there is continual need of interpreters; and I suppose in a few years, they will also be necessary in the Assembly, to tell one half of our legislators what the other half say.[35]

Franklin was not arguing for restrictions on immigration actually but rather for rapid assimilation (Anglo-conformity).

## THE SECOND WAVE: SEGREGATION AND PLURALISM

The German immigrants of the eighteenth century first settled in Pennsylvania and then in other mid-Atlantic states, but the nineteenth-century immigrants predominantly went to the Midwest, settling in the Ohio, Mississippi, and Missouri river valleys. There they became homesteaders, preserving their heritage through their schools, churches, newspapers, language, mutual-aid societies, and recreational activities. Various colonization societies in Germany also sent thousands of German settlers to the St. Louis, Missouri, region in the 1830s, to Texas in the 1840s, and to Wisconsin in the 1850s.

The failure in 1848 of an attempted liberal revolution in Germany brought many political refugees to the United States. Known as "Forty-Eighters," these Germans settled in the large cities of the East and Midwest—in particular, Baltimore, New York, St. Louis, Milwaukee, and Minneapolis. Political activists in their homeland, the Forty-Eighters quickly became active in U.S. politics. Many Germans even gave serious thought to forming an all-German state within the Union, with German as the official language. Later, some considered creating a separate German nation in North America in the event that the slavery issue caused the dissolution of the Union.

Although more dispersed throughout the country than the Irish, in the cities, they concentrated in "Germantown" communities. Here Germans owned and operated most of the businesses, and German functioned as the principal spoken language. An array of parallel social institutions—fraternal and mutual-aid societies, newspapers, schools, churches, restaurants, and saloons—like those of other immigrant groups, aided newly arrived Germans in adjusting to their new country.

Gymnastic societies and cultural centers known as *Turnvereine* provided libraries, reading rooms, discussion groups, and singing and dramatic groups for German Americans. They became controversial, however, as a result of their radical reform proposals and political activism on behalf of social-welfare legislation, direct popular election of all public officials, tax and tariff reform, abolition of slavery, and their militant opposition to prohibition.

In the Midwest, from Wisconsin to Texas, the Germans achieved success either in farming or in urban enterprises, becoming a significant part of the region's identity. By 1850, Milwaukee contained 6,000 German-born Americans and 4,000 native-born Americans. In the "German triangle"—the area defined by Cincinnati, Milwaukee, and St. Louis—the presence of hundreds of thousands of German Americans resulted in many states printing their documents in German and English and also authorizing the use of the German language in public schools for classroom instruction.[36] The use of German in the schools served an additional purpose: It was intended to preserve the whole range of German culture, much as some Hispanic leaders hope Spanish-language instruction today will bolster Hispanic culture.

# the ETHNIC experience

## Health Inspection at Ellis Island

"When I got to Ellis Island, we all had to line up and they would examine us. Some people could pass and they marked their coat. Some they marked on the left and some they marked on the right lapels. Those that were marked on one side could go through right away. Maybe they had been here before, I don't know. But I got a mark—'This is back.' So they led us through a big hall and we had to strip naked: And we met two fellas, they were doctors with stethoscopes. I didn't know what a stethoscope was—I learned that after. They tapped us on the chest and on the back and

then I had to run around. I was the only one they examined."

"All of a sudden one raised his fist. He was gonna knock the other fella down, the other doctor. I didn't know what it meant. I was told afterward. One said I had consumption and the other doctor said there was nothing wrong with me—all I needed was a bellyful of food for a couple of months, I was undernourished. Well, finally, I got passed. And when I got out, I had to go before an examiner. My brother had arranged for relatives that lived in Brooklyn. The examiner said to my cousin, 'You will have to

put up $50,000 bail, so this young man will not become a burden of the United States."

"...Then the examiner said, 'You are free to go.' And [voice breaking] when I—I tell the news 'you are free,' I choke up. The judge says, 'The boy [pause, tears streaming] may be undernourished [pause, then very emotionally] but he has a wonderful mind.' And he said again, 'You are free to go,' and we went out."

Source: German immigrant who came to the United States in 1910 at age 16. Taped interview from the collection of Vincent N. Parrillo.

## SOCIETAL RESPONSES

A diverse group in their religions, occupations, and residence patterns, German Americans came under increasing criticism for being clannish and for attempting to preserve their culture. Their large numbers added to rising tensions, which culminated in violent confrontations. One of the more notorious incidents occurred in Louisville, Kentucky, on August 5, 1855. On that day, which became known as Bloody Monday, a mob of Know-Nothings, incited by fiery articles in the Louisville *Journal*, stormed into the Germantown section intent on mayhem. When the riot was over, 22 men had been killed, several hundred wounded, and 16 houses burned.

Following the Civil War, German Americans were well positioned economically and suffered little interethnic conflict until the outbreak of World War I. As a wave of anti-German hostility and patriotic zeal swept the land, German Americans became targets of harassment, business boycotts, physical attacks, and vandalism of their property. Several states even banned the German language, and towns changed German-named street signs. Attempting to prove their loyalty to the United States, many German Americans abandoned their cultural manifestations. Between 1917 and 1920, the number of German-language newspapers dropped by one-half, and various ethnic institutions either had been shut down or had suffered major losses in membership.[37]

Since 1920, more than 1.7 million German immigrants have arrived in the United States, one-fourth of this total in the 1920s and another one-fourth in the 1950s (see the Ethnic Experience box). Such numbers gave resilience to a German ethnic subculture, but nothing like the one that flourished prior to 1914. Today, newcomers tend to assimilate fairly rapidly and few easily identifiable ethnic communities exist, although strong ethnic concentrations exist in many parts of the country, such as in south-central Texas and many Midwestern cities.

*Hundreds of Oktoberfest celebrations occur in the United States each September and October, as here in Mt. Angel, Oregon, where women in folk dresses and boys in traditional lederhosen carry the maypole. For many Americans, whether of German ancestry or not, this time of year gives everyone an opportunity to share in an ethnic celebration and beer-drinking events.*

### CULTURAL IMPACT

American speech, eating, and drinking reflect German influence. Frankfurters, sauerkraut, sauerbraten, hamburgers, Wiener schnitzel, pumpernickel bread, liverwurst, pretzels, zwieback, and lager beer were introduced by German immigrants. The words *stein* and *rathskeller* are of German origin, as are the concepts of the kindergarten and the university. Germans dominated the U.S. brewing industry, founding Anheuser-Busch, Coors, Schaefer, Schlitz, Schmidt's, Pabst, Ruppert, and many other breweries.

German immigrant industrialists who made a major mark on U.S. society included Meyer Guggenheim (mining), Frederick Weyerhaeuser (lumber), John Jacob Astor (fur trade), Bausch and Lomb (optical instruments), Henry Steinway and Rudolph Wurlitzer (pianos), and H. John Heinz (food canning). Thomas Nast, a German immigrant and the first great U.S. caricaturist and political cartoonist, created the Democratic donkey, the Republican elephant, and Uncle Sam.

## Irish Americans

Most pre-revolutionary immigrants from Ireland were Ulster Irish, Presbyterian descendants of Scottish immigrants who had migrated to Northern Ireland a generation earlier. Settling chiefly in New England at first (around 1717), they clustered together, preserving their ethnicity and seldom mingling with the English Americans. The latter regarded these newcomers contemptuously, labeling them ill-tempered ruffians who drank and fought too much. Soon the friction escalated into Boston newspaper denunciations, the destruction of an Irish Presbyterian meetinghouse, and a mob blocking the disembarkation of Irish ship passengers. By 1784, a decline in the linen trade and poor harvest had prompted the exodus of approximately 400,000 Irish Protestants to the beckoning colonies. Only the English were a larger ethnic group at that time.[38]

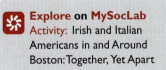

**Explore on MySocLab**
Activity: Irish and Italian Americans in and Around Boston: Together, Yet Apart

William Penn's recruitment in Europe for his colony led the next wave of Scots-Irish immigrants to choose Pennsylvania as their preferred destination. However, the tendency of the newcomers to be squatters without paying for the land and their frequent conflicts with the Germans living there spurred Pennsylvania authorities to discourage further immigration. In four waves during the eighteenth century, between 200,000 and 400,000 Scots-Irish emigrated to the colonies, a great many of them settling in the frontier regions, from Pennsylvania to Georgia, in the area known today as Appalachia. By the end of the eighteenth century, cultural assimilation had occurred, but structural and marital assimilation lagged behind.[39]

Unlike the Scots-Irish Protestants, the Irish Catholics fared poorly. Their religion, peasant culture, and rebelliousness against England marked them as strangers to the dominant culture and set the stage for the most overt discrimination and hostility any ethnic group thus far had encountered. Originally unwelcomed in the New England settlements, most of the early Irish Catholic immigrants settled in Pennsylvania or in Maryland. The latter, founded as an English Catholic colony in 1634, fell under Protestant control by the mid-eighteenth century and then prohibited Catholics from holding elected office.

By 1790, Irish Catholics accounted for nearly 4 percent of the almost 3.2 million total population. Their growing numbers became a source of increasing concern to the Federalists, especially during the presidency of John Adams. Fearing that "wild Irish" rebels would attempt to turn the United States against England and that they would join the Republican Party, the Federalists strongly opposed the incoming "hordes of wild Irishmen." Rufus King, U.S. ambassador to England, was among the foremost opponents of Irish emigration to the United States. He expressed to Secretary of State Timothy Pickering his fear that the disaffected Irish would "disfigure our true national character," which was purest in untainted New England. Future President John Quincy Adams agreed that the United States had "too many of these people already."[40]

After 1820, emigration to the United States became increasingly essential to the Irish Catholics, who suffered under oppressive British rule in their native land. Failure of the potato crop in successive years and the resulting famine during the late 1840s accelerated the exodus. Approximately 1.2 million Irish emigrated between 1847 and 1854; in the peak year of 1851, almost a quarter of a million Irish Catholics arrived. Irish immigration had its greatest impact on U.S. society between 1820 and 1860 (36 percent of the total in the 1820s, 35 percent in the 1830s, 46 percent in the 1840s, and 35 percent in the 1850s).[41]

The immigrants settled mostly in coastal cities. Their living conditions in these overcrowded "Dublin Districts" were deplorable. With many families living in poorly lighted, poorly heated and badly ventilated tenements, contagious, deadly diseases—such as cholera—were widespread. Moreover, when the immigrants were drawn elsewhere to work in mines or to build canals and railroads, shantytowns sprang up in many locales, their presence serving as a symbol to native-born U.S. residents that an "inferior" people had appeared in their midst.

## CULTURAL DIFFERENTIATION

The Irish attracted attention because of their sheer numbers, their Catholicism, and their strong anti-British feelings. These factors weighed heavily against them in Anglo-Saxon Protestant America. In addition, they were a poverty-stricken rural people who settled in groups mainly in the slum areas of cities on the East Coast. Because they could find only unskilled jobs, they began life in the United States with a lower-class status, bearing that stigma at a time when the country was becoming increasingly class conscious.

The Irish were the first ethnic group to come to the United States in large numbers as a minority whose culture so differed from the dominant culture. They were the first of many immigrant groups yet to come with a peasant culture. Other nineteenth-century immigrants—Dutch, English, French, Germans, Scots, and Scandinavians—were mostly townspeople or skilled in crafts or farming management, unlike the Irish tenant farmers long exploited by the English landholding system. As a result, many flagrantly discriminated against the Irish, although some welcomed them as a necessary working-class contingent. Yet even those who welcomed the Irish as people to fill working-class jobs did so with an ethnocentric attitude of superiority over such a lowly breed of people, as typified by these comments of a Massachusetts senator in 1852:

> That inefficiency of the pure Celtic race furnishes the answer to the question: How much use are the Irish to us in America? The Native American answer is, "none at all." And the Native American policy is to keep them away.
>
> A profound mistake, I believe....We are here, well organized and well trained, masters of the soil, the very race before which they have yielded everywhere besides. It must be, that when they come in among us, they come to lift us up. As sure as water and oil each finds its level, they will find theirs. So far as they are mere hand-workers, they must sustain the head-workers, or those who have any element of intellectual ability. Their inferiority as a race compels them to go to the bottom; and the consequence is that we are, all of us, the higher lifted because they are here.[42]

## SOCIETAL REACTION AND FINDING JOBS

Americans blamed the Irish for their widespread poverty and resented the heavy burden they placed on charitable institutions. They also stereotyped the Irish as inherently prone to alcoholism, brawling, corruption, and crime—and derisively dubbed the police vans carting them to jail as "paddy wagons." Viewed as an unwelcome social problem, the Irish served as the rallying point for opponents of immigration.

Nativism, briefly evident in the immediate post–Revolutionary War period, now swept across the land in a shameful display of bigotry and intolerance. Aiding the growth of anti-Irish feeling was anti-Catholicism. Fears of "Popery" arose, partly in response to the influx of priests to minister to the needs of the Irish Catholics. Know-Nothing violence targeted the Irish far more than it did the Germans, as destruction of property, brutal beatings, and loss of life occurred in the Irish sections of many cities. Besides starting frequent street brawls, anti-Catholic mobs sometimes burned churches and convents.

THE AMERICAN RIVER GANGES.

THE PRIESTS AND THE CHILDREN.—[SEE PAGE 915.]

*Many consider this the most vicious anti-Catholic, anti-Irish cartoon ever printed in a mass-circulation magazine. It illustrates the belief that Irish Catholics were endangering public education (symbolized by the upside-down American flag). Notice the Irish harp and papal tiara flying above Tammany Hall, the teachers being led to the gallows, and the children being thrown to the riverbank by Democratic politicians. One Protestant teacher (the Bible tucked into his jacket) is protecting children from the crocodiles, which represent Catholic bishops. Their jaws are mitres, their scales are vestments, and their faces are Irish stereotypes. This cartoon by German immigrant Thomas Nast appeared in* Harper's Weekly *on September 30, 1871.*

**CHAPTER 5** NORTH AND WEST EUROPEAN AMERICANS **135**

Nonviolent antagonism toward the Irish was most obvious in social and job discrimination. For a long time, job advertisements in Boston and elsewhere included the words "No Irish Need Apply" or the acronym "NINA." Consequently, most Irish men only could find work in such demanding but low-paying jobs in construction (ditch diggers and road, railroad, or canal building) or as miners or dock workers. This nineteenth-century job discrimination and segmentation would have some similarities to the twentieth-century experience of blacks in urban America. As time passed, Irish American men became business entrepreneurs, store clerks, salesmen, and teachers, first within the Irish communities and then elsewhere in northeast urban centers.[43]

Large-scale Irish immigration continued between 1871 and 1910, with the arrival of approximately 1.9 million newcomers. Unlike many other arriving groups, most Irish immigrants were young, unmarried women, migrating with sisters or female cousins, or even traveling alone in steerage class. By 1900, more than 60 percent of the Irish immigrants living in the United States were single women, many working as domestic cooks, maids, or caregivers. So common was the presence of young Irish women, ranging in age from late-teens to late-twenties, that the name "Bridget" became the generic name applied to all Irish servants. Those who did not work as domestics sought work in textile mills or clothing factories.[44]

## MINORITY RESPONSE

The experience of the Irish was the prototype for the experiences of later immigrants, not only in their hostile reception by the host society but also in their reaction to the prejudice and discrimination they frequently encountered. We should not underestimate the hardship involved in leaving one's native land—alone or with family—journeying to a distant country, feeling both anxieties and hopes, and then finding oneself an unwanted stranger in a strange land.

**ACTIONS AND REACTIONS.** The response of the Irish was retreatist in social interactions but aggressive in their involvement in the labor movement and in the urban political machine. Because these activities frequently offended U.S. norms of behavior, they confirmed the suspicions of native-born Americans, thereby reinforcing the stereotypes of the Irish and prolonging the vicious circle. Socially segregated from participation in normal local and associational affairs, the Irish created their own organizations and social events. In building their parallel social institutions, the Irish succeeded in helping one another, although at first they primarily interacted only with others from the same county of origin.

Besides offering informal aid for kin and neighbors, the Irish created their own mutual-welfare system through trade associations (the predecessor of labor unions), fraternal organizations, and homes for the aged that were staffed by nuns. These efforts assisted and protected the Irish from societal indifference and hostility, but they also isolated them and slowed their acculturation. The Irish community further was united through family, church, and school, as well as through social and recreational activities. Such "clannishness" added fuel to the fires of resentment among assimilationists.

Their lack of social contact with the larger community and the forced interactions among themselves made the group become more aware of its ethnic identity. Also, because the host society branded all of them as "Irish Catholics," a communal solidarity evolved in which they identified less with their local homeland regions and more with a national group identity.[45] Whereas before they might socialize only in, say, the dance hall for their home Irish county (Donegal, Kilkenny, etc.), they began to intermingle, such as in Irish Athletic Clubs that sponsored team competition in hurling (a Gaelic form of field hockey), football, and track and field.[46] In recognizing and acting on their shared ethnic identity, they developed a common subculture that would have an impact on the new society.[47]

The small degree of intermarriage both reflected and reinforced the distinction between the Irish American and other U.S. residents. Irish religious and social considerations encouraged a tendency to marry their own kind. Priests repeatedly warned that union with Protestants was tantamount to loss of faith, and the great majority of non-Irish in the city considered marriage with them degrading. As a result, the percentage of Irish marrying outside their ethnic group was extremely low.

In Irish households the mother was an important figure, providing strength and stability in the family, with the father often absent, either at work or literally. Her years of economic independence before marrying later than other ethnic women carried over into her matriarchal role, even in old age. That earlier experience in self-sufficiency also led Irish families to encourage the education of daughters as well as sons, even if family resources first went to the boys.[48]

**LABOR CONFLICT.** Irish labor was diversified and played a key role in the industrial expansion of the United States, particularly in building the great systems of canals, waterways, and railroads. Heavily concentrated in low-status unskilled or semiskilled occupations, the Irish worked at the hard, physical jobs in the cities, in the mines of Appalachia, or in construction from the Alleghenies to the Rockies. With their knowledge of the English language, the Irish provided strong, articulate membership and leadership in such early labor movements as the Knights of Labor, where they became activists for better pay and working conditions.

Their greatest notoriety came from the violence and murders committed by the Molly Maguires, a secret terrorist group that aided Irish miners in their struggles with mine owners. Following infiltration of the group by a secret agent for the Pinkerton Detective Agency and a highly questionable court proceeding, the Molly Maguire movement ended in the hanging of 20 men, one of the largest mass executions in U.S. history.

The split-labor-market theory (discussed in Chapter 4) helps explain much of the conflict involving the Irish. Irish-German conflict, particularly in Pennsylvania, was intense in the late eighteenth and early nineteenth centuries because of economic competition and the use of Germans as strikebreakers.[49] On the West Coast, Irish workers held meetings and demonstrations to demand the curtailment of further Chinese immigration, viewing the lower-paid Chinese as a serious economic threat.[50] The Irish also fiercely resisted abolition, fearing labor competition from released slaves. Anti-black riots in Chicago, Cincinnati, and Detroit followed. Most notorious was the so-called Draft Riot of 1863 in New York City, in which approximately 100 rioters were killed (13 of them blacks), 300 injured, 50 buildings burned to the ground, including two Protestant churches and the Colored Orphan Asylum on Fifth Avenue looted and completely destroyed. This riot, one of the worst in U.S. history, was the result of angry Irish longshoremen opposed to the recent use of black strikebreakers to undermine their efforts to secure better wages and of other angry Irish opposed to being drafted to fight in the Civil War.[51]

## UPWARD MOBILITY

Unlike other immigrant groups in the nineteenth century, the Irish then experienced at first occupational or social **upward mobility**. Grassroots politics gave them a power base, however, triggering a nativist concern about Catholic priests controlling U.S. politics. Through political machine organization, the Irish controlled Tammany Hall in New York by the 1860s and the Brooklyn Democratic Party by the 1870s. By the 1890s, they also controlled city governments in Boston, Buffalo, Chicago, Philadelphia, St. Louis, and San Francisco. Through a tightly organized patronage system, the boss-controlled urban political machine offered economic and political opportunities, as well as social-welfare provisions for the Irish community.[52]

Irish Catholics made slow but steady progress in entering the societal mainstream (see the Ethnic Experience box). Antipathy against them gradually declined as their command of English, improved economic position, and physical appearance made them less objectionable to English American Protestants than were the new immigrants arriving

# the ETHNIC experience

## Immigrant Expectations

"Like many more immigrants like myself, I came to this country to seek a living because living over there was very, very poor. Work was scarce and hard. I decided that I ought to try the United States to make a living."

"I left home in Ireland on a Friday morning. I went to a place then called Queenstown in County Cork. I was there for the greater part of Friday and Saturday because you had to go through quite a number of tests and screening to be allowed to board ship. On Sunday morning around eight o'clock, I boarded the ship."

"We arrived in the United States a week from that Monday, around two o'clock in the afternoon in the harbor of New York. The nicest thing I saw after being so seasick—and I might say I was very, very seasick—the nicest thing I ever experienced was seeing the Statue of Liberty. It meant we were here and we were all right. We had landed and we were safe. Then, of course, I had to go through customs and things like that."

"I had heard a great deal about the United States, that it was a good country, and I might very well say that it was a good country, although at that time I was disappointed because I wasn't the one to find the gold in the streets. I really had to go out and look for a job. I worked for awhile in a doctor's office and from there I went to work for a chemical company. There was disappointment. There were loans from my family and my friends. It's something you wonder if you can make it. Thank God I did."

Source: Irish immigrant who came to the United States in 1920 at age 18. Taped interview from the collection of Vincent N. Parrillo.

from other parts of Europe. As the Irish began to assimilate, they often served as a middleman minority, aiding new European immigrant groups in work, church, school, and city life. The new wave of immigrants helped Roman Catholicism evolve into a major faith in a predominantly Protestant country and the Irish, finding power in the church hierarchy that continues to this day, exerted great moral force on the nation.

## THE NEW IRISH

Driven by a high unemployment rate in Ireland, in the 1980s, a new wave of emigrants—more than 65,000—left their native land and entered the United States legally in the 1990s. Faced with a two-year waiting list, perhaps 50,000 more came illegally.[53] Greatly improved economic conditions in Ireland in the twenty-first century and a low birth rate reduced emigration to the United States to a current average of 1,500 annually.[54] However, the global recession of recent years affected Ireland as well as the United States, prompting the arrival of thousands of new Irish undocumented immigrants. In typical chain-migration style, they have gone to tight-knit Irish enclaves, such as those in New York's Bronx and Queens neighborhoods.[55]

Like their predecessors, the new Irish cluster in the big cities, working in construction or in the care of children and the elderly. Reflecting the chain-migration pattern, Boston receives immigrants from the west of Ireland, whereas those from Donegal, Fermanagh, and other northern counties go to Philadelphia. Cleveland attracts newcomers from Achill Island, off the coast of Mayo. Other Irish settle along Bainbridge Avenue in New York City's borough of the Bronx, known as the "Irish Mile."

Well represented in the professions, in financial services, and in the executive suites of corporate America, the old Irish—the 34.5 million descendants of earlier immigrants—now live mostly in suburbia, enjoying higher incomes and status. Once a despised minority group and victims of blatant discrimination, the Irish now are part of the American

*Traditional Irish step dancing, notable for its rapid leg movements while body and arms are kept largely stationary, is a popular expression of ethnic heritage, whether at the annual festivals throughout the United States, such as this one in Savannah, Georgia, or in Irish dance schools, or in professional theatrical productions, such as Riverdance.*

mainstream. Even many non-Irish share in the St. Patrick's Day celebrations, enjoy Irish step-dancing performances, and concerts by such Irish singing groups as Celtic Woman and Celtic Thunder.

## Scandinavian Americans

Some Swedes came to what is now the United States as early as 1638, making their landfall at the mouth of the Delaware River. They established a colony, New Sweden—a land encompassing parts of modern-day Delaware, Pennsylvania, and New Jersey—and there constructed the first log cabin in the New World.

Although small numbers of Norwegians, Swedes, and Danes continued to immigrate to the United States throughout the next 200 years, they did not come in substantial numbers until after 1865. Thereafter, motivated by religious dissension, voting disenfranchisement, crop failures, and other economic factors, the Scandinavians emigrated in large numbers, totaling nearly 2 million between 1870 and 1920.

Many of these immigrants settled in fertile soil regions of the northern Midwest and established rural communities where they could enjoy social and political equality. These farmland settlements became strongholds of Norwegian and Swedish traditions that revolved around the Lutheran church. Isolation from the dominant drift of U.S. social patterns permitted widespread, long-lived retention of old country lifestyles, which continue in some measure to this day.[56] Ole Rölvaag presented an eloquent and poignant saga of late-nineteenth-century Norwegian pioneers in the Dakota Territory in *Giants in the Earth,* a vivid socio-psychological portrait of pioneer life. Capturing the exuberant hopes, fears, despair, struggles, and interactions of the immigrants in the heartland of the United States, he offered vivid testimony to the human quest of a dream:

And it was as if nothing affected people in those days. They threw themselves blindly into the Impossible, and accomplished the Unbelievable. If anyone succumbed in the struggle—and that happened often—another would come and take his place. Youth was in the race; the unknown, the untried, the unheard-of, was in the air; people caught it, were intoxicated by it, threw themselves away, and laughed at the cost. Of course, it was possible—everything was possible out here. There was no such thing as the Impossible any more. The human race had not known such faith and such self-confidence since history began....And so had been the Spirit since the day the first settlers landed on the eastern shores; it would rise and fall at intervals, would swell and surge on again with every new wave of settlers that rolled westward into the unbroken solitude.[57]

## INGROUP SOLIDARITY

Like other immigrant groups, the Scandinavians attempted to resist Americanization and cling to their Old World traditions. They discouraged intermarriage, even far into the twentieth century. An ethnic newspaper's 1897 lament about exogamy expressed the concern "that the national spirit is not particularly strong among the Danes of this region" and that intermarriage would "strike out our mother tongue and all we received as a heritage from our fathers."[58]

As greater numbers of Norwegians settled in Minnesota and Wisconsin, they eventually outnumbered the native-born population, creating social tensions and political competition. A typical example occurred in 1878 in Trempealeau County, Wisconsin, a beautiful region of wooded hills and valleys. When the Norwegians practiced their custom of picnicking and drinking on Sunday afternoons, their neighbors increasingly censured them. When a Norwegian running as an independent was elected sheriff on a vote split along party lines, the Sunday custom continued without further interference; political party leaders then realized they no longer could ignore or dictate to this ethnic majority.[59]

Ethnicity, however, is an ever-changing dialogue between immigrants and the host society. When Presidents Theodore Roosevelt and Woodrow Wilson launched attacks, prior to U.S. entry into World War I, on hyphenated Americans for their language retention, ethnic press, and ethnic organizations, local attacks on Scandinavian ethnicity followed. (Less so today, the past use of hyphens was common, such as, for example, "Scandinavian-American.") In 1915, the *Minneapolis Journal* published an editorial titled "The Hyphen Must Go!" It argued that in the upper Midwest the melting pot was not functioning properly because immigrant communities were retaining too much of their Old World cultures, and too many "hyphenated" newspapers, schools, and societies still were using the immigrant languages.[60]

## ETHNIC IDENTITY

Norwegians, Swedes, and Danes came to the United States from lands with different governments, different traditions, and different languages. Nonetheless, because of physical similarities among the three groups and because they frequently settled together in the new land, none of the three nationalities originally was strong enough to make a separate impact on the host society, and group members often resented being called by another nationality, such as when a Swede objected to being called a Norwegian. As a result of the mixing of these three immigrant groups, the term *Scandinavian* to describe them came into common usage, such as the organization in 1860 of the Scandinavian Synod of the Evangelical Lutheran Church, whose members were Norwegians and Danes. The use and acceptability of this word grew steadily, leading to the ethnic daily newspaper in Chicago adopting the name *Skandinaven* and representing all three nationalities.[61]

In addition to farming, the Scandinavians primarily worked as lumberjacks, sailors, dock workers, and craftsmen in the building and machine trades. Because they came from countries with compulsory education, their literacy rate was high, and a significant

*Unless Norwegian Americans themselves, today's college students seldom think of this ethnic group, since only about 400 new immigrants arrive each year. Yet more than 4.4 million Americans claim this ancestry and, like many others, they also celebrate their heritage, such as with this Norwegian-American Day parade in Bay Ridge, Brooklyn.*

percentage acquired U.S. citizenship. Danes tended to spread out more and to downplay the role of the church and fraternal organizations in comparison to Norwegians and Swedes. For that reason, the Danes assimilated more quickly, although all groups succeeded in blending into the social fabric fairly easily. The Swedes hit their peak year of immigration in 1913, and the Norwegians hit their peak in 1924.

Today, more than 10 million Americans claim Scandinavian ancestry. The largest concentrations of Danish Americans live in California (more than 200,000). Norwegian Americans still live in the Midwest (approximately 2.5 million), whereas many Swedish Americans live in Minnesota and California (more than 450,000 each).

## Social Realities for Women

Social class and ethnic background were important variables in determining women's places in the social order in the nineteenth century. Women in affluent families had servants to do menial tasks, while they themselves could devote their free time to such activities as playing a musical instrument, creating fine embroidery, or perhaps reading good books, particularly Scripture. Working-class women would likely either produce goods for sale (cheese, cloth, shoes, or yarn) or render services (working as cooks or domestics or possibly as servers at inns, restaurants, or taverns).

Among those ethnic groups living even a short distance from cities—especially the Germans, Scots-Irish, and French Canadians—women normally would perform a variety of agricultural tasks, working in barns, fields, meadows, stables, or wherever they were needed.[62]

Many Irish were single women taking jobs as domestics or nannies for the native-born urban elite. In 1800, there was one domestic servant for every 20 families, but by 1840, the ratio had dropped to one servant for every 10 families. Young unmarried Irish (and Scandinavian) women often came first and worked in U.S. homes. Their daily typical workload was 16 hours of cooking, cleaning, tending to the children, and nursing the sick, six days a week. With little time to themselves, these women saved their earnings for passage money for other family members. Records from the Boston Society for the Prevention of Pauperism offer one illustration of the difficulties women had seeking

**5-4** Describe social realities for women in past centuries.

jobs in a household compared to men finding work in labor gangs. Between 1845 and 1850, it received employment applications from 14,000 female foreigners in contrast to 5,034 male applications.

The loss of husbands through accident, desertion, or sickness left many women without means to support large families except perhaps by taking in boarders or hiring out to do others' laundry or sewing at home. Among working-class, rural, and frontier families, women continued working at many tasks that genteel ladies of the mercantile and upper classes did not do. However, one commonality almost all women shared, regardless of social class or residence, was that they married at a young age, had many children, and were usually grandmothers by the time they were 40.

By 1820, the number of children under age 5, per 1,000 women between the ages of 20 and 44, was 1,295, approximately three times what it is today. Child rearing, keeping of home and hearth, and working in the fields if a farmer's wife, were the areas of responsibility for most women. Only about 6 percent of the women were in paid employment outside the home. For most women, the house or perhaps the farm was their world, their reality, and their fate.[63]

# Assimilation

Compare and contrast the assimilation paths followed by these immigrants.

The differing experiences of northern and western European Americans illustrate the roles that ethnocentrism and social distance play in the assimilation process. At first, cultural and religious differences kept the groups socially segregated for the most part, but eventually those with greater similarities (the English, Scots, Welsh, and Ulster Irish) coalesced into what became the mainstream group. Such was not the case with many other groups with pronounced ethnic differences, and this difference often was sharpened even more by their numbers and geographic isolation:

> In 1890, the "melting pot" had not yet absorbed the 80,000 Dutch, 200,000 Swiss, or 1.2 million Scandinavians in the Midwest, most of whom had arrived after 1870. Likewise, the 150,000 French immigrants, 200,000 Cajuns in Louisiana, and 500,000 French Canadians in New England and the Great Plains remained

# REALITY check

## Places and Politics: A Geo-Political Profile

Northern and western European immigrants continue to arrive every year, of course, but the present-day U.S. portrait of these nationality groups primarily lies in the descendants of earlier immigrants. The new arrivals once clustered in geographic regions—such as the Dutch in New York and New Jersey, the French in Louisiana and the French Canadians in New England, the Germans in Pennsylvania and the Midwest, the Irish in major cities in the Northeast, and the Scandinavians in the northern Midwest.

Today, their descendants are scattered throughout all 50 states. Still, as shown in Figure 5.2, certain concentrations still exist. Some are continuations of the concentrations just mentioned. Others are concentrations in new areas. Together, the patterns show that distinctive ethnic concentrations still exist even if the ethnicity itself is muted in visibility because of multigenerational residence in the United States.

One attribute of a minority group is lack of political power and that certainly is not the case for those whose ancestry groups are among the northern and western Europeans. Both the German and Irish vote long has been an important element in local, state, and national elections. All five ethnic groups long have enjoyed a strong political voice and elected thousands of their own at all levels.

At the national level, the long list includes Presidents Martin Van Buren, Theodore Roosevelt, and Franklin Roosevelt (Dutch); Herbert Hoover and Dwight Eisenhower (German); and Jimmy Carter, Bill Clinton, and John F. Kennedy (Irish). Among the other prominent names are U.S. Senators Lloyd Bentsen (Danish); Thomas Daschle and Chuck Hagel (German); Kirsten Gillibrand and Edward Kennedy (Irish); and Walter Magnuson (Swedish). Other influential individuals have been U.S. Attorney General Janet Reno (Danish); Vice President Al Gore and Senator Robert LaFollette (French); Secretary of State Henry Kissinger and Governor Sarah Palin (German); and U.S. Senators Eugene McCarthy and Daniel Patrick Moynihan (Irish).

Once outsiders, all five of these ethnic groups have merged with English Americans into the mainstream, not only politically but economically and socially as well. In no sense of the word are they minorities any longer as they once were.

---

culturally, linguistically, and religiously separated from the larger society. So too did many of the 8 million Germans in the rural Midwest or concentrated in many large cities. Their poverty and Catholic faith kept 6 million Irish in the Northeast...in social isolation....

Race, culture, and/or social class shaped group relations in the United States in 1890, keeping the nation a patchwork quilt of cultural diversity. All three variables influenced perceptions, receptivity, and interactional patterns.[64]

Their ingroup solidarity strengthened by social isolation, endogamy, and vibrant ethnic communities, these groups remained pluralistic entities throughout much of the nineteenth century, even if some of their number had assimilated.

By the end of the nineteenth century, however, an industrializing America lured millions of new immigrants, vastly different from the ethnic groups already here. Mainstream Americans would view these new white ethnics as so culturally and physically different as to be even farther removed on the social distance scale than the "old" immigrants. Consequently, Anglo-Americans judged these previously excluded older groups as more like themselves and thus more socially acceptable. A redefined mainstream American identity emerged, bringing people of northern and western European origins into this classification in contrast to the newer, "less desirable" newcomers, even though it took decades for this redefinition to become fully operative (see the Reality Check box and Figure 5.2).[65]

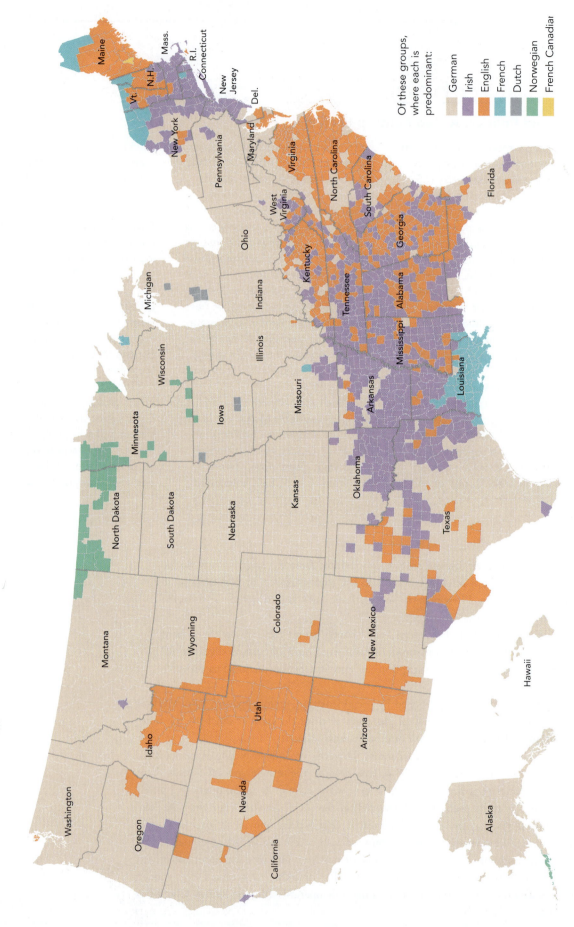

**FIGURE 5.2** Largest North and West European Ancestry: 2010

Of these groups, where each is predominant:

- German
- Irish
- English
- French
- Dutch
- Norwegian
- French Canadian

# Sociological Analysis

Thus far, we have examined the experiences of northern and western European immigrants within a sociohistorical context and studied the specific patterns of dominant–minority interaction. To understand better the meaning of those patterns, we now appraise them within the conceptual frameworks of the three major sociological perspectives: functionalist, conflict, and interactionist.

## THE FUNCTIONALIST VIEW

With their emphasis on a societal network of interrelated parts working cooperatively for survival or stability, functionalists see as highly desirable the arrival of large groups of people to forge a civilization out of a vast, undeveloped country rich in natural resources. The New World offered the new arrivals economic opportunity and freedom from religious and political oppression, while benefiting from their presence. Unskilled newcomers helped build cities, canals, and railroads; cleared land for farming; and created demand for goods and services. Others used their entrepreneurial skills or craftsmanship to supply the growing nation with needed commerce. An open social system enabled the evolution of an independent U.S. society through the efforts of poor, unskilled immigrants. To use the metaphor of Crèvecoeur, useless and withered plants took root and flourished.[66]

Sometimes the large numbers of Irish and Germans entering the country led to dysfunctions because the society could not absorb them quickly enough. They clustered together, culturally distinct from the dominant English American model, and their presence generated prejudice and discrimination against them. The ensuing conflict, like that involving French Americans in earlier years, disrupted the social system, obstructed cooperative efforts toward common goals, and prevented many newcomers from attaining personal goals. In time, the necessary adjustments occurred; education and upward mobility through economic growth and civil service (in the case of the Irish) allowed both acceptance and assimilation.

**STUDENTS SPEAK** "The functionalist view was more relevant to me because in the past, just like now, immigrants found a way into the United States because this was the land for better opportunities. They wanted a better quality of life, so they came here. But, when they arrived in the United States, they took the low-paying jobs that nobody else wanted and got paid a lower salary to do them. Most immigrants came in unskilled and still helped to build America by doing its dirty work."

**—Levi Still**

## THE CONFLICT VIEW

The beginning point of the conflict perspective is the dominance of English Americans in the new nation. Not only did they influence the adoption of language, customs, and social institutions derived from Great Britain, but they also held economic and political power. In this context, Federalist hostility toward the French and the Irish became more than ethnic antagonism. The propertied elite saw the influx of so many "common" people and the possible spread of Jacobin (French radical) revolutionary ideas as threats to their power, and they took various actions to safeguard their interests (for example, passing the Alien and Sedition Acts and forming the Native American Party). Political considerations also weighed heavily in dealings with the Irish and the Germans. The rise in power of Irish city politicians and the political activism of the Forty-Eighters caused nativist reactions through mob violence, political movements, and state legislative countermeasures.

Economic exploitation, particularly in the case of the Irish, brought prosperity to the owners of mines, factories, and railroads. Working under brutal conditions in physically demanding jobs, many Irish struggled to survive in the slums where their subsistence wages obliged them to reside. The captains of industry, when confronted with strikes or labor organization efforts, used their power to thwart such efforts through the courts, through law enforcement personnel or vigilante groups to break up demonstrations, or by

STUDENTS SPEAK "I think that the experience of the Irish immigrants is best viewed from the conflict perspective and goes a long way in vindicating the power-differential theory. Only the conflict theory perspective can truly explain what happened to the Irish. What power (financial, labor, cultural, and educational) they brought with them and the dominant power structure that was in place were the determining factors in their early hardship. Any of these theories could explain anything in terms of itself but, to my mind, only conflict theory makes the correct analysis about the Irish experience."

**—Andrew Berg**

**STUDENTS SPEAK** "The theory most relevant for me when applied to these minority groups was the interactionist theory. I learned about these three theories in another class but only their exact definitions. Here, the portrayal of the way different groups had a distinct response for immigrants gave me a better grasp of interactionist theory. Cultures are either okay with diversity or not. This was seen in the Dutch and the Quakers having a higher tolerance for those in comparison to the English and French who preferred to stay within their own culture."

**—Destiny Rojas**

hiring other workers. Much of the industrial expansion in the nineteenth century, conflict theorists maintain, came at the expense of the immigrant workers who made it possible. The resulting conflict did bring about change eventually, as Irish and Germans organized and gained a greater share of the nation's wealth.

Lieberson's power-differential theory (Chapter 2) seems quite appropriate for the Irish in particular. As unskilled, peasant migrants, the Irish were subordinated to the English Americans. The conflict was sporadic and limited, with the Irish locked into their subservient role until they, too, gained a share of power.

## THE INTERACTIONIST VIEW

Understanding how people perceive and define the strangers in their midst is the basis of interactionist analysis. The Dutch in New Amsterdam and the Quakers in Philadelphia, for example, were receptive to cultural pluralism. As a result, harmonious relations ensued between them and the diverse peoples in their respective colonies. In contrast, the Puritans were intolerant of anyone different, which resulted in the expulsion of such religious dissidents as Roger Williams and his followers. Longstanding violent conflict in Europe between the English and the Irish and between the English and the French partially explains the negative perceptions English Americans had of French Americans and Irish Americans. Cultural prejudices, transmitted from generation to generation, helped foster ethnic antagonism in the United States, often on both sides.

In a country predominantly Protestant throughout its colonial and early national periods, the arrival of large numbers of German and Irish Catholic immigrants disturbed the native population. The Protestants interpreted the presence of these groups as a threat to the "American" way of life, labeling them as inferiors and worse. Note the earlier mentioned use of *hordes* (William Shaw) and *swarm* and *herding* (Benjamin Franklin)—words used frequently by other dominant-group commentators as well. Words are symbols, and here they connote both animalistic qualities and massive numbers, the latter often considered a contaminating menace to society. With this social interpretation of reality, confrontations and conflict were inevitable.

## Retrospect

Structural and cultural differentiation played important roles in determining the nature of intergroup relations among northern and western European immigrants in the United States. Generally, even though the social structure remained in its formative (and thus very fluid) period, the ethnic groups did not experience discrimination or low status for long. Living in relative isolation from European influences and sharing the commonality of forging a new life in the wilderness helped reduce nationalistic biases. Although sporadic flare-ups occurred because of Old World rivalries, the different ethnic groups usually were hospitable to one another, welcoming strangers coming to settle because they themselves would benefit from the community's growth.

As life became more settled, residential patterns more densely clustered, and the social structure more solidified, new arrivals became more conspicuous. Their relative poverty drew even greater attention to their cultural differences. German and Irish immigrants of the nineteenth century, for example, encountered hostility not only because of their religion and culture but also because of their lack of power. Many settled in established areas and so started a new life in a region already dominated by others, who looked on them with scorn. Immigrant subgroups who kept to themselves by settling in rural areas—the Scandinavian, the French, and some German immigrants—fared better than those who tried to settle in already urbanized areas.

Prevailing attitudes were crucial to a minority group's experience. The Dutch and Quakers, tolerant of people who differed from themselves, encouraged religious and cultural diversity within their settlements. Cultural diffusion and assimilation were least likely among the religiously orthodox. This was true not only for the dominant groups in most New England colonies—who expelled or denied welcome to dissenters, Quakers, Catholics, and Jews—but also for minority groups who resisted intermarriage and assimilation, such as the nineteenth-century Dutch, Scandinavians, and Irish.

Cultural diversity was a reality from the outset. Each settlement was an ethnic enclave in which people of similar beliefs and values clustered together and helped one another to adjust in a new land. As the settlements became more populous, growing into towns and cities, the ethnic enclaves formed by newer immigrants became subcommunities within a larger society. Although not as physically isolated as earlier ethnic groups, they were, nonetheless, socially and spatially segregated—often voluntarily—from those unlike themselves.

All immigrants faced varying degrees of hardship in adjusting to the strangeness of a new land and people. To ease that adjustment, they tried to recreate the familiar old country in the new, through their churches, schools, newspapers, and fraternal and mutual-aid societies. These efforts to preserve their language and culture helped them gain a measure of security, but the attempts also often led to suspicion, dissension, and hostility between the dominant and minority cultures.

Discrimination and xenophobia occur especially when the dominant group views the size and influence of the minority group as posing a threat to the stability of the job market, the community, or the nation itself. The nativist movements against the French and the Irish during John Adams's presidency and against the Germans and the Irish during the mid-nineteenth century testify to that pattern. Through legislative efforts and violent actions, the dominant group's members sought to justify their discriminatory behavior as necessary to preserve the nation's character.

For the "old" immigrants, the Civil War brought an end to the difficulties they had encountered because of their background; they now became comrades-in-arms for a common cause. Then, too, a new threat loomed on the horizon, as "new" immigrants—shorter and swarthier, with unfamiliar dress, foods, and customs—began the second great wave of migration to the United States. These new immigrants seemed totally unlike all that U.S. citizens were or "should be." People found a new target for their fears, mistrust, prejudices, and discrimination in these "undesirable" aliens.

The functionalist perspective stresses the young nation's need for newcomers and sees the problems arising from the arrival of large numbers of Irish and German immigrants resulting from the sheer size of the influx, which hampered more rapid absorption. Conflict theorists emphasize English American dominance and the economic exploitation of other nationalities. Interactionists discuss how differing social interpretations of strangers—Dutch toward Puritans, Federalists toward foreigners, Protestants toward Catholics—set the stage for ethnic conflict.

# On MySocLab

 Study and Review on MySocLab

## KEY TERMS

Nativist, p. 120                          Upward mobility, p. 137

## DISCUSSION QUESTIONS

1. The beginning of the chapter offers a sociohistorical perspective. What was one striking or surprising piece of information you picked up here?
2. How is it significant that British Americans comprised 63 percent of the U.S. population at the nation's beginning?
3. What are some examples of cultural pluralism among the Dutch, French, German, and Irish peoples in the United States?
4. What similarities in dominant–minority patterns were shared by most northern and western European immigrants?
5. The end of the chapter offers three theoretical analyses. How did one of these theories become more meaningful or relevant to you in its application to the different groups' experiences?

## INTERNET ACTIVITIES

1. One of the "old" immigrant groups is the Irish but thousands of new Irish immigrants still are coming to the United States. As with virtually all immigrant groups with ethnic organizations to assist them, the Irish also receive a helping hand. If you will click on the Emerald Isle Immigration Center (http://www.eiic.org), you will find one such organization. Explore this site to learn about some of the current activities of this group.
2. *The German Americans: An Ethnic Experience* (http://www.ulib.iupui.edu/kade/adams/toc.html) is a book giving an in-depth portrait of German immigrants adjusting to life in the United States and gradually becoming part of the societal mainstream. Although all 11 chapters are fascinating reading, you might take a look at Chapter 5, which tells of social organizations, festivities, and outsiders' reactions, particularly to Germans frequenting beer gardens.
3. There are many websites about the ethnic Americans discussed in this chapter. Enter "[nationality] Americans" in your favorite search engine to explore what these sites have to offer in further information. If you enter "famous [nationality] Americans," you'll see lists of individuals of that heritage who have made their mark in U.S. society.

# South, Central, and East European Americans

# 6

Listen to Chapter 6 on MySocLab

Polish folk costumes are colorful, as seen at this outdoor folk dance festival at Lincoln Center in New York City. Throughout Canada and the United States, similar annual festivals are held with lively dancing, ethnic crafts and foods to be enjoyed, not just by those celebrating their heritage, but by many outsiders as well.

## LEARNING OBJECTIVES | After reading this chapter you will be able to:

**6-1** Describe the sociohistorical context for studying South, Central, and East Europeans.

**6-2** Describe the immigrant experiences of Slavs, Poles, Russians, and Ukrainians.

**6-3** Describe the immigrant experiences of Hungarians, Italians, Greeks, and Romani.

**6-4** Describe the work experiences of immigrant women in those times.

**6-5** Compare and contrast the assimilation paths followed by these immigrants.

**6-6** Discuss insights gained through sociological analysis.

During the colonial period, immigrants came to the United States from South, Central, and East Europe, as well as from northern and western regions of the continent. Many, in fact, played important roles in the Revolutionary War and during the early years of the new nation. Not until the late nineteenth century, however, did immigrants from this part of the world come in significant numbers. The same economic changes that earlier caused emigration from northern and western Europe (particularly industrialization) spread south and east, creating agrarian difficulties, famine, and unemployment and triggering a major shift in the source of European emigration.

# Sociohistorical Perspective

**6-1** Describe the sociohistorical context for studying South, Central, and East Europeans.

The 1870s saw a dramatic increase in the number of Russians, Italians, and Austro-Hungarians arriving in the United States (see the Appendix). By 1896, a turning point occurred, as immigrants from the rest of Europe outnumbered those from northern and western Europe. Their physical appearance and cultural differentiation easily identified the newcomers as strangers, and they often were broadly categorized as alike despite their many differences as individuals and as separate ethnic groups. They arrived in large enough numbers to be able to preserve their old-country cultures and social boundaries within the new urban subcultural setting, but this circumstance also increased the probability of prejudice and discrimination against them.

## THE PUSH–PULL FACTORS

Helpful to our understanding of why people migrate are **push–pull factors**, those forces that encourage migration from one place to another. "Push" factors are those negative elements (for example, persecution, repression, and hard economic times) that discourage one from remaining in the country of origin, and "pull" factors are positive inducements (for example, family or friends already there, freedom, opportunity, and living standards) that lure people to seek a better life elsewhere.

A number of elements contributed to the great wave of immigration from 1880 to 1920 (Figure 6.1). During that time, U.S. industry grew rapidly, requiring ever larger numbers of workers. Improved transportation—quicker, sturdier steamships with highly competitive rates for steerage ($10 or less per person)—encouraged transoceanic migration.

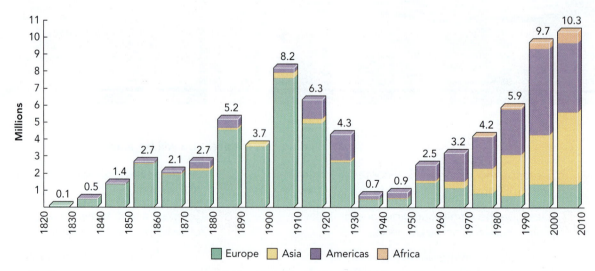

**FIGURE 6.1  Immigration to the U.S. by Region by Decade**

Peasant life especially was harsh in Europe. The ruling classes and local estate farm owners ruthlessly exploited the common people. They crushed most peasant revolts and protests instead of reforming the basic agricultural economy. Peasants saw their sons drafted into the army for periods of 12 to 31 years. Trying to eke out an existence amid poverty, unemployment, sickness, and tyranny, many of Europe's poor looked elsewhere for a better life.

Letters from friends or relatives already in the United States were read eagerly and circulated among villagers. Newspapers, books, pamphlets, transportation advertisements, and labor-recruiting agents all stimulated "America fever." Following a familiar minority pattern of avoidance, Europe's poor and persecuted peoples fled their homelands for the promise of "Golden America."

Political and economic unrest in Europe also encouraged the exodus. Old World governments faced pressures of overpopulation, chronic poverty, the decline of feudalism, dissident factions, and a changing agrarian economy. For them, large-scale emigration to the United States provided a practical means of easing societal pressures without actually addressing the root causes of many institutional problems, so they sponsored emigration drives, further increasing the European migration.

Hundreds of thousands of immigrants thus came to the United States: Italians, Portuguese, Greeks, and Armenians from the southern part of Europe; Hungarians, Poles, Czechs, Slovaks, and others from the central plains; Austrians and Swiss from the high mountain country; Byelorussians, Ukrainians, Ruthenians, and others from the western regions of Czarist Russia; and Jews from all parts of East and Central Europe (Figure 6.2). All these different peoples came, leaving behind their familiar world and seeking a new destiny.

**STUDENTS SPEAK** "The push-pull factors in the sociohistorical perspective were my own reality written down. My parents came because of both factors. Their push factor was hard economic times and the pull factor was opportunity. They came here to make a good living. They worked hard and received little, but they kept going and did not stop. The American Dream was all they heard about back in their country. My parents saw new opportunities and a better living as extremely important, but it was not for them. It was for my sister and me—their children."

**—April Rosas**

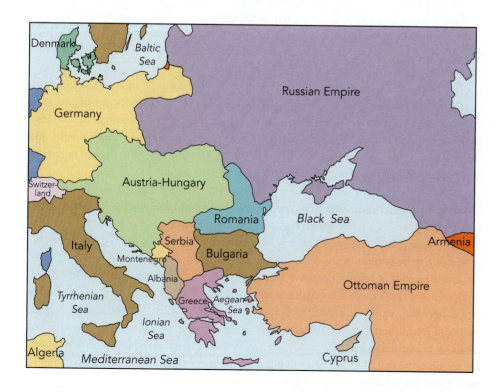

**FIGURE 6.2** Pre–World War I Southern, Central, and Eastern Europe

# the ETHNIC experience

## Immigrant Working Conditions

"Working conditions were terrible, terrible. If you have to sit two–three hours overtime for ten cents, what can I explain you? It don't get worse. But these ten cents I need. Whenever it was overtime, I was the first one to raise my hand."

"The boss watches you. You shouldn't talk to one another. He watches you between lunch and supper, you know. So you want something, you have something in your drawer like candy. He watches. No, no, no, nothing. You can't eat while you're working. So, you watch, you put the candy in your mouth."

"It was so hot in the shop, the sweat was running from the body and from the hand and the material got stained. The boss didn't care, the foreman didn't care. Once, two policemen came in. They stopped the power. They said we couldn't work in such a heat. You haven't even got a fan here to have a little coolness. Nothing! People used to faint. Big people used to faint."

"In winter—it was such a hard winter. When I opened the door in the morning to go to work, I couldn't take away my hand from the knob—the frost. Terrible. Terrible. At work in the big shop in the middle was a stove. It kept us a little warm. But, you know, young people, young blood—we put on a sweater. Yeah, the conditions was terrible. Can't be worse. Can't be worse. It was terrible. And the boss had a fresh mouth always for the workers."

Source: Austrian Jewish immigrant who came to the United States in 1914 at age 17. Taped interview from the collection of Vincent N. Parrillo.

## STRUCTURAL CONDITIONS

The United States that the immigrants came to differed considerably from the land earlier immigrants had found. The frontier was disappearing rapidly; industrialization and urbanization were changing the nation's lifestyle. The immigrants, mostly illiterate, unskilled, rural peasants, were plunged into a new cultural and social environment.

With virtually no resources, many immigrants settled in their ports of entry or in inland cities along railroad lines, such as Chicago. At the turn of the century, living conditions in cities were far worse than they are today. Overcrowding, disease, high mortality rates, crime, filth, and congestion were endemic. Crowded into poorly ventilated tenements and cellars, the immigrants often lived in squalor.

Settling in the oldest city sections, immigrants formed ethnic subcommunities, recreating the nationality quilt of Europe. Although they were neighbors out of necessity, intermarriage and joint organizational activities were rare. To find security in a strange land, they repeated the adjustment patterns of the "old" immigrants. They sought and interacted with their own people, establishing their own churches, schools, and organizations to preserve their traditions and culture.

As unskilled workers, most found employment in the low-status manual-labor jobs in the factories, mines, needle trades, and construction. At that time, workers had no voice in working conditions, for labor unions had not become effective yet. The 84-hour workweek (14 hours a day, six days a week) for low wages was common. Jobs offered no paid vacations, sick pay, or pension plans. Child labor was commonplace, and entire families often worked to provide a subsistence-level family income. Lighting, ventilation, and heating were poor (see the Ethnic Experience box). In the factories, moving parts of machinery were dangerously exposed, leading to numerous horrific accidents. There was no workers' compensation, although many laborers were injured on the job. A worker who objected was likely to be fired and blacklisted. Exploited by the captains of industry, the immigrants became deeply involved in the labor union movement, so much so that to tell the story of one without the other is virtually impossible.

Faced with these adverse circumstances, many immigrants worked hard and made sacrifices. Conditions, though bad, were better than what they had left behind. More important, the United States gave them hope and a promise of better things—if not for themselves, then surely for their children. Some, however, could not adjust to the new work discipline, became disillusioned and depressed, and returned to their native land. Others joined organizations for collective efforts to protect themselves from an uncaring system, while the more radicalized newcomers engaged in confrontational actions to change the system forcibly.

**STUDENTS SPEAK** "I could not believe the working conditions that these immigrants dealt with. It's also sad that I personally know quite a few people working for a specific company today who work similar hours and do not have any paid time off, insurance, or pension plans. It's not fair but sometimes people don't have a choice and just have to deal with it and maybe hopefully someday find something better."

**—Dana Troisi**

## SOCIETAL REACTION

Although the immigrant groups segregated themselves socially from one another, outsiders saw them mainly as unacculturated strangers and tended to lump them together. Italians and Jews stood out from others, though, because of their large numbers, residential clustering, religions, languages, appearance, and cultural practices. Although many viewed all "new" immigrants as undesirable and unassimilable, U.S. society directed the greatest antagonism against the more visible Italians and Jews (see Figure 6.3 and the International Scene box).

**RACISM.** Earlier nativist themes—anti-Catholicism, fear of "foreign radicals," and xenophobia—manifested themselves again with the so-called "new immigrants," but two new elements also emerged: anti-Semitism and actions based on physical features. Now those who had been here longer and possessed blue eyes and lighter complexions and hair claimed biological superiority over the new arrivals with their darker complexions and hair.

Probably the most influential blending of nativist and racist strains of thought during this period occurred in Madison Grant's 1916 book, *The Passing of the Great Race.* Relying on what he considered scientific truth, Grant identified race as the key factor in determining culture and behavior. He argued that interracial births can lead only to a reversion to the "lower type." As his pessimistic title suggests, Grant said the vastly superior native U.S.

**"An Interesting Question"**

*"How long will it be," asked the caption, "before the rats own the garden and the man gets out?" This cartoon shows Uncle Sam asleep in his garden, unaware of the invasion of foreign rats. Their faces are stereotyped depictions of Jews, Russians, Italians, Greeks, and other immigrants from southern and eastern Europe. This cartoon by E. M. Ashe appeared in Life on June 22, 1893. (Courtesy of Library of Congress [LC-USZ62–7386])*

# the INTERNATIONAL scene

## Anti-Immigrant Backlash in Italy

Italy attracts more illegal immigration than other European countries because its long coastline and close proximity to other countries make it especially vulnerable. The most popular clandestine sea routes for Africans are from Libya or Tunisia to the Italian island of Lampedusa (which is closer to Africa than to Italy) or to Sicily (see map in Figure 6.3). A second underground gateway is a 60-mile speedboat ride by smugglers from Albania across the Adriatic Sea. Albanians, Afghans, Kurds, Turks, and Chinese are the most frequent arrivals this way. A third route is by truck across the Slovenian border, across northern Italy, and into Milan.

With a limit of 20,000 to 30,000 legal immigrants per year, and an estimated 2 million others waiting for transit to enter, the "backdoor" of illegal entry became the only viable choice for many. Approximately 4.6 million (7.5 percent) of Italy's 60.6 million people are foreign-born, approximately half of them beneficiaries of a series of amnesties between 1986 and 2009. These amnesties, however, did not solve the problem and instead tended more to attract tens of thousands of new illegal migrants rather than to lower their numbers. Each year, hundreds drown in unsafe, overcrowded boats in attempts to reach Italy.

**FIGURE 6.3  Staging Areas for Illegal Immigration into Italy**

Africans and Asians are visible everywhere, selling cheap merchandise on the streets, trying to clean windshields at intersections, or pumping gas. Native Italians disparagingly refer to the newcomers by the ethnophaulism *vu compra*, which is a slang version of the phrase, *Vuoi comprare* (Do you want to buy?). Impacting Italy's economy is the large underground economy, an estimated 27 percent of Italy's gross domestic product (GDP) that is untaxed and thus a source of lost revenue to the local and central governments.

The arrival of so many physically and culturally distinct newcomers in so short a period created an anti-immigrant backlash, transforming Italy from a relatively open country into a closed one. The nation expelled thousands of illegal aliens and turned back tens of thousands of others at its borders and on the seas. Racial incidents, including firebombings, once commonplace now seldom occur. Even so, the growing backlash led to the formation of the *Lega Nord* (Northern League), an anti-immigration party that received 8.3 percent of the vote in the 2008 general election, forcing the ruling political party to maintain its actions against illegal immigrants. In 2010 voting, two of its leading members were elected heads of the regions of Piedmont and Veneto, capturing a third of the votes.

**CRITICAL THINKING QUESTION**

How and why does the Italian government action against illegal immigrants differ from that of the U.S. government?

Source: Drawn in part from the author's several visits to Italy and in part adapted from various news reports.

stock was disappearing (through "racial suicide") as a result of lower birth rates, which reflected their desire not to sully their racial purity:

> [Native U.S. citizens of colonial stock] will not bring children into the world to compete in the labor market with the Slovak, the Italian, the Syrian, and the Jew. The native American is too proud to mix socially with them and is gradually withdrawing from the scene, abandoning to these aliens the land which he conquered and developed. The man of the old stock is being crowded out of many country districts by these foreigners just as he is today being literally driven off the streets of New York City by the swarms of Polish Jews. These immigrants adopt the language of the native American, they wear his clothes, they steal his name, and they are beginning to take his women, but they seldom adopt his religion or understand his ideals; and while he is being elbowed out of his own home, the American looks calmly abroad and urges on others the suicidal ethics which are exterminating his own race.[1]

Grant's book struck a responsive chord with other writers and with congressional leaders. Popular magazines, such as the *Saturday Evening Post,* quoted and praised Grant. Other "scholars" followed with eugenic explanations purporting to establish a correlation between racial physique and culture:

> Previously vague and romantic notions of Anglo-Saxon peoplehood were combined with general ethnocentrism, rudimentary wisps of genetics, selected tidbits of evolutionary theory, and naive assumptions from an early and a crude imported anthropology…to produce the doctrine that the English, Germans, and others of the "old immigration" constituted a superior race of tall, blonde, blue-eyed "Nordics" or "Aryans." Whereas the peoples of Eastern and Southern Europe made up the darker Alpines or Mediterraneans—both inferior breeds whose presence in America threatened, either by intermixture or supplementation, the traditional American stock and culture.[2]

Soon, however, industrial conflict, World War I, and revolution in Russia changed societal reaction to the new immigrants. Although racist assumptions about them continued, primary concern focused on their rapid assimilation to eliminate any threat they may present to the political order. The Americanization movement, with its focus on national loyalty and stability, sought to erase cultural pluralism, stimulate civic pride and patriotism, and integrate the newcomers into the fabric of U.S. society as quickly as possible.

**AMERICANIZATION.** Without government assistance and with little knowledge of the language or customs, the immigrants were expected to fit into U.S. society quickly. Native U.S. residents expected them to speak only English, strip away their old culture, and avoid ethnic institutions or organizations. These demands often led to ethnic self-hatred or a negative self-image because of the newcomers' ambivalence about assimilation or their inability or slowness to achieve it.

To preserve the stability of the country, many people attempted to hasten the assimilation of the new immigrants already here. They looked on the schools as agents of socialization, a key force in effecting Anglo-conformity. The following 1909 quotation of Ellwood Cubberley (1868–1941), a prominent author and professor of education at Stanford University, reflects prevailing dominant-group attitudes of that period:

> These southern and eastern Europeans are of a very different type from the north Europeans who preceded them. Illiterate, docile, lacking in self-reliance and initiative, and not possessing the Anglo-Teutonic conceptions of law, order, and government, their coming has served to dilute tremendously our national stock, and to corrupt our civic life.[3]

In addition to viewing them as culturally offensive and morally degraded, as did many of his contemporaries, Cubberley also shared in the belief that they negatively impacted on democratic government and public education. Furthermore, because they "tend to settle in groups or settlements, and to set up here their national manners, customs, and observances," he saw the need to break up these groups or settlements through assimilation and for educators to teach "their children, so far as can be done, the Anglo-Saxon conception of righteousness, law and order, and popular government, and to awaken in them a reverence for our democratic institutions."[4]

Children of immigrants felt the marginality conflicts between majority-group expectations and their minority perspective more keenly than their parents. They were truly caught between two worlds. Schools vigorously promoted the shedding of cultural differences as the children grew up in a society contemptuous of foreigners. Wanting to be accepted, many children began to feel self-conscious. Many were even embarrassed to bring friends to their homes, where a foreign language, foreign cooking, and different atmosphere prevailed.

**XENOPHOBIA.** Historians point to the Haymarket Affair as perhaps the single most important factor inciting a xenophobic reaction against all immigrants. In Chicago in May 1886, at the height of a general strike for an eight-hour workday, the strike's anarchist organizers—almost all immigrants—held a rally in Haymarket Square. As nervous police approached the peaceful gathering, someone threw a bomb at them, killing an officer and wounding 70 people. The bomb thrower's identity was never discovered, but the courts sentenced six immigrants and one native-born U.S. citizen to death; another immigrant received a long prison term. Newspapers promoted a negative stereotype of immigrants as troublemakers and national hysteria and fear of anarchy mushroomed, particularly in the large cities of the Northeast and Midwest. Reflecting this public hostility, one editorial writer said,

> These people are not Americans, but the very scum and offal of Europe… long-haired, wild-eyed, bad-smelling, atheistic—reckless foreign wretches, who never did an honest hour's work in their lives…crush such snakes…before they have time to bite.[5]

A magazine writer warned Americans that anarchy was a "blood disease" unknown to the Anglo-Saxons but common to the "darker swarms" from Europe: "I am no race worshipper but…if the master race of this continent is subordinated to or overrun with the communistic and revolutionary races, it will be in grave danger of social disaster."[6]

For a long time after the Haymarket Affair, the words *foreign* and *radical* were linked. Negative stereotyping and nativist movements increased. Calls for restrictions on immigration continued until the Immigration Law of 1921 was passed.

**LEGISLATIVE ACTION.** In 1907, in response to public pressure, a presidential commission comprised of members of the Senate and House investigated the entire immigration situation. The Dillingham Commission (previously discussed in Chapter 1) issued a voluminous report in 1911, concluding that the "new" immigrants tended to congregate, slowing the assimilation process, whereas the "old" immigrants had dispersed immediately on arrival. Moreover, "new" immigrants were less skilled and less educated, had greater criminal tendencies, and were more willing to accept low wages and a low standard of living. As a solution, the commission suggested instituting either a mandatory literacy test for immigrants or tighter immigration restrictions.

Congress's first response, in 1913, was to pass a literacy bill requiring all immigrants over the age of 16 to be able to read some language. President Taft vetoed the bill, however, just as President Cleveland had vetoed a similar proposal in 1896. Finally, in 1917, Congress overrode President Wilson's veto of yet another literacy bill of the same type. This law did little to stem the tide of immigrants, however, for it exempted the many refugees fleeing religious persecution. Meanwhile, the literacy rate in Europe had risen since 1900, so the literacy test was not a serious obstacle for most. Pressures for immigration restrictions mounted because of the continual flow of immigrants from war-ravaged Europe, the fear that such political upheavals as the Bolshevik Revolution would spread to the United States, and the general U.S. mood of isolationism at the close of World War I.

Although President Wilson successfully vetoed a new congressional bill dealing with immigration, it was reintroduced in a special session of Congress and signed by President Harding soon afterward. The National Origins Quota Act of 1921, adopting a proposal that the Dillingham Commission had made a decade earlier, limited the numbers of immigrants. It imposed a quota system, allowing only 3 percent of the number of people of each nationality already in the United States in 1910. The effect of this legislation was to reduce the number of south, central, and east European immigrants from a 780,000 annual average in the years 1910–1914 to approximately 155,000 annually.

When the act expired, it was replaced by the even tougher Johnson–Reed Act of 1924, which reduced each country's annual quota to 2 percent of its emigrants already in the United States as of 1890. This change discriminated even more severely against the "newer" immigrant countries, and the worldwide quota dropped to near 165,000. In 1929, however, the quota of 3 percent was restored, with a total ceiling of 150,000 (see Table 6.1).

Sociologist Henry Pratt Fairchild summed up the ethnocentric attitudes of his time when he said that anything that impairs U.S. leadership threatens the very fabric of society.

Unrestricted immigration was such a force. It was slowly, insidiously, irresistibly eating away at the very heart of the United States. What was being melted in the great Melting Pot, losing all form and symmetry, all beauty and character, all nobility and usefulness, was the American nationality itself.[7]

*"Spoiling the broth!"* ran the caption to this February 1921 cartoon, which could also capture the sentiments of some people today, if "Europe" were changed to "Latin America." The fear of inundation by and nonassimilation of immigrants led to the passage of a quota system in a restrictive immigration law later in 1921.

**TABLE 6.1   Major Immigration Acts**

| | |
|---|---|
| 1875 | First direct federal regulation of immigration, barring criminals, prostitutes, and "coolie" labor. |
| 1882 | Established a system of central control of immigration through state boards under the Secretary of the Treasury. |
| 1882 | Chinese Exclusion Act suspended immigration of Chinese laborers for ten years, extended in 1892 for another ten years, and in 1902 for an indefinite period. |
| 1891 | Established the Bureau of Immigration. |
| 1917 | Further restricted immigration of Asian persons creating the "barred zone" (known as the Asia–Pacific triangle), natives of which were declared inadmissible. |
| 1921 | Limited immigration to 3 percent of foreign-born persons of each nationality living in the United States in 1910. |
| 1924 | Banned Japanese immigration and temporarily set other immigration limits to 2 percent of foreign-born persons of each nationality living in the United States in 1890; in 1929 returned to 3 percent in equal ratio to a total ceiling of 150,000. |
| 1952 | Set an annual quota of one-sixth of 1 percent of ancestry or national origin recorded in 1920, with a minimum quota of 100 and a ceiling of 2,000 for countries in Asia–Pacific triangle. |
| 1965 | Abolished the national-origins quota system; numerical limitations of 120,000 from Western hemisphere and 170,000 from Eastern hemisphere, with a 20,000-per-country limit for the latter only; excluded spouses, children, and parents from numerical restrictions. |
| 1976 | Added a 20,000-per-country limit to the Western hemisphere. |
| 1978 | Combined the separate hemisphere ceilings into one worldwide limit of 290,000. |
| 1986 | Granted amnesty and eligibility for permanent-resident status to undocumented aliens residing in the United States before 1982. |
| 1990 | Set an immigrant ceiling of 700,000 for 1992 through 1994, dropping to 675,000 thereafter. |

*Source:* U.S. Citizenship and Immigration Services, *Immigration Legislation* (Washington, DC: U.S. Government Printing Office, 2007).

Despite an exception to receive approximately 400,000 displaced persons following World War II, the 1929 legislation remained in effect until the McCarran–Walter Act of 1952, which passed over President Truman's veto and simplified the quota formula to one-sixth of 1 percent of the foreign-born population from each country in the 1920 census.

The Immigration and Nationality Act of 1965 ended the proportional-representation quota system. Limits of 120,000 from the Western Hemisphere and 170,000 from the Eastern Hemisphere were set, the numbers based on a complicated preference system stressing job skills and close family kinship. In 1976, a 20,000-per-country annual limit was established, followed in 1978 by replacement of hemisphere quotas with a single worldwide ceiling of 290,000; this number then changed in 1980 to 270,000, excluding refugees. Immediate relatives of immigrants were admitted above the 270,000 limit, however, bringing annual legal immigration totals to more than 500,000 annually in the 1980s. Then, 1990 legislation set a new ceiling of 700,000 through 1994, after which it dropped to 675,000.

The collapse of communism in Europe in 1989 had a major impact on immigration. In the 1990s, hundreds of thousands migrated to the United States from Central and East Europe, most particularly from Poland and the former Soviet Union. Their coming revitalized old ethnic neighborhoods and created new ones, as a once-declining white ethnic presence reasserted itself in many parts of the country.

**STUDENTS SPEAK** "What was really surprising to me was the fact that after being vetoed by three different presidents, the literacy bill was eventually signed by Harding in 1921. But, what really got me was the fact that they were only taking 3 percent of the 1910 census, which meant that there were less immigrants back then, therefore, making the amounts coming in 1921 considerably smaller. I feel bad for the people who tried to come to America but were basically wait-listed until their death. I am thankful that my great-grandmother came to America in 1920, before the bill was passed. Otherwise, who knows how long it would have taken her to come over here and how that could have changed my family's history."

**—Allison Giampapa**

# Slavic Americans

Often included under the general classification "Slavic peoples" are Belarusians, Russians, and Ukrainians (East Slavic); Czechs, Poles, and Slovaks (West Slavic); and Bosnians, Bulgarians, Croatians, Macedonians, Serbs, and Slovenians (South Slavic). Poles, Russians, and Ukrainians came to the United States in much greater numbers than the others during the 1880–1920 mass migration period, and we will discuss them separately. However, U.S. public opinion during this period usually made no distinctions among these groups; and, as a result, their experiences in this country tended to be similar.

**6-2** Describe the immigrant experiences of Slavs, Poles, Russians, and Ukrainians.

## EARLIER IMMIGRANTS

Slavic people had been in the New World since colonial times. New Amsterdam and New Sweden, for example, received Protestant refugees from this region in the seventeenth century, and Moravians (from today's Czech Republic) fled to the Quaker colony of Pennsylvania in the eighteenth century. In the mid-nineteenth century, many Slavic political refugees came to the United States, and almost all of them remained. In the post–Civil War period, Slavic people began coming in steadily increasing numbers, and this influx continued until sharply curtailed by the Immigration Act of 1921.

These "new" immigrants scattered throughout the country, although many concentrated in mining and industrial areas of Pennsylvania and the Midwest. Beginning as unskilled workers, they formed the large majority of the workers in the Chicago slaughterhouses, the coal fields, and the iron and steel factories. By 1917, they outnumbered all other ethnic groups in those places of occupation. The normal pattern was for the males to come first and their families later, if at all. Like many Greek and Italian males, numerous Slavic males came merely as sojourners to earn money for land, dowries, or just a better life, returning to their native land after a year or two. In fact, they accounted for the majority of the more than 2 million aliens who returned from the United States to Europe between 1908 and 1914.

In his book *The Slavic Community on Strike,* Victor R. Greene vividly depicted the immigrant experience in the mining industry. In the following excerpt, he described the anxiety and arrival of a newcomer to the Pennsylvania coal region:

> The typical greenhorn would have alighted from the immigrant train in the Pennsylvania hard-coal region undoubtedly apprehensive if he had not yet met his correspondent. With luck, one or both had a photograph to aid in recognizing the other. Otherwise, the weary traveler at the depot asked or shouted the name of his sponsor. One can imagine the tears of joy on both sides when to the immigrant's call his countryman responded, and their relief was expressed in a demonstrative embrace….
>
> The sponsor then led his charge to a group of shacks usually at the edge of town. This ghetto was separated from the rest of the populace, just as in other places in America where the East Europeans lived…. If he arrived at night, the bundle-laden traveler would have to grope through the darkness, as no street illumination, paved roads, or signs (even if he could have read them) facilitated this last, short trip.[8]

Here, we can visualize the social segregation and the resulting ethnic enclave so common in immigrant groups. Although their languages and customs varied, the Slavic peoples all experienced economic hardship. Children often worked to help the family

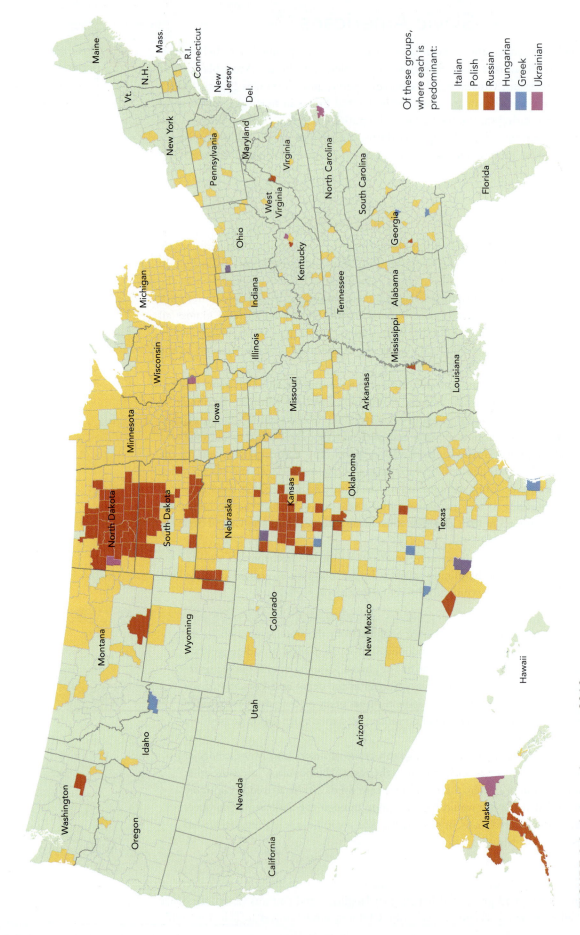

Of these groups,
where each is
predominant:

Italian
Polish
Russian
Hungarian
Greek
Ukrainian

**FIGURE 6.4** Largest Ancestry: 2010

survive, instead of going to school, thus depriving these immigrant youngsters of a "normal" childhood:

> The sight of so many children employed in mining along with their fathers appalled many Americans.... Some child labor reformers announced that they had found boys as young as six working at the mines; nine or ten was probably the actual minimum.... The value placed by Americans on educating the young little interested the Slav, for the valuable child was the working one. Above a minimum education was useless, and the pressing need for income forced sons into the pits at or before their teens.... All of the workers here, men and boys, labored the normal ten-hour, six-day week, when at full time.[9]

A combination of factors—their peasant background, economic deprivation, child labor, and little education—slowed the upward mobility of Slavic Americans. A high proportion of the second and third generation, for example, had lower income and educational levels than did Greek and Jewish Americans through the 1960s.[10] Many Slavic Americans today are middle class and less recognizable as a distinct ethnic subgroup because of high rates of intermarriage.

### RECENT IMMIGRANTS

Slavic migration to the United States has been substantial, boosted in great part by the flight of refugees that added to a normal flow of immigrants. For example, approximately 20,000 refugees came from Nazi-occupied Czechoslovakia, most of them professionals, scholars, and artists. When the communists seized control in the late 1940s, thousands more sought refuge in the United States. Still other Czech refugees were admitted into the United States in 1968 after the Soviet invasion ended their country's brief flirtation with liberalization.

After the breakup of Yugoslavia, the tragic violence that raged in the 1990s among Serbs, Croatians, and Bosnians sparked a large refugee exodus, with more than 137,000 refugees from this strife-torn land fleeing to the United States, although far more of the displaced sought refuge in nearby European countries.

Since 2002, more than 600,000 Slavic immigrants and refugees have settled in the United States. Poland and Russia together account for approximately 40 percent of that total, but Ukrainians, Bosnians, Serbians, and Bulgarians in that order constitute another 50 percent (see Figure 6.4). The Slavic foreign-born presence is greater than many Americans realize. Furthermore, more than 18.8 million Americans claimed Slavic ancestry in 2012.[11]

# Polish Americans

Included among other Slavic groups until 1899, when immigration officials began counting them separately, the Poles constituted the third largest ethnic group of early twentieth-century immigration. With their homeland partitioned among Germany, Russia, and Austria-Hungary, one million Poles came to the United States between 1899 and 1914, fleeing poverty and seeking economic opportunity. In fact, the desire for economic improvement was so common to almost all the new immigrants that the English expression "after bread" is found in the vocabularies of most Central and East Europeans who migrated to the United States.

Nobel Prize–winning Polish writer Henryk Sienkiewicz, who visited the United States from 1876 to 1878, illustrated this point in his classic observation of the difficulties

One store found in any Polish neighborhood is the deli, where customers commonly purchase kielbasy, pierogis, golabki (stuffed cabbage leaves), and paczki (doughnuts). Chicago has been home to the largest Polish-American population in the United States for more than 100 years, and Milwaukee Avenue is the heart of that community.

his people first encountered here. Notice also the traces of ethnocentrism in his observation of Americans:

> Their lot is a severe and terrifying one and whoever would depict it accurately would create an epic of human misery.... Is there anyone whose hand is not against them? Their early history is a tale of misery, loneliness, painful despair and humiliation.... They are primarily peasants and workers who have come in quest of bread. Thus, you will easily understand that in a country inhabited by a people who are not at all sentimental, but rather energetic, industrious, and whose competition it is difficult to survive, the fate of these newcomers, poorly educated, unfamiliar with American conditions, ignorant of the language, uncertain how to proceed, must be truly lamentable.[12]

Elsewhere, Sienkiewicz found vibrant Polish communities in Radom, Illinois; Krakow, Missouri; Polonia, Wisconsin; and Panna Maris, Texas.[13] Buffalo, Detroit, and Milwaukee all also had sizable Polish populations; and Chicago had the largest Polish community.

### CULTURE SHOCK

The effects of culture shock—bewilderment and disorganization, particularly in family life—become apparent in many immigrants' writings and in the records of courts and social-service agencies. One of the early sociological classics, *The Polish Peasant in Europe and America,* by William I. Thomas and Florian Znaniecki, explored this theme and influenced subsequent studies of Polish American life.[14]

Leaving behind a *gemeinschaft* society with behavior regulated by custom and habit, the Polish immigrants continually encountered unsympathetic, even hostile, people whose language and customs they did not comprehend. Thomas and Znaniecki maintained that, even if active demoralization and antisocial behavior did not result, those who made the transition suffered a "partial or general weakening of social interests, a growing narrowness or shallowness of the individual's social life." In fact, many immigrant families found the adjustment too difficult, and so crime, delinquency, divorce, desertion, prostitution, and economic dependence were the by-products of family disorganization. Such tendencies also occurred in other immigrant communities caught in a web of economic and social instability.

## COMMUNITY ORGANIZATION

The values and forms of village life in rural Poland were reintegrated, although not completely, in the U.S. parish structure of the urban Roman Catholic Church. For example, St. Stanislaus Kostka Church in Chicago by 1897 became the world's largest parish with 8,000 families totaling 40,000 people.[15] Similar to other Polish churches, it blended staunch Roman Catholicism, Polish culture, and a full range of social services to help the immigrants become acculturated.

Not all Poles desired assimilation, however, and many wanted the church to reflect Polish culture. Frustrated also by futile attempts to have Polish priests elevated in a church hierarchy dominated by Irish and German prelates, representatives from various "independent" parishes formed the Polish National Catholic Church; Lithuanians formed a similar church. Both church groups used their native languages in the Mass rather than Latin. They added other elements of their culture (patriotic songs and patron saint feast days) to their church activities also.

Between 1895 and 1918, approximately 250,000 Polish Jews—fleeing a rise of anti-Semitism—migrated to the United States, followed by another 150,000 between 1920 and 1936 to escape increasing anti-Semitism in Europe.[16] That flow ended in 1939 when Germany invaded and conquered Poland. Migration resumed with passage of the 1948 Displaced Persons Act after World War II, as many Holocaust survivors sought to begin life anew in America.

Culture also affected Polish attitudes toward U.S. education. Summarizing the numerous scholarly references to this point, Helena Znaniecki Lopata reported,

> The attitudes of the Polish peasants toward education—which defined it as a waste of time at best, and as a dangerous thing undermining the traditional way of life at worst—were transplanted to the American soil. Ideally, the children of Polonia began working at an early age to help the family in its endless struggle for money. The United States Immigration Commission, which undertook an intensive study of immigrants in 17 American cities in 1911, found the children of Poles following this typical educational career: parochial school from the ages of 8 to 12, first communion, public school for two years, and then work.[17]

At that time, the Polish immigrant merely wanted the educational system to provide children with a strict moral upbringing in a well-disciplined atmosphere. A high school diploma then was far less important than a regular paycheck.

The Polish community did not fall into complete family disorganization and demoralization, as predicted by Thomas and Znaniecki. Its immigrant peasant culture was not a rigid set of norms subject to collapse from constant attack; indeed, that culture was as receptive to ethnogenesis as any other ethnic community. Still, Poles formed some of the earliest and strongest ethnic associations, such as the Polish National Alliance.

Several studies conducted in the 1960s showed the rate of Polish upward mobility lagged behind other ethnic groups.[18] Although this was true of the first two generations, changes occurred in the mid-1970s, when older Polish Americans were at the top of the blue-collar world, and most of their offspring were entering the professions and the white-collar world.[19] By 1980, Polish-American high school graduation was higher than all other European American groups.[20]

## POLISH AMERICANS TODAY

Of the 9.6 million Americans claiming Polish ancestry, approximately 80 percent are clustered in nine Northeastern and Midwestern states. Chicago still claims the world's largest concentration of ethnic Poles outside Poland. There and elsewhere, however, traditional inner-city Polish neighborhoods have yielded to other minority groups, as the better educated and more successful Polish Americans have moved to the suburbs. St. Stanislaus Kostka Church, for example, still stands, but the second language of the Mass is no longer Polish but Spanish.

New Polish immigrants still arrive—more than 172,000 in the 1990s and approximately 112,000 between 2002 and 2011. Each year, more than a third of the new arrivals choose the Chicago metropolitan area as their intended settlement area.[21] Their numbers keep Polish ethnic neighborhoods somewhat resilient, but their assimilation occurs with relative ease. Most individuals with Polish ancestry, however, are now third-, fourth-, even fifth-generation Americans. For them, the norm is structural assimilation into the same social networks shared with other European immigrant descendants, and they retain little, if any, of the cultural ethnicity found in earlier generations.

# Russian Americans

The first Russian immigrants were Mennonites, who actually were of German origin and had maintained their German language and German customs within Russian borders for a century. As they became targets of forced assimilation, military conscription, and persecution during the 1870s, they began to leave Russia and emigrate to the Great Plains of North America. Although the Mennonites never were very numerous in the United States—only 30,000 to 40,000 in total by 1900—they made a significant contribution to U.S. agriculture by introducing Turkish wheat, a hard winter wheat that, by the turn of the century, had become the leading first-class wheat product.

Of the more than 3 million Russian immigrants who arrived in the United States between 1881 and 1920, approximately 43 percent were Jewish.[22] In Chapter 12 on religious minorities, we examine the Jewish experience in the United States. This section focuses primarily on the non-Jewish Russian immigrants, who mostly were members of the Russian Orthodox Church.

The peak Russian migration occurred between 1881 and 1914, with poor, illiterate peasants emigrating for economic reasons and others seeking political or religious freedom. Forced to adjust from a rural environment to an industrial one, they joined other immigrants in grueling labor in mines and factories. Severely exploited, they often complained about the harshness of their work situation, became active in the labor movement, and sought to improve their working conditions.

Following the 1917 Bolshevik Revolution, a new type of Russian immigrant sought asylum in the United States. Czarist army officers, landowners, professional people, and political activists all fled from the new regime (see the Ethnic Experience box). Thereafter, Soviet restrictions sharply curtailed Russian emigration, except for those Russians who succeeded in coming to the United States as displaced persons (DPs) after World War II.

## LIFE IN THE UNITED STATES

During the boom immigration period, the transplanted Russian peasants stood at the bottom of the socioeconomic ladder in their newly adopted country. Two excerpts, although referring to Russian immigrants, are excellent illustrations of the recurring pattern of any minority experience. They just as easily could be applied to other groups

# the ETHNIC experience

## Immigrant First Impressions

"The closer we came to the United States the better we felt after being so dizzy and nauseous. The trip took us ten days and we landed in Ellis Island in 1924. We saw a big, big building. It was like an armory and, yes, we went through inspection. Before we went on the boat we went through inspection and the physical, and when we came to Ellis Island it was the same thing. They inspected all the clothing of ours and the physical too. Everything was all right with us. Some people didn't pass the inspection and they had to go back, with their health and all."

"All the immigrants were holding their bundles, the baggage, by them. Also we ate by huge tables and most of the food they served was herring. There were some young immigrant boys and they played the mandolin and I was dancing and I didn't think about anything. We were laughing and dancing. I didn't understand what they were saying but we had a lot of fun. We stayed in Ellis Island three days because we came in on a Friday and on the weekend they didn't let anyone out. So we stayed there three days."

"When my father came in—they told me it's my father, of course, but I didn't know him because I hadn't seen him in ten years—I was thrilled to see him. And, of course, as a young girl, I was very happy and I was giggling a lot and that worried my father because he heard a lot of girls came here in this country and they got in trouble. He asked me, "My dear daughter, why are you giggling so much?" I didn't have an answer for him then. I never saw my father and yet I saw him worry for me and giving me orders what to do, what not to do. It was very strange to me, but we were all very happy to see him and finally he took us on a subway. The subway was very new to me. This I didn't see in Europe."

"Now I see it wasn't such a big palace my father took us in. It was four rooms but everything looked so nice. It was a piece of carpet on the floor with a victrola with the letters, chairs, and a little sofa, and I thought we came into a palace and I used to correspond with my girlfriends overseas and I told them what beautiful things we have. But now when I look back it wasn't really so beautiful."

Source: Russian immigrant who came to the United States in 1923 at age 15. Taped interview from the collection of Vincent N. Parrillo.

who live or have lived in urban slums. In the first, the editor of a religious newspaper tells in 1916 of the toll exacted by long working hours under wretched conditions:

> Each working day shortens the worker's life for a few months, saps the living juice out of him, dries out the heart, dampens the noblest aspirations of the soul; transforms a living man into a sort of machine, embitters the whole life. The ragged soul and body of the worker bring forth to the world half-sick children, paralytic, idiotic—therefore the factory's poison kills not merely the unfortunate workers, but also whole generations.[23]

Closely related to inhumane working conditions were poor living conditions necessitated by low wages. This timeless commentary by a social worker of the same early period analyzes the effects of the urban ghettos' squalor and apathy on the Russian immigrants:

> Parental neglect, congestion of population, dirty milk, indigestible food, uncleaned streets, with the resulting contaminated atmosphere, the prevalence of infectious diseases, multiplied temptations to break the law.... Add a twelve-hour day, and a seven-day week, irregular, casual employment, sub-standard wages, speeding processes which have no regard to human capacities or nervous strains for which the system is unprepared, indecent housing, unsanitary conditions both in home and factory, and we have an explanation amply adequate to account for sub-normal wage earners.[24]

## XENOPHOBIA

Many Russian Americans who had worked hard to achieve some economic security in the United States found themselves jobless and unable to find other work after the Bolshevik Revolution in 1917. Employers, fearful of any threat to capitalism in the United States, fired their Russian workers lest they be Bolsheviks. Most Russian peasant immigrants probably were ignorant of the ideology of Bolshevism or, in the case of second-generation Americans, more attuned to U.S. values and attitudes, but they were nevertheless identified as "Bolsheviks" simply because of their nationality. Some may have been sympathetic to the Bolshevik regime but only because the Bolsheviks had participated in the overthrow of the hated Czarist government. The thought of spreading the Bolshevik Revolution to the United States, where the political, labor, and social conditions were so different, appears to have been in the minds of only a tiny percentage.[25]

Nevertheless, labor unrest and radical agitation during that period caused a strong xenophobic reaction. A. Mitchell Palmer, U.S. Attorney General, stepped into the federal power vacuum caused by the incapacitation of President Wilson. His first target was the Union of Russian Workers, and his men raided 11 of their meeting places in various cities. Approximately one month later, 249 immigrants were deported, many of them forced to leave their wives and children behind in most dire circumstances. The Palmer raids continued with a vast dragnet of East Europeans, primarily Russians:

> Officers burst into homes, meeting places, and pool rooms, as often as not seizing everyone in sight. The victims were loaded into trucks, or sometimes marched through the streets handcuffed and chained to one another, and massed by the hundreds at concentration points, usually police stations…. Many remained in federal custody for a few hours only; some lay in crowded cells for several weeks without a preliminary hearing. For several days in Detroit, eight hundred men were held incommunicado in a windowless corridor, sleeping on the bare stone floor, subsisting on food which their families brought in, and limited to the use of a single drinking fountain and single toilet. Altogether, about three thousand aliens were held for deportation, almost all of them Eastern Europeans.[26]

Home-grown opposition to these illegal actions arose, and many of the immigrants were freed, although more than 500 were deported; expulsion remained an effective weapon of the U.S. government. Eventually, the growing strength of the Congress of Industrial Organizations (CIO) within the labor movement brought immigrant workers a measure of economic security and domestic tranquillity.

## RECENT IMMIGRANTS

Russian immigration dropped sharply while the communists were in power. Altogether, approximately 163,000 new immigrants came to the United States between 1921 and 1990. That number easily was surpassed in the 1990s with the arrival of more than 433,000 Russian immigrants. The numbers are no longer that dramatic, but another 127,000 arrived between 2002 and 2011.[27] As a result, Russian immigrants today are the second-largest foreign-born population in the United States. More than one-half of all Russian Americans live in the New York tri-state area, with other large concentrations in California, Illinois, and Pennsylvania.[28]

One in 12 New York City residents is a Russian American.[29] In a 25-block section of Brooklyn called Brighton Beach, nicknamed "Little Odessa" after the Black Sea port, lives the nation's largest Russian-speaking population concentration, exceeding 50,000. Here the émigrés have settled just outside the central shopping district in regional ethnic neighborhoods. The community is so thoroughly Russian in its sights, sounds, smells, window signs, and spoken language that the outsider can quickly be either charmed or disoriented.

The Brighton Beach section of Brooklyn, New York, is home to over 50,000 Russian immigrants, many of them Jewish. A walk along the streets of this 25-block neighborhood will reveal numerous examples of its ethnicity in signs, cooking aromas, and spoken language. The signs offering customers a variety of ethnic and U.S. foods illustrate one form of ethnogenesis that immigrants typically experience.

Thousands of descendants of Russian immigrants belong to the Russian Orthodox Church, which has 138 parishes in the United States.[30] With more than half of them holding college degrees and working in virtually every profession and occupation, Russian Americans preserve their heritage with history centers, newspapers, publishing houses, and organizations. To illustrate one significant entry of Russian immigrants into the labor force, more than 20,000 Russian-speaking scientists now work in the United States.[31] Also, Russian-speaking software engineers have been responsible for developing 30 percent of Microsoft products.[32]

## Ukrainian Americans

Ever since the first Ukrainian, Ivan Bohdan, sailed with his friend Captain John Smith to the Jamestown colony in 1608, Ukrainians have been coming to the United States. What had been a small, steady stream changed into four large waves of new arrivals, beginning in the 1880s.

### EARLIER IMMIGRANTS

Approximately 700,000 Ukrainians immigrated to the United States by 1914, some of them settling as farmers in the western United States and Canada, but most settling in the urban industrial centers of the Northeast and Midwest, working in factories or coal mines.

> The experience of the first Ukrainian group in America contains some of the basic elements of that of other pioneers on this continent. When they landed in New York, they did not understand a word of English; their colorful attire attracted much attention, and they were regarded as a curiosity. Being unable to get lodgings, they had to leave the city. They walked to Philadelphia, being forced to sleep outdoors because people were afraid to give shelter to such curious strangers....
>
> This group of immigrants arrived in the mining communities during a labor strike. Not understanding the conditions, or probably because of necessity, they

Taste America, *an invitation-only event held under the theme of* E Pluribus Unum, *attracted more than 650 guests, primarily members of both Houses of Congress and their families. Ethnic groups presented their contributions to American history and culture. Ukrainians were one such group, offering food, drinks, and information on the Ukraine.*

went to work as strike-breakers; consequently, they brought upon themselves the hatred of old miners, mostly Irishmen. There were frequent assaults on the strike-breakers which ended in riots. The influx of fresh immigrants tended to keep the wages low, and this prolonged the racial and labor antagonism between the Ukrainian and Irish groups. In connection with this racial animosity, not infrequently, the newcomer became a victim of "accidental" injury in the mine, or even death.[33]

The second wave came in the 1920s. Better educated than their predecessors, these new arrivals also were less isolated. Living together in ethnic communities, they formed parallel social institutions (clubs and other social organizations and newspapers) to keep their own culture and language resilient in their new country.[34]

Sometimes called Carpatho-Russians or Little Russians, and until 1992 simply included as part of Soviet Union immigration and refugee statistics, the Ukrainians are among the nationalities who regained independence following the dissolution of the Soviet Union. They have a language and culture distinct from the Russians and always have maintained their own group identity. The parallel social institutions of Ukrainian Americans not only reflected this fact but became even stronger after World War II to preserve the unity and heritage of U.S.-born generations.

With the 1948 passage of the Displaced Persons Act, allowing homeless people from war-ravaged Europe to enter, the third wave arrived. Under this special legislation and with the assistance of many Ukrainian Americans, approximately 85,000 Ukrainian refugees came to the United States (see the Ethnic Experience box). The new arrivals were even better educated, more politically oriented, and better able to adapt to U.S. life than the older immigrants had been.

## RECENT IMMIGRANTS

Since the creation of the independent Ukraine nation in 1992, its citizens have led all other former Soviet "republics," including Russia, in this still-continuing fourth wave of immigrants to the United States. Between 2002 and 2011, more than 136,000 Ukrainian immigrants and 23,000 refugees arrived, making the Ukraine the largest European supplier of present-day immigrants.[35]

# the ETHNIC experience

## Education In and Out of the Classroom

"My sister and I were sent to a public school in the local town. This experience was devastating to me since I did not know one word of English. The teacher, who seemed like a friendly person, must have tried with much frustration to communicate with me, but I was frustrated too, and so did what most children do under those circumstances—I turned her off and did what my imagination led me to do. I colored, cut, played imaginary games and had an all-around good time till I finally started to put some of the sounds together and began to realize the meaning of a few English words."

"...Because we lived in Maryland, race prejudice was the first unpleasant and embarrassing situation which my family had to encounter. My father was the only white man to work in the fields. During the lunch break he was allowed to come into the farmhouse to eat while the others ate their lunch outside. Soon my father learned that dark-skinned men were not allowed to eat with fair-skinned men. I heard my parents discussing this problem. Since they did not know American history and did not speak English, they had to figure that for some reason the dark people were not liked in this country. We did not even know what they were called except that the farmer sometimes called them 'niggas,' which later I learned was niggers."

"One day the farmer became very angry because he learned that we were entertaining the other farm hands in our home. My mother, being a good neighbor, invited the other workers to our house for supper. We had pirogis and the men drank corn liquor. The Negro families reciprocated and we were invited to their homes. It seemed a very natural thing to do and we could not understand why the farmer became so excited. During our first six months stay in Maryland, our home must have been the first case of integration in the South and we were not even aware of it."

"Although I was only seven years old at the time, my observations of the treatment which the whites inflicted on the blacks had a lasting effect on me. While riding in the all-white school bus, I was shown the shabby school for the 'niggas.' I could not understand why two schools were needed in the first place. While stopping for food in the town, I saw only whites were served in most stores. No matter where I went, the Blacks were excluded.... Looking back, I guess that my education in Maryland did not take place in the segregated public school but on the farm, where I learned more about human behavior than any college course could ever offer."

Source: Ukrainian refugee who came to the United States in 1949 at age 7. Taped interview from the collection of Vincent N. Parrillo.

*A good example of a parallel social institution and keeping traditions alive in the younger generation is the International Hungarian Scouting Association, which has many chapters in the U.S. These young people participate in many events with the American Hungarian Federation, an organization dedicated to uniting the American Hungarian community.*

Many of these recent immigrants migrated to such large cities as New York, Philadelphia, Chicago, Detroit, Los Angeles, San Francisco, and Washington, DC, where they created ethnic neighborhoods, continuing a familiar settlement pattern of other immigrants. Although most Ukrainians are Orthodox Christians or Catholics, many Ukrainian Jews also have migrated since the 1990s, often settling in urban or suburban neighborhoods alongside Russian Jews, with whom they share a similar cultural kinship. Today, approximately 960,000 Americans claim Ukrainian ancestry.[36]

# Hungarian Americans

Describe the immigrant experiences of Hungarians, Italians, Greeks, and Romani.

In the nineteenth century, the Hungarians, or Magyars, were a minority in control of the Kingdom of Hungary. They began a campaign of "Magyarization"—imposing the Magyar language and culture—on all peoples living within their boundaries. As emigration to the United States increased, the Hungarian government financed both Catholic and Protestant churches and various immigrant societies in an unsuccessful effort to maintain its influence over Hungarians living in the United States.

The era of greatest Hungarian immigration to the United States was between 1880 and 1919, when approximately 1.6 million arrived, many from the middle Danube region.[37] As many as half may have returned to their homeland once they had saved enough money.

Like others before and after them, the Hungarians congregated in their own ethnic clusters. Most settled in New Jersey, New York, Ohio, Pennsylvania, Illinois, Indiana, and West Virginia. Cleveland and New York City attracted the greatest concentration of immigrants. By 1920, with more than 76,000 ethnic Hungarian residents, New York City was the third largest Hungarian city in the world.[38] Even now, New York City contains the largest concentration of Americans of Hungarian origin.

In those earlier ethnic communities, the Hungarians established their own institutions and organizations, embodying the same religious division among Catholics, Protestants, and Jews as in their homeland. They established their own social and fraternal organizations to provide benefits to the sick and to pay for funerals. They also founded their own newspapers and nationalistic cultural groups.

## LABOR CONDITIONS

The United States was seeking industrial workers, so the Hungarians forsook farming and worked instead in the mines, steel factories, and other heavy industries. The labor agitation of the late nineteenth century—which often turned violent and bloody—usually included Hungarian as well as Lithuanian and Slavic workers.

> The most violent episode occurred outside of Hazelton, Pennsylvania in 1897. A posse, headed by a sheriff who was a former mine foreman, fired several vollies [sic] into an unarmed group of 150 strikers, mostly Hungarian, who were marching to a nearby town to urge other miners to join the strike. Twenty-one immigrants were killed and another forty wounded. There was general agreement among other mine foremen that there would have been no bloodshed if the strikers had not been foreign-born.[39]

The prominence of Hungarian immigrants in such brawny occupations as mining and steel, as well as in the labor unrest, led to whites using the ethnophaulism *hunky*, an alteration of their proper name, to refer generally to all central European laborers. By the turn of the century, *hunky* had evolved into a universal term for a white roughneck laborer—a redneck—and blacks simply extended it to all whites, using the dialectal pronunciation *honky*. The term *hunky* now has fallen into disuse, but *honky* lingers on as a racial slur.[40]

A sizable number of these turn-of-the-century immigrants originally came as sojourners, but most eventually stayed. Consequently, their becoming U.S. citizens was a slower process. Members of the Hungarian-American community who were naturalized citizens totaled only 15 percent before World War I, 21.1 percent by 1920, and 55.7 percent by 1930.[41]

### RECENT IMMIGRANTS

In the mid-1950s, an entirely different group of Hungarians came to the United States for political rather than economic reasons. When the Soviet Union crushed the Hungarian rebellion in 1956, Congress passed special legislation to circumvent the restrictive national quotas of the McCarran–Walter Bill of 1952. The United States airlifted refugees—families, minors unaccompanied by parents, and students—and gave them temporary shelter at Camp Kilmer, New Jersey. Many volunteer agencies and Hungarian Americans then assisted the 30,000 newcomers (known today as the "Fifty-Sixers") in their relocation and readjustment.

About 15,000 Hungarians have come to the United States since 2000, averaging 1,100 each year.[42] The Census Bureau reports that more than 1.5 million Americans claim Hungarian ancestry.[43] Most are American-born and tend to view their ethnicity as their heritage, not their everyday reality.[44] Although active in a wider nonethnic social network, they also participate freely in ethnic activities within their community. Even so, the low birth rate in Hungary and low migration numbers to the United States suggest a future decline of Hungarian-American communities.

# Italian Americans

The first Italians to come to the New World included some important early explorers. Cristoforo Colombo (Columbus), Giovanni Cabotto (John Cabot), Amerigo Vespucci, and Giovanni de Verrazano all explored and charted the new land. Father Marcos da Nizza explored Arizona in 1539, and other Italians were among the settlers throughout the colonies. Filippo Mazzei influenced the writings and even farming of his neighbor, Thomas Jefferson. Many Italians fought in the American Revolution, the Civil War, and the other wars that followed. Antonio Meucci invented the first primitive version of the telephone 26 years before Alexander Graham Bell, and Constantino Brumidi painted the frescoes in the rotunda of the U.S. Capitol building.

Throughout the nineteenth century, parallels and relationships existed between Italians and blacks. In some pre–Civil War southern localities, futile efforts were made to replace black slaves with Italian workers. In other areas, Southerners barred Italian children from white schools because of their dark complexions. Union General Edward Ferraro commanded an all-black combat division during the Civil War. In 1899, five Sicilian storekeepers were hanged in Tallulah, Louisiana, for the crime of treating black customers the same as whites.

### THE GREAT MIGRATION

Of the nearly 5.5 million Italians who have come to the United States throughout its history, 80 percent came between 1880 and 1920 (see the Ethnic Experience box). Many Italian males engaged in "shuttle migration," going back and forth between the United States and Italy. Fleeing abject poverty and economic disaster in the harsh *Mezzogiorno* east and south of Rome, their rapid and pronounced visibility led to vicious anti-Italian bigotry.

Most Italian immigrants were peasants from rural areas and thus ill prepared for employment in an industrial nation. As a result, they labored in low-status, low-paying

# the ETHNIC experience

## Bewilderment and Adjustment

"We came here on a large ship in 1910. We had a rough time coming here with storms and all, and my big sister was deadly sick. She never lifted her head up from her berth. It was a very long trip, about thirteen days, and the waters were rough. And when we got to Ellis Island, we were so happy to get out of that ship."

"When we got there my daddy was waiting for us and we got some nice gifts from the attendants in Ellis Island—who got a doll, who got a jumping jack. But the funniest part was when they were selling bananas in the room, and my brother thought they were peppers and he wanted a pepper and discovered they were bananas."

"When my father took us down to the street, we heard a different language. We looked at each other. We went to my mother. We didn't know what they were saying, maybe they were talking about us. My father said, 'Don't worry. That's the language they speak here and you'll learn it yourself very fast.'"

"Then my dad took us on a train to Old Forge, Pennsylvania, where he had rented rooms for us and we lived there six months. They were mostly all Polish people and German, and my mother didn't feel at home with no Italians around. My mother wanted to move to Paterson, New Jersey, because there were more Italian

people there, but here she didn't understand anybody. And that's what we did. There were all Italians on the street where we lived. My dad was a musician but the other Italian immigrants worked on the trolley tracks, digging trolley tracks or to make streets."

"I got in right away with all the kids. They were all very friendly with me. As soon as recess used to come, they used to be in a playground. They would all come around me and they would talk to me in English, which helped me pick it up right away."

Source: Italian immigrant who came to the United States in 1910 at age 8. Taped interview from the collection of Vincent N. Parrillo.

manual jobs in factories or as railroad laborers, miners, and longshoremen; in construction, they dug ditches, laid sewer pipes, and built roads, subways, and other basic structures in urban areas.

## SOCIETAL HOSTILITY

Strong hostility against Italian immigrants sometimes resulted in violence and even killings. Several Italians were lynched in West Virginia in 1891. That same year, when 10 Sicilians were acquitted by a jury of killing the New Orleans police chief, an angry mob that included many of the city's leading citizens stormed the prison and executed them, adding an 11th victim who had been serving a minor sentence for a petty crime. Four years later, coal miners and other residents of a southern Colorado town murdered six Italians. In 1896, three Italians were torn from a jail in Hahnsville, Louisiana, and hanged. In a southern Illinois mining town, after a street brawl in 1914 that left one Italian and two native-born U.S. citizens dead, a lynch mob hanged the only survivor, an Italian, seemingly with the approval of the town's mayor. A few months later, another Italian was lynched in a nearby town after being arrested on suspicion of conspiracy to murder a mining supervisor. No evidence to substantiate the charge existed, other than his nationality.

In Massachusetts, Nicola Sacco and Bartolomeo Vanzetti—an immigrant shoe-factory worker and a poor fish peddler—were charged with and convicted of robbery and murder in 1920. The prosecutor insulted immigrant Italian defense witnesses and appealed to the prejudices of a bigoted judge and jury. Despite someone else's later confession and other potentially exonerating evidence, their seven-year appeals fight failed to win them retrial or acquittal; they were executed in 1927. At his sentencing in 1927, Vanzetti addressed presiding Judge Webster Thayer, saying,

> I would not wish to a dog or to a snake, to the most low and misfortunate creature of the earth—I would not wish to any of them what I have had to suffer for the things that I am not guilty of.... I have suffered because I was an Italian, and indeed I am an Italian.[45]

These incidents are extreme examples of U.S. reaction to the Italian immigrants. Because they arrived in large numbers, the public became increasingly aware of their presence, and Italian Americans quickly became stereotyped as possessing all the objectionable traits the dominant group perceived in the "swarm" of immigrants then coming to the United States. When an Italian got into trouble, newspaper headlines often magnified the event and stressed the offender's nationality.[46] Italians, like Jews, found certain occupations, fraternities, clubs, and organizations closed to them, and restrictive covenants among property owners excluded them from certain areas of the city and suburbs.

## SOCIAL PATTERNS

The Italians settled mainly in urban "Little Italys"—such as the North End of Boston, Mulberry Street in New York City's Lower East Side, the area to the northwest of Chicago's Loop, and San Francisco's North Beach district.[47] Often, families from the same village lived together in the same tenement. Earning poor wages as part of the unskilled labor force, the new Italian immigrants moved into rundown residential areas vacated by earlier arrivals whose children and grandchildren had moved up the socioeconomic ladder. Their numbers enabled them to create an Italian community abounding with Italian stores, newspapers, theaters, social clubs, parishes, and schools. Because of their regional and family orientations, however, they at first failed to establish a national social identity.

A variant of the extended-family system of southern Italian society was adapted to Italian life in the United States. Relatives were the principal focus of social life, and non-Italians usually were regarded as outsiders. True interethnic friendships rarely developed.

San Francisco's North Beach neighborhood—adjacent to Fisherman's Wharf and once actually a beach before landfill occurred in the late nineteenth century—still retains much of its Italian presence despite the influx of many non-Italian people and businesses. It attracts locals and tourists to its cafes, restaurants, and Italian specialty stores.

Moreover, individual achievement (a U.S. tradition) was not strongly encouraged. More important were family honor, group stability, social cohesion, and cooperation. Each member of the family was expected to contribute to the economic well-being of the family unit.

In the old country, absentee landowners commonly had exploited Italian tenant farmers, and priests and educators silently had supported this inequitable system, rarely welcoming peasant children in the schools. Landowner resistance to the political unification of Italy, which finally occurred in 1870, further increased the hardships of tenant farmers and small landholders. Consequently, Italian immigrants generally mistrusted priests and educated people.[48] In the United States, as in Italy, the working class—especially males—had little involvement with the church, and schooling was regarded as having limited practical value. Children attended school, for the most part, only as long as the law demanded; then they were sent to work to increase the family income. A few families did not follow this pattern, but most second-generation Italian Americans who attended college did so against the wishes of their families. As sociologist Herbert Gans explained:

> Situated on the lowest rung of the occupational hierarchy, they were exploited by their employers and by the "padrone," the agent who acted as middleman between the immigrants and the labor market. Moreover, the churches in the immigrant neighborhoods were staffed largely by Irish priests, who practiced a strange and harsh form of Catholicism, and had little sympathy for the Madonna and the local saints that the Italians respected. The caretaking agencies and the political machines were run by Yankees and other ethnic groups. As a result of the surrounding strangeness, the immigrants tried to retain the self-sufficiency of the family circle as much as they could. They founded a number of community organizations that supported this circle, and kept away from the outside world whenever possible.[49]

## MARGINALITY

First-generation Italian Americans, because so many of their compatriots lived and worked nearby, retained much of their language and customs. The second generation became more Americanized, producing a strain between the two generations. Italians who did not settle or remain long in the Little Italys assimilated much more quickly. Some changed their names and religion to accelerate the process.

In his classic study, *Street Corner Society,* William Foote Whyte commented on the problems of marginality experienced by Italian American young men:

> Some ask, "Why can't those people stop being Italians and become Americans like the rest of us?" The answer is that they are blocked in two ways: by their own organized society and by the outside world. Cornerville people want to be good American citizens. I have never heard such moving expressions of love for this country as I have heard in Cornerville. Nevertheless, an organized way of life cannot be changed overnight. As the study of the corner gang shows, people became dependent upon certain routines of action. If they broke away abruptly from these routines, they would feel themselves disloyal and would be left helpless, without support. And, if a man wants to forget that he is an Italian, the society around him does not let him forget it. He is marked as an inferior person—like all other Italians. To bolster his own self-respect, he must tell himself and tell others that the Italians are a great people, that their culture is second to none, and that their great men are unsurpassed.[50]

## SOCIAL MOBILITY

Upward mobility occurred more slowly for the Italians than for other groups arriving in the United States at approximately the same time, such as the Greeks, Armenians, and Jews. Many factors we already have discussed contributed to this situation—a retreatist lifestyle, disdain for education, negative stereotyping, and societal hostility protracted by the continuing flow of new Italian immigrants. Sheltered within their urban ethnic communities, the Italians gradually adapted to industrial society. They joined the working class and encouraged their children to do likewise as soon as they were able.

Second-generation adults, although drawn to *la via nuova*—"the new way"—through schools, movies, and other cultural influences, still adhered to a social structure centered on the extended family. Expected to contribute to the family's support early in life, they followed their parents into working-class occupations without benefit of the extended education necessary to secure higher-status jobs. Today, though, the picture has changed. Considered to be an ethnic group in poor circumstances in the 1930s, by the 1970s, Italian Americans had entered the economic mainstream.[51]

## ITALIAN AMERICANS TODAY

Although scattered throughout all 50 states, the states with the highest percentages of Italian Americans today are all in the Northeast: Rhode Island (19.3 percent); Connecticut (18.7); New Jersey (17.0); Massachusetts and New York (13.6); and Pennsylvania (12.1).[52]

Since 2002, nearly 28,000 new Italian immigrants have arrived. Today, more than 17.2 million people claim Italian ancestry, almost 6 percent of the total U.S. population.[53] Although most are native-born Americans, approximately 800,000 speak Italian daily, making it the eighth most commonly spoken language at home other than English (behind Spanish, Chinese, French, Vietnamese, German, Korean, and Tagalog, spoken by Filipinos).[54] Most third- and fourth-generation Italian Americans, however, do not speak the language of their forebears (your author is one of them).

Intermarriage, or marital assimilation, is a primary indicator of structural assimilation, the last phase of minority-group mainstreaming. Exogamy among Italian Americans, especially among those three and four generations removed from the old country, exceeds 40 percent, which is similar to that of most European American groups.[55] As structural assimilation proceeds, Richard D. Alba suggests, all Americans of European ancestry have entered "the twilight of ethnicity." Twilight, says Alba, is an appropriate metaphor because ethnic community remnants and differences still remain, with occasional flare-ups of ethnic feelings and conflicts. Even so, this ethnicity is "little more than flickers in the fading light" as social assimilation increases.[56]

Despite their assimilation and upward mobility, Italian Americans still find themselves unfairly linked to criminal activities, even though the U.S. Department of Justice estimates that less than .0025 percent of all Americans of Italian descent are involved in organized crime.[57] Nevertheless, films, television shows, and commercials continue to perpetuate this stereotype.[58] The reality is that Italian Americans now are attaining educational levels comparable to those of other white ethnic groups and are mostly middle class. Approximately two-thirds in the labor force are in such white-collar jobs as executives, physicians, teachers, attorneys, and administrators.

# Greek Americans

Most of the Greeks who came to the United States in the early twentieth century did not expect to stay long. Approximately 90 percent were male, far more than from other European countries at the time. They came as sojourners, planning to make money and then return to Greece. For many, the dowry system was an important "push" factor.

Fathers and brothers found they could earn more money in the United States than in their homeland, so these Greek men journeyed here to earn the money necessary to provide substantial dowries for the prospective brides in their families. The fact that so many Greek immigrants were male encouraged them to return home to their women.

## OCCUPATIONAL DISTRIBUTION

Many Greeks worked as laborers on railroad construction gangs or in factories. They were often under the control of a *padrone,* who, like the Italian *padroni,* acted as a labor agent and paternal figure. Abuses were common in this system. Other Greek immigrants operated small businesses of many types, although Greeks came to be identified particularly with candy stores, diners, and restaurants:

> The association of Greeks with candy and food was proverbial. Chicago became the center of their sweets trade, and in 1904, a Greek newspaperman observed that "Practically every busy corner in Chicago is occupied by a Greek candy store." After World War II, the Greeks still maintained 350 to 450 confectionary shops and eight to ten candy manufacturers in the Windy City. Most Americans still connect the Greeks with restaurants and for good reason. Almost every major American city boasts of its fine Greek eating establishments, a tradition that goes back more than half a century. After World War I, for example, estimates were that the Greeks owned 564 restaurants in San Francisco alone.[59]

For many Greeks, the restaurant provided a relatively stable economic base and higher social status. Restaurant owners enjoyed more esteem than peddlers or manual laborers. Because so many immigrants sought a career in the restaurant business (and still do), they continuously interacted with the general public. A 1901 government survey showed Greeks faring better than Poles, and by 1972, cities such as Boston were reporting no Greeks unemployed or on welfare, and with a higher-than-average income.[60]

## SOCIAL PATTERNS

Although they came from a predominantly agricultural country, Greeks settled primarily in the cities. Like so many other ethnic groups, they gathered in ethnic residential enclaves, or "Greek colonies," within the major cities. A *kinotis,* or community council, served as the governing body; it was responsible for establishing and staffing schools and churches and for promoting the general welfare of the community. The *kafeneion,* or coffeehouse, played a very important role:

> It was to the coffeehouse that the immigrant hurried after his arrival from Greece or from a neighboring community. It was in the coffeehouse that he sought out acquaintances, addresses, leads to jobs, and solace during the lonely hours....
>
> The coffeehouse was a community social center to which the men returned after working hours and on Saturdays and Sundays. Here they sipped cups of thick, black Turkish coffee, lazily drew on narghiles, played cards, or engaged in animated political discussion. Here congregated gesticulating Greeks of all kinds: railroad workers, factory hands, shopkeepers, professional men, the unemployed, labor agitators, amateur philosophers, community gossips, card-sharks, and amused spectators.[61]

Favorable working conditions induced many Greek males to remain in the United States. But because they preferred endogamous marriage, they often returned home to marry a Greek woman, or they sent money home to pay for the passage of a wife or wife-to-be. Like other immigrant peoples of this period, the Greeks maintained close family ties. The father was the unchallenged head of the household. Children were raised to be strictly obedient and had specific chores assigned to them. They studied Greek in addition to their regular classes at public schools and frequently were admonished to work hard and take advantage of the opportunities their parents had not had. Greeks placed a high value on education and encouraged their children to enter the professions.

The Greek church—the Eastern Orthodox Church—and the Greek press bolstered Greek American solidarity. In addition, many organizations encouraged cohesiveness. The most notable of these was the still-functioning American Hellenic Educational Progressive Association (AHEPA), founded in 1922. Its purpose then was to preserve the Greek heritage and to help immigrants understand the new country's way of life.

## SOCIETAL REACTION

Not all early Greek immigrants adjusted smoothly to U.S. society. Many young males, unencumbered by family discipline and village controls, got into trouble. Henry Pratt Fairchild, a prominent sociologist in those years, especially was concerned about the overrepresentation of Greek immigrants among law violators. He was pessimistic about their assimilating or even being a benefit to U.S. society, and his underlying ideas contain elements of the culture-of-poverty thesis developed in the 1960s with respect to Puerto Ricans, Mexicans, and blacks. Fairchild stated that the negative values in the Greek community would remain until elimination of their ethnic neighborhoods, forcing them to intermingle with members of the better (for example, middle) class:

> This lack of reverence for law, and every form of authority, seems to be characteristic of every race. But the Greeks appear to have it when they come. What the character of their children will be in this respect, we can only conjecture.... It has been frequently remarked in the course of the preceding discussion, that the evil tendencies of Greek life in this country manifest themselves most fully when the immigrants are collected into compact, isolated, distinctively Greek colonies, and that when the Greek is separated from the group and thrown into relations with Americans of the better class, he develops and displays many admirable qualities.[62]

Such views may surprise contemporary readers, who usually view Greek Americans as a model of a nationality group accepted by the dominant group: one that has achieved economic security, become assimilated, yet also retains a strong pride in its ethnicity.

## GREEK AMERICANS TODAY

More than 1.3 million Americans claim Greek ancestry, and their greatest numbers are in New York, California, Illinois, Massachusetts, Florida, New Jersey, Pennsylvania, Ohio, Michigan, and Texas.[63] Like most other European countries, Greece has a low birth rate and projected population decline in this century. And, similar to other European countries, it now sends fewer new immigrants (less than 1,000 each year) to the United States.[64] With few new arrivals to revitalize ethnic communities, a lessening ethnicity and culture is likely.

Until now, Greek Americans blended aspects of pluralism (fierce love of homeland, pride in their heritage, slowness to become citizens, endogamy, and institutional agencies) with aspects of assimilation (geographic and occupational dispersion, low visibility, and relatively high socioeconomic status). Cultural pluralism has been an important element in their adaptation to U.S. society, with the Greek language and culture preserved through the Greek Orthodox Church.

The Greek American community so far has retained much of its ethnic vitality. Its church and festivals provide continuing sources of ethnic pride and identity. Greek coffee shops, benefiting from the recent popularity of espresso bars, prosper, as do Greek restaurants, in many U.S. cities. Still, the demographic realities already have led to a division in the Greek-American community between those who treat their heritage only symbolically and those who wish to preserve their culture more fully.

# Romani Americans

The U.S. Roma, often negatively stereotyped in the United States and Europe and derogatively called "Gypsies," are perhaps the most elusive U.S. minority. They number up to one million, according to the Census Bureau, although that is only an estimate.[65] Several factors account for this: census and immigration authorities never have kept official statistics on them; the Roma also actively discourage any form of "snooping"; and often they do not reveal their ethnicity to outsiders.

Who are they? Their major distinguishing characteristics are language and culture. Although they trace their origins to East and Central Europe since the Middle Ages, they speak Romani, a form of Sanskrit, which has enabled researchers to trace their roots to northern India.[66] Romani culture distinguishes between the *Rom* and the *gadje* (outsiders). Words that distinguish between ingroup and outgroup in this way are quite common in tribal societies. When individual Roma assimilate into the dominant culture, the Roma no longer consider them part of their group. Thus, we must view the Roma as a persistent subculture maintaining a unique cultural system.

Sent as slaves to the Americas as early as the fifteenth century on the third journey of Columbus in 1498, Spain shipped even more to its eighteenth-century colony in Louisiana, where an Afro-Romani community of the descendants of intermarriage from the two enslaved peoples still live. Beginning in the second half of the seventeenth century and into the eighteenth century, Romani slaves from England and Scotland came to work on Virginia plantations. Records indicate that free Roma settled among the Germans in Pennsylvania, and the Dutch in New Amsterdam. Repressive actions against them in England in the 1840s prompted migration to the United States in substantial numbers.[67] The Nazis perhaps exterminated as many as 700,000 Roma, and they generally remained unwelcome throughout Europe after World War II. Many legal and illegal Roma immigrants undoubtedly came to the United States during the postwar period. Our only evidence for this, however, is their increased visibility at that time.

## CULTURAL DIFFERENTIATION

At the core of Roma culture is the family (the *familia*), which actually is a functional **extended family**. Parents, siblings, aunts, uncles, cousins, assorted other relatives, and adopted children all live and work together, caring for one another in times of joy and sorrow. The *familia* is an effective support institution for all problems, offering also a safe refuge from the *gadje*. The second unit of identity for the *Rom* is the *vitsa*, a clan or band of a few to more than a hundred *familiyi*, forming a cognitive kinship group of affiliation through which the Roma classify one another.[68]

The *familia* is strongly patriarchal, with males working for short spans of time in various trades: roofing, driveway blacktopping, auto-body repair, scrap metal, and carnival work. Women provide a valuable source of income, usually from fortune-telling, which the Roma practice only with the *gadje,* not among themselves. Parents do not force matches but are the principals in the mate-selection process, encouraging marriages within the *vitsa* beyond first-cousin relationships. A bride price, or *daro,* goes toward the bride's trousseau, wedding festivities, and household articles for the new couple.[69]

Most Roma marry between the ages of 12 and 16, seldom over 18, for a first marriage—their youthfulness perhaps contributing to the high rate of failed Roma marriages. The wife traditionally lives with her husband's family and is known as a *bori,* subject to the supervision of her in-laws. Elopements have increased and romantic love is more accepted preceding still-arranged marriages, but *Rom–gadje* intermarriages are discouraged and considered socially inferior.[70]

Romani culture, which has some differences among the three main subgroups (Vlax, Bashaldé, and Romanichals), has as its linchpin the concept of *marimé,* which extends to all areas of life. The term, which means "defilement" or "pollution," refers to rigid lines between good and bad, clean and unclean, health and disease, *Rom* and *gadje.*

Most notable is its application to the upper and lower halves of the human body. The pure and clean upper portion cannot come into contact in any way with the lower portion, which is *marimé,* or with objects that have been in contact with it. For example, each person uses soaps and towels of different colors for the two body portions. A woman brings shame on herself for exposing too much leg, but breasts unashamedly are squeezed by both men and women. A *marimé* woman—one who has recently given birth or is having her monthly period—cannot cook or serve food to men, step over anything belonging to a man, or allow her skirts to touch his things. Because the *gadje* wash face towels and tablecloths with underwear, relax with their feet on the table, and otherwise do not protect the upper half of the body, the Roma see them as defiled all over, from head to foot.[71]

Romani sexual mores concerning intimacy are very strict, an outgrowth of their normally confined living arrangements and their social structure. Premarital chastity remains highly regarded, and Romani women rarely resort to prostitution. Birth control and abortions are rare, so their high birth rate continues to increase their U.S. population size.[72] The safety valve within the social organization is the *kris,* or tribunal. Through an effective grapevine, the Roma send word to the different tribes of the time and place of the *kris.* Much like Native American chieftains at a powwow, the tribal leaders confer, settle disputes, and place restraints on more powerful members. The most potent social sanction is shunning—no longer acknowledging someone as a *Rom.* Because they spend virtually all their waking moments in group activities with other *Rom,* shunning is a feared social death that keeps the Rom effectively in line.[73] The *kris* operates with ceremonial dignity; it forms the social cement that binds their society together. Once the tribunal matters are concluded, the *kris* becomes an occasion for general feasting, renewal of friendships, bartering, and bridal matchups because such large gatherings are infrequent.

### EVASIVE PLURALISM

Although the Roma living in all 50 states have a home base—notably in Texas, California, and the Midwest—they maintain a fondness for travel. This mobility orientation rests partly on their association of travel with freedom, health, and good luck and of settling down with illness and bad luck. Job opportunities, social visits, and evasion of *gadje* authorities are other motives. Part of their avoidance pattern includes posing as Native Americans, Hispanics, or southern Europeans to obtain jobs, housing, and welfare. They are so successful in doing so that many Americans are unaware that there are any Roma in the United States at all.[74]

The Roma have kept their tribal codes and morals virtually unchanged in an urbanized and industrialized society by remaining outside the educational institutions and being passively antagonistic to the larger society. Although they are highly conscious of ritual, they survive through adaptation to their environment. Despite enormous pressure from every society in which the Roma have lived, they have retained their identity and resisted assimilation.

# Immigrant Women and Work

**6-4** Describe the work experiences of immigrant women in those times.

Within the immigrant communities, gender played an important role in the organization of economic activities. Although men sought employment in a variety of occupations, cultural norms dictated that married women should not work outside the home. Indeed, less than 5 percent did so in 1890, often only because their husbands were disabled, missing, or unemployed. Typically, the wife's role was to maintain the house. If family needs required her income because the children were too young to work, then she would take on work at home (for example, laundry, sewing, or crafts) or else care for boarders (a common practice given the high number of male immigrants).[75]

*Greek coffeehouses were an important social gathering place for Greek male sojourners in the early twentieth century. This 1919 scene on Washington Street, New York City shows the immigrants drinking coffee, playing an outi (lyre), or smoking tobacco through a hookah.*

The world of work for women thus fell mostly to the young and single. More than half of all gainfully employed women at the turn of the century were between 16 and 24 years old. These young women often were employed in factories or mills in "suitable" positions such as machine tenders or seamstresses, perhaps, or as assemblers, inspectors, packers, and the like in various types of garment, textile, tobacco, or other manufacturing plants.[76]

Approximately a third of all employed female workers at this time were blue-collar workers. Another third were domestic workers: maids, cooks, nannies, and so on. The final third of female workers usually were not first-generation Americans. Employed women in this category were in such white-collar positions as nurse, teacher, or salesclerk.[77]

An expanding economy and population and the institution of child labor laws (not applicable to agriculture) brought about an increase in jobs for women. Included in the significant rise of female participation in the nonfarm labor force were married women as well. By 1920, 1 in 5 paid workers was a woman, and 1 in 10 married women (twice that of 1890) had become a wage earner.[78]

# Assimilation

With so massive and complex a migration and settlement pattern, no general assessment of acculturation and assessment is possible for the many ethnic groups from South, Central, and East Europe. Strikingly different in appearance, culture, customs, language, and often religion, societal reaction (often negative, sometimes exploitive) was more uniform to their presence than was their adjustment to the new society. At first, most experienced the social isolation and social distance that newcomers typically do, but these also were accompanied this time by racism, as illustrated in Madison Grant's book discussed earlier in this chapter. Whether in rural or urban locales, most remained socially segregated in flourishing ethnic communities with a strong social network and where endogamy was the norm.

For many immigrants, the transition from an agrarian to an industrial society was difficult. Those who came from an urban background or had to adapt as a subordinate minority group in Europe, such as the Jews and Armenians, adjusted to city life more easily. They took advantage of educational opportunities, climbed the socioeconomic ladder when possible, and adapted to U.S. society. Others, consisting predominantly of illiterate peasants, took longer to get established. Not all the immigrants became citizens, and not all were successful; some did not even learn English.

Although educational values and opportunities aided the assimilation of Armenians, Greeks, and Jews, other groups from this part of Europe took one or two generations longer to enter the mainstream. The labor movement, filled with sacrifice and turmoil, was a significant factor in their achieving economic security, which in turn led to better education for the children and eventual entry into the mainstream. Still, by 1971, their assimilation was far from complete, leading social critic Michael Novak to call this group of Europeans the "unmeltable ethnics."[79]

Yet throughout the generations, even as they shed their ethnolinguistic marks that distinguished these white ethnics from other white Americans, those who were Catholics and Jews still encountered prejudice because of their faiths. Their continuance as the target for ethnophaulisms, ethnic "humor," and stereotyping is an unfortunate legacy from those intolerant times. Interestingly, just as their cultural and physical differences aided the social acceptance of northern and western Europeans in earlier times, so too are the cultural and physical differences of the majority of today's immigrants enhancing the social acceptance of those whose heritage is from South, Central, or East Europe (see the Reality Check box).

Except for Slavic immigrants—including Russian, Ukrainian, and Polish—the significant decline in arrivals from other parts of Europe (prompted in large measure by low

**6-5** Compare and contrast the assimilation paths followed by these immigrants.

# REALITY check

### Places and Politics: A Geo-Political Profile

Still arriving from South, Central, and East Europe are thousands of new immigrants, but any discussion of these nationality groups today lies in the much greater numbers of descendants of the earlier immigrants. Like the other European immigrants discussed in Chapter 5, these immigrants once clustered in geographic regions, mostly near factories in the older cities of the Northeast and Midwest, or near the mines of Pennsylvania and points west. A strong presence today in all 50 states, their concentrations vary as Figure 6.4 indicates.

Gaining a political voice is part of the process of moving from marginality to mainstream status. Primarily through their ethnic organizations, South, Central, and East European Americans became a political influence and courted by politicians at the local, state, and national levels. A first, most tended to vote Democratic, but in the Nixon and Reagan presidential campaigns, many voted for the Republican candidates. Presently, these ancestry groups still lean Democratic.

In areas where they had strong population concentrations, those of Greek, Italian, Polish, Russian, and Ukrainian heritage often elected some of their own to local offices, although this was less true among Hungarians. Examples of state officials are former Governors Michael Dukakis (Greek), George Pataki (Hungarian), Ella Grasso and Mario Cuomo (Italian), and Tim Pawlenty (Polish). Holding national office have been U.S. Senators Barbara Mikulski and Edmund Muskie (Polish). Wyoming, the first state to grant women the right to vote, in 2007 also became the first state in U.S. history to have two Italian American U.S. Senators, Republicans John Barrasso and Michael Enzi. Prominent outside their local venue have been New York City Mayors Fiorella La Guardia and Rudy Giuliani (Italian) and Michael Bloomberg (Russian and Polish).

Although urban ethnic neighborhoods still remain for these nationality groups, most claiming any of these ancestries are integrated fully into society, and they exercise their political power more as homogenized Americans, not as ethnics.

---

birth rates) suggests that assimilation likely will accelerate. Slavic communities, receiving a steady influx of compatriots, should continue to thrive a while longer, displaying all the attributes of everyday ethnicity. No such future awaits Hungarian, Italian, and Greek communities, however. Most likely, they will shrink and eventually disappear, as assimilation progresses unchallenged, despite futile efforts by a few to hold on to their cultures and traditions. These groups are destined to join the ranks of the North and West Europeans and become homogenized Americans with a European heritage.

## Sociological Analysis

**6-6** Discuss insights gained through sociological analysis.

**Watch on MySocLab**
Video: **Sociology in Focus: Economy and Work**

In this chapter, our examination of immigrants from diverse backgrounds necessarily has covered a wide range of material. By applying the three major sociological perspectives, however, we can identify unifying themes of common experiences in dominant–minority relations.

### THE FUNCTIONALIST VIEW

From the functionalist viewpoint, the arrival of significant numbers of immigrants served the rapidly industrializing nation well. Immigrants provided a valuable labor pool to meet the needs of an expanding economy, enabling the United States to emerge as an industrial giant. Unemployment during this era was not a problem, and the poor of Europe were able to build a better life for themselves in their adopted land. Despite nativist fears, the freedom and economic opportunities created fervently patriotic citizens among the newcomers. Later, political and war refugees, many of them talented and highly skilled people, augmented this hardworking, freedom-loving population. The U.S. social system evolved into a complex, interdependent, and prosperous society, in large measure through the efforts of its first- and second-generation European Americans.

Accompanying problems of overcrowded tenements, social disorganization, crime, harsh working conditions, labor strife, and ethnic antagonism all can be understood within the context of rapid social change. For poor immigrants unable to afford better housing, the tenements at least offered a place to begin life anew, while also providing a dense concentration of compatriots for a social support system.

For many, the abrupt change of life—language, customs, and urban living—introduced problems of adjustment resulting in various pathologies of behavior. The abuses of the industrial age—child labor, poor wages, wretched working conditions, and lack of security—caused severe hardship for many workers, but these factors were overcome in time through legislative safeguards and labor union organization. Massive immigration, especially during the first two decades of the twentieth century, further strained society's capacity to absorb the newcomers, prolonging the assimilation process and fostering negative reactions from the U.S. native-born population. Gradually, the necessary adjustments occurred through labor regulations, housing codes, acculturation, and upward mobility. With the corrective actions taken, harmonious interrelations ensued, restoring the social system to a stage of equilibrium.

## THE CONFLICT VIEW

A focus on the use and abuse of power, rather than on societal inability to cope with rapid change, marks the conflict approach. U.S. industrialists exploited immigrant workers, maximizing profits by minimizing wages and maintaining poor working conditions. When workers protested or went on strike, employers blacklisted them, hired other ethnics as strikebreakers, secured court injunctions, or used vigilantes, police, or state militia to break up the efforts. Employers possessed absolute economic power to curtail worker agitation because their position was reinforced by other social institutions aligned with the powerful against the powerless. The power-differential theory (Chapter 2) suggested by Lieberson places such actions in a conceptual framework consistent with the earlier experiences of the Irish. Bonacich's split-labor-market theory (Chapter 4) becomes applicable, for example, in the use of Hungarians and Italians as strikebreakers, generating interethnic conflict as a means of thwarting "troublemakers" in the labor force.

Upward mobility for these "white ethnics" occurred not from gradual societal adjustments but from an organized worker movement in opposition to the power structure. First- and second-generation workers fought hard through the labor union movement—often at great risk and with great sacrifice against strong pressures—to secure their share of the American Dream. Change thus resulted from conflict, from class consciousness, and from an unrelenting social movement against entrenched economic interests. With economic gains came stability and respectability, enabling these ethnic groups to gain acceptance and overcome the prejudice and discrimination directed against them.

## THE INTERACTIONIST VIEW

Imagine yourself a native-born American living in a Northeastern or Midwestern city at the turn of the twentieth century. From two-thirds to three-fourths of your city is populated by foreign-born people, most of whom are dark-skinned and dark-haired or physically distinctive because of their clothing. Everything about them—their religion, lifestyle, and behavior—seems so different, so alien. The people you associate with do not live clustered together in such crowded slums. And there are so many of them! You constantly read about them getting arrested for breaking some law or other. The city has changed—and not for the better. You worry that the country itself will lose its "true" identity as it is overrun by these European "misfits" who exhibit little appreciation for the national values and democratic principles of the United States.

Such a mental picture is not difficult to construct. Industrialization, urbanization, social disorganization, economic exploitation, and a host of other factors may have created the social problems regarding immigrants then, but the native-born tended to see only the symptoms manifest in the immigrant communities. Believing such conditions had not existed until "these people" came, members of the dominant group defined the problems as inherent in the "new" immigrants. Indeed, everything the typical U.S.-born citizen saw or heard reinforced the perception that the current flood of immigrants threatened the entire social fabric. The demands for immigration restrictions, eventually enacted, and the acts of avoidance, discrimination, and occasional violence all reflected the negative stereotyping of those who looked "different."

# Retrospect

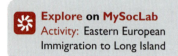

**Explore on MySocLab**
Activity: Eastern European Immigration to Long Island

The period from 1880 to 1920 was one of the greatest immigration epochs in U.S. history; 23 million people left everything behind for the promise of "Golden America." Social and economic forces at work on both continents combined to encourage this mass migration. Europe's inability to offer a decent standard of living and this country's massive need for laborers were the major push–pull factors. Recruited or attracted to the United States because of its rapid industrialization, European immigrants met an important need in the nation's growth and development.

Yet the "new" immigrants hardly were welcomed with open arms. Ethnocentric preconceptions of how an "American" should look and behave prejudiced large segments of the society against them. Their physical and cultural differences marked them as strangers and heightened nativist fears about an undesirable element populating the country. By 1900, one-third of the total population consisted of first- or second-generation Americans, a fact that spurred demands to close the "floodgates" to stem the "immigrant tide." Finally, in 1921, the first restrictive legislation against Europeans was enacted. Not until the mid-1960s would the discriminatory quota system based on national origin end.

Many theoretical considerations in majority–minority relations apply to these European immigrants. Their cultural and structural differences set the stage for stereotyping, all three levels of prejudice, and discrimination. Progressive stages of culture shock, community organization, development of subcultural areas, and marginality were common. Dominant patterns of nativism, antagonism, social and spatial segregation, and legislative controls appeared frequently, as did the minority responses of avoidance, deviance, defiance, and acceptance.

The immigrants settled in ethnic clusters and established their own institutions, and they generally followed the broad patterns of earlier groups of immigrants. The various new peoples differed from one another in language, customs, and value orientations, although many U.S. natives found indistinguishable those who were not Italians or Jews and so lumped them together. Not all of them wanted to stay and not all who did assimilated. The new immigrants in their ethnic clusters exhibited the same sort of cultural pluralism as, in more isolated settings, the "old" immigrants once had shown. But the times were different. Urbanization had introduced a greater degree of functional interdependence, a reliance of all residents on one another for the exchange of goods and services. Thus, the newcomers were less isolated than many earlier immigrants had been. Their numbers were great, and the dominant society wanted them to assimilate, although it also feared that they could not.

U.S. industry employed the immigrants because it needed them. The work was hard, the hours long, and the pay low, but most believed that the opportunities were better in the United States than in their homelands. Exploitation of workers led to labor unrest and the growth of the union movement. Some immigrants were attracted to radical movements, and others returned home, but most toiled, indoors or outdoors, to succeed in their adopted land for themselves and their children.

Today, immigrants from this part of Europe continue to arrive. The greater bulk of them are Slavic immigrants, as the low birth rate and economic situation in other countries lessen the motivation to leave. Those who do come find a more hospitable environment than did their predecessors and so their experiences are much more positive.

# On MySocLab

 **Study and Review on MySocLab**

## KEY TERMS

Extended family, p. 178                    Push–pull factors, p. 150

## DISCUSSION QUESTIONS

1. The beginning of the chapter offers a sociohistorical perspective. What was one striking or surprising piece of information you picked up here?
2. What factors aroused dominant-group antagonism against the newcomers? In what ways was this hostility expressed?
3. In what ways were the various ethnic groups' adaptations to U.S. society similar?
4. Apply the concepts of stereotyping and the vicious-circle phenomenon to immigrant experiences.
5. The end of the chapter offers three theoretical analyses. How did one of these theories become more meaningful or relevant to you in its application to the different groups' experiences?

## INTERNET ACTIVITIES

1. Did any of your family enter the United States through Ellis Island? You can trace them at the American Family Immigration History Center (http://www.ellisisland.org). At this site, you can search the records of family members and access the passenger record, ship's manifest, and a photo of their ship.
2. There are many websites about the ethnic Americans discussed in this chapter. Enter "[nationality] Americans" in your favorite search engine to explore what these sites have to offer in further information.
3. What prominent Americans claim ancestry from any of the groups discussed in this chapter? If you enter "famous [nationality] Americans" in your search engine, you'll see lists of individuals of that heritage who have made their mark in U.S. society.

# American Indians

 **Listen** to Chapter 7 on **MySocLab**

*Like many cultures, Native American values emphasize primary relationships based on kinship (the extended family and descent from a common ancestor) and community (friendship and other tribal members). This picture is of four generations of Arapahoe women on the Wind River Indian Reservation in Ethete, Wyoming.*

## LEARNING OBJECTIVES | After reading this chapter you will be able to:

**7-1** Describe Indian-White relations and perceptions within a sociohistorical context.

**7-2** Identify unique aspects of American Indian values and social structures.

**7-3** Review persistent stereotypes about American Indians.

**7-4** Evaluate inconsistent changes in government policies toward American Indians.

**7-5** Assess quality of life among contemporary American Indians.

**7-6** Analyze assertiveness and court cases in recent years.

**7-7** Examine urban American Indian life.

**7-8** Examine the cultural impact of American Indians on U.S. culture.

**7-9** Analyze the complexity of present-day assimilation and pluralism.

**7-10** Offer insights gained through sociological analysis.

Different in race, material culture, beliefs, and behavior, the Europeans and the American Indians initially were strangers to each other. The Europeans who first traded with and then conquered the natives showed little interest in understanding them. Brutalized and exploited, the American Indians experienced all the dominant-group response patterns: legislative action, segregation, expulsion, xenophobia, and—for some tribes and groups—annihilation. In turn, they reacted with varying patterns of avoidance, defiance, and acceptance, steadfastly remaining numerous and in persistent subcultures with a marginal existence.

# Sociohistorical Perspective

Most historians place the pre-European colonization number of American Indians who lived in what later became the United States at between 6 and 10 million. Divided into several hundred tribes with discrete languages and lifestyles, these original inhabitants had cultures rich in art, music, dance, life-cycle rituals, belief systems, social organization, coping strategies, and instruction of their young. Although tribes varied in their values, customs, beliefs, and practices, their cultures primarily rested on living in harmony with the land.

Early European explorers and settlers, reflecting ethnocentric views, condemned the aspects of American Indian culture that they did not understand and reacted to other aspects only in terms of their own culture. Some considered the indigenous people to be savages, even though American Indian societies had a high degree of social organization. Others idealized them as uncorrupted children of nature who spent most of their time engaging in pleasurable activities. In Europe, intellectual debate raged over how the presence of people so isolated from other human beings could be explained. Were they descended from the inhabitants of Atlantis, Carthage, ancient Greece, or East Asia? Were they the Lost Tribes of Israel?[1] Were they no better than beasts, or were they intelligent, capable beings?

In colonial and frontier days, the stereotype of American Indians often was negative, especially when they obstructed Europeans from occupying the American Indians' land. As a result of *self-justification*—the denigration of others to justify maltreating them—some whites viewed American Indians as cruel, treacherous, lying, dirty heathens. Supposedly, all they desired during the frontier period were scalps, firearms, and "firewater." Even today, many stereotype contemporary American Indians are backward, unmotivated, or continually drunk, or else are regarded as romantic relics of the past.

Outsiders frequently generalize about American Indians, thinking of the many tribes as one people even though the tribes always have differed from one another in language, social structure, values, and practices. Of the approximately 300 different American Indian languages spoken in 1492 within what became the United States, only approximately 175 still are spoken today and 55 of these only by a few elderly tribal members. English, however, is the predominant language in the home, school, and workplace. At present, there are 334 federal- and state-recognized American Indian reservations, and the Bureau of Indian Affairs recognizes 565 different tribal entities in the United States.[2]

The American Indians' experiences in the colonial period were unique in one respect: The whites, not the American Indians, were the newcomers, and the whites were the minority for many years. The relationship between American Indians and whites often was characterized by distrust, uneasy truces, or violent hostilities. Even in colonial Massachusetts and New Netherland, where peaceful coexistence initially prevailed, the situation deteriorated.

As the two peoples interacted more fully, each group grew more antagonistic toward the other. The American Indians could not understand the European settlers' use of beatings, hangings, and imprisonment as means of social control. The settlers could not understand the American Indians' resistance to Christianity and to the whites' more "civilized" way of life. These were but marginal considerations, however; the major issue was whose way of life would prevail and whether the land would be developed further or allowed to remain in its natural state, abounding with fish and wildlife.

In the mid-nineteenth century, the U.S. government adopted a policy of forced relocation of American Indian tribes to encourage westward expansion. Using military force, it displaced the many tribes and resettled them on wilderness reservations, where they remained unless new settlement plans or the discovery of oil and valuable minerals (such as gold in the Black Hills of South Dakota) caused further displacement. This program of compulsory segregation and dependence—compounded by attempts at "Americanization"—reduced the American Indians' status to that of a subordinate colonized people—wards of the government—living at a subsistence level. Reflecting changing attitudes and interests in the late nineteenth and early twentieth centuries, Congress enacted various legislative acts supposedly designed to help American Indians but that actually worked to their further disadvantage, worsening their already low and dependent status (see the Ethnic Experience box for a similar governmental interaction with the Hawaiians).

One short-lived Pan-Indian association of the twentieth century, the Society of American Indians (1910–1920), failed to unify the tribes into an effective pressure group or to generate much outside support. In 1944, a group of World War II veterans formed the National Congress of American Indians (NCAI). In the early 1960s, another organization, the National Indian Youth Council (NIYC) came into existence. New moves toward unity began in the 1960s, and new legislation and greater government sympathy helped the American Indians' cause.

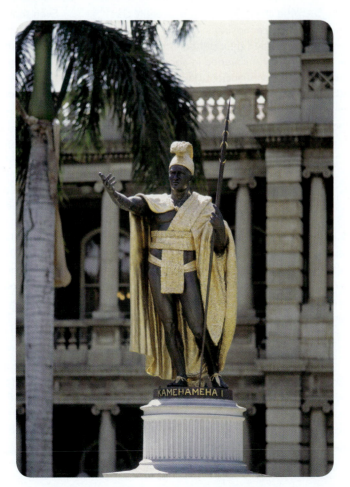

*Of the four statues honoring King Kamehameha, who united the Hawaiian Islands into one royal kingdom in 1810, the most recognizable one stands in front of Aliiolani Hale (the judiciary building). Every June 11th, on Kamehameha Day, the four statues are draped ceremoniously with long strands of flower lei to celebrate Hawaii's greatest king.*

# the ETHNIC experience

## Hawaiians Lose Their Independence

Hawaii's history—preserved in the oral tradition through chants and legends—dates back to approximately 700 BCE with migration of Polynesians from the Marquesas. As with American Indians, life changed dramatically for the indigenous people in Hawaii after European contact in 1778.

In the centuries before European contact, Hawaiian society was a highly stratified system. Under the king were the *ali'i*, or chiefs, who ruled over portions of the land at the whim of the king, who could remove and replace them according to a system of rewards and punishments. Below the chiefs in temporal power, but often far above them in spiritual power, were the *kahuna*, or priest craftsmen—specialists in such areas as canoe building, medicine, and casting and lifting spells. Most people, however, were commoners (*makaainana*) or laborers, who paid tributes to the king and chief in the form of food, clothing, and other goods, and also provided warriors for the chief's army. At the bottom were a small number of slaves known as *kauwa* and outcastes.

Social control rested on a *kapu* (taboo) system that dominated all aspects of life from birth to death, with violators swiftly punished by being strangled or clubbed to death. Commoners could not even let their shadows fall across the person of a high chief, so they quickly kneeled or lay down in the presence of such sacred persons. Commoners performed simple religious ceremonies to their personal gods (*aumakua*), and the *kahuna* performed more elaborate rituals (sometimes including human sacrifices) for the *ali'i* in the large temples (*heiau*) to the four major gods (*Ku, Kanaloa, Lono*, and *Kane*), who represented the universal forces of nature.

In the late eighteenth century, foreign ships arrived in increasing numbers, bringing domestic animals, trees, fruits, and plants never before seen in Hawaii. They also brought diseases, alcohol, and firearms. With little immunity to new diseases, the Hawaiians soon began to die in alarming numbers as survivors witnessed the destruction of their traditional way of life. By the time missionaries—mostly from Puritan New England—arrived in 1820, the Hawaiian people already had dismantled their *heiaus*, rejecting earlier religious beliefs, and soon many converted to Christianity. Early missionaries disliked the *hula*, originally a religious rite to honor the gods and the chiefs. The sight of scantily clad women moving in rhythm to poetry offended their puritan ethics, and they nearly succeeded in abolishing this aspect of ancient Hawaiian culture.

The first newcomers were of European ancestry, beginning with the English under Captain James Cook and then Americans who came as explorers, adventurers, businessmen, and missionaries. At first, all foreigners were known as *haole* (outsiders), or non-Hawaiians. Because the first foreigners that the Hawaiians saw were Europeans, the word soon came to refer strictly to persons of European ancestry. This meaning continues to this day, although sometimes it also can be used derogatorily.

Among the Caucasians who came in small groups as agricultural workers were Russians, Portuguese, Spaniards, Germans, and Norwegians. Many of these groups intermarried with Hawaiians and other racial groups. Larger waves of immigrants then came, beginning with the Chinese as plantation workers in the 1850s. Quite a few Chinese married Hawaiian women. As a result, Hawaiian Chinese families are common in Hawaii today. Throughout the next 70 years, other groups arrived, first the Japanese, then the Koreans, Filipinos, Puerto Ricans, and Samoans.

In the late nineteenth century, several Hawaiian monarchs attempted to reduce the agitation fomented by the sugar planters for annexation to the United States to secure a dependable market for their product. The divisiveness between the ruling and economic power structures was best illustrated in the legislature, though, where white legislators refused to speak Hawaiian, the kingdom's official language, and native Hawaiian members refused to use English.

Even though the annexationists were badly outnumbered, and the majority of the Hawaiian people—as well as many white residents—were against annexation, these businessmen considered the monarchy too inept to safeguard their property interests and profits. In 1893, their armed companies of militia took over government buildings and offices, supported by U.S. marines and sailors who landed the night before "to keep order." Queen Lili'uokalani was powerless and surrendered under protest. President Cleveland's administration concluded that the monarchy had been overthrown and raised the U.S. flag over Honolulu. In 1895, loyalists staged a revolt in an attempt to restore the throne, but it was quickly crushed and the queen placed under house arrest. As a condition to obtain amnesty for the Hawaiian rebels, she was forced to relinquish any claim to the throne. President McKinley then signed the resolution of annexation on July 7, 1898, to seal the fate of the forever-lost kingdom.

# the MINORITY experience

## What's in a Name?

**Indian:** Since the days of Columbus, this was the common term, but it was also confusing as to whether its reference was to the indigenous peoples of the Americas or of India. Many also viewed this term as an erroneous term used by the oppressor.

**Native American:** Introduced in the 1960s as a politically correct alternative, this term suggested an enlightened awareness and desire to avoid dehumanizing stereotypes. To some, though, this term excludes the indigenous people of Alaska, Hawaii, and Puerto Rico. Technically, anyone born in the United States is a "native American," which adds even more confusion.

**American Indian:** Once also considered a negative term, today many activists prefer this term over *Native American*, although both terms work today for the general population, and the existence of the National Museum of the American Indian reinforces this term.

**Tribal name:** Rejecting the broad generic terms of "Native American" and "American Indian," many individuals prefer to be identified by their tribal affiliation (e.g., Cherokee, Kiowa, Navajo).

The most significant factor in the American Indians' success, however, was the Civil Rights movement, which heightened the nation's social consciousness and inspired the American Indians to renew their campaign for self-determination.

Although they never had been silent, they now became more vocal, organized, and militant, while finding outsiders more receptive. A new generation of "Red Power" advocates took up the fight for American Indian rights. Some attempted to achieve their goals through a national, or Pan-Indian, movement, whereas others preferred to emphasize individual tribal culture and practices.

Throughout their 500-year history with whites, American Indians consistently rejected the notion that the whites' religions and lifestyles were superior to theirs. To understand the nature of the relations between these two groups, we must comprehend the roles of ethnocentrism, stereotyping, cultural differences, and power differentials in intergroup relations.

## Early Encounters

In the first encounters between American Indians and Europeans, two races with vast differences in culture, knowledge, and lifestyle saw each other's physical distinctions for the first time. Each group was a source of wonder to the other. Columbus's first impressions of the Arawak tribe in the Caribbean reflected his ethnocentrism:

> I knew they were a people who could be more easily freed and converted to our holy faith by love than by force…they are very well made, with very handsome bodies, and…with good faces…They should be good servants and intelligent, for I observed that they quickly took in what was said to them, and I believe that they would easily be made Christians, as it appeared to me that they had no religion.[3]

Although he admired the American Indians, Columbus essentially saw them as potential servants, and he assumed that they had no religious convictions because he found no trappings of religion or written codes such as he was accustomed to seeing in Europe.

Some Europeans romanticized American Indians and a positive mystique about the American Indians swept Elizabethan England and other parts of Europe, but others viewed them as bloodthirsty barbarians and cruelly exploited them. The early phases of Spanish military activity in the New World involved enslavement, plunder, rape, and slaughter. For example, the Spanish put the peaceful Arawak tribe of the Caribbean islands into forced labor for land clearing, building, mining, and plantation work. Because they had no weapons to match those of their conquerors, the enslaved peoples often responded by committing mass suicide and mass infanticide. Within a few decades of the European discovery of the New World, the American Indian population began to decline rapidly as a result of disease, warfare, and self-destruction.

American Indian populations in Latin America and North America were decimated by various sicknesses that resulted from earlier contact with white explorers or traders. When the early settlers in New England found deserted American Indian villages, they rejoiced, considering this to be mute testimony of the judgment of Divine Providence on these "heathens" as well as on their own undertaking. The Lord had smitten the pagan to make way for the righteous! This accidental annihilation often resulted from a serious contagion such as smallpox, tuberculosis, or cholera. American Indians were also fatally susceptible to such diseases as measles, mumps, and chicken pox because they had not developed immunities to these Old World illnesses.

Epitomizing the **dichotomy** of views of the American Indian either as a Noble Savage or as a bloodthirsty barbarian was the great debate between Bartolomé de las Casas, a bishop serving in the New World, and Juan Ginés de Sepulveda, a Renaissance scholar. The latter considered the American Indians no better than "beasts" who should be enslaved. Las Casas presented a picture of the American Indians as innocents who were artistically and mechanically inclined, and with intellectual capabilities for learning and a willingness to co-exist with the Spanish intruders. In 1550, the Council of the Indies, a panel of distinguished theologians and counselors, met at Valladolid. The council heard the arguments of the two antagonists, agreed in large measure with Las Casas, and thereupon fundamentally altered Spanish policy toward the American Indians.

*The landing of Columbus on the island of San Salvador in the Bahamas on October 12, 1492, marked the beginning of a dramatic social upheaval in the lives of the indigenous peoples throughout the Americas. Brutal conquests, subjugation, exploitation, annihilation, and the loss of centuries-old ways of life among many tribes soon followed.*

As part of his long struggle to protect the American Indians, Las Casas had returned to Spain to plead their case directly to King Charles V. In doing so, he revealed the extent of their decimation: "At my first arrival in Hispaniola [1502], it contained a million inhabitants and now there remain scarce the hundredth part of them."[4] He believed the American Indians could survive only if another labor force replaced them. By convincing the Spanish authorities that Africans were sturdier and better adapted to agricultural operations, he opened the doors for the subsequent massive slave trade of blacks to the Spanish possessions in the New World. It is cruelly ironic that the humane efforts of Las Casas on the American Indians' behalf encouraged the brutalization and exploitation of black people and he later deeply regretted his support for this alternate practice.[5]

The Indian populations in North and Latin America differ in their social, economic, and political status. Moreover, their centuries-old concentrations sometimes are irrespective of present-day national boundaries, such as the Mohawk in New York State and Canada, and the Blackfeet in Montana and Canada. Several factors—habitability of terrain, migration patterns, degree of industrialization, and especially different governmental and social attitudes—account for these differences. In the United States, the nineteenth-century policy of removal, relocation, and American Indian dependence on the federal government prevented most tribes from becoming full participants in U.S. society.

In Latin America, Spain's adoption in the sixteenth century of a benevolent policy toward the indigenous populations led to greater interaction, intermarriage, and absorption, and gradual acculturation occurred between the native peoples and the Spanish. Except for those living in the central Andes and other remote areas, the indigenous peoples became fuller participants in their society than did their counterparts in the United States and lived in relative cultural and racial harmony with the white, black, *mulatto* (of mixed black and white ancestry), and *mestizo* (of mixed American Indian and white ancestry) populations. Along with the other non-white groups, they were part of the large lower social class, in sharp contrast to the small upper class. Despite this comparative racial harmony, however, they have had little opportunity for upward mobility, and most Latin American non-whites live in economic stagnation. In contrast, most North American tribes have experienced both economic stagnation and a lack of racial harmony.

## CULTURAL STRAINS

When the white settlers were few in number and depended on American Indian assistance, intergroup relations usually were peaceful and cooperative. The American Indians along the East Coast helped the colonists by teaching them what to plant and how to cultivate their crops, as well as imparting knowledge and skills needed to survive in the wilderness. With stabilization of the settlements, relations between the two races became more strained.

At first, both sides benefited from the thriving trade in furs and hides for cloth, tools, and food provisions. Eventually, the attempt to meet the growing demand for furs and hides inevitably led to wildlife reduction. Moreover, the once self-sufficient tribes became increasingly dependent on the colonial traders for clothing, blankets, commercial rope and netting, kettles, pans, knives, hatchets, axes, guns, files, metal awls, other tools, and alcohol. An irreversible path to economic dependence ensued.

Meanwhile, a labor shortage within the ever-expanding colonial settlements encouraged some Indians to leave their tribal compounds to work as servants or laborers. Adapting to living and working in relative comfort in comparison to their former homes, these Indians came into regular contact with whites on the streets of colonial villages. As some whites accepted their presence and others looked on with disdain, other Indians—resisting such enticements and trying to retain their culture, traditional way of life, and close family and tribal bonds—viewed this racial intermingling with apprehension.

Despite the potential for further integration, population growth from natural increase and immigration created a need for more land and the Indians were in the way. Their life-style drew little appreciation and their presence even less:

> …the English colonists were being hardened in the conviction that the Indians were a graceless and savage people, dirty and slothful in their personal habits, treacherous in their relations with the superior race. To put it bluntly, they were fit only to be pushed aside and subordinated, so that the land could be occupied and made productive by those for whom it had been destined by God. If the Indians could be made to fit into a humble niche in the edifice of colonial religion, economy, and government, very well, but if not, sooner or later, they would have to be driven away or crushed.[6]

Throughout the westward movement, if contact led to cooperation between the two cultures, the resulting interaction and cultural diffusion usually worked to the disadvantage of the American Indians. They lost their self-sufficiency and became economically dependent on whites. The whites, in turn, insisted on full compliance with their demands as the price of continued peaceful relations. Even if the American Indians complied with the whites' demands, however, many whites continued to regard them as inferior people destined for a subservient role in white society.

## DIFFERING VALUES

Benjamin Franklin offered a classic example of different values in his account of a treaty signed between the whites and the Iroquois in 1744:

> After the principal Business was settled, the Commissioners from Virginia acquainted the Indians by a Speech, that there was at Williamsburg a College, with a Fund for Educating Indian Youth; and that, if the Chiefs of the Six Nations would send down half a dozen of their Sons to that College, the Government would take Care that they should be well provided for, and instructed in all the Learning of the White People…[The Indians'] Speaker began…"We are convinced…that you mean to do us good by your Proposal; and we thank you heartily. But you, who are wise must know, that different Nations have different Conceptions of things; and you will therefore not take it amiss, if our Ideas of this Kind of Education happen not to be the same with yours. We have had some Experience of it; Several of our Young People were formerly brought up at the Colleges of the Northern Provinces; they were instructed in all your Sciences; but, when they came back to us, they were bad Runners, ignorant of every means of living in the Woods, unable to bear either Cold or Hunger, knew neither how to build a Cabin, take a Deer, or kill an Enemy, knew our Language imperfectly; were therefore neither fit for Hunters, Warriors, nor Counsellors; they were totally good for nothing. We are however not the less obliged by your kind Offer, tho' we decline accepting it; and, to show our grateful Sense of it, if the Gentlemen of Virginia will send us a Dozen of their Sons, we will take great Care of their Education, instruct them in all we know, and make *Men* of them."[7]

Nearly 100 years later, George Catlin offered insight into another manifestation of differing value orientations. Catlin, a nineteenth-century artist famous for his paintings of American Indians and his sensitivity to their ways, described how each of the two cultures viewed the other:

> The civilized world look upon a group of Indians, in their classic dress, with their few and simple oddities, all of which have their moral or meaning, and

laugh at them excessively, because they are not like ourselves—we ask, "why do the silly creatures wear such great bunches of quills on their heads?—Such loads and streaks of paint upon their bodies—and bear's grease? abominable"! and a thousand other equally silly questions, without ever stopping to think that Nature taught them to do so—and that they all have some definite importance or meaning which an Indian could explain to us at once, if he were asked and felt disposed to do so—that each quill in his head stood, in the eyes of his whole tribe, as the symbols of any enemy who had fallen by his hand—that every streak of red paint covered a wound which he had got in honourable combat—and that the bear's grease with which he carefully anoints his body every morning, from head to foot, cleanses and purifies the body, and protects his skin from the bite of mosquitoes, and at the same time, preserves him from colds and coughs which are usually taken through the pores of the skin.

At the same time, an Indian looks at the civilized world, no doubt, with equal, if not much greater, astonishment, at our apparently, as well as really, ridiculous customs and fashions; but he laughs not, nor ridicules, nor questions—for his natural good sense and good manners forbid him—until he is reclining about the fireside of his wigwam companions, when he vents forth his just criticisms upon the learned world, who are a rich and just theme for Indian criticism and Indian gossip.

An Indian will not ask a white man the reason why he does not oil his skin with bear's grease, or why he does not paint his body—or why he wears a hat on his head, or why he has buttons on the back of his coat, where they can never be used—why he wears whiskers, and a shirt collar up to his eyes—or why he sleeps with his head towards the fire instead of his feet—why he walks with his toes out instead of turning them in—or why it is that hundreds of white folks will flock and crowd round a table to see an Indian eat—but he will go home to his wigwam fireside, and "make the welkin ring" with jokes and fun upon the ignorance and folly of the knowing world.[8]

These two selections sharply illustrate how culture shapes an individual's view of reality. When people use their own group as a frame of reference in judging another group, the resulting ethnocentric judgments declare the outgroup to be strange and inferior.

Many historians suggest that one American Indian nation, the Iroquois, influenced some provisions of the U.S. Constitution. Iroquois is a name given to five American Indian tribes located in New York State and the Ohio River Valley—the Cayuga, Mohawk, Oneida, Onondaga, and Seneca—that united in a league in 1570. They added a sixth tribe—the Tuscarora—in 1722 and later took other groups, including the Delaware, under their protection. The League still was expanding and maturing when it was curtailed by white settlers; by 1851, it had virtually disappeared.

In its time, the League's democratic processes were so effective that romanticists called the Iroquois the "Greeks in America," and aspects of their system served as models for the colonists. Called the Great Law of Peace, the Iroquois constitution gave each of the five tribes an equal voice, guaranteed freedom of political and religious expression, and had amendment and impeachment processes.[9]

## Values and Social Structure

Although the cultures of the many tribes differed (and still do) from one another, some marked similarities have existed among them. American Indians have lived in close and intimate relationship with nature, respecting and not abusing the land. They traditionally have maximized the use of any animal prey—using its skin for clothing and shelter, its bones

**7-2** Identify unique aspects of American Indian values and social structures.

*Throughout the American Southwest, Native Americans selling handcrafted jewelry are a common sight at numerous roadside stands or at sidewalk bazaars, such as this scene in Albuquerque Old Town. With limited occupational choices available, utilizing artistic skills of one's heritage preserves the past and helps meet present-day economic needs.*

for various tools and implements, its sinews for thread, its meat for food, its bladder for a container, and so on.

American Indian approaches toward possessing land ranged from individual to joint to tribal ownership depending on the tribe. Most frequently, the land belonged to the tribe; as tribal members, individuals or families could live on and possibly farm certain portions. Land no longer cultivated by one American Indian could be cultivated by another. However, the nominal owner could not dispose of the property without considering the land-use rights of the current user. More emphasis thus was placed on the rights of the user than on the rights and power of the nominal owner.[10] In terms of shared access, this practice resembles a law in present-day Sweden that roughly translates as "every person's right." In that country, a landowner cannot deny others access to the land because all are entitled to enjoy its beauty. Thus, campers and hikers do not encounter no-trespassing signs; because all respect the land, littering and other forms of abuse are quite rare.

American Indians established primary relationships either through a clan system (descent from a common ancestor) or through a friendship system, much like the systems of other tribal societies. Kin relationships served as the basis of their social organization, stretching from close family units to extended territorial entities.

> The Indians, in their initial attempts to establish a basis of cooperation with the immigrant whites, attempted to incorporate the newcomers into the familiar kinship system. When proffered marriage alliances were turned down by the whites, the Indians sought to establish relationships based on the reciprocal responsibilities of brother to brother, nephew to uncle, and, finally, children to father. The white man refused the proffered relationships, misinterpreted Indian speech as weakness, and increasingly imposed his will on the disheartened remnants of once proud Indian nations.[11]

American Indian children grow up under the encouragement and discipline of the extended family, not only the nuclear family. A generalized love of all children in the tribe, rather than just one's own offspring, is common among American Indians. Whether the American Indian tribe was a hunting, fishing, or farming society, the children were raised in a cooperative, noncompetitive, affectionate atmosphere. Considered from the outset as an individual, the child developed a sense of responsibility and interdependence at an early age. Unrestrained displays of affection or temper and the use of corporal punishment rarely have been part of traditional American Indian childcare practices. Instead, the means of social control are shame and ridicule, and the American Indian matures into an individual keenly aware of any form of conduct that would lead other members of the tribe to react negatively.[12]

Closely related to sensitivity to shame and ridicule is the American Indian concept of personal honor, including the honor of one's word. Once pledged, whether to a white person or to another American Indian, that word was considered inviolate. Exceptions did exist, for chiefs might lie, but only as a war measure, and later, in an attempt to please a white person. Some tribes had no word for *thief,* although an enemy's goods always were fair game. Sometimes, as among the Lakota (Sioux), Crow, and Blackfeet, young men of one tribe would steal from another tribe as a form of sport or a joke, but normally, they would not steal from one another.[13]

The American Indian woman's role differed from the man's. Women's functions were to work and to raise children. However, the notion that women held a subservient position and labored long and hard while the men idled away their time is inaccurate. Actually, a cooperative but not egalitarian arrangement existed between the sexes, with the men doing the heavy work and the women doing tasks that would not conflict with their child-rearing responsibilities. In hunting and fishing societies, the men would be away from the village for extended periods searching for food. In farming societies, the men cleared and cultivated the land, and the women tended the crops, collected edible foods, and gathered firewood while the men sought a fresh meat supply. Each member of the tribe, according to sexually defined roles, had kinship and tribal responsibilities to fulfill. Moreover, in some tribes—such as the Cherokee, Cheyenne, and Iroquois—women held high esteem and influence.

**STUDENTS SPEAK** "I didn't really know much about Native Americans, only what I saw on television and movies. I pictured them being peaceful people who are one with their environment. It kind of reminded me of the movie *Avatar.* I also found it very interesting that Native Americans are not just one group, but diverse in their languages, social structure, values, and practices.

**—Alleyah Singh**

## Stereotyping

One popular misconception was that the American Indian was a bloodthirsty savage. Some tribes, such as the Apache and Ute, were warlike, but most sought to avoid conflict if they could. Rivalries did exist among various tribes, however, and the French, English, and (later) U.S. settlers often exploited these rivalries for their own advantage. American Indians believed in retributive justice: a wrong had to be repaid, even if it took years, but not to a greater degree. Scalping, often depicted in films as a standard American Indian practice, was not common. Even tribes that did scalp frequently did so because of their belief in retributive justice. Some historians argue that the American Indian first learned about scalping from white settlers:

**7-3** Review persistent stereotypes about American Indians.

> Whatever its exact origins, there is no doubt that scalp-taking quickly spread over all of North America, except in the Eskimo areas; nor is there any doubt that its spread was due to the barbarity of White men rather than to the barbarity of Red men. White settlers early offered to pay bounties on dead Indians, and scalps were actual proof of the dead. Governor Kieft of New Netherland is usually credited with originating the idea of paying for Indian scalps, as they were more convenient to handle than whole heads, and they offered the same proof that an Indian had been killed. By liberal payment for scalps, the Dutch virtually cleared southern New York and New Jersey of Indians before the English supplanted them. By 1703, the colony of Massachusetts was paying the equivalent of about $60 for every Indian scalp. In the mid-eighteenth century, Pennsylvania fixed the bounty for a male Indian scalp at $134; a female's was worth only $50. Some White entrepreneurs simply hatcheted any old Indians that still survived in their towns.[14]

Another side of the American Indian stereotype is the portrayal of them as silent or aloof. This image probably grew out of normal behavior in ambiguous situations, such as those faced by American Indians transported to Europe for exhibition or to Washington, DC, for treaty negotiations and with strangers. Because they had developed from childhood a strong inclination to avoid acting in any way that might bring about shame or ridicule, American Indians often remained silent for fear of speaking or acting improperly. This practice still is common in courtship, in the greeting that parents offer to children returning from boarding school and, in the face of harsh, angry words from a white. In each instance, the practice among most tribes is to allow some time, perhaps days or months, to elapse before the uncertainty is sufficiently reduced to permit conversation. American Indian silence is a precautionary device to preserve respect and dignity on both sides.[15] It does not represent aloofness, and it is temporary, continuing only until the situation lends itself to speaking.

In a larger context, the fundamental difference in values that separates European Americans from American Indians is that the former sees the world from a linear perspective. The Western mind believes in empirical evidence, in separating and categorizing elements of experience in the belief that this process leads to ultimate knowledge. Statistical truth thus becomes the key to knowledge and to understanding human behavior and relationships. This approach has led to spectacular advances in science and technology but also to an ethnocentric attitude that dismisses other approaches as unsophisticated and inadequate. In contrast, American Indians have a holistic, or symbiotic, view of existence, seeing it as a great circle, or sacred hoop, representing unity and equality, linking all aspects of culture—art, religion, ritual, social organization, language, law, and lifestyle. Life thus is a complex matrix of entities, emotions, revelations, and cooperative enterprises, and the hallmark of the American Indian approach is to experience rather than to interpret human existence. Because everything is interconnected, American Indians believe a unified approach to life is more satisfying than a fragmentary one.[16]

**STUDENTS SPEAK** "Although from kindergarten on they teach about them, teachers never really explain to children that there are modern-day Native Americans too. I am a Penobscot and I do not hunt for my food or wear skin that I just took off an animal. Once when I was a teacher's aide, I heard seventh graders talking about Native Americans. I said, 'I am Native American; do you need help with your work?' They told me, 'You're not Native American! Your name is Alana.' I said, 'My tribal name is Ngadozig N'be.' Then they said, 'Why do you wear regular clothes? And why is your skin and hair not dark?' I explained to them that I am mixed, that my grandfather and father are dark, but not every Native American looks like Pocahontas."

**—Alana Smith**

## Changes in Government Policies

**7-4** Evaluate inconsistent changes in government policies toward American Indians.

Official European and U.S. government policy toward American Indians has changed frequently throughout the years (see the International Scene box and Table 7.1). In 1763, King George III of England issued a proclamation declaring that henceforth the American Indian tribes would be treated as independent nations and denied the colonies any jurisdiction over them. Thereafter, if the colonists wanted to obtain additional American Indian lands or negotiate trade pacts, they had to do so through the English government and not directly with the American Indians.

In addition to the delay involved in drawing up petitions, crossing the ocean back and forth, and waiting for bureaucratic processing, the colonists fumed over the fact that "heathens" were accorded higher official status than they themselves enjoyed. Yet when the colonies declared their independence from England, they adopted the same policy in 1778, and the tribes retained quasi-national status. Congress reaffirmed this policy when it passed the Northwest Territory Ordinance in 1787, declaring the federal government—and not the states—responsible for American Indian property, rights, and liberty.

# the INTERNATIONAL scene

## Aborigines in Australia

Aborigines are the first inhabitants of Australia, the first Australians. Approximately 500 Aboriginal tribes were living in the country when the Europeans arrived in the eighteenth century. They suffered severe discrimination, violence, racism, and extreme assimilationist policies for about 200 years. They were deprived of their traditional lands by the newcomers. Until the second half of the twentieth century, they were considered as a race bound for extinction. They only became Australian citizens in 1967.

Today, with approximately 200,000 people dispersed throughout this huge country, they account for only 1 percent of the total population. Heavily marginalized in Australian society, whether living in cities or in the outback, and despite public programs and aid, they still face many problems: poverty, high unemployment, poor formal education, domestic violence, alcoholism, and poor health. Their life expectancy is approximately 25 years lower than that of other Australians, with a median age at death of 53.

Yet when you travel in Australia, you also can encounter another side of Aboriginal life. Aboriginal art galleries and stores abound everywhere, featuring Aboriginal paintings and artefacts. The traditional musical instrument called *didjeridoo*, or more precisely *yidaky*, is played and sold everywhere. In many of the usual beautiful theme parks, Aboriginal dances and culture are celebrated. Furthermore, many of the country's most impressive natural wonders symbolically have been returned to the Aborigines, like the world famous sacred red mountain *Uluru*. When you visit those sites, you are asked to respect the sacred character of the place. Clearly, in touristy Australia, the label *aboriginal* is a moneymaker.

Furthermore, if you are really interested, you also can discover militant Aborigines. They are not solely victims of the system or folklorized touristy items. They organize to defend their rights, their way of life, and to struggle against discrimination and marginalization. The symbol of Aboriginal struggles is without doubt the "Aboriginal Tent Embassy"

opened in 1972 directly opposite the Old Parliament House in Canberra, with Aboriginal activists constantly occupying it ever since.

Australian politics and society certainly have changed. The position of Aborigines in Australia is probably better than it was even a few decades ago. On paper, they have the same rights as other citizens, but the country remains divided, and the first Australians continue to suffer inequality. The Aboriginal question is highly complex and nobody seems to have the solution leading to a truly mutual understanding and respect among all Australians and more equal life chances for all, whatever their skin color, religion, and ethnicity. Some of the wounds from Australia's racist past remain wide open.

### CRITICAL THINKING QUESTIONS

What parallels do you find in the experiences of the native peoples of Australia and the United States? Why do you think such parallels exist half a world away?

Source: Marco Martiniello, FRS-FNRS and CEDEM, University of Liége.

## INDIAN REMOVAL ACT

In 1830, by one vote, Congress passed the Indian Removal Act recommended by President Andrew Jackson. This act called for expulsion of all American Indians from the southeastern states and their relocation to the territory west of the Mississippi River. The legislation was prompted in part by the state of Georgia, which for several years had been annexing the fertile land of the Cherokee for its expanding cotton industry. The Cherokee had rejected Georgia's assertion of legal authority to settle disputes over all lands within its borders and petitioned the U.S. Supreme Court for protection, citing their "foreign nation" status and treaties with the federal government.

Combining two cases, *Cherokee Nation v. Georgia* and *Worcester v. Georgia*, Chief Justice John Marshall delivered the majority opinion on February 28, 1832, establishing

**TABLE 7.1 Government Actions Toward American Indians**

| | |
|---|---|
| 1763 | English Royal Proclamation: Tribes accorded independent nation status; all lands west of the Appalachian Mountains are American Indian country; the royal government must approve all land purchases. |
| 1778 | Continental Congress: Reaffirms the old British policy as U.S. policy. |
| 1787 | Northwest Territory Ordinance: Opens the Midwest for settlement; declares the U.S. government responsible for American Indian property, rights, and liberty. |
| 1824 | Bureau of Indian Affairs (BIA) is created under the jurisdiction of the Secretary of War. |
| 1830 | Indian Removal Act: Mandates all American Indians must move west of the Mississippi River. |
| 1830–1843 | Except for Iroquois and Seminole, more than 100,000 eastern American Indians are forcibly relocated westward. Approximately 12,000 die on the "Trail of Tears." |
| 1850–1880 | Most reservations are established, as forced segregation becomes the new American Indian reality. |
| 1871 | Appropriations bill rider: Declares tribes no longer are independent nations; legislation, not negotiation, is to determine any new arrangements. |
| 1887 | Dawes Act: Reservations surveyed, divided into tracts, and allotted to individual tribal members; surplus land sold. |
| 1898 | Curtis Act: Terminates tribal governments that refuse allotment; the president is to appoint tribal chiefs henceforth. |
| 1906 | Burke Act: Eliminates American Indians' right to lease their land, with the intent to force American Indians to work the land themselves. |
| 1924 | Indian Citizenship Act: Grants U.S. citizenship to American Indians. |
| 1934 | Indian Reorganization Act: Ends allotment; encourages tribal self-government; restores freedom of religion; extends financial credit; promotes the revival of American Indian culture and crafts. |
| 1952 | Relocation Program: Moves American Indians at government expense to urban areas for better job opportunities. |
| 1953 | Termination Act: Authorizes elimination of reservation systems, with an immediate end to federal services and tax immunity. |
| 1973 | Menominee Restoration Act: Revokes termination and restores the Menominee's reservation and tribal status. |
| 1974 | Indian Finance Act: Facilitates financing of American Indian enterprises and development projects through grants and loans. |
| 1975 | Indian Self-Determination and Education Assistance Act: Expands tribal control over reservation programs; provides funding for new public schools on or near reservations. |
| 1976 | Indian Health Care Improvement Act: Provides funds to build or renovate hospitals, add more personnel, and give scholarships to American Indians to enter Indian Health Service. |
| 1978 | Education Amendments Act: Gives substantial control over education programs to local American Indian community. |
| 1978 | Tribally Controlled Community College Assistance Act: Provides grants to tribal community colleges. |
| 1978 | Indian Child Welfare Act: Restricts placement of American Indian children by non-American Indian social agencies in non-American Indian homes. |
| 1978 | American Indian Religious Freedom Act: Protects religious rights of American Indians, including their use of peyote. |
| 1993 | Religious Freedom Restoration Act: Restores standards of review for American Indian Religious Freedom Act that were overturned by a Supreme Court ruling in 1990. |
| 1993 | Omnibus Indian Advancement Act: Establishes foundation for gifts to BIA schools; increases economic development opportunities for tribes; improves tribal governance. |
| 2002 | Improper Payments Information Act: Reassesses each federal agency to review annually its programs to identify erroneous payments. |
| 2004 | American Indian Probate Reform Act: Facilitates consolidation of Indian land ownership to restore economic viability to American Indian assets. |

Once the sole inhabitants of Australia, the Aborigines now constitute one percent of the total population and live a marginalized existence, facing the same problems that others living in poverty elsewhere also encounter. You can hear them play their traditional musical instrument, the didgeridoo, in the tourist theme parks or in You Tube videos.

the foundation that has shaped U.S. American Indian policy ever since. The Cherokee were not a foreign nation, the Court ruled, and therefore could not sue Georgia. They were instead a "domestic dependent nation," a "distinct community, occupying its own territory." Because of this definition, the Court said, the laws of Georgia had no jurisdiction, and the Court thus ruled in favor of the Cherokee keeping the land.

President Jackson reportedly responded, "John Marshall has rendered his decision, now let him enforce it." Indeed, two of the three branches of government favored removal of the Cherokee, and Jackson interpreted his overwhelming re-election in November as a mandate from the electorate to pursue that policy. Jackson thus moved to enforce the Indian Removal Act, launching one of the ugliest episodes in the nation's history.

**EXPULSION.** After signing the Treaty of Dancing Rabbit Creek (1830) under compulsion, the Choctaw of Mississippi were the first to face removal. The government forcibly relocated 20,000, of whom 5,000 died from famine and disease along the march to Indian Territory in Oklahoma. In 1836, the army moved against the Creek in Alabama, forcing 17,000 westward; 2,000 died from exposure, famine, and disease en route, and another 3,500 died within three months of arrival. Approximately 1,000 Chickasaw in Mississippi died during their forced march.[17] The Seminole in Florida successfully resisted expulsion by adapting guerrilla warfare tactics in the Everglades, killing nearly 2,000 soldiers and costing the U.S. Army more than $40 million before it gave up the fight.[18]

**THE CHEROKEE.** In about 1790, the Cherokee, after some 14 years of warfare with the whites, decided to adopt U.S. customs and culture. In other words, they actively sought assimilation in an effort to live harmoniously with a different civilization. During the next 40 years, their success in achieving this goal was remarkable. They converted their economy to one based on agriculture and commerce, strengthened their self-governing political system, and prospered. They cultivated farmlands in the fertile soil of the tri-state region of Georgia, Tennessee, and North Carolina and reaped bountiful harvests. The Cherokee patterned themselves after the whites and set up churches, schools, saw mills, grist mills, and blacksmith shops. They acquired spinning wheels, looms, plows, and all the other implements of white society.

Most extraordinary of all was the achievement of a Cherokee named Sequoyah. In 1821, after a determined 12-year effort, he succeeded in inventing a phonetic syllabary notation system for the Cherokee language. This immense accomplishment was unprecedented in 5,000 years of recorded history. A man, untrained in linguistics, had been able to write a language by himself and do so in a way that could be learned easily. Remarkably, within three years, nearly all the Cherokee could read and write their own language. By 1828, the tribe had its own newspaper and had adopted a written constitution, a code of laws, a bicameral legislature, and an appellate judiciary.[19]

By U.S. standards, the Cherokee were the most "civilized" tribe in the country. Driven by a desire for self-improvement, they educated themselves, converted to Christianity, and learned the whites' ways of agriculture, business, and government. They successfully acculturated. Only one problem remained: The whites wanted their rich land for growing cotton, and, consequently, the Cherokee now faced eviction, too.

With U.S. public opinion against the Cherokee, the voices of John Marshall, Daniel Webster, Henry Clay, Sam Houston, Davy Crockett, and others could not help the Cherokee cause. Georgia confiscated Cherokee lands and redistributed them to whites through land lotteries, with the state militia stationed in the region to preserve the peace should the American Indians resist:

> The premeditated brutality of the militia's daily conducts suggested their commanders' hope of provoking a Cherokee reaction, which might provide an excuse for their immediate physical expulsion. The carefully disciplined Cherokee instead patiently submitted even when the provocations extended to the burning of their homes, the confiscation of their property, the mistreatment of their women, the closing of their schools, and the sale of liquor in their churches.[20]

The Cherokee retreated into the forests and continued their desperate legal maneuvering to avoid expulsion. Although federal troops removed the Choctaw and Chickasaw in Mississippi and the Creek in Alabama, they did not move against the Cherokee, who had won worldwide sympathy and whose efforts to obtain recognition of their rights in the courts continued to be successful. Instead, the federal government intensified its efforts to promote disunity among the Cherokee through bribery, jailings, persecution, and denial of the services and support guaranteed under treaties. Most of the Cherokee remained loyal to their president, John Ross, and rejected the proposed treaty of removal and its $5 million compensation payment.

Government officials finally succeeded in getting the treaty signed on December 29, 1835, by convening an ad hoc council of President Ross's Cherokee opponents. Fewer than 500 of the 17,000 Cherokee appeared, but they signed the treaty, and the Senate ratified the pact on May 18, 1836. Ross and the Cherokee people fought this fraudulent treaty; and, in January 1838, Ross presented the Senate with a petition signed by 15,665 Cherokee repudiating the document. The Senate rejected the petition by a vote of 37 to 10. A new wave of public protest against the government's conduct toward the Cherokee swelled in the North, including an impassioned open letter to President Van Buren by Ralph Waldo Emerson, but these results did not alter the outcome. On April 10, 1838, Van Buren ordered General Winfield Scott to remove the Cherokee immediately, using whatever military force was necessary. Acting against an entire people who had willingly adapted to the changing world around them, soldiers forced them at gunpoint from their homes, first to stockades and then westward, far from all that had been theirs:

> Families at dinner were startled by the sudden gleam of bayonets in the door-way and rose up to be driven with blows and oaths along the weary miles to the stockade. Men were seized in their fields or going along the road, women were taken from their wheels, and children from their play. In many cases, on turning for one last look as they crossed the ridge, they saw their homes in flames, fired by the lawless rabble that followed on the heels of the soldiers to loot and pillage. So keen were these outlaws on the scent that in some instances, they were driving off the cattle and other stock of the Indians almost before the soldiers had fairly started their owners in the other direction. Systematic hunts were made by the same men for Indian graves, to rob them of the silver pendants and other valuables deposited with the dead. A Georgia volunteer, afterward a colonel in the Confederate service, said: "I fought through the Civil War and have seen men shot to pieces and slaughtered by thousands, but the Cherokee removal was the cruelest work I ever knew."[21]

The Cherokee suffered extensively during this mass expulsion. Beginning in October 1838, army troops marched the Cherokee westward along what the Cherokee later called the Trail of Tears: 10 to 20 American Indians died each day from exposure and other miseries. By March 1839, fewer than 9,000 of the 13,000 who had set out survived to reach the Indian Territory, which is now Oklahoma. At the midpoint of this sad episode—December 3, 1838—in his State of the Union report to Congress, President Van Buren announced,

> It affords me sincere pleasure to apprise the Congress of the entire removal of the Cherokee Nation of Indians to their new homes west of the Mississippi. The measures authorized by Congress at its last session have had the happiest effects....They have emigrated without any apparent reluctance.[22]

In one of the saddest chapters in U.S. history, the federal government expelled the Cherokee from their land in the western Georgia region and forced them to move 1,000 miles westward on a journey known as the "Trail of Tears," because of its devastating effects. Facing hunger, disease, and exhaustion, more than 4,000 died along the way.

## RESERVATIONS AND DEPENDENCE

A shift in U.S. government policy in the mid-nineteenth century changed American Indian lifestyles to such an extent that its after effects remain visible today on any reservation. Switching from using annihilation and expulsion to deal with the American Indians, the government embarked on a policy of segregation and isolation, establishing, between 1850 and 1880, most of the nation's Indian reservations.

In 1871, Congress ended federal recognition of the American Indian tribes as independent, **sovereign** nations—or "domestic dependent nations," for that matter—and made them wards of the government instead. Bureaucrats became responsible for the welfare of the American Indian peoples, issuing them food rations and supervising every aspect of their lives. The results were devastating. Proud and independent people who had been taught self-reliance at an early age now depended on outsiders for their welfare. Many of the tribes, once nomads, found it difficult to adjust to reservation life. Such problems as inadequate administration by government agents and irregular delivery of food, supplies, and equipment made matters worse.

The government was not restructuring American Indian lifestyles. Americanization became the goal. This meant destroying tribal organizations, suppressing "pagan" religions and ceremonies, allowing only English as the language of instruction in the schools, requiring "white" clothing and hair styles, and teaching only the dominant (white) group's culture and history:

> Most of the attention of the Americanizers was concentrated on the Indian children, who were snatched from their families and shipped off to boarding schools far from their homes. The children usually were kept at boarding school for eight years, during which time, they were not permitted to see their parents, relatives, or friends. Anything Indian—dress, language, religious practices, even outlook on life (and how that was defined was up to the judgment of each administration of the government's directives)—was uncompromisingly prohibited. Ostensibly educated, articulate in the English language, wearing store-bought clothes, and with their hair short and their emotionalism toned down, the boarding-school graduates were sent out either to make their way in a white world that did not want them, or to return to a reservation to which they were now foreign.[23]

One extensively taught value was the rugged individualism of white society rather than the cooperative, noncompetitive approach of the American Indian. This was the purpose of the General Allotment Act of 1887. Its sponsor, Senator Henry L. Dawes, genuinely believed that the law would inspire American Indians with the spirit of self-interest that he considered the major force in white civilization.

In reality, this legislation deprived American Indians of even more land. Its goal was to break the backbone of American Indian culture by ending communal ownership of reservation lands and instead giving each American Indian a private parcel of land. Many American Indians had no technical knowledge of farming and neither the cash nor credit to obtain farm implements. Some American Indian peoples believed it was sacrilegious to plow the earth. Loopholes in the Dawes Act enabled unscrupulous whites to plunder the American Indians' lands, either through low-cost, long-term leases or by convincing American Indian owners to write wills leaving their property to white "friends." This practice was widespread, and a mysterious increase in the number of American Indian deaths followed; some of these deaths later were proved to have been murders.[24]

In 1898, faced with tribes that refused to accept the allotment policy, the government passed the Curtis Act. This law terminated the tribal governments of all tribes that resisted allotment, and it made their tribal chiefs presidential appointees thereafter. By 1914, the 138 million acres of American Indian holdings had been reduced to 56 million acres of eroded, poor-quality land.[25]

## INDIAN REORGANIZATION ACT

After 1933, Franklin Roosevelt's administration shifted from a policy of forced assimilation to one of pluralism. The Indian Reorganization Act of 1934 ended the land-allotment program, encouraged tribal self-government, extended financial credit to the tribes, gave preference in Bureau of Indian Affairs (BIA) employment to American Indians, and permitted consolidation of American Indian lands split up through inheritance. Furthermore, American Indians were encouraged to revive their ancient arts and crafts, their languages, their religions and ceremonies, and their customs and traditions. In keeping with an administrative philosophy of treating American Indians with dignity, the act was permissive, not mandatory; each tribe could vote to accept or reject the new law. Most chose to accept it.

In the 1950s, new top administrative personnel in President Eisenhower's Interior Department and the BIA advocated a different philosophy and shifted the BIA back to assimilationist policy. Critics of the 1934 legislation considered it regressive. Believing that the only way to end the chronic poverty, disease, overpopulation, and despair among the American Indians was to end the isolation of reservation life, the new administration tried other approaches.

## THE RELOCATION PROGRAM

Beginning in the 1950s, the Bureau of Indian Affairs offered assistance to individuals or families who wanted to relocate in urban areas to obtain jobs and living accommodations. For many American Indians, the word *relocation* had terrible connotations. That was the euphemism used a few years earlier for the internment camps in which 110,000 Japanese Americans had been placed during World War II. Furthermore, Dillon S. Myer, the government administrator who had been in charge of those camps, was now in charge of the American Indian relocation program.

Most of the 40,000 American Indians who enrolled in this program went to work in low-status, unskilled or semi-skilled jobs and found housing in the poorer sections of the cities. Some adjusted and became acculturated; others felt uprooted, became alcoholics, and fared poorly. As a result, more than one-fourth of the total number returned to the reservations. The program tapered off after 1960, due mostly to other efforts to improve American Indian life.

## THE TERMINATION ACT

Legislative acts passed in 1953–1954 sought to end federal responsibility for welfare and administration of American Indians by ending all federal services and liaison with tribal organizations and by selling reservation land and giving that revenue to the tribes. Medical care, schools, road maintenance, and other federal services guaranteed under treaty obligations immediately were halted, instead of gradually withdrawn to allow a period of transitional adjustments. The termination acts affected 109 tribes and bands, as 12,500 American Indians lost tribal affiliations, and approximately 2.5 million acres of trust land removed from protected status.[26]

Two of the more prosperous tribes—the Klamath of southern Oregon and the Menominee of Wisconsin (both of whom owned considerable tracts of valuable timberland)—as well as some Paiute and Ute in Utah and several other tribes, were among the

**TABLE 7.2** Formerly Terminated American Indian Tribes Now Restored

| TRIBE OR BAND | STATE | POPULATION | ACRES |
|---|---|---|---|
| Alabama-Coushatta | Texas | 450 | 3,200 |
| California Rancherias (37–38 rancherias) | California | 1,107 | 4,315 |
| Catawba | South Carolina | 631 | 3,388 |
| Coyote Valley Ranch | California | NA | NA |
| Klamath | Oregon | 2,133 | 862,662 |
| Lower Lake Rancheria | California | NA | NA |
| Menominee | Wisconsin | 3,270 | 233,881 |
| Ottawa | Oklahoma | 630 | NA |
| Peoria | Oklahoma | 640 | NA |
| Ponca | Nebraska | 442 | 834 |
| Southern Paiute | Utah | 232 | 42,839 |
| Western Oregon (61 tribes and bands) | Oregon | 2,081 | 3,158 |
| Wyandotte | Oklahoma | 1,157 | 94 |

*Note:* NA = not available.

*Source:* Bureau of Indian Affairs.

first to suffer from this legislation. For the Klamath, a tribe of 668 families totaling some 2,000 individuals, termination threatened to obliterate their tribal identity.

In the case of the Menominee, the new policy brought economic disaster. In the rapid transformation of federally funded Menominee reservation into an independent, self-supporting county, the tribe suddenly was financially responsible for all public services (such as maintenance of roads and bridges, police, and hospital). Also obliged to pay taxes on its sawmill and forests, soon many Indians faced the loss of their homes and life savings. Wisconsin soon had a serious welfare crisis it could not fund and desperately sought help from the federal government, which was chagrined to realize it was not freed of the Menominee as it had planned.[27]

The standard of living dropped sharply as the tribe lost its ability to furnish water, electricity, and health care. Shortly after termination, a tuberculosis epidemic swept through the Menominee. Washington's reckless policy shift cost the Menominee their hospital, their sawmill, and some of their best land—lakefront property, which they had to sell because they could not afford the taxes on it. President Nixon officially repudiated the termination policy in 1970, and Congress reversed the termination of the Menominee in December 1973. The Restoration Act recreated their reservation, but the Menominee never got back their old hospital or sawmill. Between 1977 and 1990, most of the other tribes that had been terminated also had their federal recognition restored (Table 7.2) but, in many cases, not their land.

**7-5** Assess quality of life among contemporary American Indians.

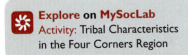

**Explore on MySocLab**
Activity: Tribal Characteristics in the Four Corners Region

# Present-Day American Indian Life

Of all the minorities in the United States, according to government statistics on income, employment, and housing, American Indians are "the poorest of the poor." It is cruelly ironic that most of the American Indians' problems are due not only to their subordinate position as a result of conquest but also to their insistence on their right to be different, to continue living as American Indians. In a society that has long demanded assimilation, this insistence has not been popular.

| American Indian Population | | | Age | Total U.S. Population | | |
|---|---|---|---|---|---|---|
| Males | | Females | | Males | | Females |

| | Males | Females | | | Males | Females | |
|---|---|---|---|---|---|---|---|
| *Median age 29.4* | 1.8 | 2.5 | *Median age 31.0* | 70+ | *Median age 35.8* | 3.7 | 5.3 *Median age 38.5* |
| | 3.2 | 3.5 | | 60–69 | | 4.5 | 4.9 |
| | 5.7 | 6.1 | | 50–59 | | 6.6 | 6.9 |
| | 6.8 | 6.9 | | 40–49 | | 7.0 | 7.1 |
| | 6.9 | 6.7 | | 30–39 | | 6.5 | 6.5 |
| | 8.1 | 7.7 | | 20–29 | | 7.0 | 6.8 |
| | 8.9 | 8.5 | | 10–19 | | 7.1 | 6.7 |
| | 8.4 | 8.2 | | 0–9 | | 6.7 | 6.4 |

9 8 7 6 5 4 3 2 1 0 1 2 3 4 5 6 7 8 9
Percentage

9 8 7 6 5 4 3 2 1 0 1 2 3 4 5 6 7 8 9
Percentage

**FIGURE 7.1** American Indian Population, 2010 (in percentages)

## POPULATION

The Census Bureau reported in 2012 that the American Indian and Alaska Native population was 2.5 million for those claiming only that race, and more than 5.1 million if combined with two or more races. They have a lower fertility rate (48.6 births per 1,000 women ages 15 to 44, compared to Asians (59.2), blacks (66.3), and whites (64.4)).[28]

As Figure 7.1 indicates, the age distribution of the American Indian population (including Alaska Natives) is weighted toward the younger years to a much greater extent than that of the total U.S. population. The greater ratio of the population in childbearing age groups suggests continued faster rates of population increase among American Indians. They are far from being the "vanishing Americans" some observers once claimed.

Watch **on** MySocLab
Video: The Basics: Health and Medicine

Read **on** MySocLab
Document: Playing the Political Slots: American Indians and Casinos

## EDUCATION

Significant changes have occurred since 1976, when the American Indian Policy Review Commission criticized the BIA for failing to resolve any of the problems in the BIA school system. Singled out for especially sharp condemnation were the 19 boarding schools described as "dumping grounds for students with serious social and emotional problems," which "do not rehabilitate" but "do more harm than good." Moreover, it accused the BIA of violating official policy by not sending students to the school closest to their homes, but often hundreds of miles away.[29] The intent of this deliberate action was to force a separation between children and their parents and between "children and the idea of the reservation."[30] (See the Ethnic Experience box.)

The Educational Amendments Act of 1978 gave substantial control over school policy and programs to the American Indian communities. As a result, local school boards and school authorities now ensure that the curriculum addresses the unique aspects of American Indian culture and heritage. Further, bilingual American Indian language programs in 17 states help preserve ancestral languages and teach English to children who were raised in households where only their tribal language was spoken.

**IMPROVEMENT.** Significant improvements in educational achievement have occurred in recent years, but American Indians still lag behind the rest of the U.S. population. Fewer American Indians graduate from high school (79 percent), and fewer still complete college (13 percent).[31] On average, if 100 American Indian students enter the ninth grade,

# the ETHNIC experience

## Boarding School Experiences

"We lived for a few years on Devil's Lake Reservation in North Dakota... I spoke no English until I was four years old. Everything we spoke in the house was Sioux. The religion that my mother and my father both professed was that of their respective tribes. My father had taken on the Sioux religion and my mother was Mohawk..."

"I can tell you more about the actual life of a reservation-born Indian, drawing from my mother's experience, than on my own. When my mother was eight years old, economic pressures and also family pressures from the point of view of social justice forced all of the five children of her family to be sent to the Haskell Indian Institute for their education. There was so little future for them if they remained on the reservation, so little possibility of an education..."

"My mother was still on crutches. She had had a very serious operation and she was six years between crutches and wheelchair and had to have the operation repeated. Yet she was never excused from any one of the regimental disciplines that were rampant at Haskell. For example, the first statement off the bus was, 'You will

be up at five o'clock in the morning. From this moment on, there is to be no Indian spoken and the punishments are very severe for anyone who violates this law. You must speak English.'"

"My mother had learned first Indian and then some French. She knew not a word of English and yet no one was allowed to ask any companion [for] even the slightest translation. My mother saw severe punishments inflicted on my aunts and uncles, but she herself, because she was so sick, was never punished. However, she was very careful not to violate the rules. Despite the fact she was still in a wheelchair, she had to be out at reveille in the morning. They were up at five o'clock. By five-fifteen, they had reveille: You had to be dressed, your face washed, and you had to be standing in military formation. Then the roll call was called. It was all with the viewpoint of checking who had escaped during the night, because escape was rampant. There was actually some kind of barbed wire around the enclosure at that time..."

"The absolute cutoff and isolation from the tribal customs and from the language brought about a lot of

culture shock. And the big thing at Haskell was to try to fool the white folks. The Indians always felt that they were on the other side of the line and that nothing would ever overcome that barrier..."

"The Indians were forced to take on a Christian religion. Either you adhered to a Christian religion or you were assigned to heavy duty on Sunday mornings, and nobody wanted that. So my mother simply joined the Methodist Church not out of any conviction whatsoever, but because she had had a delicate operation on the hip; and when she saw that the Catholics were bundled off in a pickup truck whereas those who went to the Methodist church had a comfortable, plush school bus, that was the cause for her choice of religion. She never, however, really joined the church, was never baptized. She simply conformed because she said that was the way to keep the white people off her back."

"Now they say that the whole setup has changed a lot and there is none of that rigid discipline."

Source: Sioux–Mohawk woman whose mother went to boarding school in the 1940s. Taped interview from the collection of Vincent N. Parrillo.

only 79 will graduate from high school. Of these graduates, approximately half will enter college, and only approximately 13 will earn a degree (see Figure 7.2).

**TRIBAL COLLEGES AND UNIVERSITIES.** Tribally controlled colleges came into existence in 1968 when the Navajo Nation established the first such institution, Navajo Community College, in Arizona (now called Diné College). Accelerating this movement was federal legislation in 1978 that provided funding for the establishment and continued operation of such colleges. Then, in 1996, President Clinton issued the Tribal Colleges Executive Order—renewed by President Bush in 2002—that directed federal agencies to provide more resources to tribal colleges. Yet the tribal colleges have an uneven growth. While 17 new ones have opened in the recent decades, seven others have closed.[32] In Fall 2010, approximately 30,000 American Indian students were enrolled

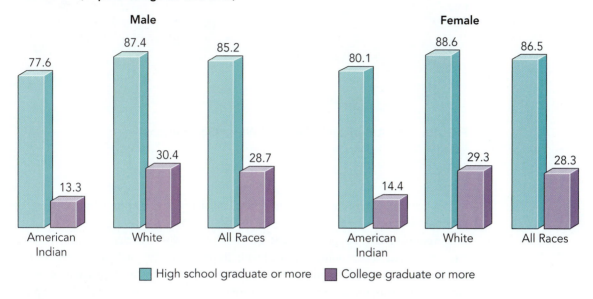

**Age by percent**

28.9 — American Indian or Alaska Native (Under 18 years)
7.8 — American Indian or Alaska Native (65 years & over)
21.8 — White (Under 18 years)
15.2 — White (65 years & over)
23.7 — All Races (Under 18 years)
13.3 — All Races (65 years & over)

☐ Under 18 years
☐ 65 years & over

**Education (of persons age 25 and over)**

Male

77.6 — American Indian (High school graduate or more)
13.3 — American Indian (College graduate or more)
87.4 — White (High school graduate or more)
30.4 — White (College graduate or more)
85.2 — All Races (High school graduate or more)
28.7 — All Races (College graduate or more)

Female

80.1 — American Indian (High school graduate or more)
14.4 — American Indian (College graduate or more)
88.6 — White (High school graduate or more)
29.3 — White (College graduate or more)
86.5 — All Races (High school graduate or more)
28.3 — All Races (College graduate or more)

☐ High school graduate or more   ☐ College graduate or more

**Economic Status**

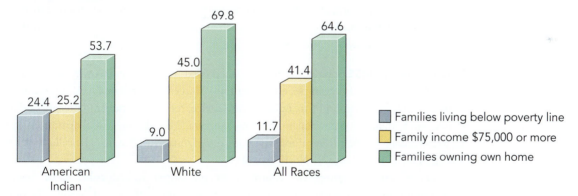

American Indian: 24.4, 25.2, 53.7
White: 9.0, 45.0, 69.8
All Races: 11.7, 41.4, 64.6

☐ Families living below poverty line
☐ Family income $75,000 or more
☐ Families owning own home

**FIGURE 7.2   Social Indicators about American Indian Progress (in percentages)**

*Source:* U.S. Census Bureau, *2011 American Community Survey.*

full- or part-time in 36 institutions in 14 states.[33] Tribal colleges and universities offer a family-like support system, reaffirming their cultural identity while preparing them to succeed in the larger society.

## EMPLOYMENT

Chronic unemployment remains a serious problem, exceeding 50 percent on many reservations and sometimes as high as 83 percent at the Pine Ridge and Rosebud reservations in South Dakota.[34] However, as educational attainment improves, so do employment opportunities. American Indian workers, in comparison to non-Hispanic

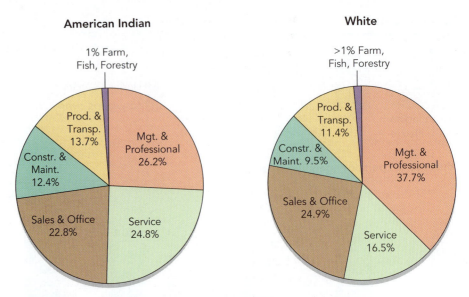

**American Indian**

1% Farm, Fish, Forestry

Prod. & Transp. 13.7%

Mgt. & Professional 26.2%

Constr. & Maint. 12.4%

Sales & Office 22.8%

Service 24.8%

**White**

>1% Farm, Fish, Forestry

Prod. & Transp. 11.4%

Mgt. & Professional 37.7%

Constr. & Maint. 9.5%

Sales & Office 24.9%

Service 16.5%

**FIGURE 7.3** American Indian and White Occupations

Source: U.S. Census Bureau, *2011 American Community Survey.*

whites, have a higher representation in blue-collar or lower-paying white-collar occupational fields.

Approximately 26 percent ages 16 and older work in management, business, science, and arts occupations, compared with 38 percent of the total population. Another 23 percent work in sales and office occupations, compared with 25 percent of whites. American Indians also are employed in a variety of other occupations, including approximately 25 percent in service occupations; 12 percent in construction, extraction, and maintenance occupations; and approximately another 14 percent in production, transportation, and material moving occupations, which are higher percentages in each field than for the total population (Figure 7.3).[35]

**TRIBAL ENTERPRISE.** Some tribes have succeeded through their own efforts. The Mississippi Choctaw, for example, are one of the 10 largest private employers in that state, with a diversified portfolio of manufacturing, service, retail, and tourism enterprises that employ more than 6,000 permanent full-time workers.[36] Similar successful operations can be found among the Salt River Pima Maricopa of Arizona, New Mexico's Jicarilla Apache, and the Devil's Lake Sioux of North Dakota.

The Cherokee Nation, the country's second largest Indian tribe, earns nearly $100 million in profits each year from commercial ventures through Cherokee Nation Industries, with companies in gaming, manufacturing, telecommunications, and environmental services industries.[37] The Maine Passamaquoddy maintain approximately 135,000 acres of harvestable timber, as well as an 1,800-acre blueberry farm, the third largest in the world, making them one of the nation's largest blueberry producers. Harvesting approximately 3.2 million pounds each year pumps approximately $500,000 into each of the Passamaquoddy's two reservations, where poverty is common and unemployment can reach 50 percent.[38]

**THE "NEW BUFFALO."** Because federal law permits them to offer any form of gambling not prohibited in other parts of the state, 242 tribes operated casinos in 28 states in 2011. They generated more than $9 billion in federal taxes and revenue savings through reduced welfare and unemployment benefit payments.[39]

Nicknamed the "new buffalo" because of their role in providing for the tribes' well-being, most of these casinos barely break even because they are too small and too remote.

To illustrate, five states—Montana, Nevada, North Dakota, Oklahoma, and South Dakota—contain nearly half the total American Indian population but generate less than 3 percent of all casino proceeds. In contrast, casinos in California, Connecticut, and Florida—totaling only 3 percent of the total American Indian population—take in 44 percent of all revenue, approximately $100,000 per tribal member. Thus, only a few wealthy tribes benefit from lucrative casinos. For hundreds of thousands of American Indians living in poverty, the casinos do nothing. Meanwhile, the white backers of the casinos are earning billions of dollars on their investments.[40]

## HEALTH CONCERNS

Demographic statistics (see Table 7.3) testify to the harshness and deprivation of reservation life and the despair accompanying it. The Indian Health Service reports that American Indians born today have a life expectancy that is 5.2 years less than the national average, and their infants die at a rate of 8.4 per every 1,000 live births, as compared to 6.9 per 1,000 for all races. Moreover, they die at higher rates than other Americans from tuberculosis (500 percent higher), alcoholism (514 percent higher), diabetes (177 percent higher), unintentional injuries (140 percent higher), homicide (92 percent higher), and suicide (82 percent higher).[41]

Why have American Indians long experienced lower health statuses in comparison to other Americans? In the words of the Indian Health Service:

> Lower life expectancy and the disproportionate disease burden exist perhaps because of inadequate education, disproportionate poverty, discrimination in the delivery of health services, and cultural differences. These are broad quality of life issues rooted in economic adversity and poor social conditions.[42]

In an extensive review of the American Indian healthcare system and the role of the federal government, the U.S. Commission on Civil Rights concluded "that persistent discrimination and neglect continue to deprive American Indians of a health system sufficient to provide health care equivalent to that provided to the vast majority of Americans."[43]

**SUICIDE AND VIOLENCE.** The number of deaths by suicide among American Indians generally is higher than for all other groups. Suicide among American Indian males ages 15 to 24 (30.6 per 100,000) is three times that of the general population's youth

**TABLE 7.3** Age-Adjusted Death Rates in the United States per 100,000 Population 2010

| CAUSE OF DEATH | AMERICAN INDIANS | ALL RACES | RATIO |
|---|---|---|---|
| Heart disease | 65.5 | 193.6 | 0.3 |
| Malignant neoplasms (cancer) | 69.5 | 186.2 | 0.4 |
| Accidents | 39.9 | 39.1 | 1.0 |
| Diabetes mellitus | 20.1 | 22.4 | 0.9 |
| Chronic liver disease and cirrhosis | 18.5 | 10.3 | 1.7 |
| Chronic lower respiratory diseases | 16.5 | 44.7 | 0.4 |
| Cerebrovascular diseases | 13.1 | 41.9 | 0.3 |
| Suicide | 11.0 | 12.4 | 0.9 |
| Influenza, pneumonia | 7.6 | 16.2 | 0.5 |

*Source:* National Center for Health Statistics, "Deaths: Final Data for 2010," National Vital Statistics Reports, 61 (2013): Table 15.

*The Pequot tribe in Mashantucket, Connecticut, owns Foxwoods, a spectacularly successful gambling casino bringing great wealth to its members. However, it is the exception; most tribal casinos are small-time bingo or poker gambling halls, whose revenues do little to combat the poverty plaguing so many reservations.*

(10.5 per 100,000).[44] Recent studies reveal that risk factors for suicide among American Indian youth include strained interpersonal relationships, family instability, depression, low self-esteem, alcohol use or substance abuse, negative school attitudes, and perceived discrimination.[45]

Suicide is not the only violence in the world of American Indians. The U.S. Justice Department reports that they experience violence far more than any other racial or ethnic group and at more than twice the national average. They are nearly three times as likely as whites and nearly twice as likely as blacks to be victims of rape or aggravated assault. Alcohol abuse, tensions with non–American Indians, poor law enforcement services, and other factors all may play a part in generating such high rates of violent crime.[46]

Sadly, gang violence is another problem on some reservations and is increasing. On the Pine Ridge Indian Reservation, for example, at least 39 gangs exist and officials blame them for the increase in vandalism, theft, violence, and fear that is altering the texture of life in Indian country. The gangs are luring youth from broken, alcohol-ravaged homes by offering brotherhood and protection from other gangs. Like any urban ghetto, gang tags are sprayed on buildings and fights break out among rival gangs.[47]

**ALCOHOL ABUSE.** A serious social problem facing American Indians today is alcohol abuse, which also is a major factor in their high **mortality rate**. American Indians have a rate of terminal liver cirrhosis twice the national rate, and the majority of American Indian suicides and motor vehicle deaths involve the use of alcohol.[48] Crimes related to consumption of alcohol and other drugs occur more often among American Indians than among whites in the same geographic areas.[49]

A myth exists that American Indians are more susceptible to alcohol problems. However, alcohol metabolism and alcohol genetics are traits of individuals, and there is more variation within any ethnic group than there is between ethnic groups.[50] In addition, one national study revealed that American Indians actually may drink less than the total U.S. population. Surveyed tribes reported a 40 percent drinking rate compared to the national rate of 70 percent. This suggests that those American Indians who do drink may experience more adverse consequences than others, and that perhaps alcoholism among American Indians is not innate.[51]

Still, drinking problem sets in early among American Indian youths. Age at first involvement with alcohol is younger than all other groups, the frequency and the amount of drinking are greater, and the negative consequences are more common. Although white youths' alcohol consumption begins to diminish after age 22, no comparable decline occurs among American Indian youths.[52] However, research shows that positive, pro-social development through parental support/involvement and school bonding facilitates youths' refusal skills against the temptations of substance abuse.[53]

Cultural marginality is an important factor in understanding alcohol and drug abuse, as studies have shown that American Indians with a stronger sense of ethnic pride are more likely to adhere to antidrug norms than those with little pride.[54] On the one hand, American Indians seek to maintain their tribal identity and traditional cultural heritage, even though they are not always certain what their heritage means in the context of modern life; on the other hand, they desire respect, success in the world of work and careers, and the standard of living enjoyed by the dominant society. Inner conflict occurs because the two sets of standards that American Indians attempt to reconcile are not always consistent. What mainstream society deems appropriate may be undesirable according to tribal values, and vice versa.[55]

### HOUSING

One of the most visible signs of American Indians' economic deprivation is reservation housing, called "open-air slums" by some critics. Mostly located down back roads and therefore rarely seen by reservation visitors, the various tribes often live in small, over-crowded western-style houses, in mobile homes, or in hogans—traditional one-room, eight-sided log houses with sod roofs. Fourteen percent of Native households have no electricity, nearly 12 percent lack plumbing, and 11 percent lack kitchen facilities. In some areas, up to 50 percent of Native homes are without phone service.[56]

Because many American Indians live in crowded dwellings, have limited sanitation facilities, and are exposed to smoke from wood-burning stoves, they are more likely to suffer from respiratory and other infectious diseases than other minority groups.[57]

## Natural Resources

Encroachment on American Indian land to obtain natural resources or fertile land continues. The need for water and energy has led government and industry to look covetously at reservation land once considered worthless. Moreover, many American Indians have serious concerns about use of their lands as dumping grounds. Another issue that divides the Indian community is balancing their environmental concerns against the need for economic development.

Read on MySocLab
Document: Women of Color on the Front Line

### ENVIRONMENTAL ISSUES

Underneath the 53 million acres held by 22 western tribes lie some of the nation's richest reserves of natural gas, oil, coal, and uranium, worth billions of dollars. In fact, one-third of the nation's low-sulfur coal and at least half of its uranium deposits are on tribal land. Some tribes, such as the oil-rich Osage in Oklahoma, benefit from the sale of these resources. Only 14 percent of American Indians, however, live on reservations that receive natural-resource revenues.

Even when a tribe thinks its timber, mining, or fishing royalties have secured it a measure of financial stability, such may not be the case. The BIA leased large tracts of Indian land to gas and oil companies but failed to collect any money from them. Even when the Department of the Interior received many millions of dollars of royalty payments, it sent the money to the Department of the Interior without instructions. As a result, Treasury officials put the money in a general fund where it was used for various government expenditures and to reduce the national debt.[58] None went into the Indian

Trust Fund. Such irresponsibility led to a class-action lawsuit a few years ago charging the government mismanaged more than $100 billion in oil, timber, grazing, and other royalties on land owned by some 500,000 individual Indian beneficiaries. A 2010 settlement approved by Congress provided $1.4 billion to be shared among the plaintiffs (yielding just $1,000 per plaintiff) and included creation of a $60 million federal Indian Education Scholarship fund to improve access to higher education for Indian youth.[59]

**BLACKFEET.** The Sweet Grass Hills are 1,000-foot-high volcanic pyramids standing on the plains of Montana. The hills receive twice the rainfall the plains do, and some observers say the grass grows sweeter in the meadows of these hills than anywhere else. American Indians from across the continent travel here to collect it for their ceremonies, braiding and drying it, then burning it to "smudge" (purify) people and objects with its sweet, sacred smoke.

As both a burial ground and a place where the Blackfeet of Montana have practiced their religion, the hills are sacred to this tribe, once the fiercest of the northern Plains peoples. In 1995, the land faced the threat of strip mining for gold under the Mining Act of 1872. Approximately 150 miles east-southeast of the Sweet Grass Hills are the Little Rocky Mountains, where previous gold mining has scarred the land, silted in the creeks, and leached cyanide (used by miners to bond and remove finely disseminated gold) into the water. Because the hills are a critical source of water for surrounding ranches and farms, an unusual coalition of environmentalists, farmers, ranchers, and the Blackfeet fought to stop two mining companies from changing the Sweet Grass Hills forever. In 1997, the Bureau of Land Management placed a ban on new oil and gas drilling in this region for 20 years, but this moratorium does not impact valid existing mineral rights, and so the hills are not protected until the claims of the two mining companies are purchased or exchanged. Moreover, the mining companies have an appeal pending in federal court to void this settlement.[60]

**NAVAJO.** More than 175,000 Navajo, 33 percent of them younger than 18 years old, live on the nation's largest American Indian reservation. Larger than the state of West Virginia, its 27,000 square miles surround the four-corner junction of Arizona, New Mexico, Colorado, and Utah. Beneath this harsh, barren land, an estimated 2.5 billion tons of coal and 55 million pounds of uranium deposits lie untouched in the ground.[61] Ironically, high-voltage wires run across vast tracts of the Navajo Nation, carrying

*Strip mining is an irreversible abuse of land, removing all soil and vegetation, polluting groundwater with heavy metals, and permanently altering the ecosystem. These peaks, north of Flagstaff, Arizona, are sacred to the Navajo, who succeeded in getting the mine closed in 2000, when the U.S. government paid the mine owners $1 million to shut down. However, the scarring of the land in the foreground is permanent.*

electricity to California but not to many of the Navajo living under them. An estimated 16,000 homes, one-third the total on the reservation, currently are without electricity, and many more homes and families are without access to basic infrastructure, such as telephones, water, wastewater, and natural gas. The Navajo Tribal Utility Authority is currently working to provide hybrid solar array and small wind turbine units to generate electricity for these homes.[62]

Perhaps the Navajo will fare better securing alternative energy than they did with coal. When the 20-year coal lease expired in 1984, the Navajo asked the Secretary of the Interior to exercise his power to increase the royalty rate, as recommended by the BIA Director for the Navajo Area, to 20 percent of gross proceeds. Instead, the rate was set significantly lower. After decades of trying to reset the royalty rate and get back royalties in excess of $600 million, the Navajo lawsuit reached the U.S. Supreme Court. In a 2009 ruling, the Court rejected their claim of a breach of fiduciary responsibility, with Justice Antonin Scalia saying, "This case is at an end."[63]

Between 1944 and 1986, companies extracted approximately 4 million tons of uranium ore from reservation land under leases with the Navajo Nation. Many Navajo worked in those mines, often living and raising families in close proximity to them. Today, those 500-plus abandoned mines still hold a legacy of uranium contamination affecting homes and approximately one-fifth of all drinking-water sources with elevated levels of radiation. Potential health effects include lung cancer from inhalation of radioactive particles, as well as bone cancer and impaired kidney function from radioactive elements in drinking water. Some Navajo have been sickened and died from these contaminants. Although the Environmental Protection Agency (EPA) is in the midst of a five-year cleanup process, it has warned children and pregnant women not to eat the carp and catfish in the San Juan River that passes through the reservation.[64]

**SOUTHERN UTE.** In pleasant contrast, the Southern Ute tribe, located on a 700,000-acre reservation in southwest Colorado, have become an energy powerhouse and a model for other resource-based tribes. Sitting on top of one of the world's richest deposits of methane, they control the distribution of approximately 1 percent of the nation's natural gas supply, after buying back the drilling rights in the 1990s. With a net worth of approximately $4 billion and wisely diversifying, mostly through real estate investments, they have donated land for a new county hospital, built a new elementary school and a plush $9.4 million recreation and community center, and offer full scholarships and living stipends for the tribe's college students.[65]

**COUNCIL OF ENERGY RESOURCE TRIBES.** Twenty-five American Indian tribes formed the Council of Energy Resource Tribes (CERT) in 1975. Modeling itself after the OPEC (Organization of Petroleum Exporting Countries) oil cartel, American Indian leaders believed their organization could prevent further exploitation and secure far greater revenues in return for tribal mineral resources. In 2013, the number of CERT member tribes totaled 53 in the United States and 4 in Canada.[66] The organization offers technical assistance, focuses on internal energy needs of the tribes, and seeks to increase the employment of American Indian youths by increasing their engineering and technical skills and by developing proposals to industrialize reservations with royalties from development of energy resources, including wind. Critics, including other American Indians, worry about environmental destruction and disruption of traditional values and culture caused by tapping into the natural resources.

## ENVIRONMENTAL RACISM

With landfills filling up or shutting down because pollutants are leaching into groundwater, disposal companies are looking for cheap new sites for the billions of tons of solid-waste materials and 40 million tons of hazardous-waste materials produced annually in the United States.[67] American Indian lands are not subject to the same set of environmental regulations as the rest of the country. Poor, but possessing large tracts of isolated land, American Indians in recent decades have seen their reservations recommended as radioactive waste dump sites.

Such proposals and the examples given earlier are examples of **environmental racism**, the disproportionate impact of hazardous substances on low-income minority groups, particularly people of color. Its opposite is **environmental justice**, a movement to abolish environmental harms to all people.[68] Both the antinuclear and environmental justice movements, working with members of these Native communities, have stopped every such proposal so far. At Prairie Island, Minnesota, however, Indian land involuntarily hosts a massive storage facility for spent fuel rods only 600 yards from the tribal day-care center. In 2012, the facility had separate toxic chemical and radiological spills in less than a week.[69]

The tribes find themselves torn between economic development to generate badly needed revenue sources and violating their beliefs about the sacredness of the land. Called everything from hapless victims of environmental racism to unscrupulous opportunists selling out their heritage by despoiling Mother Earth for profit, tribal leaders reject such criticism, seeing these projects as a means to fight high unemployment rates and gain millions of dollars of annual tribal income.

Another tribe had little choice about its contact with waste. The St. Regis Mohawk reservation on the St. Lawrence River near Massena, New York, home to 10,000 people, was inundated with chemical pollutants for decades. Located downstream and downwind in an industrial corridor extending 100 miles west to Lake Ontario, the reservation suffered from both aquatic poisoning and airborne toxins and experienced a high number of birth defects, thyroid disease, and diabetes.[70] Its water and land food chains are permeated with PCBs (polychlorinated biphenyls) discharged by General Motors (GM), Reynolds Metal, and other corporate polluters. Despite fines, EPA dredging of 30 tons of contaminated soil from the river and hauling toxic sludge from lagoons on company property, problems still remain. Twelve abandoned GM sites, including a 270-acre site along the river that possesses a "significant threat to human life," contain contaminants that could cost as much as $225 million to clean up. However, when GM emerged from bankruptcy in 2009, it was freed of obligations for these polluted properties.[71]

### WATER RIGHTS

Nevada's Pyramid Lake, a spectacular 30-mile expanse of water, belongs to the Paiute, whose water rights the federal government is supposed to protect. Instead, in 1906, the government developed an irrigation project to divert 9.8 billion gallons of water each year before it reached the lake. By the 1940s, the water level had dropped 80 feet, killing the trout on which the Paiute depended. In 1944, the U.S. Supreme Court decided the water rights case, awarding the tribe $8 million in damages. However, in settling the case on their behalf, the Department of Justice did nothing about the fish crisis, the water level in the lake, or imposing restrictions on future irrigation. Finally, the Department of Justice, formally confessing its "breach of faith with the Indians," petitioned the Supreme Court in 1983 to reopen the case to allow the Paiute to refill their lake. A 1996 agreement settled the lawsuit, as three localities and the Department of the Interior agreed to fund a $24 million program to improve river flows, water levels, and wildlife conditions over a five-year period. Today, the Paiute economy centers on permits it issues for fishing, camping, and recreational activities at the lake.

Water disputes are sharpest in the West, where the water table is the lowest. For decades, farmers and ranchers have tapped into rivers and streams on or near Indian reservations. Urban sprawl and agribusiness have prompted others to sink deep wells around reservations, siphoning off the water reserves of several tribes. In New Mexico, for example, farmers undermined a viable water system the Pueblo Tribe had built 200 years before the Spanish arrived, leaving that tribe without an adequate water supply. In 2006, a water rights settlement agreement was reached between the Taos Pueblo, the state of New Mexico, and affected non-American Indian parties that mutually resolved Pueblo water rights claims and provided basic rules for groundwater production without injuring surface water supplies or underground aquifers.

Water rights are the western tribes' most valuable rights, providing a basis for achieving economic independence. Loss of water dooms them to an even worse existence. On the bright side, since the 1980s, most water rights cases were settled in favor of the affected tribes, resulting in tens of millions of dollars awarded in each case. In 2001, the U.S. Supreme Court supported claims by five tribal reservations to water rights for the Colorado River, reflecting the continuing struggle for water in the Southwest.[72]

States and tribes must negotiate how much the tribes have coming before the federal rights are exercised. After reaching an agreement with the states, the tribes ask Congress to ratify the water rights deals, which it has done about two dozen times in the past three decades. Among the tribes seeking millions of federal dollars to build reservoirs and pipelines have been the Blackfeet in Montana, the Shoshone and Paiute in Idaho–Nevada, and the Soboba Band in California.[73]

In 2008, through the largest-ever water rights settlement in Indian country after 30 years of litigation ($2.4 billion), the 372,000-acre Gila River reservation south of Phoenix finally began getting water again. In the late nineteenth century, the water had been siphoned off by farmers upstream, ending centuries of farming by the Indian community and plunging them into starvation and poverty.[74]

Suburban sprawl is not only impacting water usage. As it encroaches on the nation's green spaces, a growing number of sacred American Indian sites are under threat from housing developments and industrial plants. From North Dakota and Minnesota to Arkansas, from Florida to Nevada, American Indian groups are fighting battles with state and federal governments to protect places, including burial sites, to prevent construction from destroying the cultural integrity of these locations.[75]

# Red Power

American Indians never have been silent about their needs and wishes.[76] Beginning with Seneca Chief Red Jacket's visit to Washington, DC, in 1792, American Indians repeatedly told the federal authorities what their people wanted and what was acceptable to them. Because they were seen as "savages," American Indians found that government representatives usually ignored their views. After the forced-removal programs and the bloodshed came to an end in the late nineteenth century, the government tried to change the reservation American Indians' way of life, to eliminate their poverty, and to encourage further integration.

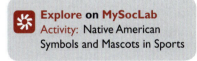

**Explore on MySocLab**
Activity: Native American Symbols and Mascots in Sports

In the twentieth century, American Indian militancy was quite rare until the 1960s. In the mid-1960s, American Indians changed their approach, partly because the social climate was different. Many social forces were at work—the Civil Rights movement, the Vietnam protests, the idealism of the Great Society, and a growing social awareness within mainstream society itself. Perhaps taking their cue from other movements, a new generation of American Indian leaders asserted themselves.

## PAN-INDIANISM

**Pan-Indianism**—a social movement attempting to establish an American Indian ethnic identity instead of only a tribal identity—has its roots in the past. The growing Iroquois Confederation of the seventeenth century, the mobility and social interaction among the

Plains Tribes in the nineteenth century, and the spread of the Ghost Dance religion in the nineteenth century are earlier examples of Pan-Indianism. As American Indian youths found comfort in one another's presence, first in boarding schools and later in urban areas, they discovered a commonality in their identity as American Indians.

Several organizations dedicated to preserving American Indian identity and gaining greater political clout evolved from this emerging group consciousness. First organized in Denver in 1944, the National Congress of American Indians (NCAI) effectively lobbied for creation of the Indian Claims Commission (1946), a judicial body allowing the tribes to sue the U.S. government. Like the NAACP (National Association for the Advancement of Colored People), it remains a major civil rights organization acting on behalf of its people. Subsequently, the National Indian Youth Council (NIYC), founded in Gallup, New Mexico, in 1961, and the American Indian Movement (AIM), founded in Minneapolis in 1968, attracted many young people who objected to discrimination and white domination. Both began with militant activism, but the NIYC—with funding support from the Department of Labor—works within the system to improve American Indian quality of life, while AIM remains confrontational, with an internal ideological rift among its leaders—most prominently Leonard Peltier and Arlo Looking Cloud—in prison on murder convictions.

AIM and most other American Indian organizations have been active for years in their opposition to the use of caricatures as mascots for sports teams, whether high school, college, or professional, such as the Atlanta Braves, Chicago Blackhawks, Cleveland Indians, and Washington Redskins. The NCAA in 2005 banned the use of American Indian mascots in post-season tournament games. However, some college teams—the Central Michigan Chippewas, the Florida State Seminoles, and the Utah Utes—use positive images in portraying Indian mascots and do so with the approval of the American Indian organizations. In 2012, under pressure from the NCAA, voters voted to drop the nickname "Fighting Sioux" for the University of North Dakota, and the Oregon State Board of Education gave its public schools five years to remove their American Indian mascots or lost state funding.[77]

At the macro level, Pan-Indian organizations address broader issues shared by the different tribes. Many American Indians prefer a micro-level emphasis that preserves their tribal identities and works for the cultural enrichment and social betterment of their own tribe rather than to engage in a national movement. As part of this tribal emphasis, these individuals also learn and teach their people silversmithing, pottery and blanket making, and other traditional crafts. In an effort to increase tribal pride and economic welfare, they also establish cultural centers to exhibit ceremonial dances and to sell their artistic works and wares.

**STUDENTS SPEAK** "Many people do not realize that every time they wear a Cleveland Indians hat, they are wearing a logo that was made to insult and poke fun at Indians, especially Louis Sockalexis, a baseball player from my tribe. He was one of the first Native American baseball players and signed with the Cleveland Spiders. However, when he was on the team, the audience multiplied just to see the 'Indian' and mock him. After a few years he left the team and eventually they changed its name to the Cleveland Indians. Back on the Penobscot reservation, he taught baseball to young boys but suffered from alcoholism and tuberculosis, and died at age 42."
**—Alana Smith**

## MILITANCY

November 20, 1969, marked the first in a series of staged media events to draw public attention to American Indian complaints and issues. On that day, a group of 78 American Indians under the name "Indians of All Tribes" temporarily occupied Alcatraz Island, a former federal prison, claiming its isolation, lack of running water and facilities of any kind, its barren land, and past prison population dependent on others duplicated that found on Indian reservations.

Other similar actions followed. In 1970, the 350th anniversary of the Pilgrim's landing, AIM activists seized the *Mayflower* replica. In 1972, AIM occupied Mount Rushmore and, in 1972, staged the Trail of Broken Treaties and takeover of the Bureau of Indian Affairs headquarters in Washington, DC. On February 27, 1973, approximately 200 AIM members seized control of the village of Wounded Knee, South Dakota, taking 11 hostages. The location was symbolic as the site of the last American Indian resistance in 1890, when 150 Miniconjou Sioux from the Cheyenne River reservation, including men, women, and children, were massacred by the U.S. Cavalry. Many were killed from behind, and the wounded were left to die in a blizzard the following night.[78] AIM's 71-day siege ended May 8, 1973, with two American Indians killed, injuries on both sides (including a U.S. marshal paralyzed), and $240,000 in damage to property.[79]

The militants had demanded, among other things, that the government deal with the Sioux on the basis of an 1868 treaty that guaranteed them dominion over the vast northern Plains between the Missouri River and the Rocky Mountains, land that the U.S. government confiscated in 1876. Sioux representatives describe their land claim as the "largest, most historically and socially significant and, in terms of time taken in the courts, the oldest American Indian land claim on record."

## The Courts

In 1980, the U.S. Supreme Court reaffirmed a lower court's award of $105 million to compensate 60,000 Sioux living on eight reservations in South Dakota, Montana, and Nebraska for the government's illegal seizure of their sacred Black Hills (*Paha Sapa*), part of the aforementioned Sioux land claim. Nearly all Sioux members were against accepting the money and their leaders followed the wishes of their people. Why did they reject millions of dollars? They viewed the land stolen from them as sacred and said, "One does not sell their mother." With the award held in trust and earning interest, that amount today is approaching $1 billion, but the Oglala Sioux, Crow Creek Sioux Tribe, Lower Brule Sioux Tribe, Rosebud Sioux Tribe, Cheyenne River Sioux Tribe, Standing Rock Sioux Tribe, Santee Sioux, and Sioux Tribe of Fort Peck have been united in their stand against accepting the money. They simply want their land back instead.[80]

The cash settlement offer for the Black Hills rested in part on a 1950 precedent, when the U.S. Court of Claims awarded $31.2 million (or approximately $10,000 for each tribal adult and child) to the Colorado Ute for lands illegally taken from them.

**7-6** Analyze assertiveness and court cases in recent years.

In a 2004 act of reconciliation, the mayor of Eureka, California, and the Wiyot tribal chief sign a deed returning 40 acres of Indian Island, the tribe's former land and burial ground. In 1860, white intruders—using hatchets, clubs, and knives— massacred up to 100 tribal members there, an act then condemned by the American writer Bret Harte. In 2006, the city ceded an additional 60 acres of the island to the tribe.

A precedent also existed for the return of land. The Taos Pueblo of New Mexico had regarded the lands at and near Blue Lake as sacred since the fourteenth century. Demanding the land back from the Forest Service instead of a proffered cash settlement, the Taos ultimately regained 48,000 acres in 1970 through congressional action at President Nixon's urging.

In 1977, the Passamaquoddy and Penobscot laid claim to approximately 5 million acres, or nearly one-third of Maine. In a 1978 out-of-court settlement, the federal government made a lump-sum payment of $25 million cash, agreed to an additional $1.7 million a year for 15 years, and sold 300,000 acres to the two tribes at a token $5 an acre. The basis for the claim was that the American Indian land had been bargained away in violation of the Nonintercourse Act of 1790, which reserved only to Congress the power to negotiate with American Indian tribes. As mentioned in an earlier section on tribal enterprise, these tribes still have extensive poverty.

In 2009, a 19-member tribal consortium brought federal litigation against the State of Washington to speed up the pace of removing fish barriers associated with state highways that block more than 3,000 miles of potential stream habitat for salmon. A 2007 U.S. District Court decision had held that treaties signed in the 1850s imposed a duty on the state to do so. Although the state legislature has funded culvert replacement since 1991, the current pace of construction could take up to 100 years to fix the problem.[81] This still-unresolved lawsuit, driven by frustration at the slow pace, is unusual because after losing many court battles with various American Indian tribes, the states of Washington, Wyoming, Colorado, and New Mexico generally prefer to negotiate directly with tribes to avoid costly and possibly losing court battles.

Other court actions take place in many locales. For example, in New York State, the Mohawk, Oneida, Cayuga, Onondaga, Seneca, and Tuscarora nations of the Iroquois Confederacy filed sizable land claims, given impetus by a 1985 Supreme Court ruling that New York's treaty with the Oneida also violated the Nonintercourse Act. In 2007, however, a federal judge ruled that the Oneida cannot take back land they sold more than a century ago, but that they may be entitled to profits the state made in reselling the land. With interest that amount could be as high as $500 million. The decision remains under appeal in the courts.[82]

# Bureau of Indian Affairs

The Bureau of Indian Affairs, created in 1824, has many critics among federal officials, sociologists, anthropologists, and American Indians (see the Ethnic Experience box). Some observers view it as a bureaucracy staffed by able, dedicated people (90 percent of them American Indians) whose ability to act is frustrated by an inefficient organization. Others see it as an inept agency that "loses" trust funds, administers ineffective programs that are supposed to reduce unemployment and poverty, and maintains a paternalistic trustee relationship with the tribes, with non-American Indians holding many of the top positions.

American Indian hostility toward the BIA goes beyond complaints about unsympathetic, incompetent, or patronizing personnel; it is directed against the bureau's very structure. Although different government agencies touch all Americans in some ways, few non-American Indians realize how thoroughly the BIA dominates the lives of American Indians residing on reservations. The agency is in charge of everything, from tribal courts and schools to social services and law enforcement. It must approve virtually every tribal decision regarding the use of tribal resources—even the disposition of cash settlements that the Navajo and other tribes have won in lawsuits against the BIA itself.

# the ETHNIC experience

## A Formal Apology to the Indian People

"The works of this agency have at various times profoundly harmed the communities it was meant to serve. From the very beginning, the Office of Indian Affairs was an instrument by which the United States enforced its ambition against the Indian nations and Indian people who stood in its path..."

"As the nation looked to the West for more land, this agency participated in the ethnic cleansing that befell the western tribes...In these more enlightened times, it must be acknowledged that the deliberate spread of disease, the decimation of the mighty bison herds, the use of the poison alcohol to destroy mind and body, and the cowardly killing of women and children made for tragedy on a scale so ghastly that it cannot be dismissed as merely the inevitable consequence of the clash of competing ways of life. This agency and the good people in it failed in the mission to prevent the devastation..."

"Nor did the consequences of war have to include the futile and destructive efforts to annihilate Indian cultures. After the devastation of tribal economies and the deliberate creation of tribal dependence on the services provided by this agency, this agency set out to destroy all things Indian."

"This agency forbade the speaking of Indian languages, prohibited the conduct of traditional religious activities, outlawed traditional government, and made Indian people ashamed of who they were. Worst of all, the Bureau of Indian Affairs committed these acts against the children entrusted to its boarding schools, brutalizing them emotionally, psychologically, physically, and spiritually. Even in this era of self-determination, when the Bureau of Indian Affairs is at long last serving as an advocate for Indian people in an atmosphere of mutual respect, the legacy of these misdeeds haunts us. The trauma of shame, fear, and anger has passed from one generation to the next, and manifests itself in the rampant alcoholism, drug abuse, and domestic violence that plague Indian country. Many of our people live lives of unrelenting tragedy as Indian families suffer the ruin of lives by alcoholism, suicides made of shame and despair, and violent death at the hands of one another. So many of the maladies suffered today in Indian country result from the failures of this agency. Poverty, ignorance, and disease have been the product of this agency's work."

"And so today, I stand before you as the leader of an institution that in the past has committed acts so terrible that they infect, diminish, and destroy the lives of Indian people decades later, generations later. These things occurred despite the efforts of many good people with good hearts who sought to prevent them. These wrongs must be acknowledged if the healing is to begin."

"Let us begin by expressing our profound sorrow for what this agency has done in the past. Just like you, when we think of these misdeeds and their tragic consequences, our hearts break and our grief is as pure and complete as yours. We desperately wish that we could change this history, but of course we cannot. On behalf of the Bureau of Indian Affairs, I extend this formal apology to Indian people for the historical conduct of this agency..."

"Never again will this agency stand silent when hate and violence are committed against Indians. Never again will we allow policy to proceed from the assumption that Indians possess less human genius than the other races. Never again will we be complicit in the theft of Indian property. Never again will we appoint false leaders who serve purposes other than those of the tribes. Never again will we allow unflattering and stereotypical images of Indian people to deface the halls of government or lead the American people to shallow and ignorant beliefs about Indians. Never again will we attack your religions, your languages, your rituals, or any of your tribal ways. Never again will we seize your children, nor teach them to be ashamed of who they are. Never again."

"We cannot yet ask your forgiveness, not while the burdens of this agency's history weigh so heavily on tribal communities. What we do ask is that, together, we allow the healing to begin: As you return to your homes, and as you talk with your people, please tell them that the time of dying is at its end. Tell your children that the time of shame and fear is over. Tell your young men and women to replace their anger with hope and love for their people. Together, we must wipe the tears of seven generations. Together, we must allow our broken hearts to mend. Together, we will face a challenging world with confidence and trust. Together, let us resolve that when our future leaders gather to discuss the history of this institution, it will be time to celebrate the rebirth of joy, freedom, and progress for the Indian Nations. The Bureau of Indian Affairs was born in 1824 in a time of war on Indian people. May it live in the year 2000 and beyond as an instrument of their prosperity."

Source: Excerpts from a speech by Assistant Secretary of the Interior for Indian Affairs Kevin Gover at a ceremony on September 8, 2000, commemorating the BIA's 175th anniversary, at the BIA in Washington, DC.

In 2006, the Seminole of Florida, buoyed by income from government compensation for seized lands and casino revenues, diversified their new wealth and became the first Native American tribe to acquire a major international corporation, paying $965 million for 124 Hard Rock Cafés in 45 countries. Many Americans remain unaware of this fact.

Yet the BIA continues with its sorry record of waste, corruption, and fiscal mismanagement. A 1999 study by the National Academy of Public Administration (NAPA) detailed acute shortcomings in the agency's ability to manage finance, information technology, records, and procurement operations. Its overall ranking by the Federal Performance Project in 2000 was a "D." In 2001, the executive director of the Harvard Project on American Indian Economic Development said, "We can't find a single case of sustained economic success where the BIA is in control."[83] After a series of meetings with tribal leaders in 2002, the BIA announced changes to improve its asset management.[84] Years of fiscal mismanagement continued, as a 2007 audit by the inspector general's office of the U.S. Department of Education revealed that the BIA could not adequately account for more than $100 million in funding for students at special education schools on the reservations and expressed concern about an additional $217 million in other education funding.[85]

## Urban American Indians

**7-7** Examine urban American Indian life.

Approximately 78 percent of all American Indians live in urban areas or away from reservations (Figure 7.4).[86] New York claims the largest concentration (nearly 58,000), but that constitutes only 0.7 percent of the city's total population. The American Indian population in Los Angeles is nearly 27,000, also 0.7 percent of the total. Other cities with sizable numbers are Anchorage, Albuquerque, Chicago, Dallas, Detroit, Houston, Oklahoma City, Phoenix, San Antonio, and Tucson.[87]

Often lacking job skills and adequate education, urban American Indians generally experience the same poverty they left behind on the reservation but without the familiar environment and tribal support system. Researchers have found that urban migration does not immediately improve American Indian well-being. Findings consistent with those of other studies show that, although urban American Indians are more likely to be employed than those who remain behind on the reservations, they do not achieve any improved income earnings, on average, until after five years of residence in the city.[88]

One unfortunate consequence of migration to cities has been an increase of Native American street gangs that imitate and sometimes partner with the longer-established African-American or Latino gangs. Situated in an urban social arena where they constitute

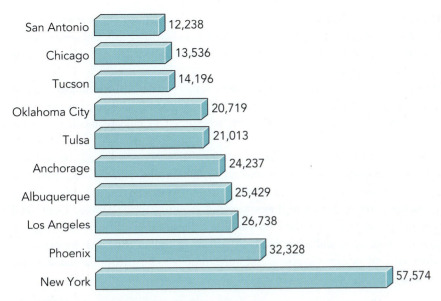

**FIGURE 7.4**  Major Cities with Largest American Indian and/or Alaskan Native Populations, 2010

*Source: U.S. Census Bureau, 2011 American Community Survey.*

a minority, new arrivals experience the culture shock of urban living away from the solidarity of the tribe. This shock sometimes leads to personal disorientation, and American Indians seldom get relief or assistance from the dominant society. These appear also to be reasons that American Indian college enrollment is so low outside the tribal colleges.

Members of urban American Indian populations generally drink more and have a higher rate of problem drinking than do most members of reservation populations. Such heavy drinking is most common among the lower social strata of urban American Indians and relates highly to such occupational considerations as prestige and satisfaction.[89] Despite some improvement in recent years, health disparities remain high among urban American Indians and Alaska Natives compared to the general population.[90]

American Indians who succeed in adapting to urban living, usually during a two- to five-year period, settle into semiskilled or skilled jobs. Once they have gained some economic security, they frequently move out of the city to racially mixed suburban areas. Although this shows some degree of acculturation and convergent social adaptation, the trend appears to be limited. Many middle-class, urban-adapted American Indians form their own ethnic institutions, including churches, powwow clubs, social centers, and athletic leagues.[91]

## Cultural Impact

Perhaps no other ethnic group has had as great an impact on U.S. culture as the American Indians, primarily because they already were here when the first Europeans arrived. The whites, who had to adapt to a new land, found it advantageous to learn from those **indigenous** people. Cities, towns, counties, states, rivers, lakes, mountains, and other geographic entities by the thousands bear American Indian names today. More than 500 words in our language are American Indian, including *wigwam, succotash, tobacco, papoose, chipmunk, squash, skunk, toboggan, opossum, tomahawk, moose, mackinaw, hickory, pecan, raccoon, cougar, woodchuck,* and *hominy.*[92]

The American Indians' knowledge of wild herbs and the more than 80 plants they domesticated brought whites a wide variety of new tastes. American Indians introduced

**7-8**  Examine the cultural impact of American Indians on U.S. culture.

the Europeans to corn, white and sweet potatoes, kidney beans, tomatoes, peanuts, peppers, pumpkins, avocados, pineapples, maple sugar, chicle (as chewing gum), and cacao, as well as tobacco and long-fiber cotton. The American Indians' knowledge of medicinal plants also is part of their legacy.

At least fifty-nine drugs, including coca (for cocaine and novocaine), curare (a muscle relaxant), cinchona bark (the source of quinine), cascara sagrada (a laxative), datura (a pain-reliever), and ephedra (a nasal remedy), were bequeathed to modern medicine by the Indians.[93]

American Indians also made various articles that many people still use today— canoes, kayaks, snowshoes, toboggans, moccasins, hammocks, pipes, parkas, ponchos, dogsleds, and rubber syringes, among other items. American Indian influence on jewelry, clothing, art, architecture, literature, and scouting is substantial. Traditional American Indian reverence for the land parallels beliefs that conservationists support. In addition, appreciation and adaptations of American Indian child-rearing practices, group-directed activities, cooperatives, and ministrations to a patient's mental state are common today.[94]

# Assimilation

**7-9** Analyze the complexity of present-day assimilation and pluralism.

That hundreds of thousands of American Indians are not assimilated into mainstream society certainly has not been through lack of effort by the dominant group. After following a policy of frontier genocide, expulsion, and forced segregation on reservations, the federal government adopted other methods to "kill the Indian, but save the man," according to a popular saying between 1860 and 1930.[95]

As mentioned earlier in the "Reservations and Dependence" section, a concerted effort at forced assimilation through authoritarian boarding schools attempted to "civilize" American Indian youth into mainstream society. On the reservations, meanwhile, the Dawes Act of 1887 disrupted their traditional approach to communal landholding in an attempt to force them to conform to the social and economic structure of the dominant society. Another dimension to this cultural onslaught occurred in the 1890s with the outlawing of indigenous religions. In the 1950s, the termination and relocation programs represented another federal effort to get American Indians to assimilate.

These efforts had a major impact on the American Indian way of life, much of it negative. Earlier sections of this chapter, for example, offered statistics about rates of suicide, alcoholism, violence, disease, poverty, educational attainment, and unemployment. Today, many live in two worlds—their own ethnic community and the mainstream community—forcing them to maintain a bicultural ethnic identity.

American Indians are not a homogeneous group and differ greatly in their level of acceptance of, and commitment to, tribal values, beliefs, and practices through a variance of customs, language, and family structure. Moreover, their socioeconomic status and geographic setting (urban, rural, or reservation) affect other individual differences.[96] Michael Garrett and Eugene Pichette suggest that a five-level continuum of acculturation would best describe American Indians:

- **Traditional:** May or may not speak English but generally speak and think in their native language; hold only traditional values and beliefs and practice only traditional tribal customs and methods of worship.

- **Marginal:** May speak both the native language and English; may not, however, fully accept the cultural heritage and practices of their tribal group; may not fully identify with mainstream cultural values and behaviors.

# REALITY check

## Places and Politics: A Geo-Political Profile

Although they live in all 50 states, American Indians primarily remain concentrated in the West, especially in Alaska, Arizona, New Mexico, and North and South Dakota (see Figure 7.4). In states with reservation lands, they are more visible because many live not only on the reservations themselves but in nearby towns as well.

In the past, the tribes each had their own political governance system and, in the case of the Iroquois and Sioux, a confederation of tribes existed for intertribal cooperative initiatives and peaceful mediation. Denied U.S. citizenship until 1924 and autonomy even longer, political power outside the reservations virtually has been nonexistent. Through the Red

Power movement, Pan-Indian organizational lobbying, and court litigation, they have had some success in flexing their muscles to improve their quality of life.

Few American Indian politicians have held national office. Three served in the U.S. Senate. Ben Nighthorse Campbell, a Northern Cheyenne from Colorado (1993–2005), spent part of his youth in a boarding school and later served in the U.S. House of Representatives (1987–1993) before election to the Senate; Robert Latham Owen, a Cherokee from Oklahoma (1907–1925); and Charles Curtis of Kansas, who was three-eighths American Indian (1907–1913 and 1915–1929), who also was the first and only vice president, serving under

President Herbert Hoover. Today, the only American Indian serving in Congress is Representative Tom Cole, a Chickasaw from Oklahoma, who has been there since 2003.

A growing political engagement of American Indians is more evident in the number of elected local and state officials. None has served yet as governor but 80 (18 of them female) currently are elected representatives in state legislatures. That number may well grow, thanks to the efforts of the Indigenous Democratic Network, a grassroots political organization devoted to recruiting and electing American Indian candidates at all levels and mobilizing the Indian Vote throughout America on behalf of those candidates.

- **Bicultural:** Generally accepted by dominant society and tribal society/nation; simultaneously able to know, accept, and practice both mainstream values/behaviors and the traditional values and beliefs of their cultural heritage.

- **Assimilated:** Accepted by dominant society; embrace only mainstream cultural values, behaviors, and expectations.

- **Pan-traditional:** Assimilated American Indians who have made a conscious choice to return to the "old ways." They generally are accepted by dominant society but seek to embrace previously lost traditional cultural values, beliefs, and practices of their tribal herbal heritage. Therefore, they may speak both English and their native tribal language.[97]

Caught between two cultures, many American Indians experience pressure to compromise their basic cultural values and behaviors to meet societal expectations and standards. When American Indian and Alaskan Native students feel alienated within a school environment because of a clash of cultures, the failure to reconcile cultural differences leads to a high percentage of school dropouts.[98] The challenge remains to find ways for American Indians to establish a healthy and meaningful cultural identity through bicultural competence (see the Reality Check box and Figure 7.5).

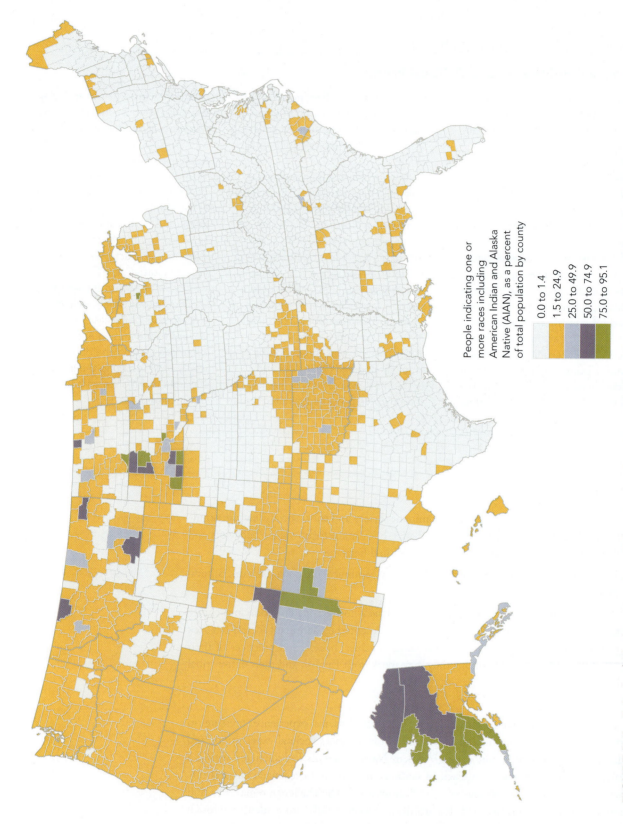

**FIGURE 7.5   Principal Native American Tribes in the Continental United States (Where They Live Today)**

*Source:* Based on data from U.S. Department of the Interior, Bureau of Indian Affairs, "Indian Land Areas, General" (map), (Washington, DC: U.S. Government Printing Office, 2001).

People indicating one or more races including American Indian and Alaska Native (AIAN), as a percent of total population by county

0.0 to 1.4
1.5 to 24.9
25.0 to 49.9
50.0 to 74.9
75.0 to 95.1

# Sociological Analysis

Both Hollywood and the public rely on stereotypes in their characterization of American Indians, even though extensive differences among tribes always have existed. In this chapter, we looked at their similarities and differences, noting changes in attitude and public policy throughout the years. Our three theoretical frameworks not only provide a coherent approach to understanding the experiences of American Indians but also provide insights into their problems.

**7-10** Evaluate insights gained through sociological analysis.

## THE FUNCTIONALIST VIEW

Outsiders never may have fully understood the traditional American Indian social system, but anthropologists have found that these tribal societies functioned with a high degree of social organization. Kin relationships, from the nuclear family to a vast clan system, formed the basis of interaction. For young and old, male and female, their clearly defined interdependent work roles in cooperative tasks of living fostered a rather stable society. Living off the land and espousing a pantheistic belief system, they were conservationists, maintaining a harmonious relationship with their natural environment. They were self-sufficient people with institutionalized practices of gift giving and property control—such as the willful destruction of personal property in a competitive display of wealth among some Pacific Coast tribes—which helped sustain a fairly equitable society without great extremes of poverty or riches.

Early contacts with white explorers, trappers, and settlers mostly were harmonious, with both sides benefiting from what each had to offer the other. Dysfunctions occurred as American Indians slipped into economic subservience, their way of life further threatened by encroachment on their land by steadily increasing numbers of white settlers. Whites saw American Indians as a hindrance to their making the land productive, so they forcibly removed them. Forced segregation on nonproductive reservations completely destroyed American Indian society as a self-sufficient entity while reinforcing other cultural aspects. The systemic disorganization of the society—entrenched for more than 100 years—restricted life opportunities. Continued poor education, low income, bad housing, poor health, alcoholism, and other pathologies are costly to any society and the people who endure them.

Functionalists stress that the most effective method of resolving these problems is to reorganize our own social institutions to put the American Indian social system back into balance. However, the plight of the American Indians is functional to the few reservation American Indians employed by government agencies to provide services and to BIA employees whose jobs rest on continued paternalistic control, as well as to whites living near reservations who dominate these regions' economy. These individuals, American Indian and white alike, would find adjustments in the system dysfunctional to themselves and therefore oppose such changes.

## THE CONFLICT VIEW

Lieberson's power theory provides an obvious model for studying American Indian–white relations. As discussed in Chapter 2, the white newcomers, superior in technology compared to the indigenous population, engaged in early conflict. The native population suffered numeric decline from warfare, disease, and disruption of sustenance activities, and its social institutions were undermined. Westward expansion, the nation's "Manifest Destiny," occurred by pushing aside the people who already possessed the land without regard for their rights or wishes. Formal government agreements and treaties became meaningless to those in power if further land confiscation or exploitation for natural resources offered profits.

What about today? Who benefits from American Indian deprivation now? The battle over the precious commodity of water in the West offers one answer. Water might enable these tribes to gain some income, but it has been stolen out from under them by mining companies, farmers, and land developers. Prolonged court battles enable powerful business interests to maintain their dams, wells, and aqueducts at the expense of the American Indians. You have read of abuses of other natural resources as well.

Why doesn't Congress do something? Legislators respond to public pressure. Those not living near American Indians are not motivated or sufficiently concerned to insist on corrective action. Those living near American Indians have a vested interest in maintaining the status quo, and they are the constituency with the power to influence their legislators.

Yet American Indians have achieved some positive results. They did so through an emerging group consciousness, whether tribal or Pan-Indian (involving all American Indians). Protest marches and demonstrations, militant acts of defiance—the Alcatraz, Wounded Knee, and BIA occupations—all brought public attention and some efforts to remedy their situation. Class-action lawsuits often have been effective. Conflict theory suggests that organized social movements by the exploited can bring about social change. American Indians increasingly are discovering that redress of their grievances will not occur without concerted public pressure and legal action.

## THE INTERACTIONIST VIEW

Consider again the words of Columbus, Franklin, and Catlin earlier in this chapter. Ethnocentric views of American Indian culture prompted a definition of the native population as inferiors, savages, and even nonhumans! Once you create such social distance between groups by dehumanizing them, it is easy to justify any action taken against them. Compounding the negative labeling process was racial differentiation. European Americans viewed even acculturated American Indians working as servants or laborers in colonial villages, or the entire Cherokee people, as members of an inferior race fit to be subordinated and relegated to a noninterfering, humble role in society.

For their part, the American Indians at first found whites' customs, fashions, and behavior outlandish and astonishing. Later, they perceived the whites as threats to their existence and as liars and treacherous people. The ensuing hostilities reaffirmed each group's negative view of the other, and the conflict ended with total subjugation of the American Indians.

Government policy often mistakenly interpreted the needs of all tribes in broad terms and treated all tribes alike: the biggest and smallest, the agrarian and fishing, the ones with economic land bases and the ones without. Many dominant-group people in the United States view American Indians as perpetuating their own problems by remaining on reservations, depending on government support, and refusing to blend in with white society. Growing up on reservations, American Indians find security in tribal life, viewing the outside world as alien and without promise. Now the strangers in their own land, they believe they have the right to preserve their culture and to receive government assistance because of past abuses, including broken treaties. With so many different interpretations of the current situation, the problems of the reservation appear difficult to resolve.

High levels of prejudice against American Indians still exist in the West, especially on the edges of the reservations where there is a climate that tolerates violence, say the experts. As stated earlier, American Indians are the victims of violent crime at a rate nearly twice the national average for blacks. Unlike blacks and whites, they most likely are to be the victims of violent crimes committed by members of a race other than their own. Clearly, the negative labeling and dehumanizing processes that led to past acts of violence against American Indians remain problems today.

# Retrospect

The white strangers who appeared among the American Indians eventually outnumbered them, overpowered them, and changed their way of life. Once a proud and independent people, the American Indians were reduced to a state of poverty, despair, and dependence. The land they had known so well and roamed so freely was no longer theirs. Forced to live within an alien society that dominated all aspects of their lives, they became strangers in their native land. Misunderstood and categorized as savages, they observed the taken-for-granted world of the whites more keenly than most whites did theirs.

Physical and cultural differences quickly became the basis for outgroup hostility as the groups competed for land and resources. Like other groups, the American Indians faced the familiar patterns of stereotyping, prejudice, discrimination, and conflict because of their alleged inferiority and actual lack of power. Isolation on the reservations not only prevented assimilation (which most American Indians did not desire anyway) but also created for them a world of dependence and deprivation. Subsequent efforts at forced assimilation—boarding schools, relocation, and termination of the reservations—failed because of American Indian resilience and the Bureau of Indian Affairs' lack of thoroughness in personal preparation, assistance, and follow-through.

The American Indians still are misunderstood and exploited. One, two, or three hundred years ago, people who lived far from the American Indians idealized them, and those who lived nearest often abused and exploited them. It is no different today. Many people are oblivious to their problems and consider them quaint relics of the past; others find them either undesirable or in the way. Some want their land and will use almost any means to secure it. American Indians still encounter discrimination in stores, bars, and housing, particularly in cities and near the reservations. They frequently are beaten or killed, and their property rights infringed on.

Since the 1960s, some American Indians have become more assertive. Many young, better-educated American Indians are forgetting tribal differences and finding a common bond—Pan-Indianism—uniting in the struggle to protect what they have and to restore what they have lost. Others prefer a more individualistic approach within the tribe. Some gains have been made, and more non-American Indians are becoming aware of the situations; however, at present, the American Indians still are one of the poorest minorities in the United States.

**Read on MySocLab**
Document: Rape and the War Against Native Women

# On MySocLab

 **Study and Review on MySocLab**

## KEY TERMS

Dichotomy, p. 192
Environmental justice, p. 216
Environmental racism, p. 216

Indigenous, p. 223
Mortality rate, p. 212

Pan-Indianism, p. 217
Sovereign, p. 204

# DISCUSSION QUESTIONS

1. The beginning of the chapter offers a sociohistorical perspective. What was one striking or surprising piece of information you picked up here?
2. Why is the power differential so crucial in understanding the American Indians' past and present problems?
3. Why have most government efforts to "help" the American Indians failed?
4. In what ways has little changed in the exploitation of the American Indians?
5. How many American Indian names of cities, towns, counties, states, rivers, lakes, mountains, and other geographic entities are there in your area?
6. The end of the chapter offers three theoretical analyses. How did one of these theories become more meaningful or relevant to you in its application to the different groups' experiences?

# INTERNET ACTIVITIES

1. The Center for Multilingual, Multicultural Research at the University of Southern California maintains an excellent site on American Indian Resources (http://www.bcf.usc.edu/~cmmr/). Here you can access the home pages of many tribes and native organizations, as well as tribal colleges, Native Studies programs, native journals and newspapers, powwow and festival schedules, and links to American Indian language resources. This site also contains many excellent, full-text articles on education and language.
2. The Census Bureau is steadily releasing new facts and demographic profiles from the 2010 Census about the American Indian and Alaskan Native population. You can access this information at http://www.census.gov/newsroom/minority_links/aian.html.

# Asian Americans

8

((• Listen to Chapter 8 on MySocLab

*Their education level and occupational skills enable many first- and second-generation Asian Americans to afford home ownership in middle-class suburbs. Often called the "model minority" for this reason, the reality is that Asians are not a homogeneous group economically, and others do struggle in poverty or live less affluent working-class lives.*

## LEARNING OBJECTIVES | After reading this chapter you will be able to:

**8-1** Describe the sociohistorical context for studying Asian Americans.

**8-2** Identify common cultural attributes shared by Asian Americans.

**8-3** Describe the immigrant experiences of Chinese, Japanese, Filipinos, and Koreans.

**8-4** Describe the immigrant experiences of Asian Indians, Pakistanis, Vietnamese, and others.

**8-5** Examine problems in usage of a model-minority stereotype.

**8-6** Compare and contrast the assimilation paths followed by Asian Americans.

**8-7** Discuss insights gained through sociological analysis.

With high immigration doubling their numbers from 6.7 million in 1970 to 15 million in 2011, Asians and Pacific Islanders are transforming the face of America. In fact, Asian immigration in 2012 was greater than the total of immigration from the entire Western Hemisphere, 42 to 40 percent of the total.[1] In California, nearly one in seven residents is now Asian; in San Francisco County, one in three residents is Asian.[2] Throughout the United States, the Asian American population is increasing noticeably, sometimes generating resentful, even hostile, reactions from other local residents. In this chapter, we look at both past and present immigrant ethnic groups from Asia (Figure 8.1).

## Sociohistorical Perspective

**8-1** Describe the sociohistorical context for studying Asian Americans.

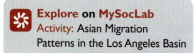

**Explore on MySocLab**
Activity: Asian Migration Patterns in the Los Angeles Basin

The Chinese first came to the United States during the California gold rush in the 1850s. Japanese, Koreans, and Filipinos began to arrive on the West Coast between 40 and 60 years later to seek their fortune. Some came to stay, but many came as **sojourners**, intending to return home after earning enough money. This view of the United States as a temporary overseas job opportunity—together with the racism they faced—led the early Asian immigrants to form subsocieties. Throughout the first third of the twentieth century, this social organization enabled Asians to overcome the structural discrimination that sharply limited their work and life opportunities.

The Chinese encountered racial hostility almost as soon as they arrived in California, despite the overwhelming need for manual labor in the mid-nineteenth century. They

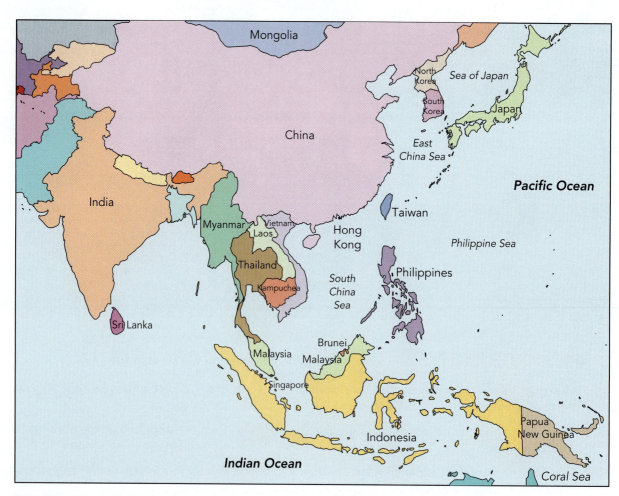

**FIGURE 8.1   Asia from India to Japan**

often were expelled from the mining camps, forbidden to enter schools, denied the right to testify in court, barred from obtaining citizenship, and occasionally murdered. After the Civil War, anti-Chinese tensions increased, culminating in the Chinese Exclusion Act of 1882. Japanese, Koreans, and Filipinos who came to the West Coast later encountered racism and discrimination similar to what the Chinese had faced. Many of them went to work as farm laborers in rural areas or as unskilled workers in urban areas.

A major social problem affecting most Asian immigrants through the 1940s was the shortage in this country of Asian women. Not only was this imbalance in the sex ratio significant in their personal, social, and community life, but also it provided the basis for racist complaints about prostitution and miscegenation. For the Chinese sojourner, both the custom that wives should remain in the household of the husband's parents and subsequent immigration restrictions help explain this disproportionate sex ratio, which in turn led to the rise of brothels in Chinatowns and public condemnation. The Filipinos also were mostly male and similarly affected by the shortage of same-ethnicity women. Whether the Asians patronized prostitutes or sought the company of white women who were not prostitutes, racist whites expressed moral indignation, and negative racial stereotypes resulted. Legislators in 14 states passed laws against **miscegenation** (interracial marriage) to prevent Asians from marrying whites.

By 1920, the Japanese sex ratio was largely balanced. Following World War II, a greater number of Asian women migrated to the United States, and the sex ratio for other Asian immigrant groups improved as well. Refugees and war brides from the Japanese, Korean, and Vietnam wars account for part of the change, as do the brides of servicemen stationed overseas during the intervening years. The Immigration Act of 1965, which gave preference to relatives of U.S. residents, finally ensured both sexes equal opportunity to enter the United States.

After World War II, immigrants from these countries and from other parts of East and Southeast Asia entered a much more industrialized society. Many also came from lands affected by Western contact. Some were political refugees, better educated and more skilled than earlier Asian immigrants. Many preferred living in California, and others moved to the East Coast or elsewhere. Entering various occupations, these postwar immigrants were spared the violent hostility of previous times, although many encountered resentment and discrimination nonetheless.

## Cultural Attributes

The social distance between themselves and Asians often causes white and black Americans to view Asians as a homogeneous group. They are not. Not only do they differ in their nationality, language, religion, and culture, but they also are diverse within each of their own cultures. Consequently, no single model can reflect the wide disparities in occupational choices or acculturation and acceptance experiences.

Although we need to look beyond racial stereotypes to understand the different Asian immigrant groups more fully, we can identify certain cultural hallmarks that Asians tend to share. The degree to which individuals internalize these norms and values depends significantly on social class, length of residence in the United States, and acculturation.

Generally, traditional Asian values emphasize appropriate behavior, strict control of aggressive or assertive impulses, and a self-conscious concern for conduct in the presence of others. Sibling rivalry is discouraged, and older children are socialized to set an example for younger siblings in politeness, gentleness, and unselfish sacrifices for another's pleasure. Unlike U.S. children, who are encouraged to develop an inner sense of guilt as a social-control mechanism, Asian children experience the external sanctions of shame, or losing face—of bringing disgrace or dishonor to the family name.

8-2 Identify common cultural attributes shared by Asian Americans.

**Read on MySocLab**
Document: **Asian and African Values: The problem of human rights**

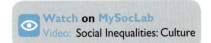

**Watch on MySocLab**
Video: **Social Inequalities: Culture**

"Although the Asian cultures are different from other cultures, I can relate to parts of them. Their children must avoid bringing shame or disgrace to their family, and that's somewhat similar to my culture as well. My parents are from Sierra Leone, and my country's culture stresses that children should not bring any shame to the family's name because of what other people might say. Also, like the Asians, our elderly people demand respect. This particular reading made me realize how dissimilar cultures can still have similarities with each other."

**—Christine Kebbie**

**8-3** Describe the immigrant experiences of Chinese, Japanese, Filipinos, and Koreans.

Within the family, open displays of emotion or affection are rare, except with infants and small children. Uniting the family is the important value of **filial piety**. Elders in the family (even those only slightly older) command respect and obedience; younger family members never talk back to them. Traditional sex-role definitions require the men to provide for and protect the women and the women to submit to the decisions of the men. Fathers and eldest sons thus are the most powerful family members.

As in most immigrant groups, the extended family is predominant among Asian Americans. A cohesive structure exists, encouraged in part by the sense of duty and responsibility arising out of filial piety but also by values stressing ancestor worship and the importance of the family name. Loneliness and isolation for the unmarried or aged seldom occur because the extended family embraces and absorbs them. No typical Asian American family model exists, however, and the blending of U.S. and Asian cultures affects the family structure, especially in promoting a more egalitarian role for women.

# Chinese Americans

U.S. residents on both coasts of North America knew something about the Chinese long before they first came to the United States. The United States had established trade relations with China as early as 1785, and many Protestant missionaries went there after 1807. Newspaper reports and magazine articles, inspired by the Anglo-Chinese War (1839–1842)—the so-called Opium War—and subsequent rebellions and incidents, featured lurid descriptions of filth, disease, cruel tortures, and executions. Americans gradually developed an unfavorable image of the Chinese based on these ethnocentric distortions and exaggerations. In 1842, seven years before the gold rush, the *Encyclopaedia Britannica* offered this unflattering portrait of the Chinese people:

> A Chinaman is cold, cunning, and distrustful; always ready to take advantage of those he has to deal with; extremely covetous and deceitful; quarrelsome, vindictive, but timid and dastardly. A Chinaman in office is a strange compound of insolence and meanness. All ranks and conditions have a total disregard for truth.[3]

## STRUCTURAL CONDITIONS

Most Chinese who came to the United States in the nineteenth century were farmers, artisans, craftsmen, political exiles, and refugees. The discovery of gold in California proved to be an opportunity not only for easterners and Europeans but also for the Chinese from Kwangtung Province, who could reach the gold rush country easily and who sought to recoup their losses from flood, famine, and the Taiping Rebellion (1850–1864). A combination of push–pull factors thus brought the Chinese to the United States. The first wave of migrants came as sojourners, intending to earn some money and then return home.

Visible because of their race, appearance, and behavior, the Chinese aroused both curiosity and suspicion. The sounds and characters of their language seemed most peculiar to the non-Chinese, as did their religion. Their "strange" clothes and hair worn in *queues* (a braid of hair in the back of the head) also seemed out of place in the crude pioneer surroundings. With little or no command of English, they mostly kept to themselves and viewed California as a temporary workplace. As a result, the Chinese remained an enigma to most Americans.

By 1860, California's population included a large and varied ethnic segment. Approximately 38 percent were foreign born, and many others were Spanish-speaking natives or children of European immigrants. The Chinese constituted approximately 9 percent of the state's population in 1860, but because they were mostly adult males, they accounted for close to 25 percent of the labor force. As the general population increased, however, the percentages of the total and working populations that they represented decreased.[4]

Hired as laborers who worked in gangs, the Chinese built much of the western portion of the transcontinental railroad for the Central Pacific. As many as 9,000 Chinese a year toiled through the High Sierra country, digging tunnels and laying tracks, and the task was completed sooner than expected. Leland Stanford, then president of the Central Pacific Railroad, described the Chinese as "quiet, peaceable, industrious, economical." Although Chinese laborers received the same wages as non-Chinese, they fed and housed themselves, unlike the white workers, and thus cost the railroad company two-thirds as much as whites to maintain.[5] The Chinese, however, did not pose an economic threat to the non-Chinese workers:

> Hiring Chinese resulted not in displacement of non-Chinese but in their upgrading. To the unskilled white railroad laborer of 1865, the coming of the Chinese meant his own advancement into that elite one-fifth of the labor force composed of straw-bosses, foremen, teamsters, skilled craftsmen. And one final reason was perhaps more cogent than all the others. No man with any choice would have chosen to be a common laborer on the Central Pacific during the crossing of the High Sierra.[6]

The end of the Civil War, however, brought veterans seeking jobs and eastern manufacturing concerns seeking West Coast markets, helped by efficient, low-cost shipment of goods over the transcontinental railroad. Fired when their work was completed, Chinese railroad laborers sought other jobs, but economic conditions worsened across the nation, culminating in the Panic of 1873. Labor supply exceeded demand, and laborers, union organizers, and demagogues mounted racist denunciations of Chinese "competition."

Among the most popular ethnophaulisms directed against the Chinese during this period of labor agitation were accusations of their being "dirty" and "disease-ridden." These epithets had originated decades earlier. In the 1840s, Americans first became aware of the relationship between germs and dirt and disease. Negative stereotypes about the supposed Chinese preference for eating vermin and the crowded, unsanitary Chinatowns caused whites to associate the Chinese with leprosy, cholera, and bubonic plague. By the 1870s, the labor issue had become predominant, but as the labor unions closed ranks against the Chinese, they labeled them a menace to both the economy and the health of U.S. society. The *real* issue by 1877, however, was race, disguised as labor conflict.

## SOCIETAL REACTION

Racist attacks against the Chinese continued throughout the remainder of the nineteenth century. Some antagonists compared them with blacks in terms of "racial inferiority." Others attacked the "vices" of the "Oriental" race. In the 1850s, one antislavery southern U.S. senator attempted to draw parallels among several groups that supposedly were inferior:

> No inferior race of men can exist in these United States without becoming subordinate to the will of the Anglo-Americans....It is so with the Negroes in the South; it is so with the Irish in the North; it is so with the Indians in New England; and it will be so with the Chinese in California....I should not wonder, at all, if the copper of the Pacific yet becomes as great a subject of discord and dissension as the ebony of the Atlantic.[7]

Cries for restrictions on Chinese immigration increased as racial antagonism rather than economic competition came to the forefront. In particular, the myth of an Asian inclination for despotic government was propagated by hostile Western media. "Oriental despotism" soon became as much a catch-phrase as "heathen Chinese." In 1865, the *New York Times* expressed alarm at the supposed negative effect of increased Asian immigration on U.S. civilization:

Now we are utterly opposed to the permission of any extensive emigration of Chinamen or other Asiatics to any part of the United States. There are other points of national well-being to be considered beside the sudden development of material wealth. The security of its free institutions is more important than the enlargement of its population. The maintenance of an elevated national character is of higher value than mere growth in physical power.

…We have four millions of degraded negroes in the South…and if there were to be a flood-tide of Chinese population—a population befouled with all the social vices, with no knowledge or appreciation of free institutions or constitutional liberty, with heathenish souls and heathenish propensities, whose character, and habits, and modes of thought are firmly fixed by the consolidating influence of ages upon ages—we should be prepared to bid farewell to republicanism and democracy.[8]

In 1867, California Democrats used an anti-Chinese platform to such advantage that they swept the state elections, including governor. Democrats elsewhere saw a bonanza in this issue because many Republicans were identified with the railroads and with companies that recruited and employed the Chinese. Moreover, the Democrats—identified with the defeated Confederacy and slavocracy—could not use Negro-baiting effectively outside the South after 1865. Republicans secured the Burlingame Treaty of 1868 between China and the United States, providing for unrestricted travel between both countries "for the purpose of curiosity, or trade, or as permanent residents." Still, public hostility in the United States against the Chinese continued to grow.

To some, the Chinese posed a serious immigrant threat to the idealized concept of the melting pot. Individuals who held this belief argued that German and Irish Catholics, at least, were physically similar to the Protestant northern and western Europeans. An 1868 *New York Times* editorial offered this display of racial bigotry:

Although they are patient and reliable laborers…they have characteristics deeply imbedded which make them undesirable as part of our permanent population. Their religion is wholly unlike ours, and they poison and stab. The circumstances would need be very favorable which would allow of their introduction into our families as servants, and as to mixing with them on terms of equality, that would be out of the question. No improvement of race could possibly result from such a mixture.[9]

As the prejudices of the 1850s distilled into the almost hysterical **sinophobia** (fear or dislike of China, its people and culture) of the 1870s and 1880s, the negative stereotype of the "yellow peril" emerged. In 1879, Senator James G. Blaine of Maine, a Republican Party leader and presidential hopeful, even attacked Chinese family values because of the sojourner orientation:

The Asiatic cannot go on with our population and make a homogeneous element. This idea…comparing European immigration with an immigration that had no regard to family, that does not recognize the relation of husband and wife, that does not observe the tie of parent and child, that does not have in the slightest degree the enabling and civilizing influence of the hearthstone and the fireside.[10]

His erroneous comments ignored not only the intense cohesiveness of Chinese family structure but also the common practice of European males coming to the United States ahead of their families.

## LEGISLATIVE ACTION

More than 225,000 Chinese came to the United States between 1850 and 1882. As Chinese sojourners came to the United States and returned to China in steady numbers, steamship companies found passenger trips a highly profitable operation and so encouraged Chinese immigration. In 1881, approximately 12,000 Chinese disembarked; in 1882, the number jumped to nearly 40,000.[11]

Another cycle of economic woes and labor agitation against the Chinese led to increasing pressures for restrictions. President Chester Arthur vetoed the first restriction bill, which would have barred all Chinese immigration for 20 years. A few months later, however, he signed a revised bill that barred Chinese laborers for a 10-year period but permitted Chinese businessmen, clergy, students, and travelers to enter. The Chinese Exclusion Act of 1882 marked a significant change in national policy toward immigrants. For the first time in the nation's history, the federal government enacted a human embargo on a particular race of laborers. Sufficient exceptions remained to allow 8,000 legal Chinese immigrants in 1883, but legislative action in 1884 tightened the restrictions further, and in 1885, the number of Chinese immigrants dropped to 22.[12]

Violence directed against Chinese immigrants, which sporadically had flared up prior to the legislation, continued. In 1871, 21 Chinese had been massacred in Los Angeles, and anti-Chinese riots had occurred in Denver in 1880. Such hostile actions became much more widespread after 1882. For example, at Rock Springs, Wyoming, in September 1885, a mob attacked and murdered 28 Chinese, wounded many others, and drove hundreds from their homes. Labor unions and politicians took action against the Chinese in various localities across the western United States. In Tacoma, Seattle, Oregon City, and many smaller towns, angry mobs expelled hundreds of Chinese residents, with considerable loss and destruction of property.

Congress extended the Chinese Exclusion Act for another 10 years in 1892, and then extended it indefinitely in 1902. Other Anglo-Saxon–dominated countries on the Pacific Rim also restricted Chinese immigration. Australia passed legislation in 1901, but Canada

This 1882 political cartoon—the year of passage of the Chinese Exclusion Act—depicts an Irishman, African American, Civil War veteran, Italian, Frenchman, and a Jew—most victims of prejudice themselves—building a wall against the Chinese, using blocks of prejudice. Across the sea, an American ship enters China, as the Chinese tear down their own wall to permit trade of such goods as rice, tea, and silk. (Source: The Library of Congress [LC-USZC4-4138]).

did not take such action until 1923. Before then, Americans frequently criticized Canada, especially the province of British Columbia, because Chinese entered the United States from there. Reverse migration also occurred after 1858, when the United States served as a point of entry into Canada for many Chinese.

Illustrating organized labor's instigation of the anti-Chinese issue is an 1893 American Federation of Labor (AFL) convention resolution, which held that the Chinese brought to the United States "nothing but filth, vice, and disease." It also maintained they had corrupted "a part of our people on the Pacific Coast to such a degree that could it be published in detail, the American people would in their just and righteous anger sweep them from the face of the earth."[13] These wild, racist charges had little basis in fact except that filth and disease did exist in some Chinatown districts—indeed, as they did in Irish, Italian, and other ethnic urban slums.

## AVOIDANCE AND SEGREGATION

How did the Chinese immigrants react to all the abuse, vilification, and discriminatory legislation? Some reluctantly returned to China. Some sought redress in the courts, winning all cases involving state immigration restrictions but few based on assault or property damage complaints. The latter were difficult to maintain in California, at least, because from 1854 to 1870, the California courts did not allow the Chinese, as noncitizens, to testify against whites.

Expelled from various trades and occupations as well as from many residential areas, Chinese immigrants had little choice but to congregate in Chinatowns and rely on their own benevolent and protective associations for assistance. A large number congregated in San Francisco, but others moved to the larger eastern and midwestern cities and formed ethnic enclaves. These Chinatowns were in low-rent ghetto areas, usually situated close to major means of transportation, which at least gave the Chinese ready access to friends and relatives. For example, in New York City and San Francisco, they were near the

*In a 1912 scene, U.S. flags fly in New York City's Chinatown. This blend of the distinctive features of an ethnic community and the U.S. influence illustrates the ongoing processes of acculturation and ethnogenesis—the absorption of some cultural elements of the host society while elements from one's own cultural heritage are retained or adapted.*

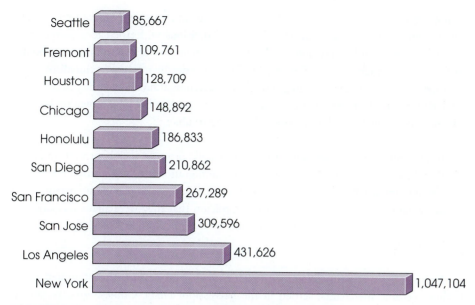

**FIGURE 8.2** Cities with Largest Asian Populations, 2011

Source: U.S. Census Bureau, *2011 American Community Survey.*

docks, and those in Boston, Pittsburgh, and St. Louis were near the railroad stations (Figure 8.2).

In seeking redress of grievances through the courts, the Chinese petitioned for equal rights. They won the right to have their children attend public schools, and then they fought to desegregate the schools. Housing codes, however, kept them in the ghetto, where they found themselves segregated both socially and spatially.

Securing jobs through the associations or from Chinese merchants, most entered occupations that either did not compete with whites (for example, in art and curio shops or Chinese restaurants) or that involved serving only their own people. They settled disputes among themselves, partly because this was their custom and partly because they distrusted the white people's court. The traditional associations and the family clan offered them the familiarity and protection they needed. Chinese temples, newspapers, schools, and Old World festivals all represented efforts to preserve their cultural and traditional practices.

Albert Palmer drew on his firsthand experience as a white growing up near San Francisco's Chinatown in the late nineteenth century to analyze what was and was not the reality of life in that enclave:

Those who know only the picturesque Chinatown of today can hardly realize what the Chinatown of the eighties and nineties was like. It was dirty, over-crowded, rat-infested, and often diseased....And Chinatown was accounted vicious because it was the haunt of gambling, opium smoking, lotteries, tong wars, and prostitution, where helpless little slave-girls were bought and sold...

Now, fear is a great disturber, and it largely created the old Chinatown. It did this partly, in fact, by herding Chinese into narrow, squalid quarters and surrounding them by hatred and suspicion; and partly in imagination, by creating the weird and distorted picture of their outlandish character...Chinatown was never quite so bad as the prejudice and fear imagined it.[14]

San Francisco's Chinatown in the nineteenth century was not necessarily a safe haven for the Chinese because the traditional associations were in conflict with one another. As the clans (lineage bonds), *hui kuan* (ethnic or regional bonds), and secret societies (outlaw or protest bonds) fought to secure the allegiance of immigrants and to dominate the community, the Chinese faced strife from both inside and outside their community. The combination of pressures outside the ghetto and divisions within led to a pattern that fluctuated between order and violence. By 1910, residents in the community were bound tightly to one another because of external hostility *and* deadly internal factionalism.[15]

One constant of Chinese immigrant life was discrimination and hostility in the white world. Regardless of education, the Chinese remained confined to Chinatown for housing and jobs. Going outside its boundaries only invited trouble:

> If one should go out, dressed casually for a walk, or go to a club, or even to a church, he was liable to be picked up by the immigration officers on suspicion of illegal residence. For many years, officials made a practice of picking up persons in the street or in public places on the suspicion that they were aliens illegally in this country. Such arrests were reported to be very common, especially in the late 1920s.[16]

Not all Chinese remained in crowded Chinatowns of the cities. A few hundred, many of whom became merchants, settled in the Mississippi Delta. Chinese grocers catered mostly to blacks, extending them credit and providing other essential services (for example, assisting illiterate rural blacks with government forms and making telephone calls). Some Chinese married black women; others brought over their families from China.

In this transition from sojourner to immigrant, Chinese men with families tried to evade their "black" status and avoid discrimination against their children, who were attending white public schools. In the 1920s, segregationists expelled Chinese children from the white schools, and the courts upheld this action "to preserve the purity and integrity of the white race, and prevent amalgamation." In response, the Mississippi Chinese established their own schools, parallel institutions that remained until the 1950s when white churches and schools were opened to them.

## SOCIAL FACTORS

In the nineteenth century, single Chinese women rarely ventured alone to the United States in search of economic opportunity, and Chinese tradition demanded that the wife remain with her husband's parents, even if he worked far from home. Approximately half the Chinese sojourners were married, making for a significant imbalance in the male–female ratio in the United States: 1,858:1 in 1860; 2,106:1 in 1880; 2,678:1 in 1890; and 1,887:1 in 1900. By 1920, the gender ratio, although still heavily out of balance, had lessened to 695:1.[17] The ratio continued to decline steadily thereafter. By 1990, Chinese immigration had reached parity in sex distribution: 49 percent male and 51 percent female from mainland China, and 47 percent male and 53 percent female from Taiwan.[18]

In earlier years, however, the overabundance of Chinese males and the scarcity of Chinese females led to organized prostitution in Chinatowns. Numerous brothels dotted the Chinatowns, some of them run or protected by the secret societies and staffed with young women kidnapped from their villages, sold by impoverished parents, or lured abroad by the deceit of a proxy marriage.[19]

> With the vast Pacific Ocean separating him from domestic joys and companionship, the Chinese sojourner relied on the tong-controlled brothels for sex, attending the gambling and opium dens for recreation and respite from the day's toil, and paid homage and allegiance to his clansmen, *Landsmänner*, and fraternal brothers to secure mutual aid, protection, and a job.[20]

Intermarriage was extremely difficult for the Chinese; indeed, 14 states had passed laws expressly forbidding miscegenation. Furthermore, in 1884, a federal court ruled that only wives of those males exempt from the Chinese Exclusion Act of 1882—namely, merchants and businessmen—could immigrate to the United States. For nearly all the Chinese laborers in the United States, establishing a family was impossible. By 1890, 40 years after the Chinese first had arrived, only 2.7 percent of the total Chinese population was U.S.-born. The figure climbed to 30 percent by 1920. Legislation in 1943 allowed Chinese women to enter the country, enabling the U.S.-born Chinese population to pass the halfway point in 1950. By 1960, U.S.-born Chinese accounted for approximately two-thirds of the total Chinese American population.[21]

## RECENT IMMIGRANTS

Congress ended the ban on immigration from China in 1943 and in its place instituted a quota system despite lingering anti-Chinese feeling. Speaking against the repeal, however, Congressman Compton White of Idaho in 1943 condemned the Chinese as a race unable to accept U.S. standards, citing the actions of a few to create a false stereotype (especially about education) of an entire group:

> The Chinese are inveterate opium-smokers most of the day. They brought that hideous opium habit to this country....There is no melting pot in America that can change their habits or change their mentality....If there are any people who have refused to accept our standard and our education, it is the Chinese.[22]

The 1943 legislation permitted only 105 Chinese immigrants to enter the United States each year, and that quota included anyone in the world of Chinese descent, not only citizens of China. Special and separate legislative acts covering refugees, displaced persons, and brides allowed more Chinese to enter. But not until the passage of the Immigration Act of 1965, however, could the Chinese enter under regular immigration regulations.

Chinese Americans have increased rapidly in population, growing more than four-fold since 1980 to nearly 3.4 million in 2011 (Table 8.1). As a result, the Chinatowns in San Francisco, Los Angeles, and New York doubled in size, spilling over their traditional boundaries and into adjacent neighborhoods. The arrival of so many "FOB" (fresh off the boat) immigrants and refugees has raised commercial rents, squeezing out old-line shops. With the Chinatowns unable to absorb all the newcomers, Chinese are flourishing in

**TABLE 8.1   Asian American Populations**

| NATIONALITY | 1980 | 1990 | 2000 | 2011 |
|---|---|---|---|---|
| Chinese (except Taiwanese) | 806,000 | 1,645,000 | 2,423,000 | 3,361,900 |
| Asian Indian | 387,000 | 815,400 | 1,678,800 | 2,908,200 |
| Filipino | 775,000 | 1,407,000 | 1,864,000 | 2,538,300 |
| Vietnamese* | 262,000 | 615,000 | 1,110,000 | 1,669,400 |
| Korean | 355,000 | 799,000 | 1,073,000 | 1,449,900 |
| Japanese | 701,000 | 848,000 | 795,000 | 756,900 |
| Cambodian* | 16,000 | 147,000 | 178,000 | 253,800 |
| Hmong* | 15,000 | 90,000 | 170,000 | 241,300 |
| Laotian* | 148,000 | 149,000 | 168,000 | 186,000 |
| Thai* | 45,000 | 91,000 | 111,000 | 189,900 |
| Bangladeshi* | 5,800 | 12,000 | 57,000 | 62,000 |

* Virtually all have entered the United States since 1970.
Source: U.S. Census Bureau, *2011 American Community Survey*, Table B02015.

outlying areas as well—such as the Corona, Flushing, and Jackson Heights sections of Queens in New York City and the Richmond and Sunset neighborhoods of western San Francisco. Upward mobility and outward migration have converted Monterey Park, east of Los Angeles, from an almost entirely white residential suburb into "Little Taipei," where the majority of people are now Chinese Americans.[23]

The San Francisco, Los Angeles, and New York Chinatowns, paradoxically, are both tourist attractions and slum communities. They are filled with overcrowded, dilapidated buildings and troubled by the problems of youth gangs and high tuberculosis rates.[24] Nonetheless, they retain historical, picturesque, and commercial importance. Less evident to tourists are the Chinese garment shops, or sweatshops, notorious for their long hours and meager compensation.[25] Also hidden above and behind the street-level storefront facades is a population density that is 10 to 12 times the city average.[26]

A Chinatown concern in recent years has been the increasing rebelliousness, criminality, and radicalism of many Chinese American youths. The rise of youthful militancy and delinquency appears to reflect the marginal status of those in the younger generation, who experience frustration and adjustment problems in the United States. Many recent arrivals from Hong Kong are unfamiliar with the language and culture; they either are unemployed or in the lowliest of jobs, and they live in overcrowded, slumlike quarters with no recreational facilities. For some youths, gang behavior helps fulfill status and identity needs.[27]

Compounding the problem are crime syndicates in China, known as *triads*, that smuggle perhaps as many as 30,000 Chinese into the United States each year (only approximately 10 percent are caught). Estimates place the number of illegal aliens in big-city Chinatowns as one in five residents.[28]

Within the Chinatowns, streets mark off the sections containing residents of different regional origins and dialects, much as in an early twentieth-century Little Italy. In New York City, for example, which is the largest Chinese enclave in the Western Hemisphere, Burmese Chinese concentrated on Henry Street, Taiwanese on Centre Street, Fujianese on Division Street, and Vietnamese Chinese on East Broadway. Once, those from Canton Province were the primary economic leaders of Chinatown, but now it is the Fujianese with their own regional associations, which has resulted in tensions with the older establishment.[29]

### SOCIOECONOMIC CHARACTERISTICS

Chinese Americans present a bipolar occupational distribution: 49 percent occupy management, business, science, and arts positions as compared to 36 percent of the white labor force, but many Chinese males are service workers, at 17 percent as compared to 14 percent among non-Hispanic white males. Such employment characteristics reflect in part educational and immigration patterns. For example, three-fifths of employed Chinese are college graduates, a high percentage that is reflected in a higher median family income for Chinese Americans than for blacks, whites, and most other U.S. ethnic groups except Japanese. (Figure 8.3).[30]

# Japanese Americans

When Commodore Matthew Perry sailed into Tokyo Bay in 1853, his arrival marked the beginning of a new era for Japan. For more than 200 years, the Japanese had lived in government-enforced isolation. The emperors had prohibited travel and foreign visitors, although castaways were treated hospitably and allowed to leave unharmed. No one was permitted to build large boats though, and any attempt to emigrate was punishable by death.

**Explore on MySocLab**
Activity: Japanese Americans:
A Mixed Heritage

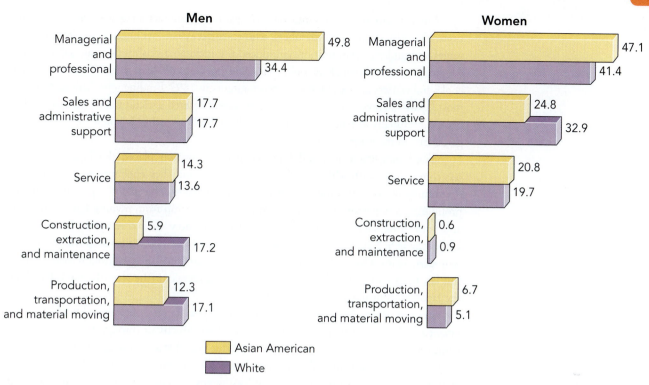

**FIGURE 8.3** **Occupational Distribution of the Employed Civilian Labor Force by Sex: 2011**
*Source:* U.S. Census Bureau.

The situation began to change in 1860, when the Japanese government sent its first official emissaries to Washington, DC. U.S. observers thought the Japanese lacked emotional expression:

[A San Francisco reporter wrote:] "This stoicism, however, is a distinguishing feature with the Japanese. It is part of their creed never to appear astonished at anything, and it must be a rare sight indeed which betrays in them any expression of wonder."

In the eighty-five years that passed between the arrival of Japan's first embassy and the end of the Second World War, this "distinguishing feature" of the Japanese became the cardinal element of the anti-Japanese stereotype. Characterized by journalists, politicians, novelists, and film-makers as a dangerous enemy, the Japanese were also pictured as mysterious and inscrutable.[31]

Beginning in 1868, the Japanese began emigrating, first as laborers and eventually as permanent settlers. Their numbers on the U.S. mainland were small at first. U.S. Census Bureau records show only 55 in 1870 and 2,039 in 1890. After that, they came in much greater numbers, reaching 24,000 in 1900; 72,000 in 1910; and 111,000 in 1920.

## ECONOMIC COMPETITION

Because many families in Japan still followed the practice of **primogeniture** (in which the eldest son inherits the entire estate), many second and third sons came to the United States to seek their fortunes. They settled in the western states, where anti-Chinese sentiment was strong still, most of them becoming farmers or farm laborers. Their growing numbers, their concentration in small areas, and their racial visibility led to conflict with organized labor, vegetable growers, and shippers in California.

Early Japanese immigrants entered various manufacturing and service occupations. Hostility from union members, who resented Asians' willingness to work for lower wages and under poor conditions, produced the inevitable clashes in a split labor market. Members of the shoemakers' union attacked Japanese cobblers in 1890, and unionized cooks and waiters attacked Japanese restaurateurs in 1892. Finding jobs difficult to obtain, most Japanese gravitated to the outlying areas and entered agricultural work, first as laborers and eventually as tenant farmers or small landholders; other Japanese became contract gardeners on the estates of whites.

Their industriousness and knowledge of cultivation placed the Japanese in serious competition with white and Hispanic farmers, and they encountered further acts of discrimination. In 1913, the California legislature passed the first alien landholding law, prohibiting any person who was ineligible for citizenship from owning land in the state and permitting such persons to lease land for no more than three years in succession. Under the U.S. Naturalization Act of 1790, then still in effect, citizenship was available to "any alien, being a free *white* person" (italics mine). In 1868, the government had modified this law to extend citizenship to persons of African descent (the recently freed slaves), but the Japanese continued to be excluded.

Because their children born in this country automatically were U.S. citizens, the Japanese held land in their children's names, either directly or through landholding companies whose stock they owned collectively. After World War I, new agitation arose against the Japanese. In 1920, the California legislature passed a law prohibiting aliens from being guardians of a minor's property or from leasing any land at all. The U.S. Supreme Court upheld the constitutionality of this law in 1923, and New Mexico, Arizona, Louisiana, Montana, Idaho, and Oregon passed similar statutes. Because their opportunities still were best in agriculture, many Japanese continued to work as tenant or truck farmers and, by 1941, were raising 42 percent of California's truck crops. In all likelihood, that helps to explain why white vegetable growers and shippers pressed for Japanese evacuation during World War II.[32]

## NATIONAL POLICY

Most non-Californians had no strong feelings about Japanese immigrants, but they were aware of Japan's growing military power when the Japanese defeated Russia in 1905 after two years of warfare. The catalyst that triggered a change in national policy toward the Japanese was a local incident. In 1906, the San Francisco Board of Education passed a resolution transferring 93 Japanese children scattered throughout the city's 23 schools into a segregated "Oriental" school in Chinatown. This action made national headlines and had international ramifications. Under pressure from the Japanese government, President Theodore Roosevelt instructed the attorney general to initiate lawsuits challenging the constitutionality of this action.

As a compromise, the school board rescinded its resolution, the government dropped its legal action, and Roosevelt issued an executive order (which remained in effect until 1948) barring the entry of Japanese from a bordering country or U.S. territory. Thus, Japanese who stayed even briefly in Hawaii, Canada, or Mexico no longer could enter the mainland United States. In addition, President Roosevelt secured the so-called Gentlemen's Agreement of 1908, whereby Japan agreed to restrict, but not eliminate altogether, the issuance of passports. The big loophole in this agreement was permission for wives to enter. Many Japanese married by proxy and then sent for their "picture brides." Several thousand Japanese entered the United States every year until World War I, and nearly 6,000 a year came after the war.

As men brought their wives here and children were born, fearful nativists made exaggerated claims that the Japanese birth rate could lead to the Japanese "overrunning" the country. Questions about Japanese immigration began to shift from economic competition to the "assimilability" of the Japanese because of their race, lifestyle, and alleged birth rate. The anti-Japanese stereotype, long a part of dominant-group attitudes, played a key role:

> The anti-Japanese stereotype was so widespread that it affected the judgments of sociologists about the possibilities of Japanese assimilation. Thus, in 1913, Robert E. Park was sufficiently depressed by anti-Japanese legislation and popular prejudice to predict: "The Japanese…is condemned to remain among us an abstraction, a symbol, and a symbol not merely of his own race, but of the Orient and of that vague, ill-defined menace we sometimes refer to as the 'yellow-peril.'" Although Park later reversed his doleful prediction, his observations on Japanese emphasized their uncommunicative features, stolid faces, and apparently blank character.[33]

The Immigration Law of 1924—which severely restricted the number of southern, central, and eastern Europeans who could enter the United States—specifically barred the Japanese because it denied entry to all aliens ineligible for citizenship. The bill passed by large majorities (323 to 71 in the House and 62 to 6 in the Senate), indicating widespread support for limiting immigration to the supposedly "assimilable" peoples. The Japanese government vehemently denounced this legislation, taking it as a national affront, a violation of the terms of the Gentlemen's Agreement, and an insult to a world power only recently courted by the United States. Nevertheless, the legislation remained in effect until 1952 (see the International Scene box about a latent function of Japanese national policy on immigrants).

## EXPULSION AND IMPRISONMENT

By 1940, approximately 127,000 ethnic Japanese lived in the United States, 94,000 of them in California. Approximately 63 percent were U.S.-born, and only 15 percent were of voting age. Japan's attack on Pearl Harbor in 1941 and the subsequent war led to what subsequently was referred to as "our worst wartime mistake."[34] More than 110,000 Japanese, many of them second- and third-generation Americans with as little as one-eighth Japanese ancestry, were removed from their homes and placed in "relocation centers" in Arkansas, Arizona, eastern California, Colorado, Idaho, Utah, and Wyoming.[35]

> The evacuees loaded their possessions onto trucks….Neighbors and teachers were on hand to see their friends off. Members of other minority groups wept. One old Mexican woman wept, saying, "Me next. Me next."
>
> …People were starting off to 7 o'clock jobs, watering their gardens, sweeping their pavements. Passers-by invariably stopped to stare in amazement, perhaps in horror, that this could happen in the United States. People soon became accustomed to the idea, however, and many profited from the evacuation. Japanese mortgages were foreclosed and their properties attached. They were forced to sell property such as cars and refrigerators at bargain prices.[36]

The mass expulsion of the Japanese from the West Coast was unnecessary for national security, despite claims to the contrary. The traditional anti-Asian sentiment on the West Coast, fear of the so-called "treacherous" character of the Japanese, and opposition to Japanese American success in agriculture all may have been factors. No mass evacuation of the 150,000 ethnic Japanese occurred in Hawaii, which was much more strategically important and vulnerable to attack because of its location. The differences

# the INTERNATIONAL scene

## The Difference Between Race and Culture

After decades of Japanese refusal to let in unskilled foreigners, tens of thousands of Bangladeshis, Pakistanis, Thais, and other Asians entered Japan in the 1980s on tourist visas and stayed illegally. Worried that it might be flooded by foreigners, as France and Germany had been, Japan enacted tougher immigration curbs on unskilled workers in 1989 and began expelling the estimated 100,000 illegal immigrant Asians. Still needing a labor pool and not wanting to open its doors to outsiders, Japan next changed its immigration laws in 1990 to encourage immigration of foreigners whose parents or grandparents already lived in Japan, expecting a homogeneous blending.

Approximately 150,000 unskilled ethnic Japanese fleeing the then-troubled economy of Brazil quickly entered Japan to take dirty, difficult, and dangerous jobs at construction sites, factories, and foundries or low-status jobs in restaurants and shops unwanted by native-born Japanese. But what at first appeared to be a mutually beneficial arrangement created numerous adjustment problems for both sides, neither of which was prepared for the resulting culture shock.

The Japanese expected the Brazilians to be Japanese, but culturally, they were not. They spoke Portuguese—and little or no Japanese—when they arrived and for a long time afterward. They dressed differently, talked more noisily, and laughed and embraced one another in public, all unlike the native-born Japanese.

Their ethnicity became more visible with the advent of numerous Portuguese-language radio programs and newspapers, restaurants, stores, and social clubs. Brazilian street festivals in Tokyo flavored with samba and salsa attracted large crowds.

The immigrants complained that they were looked down on and treated with suspicion. They said they suffered discrimination in stores and restaurants, where they were either made to feel unwelcome or treated as probable shoplifters. Another problem they faced was the lack of health benefits and worker's compensation if they were injured at work. The government, meanwhile, opened a dozen centers to assist the foreign-born laborers.

Today, two decades later, approximately 317,000 Brazilians live in Japan. Illustrative of the cultural pluralism within a once homogeneous society is Homi, a large ethnic enclave within Toyota City. Street signs are in Japanese and Portuguese; the restaurants in the shopping complex serve Brazilian dishes; a convenience store displays Brazilian magazines; and a Japanese supermarket gave way to a Japanese-Brazilian one. Even the parking lots, once filled with white or gray cars preferred by the Japanese, now contain numerous purple cars retrofitted into low-riders.

### CRITICAL THINKING QUESTION

What similarities to the above situation, if any, do you find between native-born African Americans and immigrants from Africa?

in the Japanese experience in Hawaii and on the mainland perhaps are best understood by looking at the differences in structural discrimination. In Hawaii, the Japanese were involved more fully in economic and political endeavors, partly because they lived in an environment of greater racial harmony. On the West Coast, the Japanese were more isolated from mainstream U.S. society, and certain labor and agricultural groups saw them as an economic threat. Also, anti-Asian attitudes and actions had prevailed in that area for nearly 100 years.

Besides the trauma that resulted from being uprooted and interned, the Japanese had to adjust culturally to their new surroundings. Instead of their preferred deep hot baths, for example, they had only showers and common washrooms. Central dining halls prevented families from eating together intimately as a family unit. Outside and sometimes distant toilet facilities, not partitioned in the early months, were a hardship for the old and for the parents of small children. Nearly 6,000 babies were born at these centers and proper hospital facilities were not always available. Only partial partitions divided rooms occupied by different families in the same barracks, permitting minimal privacy.

In 1943, an American soldier, bayonet affixed to his rifle, guards a Japanese internment camp at Tule Lake,, California. The Japanese American National Museum has an online archive of personal stories from community members who survived the camps. Only in 1988 did the government make token reparations payments to those still living for losses sustained by this wartime imprisonment.

Ted Nakashima, a second-generation Japanese American, offered a disheartening portrait of what the early months of life in the Tule Lake, California, camp were like:

> The resettlement center is actually a penitentiary—armed guards in towers with spotlights and deadly tommy guns, fifteen feet of barbed wire fences, everyone confined to quarters at nine, lights out at ten o'clock. The guards are ordered to shoot anyone who approaches within twenty feet of the fences. No one is allowed to take the two-block-long hike to the latrines after nine, under any circumstances. The apartments, as the army calls them, are two-block-long stables, with windows on one side. Floors are…two-by-fours laid directly on the mud, which is everywhere. The stalls are about eighteen by twenty-one feet; some contain families of six or seven persons. Partitions are seven feet high, leaving a four-foot opening above…
>
> The food and sanitation problems are the worst. We have had absolutely no fresh meat, vegetables, or butter since we came here. Mealtime queues extend for blocks; standing in a rainswept line, feet in the mud, waiting for the scant portions of canned wieners and boiled potatoes, hash for breakfast or canned wieners and beans for dinner. Coffee or tea dosed with saltpeter and stale bread are the adults' staples. Dirty, unwiped dishes, greasy silver, a starchy diet, no butter, no milk, bawling kids, mud, wet mud that stinks when it dries, no vegetables—a sad thing for the people who raised them in such abundance…
>
> Today, one of the surface sewage-disposal pipes broke and sewage flowed down the streets. Kids played in the water. Shower baths without hot water. Stinking mud and slops everywhere.
>
> Can this be the same America we left a few weeks ago?…What really hurts most is the constant reference to us evacuees as "Japs." "Japs" are the guys we are fighting. We're on this side and we want to help.
>
> Why won't America let us?[37]

Although the harsh physical conditions and sanitation problems improved, the Japanese Americans remained prisoners. They tried to make life inside the barbed wire fences a little brighter by fixing up their quarters and planting small gardens. However, these "residents" of the "relocation centers" still lived in what actually were concentration camps. Approximately 35,000 young Japanese Americans left these centers by the end of 1943, going voluntarily to the East and Midwest for further schooling or a job. For those obliged to remain in the camps, life was monotonous and unproductive. The evacuation brought financial ruin to many Japanese American families; they lost property, savings, income, and jobs for which they never were adequately compensated.

By weakening Japanese subcommunities and institutions, the evacuation program encouraged acculturation. The traditional authority of the first-generation Japanese Americans (*Issei*) declined; family structure and husband–wife roles underwent changes and became more equal because of camp life; and the second-generation Japanese (*Nisei*) who resettled found new opportunities. Of the Japanese who relocated to the Midwest and to the East Coast, a large number later returned to the West. Many integrated into U.S. society in the postwar period because they had been forced to do so.

In 1944, the Supreme Court upheld the Japanese evacuation by a 6 to 3 vote (*Korematsu v. United States of America*), although the dissenting justices gave strong minority opinions. Justice Francis Murphy called approving the evacuation "the legalization of racism." Justice Robert H. Jackson, who later prosecuted the Nazi war criminals at Nuremberg, wrote,

> But once a judicial opinion rationalizes such an order to show that it conforms to the Constitution, or rather rationalizes the Constitution to show that the Constitution sanctions such an order, the Court for all time has validated the principle of racial discrimination in criminal procedure, and of transplanting American citizens. The principle then lies about like a loaded weapon ready for the hand of any authority that can bring forward a plausible claim of an urgent need. Every repetition imbeds that principle more deeply in our law and thinking and expands it to new purposes.[38]

Soon after, another case, *Endo v. United States*, brought an end to this forcible detention—as of January 2, 1945—when the U.S. Supreme Court unanimously ruled that all loyal Japanese Americans be set free unconditionally. Justice Jackson's 1944 dissenting opinion seemed prophetic 35 years later, when the seizure of U.S. hostages at the U.S. Embassy in Iran prompted calls by some politicians for Iranian students then attending U.S. colleges to be rounded up and detained in the very same concentration camps.

After their release, Japanese Americans sought redress through the Japanese American Citizens League (JACL). This organization fought to restore and reopen individuals' frozen bank deposits, obtain compensation for owners of confiscated land, and regain lost retirement benefits owed to civil service workers. The Evacuation Claims Act of 1948 brought token repayment of approximately 10 percent of actual Japanese American losses.[39] The Civil Liberties Act of 1988 offered a formal apology to the former internees for violating their "basic civil liberties" because of "racial prejudice" and awarded a tax-free reparations payment of $20,000 to each of the 60,000 surviving detainees.[40]

## RECENT IMMIGRANTS

Traditionally, Japanese parents have encouraged their children to get a good education; and, since the 1940s, Japanese American males and females have performed well above the national norms of those completing high school and college. The culture's emphasis on conformity, aspiration, competitiveness, discipline, and self-control helps to explain the high educational attainments of Japanese Americans.[41] Encouraged by their *Nisei* (second-generation) elders and the upwardly mobile *Sansei* (third generation), the *Yonsei* (fourth generation) and *Gosei* (fifth generation) increasingly have entered professional fields, especially engineering, pharmacy, electronics, and other technical fields. Approximately

3 in 5 Japanese Americans are U.S.-born (the highest among Asian American groups) and, in 2011, they had one of the highest percentages of college graduates.[42]

Japanese Americans have become arguably the best-assimilated of all Asian Americans. One of Hawaii's current U.S. senators, Mazie Hirono, and two immediate past U.S. senators, Daniel Akaka and Daniel Inouye, have been of Japanese ancestry. On the mainland, structural assimilation, for example, is evident among the *Sansei* and *Yonsei,* whose outgroup dating and exogamy significantly exceed all other races and Asian American groups.[43] Japanese Americans are the first non-white group to merge biologically so fully into the dominant U.S. society.

Japanese immigration to the United States amounted to 98,400 between 2000 and 2011—far less than the totals of most other East Asian countries.[44] Consequently, the Japanese American population represents a steadily declining proportion of the Asian American community (5 percent in 2010). More than half of all Japanese Americans live either in California (33 percent) or Hawaii (24 percent). Approximately half of all new arrivals are skilled and professional workers who find many similarities between U.S. society and their homeland. Most are adherents of Buddhism, a religion whose U.S. membership is growing because of the continuing entry of Japanese and other Asian believers in this faith.

One special group in the United States is comprised of businesspeople and employees of the *kaisha* (large corporations) on two- or three-year assignments with their companies' U.S. branch offices. Comparable in a way to the sojourner presence of Chinese laborers in the nineteenth century, these Japanese corporate employees often live in suburban towns near large urban centers.

## Filipino Americans

The Filipinos came to the United States with a unique status. In 1898, when the Philippines became a U.S. possession, the inhabitants were U.S. nationals, although not U.S. citizens. Not therefore designated as aliens, they faced no quota restriction on their entry until 1935. The geographic locale of their homeland and their Spanish heritage complicated their status, however, because the federal government argued that they were not whites. The U.S. Supreme Court upheld this official position in a 1934 ruling on a case challenging the 1790 naturalization law limiting citizenship to foreign-born whites:

> "White persons" within the meaning of the statute are members of the Caucasian race, as Caucasian is defined in the understanding of the mass of men. The term excludes the Chinese, the Japanese, the Hindus, the American Indians, and the Filipinos.[45]

### EARLY IMMIGRANTS

Like so many other immigrant groups, the early Filipino immigrants did not think of themselves in nationalist terms. Instead, they placed themselves in one of several native language subgroupings: the Tagalogs, Visayans, or Ilocanos. Their social hangouts—the clubhouse, bar, or poolroom—often reflected that separation. U.S. society lumped them together, however, and in time, societal hostility forged a common ethnic identity among them.

After the Gentlemen's Agreement of 1908 curtailed Japanese emigration, the Hawaiian Sugar Planters' Association recruited laborers from the Philippines to work the plantations. Fifteen years later, the modest number of Filipinos in the continental United States (5,603 in 1920) began to increase. Why? California growers, faced with the loss of Mexican labor because of quota restrictions in the pending Immigration Act of 1924, turned to the Filipinos as an alternative labor source. By 1930, the number of Filipinos in the continental United States had increased to more than 45,000, with more than two-thirds living in California.

Many Filipinos worked in agriculture at first, particularly in California and Washington. However, the lure of the city attracted many young Filipino males to urban areas, where they sought jobs. Discrimination, along with lack of education and job skills, resulted in their getting only low-paying domestic and personal-service work in hotels, restaurants, other businesses, and residences. They were employed as bellboys, waiters, cooks, busboys, janitors, drivers, house boys, elevator operators, and hospital attendants. By 1940, their employment in these areas peaked, with 9 of 10 Filipinos so employed.[46] Feeling exploited by their employers, they often joined unions (or formed their own unions when denied membership in existing unions) and went on strike, intensifying management resentment. Ironically, the union hierarchy also disliked them and later joined in efforts to bar them from the United States.

Race riots erupted in Exeter, California, on October 24, 1929, and in Watsonville, California, on January 19, 1930, when one Filipino was killed. In both instances, several hundred white men beat Filipinos, shattered windows in cars and buildings, and wrecked property. As the Depression of the 1930s worsened and jobs became scarcer, critics increased their objections to the presence of the Filipinos. Other clashes occurred in San Jose and San Francisco, followed on January 28, 1930, with the bombing of the Filipino Federation of America Center in Stockton, called "the Manila of California" because of its large Filipino population.

### THE SCARCITY OF FILIPINO WOMEN

Of every 100 Filipinos coming to California between 1920 and 1929, 93 were male, nearly 80 percent of them single and between 16 and 30 years of age. With few Filipino women available, these males sought the company of women of other races, thereby enraging many white men, as the following racist statement illustrates:

> The Filipinos have…demanded the right to run dance halls under the alias of clubs, with white girls as entertainers. And the excuse they have openly and brazenly given for their demand is that the Filipinos "prefer" white women to those of their own race and that besides, there are not enough Filipino women in the country to satisfy their lust.…If that statement is not enough to make the blood of any white man, of any other decent man boil, then there is no such thing as justified indignation at any advocacy of immorality.[47]

This rabble-rousing statement reflects the sort of sexually oriented charges often directed against minority racial groups. Filipino men's association with white women through intermarriage, dance hall encounters, and affairs led to increased tensions in Filipino–white relations. The Filipinos' reputation as great lovers emerged as a stereotype and probably was enhanced when a San Francisco judge commented:

> Some of these boys, with perfect candor, have told me bluntly and boastfully that they practice the art of love with more perfection than white boys, and occasionally, one of the girls has supplied me with information to the same effect. In fact, some of the disclosures in this regard are perfectly startling in nature.[48]

Filipino responses followed quickly. Sylvester Saturday, editor of the Filipino Poets League in Washington, DC, stated,

> We Filipinos are tickled at being called "great lovers." Surely, we are proud of this heritage. We love our women so much that we work ourselves to death to gain and keep their affections.[49]

A Filipino from Chicago chided,

> And as for the Filipinos being "great lovers," there is nothing surprising about that. We Filipinos, however poor, are taught from the cradle up to respect and love our women. That's why our divorce rate is nil compared with the state of which Judge Lazarus is a proud son. If to love and respect our womenfolks is savagery, then make the most of it, Judge. We plead guilty.[50]

Whites were not amused. Several western states passed laws prohibiting marriages between Filipinos and whites. The Tyding–McDuffie Act of 1935 granted deferred independence to the Philippines and imposed an immediate rigid quota of 50 immigrants a year. Repatriation efforts from 1935 to 1937 succeeded in returning only 2,190 U.S. residents to the Philippines.[51]

Because of the lack of Filipino women and legal restrictions on intermarriage, many Filipino males remained single. These early immigrants became lonely old men with no family ties, living in poverty after years of hard work, although a small number did intermarry with Mexicans, Native Americans, mulattos, Asians, and whites.[52]

Unlike the Chinese, who had a tradition as sojourners and who formed benevolent and protective associations, the Filipinos did not establish the support institutions usually found in immigrant communities. Their lack of families and the seasonal, transitory nature of their employment were primary reasons for this. As a result of housing discrimination, they lived in hotels and rooming houses in less desirable sections of town. The pool hall and taxi-dance hall became their recreational outlets.[53]

**STUDENTS SPEAK** "I was shocked to read about what the Filipinos went through. What stood out to me was the social problem of not enough Asian women in America, which had a huge impact on their social, personal, and community lives. This led to the males patronizing prostitutes or seeking white women. Soon the majority became even more racist, with 14 states passing miscegenation laws. After reading this, I thought to myself how history always repeats itself. When new immigrants come to America to start a better life for themselves, the majority often tries to put them down."

**—Andrea Kirkconnell**

## RECENT IMMIGRANTS

With the Philippines a strategically important ally during World War II, the social climate in the mainland United States became more liberal toward Filipinos. In January 1942, legislation enabled Filipino residents to become naturalized U.S. citizens. They could

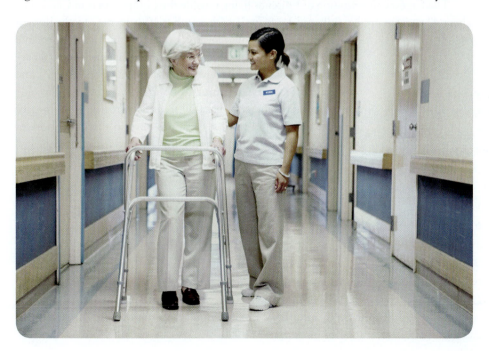

*Filipinos are most visible to other Americans in health care. They are the largest ethnic group among nurses at many hospitals in East Coast and West Coast metropolitan areas, but they also hold other positions in health care in hospitals, labs, and nursing homes. Others pursue other professional careers, but many hold working-class jobs as well.*

**FIGURE 8.4** Asian Group Populations, 2010

Source: U.S. Census Bureau.

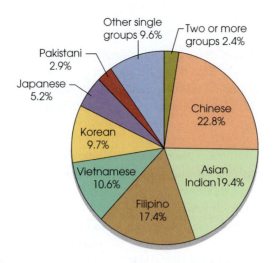

Other single groups 9.6%

Two or more groups 2.4%

Pakistani 2.9%

Japanese 5.2%

Korean 9.7%

Vietnamese 10.6%

Filipino 17.4%

Chinese 22.8%

Asian Indian 19.4%

buy land in California, and many did—often from Japanese Americans who were being removed from certain areas, such as Los Angeles. Many Filipinos bought farms in the San Fernando Valley, the San Joaquin Valley, and the Torrance–Gardena area.[54]

Since the Immigration Act of 1965, Filipino immigration has been quite high. An unstable political situation at home toward the end of the Marcos regime (which was overthrown peacefully in 1986) and continuing economic deprivation in the Philippines have served as the major push factors. Like the Japanese, new Filipino arrivals tend to have better educational and occupational skills than most of their ethnic cohorts born in the United States. More than half are professional and technical workers in medicine, law, engineering, and education. Because of licensing and hiring problems, however, many are unable to secure jobs commensurate with their education, skills, and experience.[55]

Filipinos are fragmented socially, linguistically, and politically. Unlike the Koreans, few are entrepreneurs, and seldom do Filipinos form cooperative credit associations to raise business capital. Filipino youths, unlike other East Asian American youths but like the Indochinese, often reject traditional family discipline and become assimilated. Two thirds of all Filipino Americans speak a language other than English at home.[56]

The largest concentration of Filipinos living outside the Philippines is in California, where 43 percent reside, followed by Hawaii with another 10 percent. Mostly Roman Catholics, with a strong loyalty to family and church, today's Filipino Americans otherwise present diverse socioeconomic characteristics of education, occupation, income, and residence. Time of immigration and age appear to be the key variables. The old-timers—retired laborers—usually are single males with meager incomes. Second and third generations born in the United States typically share such problems as lack of social acceptance, low income, low educational achievement, and negative self-image. In contrast, new arrivals often are college graduates seeking white-collar jobs in the economic mainstream.[57]

Filipino Americans more than doubled in number between 1970 and 1980, going from 343,000 to 775,000, and doubled again—to nearly 1.9 million—by 2000. Today, at more than 2.5 million, they are the third-largest Asian and Pacific Islander ethnic group in the United States, comprising 17 percent of the total U.S. Asian population (Figure 8.4). Averaging 57,000 new arrivals annually, Filipino immigrants between 2000 and 2012 totalled more than 714,000.[58]

**STUDENTS SPEAK** "This chapter was very interesting. My background is of Filipino descent, although I was raised and born here in the United States. I have never read anything like I did in this chapter regarding the Asian races. Growing up in a predominantly white town, I did not know my own history. The miscegenation law that was passed definitely surprised me and so did other things about my own cultural heritage. It was interesting to learn this perspective. It's very true that many Filipinos are in the healthcare field, although I am not."

**—Rajh Odi**

# Korean Americans

The United States became the first Western nation to sign a treaty with Korea, when it formalized a relationship of friendship and trade in 1882. Other nations quickly followed suit, and all attempted to displace China as the then-preeminent foreign power in Korea.

Despite various treaties and declarations by the different nations purporting to guarantee Korea's independence, emerging Japanese hegemony (both political and economic) became the reality. Japan's victory over Russia in 1905 solidified Japanese domination of Korea, and Japan exercised colonial control until the end of World War II. Even then, Korea did not gain national independence, for an Allied military agreement in 1945 mandated that Soviet troops accept the Japanese surrender in the region north of the 38th parallel and U.S. troops do the same in the region south of it. This temporary line, created out of military expediency, became a permanent demarcation that still defines the split between North and South Korea.

> **Read on MySocLab**
> Document: Intimacy at a Distance, Korean American Style: Invited Korean Elderly and Their Married Children

## EARLY IMMIGRANTS

The Hawaii Sugar Planters' Association, needing laborers to replace the Chinese, who were excluded by the 1882 legislation, recruited 7,226 Koreans, 637 of them women, between 1903 and 1905. This was the first large group of Koreans to migrate to the United States. The Koreans, mostly peasants, sought economic relief from the famines plaguing their country at the turn of the century. In Hawaii, they worked long hours for meager wages under harsh conditions. Of the original group, approximately 1,000 returned to Korea, but 2,000 males and 12 women went on to the mainland United States, and the rest remained in Hawaii. The males were almost all between the ages of 20 and 40 (see the Ethnic Experience box).[59]

Between 1907 and 1924, several thousand more Korean immigrants—mostly "picture brides," political activists fighting Japanese oppression, and students—migrated to the United States. As a result of the age disparity between the picture brides and the older males, many second-generation Korean Americans spent a good portion of their formative years with non–English-speaking widowed mothers who had limited formal schooling.[60]

## RECENT IMMIGRANTS

Not until the end of the Korean War and passage of the Refugee Relief Act in 1953 did Koreans emigrate in substantial numbers. As refugees or war brides, Koreans came to the United States in growing numbers beginning in 1958. The continued presence of U.S. troops in South Korea and the cultural influence on South Korea that resulted were constant inducements to intermarry or contemplate living in the United States. The liberalized immigration law of 1965 opened the doors to Asian immigrants and allowed relatives to join family members already in the United States. This chain-migration pattern resulted in an impressive fivefold population increase in 10 years, from 70,000 in 1970 to 355,000 in 1980, and in a doubling of that number to 799,000 in 1990. Since then, the Korean population has grown to more than 1.4 million.

## THE ROLE OF THE CHURCH

Nearly 70 percent of the Korean-American population identifies itself as Christian, a significantly higher proportion than the 26 percent Christian population living in Korea. Mostly Presbyterian and Methodist, Korean American congregations now exceed 2,000, compared to fewer than 75 in 1970. Ethnic churches, including Korean ones, make important contributions to immigrant communities, serving more than religious purposes. The

# the ETHNIC experience

## The First Korean Women in the United States

*The following comments, through the courtesy of Harold and Sonia Sunoo, are a composite of taped interviews with three of the first 12 Korean women to come to the U.S. mainland:*

"We left Korea because we were too poor. We had nothing to eat...There was absolutely no way we could survive."

"At first, we were unaware that we had been 'sold' as laborers...We thought Hawaii was America in those days...We cut sugar canes, the thing you put in coffee...."

"I'll never forget the foreman. No, he wasn't Korean—he was French. The reason I'll never forget him is that he was the most ignorant of all ignoramuses, but he knew all the cuss words in the world...[I] could tell by the sound of his words. He said we worked like 'lazy.' He wanted us to work faster...He would gallop around on horseback and crack and snap his whip...He was so mean and so ignorant!"

"...If all of us worked hard and pooled together our total earnings, it came to about fifty dollars a month, barely enough to feed and clothe the five of us. We cooked on the porch, using coal oil and when we cooked in the fields, I gathered the wood. We had to carry water in vessels from water faucets scattered here and there in the camp area..."

"My mother and sister-in-law took in laundry. They scrubbed, ironed, and mended shirts for a nickel apiece. It was pitiful! Their knuckles became swollen and raw from using the harsh yellow laundry soap...but it was still better than in Korea. There was no way to earn money there."

*On the mainland, the Koreans encountered even worse problems than in Hawaii because of the more highly charged racial tension and the severe weather conditions, as the following account indicates:*

"We had five children at that time—our youngest was three and a half. I was paid fifteen cents an hour for weeding. Our baby was too young to go to school, so I had to take him along with me to the fields—it was so early when we started that he'd be fast asleep when we left so I couldn't feed him breakfast. Returning home, he'd be asleep again because he was so tired. Poor child, he was practically starved. He too suffered so much...[In February] the ground...was frozen crisp and it was so cold that the baby's tender ears got frozen and blood oozed from him...For all this suffering, I was paid fifteen cents an hour."

Source: Three Korean immigrants who came to Hawaii between 1903 and 1905 at ages ranging from 19 to 25. Taped interviews from the collection of Vincent N. Parrillo.

church becomes a social organization, providing religious and ethnic fellowship, a personal community, and a family atmosphere within an alien and urban environment.[61]

One study of the role of Korean churches in the ethnic community of Chicago, where more than 100,000 Koreans live, found patterns reminiscent of those of earlier European immigrants.[62] Their church involvement—much higher than in Korea—was strongly motivated by their sense of marginalization from the larger society. Providing institutional transmission of Korean culture, the ethnic church thus legitimizes traditional ethnic values and moral standards. For many second-generation Korean Americans who believe that complete assimilation is not possible because of their race, the Korean ethnic church—particularly the evangelical Protestant church—provides a significant sense of belonging and group identity. Because the greater the participation, the greater the identification with homeland and culture, Korean American churches, like similar institutions in other ethnic communities, serve as a focal point for enhancing ethnic identity.

## OCCUPATIONAL ADAPTATION

Korean Americans have one of the highest self-employment rates of all ethnic or racial groups, including whites, although they want their children to find "good jobs" elsewhere in the open labor market. Whereas approximately 1 in 9 Korean Americans is a business owner; for blacks, it is 1 in 28; for Hispanics, 1 in 16; and for non-Hispanic whites, 1 in 15.[63] In many cities and **exurbs**, Korean small businesses and firms especially are conspicuous.

At first, these business owners followed the usual immigrant practice of hiring their fellow co-ethnics because such a practice was mutually beneficial to employers and employees. Lately, however, a new pattern has emerged. For example, in Los Angeles and New York City—cities with large Hispanic populations—Mexicans and Central Americans increasingly are visible as employees in Korean-owned businesses, partly as an available labor pool and partly to render customer service to the nearby Hispanic clientele with limited command of English. In another example of **minority–minority relations**, in Los Angeles, the two groups are learning each other's language to communicate before learning English.[64]

Many Korean American women also work, but such income-producing activity is not empowering in and of itself. The determination of whether their labor makes them more independent or furthers their submission to patriarchal rule depends on such other factors as their perception of work, their changed roles as working mothers, and whether or not economic downward mobility is a factor.[65]

Widespread use of rotating credit associations has greatly aided the Koreans in establishing their own businesses. Like the *hui* among the Mandarin Chinese, the *tanomoshi* among the Japanese, and the *susu* of the Caribbean Islanders, the **kye** of the Koreans provides start-up funds for their ethnic entrepreneurs. In the arrangement's simplest form, each member contributes a fixed amount monthly to a fund and has rotating access to the pot. The first borrowers pay extra loan interest. Dating back to Korean farming villages of the sixteenth century, the *kye* helps newcomers get started in business while simultaneously functioning as a social club to bind immigrants together.

Overall, Koreans have a greater proportion of college graduates than most other non-white groups and whites. Their income, however, lags behind that of native-born Americans and most other Asian American groups.[66] Koreans have fared rather poorly in social acceptance, as indicated by social distance measures, an important indicator of structural assimilation. In his 1956 and 1966 studies, Emory S. Bogardus found Koreans at or near the bottom in preference rankings, below all other East Asian peoples. In my 2001 and 2011 studies, I found that Koreans had improved in preference rankings, although they still remained in the bottom tier (see Chapter 1).[67]

As in many other U.S. churches, Korean Americans often use praise music in their worship services to appeal to the younger generation who have spent all or most of their lives in the United States. To further attract the second generation, worship services are often in English, unlike the Korean language of past years for the immigrant community.

## Asian Indian Americans

Emigration from India to the United States happened in two distinct phases. In the early twentieth century, several thousand poorly educated Indian agricultural laborers migrated to the West Coast and settled in rural regions in Washington (lumbering) and California (agriculture). Nearly all the early immigrants were Sikh males who came from the Punjab region of northern India. Distinctive in their traditionally worn beards and turbans, they soon experienced hostile racism and violent attacks. In the 1970s and 1980s, a second

**8-4** Describe the immigrant experiences of Asian Indians, Pakistanis, Vietnamese, and others.

group of immigrants—many of them middle class, college educated, or professionally trained—arrived. More recently, less educated relatives of earlier immigrants have come, typically entering such family-owned businesses as groceries, motels, and convenience stores or driving taxis or limousines.

### EARLY IMMIGRANTS

Between 1820 and 1900, fewer than 800 immigrants came to the United States from India. In the next two decades, a small wave of nearly 7,000 agricultural laborers from northern India journeyed to the West Coast of the United States, and still others entered Canada. Almost entirely male, this group—like so many other immigrant groups—intended to accumulate some savings and then return home. Between 1908 and 1920, nearly 1,700 did leave, and a few hundred were deported as undesirable aliens.[68]

### SOCIETAL REACTION

Even though the Japanese, Chinese, and Filipinos far outnumbered the Asian Indians, the latter, too, experienced discrimination and dominant-group aggression because of their visibility and identification as Asians. Near a lumber camp in Bellingham, Washington, on September 5, 1907, several hundred whites raided the living quarters of Indian workers, forcing approximately 700 of them to flee across the Canadian border. Two months later, in Everett, Washington, several hundred whites drove the Indian workers out of town. Racial prejudice manifested itself also in Port Angeles, Washington, where real estate brokers published in the local newspaper the terms of their covenant not to sell to "Hindoos or Negroes." They justified their action on grounds that wherever these groups settle, they "have depreciated [the] value of adjacent property and injured the reputation of the neighborhood, and are generally considered as undesirable."[69]

The San Francisco–based Asiatic Exclusion League quickly included Asian Indians among its targets and warned the public that these people were a "menace." League officials declared that the East Indians were untrustworthy, immodest, unsanitary, insolent, and lustful.[70] National hostility toward Asian Indians from 1908 to 1910 led immigration officials to reject 1,130 would-be immigrants from India at their ports of entry. Pro-immigration pressure from the Western Pacific Railroad in 1910 enabled 1,462 of them to enter between 1911 and 1920, but another 1,762 were denied entry, mostly on grounds that they would become public charges.[71] The popular magazine *Collier's*, influenced by the Asiatic Exclusion League's exaggerated claim that 10,000 Asian Indians already lived in California, printed an article warning its readers about the "Hindu invasion."[72]

*Hindu* was a popular ethnic epithet for Indians in those days, undoubtedly used because so much of the Indian subcontinent (including 80 percent of India's population today) was Hindu. However, these immigrant victims were mostly Sikhs, a religious minority composing only 2 percent of present-day India's population.

> In this atmosphere of marked hostility toward Asians, the few thousand East Indians gradually established themselves primarily in California and relied chiefly on agriculture as a means of livelihood. Typically, the Indians sought work in groups with a leader serving as their agent in negotiating with employers. Owing in part to the desire of many farmers to break the Japanese monopoly on the labor supply in those areas, they had little difficulty finding employment in the Sacramento and San Joaquin valleys. Also, Indians moved into the Imperial Valley, another rapidly growing agricultural area.[73]

In 1923, the U.S. Supreme Court reversed previous lower-court decisions and ruled that Asian Indians were non-whites and thus ineligible for citizenship under the terms of the 1790 Naturalization Act. The government then revoked naturalization certificates that previously had been granted to 60 or 70 Asian Indians. The decision also prevented Asian Indians in California from owning or leasing land in their own names because state legislation prohibited alien landholding. The Asian Indians thus became itinerant farm laborers. Few of them had any family life because of the migrant nature of their work and the lack of women they could marry.

## MINORITY RESPONSE

The social and economic restrictions imposed by discriminatory immigration and miscegenation laws created and magnified the social isolation of the early immigrants. Unable to travel, send for wives or future brides, or marry women outside their own group, East Indian immigrants neither could participate fully in U.S. society nor produce a second generation of U.S. citizens to aid their movement into the mainstream of American life.[74]

Approximately 3,000 Asian Indians returned home between 1920 and 1940. A few hundred more were deported. The population dwindled from 5,441 in 1920 to 2,405 by 1940.[75] A few of those who remained married Mexican American women. Most, however, lived in communal groups apart from the rest of society. Some Sikhs congregated in Stockton, California—the site of a large Filipino community—and built a temple there for worship.

In July 1946, the Luce–Celler Bill removed Asian Indians from the "barred zone" established in 1917 to prevent most Asians and Pacific Islanders from immigrating to the United States. Thenceforth, 100 Asian Indians could enter annually. In addition, males already living here could bring over their wives and children or make marital arrangements with women living in their homeland. Finally, Asian Indians were permitted to become naturalized citizens, an opportunity taken by 1,772 of them between 1948 and 1965. Because they rarely intermarried and they retained important aspects of their culture, the rural Asian Indians only slightly remained acculturated even though they had adopted certain material comforts, dress, and other features of life in the United States.[76]

Physical appearance was an important factor setting these immigrants apart. In the early twentieth century, the full beards prescribed by the Sikh religion were not fashionable. Moreover, all the men wore turbans and were sometimes belittled as "rag heads." The Indian women who arrived before the Depression—like those who have arrived since the more liberal Immigration Act of 1965—were quite distinct in wearing the *sari*, a lightweight outer garment with one end wrapped about the waist and the other draped over the shoulder or covering the head. Most cultural differences—appearance, food taboos, and social interaction—were an integral part either of the Hindu caste system or of the Sikh religion in India. Therefore, Asian Indians not only seemed strange to non-Indian U.S. natives but had difficulty assimilating because they were reluctant to abandon their customs and practices.

## RECENT IMMIGRANTS

Statistics reveal a dramatic change in the number of immigrants from India. Only 15,513 entered the United States during the 65-year period from 1901 to 1965. In the next five years, that total was easily surpassed: 24,587 immigrated between 1966 and 1970. Then the immigrant totals sky-rocketed: Approximately 148,000 newcomers from India arrived in the 1970s; 232,000 in the 1980s; and 352,000 in the 1990s. Between 2000 and 2012, that last total was surpassed easily, with nearly 790,000 new legal permanent residents.[77]

The Asian Indian presence now is substantial, exceeding 2.9 million (more than twice the number in 1990). A higher percentage of individuals age 15 and older is married (70 percent), but Asian Indians have a lower birth rate than any other Asian group. Currently, the second-largest Asian/Pacific American population (behind the Chinese),

*More than 60 percent of Asian Indians in the United States are in managerial positions in business or else have professional or technical occupations in such fields as education, health care, and science. Many others are self-employed and operate small businesses like convenience stores, gas stations, and family-managed hotels and motels.*

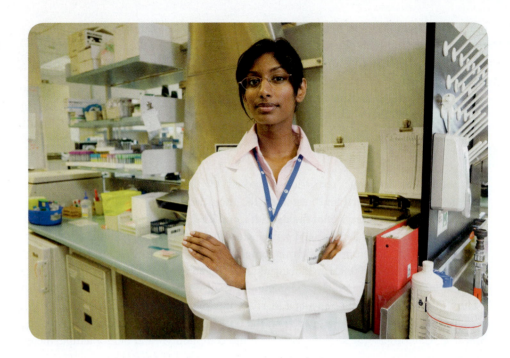

30 percent of all Asian Indians live in the Northeast, 29 percent in the South, 25 percent in the West, and 16 percent in the Midwest. They are the largest Asian group in 23 states, 13 of them in the South.[78]

Of the post-1965 immigrants from India, the largest numbers have been Hindu-speaking, followed by Gujarati, Punjabi, and Bengali speakers. Ethnic Asian Indians also emigrate from East Africa and Latin America, particularly from the Caribbean islands and Guyana, where earlier generations had immigrated as indentured plantation laborers.[79]

The Immigration Act of 1965 alone does not explain the increase in Asian Indian migration. Conditions in India are an important "push" factor. India is the world's second most populous country after mainland China, with 16 percent of the world's population occupying 2.5 percent of the world's land mass. The population density is nearly 11 times greater in India than in the United States.

The problem of overpopulation is quite serious. India's population grew from 439 million in 1960 to more than 1.2 billion in 2012. The rapid rise is not due to any increase in the birth rate but to a decline in the mortality rate. Even with a slowing population growth rate due to a gradually declining birth rate, approximately 18 million babies are born in India each year. Vast differences in access to health services, sanitary conditions, and education level result in variances in life expectancy from one area to another, ranging from 57 years in Madhya Pradesh to 74 in Kerala, for a national average of 63 years.[80]

With more than half of the population engaged in agriculture, a literacy rate of 73 percent among males and 48 percent among females, and problems of severe poverty, hunger, and inadequate resources, India offers many of its citizens little economic security.[81] However, many recent immigrants to the United States have been professionals such as physicians, dentists, teachers, and skilled workers—the very people India most needs to retain if the quality of life there is to improve. Most developing nations face this **brain drain** problem.

With their education and occupational skills, many of these newcomers achieve economic security but also experience cultural strains. For example, they are uneasy with the sexual mores in the United States. Parents have considerable difficulty convincing their children that the Indian custom of not dating before an arranged marriage has merit. Although some second-generation Indian young people still yield to their parents' traditional prerogative to arrange marriages, this is one area in which **ethnogenesis** is apparent.

# the INTERNATIONAL scene

## Asian Indians in South Africa

Of the 48.6 million people living in South Africa, nearly 1.3 million are Asian Indians. About 43 percent are Hindus and 51 percent are Muslims. They are mostly descendants of laborers recruited since the 1860s to work on the sugar estates or of traders who migrated before enactment of restrictive immigration laws in the early twentieth century.

Their heritage of struggling against white oppression began more than a century ago with the arrival of a young lawyer named Mohandas (Mahatma) Gandhi. His efforts to improve the circumstances of his compatriots living in South Africa led to the development of his strategy of *satyagraha*, or nonviolent mass defiance of discriminatory laws, later used in India's independence struggle. In 1894, Gandhi became the first secretary of the Natal Indian Congress (NIC), and before returning to India in 1914, he won concessions from Afrikaner leaders on taxes, marriage law, and rights of movement. In many respects, the NIC served as a model for the African

National Congress (ANC), whose leader, Nelson Mandela, became president of South Africa when majority rule was finally achieved.

The infamous Group Areas Act in 1950 forced 75,000 Indians and 8,500 "Coloured" (mixed-race people) to vacate what had become valuable inner suburban land for more distant settlements with rudimentary services. When the ANC was banned in 1960 and its leaders arrested or exiled, Indian leaders and the NIC played a key role in keeping the ANC together. By the 1980s, their political alliance was indicated by the presence of eight Indians on the 50-member ANC executive council.

As a middleman minority, the Indians fared better than the indigenous Africans, moving into middle-echelon jobs in accounting, sales, banking, and factory management, as well as becoming owners of many business and service enterprises. Their success then generated some African resentment and hostility. Violent attacks in 1992 against Indian

businesses in black areas forced their owners to sell out and move back to major cities.

In postapartheid South Africa, the economic success of Indians initially caused tension. In the 1990s the majority of Indian voters, a group that had previously supported the ruling ANC Party, leaned toward the National Party. This conservative shift was attributed to an Indian fear of losing economic power to the growing black business class. Since then, tensions and fears have lessened.

Finding themselves both courted and pressured by various black and white political factions in recent years, South Africa's Indians apparently felt reassured about their economic security. In the general elections, the most historically Asian Indian areas have voted for the ANC candidates.

**CRITICAL THINKING QUESTION**

How similar or dissimilar is the Asian Indian experience in the United States compared to that in South Africa?

---

Most young people tolerate their parents' introduction to eligible mates but insist that the final choice be entirely their own.[82]

More than 60 percent of Asian Indians pursue professional or managerial occupations.[83] The others typically operate convenience stores, gas stations, or family-managed hotels. In fact, with Asian Indian ownership of the latter now constituting half of all economy lodging in the United States, they have found a family-labor economic niche as ubiquitous as the Korean greengrocery.[84] (See the International Scene box for insights into the Asian Indian experience in South Africa.)

Gujarati-speaking Asian Indians gravitated toward the lodging industry partly because of widespread opportunities presented by an aging hotel-owning population leaving the business and partly because little command of English, skills, or education was needed to run the business.

Moreover, the family could live and work at the hotel which saved on expenses; and the business was a piece of real estate that appreciated over time. The factors that facilitated the entrance into and success in the business were the

# the ETHNIC experience

## Values, Identity, and Acceptance

"You ask me if I came here to settle down. Yes, I came here to settle down. I changed myself a lot. I cut my hair. I took my sari off and I wore skirts and dresses. I dressed all-American. So it hurt to go outside and have people ask, 'Are you Indian?' We don't ask a white person, 'Are you French, British, Polish?' We are all Americans."

"I made a choice when I came to this country. My choice was to become an American citizen, and I have become one. I think we are wrong going into all these labels of cultural heritage. Our main goal is to keep America strong—America No. 1. And we can do that by communicating with each other; and in order to communicate and understand each other, we need to have one channel of culture and language."

"And it is difficult for us to forget about India because it is part of our culture. I spent 29 years there. I consider India as my mother—my womb. It gave me birth and my values. America is my father: It gave me my dream. They are both equally important."

"Maybe my children won't have to fight bigotry if we stop putting these labels on government forms, job applications, and on television. We must stop that. We should want to help people be part of us. We are Americans of Asian heritage. As long as they don't classify us, it will be easier for our children to be all Americans."

"My children are completely Americanized. I believe when in Rome, do as the Romans. I never forced on them the Indian language. In fact, they don't speak one word of the Indian language. They are very strong with Indian values, but I don't think they are Indian values alone. Those are universal values. Every American, Indian, Chinese, Japanese, Black, Puerto Rican—no matter what nationality you are, what racial group, all parents want that their children are well behaved, go to school, have good careers, don't hang out in the street and get into drugs or other trouble. I don't think the values are, you know, set for any one ethnic group. I don't

find any American mother different from any Indian mother."

"The news media plays a very big role in spreading diversity. I'll give you an example. Every news media on television labels a person Black, White, Indian, and so on. Why? We are all Americans!"

"What happened with my older daughter, who graduated college, was people kept asking her all the time, 'Are you Indian?' 'Are you Indian?' 'Are you Indian?' And then, at the age of 22, she turned around and said, 'Hey, gee, if they're always asking me if I'm Indian, why don't I think about India, find something out about India.' And if you're going to see after 50 years, different pockets of different ethnic groups, we too have to blame our own television media and our news media. If we keep giving people labels then, I don't know what is going to happen in America in the future."

Source: Asian Indian woman who came to the United States in 1970 at age 29. Taped interview from the collection of Vincent N. Parrillo.

class, ethnic, and family resources that were mobilized by Gujarati hoteliers. Class resources included financial and human capital. Ethnic resources included access to training, information, labor, networks, and most importantly, capital from within the Gujarati community. It is precisely because Gujaratis were able to mobilize these resources that they were able to establish a foothold and later dominate the industry.[85]

Racial ambiguity marks the Asian Indian acceptance pattern. The skin colors of Asian Indians range from light brown to almost black, although most of the U.S. immigrants are of a light hue. Americans perceive them as racially different but have difficulty categorizing them. Defined as "white" sometimes, "Asian" at other times, and "brown" or "black" at still other times, Asian Indians tend to classify themselves as "white" and identify with the majority group (see the Ethnic Experience box).

# Pakistani Americans

More than 351,000 Americans claimed Pakistani ancestry in 2011, giving this group a significant presence in the United States—larger than, for example, the Nicaraguans or Turks.[86] Three in five are white-collar workers or professionals, and the rest are craftsmen, service workers, or laborers. Another common occupation of Pakistani immigrants in many cities is taxicab driver. In New York City, for example, immigrants from Pakistan, Bangladesh, and India made up less than 0.5 percent of the population but constitute 30 percent of its taxicab drivers.[87] Another common endeavor is family ownership of discount stores.[88]

Pakistani Americans have a widely dispersed settlement pattern, although 25 percent settle in the New York City metropolitan region. The Chicago, Washington, DC, Houston, and Los Angeles metropolitan areas are other areas of residential clustering. The Pakistanis' acculturation and assimilation patterns are similar to those of other groups considered in this chapter.

# Vietnamese Americans

In April 1975, as the Vietnam War ended, 127,000 Vietnamese and 4,000 Cambodian refugees entered the United States. As they waited in relocation centers at military bases for sponsors to materialize, public opinion polls showed that most U.S. citizens, especially members of the working class, believed the refugees would take away jobs from people already living in the United States. Labor and state officials raised serious objections to "flooding" the labor market and welfare rolls with so many aliens at a time when the economy was mired in a recession. Yet all the refugees were resettled within seven months across all 50 states with little disruption.

Like the Cuban exiles of the 1960s, many of these Vietnamese were middle class, migrating for political rather than economic reasons. Many were well educated, with marketable skills, and nearly half spoke English.[89] They were relatively cosmopolitan people, mostly from the Saigon region, and many previously had lived elsewhere, particularly in North Vietnam.

In 1979, tens of thousands of Vietnamese "boat people"—many of them actually ethnic Chinese residents of Vietnam—sought refuge in other countries, setting sail in flimsy, overcrowded boats. Many drowned or were killed by pirates, but several hundred thousand reached refugee camps in Thailand and other countries (see the Ethnic Experience box). Acting in concert with other receiving countries, U.S. President Carter authorized admitting an additional 200,000 Indochinese refugees into the United States.

Immigration from Vietnam remains significant. Approximately 275,000 Vietnamese immigrated to the United States in the 1990s, and more than 371,000 entered between 2000 and 2012.[90] From a virtual nonpresence in the United States in 1970, the Vietnamese now number more than 1.6 million, making them the fourth largest East Asian group, and constituting nearly 11 percent of the total Asian American population.[91] Most of these more recent arrivals speak little English and have few occupational skills, making their adjustment and attainment of economic self-sufficiency more difficult.

## CULTURAL DIFFERENTIATION

Unlike most people in the United States who believe in free will and self-determination, many Vietnamese believe in predestination, with very limited individual control over events.[92] Two of the more important factors that the Vietnamese believe determine a person's destiny are *phuc duc* and astrology. These are core elements within the family

# the ETHNIC experience

## A Desperate Bid for Freedom

"Our boat was kind of lucky, 'cause 70 percent of boats get captured by Vietnamese Coast Guard. That day there was no moon. It was totally dark...Luckily we make it...After one day and one night, we get out of the control of the Vietnamese. Now we know we're free!...Our boat was 30 feet long and about seven feet wide and, totally, we had about 103 people. It was so crowded, almost like a fish can, you know? Can you imagine?"

"...There was only enough water for one cup for each person in one day. So we rarely drank the water for, if we don't have water, we're going to die in the sea. The first day everyone got seasick. Nobody got used to it, the kind of high waves and ocean. So everyone got seasick and vomited...But by the second day and the third day, we felt much better."

"We kept going straight into the international sea zone and we met a lot of ships. We tried to get signal for help, we tried to burn our clothes to get their attention. We wrote the big S. O. S. letter in our clothes and tried to hang it above the boat. No matter how we tried, they just passed us by. I think they might feel pity for us, have the good compassion, but I think they're afraid their government going to blame them because the law is, if you pick up any refugee in the ocean, your country got to have responsibility for those people. So finally, we so disappointed because we got no help from anybody and our boat is now the only boat and we have only three h.p. motor."

"We have too many people and the wave is extremely high, about 5 feet. It is so dangerous. You can see the boat only maybe like one feet distant from the sea level. But we got no choice. We decide to keep going straight to Malaysia. The fifth day, the sixth day, we saw nothing. The only thing we saw is water, sun, and at night, the stars. It's just like upside-down moon. And the sea. If you look down into the ocean, you get scared, because the water—color—is so dark. It's like dark blue. If you look down into the water, you had the feeling like it invite you, say 'Go down with me.' Especially at night, the water—it's black, like evil waiting for you. Say, 'Oh, 103 people, I was waiting for you. Come down with us.' We kept going, but we don't know where we're going to be, if we have enough food and water to make it...We don't even know if we're going the right way...we just estimate by looking at the sun and the stars."

"...The sixth day, we saw the bird and a couple of floating things, so we are hoping we are almost come to the shore. We had some hope and we kept traveling one more day, the seventh day. That day is the day—our water—we have only one more day left. And the gasoline is almost gone. And we saw some fire, very little fire, very far away. And we went to that fire. One hour, two hours. And finally we saw that fire offshore drilling platform of Esso Company. Everybody's screaming and so happy because we know at least we have something we can turn to...We know we cannot go any further. Most of the women and children in my boat are exhausted, and some of the children unconscious. Some of the children had been so thirsty, they just drank the water from the sea. And the water from the sea is terrible. The more you drank, the more you got thirsty. And the children, starving, got a bad reaction from the seawater. We all got skin disease and exhausted...They took us in their boat to the refugee camp in Malaysia."

Source: Vietnamese refugee who came to the United States in 1980 at age 17. Taped interview from the collection of Vincent N. Parrillo.

infrastructure of filial piety and ancestor worship, and they provide important insights into the Vietnamese ability to adapt to a new society with minimal emotional anxiety.

The concept of *phuc duc* refers to the amount of good fortune that comes from meritorious or self-sacrificing actions. This accumulation of rewards, earned primarily by women for their family, also affects the lives of succeeding generations into the fifth generation. *Phuc duc* is quantifiable, in that improper conduct diminishes the amount one has, whereas the nature of one's actions and one's degree of personal sacrifice determine the amount one acquires:

In the West, guilt, which is related to shame, is essentially a personal matter; in Vietnam, one's transgressions have both a horizontal and a vertical dimension: they affect both the nuclear and the extended family in the current generation and the well-being of the family for generations to come. Not only is this a powerful deterrent to improper behavior, more important, it is a glue, a bonding agent (although not the only one) that holds the society together.

The accountability that *phuc duc* places upon the Vietnamese, in terms of the implications that it carries for personal conduct, is awesome. It is difficult enough being responsible for oneself and one's personal nexus of family and friends, but for this to extend for generations forward is a heavy load indeed.[93]

So strong is the Vietnamese belief in horoscopes that parents accept no responsibility for a child's personality, believing that the configuration of the celestial bodies at the moment of conception fixes the character of that individual. At the time of birth, a Vietnamese astrologer specifically predicts the personality and events to come for the newborn infant. This often becomes a self-fulfilling prophecy because the predictions influence actual behavior (the parents' child-rearing practices as well as the child's own actions, including mate selection as an adult). The Vietnamese way of life thus includes belief in a deterministic life force over which the individual has minimal control. This concept has greatly influenced the accommodation of the Vietnamese to the United States:

> Both *phuc duc* and astrology provide a rationale wherein responsibility for personal acts can be avoided, and this is supported by the belief that the *phuc duc* that parents acquire does not affect their own children. It skips a generation and is visited upon the grandchildren and beyond.[94]

Vietnamese are strongly tradition bound, revering their ancestors, homeland, and family traditions. Their culture is oriented toward achievement of group goals, primarily within the extended family. In addition, the cultural values of courage, stoicism, and adaptation through conformity helped make the refugees' adjustment somewhat easier.

## ACCULTURATION

Vietnamese refugees who possessed relatively traditional views faced the greatest culture shock and difficulty in adapting. Women were more likely than men to suffer from depression, anxiety, and tension. A greater frequency of feelings of inadequacy, anger, tension, and sensitivity occurred among these Vietnamese refugees than in the general population. Principal causes of mental stress were loneliness, lack of community life, breakup of the family, uncertainty about the future, homesickness, grief over losses in fleeing the homeland, and frustration in coping with life in the United States. As found in earlier studies of Cuban and Hungarian refugees, assuming hostile and aggressive attitudes toward the host society or fellow refugees often proved an effective adaptive style. This emotional arousal helped Vietnamese to overcome the passivity of their traditional cultural values and find better ways to survive and surmount their problems.[95]

Contributing to Vietnamese immigrants' adjustment problems was the federal government's policy of scattering the refugees throughout the United States. Intended as an integration program to accelerate acculturation, it denied the Vietnamese a social and emotional support network of ethnic communities comparable to those developed and used by other immigrant groups. Initially, no mutual assistance organizations were formed, and early studies showed varying degrees of success in the refugees' adaptation to life in the United States.

Gradually, Vietnamese Americans began to relocate near one another, particularly in California, Texas, Virginia, and New York. Here their concentrations, aided by subsequent "normal" immigration, led to the development of ethnic neighborhoods and

*Vietnamese-American enclaves exist in many states, but the oldest and largest is about 45 miles south of Los Angeles in the suburban city of Westminster, California. This "Little Saigon" is a spread-out community with numerous strip malls, but its heart is the Bolsa Avenue center where the Asian Garden Mall and Little Saigon Plaza are located.*

social networks characteristic of first-generation Americans. "Little Saigons" blossomed in numerous cities where the language, signs, shops, offices, and music all convey a distinctly Vietnamese atmosphere. The largest of these are in Orange County and San Jose, California, and in Houston. In many Chinatowns, a distinct Vietnamese presence also is visible.

As with most immigrants, age determines the degree of acculturation (see Figure 8.5). The elderly come to be with their families but show little interest in giving up their cultural values or assimilating. Youths find their traditional family values inconsistent with those of the dominant group in U.S. society. Traditionally, Vietnamese parents play a major role in determining their adolescents' social interactions. Vietnamese culture emphasizes achieving one's identity and sense of worth through close relationships with family adults and as a member of an extended family. However, U.S. adolescents are more autonomous and concerned about peer approval. These ways attract Vietnamese youths, encouraging

| Asian or Pacific Islander Population | | Age | Total U.S. Population | |
|---|---|---|---|---|
| Males | Females | | Males | Females |
| Median age 34.2 — 2.6 | 3.6 — Median age 36.3 | 70+ | Median age 35.8 — 3.7 | 5.3 — Median age 38.5 |
| 3.6 | 4.3 | 60–69 | 4.5 | 4.9 |
| 5.6 | 6.7 | 50–59 | 6.6 | 6.9 |
| 7.1 | 8.1 | 40–49 | 7.0 | 7.1 |
| 8.1 | 9.2 | 30–39 | 6.5 | 6.5 |
| 7.8 | 8.1 | 20–29 | 7.0 | 6.8 |
| 6.4 | 6.1 | 10–19 | 7.1 | 6.7 |
| 6.3 | 6.2 | 0–9 | 6.7 | 6.4 |

9 8 7 6 5 4 3 2 1 0 1 2 3 4 5 6 7 8 9
Percentage

9 8 7 6 5 4 3 2 1 0 1 2 3 4 5 6 7 8 9
Percentage

**FIGURE 8.5** Asian/Pacific Islander Population, 2010 (in percentages)
Source: U.S. Census Bureau.

them to reject parental guidance and enter into situations without parental consent. Intergenerational conflict thus is made worse by the gap between the cultural values of the adults and those learned by their children.[96]

Vietnamese—like Koreans—have lower median family incomes, higher poverty and unemployment rates, and disproportionate representation in low-skill, low-paying jobs than most other Asian American groups (Figure 8.6). These economic disadvantages particularly manifest themselves among the foreign-born population, although second- and third-generation Vietnamese Americans should fare better thanks to their higher education levels and English proficiency.[97]

**Age by percent**

21.6    21.8   15.2    23.7   13.3    9.9

Asian    White    All Races

- Under 18 years
- 65 years & over

**Education (of persons age 25 and over)**

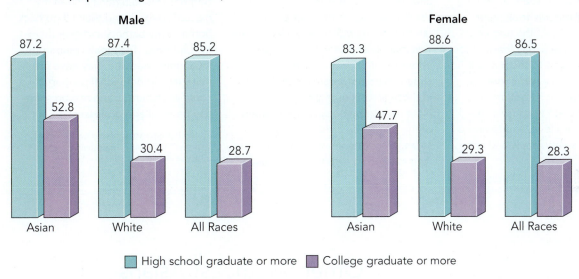

**Male**

| Asian | White | All Races |
|-------|-------|-----------|
| 87.2 | 87.4 | 85.2 |
| 52.8 | 30.4 | 28.7 |

**Female**

| Asian | White | All Races |
|-------|-------|-----------|
| 83.3 | 88.6 | 86.5 |
| 47.7 | 29.3 | 28.3 |

- High school graduate or more
- College graduate or more

**Economic Status**

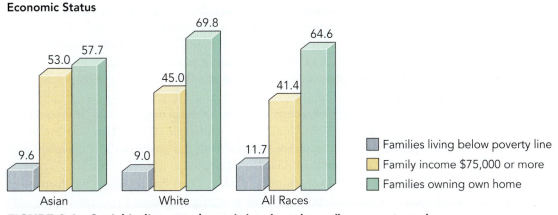

| | Asian | White | All Races |
|--|-------|-------|-----------|
| Families living below poverty line | 9.6 | 9.0 | 11.7 |
| Family income $75,000 or more | 53.0 | 45.0 | 41.4 |
| Families owning own home | 57.7 | 69.8 | 64.6 |

**FIGURE 8.6** **Social Indicators about Asian Americans (in percentages)**

*Source:* U.S. Census Bureau.

# the ETHNIC experience

## The Struggle to Adapt

"I came to the U.S. for the adventure. I had heard much about this country and seen many American films. My parents are Chinese and migrated to Thailand about 20 years before I was born. My father is a very successful businessman, having his own lumber business and a few hotels. So I really came here only to satisfy my own curiosity, but I stayed here for my undergraduate and graduate course work and I haven't returned yet.

"It's almost as if I sensed this before I left. I was going to America because I wanted to see that country, but before my parents took me to the airport, I cried. At the airport, a lot of people came to say farewell to me and I just waved to them. I had the feeling I would never come back here. Especially when I got into the airplane, I felt that I was losing the things that I really love, and I wanted to get off. It's a very lonely and scary feeling...

"Things seemed strange to me at first. Oriental people all have dark hair. Here I saw many people with different features, with blond hair, brown hair, and so on. At that time, they looked funny to me. I had seen some American soldiers in Thailand, but they were a small minority. Now everyone around me was so very different. Another thing was being driven [so fast] on the highways... We have few good highways in Thailand and this was a new experience.

"I can't describe to you how lonely and depressed I was in this country. I at first wished I had never come. The family I stayed with in New Hampshire was friendly and tried to teach me about America, but the language and cultural barriers were overwhelming in those first six or eight months. I was withdrawn because I was afraid of the people and didn't know how to do. Most people were impatient with me and so avoided me. I was sad

and didn't like this country, but I felt obliged to my parents to stay for the year even though I was very homesick.

"At the end of the school year, I went back home. I discovered I had changed. I was more independent and stubborn, and I enjoyed doing some things that Thai people thought were silly, like getting a suntan. Also, I really wanted to be somebody and make my parents proud, and I thought the best way was to get an education in the U.S. So I came back here and earned my bachelor's degree. This summer, I'll finish my master's degree and then I'll go back home to my parents and give them my diplomas. They really belong to my parents because they gave me material and emotional support. I'll come back here... and maybe someday be a college professor."

Source: Thai immigrant who came to the United States in 1971 at age 19. Taped interview from the collection of Vincent N. Parrillo.

# Other Southeast Asians

Cambodians and Laotians, like the Vietnamese, came from the area of Southeast Asia formerly colonized and administered as French Indochina. For centuries prior to the arrival of the French, however, these three groups were linguistically, culturally, and ethnically distinct from one another, and differences exist within each nationality group as well. Of the more than 2.3 million Indochinese Americans, approximately 17 percent were from Laos, 10 percent were from Cambodia (Kampuchea), and 66 percent were from Vietnam.

Thailand, formerly Siam, is another Southeast Asian nation that has sent significant numbers of immigrants to the United States. Although 180,000 Thai now live in the United States, relatively little has been written about this group, except in groupings with other Southeast Asians (see the Ethnic Experience box).

More than 203,000 Laotians now call the United States home. Like many nineteenth- and early twentieth-century European immigrants, many do not self-identify with a national identity but rather with a regional identity. They include numerous subgroups, including the Mon-Khmer, Yao, Tai Dam, and Lue. Most arrivals are the lowland Lao.

Another ethnic group, the Hmong (pronounced *mung* and meaning "free people"), however, are the most studied of all groups, although they are not Laotians because they are not of the Lao ethnic group or speak Lao.[98]

A traditional mountain people living north of the Plain of Jars in Laos, the Hmong had little exposure to the modern world—Western or Eastern—practicing slash-and-burn farming on hilltops, attributing disease to evil spirits, and relying on the stories of their parents and grandparents for their education. Their belief in spirits includes the idea that a frightening or shameful experience leads to illness caused by the individual spirit fleeing the body. To lock the soul inside so that it cannot leave, the Hmong wear copper or silver bracelets, anklets, and necklaces as special protective jewelry.[99]

Hmong society is patrilineal: The traditional role of the wife is devotion to her husband. An extremely strong extended family and clan system binds the individuals together. This is why, after initially being scattered across the country by the U.S. government, many Hmong have resettled near kin and clan members. Of the 244,000 Hmong population residing in the United States today, most reside in three states: California, Minnesota, and Wisconsin.[100] Although problems of language, economic naiveté, and lack of job skills initially plagued the Hmong, placing a large percentage on welfare, some recent studies suggest that a gradual, successful acculturation has begun.[101]

As the children become "Americanized" adolescents, cultural dissonance typically affects the Hmong family. Parents lack personal experience and role models for dealing with the adolescent experience in the United States because adolescence as such did not exist in Laos. There, succeeding generations married young and assumed parental responsibilities early. Dating without an adult chaperone, and any overt public display of affection, such as kissing or holding hands in public, violates Hmong tradition. Attracted to the U.S. way of life, Hmong teenagers often challenge their parents' authority on these matters.[102] Such intergenerational conflicts between immigrant parents and their children are common among all ethnic groups, as the younger generation identifies with the behavioral patterns of the larger society in which they live.

## Ethnoviolence

Bias-motivated hate crimes against Asian/Pacific Americans have declined throughout the years, from 355 in 1995 to 138 in 2011.[103] This is a positive and dramatic change since the wave of anti-Asian violence in the 1980s and early 1990s.

When the May 1992 Los Angeles riots erupted, leaving 50 dead, 4,000 injured, damaging or destroying approximately 2,300 Korean-owned stores, and causing losses estimated in excess of $1 billion, a nationwide pattern of black–Korean conflict already had been well established.[104] Like Jewish and Italian immigrants before them, thousands of Koreans owned inner-city retail stores, serving as a middleman minority to blacks and Hispanics in virtually every major U.S. city. Working long hours and relying on low-paid family labor to eke out a profit, they succeeded in neighborhoods where many area residents lived a marginal existence.

Black resentment stemmed partly from the Koreans' ease in borrowing through the *kye* and their mercantile success in black neighborhoods. Blacks accurately complained that Koreans took money out of the community but rarely hired non-Koreans. They also interpreted Koreans' limited English and brusque cultural interactions with customers as rudeness. Social distance, economic frustration, envy, alienation, and a sense of being exploited all help explain the racial tensions that sometimes erupted into **ethnoviolence**. A subsequent increase in the number of inner-city black entrepreneurs and concerted outreach by Korean merchants to the communities they serve has helped to lessen the problem.[105]

Despite progress, occasional incidents of harassment, intimidation, graffiti, vandalism, and assault continue to serve as painful reminders of the continuing presence of racism, bigotry, and discrimination against Asian Americans. These violent episodes may be fewer than in earlier years and echo a similar pattern of actions taken against earlier immigrant groups, but that offers no comfort for the victims or for a U.S.-born generation that considers itself more sophisticated and tolerant than past generations.

# The Model-Minority Stereotype

Read **on MySocLab**
Document: Diversity Among Asian Americans

Perhaps no idea has remained so entrenched in the public mind as that of Asian Americans as a "model minority."[106] Images of Chinese engineers, Japanese financiers, Filipino nurses, Korean entrepreneurs, and Vietnamese restaurateurs abound, helping to reinforce this positive stereotype. Asian American educational and economic successes apparently demonstrate that people of color can realize the American Dream through hard work and self-reliance. These achievements are seeming testimony to the possibility of color-free, problem-free, government-intervention–free integration into U.S. society. Moreover, advertising in mainstream news magazines helps perpetuate the stereotype by frequently depicting Asian Americans as highly educated, affluent, and proficient with technology.[107] Like all stereotypes, however, that of the model minority is misleading and ignores the diversity of the Asian American population. Many Asian Americans, in fact, are poor and poorly educated, people who need help in attaining economic and educational success.[108]

Other examples also contradict the stereotype. Many Southeast Asian refugees still require welfare aid. Not all Asian American students are strong academically.[109] The criminal activities of major Asian American drug rings, smaller-scale Asian American extortion gangs, and Asian American youth gangs are seen as an often brutal menace. Some Asian Americans live in crowded dwellings and suffer from tuberculosis or depression, and some live with dwindling hope of any improvement.

The idea of a model minority also creates a harmful and unrealistic example for the dominant group to use as a reason to blame others for their difficulties in achieving success. Commentators often unfairly criticize other minority groups for failing to attain comparable levels of achievement, ignoring that much of the success of Asian American youths is attributable to their being (in many cases) children of professionals, as well as to their coming from cultures that have prized educational achievement for many generations.

*An excellent example of an immigrant or minority group carving out an occupational niche in the labor market of an evolving U.S. society is the proliferation of Asian-owned and operated nail salons in local communities. Although other group members, such as blacks and Hispanics, also work in this area, Asians by far dominate this enterprise.*

# Assimilation

As with all groups, rates of acculturation and assimilation vary widely both among and within them, depending on various socioeconomic factors and length of residence. We, however, can make a few general observations. Because minority groups have less economic, political, and social power than the societal mainstream, such indicators as income, education, political participation, residential patterns, and intermarriage provide insights into the comparative status of Asian Americans.

As a group, Asian Americans have the highest median family income ($65,129 in 2011 compared to $55,412 for non-Hispanic whites). They have the lowest poverty rate of all minority groups, by half—and one that slightly lower than that of non-Hispanic whites.[110] Approximately 50 percent have at least a college degree, compared to 30 percent of whites and 29 percent of all races (see Figure 8.6).[111] These positive indicators suggest substantial progress in the area of civic assimilation.

Citizenship is the first step toward political participation and influence. They are second only to Europeans in the percentage who become U.S. citizens (58 to 68 percent), a pattern possibly influenced by the greater distance between their homelands and the United States.[112] Although their numbers will not give them the same political muscle as the larger black and Hispanic groups, their influence is growing.

Residential segregation is an important dimension of social relations between minority- and majority-group members. Although Asian Americans mostly are an urban population and nearly three-fourths of them live in only ten states (see Figure 8.7), they tend to live in less segregated areas than other minority groups. Moreover, they are dispersing more and more throughout the United States, as their numbers increased by at least 30 percent in every state on the mainland between 2000 and 2010.[113]

Racial intermarriages do not necessarily indicate complete acceptance between members of two groups, as racial boundaries still may exist despite their meaninglessness to those who do intermarry. Nevertheless, comparative intermarriage statistics can give us some indication of a group's social acceptance, at least with respect to other groups. Approximately 55 percent of all U.S.-born Asian Americans have a non-Asian spouse, and that proportion continues to increase.[114] As more Asian Americans outmarry, future generations of Asian Americans may increasingly blend with other U.S. racial and social groups, mirroring the experience of European ethnic groups in the last century.

**8-6** Compare and contrast the assimilation paths followed by Asian Americans.

*An important reason for such a high level of Asian American success is the high value that their cultures place on education. More than 55-percent have at least a college degree, compared to 30 percent of non-Hispanic whites and 29 percent of all races. As a result, their median family income averages $10,000 more than non-Hispanic whites.*

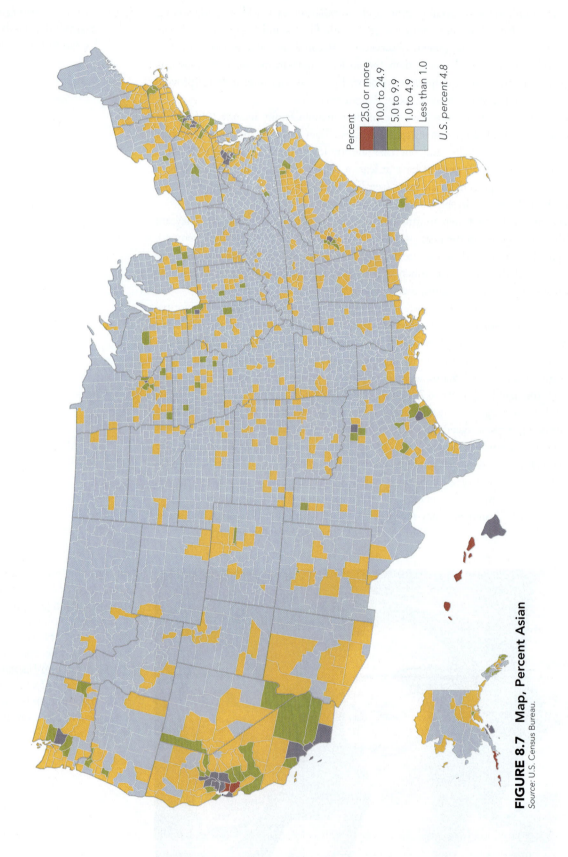

**FIGURE 8.7** Map, Percent Asian
Source: U.S. Census Bureau.

Percent

| | |
|---|---|
| | 25.0 or more |
| | 10.0 to 24.9 |
| | 5.0 to 9.9 |
| | 1.0 to 4.9 |
| | Less than 1.0 |

*U.S. percent 4.8*

Finally, certain acculturation patterns often found among Asian American families illustrate how the ethnogenesis process alters traditional family structure.[115] Frequently the balance of power between generations shifts as older parents become dependent on their children, who must translate for them. Often, more successful younger brothers usurp the position of the esteemed oldest son because they frequently immigrate before him. Women's labor force participation in the United States is an important factor in changing relations between husbands and wives and in the capital-accumulation process.

# Sociological Analysis

Some of this chapter's discussion of Asian immigrants covered events that occurred in previous generations; other parts focused on the contemporary scene. If we apply the sociological perspective to these individual group chronologies, we find that the time span involved is irrelevant to understanding the continuing patterns of intergroup relations.

8-7 Discuss insights gained through sociological analysis.

## THE FUNCTIONALIST VIEW

The Chinese who came to the United States in the nineteenth century fulfilled important social needs—working on railroads, farms, and ranches and in stores and factories. Their work contributed significantly to the building of a transcontinental transportation system, the manufacture of needed goods, and the provision of valuable services. Although racial antagonism existed earlier, nationwide economic hard times in the 1870s made the situation much worse. Economic dysfunctions set off intensified labor antagonism, culminating in a system adjustment of immigration restrictions. Despite occasional internal strife, the withdrawal of the Chinese into their Chinatowns helped to promote ethnic solidarity and to offer an interactive social network in a hostile white society. Later, these Chinatowns functioned as absorption centers for tens of thousands of new arrivals, once the immigration restrictions were lifted.

Japanese, Korean, Filipino, and Asian Indian farm laborers, both in Hawaii and on the mainland, helped agriculture expand and prosper. An urbanizing West Coast offered many domestic and personal service jobs—jobs filled mostly by Filipinos who liked city life and its educational opportunities. Major societal dysfunctions—a severe, long-lasting economic depression and the trauma of a desperate war begun with a surprise attack—triggered negative actions against the Filipinos and Japanese, respectively. Eventually, a restoration of system balance enabled these minority groups to overcome past discrimination and become assimilated more fully. Problems remaining with Filipino immigrants stem from their unemployment or underemployment and their rapid increase in population, compounded by the recent recession and the changing occupational structure of society.

Cultural traditions and family cohesiveness have been positive functions easing the adjustment of most East and Southeast Asian immigrants into U.S. society. In fact, the percentage of married foreign-born from Asia is higher (66 percent) than for all foreign-born (58 percent) or for native-born (47 percent). Furthermore, multigenerational households (three or more generations living together) were twice as likely among Asian American households, particularly with a householder born in the Philippines or Vietnam.[116] Such a presence of married couples and multigenerational families can aid in family stability and combined earnings. Also, Korean, Vietnamese, and other Asian refugees gave Americans the opportunity to act on one of their commonly held values—humanitarianism—by opening their doors to people from war-ravaged lands. Just as the U.S. host society provided freedom and opportunity for these Asian peoples, so, too, did society gain from their labors and contributions to U.S. culture.

## THE CONFLICT VIEW

When employers—railroads, farmers, urban businesses, and Hawaiian plantation owners—needed inexpensive alien labor, they recruited it and reaped the profits. When times turned bad, those with power used intergroup ethnic antagonisms to divide the working class and thereby protect their interests. So it was the series of electoral victories by the anti–Chinese Workingmen's Party in California that caused the Republican and Democratic political parties to commandeer the anti-Chinese cause to defuse this new political movement. Similarly, white California growers advocated Japanese removal in 1942 to eliminate their competition in the marketplace. Labor organizations campaigned against the Chinese in the 1870s and against the Filipinos and other groups in the 1930s to prevent their taking increasingly scarce jobs.

Originally applied to the historical example of labor antagonism against the Chinese, the split-labor-market theory (see Chapter 4) explains the experiences of several other Asian groups equally well. Coming from low-income countries, Asian workers accepted wages that, although reasonable by their standards, undermined the wage scale of the native workers. For instance, when the Chinese entered the shoemaking trade extensively in the 1870s, weekly wages in the trade dropped from $25 to $9. Complaints about unfair competition by Japanese farm laborers included their "willingness" to work for less than whites or to accept payment in crops or land instead of wages. In the late twentieth century, white shrimpers burned Vietnamese-owned boats in Galveston Bay, Texas; blacks in Harlem and Brooklyn urged boycotts of Korean stores; Hispanics in Denver housing projects attacked Indochinese refugees; and black–Filipino animosity on the East Coast occasionally manifested itself among medical service workers competing for certain hospital jobs.

Economic exploitation or competition generates other forms of ethnic antagonism. The Chinatown sweatshops exploit immigrant labor and undermine the position of unionized garment workers, who further are affected adversely by imports from developing countries. Auto workers and steel workers experience layoffs and job insecurity because of Chinese and Japanese products. Although black, white, and Hispanic workers treat Asian Americans as the enemy, the real culprits are those who benefit most—the sweatshop employers, the corporations that avoid capital modernization expenditures to maximize profits, and the U.S.-based multinational corporations that establish factories in low-income countries, marketing their products in the United States and elsewhere for higher profits.

## THE INTERACTIONIST VIEW

Westerners have used the word *inscrutable* almost exclusively to describe Asians, especially the Chinese and Japanese. The concept that Asians defy understanding rests on their markedly non-Western physical appearance, language, belief systems, customs, stoicism, and observable behavior. Consistent with the connection between the perceived similarity factor and acceptance of strangers, the wide social distance between native-born U.S. citizens and Asian immigrants becomes understandable. As groups farther from the dominant group's interaction patterns, Asians offer easy targets for negative stereotyping, prejudice, scapegoating, and discrimination. Cultural differences become intertwined with physical differences in the minds of many Americans, allowing racism to predominate in value judgments and avoidance–dominance responses.

Asian immigrants in the late nineteenth and early twentieth centuries gave the West Coast an immigrant experience similar to the European migration in the eastern United States. Hispanic Americans and Native Americans already were indigenous to the West, so Asians created new subcommunities, worked for low wages, and received the scorn and resentment of the whites. The Asian newcomers were replicating patterns already exhibited by European immigrants in the eastern United States, but people in the West interpreted these as threats to their own economic security and mainstream culture. This social interpretation of reality set in motion the interaction problems that followed. Attitudes translated into actions, setting off reactions and reinforcing attitudes on both sides; thus, the vicious circle intensified and perpetuated the ingroup's perception of the outgroup.

Recent Asian immigrants offer a bipolar model. Those who come from preliterate societies, wedded to a tradition of subsistence living, face a bewildering leap into an urban society. Schutz's observation, discussed in Chapter 1, that every taken-for-granted situation for the native presents a crisis for the stranger, overwhelmingly is true for many Southeast Asians. Their adjustment and integration into U.S. society may be long and difficult. Other Asians possess an educational background and skills that enable them to enter the economic mainstream more easily. Nonetheless, their racial and cultural differences currently limit their social integration or structural assimilation.

# Retrospect

A combination of racial and non-Western cultural differences caused a great many Asian immigrants from 1850 to 1940 to remain outside the U.S. mainstream all their lives. Lack of acceptance and social interaction in the dominant society and frequent hostile actions directed against them reinforced the Asians' awareness of the differences in the people and culture around them. Each succeeding wave of Asian immigrants, from whatever country, encountered some degree of hostility because of their racial and cultural visibility. To some Americans, the Asians posed a serious challenge to the cherished notion of a melting pot because of their race, their non-Christian faith (though some were Christians), their language and alphabet, and their customs and practices. That many chose to settle on the West Coast near their port of entry, much as European immigrants had in the East, only underscored their presence and led whites to exaggerate their actual numbers. Many also believed that these immigrants posed an economic threat to U.S. workers, which further encouraged racist reactions.

Many white Americans came to accept negative stereotypes, first about the Chinese and later about the Japanese and Filipinos. Normal ethnocentric judgments about a culturally distinct people, coupled with racial visibility that offered a distinct link to the stereotype, caused generalized societal antagonism toward the Asians. The vast differences in culture and physical appearance, augmented by racist fears and fantasies of threats to economic security or to white womanhood from "lascivious Orientals," led to sporadic outbreaks of violence and a continuing current of hostility.

Until 1940, Japanese Americans mostly settled in rural areas on the West Coast. On the mainland, racist antagonisms and fears culminated in 1942 with the militarily supervised removal of Japanese Americans from their homes and jobs. Although a few Japanese Americans were rounded up in Hawaii, no mass evacuation occurred there because Hawaii presented a less racist environment and offered fuller political and economic participation.

Filipinos, too, encountered overt racial discrimination prior to 1940. Following changes in U.S. immigration law in 1965, millions of Filipinos, Chinese and Asian Indians migrated to the United States. Although many are underemployed, they and other new arrivals encounter less hostility today than did their predecessors.

Koreans, Vietnamese, Cambodians, Laotians, and Thais are more recent East and Southeast Asian immigrants. Originally war refugees, most are now immigrants like those from other lands. They enter a country that is far less racially hostile toward Asians than in the past. Many are individuals with marketable job skills. Most come from a region of the world where patience, stoicism, quiet industriousness, and the cohesiveness of an extended family are long-standing traditions. These values aid the newcomers' transition to a new life.

Asia currently is the major source outside the Western Hemisphere of immigrants to the United States. More than two-fifths of all immigrants now come from Asia. Obviously, that part of the world profoundly is altering the ethnic composition of the U.S. population. In the years ahead, the United States will become even more a land of racial and cultural diversity.

# On MySocLab

 Study and Review on MySocLab

## KEY TERMS

Brain drain, p. 258
Ethnogenesis, p. 258
Ethnoviolence, p. 267
Exurbs, p. 255

Filial piety, p. 234
Kye, p. 255
Minority–minority relations, p. 255
Miscegenation, p. 233

Primogeniture, p. 243
Sinophobia, p. 236
Sojourners, p. 232

## DISCUSSION QUESTIONS

1. The beginning of this chapter offered a sociohistorical perspective. What was one surprising or striking piece of information you picked up here?
2. Discuss the interrelationship between labor conflict and racism with regard to the Chinese, Japanese, and Filipinos.
3. How did the Chinese immigrants of the late nineteenth century respond to hostility and discrimination?
4. What explains the different treatment of Japanese Americans in Hawaii and on the mainland during World War II?
5. How do the concepts of "ethnic church" and "middleman minority" apply to Korean Americans?
6. What are some cultural characteristics of Vietnamese Americans?
7. How do today's Asian immigrants differ from their predecessors? How and why does society respond to them differently?
8. The end of the chapter offers three theoretical analyses. How did one of these theories become more meaningful or relevant to you in its application to the different groups' experiences?

## INTERNET ACTIVITIES

Virtually every ethnic group has websites about itself. Here are a few on some of the main Asian and Pacific Islander websites in the United States. Visit any of interest to you and comment on one or more of them.

1. The Census Bureau offers demographic profiles of various groups in the United States. Go to either Asians (http://www.census.gov/prod/cen2010/briefs/c2010br-11.pdf) or Pacific Islanders (http://www.census.gov/prod/cen2010/briefs/c2010br-12.pdf).
2. Want to learn more about the Japanese internment during World War II? Go to http://caamedia.org/jainternment to find out.
3. The Korean American Historical Society (http://www.kahs.org/links.html) maintains numerous links on its culture and history, if you scroll down a bit.

4. To learn more about Filipino Americans, go to http://www.asian-nation.org/filipino.shtml.
5. "Challenges for Asian Indians in the 21st Century" (http://www.nriol.com/content/articles/article65.asp) offers interesting information for discussion.
6. The Hmong are a group that began emigrating to the United States after the Vietnam War ended. If you will click on Hmong Studies Internet Resource Center (http://www.hmongstudies.com), you will gain access to information about their history, experiences in the United States, and learn how a fairly new U.S. ethnic group is using the Internet to strengthen its ethnic community, which is scattered throughout the country.

# Middle Eastern and North African Americans

9

((•)) **Listen** to Chapter 9 on **MySocLab**

> *Many immigrant newcomers, such as this Asian businessman, possess an education level, along with occupational and/or managerial skills to get good-paying jobs in the United States with either American- or foreign-owned companies. Their incomes enable them to live in urban or suburban residences outside ethnic neighborhoods.*

## LEARNING OBJECTIVES | After reading this chapter you will be able to:

**9-1** Describe the sociohistorical context for studying Middle Easterners and North Africans.

**9-2** Identify patterns and social indicators existing among Arab Americans.

**9-3** Describe the immigrant experiences of Lebanese, Syrians, Egyptians, and Iraqis.

**9-4** Describe the immigrant experiences of Palestinians, Iranians, Israelis, and Turks.

**9-5** Compare and contrast the assimilation paths followed by these immigrants.

**9-6** Discuss insights gained through sociological analysis.

Middle Eastern and North African immigrants come from a part of the world that was the locale for some of the world's earliest civilizations. North Africa, the setting for thriving societies during the time of the ancient Greeks and Romans, fell under French and English domination in the nineteenth century, but today, Mauritania, Morocco, Algeria, Tunisia, Libya, Egypt, and Sudan all are independent nations. The Middle East—called so in part because it is situated between the area of Western thought and history on one side, and the area of Eastern thought and philosophy on the other—experienced Turkish, British, or French colonization in the nineteenth and twentieth centuries before emerging as the independent countries depicted in Figure 9.1.

From Northern Africa to Turkey (a Eurasian country bridging the continents of Europe and Asia) and onward throughout the Middle East, Islam is the predominant religion. (We will discuss religious minorities in Chapter 12.) However, many Middle Eastern and North African immigrants are not Muslims. In addition, the languages and cultures in these numerous countries are diverse as elsewhere in the world. Although some immigrants are Arabs, many others are not. Because of such religious and other ethnic differences, generalizations about the people covered in this chapter as "Arabs," "Muslims," or some other "catch-all" category ignores the reality of their diversity.

Although some Middle Easterners and North Africans immigrated to the United States before 1965 and had encounters similar to those of earlier racial and ethnic groups, most have come since the 1965 Immigration Act. The nature of their acceptance as strangers and their adjustment to U.S. life have differed from the experiences of pre-1920 immigrants because structural conditions in both the sending and the host countries have changed. As before, some immigrants today have limited job skills and educational levels. Many other newcomers, however, are professional, managerial, or technical workers. Some are underemployed, but others find employment in their occupational roles. Either way, most tend to be isolated from informal social contact with other people outside their nationality and/or religious group. As with many Asian Americans, the social distance between most first-generation Middle Eastern or North African Americans and native-born U.S. citizens is considerable.

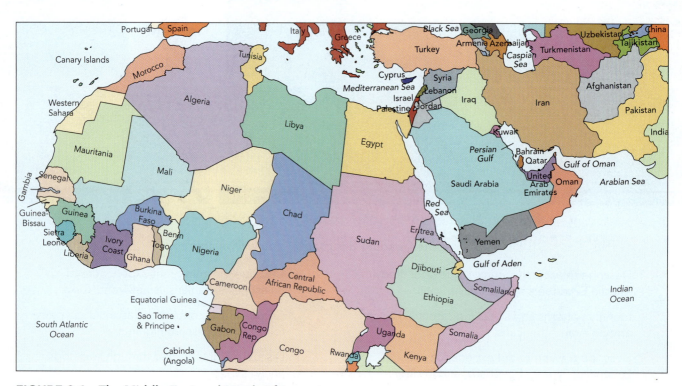

**FIGURE 9.1   The Middle East and North Africa**

# Sociohistorical Perspective

Aside from special legislation of temporary duration allowing political or war refugees to enter the United States, immigration regulations before 1965 effectively limited the number of Middle Eastern and North African immigrants. Because few had migrated to the United States prior to 1890, the year on which the 1924 immigration legislation based its quotas, few immigrants from this part of the world were able to gain approval to migrate to the United States. Eliminating this restrictive national-origins quota system thus opened the door to many different peoples previously denied entry.

**9-1** Describe the sociohistorical context for studying Middle Easterners and North Africans.

> **Watch on MySocLab**
> Video: **The Basics: Race and Ethnicity**

## THE PUSH–PULL FACTORS

For many immigrants, overpopulation and poverty so seriously limit the quality of life in their homelands that they seek a better life elsewhere. Sometimes restrictive government actions or limited socioeconomic opportunities push people to look elsewhere. The United States, with its cultural diversity, economic opportunities, and higher living standards, is influential throughout the world and a magnet to those dissatisfied with their situation. For others, the United States offers educational, professional, or career opportunities. Rapid air travel and instant communications, which reduce the psychological distance from a person's native country, are further inducements.

Since the 1965 change in the immigration laws, the "push" factors of ethnoviolence, limited life opportunities, and/or political instability have motivated growing numbers to migrate to the United States, lured by such "pull" factors as freedom, opportunity, and a better quality of life. More than 1 million foreign-born Arab Americans now live in the United States, a number that exceeds the combined foreign-born population from Germany and Italy.[1] Yet other Arab Americans are U.S. born and their ancestry is their heritage, not their everyday ethnic reality. Many do not speak Arabic, may have non-Arab partners in life, and raise their children in a nonethnic environment. Although the Census Bureau identifies approximately 1.8 million Americans of Arab ancestry, other organizations suggest the number approaches 3 million. In addition, approximately 143,000 Americans claimed Israeli ancestry in 2011.[2]

## STRUCTURAL CONDITIONS

The immigrants discussed in this chapter follow the same patterns as have other ethnic groups that immigrated to the United States. They usually settle in urbanized areas near their compatriots, with whom they develop close primary social contacts.

**IMMIGRANTS.** Because many are trained professionals or skilled technicians, however, their job situation differs markedly from that of others with less skills and education. The first group is more likely to settle in suburbia or upscale urban neighborhoods, while the second group usually settles in older city neighborhoods. The economic profile of these Americans thus ranges from the affluent to the struggling. Wherever they congregate to live and work, various support facilities have arisen: churches or mosques, grocery stores and restaurants specializing in native foods, social clubs or organizations, and perhaps their own schools and newspapers. They soon send for other members of their family or write home telling of their good fortune, prompting others to come to the United States. The chain-migration pattern of earlier immigrants thus repeats itself.

Because many of these immigrants have marketable skills, they can obtain professional and salaried jobs without first adopting a subservient role in the economy. They need not yield to pressures to assimilate fully to gain middle-class respectability. Their income is high enough to enable them to enjoy the lifestyle they want and, as a result, they are free to continue their own cultural behavior patterns. Some Americanization undoubtedly occurs, but these first-generation immigrants do not have to make substantial cultural sacrifices to "make it" in U.S. society.

**NONIMMIGRANTS.** Another sizable foreign-born segment in the United States consists of nonimmigrant (sojourner) students, workers, and businesspeople. Although they usually remain for only two to five years, their growing numbers make them a significantly visible presence. In 2011, for example, from this part of the world, more than 67,000 students and exchange visitors (11,400 from Israel) arrived in the United States and more than 317,000 temporary workers and their families (18,400 from Israel). In addition, approximately 560,000 came as tourists and business travelers, 318,000 of them from Israel.[3]

These temporary business visitors do not fit the acculturation patterns common to other immigrant groups. For instance, prosperity in oil-rich Middle Eastern countries eliminates a key "push" factor and encourages some to plan an eventual return to their native country. A Saudi Arabian, for example, might return from the United States after acquiring an advanced education or experience that will permit a better life back home. Saudi Arabia collects no taxes whatsoever, offers free education and medical care, and has a high standard of living. Although the number of immigrants from Saudi Arabia may be extremely low, a greater number of newcomers from other Arab countries is seeking permanent residence in the United States, as Table 9.1 indicates.

In many respects, these temporary visitors—visible to others in work, residential, shopping, and entertainment settings—resemble U.S. citizens who work for multinational corporations overseas. Even if assigned to another country for a considerable number of years, these Americans rarely lose their sense of ethnic or national identity. They live within the culture and enjoy the available opportunities without contemplating abandoning their own cultural ties and becoming assimilated in the host country. Similarly, many aliens working in the United States have no interest in U.S. citizenship or assimilation, whether they work for one of their own country's multinational corporations or for some U.S. employer. Today's sojourners may be more sophisticated than their predecessors, but their resistance to assimilation is just as strong.

At the same time, however, other immigrants are highly motivated to become part of U.S. society, as demonstrated by the fact that, between 2002 and 2012, more than 350,000 immigrants from the Middle East and North Africa became naturalized U.S. citizens.[4]

**TABLE 9.1   Middle Eastern and North African Immigrants to the United States**

| COUNTRY | 1971–1980 | 1981–1990 | 1991–2000 | 2001–2009 | 2010–2012 |
|---|---|---|---|---|---|
| Algeria | 1,123 | 1,511 | 6,326 | 9,442 | 4,038 |
| Egypt | 25,495 | 34,259 | 46,714 | 64,109 | 25,744 |
| Iran | 46,152 | 165,267 | 112,597 | 111,748 | 41,920 |
| Iraq | 23,404 | 22,211 | 40,749 | 45,167 | 61,357 |
| Israel | 36,306 | 43,669 | 41,340 | 42,128 | 12,494 |
| Jordan | 29,578 | 36,032 | 38,749 | 34,815 | 11,843 |
| Lebanon | 33,846 | 45,770 | 43,469 | 36,005 | 9,661 |
| Morocco | 4,431 | 7,158 | 20,442 | 39,355 | 13,068 |
| Saudi Arabia | 700 | 4,180 | 7,716 | 10,368 | 4,002 |
| Syria | 13,339 | 22,230 | 26,109 | 23,318 | 8,354 |
| Yemen | 5,170 | 5,634 | 16,319 | 21,052 | 9,572 |

*Source:* Adapted from U.S. Office of Immigration Statistics. *Statistical Yearbook 2012* (Washington, DC: U.S. Government Printing Office, 2013), Table 3.

Despite public suspicions about their loyalties, or perhaps partly because of them, Arab Americans have a higher rate of naturalization (54 percent) than the total foreign-born population (40 percent).[5]

### SOCIETAL REACTION

Approximately 325,000 Middle Easterners migrated to the United States between 1880 and 1920. These early arrivals encountered far more prejudice and discrimination in the United States than those who followed, as Americans became more tolerant of the differences in appearance and customs of non-Western immigrants. However, terrorist attacks on September 11, 2001, in New York City and Washington, DC, increased suspicions about Arab Muslims. People still often categorize others and make judgments based on visible impressions, and this often leads to stereotyping. Distinguishing racial features and distinctive apparel, such as a *hijab* (head scarf) or turban, set some of the newcomers apart. Although little overt discrimination occurs, limited social interaction takes place in most cases.

In post-9/11 surveys of social distance among various minority groups, racially distinct non-Western immigrants scored at the bottom, most notably Arab and Muslim Americans (See Table 1.1).[6] Many newcomers find themselves accepted in their professional, managerial, and technical occupational roles by members of the dominant society but excluded from outside social activities. Once the workday or workweek ends, they seldom receive social invitations from dominant-group members; thus, they interact mostly with family and compatriots. Economic mainstreaming may have occurred for many non-Western immigrants, but they yet have to achieve social integration.

## Arab Americans

*Arab* is a broad term covering people of diverse nationalities, religions, and socioeconomic backgrounds. Although Arab Americans may share a sense of peoplehood, they come from 22 nations of North Africa and the Middle East (Figure 9.2). Not surprisingly, many cultural differences separate them from one another, and their ethnic identities remain rooted in their nationalities and specific homelands.

Of the 1.8 million Arab Americans, nearly all are immigrants or descendants of immigrants who arrived since 1980. More than 190,000 Arab Americans live in southeastern Michigan, giving that area one of the largest concentrations of Arabs outside the Middle East.

**9-2** Identify patterns and social indicators existing among Arab Americans.

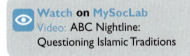 **Watch on MySocLab**
Video: ABC Nightline: Questioning Islamic Traditions

 **Read on MySocLab**
Document: The Concentration of Arab Americans

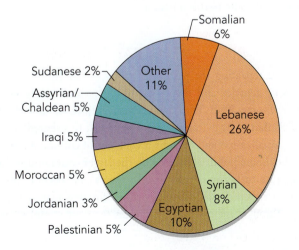

**FIGURE 9.2 Arab Americans by Origin**
*Source:* U.S. Census Bureau.

*Except for the hijab or headscarf that the woman is wearing, most people would never know this is an Arab/Muslim-American family. Obviously fans of the Detroit Pistons, the local NBA basketball team, they typify so many immigrants who cherish and keep their cultural traditions even as they embrace the American lifestyle.*

**Read on MySocLab**
Document: Growing Old in an Arab American Family

Dearborn, Michigan, a suburb of Detroit, became a favorite destination of many working-class Arab immigrants after the 1967 Arab–Israeli War. Several thousand Muslim Palestinians, Yemenis, and southern Lebanese arrived there, making it today the largest Muslim community in the United States. Because of the concentration of so many first-generation Arab Americans, Dearborn today resembles more completely a "Little Arabia" than any other Arab American community. Nearby Detroit suburbs, such as Livonia, also house large numbers of middle-class Arab Americans.

## SOCIAL ORGANIZATION

Many of today's Arab Americans are sophisticated, cosmopolitan people whose lifestyle matches that of other middle- or working-class U.S. citizens. Like many other past and present immigrant groups, Arab Americans have established institutions to help preserve their cultural heritage, strengthen their ethnic identity, and unite the community. More than four dozen Arabic newspapers are published and some 50 Arabic radio programs broadcast in such cities as Chicago, Detroit, New York, and San Francisco to aid in this effort. Religious and community organizations provide important emotional, social, and financial services to help sustain the Arab community. Among professional organizations, two of the better known are the National Association of Arab Americans and the Association of Arab American University Graduates.

As with most immigrant groups, kinship links play an important role in stabilizing community life.[7] Exchanges of letters, gifts, and family visits help maintain bonds between the immigrants and their relatives back home. Another important element is belief in an integrated economic family unit. Family members pool their income and resources in a common fund for all to share, even if the family is dispersed. Each month, many Arab Americans send vast amounts of money overseas to their relatives, helping them buy land, build homes, or purchase modern agricultural equipment such as tractors, plows, and irrigation pumps. Ironically, greater acculturation appears to be associated positively with satisfaction with life in the United States but negatively with family satisfaction.[8] Perhaps marginality and the clash of values contribute to this outcome.

## RESIDENTIAL PATTERNING

Arab Americans are repeating the pattern of many earlier European immigrants, with males outnumbering females and their settling almost exclusively in urban areas (see Figure 9.3). In fact, some Arab American activists emphasize how the Irish immigrant experience parallels that of Arab immigrants. They point to a shared history of systematic exclusion and marginalization and that the acceptance of cultural differences rests on the perception that they share political values with the larger community. Thus, they encourage Arab immigrants to become naturalized citizens and become politically active to enhance the assimilation process.[9] The proportion of males is larger than that of females in all age groups through age 64, and the largest segment is males ages 20 to 49 (see Figure 9.4).

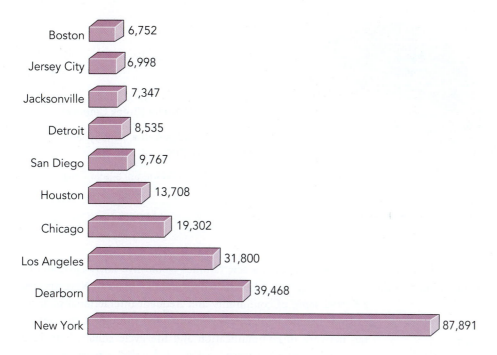

Boston 6,752
Jersey City 6,998
Jacksonville 7,347
Detroit 8,535
San Diego 9,767
Houston 13,708
Chicago 19,302
Los Angeles 31,800
Dearborn 39,468
New York 87,891

Approximately 94 percent live in metropolitan areas, with Detroit, Los Angeles, New York, Chicago, Washington, DC, and northeast New Jersey as the top metropolitan areas of Arab American concentration. They live in all 50 states, but two-thirds reside in only 10 states and half of that number live in California, New York, and Michigan.[10] Some first-generation Arab Americans live in recognizable ethnic neighborhoods in close proximity to one another, but others adopt slightly more dispersed residential patterns.

In an extensive field study of nearly 3,000 Arab immigrants living in the Paterson, New Jersey, metropolitan area, my investigators and I found them to be a religiously diverse group: 34 percent Muslim, 30 percent Orthodox Christian, 25 percent Melkite Catholic, and 10 percent Protestant. As in Paterson, most Arab Americans throughout the country are Christians (see Figure 9.5). Lebanese refugees, mostly of the middle class, tended to live in nearby suburbs; Circassians, Jordanians, Palestinians, and Syrians lived on the northern and southern peripheries of the city, spilling over into adjacent exurbs. This pattern of Arab immigrants settling on the edges of cities instead of in historically inner areas or transition zones has been found in other U.S. cities also.[11]

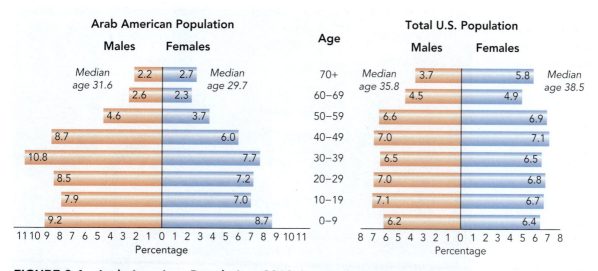

**FIGURE 9.4** Arab-American Population, 2010, in percentages
Source: U.S. Census Bureau.

**FIGURE 9.5** Religion of
Arab Americans, 2010

*Source:* Zogby International, 2010.

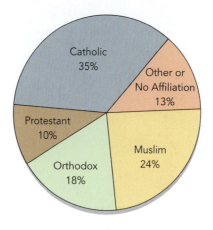

- Catholic 35%
- Other or No Affiliation 13%
- Protestant 10%
- Orthodox 18%
- Muslim 24%

Catholic includes Roman Catholic, Maronite, and Melkite (Greek Catholic).

Orthodox includes Antiochian, Syrian, Greek, and Coptic.

Muslim includes Sunni, Shi'a, and Druze.

In the Paterson area, we found that a few families would live fairly close to one another but that the next grouping would be situated several blocks away. Nevertheless, a shared sense of community and frequent interactional patterns existed. Ethnic solidarity was maintained through a cosmopolitan network of communication and life-cycle rituals, homeland concerns, political activism, or limited social situations (work, school, and nearby families). Instead of maintaining a territorial ethnic community as other immigrant groups have done, Arab immigrants often maintained an interactional community. In recent years, however, the steady influx of new arrivals has resulted in the creation of more visible Arab neighborhoods in numerous states.

In the Paterson study, racial composition of the neighborhood did not appear to be a factor in choice of residence or desire to relocate. No interracial tensions or conflicts were reported; Arab Americans shared a common assumption that those who lived where they did—white or black—were respectable people. Coming from a part of the world steeped in religious rather than racial prejudices, Arab Americans appear to be unconcerned about racial differences in the more secular society of the United States.

**STUDENTS SPEAK** "I thought it was interesting to read about Arab and Muslim Americans seldom receiving social invitations from dominant-group members. I have a good friend who is Muslim American and doesn't interact with many others in society outside of work. Whenever I'm at his house, he usually has his family over and I'm not talking just his parents, brothers, and sisters. On a daily basis, he'll have his cousins, aunts, and uncles over as well and I always wondered why they were so family-oriented compared to other American families. This chapter gave me a better idea of why that is."

**—Alexandra Schorling**

*Although many Americans think otherwise, the majority of Arab Americans are Christians, and only one-fourth are Muslims. About one-fifth are Orthodox Christians, which includes Antiochian, Coptic, and Syrian sects. This photo shows a priest leading a Sunday morning service at an Antiochian church in Syracuse, New York.*

## SOCIAL INDICATORS

Arab Americans are more likely to be married (53 percent) than the total U.S. population (48 percent) and less likely to be divorced (7 percent compared to 11 percent). Married-couple households are most frequent among Palestinian Americans (65 percent) and least likely among Moroccans (49 percent). Female-headed households among Arab Americans were less common (9 percent compared with 13 percent nationwide).[12]

As shown in Figure 9.6, Arab Americans as a group are highly educated. Approximately 46 percent has at least a college degree, compared to 29 percent of all Americans. A greater proportion of Arab Americans have a postgraduate degree (18 percent), compared to the total U.S. population (11 percent). Egyptians had the highest level of educational attainment, while Iraqis had the lowest.[13]

Educational attainment translates into occupations and income. A greater percentage (41 percent) is in management, business, science, or the arts, compared to one-third of the total population. The 28 percent in sales or office jobs is higher than the national average of 25 percent. Only 15 percent in the Arab ancestry group hold service jobs compared to 18 percent of all Americans. More than half of all Egyptian Americans worked in management, professional, science, or arts occupations, while 22 percent of all Moroccan Americans worked in service occupations, significantly higher than other Arab groups.

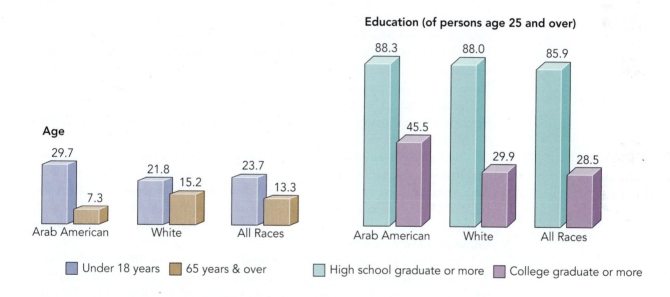

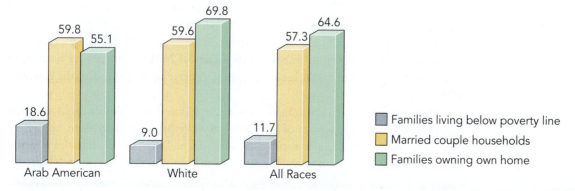

**FIGURE 9.6** 2011 Social Indicators about Arab Americans (in percentages)

*Source:* U.S. Census Bureau.

Approximately 55 percent of Arab Americans own their own homes in comparison to the national average of 65 percent.[14]

In terms of median income, both Arab men and women earn an average of $4,500 and $6,300 more than the national median for males and females, respectively. The greatest earnings gap between men and women ($13,000) was among the Egyptians, Lebanese, and Syrians. Egyptian, Lebanese, and Syrian males, in that order, had the highest median income among all Arab Americans, while Iraqi males had the lowest.[15]

Not all Arab Americans are affluent, however. Approximately 19 percent live in poverty compared to the national average of 12 percent. Two in five Iraqi American families live in poverty, while 23 percent of Lebanese and 22 percent of Palestinian American families are below the poverty threshold.[16]

## FIGHTING STEREOTYPES AND GROUP BLAME

Any discussion of Arab American problems with stereotyping or violence must distinguish conditions before and after September 11, 2001, the day of major terrorist attacks on the United States. Although Islamic radicals committed these atrocities, some Americans saw little distinction between those radicals and anyone identified as Arab, Muslim, or both.

Before those attacks, films and television shows rarely portrayed Arabs as ordinary people. More often, they were oil-rich billionaires or cold-blooded terrorists. They ranged from such broadly stereotypical TV wrestling villains as Abdullah the Butcher to cartoon villains such as Ali Boo-Boo, the desert rat in a Heckle and Jeckle animated feature. In the 1987 film *Wanted Dead or Alive,* starring Gene Simmons of the rock group Kiss, an Arab terrorist conspired with Arab Americans to poison the people of Los Angeles. The 1992 Disney film *Aladdin* gave the villainous Jaffar a distinctly Arabic accent, whereas Aladdin and Jasmine sounded like typical U.S. teenagers. In *Martial Law* (1999), Middle Eastern terrorists detonated bombs in New York City, and the federal government forced all Arab and Muslim Americans into detention camps.

Such widespread media portrayals have a cumulative, conditioning effect, and it is not a positive one. Adding to their difficulty in overcoming these stereotypical perceptions, Arab Americans have had to dissociate themselves from real-life terrorism. Bombings of the World Trade Center in 1993 and of U.S. embassies in Africa in 1998 caused the Arab American community some anxiety about the potential stigmatizing of all Arabs for the violent acts of only a few radicals.

The mass destruction and killing of nearly 3,000 people in attacks on the World Trade Center and Pentagon shocked everyone, including Arab Americans, many of whom had migrated here to get away from violence in their homelands. Although most Americans did not assign group blame, anti-Arab invective and sporadic acts of violence did occur. Such actions were remindful of the backlash that many Irish Americans felt in the 1870s over the terrorist activities of the Molly Maguires or that many immigrants experienced when a bomb exploded in the midst of police officers at an immigrant labor rally at Haymarket Square in Chicago in 1886. Perhaps, though, it is a tribute to the increased tolerance of U.S. society of 2001 that there were no calls for an action similar to that taken against Japanese Americans in 1942 after the bombing of Pearl Harbor.

However, it became more difficult to be an Arab American. Taking a flight anywhere made one an immediate subject of intense scrutiny. Verbal abuse, vandalism, and physical attacks occurred.[17] Because some of the hijackers had lived in communities a year or more, many first-generation Arab Americans found their loyalties questioned. Ingroup–outgroup boundaries solidified more between Arab and other Americans, as reported in the social distance surveys discussed in Chapter 1. Federal arrests of numerous Arab Americans also increased fear and resentment in the Arab American community.

On September 14, 2001, three days after the terrorist attacks, more than a thousand Arab-American worshipers gathered at the Passaic County Mosque in Paterson, New Jersey, where they prayed for America and all victims of the World Trade Center and Pentagon terrorist attacks. Afterwards, they lined up to donate blood for the wounded.

Presented with so much negative stereotyping and suspicions, one might falsely conclude that predominantly Arab nations are our enemy. In fact, the United States maintains friendly relations with 19 of 21 such countries, and most were allies during Operation Desert Storm in 1991. The 1.8 million Arab Americans living in the United States are normal human beings pursuing the American Dream, but the media seldom report that. Failure to grasp the humanity of the Arab people increases the social distance between non-Arabs and Arabs.

## Lebanese and Syrian Americans

Several factors contributed to a confusion of ethnic identities and a lack of accurate official U.S. statistics regarding immigrants from Syria and Lebanon. In the late nineteenth and early twentieth centuries, the entire Arabian Peninsula and the lands directly north of it were part of the Ottoman Empire, and its inhabitants were designated as Turkish citizens until the end of World War I. Although much cultural diversity existed in this geographic region, all the inhabitants spoke Arabic and, except for the Sinai Egyptians, used the term *Syrian* to identify themselves, as did the Americans. Still, the immigrants had Turkish passports, so U.S. officials identified them as Turks until 1899, when a separate category for Syrians began. Although approximately 85 percent of the immigrants came from the area now known as Lebanon, only in the 1930s did the term *Lebanese* gain acceptance. Some Lebanese resisted the change in designation, preferring to continue calling themselves Syrians, whereas some people from what is now Syria began calling themselves Lebanese.

**9-3** Describe the immigrant experiences of Lebanese, Syrians, Egyptians, and Iraqis.

### ETHNIC IDENTITY

In the past, Arab Americans tended to identify themselves by family name, religious sect, and village of origin. Rarely did they cross religious or village lines to set up common organizations. Instead, social clubs and fraternal organizations had a clannish focus, often leading to factionalism within the community. Neither political authority nor specific regional residence determined group affinity. Instead, religion defined the goals and boundaries of the "Syrian" community in the United States. The theological differences of Jews, Christians, and Muslims translated into social and structural realities keeping each community socially separate from the others.[18]

## MIGRATION AND SETTLEMENT

Although religious differences kept the three groups separate, the push–pull factors that led them to immigrate to the United States affected them similarly. Essentially, a combination of harsh living conditions—hunger, poverty, and disease—and Turkish oppression, particularly of Christians, led many to leave. The pull of the United States was the result of reports by missionaries and steamship agents of economic opportunities and religious and political freedom. Emigration to the United States began in the 1870s, reaching an estimated 100,000 between 1890 and 1914 as the harshness of Turkish rule increased. The peak years were 1913 and 1914, when more than 9,000 migrated to avoid conscription into the Turkish army on the eve of World War I.

A seven-block area along Washington and Rector Streets in lower Manhattan became a thriving Lebanese and Syrian community during the late nineteenth century. Others settled in downtown Brooklyn and elsewhere throughout the entire country. Another center for immigration was Worcester, Massachusetts. Most immigrants came either from cities or from densely populated villages. They usually chose to reside in U.S. cities of 100,000 or more and had little difficulty adjusting to urban life.[19]

Between 1890 and 1895, the New York community established three Arab Christian churches: Melkite, Maronite, and Eastern Orthodox. Before then, Syrians simply had joined U.S. churches. Maronites and Melkites usually became Roman Catholics; members of the Eastern Orthodox Church generally became Episcopalians.[20]

## CULTURE CONFLICTS

Newly arrived Lebanese and Syrians often replaced departing Irish American residents in old city neighborhoods. This is an example of the sociological concept of **invasion–succession,** in which one group experiencing upward mobility gradually moves out of its old neighborhood. Another group then replaces it, living at the previous residents' original socioeconomic level. Sometimes hostility develops between the old and new groups. In the case of the Syrians, religious tension resulted in a clash with the Irish, as this 1920 account about the Dublin District of Paterson, New Jersey, reveals:

When the Syrians came to live there, the rentals became higher. This caused hard feelings between the Irish and the Syrians, which developed into a feud between the two nationalities. The fight started in the saloon on Grand and Mill Streets, first with bitter arguments and harsh words, and then threatening fist fights. From the saloon, the fight came out to the streets. It was like two armies in opposition facing each other....The police force was called in to put an end to this fight. All they could do was to throw water on them to disperse them. These fights continued for three days in the evening. Finally, a committee of Syrians went to talk to Dean McNulty of St. John's, explaining to him that they were Christians coming from the Holy Land, not Mohammedans or Turks, as the Irish used to call them. They were good Catholics and they wanted to live in peace with everybody. Then the good Dean, at Sunday masses, urged the Irish to stop fighting with the Syrians, who were like them, Catholics. He succeeded in stopping this fighting better than the police.[21]

Another problem the Lebanese and Syrian immigrants encountered before World War I was racial classification. In 1909, the U.S. District Court in St. Louis ruled them

*Lower Manhattan was the locale of many immigrant communities in the late nineteenth and early twentieth centuries. Besides the better-known Italian and Jewish communities of the Lower East Side, a vibrant Syrian community along Washington and Rector Streets was another distinctive neighborhood filled with sights and sounds of ethnicity.*

ineligible for naturalization on the basis of the 1790 legislation, declaring them to be non-white. Many Lebanese and Syrian Christians were blond and blue-eyed, but the racial barrier was determined by their country of origin. Later, the Circuit Court of Appeals reversed this decision. Shortly thereafter, the matter came up again, this time in the U.S. District Court in New York, which also ruled that they could be naturalized.[22]

## EARLY PATTERNS

In those early years, males usually came alone and then sent for their wives and children. Although poor, most were literate and insisted that their children complete primary school. Married women were more emancipated and less dependent on their husbands than were their counterparts in other ethnic groups at that time. Both mother and children—after they completed grade school—worked together for the family's economic welfare. The family structure proved to be an important factor in their economic success.

Generally, the men preferred to work as traders and shopkeepers because trading was a time-honored occupation in their native land. Many became peddlers and traveled throughout the United States, bringing essential and exotic goods to far-flung communities. In the late nineteenth and early twentieth centuries, these peddlers filled an economic need and were welcome visitors to remote homes and communities. Approximately one in three Lebanese and Syrian men became peddlers; others tried various commercial ventures, started restaurants, or, in a few cases, worked in factories.

The choice of peddling by so many expedited their acculturation. It took them into U.S. homes, quickly teaching them the hosts' language and customs. It prevented their cultural isolation by way of ghetto settlement patterns, instead dispersing them throughout the country. By 1914, most Lebanese and Syrian peddlers had switched to being shopkeepers, with the majority operating grocery or dry goods stores.

## UPWARD MOBILITY

Lebanese and Syrian Americans achieved economic security quickly, often in the first generation. This especially is significant because less than one-fourth of those who came were professional or skilled workers. Aiding them in their adjustment, acceptance, and upward mobility were (1) wide dispersal, negating any significant opposition to their presence; (2) business expertise and self-employment, which allowed them greater rewards; and (3) cultural values of thrift, industriousness, and investment that were comparable to the middle-class values of the host society:

> Even while they were still in the lower income brackets and in working-class occupations, the "Syrians" displayed the social characteristics of the middle classes in American urban centers. Studies of these Arab immigrants in Chicago, Pittsburgh, and the South reveal a common pattern: low crime rates, better than average health, higher I.Q.'s, and more regular school attendance among the children, few intermarriages and divorces.[23]

Coming from a country in which nearly every man owned the house he lived in, was determined to be independent, and was highly motivated to succeed, Lebanese and Syrian Americans accumulated money rapidly and invested either in property or in business ventures. By 1911, Syrians worked in nearly every branch of commerce, including banking and import–export houses, and the government reported that their median income was only slightly lower than the $665 annual income of the adult native-born male.

> Unlike other immigrant groups who had to wait two or three generations to exert their independence from ghetto life and to satisfy their desire for mobility, it was the Syrian immigrants (first generation) who amassed the wealth that their sons used as a lever for bringing themselves into wider contacts with society.[24]

Rapid economic success and lack of either unfavorable stereotypes or discrimination barriers once they were known as Syrians rather than Turks allowed Syrian/Lebanese immigrants to assimilate into U.S. society quite easily, so they did not need to duplicate the host society's institutions. True, they had social organizations and their own newspapers, but their mobility, wide dispersal, differing religions, and emphasis on the extended family rather than on ethnic organizations resulted in their being assimilated rather easily (see the Ethnic Experience box).

By the mid-1950s, Lebanese and Syrian Americans had abandoned their "nomadic" occupations completely. They had entered the mainstream of U.S. economic and social life and were represented in virtually every industry and profession.[25] Because they were prosperous, their children were able to enter the sciences, the professions, politics, and the arts, and many have distinguished themselves in these fields.

## THE CONTEMPORARY SCENE

Today, their numbers and the separate nation-state identities of their homelands enable Lebanese and Syrian Americans to maintain their own ethnic identities both within and outside their communities.

Lebanese Americans are the largest of all Arab Americans groups, constituting 26 percent of the total, with more than 491,000 claiming Lebanese ancestry in 2011. Between 3,000 and 4,000 additional Lebanese immigrants arrive each year. They have the highest rate of citizenship among all Arab Americans. Three-fourths are native-born U.S. citizens and 93 percent of all Lebanese Americans are U.S. citizens.[26]

Although living in all 50 states, more than half of all Lebanese Americans are concentrated in Michigan, California, Ohio, Florida, and Massachusetts. They are the second highest educated subgroup (after the Egyptians), with 46 percent holding at least a college degree and 20 percent holding an advanced or professional degree. Approximately 8 percent of Arab Americans is of Syrian ancestry. In 2011, the number was approximately 153,000 and they are joined by an average of 2,600 additional Syrian immigrants each

# the ETHNIC experience

## First Encounters with U.S. Ethnicity and Language

"I am of Circassian origin, having been born in Syria. My father worked in government with the interior ministry. When the government changed from a moderate socialist to a radical socialist government following the Arab–Israeli War in 1968, my father was arrested as a pro-Western sympathizer. He escaped from jail, and we all fled to Jordan, where we received asylum. We migrated to West Germany, but very few Circassians live there, and so we came to the U.S. where other Circassians who had fled from Russia now lived."

"Before we came here, the idea I had about America was that the people were the same, that everybody was an American except the blacks because they were different in color. I thought everybody would be an American, but when we came

here—especially as soon as I went to high school—I found everyone identified with their parents' origin. In other words, they would call themselves Italian-American, Dutch-American, and so on. It was a little confusing to me because I expected them to say they were Americans. Instead they said their nationality first and then said American."

"Most Circassians live in northern New Jersey or in California, and so we settled in New Jersey where my father already knew some people. I did have a lot of trouble with the language here. I spoke two languages—Circassian and Arabic—but starting as a sophomore in high school, I had trouble relating to the people. You know how high school kids are. They're immature. Sometimes in class, I might say something with

a super-heavy accent, and perhaps even say it completely wrong, and they would laugh at me. I didn't have many friends in high school because I worked after school, and besides, we didn't interact very much with the Americans because the Circassian community had its own activities and clubs. Our language and culture were different and the Americans weren't so friendly. Besides, once you know you have an accent, that does stop you from even trying to make friends. It's a barrier. You're still trying to learn a language and it's hard. With my brothers, I spoke Arabic, with my parents who were so nationalistic, we had to speak Circassian, and in school, I had to learn English, and it was all very confusing."

Source: Syrian immigrant who came to the United States in 1968 at age 15. Taped interview from the collection of Vincent N. Parrillo.

succeeding year. The median incomes for Syrian males and females are higher than the national average as is their median family income.[27]

A strong emphasis on family ties, respect, and social status are important elements of Syrian American society. The newcomers, either joining friends or relatives who already are assimilated and dispersed, or coming as middle-class refugees, usually blend in easily with the rest of U.S. society in their work and residence. Lebanese and Syrian Americans maintain a strong social network of communication and interaction in social events. Although large-scale intermarriage has occurred in recent decades, their extended families continue to do things together, including vacationing and relocating to different geographic areas.[28]

## Egyptian Americans

Constituting the second largest Arab American group, Egyptian Americans numbered 216,000 in 2011. With its high birth and poverty rates as push factors, Egypt is sending an average of 8,000 emigrants annually to the United States. As a consequence, Egyptian Americans are the fastest-growing Arab American population, and approximately 10 percent of the total. Approximately 42 percent of all Egyptian Americans are native born, and another 37 percent are naturalized U.S. citizens, leaving 31 percent, mostly newcomers, who are foreign-born noncitizens. Of all the Arab American groups, Egyptians have the highest level of educational attainment: 96 percent have at least a high school diploma and 67 percent have a college degree or higher. Not surprisingly, they have the highest percentage in management, business science, or arts positions (52 percent) but trail Lebanese and Syrians in high income and low poverty levels.[29]

## A GROWING WAVE OF IMMIGRATION

Unlike the large numbers of other Arab immigrants who settled in the United States in the mid-nineteenth century, the Egyptians only began arriving in significant numbers in the last third of the twentieth century. Most left for economic or educational reasons, but many Coptic Christians and Jews emigrated over concern about the political situation in Egypt. For 10 years following Egypt's 1967 defeat in the Arab–Israeli War, approximately 15,000 Egyptians immigrated to the United States. In the past three decades, an unprecedented wave of 171,000 Egyptian immigrants came to the United States, more than 100,000 of them since 2000.[30]

Many in that first group of Egyptian immigrants were educated professionals and skilled workers, who benefited from the 1965 Immigration Act, which offered occupational preference to professionals and scientists. Although many educated and professional immigrants still come, family reunification and relative preference options under current immigration law have allowed for a greater diversity of occupational and educational backgrounds among the newer arrivals.

The majority of Egyptian Americans are Coptic Orthodox Christians, a marginalized minority group of approximately 13 percent of the total population in mostly Muslim Egypt. In the United States, about 166 parishes now exist. St. Mark's Church was the first to be founded in the late 1960s in Jersey City, New Jersey, a small city that is home to 30,000 Copts.[31]

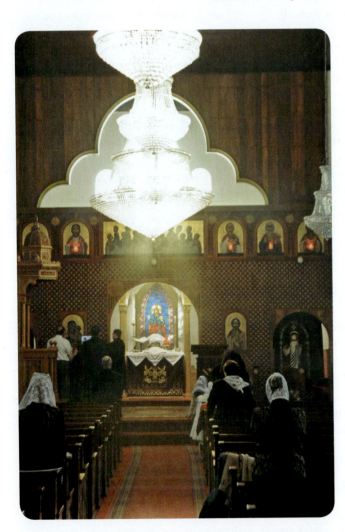

The Coptic Orthodox Church of St. Mark in Jersey City, New Jersey, was the first of this faith to take root in the United States, but it is now one of more than 200 throughout the country. Founded in the late 1960s by Egyptian immigrants, this church is the spiritual center for the estimated 30,000 Copts presently living in this city.

## SETTLEMENT AND ACCULTURATION

The largest concentrations of Egyptians live in California, New Jersey, New York, Florida, Texas, and Illinois. Increasingly, many are settling in southern states, perhaps seeking a warm climate more akin to that of their homeland. New Jersey is the only state in the nation where Egyptian Americans are the dominant subgroup (37 percent) in comparison to other Arab Americans, easily outnumbering the Lebanese (15 percent) and Syrians (9 percent) there.[32]

Because of their strong educational background, most Egyptian immigrants and their American-born children have had little difficulty adjusting to American culture. More recent arrivals tend to live within well-defined urban ethnic communities. Those of longer U.S. residence or birth do not necessarily live within an everyday ethnic reality, as they follow the time-worn path of other ethnics of assimilating and moving into nonethnic neighborhoods. Further, a growing number of Egyptian Americans have been marrying outside their ethnic community, which further has eased their assimilation.

Even so, most Egyptian Americans have lived in the United States a relatively short time, giving reason for their establishment of ethnic-based organizations, many of them with an academic, business, or professional orientation. Included among them are the Association of Egyptian-American Scholars, Egyptian American Cultural Association, Egyptian Businessmen's Association, Egyptian Physicians' Association, and Egyptian American Professional Society.

# Iraqi Americans

Even though all Iraqis are from the Arab world, we must make a distinction between the so-called Iraqi Arabs who are Arabic-speaking Muslims and the Iraqi Chaldeans and Assyrians, who are Aramaic-speaking Christians and consider themselves to have a unique ethnic identity. The latter group were among the earliest Arab immigrants to come to the United States, while Iraqi Arabs primarily have immigrated since 1965.

Coming primarily from northern Iraq in the early twentieth century at first, the Chaldeans preferred Detroit as their destination, whereas the Assyrians tended to settle in Chicago. To this day, that pattern continues, as relatives of the earlier immigrants follow the chain-migration tradition in joining family members already situated in those locales.

## HOMELAND INFLUENCE

Influencing Chaldeans living in the Detroit metropolitan area were significant pre– and post–World War II changes in their homeland influence in the evolution of Iraq into a modern nation-state and the heightened Arab consciousness caused by Arab–Israeli tensions.[33]

The early immigrants formed a community of village-oriented entrepreneurs whose religious traditions served as their self-identification. They maintained a *gemeinschaft* subsociety within U.S. society. Family orientations were strong, and many Iraqis were self-employed, operating grocery stores and other small businesses. They were, for the most part, a self-enclosed ethnic community.

Not only did the post–World War II immigrants in Detroit have different value orientations from their predecessors, because of their higher education levels and more urbanized backgrounds, but these newer orientations also had an effect on the self-perceptions and behavior of the earlier immigrants. Although Chaldeans are Christians, they felt the pull of Arab nationalist loyalties, and this national consciousness was infectious.[34] Most soon came to think of themselves as Arabs or Iraqis, not as Chaldeans or Telkeffes (a name drawn from the village of Telkaif, where many originated). These immigrants were less likely to be self-employed and more likely to interact with people of different backgrounds, including close friendship ties and intermarriage.

## THE CONTEMPORARY SCENE

Iraqis are the fourth largest group of immigrants to come to the United States from the Arab world since 1965. In 2011, approximately 112,000 Iraqi Americans and 111,000 Assyrian/Chaldean Americans resided in the United States.[35] More than 86,000 Iraqi immigrants, often departing from another Arab country, have arrived since 2000. At present, they total nearly 8,000 annually.[36] They come from a country suffering from continual violence and far-too-numerous deaths of innocents. When the violence ends, an increased stream of refugees is likely to seek refuge in the United States. In typical chain-migration patterning, they settle where other Iraqis live, most particularly in Michigan, California, and Illinois.[37]

Interestingly, neither the 1990 Gulf War against Saddam Hussein's troops nor the 2003–2011 U.S. war in Iraq generated any significant hostility against Iraqi Americans living in the United States. Several factors probably contributed to this lack of societal animosity. Given their tendency to live within the larger Arab American community, Iraqi Americans are not that visible. Furthermore, as people who fled the violence, they mostly were supportive of the military action against their homeland's dictator.

# Palestinian Americans

Describe the immigrant experiences of Palestinians, Iranians, Israelis, and Turks.

Although Palestinian migration to the United States dates back to the late nineteenth century and others arrived as refugees following the 1948 Arab–Israeli war, the largest number arrived after 1965, mostly from the West Bank and Jerusalem. This group included professionals and students who remained after college. Many Palestinian Americans are Muslims, but a significant proportion is Christian, mostly belonging to the Antiochian Orthodox Church.[38]

Approximately 97,000 Arabs of Palestinian ancestry lived in the United States in 2011, 64 percent of them born in the United States. They constitute approximately 5 percent of the Arab American population. Many Palestinian Americans live in Palestinian communities clustered in Chicago, Detroit, San Francisco, Houston, Jacksonville, New York City, and northeastern New Jersey. The largest Palestinian population is in California, but their greatest concentration is in Illinois.[39]

Some worked first as sojourners in other Arab countries and then came to the United States directly from these countries. Among these first-generation newcomers, some hope for an eventual return to the Middle East, when financially able to do so, because there they feel more culturally comfortable and believe they would have a qualitatively better social life.[40] However, 77 percent of the more than 35,000 foreign-born Palestinian Americans are naturalized U.S. citizens.[41]

The second generation is more likely to be in married-couple households (approximately 65 percent), a higher level than for most other Arab Americans. More than half (59 percent) of all Palestinian Americans own their own homes, more than most other Arab Americans except for the Lebanese (68 percent) and the Syrians (67 percent). As with many other ethnic groups, those who have resided in the United States longer tend to have higher income and education levels, along with a lower poverty rate than those who are more recent arrivals.[42]

## HOMELAND INFLUENCE

After nearly 50 years of Palestinians living as a dispossessed people with no homeland, changes in Israeli leadership and government policy culminated in the agreement signed by Palestinian leader Yasir Arafat and Israeli Prime Minister Yitzhak Rabin in 1995 that transferred control over much of the West Bank of occupied Jordanian territory to its Palestinian residents. Despite Rabin's assassination in 1996 and the subsequent impasse in Israeli–Palestinian talks, Palestinian self-rule continues to evolve, and that homeland influence has renewed the pride of Palestinian Americans in their ethnic identity.

However, many Palestinian Americans are frustrated that Palestine is still refused recognition as an independent nation, and they see the media as misrepresenting and biased against Palestinians. Further, they believe that their host country, the United States, is unfairly supportive of Israel and its military incursions on the Palestinians.[43] In addition, continued Israeli–Palestinian conflict, especially the suicide bombers, the radicalism of Hamas, and links to terrorist motivation against U.S. targets contribute to occasional strained relations between Palestinian Americans and other U.S. citizens.

## THE AMERICAN FEDERATION OF RAMALLAH

Many recent Palestinian arrivals from the Middle East lack advanced education or occupational skills for various white-collar positions, so they find employment in various working-class trades. One source of assistance is the American Federation of Ramallah, named after a Palestinian city 10 miles north of Jerusalem. It is a nationwide ethnic organization, with local and regional social clubs designed to help people of Palestinian heritage adjust to life in the United States. The organization provides financial assistance, guaranteed bank loans, and expertise to enable the newcomers to start small businesses. The newcomers gradually repay the loans, adding a small percentage to help others who follow them.

The federation also conducts many social activities, such as parties and picnics, through its local chapters. These events help maintain ethnic bonding and provide opportunities for young people to meet potential marriage partners. A youth department offers summer camp programs and cultural heritage classes.

### COMMUNITY LIFE

For middle-class Palestinian Americans, the community's mosques and churches serve many purposes. They meet religious needs, of course, but they also function as ethnic centers for social occasions, temporary hostels for new arrivals not yet situated, cultural learning centers for youths, meeting places for Arab organizations, and reception centers for visiting dignitaries.

Working-class Palestinian-American males, many of whom live in urban neighborhoods, often congregate in coffeehouses in their free hours, much as earlier Greek immigrants did. These neighborhood social centers provide places to relax, exchange news about the community or homeland, and perhaps learn of work opportunities.

## Iranian Americans

Iran, formerly called Persia, is not an Arab country. The great majority of its people speak their own language, Farsi, not Arabic, and their culture has unique qualities that set it apart from the culture of neighboring Arab states. Immigration patterns and societal reaction to Iranian immigrants have fluctuated greatly in the past 30 years depending on the political climate.

*First-generation immigrants usually maintain a strong interest in the politics of their homeland, and Iranian Americans are no exception. When demonstrators in Tehran were attacked and imprisoned for challenging what they called the rigged election of President Ahmadinejad in 2009, Iranian Americans in many U.S. cities staged public protests.*

## EARLIER IMMIGRANTS

Immigration to the United States from Iran is a relatively new phenomenon. During the reign of the westernizing Shah Mohammed Reza Pahlevi, approximately 50,000 Iranian students studied in the United States annually. They maintained a sense of community among themselves, forming associations and interacting with one another. Fear of political repression under the shah kept many from returning to their homeland until after his fall from power in 1979.

Other Iranians living in the United States in the late 1970s were skilled male professionals working as sojourners, who had no intention of remaining, or political refugees hoping to return home someday. Although physically separated from their families, typical Iranian immigrants still viewed their extended family at home as their only source of primary relations, which they maintained through regular telephone calls. These men did not form a territorially compact community or develop close ties with their compatriots.[44]

At that time, only the Iranian college students maintained an ethnic community or network. Other Iranians kept to themselves, partly for fear that members of the shah's secret police force (SAVAK) would report something about them, bringing harm to relatives still in Iran. Minority emigrants from Iran—Armenians, Baha'is, and Jews—showed great cohesiveness, intending to become U.S. citizens, but they constituted a small percentage of all Iranian immigrants.

These early Iranian immigrants fell into four self-designated categories. Only approximately 20 percent called themselves *mandegar* (settlers), or Persian Yankees. Many of these were older, former exchange students who opted to stay permanently. The majority were in the second category, the *belataklif,* or ambivalent Iranians. Torn by a nostalgic love and guilt feeling for what had been left behind, yet growing attached to what lay ahead in the United States, the *belataklif* remained undecided about staying or returning. Yet the longer one remained, the less likely one was to return, thus becoming a *mandegar.* The other two categories were the *siyasi,* political exiles who viewed their host society only as a necessary refuge, and the *cosmopolitans,* who were committed to their profession and not to their nationality—citizens of the world at home anywhere. Today, the first and fourth categories primarily describe Iranian Americans.[45]

## THE CONTEMPORARY SCENE

Born to mostly middle-class professional parents, today's second-generation Iranian Americans grow up in a child-centered family with egalitarian norms, quite unlike the patriarchal and authoritarian character of families in Iran. Nonetheless, many parents are concerned about preserving their Iranian heritage and make efforts to preserve the positive aspects of the culture, despite the inevitable Americanization process.[46]

*Nowruz* is a new year's celebration that begins on the first day of spring. A nonreligious and colorful festival dating back more than 2,000 years, it is deeply ingrained within the fabric of Iranian society. Now an institutionalized event among Iranian Americans, they also commemorate it as a Persian National Day. A highlight is the annual Persian Parade in New York City, with its floats and native costumes worn by participants attracting tens of thousands of spectators.

> The celebration of *Nowruz* is the most impressive expression of Iranian-American cultural heritage and is celebrated with great extravagance…in almost every sizable Iranian community across the United States. It is a joyful occasion for the entire Iranian community and is a manifestation of Iranian national pride, particularly for the second-generation.[47]

*Sizdah Behar* is a picnic day that marks the end of the 13-day *Nowruz* celebration. A communal event shared by family and friends, it consists of picnicking, strolling, and hiking in the open air. Perhaps the largest gathering for *Sizdah Bedar* is in Mason Park in Montgomery County, Maryland, where more than 30,000 Iranian Americans will gather. In California, similar events attract large numbers in Los Angeles, San Diego, and San Francisco. Iranian Americans also celebrate U.S. holidays as well, notably the Fourth of July, Thanksgiving, and Christmas.

Iranian immigration, which peaked in the 1980s at 98,000, dropped to 77,000 in the 1990s, then rose to 96,800 between 2000 and 2011.[48] Nearly half of all Iranian immigrants choose California as their state of intended residence. With more than 464,000 Americans now claiming Iranian ancestry, the presence of Iranian Americans is more readily noticed by outsiders. Although found in most major cities, distinct Iranian neighborhoods exist in Queens, New York; Beverly Hills, California; and in the Washington, DC–Arlington, Virginia, area. Classes in Farsi, the primary Iranian language, take place in these enclaves. Also located in these four areas are Islamic centers and mosques, further evidence of the sizable Iranian community.

# Israeli Americans

Immigration from Israel is fairly substantial—more, for example, than that of Ireland and Italy combined between 2000 and 2011. In that period, 63,600 arrived, compared to 18,785 for Ireland and 33,955 for Italy.[49] As mentioned previously, many Israeli nonimmigrants come to the United States as well. In 2011, these included approximately 11,400 students, 18,500 temporary workers and their families, and approximately 318,000 tourists and business travelers.[50]

## PUSH–PULL FACTORS

Among the push–pull factors contributing to Israeli immigration were the political unrest in the Middle East, heightened by the 1973 Yom Kippur War—begun with a coordinated surprise attack by Egypt and Syria—that shattered whatever sense of security many Israelis possessed. In addition, by the late twentieth century, the number of educated and skilled workers far exceeded the available skilled positions, leading to fierce competition in the job market. Compounding the problem was heavy taxation and the lack of available housing. Meanwhile, the close relationship between Israel and the United States had brought extensive exposure to American culture, fads, fashions, and forms of entertainment. This "Americanization" of Israel created a comfort level about living in the United States, particularly because it offered opportunities to achieve one's goals at a level not possible in Israel.[51]

The social structure of Israel served as another motivation for at least one segment of the population to migrate. Sephardic Jews (those of North African and Middle Eastern ancestry) had long been victims of ethnic discrimination by Ashkenazi Jews (those of European origin and the overwhelming majority of Israelis). Resentful of a highly stratified government that favored the majority and one that intervened rather extensively in people's lives, many Sephardic Jews and Israeli Arabs sought economic opportunities elsewhere to escape the socioeconomic discrepancies that arose from discrimination in Israel.[52]

## SETTLEMENT PATTERNS

Chain migration is an important determining factor in where the immigrants choose to live. As one might expect, Israeli Jews often select established Jewish neighborhoods, while Israeli Arabs tend to locate near other Arabs, particularly in and around such Midwestern cities as Chicago and Detroit. Popular residential choices for Israeli Jews are Queens and

Brooklyn in New York City and West Hollywood and the San Fernando Valley in Los Angeles. Together, these two metropolitan areas account for approximately half of all Israeli Jews living in the United States.[53]

Ethnic communities commonly are a re-creation in miniature of the homeland society left behind and Israeli immigrants are no different. Because they are accustomed to the closely-knit community and shared ideological experience of Israel, they compensate for this loss by forming extensive and vibrant communities within the larger American culture, particularly in the New York and Los Angeles areas. Helping Israeli Americans remain connected to Israeli culture and the Hebrew language are Hebrew newspapers, radio and television programs, and such organizations as the Israeli Flying Clubs, the Israeli Musicians Organization, and the Israeli Organization in Los Angeles (ILA).[54]

## ADJUSTMENT AND IDENTITY

Israeli Americans typically experience a smoother transition to American life than other immigrant groups. Their high educational levels and specialized job skills enable them to bypass the often frustrating experiences of less trained immigrants. The support of relatives already living in the United States, as well as a strong organizational support network, further eases the adjustment. Consequently, they usually attain a comfort level of social cohesion and financial security fairly quickly.

Even though they currently reside in the United States, unlike the Arab Israelis who strive to put down roots, some Jewish Israelis intend to remain only long enough to finish their educational or financial goals before returning to Israel, and so they are reluctant to assimilate completely into American culture. This sojourner attitude may be a defensive measure against the open hostility they have suffered from both the Israeli government and American Jews.

Although American Jews have traditionally welcomed Jewish immigrants, the Israeli immigrants represent a failure of the Zionist cause that Americans Jews have generously supported. Israeli Americans are given the derogatory label of *yordim,* which signifies that they have descended from Israel to the diaspora, as opposed to *olim,* those who have ascended from the diaspora to Israel. The

*Similar to other ethnic celebratory festivals, the Israel Independence Day Festival held at Woodley Park in Van Nuys, California, offered bands and singers, the opportunity to sing along, participate in the folk dances, and buy many kinds of food and crafts. All the booths were lined up on "streets" that were given names from those in Tel Aviv.*

negative connotations and sense of betrayal associated with immigration prevent many Israelis from openly declaring themselves permanent citizens of the United States.[55]

Even so, many Jewish Israeli immigrants—60 percent—eventually become naturalized U.S. citizens, particularly through marriage to U.S. citizens. Nevertheless, they hold onto a transnational identity by remaining active in Israeli organizations and continue to identify strongly with Israel. Fueling this dual loyalty is the above-mentioned stigma attached to their immigration, which helps explain why many prefer to refer to themselves as "Israelis" instead of "Israeli Americans."[56]

# Turkish Americans

More than 500,000 Turkish immigrants have come to the United States since 1820. Ordinarily, that number would place Turkey in the top 20 suppliers of emigrants. However, various subjugated peoples of different languages and cultures left the Ottoman Empire with only Turkish passports prior to World War I. More than 300,000 people, three-fourths of the total "Turkish" immigrants, entered the United States during this period (see the Appendix). Although immigration officials identified them as Turkish by their passports, many actually were Armenians, Syrians, Lebanese, or other nationalities. More than 104,000 ethnic Turks have immigrated since 1990, making the current era the period of their largest immigration. In 2011, the number of Americans claiming Turkish ancestry was 199,200.[57]

## FACTORS AGAINST IMMIGRATION

Several factors explain the earlier low level of emigration from Turkey in comparison with other poor, undeveloped nations during the great migration period of 1880–1930. Perhaps foremost, Muslim Turks had waged a relentless campaign against the Christians within their empire and hardly would be inclined to settle in an almost exclusively Christian country. Second, the Turks traditionally had migrated in large groups. Consequently, there was little beyond the country's borders to attract families or individuals. In 1923, Turkey barred any emigrant from ever returning, even as a visitor. This law remained in force until 1950. With laws against emigration, few Turks chose to seek a better life elsewhere. Since 1965, however, an increasing number of Turkish immigrants have migrated to the United States because Turkey has been a friendly ally of the United States for several generations.

## SOCIETAL ATTITUDES

Although relatively few Turks immigrated to the United States before World War I, feelings toward the Turks in the United States were mostly negative, primarily because of the Ottoman Empire's political and religious repression. Perhaps both that hostility and the desire to adopt a Turkish identity may explain the high level of return to Turkey after the end of the Ottoman Empire:

> Between 1890 and 1924, an estimated 25,000 to 50,000 Muslim Turks arrived in the United States....Anecdotal evidence indicates that the creation of a Turkish national identity among the "Turkish" immigrants who remained in the United States paralleled the process being carried out in the new Republic of Turkey after 1923. Given the opportunity to ascribe to a "Turkish" identity, many apparently did so in the Republican, post–Ottoman era. This question of

identity becomes more complex and therefore more intriguing when one considers that perhaps eighty percent of the Turks who arrived in the U.S. before 1924 returned....If this is true, it is one of the highest return rates recorded for any immigrant group. Certainly the high rate can, in large part, be linked to the concept of sojourning—staying to earn enough money for a better life upon return—as well as the inability to deal with the extensive cultural disconnect in the host country.[58]

The Ottoman Empire's efforts to suppress Armenian and Syrian/Lebanese Christians often were brutal. Annihilation of enemies occurred frequently, and Turkish massacres of thousands of Armenians in the 1890s and again in 1915 stirred the wrath of many Americans. To this day, many Americans of Armenian descent mark the anniversary of these Turkish pogroms. American hostility toward the Turks was common during those times, which helps explain the initial hostility Syrian/Lebanese immigrants encountered in the United States when they were misidentified as Turks. In his survey of social distance in 1926, Emory S. Bogardus found that Turks ranked 27th of 30, above only Chinese, Koreans, and Asian Indians. In the 1946, 1956, and 1966 studies, Turks remained near the bottom, whereas Armenians ranked from 5 to 11 positions above them.[59]

## SETTLEMENT PATTERNS

When the Balkan War of 1912 began, many young unmarried Turkish males came to the United States to avoid military service. When war-ravaged Europe achieved peace again in 1919, more than 30,000 returned to Turkey. The few thousand who remained settled primarily in New York, Massachusetts, Michigan, Illinois, and Indiana.

Most Turkish immigrants who came before World War II were illiterate and secured jobs as unskilled laborers. They settled mostly in New York City and Detroit, and kept to themselves. Some gradually became acculturated, while others remained segregated socially within U.S. society. Turkish Americans live now in all 50 states, but the largest concentrations are in Brighton Beach in Brooklyn, Sunnyside in Queens, and in the cities of Paterson and Clifton, New Jersey.[60]

More recent Turkish immigrants are better educated than their predecessors (see the Ethnic Experience box). More than half have a bachelor's degree (nearly twice that of the total population), and one-fourth of Turkish American adults have a graduate degree. Many are professionals or experienced businesspeople who settle in a relatively dispersed pattern. Others are working-class tradesmen and laborers who usually cluster together in urban areas in sufficient numbers to induce the establishment of bilingual programs in neighborhood schools.

> Turkish immigrants with limited skills are often dependent on community-survival strategies for finding work and housing....[They] are mainly lower-class workers in the lowest-paid wage jobs in mostly Turkish-owned businesses, such as restaurants, gas stations, and grocery stores....Such occupational concentrations play an important role in shaping their identities, as the impact of common occupational activity and interpersonal interactions in work spaces can provide a sense of difference. Many...have little or no contact with anyone outside their own ethnic community, for they work and socialize with others from Turkey.[61]

The negative image of Muslims among the U.S. public shapes the Turkish-American sense of identity. As does the government in their homeland, they consider themselves secular and declare their differences from other Muslims. In particular, they emphasize their similarities with Europeans as one means to distance themselves from the unpopular

# the ETHNIC experience

## Overcoming Reluctance by Others

"I know of many immigrants to this land who suffered a lot and enjoyed life less so that their kids could have success stories. My case was quite different as I came to America with my family as a green card winner, with no visa or work permit problems."

"When we came, my older daughter and son started 4th and 2nd grades respectively in a public school. Although my son did mingle with new friends and join their games, my daughter was excluded and she would come home unhappy. We encouraged her to try to make some friends. It did not work and, finally, my wife talked to the teacher about this problem, which helped only a little. But I never blamed those kids; they are just kids."

"As both my wife and I knew some English before we came, language was not a barrier. However, we needed some time to adjust as some people spoke fast. I developed self-confidence as a solution; I never got embarrassed to ask sometimes, 'Could you please speak slowly?' or 'Could you please repeat?'"

"Shortly after I came, I started working as Director of the Interfaith Dialog Center (IDC). Asked to contact neighboring churches, I called around 30 churches and could not get any appointment. I felt so sorry in those days. I learned later that people were suspicious because we were Muslims. Almost a month later, I went and knocked on the door of a minister in Carlstadt, whom I had talked to earlier on the phone. We had a nice conversation, then lunch on another day in a Turkish restaurant, and he next introduced me to many more pastors."

"I met many more people in the following years. They helped IDC with their ideas and feedback, to move IDC forward. IDC now has friends and supporters from all walks of life—clergy, academics, elected officials, law enforcers, etc. IDC and I were received very well by New Jerseyans, whether Christian, Jew, or other faiths. In many ways, my case is a good example of changing attitudes between Turkish Muslims and Americans."

### CRITICAL THINKING QUESTIONS

What combination of factors eased this immigrant's adjustment to American life? What makes his experience typical or atypical compared to other immigrants?

Source: Levent Koç, Turkish immigrant who came to the United States in 2004.

Arab image. Their Turkish language is one defining element of their group identity, which is strengthening through growing community organization, continuing immigration, and festival celebrations.[62]

# Assimilation

**Structural assimilation** among immigrant groups rarely is a first-generation occurrence. Because most people claiming ethnicity from this part of the world are newcomers, sufficient time has not yet elapsed to give us a full perspective on their assimilation. However, studies are emerging to give us some insights into their acculturation as immigrants. First, though, let us consider the assimilation of those who are not foreign born. This would include the descendants of Lebanese, Syrians, and Turks who arrived in the early or mid-twentieth century. For the most part, their multigenerational life in the United States means only vestiges of ethnicity remain, and they are as much a part of the U.S. mainstream as the descendants of European immigrants.

Those recent arrivals of middle-class backgrounds whose education and occupational skills enabled them to settle in upscale urban neighborhoods or suburban communities are part of the economic mainstream, but they often have not yet overcome social barriers

**9-5** Compare and contrast the assimilation paths followed by these immigrants.

**Explore** on **MySocLab** Activity: Middle Eastern Americans in the US: A Snapshot of Settlement in Brooklyn

New York City's Madison Avenue is the site for many ethnic parades in any given year. Each May, the Turkish Day Parade, initiated in the 1980s, brings thousands of Turks to the streets to participate. Immigrants from Turkey and their descendants march down the avenue in colorful costumes and waving flags in a display of their cultural heritage.

to full acceptance. Like the similarly situated Asian Americans discussed in the previous chapter, everyday ethnicity still is a real part of their lives, even though they may be living and working in a larger society. They are living in two worlds—private and public—old and new.

On a related point, researchers studying Arab American adults found that acculturation and satisfaction with life in the United States and with family life were stronger if certain factors were present. These were longer U.S. residence, younger age at immigration, no recent visits to their country of origin, and being Christian. Discrimination experiences influenced reduced satisfaction with life in the United States but not with acculturation in general.[63] Such findings would seem to reinforce assimilationist theory that length of

Enjoying a slice of pizza, these Arab-American youngsters, like most immigrant children, will likely acculturate faster than their parents. With the impact of the media, schools, everyday life, and their ability to learn a new language more easily than adults, they will identify more closely with the land where they grow up than that of their parents' youth.

# REALITY check

## Places and Politics: A Geo-Political Profile

Despite the large concentration of Arab Americans in Dearborn, Michigan, and some other urban areas, they are fairly evenly divided among the four regions of the United States (Figure 9.7). Approximately 27 percent of all Arab Americans live in the Northeast, compared to approximately 24 percent in the Midwest, 26 percent in the South, and 22 percent in the West. Arab Americans in the Northeast are more likely to be U.S.-born, whereas those in the West are more likely to be immigrants. Different Arab subgroups are fairly evenly dispersed, although Saudi Arabians are concentrated in the West, Assyrians in the Midwest, and Syrians in the Northeast.

Israeli Americans primarily are concentrated in large metropolitan areas on the East and West coasts. Many follow Israeli, not American, politics, but those who become naturalized citizens tend to vote for U.S. political candidates of either political party who support Israeli interests.

Numerous Arab Americans have held office at the national level, including U.S. Senators James Abourezk and James Abdnor (both of South Dakota), George Mitchell (Maine), and John Sununu (New Hampshire), who was also governor as well as White House Chief of Staff under President George Bush, Sr. Other governors have been Victor Atiyeh (Oregon), John Baldacci (Maine), and Mitchell Daniels (Indiana). Serving in

the President's Cabinet have been Spencer Abraham (Secretary of Energy and also a U.S. Senator) and Donna Shalala (Secretary of Health and Human Services). Approximately a dozen others have served in the U.S. House of Representatives.

The Arab American Institute, based in Washington, DC, serves as the political arm of the Arab American community. Through voter registration, education, and vote mobilization efforts, it works to secure political empowerment and move Arab Americans into the political mainstream.

Sources: U.S. Census Bureau, *We the People of Arab Ancestry in the United States* (March 2005); Nabeel Abraham and Andrew Shyrock (eds.), *Arab Detroit: From Margin to Mainstream* (Two Rivers, WI: Great Lakes Books, 2000).

residence and cultural affinity are key determinants of adjustment and acceptance (see Reality Check box and Figure 9.7).

Racial identity is an important component of the assimilation process. Many Christian Lebanese and Syrians, who think that "Arab American" does not describe them, are more likely to associate themselves with a white racial identity. Among those who believe the pan-ethnic term "Arab American" does describe them, some assume both strong ethnic and white identities, while others report a strong white identity, yet distance themselves from the pan-ethnic Arab American label.[64] In all instances, however, Arab Americans assimilate to a white identity, whether or not they subscribe to a pan-ethnic identity as well.

## Sociological Analysis

Most Middle Eastern and North African immigrants discussed in this chapter have been arriving since 1965. Because most therefore are first-generation Americans, their experiences lack sufficient historical perspective to permit full analysis. Furthermore (as noted at the beginning of the chapter), because many are educated with marketable occupational skills, not all entirely fit the theoretical framework of past immigrants. How well do the three theoretical perspectives explain their situation? As we will see, each provides a focus that promotes further understanding.

**9-6** Discuss insights gained through sociological analysis.

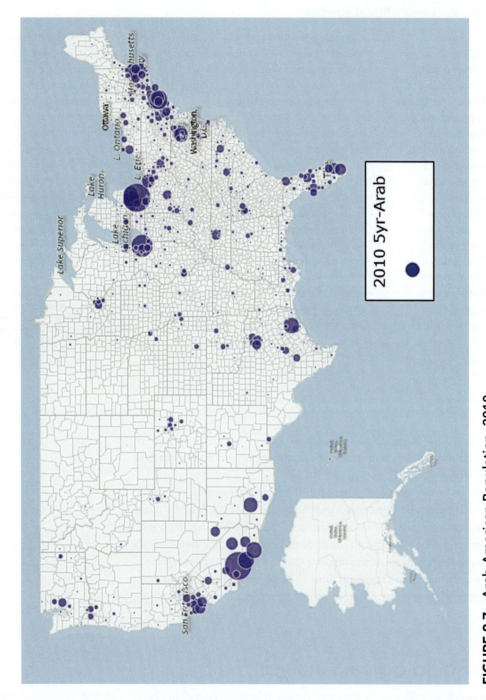

**FIGURE 9.7** *Arab American Population, 2010*

Source: U.S. Census Bureau

## THE FUNCTIONALIST VIEW

How has the social system been able to adapt relatively smoothly in absorbing the new-comers, many of whom are religiously different? Functionalists would point to the immigration laws ensuring either sufficient earning power in occupational preference (higher admission priorities for skilled workers) or a support system in relative preference (higher admission priorities for close relatives). These better educated, better skilled, and/or better connected individuals quickly adjust, contribute to the economy, and seem to integrate into society with a minimum of problems. Most currently rank low on the social distance scale, but they become functionally integrated fairly easily. Their economic power allows them to live in middle-class neighborhoods, accessible through fair-housing laws. Some may even integrate areas, their comparable values and lifestyle making their native-born neighbors more receptive to them as a culturally distinct people.

The less-skilled newcomers help fill a population void in urban and exurban neighborhoods. Although they may encounter some minor problems, these newcomers bring stability to neighborhoods, preventing their decline and helping maintain a racial balance. Urban density gives the immigrants close proximity to one another, enabling ethnic solidarity to develop and be sustained. Living near their work, these newcomers find jobs other U.S. residents are unwilling to take. They also fulfill societal needs. As they struggle to succeed in the United States, they find better opportunities than they had known in their home countries, while society benefits from their work, purchasing power, and cultural contributions.

**STUDENTS SPEAK** *"I found myself agreeing mostly with the functionalist view because it proves the point of how laws have helped immigrants in real terms to make it and survive in the United States. What I like is how there is a fair chance for those immigrants who enter the United States with an education and skills to adjust to the economy effectively and quickly. All immigrants under the law get a chance to work and be accepted."*

**—Joseph Afflerbach**

## THE CONFLICT VIEW

Early non-Western immigrants provide grist for the analytical mill of conflict theorists. Industrialists often used Syrian/Lebanese men as strikebreakers in the Northeast, particularly during the intense labor unrest in the early twentieth century. Because the Syrian/Lebanese offered factory owners a cheaper labor alternative, other workers resented their presence, fearing that the newcomers' growing numbers would jeopardize their own positions. Once again, the split-labor-market theory seems applicable. Economic competition between two wage-level groups generated ethnic antagonism and violence.

More recent arrivals suggest a different analysis. In this case, tensions arise in the United States among those African and Hispanic Americans at the bottom of the socioeconomic ladder, who see foreign-born non-Westerners leapfrogging over them. Resentment builds against the new arrivals whose hiring appears to deny upward mobility to native-born minority groups. Foreigners benefit at the expense of U.S. natives, they think. In addition, the movement of non-Western immigrants into white, middle-class apartment complexes and suburban neighborhoods changes the prior cultural homogeneity, which sometimes stirs hostilities among the old-timers against the newcomers.

Although conflict may be less intense regarding these groups than toward previous waves of immigrants, an undercurrent of tension and resentment may exist, as evidenced by occasional eruptions of public protest, such as the effort to provide bilingual education to a group of Turkish American children in an urban school (an actual incident). Fear of further terrorist attacks and racial profiling add to underlying tensions between the Arab American community and host society.

**STUDENTS SPEAK** *"The striking fact about the experiences of these immigrant populations is the relative ease with which they were able to come to the U.S. and begin lives without facing as much discrimination or marginalization as the predecessors from other parts of the world. It vindicates the conflict theorists' view that the determining factor in the relationship that immigrants have to their host country is relative power. The fact that many of the people coming from this region are educated professionals in their homeland greatly reduces the burden of rapid Americanization."*

**—Andrew Berg**

## THE INTERACTIONIST VIEW

Because visual clues are a major means of categorizing strangers, people with different clothing or physical characteristics get classified as dissimilar types. Is it surprising therefore to learn that the religiously different Muslims score lower on the social distance scale? Consider the case of the Irish in Paterson who attacked the Syrians moving into their neighborhood, supposing them to be Turks or "Mohammedans." Only when a respected religious leader from their own community redefined the situation for the Irish did the fighting stop. In recent years, Arab Americans struggled against U.S. natives who presumed they were all terrorists because of a few extremists. Misinterpretations about an ethnic group often cause problems for the group's members, and the peoples in this chapter are no exception.

Because many recent immigrants join the economic mainstream, their coworkers or neighbors assume that they have integrated socially as well. Interaction may occur in work-related relationships, but socially, the middle-class newcomers tend to become "unknown ethnics," at least in primary relationships. Socially isolated for the most part, they thus interact with compatriots and so remain a generalized entity in the minds of members of the dominant group. This social segregation appears to result more from an attraction toward similarly perceived others than from overt avoidance. Whatever the reason, Middle Eastern and North African Americans mostly are social outcasts in the leisure activities of other U.S. residents. Variety may be the spice of life, but we usually do not apply that principle to racial and ethnic personal relationships.

**STUDENTS SPEAK** *"The interactionist view helped me better understand why many Middle Eastern and North African Americans are socially isolated or segregated. When people view a certain group as different socially, the newcomers tend to gravitate towards a more familiar social life. If more Americans were educated on the differences between people from this region, they would have greater acceptance. The events of 9-11 were a setback for us in eliminating prejudice. Hopefully, people can become less judgmental of others, especially in regard to their appearance or cultural differences."*
**—Diadra Wilson**

## Retrospect

Relatively few members of the racial and ethnic groups discussed in this chapter came to the United States before 1965. The experiences of those who did generally were similar to the experiences of other non-Western peoples in the United States and depended on the then-prevailing policies and regional attitudes.

For the most part, the immigrant experience of people from North Africa and the Middle East is a current societal occurrence. Although identifiable because of physical and cultural differences, they usually experience little difficulty because of their occupational status, their urban locale, and the relaxation of U.S. norms about newcomers. Nevertheless, as strangers they are keenly aware of the society in which they find themselves, and U.S. natives generally tend to avoid interacting with them in meaningful primary relationships. These newcomers are somewhat unusual in that many are able to secure a respectable social status via education, occupation, income, and residence, but because of their cultural differences, they have minimal social participation with native-born U.S. residents. This often is a two-way arrangement.

As larger numbers of immigrants from this part of the world come to the United States, they make their presence felt more and more. One aspect of this impact is in religion. Waves of earlier European immigrants changed the United States from an almost exclusively Protestant country to one of three major faiths. Now this Judeo-Christian population composition is expanding again, as increasing numbers of Muslims arrive.

As the United States becomes more diverse in religion and value orientations, more U.S. residents are becoming aware of the differences in the people around them. Some argue that Americans today are more tolerant because of a resurgence of ethnicity and a more liberal government attitude toward cultural pluralism. Others contend that the past nativist reactions to Asians in the West and to southern and eastern Europeans in the East is finding new form today against the newest immigrants. Riots and violent confrontations may have disappeared, but more subtle and sophisticated acts of discrimination occur, including calls for increased immigration restrictions. Others dispute this claim.

Many of the recent immigrants are better educated and better trained, often speak English before they arrive, and thus enter U.S. society at a higher socioeconomic level than earlier immigrants did. Their ethnic community is more interactional than territorial for the most part, although some groups are more clustered and visible than others. They seem to adjust fairly easily to life in the United States, although ingroup socializing is quite common, as was the case with past immigrant groups. Perhaps we still are a generation away from being able to measure the full impact of their role within U.S. society.

# On MySocLab

Study and Review on MySocLab

## KEY TERMS

Structural assimilation, p. 299            *Gemeinschaft*, p. 291            Invasion–succession, p. 286

## DISCUSSION QUESTIONS

1. The beginning of the chapter offers a sociohistorical perspective. What was one striking or surprising piece of information you picked up here?
2. Why do differences in economic power between non-Western immigrants and earlier immigrants make assimilation less necessary now than before?
3. How have structural conditions in the home countries reshaped ethnic identity and attitudes among Arab immigrants in the United States?

4. Discuss problems of stereotyping and prejudice encountered by non-Westerners because of outgroup perceptions and the media.
5. The end of the chapter offers three theoretical analyses. How did one of these theories become more meaningful or relevant to you in its application to the different groups' experiences?

## INTERNET ACTIVITIES

1. Arab American Stereotypes (http://www.adc.org/index.php?id=283) will tell you about how Disney and other media portray Arabs and the effect this has on Arab American students.
2. Famous Arab Americans (http://www.aaiusa.org/arab-americans/23/famous-arab-americans) gives a list of contributors in many fields. Some of the names may surprise you.
3. The Arab-American Anti-Discrimination Committee (ADC) (http://www.adc.org) is a civil rights

organization committed to defending the rights of people of Arab descent and promoting their rich cultural heritage. ADC, which is nonsectarian and nonpartisan, is the largest Arab American grassroots organization in the United States. It was founded in 1980 by former U.S. Senator James Abourezk. Go to this site, look at its "Press Releases" section, and read some of those items in detail to learn about some current concerns. These could serve as a basis for a discussion topic.

# Black Americans

((•  **Listen** to Chapter 10 on **MySocLab**

*One false belief about African Americans is that most are poorly educated and live in or near poverty. Slightly less than 1 in 4 do fall into that category, but most live working- or middle-class lives. The lifestyle revealed in this photo is far more typical of today's African Americans than is the image of them in substandard and crowded housing.*

## LEARNING OBJECTIVES | After reading this chapter you will be able to:

**10-1** Describe the sociohistorical context for studying Black Americans.

**10-2** Examine how institutionalized racism has affected them.

**10-3** Assess peaceful and violent actions that propelled social change.

**10-4** Explain how interpretations of IQ tests and language usage perpetuate stereotypes.

**10-5** Examine what social indicators tell us about Black progress.

**10-6** Assess disagreements of whether race or class is more important today.

**10-7** Identify distinctions among African and Afro-Caribbean immigrants.

**10-8** Evaluate the integration of Blacks into the societal mainstream.

**10-9** Discuss insights gained through sociological analysis.

Most Africans who arrived in America from 1619 until the end of the slave trade in 1808 immigrated unwillingly, but in recent decades, the voluntary emigration to the United States from Africa has been substantial (Figure 10.1). Between 1899 and 1922, approximately 115,000 African blacks and more than 25,000 Afro-Caribbean blacks arrived. Then the restrictive immigration law of 1924 reduced the number of new immigrants from these groups; Africans, for example, were limited to only 122 newcomers annually. Africa sent more than 955,000 immigrants between 2000 and 2011, and more than 376,000 Afro-Caribbeans arrived in the same time period.[1]

Cultural differences have prevented any unifying racial bond from forming between black immigrants and native-born blacks. The newcomers are strangers in a new land; many native-born blacks—like Native Americans—are strangers in their own land, and both groups are strangers to each other. The new arrivals come from areas where (1) their race is the majority, (2) a tripartite color system prevails, or (3) color is not a primary factor in group life, but they enter a society where color is an important determinant of social and cultural identity. They find that white Americans associate Africans with a partially assimilated and socially restricted native black population that itself does not accept or relate well to them.

In fact, African and Caribbean immigration has raised the issue of who is "African American." Many native-born blacks consider foreign-born blacks as "not one of us" and many of the latter prefer to call themselves "Africans" or by their national origin, such as

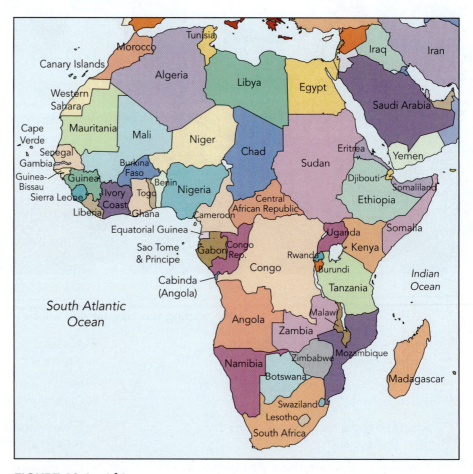

**FIGURE 10.1** Africa

# the MINORITY experience

## What's in a Name?

**Colored:** First used in the fourteenth century, the term became widely used in the United States. Although not considered derogatory, it is now outdated. It lives on in the association name, *National Association for the Advancement of Colored People*.

**Negro:** Reflecting the Latin, Italian, Portuguese, and Spanish words for *black*, this term replaced *colored* as a proper term. Used by Martin Luther King, Jr., in his famous "I have a dream" speech, it fell into disuse in the 1960s as civil rights leaders associated the word with years of slavery, segregation, and discrimination. It

lives on in the organization name, *United Negro College Fund*.

**Black:** A civil rights era replacement word, it became popular to replace the outdated "Negro," partly because it signified a racial bond between Americans of slave and free immigrant ancestry. The word *black*, like that of *white*, may or may not be capitalized, depending on a publication's style guidelines.

**Afro-American:** An alternative civil rights era word, it was favored by those wanting to identify with a cultural heritage, as other ethnic

Americans did. By the 1980s, it had yielded in popularity to the next term.

**African American:** This term, popular for more than 30 years, remains in popular usage. For some, it is an acceptable alternative to *black*. However, given its confusion in distinguishing between those American-born and those African- and Caribbean-born, many American-born individuals prefer *black* and many recent Americans prefer identification with their homeland country (e.g., Haitian, Kenyan, or Jamaican American).

---

Nigerian or Kenyan. As you have already seen in this book, we use the general term "black Americans," but in the following pages, we will make distinctions.

This chapter attempts to place black–white relations in perspective by showing their similarities with and differences from the patterns of dominant–minority interaction of other racial and ethnic groups. Other major themes are the long-lasting impact of cultural conditioning and the changes wrought by the Civil Rights movement.

## Sociohistorical Perspective

During the age of exploration, black crew members served under Columbus and under such sixteenth-century Spanish explorers as Balboa, Cortéz, Pizarro, and de Soto. The first-known group of African immigrants consisted of 20 voluntary immigrants who landed in Jamestown in August 1619, a year before the Pilgrims landed at Plymouth Rock. They came as indentured servants (as did many whites), worked off their debt, and became masters of their own destiny. They were the fortunate few, for the labor demands of the southern colonies soon resulted in the enslavement of millions of other Africans and their forced migration to the United States. Most of today's black Americans are descended from those nearly 500,000 slaves brought here from Africa and the Caribbean.

**STUDENTS SPEAK** "When we discussed whether I like to be called a Black American, African American, or just African, I automatically thought of no other way to describe myself than as African. I am in fact an African because of the way I was raised. The way I see it, if you consider yourself Black American, you can still have African descent, but I'm a second-generation African and I was taught everything about my culture in Sierra Leone, so therefore I really dislike when people refer to me as a Black American or African American, even if it's the 'correct term' to describe my ethnic background."

**—Christine Kebbie**

**10-1** Describe the sociohistorical context for studying Black Americans.

# THE YEARS OF SLAVERY

To ease their transition to a new land, other ethnic groups recreated in miniature the society they left behind, but the Africans who came to the United States were not allowed to do so. Other groups could use education to give themselves and their children a better future, but state laws in the South made educating slaves a criminal offense. Other groups may have encountered some degree of hostility and discrimination, but through hard work and perseverance, many were able to overcome nativist fears and prejudices. For blacks, however, 200 years of master–slave relations did much more than prevent their assimilation; they shaped values and attitudes about the two races that still linger today.

Indeed, some black leaders have lobbied for **slavery reparations**, similar to those given to Japanese Americans in 1988 for their incarceration in the 1940s. Arguing that if President Andrew Johnson had not stripped the freed slaves of the land given them by General William Tecumseh Sherman under Special Field Orders No. 15, their descendants now might control a much larger share of U.S. wealth, proponents seek cash payments to right an old wrong. Opponents insist that, unlike other reparation payments, no victims are alive today, the statute of limitations has long expired, and descendants of slaves are impossible to identify because such descent is not identical with racial self-identification.

As the industrial North and the slaveholding, agrarian South evolved into different societies, they developed different norms. To be sure, the institution of slavery created an inferior status for blacks and led to much prejudice and discrimination. Yet there were free blacks in the South also (nearly half a million by 1860)—people who had been emancipated by their owners, had purchased their freedom, or were descendants of free mothers. They lived in such urban areas as New Orleans, Mobile, and Charleston; in the tidewater regions of Virginia and Maryland; and in the Piedmont region of western North Carolina and Virginia. Those who lived in southern cities worked in a wide variety of skilled and unskilled occupations; some were architects, teachers, store and hotel managers, clerks, and milliners. In the North, although there was some variance, blacks faced considerable discrimination in education, housing, employment, and voting rights. Because in the North no operative caste system delineated norms and interaction patterns, many whites reacted more strongly to blacks in their midst. As a result, northern blacks had considerable difficulty achieving economic security.

## RACISM AND ITS LEGACY

Although some ancient civilizations considered themselves superior to others, they typically did on the basis of culture or special religious status, not race. Most historians agree that racism did not emerge as an ideological phenomenon until the sixteenth and seventeenth centuries.[2] This was the period of European exploration and imperialism, during which Europeans were brought into contact with many physically different, less technologically advanced peoples. The physical characteristics, values, and ways of life of these people differed from their own, so the Europeans naively concluded that there must be some relationship between how the people looked and how they behaved. This was another instance in which prejudices and stereotyping resulted from ethnocentric rationalization.

Myths about the racial inferiority of blacks emerged as a rationalization for slavery. Although slavery was by no means uncommon in earlier societies, ancient civilizations did not link skin color and social status. Statues and paintings from ancient Egypt, for example, depict slaves and rulers alike as both white and black.[3] Speculation about how racism arose includes such factors as (1) the rise of seagoing power among European nations and increased contact with red, brown, black, and yellow peoples; (2) the influence of Christianity, linking slavery and skin color with the Curse of Ham (Noah's second son, cursed by his father in Genesis 9:20–29); and (3) European technological and military superiority over native peoples throughout the world.[4] In the nineteenth century, with racism firmly implanted in U.S. culture, a mangled and scientifically unsound form of evolutionary theory emerged to support racist thinking, as some argued that the white race was more highly evolved than the others.[5]

W. E. B. DuBois interpreted the rise of racism as follows:

> Labor was degraded, humanity was despised, the theory of "race" arose. There came a new doctrine of universal labor: mankind were of two sorts—the superior and the inferior; the inferior toiled for the superior; and the superior were the real men, the inferior half men or less....Luxury and plenty for the few and poverty for the many was looked upon as inevitable in the course of nature. In addition to this, it went without saying that the white people of Europe had a right to live upon the labor and property of the colored peoples of the world.
>
> In order to establish the righteousness of this point of view, science and religion, government and industry, were wheeling into line. The word "Negro" was used for the first time in the world's history to tie color to race and blackness to slavery and degradation. The white race was pictured as "pure" and superior: the black race as dirty, stupid, and inevitably inferior; the yellow race as sharing, in deception and cowardice, much of this color inferiority; while mixture of the races was considered the prime cause of degradation and failure in civilization. Everything great, everything fine, everything really successful in human culture was white.[6]

Once established, the master–slave social system and the theory of racial inferiority supporting it conditioned values, attitudes, and the development of capacities that lasted far beyond the Civil War. Treated as if they were biologically inferior, blacks became socially inferior, first as a result of slavery and then as a result of discrimination in jobs, housing, and education. Unlike the participation in the free community by former slaves of Latin America, U.S. blacks remained trapped in a vicious circle of stereotyping, prejudice, and discrimination.

Although many laws now protect people against discrimination, racist beliefs continue to exist. They can be seen in the reasons people give for moving out of racially changing neighborhoods or in their attitudes toward cities, crime, and welfare. Fear of crime, violence, and other problems of the inner city may be justified, but some individuals incorrectly attribute such troubles to race. Deviance, it must be remembered, occurs among all groups that are poor, powerless, and victims of discrimination. The problem with racism is twofold: its legacy and its subtlety. *Legacy* refers not only to its institutionalization within society but also to its transmission from one generation to the next. Slavery and segregation may end, but some people continue to believe blacks are inferior. This is part of the subtlety of racism because people usually draw such conclusions from their observable world. They are not aware that this "objective" reality is a multigenerational social construct. The alleged inferiority is a myth, except as a social product. People primarily see the effects of prolonged racist attitudes and actions. Even a person's own attitudes, actions, and reactions unwittingly may contribute to the spread of racism.

## Institutionalized Racism

**Institutionalized racism**, which occurs when laws attempt to legitimize differential racial treatment, took a new form after the United States abolished slavery. At first, though, racial equality seemed to have some chance of developing. During the Reconstruction period and close to the end of the nineteenth century, southern blacks generally had greater access to stores, restaurants, public transportation, bars, and theaters than in the first half of the twentieth century. Back then, whites typically lived on one street in large

**10-2** Examine how institutionalized racism has affected them.

## the ETHNIC experience

### How Northerners Differ from Southerners

"I had heard so much talk about New York. People would say things were so good in New York until I felt that if I would get to New York, I would find money on the streets and wouldn't have no more worries. All my problems would be solved. When I got to New York, things were much different than that. Jobs were very hard to find, and the people were very different than in West Virginia."

"Finally, I did get a job through the State Employment Office, working as a cook in the Brooklyn Navy Yard in a private canteen. I stayed there a year and then the war closed up—was over. Then I got another job in a seafood house on 34th Street and 3rd Avenue and I stayed there a year. Then a friend of mine and I went into our own business selling raw

fish. Opened a store in Brooklyn selling raw fish. And, of course, it didn't pan out that way. The problem with that business was that we didn't have enough capital to carry us over the rough spots. And then my wife started having babies, and so I had to give up that job and seek another, which I did, and finally, I got a job right away at another seafood house."

"In the South, we had whites live here, Colored live there, and everybody would speak to you whether they knowed you or not. But when I got to the North, I'd be out on the street, maybe walking around, before I got the jobs, looking around, trying to find my way around, and I would be saying, 'Good morning,' and 'Good evening,' whichever way the situation was, and people would look at me as if

I was some dope or something. People would say, 'What's wrong with him?' People are not as friendly up here."

"And I also found out when we bought a house here, that the whites started right away moving out. They started selling their houses, putting up signs for sale. That didn't bother me any. Only thing was that I was just saying to myself that I thought New York was so great. Why should this be happening? And in the South, where I was living, it didn't happen that way. Blacks and whites lived side-by-side there, and we didn't have no problems with that. That kind of upset me that in New York, after hearing so much about it, this did go on."

Source: Black migrant from West Virginia who came north in 1944 at age 26. Taped interview from the collection of Vincent N. Parrillo.

homes, while behind them on the parallel street were the lesser dwellings of blacks, many of whom worked as domestics. Although a clear status distinction existed, in most places, only limited actual distance divided the two races. Blacks lived in close proximity to whites and frequently interacted with them in secondary relationships through their occupational roles as domestic or service workers. In education, marriage, political participation, and major economic enterprises, however, blacks did not share any commonality with whites (see the Ethnic Experience box).

### IMMIGRATION AND JIM CROW

The change in black–white relations during the late nineteenth and early twentieth centuries is an example of **cultural drift**, a gradual and pervasive change in a people's values. Economic problems, scandals, and frustrations endured by southern whites appear to be some of the factors that reshaped their attitudes. In a region where they had long been considered inferior, many blacks were achieving socioeconomic respectability and becoming economic competitors. Resentment at black upward mobility, amplified by a historical undercurrent of racist attitudes, was increased further by economic troubles (declining cotton prices and unemployment). Blacks became a convenient scapegoat for the frustrations and hostility of southern whites.

When Reconstruction ended in 1876, blacks once again found themselves in a formalized inferior status through segregation laws, voting disfranchisement, **black codes** (state laws designed to keep blacks in subservient positions), job discrimination, and occupational eviction. Not until the 1960s did many of these segregationist practices end in the South.

Less liberal attitudes in the North were another factor that led to an increased incidence of racist acts of discrimination in housing, labor, associations, unions, schools, and churches throughout the United States.[7] What caused this change in the North? The change in racial attitudes occurred just when great numbers of southern and eastern European immigrants were settling in northern urban areas. The arrival of so many dark-eyed, dark-haired, dark-complexioned newcomers set in motion a nativist reaction culminating in restrictive immigration laws. Northerners became more sensitive to the influx of foreigners and "anarchists" as well as to southern blacks coming north to seek work. The overtones of racism in the North's ethnocentric reaction to the "new" immigrants prompted greater empathy among Northern nativists for the South's reaction to blacks. As a result, the North ceased to pressure the South regarding its treatment of blacks and allowed the Jim Crow laws to emerge without a challenge.

In the 1870s and 1880s, Californians succeeded in making the Chinese question a national issue and cleverly related it to that of blacks whenever necessary. Political deals were made; and, later, southern representatives voted overwhelmingly in favor of the Chinese Exclusion Act of 1882 and the 1921 immigration bill restricting southern and eastern Europeans, most of whom were settling in the North.

In 1896, the U.S. Supreme Court ruling on *Plessy v. Ferguson* upheld the principle of "separate but equal" railroad accommodations for blacks and whites. Only a few southern states had had mandatory segregation laws covering train passengers before the turn of the century. Between 1901 and 1910, though, most southern states passed multiple, activity-specific **Jim Crow laws** as part of a rolling snowball effect of such legislation. Segregation became the norm in all areas of life—bars, barbershops, drinking fountains, toilet facilities, ticket windows, waiting rooms, hotels, restaurants, parks, playgrounds, theaters, and auditoriums. Through literacy tests, poll taxes, and other measures, the southern states also succeeded in disfranchising black voters.

## EFFECTS OF JIM CROW

The segregation laws, mostly of early twentieth-century vintage, reflected racist attitudes that remained strong throughout the South decades after slavery had ended. When the 1954 Supreme Court ruling overturned school segregation laws, 17 states had mandatory segregation: Alabama, Arkansas, Delaware, Florida, Georgia, Kentucky, Louisiana, Maryland, Mississippi, Missouri, North Carolina, Oklahoma, South Carolina, Tennessee, Texas, Virginia, and West Virginia. Four other states—Arizona, Kansas, New Mexico, and Wyoming—permitted segregation as a local option.

**THE SOUTH.** It is impossible to exaggerate the impact on society of legalizing such discriminatory norms. These laws existed for two or three generations. During that time, both white and black children grew up in a racially stratified society. Because the white world of reality was one in which differential treatment was the norm, the inferior status of blacks was taken for granted. For most whites growing up in such an environment and, in turn, transmitting values and attitudes to their children, this reflected objective reality.

*Until the 1960s, Jim Crow laws kept society in the South racially segregated, including in Florida, site of this movie theater. All public interaction, such as this rear entrance and separate seating accommodations, were structured by race. These pervasive norms socialized people into accepting a world of institutionalized discrimination as "normal."*

# the ETHNIC experience

## Adjusting to Northern Urban Life

"I came to the North not because of a lack, not being able to cope with economic situations in the South, because I was doing all right economically. I came, more or less, for a change of environment and for a higher income for the work I was doing."

"I was educated in the South and by the time I left, I was not sharecropping any longer. I was teaching and so my standard of living was different from back when I was a child growing up. I had heard many rumors about the North when I was a child. I had heard there was no segregation in the North. You were at liberty to ride buses, use all facilities, no discrimination in jobs. And I found all of this was, more or less, a fairy tale in a lot

of respects. As an adult, I had a more accurate picture of what the North was all about since I had relatives living in Detroit, Washington, and New Jersey."

"I worked at different jobs—office worker, in a nursery school, a dietician—before going to grad school and becoming a public school teacher as I was in the South."

"The biggest adjustment to me going from a rural to an urban setting was getting accustomed to rushing, rushing, rushing city life. To me, the people were always running instead of walking. There was always the hustle-bustle to catch the buses and catch subways and this kind of thing. And this was the hardest thing for me to

get accustomed to, and the rate at which people worked. The people in the North move much, much faster than people in the South."

"I lived in an apartment with my sister four months, got married, and moved to another apartment with my husband. We lived there a year and then moved to the suburbs where we bought our house. Now things here have deteriorated to the extent we have higher unemployment in the North than we do in the South. The overcrowding situation and your housing situation is badly in need of improvement, too."

Source: Black migrant from South Carolina who came north in 1954 at age 22. Taped interview from the collection of Vincent N. Parrillo.

Structural discrimination in the South was pervasive. Despite legal challenges by the National Association for the Advancement of Colored People (NAACP) and by other groups and individuals, most blacks and whites appeared to accept the situation. To whites, the inferior status of blacks in southern society appeared to justify continued differential treatment. It was, as Gunnar Myrdal concluded in his study of U.S. race relations, a perfect example of the vicious-circle phenomenon, in which "discrimination breeds discrimination."[8] Because blacks' education and job opportunities were restricted, the consequences of deprivation and limited opportunity only aggravated the situation. Blacks did not hold lucrative jobs or become educated, often living in squalor amidst poverty, disease, crime, and violence, and so they were not "good enough" to use the same facilities as whites. This gave whites more ammunition to bolster their aversion to blacks and increased their prejudicial attitudes and discriminatory actions. Myrdal called this intensification a **cumulative causation** (vicious circle), in which an almost perpetual sequence of reciprocal stimuli and responses produces complex interactive results.[9]

**THE NORTH.** But what about the North, where few segregationist laws existed? Although there had been some migration to the North earlier, prior to 1914 almost all blacks resided in the South. Then, large numbers of blacks began to migrate to the northern urban areas. Clearly, the Jim Crow laws and poor economic conditions were the major push factors for moving north, and promises of better wages, education, and political freedom were the primary pull factors (see the Ethnic Experience box).

By 1915, the North needed labor. The war was under way in Europe and Northern industry was reaping the benefits from it. The large supply of foreign immigrant labor was rapidly dwindling. In the fourteen years after 1900, over twelve million immigrants found their way to the United States. More than one million immigrants reached the United States in 1914 alone. The next year, this figure was cut to about one third; in 1916, to about one fourth; and, by 1918, only 110,618 new arrivals landed on the shores of the United States, while 94,585 left. Other sources of labor were needed and Southern Negroes appeared as an available and willing substitute....

The larger pay and increased economic opportunities in the North were heady inducements to migrants. But it was not only for economic reasons that the desire to come North existed in so many....The desire of adults to see their children able to obtain an education caused many to move North....According to a *New York Times* editorial (January 21, 1918), higher wages would have been far less attractive if the colored man had not felt, and felt for a long time and bitterly, that in the North and West, he would not, as in his southern home, be reminded of his black skin every time he met a policeman, entered a street car, railway station, or train, and in a hundred other less conspicuous ways in the course of a day.[10]

By 1925, more than 1.5 million blacks lived in the North. As their counterparts on the West Coast had done in response to Asian immigrants, labor unions in the North organized against the blacks. Seeing them either as an undesirable social element or as economic competition, many workers quickly became antagonistic toward them. Although African Americans found greater freedom in the North, the dominant group's animosity toward them led to majority patterns of avoidance and discrimination.

Race riots, basically an urban phenomenon reflecting the growing hostility in the North, swept through a number of cities during World War I. In 1917, in East St. Louis, Illinois, 39 blacks and 8 whites were killed and hundreds seriously injured in one of the worst of these riots. In 1919, the crisis became even more acute, with returning war veterans seeking jobs and more blacks moving north:

That year, there were race riots large and small in twenty-six American cities including thirty-eight killed in a Chicago riot of August, from twenty-five to fifty killed in Phillips County, Arkansas; and six killed in Washington. For a day, the city of Washington, in July, 1919, was actually in the hands of a black mob fighting against the aggression of the whites with hand grenades.[11]

The riots intensified the hostile racial feelings even more. The South had *de jure* **segregation**, but Jim Crow—as a cause of black migration and a model for northern attitudes and actions—played an important role in the development of *de facto* **segregation** in the North. With race the determinant for various life opportunities in both the North and the South, succeeding generations of blacks encountered the same obstacles to upward mobility. So, the effects of Jim Crow on black assimilation into the mainstream of U.S. society went beyond the South and lasted longer than just the first half of the twentieth century.

### THE KU KLUX KLAN

Originally organized in the South during Reconstruction, primarily to intimidate blacks so that they would not exercise their new political rights, the Ku Klux Klan (KKK) reorganized in the twentieth century with a broader range of target groups. In 1915, William J. Simmons resurrected the movement, formalized its rituals and organization, and dedicated it to white supremacy, Protestant Christianity, and "Americanism." A combination of factors—the agricultural depression, Prohibition, immigration, and isolationism—enhanced the Klan's rapid expansion. By 1923, it claimed 3 million enrolled members and operated in virtually every state in the union, with public ceremonies and parades.

*Chanting "white power" as they raise their left hand during an hour-long rally on the steps of the Defiance, Ohio courthouse, these Ku Klux Klan members seek new recruits. The Klan has a long history of opposition to minorities, not just blacks. In the 1920s, when its membership exceeded three million, it objected to Catholic and Jewish immigrants from Europe.*

At first, the Klan concentrated on maintaining white supremacy by intimidating white employers as well as black workers and potential voters. Although this remained an important theme, as the Klan spread northward, its racist orientation broadened into a more general nationalism and nativism. Fears and condemnation of Jews and foreigners, especially Catholics, led the Klan into a campaign of promoting an Anglo-Saxon version of Americanism with evangelical zeal. The hooded Klansmen used mass raids, tarring and feathering, flogging, and other strong-arm tactics to enforce their notions of moral decency or to stabilize the old order. In reality, their actions only fomented additional strife and cruelty.

The Ku Klux Klan thus evolved into a multi-xenophobic organization that saw southern and eastern European Catholics and Jews, as well as blacks, as a threat to the nation's character. The Klan's enormous popularity in the early 1920s reflected the times because these minority peoples were considered an economic threat to more established residents. As prosperity increased and immigration decreased, thereby reducing the tensions, support for the Klan ebbed. Its success, though, like the success of the Native American Party and the Know-Nothing Party of the nineteenth century, indicates that many people were receptive to its philosophy and goals.

The Ku Klux Klan is not just a relic from the past. The Southern Poverty Law Center estimates there are between 5,000 and 8,000 Klan members today.[12] Wherever racial strife occurs, its members still come to sermonize, recruit, and stir up trouble. They have harassed and intimidated blacks in southern California and Vietnamese along the Texas Gulf Coast. When unemployment rises, they seek out the vulnerable white victims, offering a convenient scapegoat for their troubles. In the backwoods of several states, they run paramilitary camps, practicing marksmanship and battle tactics for what they envision as an inevitable race war. Klan members indoctrinate their children at these camps, also, passing on a legacy of hate. Meanwhile, on websites and equal-access local cable channels, they telecast programs promoting their bigotry.

**10-3** Assess peaceful and violent actions that propelled social change.

**Read on MySocLab**
Document: Inspired by Obama

## The Winds of Change

In the past, blacks made many concerted efforts to improve their lot. The Colored National Farmers' Alliance claimed 1,250,000 members in 1891, but it faded from the scene by 1910. In the twentieth century, several black leaders—Booker T. Washington, W. E. B. DuBois, Marcus Garvey, and A. Philip Randolph—tried to rally their people. In the next three decades, the NAACP and other groups filed court cases that achieved only limited success but laid the basis for the 1954 school desegregation ruling, which produced a massive restructuring of black–white relations.

## DESEGREGATION: THE FIRST PHASE

Having experienced life outside their cultural milieu, many blacks who fought in World War II returned home with new perspectives and aspirations. The GI Bill of Rights, the Veterans Authority, and the Federal Housing Authority offered increased opportunity for education, jobs, and housing. Expectations increased, and the growing popularity of television sets brought into more and more homes tangible views of lifestyles that previously could be only vaguely imagined.

Several court cases challenging school segregation laws of Delaware, Kansas, South Carolina, and Virginia reached the U.S. Supreme Court in 1954. After consolidating the several suits, the justices ruled unanimously that the "separate but equal" doctrine was unconstitutional. Social science data, through *amicus curiae* briefs, played an important role in the decision.[13] The following year, the Court established a means of implementing its decree by giving the federal district courts jurisdiction over any problems relating to enforcement of the ruling. The Court insisted that the states move toward compliance with "all deliberate speed," but this guideline was vague enough to allow the states to circumvent the ruling at first.

Although the NAACP quickly began a multipronged challenge to school districts in the 17 states where statutorily mandated school segregation existed, its efforts met with mixed success. Many whites, perceiving their values, beliefs, and practices threatened by outsiders, resisted desegregation. State legislatures passed bills to stave off integration, whites used economic and social pressures to intimidate any blacks who attempted to integrate local schools, and the school districts themselves procrastinated in dealing with the problem. For three years, the battle of wills resulted in a stalemate, continuing the status quo despite the Supreme Court ruling.

On another front, an event occurred in Montgomery, Alabama, in 1955 that foreshadowed other minority actions in the 1960s. Rosa Parks, a tired black seamstress on her way home from work, found the seats in the black section of the bus all occupied and so sat down in an open seat in the section reserved for whites. When she refused the bus driver's demand that she relinquish the seat, she was arrested. Through the organizing efforts of the Rev. Martin Luther King, Jr., the black community staged a successful bus boycott in protest. Four months later, the NAACP argued the case in the federal district court, which ruled against segregated seating on municipal buses and the U.S. Supreme Court upheld the decision.

The confrontation in the fall of 1957 at Little Rock Central High School in Arkansas was a watershed event in desegregation. Here, the state's defiance of the Supreme Court could not be ignored because the governor called out the National Guard to forcibly block implementation of a federal court order to integrate the high school. President Eisenhower, who personally had opposed the 1954 ruling, acted decisively by federalizing the National Guard and sending regular army troops to Little Rock to ensure compliance.

With all legal avenues of appeal exhausted and the federal government insisting that all citizens, including black children, be accorded equal rights, southern resistance ebbed. Desegregation in the public schools, although sometimes slight in effect because of neighborhood-based districting plans, became the norm throughout the southern states. That is not to say that everything was harmonious. Some whites established private academies to avoid sending their children to integrated schools, and some southern leaders publicly committed themselves to upholding southern tradition at all costs. Still, Jim Crow had been dealt a severe blow, and opponents readied themselves for the next assault.

## DESEGREGATION: THE SECOND PHASE

In the 1960s, the Civil Rights movement gained momentum, attracted many followers, and moved against the remaining Jim Crow legislation. Sit-in demonstrations began in Greensboro, North Carolina, on February 1, 1960, when four freshmen from the all-black Agricultural and Technical College sat at the all-white lunch counter at the local Woolworth's store and refused to leave. During the spring of 1960, similar sit-ins occurred throughout the South. From the sit-ins evolved a fourth social organization—the Student Nonviolent Coordinating Committee (SNCC)—to compete with the NAACP, the Congress on Racial Equality (CORE), and the Southern Christian Leadership Conference (SCLC), which Dr. King had formed after the bus boycott.

The success of the sit-ins convinced many people that direct action was a quicker and more effective means of achieving total desegregation than protracted court battles. James Farmer of CORE organized Freedom Rides from Washington, DC, to selected southern locations in 1961 to challenge the segregated facilities in bus terminals. These were followed by freedom marches, voter registration drives, and continued litigation challenging the constitutionality of Jim Crow legislation.

All of these movements were symptomatic of the times. John Kennedy's election as president in 1960 and his speaking of "a new generation of leadership" had inaugurated a period of high hopes and ideals. It was a time of political commitment and societal change, of VISTA and the Peace Corps, of promise and reachable goals. As the Civil Rights movement grew, "We Shall Overcome" became the rallying theme song, and Bob Dylan's "Blowin' in the Wind" captured the spirit of the times.

Civil rights activity met with fierce resistance. Dr. King urged nonviolence, but younger black activists grew impatient with such an approach:

> The aim was "to awaken a sense of moral shame in the opponent." Such a philosophy presumed that the opponent had moral shame to awaken, and that moral shame, if awakened, would suffice. During the 1960s, many civil rights activists came to doubt the first and deny the second. The reasons for this did not lie primarily in white Southern terrorism as manifested in the killing of NAACP leader Medgar Evers, of three civil rights workers in Neshoba, Mississippi, of four little girls in a dynamited church in Birmingham, and many others. To a large extent, white Southern violence was anticipated and expected. What was not expected was the absence of strong protective action by the federal government.
>
> Activists in SNCC and CORE met with greater and more violent Southern resistance as direct action continued during the sixties. Freedom Riders were beaten by mobs in Montgomery; demonstrators were hosed, clubbed, and cattle-prodded in Birmingham and Selma. Throughout the South, civil rights workers, Black and White, were victimized by local officials as well as by nightriders and angry crowds. It was not surprising, then, that student activists in the South became increasingly disillusioned with nonviolent tactics of resistance.[14]

Two events in 1963—the March on Washington and the integration of the University of Alabama—gave Dr. King and President Kennedy the opportunity to express the mood of the times. On August 28, 1963, tens of thousands of marchers of all races from all over the country and from many walks of life gathered before the Lincoln Memorial. There Dr. King gave his famous "I have a dream" speech, in which he proclaimed that blacks could never be satisfied until they achieved full equality and justice. However, he continued, he had a dream that one day his four children would experience that reality, that they would be judged by others on their character, not by their skin color.

On April 4, 1968, an assassin's bullet prevented Dr. Martin Luther King, Jr., from seeing his dream become reality. President Kennedy had been assassinated four and a half

*Over 200,000 people jammed the area in front of the Lincoln Memorial and on either side of the Reflecting Pool all the way to the Washington Monument. The 1963 March on Washington ended with Martin Luther King's "I Have a Dream" speech, which effectively gave a vision about the goals sought by the Civil Rights movement.*

years earlier, on November 22, 1963, before Congress could pass the civil rights legislation he had proposed after sending troops to enforce the integration of the University of Alabama that same year. In explaining that action, President Kennedy had told the public in a television address:

> This nation was founded by men of many nations and backgrounds. It was founded on the principle that all men are created equal, and that the rights of every man are diminished when the rights of one man are threatened....
>
> It ought to be possible, therefore, for American students of any color to attend any public institution they select without having to be backed up by troops. It ought to be possible for American consumers of any color to receive equal service in places of public accommodation, such as hotels and restaurants, and theaters and retail stores without being forced to resort to demonstrations in the street.
>
> And it ought to be possible for American citizens of any color to register and to vote in a free election without interference or fear of reprisal.
>
> It ought to be possible, in short, for every American to enjoy the privileges of being American without regard to his race or his color.
>
> In short, every American ought to have the right to be treated as he would wish to be treated, as one would wish his children to be treated. But this is not the case....
>
> One hundred years of delay have passed since President Lincoln freed the slaves, yet their heirs, their grandsons, are not fully free. They are not yet freed from the bonds of injustice; they are not yet freed from social and economic oppression.
>
> And this nation, for all its hopes and all its boasts, will not be fully free until all its citizens are free.[15]

The Civil Rights Act of 1964 was the most far-reaching legislation against racial discrimination ever passed. It mandated that equal standards be enforced for voter eligibility in federal elections. It prohibited racial discrimination and refusal of service on racial grounds in all places of public accommodation, including eating and lodging establishments and places of entertainment, recreation, and service. It gave the attorney general broad powers to intervene in private suits regarding violation of civil rights. It banned racial discrimination by employers and unions and by any recipient of federal funds, and it directed federal agencies to monitor businesses and organizations for compliance and to withhold funds from any noncomplying state or local agency.

Congress passed additional legislation in 1965 to simplify judicial enforcement of the voting laws and to extend them to state and local elections. In 1968, further civil rights legislation barred discrimination in housing and gave Native Americans greater rights in their dealings with courts and government agencies at all levels. Congress also set stiff federal penalties for persons convicted of attempting or conspiring to intimidate or injure anyone who was exercising any of the civil rights provided by congressional action.

In 1966, Stokely Carmichael, the head of the Student Nonviolent Coordinating Committee (SNCC), advanced the slogan "Black Power"—a declaration that civil rights goals could be achieved only through concerted black efforts. It symbolized the attainment of what Kurt Lewin called a "sense of peoplehood" and what Franklin Giddings identified as a "consciousness of kind." The word *black* rather than *Negro* became the accepted way of referring to this racial group in the 1970s. Unfortunately, Carmichael also was a major force in the purge of whites from the SNCC leadership—an isolationist act that alienated many white sympathizers to SNCC's cause.

Nearly five decades later, we can readily see the gains in black power in the political arena, most especially with the election of Barack Obama as President. The number of black elected officials increased dramatically, from approximately 170 in 1964 to more than 10,500 today, approximately two-thirds of these in the southern states.[16] Blacks also improved their rate of participation in other areas, including voter registration. Perhaps "stateways" are changing "folkways," because legislation has opened doors to blacks, thereby providing long-term opportunities for the social conditioning of people's attitudes toward racial harmony.

# Urban Unrest

As the Civil Rights movement gained momentum, it spread northward as well. Protests against discrimination in employment and housing and against *de facto* segregation in northern schools began in the early 1960s, in New York City and Philadelphia, and quickly spread.

As blacks experienced some gains and some frustrations, a pattern of increased alienation, cynicism, hostility, and violence ensued. When a social movement achieves some goals, its expectations are increased and so are its frustrations, which often leads to greater militancy.[17] Militant leaders such as Malcolm X, Eldridge Cleaver, Huey Newton, and Bobby Seale emerged to speak of the grievances of northern blacks. New organizations, such as the Black Panthers, and older ones, such as the Black Muslims, attracted many followers as they set out to meet the needs of northern blacks in the ghettos.

## THE 1960s RIOTS

In the summer of 1964, blacks rioted in the tenement sections of Harlem, Rochester, and Philadelphia, attacking both police and property. The following summer, the violence and destruction were more massive; outbursts occurred first in the Watts section of Los Angeles and then in Chicago; Springfield, Massachusetts; and Philadelphia. Ghetto violence continued. In the summer of 1966, 18 different riots occurred, and in the summer of 1967, 31 cities experienced riots, of which those in Newark (26 killed) and Detroit (42 killed) were the worst.

The increase in the number and intensity of riots in 1967 prompted an in-depth study of 75 of the disorders, including those in Newark and Detroit, by the National Advisory Commission on Civil Disorders. It concluded that, although specific grievances varied somewhat from city to city, consistent patterns existed in who the rioters were, how the riots originated, and what the rioters wanted. The most intense causal factors were police practices, unemployment and underemployment, and inadequate housing. In its 1968 report, the Commission warned that the United States was "moving toward two societies, one black, one white—separate and unequal."[18]

Dr. King's assassination in 1968 prompted violence to erupt anew in 125 cities. The Department of Justice reported 46 people killed in one week of unrest. Several years of civil rights legislation now set changes in motion. Government action at all levels sought to correct the conditions that encouraged the violence, and U.S. cities experienced no further major disturbances for several years.

Several factors contributed to the cooling of black urban violence. First, a new social movement protesting the war in Vietnam, to which many black youths were sent, became a focus of public concern. Second, many black leaders were assassinated (King, Evers, and Malcolm X) or imprisoned (Carmichael, Newton, and Seale) or went into exile (Cleaver). Third, many blacks redirected their energies toward community self-help programs, some leaders were co-opted into leadership roles within the system, and other blacks began to strive for the black power goal Carmichael had enunciated. Perhaps, also, the realization that the destruction of their neighborhoods had left a trail of economic devastation without producing any tangible benefits helped stop the rioting.

### THE 1980s MIAMI RIOTS

In Miami in May 1980, black economic frustrations and resentment against the growing Cuban community—sparked by an all-white jury's acquittal of four white police officers accused of bludgeoning a black man to death—set off three days of the worst outbreak of racial violence in 13 years. When it ended, 18 were dead, more than 400 were injured, and property damages exceeded $200 million.[19] In January 1989, violence erupted in Miami again, in the Overtown section, after a policeman shot and killed a black motorcycle rider.

### THE 1992 LOS ANGELES RIOT

Five days of rioting erupted in Los Angeles in 1992, after a jury acquitted four white city police officers of criminal wrongdoing in the videotaped beating of black motorist Rodney King. In the aftermath of the prolonged riot, officials reported 58 deaths, 4,000 injuries, 11,900 arrests, and damage ranging as high as $1 billion.[20] The events seemed like a flashback to the 1960s, and some observers predicted a new wave of rioting across the United States in response to a decade of retreat by the federal government from its earlier role as a champion of the disadvantaged. But U.S. society had changed. Most of the nation's 30 million African Americans did not take to the streets. Those who did were part of a relatively small urban underclass clearly distinct from the 40 percent of all African American families now middle class or upwardly mobile working class. Moreover, whereas the 1965 Watts riot was black versus white, the 1992 riot was *multiracial* warfare: blacks preying on other blacks, Latinos on whites, blacks and Latinos on Koreans and other Asian Americans.[21] The Rodney King verdict was the spark that detonated a powder keg built of the pathologies resulting from poverty—squalid living conditions, frustration, alienation, anger, and family disintegration.

Chapter 8 discussed some aspects of the black–Korean conflict. Part of that animosity stemmed from the growing presence and economic success of Korean merchants in black neighborhoods where poverty and unemployment were widespread. Limited education was not a barrier to self-employment for Korean Americans because of their informal

*On the second day of the 1992 Los Angeles riot, one of the worst in U.S. modern history, arsonists set this Korean shopping mall ablaze. Initially triggered by reaction to the not guilty verdict of four white police officers videotaped beating a black man, the riot expanded to involve Asians, blacks, Hispanics, and whites, either as rioters or victims.*

networks of assistance and advice. Poorly educated African Americans, however, lacked similar support networks and were less likely to become entrepreneurs in the central city.[22] As these blacks witness the economic gains of strangers in their midst while they themselves are mired in deprivation, their resentment sometimes reaches the flashpoint of violence when triggered by even a seemingly insignificant incident.

How can the United States prevent such violence? The primary answer lies in taking steps to meet minority expectations and to eliminate the economic despair that fuels riots. We must focus on overcoming depressed urban economies, chronic unemployment, a poorly skilled and poorly educated labor force, substandard housing, and unsafe streets.

Reducing the social distance among urban residents through community interaction offers another promising approach. When "we" replaces "us versus them," violence becomes less likely. Still another approach is to increase the number of African American entrepreneurs in the central city. African American proprietors would act as positive role models and could provide initial employment opportunities to urban African American youths. Local mom-and-pop stores could become bonding anchors in the neighborhood, reinforcing community life around work and thereby helping generate and sustain informal associations.[23]

## The Bell Curve Debate

In 1994, a book called *The Bell Curve*, by Richard Herrnstein and Charles Murray, set off a firestorm of controversy.[24] Rejecting conventional theories about the role of environment and culture in creating dependence and crime, the authors argued that intelligence is the best single explanation of wealth, poverty, and social status. They asserted that the United States was becoming increasingly stratified by intellectual ability—with a "cognitive elite" of brilliant, highly educated business leaders, politicians, and professionals; a large cognitive middle class of approximately 125 million with IQs measuring between 91 and 110; and a growing underclass of dullards with IQs of 90 or below.

The authors also contended that social pathologies such as poverty, welfare dependence, illegitimacy, and crime were all strongly related to low IQ. Most explosive was their argument that blacks as a group were intellectually inferior to whites as a group because the mean, or average, IQ score for blacks was 15 points lower than that for whites. Herrnstein and Murray then attacked affirmative action in college admissions and in the workplace, characterizing it as a futile policy designed to help the cognitively disadvantaged. Not-so-smart people, they implied, can never become middle class.

Another volatile theme of the book was the proposition that the cognitive elite pass on their genetic advantages to their children, while members of the low-IQ underclass pass on genetic disadvantages. Herrnstein and Murray, noting the higher birth rate among the underclass, argued that government subsidies to welfare mothers were responsible for a gradual decline in the national IQ. Therefore, they argued, such programs should be terminated.

Critics attacked the book for its selective use of data to fit its political arguments, such as ignoring the difference between actual intelligence and IQ as measured by tests. Others found factual contradictions, such as the claim that the national IQ had declined when actually group scores had been rising slowly but steadily since the 1930s. Still others attacked the book's scholarship, methodology, and analytical techniques.[25]

## EARLY IQ TESTS

Although Herrnstein and Murray offered some new wrinkles, their argument was an old, discredited one. The intelligence test, first developed by Alfred Binet in 1905, became a popular means of comparing the intelligence of different racial and ethnic groups, although that was not Binet's intention. This supposedly objective, scientific instrument was intended to measure an individual's innate intelligence, uninfluenced by any beneficial or detrimental effects of environment. As misappropriated and applied to groups of people, however, the test invited researchers to compare groups' intellectual ability. Early studies showed that northern and western Europeans—and often the Chinese and Japanese—scored consistently and decidedly higher than southern and eastern Europeans, blacks, Mexicans, and Native Americans.[26] Nativists and segregationists seized on these studies as arguments for immigration restrictions against "inferiors," for the forced assimilation of Native Americans, and for Jim Crow laws in the South.

Gradually, as nativist antipathy against the "new" immigrants abated, the argument shifted primarily to intelligence differences between blacks and whites. The disparity in the test results, which most authorities believe actually reflects a cultural bias within the tests, became a basis for claiming white intellectual superiority.

An earlier book, *The Testing of Negro Intelligence* (1958), similarly caused a furor. Its author, Audrey Shuey, surveyed some 240 studies of 60 different intelligence tests that had been given throughout a 44-year span to hundreds of thousands of servicemen from World Wars I and II and thousands of schoolchildren of all ages through college, from all regions of the country. She concluded that the "remarkable consistenc[ies] in test results…all point to the presence of some native differences" between blacks and whites "as determined by intelligence tests."[27]

For any scientist, the interpretation of findings is as crucial as the findings themselves and the methods employed to obtain them. Shuey was accurate in observing the consistent lower scoring of blacks on intelligence tests. However, many scientists disagreed with her conclusion that this was due to racial intellectual inferiority. The conclusion of innate or genetic differences was a quantum leap from her findings, which did not prove any such thing.

In the late 1960s, the IQ controversy centered on claims made by two California professors: Arthur R. Jensen, an educational psychologist at the University of California (Berkeley), and William B. Shockley, a Nobel Prize–winning physicist at Stanford University. Jensen argued that the 10- to 20-point IQ differential between blacks and whites involved only certain mental functions. He pointed out that blacks and whites tested equally well in such brain functions as rote learning and memory but that blacks did more poorly in problem solving, in seeing relationships, and in abstract reasoning. Because this material does not depend on specific cultural information, he maintained, the blacks' lower scores must be due to their genetic heritage.[28] Shockley declared that the conceptual intelligence of blacks, as measured by many different IQ tests, was significantly lower than that of whites and that some of this variance was genetically caused and therefore not correctable.

## IQ TEST PERFORMANCE BY OTHER GROUPS

**10-4** Explain how interpretations of IQ tests and language usage perpetuate stereotypes.

Refuting this position, Thomas Sowell argued that, on average, white ethnic groups, such as the Poles, Jews, and Italians, scored in the 80s on IQ tests administered during the 1920s but as a group had gained 20 to 25 points by the 1970s after experiencing upward mobility.[29] Groups of European ancestry who have not experienced upward mobility, as well as Mexican Americans and Puerto Ricans, continued to score in the 80s on IQ tests. Most significantly, at various times and places, other low-IQ groups also have done poorly on the abstract portions of mental tests. Studies of immigrant groups in 1917, of white children in isolated mountain communities, of working-class children in England, and of early Chinese immigrants all show marked deficiencies on the abstract sections. Concerning the Chinese Americans, recent studies show them to be strongest on the abstract portions of the mental tests, suggesting that upward mobility helps to improve powers of abstract reasoning. Other patterns—children's IQ scores declining as they become adults and females consistently scoring higher than males—also are frequent among low-IQ groups, not only blacks. Again, these results change once the group achieves a higher socioeconomic status.

Another problem with IQ tests is that they measure only some forms of intelligence—analytical, conceptual, and verbal (see Table 10.1). We still are learning how and why the brain functions as it does. Until we know more, any assumption of intellectual superiority or inferiority based on IQ scores is conjectural. Moreover, the only demonstrated value IQ scores have is in predicting how well students will do in a traditional school setting. They do not predict performance in nontraditional approaches to education or in any job situation. Does a professor with a 135 IQ teach better than one with 120? Not necessarily, and that is another reason IQ scores should not be a factor in questions of social interaction.

**TABLE 10.1   Black Intelligence Test of Cultural Homogeneity**

The purpose of this tongue-in-cheek "test" was to demonstrate the subcultural language or understandings of a group and also the unfairness of culture-loaded IQ tests on low-income people. Many of you will probably do badly on these questions, regardless of your ability, if the questions are alien to your cultural background, and that is the point of demonstrating cultural bias in tests.

1. Alley Apple is a (a) brick, (b) piece of fruit, (c) dog, (d) horse.
2. CPT means a standard of (a) time, (b) tune, (c) tale, (d) twist.
3. Deuce-and-a-Quarter is (a) money, (b) a car, (c) a house, (d) dice.
4. The eagle flies means (a) the blahs, (b) a movie, (c) payday, (d) deficit.
5. Gospel Bird is a (a) pheasant, (b) chicken, (c) goose, (d) duck.
6. "I know you, shame" means (a) You don't hear very well. (b) You are a racist. (c) You don't mean what you're saying. (d) You are guilty.
7. Main Squeeze means (a) to prepare for battle, (b) a favorite toy, (c) a best girlfriend, (d) to hold up someone.
8. Nose Opened means (a) flirting, (b) teed off, (c) deeply in love, (d) very angry.
9. Playing the dozens means (a) playing the numbers, (b) playing baseball, (c) insulting a person's parents, (d) playing with women.
10. Shucking means (a) talking, (b) thinking, (c) train of thought, (d) wasting time.
11. Stone fox means (a) bitchy, (b) pretty, (c) sly, (d) uncanny.
12. T. C. B. means (a) that's cool baby, (b) taking care of business, (c) they couldn't breathe, (d) took careful behavior.

Answers 1-a, 2-a, 3-b, 4-c, 5-b, 6-d, 7-c, 8-c, 9-c, 10-d, 11-b, 12-b.

*Source:* Robert L. Williams, Ph.D.

# Language as Prejudice

Words are symbols connoting meanings about various phenomena in the world around us. That the very words used to describe the two races—*white* and *black*—usually convey positive and negative meanings, respectively, is unfortunate. For example, *white* often symbolizes cleanliness, purity, or heroes (clothes, armor, hats, and horses), and *black* often stands for dirt, evil, or villains. A snow-covered landscape is beautiful, but a sky laden with black smoke is not. Black clouds are seen as threatening, but white clouds are not.

The power of words is such that the pervasiveness of positive and negative meanings for these two words easily can influence minds and attitudes. Ossie Davis had such concerns in mind when he said,

A superficial examination of Roget's *Thesaurus of the English Language* reveals the following facts: the word "whiteness" has 134 synonyms, 44 of which are favorable and pleasing to contemplate. For example: "purity," "cleanness," "immaculateness," "bright," "shiny," "ivory," "fair," "blonde," "stainless," "clean," "clear," "chaste," "unblemished," "unsullied," "innocent," "honorable," "upright," "just," "straight-forward," "genuine," "trustworthy," and only 10 synonyms of which I feel to have been negative and then only in the mildest sense, such as "gloss-over," "whitewash," "gray," "wan," "pale," "ashen," etc.

The word "blackness" has 120 synonyms, 60 of which are distinctly unfavorable, and none of them even mildly positive. Among the offending 60 were such words as "blot," "blotch," "smut," "smudge," "sullied," "begrime," "soot," "becloud," "obscure," "dingy," "murky," "low-toned," "threatening," "frowning," "foreboding," "forbidding," "deadly," "unclean," "dirty," "unwashed," "foul," etc. In addition, and this is what really hurts, 20 of these words—and I exclude the villainous 60 above—are related directly to race, such as "Negro," "Negress," "nigger," "darkey," "blackamoor," etc.

If you consider the fact that thinking itself is subvocal speech (in other words, one must use words in order to think at all), you will appreciate the enormous trap of racial prejudgment that works on any child who is born into the English language.[30]

When *black* has so many negative connotations—blackening the reputation, being black-hearted, blacklisting or blackballing someone, using black magic, running a black market, and so on—it is easy to see how language by itself can precondition a white person's mind against black people and can lead a black person's mind into possible self-hatred.

**Ebonics**, sometimes called *Black English* or *African American Vernacular English*, survives as a cultural vestige of the West African origins of many black American slaves. It is not slang, as some say, but a systematic language dialect in terms of its grammar, pronunciation, and vocabulary. Ebonics today continues in the speech patterns of low-income or rural blacks, and in rap music.[31]

## Social Indicators of Black Progress

As Figure 10.2 shows, a larger percentage of blacks than the total population are young. This demographic fact suggests both a more rapid future population growth for blacks and the importance of the socioeconomic environment in which young people grow up. The more enriched their childhood socialization, the greater their adult life opportunities. The more deprived their environment, the more limited their adult life opportunities.

Where are we today? Without question, the election of President Barack Obama was a defining moment in U.S. race relations (see the Reality Check box).

**10-5** Examine what social indicators tell us about Black progress.

**Explore on MySocLab**
Activity: Going the (Social) Distance: Blacks and Whites Together and Apart

**Explore on MySocLab**
Activity: Migration Patterns around Atlanta, Georgia

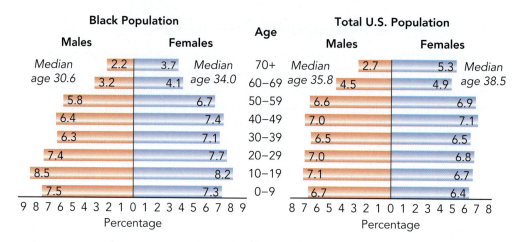

**FIGURE 10.2** Black Population, 2010 (in percentages)

*Source:* U.S. Census Bureau.

# REALITY check

### Does the Twofold Election of President Obama Mean Race Relations Are Better?

In one word, "yes," although there is a "but." Certainly, the election of a person of color to the presidency was historically significant and a major step forward in race relations. Moreover, a higher percentage of whites voted for Obama than for John Kerry, the white Democratic candidate in 2004. Obama even did better than Kerry in nearly every possible demographic: race, religion, gender, and income level. Despite the consistency of that across-the-board strong performance, in the 2012 election, he only garnered about 40 percent of the white vote.

It is likely that, in addition to differing political beliefs and/or disillusionment because of the economy, some people did not support Obama because of his race. He significantly outperformed challenger Mitt Romney among women (55 percent), African Americans (93 percent), Asians (73 percent), and Latinos (71 percent). Obama also did well among religious voters of non-Christian religions, including Muslims, Buddhists, Hindus, Jews, and pagans (74 percent). The

vote was evenly split among Catholics, but Protestants favored Romney (57 percent). The majority of those over age 40 favored him as well, while those 39 and under preferred Obama. Nevertheless, in addition to differing political beliefs, some people did not support Obama because of his race. The United States—a multicultural, multiracial society—coalesced sufficiently around a multicultural, biracial candidate to give him a 4.7 million vote margin of victory in 2012.

Yet, it would be a mistake to conclude that Barack Obama's victory has lessened the scope of the problem, for it by no means ended racism. Today, many African Americans still lack economic opportunities; many black communities are without basic services and amenities like parks and police protection that most middle-class Americans take for granted; racial profiling still exists; and unfairly harsh penalties for first-time nonviolent offenders are meted out to minorities.

Obama always has defined himself as a president who happens to be

black, deliberately playing down race as a factor. Racism nonetheless finds expression in reference to President Obama, such as the poster of him dressed as an African witch doctor above the slogan "Obamacare: Coming Soon to a Clinic Near You." It also is the underpinning of conspiracy theories questioning his place of birth and presidential eligibility.

Others are upset about the thought of a "black" man (and family) in the White House. The Southern Poverty Law Center reports an increase in memberships in hate groups and militias, partly driven by anger toward the federal government (which they see as the enemy) headed by a black man. Since 2008, the Internet has been filled with hundreds of anti-Obama racist websites (cartoons, jokes, pictures, and commentary), although many of the offending images have since been removed due to public protest.

We may have come a long way in recent generations, but the journey to interracial harmony is far from over.

Commonly viewed as an African American even though he is biracial, for that reason his presence in the White House has been a source of hope and inspiration to many, no matter what their race. As significant as that achievement is, what about the rest of black America?

How far has the United States gone toward true equality for blacks and whites? Sociologists use quantifiable measurements of social indicators to identify specifically a group's achievements in comparison with others, as well as its mobility within the stratification system. Three of the most common variables—education, income, and occupation—offer an objective portrait of what gains have been made and of how much the gap between the two races has narrowed.

## EDUCATION

An increasingly greater proportion of the population stays in school longer, and so the percentage gap between blacks and whites completing four years of high school or beyond has steadily lessened for both males and females. At one time, the achievement gap between black and white elementary students was widest in Southern states, where the legacies of slavery and segregation were reflected in low mathematics and reading scores. However, black students have made important gains in that region in the past two decades, so the widest gaps no longer are there. That dubious distinction now occurs in Wisconsin, Nebraska, Connecticut, and Illinois, where black student scores are lower than in Alabama and Mississippi.[32]

At the college level, more blacks than ever before are completing four years of college or more, but proportionately, the gap between black attainment compared to white attainment has widened a bit (see Figure 10.3). Improvement in high school completion also manifests itself in the changed dropout rates. From a dropout rate twice that of white students in 1970, the black student dropout rate fell considerably and now the rates are extremely close to one another (see Table 10.2). These statistics offer a hopeful sign for the next generation's socioeconomic progress but also suggest the need for further improvement.

Another barometer is comparative test scores. The College Entrance Examination Board, which administers the Scholastic Assessment Test (SAT), reported in 2012 that

*One reason for the growing black middle class is the growing proportion of young adults getting a college education and becoming qualified for better-paying jobs. However, a significant gap remains between black and white educational attainment, and not as many black males are enrolled in college degree programs as are black females.*

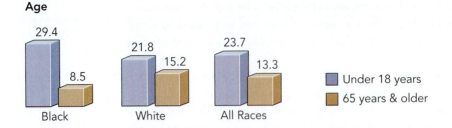

**Age**

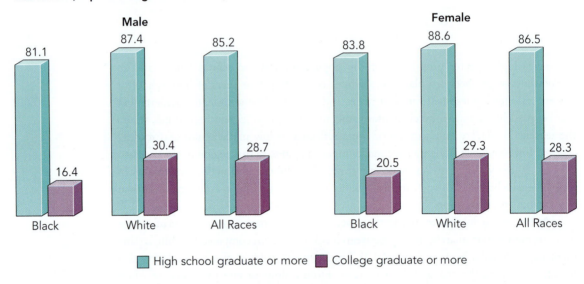

**Education (of persons age 25 and over)**

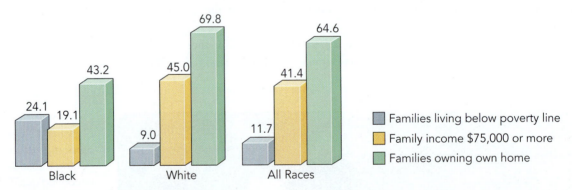

**Economic Status**

**FIGURE 10.3** Social Indicators about Black Americans (in percentages)

*Source:* U.S. Census.

a significant difference in scores still remains: 527 to 428 in critical reading mean scores, 515 to 417 in writing scores, and 536 to 428 in mathematics scores for whites and blacks, respectively.[33]

## INCOME

Historically, black family income always has been significantly lower than white family income. Civil rights legislation and the War on Poverty began to create a slow, steady improvement until the 1980s, when economic problems and a reduction in federal support

**TABLE 10.2** High School Dropouts, Ages 16–24, by Race and Gender (in percentages)

|  | 1970 | 1980 | 1990 | 2000 | 2011 |
|---|---|---|---|---|---|
| *Blacks* | 27.9 | 19.1 | 13.2 | 13.1 | 7.3 |
| Black females | 26.6 | 17.7 | 14.4 | 11.1 | 6.4 |
| Black males | 29.4 | 20.8 | 11.9 | 15.3 | 8.3 |
| *Whites* | 13.2 | 11.4 | 9.0 | 6.9 | 5.0 |
| White females | 14.1 | 10.5 | 8.7 | 6.9 | 4.6 |
| White males | 12.2 | 12.3 | 9.3 | 7.0 | 5.4 |

*Source:* National Center for Education Statistics, *Digest of Education Statistics: 2012,* Table 128.

for remedial programs eroded some of the gains. As Table 10.3 indicates, the 2011 median family income was $66,025 for whites and $40,140 for blacks. Put differently, the average black family earned 61 cents for every $1 the average white family earned. It appears that the income gap virtually has disappeared in the public sector, but remains in the private sector and so, overall, the actual income gap between the two groups has increased since 2000.[34]

An important social indicator is the poverty rate among blacks. After its significant drop from 48.1 percent in 1959 to 29.5 percent in 1970, it has held fairly constant in recent years after dropping a few more percentage points in the 1990s. Today, approximately 1 in 4 blacks live in poverty compared to approximately 1 in 8 whites. Through good times and bad, the black poverty rate consistently has remained approximately more than twice that of the white rate.

One significant factor has been the **feminization of poverty**—the high percentage of impoverished families headed by women. Many women lack education and job skills, and their earning potential is limited further by the unavailability or unaffordability of child-care centers, making families headed by women especially vulnerable to living in poverty. Among female-headed households, 31 percent lived in poverty in 2011. Approximately 51 percent of all black children under 18 lived in a female-headed household in 2011, a consistent percentage for five years and a matter of grave concern to African American leaders and government officials alike.[35]

For black Americans, progress and regression have occurred simultaneously. A larger segment than ever before has better-paying positions and greater economic stability. At the same time, stagnation continues among a multigenerational poor underclass residing in urban ghettos and habitually unemployed or underemployed.

**TABLE 10.3** Median Family Income, 1950–2010, Selected Years

| YEAR | WHITE INCOME | BLACK INCOME | BLACK INCOME AS A PERCENTAGE OF WHITE INCOME | ACTUAL INCOME GAP |
|---|---|---|---|---|
| 1950 | $ 3,445 | $ 1,869 | 54.3 | $ 1,576 |
| 1960 | 5,835 | 3,230 | 55.4 | 2,602 |
| 1970 | 10,236 | 6,279 | 61.3 | 3,957 |
| 1980 | 21,904 | 12,674 | 57.9 | 9,230 |
| 1990 | 36,915 | 21,423 | 58.0 | 15,492 |
| 2000 | 45,904 | 30,439 | 66.3 | 15,465 |
| 2010 | 66,025 | 40,140 | 60.8 | 25,885 |

*Source:* U.S. Census Bureau, *2011 American Community Survey,* Table S0201.

Yet, a sizable African American middle class has evolved. Approximately 36 percent of U.S. black families have incomes of $50,000 or more. At the same time, we have witnessed the collapse of inner-city neighborhoods. Entry-level urban manufacturing jobs are gone mostly, as are black middle-class role models in those areas. Instead, a welfare and underground economy exists, where the only successful people with money are drug pushers, pimps, and prostitutes. It is a world where the men often lack jobs and the women often lack husbands. A large proportion of the African Americans living in poverty make up this hard-core poor, trapped in a seemingly unending cycle of broken homes, joblessness, welfare, drugs, crime, and violence—a reality that culture-of-poverty advocates cite in support of their position.

Blauner's internal-colonialism theory (see Chapter 2) certainly applies to this trapped segment of the black population. The segregated black ghetto appears to be a more permanent phenomenon than those of European immigrants, with few individuals able to escape it. Until some large-scale improvement occurs—and none seems imminent—our urban ghettos will remain sinks of despair, decay, and fear.

## OCCUPATION

Because the nature of a person's work provides an important basis for societal esteem, the occupational distribution of an entire group serves as a comparative measure of its status in the larger society. Table 10.4 offers a statistical breakdown of this measure. Although African American representation in managerial, professional, technical, and white-collar occupations has grown slowly but steadily, significant differences remain.

In recent years, black men slowly have increased their proportion working in management or professional position to 23 percent, but white men also have increased their percentage, which stood at 34 percent in 2011. Black men also were more likely than white men to work in service occupations (23 versus 14 percent). These occupations include police, firefighters, food service workers, health aides, social welfare aides, and cleaning and building service workers. Approximately 36 percent of black males are physical laborers (combined bottom two categories) compared to approximately 34 percent of whites.[36]

Both black and white women were fairly evenly employed in sales and office support occupations (31 percent and 33 percent, respectively). Black women were more likely to work in service occupations (28 versus 20 percent); meanwhile, 41 percent of white women were employed in managerial and professional occupations compared to 33 percent of black women.[37]

## HOUSING

To a large extent, the quality of one's housing reflects one's occupation and income. Moreover, despite the drop in housing prices because of the 2008–2011 recession, houses usually increase in value during the years of home ownership, thereby increasing one's

**TABLE 10.4   Occupational Distribution by Sex and Race, 16 Years and Over, 2011 (in percentages)**

| OCCUPATION | MALE | | FEMALE | |
|---|---|---|---|---|
| | BLACK | WHITE | BLACK | WHITE |
| Managerial, professional | 22.8 | 34.4 | 32.8 | 41.4 |
| Sales and office | 18.6 | 17.7 | 31.2 | 32.9 |
| Service | 23.0 | 13.6 | 28.4 | 19.7 |
| Construction, extraction, repair | 11.3 | 17.2 | 0.6 | 0.9 |
| Production, transportation, moving | 24.2 | 17.1 | 7.0 | 5.1 |

*Source:* U.S. Census Bureau, *2011 American Community Survey,* Table S0201.

net worth. In 2011, 43 percent of all blacks were homeowners, compared to 70 percent of whites, figures that have remained fairly constant in recent years.[38] However, racial discrimination continues to affect urban neighborhoods and population distribution. The 1968 Fair Housing Act made it unlawful to refuse to sell or rent a dwelling to any person because of race, color, religion, or national origin, but more than three decades later, *de facto* segregation persists in U.S. metropolitan areas.

**REDLINING.** One continuing problem is **redlining**—the refusal by some banks to make loans on property in lower-income minority neighborhoods, which they indicate on secretive city maps with red pencil lines. Such a practice accelerates the deterioration of older housing because owners have difficulty obtaining funds to improve buildings and potential buyers cannot secure mortgages. To overcome this problem, the Community Reinvestment Act (CRA) of 1977 stipulated that banks have an "affirmative obligation" to lend in lower-income neighborhoods. When seriously applied, the CRA proved effective in helping turn neighborhoods around and enabling thousands of lower-income people to become home owners.[39]

Redlining led banks to close branch offices in poor neighborhoods, thereby removing a crucial financial anchor from many communities. One study found that, in 12 major U.S. cities, three times as many banks per 100,000 residents existed in white areas as in minority areas; but, in 1970, the areas had been fairly equal in their number of banks per 100,000 residents. Moreover, banks are far more likely to reject mortgage applications for higher-income blacks or Hispanics than lower-income whites.[40]

**RESIDENTIAL SEGREGATION.** Most African Americans now live outside central cities (Figure 10.4), continuing an outmigration to the suburbs that began several decades ago.

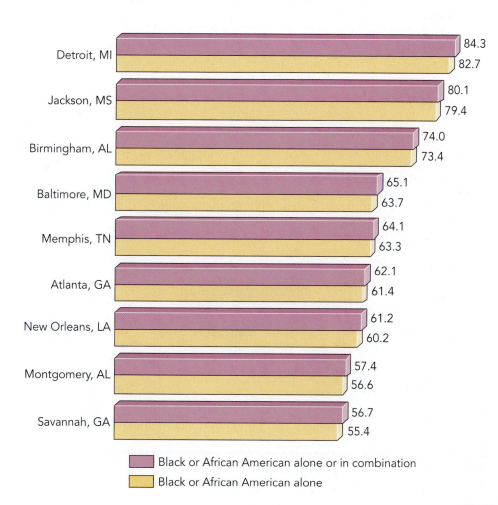

Detroit, MI — 84.3 / 82.7
Jackson, MS — 80.1 / 79.4
Birmingham, AL — 74.0 / 73.4
Baltimore, MD — 65.1 / 63.7
Memphis, TN — 64.1 / 63.3
Atlanta, GA — 62.1 / 61.4
New Orleans, LA — 61.2 / 60.2
Montgomery, AL — 57.4 / 56.6
Savannah, GA — 56.7 / 55.4

Black or African American alone or in combination
Black or African American alone

**FIGURE 10.4 Major Cities with Largest Black Populations, by Percent**

*Source:* U.S. Census Bureau.

Does this mean there is less black–white residential segregation? Analysts, using two measurement tools called a *dissimilarity index* and a *hypersegregation index,* reported that census data show that, although blacks remain the most segregated group, a slow but steady decline in residential segregation between blacks and whites continued at the same pace between 2000 and 2010 as in the 1990s. Even so, black–white segregation remains quite high.[41]

Nationally, the typical white lives in a neighborhood that is 75 percent white, 8 percent black, 11 percent Hispanic, and 5 percent Asian. In contrast, the typical black lives in a neighborhood that is 45 percent black, 35 percent white, 15 percent Hispanic, and 4 percent Asian.[42] Only in the Midwest do the majority of blacks live in nearly all-black neighborhoods. The lowest levels of black–white segregation are in the high-growth Sunbelt, which attracts both whites and minorities, thereby generating a growing share of Americans living in areas where the two races mix freely.

Racial segregation remains stubbornly rooted in the nation's older cities, where blacks and whites always have lived apart. Of the 50 metropolitan areas with the largest black populations, those with the highest levels of segregation (in descending order) are Detroit (Figure 10.5), Milwaukee, New York City, Newark, Chicago, and Philadelphia.[43] Such urban residential segregation limits job opportunities for minorities and prevents them from moving closer to suburban jobs.[44] Suburbia also is becoming more integrated, although its outer rings still are mostly white. Despite the notion advanced by some that middle-class blacks are almost as segregated from whites as are poor blacks, researchers, controlling for numerous socioeconomic characteristics, found that they are not. These suburban blacks have far more white neighbors than do low-income, inner-city blacks, although their white neighbors often are less affluent than they are. It would appear that race still powerfully shapes their residential options, even if they are less segregated than poor blacks.[45]

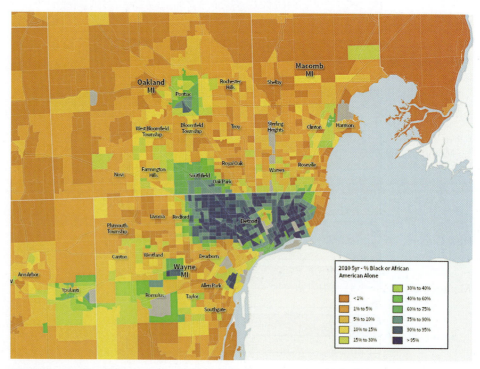

**FIGURE 10.5  Percent of Persons Who Are Black in Detroit, 2010.**

Source: U.S. Census Bureau

# Race or Class?

Despite economic gains made by many African Americans, one in four remains mired in poverty. This means that three in four are of working-class status or higher, enjoying varying measures of economic security and quality of life. Educated blacks can compete equally with whites, enjoying unprecedented opportunities for better-paying jobs. At the same time, increasingly stringent job qualifications in this high-technology age permanently may trap the black underclass in an economic subordination from which they cannot escape. The causes of this split, or **bipolarization**, within the black community have stirred heated debate for three decades. Is it the result of continuing racial discrimination or of socioeconomic conditions?

Some social scientists argue that the life chances of blacks—their economic opportunities—now are determined far more by their social class than by their race. Although race is not insignificant, they stress that social class, not racial discrimination, denies upward mobility to the black poor. Affirmative action helps middle-class blacks, not the poor. A preoccupation with either blaming the victim for individual or cultural inadequacy or attributing black poverty as the result of social forces like segregation and middle-class flight from urban centers does little to address the problem. Until we recognize the dependent nature of welfare and the need to provide skills and good education to the urban poor, we effectively cannot attack the problem of inequality.[46]

Other social scientists maintain that economics is but one facet of the larger society and therefore should not be considered in isolation. Institutional racism permeates society, controlling entry to desirable positions in education, employment, earnings, housing, and social status. By surrendering their cultural identity, blacks may gain middle-class status but they still must function in a white world that permits only limited entry while retaining actual power, control, and wealth.[47]

One example of racism pervading our social institutions was how the media portrayed New Orleans flood victims after Hurricane Katrina in 2007. Most of the "heart-breaker" stories were disproportionately about whites, even though most victims were blacks, but the clearest examples of bias were differing captions to photos of survivors foraging for food. One caption read, "Two white residents wade through chest-deep water after finding bread and soda from a local grocery store." A second photo of a black resident read, "A young man walks through chest-deep water after looting a store."[48]

## THE BLACK MIDDLE CLASS

In 1910, the black middle class constituted approximately 3 percent of the black population and consisted mostly of a mulatto elite who owned businesses in service industries (barbers, caterers, tailors), often serving a white clientele.[49] By 1960, this population segment had grown to approximately 13 percent, entering the professions (accountants, doctors, lawyers, undertakers) but serving mostly a black clientele and living within the black community.[50] After the Civil Rights movement, a new black middle class emerged, employed in the predominantly white corporate world, universities, and government agencies, and with few ties to the black community. Using occupation and income as determinants, approximately 45 percent of African Americans today are middle class.[51]

Despite this improvement, the average earnings of the black middle class remain lower than those of the white middle class. Also, black entrepreneurs often have limited cash resources, making their businesses riskier ventures and thus more susceptible to economic recessions and failure. Racism also remains a factor, whether in the form of a glass ceiling limiting blacks to middle-range managerial positions or in verbal epithets from strangers, harassment from police, poor restaurant service, or difficulty hailing a cab.[52]

Although some would argue that black identities are a liability in a racialized society, even for the black middle class, research shows that this group finds positive

---

**10-6** Assess disagreements of whether race or class is more important today.

**Read on MySocLab**
Document: Black Spaces, Black Places: Strategic Assimilation and Identity Construction in Middle-Class Suburbia

**Explore on MySocLab**
Activity: Improvement Is Better than Assistance? Race, Spending, and Patterns of Inequality

**Watch on MySocLab**
Video: Sociology on the Job: Social Class in the US

**Read on MySocLab**
Document: The Code of the Streets

*A suburban lifestyle was once almost the domain of middle-class white Americans. Thanks to advances beginning with civil rights legislation in the 1960s that opened new opportunities in education, housing, jobs—all leading to upward mobility—a steadily increasing number of blacks also can partake of this piece of the American Dream.*

elements in both their black identity and participation in a community of blacks, and so are motivated to maintain it.[53]

## THE BLACK POOR

Another component of the black population is the poor. Today's inner-city neighborhoods face greater social isolation than past urban communities. The flight of middle- and working-class black families from inner-city neighborhoods removes essential role models and undermines supportive social institutions. Furthermore, outsiders avoid these communities, which are plagued by massive unemployment, crime, and substandard schools. Consequently, area residents—women and children on welfare, school dropouts, teenage mothers, and aggressive street criminals—are cut off from mainstream society. Associated with their isolation and neighborhood poverty are inequalities in public schools, safety, environmental quality, and public health.[54]

Current social indicators about this segment of the black population do not provide any cause for optimism that significant improvement will occur in the near future. Unless some bold, innovative action addresses the multiple problems of limited education and job skills, high unemployment, and single-parent, welfare-dependent families, the situation shows every sign of perpetuating the black underclass.

## THE RACIAL DIVIDE

Although African Americans have made significant gains since the 1960s, few sociologists would argue that racism is a thing of the past. It may be less prevalent and overt, but it still exists. Numerous political conservatives, opposed to any racial preference system or racial categorization as a "rational discrimination," have argued for the end of affirmative action and the implementation of "color blindness" in attitudes and laws. Such a viewpoint may indicate either an egalitarian desire that all races share equally in resources and opportunities, or else a less altruistic concern to protect one's status by opposing any program that threatens it.[55]

In stark contrast, Stephen Steinberg attacked the so-called arrival of a color-blind society as a "spurious justification for maintaining the racial status quo."[56] His contention—in essence, the liberal position—is that programs such as affirmative action are necessary to "confront the legacy of slavery and resume the unfinished racial agenda" because part of that legacy is the continued existence of racist institutions and practices.

As these arguments rage along ideological lines among intellectuals, minority leaders, and politicians, the general public seems divided more along racial lines. Many whites believe either that a level playing field now exists—thanks to changed attitudes, majority-group enlightenment, and antidiscrimination laws—or that an uneven playing field tilted in favor of minorities exists. Many African Americans believe systemic racism against black people permeates all social institutions and everyday life.

Starkly illustrating the vastly differing racial perceptions between whites and blacks was a 2009 national poll about social conflict between blacks and whites. A majority of blacks (53 percent) but only slightly more than a third of whites (35 percent) say major conflicts exist between the two races. Hispanics (47 percent) also are more likely than whites to see serious disagreements between blacks and whites.[57] Apparently, we still have a long road to travel to achieve better interracial understanding and cooperation.

**STUDENTS SPEAK** *"It's strange being an African American and reading about the African American experience. Every action, every step I take in my life to do better and attain more comes after the deaths of those who fought and came before me and gave me these opportunities. I will be the first in my family to get a college degree. In fact, I am the first to do lots of things in my family, but I had to strive for all I have achieved and will achieve. The world for African people is really a crazy one. Our family history is unknown. Often, we as people do not know who we are. We know nothing beyond enslavement long ago, although some of us did have free-born ancestors."*

**—John Futrell**

# African and Afro-Caribbean Immigrants

Although many non-blacks simply use Negroid racial features as the basis of group classification, much cultural diversity exists among blacks in the United States. Generalizing about them is just as inaccurate as generalizing about whites. Regional and social-class differences create distinctions among U.S. blacks, and cultural differences make Afro-Caribbean black immigrants unlike native-born blacks. In addition, black immigrants from Africa are distinct culturally not only from the two former groups but also from one another when they have different countries of origin. Further complicating matters is the tendency of many native-born U.S. blacks to call themselves African Americans, even though a wide cultural gulf separates them from the more recent African immigrants. Approximately one-fourth of black population growth since 1990 has resulted from immigration. Such demographic changes are complicating what it means to be African American.

**10-7** Identify distinctions among African and Afro-Caribbean immigrants.

## AFRO-CARIBBEAN AMERICANS

The number of Americans claiming Afro-Caribbean ancestry totaled more than 2.7 million in 2011, quite a sizable number for people from that part of the world.[58] Primarily concentrated on the East Coast, 6 out of 10 live in the New York, Miami, or Fort Lauderdale metropolitan regions. In Miami, Haitians constitute more than half of this population, while Jamaicans are the majority of this population in New York and Fort Lauderdale, both of which also have large Haitian populations.[59]

Residential segregation is high among Afro-Caribbean Americans in virtually all U.S. cities. Because their neighborhoods tend to overlap with African Americans, segregation from them is only moderate. However, Afro-Caribbean segregation from Africans, though still in the moderate range, is significantly higher, and their segregation from whites is the highest among all black groups.[60]

Although fewer Afro-Caribbean men have white partners than African American men, interracial marriages are far more likely to occur among Afro-Caribbean women than African American women, particularly those who arrived as children or were born in the United States.[61] Another study found that, irrespective of ethnicity, blacks in England were far more likely to have a native-born white partner than were their U.S. counterparts.[62]

**HATIAN AMERICANS.** Most members of the first wave of approximately 4,400 Haitian immigrants, who came to the United States in the 1950s, were well-educated members of Haiti's upper class fleeing from the harsh regime of President François Duvalier. In the 1960s, nearly 35,000 Haitians, mostly of the middle class, arrived in the United States. The third wave, primarily illiterate peasants and unskilled urban workers with little or no education, has been emigrating since the mid-1970s. Since 1990, more than 425,000 Haitian immigrants entered the United States, 248,000 of that total between 2000 and 2011.[63]

In the 1990s, in an action reminiscent of the Vietnamese "boat people," thousands of Haitians fled their homeland in overcrowded, flimsy boats and attempted to enter the United States. Federal policy, consistent through Republican and Democratic administrations, has been to deny refugee status to most, discourage their entry, treat them as **undocumented aliens**, and deport them. A 1992 Supreme Court ruling supported this government policy of forced repatriation, and the 1997 Nicaraguan Adjustment and Central American Relief Act failed to include Haitians among the undocumented aliens it made eligible for permanent status.

Emigration from Haiti probably will continue for a long time. In their homeland, hunger is widespread, and less than one-fourth of the population has access to clean drinking water. Moreover, the devastation wreaked by the 2010 earthquake has worsened further the quality of life. Rates of infant mortality, tuberculosis, and HIV are among the highest in the world. Only one-third of the land is arable, but two-thirds of the population farm the land. The struggle to eke out a living through subsistence agriculture has led to over-cultivation, soil erosion, and deforestation. Haiti's forests and woodlands now only cover 1 percent of the total land area.[64]

Haiti has some of the highest rates of birth, death, and natural increase in the Western Hemisphere. With a population of 9.8 million in a land area only slightly larger than Maryland, its population density measures 966 inhabitants per square mile. Some 53 percent of all Haitians over the age of 15 are illiterate.[65]

Many of today's Haitian arrivals speak Haitian Creole although French is the language of the educated elite in Haitian government, commerce, and education. Fluency in one language does not mean comprehension of the other. Nevertheless, because of the prestige attached to things French and the assumption by many U.S. residents that all Haitians speak French, Haitians often pretend to be able to speak it to enhance their status.[66]

Most Haitians are Roman Catholics, with an increasing segment attracted to evangelical Protestantism. A significant minority practice *voudou*, a religion with African roots that combines belief in the existence of a *bon Dieu*, or good God, and *lwas*, spirits who offer protection, advice, and assistance in resolving spiritual and material problems.[67]

The largest concentration of Haitians (437,000) is in Florida. Like children of all immigrants, Haitian youth assimilate fairly easily but face a conflict as they do. High school students distinguish between "just come" Haitians (those whose clothing, use of Creole, and self-segregation make them visible to others and targets for derision) and "undercover" Haitians (those whose clothing, language, and interactions closely resemble native-born black Americans in their desire to "fit in"). Those with sufficient resources to live in African American or ethnically mixed, middle-class suburbs encounter far less anti-Haitian prejudice and so are more likely to retain pride in their heritage and openly become Haitian Americans.[68]

An ethnographic study conducted for the U.S. Census Bureau found that Haitians put their trust only in family and church. Civic participation was an alien concept to most respondents, probably due to the fact that their homeland has virtually no democratic heritage. Even Haitians active in their church do not conceive of participating in a community outside of church. The study also revealed that, on the one hand, their experiences of societal racism led Haitians to identify with African Americans, but at the same time, prejudice specifically against Haitians and some of it on the part of African Americans, impelled many to cling to a specifically Haitian identity.[69]

**JAMAICAN AMERICANS.** Jamaicans constitute the largest non-Hispanic immigrant population from the Caribbean. Of the 1 million Jamaican Americans living in the United States in 2011, 60 percent were foreign born. California by far has the largest concentration of Jamaican Americans west of the Appalachian Mountains, but most Jamaicans settle on the East Coast in urban environments, particularly in New York, Florida, Connecticut, and New Jersey. At present, about 61 percent of all Jamaican immigrants have become U.S. citizens.[70]

Between 2000 and 2011, more than 211,000 new Jamaican immigrants arrived, this continual large influx augmenting the Jamaicans' ethnic communities and cultural vitality.

*As Afro-Caribbean immigration increased in the past several decades, so too did black ethnic restaurants and stores, often providing community services beyond their specific roles. This Jamaican restaurant and bakery on Flatbush Avenue in the "Little West Indies" neighborhood of Brooklyn, New York, also provides a community anchor for its local first-generation clientele.*

The presence of Jamaicans perhaps is most visible to other Americans through West Indian food stores and reggae music. Speech is another indicator because Jamaicans speak English but in a *patois* characterized by rapid speech patterning and a clipped accent, which sometimes causes difficulty for a first-time listener.

Unlike the Haitians, Jamaicans come from a strongly democratic country, and so their notions of civic engagement are similar to those in the United States. However, their sense of community in the United States tends to be limited to the people with whom they share a neighborhood. Many nuclear families are separated, with one partner still in Jamaica, while respondents who come to the United States to pursue their education commonly live in female-headed households or with relatives whom they previously did not know very well.[71]

Besides adjusting to a new home environment, immigrants also face difficulties adjusting to big-city life, often in tough neighborhoods and high schools where cultural clashes cannot be avoided. In New York City, for example, violence between Jamaican and Haitian students, or between Afro-Caribbeans and African Americans, was common, as were tensions between adults trying to become active in the local political process.[72]

Economic and educational opportunities are the primary motivations for immigration. Speaking English and adapting fairly easily to U.S. society, many first-generation Jamaican Americans find jobs, especially in various healthcare positions, earning better wages than back home, where they may send money to support their families. Second-generation Jamaican Americans are not descending into an urban underclass as some feared but instead rapidly moving into the mainstream—working in jobs comparable to those held by native New Yorkers their age. By blending their ethnic culture and norms with American ones, they have an advantage in avoiding some of the obstacles that native minority groups cannot.[73]

### AFRICAN-BORN AMERICANS

In only six years, 2006 to 2011, more than 400,000 non-Arab Africans arrived, six times the number in the peak years of the slave trade. In fact, since 1990, more sub-Saharan Africans have migrated to the United States than in nearly the entire preceding two centuries.[74] As a result, 91 percent of all foreign-born blacks (approximately 1.1 million) were born in Africa.[75] Unlike the Afro-Caribbean population, Africans are widely dispersed throughout the United States, with their largest numbers in Washington, DC, and New York City (see Figure 10.4). Most are from Nigeria and Ethiopia. Another large contingent hails from Somalia or Ghana. Because of their stronger socioeconomic status, African-born Americans tend to live in neighborhoods with higher education and income levels and have a greater percentage of home ownership than African Americans and Afro-Caribbeans.[76]

Many African immigrants are well educated; 31 percent have a bachelor's degree or higher. Others possess occupational skills that enable them to achieve economic security fairly quickly. Having achieved middle-class socioeconomic status, or at worst working-class stability, these first-generation Americans usually prefer to retain their African identity rather than to blend in with the black American community. Keeping their homeland ties, they send back more than $1 billion annually to their families and friends in Africa.[77]

Nationwide, many Americans may not know much about Cape Verdean Americans, but many music fans are aware of Elle Varner, a guitarist, songwriter, and recording artist. "Refill," a single from her first album "Perfectly Imperfect," earned a 2013 Grammy nomination as best R & B song.

**CAPE VERDEAN AMERICANS.** Approximately 400 miles off the coast of West Africa, near the equator, are 10 islands and five islets known as the Cape Verde archipelago. Until 1975, these islands were a Portuguese colony and their opportune location relative to trade winds and ocean currents made them strategically important for maritime traffic. From the early eighteenth to the mid-nineteenth century, whalers from the United States often sought shelter or fresh provisions there and sometimes took on Cape Verdeans as crew members. Some remained as crew members or became harpooners, captains, and even ship owners, but most worked to pay their passage to the United States to escape the poverty and intermittent famines they faced on the islands. Once the textile mills opened in the United States in the mid-nineteenth century, the number of Cape Verdean immigrants to New England increased from a steady trickle to hundreds, sometimes thousands, annually.

Cape Verdeans, a mixture of African and European ancestry, vary widely in their physical appearance, even within the same family. Although U.S. residents classified them as "black," they saw themselves as "Portuguese," believing that their sociocultural identity set them apart from Africans and American blacks. However, rejection by the more numerous white Portuguese in New England and simplistic racial stereotyping by other U.S. natives resulted in Cape Verdeans identifying themselves as a separate social category—as non-black Portuguese Cape Verdeans.[78] Those arriving since the late 1980s tend to identify themselves as black, perhaps because they are more visibly African than the earlier mostly light-skinned arrivals.[79]

The pursuit of a non-black identity, despite a physical appearance suggesting otherwise to many U.S. outsiders, encouraged continuance of such "ethnic markers" as language (*Crioulo*), music, and cuisine. Musical sounds come from the guitar, mandolin, and drums. Cape Verdean festivities attract friends and family who have moved away from the community clusters. Through communications and transportation technology, a strong interactional network remains. Any family crisis (childbirth, illness, and death) demands social visits. Endogamy remains the norm, with marriage to a U.S. black often treated as grounds for social ostracism.[80]

More than 15,000 Cape Verdean immigrants arrived in the United States between 2000 and 2011. Approximately 103,000 Americans claim Cape Verdean ancestry, making them the third largest group of recent arrivals from sub-Saharan Africa, behind Nigerians and Ethiopians. Massachusetts is home to nearly 53,000 Cape Verdean Americans, 18,000 live in Rhode Island, and another 4,000 live in Connecticut. Small numbers can be found in all states except Idaho and South Dakota.[81]

Half of all Cape Verdeans work professional, sales, or office positions, and another fourth are in service occupations. Increasingly, second- and third-generation Cape Verdean Americans are graduating from college (now 14 percent of all Cape Verdean Americans). Once living primarily in well-established communities in New England, Cape Verdean Americans are now scattered throughout the United States, as well as settling in newer clusters in the Atlanta and Southern California regions.[82]

**NIGERIAN AMERICANS.** Nigeria is Africa's most populous country and ranks eighth in the world in population, exceeding 170 million people in 2012. It has one of the highest growth and fertility rates in the world and 13 percent of the world's black population lives there. With 44 percent of this population under the age of 15, Nigeria's annual growth rate should continue to rise rapidly in the near future.[83]

Population pressures, economic difficulties, and political unrest are the push factors that caused immigration to the United States

**STUDENTS SPEAK** "The case of examining Africans becomes a very difficult one, seeing that Africa has 54 countries, with each country having many different ethnic, cultural, linguistic, and genetic differences. There is also a wide social distance from African Americans, especially in suburban areas. As an Ethiopian/Eritrean, I have noticed that my community and other African communities tend to stick to their own group. There is a common misconception that Africa is a country, which is sad, of course, given the vast diversity in one part of the continent, let alone the whole continent. Tribal and ethnic differentiations are the norm in Africa and are not understood in the U.S. and other English-speaking countries."

**—Feven Ghebremeskel**

to increase significantly. The number of Nigerian immigrants quadrupled from approximately 8,800 in the 1970s to 35,400 in the 1980s. Approximately 128,000 immigrants arrived between 2000 and 2012 (about 39,000 between 2010 and 2012), making this the period of greatest Nigerian immigration.[84]

More people (271,000) claim ancestry from Nigeria than from any other African country. The primary states of residence of Nigerian Americans are Texas, California, New York, Maryland, Georgia, Illinois, and New Jersey.

Approximately two-thirds of these immigrants enter professional, sales, and office occupations, and another 21 percent enter service occupations. A fairly even proportion of both men and women—approximately three-fourths—are in the labor force. One-third hold a bachelor's degree and 28 percent have an advanced degree.[85] In fact, pursuing a college education to attain professional careers is the cornerstone for many Nigerian-American families, while others establish small businesses as they adjust to a new life. Virtually all go through the same identity struggle as other black immigrants, caught between race and ethnicity, while maintaining relationships with family and friends in Nigeria.[86]

# Assimilation

10-8 Evaluate the integration of Blacks into the societal mainstream.

Any discussion on the subject of black American assimilation must first consider the diversity of the black population in the United States (see Figure 10.6). Native-born blacks face racial issues in their social acceptance, but they grow up and live within the American culture. However, they by no means are a single entity. Socioeconomic differences affect whether they live within the mainstream or margins of society. Moreover, those raised in the Northeast are likely to differ in lifestyles and interaction patterns from those raised in the South.

Race obviously is an important factor in the U.S. experiences of Afro-Caribbeans and Africans also, but compounding theirs are the adjustment and acculturation processes all immigrants undergo. Today's first-generation black Americans thus illustrate many of the everyday ethnic realities and patterns of other immigrant groups: chain migration, residential and occupational patterning, parallel social institutions, ingroup solidarity, and endogamy.

In addition, cultural and socioeconomic differences among U.S.-born African, Afro-Caribbean, and African-born Americans can lead to their limited social interaction with one another. For example, African or Afro-Caribbean youths with immigrant parents place greater emphasis on family interdependence than do black youths with U.S.-born parents.[87] Because the self-selection process results in a disproportionate number of highly skilled immigrants, African-born and Afro-Caribbean Americans have fared better than U.S.-born African Americans.[88] This socioeconomic differential not only has resulted in significant lifestyle variations but also in some inter-minority tensions.[89] Recently, some black scholars complained, for instance, that increasing numbers of African-born or Afro-Caribbean immigrants are getting accepted to the nation's top colleges at the expense of U.S.-born African Americans.[90] Yet, ethnic heterogeneity among immigrant blacks commonly yields to racial hegemony. In what still remains a color-coded society, the dominant group views them as undifferentiated "blacks" and therefore relegates all to a separate, minority status.[91]

Kenneth Chenault, the Chief Executive Officer (CEO) of American Express, is one of five blacks currently holding this top management position in one of the 500 largest corporations in the United States, known collectively as the Fortune 500 companies. In 2009, Ursula Burns of Xerox Corporation became the first black female CEO.

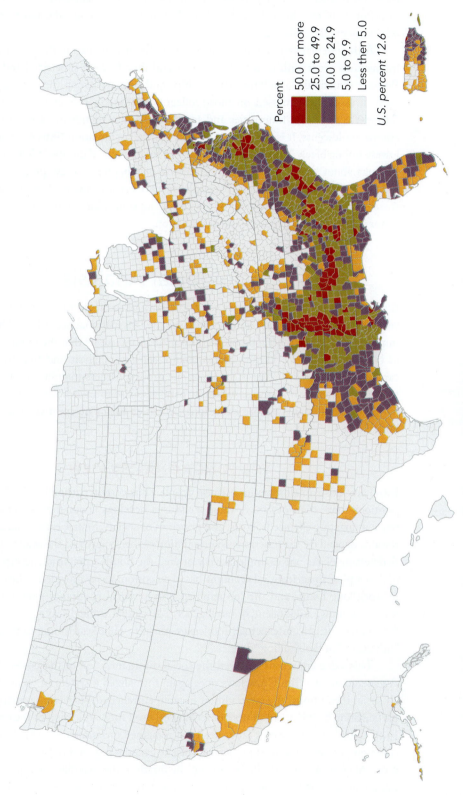

**FIGURE 10.6** Black or African American Population, 2010 (in percentages)

Source: U.S. Census Bureau.

Black American culture remains a resilient component of U.S. society, despite the high level of cultural assimilation among most native-born blacks. Although gaps remain, secondary structural assimilation (education, income, occupation, and housing) is greater than ever before, as detailed earlier. Of course, not all have benefited. More black men are in prison than ever before, more young, black men commit suicide, and black academic achievement still trails that of whites.

Although blacks and whites interact more frequently than in the past, most of these interactions occur within secondary groups and therefore are superficial and segmented. Primary structural assimilation (friendships and primary-group memberships) remains limited, as easily witnessed on most college campuses in cafeterias or other informal settings, as well as in fraternities and sororities. And as friendships are segregated, even among adolescents, it is not surprising that marital assimilation (intermarriage) remains lowest among black Americans in comparison to other racial groups.[92] My social distance findings about African Americans, discussed in Chapter 1, show progress, though, in the narrowing social distance between the races. Certainly, many changes have occurred since the Civil Rights movement of the 1960s, but skin color still remains an unfortunate factor in full social acceptance and assimilation.

# Sociological Analysis

**10-9** Discuss insights gained through sociological analysis.

**Read on MySocLab**
Document: African American Families: A Legacy of Vulnerability and Resistance

Blacks have been victims of slavery, restrictive laws, or racial discrimination for most of the years they have lived in the United States (see the International Scene box). Despite many improvements since the 1960s, problems remain. Some argue that the unique experiences of black people in the United States require separate analysis and that their situation cannot be compared to that of other ethnic groups. Others maintain that, despite certain significant dissimilarities, sufficient parallels exist to invite comparative analysis in patterns of dominant–minority relations. All three major perspectives will incorporate both views.

## THE FUNCTIONALIST VIEW

Inequality exists in all societies because people value certain occupational roles and social positions more than others. A value consensus develops about their functional importance in meeting the needs, goals, and priorities of society. Status, esteem, and differential rewards depend on the functionalist orientation of the society and the availability of qualified personnel. As one example, slavery offered the South a practical and effective means of developing an agricultural economy based on cotton; slaves provided a cheap labor force to work long hours; and the job required only physical endurance—no unusually high level of training, skills, talent, or intelligence. The system worked, leaving slave owners free for "genteel" artistic, intellectual, and leisure pursuits while reaffirming in their minds the "inferiority" of their toiling "darkies."

This value consensus survived the social disorganization of the post-bellum South. A generation later, Jim Crow laws once again formalized a system of inequality through all social institutions. A new tradition became entrenched, restricting opportunities and participation based on old values but feeding on itself for justification of the existing order. In the North, blacks filled a labor need but remained unassimilated. This lack of societal cohesion and the continued presence of blacks generated prejudice, avoidance, and reciprocal antagonism. In both the North and the South in the twentieth century, these system dysfunctions—the waste of human resources and lost productivity—produced social problems of poor education, low income, unemployment, crime and delinquency, poor housing, high disease and mortality rates, and other pathologies.

# the INTERNATIONAL scene

## The Perception of Race in Brazil

Like the United States, Brazil was colonized by Europeans (primarily, the Portuguese) who subjugated the native population and imported about 4 million Africans as slave laborers. In fact, Brazil today is second only to the United States in the number of its citizens of African descent outside Africa itself. Despite these similarities, race relations in Brazil have followed a different path from that in the United States.

The United States maintains a fairly rigid biracial system, classifying people as white or non-white, despite its multiple-race categories first used in the 2000 census. This simplistic "us" and "them" categorization has long promoted racial prejudice, segregation, and hostility. Moreover, it is becoming increasingly unrealistic. The Census Bureau says there were about 2.4 million interracial married couples in 2010, up from 310,000 in 1970. Furthermore, approximately 8.7 million Americans identify themselves as belonging to two or more races. With such numbers, how well do simplistic U.S. racial categories serve the nation's emerging multiracial society?

In Brazil, a multiracial classification system exists. In its broadest categories, the society has three population types: *pretos* (blacks), *brancos* (whites), and *pardos* (mulattos). The racial mixture is 54 percent white, 6 percent black, 39 percent mulatto and mestizo, and 1 percent Asian or Amerindian.

Mulattos in the United States are classified with blacks, but they constitute a separate group in Brazil. Moreover, Brazilian mulattos may be categorized further into about 40 subclassifications of color variations. To identify each of these separate racial categories, Brazilians use dozens of precise terms reflecting minute distinctions in skin shading, hair, and facial features.

Since the first days of Portuguese settlement, miscegenation has been common, although usually within similar color gradients rather than between couples at opposite ends of the color line. Brazil's more fluid color continuum deters formation of a racist ideology or segregated institutions, although whites remain traditionally in a higher social class than most of the people of color.

### CRITICAL THINKING QUESTIONS

Should the United States adopt a multiracial classification system? Why or why not?

---

System corrections, in the form of federal judicial and legislative action, helped restore some balance to society, reorganizing social institutions and eliminating barriers to full social, political, and economic opportunities. Other dysfunctions—the Vietnam War, structural blue-collar unemployment, and economic downturns—curtailed some gains by blacks. Further adjustments are necessary to overcome the remaining problems, most especially those in the inner city.

## THE CONFLICT VIEW

Slavery is an obvious example of past economic exploitation of blacks, but recent practices may be less obvious. Job discrimination, labor-union discrimination—particularly in the building trades—and prejudices in educational institutions leading to low achievement and high dropout rates force many blacks into low-paying, low-status, economically vulnerable jobs. For many years, confining blacks to marginal positions preserved better-paying job opportunities for whites. Maintaining a low-cost surplus labor pool not in competition for jobs sought by whites benefited employers and the dominant society.

Such a pool provided domestic and sanitation workers and seasonal employees, as well as job opportunities for others in social work, law enforcement, and welfare agencies.

Both *de jure* segregation and *de facto* segregation illustrate how successfully those with power protected their self-interests by maintaining the status quo. Control by whites of social institutions confined blacks to certain occupations and residential locations, away from participation in the political process and out of the societal mainstream. Although a black and mulatto elite did arise and some positive white actions occurred, such as President Roosevelt's 1941 executive order banning racial discrimination in defense industries, blacks mostly remained severely oppressed.

Blauner's internal-colonialism theory is appropriate here (see Chapter 2): The outside control of black segregated communities was by employers, teachers, social workers, police, and politicians who represented the establishment, and made the administrative, economic, and political decisions that governed the ghetto. Unlike European groups, blacks did not gain control and ownership of their own buildings and commercial enterprises within a generation, remaining instead a subjugated and dependent colonized population.

The Civil Rights movement of the 1960s, a culmination of earlier efforts and court decisions, fits the Marxist analysis of social change. Blacks developed group cohesiveness, overcame a false consciousness that equality was unattainable, and formed an effective social movement. Sweeping changes through civil rights legislation, punctuated by urban violence from 1964 to 1968, brought improved life opportunities to blacks and other minorities.

A more recent and controversial perspective, **critical race theory**, is a Marxist position that racism is so ingrained in the social system that equal protection under the law is impossible. Instead, only unequal measures on behalf of racial minorities can compensate. This viewpoint is not one-dimensional in an emphasis on race alone, however, as it argues that disempowerment or aggression must be understood in the context of the intersectionality of race with ethnicity, social class, gender, and sexual orientation.[93]

## THE INTERACTIONIST VIEW

Just as our attraction to strangers is based on perceived similarities, our antipathy to strangers can be based on learned prejudices. In the United States, skin color often triggers negative responses about busing, crime, housing, jobs, and poverty. Where did such attitudes originate? Earlier, we examined multigenerational stereotyping and social isolation of blacks as the legacy of racism. If beliefs about people—culturally transmitted and reinforced by external conditions—center on their differences or alleged inferiority, then avoidance, exploitation, and subjugation can become common responses.

The opposition to integration efforts usually comes from fear of these "unlike" strangers. Although expressed reasons may include preserving neighborhoods or neighborhood schools, the real reason often is concern that blacks will "contaminate" the area or school. Beliefs that a black presence adversely affects the crime rate, school discipline, property values, and neighborhood stability often prompt whites to resist proposed integration. Similarly, unfounded beliefs that blacks are less reliable, less honest, and less intelligent than whites frequently influence hiring and acceptance decisions. The unfairness and inaccuracy of such sweeping generalizations are less significant than the fact that people act on them. Too many white people have spun a gossamer web of false reality and believe it.

Black racism works in much the same way. Black racists see all whites as the enemy and all blacks as right, and they respond with suspicion to any friendly action by whites or any white criticism of a black person. Because both sides define situations in a particular way, the interpretation they assign usually reinforces their original biases. Upward mobility—in education, occupation, and income—does much to alter people's interpretations. Eliminating residential segregation and encouraging more primary interactions will further that process.

# Retrospect

Through 200 years of slavery and 100 additional years of separate-and-unequal subjugation, blacks found society unresponsive to their needs and wants. Negatively categorized by skin color, they clearly saw that two worlds existed in this country: the white and the non-white. Many blacks still remain trapped in poverty and isolated in urban ghettos. Many who have achieved upward mobility find that they still are not accepted in white society, at least in meaningful primary relationships.

Numerous similarities exist between the black experience in the United States and the experiences of other minority peoples. Like Asians and Native Americans, blacks frequently are judged on the basis of their skin color and not their individual capabilities. They experience, as have many immigrant groups, countless instances of stereotyping, scapegoating, prejudice, discrimination, social and spatial segregation, deprivation, and violence. When they become too visible in a given area or move into economic competition with whites, the dominant group often perceives them as a threat and reacts accordingly. All this is a familiar pattern in dominant–minority relations.

More than 200 years of slavery exacted a heavy toll on U.S. blacks, and the exploitation and discrimination did not end with the abolition of slavery. As a result of generations of social conditioning, many whites preserved a master–slave mentality long after the Civil War. Two generations later, when blacks had made some progress, Jim Crow laws eliminated those gains and re-established unequal treatment and limited life opportunities, thereby increasing prejudice.

A change in values and attitudes became evident with the historic Supreme Court decision of 1954 on school desegregation. Although school integration was slow, it did come about, and both blacks and whites were encouraged to seek even more changes. The resurgent Civil Rights movement peaked in the mid-1960s, with passage of a broad range of laws guaranteeing black people a more equitable life experience.

More than a half century has elapsed since the 1954 court decision, with a great many changes taking place in the land and observable improvements occurring in all aspects of life for many African Americans. Still, problems remain. A disproportionate number of non-white poor continue to be concentrated in the cities, frequently trapped in a cycle of perpetual poverty. *De facto* segregation remains a problem, also, with the majority of whites living in suburbs farther away from the city and the majority of blacks living in more adjacent ones.

The growing numbers of African-born and Afro-Caribbean immigrants have brought greater diversity to black America. Differing cultures and value orientations, along with a higher level of education and marketable skills among the newcomers, have created a black ethnic mosaic remindful of the white ethnic mosaic of 100 years earlier. Until assimilation further reduces the social distance among U.S.-born, African-born, and Afro-Caribbean black Americans, interethnic tensions and race-based coalitions will likely continue.

Greater interaction occurs between the two races in places of public accommodation, and this eventually may reshape white and black attitudes. That, together with improved educational opportunities, may lead to greater structural assimilation for African Americans. One element crucial to any such progress is the condition of the economy. Its ability to absorb African Americans into positions in the labor force that permit upward socioeconomic mobility, in large measure, will determine their future status in U.S. society.

# On MySocLab

Study and Review on MySocLab

## KEY TERMS

Bipolarization, p. 333
Black codes, p. 312
Critical race theory, p. 344
Cultural drift, p. 312
Cumulative causation, p. 314

*De facto* segregation, p. 315
*De jure* segregation, p. 315
Ebonics, p. 325
Feminization of poverty, p. 329
Institutionalized racism, p. 311

Jim Crow laws, p. 313
Redlining, p. 331
Slavery reparations, p. 310
Undocumented aliens, p. 336

## DISCUSSION QUESTIONS

1. The beginning of the chapter offers a sociohistorical perspective. What was one striking or surprising piece of information you picked up here?
2. What similarities exist among the experiences of blacks, Native Americans, and Asians in the United States?
3. What similarities are there between the responses of blacks and of European immigrants to prejudice and discrimination?
4. Pages 325–332 offer various social indicators by which we measure the degree of mainstreaming that has occurred for any minority group (in this case, black Americans). What conclusions can you draw from these data? Have we made progress in recent decades? Where do the main problems still remain? What would you expect future data to show? Why?
5. Various black ethnic groups are discussed in addition to American-born blacks. From reading about this heterogeneity among blacks, what observations can you make about non-blacks' perceptions of that race?
6. The end of the chapter offers three theoretical analyses. How did one of these theories become more meaningful or relevant to you in its application to the black experience?

## INTERNET ACTIVITIES

1. Want to see the Census Bureau's latest report on U.S. blacks? Go to http://www.census.gov/prod/cen2010/briefs/c2010br-06.pdf, and you will find a wide range of facts about them.
2. A decade-long controversy exists about ebonics, the African American vernacular English. At the website for the Center for Applied Linguistics (http://www.cal.org/topics/dialects/aae.html), you'll find numerous articles about this issue.
3. Pages 322–323 discuss the highly controversial book, *The Bell Curve*, by Richard Herrnstein and Charles Murray. There are many articles on the Internet about it, most of them highly critical. Using your favorite search engine, type "Bell Curve Debate" in the search box. You'll get a good list of articles. Select two and compare their comments and arguments.
4. You know the names of many black athletes and entertainers, but how many black inventors' names do you know and what did they invent? Go to http://inventors.about.com/od/blackinventors/a/black_inventors.htm and find out.

# Hispanic Americans

# 11

((◊ **Listen** to Chapter 11 on **MySocLab**

With the Honduran flag in the background, this girl in a traditional dress typifies the many second-generation Hispanic Americans who celebrate their heritage at the annual festive events throughout the United States, and thus reaffirm their specific ethnic group identity within a larger Hispanic-American cultural framework.

## LEARNING OBJECTIVES | After reading this chapter you will be able to:

**11-1** Describe the sociohistorical context for studying Hispanic Americans.

**11-2** Examine what social indicators tell us about Hispanic progress.

**11-3** Describe the immigrant experiences of Mexicans, Puerto Ricans, and Cubans.

**11-4** Describe the immigrant experiences of Caribbean, Central and South Americans.

**11-5** Compare and contrast assimilation paths followed by Hispanic Americans.

**11-6** Discuss insights gained through sociological analysis.

Perhaps no ethnic group attracts more public attention these days than do the Hispanic people. Their large numbers, their residential clustering, and the bilingual programs and signs associated with them make them a recognizable ethnic group. Although those who live in poverty or the small number involved in gangs, drugs, or other criminal activity get attention and generate negative stereotypes, most Hispanic Americans live in the societal mainstream as members of the working or middle class. Their cultural backgrounds, social class, and length of residence in the United States may differ, but Hispanic Americans share a common language and heritage. Because of this commonality, outsiders often lump them all together despite their many differences.

# Sociohistorical Perspective

**11-1** Describe the sociohistorical context for studying Hispanic Americans.

Spanish influence in what is now the United States is centuries old. Long before the English settled in their colonies in the New World, Spanish explorers, missionaries, and adventurers roamed through much of the Western Hemisphere, including Florida and the Southwest. In 1518, the Spanish established St. Augustine, Florida, and in the same year that the first permanent English settlement (Jamestown) was established (1609), the Spanish founded Santa Fe in what is now New Mexico. Spanish cultural influence was extensive throughout the New World in language, religion, customs, values, and town planning (for example, locating church and institutional buildings next to a central plaza).

The nation's largest Hispanic groups—Mexicans and Puerto Ricans—became involved with the United States through two nineteenth-century wars 50 years apart. Through the fortunes of war, the places where they lived became part of the United States, requiring them to live under a different set of laws in a country where they now were a minority.

For the Mexicans, the Treaty of Guadalupe Hidalgo ended the Mexican–American War in 1848, brought Texas, New Mexico, Arizona, and California into the United States, and gave U.S. citizenship to approximately 75,000 Mexican nationals still living there one year after the treaty. Viewed as a conquered and inferior people, they soon lost title to the land where they and their ancestors had lived because they could not prove ownership in the Anglo court system. By 1892, official policy toward Mexican Americans was so biased against them that the federal government allowed anyone except them to get grazing privileges on public lands in the Southwest. Nor did the violence end. In fact, the interethnic violence between Anglos and Mexican Americans thereafter was so extensive that some experts believe there were more killings of Mexican Americans than black Americans lynched between 1850 and 1930.[1] Experienced in farming, ranching, and mining—concentrated along the fertile river valleys—the Mexican Americans proved a valuable labor pool and were incorporated within the white economy as lower-strata laborers.

Ruled by Spain for more than 400 years, Puerto Ricans became U.S. nationals when the Treaty of Paris in 1898 ended the Spanish–American War and made their land U.S. territory. Until 1948, when Puerto Rico became a commonwealth with full autonomy and its people could elect their own governor, the island was a colony with appointed governors and its legislative actions subject to annulment by the U.S. Congress, which reserved the right to legislate for the island if it wished. As only one example of the island's colonial status, U.S. officials decreed that all education was to be in English. That edict remained in effect until 1991, when Puerto Ricans voted to restore Spanish as the island's official language.

## STRUCTURAL CONDITIONS

The Hispanic American experience varies greatly, depending on the particular ethnic group, area of the country, and period involved (Figure 11.1). In the Southwest, agricultural needs and the presence of Central and Mexican Americans are crucial factors in

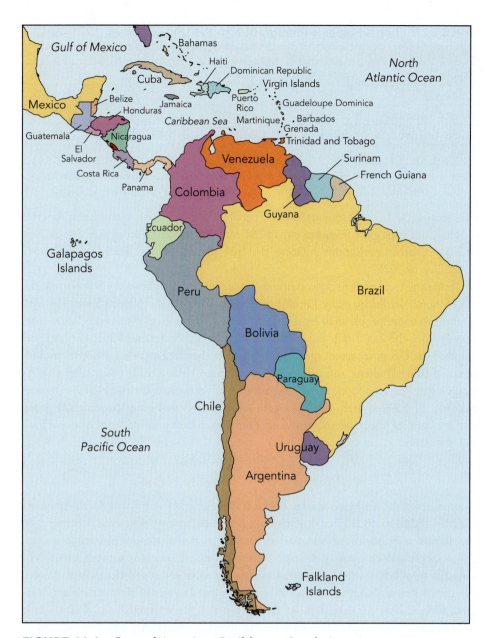

**FIGURE 11.1** Central America, Caribbean, South America

dominant–minority relations. In the East, industrial employment, urban problems, and the presence of Cubans or Puerto Ricans provide the focal points of attitudes and actions.

In the past, low-skilled immigrant groups—including Puerto Ricans and Mexicans—typically obtained jobs such as unskilled factory work that had low status, low pay, and little mobility but at least provided sufficient income to achieve some degree of economic security. Unlike past groups from less industrialized nations, however, today's Hispanic immigrants enter a post-industrial society where fewer unskilled factory jobs are available. Instead, they find work in other physical labor fields such as agriculture, construction and home improvement (demolition, flooring, framing, masonry, painting, and roofing), food service, and landscaping.

Overpopulation throughout Latin America is a significant factor in the continued migration of large numbers of Hispanics to the United States (Table 11.1). High birth rates, improved sanitation, reduction of child mortality, and negative cultural and religious attitudes toward birth control have led to population booms in countries whose resources

**TABLE 11.1** Legal Hispanic Immigration to the United States, 1971–2012

| | 1980–1989 | 1990–1999 | 2000–2009 | 2010–2012 |
|---|---|---|---|---|
| Mexico | 1,009,586 | 2,757,418 | 1,704,166 | 426,866 |
| Caribbean | 789,343 | 1,004,114 | 1,053,357 | 399,016 |
| Central America | 339,376 | 610,189 | 591,130 | 126,683 |
| South America | 399,803 | 570,596 | 856,508 | 248,218 |
| Total | 2,538,108 | 4,942,317 | 4,205,161 | 1,200,783 |

*Source:* U.S. Office of Immigration Statistics, *Yearbook of Immigration Statistics: 2012*, Table 2.

and habitable land cannot support so many people. The total population of Latin America and the Caribbean grew from more than 285 million in 1970 to more than 599 million in 2012. Current projections indicate that the population will reach approximately 672 million by 2025.[2]

Suffering from poor living conditions, inadequate schools, limited job opportunities, and economic hardship, many Latinos seek a better life in the United States—indeed, significantly more people than legal channels can accommodate. As a result, some enter illegally along the 2,000-mile border between the United States and Mexico or into port cities by boat. U.S. government agents have been apprehending more than 640,000 **undocumented (illegal) aliens** annually. Most come from Mexico, with other large clusters from Guatemala, Honduras, and El Salvador.[3] Undocumented aliens, by some estimates exceeding 11 million, strain local and state social services and generate dominant-group hostility, but they also make substantial economic contributions as consumers and as low-skilled workers.

## CULTURAL DIFFERENTIATION

The cultures of the peoples from the various Caribbean and Central and South American countries differ. Value orientations within a particular country also vary, depending on such factors as degree of urbanization and industrialization, amount of outside contact, and social class. With these qualifications in mind, we will examine some cultural traditions that most Latinos share to a greater or lesser degree and that differ from traditional U.S. values. Before doing so, we should recognize that in areas of considerable acculturation, such as New Mexico, some of these cultural traits are muted, and Latinos have adopted many Anglo (the Latino term for "mainstream white U.S.") behavior patterns.

**THE COSMIC RACE.** One cultural concept associated with older Hispanics—especially Mexicans—is that of *La Raza Cosmica,* the cosmic race. The Mexican intellectual José Vasconcelos coined the term in 1925 to refer to the amalgamation of the white, black, and Indian races that he believed was occurring in Latin America.[4] In his old age, he dismissed the idea as a juvenile fantasy, but the concept evolved into a group categorization similar to what Kurt Lewin calls the recognition of an "interdependence of fate." In essence, *La Raza Cosmica* suggests that all the Spanish-speaking peoples in the Western Hemisphere share a cultural bond and that God has planned for them a great destiny that yet has to be realized.

From this mythic construct, activists sought to unify compatriots around a common political goal based on the nationalism of an imagined community. Although those cultural resources remained dormant for much of the late twentieth century, *La Raza* lived on as the name of an influential newspaper and of a strong political organization representing Chicano interests. On a broader scale, the realization of that common political goal occurred in the major role played by Hispanic voters in re-electing President Obama. The Latino impact reverberated after the election, causing elected officials of both parties to focus more fully on immigration reform and other issues of concern to this growing segment of the electorate.[5]

**MACHISMO.** Overstated in the Anglo stereotype, *machismo* is a basic value governing various qualities of masculinity. To Hispanic males, such attributes as inner strength in the face of adversity, personal daring, bravado, leadership, and sexual prowess are measures of one's manhood.[6] The role of the man is to be a good provider for his family, to protect its honor at all times, and to be strong, reliable, and independent. He should avoid indebtedness, accepting charity, and any kind of relationship, formal or informal, that would weaken his autonomy. Traditional culture and the family system are male dominated. The woman's role is within the family, and women are to be guarded against any onslaught on their honor. Machismo also may find expression in such forms as perceived sexual allure, fathering children, and aggressive behavior. *Marianismo* is the companion value, describing various qualities of femininity, particularly acceptance of male dominance, emphasis on family responsibilities, and the nurturing role of women.

The concept of machismo is not strictly Latin American. Such traditional gender role orientations are common throughout most developing countries, whether African, Eastern, Middle Eastern, Western, or Pacific Island. For Latinos, machismo diminishes with increasing levels of education, assimilation, and multigenerational residence in the United States.

The result of these values not only can be a double standard of sexual morality but also a difficulty adjusting to U.S. culture, as women have more independence in the United States than in most Hispanic countries. Instead of men being the sole providers, women also can find employment, sometimes earning more money than the men of the family. The participation of Hispanic women in the labor force seems to be related to educational level. More highly educated Cuban, Central American, and South American women participate in the labor force at rates similar to those of white women in the United States, whereas Mexican and Puerto Rican women have lower rates. Overall, the participation of Hispanic women in the labor force is about the same as the national average for all women, although more are in less-skilled positions.[7]

**DIGNIDAD.** The cultural value of *dignidad* is the basis of social interaction; it assumes that the dignity of all humans entitles them to a measure of respect. It is a quality typically attributed to all, regardless of status, race, color, or creed.[8] Regardless of status, each person acknowledges others' *dignidad* in a taken-for-granted reciprocal behavior pattern. Therefore, Hispanics expect to be treated in terms of *dignidad*. Because it is an implicit measure of respect, one cannot demand it from others. Instead, one concludes that others are rude and cold if they do not acknowledge one's *dignidad*. More broadly, the concept includes a strong positive self-image.

**STUDENTS SPEAK** "Just like any other minority group, Hispanics are not all the same. Each Hispanic country has uniqueness in land, language, people, food, music, government, economic status, education, history, beliefs, and values. What you find in Puerto Rico or Guatemala, you will not find in the Dominican Republic or Mexico. A small example is the *cocui*, a small frog found only in Puerto Rico. Many times Hispanics are categorized as Hispanic just for speaking Spanish but, in truth, it's way beyond that. Spanish culture is an enormously broad range of beauty with many variations. Latinos have much pride of where they come from and even though Hispanic Americans become Americans and assimilate, they never forget where they come from."

**—Emna Solares**

## RACIAL ATTITUDES

In most Latin American countries, skin color is less important than social class as an indicator of social status. An apparent correlation exists between darker skin color and lower social standing, but the racial line between whites and blacks that is drawn sharply in the United States is less distinct in Latin America. A great deal of color integration occurs in social interaction, intermarriage, and shared orientations to cultural values. There also is a much wider range of recognized color gradations, which helps to blunt any color prejudice. Still, in some places, such as Puerto Rico, color prejudice has increased, perhaps as a result of social and economic changes from industrialization.[9]

Color often serves as an unexpected basis of discrimination for Latinos coming to the United States. Being stereotyped, judged, and treated on the basis of one's skin color is

# the MINORITY experience

## What's in a Name?

What makes someone a Latino? Is it genetics (your blood lines) or geography (where you were born)? For example, a child born in the United States to Dominican immigrant parents would be called "Dominican American." Pope Francis is a native Spanish speaker born and raised in Argentina. However, his parents were born in Italy.

Because of his European heritage, some argue that, even though Pope Francis may be from Latin America and a special inspiration to Spanish-speaking Catholics around the world, he is not a "Latino." Others argue that if you are born in Latin America, and share its language, history and culture, then you indeed are a Latino. The issue rests on whether or not to make a distinction between Latin American (geography) and Latino (genetics).

A related issue is the use of *Hispanic* or *Latino/Latina*. Although *Hispanic* is a long-used governmental term, many people falling under this label reject it because of its association with European conquest of the Americas and/or recent immigrants who speak only Spanish. Instead, they prefer Latino/Latina to identify more accurately their mix of indigenous, African, and European ancestry.

essentially unknown to these brown-skinned peoples in their homeland, so encountering racial prejudice and discrimination can be a traumatic experience. Before long, they realize the extent of this ugly aspect of U.S. society. Some adapt to it, others forsake it and return home, but all resent it.

## RELIGION

Throughout Latin America, Catholicism typically means personal relationships with the saints and a community manifestation of faith, and less the individual actions and commitments expected in the United States. Another aspect of religious life in Puerto Rico, Brazil, and other parts of Latin America is the widespread belief in spiritualism and superstition. These practices, which constitute remnants of earlier folk rites, continue to be observed by various cults as well as by many Catholics.[10]

For many people, especially in the lowest socioeconomic class regardless of their racial or ethnic background, religion serves as an emotional escape from the harsh realities of everyday life. **Pentecostalism**, a form of evangelical Christianity, inspires a strong sense of belonging through openly expressive worship participation, thus offering to some a greater attraction than Catholicism. Pentecostal churches represent the largest Hispanic Protestant religious movement in Puerto Rico and the U.S. mainland, as well as throughout Latin America. In the United States, hundreds of such churches, with small and intimate congregations of approximately 60 to 100, offer their largely immigrant members a renewalist Christianity that emphasizes God's ongoing day-to-day intervention in human affairs. Hispanic Catholics practice a distinctive form of Catholicism—a blend of many beliefs and behaviors that constitute Pentecostal or Renewalist Christianity with the main features of traditional Catholic teaching.[11]

Approximately 15 percent of all Latinos identify themselves as evangelical Protestants, while 68 percent are Roman Catholics. Hispanic churches, as other ethnic churches before them, provide both a spiritual haven and a sense of community. As the proportion of Hispanic Catholics increases, the Latino influence on U.S. religious institutions is becoming more pronounced.[12] The 2013 election of Pope Francis, hailed as "the first Latino pope," generated enthusiasm and pride among Hispanic Americans, but also raised questions about determining ethnic identity (see the accompanying box).

## OTHER CULTURAL ATTRIBUTES

Hispanics generally have a more casual attitude toward time than do others in the United States, and they hold a negative attitude toward rushing, believing it robs one of dignity. Another cultural difference—one that easily could lead to misunderstanding—is their attitude about making eye contact with others. To them, not looking directly into the eyes of an authority figure, such as a teacher or police officer, is an act of respect, but native U.S. residents may interpret it as shyness, avoidance, or guilt. Like southern Europeans, Hispanics regard physical proximity in conversation as a sign of friendliness, but Anglos are accustomed to a greater distance between conversationalists. One can envision an Anglo made uncomfortable by the seemingly unusual nearness of a Hispanic person and backing away, the latter reestablishing the physical closeness, the Anglo again backing away, and the Hispanic concluding that the Anglo is a cold or aloof individual. Each has viewed the situation from a different cultural perspective, leading to very different interpretations of the incident.[13]

## CURRENT PATTERNS

Hispanics are the largest ethnic group in the United States and steadily are increasing in number all the time. At 51 million residents in 2010 (a 43 percent increase over the 35.3 million in 2000, compared to an overall 10 percent increase), they now constitute approximately 17 percent of the total U.S. population. As the nation's largest minority group, their proportion of the total population will increase, given their higher birth rate than other groups, a high immigration rate from Spanish-speaking countries, and a low average age of these immigrants (36 percent are under age 18).[14]

More than half of all Hispanics live in only three states: California, Texas, and Florida. More than three-fourths live in eight states with Hispanic populations of 1 million or more (California, Texas, New York, Florida, Illinois, Arizona, New Jersey, and Colorado). The Hispanic percentages of some of the nation's nine largest cities are Miami (70 percent), San Antonio (63 percent), Los Angeles (49 percent), Houston (44 percent), Dallas (42 percent), San Jose (33 percent), Chicago, New York, and San Diego (29 percent each).[15]

What do these growing numbers and extensive population clusters suggest for future dominant–minority relations? No simple answer exists because of the variance in Hispanic education, socioeconomic background, and occupational skills. Despite nativist

*A common sight in Hispanic neighborhoods is bodegas or stores catering to the needs of the local community, with familiar products and signs in the residents' native language, such as this grocery store on Broadway's Sugar Hill section of New York City.*

# the INTERNATIONAL scene

## Cultural Diffusion in Argentina

Because nearly all Argentinians are descendants of relatively recent immigrants from Europe, their culture has a stronger European orientation than is found in neighboring Latin American countries. The people of Buenos Aires, the *porteños*, often call their city the Paris of South America, and with its culture and glamour, it probably earns that name. Buenos Aires often is described as Latin America's most European city. The population consists largely of the descendants of immigrants from Spain and Italy who came to Argentina in the late nineteenth or early twentieth century. There also are significant minorities of Germans, British, Jews from central and eastern Europe, and Middle Eastern peoples, who are known collectively as *turcos*.

Since the 1930s, most migrants to the city have come from the northern portion of Argentina, where the population predominantly is *mestizo* (mixed Indian and European). Today, the *mestizos* make up between one-fourth and one-third of the population in the metropolitan area; they tend to live in the poorest sections of the city, in the *villas miserias* and the distant suburbs. The area's black and mulatto population is of negligible size.

There are no ethnic neighborhoods, strictly speaking, but many of the smaller minorities typically settle close to one another in tightly knit communities. Villa Crespo, for example, is known as a Jewish neighborhood; the Avenida de Mayo is a center for Spaniards; and Flores is the home of many *turcos*. The assimilation of these groups has been less than complete, but the Argentinian identity has been flexible enough to allow ethnocentric mutual aid societies and social clubs to emerge. Even the dominant Spanish language has been affected by other European cultures and has undergone changes. In the slums and waterfront districts, an Italianized dialect has emerged, and Italian cuisine is popular in the city.

Another hybrid of the Old and New Worlds is the tango, which emerged from the poor immigrant quarters of Buenos Aires toward the end of the nineteenth century and quickly became famous around the world as Argentina's national dance. Influenced by the Spanish tango and, possibly, by the Argentinian *milonga*, it originally was a high-spirited local dance but soon became an elegant ballroom form danced to melancholy tunes.

The combination of Old and New World cultures also is seen in the Argentinian diet. Southern European influences appear especially in the city where breakfast often is a light serving of rolls and coffee, and supper is taken, in the Spanish tradition, after nine o'clock at night. The Italian influence is seen in the popularity of pasta dishes. But the New World asserts itself in the Argentinian passion for beef, which is overwhelmingly preferred to other meats and fish. *Maté*, a native tea-like beverage brewed from *yerba maté* leaves, is popular in the countryside.

### CRITICAL THINKING QUESTION

What examples of Hispanic cultural diffusion in the United States can you name?

---

fears, however, English language mastery is a common goal of Hispanic parents for their children; few in the second generation and hardly any in the third generation are Spanish dominant in their daily conversations.[16] Concerns about ethnic tribalism or about the need to enshrine English as the "official" language of the United States seem unfounded, as we will discuss in the last chapter.

Cultural vitality, long an attribute among Mexican Americans in the Southwest living so near their homeland, likely will remain within other Latino communities also. The dynamics of cultural pluralism are fueled by the large Hispanic presence, current migration patterns, psychological ties to the homeland, rapid transportation and communications, government policy, and societal tolerance. Acculturation and mainstreaming no doubt will occur for most Hispanics, as they have for members of other groups, but the dynamics of cultural pluralism suggest that the Hispanic influence will be long-lasting in U.S. society. Although Hispanics may blend in with the rest of society, like the French who influenced the Louisiana region, they well may fundamentally affect U.S. culture itself (see the International Scene box).

# Social Indicators of Hispanic Progress

As Figure 11.2 shows, a much larger percentage of Hispanics than non-Hispanics are young, with proportionately more children and fewer elderly. Higher fertility, particularly among the foreign born, and the high percentage of young adult immigrants in their reproductive years create this differential. However, Hispanic groups vary in their migration and fertility patterns. For example, 21 percent of Cuban Americans are under 18, compared to 36 percent among Mexican Americans. In contrast, children under 15 constitute 22 percent of whites.[17]

Diversity among various Hispanic cultural groups also manifests itself in such social indicators as education, income, and occupation (see Figure 11.3). These indicators support mixed findings on the status of Hispanic Americans and provide some cause for concern.

**11-2** Examine what social indicators tell us about Hispanic progress.

**Read on MySocLab**
Document: The Hispanic Dropout Mystery: A Staggering 30 Percent Leave School, Far More Than Blacks or Whites. Why?

## EDUCATION

Perhaps the most important indicator of societal mainstreaming is education, for it provides the means for greater job opportunities. Unfortunately, far more Latinos ages 25 or older never finished high school compared to the total population (37 to 14 percent). The comparison for holding at least a bachelor's degree is 13 to 28 percent.[18] All Hispanic groups significantly lag behind the non-Hispanic population in producing high school graduates, especially Central Americans and Mexicans.

Reasons cited for the education gap between Hispanics and non-Hispanics include the limited formal education of parents, less preschool experience for Hispanic children compared to whites and blacks, and cultural/linguistic differences encountered in school. Also important is the increased proportion of immigrants in the U.S. Hispanic population. Few educational differences exist between males and females. South Americans and Cuban Americans have the highest percentage of college graduates, and Mexican Americans have the lowest.

We can find two promising notes within other educational data. U.S.-born Hispanics in all ethnic groups are more likely than the foreign born to have higher percentages of high school and college graduates. Approximately 44 percent of foreign-born Hispanic adults are high school graduates compared with 73 percent of U.S.-born Hispanic adults. Further, second-generation Latinos get better grades and their dropout rate is approximately 15 percent compared

**STUDENTS SPEAK** "Many foreign-born Hispanic parents don't speak English, making it impossible to be involved in their children's schools and their school work. New Hispanic immigrants are coming every day and if this trend of dropouts and parental non-involvement persists, they are going to fall into the poverty cycle as well. As a foreign-born Hispanic myself, I know it is difficult, but we have to look for changes. The Spanish-speaking channels reach people easily and they encourage education, but it is not enough. We have to find other ways to break this cycle."

**—Sylvia Barrera**

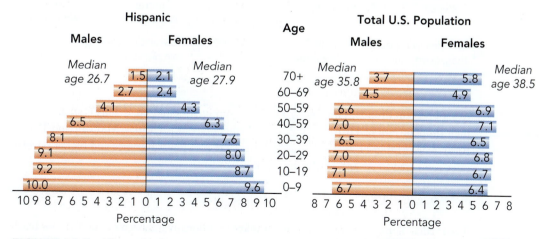

**FIGURE 11.2** Hispanic-American Population, 2010, in percentages

Source: U.S. Census Bureau.

**FIGURE 11.3** Social Indicators about Hispanic Subgroups in 2011 (in percentages)

*Source:* U.S. Census Bureau.

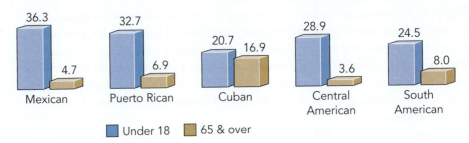

Age

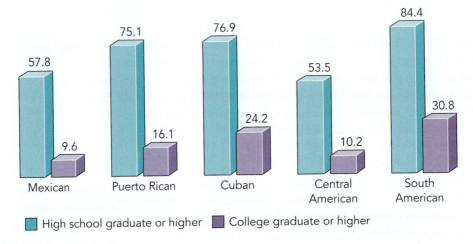

Education (of persons age 25 and over)

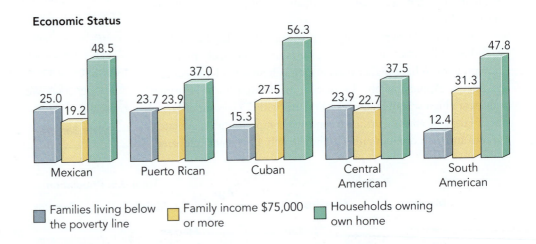

Economic Status

to a 44 percent dropout rate among Hispanic immigrant children.[19] This is an alarmingly high dropout rate of Hispanic high school students—in particular, Mexican and Puerto Rican teens (Table 11.2). These statistics translate into lower incomes and higher poverty rates compared to Asians, blacks, and whites.

## INCOME

The median family income for Latino families traditionally has been higher than for black families (Table 11.3). Moreover, the real income gap is growing. Despite a strong Hispanic middle class—22 percent of Hispanic families have incomes of $75,000 or more—another

**TABLE 11. 2**  High School Dropouts, Ages 16-24, by Race/Ethnicity and Gender (in percentages)

|  | 1980 | 1990 | 2000 | 2010 |
|---|---|---|---|---|
| *Blacks* | 19.1 | 13.2 | 13.1 | 8.0 |
| Females | 17.7 | 14.4 | 11.1 | 6.7 |
| Males | 20.8 | 11.9 | 15.3 | 9.5 |
| *Whites* | 11.4 | 9.0 | 6.9 | 5.1 |
| Females | 10.5 | 8.7 | 6.9 | 4.2 |
| Males | 12.3 | 9.3 | 7.0 | 5.9 |
| *Hispanics* | 35.2 | 32.4 | 27.8 | 15.1 |
| Females | 33.2 | 30.3 | 23.5 | 12.8 |
| Males | 37.2 | 34.3 | 31.8 | 17.3 |

*Source:* National Center for Education Statistics, *Digest of Education Statistics: 2011*, Table 116.

**TABLE 11.3**  Median Income of Hispanic, Black, and White Families for Selected Years, 1970–2011

| YEAR | HISPANIC | BLACK | WHITE | HISPANIC INCOME AS PERCENT OF WHITE |
|---|---|---|---|---|
| 1970 | NA | $ 6,279 | $10,236 | NA |
| 1980 | $14,716 | $12,674 | $21,904 | 67 |
| 1990 | $23,431 | $21,423 | $36,915 | 64 |
| 2000 | $33,447 | $30,439 | $45,904 | 73 |
| 2011 | $40,982 | $40,140 | $66,025 | 62 |

*Note:* NA = not available.
*Source:* U.S. Census Bureau, *2011 American Community Survey*, Table S0201.

22 percent live in poverty. Generally, Hispanics consistently have had a lower percentage of impoverished families than blacks. A higher percentage of Mexican and Puerto Rican Americans live in poverty than other Hispanic groups, whereas Cuban and South Americans are the least likely of all Hispanic subgroups to live in poverty (Table 11.4). Also, Puerto Ricans have lessened their poverty numbers slightly in recent years.

**TABLE 11.4**  Persons below Poverty Level, 2011 (in percentages)

| | |
|---|---|
| White | 10.4 |
| African American | 25.6 |
| All Hispanic | 22.4 |
| Mexican American | 23.8 |
| Puerto Rican | 25.3 |
| Cuban American | 15.8 |
| Dominican American | 27.5 |
| Central American | 18.9 |
| Salvadoran American | 17.1 |
| South American | 14.0 |

*Source:* U.S. Census Bureau, *2011 American Community Survey*, Table S0201.

*Education, as stated in earlier chapters, is the means by which minorities can achieve upward mobility by qualifying for better-paying jobs. Although some Hispanic young adults are graduating from college, the sad reality is that a higher percentage drop out of high school and/or do not attend college in comparison to other U.S. minority groups.*

As with the education data, we again must note the impact of immigration on these income and poverty statistics. New entrants into the U.S. labor force typically earn less than those with longer residence because they often lack the education, training, experience, and seniority of other workers. Therefore, they tend to take lower-skill jobs at entry-level salaries. Like past European peasant immigrants, economic survival is their immediate goal. The United States for them is, as William Bradford described North America for the English Puritans in the early seventeenth century, a place "where they must learn a new language and get their livings they knew not how."

## OCCUPATION

Occupation provides an important basis for personal esteem, and the occupational distribution of an entire ethnic group thus serves as a comparative measure of its status within the larger society. Table 11.5 addresses this aspect of Hispanic structural assimilation. As might be expected from the educational data, most Hispanic males (except Cuban, Puerto Rican, and South Americans) are heavily underrepresented in managerial and professional occupations, and an unusually high number of Mexican and Central Americans work in unskilled blue-collar occupations. Reflecting the typical gender occupational distribution in U.S. society, Hispanic females tend to be just as likely to work in sales and administrative support positions as non-Hispanic females. Hispanic women are less likely than non-Hispanics, however, to occupy managerial and professional positions, although Cuban, Puerto Rican, and South American women are more strongly represented in these jobs than are other Hispanic women. All Hispanic women are more likely than non-Hispanics to work in service occupations as well as in unskilled blue-collar positions as operators, in transportation, and as laborers.

**TABLE 11.5  Occupational Distribution, 2011**

|  | NON-HISPANIC | MEXICAN | PUERTO RICAN | CUBAN | CENTRAL AMERICAN | SOUTH AMERICAN |
|---|---|---|---|---|---|---|
| **Males** | | | | | | |
| Managerial, professional | 36.0 | 12.5 | 22.7 | 30.3 | 11.2 | 24.7 |
| Sales and office occupations | 18.5 | 13.6 | 20.8 | 18.5 | 10.9 | 19.7 |
| Service occupations | 11.3 | 22.7 | 23.0 | 19.4 | 19.1 | 15.5 |
| Production, transportation | 16.7 | 22.9 | 20.0 | 18.0 | 22.0 | 19.3 |
| Construction, extraction, maintenance | 16.7 | 28.3 | 13.5 | 13.5 | 35.6 | 20.7 |
| **Females** | | | | | | |
| Managerial, professional | 41.5 | 22.1 | 31.9 | 37.6 | 16.2 | 31.5 |
| Sales and office occupations | 35.3 | 32.0 | 37.0 | 30.1 | 28.2 | 33.2 |
| Service occupations | 17.5 | 32.3 | 23.7 | 21.3 | 41.1 | 28.3 |
| Production, transportation | 4.9 | 10.9 | 6.7 | 9.4 | 13.0 | 6.7 |
| Construction, extraction, maintenance | 0.7 | 2.7 | 0.8 | 1.7 | 1.0 | 0.3 |

*Source:* U.S. Census Bureau, *2011 American Community Survey.*

# Mexican Americans

Most of the 33.6 million Mexican Americans live in the southwestern states, with more than three-fourths in California, Texas, Arizona, Illinois, and Colorado. The largest population concentrations live in Los Angeles, Chicago, Houston, San Antonio, and Phoenix.[20]

Much diversity exists within this ethnic group in degree of assimilation and socioeconomic status, ranging along a continuum from the most newly nonacculturated arrivals to the *Hispanos* of northern New Mexico and southern Colorado who trace their ancestry in that region to the days of the Spanish conquest of what is now the southwestern United States.

Throughout New Mexico—which, unlike Texas and California, has limited contact with Mexico through border crossings—the employment pattern is bright. In fact, most Hispanic Americans there hold economically secure jobs and are heavily represented in civil service occupations at the local, state, and federal levels. Like many recent non-Western immigrants, they retain a cultural heritage that includes their diet, child-rearing philosophy, emphasis on the family, and extended family contacts.

Second-generation Mexican Americans living in large cities typically display greater structural assimilation as evidenced by separate residences for nuclear families, English-language competence, fewer children, and comparable family values, jobs, and income than those living in border towns or agricultural regions.[21] However, most present-day Mexican Americans, whether they live in an urban setting or a rural area, lag far behind the rest of the U.S. population on every measure of socioeconomic well-being: education, income, and employment status.

### RECRUITING MEXICANS

In the second half of the nineteenth century, Mexicans from south of the border helped fill U.S. labor needs for the construction of railroad lines and the expansion of cotton, fruit, and vegetable farms. Thereafter, the Chinese Exclusion Act of 1882 curtailed one source of laborers, and later the Immigration Acts of 1921 and 1924 curtailed another. However, the demand for labor—especially for agricultural workers—increased, and Mexicans left their poverty-stricken country for the opened economic opportunities in the United States.

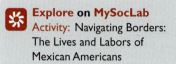

**11-3** Describe the immigrant experiences of Mexicans, Puerto Ricans, and Cubans.

**Explore on MySocLab**
Activity: Navigating Borders: The Lives and Labors of Mexican Americans

**Watch on MySocLab**
Video: The Basics: Economy and Work

*Once the bracero program (1942–1964) provided U.S. farmers with the seasonal help they needed to harvest their crops by allowing Mexicans to enter the United States on temporary visas. Today, mostly Hispanic migrant workers, both legal and illegal immigrants, fill this need, as in this cauliflower field near Santa Cruz, California.*

Despite U.S. government restrictions on immigration, it was easy for Mexicans to cross the largely unpatrolled border and enter the United States illegally, and many did so. The ones who crossed into Texas were known as "wetbacks" because they had crossed the Rio Grande. Some Mexican aliens also entered the United States legally as contract laborers. Under this *bracero* program, Mexican aliens entered the United States on temporary visas and then returned to Mexico after the harvest. This system provided needed workers without incurring the expenses of educating their children and of extending welfare and other social services to them during the off-season. The program lasted from 1942 until 1964, when farm mechanization, labor shortages in Mexico, and the protests of native Hispanics in the United States ended it.

## EXPULSION

Although cheap Mexican labor was a boon to the southwestern economy, Mexicans usually found themselves unwelcome during downturns in the U.S. economy. One such time was the 1930s, when many U.S. citizens were jobless. Some Mexicans returned home voluntarily, and others did so under pressure by local residents. Hundreds of thousands who did not leave willingly were rounded up and deported from southern California, from cities throughout the Southwest, and as far north as from Chicago and Detroit:

> In Los Angeles, official trucks would grind into the barrios—the Mexican American neighborhoods—and the occupants would be herded into them. There was little or no determination of national origin. Citizenship or noncitizenship was not considered. Families were divided; the bringing of possessions was not permitted....
>
> "They pushed most of my family into one van," one of the victims, Jorge Acevedo, remembers bitterly. "We drove all day. The driver wouldn't stop for bathroom, nor food nor water. Everyone knew by now we had been deported. Nobody knew why, but there was a lot of hatred and anger....We had always known that we were hated. Now we had proof."[22]

During the recession of the mid-1950s, the U.S. Immigration and Naturalization Service launched "Operation Wetback" to find and return all undocumented Mexican aliens. Between 1954 and 1959, concentrating on California and Texas but ranging as far north and east as Spokane, Chicago, Kansas City, and St. Louis, government officials found and expelled 3.8 million Mexicans, less than 64,000 of whom ever received a formal hearing. Not all were undocumented aliens. INS agents stopped and questioned many U.S. citizens if they "looked Mexican." Those unable to prove their legal status on the spot found themselves arrested and sent "home" without any further opportunity to defend themselves.[23]

## VIOLENCE

One infamous incident in which prejudices against Mexicans erupted into violence was the Zoot Suit Riot of 1943. The name came from the popularity among Mexican American youths at that time of wearing long, loose-fitting jackets with wide shoulders; high-waisted, baggy trousers with tight cuffs; and flat-topped hats with broad brims. The gamblers in the original show and the film version of *Guys and Dolls* dressed in this fashion.

On June 3, 1943, two events triggered the riot. Some Mexican boys, returning from a police-sponsored club meeting, were assaulted by a group of non-Mexican hoodlums from the neighborhood in Los Angeles. That same evening, 11 sailors on leave were attacked, and 1 sailor was badly hurt. The sailors said that their assailants were Mexican youths who outnumbered them 3 to 1. When the police, responding late, found no one to arrest in the area, approximately 200 sailors decided to settle the matter themselves the following evening. Cruising through the Mexican section in a caravan of 20 taxicabs, they savagely beat every Mexican they found. The police did nothing to stop them and, as Carey McWilliams reported, the press gave this event and its aftermath wide publicity:

> The stage was now set for the really serious rioting of June seventh and eighth. Having featured the preliminary rioting as an offensive launched by sailors, soldiers, and marines, the press now whipped public opinion into a frenzy by dire warnings that Mexican zoot-suiters planned a mass retaliation. To ensure a riot, the precise street corners were marked at which retaliatory action was expected and the time of the anticipated action was carefully specified. In effect, these stories announced a riot and invited public participation....
>
> On Monday evening, June seventh, thousands of *Angelenos,* in response to twelve hours' advance notice in the press, turned out for a mass lynching. Marching through the streets of downtown Los Angeles, a mob of several thousand soldiers, sailors, and civilians proceeded to beat up every zoot-suiter they could find. Pushing its way into the important motion picture theaters, the mob ordered the management to turn on the house lights and then ranged up and down the aisles dragging Mexicans out of their seats. Street cars were halted while Mexicans, and some Filipinos and Negroes, were jerked out of their seats, pushed into the streets, and beaten with sadistic frenzy....

Here is one of the numerous eyewitness accounts written by Al Waxman, editor of *The Eastside Journal:*

> Four boys came out of a pool hall. They were wearing the zoot-suits that have become the symbols of a fighting flag. Police ordered them into arrest cars. One refused. He asked: "Why am I being arrested?" The police officer answered with three swift blows of the night-stick across the boy's head and he went down. As he sprawled, he was kicked in the face. Police had difficulty loading his body into the vehicle because he was one-legged and wore a wooden limb....
>
> At the next corner, a Mexican mother cried out, "Don't take my boy, he did nothing. He's only fifteen years old. Don't take him." She was struck across the jaw with a night-stick and almost dropped the two-and-a-half-year-old baby that was clinging in her arms....
>
> A Negro defense worker, wearing a defense-plant identification badge on his work clothes, was taken from a street car and one of his eyes was gouged out with a knife. Huge half-page photographs, showing Mexican boys, stripped of their clothes, cowering on the pavements, often bleeding profusely, surrounded by jeering mobs of men and women, appeared in all of the Los Angeles newspapers....
>
> When it finally stopped, the Eagle Rock *Advertiser* mournfully editorialized: "It is too bad the servicemen were called off before they were able to complete the job....Most of the citizens of the city have been delighted with what has been going on."[24]

This bloody incident, like earlier Know-Nothing riots, anti-Chinese race riots, black lynchings, and many other acts of violence, was the result of increasing societal tensions and prejudices against a minority that erupted into aggression far in excess of the triggering incident. Whatever Mexicans thought about Anglo society before this wartime incident, they long would remember this race riot waged against them with approval from the police, the newspapers, and city hall.

## URBAN LIFE

In some places, such as Los Angeles and New Mexico, Mexican Americans often are better integrated into the mainstream of society than their compatriots elsewhere. There, they have higher intermarriage rates, nuclear instead of extended family residence patterns, and less patriarchal male roles. They enter more diverse occupations, and many attain middle-class status and move from the barrio to the suburbs and outskirts of the city. Yet in East Los Angeles and in other areas of the Southwest, particularly in smaller cities and towns, Mexican Americans reside in large ethnic enclaves, virtually isolated from participation in Anglo society. Even some *Hispano* middle-class individuals whose families have lived in the United States for generations choose to live among their own people and interact mostly with them.

Many Mexican Americans live in substandard housing under crowded conditions. In the southwestern states where most Mexican Americans live, their housing is more crowded than that of non-whites; in Texas, twice as many Mexicans as blacks live in over-crowded housing. Segregated in the less desirable sections of town, with their children attending schools that warrant the same criticisms as inner-city schools in major cities, they experience many forms of discrimination.

The large influx of Mexican Americans and their residential clustering in urban areas have resulted in a high level of increasingly segregated schools. This trend toward isolation of schoolchildren holds for most urban Hispanics but is pronounced particularly in the Southwest. For example, the percentage of white students in Los Angeles County high schools attended by Mexican American students has dropped from 45 percent in 1970 to less than 15 percent today.[25]

## STEREOTYPING

Currently, the two most common stereotypes that Mexican Americans have had to combat involve their identification as undocumented aliens or youth gang members. "Looking" Mexican often raises suspicions about legal residence or makes prospective employers wary of hiring a possible undocumented alien, even if the individual is a legal U.S. resident. In the poor urban barrios of Los Angeles, San Antonio, and El Paso, youth gangs are an integral subculture within the community. Gang fights and killings—particularly in

*Olvera Street is located in the oldest section of Los Angeles. Once the residential locale of Mexican Americans, it fell into a seriously deteriorated state until it was revitalized in the late 1920s. Today, it flourishes as a successful commercial area that attracts millions of tourists each year and is LA's center for Cinco de Mayo festivities.*

East Los Angeles—and the associated drug scene create a lasting, negative picture of all Mexican Americans in the minds of many Anglos.

Like blacks and Puerto Ricans, Mexican Americans suffer from culture-of-poverty beliefs held by the dominant society. All too often, outsiders blame their low socioeconomic standing on their supposed cultural values. In reality, Mexican Americans have a participation rate in the labor force comparable to, or higher than, other groups—white, black, Asian, or other Hispanic.[26] Furthermore, the percentage of Mexican Americans receiving welfare assistance is only approximately one-sixth that of blacks and of other Hispanic groups and approximately one-half that of whites. Because Mexican Americans have a large proportion of immigrant workers, the usual pattern of lower wages for the foreign-born wage earners impacts significantly on the median income reported for all Mexican Americans. Studies show that, as their length of time in the United States increases, Mexican immigrants close the earnings gap with U.S.-born Mexican Americans but not with non-Hispanic whites. The gains in earnings associated with age, time in the United States, and English proficiency differ by gender, as women do not close the gap that much.[27]

## CHICANO POWER

Until the 1960s, the term *Chicano* was a derogatory name applied in Mexico to the "lower"-class Mexican Indians rather than to the Mexican Spanish. Then, as an outgrowth of the Civil Rights movement and in direct contradiction to the stereotype of the passive, apathetic Mexican community, the Chicano movement emerged. Seeking to instill pride in the group's *mestizo* heritage (mixed Spanish and Indian ancestry), activists adopted the term in their efforts to promote political activism and demands for economic and educational quality. Prominent leaders emerged—César Chávez and his United Farm Workers Union, Rodolfo Gonzales and his *La Raza Unida* political third-party movement, Reies Lópes Tijerina and his Alianza group seeking to recover land lost or stolen throughout the years, and David Sanchez and his militant Brown Berets, who modeled themselves after the Black Panthers. These past militant leaders have been replaced by a new generation of Chicano advocates, such as Janet Murguía, executive director of the National Council of La Raza. Another significant entity is the Mexican-American Legal Defense and Education Fund (MALDEF). This civil rights organization effectively uses its influence in the public arena to address such issues as bilingualism, school financing, segregation, employment practices, and immigration reform.[28]

Before this national movement dawned, rapid expansion in Sunbelt cities in the 1950s and 1960s had generated problems and tensions that led to the formation of community groups opposed to urban renewal plans threatening Mexican American neighborhoods. These organized neighborhood protests were the vanguard of what became known as the Chicano movement. In San Jose, for example, activists of diverse origins and agendas united in opposition to the effects of urban development on the barrios, and this city later became a center for the Chicano movement during its time of phenomenal growth.[29]

Older organizations, such as the League of United Latin American Citizens and the American G. I. Forum, once focused on assimilation and the Anglo world, with a primary emphasis on social functions. Newer groups—such as *La Raza Unida* and *Movimiento Estudiantil Chicano de Aztlán*—served as synthesizers, bringing the two cultures together. The newer groups have focused on political issues, such as the farm workers' plight, while promoting a sense of peoplehood.

Turning away from the third-party politics of the past, Chicanos are integrating into the two main political parties. In states where they are heavily concentrated, Chicanos are developing a powerful political base, now including nearly 6,000 elected and appointed local and state Hispanic public officials, most of whom are in Texas, California, New Mexico, Arizona, and Colorado.[30]

## CURRENT PATTERNS

Illinois is now the third highest state of intended residence among new Mexican arrivals, after California and Texas. The Census Bureau reported that in 2011, nearly 1.7 million Mexican Americans lived in Illinois (thanks in large measure to the lure of its meat-packing industry), making it the fourth highest in Mexican American population behind California, Texas, and Arizona. Nearly three times as many Mexican Americans live in Illinois as in New Mexico.[31]

Mexican immigration continues into both rural and urban areas, but most immigrants are settling in urban neighborhoods, although not necessarily in inner cities. In 2011, 76 percent of the Mexican American population was third generation or higher, and thus hardly the newcomers so many Americans assume most of this group to be.[32] Many of the central-city residents are of a low socioeconomic status and live in areas where the school dropout rate of Mexican American youths runs as high as 45 percent, with student alienation serving as a major cause.[33]

# Puerto Rican Americans

Originally inhabited by the Arawak and Caribe indigenous tribes, Puerto Rico came under Spanish domination in 1493 and remained so for 400 years. With the decimation of its native population, Spaniards replaced them with African slaves. **Miscegenation** (interracial marriage) was common, resulting in a society that de-emphasized race. Reflecting the high degree of color integration are such words as *moreno, mulatto, pardo,* and *trigueño,* indicating a broad range of color gradations. Today, structural assimilation in the island's multiracial society extends to housing, social institutions, government policy, and cultural identity.[34] A high degree of intermarriage often means that people classified in one racial category have close-kin relationships with people in other racial categories, either by bloodline or by adoption.

Many Latinos—including Puerto Ricans—primarily regard themselves in cultural terms. However, because so many are influenced by the racial categorization of mainstream U.S. society, some usually will answer—when asked about their race—in standard U.S. terms and identify themselves as black, white, or Indian. Others, though, see themselves as a mixture of race and ethnicity and may identify themselves as Afro-Latinos or white Hispanics. In fact, the Latino view of race differs within Latin American countries, social classes, and even families. Not surprisingly, in the 2010 Census more than 18 million Latinos identified themselves as "other," apparently unwilling to accept the government's rigid racial classifications.[35]

Several cultural and historical factors led to the more tolerant racial attitudes found in Puerto Rico (and in other Latin American countries). Spain long ago had experience with dark-skinned people (Moors), who often married white women. Second, in the wars of Christians against Moors and Saracens, captured whites also became slaves, resulting in laws to protect certain fundamental rights of all slaves, a tradition that carried over to the Spanish colonies in the New World. Upper-class men in these colonies recognized their illegitimate children by women of color, frequently freeing the babies at their baptism. Furthermore, through the practice of *compadrazgo* (ritual kinship), leading white members of a community often became godparents of a child of color at baptism. Even in cases where the child's real father was unknown, the *padrino,* or *compadre,* was well respected and became a significant person in the child's life.[36]

## EARLY RELATIONS

After the United States annexed Puerto Rico in 1898 after the Spanish–American War, it attempted forced Americanization. Authorities discouraged anything associated with the Spanish tradition and mandated the use of the English language. Presidents appointed governors, usually from the mainland, to rule the territory. The inhabitants received U.S. citizenship in 1917, but otherwise, the island virtually remained an ignored, undeveloped, poverty-stricken land. Citizenship brought open migration because it eliminated the need for passports, visas, and quotas, but it did not give the people the right to vote for president or to have a voting representative in Congress. By 1930, approximately 53,000 Puerto Ricans were living on the mainland. During the Depression and the war years, migration effectively stopped, but then a mass migration occurred during the post–World War II era.

In the 1940s, several improvements occurred. Puerto Rico became a commonwealth, with the people writing their own constitution and electing their own representatives. In addition, the island gained complete freedom in its internal affairs, including the right to maintain its Spanish heritage and elimination of all requirements to use English.

To help the island develop economically, the U.S. government launched Operation Bootstrap in 1945. U.S. industries received substantial tax advantages if they made capital investments in Puerto Rico. These tax breaks and the abundant supply of low-cost labor encouraged businesses to build 300 new factories by 1953 (increasing to 660 by 1960), creating more than 48,000 new jobs. As a result, Puerto Rico became the most advanced industrialized land, with the highest per capita income, in the Caribbean and in most of Central and South America.

By the 1980s, however, expiring tax exemptions prompted numerous industries to leave the island in search of cheaper labor and tax exemptions elsewhere, thereby reducing available job opportunities. Since then, Puerto Rico's unemployment rate consistently has been approximately twice that of the mainland, rising and falling in response to main-land economic conditions. The island's unemployment rate, which peaked at 23 percent in 1983, stood at 13.7 percent in April 2013.[37]

## THE PUSH–PULL FACTORS

Despite the creation of thousands of factory jobs through Operation Bootstrap, the collapse of the Puerto Rican sugar industry in the 1950s triggered the beginning of *La Migracion*, one of the most dramatic voluntary exoduses in world history. One of every six Puerto Ricans migrated to the mainland, driven by the island's stagnant agrarian economy and encouraged by inexpensive plane fares and freedom of entry as U.S. citizens. Many were rural people who settled in metropolitan urban centers, drawn by the promise of jobs. The greatest period of Puerto Rican migration was 1946–1964, when approximately 615,000 moved to the mainland. Only the Irish migration of the mid-nineteenth century offers a close comparison, but that was forced in part by the Potato Famine (see the Ethnic Experience box).

After 1964, a significant drop in Puerto Rican migration occurred, aided in part by a revived Puerto Rican sugar industry after a U.S. boycott of all Cuban trade. Other factors contributed to this drop. The pull factor lost its potency, as cities such as New York City lost hundreds of thousands of manufacturing jobs and thus its promise as a job market. An island population of less than 2.4 million at that time and a declining fertility rate made sustaining the previous high exodus rate impossible. Furthermore, the earlier exodus relieved pressure on the home job market as well as increases in U.S. government welfare support, combined with remittances from family members on the mainland, encouraged many to stay on the island. In the 1970s, migration dropped to 65,900, before rising dra-matically to 333,000 in the 1980s, prompted in large measure by the high unemployment rates mentioned earlier.

High migration rates and birth rates resulted in an 82 percent increase in the Puerto Rican population living on the mainland—from 2.7 million in 1990 to approximately 4.9 million today.[38] That number exceeds the 4 million currently living on the island.

Like members of most ethnic groups, some Puerto Ricans return to their home-land to visit, and others to stay. Close proximity to the island is an obvious inducement,

# the ETHNIC experience

## Harassment Against Early Migrants

"My husband and I bought our own house in Brooklyn after the Second World War, and a few years later, we bought other property on Long Island, where we moved to raise our family. In 1956, we were employed by the U.S. Military Academy, West Point, and purchased a lovely home in a so-called exclusive area not too far away. This was a quaint neighborhood where custom-built homes ranged from $40,000 up to $100,000."

"Shortly after we moved in, we went down to Florida on vacation. When we came back, the house was empty. We slept on the floor and the following day, our attorney by telephone searched every place high and low until he found our possessions in a warehouse in Nyack. Some of our neighbors had learned we were originally from Puerto Rico, were unhappy to have us as neighbors, and had plotted this against us. The harassment continued for a long time. They threw their garbage every night on our lawn. They even sent the police to intimidate us and even tried to buy us out. We told them they couldn't afford the luxury of buying us out. We felt we had all the rights in the world to enjoy all the privileges others had. We were honest, hard-working, respectable citizens, too. So we took legal action and demanded for damages. The judge was fair and ruled for us."

Source: Puerto Rican woman who came to the mainland in 1946 in her 20s. Taped interview from the collection of Vincent N. Parrillo.

although the reasons for moving back vary. For some, the return migration stems from retirement or the desire for the more family-oriented society without discrimination and urban crime found more often on the mainland. Researchers investigating the motives for this circular migration also found that economic marginality is an important factor. That is, some migrants fail to succeed economically on the mainland and return to the island. The children of these less successful returning migrants are more likely to be impoverished than the children of migrants who remain on the mainland and the children of natives who never left the island. This outcome also could be caused by migration-related disruptions in employment.[39]

## THE FAMILY

In Puerto Rico, as in all Latin American countries, an individual's identity, importance, and security depend on family membership. A deep sense of family obligation extends to dating and courtship. Family approval is necessary because of the emphasis on marriage as a joining of two families, not only a commitment between two individuals. An indication of family importance is the use of both the father's and mother's surnames, but in reverse order to the U.S. practice. José Garcia Rivera, whose father's last name is Garcia and whose mother's is Rivera, should be called Mr. Garcia, not Mr. Rivera. Erroneous interpretation of these names in the United States by non-Hispanics can be a source of intercultural awkwardness for Spanish-speaking people.

One common form of Puerto Rican household is the extended family residing either in the same household or in separate households with frequent visits and strong bonds. Another is the nuclear family, increasingly common among the middle class. A third type is the female-headed household, with children of one or more men but with no permanent male in the home.[40] The last type frequently is found among welfare families and thus is the target of much criticism.

## RELIGION

The Catholic Church traditionally played an important role with immigrant groups, assisting in succession the French, Irish, Germans, Italians, Slavics, Poles, Syrians, Lebanese, and others.[41] This pattern at first did not repeat itself with the Puerto Ricans, at least in terms of representation in the church hierarchy, church leadership in the ethnic community, or immigrant involvement in the church. In 1970, Nathan Glazer and Daniel P. Moynihan observed,

> The Puerto Ricans have not created, as others did, national parishes of their own. Thus, the capacities of the Church are weak in just those areas in which the needs of the migrants are great—in creating a surrounding, supporting community to replace the extended families, broken by city life, and to supply a social setting for those who feel lost and lonely in the great city....
>
> Most of the Puerto Ricans in the city are Catholic, but their participation in Catholic life is small.[42]

Several factors contributed to this departure from the usual pattern. Because the island was a colony for so long, first Spanish and then U.S. priests predominated within the church hierarchy on the island. Few Puerto Ricans became priests, and the few who did rarely came to the mainland with the immigrants. The distant and alien nature of the church in Puerto Rico caused Puerto Ricans to internalize the sense of their Catholic identity without formally attending mass and receiving the sacraments. Baptisms, weddings, and funerals all became important as social occasions, and the ceremony itself was of secondary importance. On the mainland, a few other factors weakened any possibility that the Puerto Ricans would develop a strong ethnic church. The movement of white Catholic ethnics out of the cities left behind clusters of old national churches with few parishioners. Church leaders decided to use these existing churches, schools, and other buildings to accommodate the newcomers. Thus, instead of having their own churches, the Puerto Ricans had the services of one or more Spanish-speaking priests, with special masses and services performed in a basement chapel, school hall, or other area of the parish. Although this practice was cost-effective for the Catholic Church, it prevented the parish from becoming the focal point for a strong, stable community because the group could not identify with it.

As the integrated parishes became more Hispanic throughout the years, the New York archdiocese added more Spanish-speaking priests. In time, the annual *Fiesta de San Juan* each June became a widely observed religious festival in New York City. Religious/civic organizations such as the *Centro Católico Puertorriqueño* in Jersey City and the *Caballeros de San Juan* in Chicago became effective support organizations, further uniting the Puerto Rican community.[43]

## PUERTO RICAN COMMUNITIES

More than half (53 percent) of all Puerto Ricans live in the Northeast, with another 30 percent residing in the South. Two states—New York (with 1.1 million) and Florida (with 848,000)—account for the lion's share of that total, comprising 41 percent of the Puerto Rican population on the mainland. Puerto Ricans, of course, live in all 50 states, with other large concentrations (more than 266,000) found in New Jersey, Pennsylvania, and Massachusetts.[44]

For many years, the continuous **shuttle migration** prevented an organized community life from fully developing. Hometown clubs—voluntary organizations based on one's place of birth—provided a place to celebrate weddings, birthdays, first communions, and confirmations. However, because they drew members from scattered New York neighborhoods, they did not serve as community centers, nor did any other social institution. Only

*Hispanics fuel the growth of Pentecostalism, an energetic form of evangelical Christianity less structured than traditional Christian worship. Already changing their lives by migrating, perhaps, like these worshipers in Tucson, they also seek a worship style more intimate and participatory than ritualistic Catholic masses.*

the annual Puerto Rican Day Parade, begun in 1958, served to galvanize group identity. By the late 1970s, however, increased ethnic neighborhood organization was evolving with the establishment of various social institutions. Some were informal, like the *bodega,* or local grocery store, which still serves as more than a source of Hispanic foods. It is a social gathering place where social interaction, gossip, and neighborliness create a rich community center. Here, one can obtain advice on finding a home, getting a job, or buying a car. The *bodega* thus functions as an important part of the community's infrastructure.[45]

Other community institutions are civic and social organizations. Most notable is *Aspira,* founded in 1961. Through guidance, encouragement, and financial assistance, *Aspira* seeks to develop cultural pride and self-confidence in youths and to encourage them to further their education and enter the professions, technical fields, and the arts. Begun in New York City, its grassroots program achieved national fame and expanded to other cities. Another organization begun in New York City is the Puerto Rican Family Institute, which provides professional social services to Puerto Rican families. Parent action groups, athletic leagues, cultural organizations, and social clubs also exist, providing services and fulfilling community needs. Because of their limited political involvement, Puerto Ricans have had less electoral influence than other ethnic groups. Although they have been U.S. citizens since 1917, island Puerto Ricans cannot vote in federal elections.

## SOCIOECONOMIC CHARACTERISTICS

Along with Mexican Americans, Puerto Ricans have a higher poverty rate than other Hispanic groups. However, theirs has been declining steadily in recent years, while that of the Mexicans has been increasing steadily. Helping to improve their economic standing is the increased educational attainment of Puerto Ricans. They have more college graduates than Mexican Americans (16 to 10 percent) and a greater percentage of high school graduates (75 to 58 percent).[46]

Approximately the same percentage of Puerto Rican families lives in poverty as do African American families. Even though blacks have a higher educational level (83 to 75 percent high school graduates or more; 18 to 16 percent bachelor's degree or more), Puerto Ricans have a similar proportion below the poverty line.[47] One explanation for this may lie in family structure. A total of 17 percent of all African American families have a

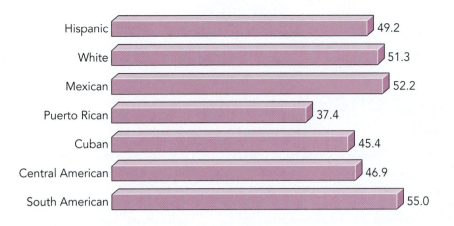

**FIGURE 11.4** Hispanic Married-Couple Families, by origin, in 2011 (in percentages)

Source: U.S. Census Bureau.

female head of household with children under age 18, as do 18 percent of Puerto Rican families (see Figure 11.4).[48] As discussed in Chapter 10, female-headed households are more vulnerable to living in poverty, and this especially is true for minority women who often lack sufficient education and job skills.

Although these statistics offer cause for concern, at the same time, it would be a mistake to generalize that most Puerto Ricans live in poverty. In fact, many are doing quite well. In 2009, the annual income of 18 percent of Puerto Rican families exceeded $50,000, while the annual income of an additional 24 percent exceeded $75,000.[49]

# Cuban Americans

Although the United States granted Cuba independence after the 1898 war with Spain, it continued to exercise *de facto* control over the island. The United States pressured Cuba to relinquish the large naval base it still operates at Guantánamo Bay, and through the Platt Amendment of 1902, it reserved the right to intervene in Cuba if necessary to protect U.S. interests. The Cubans resented these infringements on their newly achieved sovereignty until, in the 1930s, Franklin Roosevelt's Good Neighbor Policy helped ease relations between the two countries.

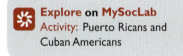

**Explore on MySocLab**
Activity: Puerto Ricans and Cuban Americans

## MIGRATION

Because the U.S. government did not differentiate Cuban immigrants from others listed as originating in the West Indies until 1950, we do not know the exact numbers of Cuban immigrants prior to that time. Although 500,000 people came to the United States from the West Indies between 1820 and 1950, the Cubans appear to have had little impact on the U.S. scene during that period. Still, a few legacies persisted, such as the Cuban community in northern New Jersey that dates back to 1850 and attracted many immigrants in the 1960s.

Since 1960, more than 1.1 million Cubans have entered the United States. Touched off by Castro's rise to power, Cuban immigration surged in the first years of the Cuban revolution, then ebbed and flowed with shifts in both U.S. and Cuban government policies (see the Ethnic Experience box). In the 1960s and 1970s, the first waves of post-revolutionary refugees (approximately 459,000) were "displaced bourgeoisie"—well-educated middle- and upper-class professionals and businesspeople alienated by the new regime. Sympathetically received as resisters against, and refugees from, the first communist regime in the Western Hemisphere, these Cubans concentrated in several major cities, notably Miami and New York. Initial concern in those cities that the new immigrants might overburden the educational, welfare, and social services systems quickly dissipated as the Cubans made rapid economic progress and became a part of the community.

# the ETHNIC experience

## Brotherhood in Talk and in Deed

"I have to tell you that the Spanish-speaking people are always talking about brotherhood and the brotherhood of the Latin American countries. They say our brother country Mexico and our brother country Venezuela, and every time they mention a Latin American country, they say the brother country. Well, in reality, it is wrong. When we needed an escape from Cuba, we only had America. America was the only country that opened the door. America is the only place where you can go for freedom and where you can live as a human being."

"I love Cuba very much, but I can tell you that we never had the freedom that we have here. I can sincerely say that the opportunities in this country—America—are so great and so many, that no matter how bad they say we are as far as economics right now—they're talking about recession and everything—no matter how bad they say, it will never be as bad as it was and it is, actually, in Cuba."

"America took us in and we are grateful to America and to the Americans. And remember, when we came over, we were looking for freedom and liberty. Now we have freedom, we have liberty, and we have the chance to make money. Many Cubans are doing very well, better than me.

I make enough to support my family and to live decently. I am very happy and grateful."

"Believe me, I am not only speaking for myself, but for a large group of Cubans who feel the same way I feel. We are happy here. We miss Cuba. Sometimes we get tearful when we think about the old friends and the old neighborhoods, but we are lucky. We are lucky because we still can say what we want to say, and we can move around wherever we want, and be what we want to be."

Source: Cuban refugee who came to the United States in 1960 at age 18. Taped interview from the collection of Vincent N. Parrillo.

The next influx of Cubans (132,000) occurred in 1980 and was more controversial. Arriving in a so-called "freedom flotilla" of small boats, many chartered by Cuban Americans to bring in other family members, most were urban working-class and lower-class people. However, Castro also forced the departure of several thousand mental patients and prisoners among them—which triggered an unfavorable U.S. response. Called *Marielitos* because they had left Cuba from the port of Mariel, the term became a stigma attached to all these refugees either because of the dubious background of some or the limited education and job skills of many. At first, this group had difficulty adjusting, due partly to their lack of familiarity with a less rigid society in which they must make their own way and find work. Gradually, with help from the longer-established Cuban community, they also were able to acculturate.[50]

## ETHNIC COMMUNITIES

Cubans often settled in blighted urban areas, but their motivation, education, and entrepreneurial skills enabled them to bring color, vitality, stability, and improvement to previously declining neighborhoods. Long-time residents of areas heavily populated by Cubans often credited them with restoring or increasing the beauty and vigor of the community.

Miami offers an excellent example. Its climate and nearness to Cuba made it the ideal choice of many exiles, but increased the fears of residents about having so large an ethnic group in their midst. Yet, in the 1960s, the Anglos realized that the Cubans had sparked a real-estate boom, even while other major cities experienced a depressed housing market. Cuban entrepreneurs brought a new commercial vigor to the downtown area, as they created shoe, cigar, and cigarette manufacturing establishments, import houses, shopping centers, restaurants, and nightclubs. Northwest of Miami, others set up sugar plantations and mills. All this activity marked the beginning of a still-continuing boom period for Miami.[51]

In the early 1980s, however, a series of ethnic-related traumas—labor union restrictions, negative newspaper and public responses to the *Marielitos*, voter approval of a harsh Dade County anti-bilingual ordinance, and four days of anti-Cuban rioting by African Americans—prompted a Cuban reaction that quietly reshaped Miami's political, social, professional, and architectural landscape. Cubans responded to discrimination against them by forming their own economic enclave and entering local politics. Unlike the classical assimilation model of integration and absorption within the dominant society, this movement toward economic and political empowerment enabled Cubans to assert themselves and *then* enter the societal mainstream. Significantly, studies show that Cuban entry into the labor force did *not* negatively affect the city's black population.[52]

## THE CONTEMPORARY SCENE

By 2011, the Cuban American population numbered 1.9 million, making them the third largest Hispanic nationality group, after Mexicans and Puerto Ricans. As shown in Figure 11.4 and Tables 11.3, 11.4, and 11.5, Cuban Americans are doing well according to all social indicators.

It would be a mistake, however, to assume that there is a single Cuban American entity, for within that general patterning are multiple lifestyles. The ethnocultural identity of the first generation, whether early or recent arrivals, remains embedded in Cuban culture, interested in events in Cuba, and fiercely anti-Castro. The Americanized second generation is bilingual but far less active in sociopolitical activity and more interested in the same pop culture, sports, and other matters that appeal to nonethnic young people.[53] Moreover, black Cuban Americans live between two worlds, belonging to both a successful immigrant group yet experiencing the hardships and discrimination of their race.[54]

Because two of every three Cuban Americans live in Florida, the Cuban impact on Miami, now dubbed "Little Havana," has been significant. The city is now 70 percent Hispanic, and Cubans comprise half of that population. More than half of all Cuban Americans live in Miami–Dade County, where Cuban influence has transformed Miami from a resort town to a year-round commercial center with linkages throughout Latin America and has turned it into a leading bilingual cultural center. Approximately 62 percent of Miami–Dade County now is Hispanic, including 894,000 Cubans, 94,000 Puerto Ricans, 56,000 Mexicans, and 236,000 from Central America, and 264,000 from South America.[55]

California has the second-largest Cuban American concentration (84,000), followed by New Jersey (79,000) and New York (75,000). Other Cuban Americans are scattered among the remaining states.[56]

## CULTURAL VALUES

In addition to sharing a commonality of values with other Latinos, Cubans share certain subcultural values that differ from those of the dominant U.S. culture.[57] Among these are attitudes toward work, personal qualities, and the role of individuals in society.

Dominant-group values in the United States stress hard work as a means of achieving material well-being, whereas the Cuban orientation is that material success should be pursued for personal freedom, not physical comfort. Cubans do not consider work an end in itself, as they believe Anglos do. Instead, they think one should work to enjoy life. Intellectual pursuits are highly valued; idleness is frowned upon.

Cubans are fervent believers in collective generosity, in contrast to the old Anglo Puritan values of thrift and frugality. Common group traits include sharing good fortune,

In Miami's "Little Havana," some retired Cuban American men, many of them from the first wave of Cuban migration, spend the afternoon playing dominoes in Maximo Gomez Park. This activity is an institutionalized form of ethnic solidarity and social interaction, as card games once were in Italian social clubs a few generations ago.

maintaining a warm open-house policy, and reaching out socially to others. Cubans believe that one of the worst sins is to be a *tacaño*, a cheapskate who does not readily show affection and friendship through kindnesses and hospitality.

Individualism is a value best shown through national and personal pride, which Anglos often misperceive as haughtiness. Yet Cubans believe in expressing individualism not so much through self-assertiveness as through attitudes and actions oriented toward a group, sometimes a large number of people. Hostility needs to be directed through *choteo* and *relajo,* the continuous practice of humor, jokes, and wit, and accepted by others in good part. This is because one should avoid being a *pesado*—someone unlikeable, disagreeable, and without wit—which is the worst of all cultural sins. Cuban Americans thus value *personalismo* (personalized social interactions) more than their Anglo-American counterparts and so tend to spend more leisure time in social activities.

Although they remain the most metropolitan of all Hispanic American groups, Cubans today are as likely to live in such well-groomed suburbs as Coral Gables or Hialeah in Miami–Dade County, Florida—or others in California, New Jersey, or New York—as they are to live in the nearby cities. Except for South Americans, Cubans have a lower fertility rate, lower unemployment rate, higher median family income, greater education rate, and greater middle-class population composition than other Hispanic groups. As Table 11.5 shows, 22.7 percent of males and 31.9 percent of females are in managerial or professional occupations, a higher proportion than for most other Hispanic groups.

# Caribbean, Central and South Americans

**11-4** Describe the immigrant experiences of Caribbean, Central and South Americans.

Several push factors—overpopulation, acute shortage of farmland, economic hardship, and political turmoil—triggered a significant increase in **emigration** from several Latin American countries in recent decades. Central and South Americans constitute 13.5 percent of all Hispanic Americans (Figure 11.5). After Mexico, the largest contingents come from Cuba, the Dominican Republic, El Salvador, Colombia, Guatemala, Ecuador, Peru, and Nicaragua (Figure 11.6). More than 1.3 million Caribbean immigrants arrived since

**Read on MySocLab**
Document: Immigrant Highway

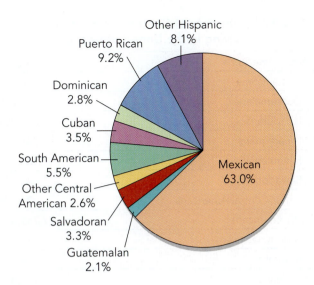

**FIGURE 11.5** Hispanic Americans by Origin, 2010

*Source:* U.S. Census Bureau.

2000, along with 678,000 from Central America and more than one million from South America.[58]

More than a half-million Central Americans live in Los Angeles. Substantial numbers also reside in San Francisco, Houston, Washington, DC, New York, Chicago, New Orleans, and Miami. As the largest Central American group in the United States, Salvadorans usually constitute the majority of Central Americans in most cities, followed by Guatemalans (Table 11.6). Among Central Americans, Nicaraguans predominate in Miami, however, and Hondurans in New Orleans.

## DOMINICAN AMERICANS

Nearly 1 million Dominican immigrants have left their Caribbean homeland for the United States since 1980, in recent years averaging more than 46,000 annually—which makes the Dominican Republic second only to Mexico as a source of Spanish-speaking immigrants to the United States. Of the 1.6 million Dominican Americans, approximately

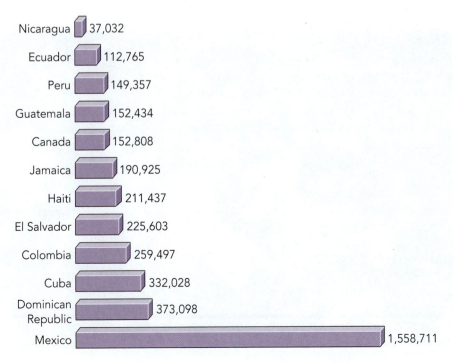

**FIGURE 11.6** Leading Western Hemisphere Countries for Immigrants, 2003–2012

*Source:* U.S. Office of Immigration Statistics.

**TABLE 11.6** Number of Central and South Americans Living in the United States, 2010

| | |
|---|---:|
| *Central Americans* | 3,998,280 |
| Costa Ricans | 126,418 |
| Guatemalans | 1,044,209 |
| Hondurans | 633,401 |
| Nicaraguans | 348,202 |
| Panamanians | 165,456 |
| Salvadorans | 1,648,968 |
| Other Central Americans | 31,626 |
| *South Americans* | 2,769,434 |
| Argentineans | 224,952 |
| Bolivians | 99,210 |
| Chileans | 126,810 |
| Colombians | 908,734 |
| Ecuadorians | 564,631 |
| Paraguayans | 20,023 |
| Peruvians | 531,358 |
| Uruguayans | 56,884 |
| Venezuelans | 215,023 |
| Other South Americans | 21,809 |

*Source: U.S. Census Bureau, 2011 American Community Survey.*

two of every three live in New York State. Most live in New York City, particularly in Washington Heights in Manhattan and in the Bronx, where Dominicans are a majority in the borough. Other primary areas of residence are New Jersey, Florida, and Massachusetts.

Dominicans more likely are to live and interact within their own ethnic neighborhoods than to integrate into mixed Hispanic neighborhoods. A common pattern is to co-exist alongside Puerto Ricans, each ethnic group keeping mostly to itself. As Puerto

*More than one million Dominican Americans live in the greater New York metropolitan region. Especially concentrated in New York City's Washington Heights area in Manhattan and in the Bronx, they comprise approximately one-eighth of the city's population, where the Dominican Independence Day parade along Grand Concourse is one of the city's largest.*

Ricans move out of ethnic neighborhoods into urban or suburban neighborhoods with a significant white or multiethnic presence, Dominicans have replaced them in the older, more segregated neighborhoods.[59]

Most Dominicans are people who have fled the poverty of their land. Because many lack specialized skills, they have a high unemployment rate and often live in poor urban neighborhoods, suffering the deprivation and family disruption so common among people with low levels of education and job skills. More than one in four lives in poverty. Second-generation Dominican Americans, however, tend to be more educated, be employed in skilled or professional occupations, and earn higher incomes. Fifteen percent have college degrees or higher, slightly below Puerto Rican Americans but higher than that for Mexican Americans.[60]

## SALVADORAN AMERICANS

Several push factors account for the large-scale Salvadoran emigration to the United States. Agricultural modernization and expansion of property holdings by the landowning oligarchy displaced tens of thousands of rural peasants. Relocating to such urban centers as San Salvador, many of these dispossessed poor could not find work despite the growing industrialization. Conditions deteriorated when the Salvadoran government responded to protests and demonstrations with severe repression. Paramilitary death squads composed of members of the ruling elite, as well as regular security and military forces, targeted peasant leaders, union militants, and political activists. Revolutionary movements arose, and guerrilla offensives in the 1980s prompted escalating violence by the security and military forces and the death squads. Large-scale attacks against civilian populations in rural areas occurred, including massacres of entire villages believed to be sympathetic to the guerrillas. As a result, 20 to 30 percent of the population fled the country.[61]

As a stream of undocumented Salvadorans fled into the United States, immigration agents sought to apprehend and return them, denying them refugee status. The Reagan-era State Department argued that, although El Salvador might be a war-torn country, none of those who left could prove that they specifically had been singled out for persecution and thus did not have the necessary "well-founded fear of persecution" to qualify for political amnesty. Out of this conflict was born the **sanctuary movement** in the United States: Clergy defied the government, hiding Salvadoran refugees in churches and homes. The clergy and members of their congregations provided food, shelter, and clothing and secretly helped the refugees get to safe locations. At first living as a "secret" population, these refugees were among the 143,000 Salvadoran successful applicants for amnesty and permanent residence in the United States.[62]

Although the political situation improved in El Salvador in the 1990s, most Salvadorans in the United States remained, putting down roots and enjoying the support system within their tight-knit ethnic communities. Through chain migration, other relatives and friends join them, continuing a steady migration flow that ranks El Salvador third among Western Hemisphere countries providing immigrants to the United States in recent years. Approximately 2 million Salvadorans live in the United States, with large population clusters in California, Texas, and the New York and Washington, DC, metropolitan areas.[63]

## NICARAGUAN AMERICANS

Nicaraguans have entered the United States as immigrants, refugees, asylees, and undocumented aliens. A **refugee** is an alien outside the United States who is unable or unwilling to return to his or her country because of persecution or a well-founded fear of persecution. An **asylee** is similar to a refugee but physically is in the United States or one of its embassies, or at a port of entry when requesting refuge.

*Worldwide, professional soccer is extremely popular, but in the United States it appeals primarily to ethnic Americans, for whom it serves as a rallying point for ethnic identity and pride to cheer for one's homeland. Here, enthusiastic El Salvador fans celebrate their team's victory over Costa Rica in a 2009 Gold Cup game in Los Angeles.*

After the Sandinistas came to power in Nicaragua and the Contras undertook a guerrilla war against the new government, more than 46,000 middle-class refugees entered the United States between 1980 and 1990. Simultaneously, another 79,000 Nicaraguans streamed into Texas, filing asylum applications. Most of this latter group, unlike the refugees, consisted of poor, unskilled, and illiterate *campesinos* from the countryside.[64]

Drawn by the Latin American population and the already established Nicaraguan communities in Miami and southern California, most refugees chose one of those two destinations. Miami–Dade County schools, for example, experienced almost a quadrupling of their Nicaraguan student enrollment. With no previous educational experience, most of the 13- to 15-year-olds were illiterate and had to be taught the basics of reading and arithmetic.[65] Sweetwater, a western suburb of Miami, almost completely became Nicaraguan, earning the nickname "Little Managua."

When the Sandinista regime ended in 1990 and the Contra war fizzled out, the 11-year-long exodus of refugees subsided. Some Nicaraguans returned to their homeland, but most chose to stay in the United States.[66] All Nicaraguan refugees and asylees since have received permanent resident status. The immigrant stream in recent years is steady, approximately 3,500 annually, and more than 387,000 now claim Nicaraguan ancestry. About 21 percent hold a bachelor's degree or higher, while 19 percent lived in poverty in 2011.[67] Most live either in Florida or California. Other states with sizable population concentrations include New York, Texas, New Jersey, Maryland, and Virginia.

### COLOMBIAN AMERICANS

Among South American countries, Colombia supplies the most immigrants to the United States—more than 280,000 since 2000.[68] Population pressures, the promise of better economic opportunities abroad, and chain-migration networking have increased the annual immigration totals, which now are in the tens of thousands yearly. Of the 995,000 Colombian Americans now residing in the United States, approximately 64 percent are foreign born. Most of the remainder are children born to these first-generation Colombian Americans.[69]

Socioeconomically, Colombians are a mixture of educated professionals and low-skilled peasants seeking a better life (see the Ethnic Experience box). Both their 13 percent poverty rate and 31 percent holding bachelor's degrees or higher are slightly

# the ETHNIC experience

## Cultural Traits and Adjustment

"The Colombians here are the poor people. They are the ones who had no chance for an education in Colombia. They are the ones who—because they had no education—their pay was very meager. And so over here, they have a better life than they would in Colombia. So over here, they really—if you can call it the American Dream—has been fulfilled in them."

"Emotionally they're very attached to their country. See, this is the thing that is very hard for people to understand. They want them to become American and to forget everything. You can't! The ties—the blood ties—are too strong! You just can't become—as I said, I cannot even become an American. I can't! Even if I wanted to. You would have to make me all over again. And I love this country and I choose to stay in this country."

"Now with these people—take some of them. They have come because of necessity—sheer necessity. We criticize them because they don't love America, but I don't think that is the fact. Also, if you notice the kind of people that come here. For instance, I had students who were the children of my father's workers on the coffee plantation. Now in my country, they were tilling the soil. You know, the children of the owner go to school. The children of the worker go to till the soil. They had no chance of an education. They had huts up in the mountains where they had no running water, no electricity. Now they come here and they have all the conveniences. If they live poorly, Americans criticize them, but they don't realize where they were living before. If they're not clean and spotless, and they don't keep the shades the right way—but these people have been doing this for a hundred years! The people who just came in never even had a shade to talk about. They never had a venetian blind. They never even had a window to talk about!" [Laughs.]

"I think we have to be careful because we often make the mistake of imposing our way to the people. Now you could say, we're not going to them, they're coming here. But if you accept them in the country, I think you also have to accept a big risk. I think the melting pot idea is not the prevalent idea. It is not a workable idea. Each one has a culture. Each people has a culture and if you want them in America, if you allow them to stay here, you have to work something by which each one is able to live. I don't mean to say that we have independent little countries, but that they are comfortable. Because you cannot remove—those are strong things that you cannot remove from a person."

Source: Colombian immigrant who came to the United States in 1952 at age 16. Taped interview from the collection of Vincent N. Parrillo.

---

above the national norm.[70] Living mostly in urban neighborhoods near other Hispanics, they form their own social clubs, institutions, and celebrations, attempting—as all first-generation Americans do—to preserve their culture. Colombian Americans mostly are concentrated in New York City (especially in Queens), South Florida, Northern New Jersey, Washington, DC, and California.

A minuscule percentage of Colombians are involved in the cocaine trade and in related drug-war killings. The high profile of this small number of criminals unfortunately smears the rest, just as Italian Americans have suffered from a nationality stereotype because of the Mafia. In reality, nearly all Colombian Americans are decent, law-abiding people who work hard to make a life for themselves in their adopted country. As is the case with many Central and South Americans, the Colombian population can have ancestry that is *mestizo* (mixture of European and indigenous), Spanish, Afro-Colombian, indigenous, and Syrian or Lebanese.

**STUDENTS SPEAK** "I came to the USA in 2006 when I was 17 years old. Ever since I was five, my grandmother had been telling us we would go to the USA, so this thought was long in my head. I dreamed to be here and I wanted to get out of Peru. Once here, the first problem was assimilating. Everything was new and different: the streets, the housing, the way people drive, the weather, and the radio and TV stations. So, yes, it was definitely very hard to adapt to a new country, but if I'm here, it is for a reason. I have to take advantage of the opportunity life is presenting me."

**—Erick Gonzales**

# REALITY check

## Places and Politics: A Geo-Political Profile

As discussed earlier, Hispanics are settling in all 50 states although three-fourths of them live in only seven states (see Figure 11.7). However, something else also is occurring. The Hispanic settlement pattern most closely resembles that of the nineteenth-century Germans. In both instances, large numbers settled in cities, creating vibrant neighborhoods with strong ethnolinguistic marks, and in rural areas, bringing a significant ethnic presence to areas long dominated by non-Hispanic whites, and fueling population growth in some of these areas or offsetting population decline in others.

Although mainly living in urban areas, Hispanics now are the fastest-growing group in rural and small-town America. Doubling their numbers in nonmetropolitan areas in the past two decades, most are recent U.S. arrivals, some undocumented, with limited English proficiency and low-education levels. Changing from their traditional pattern of settling in the Southwest, many live elsewhere, such as North Carolina, Georgia, Minnesota, Nevada, and upstate New York. Approximately one in seven works in agriculture; many others are employed in such industries as animal slaughtering and processing, carpet and rug manufacturing, and construction.

Long an influential minority in California and New Mexico, Hispanics continuously have been represented in the U.S. Congress since 1931. Nearly all have been Mexican Americans throughout the years, but Puerto Ricans and Cuban Americans also have served in one or both houses. Hispanics, now 16 percent of the total population, constituted 10 percent of U.S. voters in 2012, and have three U.S. senators and 28 congressional representatives in the 113th Congress, an all-time high in both houses. At the state level, Latinos currently have a combined total of 70 state senators and 206 representatives in 36 state legislatures. Courted by politicians from both political parties, the Latino vote is a greater voice in those seven states where their greatest population concentrations are, but it is only a matter of time before Latino political power is an even more widespread and influential force.

Sources: Adapted from Huffington Post, "Latino Congress Members: 2012 Election Sets a New Record with the Most Latinos Elected to U.S. Senate, House In History." (http://www.huffingtonpost.com ); PRNewswire, "Latinos to Serve in State Legislatures of 36 States." (http://www.prnewswire.com); U.S. Census Bureau, The Hispanic Population:2010 (May 2011).

# Assimilation

**11-5** Compare and contrast assimilation paths followed by Hispanic Americans.

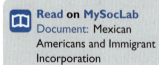
**Read on MySocLab**
Document: Mexican Americans and Immigrant Incorporation

As with all immigrant groups, any discussion of assimilation must take into account the cultural diversity among the groups identified as "Hispanic," as well as other variables such as length of residence, place of residence, social class, family structure, and education of parents (see the Reality Check box and Figure 11.7). Those differing socioeconomic characteristics among the various Latino groups, as discussed in earlier sections, affect integration into the societal mainstream. Because Hispanics can be of any race, we also must consider that variable in any discussion of assimilation. Consequently, Hispanic Americans can be found at all stages along the pluralism–assimilation continuum. Within the broad range of areas of assimilation, the social institutions of education and family provide valuable insights.

**EDUCATION.** One means of interpreting rapid assimilation to the United States is educational attainment. Unfortunately, high school age immigrant youths are far more likely than their native-born ethnic peers to drop out of school; some Hispanic groups have above-average levels of school attrition. The most serious problem exists among Mexican teenagers, where nearly half of Mexican-born 15- to 17-year-olds are not in school. Central American youths, especially those from El Salvador and Guatemala, also have

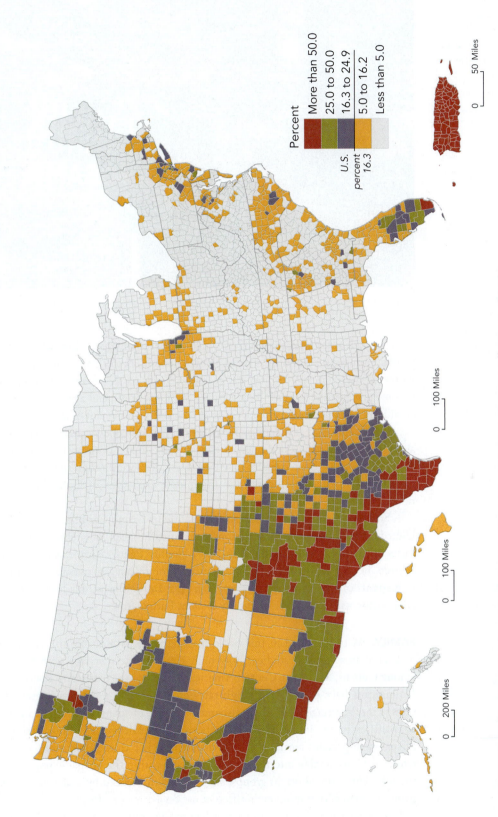

**FIGURE 11.7** Percentage of Population, Hispanic or Latino Origin, All Races, 2010

Source: U.S. Census Bureau.

Percent

More than 50.0
25.0 to 50.0
16.3 to 24.9
5.0 to 16.2
Less than 5.0

U.S. percent 16.3

0   50 Miles

0   100 Miles

0   100 Miles

0   200 Miles

In the 2012 presidential election, the growing political power of Latinos was evident, as a record 11.2 million voted, a 15 percent increase over 2008. In battleground states like Colorado, Florida and Nevada, the Latino electorate was particularly decisive, providing the margin of victory in a number of key municipal, state and federal elections.

high dropout rates (less than half are high school graduates). However, if any of these youths immigrate before the start of their schooling, then they are no more likely than native-born Americans to drop out of high school, partly because the younger arrivals become proficient in English more easily.[71] National origin and age of entry therefore are significant variables in the effectiveness of education as an agent of assimilation.[72]

An exception to this pattern occurs among groups concentrated in central cities and attending schools with a demoralized educational climate. In this setting, longer duration of residence in the United States may lead to greater acculturation to U.S. society but not necessarily to better enrollments and the middle-class ideal of high educational aspirations among these groups.

Some analysts argue that the social position of Latino Caribbean populations in the United States today continues relationships rooted in racial hierarchies produced by centuries of European colonialism. Thus, they identify Puerto Ricans as colonial racialized subjects in the Euro-American mindset but Dominicans as transformed into colonial immigrants in the New York metropolitan area. In their view, this legacy of colonialism affects the social acceptance of racially distinct Latino Americans.[73]

**FAMILY.** As often stated in this book, intermarriage patterns are important indicators of assimilation. Recent studies show high rates of intermarriage with non-Hispanics among Cubans, Mexicans, Central Americans, and South Americans. Puerto Ricans and Dominicans have exceptionally high rates of intermarriage with each other, but lower rates of intermarriage with other Hispanics and non-Hispanics.[74] About 15 percent of all Hispanic marriages in recent years have been to non-Hispanics.[75] Third-plus-generation Hispanics especially are increasingly marrying other third-generation co-ethnics and whites.[76] Considerable intermarriage also occurs within the Hispanic population among the different national origin groups, significantly influenced by a pan-ethnic identity of being "Hispanic" that transcends different national origins.[77] Puerto Ricans, though, tend to have greater self-esteem if more attached to their culture and so resist this pan-ethnic identity.[78]

Language acquisition is an obvious factor in the assimilation process. As with past European immigrants, the continual influx of large numbers of new Hispanic immigrants serves to reinvigorate the use of Spanish in everyday life. Its presence has triggered English-only and Official English movements, a subject we will discuss in Chapter 15. Nevertheless, even as recently arrived adults have limited English proficiency, Hispanic children—as youngsters always do—learn the new language easily and assimilate more readily than their parents.

Without question, cultural pluralism is an everyday reality among many Latinos and Latinas whose ethnic identity is a vibrant dynamic. A steady influx of newcomers and the presence of many first-generation Hispanic Americans mean continuance of that pattern. However, it would be a mistake either to conclude that the forces of assimilation are not at work, especially among the second generation, or to ignore the assimilation of many Hispanic Americans because of their length of residence and socioeconomic status.

# Sociological Analysis

Like other immigrant groups before them, the new arrivals from Latin America are changing the face of the United States, making their distinctive contributions to the neighborhoods in which they live. But with their growing numbers, they also are encountering the hostility historically accorded to almost all newly arriving ethnic groups. Applying sociological perspectives can place their current experiences in a comparative context.

**11-6** Discuss insights gained through sociological analysis.

### THE FUNCTIONALIST VIEW

Rapid population growth has been a mixed blessing for these newcomers. They have been able to develop supportive ethnic subcommunities, providing social institutions and an interactive network that ease adjustment to a new country. Cuban settlement in deteriorated urban neighborhoods revitalized those areas and inevitably brought interethnic assistance to other Hispanic groups. Currently, Hispanics are increasingly moving to rural areas, attracted by the low cost of living outside metropolitan areas, and so are helping offset population losses in those communities and transforming the social and economic fabric of many small towns.[79] Because approximately four-fifths of all Hispanics live in nine states (California, Arizona, Colorado, New Mexico, Texas, Illinois, New York, New Jersey, and Florida), they quickly are realizing their potential political power, enabling them to improve their life situation. Concern exists that their numbers and common language may be dysfunctional, delaying assimilation and creating an "Hispanic Quebec" within the United States.

Immigrants with lower levels of educational attainment often fill the needs of industries on the periphery, such as garment factories, restaurants, and hotels, which depend on low-skilled workers, even undocumented aliens and minors. This segment of the labor market prefers to hire immigrants with less than a high school education, as evidenced by the fact that immigrants with less than a high school diploma (except Dominicans, Puerto Ricans, and Russians) have higher rates of labor-force participation than U.S.-born people in the same category and slightly higher earnings. These advantages decrease with increased education, suggesting that, in the less competitive, lower-status jobs, Latin American immigrants have become the highest earners as they fill manual labor jobs needed by labor-intensive industries.[80]

Rapid social change is the key to functional analysis of existing problems. The rapid influx of large numbers of immigrants and the changing occupational structure of U.S. society have prevented the social system from absorbing so many low-skilled workers right away. How can we ease Hispanic newcomers into the societal mainstream? We can either take a *laissez-faire* attitude, allowing the passage of time to produce acculturation and economic improvement, or we can seek an interventionist means of resolving the problems. Advocates of the latter approach argue that, through bilingual and other educational programs, job-training programs, and business investment incentives for more job opportunities, we can improve the system to help newcomers realize the American Dream that brought them here.

## THE CONFLICT VIEW

Although Robert Blauner first applied the concept of internal colonialism to the black ghetto (see Chapter 2), Chicano activists found the idea appealing because it coincided with the legacy of Anglo takeover and domination of the Southwest in 1848 and continued Anglo control of the barrios in the cities of the region since that date. They readily embraced the concept of the barrio as an internal colony, dependent on Anglo investment and subservient to Anglo domination of municipal government and commerce. They criticized the concentration of the Mexican American working class in poor urban barrios and the exodus of the Anglo and Latino middle class to the suburban fringe. In these economically weakened barrios, Mexican Americans struggled against larger economic and political trends.

Analysts of internal colonialism maintain that the continued residential segregation of Hispanic Americans in ghetto areas of many U.S. cities is unlike the pattern experienced by European immigrants to the United States. In the case of Europeans, the level of segregation declined with length of residence in the United States. However, with the newer immigrants, instead of seeing a gradual acculturation or structural assimilation process, these analysts see the persistence of subordination, with Latinos confined to certain areas of rental properties controlled by absentee landlords and restricted to low-paying job opportunities, inferior schools, and many other forms of discrimination.

Economic exploitation is another dimension of conflict analysis. Mexicans, Central Americans, and other Latinos work as migrant farm laborers in many places under abysmal conditions for meager pay despite repeated exposés. City sweatshops employing thousands of undocumented aliens, refugees, and low-skilled legal immigrants operate in clandestine settings, prospering from the toil of low-wage employees. The rise of an ethnic bourgeoisie—the *padrino* in urban or farm settings, the token elite among the Chicano population, or the small middle class with other Hispanic groups—only helps control the rest and does not signal an economic upgrading and assimilation of the remaining group members.

Resolving the problem of this low social status of millions of Hispanic Americans, according to this view, will occur only through protest movements, organized resistance to exploitation, and the flexing of ever-strengthening political muscle. New citizens need to realize more fully their commonalities, taking a lesson from the Irish and using their ballot power to create the necessary changes to benefit themselves. If they effectively wield their political clout, as demonstrated in the 2012 presidential election, they can overcome the power differential that exists in the social and economic spheres as well.

## THE INTERACTIONIST VIEW

Anglo–Hispanic relations often are strained by inaccurate perceptions. Members of the dominant group tend to think that there is but one Spanish-speaking public, when actually a variety exists, each preferring different foods, music, and recreation and having different cultural attributes. Too many Anglos view Hispanic ethnic subcommunities, parallel social institutions, and limited command of English as detrimental to the cohesiveness of U.S. society, failing to realize that more than one-third of Hispanics are first-generation Americans repeating a resettlement pattern of earlier European immigrants. Extensive poverty among many Hispanics often invites outsiders to blame the victim or to engage in culture-of-poverty thinking. Instead of confronting the problems of poor education and lack of job skills and job opportunities, some find fault with the group itself, reacting with avoidance, indifference, or paternalistic behavior.

In our earlier discussion about eye contact, physical proximity, the notion of hurrying, and the relevance of time, we identified a few areas of potential cultural misunderstanding. Add to this Anglo impatience with language problems, African American concerns about economic competition, taxpayer resistance to welfare costs, labor union fears that wages will be undermined by cheap labor, and nativist alarm at the failure of the melting pot to "melt" the Hispanics, and you have further reasons for non-Hispanics to stereotype Latinos as an increasing social problem. Because perceptions influence interaction patterns and social policy, the potential for tensions and conflict is strong.

Witnessing extensive Spanish-language usage no doubt is the main "hot button" that triggers nativists' ire more than any other ethnic manifestation by Hispanics. Similar reactions once occurred when German and Italian newcomers concentrated in large clusters and their languages were everyday commonalities. As discussed in Chapter 2, language and culture share an interdependent relationship; each fosters the other, with both usually ebbing through the assimilation process throughout the generations. In Chapter 15, we examine the issues and concerns involving language retention and English literacy.

For Hispanics, clinging to the old country's culture and ethnic identity is a matter of pride and personal commitment to a rich heritage. Some find it their only solace against discrimination, and even those who achieve economic mobility retain a strong ethnic identification. Washed afresh with new waves of Hispanic immigrants, the ethnic communities retain their vitality, prompting even successful Hispanics to hold onto their ethnic traditions. Interactionists thus point to the resilience of an ethnic self-definition, which is somewhat at odds with assimilationist views.

# Retrospect

In many ways, recent Hispanic immigrants repeat the patterns of earlier racial and ethnic groups. Coming in large numbers from impoverished lands, many enter the lowest strata of society, cluster together in substandard housing units, and face the problems of adjustment, deprivation, frustration, and pathology (sickness and crime). Marked as strangers by their language, customs, and physical appearance, they face difficulty in gaining acceptance and achieving economic security. The Hispanic poor face the same problems and criticisms as earlier groups. They also are criticized for failing to overcome these problems immediately, even though other groups often took three generations to do so. The dominant–minority response patterns in this case thus are quite similar to those of earlier immigrant peoples.

Particularly significant for the Hispanic immigrants, in comparison to other groups, are the changed structural conditions. The restrictive immigration laws of the 1920s drastically curtailed the great influx of southern, eastern, and central Europeans. Consequently, the immigrants already here did not receive continuous cultural reinforcement from new arrivals. But among Hispanics, there is a sizable flow of new arrivals, and rapid and inexpensive communications and transportation encourage return trips to the not-so-far-away homeland. In addition, earlier European immigrants sometimes encountered heavy-handed attempts at Americanization, whereas today's immigrants live in a time when pluralism and ethnic resurgence are common among members of the dominant group.

Other crucial changes in structural conditions are in technology and the job market. When the European poor came to the United States, they could find many unskilled and semiskilled jobs. Despite many evils and abuses in industry, an immigrant could secure a little piece of the American Dream through hard physical labor. The immigrant today enters a labor market where technology has eliminated many of those types of low-skill jobs, but others remain or have taken their place: construction, installation, home maintenance, and service industries. Through hard work, they follow a path that many other immigrants pursued to gain economic security.

During the mass European migration, the fledgling labor unions successfully struggled to improve the economic condition of the immigrant workers. Nowadays, unions have limited means to help newcomers, and the federal government is less inclined to offer welfare aid than in the 1960s, when the government encouraged individuals to apply for welfare by liberalizing eligibility requirements. With structural unemployment leaving no alternative, the system maneuvers many Hispanic newcomers into a marginal existence.

Highly visible because of their numbers, language, culture, and poverty, many Latinos find themselves the objects of resentment, hostility, and overt discrimination from the dominant society. The familiar pattern of blaming the victim results in negative stereotyping, social segregation, and all shades of prejudice and discrimination against the Hispanic and Caribbean poor.

Not all are poor, of course. For those who are not, attaining economic security means a very different life experience. Other positive factors offer some promise of easing the transition to life in the United States: bilingual education, increased public awareness, a greater tolerance for cultural pluralism, and civic and government programs. Serious problems remain for a disproportionate number of Hispanic Americans, however, and it is too soon to tell whether new legislation designed to control the influx of undocumented aliens will have any positive impact on the Hispanic poor.

# On MySocLab

✓ **Study** and **Review** on MySocLab

## KEY TERMS

Asylee, p. 375

*Dignidad*, p. 351

Emigration, p. 372

*Machismo*, p. 351

*Marianismo*, p. 351

Marielitos, p. 370

Miscegenation, p. 364

Pentecostalism, p. 352

Refugee, p. 375

Sanctuary movement, p. 375

Shuttle migration, p. 367

Undocumented alien, p. 350

## DISCUSSION QUESTIONS

1. The beginning of the chapter offers a sociohistorical perspective as well as information on racial attitudes and cultural differentiation. What was one striking or surprising piece of information you picked up here?

2. Pages 355–358 offer various social indicators by which we measure the degree of mainstreaming that has occurred for any minority group (in this case, Hispanic Americans). What conclusions can you draw from these data? Have we made progress in recent decades? Where do the main problems still remain? What would you expect future data to show? Why?

3. Various Hispanic ethnic groups are discussed in the remainder of the chapter. From reading about them, what observations can you make?

4. A common criticism of Hispanic Americans centers on their not assimilating. Based on the material on pages 378–380, what comments can you make?

5. The end of the chapter offers three theoretical analyses. How did one of these theories become more meaningful or relevant to you in its application to the Hispanic experience?

# INTERNET ACTIVITIES

1. Want to see the Census Bureau's latest report on U.S. Hispanics? Click on "Hispanic Population in the United States" at http://www.census.gov/prod/cen2010/briefs/c2010br-04.pdf, and you will have access to the latest information on their demographic and socioeconomic characteristics.

2. Explore the Internet a little and see what's out there offering information, support, and assistance to the Hispanic American community. For example, click on "Latino/Hispanic Resources" at http://www-bcf.usc.edu/~cmmr/Latino.html, and then check out some of the links. What are you finding? Do you see some common themes or patterns? What groups are better represented than others? What are the primary resources offered?

# Religious Minorities

🔊 **Listen** to Chapter 12 on **MySocLab**

# 12

At the Sunday worship service at Lakewood Church in Houston, Pastor Joel Osteen preaches to some 25,000 people each week. He reaches many more through television, stadium rallies, and best-selling books. More than 800 mega churches host an excess of three million people on any given Sunday. Mega churches are loosely defined as non-Catholic churches with at least 2,000 weekly attendants.

## LEARNING OBJECTIVES | After reading this chapter you will be able to:

**12-1** Describe the sociohistorical context for studying religion in America.

**12-2** Compare and contrast the experiences and attributes of Catholics, Jews, Mormons, and Muslims.

**12-3** Compare and contrast the experiences and attributes of Amish, Rasta, Santeríans, and Hindus.

**12-4** Explain civil religion in the United States.

**12-5** Examine current controversies involving religious beliefs.

**12-6** Discuss the integration in U.S. society of these religious groups.

**12-7** Discuss insights gained through sociological analysis.

387

Any study of minority groups must also include religion because it can generate ingroup–outgroup stereotyping, misunderstandings, and conflict, just as race and ethnicity sometimes do. For some immigrant groups—for instance, such earlier groups as German and Russian Jews or Irish and Italian Catholics, or such present groups as Arab Muslims or Asian Indian Hindus—religion and ethnicity heavily intertwine, providing a basis for understanding both group solidarity and initial hostile societal reaction toward the group. Sometimes the religious group itself is an ethnic group—the Amish, for example.

Unlike most nations, in which one or a few faiths dominate, the United States has an immense diversity of faiths. Within the United States, more than 1,500 religious groups exist, 200 of them conventional Christian and Jewish denominations, and 29 of these have a membership exceeding 1 million.[1] That religious pluralism has expanded so dramatically in recent decades that the United States, once a Christian country, now is the most religiously diverse country in the world.

Although the country remains mostly Christian (82 percent claim this faith), immigration, intermarriage, and a growing disenchantment with some of the oldest religious institutions are redefining its religious composition. For example, the United States today contains 7 times more Muslim Americans (6 million), 10 times more Buddhists (2 million), 9 times more Hindus (1 million), and 220 times more Sikhs (220,000) than it did in 1970. Religions once on the margins of mainstream Christianity are growing the most vigorously: Jehovah's Witnesses by 175 percent, Mormons by 179 percent, and the Pentecostal Assemblies of God by 354 percent. In contrast, the once dominant Episcopal, Presbyterian, and Congregational churches have declined in membership by 20–40 percent.[2] Furthermore, many people leaving mainstream churches in droves are joining a **nondenominational** megachurch that is less dogmatic and bureaucratic.[3] Another significant group are those who defined themselves in 2012 as "unaffiliated," who numbered 46 million Americans, or nearly 20 percent of all U.S. adults.[4] And, virtually in all religions, we find considerable racial and ethnic diversity (Figure 12.1).

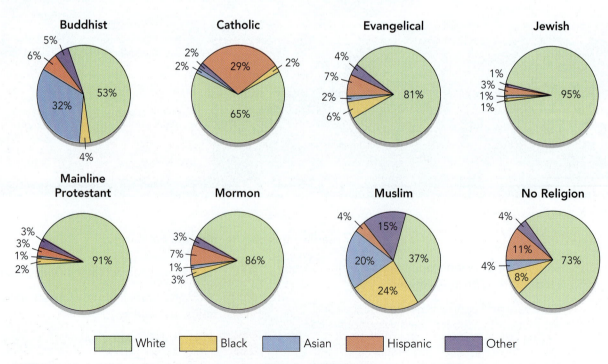

**FIGURE 12.1** Ethnic/Racial Composition of Selected Religions

Source: Pew Forum on Religion & Public Life, *U.S. Religious Landscape Survey,* 2008.

The United States today is a more secular society than ever before. Religious differences no longer fan the flames of intense bigotry and acts of mob violence. The terrorist attacks of September 11, 2001, did prompt a backlash of sporadic violence against Muslims, Sikhs, and Hindus, but most Americans did not act against members of non-Western religions. However, even though this country may not be torn apart religiously as Iraq or the Balkans have been in recent years, it would be a mistake to assume that religious harmony prevails throughout the land. Religious conflicts still occur, false stereotypes still find acceptance, and religious prejudice still exists. Because of their beliefs, some religious minorities—such as the Amish, Rastafarians, and Santeríans—encounter conflicts with the dominant society. In addition, issues such as abortion, birth control, and school prayer continue to bring people of varying religious beliefs into conflict with one another.

In this chapter, we examine both past and present patterns of religious tolerance and conflict in the United States. Specifically, we look at some groups that either have experienced problems similar to those confronted by racial or ethnic groups discussed in previous chapters or continue as viable religious subcultures in this pluralistic society. Because of this orientation, we do not look at other religions lacking a prominent display of ethnoreligious cultural marks and minority-group status, although in some cases, such religions may have a larger population base.

## Sociohistorical Perspective

Since the time of the Pilgrims, this nation has been the haven for many religious groups fleeing persecution and seeking religious freedom. Even during colonial times, however, instances of religious intolerance occurred, such as when Massachusetts expelled Anne Hutchinson, Roger Williams, and their followers and when Maryland denied Catholics the right to hold political office. As the isolated settlements—many of a single religious persuasion—evolved into interactive colonies, Anglo-Saxon Protestantism dominated. Nevertheless, the Founding Fathers built into the Constitution two fundamental principles: separation of church and state and freedom of religion. Those two guarantees bestowed a unique legacy on U.S. culture that continues to the present day.

For nearly all immigrant groups, religion has played a significant role. The church, synagogue, temple, or mosque typically became the central social institution of their ethnic communities, functioning both as a spiritual bond reinforcing group identity and as the social, educational, and even political base of their activities. That colonial legacy remains visible today in many older New England towns, where a church stands prominently beside the village green, in the center of the community—the place in which town meetings made participatory democracy a reality. Similarly, in the remnants of white ethnic neighborhoods in northern cities, in midwestern farming communities, in southwestern states, and in specific places such as St. Augustine, Florida, or New Orleans, still-standing religious edifices and recorded ethnic community histories and studies offer abundant testimony to the role religion played among first- and second-generation residents.

The clergy always have provided important leadership among racial and ethnic groups. In addition to spiritual guidance, they often served as a rallying force to enhance community cohesiveness as well as the economic and social welfare of their people. Frequently, priests, rabbis, and ministers also have been in the forefront of concerted efforts to ease immigrants' transition to U.S. life and their entry into the economic mainstream. Black ministers—such as Dr. Martin Luther King, Jr., and Jesse Jackson—consistently have been in the vanguard of the movement for civil rights and equality. Religious leaders throughout U.S. history have played an important role not only in shaping the values and moral behavior of their congregations but in influencing public policy, encouraging charitable activities, and implementing the spirit of the Constitution.

**12-1** Describe the sociohistorical context for studying religion in America.

**Explore on MySocLab**
Activity: A Brief Tour of the Religious Pluralism of the US

**Watch on MySocLab**
Video: The Big Picture: Religion

Unfortunately, not all religious leaders have been magnanimous in promoting equality, nor have all religions experienced tolerance in the U.S. experience. Some—Catholics, Jews, and Mormons, for example—have been victims of discrimination, persecution, and even violence. Others—such as the Amish, Christian Scientists, Jehovah's Witnesses, Native Americans, and Rastafarians—have come into conflict with society over their religious beliefs. Even though the ideal culture stresses freedom of religion, in practice, religious bigotry and intolerance have caused suffering and hardship to some religious minorities in the United States.

# Catholic Americans

**12-2** Compare and contrast the experiences and attributes of Catholics, Jews, Mormons, and Muslims.

Catholicism did not gain easy acceptance in the United States. By the mid-seventeenth century, all the colonies had passed laws designed to thwart Catholic immigration, most of them denying Catholics citizenship, voting rights, and office-holding rights.[5] The nation almost exclusively remained a Protestant domain until 1830. Throughout the next 30 years, immigration had a profound political and social impact on the nation. More than 500,000 immigrants in the 1830s, 1.7 million in the 1840s, and 2.6 million in the 1850s—the great bulk of them Roman Catholics, mostly Irish and German peasants—entered the country. As they did, a feeling of alarm spread among U.S. Protestants, many of whom believed that Catholics would subvert the nation.

## SOCIETAL HOSTILITY

Samuel F. B. Morse, inventor of the telegraph and son of a militant minister, railed against an alleged papist conspiracy to take control of the U.S. government through Catholic immigration. He exhorted Protestant citizens not to be "deceived by Jesuit-controlled immigrants." Instead, they should "fly to protect the vulnerable places of your Constitution and Laws. Place your guards; you will need them, and quickly too.—And first, shut your gates."[6]

Lurid, best-selling exposés of the Catholic Church appeared. Rebecca Reed fabricated a story about her life in a convent in Charlestown, Massachusetts, that resulted in the burning of that Ursuline convent in 1834. Two years later, the most infamous of these inflammatory works appeared: *Awful Disclosures of the Hotel Dieu Nunnery of Montreal* by Maria Monk. The author claimed to be an escaped nun who had been kept prisoner in the Montreal convent and forced to have sexual relations with priests. Resisting nuns were killed, she reported, as were any babies born, their bodies then thrown into a lime pit. Although Maria Monk later was discredited as a prostitute and fraud after investigations uncovered no evidence to support her charges, many religious bigots continued to believe her story. The monograph frequently was reprinted, selling hundreds of thousands of copies and spawning a sequel and many imitators.

Throughout the 1850s, nativist hostility against Catholics intensified, with the Know-Nothing movement spearheading the agitation. Predictably, violence erupted. Mobs rioted, burning Catholic churches, schools, convents, and homes.

One particularly effective diatribe against Catholics was Josiah Strong's *Our Country* (1855), which accused Catholic immigrants of immorality, crime, corruption, and socialism. Reprinted in numerous editions, it incited public antipathy toward Catholicism for decades. The Reverend Justin H. Fulton also was an effective demagogue; his anti-Catholic books *Rome in America* (1887) and *Washington in the Lap of Rome* (1888) warned of a Catholic threat to America's liberty through the school system and through control of the government. Another Maria Monk–type, Margaret Lisle Shepherd, published her autobiography, *My Life in a Convent* (1887), claiming to be an escaped nun who had fled priests' carnal lust. Her story, although false, was widely believed and added to the anti-Catholic chorus.

In 1887, a short-lived but highly successful anti-Catholic organization, the American Protective Association (APA), emerged out of Iowa to become a national force with approximately 500,000 members.[7] Dedicated to keeping Catholics out of office, employing only Protestants, and refusing to cooperate with Catholics in any strikes, the APA struck a responsive chord among working-class U.S. Protestants who believed Catholic immigrants were coming to take their jobs, particularly after the Panic of 1893 and the ensuing high rate of unemployment. Enjoying some success in recruiting members in the East but none in the South, the APA was strongest throughout the Midwest. Although its endorsed candidates gained control of city governments in Detroit, Kansas City, and Milwaukee—causing the firing of all Catholic officials in those cities—the APA sowed the seeds of its own destruction. Internal conflicts, charges of corruption and embezzlement of funds, and a reputation for violence combined to torpedo the APA; it had no power after 1896.[8]

Anti-Catholicism did not end with the APA's demise, however. In 1911, General Nelson Miles, former Army Chief of Staff and Congressional Medal of Honor recipient, organized the Guardians of Liberty in upstate New York. Dedicated to keeping Catholics out of office because they supposedly would take their orders from Rome, this group never wielded any real political clout. An anti-Catholic publication, *The Menace*, gained more than 1.5 million readers, mostly rural. The Catholic Church unsuccessfully sued to revoke *The Menace*'s mailing privileges on the ground that the periodical's graphic depictions of the alleged immorality of the Catholic Church violated federal obscenity laws. But *The Menace* was not alone; a total of 61 anti-Catholic periodicals appeared prior to World War I.[9]

The post–World War I period saw the resurrection of the Ku Klux Klan (KKK), this time dedicated to the theme that Catholicism and Judaism were alien to Americanism. As described in Chapter 10, the KKK grew to a membership of 2 to 3 million and was partly responsible for passage of the restrictive immigration laws of 1921 and 1924. Thereafter, it declined in numbers and influence, and its final hurrah was a slanderous campaign in 1928 against Democratic presidential candidate, Al Smith, the Catholic governor of New York.

## VALUES AND PRACTICES

Several factors help explain nativist hostility against U.S. Catholics in the eighteenth, nineteenth, and early twentieth centuries. First, religion then played a far greater role in people's lives, which made religious differences a matter of greater concern. Generations of Catholic–Protestant conflict in Europe had created a legacy of latent antagonism among European Americans. Furthermore, U.S. culture and Protestantism had evolved along parallel lines, stressing individualism and self-reliance, whether in making one's fortune or in gaining salvation through the teachings of the Bible.

**RELIGION.** Because Catholics followed Church dogma, or prescribed doctrine, and operated their local churches as part of a vast bureaucracy whose hierarchy of authority reached back to the pope in Rome, many U.S. Protestants feared that this structure would undermine their way of life. They envisioned millions of Catholic immigrants, obeying a foreign ruler (the pope) like an unthinking, indoctrinated army. If such people gained political office, some Protestants feared, control of the country would move to Rome. The physical presence of priests and nuns and the building of churches, convents, and parochial schools—virtually all nonexistent in the United States before—served to confirm the worst Protestant fears.

Other Catholic practices puzzled and disturbed many U.S. Protestants. They considered vows of **celibacy** among priests and nuns unnatural, which encouraged them to believe the lurid fabrications that were printed about sordid sexual practices within the religious orders and the priesthood. Mandatory attendance at the weekly repetition of the same mass ceremony, then spoken in Latin, seemed to them both un-American and repressive of individual thought. Use of a private confessional booth to tell one's sins to a priest, unlike the usual Protestant practice of silent confession during worship services, seemed bizarre to some. Although Catholics themselves understood and accepted the context of their own beliefs and practices, to Protestants many generations removed from familiarity with them, these outgroup differences seemed strange and threatening.

**EDUCATION.** Catholic education perhaps generated the most conflict between Catholics and Protestants. Daily readings from the King James Bible in public schools constituted one of several factors prompting Catholics to establish parochial schools to provide appropriate religious training and moral guidance for their children. Efforts in the 1840s to obtain public funding for parochial schools or to substitute the Catholic version of the Bible for Catholic students in public schools generated fierce controversy in Boston, New York, Philadelphia, and Cincinnati.[10]

The issue of public funding for parochial schools flared up again in the 1870s, but the opposition of President Grant and the Republican Party neutralized organized nativist opposition. Efforts in the 1880s in Massachusetts and in three midwestern states (Ohio, Illinois, and Wisconsin) to regulate parochial schools also generated intense controversy.[11] Throughout this period, Protestant periodicals argued that the public school system would end the "ignorance and superstition" of Catholic children and so campaigned not only against public funding of parochial schools but in favor of eliminating them altogether.[12]

## THE CONTEMPORARY SCENE

Today, Roman Catholics in the United States number more than 68 million, making their religion the largest single denomination in the country and growing rapidly due to immigration. Overt discrimination against them has ended; and, except for recent Filipino, Haitian, and Hispanic Catholic immigrants, most are assimilated into the economic and political mainstream. They can be found in all occupations and in many leadership roles. John F. Kennedy became the first Catholic president in 1960; in Congress, Catholics ranked first in 2013 among the denominations with 161 legislators (30 percent). In 2013, six of the nine U.S. Supreme Court justices were Catholics.[13]

Greater dialogue occurs between Protestant and Catholic religious leaders, an outgrowth of the **ecumenical movement** initiated by Pope John XXIII five decades ago. The change from saying Mass in Latin to English in the United States helped make Catholicism seem less strange to outsiders. Also, an acute shortage of priests obliged the laity to become more active: reading scripture, leading music, distributing communion at services, and taking leadership positions in nearly every phase of the church's life, including religious instruction, family life bureaus, and financial and administrative positions. With both men and women handling these church tasks, Catholicism in some ways has become more like several Protestant denominations and thus less "different" to outsiders. Mainstream U.S. Catholic social views tend to agree with those of conservative U.S. Protestants on various subjects, including pornography, abortion, birth control, and school prayer.

Perhaps the best evidence of greater religious and ethnic tolerance, however, lies in the rise in the religious intermarriage rate, which is currently at 22 percent.[14] Group size is an apparent factor. The larger the percentage of Catholics in a given area, the more likely that Catholics will marry within their group, but the smaller the percentage, the more likely they will marry someone not of their faith.[15]

In recent decades, non-Hispanic Catholics have been upwardly mobile in wealth accumulation. Catholic values related to work and money—together with smaller nuclear families, high rates of marriage stability, and higher educational achievement—led to achievement of a wealth level comparable to that of mainline Protestants.[16]

Problem areas remain, however, including surveys showing that as many as 85 percent of Catholic Americans reject the Church's teaching on birth control and that they divide

Nearly one-fourth of Americans are Catholic. When Pope Benedict XVI visited New York City and Washington, DC, in 2008, he attracted hundreds of thousands. At Yankee Stadium in New York City, approximately 60,000 people filled the ballpark to witness his celebrating Mass. He was the third pope, after Paul VI and John Paul II, to visit the United States.

equally on the antiabortion position of the Church. At the height of the sexual abuse cases involving priests in 2002, Catholic participation in church life and satisfaction with church leadership dropped noticeably, but it since has rebounded to pre-scandal levels.[17]

# Jewish Americans

Jewish people are a unique minority because they are not a specific religious grouping and need not even be religious. Although religion has been an important bond among Jews, it is not a cohesive force in that three main branches of Judaism exist in the United States—Orthodox, Conservative, and Reform. In addition, many agnostics and atheists also identify themselves as Jews; for these secular Jews, the emphasis is on Jewish culture and history rather than a belief in God. And with large variations in physical appearance, native languages, and cultural attributes, Jews possess that elusive quality Franklin Giddings called "consciousness of kind."[18] In 1946, Jean-Paul Sartre wrote that a Jew is someone whom other people identify as a Jew. Perhaps then, our best informal definition of the Jewish people is that they consist of all those who think of themselves as such, with outgroup members treating them accordingly. However, conservative factions within Judaism limit Jewish identity to those who are born of a Jewish mother or who are converts.

**Read on MySocLab**
Document: How Did Jews Become White Folks?

### IMMIGRATION BEFORE 1880

Although we have archaeological evidence of earlier Jewish presences in New Mexico and Tennessee, the first recorded group of Jewish immigrants—4 men, 6 women, and 13 younger people—arrived in New Amsterdam in 1654 as refugees from the Portuguese takeover of previously Dutch-ruled Brazil. Benefiting from tolerant Dutch rule, Jews enjoyed open acceptance in this settlement. Later, many Jewish refugees of Spanish and Portuguese origin, fleeing the Spanish Inquisition, came to the United States by way of Holland, the Caribbean, or South America. By the end of the eighteenth century, approximately 2,000 to 3,000 Sephardic Jews were living in America.[19]

Most of the earlier discussion about nativist hostility toward Catholics applies with equal validity to Jewish immigrants. All the English colonies discouraged Jewish immigration and passed laws to keep Jews from voting or holding office. When Jews were permitted to vote in New York in 1736, a group of residents claimed the election was fraudulent on that basis. When the Know-Nothing movement reached its height in the 1850s, the Know-Nothings singled out "this peculiar race of people" for criticism and discriminatory treatment. During the Civil War, former Know-Nothing member Ulysses S. Grant, acting on unfounded charges that Jews were profiteering through smuggling and cotton speculation, issued General Order Number 11, expelling all civilian Jews from his military jurisdiction. On January 4, 1863, Lincoln revoked this order.[20]

By the mid-nineteenth century, the second wave of Jewish migration began. In this wave came Ashkenazi Jews, mostly from the German provinces. They were more prosperous and better educated than earlier German Jewish immigrants and represented the first mass Jewish immigration—groups of entire families coming from a single locality or community. From an 1840 Jewish population of 15,000, Jewish Americans increased to 250,000 in 1880. At that point, Jewish American communities almost exclusively were German.

## NEWCOMERS AND TENSION

The third wave of Jewish migration was the most significant—in numbers, cultural influence, work contributions, and dominant-group reaction. From 250,000 in 1880, the U.S. Jewish population rose to nearly 3 million before generally restrictive immigration laws were enacted in the 1920s. The initial impetus for this massive migration was a **pogrom** (organized massacre) that followed the assassination of Czar Alexander II (1881). Although no Jews were involved in the regicide, the czarist government used them as a scapegoat to divert people's attention from long-festering social, political, and economic grievances. This marked the beginning of a long series of pogroms, with many attacks, loss of lives, and extensive property damage in Jewish communities throughout the Russian Empire's Pale of Settlement region (an area at the western edge of Russia). In addition to the need to escape government-incited violence, powerful economic incentives encouraged emigration. Some people came to escape destitution. Others fled from the economic instability that resulted from government efforts to industrialize Russia.

Considerable cultural tensions developed among Jews from different areas of Europe. Sephardic Jews, the first arrivals, considered themselves superior to the nineteenth-century German newcomers (Ashkenazi Jews), who in turn later looked with disdain on newcomers from eastern Europe. Although a few Jewish immigrants from Central and East Europe had arrived as early as the eighteenth century, for some Jewish ethnics, the distinctions based on place of origin and time of arrival in the United States persisted well into the mid-1940s, as this report indicates:

> The earlier arrivals scarred the later ones as crude, superstitious, and economically indigent, and the latter despised the former as snobs and religious renegades. As recently as 1925, one student of immigrant groups asserted that "intermarriage between a Sephardic Jew and a Russian Jew, for instance, is as rare, if not rarer, than intermarriage between Jew and Gentile." Even within each of these divisions of Jews, there was at first aversion to marriage with some of the subdivisions. Bavarian Jews hesitated to marry with those German Jews who came from the area near the Polish border, derisively labelled "Pollacks." The Russian Jew looked down on the Polish and Galician Jews and refused to marry them or permit his children to do so.[21]

Thus, ethnic prejudices, as well as cultural and class differences, led to strain between the "old" Jewish population and the "new" Jewish arrivals. German Jews, who by this time had supplanted the Sephardic Jews as an ethnic elite, were embarrassed by their lowly co-religionists with their "strange" appearance, Yiddish language, and orthodox religious practices. At first, many rejected the new arrivals, partly out of fear that growing anti-Semitic feeling would place all Jews—old and new—into one negative category. Soon, however, these Americanized Jews created community organizations to help the newcomers adjust to their new country.

## ANTI-SEMITISM

Anti-Jewish stereotyping spread in the arts and the media as it had for other immigrant groups, such as the Irish and Asians. On stage, Jews sometimes were depicted either as scoundrels or as comic characters. Newspapers and magazines at times ran cartoons and editorials that were openly anti-Semitic. One example was *Life* magazine, published in New York City, where the Jewish population rose from 4 percent in 1880 to 25 percent in 1910. The magazine called the city "Jew York" and attacked supposed Jewish clannishness, pushiness, and domination of the theater. In the early twentieth century, approximately half of the actors, songwriters, publishers, and entrepreneurs in New York City were Jewish; this included those who worked in the flourishing Yiddish-language theater that served the immigrant community. *Life*'s editors launched a 10-year attack on the "Jewish Theatrical Trust," accusing it of poisoning U.S. values and of lowering the moral tone of the theater by running lascivious plays for profit. The accusations were false or distorted. By catering to a specific ethnic group, the Yiddish theater was "different," but the plays were not lewd or lascivious.

Two notorious incidents emphasize the heights anti-Semitic feelings reached in the late nineteenth and early twentieth centuries. In the first instance, Joseph Seligman, an eminent banker and frequent guest of President Grant at the White House (who declined an offer to become Secretary of the Treasury), was denied accommodations in 1877 at a fashionable resort hotel in Saratoga Springs, New York. Although he and his family had stayed there several times before, the hotel's new policy of "not accepting Israelites" made headlines across the country. This incident brought latent anti-Jewish attitudes into the open, and many other establishments quickly followed suit.

The second incident concerned Leo Frank, the manager of an Atlanta pencil factory, who in 1913 was convicted hastily on flimsy evidence of murdering a young factory girl. Many felt he was convicted because he was a Jew, and his case spurred the formation of the B'nai B'rith's Anti-Defamation League. With prominent Georgia newspapers and clergymen calling for a new trial and many Jews contributing money to Frank's legal appeal, the state's governor commuted his scheduled execution to life imprisonment, an act praised by the Georgia press. However, some of the dead young woman's friends and neighbors abducted Frank from the state prison, transported him 175 miles to her hometown, and lynched him. It was more than a local episode. Nationwide press coverage of the incident included comments about the "Parasite Race," helping fan the flames of prejudice.

Anti-Semitism of varying intensity has continued to the present day. The Silver Shirts, led by William Pelley, and the National Union for Social Justice, headed by the "radio priest," Father Charles Coughlin, were two of the most active

The Holocaust Museum in Washington, DC, is adjacent to the National Mall, and is the official U.S. memorial. The "Tower of Faces" pictured here is a tribute to the millions who lost their lives and a reminder of the incredible evil of that time. Of its 30 million visitors since its opening in 1993, more than ninety percent were not Jewish.

movements against the Jews in the late 1930s. Anti-Semitic behavior declined after World War II, however, partly because of revulsion against Nazi genocide and partly because pluralism became more generally accepted. Still, isolated incidents occur, mostly acts of vandalism or desecration. Some analysts suggest that the roots of anti-Semitism can be found in the teachings of Christianity (now renounced in the Catholic Church by Vatican II), which for centuries blamed the Jews for the death of Christ.[22] Latent anti-Semitism also may manifest itself for other reasons, including status and economic rivalries.

Although the number of anti-Semitic incidents in the United States is no longer as high as in 1994 (with nearly 2,100 anti-Semitic incidents, including 143 on college campuses), they still occur. In 2011, they reached their lowest level in two decades, with a total of 1,080 such incidents of vandalism (330), harassment (731), and physical assault (19). States with the most anti-Semitic incidents were California (235), New York (195), New Jersey (144), Florida (111), and Massachusetts (72).[23] One encouraging note is increasing community activism against such incidents. For example, a few years ago when a Jewish family's home in Billings, Montana, was vandalized after displaying a Menorah in the window, the entire town—Jews and Christians alike—held marches and candlelight vigils. The local newspaper printed full-page Menorahs and nearly 10,000 homes displayed them. Since then, no serious acts of hate violence have occurred in that town.

### UPWARD MOBILITY

Like many other immigrants, most East European Jews who came to the United States were poor. Most, therefore, settled in or near the large cities that were ports of entry (Boston, New York, and Philadelphia). Many went to work in the garment industry, while others became street peddlers until they saved enough capital to open their own stores. Because two-thirds of the Jewish male immigrants were skilled workers, compared to an average of one-fifth of the males from other immigrant groups, their absorption into the U.S. economy proceeded relatively smoothly.[24] As a result, they climbed the socioeconomic ladder more quickly and in larger proportions than most other groups (except not into middle-management positions in much of the corporate world).[25]

Several cultural factors contributed to the success of some first- and many second-generation Jewish Americans. First, because of generations of discrimination in Europe, they had been relegated to such self-sustaining occupations as merchant, scholar, and self-employed artisan. Thus, they brought with them skills and knowledge useful in an industrial society, together with values that encouraged deferred gratification, seriousness of purpose, patience, and perseverance—precisely the virtues stressed by the U.S. middle class and the Protestant ethic (see the Ethnic Experience box).

Second, during the period of great immigration, 1880 to 1920, most Jews came with their entire families; in many other ethnic groups, males usually came first and then either returned to the old country or sent for their families. Having the entire family unit together from the outset gave Jewish newcomers greater emotional stability against the psychological strain of the immigrant experience and an advantage in cooperative economic efforts.

A third factor was the Jewish people's traditional emphasis on learning—especially for boys. Even if the children were illiterate in the language of their country of origin—and this often was less true for Jews than for many other immigrant groups—they had learned Hebrew and, as a result, the discipline of study. By the time he was 13, a Jewish boy, if raised in a religious family, was prepared to read from the Torah for his bar mitzvah. Today, a large number of Jewish girls also participate in this ceremony (known as a bat mitzvah). In Jewish culture, this positive orientation toward learning carried over to public education and secular studies. Although parents toiled in low-status factory jobs, they encouraged their children to further their education and then enter the professions. The high percentage of Jewish youths attending public and private colleges in the first few decades of the twentieth century is all the more remarkable because of their limited

# the ETHNIC experience

## My American Dream

"I heard a lot about the streets in America being paved with gold, but I knew one thing, because I came in contact with GI's and I saw they came from different backgrounds in different parts of the country, and I knew one thing—that I was going to have to work in the United States. People didn't actually still say the streets were paved with gold, but this was still the belief in Europe because, you know, the dollar was the Almighty. In Europe, you could buy five, six times with the dollar what you could buy in the United States. So this was why people still believed the streets were paved with gold. All what you needed was a shovel. But I knew. I was prepared. I never was disappointed in coming here to the United States."

"What is to me the American Dream? To some people, maybe it's a bigger car or a bigger house. This is their dream. Take more vacations. Sure, we need vacations, but I think our way of life should be to practice just what we preach, just what we have in our Constitution. I mean, not to discriminate against people of all kinds, because this country—if it really is a melting pot—for this one reason, because it is so great this country, because from so many countries, the idea can be put together."

Source: Polish Jewish immigrant who came to the United States in 1948 at age 35. Taped interview from the collection of Vincent N. Parrillo.

residence in the United States and because most U.S. citizens placed less emphasis on a college education in those times.[26]

By the 1940s, the occupational distribution of Jews was comparable to that of members of high-status Protestant denominations, although they remained significantly underrepresented in some industries, such as steel, oil, banking, and insurance for many years thereafter.[27] Not all experienced upward mobility though. Thousands of Jewish poor, especially among the aged, existed on a level far from the stereotypical portrait of successful Jews.

## SOCIAL INTERACTION

**Social ostracism** often accompanied their economic successes. Higher economic status did not necessarily mean a comparable increase in social prestige. Even when Jews gained positions with higher levels of income, they still found themselves excluded from social and recreational clubs and had to establish parallel social and recreational organizations for themselves. They also encountered restrictions in housing; admissions quotas for colleges, universities, and professional schools; and other obstacles designed to keep them at a social, economic, and educational distance from white Protestants.

Although many Jewish middle-class families moved to the suburbs after World War II, they continued to be socially segregated in the 1950s and 1960s. Numerous studies at the time found the frequency of social interactions and close associations between Jews and non-Jews in Detroit declining after adolescence, particularly at the time of choosing a mate. Jewish suburbanites might take part in day-time social activities of the entire neighborhood but in the evening and on weekends, they usually experienced relative isolation and found their social relationships confined to other Jews, and not necessarily voluntarily.[28]

These observations seem less true today. U.S. interfaith marriages among Jews and non-Jews were 47 percent between 1996 and 2001. Today, approximately one-third of all married Jewish Americans are intermarried.[29] Although some experts argue that religious intermarriage simply is personal choice and does not reflect values emphasizing assimilation, others see it as one of the final stages of assimilation. At the very least, such

*This interfaith marriage between an Episcopalian bride and a Jewish groom, performed by a rabbi and a priest, shows a continuing trend in marital assimilation along ethnic and religious lines. Recent studies show many children from these marriages are not raised in the Jewish faith, suggesting a further decline of the U.S. Jewish population.*

a pattern reveals a significant increase in meaningful primary relationships between Jews and non-Jews.

Significantly, only 28 percent of the children of mixed marriages are brought up as Jews, 31 percent are reared in no religion at all, and 41 percent are reared in another faith or in an amalgam of Judaism and other beliefs. This finding, coupled with a low birth rate and a low immigration rate, has led Jewish traditionalists to be fearful about the future of Judaism in the United States, including predictions that the Jewish American population will decline significantly from its present 5.2 million.[30] One organization, the Jewish Outreach Institute, promotes the inclusiveness of intermarried families by offering its resources and educational and networking programs for parents raising children in an interfaith marriage and for grandparents whose adult children have intermarried.[31]

### JEWISH IDENTITY

For the large numbers of Jewish immigrants in the late nineteenth and early twentieth centuries, the synagogue played a significant role in the community. At the same time, it competed with various cultural, ideological, and self-help organizations supported by many Jews. Classes offered by such organizations as the Educational Alliance on New York City's Lower East Side, for example, provided opportunities for acculturation. Together, the synagogues and organizations provided cohesive bonds, laying the foundation for community organization, social activities, and a feeling of belonging.[32]

As Jews became more highly educated and assimilated, the ethnicity that had closely secured European immigrants to their religious traditions lost its hold. New focal points of Jewish identity became building and supporting the nation of Israel, as well as involvement in politics and social concerns within the United States. In 2013, Jewish legislators numbered 22 out of 435 in Congress and 10 of 100 in the U.S. Senate.

Many Jewish Americans today see religion less as an inherited ethnic identity and more as a personal choice of belief and practice.[33] Jewish survey data show that only 20 percent of Jews in the United States (half of them Orthodox) are seriously religious.[34]

# the INTERNATIONAL scene

## Religious Diversity in Israel

Religious diversity is not a concept most people associate with Israel, a nation founded in the mid-twentieth century as the Jewish state. To many outsiders, Israel seems monolithic and homogeneous, consisting mostly of Jewish inhabitants with a small Palestinian minority. This, however, is far from the reality. In 2012, Jews constituted 76 percent of the total population, with Muslims (mostly Sunni) next at 17 percent, Christians at 2 percent, Druze at 1.7 percent, and other faiths at 4 percent. With its population becoming even more diverse from a continuing influx of immigrants and a growing Arabic population, Israel faces a growing challenge of inclusion.

Despite popular belief that most of Israel's Arab population lives on the West Bank, 60 percent live in the Sea of Galilee and northern regions. Still others live in the inland area and in seven mixed-religion cities throughout the country. Since the 1967 reunification of Jerusalem, for example, that city's Arab Muslim population has increased faster than its Jewish population.

The Druze—a relatively small Middle Eastern sect centered in Lebanon, with a turbulent near-1,000-year-old history—cloak their religion in secrecy and maintain a close-knit identity and loyalty. Their prohibitions against intermarriage and conversion, either away from or into their religion, make their survival and continuity across nearly a millennium all the more remarkable.

In the city of Haifa is a small community of Baha'i, whose religion was founded in the mid-nineteenth century by Baha' Ullah. The Baha'i—with houses of worship in Africa, Australia, Central America, Europe, and the United States—believe in a universal faith. No preaching occurs in their temples; instead, services consist of the recitation of scriptures of all religions.

The mostly Jewish population itself hardly is a single entity. The majority are secular but retain some loyalty to religious traditions, particularly during Yom Kippur and Passover. Approximately 25 percent would classify themselves as devoutly Orthodox. Not only does Israel's Jewish population range from ultra-Orthodox to secular, but it also contains great diversity because of immigration. Gaps between second- and third-generation Jews of European descent (Ashkenazim) and those of North African and Middle Eastern descent (Mizrahim), who each comprise approximately half the Jewish population, have narrowed throughout the years but still remain. The Ashkenazi are the dominant elite and tend to be more affluent, secular, and Westernized, whereas the Mizrahi are more traditional, conservative, and religious. Occasionally, tensions between the two groups spill over into violence.

### CRITICAL THINKING QUESTION

What do you know of religious diversity among Jews in the United States?

---

Affixed to their Jewishness culturally but secular in their beliefs, such people are more likely to intermarry and assimilate. It is to them that rabbis and leaders in the Reform branch of Judaism have been reaching out in an effort to maintain the Jewish community. Yet rabbis and leaders in the more traditional Conservative and Orthodox branches view welcoming interfaith couples into the religion as diluting Judaism. This emotional issue continues as all these groups struggle to ensure the survival of American Jewry and somehow maintain the integrity of Jewish thought, values, and institutions.

Since 1990, more than 105,000 Israelis have migrated to the United States, thus augmenting the Jewish American population. Eight percent of today's Jewish adults are immigrants, and two-thirds of these emigrated from one of the republics of the former Soviet Union.[35] The most favored settlement areas have been the New York and Los Angeles metropolitan regions. (For information on religious diversity in Israel, see the International Scene box.)

**STUDENTS SPEAK** "The section discussing Jewish Americans is something that I know about first hand. In 1984, my parents were married. My father came from a strict Irish-Catholic background. He grew up going to church every Sunday and going through the entire Catholic school system. On the other hand, my mom grew up in a not-so-strict-but-still-religious Jewish family. When they got married, there wasn't much acceptance of an interfaith marriage. Even though my mom and dad were happy and in love, they still had to deal with disapproval, not only from outsiders but also from their own families."

**—Haley O'Sullivan**

# Mormon Americans

The Church of Jesus Christ of Latter-Day Saints offers a fascinating portrait of a religious group evolving from a despised and persecuted people into a highly successful and respected church. This group is unique as a minority group because its principal migration was to leave what was then the United States. Its series of relocations westward, ultimately ending with permanent settlement in the Rocky Mountains during the 1840s, gave it an enduring sense of territoriality and shared tradition.[36]

## THE EARLY YEARS

At age 18, by his own account, Joseph Smith received the first of several visitations from the angel Moroni, who guided him to a hidden stack of golden plates, each eight inches square.[37] Aided by two stones called the Urim and Thummin, Joseph Smith translated the hieroglyphics into the *Book of Mormon*, a massive and controversial work. Mormons consider it the true word of God, providing one of the foundations of their faith along with the Bible. In 1830, two years after completing his translation of the book, Joseph Smith—now 25 years old—founded the Mormon faith in the western New York State region where he then lived. Within a year, the church had more than 1,000 members.

As the church continued to grow rapidly under Smith's charismatic leadership, it attracted enemies. Fleeing harassment in New York and then Ohio, the Mormons resettled in Missouri, incurring further hostility because of their antislavery views, growing political power, and cooperative communities. Their more individualistically oriented neighbors found such communities threatening on the sparsely settled frontier. Expelled by the governor in 1838 following some officially sanctioned killings, the Mormons moved to Illinois, where they faced their worst clashes as the church's encouragement of polygamy, together with the Mormons' growing numbers and strength, inflamed societal hostility into frequent acts of violence. In 1844, Joseph Smith and his brother, Hyrum, were killed by a mob storming the jail in which they had been incarcerated. Thereafter, raids, pitched battles, burned homes and temples, the rape of Mormon women, and even the use of artillery pieces by both sides brought Mormon existence to a crisis stage.[38]

Faced with extermination or forced assimilation, most of the Mormons (approximately 30,000), under the leadership of Brigham Young, migrated westward until they reached the Great Salt Lake Valley in 1847. Intergroup conflict had strengthened their group identity and cohesiveness, and now the Mormons experienced steady and rapid growth in the isolated Salt Lake region. Part of this growth was due to the arrival throughout the nineteenth century of tens of thousands of converts from England and Scandinavia. The discovery of gold in California ended Mormon isolation, however, because their settlement was located along one of the best routes to the California gold fields.

Mormon theocratic political power threatened federal control of the Utah territory and thus control of a key route to California, generating several decades of government attempts to alter Mormon economic, political, and social institutions. In such instance, President Buchanan sent troops to Utah in 1857 to ensure the peaceful installation of Alfred Cumming, a non-Mormon, as territorial governor.

Government efforts next shifted to an attack on **polygyny**, the Mormon practice of men having more than one wife. Although permitted by church doctrine, polygyny occurred among only 20 percent of the eligible males, two-thirds of whom had one additional wife.[39] Lurid newspaper stories about alleged Mormon depravity inflamed public opinion and created a stereotype of Mormon males as evil, seductive, promiscuous, sexually virile libertines. Non-Mormon opportunists produced such products as Brigham Young Tablets and Mormon Bishop Pills that supposedly were able to increase a man's sexual desire or ability.[40] In 1862, Lincoln signed the Morill Act, forbidding bigamy in U.S. territories. Continually harassed by federal agents after the Civil War, the Mormons challenged the law as an infringement on their religious freedom, but in 1878, the U.S. Supreme Court ruled in *Reynolds v. United States* that the law was constitutional.

Unable to gain access to church records to prove the multiple marriages, the government passed a new law in 1882 forbidding anyone from living in "lewd cohabitation," which resulted in the jailing of hundreds of Mormon polygamists. In 1887, the Edmunds–Tucker Act dissolved the Mormon Church as a legal entity and provided for the confiscation of church property. When this law was upheld by the Supreme Court in 1890 as constitutional, church president Wilford Woodruff issued a manifesto ending the open practice of plural marriage. President Benjamin Harrison then granted pardons to all imprisoned polygamists. In 1896, Utah became a state, beginning a new era of relations between Christians and Mormons.

## VALUES AND PRACTICES

Following the behavioral code established by Joseph Smith, whom they believe was a prophet of God, Mormons typically do not smoke or drink any form of alcoholic beverages, coffee, tea, or caffeinated soda beverages. Emphasis is on group rather than individual activities, promoting group identification. Especially encouraged are the performing arts, team sports, and organized recreational activities. Other aspects of the Mormon faith, described in the following sections, are deeply embedded in the group's social institutions.

**FAMILY.** Mormons place heavy emphasis on the family, both as the primary agent for socializing people into the Mormon belief system and as the basic social organization in the eternal Kingdom of God. Anything undermining family growth or stability is discouraged—for example, premarital and extramarital sex, indecent language, immodest behavior, abortion, birth control, intermarriage, and divorce. These problems occur far less often among active, observing Mormons than among those who are less religiously involved. Drugs and premarital sex are a much smaller problem among Mormon teenagers and young adults than nationally.[41]

Unlike typical U.S. families, in which each person pursues individual interests and activities, Mormon families do many things together. Monday is set aside as Family Home Evening. At other times, families attend social and sporting events together, with the emphasis on the intermingling of different age groups. Among older Mormon families of pioneer stock, the kinship network manifests itself in annual summer reunions. All families engage in the genealogical search for ancestors to secure for them a proxy baptism or sealing ceremony in a Mormon temple to enter God's presence in the Celestial World. Through the Mormon Genealogical Society, more than 2 billion names have been preserved on microfilm—obtained from vital statistics, census materials, church records, and other official records. Each year, this extensive collection increases, and it is available to Mormons and non-Mormons alike for genealogical investigation.

**EDUCATION.** Because of Joseph Smith's revelation in 1833 that intelligence reflects the glory of God, Mormons place great stress on education. Mormons founded both the University of Utah (the oldest university west of the Mississippi) and Brigham Young University (the nation's largest church-related university, with more than 33,000 students enrolled in 2012–2013). Utah is in the top 25 percent of states in literacy and in the percentage of enrolled college students and college graduates.[42]

**RELIGION.** A vigorous and systematic missionary program involves more than 50,000 young missionaries, ages 19–25, or retired couples as unpaid volunteers serving in nearly 350 missions throughout the world.[43] With approximately 6.1 million U.S. members, the Church of Jesus Christ of Latter-Day Saints is the fourth-largest religious body in the United States, more than the combined membership of the Episcopal and Lutheran churches—two pillars of the U.S. religious establishment.[44] Another significant factor in the spectacular growth of the church is its members' practice of tithing—giving 10 percent of their gross income to the church. Income from tithing supports meeting house construction and maintenance, its educational system, religious institutes for students, missionary work, curriculum materials, and world relief efforts. Worldwide, Mormon membership now is more than 14.4 million, although critics argue the number is much lower. Whatever the number actually is, U.S. residents account for less than half of this American-created faith that now is worldwide.

**ECONOMICS.** Mormons take care of their own poor, without public-welfare assistance. Through a national exchange program to bishops' storehouses (resembling small supermarkets), the Mormon poor receive their needed foodstuffs. Other items—clothing, toiletries, and household items—also are available there, provided through monthly cash donations by other Mormons.

The Mormon Church, with assets estimated at $40 billion, generates an estimated $8 billion in tithing and billions more from its for-profit enterprises. That income goes toward massive foreign construction projects, charitable spending, and investments. Most of its investments go not into stocks or bonds but directly into church-run agribusiness, insurance, media, real estate, and retail-store companies. Deseret Management Corporation—the company through which the church holds nearly all of its commercial assets—has vast real estate holdings both in the United States and abroad, including a $2 billion megamall in Salt Lake City, and properties in Britain, Canada, Australia, Mexico, Argentina, and Brazil worth untold hundreds of millions. The church's Polynesian Cultural Center is Hawaii's foremost paid visitor attraction, attracting more than 1 million visitors annually and employing 1,100 workers. In addition to 49 other farms and ranches, it owns and operates the largest cattle ranch in the United States—the 290,000-acre Deseret Ranch outside of Orlando, Florida, with an estimated real-estate value of more than $858 million. Other commercial ventures include a sizable chain of bookstores, the Beneficial Life Insurance Company, AgReserves, Inc. (the largest producer of nuts in the United States), and Bonneville International Corporation (owner of 25 radio stations and a television station).[45]

## THE CONTEMPORARY SCENE

Although the Mormons incurred the wrath of many whites for their opposition to slavery in the 1840s, by the 1960s, they were under attack for "racist" church doctrine. Blacks could become church members (as indeed some did throughout the nineteenth century), but they could not join the priesthood. Then, in June 1978, church president Spencer W. Kimball announced a divine revelation that blacks could become priests. Four other revelations—Brigham Young's guidance to Utah, Wilford Woodruff's instruction to end plural marriage, and two concerning life after death—are part of Mormon history since Joseph Smith's death. Widespread acceptance and adaptation quickly followed each of them.

Although the church championed women's suffrage in the nineteenth century, it came under fire in the late twentieth century for being sexist. The church always has encouraged higher education for women and never prohibited them from working, but it did not permit them to become elders in the church leadership or to espouse feminist causes. Feminist advocates found themselves excommunicated for expressing their views publicly.[46]

Supporters maintain that women fill numerous positions in the church, such as the efforts of the Relief Society, teaching doctrinal study classes, directing choirs and dramatic productions, officiating in temple ceremonies, and serving at all levels on welfare committees. They also argue that the doctrine of the Church of Jesus Christ of Latter-Day Saints converges in some areas with ideals of feminism, such as equality between men and

*The Salt Lake Temple is the largest of more than 130 around the world and the best-known temple of The Church of Jesus Christ of Latter Day Saints. Dedicated in 1893, the neo-Gothic granite structure has six majestic spires, and it serves as a sacred place of worship, augmented by the 360-member Mormon Tabernacle Choir, all volunteers.*

women, but it is at odds with versions of feminism that emphasize female sufficiency apart from men and the radical feminist critique of the family as an institution for the repression of women. Although some individual families may be repressive and dysfunctional, most Latter-Day Saints believe that the defect is not inherent in the structure. Indeed, they consider the family the source of both men's and women's greatest work and joy.[47]

In recent years, the Mormons have been downplaying their differences with mainstream Christianity. Beginning in 1982, editions of the *Book of Mormon* began carrying the subtitle "Another Testament of Jesus Christ." The official letterhead and website for the Church of Jesus Christ of Latter-Day Saints now have "Jesus Christ" in much larger letters. Officials prefer the media to use the term "the Church of Jesus Christ" instead of "the Mormon Church." As it continues to attract new members and achieve more mainstream acceptance, the Church of Jesus Christ also serves as a conservative repository of old-fashioned values and as a home-grown religion success story.

## Muslim Americans

Although Westerners may think of Islam (the religious faith of Muslims) as an Arab religion, most Muslims throughout the world are not Arabs. Indonesia contains the largest Muslim population (approximately 214 million). Other non-Arab countries with large Muslim populations include India (approximately 161 million), China (approximately 26 million), Malaysia (approximately 17.6 million), and Kazakhstan (approximately 8.2 million). Throughout the many black African countries, Islam has millions of adherents. Worldwide, Islam embraces more than 1.6 billion people, making it second only to Christianity in membership (see Figure 12.2 on the ethnicity of U.S. Muslims).

Although exact numbers are impossible to determine, given the areas of Africa from which slaves were obtained, experts estimate that as many 40,000 African Muslims were enslaved in America, including Kunta Kinte, Alex Haley's ancestor that he talked about in his Pulitzer Prize–winning book, *Roots* (1977). Many of the first Muslim Americans, therefore, were unwilling immigrants, enslaved people of color.[48]

Approximately 10 percent of the early Syrian immigrants to the United States were Muslims and Druze. After 1908, the Ottoman government began drafting Muslim Arabs

**Read on MySocLab**
Document: Hijab on the Hardcourt

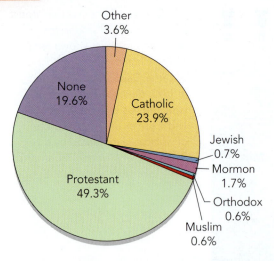

**FIGURE 12.2A   Religious Affiliation, 2012**

*Source:* Pew Forum on Religion and Public Life.

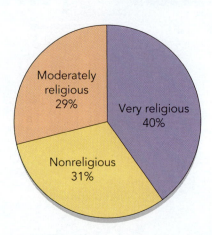

**FIGURE 12.2B   American Religiousness, 2012**

*Source:* Gallup.

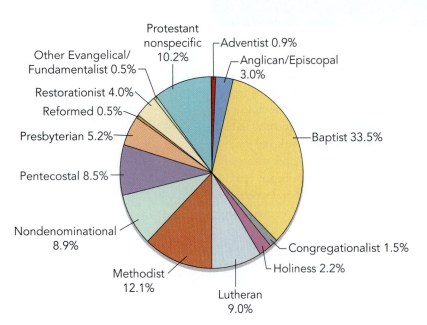

**FIGURE 12.2C   Composition of American Protestantism**

*Source:* Pew Forum on Religion and Public Life.

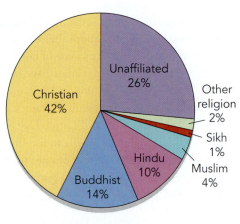

**FIGURE 12.2D   Religious Affiliation of Asian Americans**

*Source:* Pew Research Center.

into the Turkish army, and several thousand immigrated to the United States to escape military service. In 1916, a large group of Muslim Arabs settled in Dearborn, Michigan, to work at the nearby Ford Motor Company plant. That legacy continues today, as Dearborn still boasts the largest Muslim community in the United States.[49]

Because their numbers were relatively few and because few Muslim women came to the United States before World War II, only four mosques were built until that time. Without women, stable communities and institutions had little chance to develop.

Since World War II, however (and especially after 1965) many Muslim immigrants from all parts of the world have come to the United States (see the Ethnic Experience box). More Muslims now live in the United States today than in Afghanistan or Libya. More than 2,100 mosques now dot the U.S. landscape, most of them in cities but 28 percent in the suburbs. Today, Muslim Americans number approximately 2.6 million, of whom approximately 24 percent are black.[50]

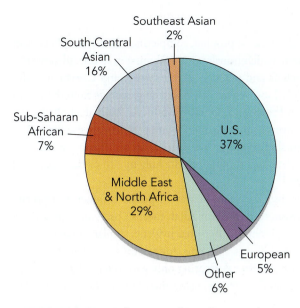

**FIGURE 12.2E  Ethnicity of Muslims in the United States**

*Source:* Pew Research Center.

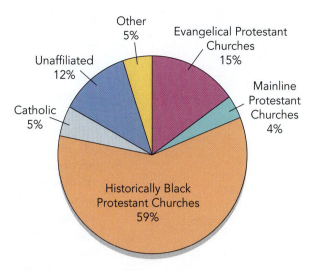

**FIGURE 12.2F  Religious Affiliation of Black Americans**

# the ETHNIC experience

### A Muslim Among Christians

"When I was in high school, I was interested to know about the United States. There was an American Cultural Center in Kabul that offered a lot of books, magazines, and journals for the people of Afghanistan to study and learn about the United States. Also there had been shown films about the United States. I studied them and learned and knew about how the people lived and how they improved their country. I wished and I prayed that I could go there for my education and see this great country. But it was not to be for many years later when my family and I escaped from the communists and the United States took us in...."

"The culture is so very different in this country. When we first came here, there were hardly any Muslims in Paterson and virtually no Afghans.

We did not then have a mosque for worshiping or an Islamic religious community to offer us any spiritual support. As we struggled to improve our English and make some money not just for the basics of food, clothes, and rent, but also for a set of dishes, lamps, tables, and other housing needs, we had to sustain ourselves spiritually by ourselves, praying alone. Fortunately, my brother and his family lived nearby (he was my sponsor), and our families got together once a week to pray."

"I must tell you, though, how wonderful this country is for people of different religions. Two Salesian Sisters befriended me just a few days after I arrived here. When they heard that I had a science background but had no job, they helped me find one teaching science in a Catholic school

even though my English then was not as good as now. Here I was, a new Muslim immigrant teaching in an American Catholic school! The religious freedom and acceptance is one of the beautiful things I love about this country."

"There are many more Muslims here now and a half-dozen mosques in this area. I don't feel so alone any more in my faith; but you know, I was so accepted by the Christian people around me, I never found any negative attitudes. My new American friends helped me find a better life for myself and my wife and children, so we may have once been alone in our faith, but we never felt isolated from the Americans."

Source: Afghan refugee who came to the United States in 1980 at age 40. Taped interview from the collection of Vincent N. Parrillo.

## VALUES AND PRACTICES

In Islamic belief, Muhammad was the greatest prophet, completing a line of prophets from Adam through Moses to Jesus. Islam, which translates to "submission to one all-powerful God," incorporates many of the beliefs and practices of the Jewish and Christian faiths. Muslims subscribe to a rigorous Holy Law, or Shari'ah, based on teachings from the *Quran* (Koran). They keep the Sabbath on Friday and do not eat pork or drink alcoholic beverages. Uniting all Muslims, despite diverse cultural contexts and practices are the five pillars of Islam: the profession of faith, worship or prayer five times a day, almsgiving to the poor and needy, fasting during the daylight hours throughout the holy month of Ramadan, and a pilgrimage to Mecca at least once.[51]

To Muslims, religious beliefs and the social mores of public conduct and private experience are inseparable. Submission to the will of Allah means observing a prescribed code of conduct in every facet of life, including personal hygiene, similar in concept and practice to the Bengali, Gujarati, and Hindus. Muslims, for example, eat their food only with the right hand and clean their body after defecating only with the left hand. Thus, a reprehensible sight to them is to witness Westerners using their left hand to place food in their mouths.

Conservative in their values and attitudes, Muslims also reject the dominant U.S. group's preoccupation with materialism and self-indulgent pleasures at the expense of obligations to family and community. Female immodesty, societal sexual permissiveness, pornography, high rates of alcohol and drug abuse, illegitimate births, abortions, and divorce all concern U.S. Muslims who are attempting to maintain the integrity of their way of life.

Muslims, of course, are but one of many conservative religious groups in the United States who nonetheless identify themselves as loyal Americans and as part of U.S. society. No one should confuse them with radical Muslims who pervert the teachings of the *Quran* to justify violence and killing.

*Just as the past influx of Catholic and Jewish immigrants resulted in construction of many new churches and temples, so too has the arrival of hundreds of thousands of Muslims prompted the building of mosques for the new ethnic communities. Opened in 2005, the Islamic Center of America in Dearborn, Michigan, is one of the largest in North America.*

# the INTERNATIONAL scene

## Fear Overcomes Tolerance in Switzerland

After decades of migration to the European continent, millions of Muslims have accepted Western norms, but millions of others have not. Often living on the margins of society, Muslims experience a wide social distance gulf between mainstream society and themselves. Ongoing tensions, occasional outbreaks of violence, voter backlash, and internal restrictions through enacted or proposed legislation have both sides feeling threatened by the other.

In the midst of all this, a surprising action occurred in 2009 in Switzerland, a country with a long history of neutrality, pluralism, and religious tolerance. A nationwide referendum passed to ban the building of minarets (towers attached to mosques from which a muezzin or crier calls the faithful to prayer).

The measure passed with 58 percent of the vote and carried in 19 of 23 cantons, although it was defeated in the four largest Swiss cities. Nevertheless, the measure became law and plunged the country into controversy. Arguing that the ban violates the freedom of religion guaranteed in the Swiss constitution, the Swiss Green Party has appealed to the European Court on Human Rights on the matter.

That outcome, while important, is less significant than is the xenophobia in a liberal, multicultural society that led to such a vote, despite the Federal Assembly voting 129–50 for the public to reject the ban and by Catholic, Protestant, and Jewish clergy and organizations also speaking out against it. Fear is an irrational motivator, however. Yet actions

have consequences, and now many Swiss worry that they may have made themselves a target for Islamic terrorism.

Of a total population of 8 million, there are approximately 344,000 Muslims, mostly from Turkey and Kosovo, living in Switzerland. Most do not follow the codes of dress and conduct associated with conservative Muslim countries like Saudi Arabia. Of the 150 mosques in Switzerland, only four presently have minarets, and none conduct the call to prayer.

### CRITICAL THINKING QUESTION

What can be done to reduce mutual distrust between groups to prevent such actions or to undo them if they occur?

## CONFRONTING PREJUDICE AND DISCRIMINATION

You will recall from earlier chapters how French Americans in 1798 and German Americans during World War I faced overt prejudice, even violent acts of discrimination under the guise of patriotism. Following the terrorist attacks of September 11, 2001, Muslim Americans similarly faced hostility that unfortunately still continues, not only in the United States but in Europe as well (see the International Scene box). Individual violent actions, such as the deaths, maiming, and injuries caused by bombs set off in 2013 in Boston by two Muslim-American brothers, provoke anti-Muslim rhetoric, but they also generate condemnation from American Muslim religious and community leaders, and pleas not to blame an entire group for the actions of two individuals.[52]

U.S. public views of Islam remain divided. A 2013 CBS News/New York Times public opinion poll revealed that 39 percent of Americans thought Islam is no more likely to encourage violence than other faiths, whereas 43 percent thought it did, and 18 percent said they did not know. Respondents with a negative view were more likely to be conservative Republicans or evangelical Protestants.[53] Another poll, this one in 2011 and conducted by Fox News, found that 43 percent of respondents considered mainstream Islam a peaceful religion and 38 percent thought it encouraged violence.[54] In both polls, the results revealed greater trust in the peacefulness of Islam than in previous years.

Interestingly, the polls find that the more familiar Americans are with Islam, especially if they know someone who is Muslim, the more positive view they will have toward the religion and vice versa.[55] Such findings support the intergroup contact hypothesis discussed in Chapter 3 and serve as a prime motivator for the many interfaith initiatives throughout the country.

Several Muslim-American nonprofit organizations actively work to promote understanding and counter the negative stereotyping, prejudice, and discrimination. The Council on American-Islamic Relations is the nation's largest Islamic civil rights advocacy group that seeks to enhance an understanding of Islam and works to empower the U.S. Muslim community by encouraging their political and social activism. The American Muslim Alliance is a political organization dedicated to involving Muslim Americans in the mainstream political process through such political empowerment efforts as coalition building, fielding Muslim candidates, and generating voter turnout.

# Amish Americans

**12-3** Compare and contrast the experiences and attributes of Amish, Rasta, Santeríans, and Hindus.

**Read on MySocLab**
Document: The Amish: A Small Society

The Amish—like the Mennonites and the Hutterites—are a sect descended from the Swiss Anabaptists, who believe in voluntary adult baptism only, as practiced by the early Christians. Their founder, a Mennonite bishop named Jakob Ammann, began a sectarian movement when a schism arose in 1693 over enforcement of the still-practiced *Meidung*, or **shunning**—a powerful social control mechanism that enables the Amish to maintain their way of life.

When a bishop, acting on the vote of the congregation, imposes the *Meidung* on an errant member, others, including family members, cannot interact with that person without also being placed under the ban. Informal sanctions such as ridicule and group disapproval, followed by a formal admonition from a minister or deacon, if necessary, precede such an action. Unusual but not altogether rare, the *Meidung* also can be revoked if the transgressor publicly confesses and personally asks the congregation for forgiveness. Considered an act of "tough love," shunning also strengthens the chain of community by removing the weakest link.[56]

Although some Amish may have come earlier, their first documented arrival in America is 1727, when a few families left Switzerland and settled in Pennsylvania. Migration continued from this region and from Germany between 1727 and 1780, with large numbers of Alsatian and Bavarian Amish migrating between 1815 and 1840 and establishing communities in Ontario (Canada), Illinois, and Ohio. With an intensive agricultural orientation, the Amish found the unlimited availability of land in the New World so attractive an inducement that they completely transplanted themselves to North America. Their subculture became extinct in Europe, as the Amish who remained there were absorbed into the dominant society.

## VALUES, SYMBOLS, AND PRACTICES

Forming *gemeinschaft* communities—intimate, homogeneous, and characterized by strong religious tradition—the Amish remarkably have remained constant in a continually modernizing dominant society. Their communities are highly integrated because their social institutions—family, school, church, and economic endeavors—are complementary and consistent in values and expectations. Young and old live similar lives. The entire group shares the same lifestyle and restrictions, accepting them as the will of God.

Pride is a major sin, so wearing jewelry—even wedding bands—and making other efforts at promoting physical attraction are forbidden; boasting is rare, and seeking a leadership role is frowned upon. No Amish seeks political office and many do not register to vote. Here, we must distinguish between the more conservative Old Order Amish—highly concentrated in Indiana, Ohio, and Pennsylvania—and other Amish communities such as the Beachy Amish (who own and drive cars), Swiss Amish, Nebraska Amish,

Weaver Amish, New Order, or Swartzentruber (who drive black buggies with kerosene lanterns). Amish in the Midwestern states tend to vote Republican and adamantly oppose farm subsidies, believing they would undermine their self-help social system.

Clothing is an important symbol of group identity that helps maintain separatism from outgroups and continuity within the community. In an unchanged, three-centuries-old tradition, the men wear low-crowned wide-brim hats; coats without collars, lapels, and pockets; and trousers with suspenders but without cuffs or creases. Belts and gloves are not permitted, even in cold weather. Women wear solid-color one-piece dresses, with long skirts and aprons, and keep their heads covered at all times, whether indoors or outdoors. Clothing thus expresses a common understanding among those sharing similar traditions and expectations. Other aspects of appearance—beards, but not mustaches, for all married men and a special braided hairstyle for females—further reinforce this orientation.

Language serves as another symbolic attribute of the *unser Satt Leit* (our sort of people). Pennsylvania Dutch is a German dialect resembling Palatine German folk speech and is common to all Amish, regardless of where they live. English is the group's second language, usually introduced to children when they enter school and learned without difficulty, enabling them to communicate effectively with their English-speaking neighbors. Interestingly, the Amish refer to all non-Amish people as "English," regardless of their nationality or race. German is used exclusively for the preaching service and formal ceremonies; the families teach German to their children so that all can understand it when it is used in sermons and hymns.[57]

Conservative Amish farmers use teams of horses instead of tractors and gain an additional benefit from the natural supply of fertilizer, unlike their less conservative co-religionists who use tractors. Most Amish homes may be lacking in modern conveniences, but they are clean, solid, kept in good repair, and, like the farms, well run:

> Newer Amish houses differ from the traditional variety in a number of ways. They tend to be smaller, and many do not have a "farmhouse" appearance at all. In fact, except for such items as no electrical wiring and the lack of curtains, they often look much like non-Amish houses. In the matter of modern appliances and equipment, the differences between "traditional" and "new" are even more significant.

*Clinging to their traditional values and lifestyle as a persistent subculture, the Amish continue to thrive both culturally and economically, even as their numbers grow. One obvious sign of their contrast to modern society is a horse and buggy traveling down a roadway surrounded by diesel- and gas-driven vehicles, as here in Shipshewana, Indiana.*

The Amish have never permitted their members to use electricity furnished by public power lines. The church has been unyielding on this point, and the prohibition has served to restrict the kinds of devices and appliances available to members. Over the years, however, the followers of Jacob Ammann have come up with some rather interesting alternatives: bottled gas, batteries, small generators, air pressure, gasoline motors, hydraulic power. The net result has been a variety of modern devices that have become available to the Amish, not only in their homes, but in their barns, workshops, stores, and offices....

Amish homes in the Lancaster area, though surprisingly modern in certain respects, are without electricity. There are no light bulbs, illumination being provided by oil lamps or gas-pressured lanterns. And the list of prohibitions remains long: dishwashers, clothes dryers, microwaves, blenders, freezers, central heating, vacuum cleaners, air conditioning, power mowers, bicycles, toasters, hair dryers, radios, television—all are taboo.[58]

Even for some of the Old Order Amish, however, the modern world forces compromises. A combination of growing population and limited land availability oblige some to enter occupations other than farming. A half century ago, virtually all the Amish were farmers, but now it is less than half. As they become business **entrepreneurs**, they adapt as they must to maintain their way of life.[59]

The Amish consider adolescence the most dangerous period of an individual's life. Because of physical and emotional changes and peer-group influence exceeding family control, adolescents strain for independence, to be free of Amish restraints. Interestingly, the Amish keep most of their young people willing to adopt the Amish way of life by first experiencing *rumspringa* ("running around"). They allow their youth to experiment with the larger world and its temptations: regular clothing, cell phones, movies, drinking, smoking, cruising in cars, dancing, flirting, and wild parties. The teens may "go away" on a Friday night and not return until Sunday evening. *Rumspringa* takes place while the youngsters live at home and carry on their ordinary work activities, on family farms or in factories. It is limited to their free times, in the evenings and weekends away from the Amish homes.[60]

However, exposure to high school worldliness is forbidden; formal education ends with the eighth grade, and teens receive vocational training at home thereafter. Because baptism does not occur until a person's late teens or early twenties, adults are more tolerant of discreet adolescent *rumspringa* activities, hoping that their teenagers will learn enough to give up worldly ways forever and become baptized in the Amish church or else remain in the outside world. Most young people do return to Amish ways, get baptized, and assume adult responsibilities. Approximately 20 percent of Amish youths may leave, often joining a more liberal Mennonite group, but only a very small percentage of baptized Amish ever leave.[61]

If an individual wishes to remain part of the community, the Amish insist on an endogamous marriage. The Amish do not practice birth control and so have a high birth rate, with an average family of six to seven children. They have grown from 59,000 in 1970 to more than 250,000 today, and now reside with 456 autonomous settlements in 29 states, stretching from Montana to Florida.[62] Social class has no meaning to the Amish, and all share a strong sense of social obligation to one another. This includes helping others when disaster or tragedy strikes and providing home care rather than institutionalization for the aged.

## CONFLICTS WITH SOCIETY

The Amish oppose social security and all other forms of insurance, believing the Christian brotherhood is responsible for its own people. Besides rejecting social security payments from the government, they refused to pay the mandatory self-employment social security tax. During years of conflict with the government about this issue, the government confiscated some Amish farms and horses to collect owed taxes. Finally, Amish leaders went to Washington, astounding the legislators by their request to be exempted from government benefits. Consequently, a law was passed, exempting them from both payments and benefits.

State laws making school attendance compulsory until age 16 provided another arena of conflict for the Amish with society. Because the Amish refused to send their children to high school, some were harassed and arrested by state officials. A Wisconsin case ultimately reached the U.S. Supreme Court, resulting in a ruling in favor of the Amish. For them, an eighth-grade education is sufficient, with farm vocational training occurring thereafter.

Under Amish tradition, youngsters work as apprentices after the eighth grade. For years, that didn't conflict with federal law because the Amish community's livelihood was rooted in agriculture, and farms are exempt from child-labor laws. With the growing costs of farming and land in the past decade, many families turned to woodworking and other trades, then bringing them into conflict with these laws. Some businesses were fined thousands of dollars for employing youths, usually their own children. Claiming the laws threaten their religious and work values, the Amish sought an exemption. Finally, in 2004, President Bush signed legislation exempting the Amish from child-labor laws.[63]

Tourism annoys the Amish, especially in Lancaster County, Pennsylvania. Approximately 5 million tourists visit Lancaster County each year, 350 visitors for every Amish individual. Ignoring Amish religious beliefs against having their pictures taken, camera-wielding tourists routinely take such pictures. Guided bus tours (as many as 50 a day) clog the narrow roads, block Amish vehicles, and park in front of the Amish schools and farms. Motels, restaurants, antiques, handicraft and souvenir outlets, and many other commercial enterprises cover the region, generating hundreds of millions of dollars from tourists, of which only a small portion actually goes to the Amish.[64]

Despite these problems, the Amish thrive. Non-Amish neighbors and leaders praise their integrity, work ethic, and neighborliness. Their birth rate, ingroup solidarity, and resistance to outside influences suggest that not only will they continue as a persistent subculture for many years to come, but also will dramatically increase in number.

**STUDENTS SPEAK** "I found the Amish Americans interesting. They can be conservative, such as not wearing any jewelry or promoting any physical attraction, but they allow their adolescents to experiment with temptations in life. This just surprised me because, after reading about what they value and some of their practices, the adolescent age just doesn't seem to fit into this religion. I can see why they may practice this period of experimenting with temptations though, because it gives them some independence at this young age to be able to make some of their own decisions in life."

**—Alexandra Schorling**

# Rastafarian Americans

Rastafarians provide a contemporary example of a misunderstood religious minority group that frequently experiences prejudice and harassment. They fulfill the characteristics of a minority group: unequal treatment, easy identification, self-conscious identity, real or assumed common ancestry, and **endogamy**. Factors that direct attention to them are their skin color, distinctive hairstyling, and use of *ganja* (marijuana) for religious purposes, much as Navajos and Huicholes use peyote in their religion.

## THE EARLY YEARS IN JAMAICA

Marcus Garvey, Jamaican-born founder of the Back to Africa movement of the early twentieth century, was influential in Jamaica before leaving the island for the United States in 1916. On his departure, he is supposed to have said, "Look to Africa, where a black king shall be crowned, for the day of deliverance is near." When Ras Tafari was crowned as

Emperor Haile Selassie in Ethiopia in 1930, he added the titles "King of Kings" and "Lion of the Tribe of Judah," placing himself in the legendary line of King Solomon. The coronation of the young Ethiopian emperor reminded Garvey's followers of his words and seemed to fulfill the biblical prophecy of Revelation 5:2–5:

> And I saw a mighty angel, who announced in a loud voice, "Who is worthy to break the seals and open the scroll?" But there was no one in heaven or on earth or in the world below who could open the scroll and look inside it....Then one of the elders said to me, "Don't cry. Look! The Lion from Judah's tribe, the great descendant of David, has won the victory, and he can break the seven seals and open the scroll."

Finding other corroborating scriptural passages (Revelation 19:16, Psalm 68:4, and Daniel 7:9 describing the king's hair as being "like pure wool"), the Rastas believed themselves to be the black Israelites of the Diaspora. Four ministers—Leonard Howell, Joseph Hibbert, Archibald Dunkley, and Robert Hinds—spread the message, attracting many followers. To black Jamaicans experiencing both economic frustration at the time of a worldwide depression and white colonial rule, the movement offered hope and the promise of a better day coming.[65]

Three major assumptions dominated the early phase of the Rastafarian movement: the innate wickedness of whites, the racial superiority of blacks, and the eventual revenge of blacks against whites by means of enslavement. Living at the bottom of the ladder in a highly stratified society, Jamaican blacks thus protested against white racism and economic exploitation through the Rastafarian movement. Since then, most Rastafarians have taken a more conciliatory stance toward whites, no longer condemning them en masse.[66]

Believing the colonial social institutions enchained them, the Rastas flouted the laws, denying the jurisdiction of the rulers. Because working for taxpayers or social institutions implied recognition and thus tacit approval of the existing social structure, the Rastas refused to do so. Instead, they eked out an existence off the land, living as squatters in temporary shacks. Because the Rastas were poor, these attitudes provided them with coping mechanisms while they awaited the end of their exile from Africa.

## FROM OUTCASTS TO SOCIAL ACCEPTANCE

The Rastas' rebelliousness, although passive, brought quick condemnation in the early years of the movement. Jamaican newspapers called the Rastas unpatriotic, despicable, *ganja*-smoking criminals. Some schools refused to admit their children, and the government disrupted their meetings, arrested members, and raided and burned their homes. Dominant-group persecution served only to unify the Rastafarians further. Finally, the Rastas invited the University of the West Indies (UWI) to conduct an impartial investigation of their movement. The UWI report rehabilitated their public image, and a new period of reciprocal cooperation began between the Rastas and the dominant society. A high point was reached on April 21, 1966, when Haile Selassie visited Jamaica and some Rastas were invited to the residence of the governor general for the first time to meet with the emperor in private. Each year, on that date, Rastafarians in Jamaica and the United States celebrate the event.

In the past few decades, Rastas have become more assimilated into the sociocultural milieu of the island society. Their expressive art forms have been featured in public exhibitions and at the annual National Festival; their imprint on Jamaican music, popularized by Bob Marley and ranging from ska to reggae, has been significant. Their widened appeal now includes numerous groups among the U.S. public as well in Jamaica. As a socially recognized group, Rastafarians in Jamaica also attract members from the middle and upper classes as well.

Dreadlocks hairstyling among Rastafarian men helps establish social distance, setting them apart from outgroup members while creating a recognizable ingroup bond. In contrast, their unique reggae music has attracted a large following among various age groups throughout most of U.S. society and other countries as well.

## VALUES, SYMBOLS, AND PRACTICES

Although some Rastafarians do not wear their hair long, most do so as a symbol of unity, power, freedom, and defiance to outgroups and in accordance with biblical custom.[67] Because they reject nearly all chemically processed goods, Rastafarians do not use soap, shampoo, or combs. They are far from unsanitary, however, instead frequently washing their hair and body in water and herbs. The hair grows long and is braided into dreadlocks.

Food is another symbol of religious identification. Rastafarians rarely eat meat, abhorring pork and favoring small fish and vegetables. They will not drink liquor, milk, or coffee, preferring instead herbal tea. No manufactured foods, salt, or processed shortening is used; natural foods and oil from dried coconut are the staples in *I-tal* food and cooking, the name signifying the Rastafarian diet.

Smoking *ganja* (marijuana) originally gave the Rastas *communitas*—a sense of cohesive unity. By producing an altered state of consciousness, they could gain temporary escape from their lives of hardship. Gradually, smoking *ganja* became identified with seeking communion with the supernatural, experiencing the self as God.[68]

The Rastafarians' language also symbolizes their philosophy and perception of reality. A form of Creole English, Rastafarian speech is nearly devoid of subject–object opposition; *you* and *me* almost are never used, but an *I and I* primary combination used instead, even to outgroup members. Shedding the cognitive shell and asserting a new self-concept and world view that they believe to be their natural, African state, Rastafarians use *I and I* to identify soulfully with others at a higher level than I–Thou or I–It relationships. *I and I* is a special communal term meaning "I and myself," "I and my brothers," or "I and God."[69]

## THE CONTEMPORARY SCENE

Rastafarianism survives because of its adaptive capabilities. An existential interpretation of their doctrines has enabled the Rastas to adjust to industrialism and to U.S. society without sacrificing their naturist ethic. Exact numbers in the United States are difficult to determine, partly because many follow the lifestyle but not the religion. One estimate places the number of Rastas and Rasta supporters at 800,000, with 80,000 of them living in Brooklyn.[70] Others argue that the numbers are much lower.

Mostly poor, unskilled workers, the Rastafarians tend to live in low-rent urban neighborhoods. Their cultural orientations isolate them from both white and black Americans, the social distance forging a small, cohesive subculture. Rastafarians frequently encounter problems with the police, their appearance and regular use of marijuana inviting harassment. Their ingroup solidarity, adaptability, and social distance from the dominant society make the Rastafarians likely to remain a persistent subculture, much as the Romani have been.

# Santerían Americans[71]

A fairly new religion in the United States is Santería or *La Regla Lucumí*, which originated in the region of West Africa now divided between Nigeria and Benin. Because it evolved from preliterate communal experiences of the Yoruba people into a traditional religion, the belief structure of Santería flows from an oral tradition. There is no written scripture or body of sacred texts, although written versions of the practices, traditions, and stories do exist.[72]

Santeros believe in one god known as Olorun or Olódùmarè. Olorun is the source of *ashé,* the spiritual energy that makes up the universe, all life, and all things material. Olorun interacts with the world and humankind through head guardians called *orishas.* The *orishas* rule over every force of nature (for example, wind, water, storms, and forests) and every aspect of human life (for example, love, illness, maternity, and fate). Fans of popular Latin jazz musicians Tito Puente, Celia Cruz, and Eddie Palureri know that some of their music mentions the *orishas.* Communication between *orishas* and humankind occurs through ritual, prayer, divination, and *ebó* or food offerings in the form of animal sacrifice (most commonly, chickens). Song, rhythms, and trance possession are other means of interacting with the *orishas* and of learning how to develop deeper and fuller lives during one's stay in this world.[73]

From 1511 until the mid-nineteenth century, approximately 702,000 African slaves were brought to Cuba, compared to approximately 427,000 African slaves brought to the United States.[74] Prohibited from practicing their religion openly in Cuba, the Yoruba hid much of their religion beneath a facade of their captors' and owners' Catholicism. Yoruba spirits, or *orishas,* received devotion through the recognized images of Catholicism by being accorded dual identity with Catholic saints. The *orisha* Shangó (or Changó), for example—who represents the natural/cosmic forces of fire, thunder, and lightning and whose functions/power are passion, virility, and strength—became associated with St. Barbara, patron saint of artillery. Thus, the Yoruba people began to practice "Santería"—"the way of the saints." The memory of this subterfuge period of their religion's history is why many practitioners today consider the term *Santería* derogatory.[75]

Santería flourishes in Cuba today. Experts estimate that 70 percent of all Cubans practice Santería, whether through an occasional offering or rigorous practice. It is woven into the cultural and spiritual fabric of Cubans' lives and an intrinsic part of Cuban music, religious practices, and social structure. In fact, each year on September 8 at St. Patrick's Cathedral in New York City, a high mass is said in honor of the patron saint of Cuba, at which many santeros wear yellow, the color associated with the orisha Oshún.[76]

## VALUES, SYMBOLS, AND PRACTICES

Santeros (male priests) and santeras (female priests) fiercely preserve the traditions of Santería and full knowledge of the rites, songs, and language is prerequisite to any deep involvement in the religion. Because *orishas* each have a distinctive *ashé* that humans need, a believer must give an *ebó* for that specific *orisha* to take and, through its magical powers, transform into the type of *ashé* necessary to achieve what the petitioner wants. Specific colors, numbers, and natural objects are symbols associated with *orishas.* For example, red and white, the numbers 4 and 6, apples, bananas, roosters, and rams are attributes for Changó.[77]

Animal sacrifice is only one of many categories of *ebó* in the religion. Offerings such as *addimú* include candles, fruits, candy, or any number of items or actions that may be appreciated by the *orishas* in the religion. In divination (a basic Santería ritual), the *orishas* may ask (through the santero or santera) for a favorite fruit or dish, or they may call for the person to heed advice given. At times, they may demand that a person give up drinking or other practices that are unwise for that individual. They may request that a person wear certain jewelry, receive initiations, or perform any number of other actions. Or they may request sacrifice of an animal—usually a chicken or a dove—before coming to that person's aid. As a rule, animal sacrifice is called for only in major situations such as sickness or serious misfortune. And to critics who complain about these animal sacrifices, the santeros answer that the U.S. poultry industry kills more animals in one day than the religion has sacrificed worldwide in the last several hundred years.[78]

Trance possession is an important aspect of Santería. During a *bembé* or drumming party for the *orishas*, an *orisha* may be persuaded to join the party by entering the body of one of the participants. This is referred to as being "mounted" by the *orisha*, or the *orisha* is described as having "come down" from heaven to be with humans. When the songs, rhythms, and dances—deliberately calculated to entreat the *orishas* to come down—result in a trance possession, it is a time of great joy, as believers feel blessed by the spirits' counsel, cleansings, and sheer presence.

## SANTERÍA IN THE UNITED STATES

Because of the secrecy associated with Santería, no one knows exactly how many practitioners live in the United States, although estimates run as high as 800,000. The largest concentration, perhaps 300,000, live in New York City. Another 70,000 may live in South Florida.[79] Their presence partly is evidenced by the many store-front *botanicas* in Miami and the Northeast providing Santería figures, incense, and herbs for the faithful. Approximately a dozen websites also spread the word.

Santería has evolved from a black Cuban folk religion to a more widespread religious practice across the United States, attracting many non-Cubans, both blacks and whites, and people from various social classes. This wider appeal and a declining reliance on the use of Spanish reduce its "ethnocentric, cliquish character."[80] As it attracts more U.S. converts, its beliefs, rituals, and structure are changing. Santería is moving away from a mythological structure to a belief system incorporating some principles of psychology and Christian ethics. Initiation rituals now involve shorter periods of time (three months instead of three years), are open to all (not only to a select few who have been touched by an *orisha*), and consecrated *bata* drums no longer are necessary, either because of their unavailability or to avoid complaints from neighbors. In urban areas with large Puerto Rican populations—such as New York City and northern New Jersey—Santería is blending with Puerto Rican spiritism to take on yet another new form.[81]

As Santería became more visible, local officials sought to ban its animal sacrifices. Animal-rights activists received a setback in 1993, however, when the U.S. Supreme Court ruled in *Lukumi Babalu Aye v. City of Hialeah* that a Florida city could not outlaw the ritual animal sacrifices of Santería. In 2009, a similar legal battle in Euless, Texas (a suburb of Forth Worth) ended when the Fifth Circuit Court of Appeals reversed a lower court ruling, thereby allowing a Santerían priest to conduct ceremonial animal sacrifices near his home-based shrine.[82]

# Hindu Americans

Most people think of Hinduism as a religion, but more accurately, it reflects a whole set of practices and a range of philosophical and metaphilosophical concepts called *Santana Dharma* (which roughly translates to "everlasting religion"). Unlike most Western religions, Hinduism does not have a single founder, a specific theological system, a single system of morality, or a religious organization. Its roots are traceable to the Indus Valley civilization circa 4000 to 2200 BCE.[83] Over thousands of years, numerous cultural and military invasions shaped its development. Most influential was the arrival in northern India (circa 1500 to 500 BCE) of Indo-Europeans from the steppes of Russia and Central Asia, who brought with them the religion of Vedism. These beliefs became mixed with the indigenous Indian native beliefs.[84] Since then, Hinduism has grown to become the world's third largest religion, claiming more than one billion believers, or 15 percent of the world's population.[85] It is the dominant religion in India and has many adherents in Malaysia and Sri Lanka.

The most important of all Hindu texts is the *Bhagavad Gita*, a poem describing a conversation between a warrior Arjuna and his charioteer Krishna. Vedism survives in the *Rigveda*, a collection of more than 1,000 hymns. Other sacred texts include the *Brahmanas*, the *Sutras*, and the *Aranyakas*.[86] Because Hinduism is not a religion in the strict sense, it does not have converts; one can be a Catholic, Jew, Muslim, or Protestant and still practice Hinduism.

## VALUES, SYMBOLS, AND PRACTICES

At the heart of Hinduism is the monotheistic principle of Brahman, that all reality is a unity; the entire universe is one divine entity. Hindus visualize that deity as a triad consisting of Brahman, the Creator, who continually creates new realities; Vishnu, the Preserver, who sustains these new creations by traveling from heaven to earth in 1 of 10 incarnations whenever dharma (eternal order, righteousness, religion, law, and duty) is threatened; and Shiva, the Destroyer, who at times is compassionate, erotic, and destructive.

Cattle slaughter is a sacrilege, as Hindus revere the cow as a mother to all humankind for the nourishing milk it provides. The origins of this value orientation probably rest on a largely agrarian Indian society that depended on the cow for milk, for carting, and even for the practical use of cow dung as a fertilizer, a disinfectant, and a fuel. Hindus are not necessarily vegetarians, however; most, in fact, eat meat other than beef.

The *Rigveda* defined five social castes. Normally, people were assigned to the same caste as their parents, and marriages occurred within the same caste. Caste determined the range of possible jobs or professional choices among which a person could decide. In decreasing status, the five castes are Brahmins (the priests and academics), Kshatriyas (the military), Vaishyas (farmers and merchants), Sudras (peasants and servants), and Harijan (the outcasts, commonly known as the untouchables). Although India formally abolished the caste system in 1949, it remains a significant force, particularly in southern India.

Hindus believe in transmigration of the soul, resulting in reincarnation. They perceive humans as being trapped in *samsara*, a meaningless cycle of birth, life, death, and rebirth. *Karma* is the accumulated sum of one's good and bad deeds, which determines how you will live your next life. Through dedication to pure acts, thoughts, and devotion, one can be reborn at a higher level. Eventually, one can escape *samsara* and achieve enlightenment. Conversely, bad deeds can cause a person to be reborn at a lower level or even as an animal. Hindus thus accept society's unequal distribution of wealth, prestige, and suffering as natural and just consequences for people's previous acts, both in this life and in previous lives. Meditation, particularly yoga, is a common practice. Other activities may include daily devotions, public rituals, and the ceremonial dinner, *puja*.

*In a 500-acre religious community in West Virginia, known as New Vrindaban, stands this elaborate and ornate Hindu temple known as the "Palace of Gold." Combining architectural elements from the East and West, it is made of marble, gold, and carved teakwood. Opened in 1979, it attracts 50,000 tourists and religious pilgrims each year.*

Just as wearing a cross (for Christians) or a Star of David (for Jews) is an identifying symbol of one's faith, wearing a *pottu* (a dot on the forehead) is an ethnoreligious symbol for Hindus. An unmarried female wears a black dot, and a married woman, a red one. The *pottu*, also called a *bindi*, symbolizes the third eye mentioned in Hindu scriptures. These teach that the ultimate end of human life is liberation (*moksha*) from the finite human consciousness in which we see all things as separate from one another and not as part of a whole. When a higher consciousness dawns on us, we see the individual parts of the universe as deriving their true significance from the central unity of spirit. The Hindu scriptures call the beginning of this experience the second birth, or the opening of the third eye or the eye of wisdom.[87]

Approximately 80 percent of Hindus are Vaishnavites, who worship Lord Vishnu. Others follow various reform movements or neo-Hindu sects. Various sects of Hinduism have evolved into separate religious movements, including Hare Krishna, Sikhism, Jainism, and Theosophy. Two recent popular variations in the Western world—Transcendental Meditation and the New Age movement—both use Hindu techniques and concepts.[88]

### HINDUISM IN THE UNITED STATES

Approximately 1.5 million Hindu Americans live in the United States.[89] Most of that number consists of Asian Indian immigrants arriving since 1965 and their descendants. Their greatest concentrations are in the New York–New Jersey metropolitan area, California, Illinois, Texas, Pennsylvania, Michigan, Maryland, and Ohio.

While seeking to preserve their ethnoreligious distinctiveness and connectivity to India, Hindus also desire integration into mainstream U.S. society. In putting down roots and building their temples around the country, they also formed regional and national Hindu organizations to reaffirm their ethnic identity, unite the community, and advance their interests. The latter included, in an action reminiscent of Jewish Americans, an early effort to defend Hinduism against commercialization, defamation, and misuse through formation of antidefamation groups. The American Hindus Against Defamation

**STUDENTS SPEAK** *"The section that most intrigued me was the section on Hinduism. It was a real eye opener. I did not know that you could be from another religion and still practice Hinduism. I also believed that they could not eat any kind of meat, but to my surprise they do. I thought, since the cow was sacred to them, that Hindus were all vegetarians. I also found it interesting that they believe in reincarnation. This entire chapter and section showed how beautiful and interesting all religions are."*

**—Yessenia Alvarado Diaz**

(AHAD), formed in 1997, initiated several successful protest campaigns to stop American businesses and the entertainment industry from using Hindu deities, icons, and texts. Soon, several other antidefamation groups came into existence, including the Hindu International Council Against Defamation (HICAD) based in New Jersey and the Internet-based India Cause.[90]

As already indicated with several other groups, the complex interplay of race and ethnicity, including religion and sometimes especially religion, is of great significance in the identity formation of new Americans. Race and/or religion could marginalize a group and negatively impact its assimilationist goals. Among second-generation Hindu Americans, some evidence exists to suggest an increased cultural nationalism on the one hand, but also a belief in professional education as the way to overcome racial and ethnic barriers in the United States.[91]

# Religion and U.S. Society

**Read on MySocLab**
Document: **Christian Fraternities**

**Read on MySocLab**
Document: **Evangelical Elites in the U.S. Military**

Religion is an important aspect of U.S. culture. In a 2011 Gallup survey, 92 percent of U.S. respondents said they believe in God; 58 percent said religion was "very important" in their lives in a 2012 Pew Research Center poll. Such responses have been fairly consistent for decades and are two to three times higher than in other Western nations.[92] Approximately half of the population of the United States belongs to a church or synagogue (Figure 12.3). Although 37 percent attendance at weekly worship service may appear low, it is by far the highest of all developed countries; for example, only 18 percent of Canadians and 10 percent of the British attend church weekly.[93]

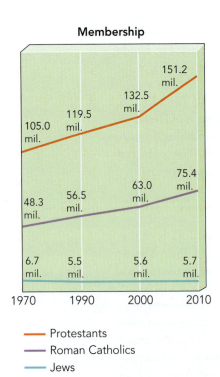

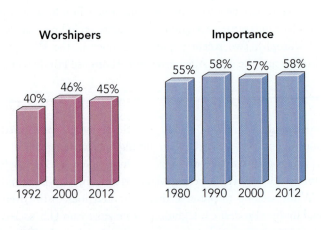

**FIGURE 12.3** Vital Signs of Religion in the United States, 2012

*Source:* Pew Forum on Religion & Public Life

Undoubtedly, some Americans use religion for social rather than religious purposes, finding in their church a source of community and a reaffirmation of the values of humanitarianism, work, individualism, and group conformity. Nevertheless, religiosity is an important element in society. Religiosity tends to be highest among African Americans and Afro-Caribbean Americans in comparison to Asian Americans, Hispanic Americans, and European Americans. African Americans are most likely to be active church members, while Afro-Caribbean Americans tend to read religious materials more frequently than African Americans. These research findings appear mainly due to specific cultural elements within these black communities.[94]

As we mentioned earlier, much religious diversity exists in the United States. Even Catholicism and Protestantism have great diversity within their churches; they are not the monolithic entities some assume them to be. The ethnic diversity of subgroups of the Catholic Church—French, German, Haitian, Hispanic, Irish, Italian, and Polish, to name but a few—promotes varying forms of religious behavior among these subgroups.[95] The Irish—as ethnic Italians and Poles have long recognized—dominate Catholicism in the United States. At present, Irish Americans represent less than 15 percent of the Catholic population but approximately half of the U.S. bishops. Protestants range from the more liberal Congregationalists and Episcopalians with their formal religious ceremonies to the more conservative American Lutherans and American Baptists with their less elaborate worship services. The Assemblies of God and Jehovah's Witnesses are but two of the many different Protestant faiths, as are such fundamentalists as the Missouri Synod Lutherans and Southern Baptists, with their strict interpretations of the Bible.

### CIVIL RELIGION

Some social analysts suggest that the United States has a **civil religion**, a shared belief system incorporating all religious elements into a sanctification and celebration of the American way of life.[96] Since the 1950s, our Pledge of Allegiance has identified us as a nation "under God." All our coins and paper money declare "In God We Trust." Congress begins each session with a prayer; presidents regularly schedule prayer breakfasts with government leaders, and they mention God in nearly all their state of the union and inaugural

**12-4** Explain civil religion in the United States.

*Despite the constitutional separation of church and state, a major component in the inauguration of all presidents, that which formally begins the term of office, is the swearing-in ceremony, with one hand resting on a Bible. Usually, it is a family Bible, as in 1985 with President Ronald Reagan, with First Lady Nancy Reagan watching.*

addresses. Religion is an important element in oaths of office, in courtroom procedures, and on most formal public occasions. The Boy Scouts and Girl Scouts both emphasize "God and Country" in their philosophies and oaths/promises and in various awards and badges. The list is virtually endless.

## CURRENT CONTROVERSIES

**12-5** Examine current controversies involving religious beliefs.

The U.S. Supreme Court often issues controversial decisions interpreting the First Amendment's stipulation about the separation of church and state. In its efforts to avoid any appearance of an "establishment of religion," the Court sometimes has outraged religious advocates of particular moral issues. From a religious perspective, its most controversial decisions have been those banning prayer in public schools and permitting abortion in the first two trimesters of pregnancy. Other decisions—for example, upholding the Amish exemption from compulsory-education laws and allowing certain forms of federal assistance to faith-based charities and parochial schools (lunches, books)—encourage certain religious activities while still striving to maintain First Amendment principles.

School prayer and abortion continue to be controversial issues. Proposed constitutional amendments have lacked sufficient support for adoption, but religious groups persist in their efforts. Catholics, Mormons, Lutherans, Baptists, and other conservative sects and denominations have combined their efforts to overturn the abortion ruling through lobbying and support of sympathetic legislators. School prayer does not generate the same degree of emotion, but it also unites people of different faiths to affect a change. Opposing them are strict constitutionalists, secularists, and people of more liberal religious persuasions.

Creationists' support for a literal interpretation of the Bible puts them in conflict with an array of scientific theories with implications of a non-Biblical origin of the world. These include Big Bang theory, the red shift, isotope decay and carbon dating, plate tectonics, stratigraphy (the study of rock strata), and evolutionary theory. In recent years, creationists have been crusading for "balanced treatment" about the origins of life. Objecting in particular to textbooks and curriculums on the subject of evolution, Christian fundamentalists insist that the book of Genesis be included as well. Arkansas, Louisiana, and Mississippi passed legislation requiring such an approach, and 18 other states were considering similar laws when a federal district court in early 1982 struck down the Arkansas law as a violation of the First Amendment. Since then, creationists have continued their battle against the orthodox sciences and the courts continue to rule that mandated creationist teaching in the schools is unconstitutional.[97]

# Assimilation

**12-6** Discuss the integration in U.S. society of these religious groups.

The assimilation of religious minority groups in the United States depends heavily on prevailing societal attitudes, degree of dissimilarity, and length of residence. For example, in the seventeenth and eighteenth centuries, this mostly was a Protestant land. Even so, the social distance among the various sects and denominations was significant. The religious intolerance of the seventeenth century—for example, continued persecution of Baptists in New England—then yielded by the eighteenth century to greater tolerance among the various Protestant faiths. However, members of the different faiths mostly continued to look on one another with disdain. One common ground did unite them though: their dislike of Catholics, whose integration into the mainstream they considered impossible.

Extensive Catholic immigration in the nineteenth century, as discussed earlier, sounded alarm bells in Protestant America. Jewish immigration, particularly in the second half of the century, added to nativist concerns. As the multigenerational assimilation process brought the once-contentious Protestant sects and denominations into

# REALITY check

## Places and Politics: A Geo-Political Profile

Because the United States is a religiously diverse country, each of the 50 states contains a wide variety of religious groups. However, because of the strong connection between ethnicity and religion, the residential patterning of immigrants and their descendants results in more numerous religious adherents of one faith over others in different counties. As Figure 12.4 shows, the prevalence of Catholics closely parallels where many Hispanics, Irish, or Italians settled. Baptists are predominant among black and white Southerners. Lutherans are the largest group in the northern Midwest where many Germans and Scandinavians settled, while Mormons prevail in Utah and adjoining counties, reflecting the continuing pattern first established in the Great Salt Valley in 1847.

The firmly established principle of the separation of church and state means that there are no religious political parties or candidates. Of course, most people who hold elected office are religious practitioners. For example, the 113th Congress (2013–2014) is the most religiously diverse in U.S. history. Among those serving are Catholics (163), Baptists (74), Methodists (46), Presbyterians (43), Episcopalians (38), Jews (33), Lutherans (23), Mormons (15), Orthodox Christian (5), Buddhists (3), Muslims (2), Pentecostals (1), and Hindu (1).

Certain religious groups (Catholics, Episcopalians, Jews, Methodists, and Presbyterians) have higher congressional representation than their share of the national population, while Baptists are underrepresented. Protestants dominate both political parties. Catholics and Jews are more likely to be Democrats, while Mormons tend to be Republicans.

Despite the official separation of church and state, in recent years, religion sometimes has been a shrill part of partisan politics. Churches and clergy were active for past social issues (abolition, women's suffrage, and civil rights) and today's issues of abortion, the death penalty, and same-sex marriage similarly have galvanized organized religious organizational muscle and action. In the foreseeable future, we can expect more of this mixture of religion and politics.

Sources: The Pew Forum on Religion and Public Life, "Faith on the Hill: The Religious Composition of the 113th Congress." Retrieved April 19, 2013 (http://www.pewforum.org/Government/Faith-on-the-Hill--The-Religious-Composition-of-the-113th-Congress.aspx).

a shared mainstream, Catholic and Jewish Americans remained on the periphery well into the twentieth century. As white ethnics, the ethnolinguistic cultural marks of these white ethnics disappeared and so too did the social distance between them and Protestant Americans. Today, some religious bias still remains with pockets of bigotry and sporadic bias incidents, but few would argue that Catholic and Jewish Americans continue to live outside the societal mainstream. Similarly, Mormons easily function within the societal mainstream and Amish traditions may keep them a persistent subculture, but others nevertheless accept them fully as a distinct part of U.S. society (see the Reality Check box and Figure 12.4).

On the edge of the mainstream today are other religious minorities, primarily consisting of first- and second-generation Americans of non-Western faiths. They therefore face more than just the difficulties of adjustment and acceptance all foreigners face. Representing cultures and faiths outside the Judeo-Christian mainstream of most black and white Americans, their full assimilation may be a slow process.

For assimilation to occur, three steps are necessary. First (and easiest through the generations), Americanization must significantly reduce the ethnolinguistic marks that make religious practitioners a visible minority. As with past religious minorities in other convergent subcultures, this is a normal process. Second, just as the United States went from a single melting pot for Protestants into a triple melting pot to absorb Catholics and Jews before merging back into a single melting pot, we significantly will need to expand our melting-pot concept into a society of more than three major faiths. Third, because

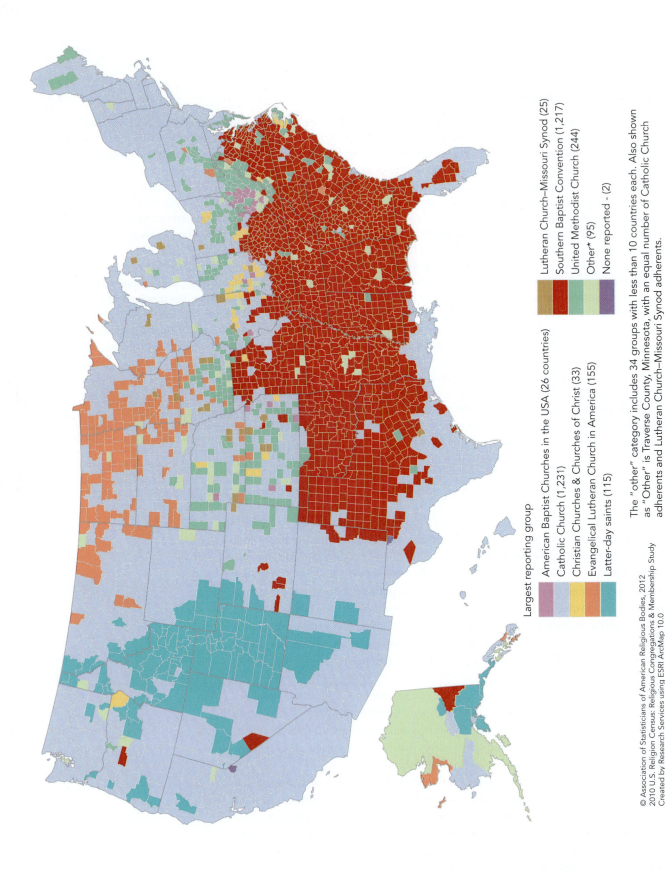

Largest reporting group

American Baptist Churches in the USA (26 countries)
Catholic Church (1,231)
Christian Churches & Churches of Christ (33)
Evangelical Lutheran Church in America (155)
Latter-day saints (115)

Lutheran Church–Missouri Synod (25)
Southern Baptist Convention (1,217)
United Methodist Church (244)
Other* (95)
None reported - (2)

The "other" category includes 34 groups with less than 10 countries each. Also shown as "Other" is Traverse County, Minnesota, with an equal number of Catholic Church adherents and Lutheran Church–Missouri Synod adherents.

© Association of Statisticians of American Religious Bodies, 2012
2010 U.S. Religion Census: Religious Congregations & Membership Study
Created by Research Services using ESRI ArcMap 10.0

**FIGURE 12.4   Participating Religious Group with the Largest Number of Adherents, 2010**

many of these religious adherents are people of color, we need to eliminate the racial barrier in our melting-pot concept.

Perhaps one aftermath of the 9/11 terrorist attacks and subsequent terrorist actions by radical Muslims may be an accelerated assimilation process among Muslim Americans. That's what happened following the tragic, wrongful internment of 110,000 Japanese Americans in 1942 and with German Americans during World War I. So too may the desire of Muslim Americans to dissociate from Islamic terrorists and be identified as "Americans" speed up their social integration into the fabric of U.S. society.

Even as they struggle for full integration into U.S. society, Muslim Americans already are a socioeconomic success story. They are the "most affluent, integrated, politically engaged Muslim community in the Western world."[98] A major 2007 study by the Pew Research Center revealed that their income and educational levels are approximately the same as native-born Americans and that an overwhelming number (71 percent) believed that one can get ahead in America with hard work.[99] Furthermore, Muslim American women report incomes nearly equal to their male counterparts, no doubt due in large measure to the fact that more women have college and postgraduate degrees than the men. In fact, as a group, Muslim American women are more highly educated than women in all other religious groups except Jews.[100]

# Sociological Analysis

Each of our three theoretical frameworks provides a means of understanding the significance of religion in intergroup relations and within the activities of convergent and persistent subcultures. Although different in emphasis, these perspectives offer unifying themes about religious pluralism in the United States.

**12-7** Discuss insights gained through sociological analysis.

## THE FUNCTIONALIST VIEW

In *The Elementary Forms of Religious Life* (1912), Émile Durkheim identified religion as an integrative bond for society, a theme elaborated on by modern functionalists. Religion, they maintain, serves as social "cement," uniting people with shared values and beliefs to celebrate harvests and life-cycle events. Religion gives meaning and purpose to people's lives, offering emotional and psychological support to individuals in both good and bad times. Religious teachings also help maintain social control, reinforcing important values and norms and providing moral standards.

Each of the groups discussed in this chapter—Catholics, Jews, Muslims, Mormons, Amish, Rastafarians, Santeríans, and Hindus—used their religious bonds as a means of strengthening their resolve and identity in a pluralistic and sometimes harsh society. Catholic and Jewish immigrants usually lived in ethnic neighborhoods with their church or synagogue as the focal point of their community activities, easing their transition to the U.S. lifestyle. Experiencing acts of hostility, Mormons and Rastafarians (and often Catholics and Jews) drew closer to other ingroup members and sustained hope through their faith. Mormons, Muslims, and Rastafarians, in particular, function in the secular world but maintain their sense of identity and purpose through adherence to specific religious tenets. Because of their strong religious convictions, the Amish and the Hasidic Jews remain constant in their ways despite the changing world around them.

As separatist minorities, the Amish and Hasidim developed economic and social interaction patterns that intensified their values and beliefs. All aspects of their daily lives have functioned together in harmony, eliminating stress and conflict between religion and daily living. Amish institutionalization of adolescent rebelliousness operates as a safety release for otherwise strict communes. The socialization efforts by Amish, Catholics, Hindus, Jews, Mormons, and Muslims of children and youths, although varying greatly in approach and intensity, serve to transmit and sustain throughout generations a continuing social system organized around specific religious beliefs and practices. Language, symbols, and rituals further instill a shared religious identity and social bond.

## THE CONFLICT VIEW

Karl Marx and later conflict theorists considered religion a social control mechanism designed to protect the interests of those in power. The dominant religion of a society represents the ruling economic and political class, and it legitimizes the existing social structure, blunting people's frustration, anger, and pain with the promise of an after-life reward. Religion can be a divisive factor, breeding dissension and violence, though conflict theorists suggest that the real reasons behind such upheavals are economic and political. What appears to be religious bigotry or fanaticism usually is a struggle for power and control disguised as a religious matter. Even the participants may be unaware of the reality of the situation, caught up as they are in the religious justification given for the conflict.

Notice how nativist alarm about mid-nineteenth-century Catholic immigrants centered on their perceived growing political strength. Fears of papal rule of the United States were very real then. Loss of political control still haunted Protestant Americans 30 years later. The American Protective Association even dedicated itself to keeping Catholics out of office. Problems arose for Rastafarians in Jamaica because they challenged the political status quo, and the Mormons in Illinois and Missouri made enemies because of their political strength in those states. The Amish, on the other hand, sought no political leadership or economic dominance and so encountered little hostility for those reasons.

Economic competition did create religious antagonism against Catholics and Jews. The rebelliousness of striking Irish laborers against mine and factory owners sparked anti-Catholic reactions, as did the recessions in the 1870s and 1890s, causing workers to fear that Catholics would take away their jobs. Similarly, rapid upward mobility among Jewish Americans ignited fears of their dominance, resulting in unflattering Shylock stereotyping and exclusion from organizations and establishments of affluent Christians. Such actions support conflict-theory argument that the roots of religious confrontation, whether peaceful or violent, actually lie in political and economic distributions of resources.

## THE INTERACTIONIST VIEW

Appearance is a key element in perceptions of those of different religions. Away from their worship services, most U.S. residents offer few clues about their religious preference; some do, however. When an outsider sees a physically distinct believer—a Hasidic Jew, a Hare Krishna follower, an Amish person, a Rastafarian, or a devout Muslim, for instance—the dissimilarities announce a social distance and tend to reduce the chances of close interactions. Those physical clues may even foster negative responses. Conversely, outward appearance becomes a source of comfort and reinforced religious identity to a fellow believer. The wearing of religious symbols—perhaps ashes or a dot on one's forehead or a cross or a Star of David on a necklace—also may induce positive or negative reactions.

Self-identity emerges out of the orderliness of day-to-day accomplishments of individuals interacting face to face, interpreting and reinterpreting their ways of doing things. Under insulated conditions, these shared definitions become more solidified, and the group members grow into a more cohesive unit. Amish and Hasidic Jews living in their separate communities, and the Mormons in the Utah Territory, succeeded in developing their own social systems encompassing all aspects of daily life, thereby reinforcing the precepts of their religious beliefs. Rastafarians, in rejecting the dominant economic system and language syntax, created a symbolic world so differentiated from the dominant society that their everyday interrelationships with one another reinforced their group solidarity. Even Catholics and Jews, as well as the Mormons of modern times, benefit from such cooperative interpretation with one another because studies show each tends to interact in primary-group relations outside religious settings with members of the same faith.[101] For members of all faiths, the religious bond serves both to unite and insulate; it is preserved and maintained through daily interactions with like-minded individuals.

Societal labeling of dissimilar religious minorities often results in negative attitudes and actions toward them, with an avoidance response promoting subcultural insularity. If Catholics are attacked as "docile and superstitious," Jews as "mercenary," Mormons as "chauvinistic," Amish as "backward," Rastafarians as "potheads," and Santeríans as "weird," group members are likely to turn inward to achieve the sense of personal worth denied them in the outside world.

# Retrospect

Founded on the principle of religious freedom, the United States became a place of refuge for people of many faiths. Yet religious tolerance has not always prevailed; some groups have been harassed both verbally and physically as they have sought the right to follow their beliefs.

Throughout much of the nation's history, Catholics have been vilified and abused. Anti-Catholic actions included colonial statutes against their political participation, vicious pamphlets and books, hostile political party platforms, Know-Nothing and Ku Klux Klan demonstrations and violence, and American Protective Association activities. Proposed aid to parochial schools and faith-based charities remains controversial, as do various religions' positions on abortion, birth control, and nuclear arms. Catholics, once a discrimination target in Protestant America, today are the largest single religious denomination in the country.

Jewish Americans encountered many of the same problems as Catholics, often from the same nativist groups. Overt anti-Semitic stereotyping and actions continued well into the twentieth century. Upward mobility occurred more quickly for Jews than for most other immigrants because more of them entered the United States as skilled workers with families intact, and their religious emphasis on learning encouraged secular education and entry into better-paying jobs. A high intermarriage rate—a cause for concern among many Jewish leaders—is seen by others as irrelevant to continued vitality in the Jewish community.

The Latter-Day Saints (Mormons), a persecuted minority expelled from several states, grew into a large, successful, and respectable church. Their emphasis on family and education earns the Mormons high praise, as do their economic investments and assistance to their poor. Although criticisms directed toward plural marriages and perceived racism have ended through changes in church doctrine, charges of sexism remain, though most Mormon women appear satisfied with their role in the church.

U.S. Muslims are growing in number, and mosques now are common throughout the United States. Many of their conservative views parallel those of members of the Catholic and Mormon faiths, and they face difficulty in dissociating themselves from Islamic terrorists. The Amish are a good example of a persistent subculture, and they remain a vibrant and growing community. Rastafarians, Santeríans, and Hindus are becoming more numerous in the United States because of immigration, and each group's religious practices have brought the nation greater cultural diversity.

Today, religion remains an important aspect of culture in the United States, as indicated by public-opinion polls and church attendance. A civil religion arguably exists, and religion-based controversies over abortion, school prayer, and the teaching of evolutionary theory continue.

Functionalists stress the integrative aspects of religion, whereas conflict theorists focus on economic and political power struggles as the basis for religious conflict. Interactionists examine how social interpretations foster ingroup solidarity and outgroup acceptance or hostility.

# On MySocLab

 ✓ **Study** and **Review** on MySocLab

## KEY TERMS

Celibacy, p. 391
Civil religion, p. 419
Ecumenical movement, p. 392
Endogamy, p. 411

Entrepreneurs, p. 410
Nondenominational, p. 388
Pogrom, p. 394

Polygyny, p. 400
Shunning, p. 408
Social ostracism, p. 397

## DISCUSSION QUESTIONS

1. What new insights did you gain into the religious faiths already familiar to you in terms of dominant–minority relations and their values, practices, and symbols?
2. Of the religious faiths discussed about which you were unfamiliar, what insights did you gain in terms of dominant–minority relations and their values, practices, and symbols?
3. Discuss the similarity–attraction bond in the societal response to the Mormons.
4. What similarities and differences can be found between Islam and other major religions in the United States?

5. How do the Amish illustrate a persistent subculture?
6. Discuss the similarity–attraction bond in the societal response to the Rastafarians.
7. What unique features of the Santería religion attract followers and upset municipal officials?
8. What unique features of Hinduism allow its followers to adapt to U.S. society?
9. Discuss the role of religion in present-day U.S. culture.
10. How do the three sociological perspectives help us to understand religion?

## INTERNET ACTIVITIES

1. On the "The Amish & The Plain People" website (http://www.800padutch.com/amish.html), you will find an excellent, highly informative set of questions and answers about the historical traditions, weddings, schooling, and lifestyle of the people living of the Pennsylvania Dutch Country.
2. If you want to know more about the provocative Amish approach to handling adolescent rebelliousness, go to http://www.amazon.com, enter "books," and type in "Shachtman Rumspringa." This will take you to *To Be or Not Be Amish*. Click "Search inside this book," and then click "first pages" to read a few pages about this astonishing adolescent behavior.
3. The Anti-Defamation League (http://www.adl.org) is the world's leading organization fighting anti-Semitism,

as well as all targets of prejudice, hate, and violence. At this website, you will find many information sources on current events, hate groups, what to tell children about prejudice, and ways to overcome it.
4. If you go to your favorite search engine and enter either "abortion articles" or "school prayer articles" in the search box, you will discover a good number of Internet articles on both sides of these religiously influenced controversial issues.
5. Go to the "U.S. Religious Landscape" (http://religions.pewforum.org/pdf/report-religious-landscape-study-full.pdf) site to learn detailed information about the extent and changes in religious membership and interfaith marriages. Were you surprised by anything? What was most interesting to you on this website?

# Women as a Minority Group

# 13

🎧 **Listen** to Chapter 13 on **MySocLab**

*Although women have always been underrepresented in Washington, the 113th Congress (2013–2014) reached an all-time historic high with 20 female Senators (including the first-ever Asian American woman) and 78 voting female members in the House of Representatives.*

## LEARNING OBJECTIVES | After reading this chapter you will be able to:

**13-1** Describe the sociohistorical context for studying women in America.

**13-2** Explain how socialization influences gender roles.

**13-3** Examine issues involving immigrant and minority women.

**13-4** Explain what social indicators tell us about women's status today.

**13-5** Examine sexual harassment and sexism as issues today.

**13-6** Discuss insights gained through sociological analysis.

At first, one might question the inclusion of women as a minority group, given that they outnumber males in society and even more so in college enrollments. However, as stated in Chapter 1, a key attribute of a minority group is its subordinate status to a more powerful group. As this chapter will reveal, women lack equal access to power in many fields of endeavor and an income gap persists despite numerous efforts to correct the situation.

A good part of these circumstances result from **sexism**—an ideology, or set of generalized beliefs, that one gender is superior to the other. For centuries, the presumption of male superiority led to patterns of prejudice and discrimination against women, and many of those patterns still persist despite numerous advances in gender equality. For many generations, women were subordinate to men in virtually all societies throughout history. Aristotle, for example, thought women had an inferior brain because it was smaller, which he assumed meant that it was less developed and thus in less control of their emotions, an assumption that is scientifically wrong.[1] In 1879, Gustav LeBon, a founder of social psychology, made a similar observation:

> In the most intelligent races, as among the Parisians, there are a large number of women whose brains are closer in size to those of gorillas than to the most developed male brains. This inferiority is so obvious that no one can contest it for a moment; only its degree is worth discussion. All psychologists who have studied the intelligence of women, as well as poets and novelists, recognize today that they represent the most inferior forms of human evolution and that they are closer to children and savages than to an adult, civilized man. They excel in fickleness, inconstancy, absence of thought and logic, and incapacity to reason. Without doubt, there exist some distinguished women, very superior to an average man, but they are as exceptional as the birth of any monstrosity, as, for example, of a gorilla with two heads; consequently, we may neglect them entirely.[2]

In the twentieth century, Sigmund Freud advanced notions that sexual differences affected behavior. He believed that the fact that males have a penis made them more aggressive, whereas "penis envy" made females feel shame and a sense of inferiority. Erik Erikson suggested that male genitalia influenced boys to be questing, aggressive, and outward-thrusting and that female genitalia directed girls to be concerned about boundaries, limits, and "interiors." Subsequent cross-cultural studies disproved such false claims, instead demonstrating how the socialization process and societal expectations of men and women produce variances in gender-role norms and behavior.

Not everyone had been so blind to the effects of male domination. In an appendix to his classic and influential analysis of black–white relations, *An American Dilemma* (1944), Gunnar Myrdal noted a parallel between the position of women and blacks in U.S. society.[3] In fact, he observed, the legal position placing women and children under the control of the male head of the household had supplied the basis for the legal position of black servants in the seventeenth century. In 1951, sociologist Helen Hacker identified major areas of sexual discrimination in U.S. society and described women as marginal in a masculine society.[4] Not until the 1960s, however, did the feminist movement make any headway, launched in part by Betty Friedan's consciousness-raising book *The Feminine Mystique* (1963). In fact, she called it "the problem that has no name" as the term *sexism* had not yet come into popular usage.[5]

As public awareness about women as an oppressed group increased, the parallels of their status to that of racial and ethnic groups became more obvious. For example, the minority-group characteristics discussed in Chapter 1 clearly apply to women also. Women are born into their sexual identity (**ascribed status**), and most are easily identifiable by physical and cultural characteristics. In addition, women now recognize their

# the GENDER experience

## An Early Plea for Equal Rights

"I long to hear that you have declared an independency—and by the way, in the new Code of Laws which I suppose it will be necessary for you to make, I desire you would Remember the Ladies, and be more generous and favorable to them than your ancestors. Do not put such unlimited power into the hands of the Husbands. Remember all men would be tyrants if they could. If particular care and attention is not paid to the Ladies, we are determined to foment a Rebellion, and will not hold ourselves bound by any Laws in which we have no voice, or Representation.

"That your Sex are Naturally Tyrannical is a Truth so thoroughly established as to admit of no dispute, but such of you as wish to be happy willingly give up the harsh title of Master for the more tender and endearing one of Friend. Why then, not put it out of the power of the vicious and the Lawless to use us with cruelty and indignity with impunity. Men of Sense in all Ages abhor those customs which treat us only as the vassals of your Sex. Regard us then as Beings placed by Providence under your protection and in imitation of the Supreme Being make use of that power only for our happiness."

Source: Letter from Abigail Adams to John Adams, March 31, 1776. Retrieved June 8, 2013 (http://www.teachingamericanhistory.org/library/index.asp?document=278).

commonality with one another as victims of an ideology (sexism) that, like racism, attempted to justify their unequal treatment.

Yet another characteristic, the minority-group practice of **endogamy**, may seem inapplicable, but in marriage, the domination–subordination lines also are manifest. Traditional marriage ceremonies provide for the man to cherish his wife while she promises to obey her husband, and when the traditional ceremony ends, they are pronounced not "husband and wife," but "man and wife," grafting the woman's identity and maiden name onto her relationship to her husband. For many decades, property laws, credit regulations, social security benefits, divorce laws, and even telephone listings reinforced this less than equal status until recent changes occurred in most of these areas.

## Sociohistorical Perspective

Early colonists in the New World, recreating in miniature the social systems of their homelands, continued male-dominance patterns. In settlements and on the advancing frontier, women were valuable "commodities," both for their skills and labor in the battle for survival and as sexual property in a region with a shortage of women. Although some instances of female independence in land ownership, inheritance, and voting rights did arise in those early years, for the most part, women remained subordinate to men, with few legal rights except as appendages to their husbands (see the Gender Experience box). The U.S. Constitution did not give voting rights to women until ratification of the Nineteenth Amendment in 1920, and the courts did not interpret its other provisions regarding full and equal participation as applying to women until many decades later.[6]

The status and power of Native American women varied considerably from one tribe to another, depending on cultural orientations and patrilineal or matrilineal structure. In **matrilineal** and **matrilocal** societies, women had considerable power because property (housing, land, tools) belonged to them and passed from mother to daughter. Because the husband joined his wife's family, he was more of a stranger, yielding authority to his wife's

**13-1** Describe the sociohistorical context for studying women in America.

eldest brother, and thus was unlikely to become an authoritative, domineering figure. Among such peoples as the Cherokee, Iroquois, Pueblo, and Navajo, a disgruntled wife could divorce her husband simply by tossing his belongings out of their residence. Also, in matrilineal societies such as the Iroquois, women were influential in tribal governance because important civil and religious offices stayed within matrilineal lineages. If the actions of a tribal delegate displeased the women, they removed him from office.[7]

## RESTRICTIONS ON WOMEN

As the United States grew and prospered—and as the Industrial Revolution changed the very nature of society—a dichotomy emerged in the roles of women. Poor women, mostly from immigrant families, went to work in factories at low-skill jobs for wages lower than men's. Middle- and upper-class women (usually native born) from families of prosperous merchants and industrialists were figuratively placed on a pedestal as towers of moral strength, refinement, and soothing comfort to their world-weary males. Prevailing values in the nineteenth and early twentieth centuries held that the nature of women was to please and the nature of men was to achieve.[8]

Legal restrictions denied U.S. women any right to self-determination. They could not vote, own property in their own name, testify in court, make a legal contract, spend their own wages without their husband's permission, or even retain guardianship over their own children if their husband died or deserted them. Because men supposedly were active and women passive, only men were thought to enjoy sex; any woman who also enjoyed it was considered deviant and degenerate. A double standard in sexual conduct thus emerged. In a similar vein, it was taboo for women to give public speeches because a passive, refined lady would not behave so crudely.

Did everyone think and act this way in the nineteenth century? Certainly not, but these were the prevailing norms. Still, the abolitionist movement attracted female activists to fight against the continuance or expansion of slavery. The New York State legislature in 1848 acted to protect the property rights of married women; and, in 1869, Wyoming Territory gave women the right to vote, continuing that practice after it became a state in 1890—the first state to do so.

STUDENTS SPEAK "This section made me upset to think that in the 1800s we as women were restricted in everything that we did. Our husbands were like our fathers. We weren't allowed to do anything without their permission. Women even might not maintain guardianship of their own children after their husband passed. This was one thing that surprised me the most because nowadays it is hard to keep a mother and child apart and it is harder for a man to get custody of a child than for a woman."

**—Stephanie Zeron**

## THE SUFFRAGE MOVEMENT

Efforts to give all women the right to vote met with fierce resistance. As the suffragists held rallies, protest marches, and demonstrations, they were ridiculed, insulted, and abused—slapped, tripped, and pelted with overripe fruits and vegetables and burning cigar stubs. Chaining themselves to the posts, fences, and grillwork of public buildings, these early feminists endured arrest and jail. In 1913, in Washington, DC, federal troops were brought in to quell the unrest. In 1916, six months of picketing at the White House ended with mass arrests and imprisonment when the women refused to pay what they labeled "unjust" fines. Hostility against such challenges to the male establishment is indicated by this eyewitness account of how the prison guards maltreated the demonstrators:

I saw Miss Lincoln, a slight young girl, thrown to the floor. Mrs. Nolan, a delicate old lady of seventy-three, was mastered by two men....Whittaker the prison superintendent in the center of the room directed the whole attack, inciting the guards to every brutality. Two men brought in Dorothy Day, twisting her arms above her head. Suddenly, they lifted her and brought her body down twice over the back of an iron bench....The bed broke Mrs. Nolan's fall, but Mrs. Cosu hit the wall. They had been there a few minutes when Mrs. Lewis, all doubled over like a sack of flour, was thrown in. Her head struck the iron bed and she fell to the floor senseless. As for Lucy Burns, they handcuffed her wrists and fastened the handcuffs over her head to the cell door.[9]

Finally, in 1919, Congress passed the Nineteenth Amendment, giving women the right to vote. Ratified a year later, it became the law of the land. Yet other feminist reforms did not follow. Women did not use their newly gained political power much, and few won elective office despite their numbers among the electorate. Approximately 90 percent of the suffragists ceased further activist measures as the feminist movement faded—until it was resurrected some 40 years later. Anti-suffrage groups remained active, though, campaigning against local laws that prevented women from serving on juries, holding elected office, or getting jobs competitive with those of men.

Following passage of the Nineteenth Amendment, labor force participation by women increased to approximately 25 percent, although job discrimination continued. Women rarely held decision-making positions and were the first fired during the Great Depression. Society still frowned on the career woman, tolerating only women who worked for needed supplemental income. The approved female role still was as the good wife and mother; the woman's primary responsibility was taking care of the home.[10]

World War II changed all that—temporarily because of the need for women in all work areas to contribute to the war effort while the men went overseas to fight the enemy. The percentage of women working increased to 36 percent, with training programs and childcare centers often available to them. A postwar recession and the return of GIs to their former jobs resulted in the firing of 2 million women within 15 months after the war ended. As childcare centers were dismantled, propaganda encouraged women to leave their jobs and return to their home responsibilities full time. Nevertheless, the proportion of women working soon increased again and, by the 1980s, it exceeded 50 percent.

SAVAGERY TO "CIVILIZATION"

THE INDIAN WOMEN: We whom you pity as drudges reached centuries ago the goal that you are now nearing

*Joseph Keppler drew this editorial cartoon for the May 16, 1914, issue of Puck, using Indian women as an exemplar of feminist liberty. Here, Iroquois women observe Susan B. Anthony, Anne Howard Shaw, and Elizabeth Cady Stanton leading a parade of women seeking the same rights that tribal women had enjoyed for centuries.*

*Since the late 1960s, Gloria Steinem has been a prominent activist, journalist, author, and media spokesperson for the women's liberation movement. She co-founded* Ms. *magazine and the Women's Media Center. Active in politics, a commentator and lecturer, she has been the recipient of numerous awards and honors.*

**13-2** Explain how socialization influences gender roles.

**Listen on MySocLab**
Audio: Study Finds Link Between Daycare, Aggression

**View on MySocLab**
Document: Men's and Women's Athletic Performance

## THE WOMEN'S LIBERATION MOVEMENT

The 1960s was a decade of social activism inspired by many factors, including President Kennedy's appointment of a Presidential Commission on the Status of Women, which documented extensive sexual discrimination in the country. Passage in 1963 of the Equal Pay Act prohibited capricious discrimination against women in payment of wages. When Congress failed to act on other commission recommendations, some feminist advocates formed the National Organization for Women (NOW) in 1966, and a new phase of the feminist movement began. Resisted at first by most other women's groups, the New Left, and even civil rights groups, the women's liberation movement eventually gained acceptance, succeeding in its efforts to end many forms of sexual discrimination, particularly economic ones.

# The Reality of Gender Differences

Men and women differ biologically, but do they differ in other ways also? Are women naturally more tender, loving, nurturing, and passive? Are men more aggressive, intelligent, and dominant? When Freud argued that biology was destiny, he simply was restating a prevailing belief that had existed for centuries. Abundant evidence almost everywhere demonstrated the lower socioeconomic status for women, leading to a social construction of reality that their inferiority rested on biological differences. Yet how many of these "natural" differences actually result from sociocultural factors and how many are truly innate? We still do not know completely because of the difficulty in untangling the impact of cultural conditioning from inherent capabilities. Nevertheless, we do have some clues from research investigations.

## BIOLOGICAL EXPLANATIONS

Aside from physical and reproductive differences, males and females are biologically distinct in other ways. Females tend to have a lower infant mortality rate, a higher tolerance for pain, and greater longevity. Males tend to have greater physical strength. Scientists studying newborn infants, however, have not detected any significant differences in personality traits between the sexes.

Numerous studies show gender-specific differences in brain function.[11] For example, men have fewer fibers connecting the verbal and emotional areas of the brain, perhaps making it more difficult for them to express emotions. Because they have more fibers in the reasoning area of the brain, however, they demonstrate a superior ability to understand abstract relationships, which may make them more naturally suited to disciplines such as mathematics and engineering. Brain–gender researchers continue to examine the differences in male and female abilities. Some of these gender-specific differences may be due to differing structures and activities in the brain's lobes and to the exposure of fetuses to hormones in the womb.[12]

Thought processes are not the same as differences in behavior and social status, however. In fact, cross-cultural comparisons show the weakness of the biological argument. Why, for example, are women often physical laborers in Russia, as well as accounting for approximately one-third of the engineers and three-fourths of the physicians? The answer may lie in society's definitions of gender identity and of the appropriate behavioral roles within that identity.

## SOCIALIZATION AND GENDER ROLES

Although gender identity is an ascribed status, society shapes that identity through socialization. In the process of learning traits and activities that are desirable and correct, individuals internalize approved gender-role behavior as a real part of themselves. These cultural dictates of appropriate male–female conduct sometimes vary from one society to another. Anthropologist Margaret Mead found, for example, variations among three tribes in New Guinea: The Arapesh culture produced both men and women with decidedly feminine traits, whereas the Mundugamor produced both men and women with pronounced masculine traits. Among the Tchambuli, however, the usual gender-role behavior of Western society was completely reversed.[13] Mead's findings emphasized the influential role of culture and socialization in developing sexual differentiation.

In much of the world, male dominance has long existed, reinforced by the writings of male philosophers and religious leaders. Even the sacred books of the world's three major religions promote sexist ideology, evoking supernatural justification for male supremacy. Islam's Koran states, "Men are superior to women on account of qualities in which God has given them pre-eminence." In the New Testament, Saint Paul proclaims, "Let the woman learn in silence with all subjection. But I suffer not a woman to teach, nor to usurp authority over the man, but to be in silence…she shall be saved in childbearing, if they continue in faith and charity and holiness with sobriety." Finally, the morning prayer of male Orthodox Jews includes the line, "Blessed art Thou, oh Lord our God, King of the Universe, that I was not born a woman."

**CHILDHOOD SOCIALIZATION.** Influenced by value pronouncements such as those described in the preceding section, but even more so by their own upbringing, parents convey their expectations to children in thousands of ways. Studies show mothers and fathers touch, handle, speak to, play with, and discipline children differently depending on the child's gender. Children learn to play differently, girls more often in exclusive dyadic relationships and boys more often in larger groups. Boys usually grow up experiencing more expansive territory on their bikes or hikes, requiring numerous adaptive decisions, while girls generally experience a more structured, narrower world, which limits their opportunities to develop self-reliance. Children also learn from parents and other adult role models, assuming their attitudes and evaluations.[14]

The impact of parents, family, friends, school, and the media in shaping differences in sexual behavior extends to personalities as well. Through their childhood experiences, boys tend to become inquisitive, self-assured, and convinced that they can control things, whereas girls tend to become passive, timid, and fearful of new situations. Although individuals vary in personality and temperament, this pattern

*Just a few generations ago, women's sports activities were restricted to such "genteel" and segregated activities as golf and croquet. Now, especially after passage of Title IX legislation barred sexual discrimination in institutions receiving federal funding, women have enjoyed and excelled in many sports, including the championship Connecticut team.*

# the GENDER experience

## A Feminist's List of "Barbarous Rituals"

Woman is:

- kicking strongly in your mother's womb, upon which she is told, "It must be a boy, if it's so active!"
- being confined to the Doll Corner in nursery school when you are really fascinated by Tinker Toys.
- being labeled a tomboy when all you wanted to do was climb that tree to look out and see a distance.
- seeing grownups chuckle when you say you want to be an engineer or doctor when you grow up—and learning to say you want to be a mommy or nurse, instead.
- dreading summertime because more of your body with its imperfections will be seen—and judged.
- liking math or history and getting hints that boys are turned off by smart girls.

- discovering that what seems like everything worthwhile doing in life "isn't feminine," and learning to just delight in being feminine and "nice"—and feeling somehow guilty.
- swinging down the street feeling good and smiling at people and being hassled like a piece of meat in return.
- brooding about "how far" you should go with the guy you really like. Will he no longer respect you? Will you get—oh God—a "reputation"? Or, if not, are you a square? Being pissed off because you can't just do what you feel like doing.
- finding that the career you've chosen exacts more than just study or hard work—an emotional price of being made to feel "less a woman."
- being bugged by men in the office who assume that you're a virginal

prude if you don't flirt, and that you're an easy mark if you are half-way relaxed and pleasant.

- wanting to go back to school, to read, to join something, do something. Why isn't home enough for you? What's wrong with you?
- feeling a need to say "thank you" when your guy actually fixes himself a meal now that you're dying with the flu.
- being widowed, or divorced, and trying to get a "good" job—at your age.
- getting older, getting lonelier, getting ready to die—and knowing it wouldn't have had to be this way after all.

Source: From Robin Morgan, *Going Too Far: The Personal Chronicle of a Feminist*. New York: Vintage Books, 1978, pp. 107–13.

emerges through the socialization process to match self-evaluations with the unequal rewards of the system, thereby reinforcing the social construction of reality (see the Gender Experience box).[15]

The **gender-role expectations** set by society impact heavily on the development of males and females. Conformity to them serves as a basis for status and popularity, even in elementary school.[16] Culturally influenced behavioral differences between boys and girls become the social norm as a child grows older. Studies typically show that, in the passage of time between preschool years and second grade, girls usually demonstrate a higher frequency of domestic and gender-role exploring behaviors, in contrast to boys, who tend to engage in explorative acting and information-seeking behaviors.[17] Socialization is a lifelong process; throughout one's childhood, adolescence, and adulthood, a continuous array of experiences reinforces early influences.[18] Toys, games, textbooks, teachers' attitudes and actions, and peer influence all help maintain gender stereotypes. Most influential is the role of the media, particularly television commercials and programming. If we are to believe television, only men live life with gusto, buy cars, and have group fun, whereas women use the right shampoo to be more alluring, wear a seductive perfume, or get their floors to shine brightly.[19] A content analysis of the lyrics of many of today's hit songs and the images conveyed in many music videos reveal the continuance of gender stereotyping.[20]

**ADVERTISING.** The impact of advertising in reinforcing traditional gender roles and stereotypes is very pervasive. Jean Kilbourne argues,

> There is no doubt that flagrant sexism and sex role stereotyping abound in all forms of the media. There is abundant evidence about this. It is far more difficult to document the effects of these stereotypes and images on the individuals and institutions exposed to them because, as I've said, it is difficult to separate media effects from other aspects of the socialization process and almost impossible to find a comparison group (just about everyone in America has been exposed to massive doses of advertising).
>
> But, at the very least, advertising helps to create a climate in which certain attitudes and values flourish, such as the attitude that women are valuable only as objects of men's desire, that real men are always sexually aggressive, that violence is erotic, and that women who are victims of sexual assault "asked for it."[21]

Research on television advertising reveals four significant patterns: Men do most of the commercial voiceovers; women tend to perform typical family activities, usually in the home and benefiting men, but men carry out a wide variety of activities; women are younger than men; and fewer girls and women appear than boys and men.[22] Moreover, as Erving Goffman observed, subtle forms of sexism are common in print advertising as well:

> (1) Overwhelmingly, a woman is taller than a man only when the man is her social inferior; (2) a woman's hands are seen just barely touching, holding, or caressing—never grasping, manipulating, or shaping; (3) when a photograph of men and women illustrates an instruction of some sort, the man is always instructing the woman—even if the men and women are actually children (that is, a male child will be instructing a female child); (4) when an advertisement requires someone to sit or lie on a bed or a floor that someone is almost always a child or a woman, hardly ever a man.[23]

Advertisers long ago discovered the effectiveness of using women as sex objects to get the viewers' attention and to sell a product, as here in New York City. In the past few years, billboards and advertisings in public spaces have increased in numbers, prompting neighbors and public advocate groups to protest the sexual nature of many ads.

"I was very interested in this socialization and gender roles portion. One aspect of our society that interests me a lot is how far women's sports have come. From what I learned in reading articles about the past, it seemed as if it was basically impossible to ever find any women's sport on television. But nowadays, one can find women playing professional and college basketball, collegiate and Olympic volleyball, golf, and other sports as well. Just in recent times, the amount of publicity women's sports gets has been remarkable and I personally am for it because it is great for our society."

**—Connor Healy**

In today's world, women continue to make gains in all areas. Yet we remain in a transitional stage, and socialization inequities continue. Sometimes advertisers emphasize the strengths of emancipated women to sell their products, but more often, they contribute to **role entrapment** by depicting women in stereotypical or sex-object ways. Many writers and educators at all grade levels emphasize women's rights and the ideals of gender equality, and many parents seek to maximize their daughters' future possibilities, but gender differentiation remains deep-rooted in all our social institutions, including the family and education. During the 2010–2011 prime-time television season, women accounted for 41 percent of all characters (and remained significantly younger than their male counterparts) and, among the major news networks (ABC, CBS, NBC), women correspondents reported only 28 percent of the news stories, although that was the highest level of visibility ever.[24]

# Immigrant and Minority Women

**13-3** Examine issues involving immigrant and minority women.

No examination of women as a minority group is complete without an understanding of the many intersections existing among race, ethnicity, social class, and gender. Whatever difficulties women may encounter because of sexism can multiply because of an interlocking matrix of other socially constructed forms of differentiation, especially race. Women of color face a double barrier that can more intensely limit their full participation in society. Then again, the life chances of an African American male today are less optimistic that those of their female counterparts. Clearly, many complexities exist when considering the connections between race and gender.

With regard to ethnicity, nearly all immigrants, past and present, have come from traditional societies with clearly defined gender-role models of behavior and responsibility. Those internalized self-concepts and expectations were not only part of everyday life in their homeland but a source of continuing norms within their ethnic communities after immigration. In culturally insulated neighborhoods with parallel social institutions, women seldom worked outside the home, performing instead their traditional roles for their families within the home, a pattern still evident in many immigrant communities today.

## VESTIGES OF WHITE ETHNIC ORIENTATIONS

In many northeastern U.S. cities, numerous elderly immigrant poor live on meager fixed incomes, struggling to survive in decaying neighborhoods that are no longer cohesive or homogeneous. Most of these elderly are female, with a limited command of English, because their traditional role in the old ethnic community did not necessitate fluency in English and because most arrived in the United States long before the advent of the feminist movement. Lacking job skills and with limited formal education, they cling to the remnants of their familiar world. As women who are advanced in years and unprepared for independence, life presents daily challenges. Among many first-generation immigrant women today, the traditional view of gender identity—with women primarily in a subservient, nurturing role—manifests itself in everyday life.

Often overlooked in discussions of ethnicity are second-generation adult Americans. Yet their primary socialization came from parents with homeland value orientations and traditional gender-role models, which shaped their children's perceptions of the world somewhat differently from those of children of native-born parents. Studies of working-class Americans—many of them second-generation U.S. residents of central, southern, and eastern European heritage—revealed some of these continuing values. In a now-classic study, Lillian Rubin offered a portrait of working-class women who defined themselves as wives and mothers, even if they worked, and who rejected the notion of work as liberating and considered the issues of the feminist movement as irrelevant to them.[25]

Economic transformation (disappearing jobs, declining incomes, and the need for wives to work) brought the struggle to reorder gender roles into the consciousness of women at all class levels. White ethnic working-class women no longer thought that women's issues had nothing to do with them. Yet even if they worked full time, these women found themselves working a **second shift** for, when they came home, there was little to no new division of family labor with husbands in sharing domestic duties.[26] The traditional gender roles and rules remained deeply internalized. If, however, the wives had high-status jobs, then their husbands' gender egalitarianism increased as their traditional gender attitudes changed.[27]

For many minority working-class families, however, their traditional gender-role orientations apparently serve as a barrier to any change in the household division of labor, even in today's economy if the men lose their jobs and thus have greater time availability. In addition, although women's wages are necessary for working-class families' survival, the educational and employment histories of most of these women often limits their options for well-paid work that would enable them to outsource some of their housework chores.[28]

## TODAY'S MINORITY WOMEN

*Machismo,* the pervasive value orientation of the male as provider and dominant force in the family, has a major effect on the daily lives of lower-income Hispanic women. Problems arise among low-income Hispanic Americans when only the woman is able to find work or when she earns more than her spouse. This situation creates family strain and gender identity instability as economic reality collides with the internalized male self-image and culturally prescribed role behavior.

Generally, foreign-born Asian American women maintain traditional family and gender roles, although their status and roles do vary, depending on their nationality and educational levels. The higher their education and the more Americanized the women are, the higher their status. Although more Asian women are combining career and family roles, they continually find themselves forced to resolve the contradictions between host and home cultures by choosing one over the other. For many, it is a "lose-lose" situation with the inevitable criticism on one side for betraying their cultural roots or on the other for refusing to assimilate.[29] Income-producing work does not in and of itself empower immigrant Asian American women. That shift also depends on their positive reconciling of work and mother roles, by seeing themselves as active agents of change rather than as locked into subordinate domestic responsibilities.[30]

The dichotomy among African Americans, discussed in Chapter 10, relates directly to the status and role of African American women in U.S. society. College-educated African American women are more likely to do well in employment, income, and egalitarian marriages, although their greater numbers compared to African American male college graduates can be a disadvantage in finding a spouse of the same social class and race.[31] In contrast, low-income African American women often do not identify with the feminist movement because many of its demands seem irrelevant to their needs. Their focus has been on economic stability, a better future for their children, and racial discrimination, thereby making sexism a lower priority.[32]

**COMMONALITIES.** One common theme that occurs when we study minority women in various racial and ethnic subgroups is how often cultural attributes intensify their subordinate status. Not only do immigrant groups recreate in miniature their old familiar worlds to establish a secure place in an alien country, but their evolving ethnic self-consciousness and community organization encourage the maintenance of accompanying male dominance patterns as well. These traditional gender roles within the minority subgroup deflect recent advances in sexual equality in the larger society. Moreover, as both a woman and a minority-group member, an individual is at a double disadvantage, encountering prejudice and discrimination on two fronts—because of her gender and because of her race or ethnicity.

Shared concerns of lower-income minority women, beyond sexual oppression, include high infant and maternal mortality rates, child care and health care, segregated housing and schools, quality education programs, gang activity and safe streets, unemployment and underemployment, declining welfare programs, and family stability.

**THE NEW FEMINISM.** Feminist scholars now speak of a "third wave" that takes multiple perspectives and rejects grand narratives in favor of personal narratives to create a feminism that emphasizes an inclusive and nonjudgmental approach.[33] Previously, many women of color who were legal scholars felt excluded by white feminist legal scholars and so they focused instead on critical race feminist theory.[34] This new approach encompasses different social contexts and from these differing standpoints, a more realistic understanding emerges about the intersection of gender, race, and class so that feminists of color do not have to choose between their race and gender to advance their scholarship or their advocacy. Racism is a woman's issue and sexism therefore is not an unrelated issue.[35]

Issues of gender, race, and class also combine in complex ways to produce numerous role conflicts among professional minority women. The dual burden of career and family affects their experiences and career development, just as it does with their white counterparts. However, they also live in a bicultural world that produces unique experiences and stresses as they defy both organizational stereotypes and the traditional gender roles of their own communities, which appear to be more durable than in the Anglo community. Furthermore, there is little room for their own ethnic or cultural identity within the organizations in which they work. Indeed, minority women face stereotypical and prejudicial perceptions about such identities in organizations where few or no role models exist. The need to balance their organizational and cultural identities is an ongoing and challenging activity.[36]

13-4 Explain what social indicators tell us about women's status today.

# Social Indicators of Women's Status

The justification for considering women as a minority group and for speaking of the existence of sexism becomes more understandable through scrutiny of leading social indicators. As with other minorities in earlier chapters, we now examine the comparative status of women in terms of education, employment, and income. In addition, we look at sexual harassment, law, and politics (see also the International Scene box).

## EDUCATION

For many generations, education was segregated by gender. Males and females often attended different schools or were physically and academically separated in "coeducational" schools. For example, the still-standing Henry Street grammar school on New York's Lower East Side—a well-known white ethnic area for more than a century—contains the word *Boys* engraved above one of its two opposite-end entrances and the word *Girls* above the other. Women were once taught only the social graces and morals. Teaching academic subjects to females was considered a waste of time; a Harvard professor, Barrett Wendell, in 1911 even proclaimed that such an attempt would "weaken the intellect of the teacher."[37]

Even after females overcame these prejudices and took academic subjects alongside males, the educational system maintained sexism in both obvious and subtle ways. Teachers and counselors with traditional gender-role expectations often encouraged students to

# the INTERNATIONAL scene

## Women's Status in Canada

In many ways, the social indicators on Canadian women reveal comparable socioeconomic circumstances to U.S. women, although a few differences exist. In 1929, less than 4 percent of women worked outside the home, but now 62 percent are in the labor force, and 12 percent of all female workers are self-employed. Although most families have dual-income-earner couples, only 17 percent of families have the father as the sole breadwinner.

For more than a decade, Canadian law has mandated equal pay for equal work ("comparable worth"). These laws seek to create pay equity through job evaluations that take into account the skill, effort, and responsibility required to do a job and the conditions under which the work is performed. Nevertheless, a wage gap persists between men and women. On average, women working in full-time, full-year jobs earn 71 percent of what men earn.

Canada's problem with the feminization of poverty problem has been decreasing. Approximately 18 percent of all families in the nation with children under age 24 are headed by women. Women who head single-parent families are among Canada's poorest; 21 percent of such families live in poverty, but this is a drop from 34 percent in 2001. One in ten women (1.7 million) lives in poverty.

Education data offer hopeful signs. Women make up more than 56 percent of full-time undergraduates at Canadian universities. Currently, 91 percent of all women ages 25 and older have a high school diploma or better, and more than 28 percent hold a bachelor's degree or higher.

In the Canadian House of Commons, 76 of the 308 members of Parliament (25 percent) in 2013 were women. In the Senate, 39 of 105 seats (38 percent) were held by women. Three of the nine Supreme Court justices are women and, for the first time, a woman is the Chief Justice.

All jurisdictions in Canada give women a statutory right to take maternity leave without penalty, usually for a period of 17 weeks. An additional 24 weeks of parental leave, which may be taken by either parent, is available to certain workers, mostly employees of the federal government, banks, and transportation and communications companies. Although these rights are for unpaid leave, the Employment Insurance Program also provides 15 weeks of maternity benefits for mothers and 10 weeks of parental benefits for natural or adoptive parents. Families with children under age 13 are eligible for tax deductions and allowances for childcare support while the parents work.

### CRITICAL THINKING QUESTION

In what ways does Canada differ from the United States in various statistics and in addressing women's issues relating to family and work?

Source: Data are from *Statistics Canada* (http://www.Statcan.ca), accessed June 8, 2013.

---

have gender-linked aspirations and career choices. Children's books and textbooks reinforced sexual stereotypes, with male characters heavily outnumbering female characters and males portrayed as active and adventuresome in contrast to the more passive females. Stereotypical activities—boys creating things or earning money and girls shopping, cooking, and sewing—existed in all texts, even in mathematics books. In Standard English usage, male pronouns identified any unidentified individual, further biasing children's education and the culture in general. Many of these stereotypical depictions no longer exist through pressure on publishers to adopt gender-neutral language.

In 1998, the American Association of University Women Educational Foundation issued a report about the gender bias still existing in schools despite decades of progress.[38] Even now, some of these problems still remain. Girls may enter the first grade with the same skills and ambitions as boys, or even higher ones, but classroom sexist conditioning can still result in lower self-confidence and aspirations by the time they graduate from high school. Two-thirds of the nation's teachers may be women, but they tend to favor sexual stereotypes, recalling more positively the assertive male students while liking least the assertive females. Teachers tend to call on boys more often, give them more detailed

*Americans have long relied on education as one of the best means of achieving greater equality in our society. With increasing percentages of women earning bachelor's degrees in a wider range of majors, as well as their greater representation in advanced degrees in professional fields, further progress in gender equality looks promising.*

criticism, and praise the intellectual content of boys' work more than girls' work, while tending to praise girls for their neatness.[39]

Teachers also allow boys to shout out answers and take risks, but they reprimand as rude girls who do the same thing. In addition, few educators encourage girls to pursue careers in mathematics or science. Single-sex classrooms evolved as an answer to these problems, but although research indicates that they tend to produce girls with more self-confidence and higher grades, critics charge that they are a "bogus" solution that sets back the cause of gender equity and true coeducation.[40] Perhaps the inclusion of gender studies in teacher preparation courses will help resolve these forms of school bias.

As Table 13.1 shows, the number of school years males and females complete is very close when controlled for race, although Asian and Pacific Islander males and Hispanic

**TABLE 13.1** Educational Attainment by Race, Ethnicity, and Sex, Ages 25 and Older, 2011 (in percentages)

|  | COMPLETED FOUR YEARS OF HIGH SCHOOL OR MORE | COMPLETED FOUR YEARS OF COLLEGE OR MORE |
|---|---|---|
| *All Races* | | |
| Male | 85.2 | 28.7 |
| Female | 86.5 | 28.3 |
| *African American* | | |
| Male | 81.0 | 16.2 |
| Female | 83.7 | 20.3 |
| *Asian/Pacific Islander* | | |
| Male | 87.2 | 52.8 |
| Female | 83.3 | 47.7 |
| *Hispanic* | | |
| Male | 61.8 | 12.1 |
| Female | 64.6 | 14.4 |

*Source:* U.S. Census Bureau, *2011 American Community Survey*, Table S0201.

**TABLE 13.2** Female-Earned Bachelor's Degrees by Field of Study (in percentages)

| | 1980 | 2010 |
|---|---|---|
| Business | 33.6 | 57.2 |
| Communications | 52.1 | 62.8 |
| Computer and information sciences | 30.4 | 18.1 |
| Education | 73.2 | 79.5 |
| Engineering | 9.3 | 16.8 |
| Foreign languages | 75.7 | 69.3 |
| Health professions | 82.8 | 85.1 |
| Physical sciences | 23.6 | 40.7 |
| Psychology | 63.3 | 77.1 |
| Social sciences | 43.6 | 49.4 |

*Source:* National Center for Education Statistics, *The Condition of Education 2012*, Table A-38-1.

females are slightly higher. Women not only have achieved parity in the level of educational attainment, but also are doing so in most academic fields of study (see Table 13.2). However, women continue to be underrepresented in such male-dominated majors as computer and information sciences and engineering, and they are overrepresented in the traditional female career areas of education, health sciences, and psychology. Advanced degrees conferred in medicine, dentistry, law, and theology show a steady lessening of the sex-ratio imbalance (see Table 13.3).

Since 1990, the proportion of women enrolled in college has exceeded that for men, and that gap is widening steadily. Currently, approximately 68 percent of women ages 18 to 24 are enrolled in college, compared to 66 percent of men in that age range. At the college level, the gender gap is widest among African Americans. Among all black college students, 41 percent are males and 59 percent are females. Only among Asian Americans does the male enrollment rate exceed that for women.

**TABLE 13.3** Degrees Conferred in Selected Professions (in percentages)

| TYPE OF DEGREE | 1960 | 1970 | 1980 | 1990 | 2000 | 2009 |
|---|---|---|---|---|---|---|
| *Medicine (MD)* | | | | | | |
| Men | 94.5 | 91.6 | 76.6 | 65.8 | 56.7 | 51.1 |
| Women | 5.5 | 8.4 | 23.4 | 34.2 | 43.3 | 48.9 |
| *Dentistry (DDS, DMD)* | | | | | | |
| Men | 99.2 | 99.1 | 86.7 | 69.1 | 61.4 | 53.6 |
| Women | 0.8 | 0.9 | 13.3 | 30.9 | 38.6 | 46.4 |
| *Law (LLB, JD)* | | | | | | |
| Men | 97.5 | 94.6 | 69.8 | 57.8 | 52.7 | 54.2 |
| Women | 2.5 | 5.4 | 30.2 | 42.2 | 47.3 | 45.8 |
| *Theology (BD, MDV, MHL)* | | | | | | |
| Men | NA | 97.7 | 86.2 | 75.2 | 67.0 | 66.9 |
| Women | NA | 2.3 | 13.8 | 24.8 | 32.0 | 33.1 |

*Note:* NA = not available.
*Source:* U.S. National Center for Education Statistics, *Digest of Education Statistics,* annual.

**FIGURE 13.1** Labor Force Participation Rates for the Population Ages 25 and over, 2013

*Source:* U.S. Bureau of Labor Statistics

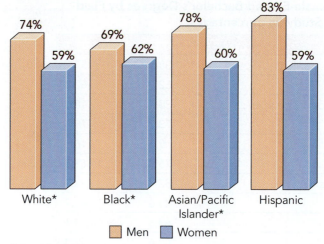

White*  74%  59%
Black*  69%  62%
Asian/Pacific Islander*  78%  60%
Hispanic  83%  59%

■ Men  ■ Women

*Non-Hispanic

## EMPLOYMENT

Approximately 59 percent of all women are in the civilian labor force, up from 52 percent in 1980.[41] The greatest increase in working women has been among wives with school-age children. In 2010, approximately 71 percent of mothers with children ages 6 to 17 were employed, up from 57 percent in 1980. Approximately 64 percent of all women with children under age 6 were employed, up from 37 percent in 1975.[42] In all categories, the percentages of African American working mothers were higher than the national averages and the percentages of whites (see Figure 13.1 and Table 13.4).

Despite the increase in the rate of women's participation in the labor force and in women's proportional representation in previously male-dominated occupations, significant differences in male–female career categories remain. First, a female occupational ghetto exists, with many women in traditional low-paying, low-status jobs. Such "pink-collar" jobs include those of speech pathologists, dental hygienists, bank tellers, bookkeepers, health technicians, librarians, sales clerks, secretaries, and insurance underwriters. Approximately 60 percent of all working women are mired in lower-paying clerical and sales jobs. Male-dominated occupations, on the other hand, tend to be the higher-paying, higher-status positions (see Table 13.5 and Figure 13.2).

Another problem is the **glass ceiling**, a real but unseen discriminatory policy among companies that limits the upward mobility of women, keeping them out of top management positions, high-profile transfers, and key assignments. Research shows that this may be due partly to gender-role expectations and behavior. Masculine-typed impression management tactics (for example, assertiveness, self-promotion) in a corporate environment tend to lead to better performance evaluations and salary, but feminine-typed impression

**TABLE 13.4** Labor-Force Participation by Women, by Age of Children, 2011 (in percentages)

|  | TOTAL | ASIAN | BLACK | HISPANIC | WHITE |
|---|---|---|---|---|---|
| No children under 18 | 53.5 | 52.1 | 52.8 | 52.6 | 53.6 |
| With children under 18 | 71.3 | 68.2 | 74.9 | 61.9 | 70.9 |
| Children 6 to 17 | 77.2 | 75.1 | 78.7 | 70.4 | 77.1 |
| Children under 6 | 64.2 | 60.6 | 70.3 | 53.9 | 63.5 |

*Source:* U.S. Department of Labor, *Women in the Labor Force: A Databook*, February 2013, Table 5, pp. 16–17.

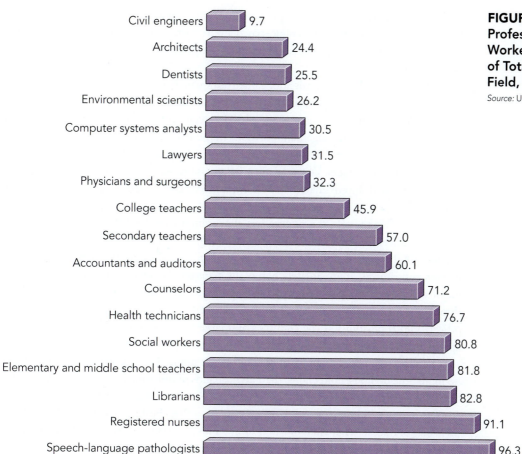

**FIGURE 13.2** Female Professional and Technical Workers, by Percentage of Total Workers in Each Field, 2010

*Source:* U.S. Bureau of Labor Statistics.

| Field | Percentage |
|---|---|
| Civil engineers | 9.7 |
| Architects | 24.4 |
| Dentists | 25.5 |
| Environmental scientists | 26.2 |
| Computer systems analysts | 30.5 |
| Lawyers | 31.5 |
| Physicians and surgeons | 32.3 |
| College teachers | 45.9 |
| Secondary teachers | 57.0 |
| Accountants and auditors | 60.1 |
| Counselors | 71.2 |
| Health technicians | 76.7 |
| Social workers | 80.8 |
| Elementary and middle school teachers | 81.8 |
| Librarians | 82.8 |
| Registered nurses | 91.1 |
| Speech-language pathologists | 96.3 |

**TABLE 13.5** Women and Men Employed in Selected Occupations, 2011 (in percentages)

| FEMALE | | MALE | |
|---|---|---|---|
| Dental hygienists | 97.5 | Automobile mechanics | 98.6 |
| Secretaries, administrative assistants | 95.9 | Electricians | 98.5 |
| Speech pathologists | 95.6 | Carpenters | 98.1 |
| Receptionists | 92.1 | Aircraft pilots, flight engineers | 95.7 |
| Occupational therapists | 92.0 | Firefighters | 95.5 |
| Registered nurses | 91.1 | Truck and tractor operators | 93.3 |
| Dieticians and nutritionists | 90.6 | Police and sheriff's patrol officers | 88.0 |
| Bookkeepers, auditing clerks | 89.9 | Civil engineers | 86.9 |
| Health information technicians | 89.7 | Cost estimators | 85.0 |
| Nursing and home health aides | 87.8 | Detectives, criminal investigators | 83.3 |
| Librarians | 86.2 | TV camera operators, editors | 80.1 |
| Paralegals and legal assistants | 84.3 | Architects except naval | 79.3 |
| Elementary/middle school teachers | 81.7 | Computer programmers | 79.2 |
| Social workers | 81.6 | Lawyers | 68.1 |
| Meeting and convention planners | 76.2 | Physicians and surgeons | 66.2 |

*Source:* U.S. Department of Labor, *Women in the Labor Force: A Databook,* February 2013, Table 116, pp. 31–42.

management tactics (for example, opinion conformity, modesty) do not reap such benefits. However, if women adopt masculine-typed impression management tactics, they often are punished for violating norms rather than rewarded as were the men for using the same tactics.[43]

The Glass Ceiling Commission, a bipartisan panel created by Congress, reported in 1995 that women remain blocked from top management positions, defined as those of vice president and above. Constituting only 29 percent of the work force, white men held 95 of every 100 senior management positions in industries across the nation. Women had greater success moving into the ranks of middle management, such as assistant vice presidents and office managers. White women held close to 40 percent of those jobs, African American women approximately 5 percent, and African American men approximately 4 percent.[44]

Since 1995, though, the picture has slowly improved. In 2012, women were chief executive officers (CEOs) of 19 of the *Fortune* 500 companies and another 21 at the *Fortune* 1000 companies. These percentages are low, but they are the highest ever. With women constituting approximately half of all managers below the top 20 people in most major companies, the possibilities loom large that many women soon will be breaking through to the top positions.[45] In 1995, women held only 2 percent of the chief financial officer (CFO) positions at the country's 500 largest corporate firms. In 2012, they held approximately 14 percent, a figure that has been holding firm the past few years.[46]

Working women face an additional burden at home. Their husbands typically spend no more time on household chores than do husbands of full-time homemakers. According to the University of Michigan Institute for Social Research, married women in dual-career families average 18 hours per week of housework to their husbands' 7 hours, although for men that is double what they did in 1968.[47] This imbalance of women doing approximately two-thirds of all housework constitutes what sociologist Arlie Hochschild called a "second shift."[48] Her study of married couples throughout an eight-year period found the women feeling constantly fatigued, emotionally drained, and torn by the conflicting demands of their multiple roles. Such is not the case in countries with higher levels of overall gender equality, where married couples that cohabited before marriage have a more equal division of housework.[49] Feminists argue that household labor divisions provide an excellent measure of power relationships in the home.

*Holding a master's degree from the Yale School of Management, Indra Nooyi became CEO at Pepsico in 2006. She is one of 15 women who reached the top of the corporate ladder and presently head a Fortune 500 company, and only one of three women of color. Forbes magazine ranked her the most powerful woman in business for 2006–2009.*

## INCOME

Ever since pay equity became a civil rights goal in the 1970s, minorities and women have made some progress toward it, but a significant gap still remains. Among year-round, full-time workers ages 18 and older, for example, women in 2011 earned 82 cents for every dollar earned by men.[50] Occupational distributions by gender into lower-paying and higher-paying fields of work partially explain the remaining income disparity. Another factor is the higher ratio of women on welfare.[51] However, women still earn less than men in nearly every field, including those dominated by women. For example, women chief financial officers (CFOs) earn 16 percent less than their male peers. A portion of this difference may be caused by variations in qualifications and seniority, but even when controlling for these variables, the disparity still exists.[52]

Generally, the median earnings across all educational categories of year-round, full-time workers age 25 and older are higher for men than for women and higher for whites than for African Americans. African American men with a bachelor's degree earn approximately 73 percent of the median income of non-Hispanic white men with a comparable college education. However, African American women college graduates earn 10 percent less than non-Hispanic white women with a similar educational level. Yet black female college graduates only earn 89 cents for every dollar earned by a black male college graduate, a pay inequity suggesting that sexual discrimination compounds the problems of racial discrimination in the workplace.[53]

Part of the pay inequity no doubt reflects the choice corporate women must make between the **fast track** and the **mommy track**. Those opting for the fast track to earn promotions over other candidates must make a full commitment to the management. Often, this entails 60-hour-plus workweeks, frequent travel, weekend meetings, and "drop everything" crises to resolve. To meet such demands, some women delay childbearing or forgo motherhood entirely. Even then, executives may assume that a woman's familial responsibilities will interfere with her productivity and that the company will incur additional expenses for maternity leaves.

Choosing motherhood usually forces women to lower their occupational goals and to delay, if not eliminate, their readiness for promotions. Soon, women with children fall behind childless women in earnings, as the latter group ascends the corporate ladder faster. Women thus risk their career mobility by having children. Although nine of ten male executives ages 40 and older are fathers, only one of three female executives ages 40 and older is a mother.[54]

Opting for the mommy track places the additional strain on women of juggling both family and work to find reliable **child care**. Although some companies provide on-site day-care centers or **flextime** work schedules (allowing workers to set, within limits, their own working hours), most do not. This need usually gets fulfilled through a relative or neighbor, or else through some nearby childcare center. The cost of child care is a major reason many women quit their jobs or delay entry into the workforce.[55]

When we consider the large number of households headed by women (see Figure 13.3), childcare needs and women's typically

*Childcare centers enable working mothers to provide supervised quality time for their children while also pursuing a career and generating family income. Still, they must juggle both roles, for when they return home, women often face a "second shift" of work in food shopping, cooking, cleaning, and other childcare tasks.*

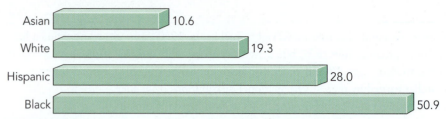

**FIGURE 13.3** Family Households with Children Headed by Women, by Percent, 2012

*Source:* U.S. Census Bureau.

lower earnings take on greater significance. More than one in four Hispanic families and half of all black families are headed by women, whose greater probability of unavailable childcare facilities and limited earning power have a negative impact on the family's economic health.[56] Thus, the number of female-headed minority households with children under 18 is an important factor in the **feminization of poverty** among blacks and Hispanics. In 2011, approximately 41 percent of all families headed by women lived in poverty. Among black female-householder-with-no-husband-present families, 47 percent lived in poverty, and among similar Hispanic families, it was 49 percent.[57]

# Sexual Harassment

13-5 Examine sexual harassment and sexism as issues today.

**Explore** on **MySocLab**
Activity: Power Dynamics in the Workforce: The Case of Sexual Harassment

For years, U.S. society ignored the issue of sexual harassment, dismissing it as an individual, personal problem. Conventional wisdom then viewed such situations simply as "natural" and unobjectionable: A man, attracted to a particular woman, made sexual advances and received a positive, negative, or "maybe" response. Until 1976, women tended to keep silent, thinking the experience an isolated encounter and not recognizing it as part of a larger pattern connected to their subordination and vulnerability in the occupational structure.

*Redbook* magazine's 1976 survey of 9,000 women defined the extent of the problem: 90 percent reported having experienced sexual harassment at work. Soon the feminist movement raised awareness of the group basis of this problem. Helping their efforts was a 1978–1980 study from the federal government's Merit System Protection Board, which reported a $189 million extra cost in hiring, training, absenteeism, and job-turnover expenses caused by harassment. It further stated that the figure probably ran into billions of dollars if private industry's costs were included and survey results also suggested that 1 percent, or approximately 9,000, female federal employees had been victims of attempted rape by supervisors or coworkers.

In 1979, Catharine A. MacKinnon wrote the first book on this subject, *Sexual Harassment of Working Women: A Case of Sex Discrimination.* She identified sexual harassment as either a single occurrence at work or a series of incidents ranging along a continuum of varying intensity, including:

> …verbal sexual suggestions or jokes, constant leering or ogling, brushing against your body "accidentally," a friendly pat, squeeze, or pinch or arm against you, catching you alone for a quick kiss, the indecent proposition backed by the threat of losing your job, or forced sexual relations.[58]

Since 1980, the courts generally have used the federal Equal Employment Opportunity Commission's (EEOC's) guidelines to protect employees from conduct considered illegal under Title VII of the Civil Rights Act of 1964. These guidelines define sexual harassment as:

> …unwelcome sexual advances, requests for sexual favors, and other verbal or physical conduct of a sexual nature…when submission is made a condition of employment, or rejection of the advance is used as the basis for future employment decision, or interfering with the individual's performance or creating an intimidating, hostile, or offensive working environment.

Other obnoxious and questionable behaviors, however, escape this definition. California's Fair Employment and Housing Department established broader guidelines: unsolicited written, verbal, or physical contacts; suggestive or obscene notes; continual leering; obscene gestures; display of obscene objects or pictures; blocking movements by physical touching; and forced involvement in obscene joking. Although these forms of sexual harassment are not specifically mentioned in Title VII, recent court decisions have declared them as such, thereby establishing judicial precedent for future cases.[59] For men uncertain about what constitutes acceptable behavior with women, a good "rough measure" of sexual harassment would be to ask yourself, "Would you be embarrassed to have your remarks displayed in the newspaper or actions described to your family?"

### COMPLAINTS AND ACTIONS

Sexual harassment in the military continually attracted media attention during the 1990s. Since the 1991 Tailhook scandal, involving U.S. Navy combat aviators molesting female officers at a convention, all branches of the military have faced serious accusations and embarrassments. Sexual harassment of females—including assault or rape complaints by recruits against platoon sergeants, by cadets against classmates, by pilots against male pilots, and by aides against superiors—revealed serious problems in the military in gender relations. Although the Department of Defense has a "zero tolerance" policy on acts of sexual harassment in all branches of the military and acts quickly on complaints, such incidents still remain a serious a problem.[60]

The military is not alone, of course, in experiencing sexual harassment charges. In recent years, numerous litigants have filed lawsuits against companies (for example, Ford, W. R. Grace Corporation, and Mitsubishi Motors), against politicians (for example, former Senator Robert Packwood of Oregon and former President William Clinton), and against universities (for example, Brown and Stanford). Part of the increase in litigation is due to greater sensitivity by workers as to the definition of sexual harassment.[61]

Although men or women can be victims of sexual harassment, the vast majority of victims are women. Two social realities contribute to this situation: (1) a culture that encourages male sexual assertiveness and female sexual responsiveness and (2) a workplace in which power is distributed unequally and where men tend to supervise the work of women. Part of the solution to sexual harassment might occur when women achieve gender equality in status and power and are treated as persons rather than as sex objects. Not to be overlooked is the fact that sexual harassment in educational institutions can be especially harmful in propagating sexism and subordination in this crucial crucible of socialization.

# Sexism and the Law

Stereotyping women as passive and in need of protection became institutionalized centuries ago in the common law of England, from which U.S. law arose. Many labor laws, originally intended to prevent the exploitation of women, became a means of restricting their job opportunities and income potential. Although many of these laws

Another advance in minority representation occurred in 2009, when Sonia Sotomayor (left) took the oath from Chief Justice John Roberts to become the Supreme Court's first Hispanic justice and only the third woman in the court's 220-year history. Her mother holds the Bible as her brother watches. Sotomayor had been a federal judge for 17 years.

since have changed, compliance does not necessarily follow. Many women do not know their legal rights, or they find the difficulties involved in securing them often outweigh the rewards.

Because changing hundreds of state laws is a long, arduous process—and because legal principles enacted by a simple majority vote can be repealed by a similar simple majority—Congress approved the Equal Rights Amendment (ERA) in 1972, intending it to extend full and equal legal rights to women. The proposed constitutional amendment's wording was brief: "Equality of rights under the law shall not be denied or abridged by the United States or by any state on account of sex." Requiring separate ratification by three-fourths of the states (a total of 38), it gained approval from only 35 in the allotted time period. The failure of the ERA resulted from the opposition of numerous groups, including many women, labor leaders, conservatives, religious groups, and insurance companies.

A significant event occurred in 1986 when the U.S. Supreme Court ruled in *Meritor Savings Bank v. Vinson* that sexual harassment by a supervisor violates the 1964 Civil Rights Act prohibiting sex discrimination in the workplace. Women's groups hailed the court's identification of harassment as a form of discrimination. In 1993, the Supreme Court further ruled that a complainant need not prove that the offending behavior caused severe psychological damage or impaired the victim's ability to perform expected work. Instead, drawing from the EEOC guidelines (quoted earlier), it defined actionable harassment as (among other things) a working atmosphere so sexually tainted by abuse that any reasonable person would find it too hostile to continue.

Although this decision gave lower courts more freedom to decide for plaintiffs who bring charges of abuse without evidence of medical or psychological injury, it did not offer detailed guidance about what a hostile environment exactly involves, nor did the 1998 court decisions that set more stringent guidelines on employer accountability. As a result, local officials have wide scope in interpreting an offensive, hostile environment compared to other abuses of power in the workplace, leading critics to complain that clearer standards of conduct are necessary. Moreover, although women tend to define sexual harassment more broadly than men, they also resist defining sexual jokes or remarks as harassment in the workplace if other hostile environment behaviors are so identified.[62]

# Sociological Analysis

Every society has had a gender-based division of labor, but this has not always meant sexual inequality. Why have many societies considered the male role as superior? Functionalists, conflict theorists, and interactionists differ both in explaining the reasons for male dominance and in identifying steps to eliminate it.

13-6 Discuss insights gained through sociological analysis.

## THE FUNCTIONALIST VIEW

In preindustrial societies, from which most immigrants to the United States have come, assigning work tasks by gender effectively created a smoothly functioning society. Such also was the case in the United States in the early nineteenth century, when distinct sex roles facilitated social stability, with women and men mostly accepting gender-specific roles in society. Sociologists Talcott Parsons and Robert Bales maintained that the efficient functioning of a society—indeed its very survival—depends on satisfying both instrumental and expressive needs.[63] Traditionally, men performed the instrumental tasks—goal-oriented activities necessary for family survival, such as earning a living and finding food to supplement what the female agriculturalists and herbalists grew or found. Women handled the expressive tasks—providing harmony, love, emotional support, and stability within the family. Today, many are questioning why these necessary tasks should be gender-linked and not shared—or reversed, if desired (see the International Scene box).

As mentioned in the section about biological explanations, the tendency of men to be larger, stronger, and more aggressive may explain their emergence as dominant in the social order. As male dominance continued throughout the generations, a sexist ideology evolved to justify the existing order as "natural." Gender role and status thus became institutionalized through socialization and practice. As long as society remained relatively unchanged, gender-role differentiation did not emerge as a concern to most people or generate among women a group consciousness and desire for change.

Social changes caused by the Industrial Revolution threw the gender-based social structure out of balance. Machines curtailed the men's advantage of greater strength for work tasks. Reductions in the infant-mortality rate and in family size—together with labor-saving home appliances—freed women from spending most of their adult lives doing chores and raising small children. Values, attitudes, and expectations about women's proper role did not change as rapidly as social and economic conditions. This cultural lag caused strain among individuals, in families, and in society itself.

Among immigrants, both past and present, family and traditions have offered two vital means of preserving identity and stability in a new country. Persons with traditional gender-role value orientations experience problems adapting to a more egalitarian society. Working Hispanic women present a conflict to the *machismo* concept of the male as the sole provider. Social activities and dating practices among teenagers challenge traditional homeland norms about adolescent male–female interaction. Higher education for women runs counter to traditional notions that women should just marry and bear children.

Achieving sexual equality, functionalists stress, requires restoration of a balance between expectations and conditions. To some, changes have been too extensive, and system harmony requires a return to the past, with clearly defined gender roles restoring a stable family life and an efficient division of labor. Most functionalists, however, call for redefined gender roles and adjustments in the family system and other social institutions to eliminate sexual discrimination. Changes in societal conditions and expectations require system adjustments if the dysfunctions are to be overcome.

# the INTERNATIONAL scene

## Women's Changing Status in Japan

Traditionally, Japanese men and women had clearly defined roles: the man was employed, and the woman stayed home with the children. In recent years, however, a battle of the sexes has been quietly escalating. National surveys reveal that most Japanese men look at married family life as part of adulthood and seek a wife who will be a good housekeeper. Women, on the other hand, are rebelling. Educated, employed, and independent minded, many no longer feel compelled to marry by age 25. The continuing increase in first marriages in the 30s age group will not help the country's already low birth rate of 1.4 children per women and Japan's subsequent shrinking population.

Even though Japanese women are among the best educated and most prosperous in the world, in 2013, only 7.9 percent of the members of the country's most powerful legislative body, the lower house of parliament (38 of 480), were women. Japanese women argue that their nation would be a different place if they had a louder political voice. Rather than endless parliamentary debates on highways and history, women might urge discussion of

job discrimination against them, and national labor laws that identify them as the "weaker" sex. One such law limits women's overtime hours, but not men's, and another entitles women to stay at home during their menstrual periods, giving male bosses an excuse to inquire into their female employees' private lives. In 2010, the World Economic Forum downgraded Japan to 101st place in its gender discrimination report, a ranking that continued in 2012.

Sexual harassment (*seku hara*) is a serious problem in the workplace. In a 1998 survey of female government workers, nearly 94 percent of respondents said they had experienced some form of sexual harassment, ranging from a display of nude posters in the office to forced sex. Approximately 6 percent said they had been raped or almost raped at work. Although complaints have been rising, sexual harassment is a fairly new concept in Japan, where such conduct was largely accepted until the 1980s. The nation's first sexual-harassment lawsuit wasn't filed until 1992, and in 1997, the parliament adopted a law that requires corporations to take steps to prevent sexual harassment.

Since then, significant progress has occurred in combating this problem, but glass ceilings preventing women from reaching high positions still exist in most Japanese companies. Interestingly, no word for "glass ceiling" exists in Japanese, making it a difficult problem to confront, as many people do not even know the concept.

Japanese women feel bias in every aspect of life. For example, Japanese law requires a married couple to choose one name. If a husband wants to keep his name, the wife cannot keep her name after marriage. Legislators argued that allowing husbands and wives to use different names would be a dangerous step toward weakening the Japanese family.

### CRITICAL THINKING QUESTION

How does the status of women in Japan compare to that in the United States, and what steps should be taken to improve conditions in both countries?

Sources: Inter-Parliamentary Union, *Women in National Parliaments*; World Economic Forum, *The Global Gender Gap: 2012*; http://www.ipu.org/wmn-e/world.htm; and http://www.weforum.org/reports/global-gender-gap-report-2012.

## THE CONFLICT VIEW

For conflict theorists, male dominance, the subordination of women, sexual inequality, and gender discrimination illustrate the universal human problems of exploitation and oppression. Substituting the words *men* and *women* for the names of dominant and minority groups, or *sex* or *gender* for *class*, enables us to incorporate women as a group in Marxist concepts of false consciousness, exploitation, awakened awareness, and organized challenges to the social order. In fact, Friedrich Engels (1820–1895) observed that the "first class oppression" in history was of "the female sex by the male."[64]

When the economic contributions of the two sexes were fairly even, as in hunting-and-gathering societies, sexual equality existed to a high degree. Women in those societies

*Former Secretary of State Hilary Clinton, shown here talking to President of Somalia Sheikh Sharif Ahmed in London in 2012, was the third female to hold this post, once a male-only cabinet position. Her serious presidential bid in 2008 and early talk in 2013 about another bid in 2014 illustrate the increased power of women in politics.*

gathered a good share of edible foods and the men were not always successful in their hunting expeditions, thus making the activities of both important. Agrarian and pastoral societies drew on male strength for needed labor in plowing, irrigation, construction, crafts, and military defense. Sexual inequality then became more marked as disparities in economic contributions—a pattern continuing into early industrial societies, with women working only in low-paying positions.[65]

In industrial societies, their role as child bearers kept females dependent on male breadwinners and thus in an inferior position. The situation continued unchallenged until increasing numbers of women entered the labor force. The fairly recent demands for sexual equality correlate with women's growing economic contributions. In other words, women's economic position determines the degree of equality in relations between men and women in society.[66] As they achieved greater economic independence, women developed a heightened awareness of their shared bond of exploitation, and the feminist movement gained momentum and many successes in eliminating sexual discrimination (see the Reality Check box and Figure 13.4).

A society's gender-based cultural characteristics, typically the product of generations of thought and reinforced patterns of behavior, live on through social institutions that perpetuate the sexist ideology that women are childlike, passive, and inferior. For centuries, the social structure of most societies placed men in controlling positions of political, economic, and social power. The subordinate role of women in society and in the family clearly benefited men, giving them little incentive to change the gender-role patterns. A prevailing male value system conferred superior status on men and an inferior one on women, defining the female role as supportive to the more highly valued male activities. In classic Marxist theory, only the social action of the subordinate group in challenging this arrangement can affect a change.

Who benefits from sexual inequality? Men do, in higher status, better jobs, higher pay, greater life satisfaction, and more leisure time at home, while their wives fulfill domestic and childcare chores. Business and industry reap higher profits by employing women at lower rates than men.[67] This exploitation of women exacts a toll from members of both sexes: denial of full human development and full use of one's talents, loss to the society of much human creativity and leadership, and individual suffering in economic deprivation and in emotional and psychological strain.

# REALITY check

## Places and Politics: A Geo-Political Profile

When women first secured voting rights, they did not use their political power immediately to improve their lives or to win a proportional share of elected offices. A combination of prevailing norms and the burden of family and home responsibilities contributed to this political inaction. Until the 1990s, women's representation in national, state, and local elected offices was disproportionately low. Men controlled the political parties and often resisted placing women in positions of organizational power or as viable candidates for "serious" offices. That situation has changed and women are slowly increasing their involvement in the political process.

Women hold 24 percent of all state legislative seats, an increase of only 4 percent in the past 20 years. However, more have served in leadership positions (Senate President, Speaker of the House, and majority or minority leader); this presently is the case in 33 states. Female legislators have their highest proportions in Colorado, Vermont, Hawaii, and Arizona, while the lowest are in South Carolina, Louisiana, and Oklahoma. Figure 13.4 shows some small geographic clusters of high and low female state legislators but no clear pattern exists, as states at or near either end of the continuum are found in all parts of the country.

A total of 34 women from 24 states have ever been a state governor. Currently, women serve as governors in five states: Arizona, New Hampshire, New Mexico, Oklahoma and South Carolina.

At the national level, women certainly have become more prominent, as evidenced by the ascendancy of Nancy Pelosi as the first Speaker of the House of Representatives, the 2008 primary presidential campaign of Hillary Clinton, and the vice presidential run of Sarah Palin. In the 113th Congress (2013–2014), women achieved their highest representation yet: 20 senators (20 percent) and 78 congressional representatives (18 percent). This progress reduces the imbalance somewhat, but a significant gender imbalance remains, with the U.S. Congress approximately 82 percent male.

Sources: National Conference of State Legislatures.

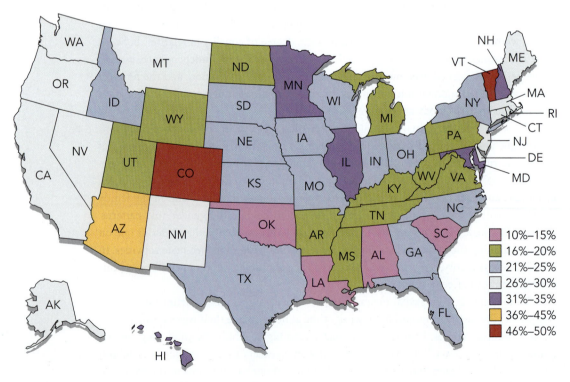

**FIGURE 13.4   Percentage of Women in State Legislatures, 2013**

*Source:* The National Conference of State Legislatures.

## THE INTERACTIONIST VIEW

Through social interaction and the internalization of others' expectations, the self emerges. From birth through adulthood, children go through a socialization process that shapes their sense of identity on the basis of cultural value orientations about gender roles. All the socialization agents—family, school, peers, church, and media—promote gender-role identity and norms in various ways, including example and reinforcement. Social definitions of appropriate behavior, emotions, and goals for boys and girls become internalized as desirable attributes for acceptance and praise. Because these social definitions begin early, are pervasive, and are accepted by those so defined, they appear to be "natural," explaining how "nature" or "God" intended us to be.

In this socially constructed reality of shared expectations about the capabilities and proper behavior of men and women, people interact with one another on the basis of their cultural conditioning. Men do not, however, consciously and deliberately subjugate women, and women do not passively submit to their masters. For the most part, both sexes have long interacted with each other in a taken-for-granted manner as to their "place" in the social structure. William I. Thomas's famous statement (made in 1911) indicates both the consequences of social definitions (including sexism) and the "male reality" of his time: "If men define a situation as real, it is real in its consequences."

Technological changes have altered our social structure and life expectations. As a result, traditional gender roles no longer find acceptance among many women. Yet a consensus does not exist about what it means to be male or female, a fact that creates an ambiguous situation. Gender roles may be blurring, but strongly held concepts of masculinity and femininity remain popular and influential. We live in a transitional period, during which society is redefining gender roles even while many aspects of traditional gender-role attitudes and practices continue. How long and difficult will this transitional period be? No one knows, although evidence from surveys on gender-role attitudes shows increased acceptance of women in nontraditional roles among both men and women.[68] As new patterns of male–female interaction become institutionalized in various social arenas, we may find greater acceptance of sexual equality.

Because the socialization process is so critical, interactionists stress the need to change its content and approach. Thus, parents can be made more aware of existing sexual biases in behavioral expectations of their children, encouraging them to develop fully all aspects of their personalities. Through education and the media, a more enlightened approach—eliminating sexual stereotypes and providing varied role models for both sexes—could do much to promote change and sexual equality. The media and the academic world also could do much to resocialize women to overcome their past conditioning and to resocialize all adults to adopt a more egalitarian value system. This perspective holds that ideas tend to have a life of their own and that, by concentrating on how we interpret the world, we can create a new social reality.

# Retrospect

A generation ago, U.S. society recognized sexism as a social problem, although it has existed for centuries. Minority-group characteristics—ascribed status, physical and cultural visibility, unequal treatment, and shared-group awareness—apply to women just as they do to various racial and ethnic groups, even though they are not a numeric minority. The practice of endogamy does not apply, but in marriage, the dominant–subordinate roles often are quite obvious. Females who accept their minority status are thus predisposed not to challenge it.

Throughout much of U.S. history, male-dominance patterns prevailed. Women lacked voting, contract, and property rights and even were denied the right to enjoy sex without being thought deviant. After a long struggle, women gained the right to vote nationally in 1919 but for a long time did not elect many women to office. During World War II, many women were employed, but peacetime brought a renewed emphasis on the home as a "woman's proper place." In the 1960s, the feminist movement began anew, fostering social awareness and still unfolding social change.

Despite some biological differences between the sexes in size, strength, and longevity, socialization primarily shapes gender identity and gender-role behavior. Entrenched value orientations result in a conditioning process that produces differential behavior patterns and life goals. The resulting gender inequality is evident throughout society and doubly so among minority women. In education, employment, income, legal status, and political power, women's status has improved but remains far from parity with men.

Functionalists contend that a gender-based division of labor was an efficient means of achieving a smoothly functioning society in the past, but they argue that technology since has thrown the social system out of balance, requiring some form of adjustment. Conflict theorists stress the oppression of women as economically based and beneficial to male status and power. Interactionists focus on the social interpretation of reality through socialization and interaction patterns, suggesting that changing the content of the socialization process will eliminate gender inequality.

# On MySocLab

 **Study** and **Review** on MySocLab

## KEY TERMS

Ascribed status, p. 428

Child care, p. 445

Endogamy, p. 429

Fast track, p. 445

Feminization of poverty, p. 446

Flex-time, p. 445

Gender-role expectations, p. 434

Glass ceiling, p. 442

Matrilineal, p. 429

Matrilocal, p. 429

Mommy track, p. 445

Role entrapment, p. 436

Second shift, p. 437

Sexism, p. 428

## DISCUSSION QUESTIONS

1. What new insights did you gain from reading this chapter? What do you know now that you didn't know before? Did anything surprise you?
2. How can we consider women a minority group if they outnumber men?
3. Discuss the biological and sociological explanations of gender-role behavior.
4. Give some examples of the problems of sexism among first- and second-generation U.S. residents.

5. Give examples of sexual discrimination in education, work, income, and law.
6. What are some consequences, both in and out of academia, of accepting the classification of women as a minority?
7. What about the sociological analysis at the end of the chapter? Did one of these perspectives help you understand this area of study better than you knew it before? How so?

# INTERNET ACTIVITIES

1. One of the best Internet resources for this chapter is the Feminist Majority Foundation (http://www.feminist.org). Go to this site and make any selection from the menu to learn more about a subject of specific interest to you. Although there are many other choices, you might want to select the "Our Work" tab, which will take you to numerous specific subject headings, or watch any of the short videos in the Resource Center. Wherever you go, read a little in that area so that you could share that information with others.

2. How do the proportions of women in the U.S. Senate and House of Representatives compare with those in other countries? At "Women in National Parliaments" (http://www.ipu.org/wmn-e/world.htm), you can find out. First, you will see the data for the world and regional averages. Clicking on "Percentage of women in each National Parliament" near the top will give you that information. Did the United States rank where you expected? What conclusions can you make about the position of women in political power in the United States compared to other countries?

# Gays, People with Disabilities, and the Elderly 14

(( Listen to Chapter 14 on MySocLab

This elderly gay couple lives in Massachusetts, which legalized same-sex marriage in 2007. They are now more fortunate than thousands of gay couples who have enjoyed long-term partnerships but who in most states are not permitted to marry or to have such marital rights relating to inheritance, medical emergency decisions, or pension benefits.

## LEARNING OBJECTIVES | After reading this chapter you will be able to:

**14-1** Describe the sociohistorical context for studying the LGBT community.

**14-2** Examine what genetic studies tell us about sexual orientation.

**14-3** Analyze LGBT numbers by racial and ethnic group.

**14-4** Analyze issues and facts about same-sex marriages and gay parenting.

**14-5** Describe the sociohistorical context for studying people with disabilities.

**14-6** Examine myths, stereotypes, and issues involving the disabled.

**14-7** Describe the sociological context for studying the elderly.

**14-8** Analyze the problem a growing elderly population creates.

**14-9** Examine myths, stereotypes, and issues involving the elderly.

**14-10** Discuss insights gained through sociological analysis.

457

People can be members of minority groups because of race, ethnicity, and gender as discussed in earlier chapters, or they may struggle as members of other minority groups against prejudice and discrimination to gain equal rights and full integration into society. Despite significant progress in improving their quality of life, the unequal treatment and life experiences of gays and lesbians, the disabled, and the elderly reveal that much more remains to be done for them to achieve equal rights that are the same as other citizens in a democracy.

As with the other minorities we have studied, to varying degrees, these three groups share the minority-group characteristics discussed in Chapter 1. This particularly is true in their receiving unequal treatment as a group and feeling a sense of group solidarity. The disabled and elderly have distinguishing physical characteristics and membership in either group is involuntary, for the most part. Moreover, in keeping with the theme and title of this book, in a very real sense, all three groups are "strangers" when it comes to being inclusive members of society. Our discussion in Chapter 1 about similarity and attraction, social distance, categoric knowing, Simmel's duality of remoteness and nearness, and Schutz's "intersubjective understanding" all are helpful in understanding more completely how these three groups compare to other minority groups in attempting to overcome their marginalization and also to learn what current issues remain to be addressed.

## Sexual Orientation

History has recorded descriptive evidence of the existence of homosexuality for millennia. Most of our knowledge of sexual behaviors and norms of past historical periods, however, comes by inference from the literature and public writings of the times. We really do not know how most people were behaving.

## Sociohistorical Perspective

Homosexuality existed without sanctions among the ancient Babylonians, Chinese, Egyptians, and Romans, as well as among Native Americans. The ancient Greeks not only accepted it as a natural expression of sexual instinct, but praised it as more genuine and tender than heterosexual love. The word *pederasty* literally means the love of boys, and most homosexuality in ancient Greece was between men and adolescents—often between a well-born teacher or mentor and his student or apprentice—not between adult males. Less well documented is homosexuality among nonaristocratic ancient Greeks, except for the mention of freeborn male prostitutes.

A series of social norms in ancient Greece set the rules of etiquette for early homosexual relationships and their subsequent replacement by heterosexual relationships. A boy approaching puberty, after a courtship, became the passive lover of one adult male until he reached the age of majority, at which time, he was expected to become an active lover with both women and boys.[1] Such practices extend beyond the Mediterranean world. For example, the Bedamini people of New Guinea believe that the sharing of semen between older and younger males is a natural means of enhancing masculinity and strength.[2]

Sappho, a popular lyric poet in ancient Greece, was born and lived on the isle of Lesbos. Although a wife and mother, her writings often sensually spoke of love for other women. She became so identified with woman-love that she inspired others to use two of the most common words that describe female homosexuality: *lesbian* and *sapphic.* She lived in a time when women more openly could express strong passions for one another, although these may or may not have been sexual.

In contrast, throughout the Middle Ages and into the eighteenth century, European society viewed homosexuality and heterosexual sodomy as sins and crimes. Governments in most of Europe, from Sweden to England to Italy, executed individuals found guilty of such acts. In 1407, for example, Venetian officials ordered 33 citizens, including 15 noblemen, to be burned alive for committing homosexual acts. In France, authorities in 1586 burned at the stake a former provost of the University of Paris for injuring a boy in the act of anal rape. The last known execution of a lesbian was a beheading in Prussia in 1721. Such events indicate the stance of the Church and of society toward homosexuality but not the prevalence of such forbidden conduct. Nevertheless, the frequent arrest of large groups and references to their favorite meeting places suggest the existence of a sizable homosexual subculture.[3]

For many years, social science researchers—influenced by societal norms that included religion-based condemnation and psychiatric labeling of homosexuality as an abnormality or mental illness—focused on homosexuality as a social problem. In fact, the psychiatric or psychoanalytical perspective that assumed homosexuality was pathological and that homosexuals were "sick" or "perverted" influenced much of the written commentary through the late 1980s.[4] In 1973, the American Psychiatric Association deleted homosexuality from its list of psychiatric disorders and began efforts to end discrimination against homosexuals. Nowadays—with homosexuality no longer labeled an illness, with an increasing body of research suggesting that sexual preference is a function of biology not choice, with growing public acceptance, and with sexual preference protected under civil rights legislation—researchers emphasize discriminatory practices against homosexuals as *the* social problem instead.

## Gay Genetics

Although many people long insisted on a biological explanation for homosexuality, it was not until the 1990s that several studies claimed the discovery of such proof. One scientist, Simon LeVay, conducted postmortem examination of brain tissues of 19 homosexual males, 16 heterosexual males, and 6 heterosexual females. In the anterior hypothalamus (a part of the brain scientists believe plays a part in sexual behavior), he found significant differences. In the homosexual males, this region was approximately the same size as those found in women's brains, whereas those of the heterosexual males were three times larger.[5] Another study disclosed size differences in a structure inside the anterior commissure (a band of nerve fibers scientists believe facilitates communication between the left and right hemispheres of the brain). This part of the brain was larger in homosexual men than in women or heterosexual men.[6]

**14-2** Examine what genetic studies tell us about sexual orientation.

Other geneticists studied 44 sets of gay male twins and found that 75 percent of them shared a unique part of the X chromosome, which is far greater than would occur by chance alone. Furthermore, they found that these men were significantly more likely to have gay male relatives on their mother's side. Because men receive the X chromosome from their mothers only, this finding would suggest a genetic link to sexual orientation.[7] However, no other scientist has been able to replicate this finding.[8] Numerous recent studies have found significant physiological and cognitive differences between gays and straights, suggesting biology does play some role. However, the American Academy of Pediatrics maintains that sexual orientation probably is not determined by any one factor but by a combination of genetic, hormonal, and environmental influences.[9]

These studies, sometimes contradictory, remain controversial, partly because of sample size and partly because they only show a biological component to homosexuality, not a cause and effect. Expression of a biological trait, such as left-handedness or temperament, depends not only on a great many social factors but also can be altered by them. At best, these studies on homosexuality suggest a partial biological explanation.

# Homosexuality in the United States

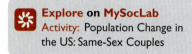
**Explore on MySocLab**
Activity: Population Change in the US: Same-Sex Couples

**Watch on MySocLab**
Video: Social Inequalities: Sex and Sexuality

Openness about being homosexual was uncommon in the United States prior to the 1960s, except in major cities, where strong subcultures thrived. For example, between 1890 and 1940, New York City's gay community had its own traditions, gathering places, and cultural and social events that sustained and enhanced gay men's communal ties and group identity.[10] Although existing laws criminalized gay men's sexual behavior and even their nonsexual association with each other, these laws were enforced indifferently. As a result, gay men formed a wide world of overlapping social networks with excellent support systems: emotional, social, and commercial. By the 1930s, popular fascination with gay culture led thousands of people to attend the city's drag balls, and newspapers published sketches of the most sensational gowns.

## STIGMA AND SANCTIONS

A shift in public attitude about alternative lifestyles occurred during the 1930s and 1940s. Prompted perhaps by a coalescing of conservative religious currents and fears of social disintegration raised by the Depression, labor unrest, and the threat of Bolshevism, more stringent enforcement of all laws took place, including the previously ignored ones against homosexuality, which society now labeled as deviant. During the Cold War of the 1950s, Communist hunter U.S. Senator Joseph McCarthy warned that homosexuals in the State Department were threatening national security. At that time, discovery or even suspicion as a homosexual could severely disrupt a person's life in any occupation. Getting fired was quite possible; getting taunted was probable. Some young adults took pleasure in going into an area known to be frequented by homosexual men or lesbians and beating them up. To most homosexuals, "passing," or carrying out their lives in such a way as to appear heterosexual, was crucial. Basically, social norms created "the closet" and forced homosexuals into it.[11]

Though not as severe as the laws in Britain (where, until 1861, anal intercourse was punishable by death), U.S. laws still were quite harsh toward homosexual men. Until only a few years ago, many sexual acts commonly practiced in the United States, such as oral–genital sex and anal sex, were considered "crimes against nature" and were illegal in many states. Municipalities invoked these laws, usually lumped under sodomy statutes, primarily to prosecute homosexual men.

## TOLERANCE AND BACKLASH

The **homophobia** (an irrational fear of gay people) of the 1950s—together with the resulting stigma and harm that could result from openness about their sexual preference—led many homosexuals to adopt a low profile despite the efforts of activist organizers in several cities. To avoid exposure, many gays hid their true selves from the straight world and quietly sought companionship in their bathhouses and bars.[12] In 1969, at one such gay bar, the Stonewall Inn in New York City, an event occurred that marked a shift in the gay community from passive adaptive goals to active militancy. The police routinely had raided the bars in the past, but on this occasion, the customers fought back rather than retreating. The event galvanized the gay community to become more assertive and to publicly acknowledge their sexual identity. As other minorities had done earlier in the 1960s, gays and lesbians joined organizations and struggled to secure equal rights and opportunities.[13]

The 1970s and 1980s saw major gains in public tolerance, including the addition of "sexual orientation" to antidiscrimination policies and statutes at local, state, and national levels. Tolerance of gay people increased as the gay rights movement gained strength. More gays "came out of the closet" and annual Gay Pride parades became part of large city celebrations. Then the AIDS epidemic of the 1980s devastated the gay community, bringing enormous personal loss and grief, but also a renewed outburst of prejudice, discrimination, and violence against homosexuals. A dramatic increase in antigay hate crimes of arson, assault, and murder marked the 1990s.[14]

Religious and political conservatives launched campaigns in the 1990s to pass local ordinances condemning homosexuality and to prevent the inclusion of sexual orientation under the protection of state antidiscrimination laws.[15] They also objected, along with military leaders, when President Bill Clinton attempted in 1993 to repeal the official ban on gays in the armed forces. The "don't ask, don't tell" (DADT) compromise sidestepped the issue of equal rights for people of all sexual orientations, but it did allow gay men and women to serve in the military without surveillance or persecution, provided they did not make their sexual preference known.[16] Such a policy, however, exacted a heavy toll. Despite a shortage of Arabic linguists to handle military intelligence, approximately 60 have been kicked out of the military for being gay, and nearly 14,000 other service members have been discharged involuntarily.[17] In September 2011, DADT officially ended, enabling gays to be open about their sexual orientation and enlist, re-enlist, or remain in the military.

A 1986 U.S. Supreme Court decision (*Bowers v. Hardwick*) said people do *not* have a constitutional right to engage in private homosexual conduct, even in their own homes. In other cases, the Court has ruled in favor of gays, such as its 1996 negation of a Colorado referendum that banned all measures protecting homosexuals from discrimination. Perhaps most important was its 2003 decision, *Lawrence v. Texas*, which overturned *Bowers* and ruled that intimate consensual sexual conduct was one of the liberties protected under due process by the Fourteenth Amendment. In effect, this decision invalidated all state laws that criminalized private homosexual activity between consenting adults, leading gay rights activists to call the decision historic, the equivalent of the 1954 *Brown v. Board of Education* desegregation ruling.

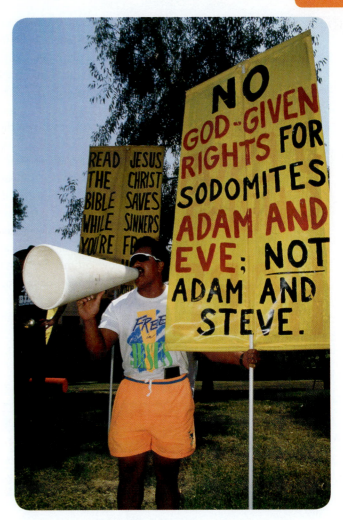

Homosexuals are a frequent target of hate groups and religious zealots. Hate crimes are violent examples of discrimination, but loud and sometimes disruptive demonstrations are "peaceful" manifestations of prejudice against gays. This Hispanic man is preaching through a megaphone to marchers in a Gay Pride parade in Irvine, California.

## HOW MANY GAYS ARE THERE?

How common is homosexuality in the United States? The exact population of homosexuals always has been difficult to determine. Until the late twentieth century, the source most often cited was the 1948 research of Alfred Kinsey, which estimated that 10 percent of all Americans were homosexuals. However, although Kinsey used a large sample, it was not a **random sample**, an objective process that allows everyone the same chance of being selected. Instead, Kinsey settled for a **convenience sample**, relying largely on college student volunteers who had attended his lectures on sexuality. Convenience samples thus may overestimate prevalence because they sample the dependent variable, in this case, young, sexually active people more likely to have diverse experiences. A truly representative cross section of the public is a more reliable probability sample and so most social scientists feel uncomfortable using a convenience sample to make generalizations. In Kinsey's case, subsequent studies showed his findings were inflated estimations.

Analyze LGBT numbers by racial and ethnic group.

Recent studies from Britain, Canada, Denmark, France, and Norway have identified the number of homosexuals in these countries to be in the 1 to 4 percent range, significantly below Kinsey's findings of 10 percent in the United States. Gay rights activists argued that the European findings were flawed because sexual orientation is not only actual behavior but also feelings—how a person falls in love—which is not measurable. This issue of proportion had political overtones because the accepted number could strengthen or weaken the impact of gays as a recognized constituency on lawmakers and other government officials.

A 1994 study, then the largest study of sexual behavior ever conducted in the United States, found that 2.7 percent of the males and 1.3 percent of the females reported having had sex with someone of the same gender within the past year. The findings were higher when the time frame extended back to puberty: 7.3 percent for males and 3.8 percent for females. When asked if they were sexually attracted to others of the same gender, 6.2 percent of the males and 4.4 percent of the females said they were. A 2012 national study, 35 times larger in the number of respondents (121,290), found higher percentages of people self-identifying as lesbian, gay, bisexual, or transgender (LGBT), with varying levels when controlled for race and ethnicity. Higher percentages occurred among younger people of color (see Figure 14.1).[18]

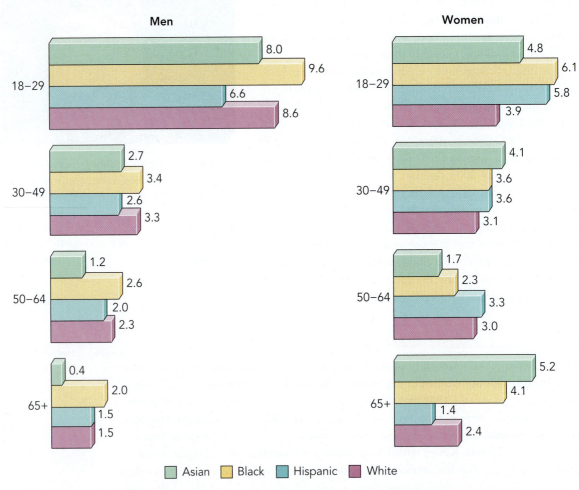

**FIGURE 14.1  Percent Identifying as Lesbian, Gay, Bisexual, or Transgender**

Source: The Williams Institute, October 2012.

These varying percentages suggest an important element about sexual behavior that Kinsey discovered in 1948. Sexual orientation is a continuum, not a simple classification of people into one of two distinct categories. Kinsey created a seven-point rating scale with exclusive homosexuality at one end and exclusive heterosexuality at the other—with desires, actions, and their frequency determining the five in-between stages. Whatever the criteria, however, the 1994 and 2012 studies suggested that the actively homosexual population is considerably smaller than Kinsey had estimated.

## PUBLIC ATTITUDES ABOUT HOMOSEXUALITY

Public opinion about homosexuality, including civil unions and gay adoptions, steadily is becoming more tolerant.[19] For example, a 2013 national poll revealed that 60 percent of Americans considered homosexuality an acceptable alternative lifestyle, compared to 35 percent in 1989. On the question of whether homosexuals should have equal rights in terms of job opportunities, an impressive 89 percent said that they should, compared to 56 percent in 1977.[20] Opinions about same-sex marriages and gay parenting were also supportive, topics that we will discuss shortly.

In recent national public opinion polls, more than four in five Americans reported that they personally knew someone who was gay (a friend, relative, or coworker). This is a dramatic increase from 1992, when pollsters found that only two in five knew a homosexual.[21] This increasing percentage augurs well. The **intergroup contact hypothesis** maintains that, when social interaction is marked by equal status (as with coworkers) or affective ties (as with friends and relatives), individuals will have more positive attitudes (for example, less antigay prejudice) and behaviors (for example, making fewer antigay comments or jokes).[22]

When responses are controlled for age, a significant generation gap becomes apparent. More than half of all Americans age 30 and older believe that homosexuality is morally wrong, compared with fewer than 4 in 10 (38 percent) among those under age 30. Approximately two in three blacks think homosexuality is morally wrong, compared to less than half of all whites and two in five Hispanics.[23]

Religion also generates differing views. Among religious groups, 76 percent of white evangelical Protestants and 65 percent of black Protestants believe homosexuality is morally wrong. Fewer mainline Protestants (40 percent), Catholics (39 percent), and the unaffiliated (29 percent) hold this view. Views also differ according to the frequency of worship service attendance. Two-thirds of regular weekly worshipers say homosexual behavior is morally wrong, compared with 43 percent of those who attend services monthly or yearly, and 31 percent of those who seldom or never attend. Among Catholics, a slim majority of weekly Mass goers (53 percent) say homosexual behavior is morally wrong, but among those going to Mass less often, a majority (65 percent) either say homosexuality is not a moral issue or say it is morally acceptable.[24]

# Current Issues

Although antidiscrimination laws, affirmative action guidelines establishing sexual orientation as a protected category, and a growing level of tolerance in society have improved conditions for gays and lesbians, it would be foolish to suggest they no longer encounter problems (see the Ethnic Experience box). In a recent poll, half of all Americans said things had "gotten better" when it comes to treating gay people with respect and courtesy, but 24 percent thought things remained about the same and 15 percent thought the situation was worse. Eleven percent said they didn't know.[25]

Read on **MySocLab**
Document: Gay Marriage Timeline

# the ETHNIC experience

## Double Marginality

"I hated being me practically my entire life. I hated being Italian American practically my entire life. I hated the negative stereotypes associated with being Italian American; I did not want to admit that I was American of Italian descent because of such negative stereotypes and images. As a young child, I wanted to change my last name to 'Carson,' or something else 'non-Italian.' I was embarrassed and ashamed of who I was and where I came from. My identity was in a crisis, and it would not be until many years later—in my adulthood—after reading much about Italian Americans, written by Italian Americans, that my identity crisis would come to an end.

Literature has amazing powers that can change the lives of the readers; literature saved my life."

"When I was a young child in elementary school—I cannot remember the exact age—I had a difficult time relating to the other students. I knew that I did not 'fit in.' I was not the only American of Italian descent, but I was one of the few in a school with mostly Jewish American and Irish American children. And, of course, I befriended the other three to five children who were also Italian American. We formed a close bond."

"Later in life, I would come to realize that my ethnicity was not the only aspect of my life that marginalized

me, and made me not 'fit in.' As a homosexual male, my sexual orientation also marginalized me, and made me feel like an outcast, made me feel less than human. And it must be stated, and known, that with its conservative and traditional ways of thinking, the Italian American community—my own community—has not always been accepting and understanding of my sexual orientation. Ironically, one marginalized community marginalizes—even minimizes and oppresses—another marginalized community."

Source: Michael Carosone, New York City. Recorded commentary from the collection of Vincent N. Parrillo.

Contentious issues heightening emotions and no doubt affecting such mixed feelings are hate crimes, same-sex marriages, and gay parenting.

## HATE CRIMES

Hate crimes remain a serious problem for the LGBT community. The FBI reported that in 2011, approximately 21 percent of all hate crimes were due to sexual orientation bias, claiming nearly 1,600 victims. Although protected under hate crime and civil rights laws, gays and lesbians only receive such protection under the Constitution on a case-by-case judicial decision after the fact.

Even though it happened in 1998, the murder of University of Wyoming student Matthew Shepard long remained the national centerpiece of proposed hate crime legislation to protect gays. At a bar, the 21-year-old Shepard met two young men who, according to their girlfriends, had gone there to rob a gay man. Shepard asked them for a ride home but instead they took him to a remote rural area, robbed him, and pistol whipped him so severely that they fractured his skull from the front to the right ear, causing severe brain stem damage. They then tied him to a fence, where he was discovered by a cyclist 18 hours later. Taken to a hospital where doctors determined his injuries were too severe for them to operate, he lay unconscious and on full life support for four days, his case prompting candlelight vigils around the world. After his death, the two murderers were found, arrested, convicted, and sentenced to life terms in prison.

In the aftermath, throughout a 10-year period, a bill was introduced in Congress each year to extend federal hate crime legislation to include gay and lesbian individuals,

THEY SAID OUR WEDDING WAS UNNATURAL! THAT IT WOULD DESTROY THE SACRED INSTITUTION OF MARRIAGE!

THEY SAID THE NEXT STEP COULD BE LEGALIZED INCEST OR BESTIALITY!

THEY SAID OUR LOVE COULDN'T PRODUCE A NORMAL HEALTHY FAMILY!

BUT I MARRIED YOUR MOTHER ANYWAY!

KEVIN SIERS ©2003 THE CHARLOTTE OBSERVER

*This editorial cartoon invokes the arguments once made against interracial marriages, which were illegal in many states until the U.S. Supreme Court ruled in 1967 that these miscegenation laws were unconstitutional. The message is clear: old, rejected reasons against mixed-race marriages have been recycled to fight legalization of gay marriages.*

women, and people with disabilities. After various setbacks, the Matthew Shepard and James Byrd, Jr. Hate Crimes Prevention Act passed and was signed into law in October 2009 by President Obama. (Byrd was an African American man who was tied to a truck by two known white supremacists, dragged from it, and decapitated in Jasper, Texas, also in 1998. Like Wyoming, Texas also had no hate crimes law protection at the time.)

## SAME-SEX MARRIAGES

**14-4** Analyze issues and facts about same-sex marriages and gay parenting.

In mid-2013, same-sex marriages were legally permissible in Belgium, Canada, Denmark, France, the Netherlands, Norway, South Africa, Spain, Sweden, and in 13 states: Connecticut, Delaware, Iowa, Maine, Maryland, Massachusetts, Minnesota, New Hampshire, New York, Rhode Island, Vermont, and Washington. Six states—Colorado, Hawaii, Illinois, Nevada, New Jersey, and Wisconsin—as well as 17 other European countries—allow gays and lesbians to enter into civil unions or domestic partnerships, entitling them to receive all benefits, rights, privileges, and obligations as heterosexual couples.[26] In the United States, the 1996 Defense of Marriage Act (1966) denied same-sex couples any and all federal benefits, such as family-related social security or veterans benefits. Moreover, they were denied well over 1,000 legal rights, such as medical emergency decisions on behalf of a partner or property inheritance from a partner in the absence of a will. In June 2013, the U.S. Supreme Court struck down this law as unconstitutional but left in place state laws banning same-sex marriage.

Until recently, national public opinion polls showed that the majority of Americans opposed same-sex marriage (SSM). The change apparently occurred in November–December 2012, when three different polls (NBC News/*Wall Street Journal*, CBS News, ABC News/*Washington Post*) each found 51 percent of respondents supporting SSM.[27] A substantial number (73 percent) of young adults ages 18 to 29 now support same-sex marriage, compared to 39 percent of those over age 65. SSM support varies by region though. That majority view prevails in New England, the mid-Atlantic states, and in those on the Pacific Coast. Majority opposition lies in the central South, while opinion is closely divided in the Midwest and the south Atlantic states.[28]

A significant shift has occurred among blacks, changing from 66 percent opposed in 2009 to 51 percent in favor in 2012. Similarly, Hispanics shifted from 53 percent opposed to gay marriage in 2009 to 52 percent in favor in 2012.[29] Among whites, political ideology affects one's view, with 69 percent of Republicans opposed and 73 percent of Democrats in favor. Religiosity is also a key factor, with 70 percent of those who attend religious services on a weekly basis opposed to SSM and an equal percentage of those who attend less often supportive.[30]

## GAY PARENTING

The controversy swirling around the issue of gay parenting comes from deep-seated religious beliefs about the morality of homosexuality and possible negative child development consequences (gender-role confusion, biased sexual orientation) for children raised by same-sex adoptive parents. However, research findings indicate that, when comparing children of same-sex parents with opposite-sex parents, no differences occur on measures of popularity, social adjustment, gender-role behavior, gender identity, intelligence, self-concept, emotional problems, interest in marriage and parenting, locus of control, moral development, independence, ego functions, object relations, or self-esteem.[31]

States vary greatly in their laws about adoption. Eighteen states and the District of Columbia allow same-sex couples to adopt through joint adoption. Only Mississippi specifically bars same-sex couples from adopting, and Utah prohibits unmarried couples from doing so, but without mention of sexual orientation. Many states' laws on same-sex couple adoptions are vague and thus left to the interpretation of judges. As individuals, gays and lesbians can adopt in almost every state. The Census Bureau reported that in 2011, 19 percent of all same-sex couples (comprising 10 percent of male couples and 24 percent of female couples) were raising children compared with 44 percent of

*Four of five children living with gay parents are adopted and the remainder has foster parents. Because of prevailing religious beliefs, Mississippi and Utah do not permit gay adoptions. Comparative studies of straight and gay families show children are equally well-adjusted in gender identity and behavior in both family types.*

opposite-sex couples.[32] An estimated 65,500 adopted children (4 percent of all adoptees) and another 14,100 foster children (3 percent of the total) live with gay or lesbian parents. California is home to the most gay parents (approximately 16,000). Same-sex couples raising adopted children tend to be older, more educated, and have more economic resources than other adoptive parents. More than half of gay men and 41 percent of lesbians want to have a child, resulting in an estimated 2 million gay and lesbian people interested in adopting.[33]

## People with Disabilities

People with disabilities have been members of all societies for thousands of years. For example, the *Rig-Veda*, an ancient sacred poem of India written between 3500 and 1800 BCE, tells of a warrior queen, Vishpla, who—after losing a leg in warfare—was fitted with an iron artificial limb and returned to battle. Despite such exceptional amputee battle heroes—Roman General Marcus Sergius (against Carthage in 218 BCE) and German mercenary knight Gotz von Berlichingen (Battle of Landshut in 1508 CE) are two others—most people with disabilities throughout recorded history lived ordinary lives but often struggled to overcome indifference, maltreatment, or pity, receiving little to nothing in the way of societal assistance.

The term *disability*, of course, refers to far more than only those who suffer loss of a limb. Definitions vary greatly, but U.S. federal law defines a "disability" as any physical or mental impairment that substantially limits one or more major life activities, such as breathing, hearing, learning, seeing, speaking, taking care of oneself, walking, or working. Such a disability may be partial or total, temporary or permanent.

Given the varying definitions and subjective nature of reporting among countries, the exact number of people with disabilities is difficult to determine. The World Health Organization estimates the total at more than 1 billion around the world.[34] In the United States, 57 million people have some type of disability; 4 million use wheelchairs, 2 million are legally blind, and 1.1 million have a severe hearing difficulty (see the Minority Experience box). These are only the visible disabilities; tens of millions more have AIDS, cancer, diabetes, epilepsy, hypertension, mental retardation, some forms of multiple sclerosis, psychiatric disorders, and traumatic brain injury.[35] This makes people with disabilities the third largest U.S. minority group, behind African and Hispanic Americans.

These numbers will continue to increase, from war casualties and from people living longer and thus becoming more susceptible to debilitating ailments. In addition, thanks to continuing advances in medicine, people who previously would have died from life-threatening illnesses or accidents now survive but do so with less than fully functioning capabilities.

## Sociohistorical Perspective

Until about the mid-nineteenth century, the prevailing view in most cultures was those with disabilities were "bad people" under punishment from God. Accordingly, families with someone with a disability typically felt embarrassment and shame and so would hide disabled family members away from school and other societal interactions, thereby

**14-5** Describe the sociohistorical context for studying people with disabilities.

# the MINORITY experience

## Deafness in a Hearing World

"A regretful irony of the telephone is that it sprang out of Alexander Graham Bell's efforts to devise speech communication instruments for deaf people. Instead, by premising human speech and hearing as the isolated means of telecommunication, the telephone served as the greatest technology disenfranchisement that deaf people ever experienced."

"Due to the inaccessibility of the telephone to us, my deaf family had to depend on the kindness of our neighbors in making only those calls deemed absolutely essential. We compensated for the lack of an inclusive design by devising the teletypewriter (TTY) as an assistive technology to enable telecommunications through telephones. Still, for more than two decades, those with TTYs were limited to calling others who also had TTYs."

"As a fledgling lawyer in the late 1980s, the only means available to me to telecommunicate with other attorneys was through a volunteer-operated relay system where I would use my TTY to call someone who would assist in my call by voicing my typewritten message to the telephone user and vice versa. I cannot begin to say how many times I was hung up on

or treated rudely as a result of a telephone user irritated with the slowness of my typed and relayed conversation. Adding injury to insult were the limitations on the charitable-based relay service, including allowance of only three calls at a time, with busy numbers counted, and queues often stretching up to an hour before my gaining access to the next available individual to relay my call."

"Fast forward to nearly two decades after enactment of the 1990 Americans with Disabilities Act (ADA). Title IV of the ADA requires common carriers (telephone companies) to establish interstate and intrastate telecommunications relay services (TRS) 24 hours a day, seven days a week. TRS enables callers with hearing and speech disabilities who use telecommunications devices for the deaf (TDDs or updated teletypewriters, the TTYs), and callers who use voice telephones to communicate with each other through a third party communications assistant. However, there is a significant disparity between the rates of typing speech versus the speed one could sign or receive someone's interpreted oral communications. In 2002, the Federal Communications Commission (FCC) recognized that a

visual telecommunications medium was needed for people whose native language was American Sign Language (ASL) and permitted the inclusion of video phones as part of the relay system, whereby deaf people can telecommunicate through a video interpreter. As a result, more than a dozen Video Relay Service (VRS) providers now provide sign language interpreting services for millions of deaf people, ushering in a new era of functional equivalency in telecommunications well more than a century after Bell patented the telephone."

"Significantly, VRS providers employ a disproportionately higher percentage of deaf and hard of hearing people in every level of the industry. The VRS model serves as a powerful example of how a civil right (Title IV of the ADA) can be leveraged by a publicly-funded, market-based approach to bring about technology that is inclusive of people with disabilities rather than us chasing technology through separate and stand-alone devices such as the TTY/TDD."

Source: Jeff Rosen is a third-generation deaf person and the General Counsel and Vice President of Governmental Affairs for a company that provides a Video Relay Service for deaf and hard of hearing people.

excluding them from any meaningful roles in society. The public, when aware of individuals with disabilities, might feel sympathy for them and a moral obligation to offer them some assistance and support as charity cases. Essentially though, this one-time prevalent viewpoint often resulted in both a negative self-image (even self-hatred) among the disabled and social ostracism.

With the evolution of modern medicine in the mid-nineteenth century, doctors sought to treat, if not cure, the problems associated with disability. The placement of individuals with disabilities into a "sick role" under the care of a medical professional meant institutionalization or confinement (exclusion) for some and a state of dependency for others. This latter social construct occurred because, when people are classified as "sick," a common assumption arises that they cannot do the things others do—learn in a regular classroom, engage in physical activities, work, or otherwise engage in normal social activities—until they get "fixed." Until then, they "need" someone to take care of them. Such an approach places individuals under the control of others. If they try to be independent and go to work, they could lose their disability status and all related benefits (including healthcare coverage).[36]

Another problem with this **medical model** is its implication that, because the disabled supposedly cannot function independently, society has no responsibility to integrate them, be it wheelchair access to buildings, sign language interpreters at important gatherings, or access to public transportation. The emphasis is that the individual is the problem and must adapt to the world as it is or else be placed in an institution or isolated at home.

Beginning in the 1960s, a new approach evolved that took note of the "differently abled," people whose physical or mental impairments may not lead to disability if society adapts to accommodate them rather than the other way around (Figure 14.2). This **social model** sought to eliminate the prejudice, exclusion, and barriers in society—whether deliberate or unintentional—that resulted in the disabled as a socially marginalized group. Efforts thus focused on changing attitudes and physical structures, on mainstreaming children in schools, and other societal restructuring that provides empowerment and equality to the disabled so that they can live lives to the fullest extent possible.

Impetus for many of these changes came from Ed Roberts—a polio victim and "father of the independent living movement"—who, together with other young adults with disabilities at Cowell (UC Berkeley Health Center), formed a group in 1970 called the Rolling Quads, who then formed the Disabled Students' Program on the campus. In 1971, they established a Center for Independent Living (CIL). Originally the CIL was a two-bedroom, roach-infested apartment, until the group received a $50,000 grant from the Rehabilitation Administration a year later. It became a model for hundreds of other similar centers throughout the United States.[37]

In the latter part of the twentieth century, a disability rights movement (led by persons with disabilities) and precedent-setting legislation (to be discussed shortly) began a profound transformation in attitudes and behaviors, a process still unfolding. As these changes take root, they are unraveling decades of social prejudice and institutional discrimination.

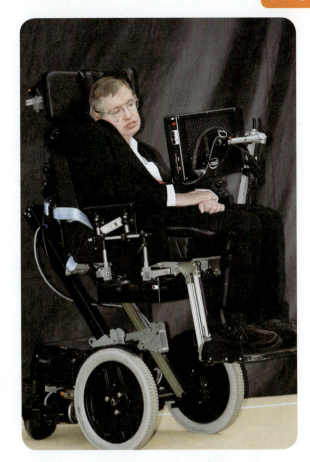

*Even though he is almost entirely paralyzed and communicates through a speech-generating device, Stephen Hawking is a brilliant theoretical physicist, cosmologist, and best-selling author, who also appeared as himself in* Star Trek: The Next Generation *(1993). He is greatly respected for his highly significant contributions to science.*

## Americans with Disabilities

The U.S. Census Bureau reports that approximately one in eight persons, age 6 and older in the civilian noninstitutionalized population, reported a severe disability. Excluded from this count are military personnel and people in nursing homes or other dependent care facilities. Within this noninstitutionalized population are 14.9 million (6.2 percent) with a sensory disability involving sight or hearing; 15.2 million (6.3 percent) with a cognitive, mental, or emotional condition causing difficulty in learning, remembering, or concentrating; 30.6 million (12.6 percent) with a condition limiting basic physical activities, such as walking, climbing stairs, reaching, lifting, or carrying; and 9.4 million (3.9 percent) with self-care limitations in dressing, bathing, or getting around inside the home. (Respondents could select more than one type of disability.)[38]

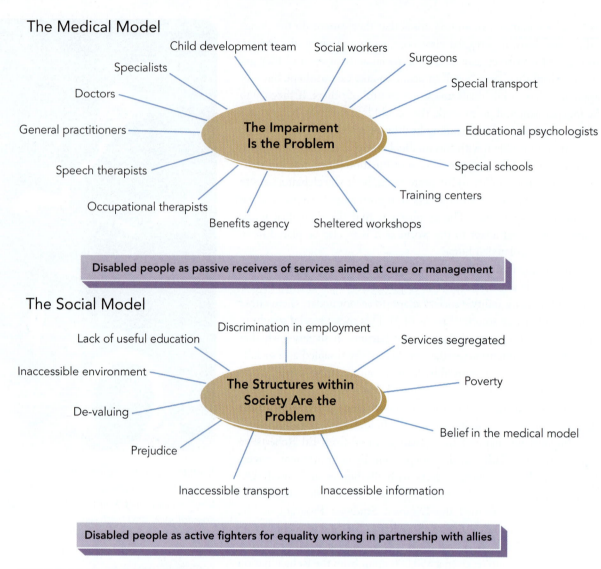

The Medical Model

The Impairment Is the Problem

- Child development team
- Social workers
- Surgeons
- Special transport
- Specialists
- Doctors
- General practitioners
- Educational psychologists
- Speech therapists
- Special schools
- Occupational therapists
- Training centers
- Benefits agency
- Sheltered workshops

**Disabled people as passive receivers of services aimed at cure or management**

The Social Model

The Structures within Society Are the Problem

- Discrimination in employment
- Lack of useful education
- Services segregated
- Inaccessible environment
- Poverty
- De-valuing
- Belief in the medical model
- Prejudice
- Inaccessible transport
- Inaccessible information

**Disabled people as active fighters for equality working in partnership with allies**

**FIGURE 14.2  Disability Models**
*Source:* Disability Equality & Education.

Disability rates rise with age, with persons 65 or older twice as likely to report a sensory, physical, mental, or self-care disability causing difficulty going outside the home. These disability rates varied somewhat among the major racial and ethnic groups, with Asians having lower rates for those under age 65, and after that age, minority groups having higher disability rates than non-Hispanic whites (see Figure 14.3).

# Legislative Actions

No doubt inspired by the civil rights and feminist movements of the 1960s, numerous advocacy groups and organizations in the 1970s combined forces to launch a powerful social movement for disability rights. Aiding their cause was the presence of 75,000 severely disabled veterans from the Vietnam War (1959–1975).

## REHABILITATION ACT OF 1973

As the first civil rights legislation in the world for people with disabilities, the Rehabilitation Act of 1973 marked a turning point in societal treatment of this minority group and prompted similar legislation in other developed countries. Of particular importance was

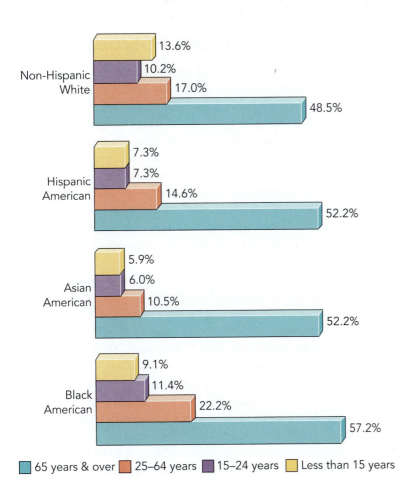

FIGURE 14.3

Non-Hispanic White — 13.6%, 10.2%, 17.0%, 48.5%

Hispanic American — 7.3%, 7.3%, 14.6%, 52.2%

Asian American — 5.9%, 6.0%, 10.5%, 52.2%

Black American — 9.1%, 11.4%, 22.2%, 57.2%

■ 65 years & over ■ 25–64 years ■ 15–24 years ■ Less than 15 years

Section 504, which stipulated that "any program or activity receiving federal financial assistance" cannot allow anyone to "be excluded from the participation in, be denied the benefits of, or be subjected to, discrimination." This meant, for instance, that airports, colleges and universities, and public libraries had to make their facilities barrier-free.

However, when the U.S. Department of Health, Education, and Welfare began watering down the regulations in 1977, a group of disabled people took over the Department's San Francisco office to protest. Their historic action, which became the nation's longest sit-in of a federal building, was successful, and the Section 504 regulations finally were signed and enacted.

## AMERICANS WITH DISABILITIES ACT OF 1990

The next significant legislation, after years of extensive lobbying, occurred in 1990. "Let the shameful wall of exclusion finally come tumbling down," said President George H. W. Bush, as he signed the Americans with Disabilities Act of 1990.[39] This legislation, the most comprehensive antidiscrimination action since the 1964 Civil Rights Act, took effect in 1992. Title I prohibits private employers with more than 25 employees, state and local governments, employment agencies, and labor unions from discriminating against qualified individuals with disabilities in job application procedures, hiring, firing, advancement, compensation, job training, and other terms, conditions, and privileges of employment. The Americans with Disabilities Act (ADA) also covers public services and public transportation (Title II), public accommodations and commercial facilities (Title III), and telecommunications (Title IV). In 2008, the law was amended to broaden ADA protection coverage for more individuals.

# Myths and Stereotypes

14-6 Examine myths, stereotypes, and issues involving the disabled.

**Read on MySocLab**
Document: Hoops and Wheels

One of the prevailing myths about disabled people is that they are helpless victims, requiring a dependency status, so they need someone to take care of them. This paternalistic view, although it may be justified toward those who have a serious mental or physical impairment, does a disservice to all other disabled individuals. Too many people make simplistic assumptions about that one physical characteristic (for example, blindness, deafness, paralysis, or loss of limb) and ignore the totality of each complex human being. Focusing on only one characteristic of a person and disregarding all others is a typical element of prejudice that leads to various behaviors that reinforce this attitude. Limitation in one area does not mean limitation in others. Some people foolishly assume, for example, that individuals with physical disabilities also have mental disabilities as well, leading them to talk to them in a condescending manner or even talk about them in their presence.

Such a social construct can lead even well-intentioned people to create other uncomfortable situations for the disabled. Whether it takes such forms as staring, continual questions, inane comments about some noteworthy disabled individual, or simply awkward silences in conversations, the result is to remind disabled people that they are "different," whether they are children or adults.[40] Sometimes, then, the *reaction* of society becomes as great a difficulty to overcome as the *actual* disability.

Before passage of the Americans with Disabilities Act, these reactions included job discrimination, institutional discrimination in the form of access to buildings and public transportation, and media portrayals of disabled as overachievers or pitiful and/or childlike objects, as well as social exclusion from all kinds of activities. Although media portrayals are still problematic (particularly with otherwise well-meaning charity telethons), significant improvements have occurred in the other areas, but progress is slow and wide gaps still remain, as we discuss in the next section.

*These wounded soldiers at the Brooke Army Medical Center in San Antonio are just a few of the many veterans of wars in Iraq and Afghanistan coming home with damaged bodies, as did veterans of previous wars. The surging increase in disabled veterans will cost the nation billions of dollars for their rehabilitation in the decades to come.*

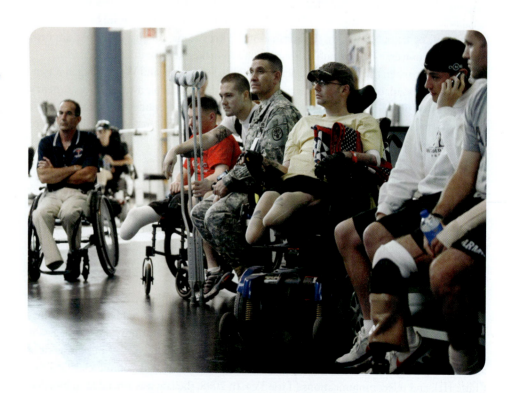

# REALITY check

## Places and Politics: A Geo-Political Profile

People with disabilities live throughout the United States, but Figure 14.4 reveals a large cluster of higher percentage states in the South and another large cluster of lower percentage states in the northern Midwest and Rocky Mountain states. Why is this? We don't know for certain, but an educated guess might consider race, age, and poverty (nutrition and birth defects).

Blacks have a higher prevalence of disability (20.3 percent) than other minorities (Asians 13.0 percent and Hispanics 13.2 percent), and they are highly concentrated in the South. Florida and West Virginia have some of the highest proportions 65 and older. Kentucky has a higher ratio of people living in poverty than the national average. In contrast, Iowa, South Dakota, and Wyoming are lower than the national average in one or more of the three variables and are approximately average in the others.

An important part of the political process is pressuring legislators to introduce and pass bills to help constituents. That not only is the story behind passage of the 1990 ADA but also is about the ongoing advocacy of organizations continually working on behalf of the disabled. Some work on behalf of military personnel, such as the Disabled American Veterans and the Paralyzed Veterans of America. Others act for specific disability causes such as the National Association of the Deaf or more broadly serve all people with disabilities, such as the National Organization on Disability.

Numerous disabled Americans have made distinctive contributions in politics. At the national level, these include former U.S. Senators Max Cleland of Georgia (lost both legs and one arm from a grenade blast in the Vietnam War); Bob Dole of Kansas, also a 1996 presidential candidate (paralyzed right arm from a World War II injury); John Porter East of North Carolina (paraplegic due to polio); Daniel Inouye of Hawaii (lost his right arm due to grenade shrapnel in World War II); and Bob Kerrey of Nebraska, also its governor (lost one leg below the knee due to combat injury in Vietnam). Currently serving in Congress are Tammy Duckworth of Illinois (lost both legs in a grenade attack in the Iraq War) and John McCain of Arizona (limited use of arms due to torture during the Vietnam War). Two former governors were David Paterson of New York (legally blind) and George Wallace of Alabama (paraplegic from a bullet wound from an assassination attempt).

Source: Matthew W. Brault, "Americans with Disabilities: 2010," *Current Population Reports,* July 2012.

## Current Issues

The most recent Kessler Foundation/National Organization on Disability national poll revealed findings consistent with five previous studies, that Americans with disabilities remain at a critical disadvantage compared to other Americans (see the Reality Check box and Figure 14.4). Among the findings were:

- Only 21 percent of working-age people with disabilities reported being employed full or part time, compared to 59 percent of those who do not have disabilities.
- More than twice as many live in poverty, with annual household incomes below $15,000 (34 percent versus 15 percent).
- People with disabilities are more likely to drop out of high school (17 percent versus 11 percent).
- They are twice as likely to have inadequate transportation (34 percent versus 16 percent), and a much higher percentage go without needed health care (19 percent versus 10 percent).

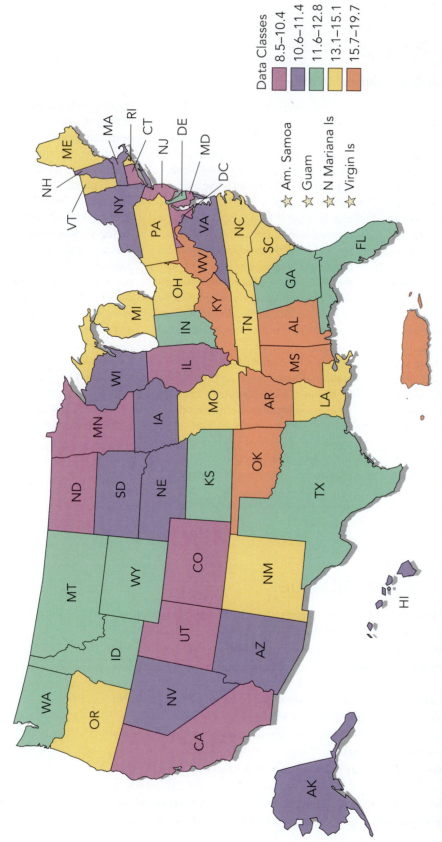

**FIGURE 14.4** Noninstitutionalized Population with any Disability, by State in percentages

Source: U.S. Census Bureau.

Data Classes
- 8.5–10.4
- 10.6–11.4
- 11.6–12.8
- 13.1–15.1
- 15.7–19.7

- ☆ Am. Samoa
- ☆ Guam
- ☆ N Mariana Is
- ☆ Virgin Is

- People with disabilities are less likely to socialize with friends, relatives, or neighbors than are their nondisabled counterparts (79 percent versus 90 percent).
- Just 54 percent of disabled adults have Internet access, compared to 85 percent of adults without disabilities.

Not surprisingly, given the persistence of these gaps, life satisfaction for people with disabilities also lags, with only 34 percent saying they are very satisfied compared to 61 percent of those without disabilities.[41]

Clearly, much remains to be done in all of these areas. Unlike the United Kingdom and other European countries with government policies that treat the disabled as automatically eligible for entitlement benefits, the United States takes a civil rights approach to advocate inclusion and equality to address these concerns. Between 1997 and 2008, the Equal Employment Opportunity Commission (EEOC) resolved nearly 5,400 complaints, resulting in more than $1.3 billion in payments to people with disabilities whose rights had been violated.[42]

Closely related to the U.S. viewpoint is the insistence of disability rights activists that they not only wish to challenge negative societal views and to promote full integration into mainstream society, but they also want the disabled to have a voice in all policy decisions that affect them. Accordingly, they make a distinction between organizations *for* the disabled (charitable organizations, parents' groups, and service providers) and self-help organizations *of* disabled people in which they can be their own advocates for independence.[43]

**STUDENTS SPEAK** *"My friend joined the Marine Corps after his high school senior year. After basic training, he went to Afghanistan. While patrolling with his squad one day, he stepped on a roadside mine. He doesn't remember anything until after they rushed him to an army medical center in Germany for intensive medical care. They ended amputating both of his legs from the knee down, and removing one kidney and testicle. The kid is now nineteen years old and has to live the rest of his life without his own legs. There are tremendous amounts of people getting hurt or killed. Even if they are not hurt, many still have PTSD."*

**—Erdem Ozeb**

## Old Age

One unique aspect about the elderly is that, assuming a normal life span, everyone eventually becomes a member of this minority group. For most readers of this book, that time is in the distant future. Until then, more immediate needs and concerns require one's attention. Even so, unlike most other minority groups, the problems of the elderly have an interconnectiveness that affects, in many ways, the lives of nongroup members. For example, the economic reality of increasing payroll deductions for social security and Medicare impact everyone's earning power. Also, many families experience severe strain over the time demands and costs of caring for aged parents. And, unless we improve the quality of life for the elderly when we have the power and influence to do so, their current situation becomes ours in old age when we no longer can be an agent for change.

## Sociohistorical Perspective

Rapid social change in industrial societies generated a shift in value orientations toward the aged. Preindustrial societies (including colonial America), rooted in tradition, usually looked to old people as the source of wisdom and experience, deferring to their judgment on any problems facing the family or community. With a large **extended family** (two or more kinship families sharing economic and social responsibilities) and with property ownership generally passed on to the oldest male (primogeniture), older people typically were the more powerful and affluent. Industrialization and technology revolutionized the existing social order, bringing about the pre-eminence of the **nuclear family**, a unit of parents and their children living apart from other relatives.

**14-7** Describe the sociological context for studying the elderly.

Land ownership no longer was the only main source of wealth. Increased mobility was possible, and one had to keep abreast constantly of new discoveries and developments to remain competitive.

Before the industrial age, the aged still worked, had clearly defined roles, were held in high esteem, and continued to make valuable contributions to the family and community. In an industrial society where work determines one's status or worth, people tend to view the aged as outmoded or obsolete, no longer productive, necessary, or important. This "Detroit Syndrome" whereby people, like cars, are assigned a limited useful life to be replaced by newer models (younger workers) is an unfortunate by-product of an industrial society coming to believe that "new" means "better." As a result, age prejudice became institutionalized in our society in laws, employment practices, advertising, media portrayals, and intergenerational interaction.[44]

Long a neglected segment of U.S. society, problems of senior citizens have drawn increased public attention in recent years. Several factors explain this heightened awareness, including demographic changes in the population composition, increased group cohesiveness, and political clout among older citizens. Senior citizens have powerful advocacy groups, such as the American Association of Retired Persons (AARP), and they have the highest voter registration and voter turnout rates of any age group, making them a voice that politicians heed.

**Watch on MySocLab**
Video: The Basics: Aging and the Elderly

*Many elderly people—especially those in their 60s and 70s— lead energetic, imaginative, and active lives, thereby giving countless daily examples to refute the false stereotypes of their so-called frailty. This 800-meter run for women age 60 and over at the Senior Olympics in San Antonio, Texas, is but one example.*

## The Graying of America

In 1900, 3 million persons (4 percent of the total population) were 65 or older; in 2012, this age group numbered 43.1 million (13 percent of the total). The number of senior citizens will continue to increase even more dramatically as the baby boomers of the late 1940s and 1950s turn 65, initiating a "senior boom" that by 2050 will be more than double, as the older population grows from to 92 million. At that point, one in five Americans (21 percent) will be 65 years or older.[45]

Every day, approximately 10,000 Americans reach the age of 65. Three-fourths of the population reaching that age live, on average, for another 17 years to age 81. Because of the increasing proportion of older citizens in our society, social scientists now utilize three subcategories for this group: those 65–74, those 75–84, and those 85 or older. In 2010, the 65–74 age group numbered approximately 21.5 million; those 75 or older totaled approximately 18.8 million. By 2030, 46 percent of the elderly will be 75 or older, with well over half this group over 80. The oldest-old, those 85 or older, will increase from 5.8 million in 2010 to approximately 8.7 million in 2030, and then double to 19 million in 2050 (see Figure 14.5 for worldwide comparisons).[46]

The importance of all these statistics is the responsibility placed on the **sandwich generation**, the elderly's adult children still providing for their own dependent children (including those in college) and simultaneously caring for aging parents who are slowly deteriorating and becoming less and less independent, particularly after age 75.

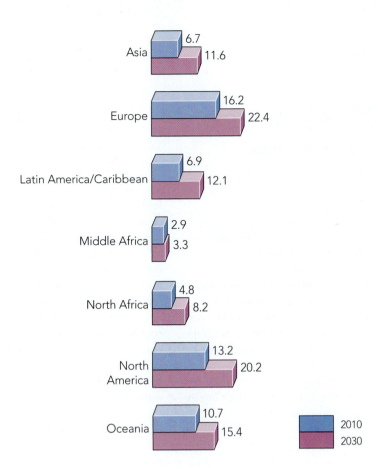

**FIGURE 14.5** Percent of the Population Age 65 and Over for Regions of the World, 2010 and 2030

Source: U.N. Population Division, *World Population Prospects: The 2010 Revision.*

## GROWING DIVERSITY OF THE OLDER POPULATION

As the older population grows larger, it also will grow more diverse, reflecting the demographic changes in the U.S. population as a whole over the last several decades. In 2010, non-Hispanic whites accounted for 80 percent of the U.S. older population, followed by blacks (8.5 percent); Hispanics, who may be any race (7 percent); and Asians (3 percent). Projections suggest that by 2030, the composition of the older population will be 72 percent non-Hispanic white, 11 percent Hispanic, 10 percent black, and 5 percent Asian (see Figure 14.6 and also the International Scene box, Tables 14.1 and 14.2 for worldwide comparisons).[47]

All these groups will experience growth in their older populations. Both Asian and Hispanic American older populations will increase fourfold by 2030. The older Asian population will grow from 1.3 million in 2010 to 3.9 million, while projections show the older Hispanic population growing from 2.9 million to 8.6 million. By 2030, the Hispanic older population will be proportionately larger than the older African American population.[48]

The geographic distribution of the U.S. elderly varies by race and ethnicity. Nearly three-fourths of all older Hispanics (1.4 million) live in only four states: California, Florida, Texas, and New York. Approximately two-thirds of all older Asians live in the western states. More than half of older blacks live in the South. More than one-third of non-Hispanic white elderly live in the South, with the remainder distributed fairly evenly throughout the rest of the country.[49]

**14-8** Analyze the problem a growing elderly population creates.

# the INTERNATIONAL scene

## Aging in Developed and Less-Developed Countries

The age structure of societies—their distribution of people into various age categories—varies according to birth and longevity rates. A higher birth rate results in smaller proportions of an elderly age cohort, but as the birth rate drops, the aged population proportion increases. In less-developed countries (excluding China), the **total fertility rate** (TFR), which is the average number of children born per woman in her lifetime, was 3.0 in 2012, compared to a TFR of 1.6 in more developed countries (see Table 14.1). As a result, individuals age 65 and older in less-developed countries in 2012 constituted 5 percent of the total population, compared to 16 percent in more developed countries. Demographers project those percentages to increase by 2030 to 10.1 percent and 22.8 percent, respectively.

Table 14.2 shows the current and projected proportions of elderly people by selected countries. In many developed countries, the proportion of the elderly citizenry will increase from one in four or five to one in three or less, further increasing the pressures and problems about their needs in relation to other groups.

Countries with greater proportions of older adults face funding problems for their social security and medical coverage because they have a smaller labor force to pay taxes or contribute to pension plans. Many European nations have sought foreign workers to meet labor shortages, creating problems in multicultural relations in what had been mostly homogeneous countries. Even so, many countries below a TFR of 2.1—the minimum rate to maintain population stability—will shrink in total population size within the next few years.

## DEMOGRAPHIC FACTORS

Two major reasons for the growing proportion of older people are the increasing life expectancy (average number of years a newborn can expect to live) and the declining birth rate. Reductions in infant mortality, improved nutrition, and advances in health care, particularly for heart disease, have increased life expectancy significantly. Boys born today can expect to live to be 76, and girls to be 81, although African Americans average three

**FIGURE 14.6** Population Age 65 and Older, by Race and Hispanic Origin, 2010, 2030, and 2050 (in percent of total population age 65 and over)

Source: U.S. Census Bureau, *The Next Four Decades: The Older Population in the United States: 2010 to 2050*, p. 7, May 2010.

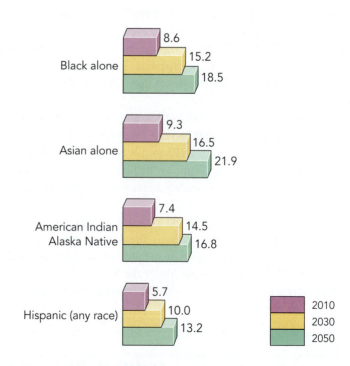

**TABLE 14.1** Total Fertility Rate in More Developed Countries, 2012

| | | | |
|---|---|---|---|
| Belgium | 1.8 | Lithuania | 1.5 |
| Bulgaria | 1.5 | Netherlands | 1.7 |
| Canada | 1.7 | Norway | 1.9 |
| Czech Republic | 1.4 | Poland | 1.3 |
| Denmark | 1.8 | Portugal | 1.3 |
| Estonia | 1.5 | Romania | 1.3 |
| Finland | 1.8 | Russia | 1.6 |
| France | 2.0 | Serbia | 1.3 |
| Germany | 1.4 | Slovakia | 1.4 |
| Greece | 1.5 | Slovenia | 1.5 |
| Hungary | 1.2 | Spain | 1.4 |
| Iceland | 2.0 | Sweden | 1.9 |
| Ireland | 2.1 | Switzerland | 1.5 |
| Italy | 1.4 | Ukraine | 1.5 |
| Japan | 1.4 | United Kingdom | 2.0 |
| Latvia | 1.1 | United States | 1.9 |

*Source:* Population Reference Bureau, *2012 World Population Data Sheet.*

years less than whites.[50] Increased life expectancy for all has emerged through the medical profession's success in reducing major causes of death for those over 55 (open-heart surgery, coronary bypass operations, kidney transplants, etc.).

Since industrialization began in the nineteenth century, the U.S. birth rate has been dropping, interrupted only in the 1940s and 1950s by the baby boom. Since 1972, we have experienced a 2.1 or lower birth rate which, if sustained for five decades, will result in zero

**TABLE 14.2** Population Age 60 and Older, 2012 and 2050 (by percent)

| COUNTRY | 2012 | 2050 | COUNTRY | 2012 | 2050 |
|---|---|---|---|---|---|
| Australia | 19.8 | 27.6 | Italy | 27.2 | 38.7 |
| Belgium | 24.0 | 31.8 | Japan | 32.3 | 42.7 |
| Canada | 21.2 | 30.7 | Mexico | 9.5 | 25.9 |
| China | 13.9 | 32.8 | Netherlands | 23.4 | 32.9 |
| Czech Republic | 23.7 | 33.2 | Norway | 21.6 | 28.1 |
| Denmark | 24.1 | 28.5 | Philippines | 6.4 | 13.7 |
| Finland | 26.3 | 31.5 | Poland | 21.1 | 36.7 |
| France | 24.1 | 31.0 | Romania | 21.0 | 36.7 |
| Germany | 27.1 | 39.6 | Russian Federation | 19.0 | 28.5 |
| Greece | 25.7 | 37.9 | Spain | 23.1 | 40.2 |
| Hungary | 23.9 | 32.7 | Sweden | 25.5 | 28.5 |
| Iceland | 18.0 | 29.8 | Switzerland | 23.4 | 30.4 |
| India | 8.3 | 18.3 | Ukraine | 21.3 | 30.8 |
| Ireland | 16.9 | 29.7 | United Kingdom | 23.2 | 30.7 |
| Israel | 15.3 | 22.5 | United States | 19.7 | 27.0 |

*Source:* UN Population Division, *World Population Prospects: The 2012 Revision*, Table S.6, pp. 23–26.

population growth, a stable population size. This means a continued rise in the median age of the population, with fewer young people and a greater proportion of older people. To illustrate, the median age rose from 22.9 in 1900 to 36.9 in 2010, and it is projected to be 38.7 by 2030.[51]

Some states—like Florida, Arizona, Nevada, New Mexico, and Hawaii—are rapidly increasing their proportion of senior citizens, who are attracted by the climate and recreational opportunities. However, fewer than 5 percent of the retired elderly move away to such locales, either because they cannot afford to do so or because they prefer to remain near family and friends. Three-fourths of Americans 65 or older actually live in metropolitan areas, many of them in metro suburbs. Senior citizens also constitute the highest proportion of small town and rural populations. Many of the snowbelt states have the greatest percentages of the nation's older and poorer senior citizens, which places even greater demand in these economically depressed areas for economic, health, and social assistance for the aged.[52]

## Values about Age

**14-9** Examine myths, stereotypes, and issues involving the elderly.

We can better understand the position of the aged in U.S. society if we examine how the social construction of reality affects the perception of old people by others, as well as their own self-perceptions. Americans are products of a youth-oriented culture in which physical attraction, productivity, sexuality, usefulness, and worth rarely are attributed to the old. So pervasive is this orientation that it has resulted in **ageism**, the manifestation of prejudice, aversion, or even hatred toward the old.[53] Like the ideologies of racism and sexism, this generalized set of beliefs abounds in negative stereotypes, ignores individual differences, and assumes the subordinate status of the aged lies in a biological rather than social explanation.

To sell their products, advertisers subtly reinforce people's uneasiness about growing older. Cosmetics, lotions, creams, baby oil, and even dishwashing liquid are marketed as products to smooth and soften skin and keep mothers looking as young as their teenage daughters. Hair coloring, cosmetics, and cosmetic surgery promise to help any who wish to defy at least the appearance of growing old. However, when we are "past our prime," other commercials alert us to the supposed preoccupations of old age: bladder control, constipation, hemorrhoids, loose dentures, and baldness.

Many of us also greatly limit our interaction with the healthy elderly, perhaps because they are living testimony to a part of the life cycle we don't want to think about. For those living alone—the 36 percent of those age 65 to 74, and the 54 percent age 75 or older—this limited interaction means isolation and loneliness are distinct possibilities.[54] No doubt this is a partial reason, in addition to physical debilitation, for the high suicide rates among the elderly. In 2010, the average suicide rate for all ages was 12.1 per 100,000, but for those age 65 to 74, it was 13.7; for those age 75 to 84, it was 15.7; and for those 85 and older, it was 17.6. Older blacks have the lowest suicide rates, while older whites have the highest, three times greater than blacks among males and four times greater among females (Figure 14.7).[55]

## Myths and Stereotypes

Closely interrelated to the prevalence of ageism in our society are the myths and stereotypes that all too commonly are believed. Because people tend to address a social problem in terms of perceptions, examining both the false and accurate portrayals of the U.S. elderly is important.

Listen on MySocLab
Audio: Older Love

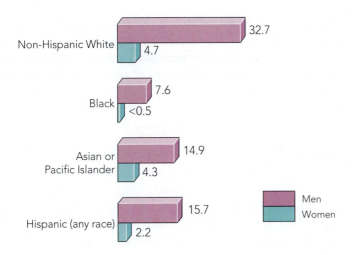

**FIGURE 14.7** Death Rates for Suicide among People Age 65 and Over, by Race and Gender, 2010 (Deaths per 100,000 population)

Note: The reference population for these data is the resident population.
*Source:* National Center for Health Statistics, 2012, Table 35.

Non-Hispanic White — 32.7 / 4.7

Black — 7.6 / <0.5

Asian or Pacific Islander — 14.9 / 4.3

Hispanic (any race) — 15.7 / 2.2

Men
Women

## MENTAL CAPACITIES

One of the most commonly held beliefs and, in large measure, the one responsible for much ageist prejudice and discrimination is that advancing age occasions a decline in one's mental faculties. Many people believe that intelligence, memory, and learning ability become less than in earlier years. "You can't teach an old dog new tricks" is the traditional folk saying. Old people often are thought of as slow-thinking or senile, incompetent, and out of touch with reality.[56] Such beliefs often result in discriminatory practices in hiring or promotions or in a reluctance to train or educate older people in new areas. Despite such popular notions, research studies—including longitudinal studies of the same persons throughout many years—show little overall decline in mental ability with age. Certain physiological changes may occur in one's outward appearance, and reflexes and responses may slow down a little, but intellectual capabilities remain constant or increase with age even into and past the seventies.[57]

The view that many seniors are senile and/or childlike is just not true. Approximately 5 percent of those over age 65 may become senile. Alzheimer's disease, which is the most progressive organic brain impairment, strikes one in five people by age 80. Still, that means the vast majority of 80-year-olds don't have the disease nor do they experience any significant mental decline. Although the average 80-year-old may receive and process information more slowly than the average 30-year-old, the differences are modest and can be offset by an older person's experience and wisdom. Furthermore, the age-linked memory decline appears limited to the storing of new information, with virtually no decline in the ability to recall, recognize, or perform things previously seen, heard, or learned. Studies also show that when the elderly are socially integrated, whatever memory loss they may experience is delayed in comparison to those who are socially isolated.[58]

However, approximately 100 treatable and reversible disorders can mimic Alzheimer-type disease, and, tragically,

*Contrary to the common ageist assumption that most old people experience an overall decline in mental ability, most do not. In fact, many countries have benefited from the leadership of their elderly statesmen, such as the world's oldest, Shimon Peres, born in 1923, and the only former prime minister to be elected as President of Israel.*

many of these are attributed to old age and are neglected. Also, what passes for senile behavior actually can result from misuse or overuse of prescription drugs or even vitamin deficiencies because old people may react quite differently than young people to certain drugs. The reality is that more than 80 percent of the elderly do not experience any significant mental impairment.

### SEXUALITY

Another misconception about older people is that they are sexually inactive because of a lack of interest and/or ability. Considering our youth-oriented society, it is not surprising that people mistakenly view the aged as asexual. Supposedly, romance is for the young, sexual attraction means good-looking bodies, and sex is a young person's "thing." Old people should "act their age"; if they don't, they're "dirty old men" or "horny old women." All forms of media reinforce this thinking through emphasis on young people in love. Older people, either because of their more conservative sexual values or societal disapproval, tend to avoid public displays of sexual interest in another person.

Research findings, however, present a different reality about sexual interest and capacity among old people. In the most comprehensive sex survey ever done among 57- to 85-year-olds, involving more than 3,000 face-to-face, two-hour interviews, as well as taking samples to measure hormone levels, researchers found that many older people indeed are sexually active, that elder sex is a reality for many seniors. In the previous year, 73 percent of those ages 57 to 64 reported sex with a partner, as did 53 percent of those ages 64 to 75, and 26 percent of people ages 75 to 85. Of those who were active, most said they did it two or three times a month.[59] Availability of a partner is a major factor, however, so those living alone are far less likely to engage in sexual activity than those living with someone.[60]

Sexuality among the aged is more a matter of attitude than of physiology. Societal values affect individual attitudes, though, and numerous social critics maintain that a double standard of aging exists. Society allows men to age more gracefully than women, for whom the calendar suggests when they become "sexually disqualified."[61] Although both men and women may suffer lowered self-esteem if their sexual function physiologically begins to fail, society tends to assume increased aging in women *must* be accompanied by diminished sexual capacity, and this societal perception in turn tends to diminish the older woman's sense of self-worth. Because the older man's sexual capacity is not necessarily expected to diminish, it is easier for him to maintain a higher level of self-esteem.

## Current Issues

The elderly are by no means a homogeneous group. They vary greatly among themselves in educational levels, income, living arrangements, health, and quality of life. Three areas of concern to all members of this diverse group, however, are age discrimination, economic security, and health care.

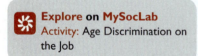

Explore on MySocLab
Activity: Age Discrimination on the Job

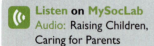

Listen on MySocLab
Audio: Raising Children, Caring for Parents

### AGE DISCRIMINATION

Even before retirement age, older workers often are victims of job discrimination. Companies prefer to hire people under 40, and unemployed workers above that age may encounter great difficulty finding new jobs. The 1967 Age Discrimination in Employment Act (ADEA) was intended to protect workers age 40 to 65, making it illegal to advertise positions with age restrictions or to deny employment for reasons of age. In practice, however, employers easily can circumvent the law by stating older workers are "over qualified" because of their extensive experience or "under qualified" because of their educational background. This legislation also protected older workers from being fired as a cost-saving practice in order to hire younger workers at lower salaries. In 1996, the Supreme Court reduced the burden of legal proof, ruling that a claimant need not prove replacement by someone under 40 years of age. However, a 2009 Supreme Court ruling changed the standard and increased the burden of proof an older worker must meet to prove an employer violated the ADEA.

Prior to passage of the ADEA legislation, discrimination against older workers in hiring, training, promotions, and other areas was common, and experts fear a return to those times, given the most recent court action.[62] Meanwhile, the number of older workers in the workforce has increased steadily, in fact doubling between 1977 and 2007, and then jumping 27 percent in the next five years.[63] This seeming contradiction is because many senior workers have delayed retirement. Age discrimination continues nonetheless, although exact statistics are difficult to obtain. Analysts identify its continued existence through the longer period of time that it takes for older men and women to find employment, the lower income many receive on reemployment, and the size of court awards to age discrimination victims.[64]

Another area of past age discrimination was mandatory retirement at age 65, which was the norm in U.S. society until 1978, when Congress raised the age limit to 70. In 1986, with passage of the Age Discrimination Act, Congress abolished mandatory retirement altogether in most occupations. Among the exceptions were police and fire-fighters, airline pilots, and air traffic controllers.

Even though mandatory retirement no longer is permitted in business, companies often force their older workers to retire by other means. They do so because of assumptions that older workers are less productive and more costly to retrain, more accident prone, and more likely to be absent for health reasons. Also, older workers earn higher salaries and affect coverage costs for company healthcare plans. Older workers indeed may cost companies more money in salaries and healthcare plans, but otherwise their value is significant. They offer experience and insights younger workers lack, actually have lower absenteeism, greater job loyalty, a more positive job attitude than younger workers, and can relate well to older customers.[65]

As a cost-cutting device on both salaries and retirement plans, companies often terminate employees before they reach retirement age by eliminating positions through layoffs, restructuring, or other means. Because the courts previously upheld an employer's right to lay off older workers for economic reasons, abuses of this tactic with the subsequent hiring of younger, cheaper workers have not been unusual. However, in 2008, the U.S. Supreme Court ruled in favor of older workers in an age discrimination case. Previously, workers had to prove age discrimination, but the Court placed the burden on employers to prove a layoff or other action that hurts older workers more than others was based not on age but on some other reasonable factor, a decision hailed by AARP as helping create a workplace that is fair and free of age bias.[66]

Another employer approach is to offer bonus pension incentives or attractive early retirement programs to older workers so that either younger workers can be brought in or the company can downsize. Such incentives are effective; typically, one-third of all workers age 55 to 64 take early retirement.[67]

## ECONOMIC SECURITY

Generally, the economic picture for the U.S. elderly has improved significantly. During the 1960s and 1970s, they had the highest poverty rate of all age groups. In 1959, for example, 35.2 percent of older people lived in poverty; in 1966, their poverty rate had decreased to 28.5 percent, still an unusually high percentage. Since then, various government programs designed to ease the financial burdens of the older population have led to a downward trend, with minor fluctuations, so that the poverty rate for those 65 and older in 2011 was 8.7 percent, lower than for any other age group.[68]

Another economic indicator is **net worth**, the difference between assets and liabilities that a person or household has at any given time. In 2010, the median net worth of all U.S. households was $77,300 and that of households with householders age 65–74 was $216,800. Home equity often represented a major portion of that net worth.[69]

Such statistics can be misleading, however. Many older Americans squeak by on fixed incomes just to meet normal living expenses. One-third of them entirely depend on Social Security benefits, while another third rely on Social Security for anywhere from 50 to 89 percent of their income. Constituting 12.6 percent of the population, Americans 65 or older receive 51 percent of all government expenditures for social services, from education to pensions. And, without Social Security and its cost-of-living increases, another 48 percent, or 17 million elderly, would fall below the poverty line.[70]

Although 1 in 11 people over age 65 live in poverty, women and minorities are heavily overrepresented. Among all races, 10.7 percent of older women were in poverty in 2011, compared to 6.2 percent of older men. Elderly poverty rates in 2011 also varied by race and Hispanic origin, with whites living in poverty at 7.8 percent, blacks at 18.9 percent, and Hispanics at 19.4 percent.[71] Differences in poverty rates become pronounced even more when factoring in living arrangements. As Figure 14.8 shows, older householders living alone are at greater risk of living in poverty, women far more so than men, and minorities at least twice as likely as non-Hispanic whites.

More than 11.8 million older Americans live alone, 71 percent of them women. This is not surprising for, as age increases, so does widowhood, with women living longer than men. However, an important cultural factor comes into play, as older Asian, black, and Hispanic women are far more likely than older, non-Hispanic white women to live

**FIGURE 14.8** Percent of People Age 65 and Over in Poverty, by Living Arrangement, Race, and Hispanic Origin, 2011[1]

*Source:* U.S. Census Bureau, 2012, Table POV2. Note: The reference population for these data is the civilian noninstitutionalized population.

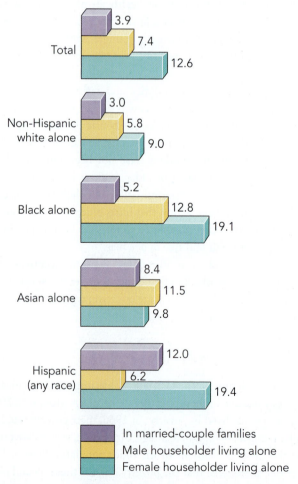

Total
3.9
7.4
12.6

Non-Hispanic white alone
3.0
5.8
9.0

Black alone
5.2
12.8
19.1

Asian alone
8.4
11.5
9.8

Hispanic (any race)
12.0
6.2
19.4

■ In married-couple families
■ Male householder living alone
■ Female householder living alone

[1]Does not include people living with other relatives and nonrelatives.

with relatives. This pattern also holds true among immigrant families.[72] Although the potential for social isolation certainly exists, government studies reveal that approximately 29 percent of those 65 and older living alone are in good health and live close to family with whom they have frequent contact. The paradox is that, although older, unmarried people living alone (most of them widowed) generally are in better health than those who do not live alone, they also are more likely to live in poverty than those who live with their spouses.[73]

Concentrated primarily in the north central and southern regions, the rural elderly (nearly 30 percent of the total elderly population) experience perhaps the greatest deprivation.[74] Many lack health services and live in older substandard, poorly insulated, poorly heated dwellings. Because of low population density, the rural elderly also tend to live isolated, lonely, and limited lives.

Thirty-six percent of Americans age 65 and older live in cities.[75] For the urban elderly, urban life often is a combination of insecurity, fear of crime, and subsistence. For the suburban elderly, housing problems usually center on meeting rising property taxes, fire insurance rates, and maintenance costs, as well as getting around because many do not drive and public transportation is quite limited in the suburbs.

## HEALTH CARE

A primary concern of the elderly is health care because they experience greater health problems than other age groups. Most people age 65 to 74 are healthy, active, and have a positive self-image, but serious physical decline and illness becomes a greater reality from age 75 onward. Illustrative of this point is the fact that only approximately 10 of 1,000 of those age 65 to 74 are in nursing homes, compared to approximately 140 of 1,000 of those age 85 and older.[76]

In the area of health care, of greatest concern to older persons is access and cost. Although they constitute approximately 13 percent of the total U.S. population, the elderly represent one-third of the hospital population and use one-fourth of the prescribed drugs. Their medical expenses are three times greater than those of middle-aged adults and six times greater than for young adults, yet the income of the elderly usually is far less than that of young and middle-aged adults. Obamacare, Medicare, Medicaid, and prescription drug programs have greatly reduced the personal health costs to the elderly, but, because they do not cover all expenses, the elderly average twice the personal health costs of those under 65.[77]

With increased age, older people also become less mobile, driving themselves less because of high automobile costs, including insurance, fuel, and maintenance, as well as the infirmities of old age. Many therefore become more dependent on others to travel to clinics, doctor's offices, and hospitals. Many physicians tend to take less interest in treating elderly patients because of ageist biases, their preference for specialization instead of primary care, and, among many, their lack of preparation in geriatrics. Although geriatric medicine programs exist at most U.S. medical schools and osteopathic schools for future practitioners, this remarkable growth during the past three decades still is not enough to provide the projected needed numbers of geriatricians.[78]

The AARP is a powerful special interest group with considerable political clout. It directs its lobbying efforts toward quality of life issues, including financial security and health care. It also helps organize protest demonstrations, such as this rally against Michigan Governor Rick Snyder's plan to tax pensions and use the revenue generated for a corporate tax cut.

# the ETHNIC experience

## Isolation and Loneliness

"I grew up in India. There were a total of 14 in our family and the days were constantly filled with noise, sometimes laughter and sometimes not, but always with love and family connections. Now, I live alone, in a silent room unless I turn on the television. If I didn't go each day to the mall nearby to sit and talk with others like me, I would have sealed lips, no one to talk to."

"After my wife died, I came to the United States to live with my son and his family. I spent most of my time with my grandchildren. I would pick them up after school and take them to soccer practice and other things. Then my son and daughter-in-law told me they wanted more privacy. I decided that I should respect their wishes and so I moved out, even though I really didn't want to."

"I now live in a rented room in a house that I found on Craig's List. I'm 76 now and bothered by arthritis.

I still see my son and grandchildren from time to time, but otherwise each day and night can be terribly lonely. Back in India, this would never happen. Family members take care of the old ones. But my family is here and in America, where people concern themselves with what is convenient for them, not what is inconvenient for others."

Source: Recorded commentary from the collection of Vincent N. Parrillo.

**STUDENTS SPEAK** "The thing that interested me the most about this chapter was the poverty rate for elderly people, especially Latinos and African Americans. With the track we are on now, Social Security may be gone before this generation is able to retire. This is a huge problem because many elderly people rely on it to survive. If there is no Social Security, the rates of poverty for older people will skyrocket, creating many problems. It will be interesting how this all pans out over the next couple of decades."

—**Daniel Penett**

## IMMIGRANT ELDERLY

One of America's fastest-growing immigrant groups are the elderly. Between 1990 and 2010, the nation's foreign-born people over 65 almost doubled, from 2.7 million to nearly 5 million, and demographers predict their numbers will exceed 10 million by 2050. In California, 27 percent of all seniors are foreign born.[79]

Sociologists call immigrant elders who come to the United States the "**.5 generation**" in contrast to the **1.5 generation**, who are under 10 years old when they arrive and easily become acculturated through school, the media, and social interactions. The immigrant elderly particularly are vulnerable, as they are reliant on their families who may be unwilling to care for them as commonly done in their homeland (see the Ethnic Experience box). In 2009, approximately 19 percent of immigrant seniors lived below the poverty line, compared to 14 percent of native-born elderly.[80]

Approximately 70 percent speak little or no English and are at an age when the language barrier is difficult to overcome. Because most do not drive, have only a limited social network, and experience a disconnect from American values and culture, social isolation and depression are unintended consequences of their migration.[81]

## Sociological Analysis

**14-10** Discuss insights gained through sociological analysis.

Instead of simply examining the statistics and data about homosexuals, the disabled, and the aged and the problems they face, social scientists attempt to formulate a theoretical framework in which to understand the causes and possible solutions to the social situation. Our three theoretical viewpoints once again offer different approaches to these insights.

## THE FUNCTIONALIST VIEW

For centuries, most societies placed sexuality primarily within the context of marriage and so viewed some form of social control of sexuality as necessary for preservation of the family and for a stable society. Consequently, traditional family values, religious teachings, and cultural norms all emphasized heterosexuality as "correct," and homosexuality as "deviant." Deviation was not socially acceptable. Instead, it was seen as a symptom of social disorganization and the breakdown of society's institutions, resulting in the stigmatization and social ostracism of gays and the implementation of many forms of discrimination. Society currently is in the midst of social change, with government policies, laws, and activists promoting equal rights for all, regardless of sexual orientation. Because traditionalists consider some of these areas—such as same-sex marriage and gay parenting—as dysfunctional to the family and a violation of social mores, they condemn such alternate lifestyles and strive to stop them, even as some states adopt more inclusive laws.

Similarly, activism for disability rights means fighting entrenched attitudes and behaviors. However, these patterns are not wrapped in moral values and so change is not as contentious an issue, although critics do maintain disability criteria and access stipulations "go too far." On the other hand, efforts to integrate the disabled into society to participate fully is seen as a functional approach, whether it be doorway and elevator access, curb ramps, traffic lights with sound signals, or other access amenities.

Demographic social changes have created social disorganization and dysfunctions in society concerning the elderly. The lower birth rate and longer life span have resulted in a greater proportion of older people than ever before, but they have fewer functions to perform in an industrial society. Gone are their respected roles as senior members of the extended family, and as discussed earlier, societal attitudes and social policy have built in an obsolescence to their occupational roles. Within this context, we may consider two major conflicting middle-range theories in social gerontology: activity and disengagement.

**ACTIVITY THEORY.** The dominant theoretical perspective known as **activity theory** holds that people of all ages require adequate levels of social activity to remain well adjusted. In the 1940s the writings of Ernest Burgess, one of the first social gerontologists,

*Because Americans live longer but may not be able to handle the daily routines of food shopping, cooking, cleaning, and washing, assisted living facilities have been one answer. They also offer many activities and programs to meet people's interests and abilities, such as this Wii bowling team competition at a facility in Hopkinsville, Kentucky.*

explained that a lack of social functions needlessly excluded the aged from socially mean-ingful activity, resulting in their having a "roleless role." Activity theorists maintain that if new activities replace those an aging individual is forced to give up, that person more likely is to be better adjusted mentally, physically, and socially. However, the new activi-ties need not be at the same level of action as in middle age to maintain the same high degree of life satisfaction, as studies show that older Americans do prefer a somewhat more relaxed lifestyle.[82]

**DISENGAGEMENT THEORY.** In contrast, this school of thought argues that the usual and even inevitable pattern is for people to become more passive and decrease their activity as they reach old age. To maintain optimal functioning, a modern society requires persons with new skills and energy. So a mutual withdrawal occurs, its time and form dependent on the individual. Social interaction and social ties weaken as society seeks out "new blood" and aging individuals recognize their own diminishing capacity and seek escape from the stress of daily life encounters.

Heavily criticized, **disengagement theory** stimulated much research, some of which supports the theory whereas most does not. Some aged do disengage, but stud-ies demonstrate that disengagement is not inevitable with old age.[83] Society more likely is to withdraw roles from the aged than they themselves are likely to relinquish them. Disengagement, in other words, is not what the majority of older people want, but it is what they get.[84]

## THE CONFLICT VIEW

Conflict theorists focus on gays, the disabled, and elderly as disadvantaged minority groups suffering at the hands of the rest of society. Whether treated with hostility or indifference, members of all three groups—once extensively denied fair treatment and equal opportunity—still struggle to gain full acceptance despite the significant progress achieved by each group.

For gays and lesbians, the struggle—through the gay rights movement and advo-cacy groups—includes challenges to laws about same-sex marriage, benefits to same-sex couples, and gay adoptions and parenting. For the disabled, the struggle includes the right to work without loss of benefit and wider access to all buildings and activities. For older Americans, the struggle includes elimination of the remnants of age discrimination and greater economic security.

In the struggle for more resources and wider acceptance, conflict is inevitable. Organized social movements challenge the status quo to correct the inequality. For more than a quarter of a century, these groups have formed organizations, hired lobbyists, and used their political clout to pressure elected officials. Their heightened group conscious-ness and cohesiveness influenced the passage of laws to protect their interests and advance their causes. In turn, their actions sparked backlashes from various quarters, depending on the group and its goals. Religious advocates challenge the morality of homosexuality, determined not to allow any form of official recognition of this minority group's demands. Numerous local public officials, business leaders, and organizations claim the Americans with Disabilities Act is being interpreted too broadly, creating extensive expenses for compliance in building and program access. Younger workers chafe under the sizable payroll deductions for Social Security and Medicare for retired workers and wonder if such programs will even be available for them when they themselves retire.

## THE INTERACTIONIST VIEW

Social scientists draw heavily on the idea of socially determined **sexual scripts** for explain-ing both heterosexual and homosexual development.[85] Because our sexual urges find expression in socially determined ways, whether heterosexual or homosexual, the process by which one choice becomes "normal" and the other "deviant" can be more readily understood through **labeling theory**, which explains how conformity and deviance result from the responses of others.

If, for example, a person who is a conformist in the rest of his or her life commits a random and isolated homosexual act that becomes known and the person thus is labeled as a homosexual, a process may begin that changes the original deviance from primary deviance to secondary deviance, a persistent pattern of behavior that leads to deviant status and eventually membership in a deviant subculture with its own norms and patterns.[86] Often, stigmatized individuals reject the negative views others hold of them, create a new in-group ethic that affirms their worth as equal members of society, and hence reject accommodative strategies of stigma management.

The positive aspects of homosexual identity often are found in the group's most prestigious publications. A content analysis of articles and stories published in the *Ladder*, a well-known lesbian publication, shows a change from secondary to tertiary deviance. For example, during its early years, the *Ladder* advocated an accommodative stance. Lesbians were urged to fit in as well as possible, to conceal any outward differences between themselves and straight women. The change to tertiary deviance began when the *Ladder* changed from a lesbian periodical to a feminist magazine openly supportive of lesbians. Increasingly, lesbianism was defined as a choice made by women in response to a sexist society. It was defined as a sensible choice, and a radical political statement, not a deviation for which a person was labeled and rejected.

People learn social behavior in interactions with other people and through these interactions they form self-concepts about being gay, disabled, or old. For generations, Western society stigmatized gays, pitied the disabled, and dismissed the old. Members of each of these groups increasingly depended on external cues because of diminished ego strength, uncertain identity, lack of role models, and specific norms. Told they were deviant, incompetent, or obsolete, they internalized these negative societal attitudes and adopted the role assigned to them. In this role, they learned new appropriate behaviors and skills, which undermined their sense of self-worth and self-confidence. This negative cycle of events then intensified as they became even more susceptible to feelings of uselessness, which society or even other family members helped reinforce.

In other words, the societal definition of the situation results in the social reconstruction of reality, causing negative changes in the individual's self-concept. To break this cycle of events, intervention needs to focus on changing societal attitudes, especially in terms of work determining personal worth. Another possibility is helping these minority group members develop greater self-confidence and coping mechanisms through their own self-determination.

# Retrospect

Homosexuality existed in ancient civilizations without sanctions and was institutionalized among ancient Greeks and Asians as a natural expression of sexual instinct. During the Middle Ages and Renaissance, European society viewed homosexuality and heterosexual sodomy as sinful and criminal, with the guilty often executed. Twentieth-century social scientists changed from viewing homosexuality as a mental illness and social problem to emphasizing instead the discrimination against homosexuals as the problem.

A 1994 U.S. study identified 3 percent of males and 1 percent of females as active homosexuals. A 2012 study found higher percentages of young people of color self-identified as part of the LGBT community. Although the public has grown more tolerant toward sexual orientation than in the past, and although antidiscrimination laws now exist, Americans remain divided on the morality of homosexuality, which in turn affects their attitudes about same-sex marriage and gay parenting.

Approximately one in five Americans reports some disability and approximately 31 million have a condition that limits their daily physical activities. The Americans with Disabilities Act has provisions requiring their inclusion in public activities and easier access to buildings. Its underpinning motivation is to focus on what the disabled *can* do, instead of what they cannot do. Too often, society reacts to the disabled as one-dimensional, focusing only on the limitation and not on the many other capabilities of each human being. Despite recent gains, national surveys continue to show disabled persons at a critical disadvantage to other Americans in virtually every aspect of life.

Most people eventually become part of the elderly minority group. More developed countries, including the United States, have low birth rates, and their elderly populations are growing in proportion to the rest of their populations. Despite significant gains in economic security for the U.S. elderly, problems still remain in this area, particularly for racial and ethnic minorities. False stereotypes about ability, mental capacity, and sexuality are all factors in the still-continuing age discrimination many elderly face. Healthcare and medical expenses—despite Medicare, Medicaid, and prescription drug programs—remain a major concern for many.

Various theoretical approaches are valuable for analyzing the minority-group status of homosexuals, the disabled, and the aged. The functionalist viewpoint offers helpful insights, particularly through utilization of activity or disengagement theory. Issues of exploitation, organized social movements, and intergroup tensions are best examined through conflict theory. The interactionists' employment of labeling theory furthers our understanding of the challenges faced by all three groups.

# On MySocLab

 Study and Review on MySocLab

## KEY TERMS

## DISCUSSION QUESTIONS

1. How do members of groups categorized as gay or lesbian, disabled, or elderly fit the sociological concept of the stranger as a social phenomenon?

2. What dominant and minority response patterns, discussed in Chapter 4, can offer some sociological insights into the experiences of gays, the disabled, and the aged in comparison to the other groups we studied?

3. How do conflicting values about equality and morality impact the issue of homosexuality?

4. On the subject of the disabled, what are the differences between entitlement programs and civil rights issues, and how might they differently affect societal attitudes?

5. What are the stereotypes about older Americans, and why do they persist?

6. If age discrimination is illegal, why does it continue?

7. What theoretical perspective do you find most helpful for analyzing the experiences of each group in this chapter? Is it the same one or different ones? Why?

# INTERNET ACTIVITIES

1. A personal essay, "Homophobia: The Fear Behind the Hatred" (http://www.bidstrup.com/phobia.htm), offers the gay perspective. Do you think the author makes a good case for the rights of this minority group?

2. A one-minute conservative commercial on YouTube called "The Gathering Storm" (http://www.youtube.com/watch?v=Wp76ly2_NoI) presents "homosexuality as a threat second only to terrorism." Take a look. What is your reaction?

3. The U.S. Census Bureau maintains a Disability Data Site (http://www.census.gov/people/disability). Each link takes you to various links for you to explore.

4. The National Council on Aging (http://www.ncoa.org) is an advocacy group promoting the dignity, self-determination, and well-being of older persons. At this site, you will find many dozens of links on how they go about doing so.

# The Ever-Changing U.S. Mosaic

# 15

Listen to Chapter 15 on MySocLab

The faces of America are of different colors and hues. They are of different cultural backgrounds and religions. Some have lived in the United States for generations and others were born elsewhere. Some speak only English and others are trying to learn the language. Together though, they constitute just one group: Americans (e pluribus unum).

## LEARNING OBJECTIVES | After reading this chapter you will be able to:

**15-1** Explain how one's homeland affects ethnic consciousness.

**15-2** Contrast multi-generational varieties in self-identity.

**15-3** Examine transnationalism and social capital as factors in societal integration.

**15-4** Explain how segmented assimilation reveals differences within groups.

**15-5** Analyze differences in naturalization rates among immigrants.

**15-6** Explain how symbolic ethnicity preserves one's heritage.

**15-7** Examine fears and realities regarding all forms of immigration today.

**15-8** Examine fears and realities about language usage and multiculturalism today.

**15-9** Examine what social indicators tell us about change in population diversity.

**15-10** Evaluate projections about U.S. society in 2060.

As a nation of immigrants, the United States has seen many different groups of strangers arrive and interact with its people. The strangers perceived a different world that the native population took for granted, and their reactions ranged from wonder to bewilderment to dismay, from fulfilled expectations to culture shock. Because their language, appearance, and cultural background often made them conspicuous, the newcomers were categorically identified and judged as a group rather than as individuals. Native-born U.S. residents' responses ranged from receptive to impatient and intolerant, while their actions ranged from indifferent to helpful to exploitative.

Throughout the nation's history, then, varied patterns of majority–minority relations existed. Ethnocentric values prompted the natural development of ingroup loyalty and outgroup hostility among both indigenous and migrant groups. Competition for scarce resources, colonialism, and political dominance by the Anglo-Saxon core groups also provided a basis for conflict. However, the resulting prejudicial attitudes and discriminatory actions varied greatly in intensity. In addition, changes in attitudes and social and economic conditions in this country throughout the years affected the newcomers' experiences.

Not all groups came for the same reasons or from the same backgrounds. Because of variations in social class, education, and occupational skills, not all immigrants began at the bottom of the socioeconomic ladder. Some came as sojourners, intending to stay only long enough to earn enough money for a better life back in their homeland. Some came with the desire to become U.S. citizens in every sense of the word; others insisted on retaining their own culture.

Prevailing attitudes about immigration, minority adaptation, pluralism, and assimilation greatly influence dominant–minority relations. For example, if assimilation is held to be the "proper" goal, then evidence of pluralism probably will draw negative reactions, even though pluralism is a normal manifestation among first- and second-generation Americans. In recent years, the growing presence in U.S. cities and suburbs of Spanish-speaking peoples and of people of color from non-Western cultures has led many other U.S. residents to question the country's immigration policies. Although race and economics undoubtedly are influencing factors, genuine concerns about widespread pluralism overwhelming the "melting-pot" capabilities of the United States is another important influence.

Stir in words such as *affirmative action, illegal aliens,* and *multiculturalism,* and the debate often reaches "white heat" temperatures (the double meaning of that adjective is deliberate). These aspects of intergroup relations suggest that the majority group and the dominant culture may feel seriously threatened. In some parts of the country, the level of intolerance for any manifestation of pluralism has risen to alarming proportions.

How important is ethnicity today? Are immigration and assimilation concerns justified? What is the future of race and ethnicity in the United States? In this chapter, we attempt to answer these questions as we examine concepts of ethnic consciousness; evolutionary changes in ethnicity; and issues of legal and illegal immigration, bilingual education, and multiculturalism.

## Ethnic Consciousness

**15-1** Explain how one's homeland affects ethnic consciousness.

Sociologists have long been interested in the attitudinal and behavioral patterns that emerge when people migrate into a society with a different culture. For example, what factors encourage or discourage ethnic self-awareness or culture preservation? If succeeding generations supposedly identify less with their country of origin, how do we explain the resurgence of ethnic consciousness among multi-generational Americans in recent years? Are there ethnic differences in social mobility, social change, and behavior patterns even among third- or fourth-generation U.S. citizens? Sociologists frequently raise these questions and offer a number of sociological explanations in an effort to describe scientifically the diversity of ethnic experience.

## COUNTRY OF ORIGIN AS A FACTOR

Immigrants arrive with cultural baggage as well as with their packed belongings. In adjusting to a new life in a new land, those distinguishing aspects of their ethnic identity (customs, language, values, and practices) are the everyday underpinnings of their ethnic consciousness. Once interacting with similar others in the old country, they quickly develop an awareness of how different they now are from the mainstream group and so they find comfort in interacting with fellow ethnics. The continuing vibrancy of that ethnicity depends partly on conditions in the receiving country, such as size of the ethnic community, the arrival of new immigrants, and the assimilation process.

Another powerful element in the maintenance of ethnic consciousness is homeland influence. For some, the memories and emotional ties to one's native land are too strong, and homesickness and yearnings prompt a permanent return. For others, frequent contact with family and friends back home, and/or events occurring there that make the news, and/or an ongoing inflow in fellow nationals migrating, all ease the transition to a new life while also keeping strong one's ethnic identity. In contrast, a lessening of migration and interaction gradually will reduce ethnic consciousness.

To illustrate, in the early twentieth century, the United States experienced, as we discussed in Chapter 6, such an enormous influx of immigrants that ethnicity was the norm in our cities, with first- and second-generation Americans often outnumbering native-born Americans of other backgrounds. Immigration restrictions in the 1920s sharply curtailed the number of new immigrants, leaving homeland contact primarily by letter, which took a few days once airmail delivery became a reality. The resulting limited contact and physical distance created a barrier that gradually reduced ethnic identification and aided the assimilation process, as fewer newcomers arrived to reinforce the language and customs of the old country.

In today's world, however, an immigrant group can maintain instant and continuous contact with the country of origin through telecommunications, rapid transportation, and the continued arrival of newcomers. Mexican and Caribbean immigrant communities,

Immigrants leave their native lands and put down roots in their adopted country, but the homeland connection remains strong, especially in times of political unrest and disasters affecting friends and families back there. The 2010 earthquake that struck the Haitian capital, Port-au-Prince, touched all hearts but none more than the Haitian Americans.

for example, benefit from geographic proximity. With instant communications, a stronger connection to the homeland remains than in years past, and where greater social contact occurs, cultural influence is also greater.

Such contact with one's country of origin also affects politics. In an analysis of the political activities of Asian Americans, three general and overlapping phases of acculturation were identified in their political activities. These were (1) the *alien phase,* when the political locus remains with the country of origin; (2) the *reactionary phase,* when they form political organizations to protect their interests and fight discrimination; and (3) the *acceptance phase,* when they display a greater degree of cultural and structural assimilation.[1] In other words, the homeland influence among Asian Americans initially affected their U.S. political noninvolvement until the acculturation process firmly took root.

Similarly, the political activities of immigrants from the Dominican Republic, Haiti, and El Salvador also manifest that first phase. Their involvement varies though, depending on the government structure and political parties in the country of origin. Affecting the immigrants' political orientation to the homeland is the home country's need for a steady flow of remittances, ethnic organizations in the host country, and competitive politics in democratic regimes.[2]

An immigrant community whose country of origin has a stable or gradually changing culture is more likely to promote retention of that ethnic culture. If that culture holds pro-education values—such as Armenian, Chinese, Greek, Japanese, and Vietnamese—then ethnic retention is a reliable predictor of higher academic achievement.[3] In turn, educational achievement appears to influence both ethnic identity and assimilation. A longitudinal study of the children of Latin American and Caribbean immigrants found that educated adults identify both with the United States and with their country of origin.[4]

In contrast, an immigrant community whose country of origin has experienced drastic changes in a short period of time may either change as well or, if the changes are unwelcome, seek to preserve the old traditions and a fantasy of the homeland. The former can be illustrated by the Chaldean immigrants from Iraq who settled in Detroit both before and after World War II. Afterward, Iraq evolved from a colonial land of different tribes into a modern nation-state. More recent immigrants, with more education and experience with urban settings and bureaucracies, were more likely to interact with members of other groups, making them a more assimilable group than the earlier arrivals.[5] Examples of communities ignoring change and constructing an imagined ethnic reality unlike the homeland would be some of today's German and Iranian enclaves.[6]

## THE THREE-GENERATION HYPOTHESIS

15-2 Contrast multi-generational varieties in self-identity.

Pulitzer Prize winner and historian Marcus Hansen conceptualized a normal pattern of ethnic revival in what he called the "Law of the Return of the Third Generation."[7] The third generation, more secure in its U.S. identity and socioeconomic status through **intergenerational mobility**, becomes interested in the ethnic heritage that the second generation neglected in its efforts to overcome discrimination and marginality. Simply stated, "What the child wishes to forget, the grandchild wishes to remember." Hansen, who based his conclusions mainly on midwestern Swedish Americans, reaffirmed his position several years later:

> Whenever any immigrant group reaches the third-generation stage in its development, a spontaneous and almost irresistible impulse arises, which forces the thoughts of many people of different professions, different positions in life, and different points of view to interest themselves in that one factor which they have in common: heritage—the heritage of blood.[8]

Hansen suggested a pattern in the fall and rise of ethnic identity in succeeding generations of Americans. His hypothesis generated extensive discussion in the academic community, resulting in studies and commentaries that both supported and criticized his views.

**Hansen's law** assumes that the second generation perceives its ethnicity as a disadvantage in being accepted in U.S. society. However, not all second-generation Americans respond that way. Hansen's law may be flawed as a precise predictor of generational differences within specific ethnic groups, but his basic insight remains valid. Assimilation is not simply a linear progression but instead a process that moves back and forth across the generations. Moreover, assimilation is not irreversible. Subsequent generations, even those who are the product of intermarriages, may emphasize their ethnic identity and learn the language of their cultural heritage[9]

Just as earlier research found lower levels of attitudinal ethnicity throughout several generations of European Americans, newer studies of more recently arrived groups also find a similar decline in ethnicity among second-generation Asian and Hispanic Americans as they seek to assimilate. Among Hispanic college students, the greater their cultural assimilation, the less prominent becomes their Hispanic self-identity; the acculturation process functioned as a trade-off between traditional Latino tendencies and mainstream Anglo-American practices.[10] Similarly, immigrant children from south Florida and southern California who adopt the "Hispanic" label are the least well assimilated; these children had poorer English skills, lower self-esteem, and higher rates of poverty than those who identified themselves as Americans or as hyphenated Americans.[11]

Among Asian Americans, studies reveal that second-generation Chinese, Japanese, and Korean Americans usually recognize a sense of a shared Asian American values in their socialization regarding education, family, hard work, and respect for elders. In this instance, an acknowledgment exists about some commonalities despite awareness of cultural differences among the various Asian groups.[12]

Although most Asian and Hispanic Americans are too recently part of U.S. society to apply the three-generation hypothesis, the experience of Japanese Americans—among whom many are third-, fourth-, and even fifth-generation Americans—may offer an insight. With above-average educational, occupational, and income levels, as well as high intermarriage rates, they arguably are the most assimilated of all Asian Americans. Still, they retain symbolic vestiges of their heritage and cling to the aforementioned values as part of their sense of self and group identity.[13] Perhaps a similar future awaits our newest groups, although their racial experiences may mediate their identity formation.

Another dimension in examining both intergenerational assimilation and mobility lies in a fairly new social science concept, the **1.5 generation**, which refers to immigrants who arrive under the age of ten.[14] The term recognizes that their socialization began in the home country, inculcating them with certain cultural characteristics, but their socialization continues in the host country, resulting in a blended cultural identity of the old and new. Although many factors will affect their sense of group identity, their bilingualism and biculturalism generally serve as a bridge for their parents in their own acculturation.

Further refining the ethnic dimensions of family is the concept of the **2.5 generation**, which deals with those who have a U.S.-born parent and a foreign-born parent. Currently, approximately one in three Asian and Hispanic Americans born to immigrant parents belongs to the 2.5 generation. For Australian and Canadian Americans, it is four in five, whereas for European Americans more

**STUDENTS SPEAK** "I am part of what the book calls the 1.5 generation. I came to the United States when I was nine years old, alongside my siblings and parents. We did not speak English, and our culture was vastly different than the American one we encountered. However, the transition period was not too difficult; we had a lot of support from close friends already established in the United States, as well as church programs that introduced us to many aspects of American life. As a child, I was able to assimilate rapidly due to my constant contact with the American culture in school. I was very comfortable with English within a couple of months, and I was able to adjust my personality to match those of my peers. My parents, however, were not so fortunate. They had, and still have, an extremely difficult time adjusting."

**—Eduardo Avila**

than half fit this category, as do slightly less than half of Middle Eastern Americans. In total numbers, the 2.5 generation is only slightly less than those identified as part of the 2.0 generation. Among the many considerations about ethnicity and adaptation is how a native-born parent may offer the 2.5 generation advantages over the 2.0 generation.[15]

**Watch on MySocLab**
Video: Social Inequalities: Race and Ethnicity

**Listen on MySocLab**
Audio: Stay or Go? Shrinking Cities Raise Questions

**15-3** Examine transnationalism and social capital as factors in societal integration.

# The Changing Face of Ethnicity

We can gain helpful insights into the complex, varied experiences and adjustments of different racial and ethnic groups by considering three important concepts: transnationalism, social capital, and segmented assimilation.

## TRANSNATIONALISM

Despite some exceptions, past immigration of even a generation ago typically resulted in a sharp, total, and rather permanent change in focus and orientation as the new ways replaced the old ways. Today, the ease of e-mail and telephone communication, the Internet, and relatively inexpensive air travel have changed that. Even as they put down roots and establish new relationships, they easily can maintain connections back home, keeping business, political, and social networks strong, and also sending money home to support those left behind. Their culture and community no longer confined to one locale, many immigrants live in both worlds simultaneously. Whereas past immigrants found themselves caught between two worlds and not fully part of either, many of today's immigrants—thanks to a shrinking world created by technology and a globalized economy—have plural identities, even dual citizenships, with one foot planted in the old country and one in the new.[16]

We have long recognized the fact that immigrants, even when intent on blending into the societal mainstream of the host country, nevertheless retain much of their "cultural baggage" that affects not only their adjustment to their new land but also serves as a stabilizing link to their homeland and sense of self.[17] Despite that "old world" influence, the traditional view of social scientists was that the political and social behavior of the newcomers occurred within the cultural/structural framework of the host society. However, the new realities just described have led scholars in recent years to revise traditional migration theory in recognition of a changed interaction pattern between immigrants and the host society.[18]

This revised orientation recognizes that recent global transformations have led to the creation of social ties and support networks no longer restricted by national boundaries. **Transnationalism** thus refers to sustained ties of persons, networks, and organizations across national borders that result from the current international migration patterns and refugee flows. The easy flow of people and their ideas back and forth between two countries has given many people the ability to maintain dual identities, with strong cultural ties and the capacity to make contributions to both places.

Instant electronic transactions and communications have compressed time and space, allowing populations to be culturally and socially anchored at multiple sites. Instead of a permanent move from one country to another, today's immigrant retains more intense, interconnected, even legitimized links (cultural, economic, familial, and political) than ever before (see the Ethnic Experience box). Some scholars therefore argue that transnationalism makes obsolete the traditional terms of assimilation, integration, or segregation of immigrants.[19]

**STUDENTS SPEAK** "My immigrant parents are always staying in contact with our family in the Dominican Republic. They continually use Blackberries to text each other, and my parents have phone plans so they call DR whenever they want. My dad uses Skype a lot as well to get a more person-to-person communication. My parents still follow DR politics just as much, if not more, than they follow the politics here in the U.S. At home, we also get a TV channel from DR that my parents watch all the time, and it provides them with everything, such as news, latest events, and TV shows. I came at age three, so I have little interest in politics or any current events there. I believe that transnationalism highly depends on the age when a person leaves one's birth country."

**—German Decena**

# the ETHNIC experience

## Transnationalism on a Personal Level

"I am a child of immigrants, as both my parents are from Ghana in West Africa. Transnationalism is a reality in my family. My father is a businessman and he runs his business both in Ghana and America, and so in a year, he makes about six trips from the States to Ghana back and forth. I keep asking him to move here and just take care of his business here in the States, but he insists that he cannot leave his other business at home and come here to stay."

"Because plane tickets are very expensive, my siblings and I do not travel back and forth. As a matter of fact, ever since I left Ghana, when I was 15 years old, I have never visited there although I plan to do so next year. I was in the U.K. for four years and then moved here to the U.S. Even though the U.K. is not my country, since I came to America, I have traveled there several times."

"Transnationalism is not something new. Most immigrants have dual identities, and they do this in order to be able to travel back forth. And I think that is really good because you enjoy both cultures, and it does not make you forget about your culture or your language because when you are in America, you have to speak English and when you go back to your country, you speak the language spoken there. The only thing is that not all countries permit you to have dual identities. In some African countries, once you become a citizen of another country, you have to give up your citizenship in your native country. But even with that, people still steel themselves to have dual identities."

"And if you're a permanent resident and you are a Green Card holder, which means you are not yet a citizen of the U.S., you have no choice but to the stay in the country for at least the first six months before you can travel. If you want to travel back and forth, what you have to do is, at least every year, you have to come to the U.S. for three months in order to keep your Green Card. That is only if you want to be traveling back and forth, but if you have decided to stay in America forever, then you can stay in the States, but you cannot stay in your native country for a year without visiting the states, or else your Green Card will [be] collected from you. I know this because my mother is going through that right now with the immigration."

Source: Ghanaian immigrant who came to the United States in 2003 at age 15. Taped interview from the collection of Vincent N. Parrillo.

## SOCIAL CAPITAL

The term **social capital** refers to actual or virtual resources available to an individual or group through social relationships, networks, and institutions. Social capital thus is a collective asset in the form of shared norms and values, mutual trust and reciprocity, information, social support, and personal connections within social network relationships that aid immigrants in achieving social, economic, and political goals. Also, the linguistic resources of the immigrant network can offer access to necessary information for otherwise linguistically isolated individuals.[20]

When we examine ethnic communities in terms of social capital, we can determine how community-based support systems and cultural orientations do or do not assist first- and second-generation Americans in their quest to share in the American Dream. Social capital is not a fixed object but rather a socially constructed, episodic, and value-based means that facilitates access to benefits and resources that best suit the goals of specific immigrant groups.[21]

Essentially, social capital offers resources to racial or ethnic minorities that are beyond their individual reach by creating connections and support. The presence of these networks cultivates hope, trust, communication, mutual assistance, and problem solving through cooperative, collective action. Although the presence of strong social capital does

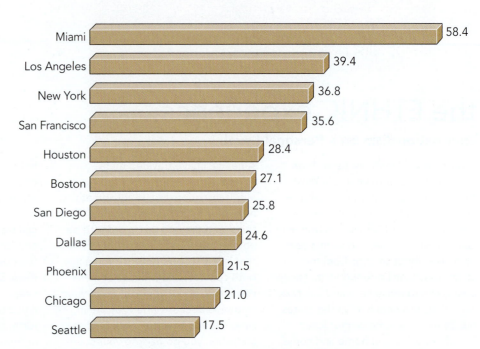

**FIGURE 15.1** **Percentage of Foreign-Born in Largest U.S. Cities, 2011**
*Source:* U.S. Census Bureau.

not guarantee a minority group's successful integration into the economic and political mainstream, it certainly makes life easier than in a community lacking it.

Ethnic communities with strong social capital can offer help to new arrivals in securing informal sources of credit, insurance, child support, English language training, educational assistance, and job referrals (see Figure 15.1). Ethnic resources feed on the vitality of supportive ethnic social structures though. For example, although Koreans and Latinos share the same neighborhood in Los Angeles's Koreatown, they live within two entirely different social environments. Unlike the Latinos, Korean children benefit from a cultural emphasis on the value of education, various afterschool institutions, and a strong social network in which coethnic friends reinforce academic goals. As a result, more graduate high school and go on to college.[22]

## SEGMENTED ASSIMILATION

15-4 Explain how segmented assimilation reveals differences within groups.

Building on the concept that immigrant groups possess different levels of social capital is the theory of **segmented assimilation**. As its name implies, this hypothesis suggests a variety of outcomes among, and even within, contemporary immigrant streams. Instead of a single or common adaptation process that becomes more successful with longer residence in the United States, new immigrant groups may follow different assimilation paths. Besides the variants in available social capital, such factors as country of origin, settlement area, social class, race, and education also play an important role.[23]

In a positive scenario, groups that are received favorably and possess high levels of human capital may quickly move up the socioeconomic ladder and integrate into the societal mainstream. In contrast, a second scenario depicts groups with limited resources as more likely unable to find stable employment to earn enough income to support their children's education. Moreover, longer residence in an inner-city environment may result in their children's acculturation to other minority peers, leading to lower educational aspirations and downward mobility, somewhat of a "new rainbow underclass."[24] Yet a third scenario is limited assimilation, in which immigrant parents support their children's educational success but reinforce traditional cultural values and thus limit their acculturation into the U.S. youth subculture.[25]

The segmented-assimilation hypothesis provides a lens for understanding the discrepancy in research findings on the educational enrollment of recent immigrants and the children of immigrants in the United States. One study, for example, reported significant intergenerational progress in educational attainment for many second-generation groups. Indeed, some surpassed those of third-generation or higher whites and African Americans. However, those of Mexican and Puerto Rican heritage languished behind the other groups.[26] A downward mobility pattern for Hispanic Caribbean youths, found in another study, was consistent with the second possible outcome of the segmented-assimilation hypothesis, whereas Afro-Caribbean youths appeared to illustrate the third type of outcome.[27] In contrast, a study of Mexican American youth found that those more successful in school were those with a facility for the English language and traditional values on familism.[28] Some resistance to racial assimilation occurs among many Caribbean immigrants who encourage an immigrant or ethnic identity in their children rather than acculturating into the African American community.[29]

If, therefore, we are to understand more completely the acculturation patterns among today's immigrants, the segmented-assimilation hypothesis informs us that one model does not fit all groups or even all members of any group. Groups differ in their incorporation into the U.S. stratification system, and this theory attempts to explain how and why they do.

## NATURALIZATION

After five years of continuous legal residence in the United States, immigrants are eligible to become naturalized citizens, provided they are of good moral character and demonstrate a command of English and knowledge of U.S. history and government. We can reasonably assume that those who become U.S. citizens are demonstrating a desire to join fully in U.S. society through this formal process.

**15-5** Analyze differences in naturalization rates among immigrants.

As Figure 15.2 shows, the longer the residence in the United States, the higher the percentage of naturalized citizens. Those who arrived in the 1970s, for example, have a greater proportion of naturalized citizens than those who arrived in the 1980s, who in turn exceed those who arrived in the 1990s, who surpass those who arrived in the last decade. Moreover, Asian immigrants lead all other groups in most time periods in the percentage of those who became U.S. citizens. How much of a role transnationalism or segmented assimilation play in these levels of naturalization among groups is a matter of great interest to social scientists.

We must be careful in analyzing the citizenship data. At first glance, the smaller proportion of newer arrivals compared to earlier immigrants in becoming naturalized citizens would seem to support the argument that newcomers are less likely to "become Americans." However, the correlation between length of U.S. residence and the proportion of those becoming citizens has been fairly constant for many decades. For example, although 8 in 10 of all immigrants who arrived in the 1970s are citizens now, less than half of them were citizens in the early 1990s.

In recent years, the number of naturalized citizens has averaged 685,000 annually. In 2011, the leading countries of birth of new citizens were Mexico (97,783), India (45,985), the Philippines (42,520), the People's Republic of China (32,864), Colombia (22,693), Cuba (21,071), and Vietnam (20,922).[30]

**FIGURE 15.2** Percentage of Naturalized Citizens by Period of Entry, 2010

*Source:* U.S. Census Bureau, *The Foreign-Born Population in the United States: 2010* (May 2012).

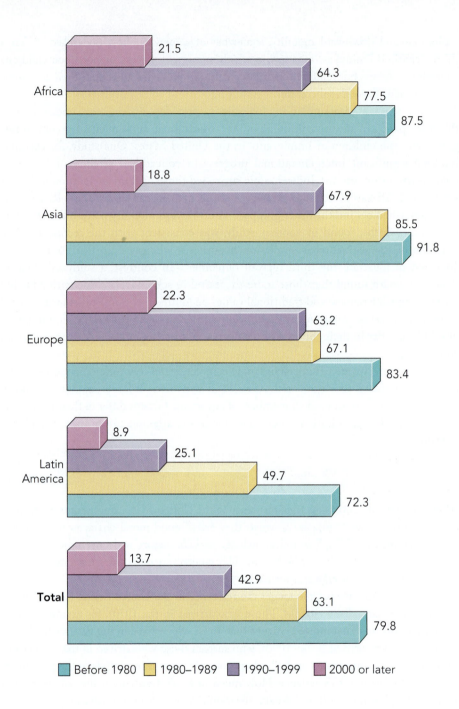

Before 1980   1980–1989   1990–1999   2000 or later

## ETHNICITY AS A SOCIAL PROCESS

Ethnicity is a creation of a pluralistic U.S. society. Usually, culture shock and an emerging self-consciousness lead immigrant groups to think of themselves in terms of an ethnic identity and to become part of an ethnic community to gain the social and emotional support they need to begin a new life in their adopted country. That community is revitalized with a continual influx of new arrivals.

Many sociologists insist that ethnicity should be regarded not as an attribute with only the two distinct categories of assimilation and pluralism, but as a continuous variable. Affecting variations in ethnic behavior are occupation, residence, and institutional affiliation, in other words, the structural situations in which groups have found themselves.[31] Preindustrial age immigrants had a more dispersed residential pattern than did industrial age immigrants, who bunched together because of concentrated large-scale factory employment and the need for low-cost housing near their place of employment. Furthermore, these immigrants were drawn to areas of economic expansion, and the migration chains—the subsequent arrival of relatives and friends—continued their concentrated settlement pattern.

Just as German, Irish, Italian, Jewish, and Polish immigrants once concentrated in urban areas where the availability of skilled or unskilled jobs matched their abilities, so too do today's Asian and Hispanic immigrant settlement patterns reflect the pursuit of potential opportunities. The complex nature of these geographical choices at the local and regional levels nationwide is another reason for the impracticality of a simplistic approach to understanding present-day ethnicity.[32]

Group consciousness thus arises and crystallizes within work relationships, common residential areas, interests, and lifestyles in working-class conditions. Moreover, normal communication and participation in ethnic organizations on a cosmopolitan level can reinforce ethnic identity even among residentially dispersed groups.

## MIGRATION PATTERNS

The longer a group is in the United States, the less geographically concentrated it is. Although this hardly may be a surprising finding, ethnicity still plays a role in the changing spatial patterns. Distinctive geographic ethnic concentrations remain in the nation because groups differ in their inclination to enter or leave an area according to the existing ethnic compositions of those areas. At least for the present, ethnic linkage to certain regions remains strong.[33]

A numerically small group, if highly concentrated in a small number of localities, possesses greater political and social influence than one dispersed more uniformly. Thus, the linkage between demographic size and location influences visibility, occupational patterns, interaction patterns, intermarriage, and assimilation.

In 2011, 62 percent of the nearly 1.1 million immigrants who came to the United States entered through only six states.[34] At the same time, three of these gateway states—California, New York, and Texas—had considerable net outmigration of their foreign-born populations to other states. In 2011–2012, the Northeast, Midwest, South, and West all had an extensive outmigration of the foreign-born to other regions, but only the Northeast experienced a net loss overall.[35]

Just as chain migration is an important factor in migration from abroad, so too does it appear to play an important role in this population redistribution of the foreign-born to other states (see Figure 15.3). As a result, the ethnic dimension in internal migration patterns remains significant. By far, the greatest numbers of interstate movers have been Asians, followed by Mexicans and other Latin Americans. States where this internal migration had the most dramatic impact on population composition were Nevada, North Carolina, Georgia, Arkansas, Minnesota, Nebraska, and Indiana.[36]

Focusing on ethnic and racial settlement patterns is helpful in understanding part of the assimilation process. In his influential ecological model of Chicago's growth and development, Robert Park noted the linkage between social and spatial mobility. Where

So many immigrants are becoming U.S. citizens that courtrooms, where naturalization ceremonies once were common, are often inadequate. On September 17, 2008, for example, more than 3,000 people took the oath of citizenship at Fenway Park, the first time ever this occurred at the home of the Boston Red Sox baseball team.

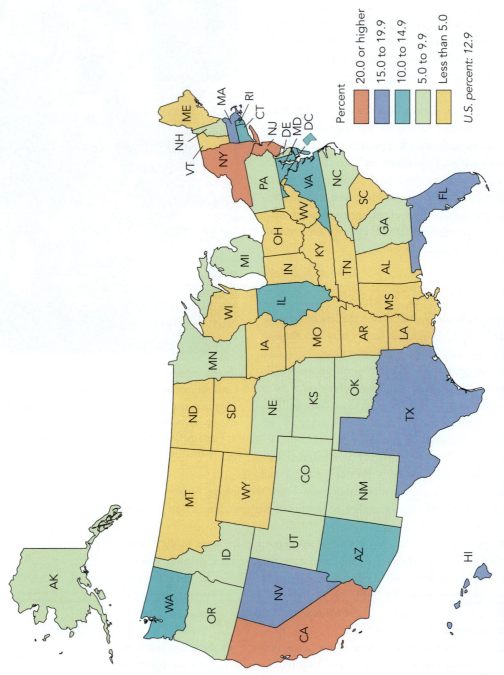

**FIGURE 15.3** Foreign-Born Population as Percent of State Population, 2010

Source: U.S. Census Bureau.

one lives is as valid an indicator of upward mobility as are income, education, and occupation.[37]

Housing markets are segmented along class and racial lines, and because the most desirable neighborhoods tend to be inhabited by whites, the relocation by minority members typically suggests a process of integration. Because such spatial mobility implies greater access to cultural, economic, physical, and social resources and is indicative of social and economic assimilation, the term **spatial assimilation** often is used to identify this process. What we are witnessing is the reduction in differences in the residential patterns across groups, although its extent and pace among immigrants is affected by their social class more than their race and ethnicity. Higher educated immigrants, for example, tend to be less segregated than less educated ones, who also are likely to be poorer.[38]

## SYMBOLIC ETHNICITY

Among first-generation U.S. immigrants, ethnicity is an everyday reality that everyone takes for granted. For most immigrants living within an ethnic community, shared communal interactions make ethnic identity a major factor in daily life. Not yet structurally assimilated, these immigrants find that their ethnicity provides the link to virtually everything they say or do, what they join, and whom they befriend or marry.

What happens to the ethnicity of subsequent generations depends on the immediate environment. As one would expect, the presence of ethnic neighborhoods or organizations in the vicinity helps sustain a strong sense of ethnic identity.[39] For most whites of European origin, living away from visible ethnic links and becoming part of the societal mainstream reduce the importance of their ethnic identity in comparison to their occupational and social identity. At this point, European ethnicity mostly rests on acknowledging ancestry through attachment to a few ethnic symbols not pertinent to everyday life.

Sociologist Richard D. Alba first spoke about a "twilight" stage of ethnicity among white ethnics, an ebbing of those visible ethnic markings of language, parallel social institutions, and residential clusters.[40] Aside from assimilation resulting in a lessening of ethnicity, high ethnic intermarriage rates also have reduced the intergenerational transmission of distinctive cultural traits and diversified the ethnic ancestry of third- and

**15-6** Explain how symbolic ethnicity preserves one's heritage.

*Many native-born U.S. residents reaffirm their cultural heritage through symbolic ethnicity, most commonly through holiday celebrations. Sometimes these activities are carryovers from the old country, but sometimes they are of U.S. origin, as with Kwanzaa, a fairly recently developed observance based on traditional African harvest celebrations.*

"My parents are from Ghana and Liberia. It was close to Christmas time and we were learning about Kwanzaa in the second grade. The teacher automatically assumed that I knew what it was because I was black, and she told me to explain it to the class. She was shocked to find out that I had no idea and told me to bring some things that our family uses when we celebrate, so the class could see. My mother didn't know either. She was really upset and went to school the next day to speak to the teacher, who then apologized to me. Because Kwanzaa is an African American ceremony, she thought all blacks celebrated it and was surprised to learn otherwise."

**—Sammaica Osei**

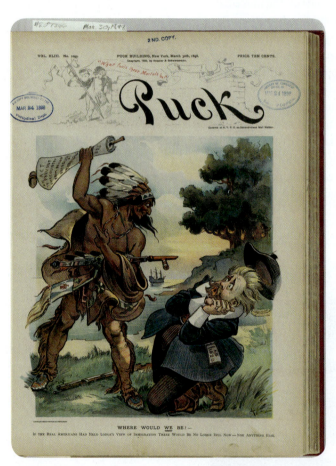

*This political cartoon from an 1898 issue of Puck, shows a 1620 Pilgrim, portrayed as U.S. Senator Henry Cabot Lodge—who advocated literacy bills to reduce immigration—cowering before an American Indian, who is about to hit him with a club around which a paper is wrapped that states, "An Act to Prevent the Country from being Overrun by Foreigners." The caption reads "Where would we be now?"*

fourth-generation European Americans. A coalesced new identity group, European Americans, has emerged. Nationality group ethnicity is muted and symbolic through a personal and voluntary identity that finds occasional expression in observing ethnic traditions during festivals, holidays, or other special times connected to one's heritage. It might also include supporting a political or humanitarian cause associated with the country of origin.

Although socially assimilated and integrated into middle-class society, third- and fourth-generation European Americans maintain this quiet link to their origins. It can find form in small details, such as objects in the home with an ethnic meaning, occasional participation in an old-country ritual, or a fondness for ethnic cuisine, even the use of religious symbols without regular participation in a religious culture or organization.[41] Individuals may remain interested in the immigrant experience, participate in ethnic political and social activities, or even visit the ancestral homeland. All these private, leisure-time activities help preserve ethnicity in symbolic ways, giving people a special sense of self and heritage in the homogenized world of U.S. culture.

African Americans express symbolic ethnicity through such elements as musical styles, fashion and dress styles (Afros, braids, dreadlocks, tribal symbols cut into the hair, bandanna headbands, Kufi hats, harem pants, African beads), cuisine (soul food), and festivals (such as Kwanzaa, a week-long festival honoring African American heritage that is celebrated primarily in the United States). Sometimes called *manifestations of cultural nationalism*—a movement toward African American solidarity based on encouraging African culture and values—these activities resemble those of the descendants of other ethnic groups proudly recalling their heritage. Interestingly, African-born Americans typically do not celebrate Kwanzaa.

# Current Ethnic Issues

Two highly controversial issues punctuate race and ethnic relations in the United States: immigration and bilingual education. Contemporary arguments against both repeat objections that were hotly asserted in the late nineteenth and early twentieth centuries. Nativist fears of being overrun by too many "non-American types" and losing societal cohesion as a result of their cultural pluralism are quite similar to concerns raised by dominant-group members of past generations. Closely related to these two issues is a third one: multiculturalism. This subject causes ongoing debates between its advocates and those insisting on assimilation.

## IMMIGRATION FEARS

The ebb and flow of immigrant waves have an impact on the host nation in many ways. Their cultural impact can enrich the society—in architecture, art, foods, and music, to name just a few—but some fear language retention and nonassimilation

**TABLE 15.1** Leading Suppliers of Immigrants to the United States, 1820–2012

| | | |
|---|---|---|
| 1. | Mexico | 8,067,025 |
| 2. | Germany | 7,304,191 |
| 3. | Italy | 5,472,088 |
| 4. | United Kingdom | 5,466,514 |
| 5. | Ireland | 4,798,810 |
| 6. | Canada and Newfoundland | 4,766,584 |
| 7. | Russia | 3,988,365 |
| 8. | Philippines | 2,179,764 |
| 9. | Austria* | 1,875,503 |
| 10. | China | 1,772,212 |
| 11. | Hungary* | 1,690,465 |
| 12. | India | 1,550,568 |
| 13. | Cuba | 1,302,577 |
| 14. | Sweden | 1,289,328 |
| 15. | Dominican Republic | 1,253,310 |

\* Data for Austria/Hungary were not reported until 1861. Austria and Hungary have been reported separately since 1905. From 1938 to 1945, Austria was included in figures for Germany.

*Source:* U.S. Department of Homeland Security, *2012 Yearbook of Immigration Statistics.* Washington, DC: U.S. Government Printing Office, 2013, Table 2.

will undermine societal cohesion. Immigrant labor can be a boon to the economy, but critics express concern about the lowering of wages and loss of jobs for native workers. Because most immigrants now are people of color and have a higher birth rate than native-born Americans, some worry about the changing racial demographics. Moreover, with developing countries now the primary sending areas, the interests of the newly naturalized citizens—and in turn, U.S. foreign policy—become increasingly involved in developments in those parts of the world (see Table 15.1).

Many immigrants still come from European countries, but they have accounted for less than 10 percent of the total number in recent years, due to the large increase in Asian and Hispanic immigrants (see Figure 15.4). Given the ongoing processes of chain migration and family reunification—and contrasting birth rates in Europe as opposed to Asia and Latin America—we safely can assume the continued dominance of developing nations in sending new strangers to these shores (see Table 15.2).

Approximately 10.3 million legal immigrants came to the United States between 2000 and 2009, exceeding the previous record set in 1990–1999, when 9.8 million arrived. With more than 1 million newcomers arriving annually since then, this decade may set an even higher record number of legal immigrants. Add in the millions of undocumented immigrants, estimated at 11.5 million in 2011, and the issue of immigration becomes a fiercely debated one.[42]

Some opposition to current immigration results from concern about the ability of the United States to absorb so many immigrants. Echoing xenophobic fears of earlier generations, today's immigration opponents worry that U.S. citizens will lose control of the country to foreigners. This time, instead of fears about the religiously different Catholics and Jews or the physically different Mediterranean whites who were dark-complexioned, the new anti-immigration groups fear the significantly growing presence of religiously and/or physically different immigrants of color.

**Read on MySocLab**
Document: Race in the Era of President Obama

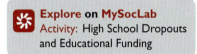

**Explore on MySocLab**
Activity: High School Dropouts and Educational Funding

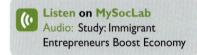

**Listen on MySocLab**
Audio: Study: Immigrant Entrepreneurs Boost Economy

**FIGURE 15.4** Percent Distribution of Foreign-Born Population by Region of Birth: 1960 to 2010

*Source:* U.S. Census Bureau.

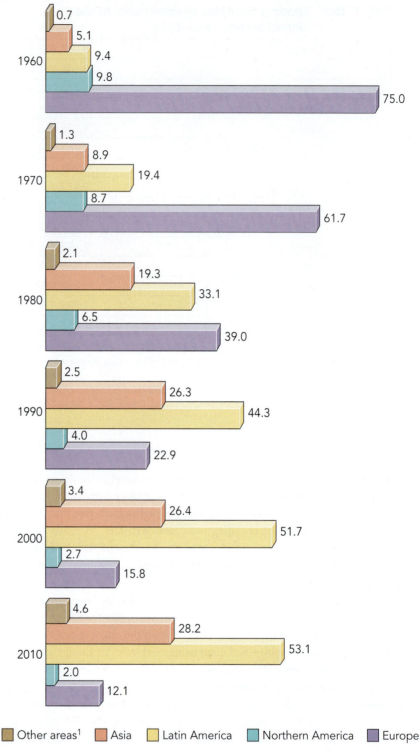

| Other areas[1] | Asia | Latin America | Northern America | Europe |

[1]Other areas include Africa and Oceania.

Visible differences, together with the prevalence of languages other than English, constantly remind native-born Americans about the strangers in their midst, whom they may perceive as a threat to U.S. society as they know it. This especially is true regarding Arab and Muslim Americans, whom anti-immigration advocates point to as illustrating the problem of too liberal an immigration policy that allowed terrorists into our midst. The reality that virtually all Arab and Muslim Americans denounce terrorism does little to reduce public fears.

**TABLE 15.2**  Major Sources of Newcomers to the United States, 1965 versus 2012

| 1965 | | 2012 | |
|---|---|---|---|
| 1. Canada | 38,327 | 1. Mexico | 145,326 |
| 2. Mexico | 37,969 | 2. China, People's Republic | 78,184 |
| 3. United Kingdom | 27,358 | 3. India | 63,320 |
| 4. Germany | 24,045 | 4. Philippines | 55,431 |
| 5. Cuba | 19,760 | 5. Dominican Republic | 41,535 |
| 6. Colombia | 10,885 | 6. Cuba | 32,551 |
| 7. Italy | 10,821 | 7. Vietnam | 27,578 |
| 8. Dominican Republic | 9,504 | 8. Haiti | 22,446 |
| 9. Poland | 8,465 | 9. Korea | 20,802 |
| 10. Argentina | 6,124 | 10. Colombia | 20,272 |
| 11. Ireland | 5,463 | 11. Jamaica | 20,300 |
| 12. Ecuador | 4,392 | 12. Canada & Newfoundland | 20,138 |
| 13. China and Taiwan | 4,057 | 13. El Salvador | 15,874 |
| 14. France | 4,039 | 14. Ethiopia | 15,400 |
| 15. Haiti | 3,609 | 15. United Kingdom | 13,938 |

*Source:* U.S. Department of Homeland Security, 2012 *Yearbook of Immigration Statistics.* Washington, DC: U.S. Government Printing Office, 2013, Table 3.

It not only is the increasing visibility of so many "strangers" in neighborhoods, schools, and workplaces that encourages this backlash. The nation's stable birth rate means that the migration and birth rates of immigrants account for a larger share of population growth than in previous years (see Figure 15.5). Demographers project that immigrants arriving since 2005 and their descendants will account for 82 percent of U.S. population growth by 2050.[43] Consequently, the U.S. Census Bureau projects that the racial composition of the United States will change dramatically in the next two generations, a prospect that displeases some people.

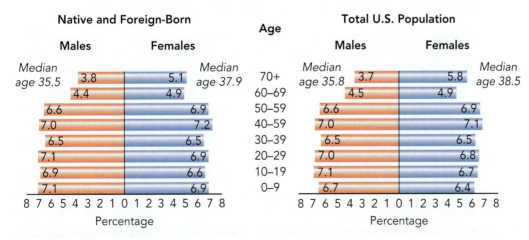

**FIGURE 15.5**  Foreign-Born and Total Population by Age and Sex, 2010 (in percent)

*Source:* U.S. Census Bureau.

*Although undocumented immigrants are an important part of the underground economy, and are seeking amnesty to become citizens, a large segment of the public wants the nation to regain control of its borders and even evict those who did not enter legally. This rally in Los Angeles is one of many such organized protests to occur in recent years.*

Another concern about immigration is economic. The public worries that immigrants take away jobs, drive down wages, and use too many government services at taxpayers' expense while not contributing sufficiently to the cost. How real are these fears?

**JOBS.** Do immigrants take jobs away from Americans? In a 2010 national poll, 62 percent of all respondents and 87 percent of Hispanic respondents thought that they mostly took jobs Americans don't want.[44] On the one hand, immigrants create many new jobs by starting new businesses (approximately 18 percent of the total). The explosion of lawn-care businesses and nail salons are only two examples. Or, consider that immigrants from Russia, Taiwan, and India founded Google, Yahoo!, and Sun Microsystems, respectively. Furthermore, immigrants increase the demand for goods and services that still others fill through these new jobs.

At the same time, the decline in native-born employment is most pronounced in states with heavier immigrant concentrations where the foreign-born increased their share of workers the most. Immigration has its biggest impact on the lower part of the labor market—particularly building maintenance, construction, and food services—where native-born unemployment numbers closely match the increase in immigrant employment increases. In other labor sectors, there appears to be far less impact.[45]

**WAGES.** The debate over immigrants lowering wages typically does not deal with skilled workers, as near-unanimous agreement exists that they give a big lift to the U.S. economy. Instead, the debate centers on the continuing arrival of millions of unskilled laborers, whom some fear take away jobs and lower wages. One study of Mexican immigration concluded that it reduced the wages of high school dropouts by 7 percent between 1980 and 2000.[46] However, even the most pessimistic economists think such downward pressure on wages affects no more than 10 percent of the labor force or that the drop has been more than 5 percent during the past 20 years.

Immigration has not lowered wages for U.S. workers because the percentage of native-born high school dropouts has fallen sharply in the past few decades, and also because immigrants and low-skilled U.S. workers fill rather different roles in the economy. To give only two examples of many, 54 percent of tailors in the United States are foreign-born, compared with less than 1 percent of crane operators, and 44 percent of plaster-stucco masons are immigrants, whereas less than 1 percent of sewer-pipe cleaners

# REALITY check

## How Immigrants Help the United States

Recent studies provide significant evidence of the benefits of immigration today:

- Immigrants are 30 percent more likely to start new businesses than U.S.-born citizens.
- Among people with advanced degrees, immigrants are three times more likely to file patents than U.S.-born citizens.
- The Congressional Budget Office projects that giving a path to legalization for unauthorized immigrants would increase federal revenues by $48 billion but would only incur $23 billion of increased costs from public services, producing a surplus of $25 billion.
- Immigrants are five times less likely to end up in prison or mental hospitals.
- More than 90 percent of the children of recent immigrants speak English.

- Every additional 100 foreign-born workers in science and technology fields are associated with 262 additional jobs for U.S.-born workers.

Sources: Michael Greenstone and Adam Looney, "Ten Economic Facts about Immigration," The Hamilton Project (September 2010); Madeline Zavodny, "Immigration and American Jobs," American Enterprise Institute (December 15, 2011); "Senate Amendment 1150 to S. 1348, the Comprehensive Immigration Reform Act of 2007," Congressional Budget Office (CBO) Cost Estimate (June 2007).

---

are foreign-born. With different skills, inclinations, and ideas, most immigrants do not seek the same jobs as U.S. workers.[47]

**COSTS AND CONTRIBUTIONS.** At the local and state levels, immigrants typically use more in services than they pay in local taxes. Those with low levels of education and job skills cost the most, particularly in health care and use of schools. In some states with large concentrations of immigrants, such as California, the newcomers consume far more in government benefits (education, health care, and social services) than they contribute in taxes (an average cost of $1,178 per native-born household in the 1990s). However, in most states, the cost per native-born household is $100 or $200 per year, but this is offset in their contributions to the states' economies in consumer spending and sales and property taxes paid.[48]

A helpful insight comes to us from North Carolina, which has one of the fastest-growing foreign-born populations in the country. Throughout the past decade, while filling one-third of the state's new jobs, their consumer spending totaled $9.2 billion. Add in the $1.9 billion they placed in savings, and North Carolina experienced a total growth dividend of $11 billion, which far exceeded the $61 million that the newcomers cost the state (or $102 per native-born taxpayer) in the difference between taxes paid and services required.[49]

On a national level, immigrants added an estimated $15 billion to the economy in 2010, according to the National Research Council.[50] Applied against their costs in education, health, and social services, economists are in general agreement that the net gain to the United States from immigration is approximately $7 billion annually.[51] Federal financial analysts say that enabling undocumented immigrants to achieve legal status could produce an additional surplus of $25 billion (see the Reality Check box).

**STUDENTS SPEAK** "Thanks to the Internet, we are able to stay in contact on a daily basis with my father's family in the Philippines. Through Skype, we are able to webcam and have conversations that feel as if we are in person. I gave birth to a daughter four months ago, and my family across the world has been able to see everything, from pictures when she was born and a video of her first laughs, to a picture of her eating her first bowl of cereal. Through technology, the world has become smaller for my family overseas and us. I am able to maintain my father's culture and values by staying in touch with my loved ones regardless of where they live, but I am also able to live the American life my father wanted for me."

**—Michelle Sucaldito**

Immigrant labor allows many goods and services to be produced more cheaply and provides the workforce for some businesses that otherwise could not exist. These include U.S. textile and agricultural industries, as well as restaurants and domestic household services. In addition, economists say, immigrants and their children bring long-term benefits for most U.S. taxpayers because—like most U.S. residents—they and their descendants will add more to government coffers than they receive during their lifetimes.

**PUBLIC-OPINION POLLS.** Statistics notwithstanding, Americans have mixed opinions about immigration. For example, in a 2009 Gallup Poll, 58 percent of respondents nationwide said they felt that, on the whole, immigration was good for the country, whereas 36 percent thought it was a bad thing. Yet, in a March 2013 Pew Research Center national poll, 49 percent said immigration strengthened the United States, but 41 percent said the opposite due to jobs, housing, and health care.[52]

These and other differing poll findings are likely reflecting the public blurring of legal and illegal immigration, as the various national polls consistently find two-thirds or more Americans think that illegal immigrants weaken the U.S. economy. When specifically asked in a 2010 CBS News/*New York Times* poll how serious a problem they thought illegal immigration was, 61 percent viewed it as "very serious," and another 27 percent said it was "somewhat serious."[53]

Back in Chapter 2, we discussed how the linguistic relativity of language may connote intended or unintended meanings. A good example is the use of the term *illegal immigrants* versus *unauthorized immigrants*. Although both mean the same thing, the first expression is more value-laden, but it is what is used in the public opinion polls. In this book, we hereafter will use the second or value-neutral term.

## UNAUTHORIZED IMMIGRANTS

**15-7** Examine fears and realities regarding all forms of immigration today.

In the aftermath of the terrorist attacks on September 11, 2001, amid concerns about insufficient screening of aliens coming to the United States and the growing presence of unauthorized immigrants, the government reorganized in 2003. Services once provided by the much-criticized Immigration and Naturalization Service now occur within the Department of Homeland Security under the U.S. Citizenship and Immigration Services (USCIS). With 18,000 federal employees working in 250 offices around the world, this office adjudicates immigrant visa petitions, naturalization petitions, and asylum and refugee applications.[54]

What fuels public debate about immigration is the high number of unauthorized foreign-born people in the United States, now estimated to be approximately 11.5 million. Recent estimates place unauthorized immigrants as 3.7 percent of the total population and 5.2 percent of the workforce. Their children, an estimated 3.2 million with nearly three-fourths of them U.S.-born, constitute 6.8 percent of the nation's elementary and secondary schools.[55]

Mexicans comprise the largest segment of undocumented migrants (estimated to be 59 percent of the total), a proportion that has remained fairly steady for the past three decades (see the Ethnic Experience box). Another 11 percent are from Central America, 7 percent from South America, 4 percent from the Caribbean, and another 4 percent from Europe and Canada. South and East Asia is another large source, sending approximately 11 percent, while the Middle East accounts for less than 2 percent.[56] A large number of people from foreign lands continue to slip across U.S. borders, but others (approximately 165,000 annually) first arrive legally as visitors (tourists, students, or businesspeople) but do not leave—and so then become visa violators.

Entering the country easily and then disappearing within it, these unauthorized immigrants usually escape detection by the Department of Homeland Security, which spends millions to patrol the borders of the United States. In the Southwest, the problem

# the ETHNIC experience

## Life as an Undocumented Person

"After completing my undergraduate studies in anthropology, I was without a job, living an economic crisis, and just separated of my wife, so I decided to try my luck 'on the other side.' I made my connection with the 'chicken farmer' or 'coyote' in Juárez City and, with great anguish, I crossed the Bravo River to arrive at El Paso, Texas. I spent five days locked up inside a house eating hamburgers and drinking Coca-Cola, without ever leaving the room. The passing sounds of sirens from border patrol cars continually filled me with a fear never before experienced."

"In the El Paso airport from where I would fly to New York, I was stopped by the Border Patrol and returned to Juárez City. I was devastated, but 5 o'clock the next morning, I repeated the passage and this time, I arrived successfully in the 'Big Apple' where friends, who had used the same networks to cross, were waiting for me. After hours of rest at night that cushioned my stress a little, I found work, at four dollars an hour, cleaning floors and public bathrooms in a gas station."

"My American Dream had been fulfilled, but it existed alongside the daily nightmare of constant realization that I was an 'illegal one,' a 'violator' of the laws of another country, a person not recognized by the United States government. The continuous dragnets by the police in public areas increased my persecution deliriums and the days and the nights became unbearable."

"The money obtained from working, the friends who shared the undocumented condition, the satisfaction to send dollars back to Mexico, the participation in sport activities, the drinking together, the attendance in courses of English in city schools, the presence of my countrymen, the celebrations of our country, the Mexican food, knowing and enjoying that beautiful city and its great cultural diversity were the best stimuli in living undocumented for four years in the capital of the world and with the daily indecision about the return to Mexico."

Eduardo Andrés Sandoval Forero returned to Mexico in 1999 to reunite with his family, earned his Ph.D. in sociology, and become a professor at the Universidad Autónoma del Estado de México.

As a further deterrent, a border patrol agent drives along the high barrier fence, built a few years ago along the Mexican border south of Sierra Vista, Arizona. This style fence, near the San Pedro River Conservation Area, completely stops all wildlife movement between countries, but not people who scale the fence or dig under it.

draws the greatest amount of public attention and generates the most apprehensions of undocumented aliens (approximately 642,000 million in 2011). Mexicans dominated the list of those apprehended, at 76 percent of the total. Other major source countries of those apprehended were, in descending order: Guatemala, Honduras, El Salvador, India, the Dominican Republic, Ecuador, Colombia, and China.[57]

Public pressure to do something about better border control and dealing with those unauthorized immigrants already here generated political debates, opposing legislative proposals for amnesty or a crackdown on "illegals," and the building of a border fence along portions of the Mexican border. Congressional hearings and mass demonstrations in many U.S. cities all illustrated the fundamental disagreements about how to deal with the situation. A divided Congress had been unable to pass any immigration reform bill but, in the second term of the Obama administration, a comprehensive bill went to the legislative branch for action.

Calls for reform come at a time when parts of the U.S. economy are dependent on the labor of undocumented migrants. Mostly Latinos, these unskilled workers have spread to a wide range of industries (see Figure 15.6). Moreover, these Mexican, Central American, and Caribbean workers annually send billions of dollars to their families back home, providing a major source of financial support there.[58]

## LANGUAGE RETENTION

One of the most divisive issues in majority–minority relations is language retention. For many native-born Americans, the presence of groups not speaking English goes to the heart of their assumptions that the newcomers are not even trying to assimilate. The large-scale presence of an immigrant group—whether on a national level such as the Hispanics or in a local area such as the Vietnamese in California—intensifies this perception. On a personal level, witnessing foreign-born parents speaking in public to their children in the language of their homeland or seeing signs or television programs in languages other than English also deepens an individual's concern about societal cohesion.

However, if we examine past language retention concerns about immigrants, we find similar patterns. Remember Benjamin Franklin's apprehension about the Germans' meager command of English and need for interpreters given in Chapter 5? Similarly, as millions of Italian immigrants in the first two decades of the twentieth century settled in the "Little Italys" of many U.S. cities, the prevalence of Italian language usage, signs, newspapers, and radio programs led many Americans to denounce these "inassimilable" Italians and to seek restrictive legislation to stop any more from coming here.

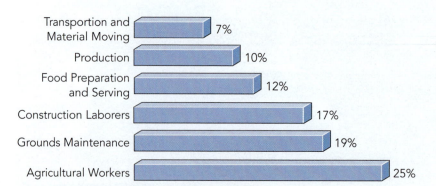

**FIGURE 15.6** **Percent of Undocumented Migrants in U.S. Labor Force: 2008**

*Source:* Jeffrey Passel and D'Vera Cohn, "A Portrait of Unauthorized Immigrants in the United States," *Pew Hispanic Center Research Report* (April 19, 2009).

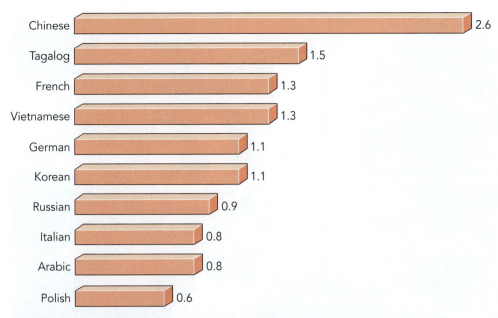

**FIGURE 15.7** Ten Languages Most Frequently Spoken at Home Other Than English and Spanish, Age 5 Years and Older, in Millions: 2009

*Source:* U.S. Census Bureau, 2009 American Community Survey (January 2011).

Although Spanish now is the second most frequent language spoken at home (approximately 34.5 million do so), other languages also have been increasing significantly. Foremost among these are Chinese, French, Tagalog (a language spoken in the Philippines), Vietnamese, Korean, Russian, Italian, Arabic, Portuguese, and Polish. In 1990, French was the third most spoken language; today, it is Chinese (see Figure 15.7).

With a million or more immigrants entering the United States each year, the extensive use of other languages alarms many nativists. The U.S. Census Bureau estimates that one in five Americans does not speak English at home. Of these, 25.3 million said they speak English less than "very well." According to experts, some of the rise is due to the fast growth of the new-immigrant population, which included millions of people who came here illegally. The share of people who speak English only is highest among those in their working years, age 18 to 64.[59]

## BILINGUAL EDUCATION

Offering **bilingual education**—teaching subjects in both English and the student's native language—can take the form of a transitional program (gradually phasing in English completely throughout several years) or a maintenance program (continued native-language teaching to sustain the students' heritage with a simultaneous but relatively limited emphasis on English proficiency). For the many U.S. residents who assume English-speaking schools provide the heat for the melting pot, the popularity of bilingual education—particularly maintenance programs—is a sore point. Some see such efforts as counterproductive by reducing assimilation, and thereby the cohesiveness, of U.S. society, while simultaneously isolating ethnic groups from one another. Advocates of bilingual programs emphasize that they are developing **bilingualism**—fluency in both English and the students' native tongue—and that many youngsters are illiterate in both when they begin school.

Public funding for bilingual education began in 1968, when Congress passed the Bilingual Education Act, designed at first for low-income families only. Two years later,

*Bilingual education continues to stir controversy over cost, effectiveness, and its alleged "threat" to societal cohesiveness, provoking some demands for its elimination. Several recent studies indicate that immersion programs have success rates comparable to bilingual programs, but contradictory findings in other studies keep the issue in dispute.*

the Department of Health, Education, and Welfare specified that school districts in which any national-origin group constituted more than 5 percent of the student population had a legal obligation to provide bilingual programs for low-income families.

In 1974, two laws significantly expanded bilingual programs. The Bilingual Act eliminated the low-income requirement and urged that children receive various courses that provided appreciation of their cultural heritage. The Equal Opportunity Act identified failure to take "appropriate action" to overcome language barriers impeding equal participation in school as a form of illegal denial of equal educational opportunity.

In 2001, passage of the No Child Left Behind Act terminated the Bilingual Education Act, as it provided no funded support for native language learning. Instead, it emphasized schools' accountability for teaching English only, and mandating annual testing of all students to measure their English language proficiency. Today, **Limited English Proficient (LEP) programs**, also known as **English Language Learner (ELL) programs**, address the challenge of children and youth mastering their new country's language. More than 11 million immigrant children who speak a language other than English at home currently are enrolled in the public schools, both urban and suburban (see Figure 15.8). Schools therefore must overcome cultural, language, and literacy barriers to provide for their education. Between 1980 and 2009, the number of school-age children (ages 5–17) who spoke a language other than English at home increased from 10 to 21 percent (from 4.7 to 11.2 million).[60]

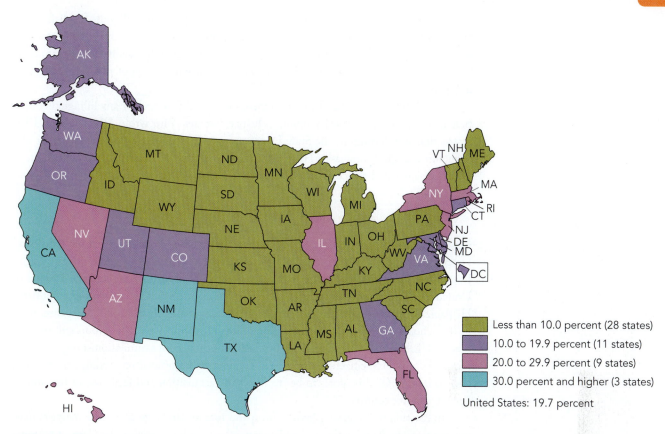

**FIGURE 15.8** Population 5 Years and Older Who Spoke a language Other Than English at Home, 2007
*Source:* U.S. Census Bureau.

Because 95 percent of all immigrant children attend urban schools, this challenge primarily falls to urban areas. This especially is the case in the six states where immigrants are most concentrated (California, New York, Florida, Texas, New Jersey, and Illinois). For example, more than one in four of the nation's students in need of English language instruction (1.5 million children) live in California. However, new immigrant patterns are doubling, even tripling the enrollment of immigrant children in such states as South Carolina, Indiana, Nevada, Arkansas, North Carolina, and Virginia.[61]

The practical value of LEP or ELL programs over native-language instruction is readily apparent because it practically is impossible to offer native-tongue classes in so many languages. As it is, urban and suburban schools struggle for funds, space, and qualified teachers for their various bilingual programs.

How effective is bilingual education in helping children learn English? Despite the many studies comparing transitional bilingual programs to structured English immersion programs, the findings are mixed. On the one hand, numerous studies, including those utilizing a *meta-analysis* (including as many other studies as possible), conclude that bilingual programs are effective, or even superior, in promoting academic achievement compared to all-English approaches.[62] Other studies have found no significant difference in academic performance, that neither bilingual education nor English immersion is superior to the other.[63] Still other studies conclude that instructional programs that teach in English are more effective than programs that provide more instruction in the students' native language.[64]

Perhaps these contradictory findings result from bilingual programs varying so widely in approach and quality. It may be reasonable to assume that students who are given enough assistance and time in any well-taught program will gain English proficiency better than those in overcrowded classrooms do or ones with limited attention given to helping students. In other words, the focus on individually helping students learn English may be a more significant factor than which type of program is used in doing so.

In a 2009 decision, the U.S. Supreme Court ruled 5–4 against any bilingual education mandate. In the majority opinion, Justice Samuel Alito wrote, "Research on ELL instruction and findings by the State Department of Education support the view that SEI [structured English immersion] is significantly more effective than bilingual education."[65] Critics disagree and the controversy continues.

## THE OFFICIAL ENGLISH MOVEMENT

Opponents of bilingual education argue that the program encourages "ethnic tribalism," fostering separation instead of a cohesive society. Their objections come in response to Hispanic leaders in such groups as the National Council of La Raza and the League of United Latin American Citizens (LULAC), who claimed that "language rights" entitled Hispanic people to have their language and culture maintained at public expense, both in the schools and in the workplace. The oldest Hispanic civil rights group still in existence, LULAC was founded in 1929. Ironically, it began as an assimilationist organization, accepting only U.S. citizens as members, conducting its official proceedings in English, and declaring one of its goals to be "to foster the acquisition and facile use of the official language of our country."[66]

In reaction to increasing immigration and foreign language usage, the nativists have pressed to make English the official language for all public business. The largest national lobbying group, U.S. English, was cofounded by Japanese immigrant S. I. Hayakawa, a former U.S. senator from California and former president of, and linguistics professor at, San Francisco State University. Its president since 1993 has been Mauro E. Mujica, an immigrant from Chile.

In 2013, the group claimed more than 1.8 million members, and its success prompted critics to attack it as being anti-immigrant, racist, divisive, and dangerous. The group counters that its goal is for official government business at all levels to be conducted solely in English. This includes all public documents, records, legislation, regulations, hearings, official ceremonies, and public meetings. It is not opposed to other languages used in everyday private lives or taught. The organization argues that the ability to speak English is the single greatest empowering tool that immigrants must have to succeed, as it will expand their opportunities greatly.[67]

As of January 2013, 31 states had official English laws. Public opinion polls strongly support making English the official language. A 2010 Rasmussen Reports poll, for example, found 87 percent of Americans saying so.[68] Since 1981, more than 50 bills have been introduced in Congress to make English the nation's official language. Six of these bills passed in one chamber but not in the other; the U.S. Senate passed such legislation in 2006 and 2007. Undaunted, proponents in both houses continue to lobby for passage.

Although proponents of official English legislation claim that such action is essential to preserve a common language and provide a necessary bridge across a widening language barrier within the country, numerous polls and studies demonstrate that the action is unnecessary. For more than 25 years, public opinion polls consistently have shown that the large majority of foreign-born Americans believe learning English is important to becoming a part of U.S. society and finding a job. For example, a 2009 national poll of immigrants revealed that 45 percent did not know English at all and 31 percent knew only a little when they arrived; 70 percent took English classes; and 84 percent said it is hard to get a good job or do well in this country without learning English.[69]

# REALITY check

## Language Acquisition: Newcomers Learning English

Critics fear the end of the historical pattern of immigrant languages dying out and yielding way to English-language dominance across the generations because the Spanish language is so prevalent today. However, recent research shows this pattern still continues, even in Southern California, with more than 50 years of continuous Mexican immigration. As the following chart reveals, native language usage drops significantly, even in the home, with each succeeding generation. Even among Mexicans, by the third generation, 96 percent prefer to speak English.

These results come from analysis of 5,703 young adults in their 20s living in Los Angeles and San Diego. Although the usage of Spanish in the home may last a bit longer, the survival curves for Mexican and other Latin American groups look quite similar to those for Asians and white Europeans.

In this study, the 1.0 generation arrived as adult immigrants and the 1.5 generation arrived in the United States as children before age 10. The 2.0 generation was born in the United States of two foreign-born parents, whereas members of the 2.5 generation were born in the United States of one foreign-born parent and one U.S.-born parent. The U.S.-born 3.0 generation has two U.S.-born parents and three or four foreign-born grandparents, whereas the 3.5 cohort has only one or two foreign-born grandparents.

Source: Rubén G. Rumbaut, Douglas Massey, and Frank D. Bean, "Linguistic Life Expectancies: Immigrant Language Retention in Southern California," *Population and Development Review*, 32, 2006: 447–60. Copyright © 2006, The Population Council, Inc. Reprinted by permission.

**Proportion of Immigrant Group Members Who Speak Mother Tongue at Home, by Generation**

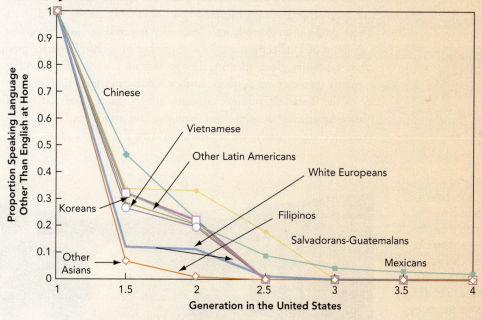

That attitude manifests itself in action. Today, first- and second-generation Americans are becoming fluent in English at a faster pace than did past immigrants (see the Reality Check box). A highly respected research organization, the Pew Hispanic Center, revealed that, while only 38 percent of Latino immigrants speak English very well, 92 percent of their adult children do so, and that figure increases to 96 percent in the next generation.[70]

In the largest longitudinal study of second-generation Americans (5,200 immigrant children in Miami and San Diego), researchers found that 99 percent spoke fluent English and less than one-third maintained fluency in their parents' tongues by age 17.[71] Similarly, another study revealed the preference by 73 percent of second-generation immigrants in Southern California with two foreign-born parents to speak English at home instead of their native tongue. By the third generation, more than 97 percent of these immigrants—Chinese, Filipino, Guatemalan, Korean, Mexican, Salvadoran, and Vietnamese—preferred to speak only English at home.[72]

On a broader scale, the U.S. Census Bureau reports that, of those U.S. residents age 18 to 64 who spoke a language other than English at home in 2007, 56 percent (31 million) reported that they also spoke English "very well." When combined with those who spoke only English at home, 91 percent of the population age 5 and older had no difficulty speaking English.[73] Often, those who do not yet speak English well or at all are disproportionately the elderly (especially those in dense ethnic enclaves), the most recently arrived, the undocumented, and the least educated.[74]

## MULTICULTURALISM

**15-8** Examine fears and realities about language usage and multiculturalism today.

In its early phase, during the 1970s, **multiculturalism** meant including material in the school curriculum that related the contributions of non-European peoples to U.S. history. Next followed efforts to change all areas of the curriculum in elementary and secondary schools and colleges to reflect the diversity of U.S. society and to develop students' awareness of, and appreciation for, the impact of non-European civilizations on U.S. culture. The intent of this movement was to promote an expanded U.S. identity that recognized previously excluded groups as integral components of the whole, both in heritage and in present actuality (see the International Scene box).

Some multiculturalists subsequently moved away from an assimilationist or integrative approach, rejecting a common bond of identity among the distinct minority groups. These multiculturalists advocate "minority nationalism" and "separatist pluralism," with a goal not of a collective national identity but of specific, separate group identities.[75] To create a positive group identity, they go beyond advocacy for teaching and maintaining a group's own cultural customs, history, values, and festivals. They also deny the validity of the dominant culture's customs, history, values, and festivals. Two examples are Native Americans who object to Columbus Day parades and Afrocentrists who assert that Western culture merely was derived from Afro-Egyptian culture.

*Although the tragedy of 9-11 prompted numerous interfaith prayer services nationwide, some places have had them for decades. A quarter-century old, the annual Interfaith Thanksgiving at a Methodist church in Austin, Texas, draws 800 people of all races and religions for the many forms of liturgical dance, chants, hymns, and prayers taking place.*

# the INTERNATIONAL scene

## Multiculturalism in France

For many generations, the French saw themselves as a seamless population bloc whose culture was directly descended from that of the tribes of ancient Gaul. Those who lived in the provinces—Alsatians, Bretons, Gascons, Provençals, and Savoyards, for example—were trained in school to become "French." Physically punished if they spoke their provincial dialects during recess, all were homogenized into the dominant culture, with the brightest students finishing their education in Paris. Even today, the French government attempts to stop the incursion of any non-French words into the language, such as its 2003 ban on the use of "e-mail" in all government ministries, documents, publications, or websites, demanding instead use of the term *courier electronique* (electronic mail).

Not surprisingly, the millions of Italian, Polish, and Spanish immigrants who entered France did not join the mainstream easily, despite their common Catholic faith with the French and their shared European heritage. At the turn of the twentieth century in southern France, for instance, a massacre of Italians occurred. Just before World War II, the French government imposed a ban against the establishment of any organizations by foreigners—a stricture that remained in effect until 1981. Assimilation, or Franco-conformity, was the allowable choice—not pluralism.

France has approximately 5 million legal immigrants (8 percent of the total population) and perhaps another million *clandestines* (illegal aliens), most coming from Muslim North Africa. Many French became concerned that their nation was losing its cultural identity because of the large influx of immigrants whose appearance, language, religion, and values were so different. Indeed, after winning a record 15 percent of the vote in 1998, the far-right, anti-immigrant National Front Party finished second in the 2002 election, with a 17 percent total. Spearheaded by left-wing parties and human rights groups, both elections sparked protest demonstrations by tens of thousands of people across France. In the streets of Paris, people chanted, "We're all immigrants."

That public chanting echoed former Prime Minister Michel Rocard's call for a new recognition of French diversity. It also recalled the encouragement of a multiculturalist viewpoint by President François Mitterrand, who, several years earlier, had observed: "We are French. Our ancestors are the Gauls, and we are also a little Roman, a little German, a little Jewish, a little Italian, a small bit Spanish, more and more Portuguese, who knows, maybe Polish, too. And I wonder whether we aren't already a bit Arab."

In the 2007 presidential election with an impressive 85 percent voter turnout, the National Front Party garnered only 10 percent of the vote. The son of Hungarian immigrants, Nicolas Sarkozy, became president, but lost a re-election bid in 2012 to a native-born rival, socialist Francois Hollande. In that election, the National Front Party received 18 percent of the vote, its strongest showing ever.

Generally, the French do not encourage cultural diversity. Instead, they stress a uniform, secularized French identity as the best guarantor of national unity and the separation of church and state. In 2004, for example, the government enacted a ban, still in effect, on religious symbols in schools, including Muslim dress (notably, the *hijab*, or women's headscarf that covers the hair and neck), Jewish *yarmulke* (skullcaps), and large crosses. The move primarily is part of French efforts to cope with the influx of North African Muslims and the challenge they present to the unofficial French creed of secularism.

### CRITICAL THINKING QUESTION

How do you think France and the United States compare in public attitudes about immigration and diversity?

Another striking example is the argument that only groups with power can be racist. This view holds that because whites have power, they are intrinsically racist, whereas people of color lack power and so cannot be racist.[76] The counter-argument is that any racial group that blames, criticizes, stereotypes, or acts against another entire racial group is guilty of racist thinking or action. Furthermore, opponents of multiculturalism argue that it undermines the assimilation ethic and that the weaker our assimilation efforts, the fewer immigrants we can accept if we are to remain a cohesive society.

# REALITY check

## The Second Generation: Assimilation and Integration

How well do immigrants integrate into U.S. society? Research findings vary, as per segmented assimilation theory, but generally they report positive findings. Perhaps the most encouraging insights come from a definitive, 10-year study, *Inheriting the City: The Children of Immigrants Come of Age* (2008), that examined five immigrant groups—Chinese, Dominicans, Russian Jews, South Americans, and West Indians—living in metropolitan New York. Importantly, the authors also conducted companion studies on native-born blacks, Puerto Ricans, and whites for a comparison.

Their study included a survey and in-person interviews of a random sample of second-generation residents ages 22 to 32 in four New York City boroughs and the inner suburbs, either in their residence, college, or workplace. What they learned contradicted the fears of some experts that these young adults would not do as well as previous waves of immigrants due to lack of high-paying manufacturing jobs, poor public schools, and

an entrenched racial divide. Far from descending into an urban underclass, the children of immigrants are using their cultural and social capital to avoid some of the obstacles that native minority groups cannot.

Repeating the pattern of the children of earlier European immigrants, this new second generation has exceeded its parents' success. The degree to which this has occurred varies, though. The children of Chinese and Russian Jewish immigrants have achieved higher levels of education and earnings than native-born whites. Those of South American and Dominican ancestry earn about as much as white Americans and have a higher education level than that of African Americans and Puerto Ricans, but their level of educational attainment is lower than that of whites. West Indians encounter the same systemic racial barriers that their darker-skinned native counterparts also face.

Overall though, the second generation is rapidly moving into the

mainstream—speaking English and working in jobs that resemble those held by native New Yorkers their age. Still, the second generation has not followed the traditional immigration model in all areas. Unlike their parents, who found economic success within ethnic enclaves, many of the second generation immigrants have moved into the mainstream economy. Yet even as they successfully integrate into U.S. society, they are able to preserve their cultural identities without feeling torn between the two cultures.

Despite their relatively high level of education and income, many have not yet become politically and civically engaged. This study, however, does leave open the question of whether New York, with its long history of incorporating immigrants into an already diverse population, provides a different context of reception than might be true elsewhere.

Source: Philip Kasinitz, John H. Mollenkopf, Mary C. Waters, and Jennifer Holdaway, *Inheriting the City: The Children of Immigrants Come of Age.* Cambridge, MA: Harvard University Press, 2008.

Another battleground for multiculturalists involves offering or eliminating courses in Western civilization. Some institutions, such as Providence College in Rhode Island, expanded such course requirements and made them interdisciplinary; other institutions, such as Stanford University, questioned their inclusion at all. At many institutions, the proposals for curriculum change ranged from making all students take non-Western and women's studies courses as part of their degree requirements to excluding all Western history and culture courses from requirements.

Regardless of their orientation, most multiculturalists are pluralists waging war with assimilationists. Neither side will vanquish the other, though, for both forces remain integral parts of U.S. society. The United States continues to offer a beacon of hope to immigrants everywhere, keeping the rich tradition of pluralism alive and well. And yet, as has been consistently demonstrated for centuries, assimilationist forces will remain strong, particularly for immigrant children and their descendants (see the Reality Check box on the second generation). Multiculturalism will no more weaken that process than did the many past manifestations of ethnic-ingroup solidarity.

Some analysts recommend the need for a common ground position that replaces the assimilationist and pluralist models with a cosmopolitan model. Exaggerating and tolerating cultural differences leaves minorities outside the mainstream and does not promote a unified national identity.[77] Insisting on cultural uniformity ignores the reality that we are all members of a culture. Instead, we might consider a "postethnic" perspective that emphasizes a shared civic nationalism that overcomes the politics of race and the politics of identity, and instead recognizes the reality of multiple identities.[78]

## Diversity in the Future

The U.S. Census Bureau—working from current demographic patterns and making certain assumptions about future births, deaths, and international migration—projects a dramatic change in the composition of U.S. society by the mid–twenty-first century. It reports that the cumulative effects of immigration will be more important than births to people already living in the United States. By the mid–twenty-first century, 82 percent of the population increase will be due to immigrants arriving since 2005 and their U.S.-born descendants.[79]

The rapid growth of the Hispanic population, says the Census Bureau, enabled Hispanics to become the largest U.S. minority group and surpass the African American population in 2000, when there were 35.3 million Hispanics and 34.7 million African Americans. By 2060, Hispanics will number 128.8 million, or 30 percent of the total population. The Census Bureau projects that non-Hispanic blacks then will number 61.8 million, or 15 percent (see Figure 15.9). All data reflect midrange projections, not high or low estimates.

The nation's Asian population will grow to 34.4 million, or 8 percent, by 2060. Native Americans will increase to 6.3 million by then, nearly 2 percent of the total. The number of non-Hispanic whites will be approximately 179 million by 2060, or 46 percent of the population.[80]

**Explore** on **MySocLab**
Activity: Issues in America: Race, Ethnicity, and Social Problems

**Read** on **MySocLab**
Document: Whites Account for Under Half of Births in U.S.

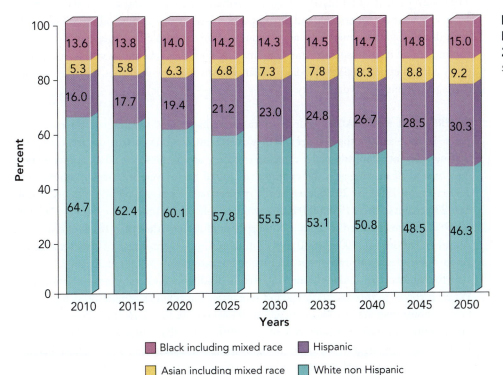

**FIGURE 15.9** U.S. Population Projections to 2050 by Percent

*Source:* U.S. Census Bureau.

Legend:
- Black including mixed race
- Hispanic
- Asian including mixed race
- White non Hispanic

Some Americans have reacted to these projections with alarm, using them to argue for immigration restrictions. Others relish the thought of U.S. society becoming more diverse. These projections, however, have some limitations, not the least of which is their assumption that current trends continue and that conditions worldwide will remain constant several decades into the future. Immigration is the most unstable demographic variable because it is affected by unforeseeable economic, political, and social forces. Certainly, four or five decades ago, no one would have predicted the current birth, death, and migration patterns that now affect the United States. A forecast about the year 2060, then, is anything but certain.

Even more significant is the high probability that these Census Bureau projections will fall victim to the **Dillingham Flaw**. Who is to say that today's group categories will have the same meaning in the mid–twenty-first century? Two generations ago, Italian, Polish, and Slavic Americans still were members of distinct minority groups that lacked economic, political, and social power. They displayed all the classic characteristics of minority groups: ascribed status, endogamy, unequal treatment, and visibility. Today, they mostly are in the mainstream, displaying traits of civic, marital, and structural assimilation. Like European Americans who intermarried earlier, those whose ancestry is Italian, Polish, and Slavic now are mostly a blend of other nationalities. Two generations from now, the same may be true of other groups, such as Hispanics. Americans will likely view one another differently from how we do now.

## SOCIAL INDICATORS OF CHANGE

**15-9** Examine what social indicators tell us about change in population diversity.

Although the demographic patterns of fertility, mortality, and migration are helpful in making projections, other patterns give reason for caution in predicting the future.

**INTERETHNIC MARRIAGES.** Our expectation that Hispanic Americans will marry outside their ethnic group, as have European Americans, finds support in the process that already is underway. In 2010, approximately 2.3 million Hispanic Americans were married to someone of non-Hispanic origin, up 92 percent from 1.2 million in 1990. That is 27 percent of all married Hispanic American couples and most notably among second-generation Americans, and the proportion is growing steadily.[81] The children born from these exogamous marriages are obviously of mixed ethnic heritage, and if this trend continues, one day, "Hispanic American" may be no more a distinctly visible ethnic category but rather one similar to today's Italian, Polish, or Slavic identities, a marker of one's heritage, not one's everyday reality.

**15-10** Evaluate projections about U.S. society in 2060.

**INTERRACIAL MARRIAGES.** For generations, we have failed to eliminate the racial barrier, so by mid-century, that barrier still may exist. However, one present-day trend suggests that our current simplistic racial categories already are obsolete. In 2010, approximately 4 percent of all marriages in the continental United States were interracial, compared to 1.3 percent in 1980. By 2010, interracially married couples numbered more than 2.4 million, 23 percent of them (558,000) black–white couples, three times more than the 167,000 in 1980. Whites married to a non-white spouse of a race other than black (most often, Asian) grew from 450,000 in 1980 to 1.72 million. Couples consisting of blacks married to a non-black spouse of a race other than white increased from 34,000 to 132,000.[82]

Researchers are making some interesting findings about interracial relationships. When it comes to interracial dating and romances, the younger generation is more open to this choice than are previous generations. However, studies show that adolescents who interracially date face a greater risk of peer difficulties than intraracially dating youth. Informal sanctions against them are strongest when the romances involve black students.[83]

Interracial relationships more often are cohabiting unions than marital unions, but in either case, among whites and blacks (including immigrant and native blacks), they are more likely to be of a black man and a white woman. Native-born African Americans are more likely than ethnic blacks to marry whites. Ethnic blacks and non-white Puerto Ricans are more likely to marry African Americans than to marry whites.[84]

Interracial marriages of all combinations (Asian, black, Hispanic, white) are no more likely to end in divorce than intraracial marriages when compared with other high-risk groups.[85] However, interracial adult couples, particularly black–white couples, often encounter negative societal reactions, much like the adolescents mentioned earlier. One study found that whites married to blacks encounter more racism directly than whites married to other non-black minorities. White women encountered more racial incidents with their black husbands (for example, inferior service, racial profiling, and racism against their children) and more hostilities from families and others they know than did other interracial pairings.[86] Despite the challenges, another study found that partners in interracial relationships reported significantly higher relationship satisfaction compared to those in intraracial relationships.[87]

Racial and interracial marriage patterns vary if we control for ethnicity. For example, West Indian men of any generation have lower exogamy rates than African American men, while exogamy rates are higher among West Indian women who arrived as children or were born in the United States than among African American women.[88] What this tells us is that both gender and racial differences in interracial marriages can exist because of ethnicity.

Interracial romantic relationships are a useful barometer of race relations and structural assimilation in U.S. society. Their increasing prevalence is an indicator of the decline in social distance among groups. Similar demographic and social factors among African, Asian, European, and Hispanic Americans help predict outdating across racial groups. Men are more likely to date interracially than women, particularly if they attend interracial schools. Neither religious preference nor geographic region is a significant factor, and neither apparently is status chasing. One study found no evidence of a pattern of majority-group members using interracial dating relationships to "trade up" by dating racial minorities with higher economic and educational attainment.[89] It would appear that, as also suggested by my social distance study discussed in Chapter 1, the racial barrier is lowering when it comes to intimate social relations.

**RACIAL IDENTITY.** In 2011, more than 8.7 million Americans were of mixed racial ancestry, 2.8 percent of the total population of 311.6 million.[90] As the number of biracial and multiracial Americans continues to grow, so does the matter of racial identity formation. As we discussed in Chapter 1, our responses to race are within a socially constructed reality, as illustrated by President Obama, a biracial man with a white mother and a black father, but whom a great many people simply classify as an African American. Even the questions raised during his candidacy about whether he was "too black" or "not black enough" revealed how fixated many were on the old racial categories.[91]

How do biracial or multiracial Americans categorize themselves? Sometimes their answer varies with the context in which it is asked—at home, in school or the workplace, or who is present at the time. The influences of family and peers also may be a factor. That identity might even change and develop throughout time as an individual matures.[92]

Self-identification also appears to depend on the relationship between physical appearance and a sense of belonging and exclusion.[93] Although more Americans than ever identify themselves as biracial or multiracial, many other biracial or multiracial Americans self-identify as monoracial. This especially is true among black biracials who tend to identify as monoracial blacks.[94] Many multiracial people growing up in a black neighborhood tend to identify themselves as black, as there is great pressure from society to choose one race.[95]

Slavery reinforced in the American mind a rigid racial classification system that has long outlived slavery itself. Once a social construct that reflected both that exploitative system and the decades of Jim Crow laws that followed, and continuing into and past the

*President Barack Obama is a splendid example of the multiple narratives becoming so common in American family life. The son of a white American mother and black African father, his extended family expands into Africa, Canada, Indonesia, Malaysia, China and slave-period America, and has Christian, Muslim, and Jewish roots. Here, he hugs his half-sister, Maya Soetoro-Ng, at her 2003 wedding to Konrad Ng, third from right, in Hawaii. From left are his daughters, Sasha and Malia; his grandmother Madelyn Dunham, seated; Konrad's parents, Joan and Howard Ng, and brother Perry Ng; and Michelle Obama.*

Civil Rights Movement, it no longer is an accurate means to describe demographic realities. Instead, say advocates, an increasingly multiracial America requires us to create a new social construct. We must deconstruct race as an "either-or" mind-set and relegate racial identity to a much less important place in our dealings with one another, perhaps like Mexico, where its census does not even ask about race.[96]

That deconstruction is underway as America's foreign-born population is challenging traditional views of race. Many are more likely to give their national origin when identifying their race or ethnicity. For example, the U.S. Census Bureau found that 87 percent of those born in Cuba and 53 percent of those born in Mexico identified themselves as white, but a majority of the more recently arrived Dominicans and Salvadorans would not describe themselves as either black or white. Both immigration and the higher birth rates among the foreign-born have driven the changing perception of race in Census 2010.[97]

**RELIGION AND MIGRATION.** Earlier immigration waves transformed the United States from an almost exclusively Protestant country into a land of three major faiths: Catholic, Jewish, and Protestant. Because religion often is closely intertwined with ethnicity, current migration patterns offer clues about the religious preferences of future Americans, if current trends continue.

Hispanic and Filipino migration may increase the U.S. Catholic adult population from the current 25 percent of the adult population to perhaps 28 percent by 2050. Migration from Africa, Asia, and the Middle East may increase the Muslim population from 1 percent of the total to 3 percent. Given current patterns, the Jewish population may decline from 2 percent to 1 percent and the Protestant population from 51 percent to 46 percent; the populations of other religions—including Buddhism, Hinduism, and Sikhism—may slightly increase from 2 percent to 3 percent. Those declaring "no religion" may grow from 15 to 20 percent. Even if these predictions turn out to be somewhat inaccurate, the future will show even greater religious diversity than the present does.

Caution is needed in accepting these predictions, of course, because the Dillingham Flaw of oversimplified generalizations and the imposition of present-day sensibilities may lead to a misreading of the eventual reality. Religious intermarriage now is increasing among followers of all faiths, and the nonreligious segment of society also is growing, so we may find a very different future with respect to religion than we accurately can project.

## BEYOND TOMORROW

*Diversity* is the word that best describes the past, present, and future of the United States. United by a core culture and shared beliefs in certain ideals, the nation's peoples have not always understood their common bond or openly accepted one another as equals. As the dual realities of assimilation and pluralism continue to pull people seemingly in two directions at once, few people recognize that they are witnessing a recurring set of historical patterns. Instead, some voices cry out again against immigration, brand the newcomers as "inassimilable," and express fear for the character and cohesiveness of society. Yet immigrants always have been important to the growth of U.S. society, and their presence has continually strengthened the country.

Despite some progress, the United States has never fully resolved its race-relations problems. As it becomes a more multiracial society than ever before, it may see a worsening of race relations. We saw some such indicators in the late twentieth century: black–Asian and black–Latino conflicts in addition to black–white conflicts. Perhaps, though, the situation will improve with deconstruction of the rigid racial categories that still promote an "us" and "them" mentality and with more sharing of power through the increased presence of people of color in elective offices and other policymaking positions. Perhaps, also, the unity of diverse peoples that occurred after the 2001 terrorist attacks will be a source of inspiration for improved race relations in the years to come. Gender equality—as well as inclusiveness and protection of rights for the aged, disabled, and homosexuals—are other areas in which some gains have occurred but in which additional concerted efforts are necessary for all to achieve their fullest potential.

As we approach the future, we do so with the educational attainment of all Americans rising. If knowledge is power, perhaps that reality will lead us to greater appreciation and tolerance for one another. This book has been an attempt to enhance that understanding. We need to comprehend the larger context and patterns within which the dynamics of intergroup relations exist. We need to realize that pluralism always has been part of the U.S. experience and does not threaten either the assimilation process or the cohesiveness of society. We need to recognize that race and ethnicity simply are other people's humanity. When we reach that level of understanding, we will be able to acknowledge that diversity is the nation's strength, not its weakness, and when that happens, our society will be even stronger.

# On MySocLab

 Study and Review on MySocLab

## KEY TERMS

## DISCUSSION QUESTIONS

1. If you are the descendant of immigrants, how realistic or unrealistic is the three-generation hypothesis in your family? If you are an immigrant or the child of immigrant parents, how realistic or unrealistic is transnationalism in your family? If you are the descendant of migrants from the rural South to the urban North, do you find any relevance to these concepts in your family?
2. What in this chapter particularly struck your interest? Why?
3. What do current immigration patterns indicate? Is immigration a problem for native-born U.S. residents? Explain.
4. What are the pros and cons of bilingual education?
5. Describe the varying viewpoints about native language retention and English language acquisition.
6. Do you have any thoughts on the projections for the future given in this chapter, or on the Dillingham Flaw warning?

## INTERNET ACTIVITIES

1. Check out this YouTube music video at http://www. youtube.com/watch?v=sEJfS1v-fU0. It's an example of what many Americans think about English as the country's language. It's very appropriate to this chapter's discussion. What do you think?
2. U.S. English (http://www.us-english.org), the organization mentioned on page 516 that is dedicated to preserving English as the common language, has its own home page. Go to it and read some of their arguments for their cause. What is your reaction?
3. Want to learn more about current immigration issues? At this site, http://www.theodora.com/debate.html, you will find a variety of discussion topics. Of particular interest may be the various "Facts of Immigration" links found when you scroll down the page.
4. How many of the biracial celebrities at http://blackflix. com/articles/multiracial.html can you recognize? Were there any surprises?
5. Take a look at the various U.S. Census Bureau projections at http://www.census.gov/population/projections/ data/national/2012/summarytables.html about race/ origin group demographics from 2015 to 2060.

# APPENDIX

## IMMIGRATION, 1820–2012

**Immigration by Region and Selected Country of Last Residence: Fiscal Years 1820–2012**

| Region and country of last residence[1] | 1820 to 1829 | 1830 to 1839 | 1840 to 1849 | 1850 to 1859 | 1860 to 1869 | 1870 to 1879 | 1880 to 1889 | 1890 to 1899 |
|---|---|---|---|---|---|---|---|---|
| **Total** | **128,502** | **538,381** | **1,427,337** | **2,814,554** | **2,081,261** | **2,742,137** | **5,248,568** | **3,694,294** |
| Europe | 99,272 | 422,771 | 1,369,259 | 2,619,680 | 1,877,726 | 2,251,878 | 4,638,677 | 3,576,411 |
| Austria-Hungary[2, 3, 4] | - | - | - | - | 3,375 | 60,127 | 314,787 | 534,059 |
| Austria[2, 4] | - | - | - | - | 2,700 | 54,529 | 204,805 | 268,218 |
| Hungary[2] | - | - | - | - | 483 | 5,598 | 109,982 | 203,350 |
| Belgium | 28 | 20 | 3,996 | 5,765 | 5,785 | 6,991 | 18,738 | 19,642 |
| Bulgaria[5] | - | - | - | - | - | - | - | 52 |
| Denmark | 173 | 927 | 671 | 3,227 | 13,553 | 29,278 | 85,342 | 56,671 |
| France[7] | 7,694 | 39,330 | 75,300 | 81,778 | 35,938 | 71,901 | 48,193 | 35,616 |
| Germany[3, 4] | 5,753 | 124,726 | 385,434 | 976,072 | 723,734 | 751,769 | 1,445,181 | 579,072 |
| Greece | 17 | 49 | 17 | 32 | 51 | 209 | 1,807 | 12,732 |
| Ireland[8] | 51,617 | 170,672 | 656,145 | 1,029,486 | 427,419 | 422,264 | 674,061 | 405,710 |
| Italy | 430 | 2,225 | 1,476 | 8,643 | 9,853 | 46,296 | 267,660 | 603,761 |
| Netherlands | 1,105 | 1,377 | 7,624 | 11,122 | 8,387 | 14,267 | 52,715 | 29,349 |
| Norway-Sweden[9] | 91 | 1,149 | 12,389 | 22,202 | 82,937 | 178,823 | 586,441 | 334,058 |
| Norway[9] | - | - | - | - | 16,068 | 88,644 | 185,111 | 96,810 |
| Sweden[9] | - | - | - | - | 24,224 | 90,179 | 401,330 | 237,248 |
| Poland[3] | 19 | 366 | 105 | 1,087 | 1,886 | 11,016 | 42,910 | 107,793 |
| Portugal[10] | 177 | 820 | 196 | 1,299 | 2,083 | 13,971 | 15,186 | 25,874 |
| Romania | - | - | - | - | - | - | 5,842 | 6,808 |
| Russia[3, 11] | 86 | 280 | 520 | 423 | 1,670 | 35,177 | 182,698 | 450,101 |
| Spain[12] | 2,595 | 2,010 | 1,916 | 8,795 | 6,966 | 5,540 | 3,995 | 9,189 |
| Switzerland | 3,148 | 4,430 | 4,819 | 24,423 | 21,124 | 25,212 | 81,151 | 37,020 |
| United Kingdom[8, 13] | 26,336 | 74,350 | 218,572 | 445,322 | 532,956 | 578,447 | 810,900 | 328,759 |
| Other Europe | 3 | 40 | 79 | 4 | 9 | 590 | 1,070 | 145 |
| Asia | 34 | 55 | 121 | 36,080 | 54,408 | 134,128 | 71,151 | 61,285 |
| China | 3 | 8 | 32 | 35,933 | 54,028 | 133,139 | 65,797 | 15,268 |
| India | 9 | 38 | 33 | 42 | 50 | 166 | 247 | 102 |
| Japan | - | - | - | - | 138 | 193 | 1,583 | 13,998 |
| Turkey | 19 | 8 | 45 | 94 | 129 | 382 | 2,478 | 27,510 |
| Other Asia | 3 | 1 | 11 | 11 | 63 | 248 | 1,046 | 4,407 |
| America | 9,655 | 31,905 | 50,516 | 84,145 | 130,292 | 345,010 | 524,826 | 37,350 |
| Canada and Newfoundland[15,16] | 2,297 | 11,875 | 34,285 | 64,171 | 117,978 | 324,310 | 492,865 | 3,098 |
| Mexico[16, 17] | 3,835 | 7,187 | 3,069 | 3,446 | 1,957 | 5,133 | 2,405 | 734 |
| Caribbean | 3,061 | 11,792 | 11,803 | 12,447 | 8,751 | 14,285 | 27,323 | 31,480 |
| Central America | 57 | 94 | 297 | 512 | 70 | 173 | 279 | 649 |
| South America | 405 | 957 | 1,062 | 3,569 | 1,536 | 1,109 | 1,954 | 1,389 |
| Other America[20] | - | - | - | - | - | - | - | - |
| Africa | 15 | 50 | 61 | 84 | 407 | 371 | 763 | 432 |
| Egypt | - | - | - | - | 4 | 29 | 145 | 51 |
| Liberia | 1 | 8 | 5 | 7 | 43 | 52 | 21 | 9 |
| South Africa | - | - | - | - | 35 | 48 | 23 | 9 |
| Other Africa | 14 | 42 | 56 | 77 | 325 | 242 | 574 | 363 |

See footnotes at end of table.

| Region and country of last residence[1] | 1820 to 1829 | 1830 to 1839 | 1840 to 1849 | 1850 to 1859 | 1860 to 1869 | 1870 to 1879 | 1880 to 1889 | 1890 to 1899 |
|---|---|---|---|---|---|---|---|---|
| **Total** | **128,502** | **538,381** | **1,427,337** | **2,814,554** | **2,081,261** | **2,742,137** | **5,248,568** | **3,694,294** |
| Oceania | 3 | 7 | 14 | 166 | 187 | 9,996 | 12,361 | 4,704 |
| Australia | 2 | 1 | 2 | 15 | - | 8,930 | 7,250 | 3,098 |
| New Zealand | - | - | - | - | - | 39 | 21 | 12 |
| Other Oceania | 1 | 6 | 12 | 151 | 187 | 1,027 | 5,090 | 1,594 |
| Not Specified[20,21] | 19,523 | 83,593 | 7,366 | 74,399 | 18,241 | 754 | 790 | 14,112 |

| Region and country of last residence[1] | 1900 to 1909 | 1910 to 1919 | 1920 to 1929 | 1930 to 1939 | 1940 to 1949 | 1950 to 1959 | 1960 to 1969 | 1970 to 1979 |
|---|---|---|---|---|---|---|---|---|
| **Total** | **8,202,388** | **6,347,380** | **4,295,510** | **699,375** | **856,608** | **2,499,268** | **3,213,749** | **4,248,203** |
| Europe | 7,572,569 | 4,985,411 | 2,560,340 | 444,399 | 472,524 | 1,404,973 | 1,133,443 | 825,590 |
| Austria-Hungary[2,3,4] | 2,001,376 | 1,154,727 | 60,891 | 12,531 | 13,574 | 113,015 | 27,590 | 20,387 |
| Austria[2,4] | 532,416 | 589,174 | 31,392 | 5,307 | 8,393 | 81,354 | 17,571 | 14,239 |
| Hungary[2] | 685,567 | 565,553 | 29,499 | 7,224 | 5,181 | 31,661 | 10,019 | 6,148 |
| Belgium | 37,429 | 32,574 | 21,511 | 4,013 | 12,473 | 18,885 | 9,647 | 5,413 |
| Bulgaria[5] | 34,651 | 27,180 | 2,824 | 1,062 | 449 | 97 | 598 | 1,011 |
| Czechoslovakia[6] | - | - | 101,182 | 17,757 | 8,475 | 1,624 | 2,758 | 5,654 |
| Denmark | 61,227 | 45,830 | 34,406 | 3,470 | 4,549 | 10,918 | 9,797 | 4,405 |
| Finland | - | - | 16,922 | 2,438 | 2,230 | 4,923 | 4,310 | 2,829 |
| France[7] | 67,735 | 60,335 | 54,842 | 13,761 | 36,954 | 50,113 | 46,975 | 26,281 |
| Germany[3,4] | 328,722 | 174,227 | 386,634 | 119,107 | 119,506 | 576,905 | 209,616 | 77,142 |
| Greece | 145,402 | 198,108 | 60,774 | 10,599 | 8,605 | 45,153 | 74,173 | 102,370 |
| Ireland[8] | 344,940 | 166,445 | 202,854 | 28,195 | 15,701 | 47,189 | 37,788 | 11,461 |
| Italy | 1,930,475 | 1,229,916 | 528,133 | 85,053 | 50,509 | 184,576 | 200,111 | 150,031 |
| Netherlands | 42,463 | 46,065 | 29,397 | 7,791 | 13,877 | 46,703 | 37,918 | 10,373 |
| Norway-Sweden[9] | 426,981 | 192,445 | 170,329 | 13,452 | 17,326 | 44,224 | 36,150 | 10,298 |
| Norway[9] | 182,542 | 79,488 | 70,327 | 6,901 | 8,326 | 22,806 | 17,371 | 3,927 |
| Sweden[9] | 244,439 | 112,957 | 100,002 | 6,551 | 9,000 | 21,418 | 18,779 | 6,371 |
| Poland[3] | - | - | 223,316 | 25,555 | 7,577 | 6,465 | 55,742 | 33,696 |
| Portugal[10] | 65,154 | 82,489 | 44,829 | 3,518 | 6,765 | 13,928 | 70,568 | 104,754 |
| Romania | 57,322 | 13,566 | 67,810 | 5,264 | 1,254 | 914 | 2,339 | 10,774 |
| Russia[3,11] | 1,501,301 | 1,106,998 | 61,604 | 2,463 | 605 | 453 | 2,329 | 28,132 |
| Spain[12] | 24,818 | 53,262 | 47,109 | 3,669 | 2,774 | 6,880 | 40,793 | 41,718 |
| Switzerland | 32,541 | 22,839 | 31,772 | 5,990 | 9,904 | 17,577 | 19,193 | 8,536 |
| United Kingdom[8,13] | 469,518 | 371,878 | 341,552 | 61,813 | 131,794 | 195,709 | 220,213 | 133,218 |
| Yugoslavia[14] | - | - | 49,215 | 6,920 | 2,039 | 6,966 | 17,990 | 31,862 |
| Other Europe | 514 | 6,527 | 22,434 | 9,978 | 5,584 | 11,756 | 6,845 | 5,245 |
| Asia | 299,836 | 269,736 | 126,740 | 19,231 | 34,532 | 135,844 | 358,605 | 1,406,544 |
| China | 19,884 | 20,916 | 30,648 | 5,874 | 16,072 | 8,836 | 14,060 | 17,627 |
| Hong Kong | - | - | - | - | - | 13,781 | 67,047 | 117,350 |
| India | 3,026 | 3,478 | 2,076 | 554 | 1,692 | 1,850 | 18,638 | 147,997 |
| Iran | - | - | 208 | 198 | 1,144 | 3,195 | 9,059 | 33,763 |
| Israel | - | - | - | - | 98 | 21,376 | 30,911 | 36,306 |
| Japan | 139,712 | 77,125 | 42,057 | 2,683 | 1,557 | 40,651 | 40,956 | 49,392 |
| Jordan | - | - | - | - | - | 4,899 | 9,230 | 25,541 |
| Korea | - | - | - | - | 83 | 4,845 | 27,048 | 241,192 |
| Philippines | - | - | - | 391 | 4,099 | 17,245 | 70,660 | 337,726 |
| Syria | - | - | 5,307 | 2,188 | 1,179 | 1,091 | 2,432 | 8,086 |
| Taiwan | - | - | - | - | - | 721 | 15,657 | 83,155 |
| Turkey | 127,999 | 160,717 | 40,450 | 1,327 | 754 | 2,980 | 9,464 | 12,209 |
| Vietnam | - | - | - | - | - | 290 | 2,949 | 121,716 |
| Other Asia | 9,215 | 7,500 | 5,994 | 6,016 | 7,854 | 14,084 | 40,494 | 174,484 |

| Region and country of last residence[1] | 1900 to 1909 | 1910 to 1919 | 1920 to 1929 | 1930 to 1939 | 1940 to 1949 | 1950 to 1959 | 1960 to 1969 | 1970 to 1979 |
|---|---|---|---|---|---|---|---|---|
| **Total** | **8,202,388** | **6,347,380** | **4,295,510** | **699,375** | **856,608** | **2,499,268** | **3,213,749** | **4,248,203** |
| America | 277,809 | 1,070,539 | 1,591,278 | 230,319 | 328,435 | 921,610 | 1,674,172 | 1,904,355 |
| Canada and Newfoundland[15, 16] | 123,067 | 708,715 | 949,286 | 162,703 | 160,911 | 353,169 | 433,128 | 179,267 |
| Mexico[16, 17] | 31,188 | 185,334 | 498,945 | 32,709 | 56,158 | 273,847 | 441,824 | 621,218 |
| Caribbean | 100,960 | 120,860 | 83,482 | 18,052 | 46,194 | 115,661 | 427,235 | 708,850 |
| Cuba | - | - | 12,769 | 10,641 | 25,976 | 73,221 | 202,030 | 256,497 |
| Dominican Republic | - | - | - | 1,026 | 4,802 | 10,219 | 83,552 | 139,249 |
| Haiti | - | - | - | 156 | 823 | 3,787 | 28,992 | 55,166 |
| Jamaica[18] | - | - | - | - | - | 7,397 | 62,218 | 130,226 |
| Other Caribbean[18] | 100,960 | 120,860 | 70,713 | 6,229 | 14,593 | 21,037 | 50,443 | 127,712 |
| Central America | 7,341 | 15,692 | 16,511 | 6,840 | 20,135 | 40,201 | 98,560 | 120,374 |
| Belize | 77 | 40 | 285 | 193 | 433 | 1,133 | 4,185 | 6,747 |
| Costa Rica | - | - | - | 431 | 1,965 | 4,044 | 17,975 | 12,405 |
| El Salvador | - | - | - | 597 | 4,885 | 5,094 | 14,405 | 29,428 |
| Guatemala | - | - | - | 423 | 1,303 | 4,197 | 14,357 | 23,837 |
| Honduras | - | - | - | 679 | 1,874 | 5,320 | 15,078 | 15,651 |
| Nicaragua | - | - | - | 405 | 4,393 | 7,812 | 10,383 | 10,911 |
| Panama[19] | - | - | - | 1,452 | 5,282 | 12,601 | 22,177 | 21,395 |
| Other Central America | 7,264 | 15,652 | 16,226 | 2,660 | - | - | - | - |
| South America | 15,253 | 39,938 | 43,025 | 9,990 | 19,662 | 78,418 | 250,754 | 273,608 |
| Argentina | - | - | - | 1,067 | 3,108 | 16,346 | 49,384 | 30,303 |
| Boliva | - | - | - | 50 | 893 | 2,759 | 6,205 | 5,635 |
| Brazil | - | - | 4,627 | 1,468 | 3,653 | 11,547 | 29,238 | 18,600 |
| Chile | - | - | - | 347 | 1,320 | 4,669 | 12,384 | 15,032 |
| Colombia | - | - | - | 1,027 | 3,454 | 15,567 | 68,371 | 71,265 |
| Ecuador | - | - | - | 244 | 2,207 | 8,574 | 34,107 | 47,464 |
| Guyana | - | - | - | 131 | 596 | 1,131 | 4,546 | 38,278 |
| Paraguay | - | - | - | 33 | 85 | 576 | 1,249 | 1,486 |
| Peru | - | - | - | 321 | 1,273 | 5,980 | 19,783 | 25,311 |
| Suriname | - | - | - | 25 | 130 | 299 | 612 | 714 |
| Uruguay | - | - | - | 112 | 754 | 1,026 | 4,089 | 8,416 |
| Venezuela | - | - | - | 1,155 | 2,182 | 9,927 | 20,758 | 11,007 |
| Other South America | 15,253 | 39,938 | 38,398 | 4,010 | 7 | 17 | 28 | 97 |
| Other America[20] | - | - | 29 | 25 | 25,375 | 60,314 | 22,671 | 1,038 |
| Africa | 6,326 | 8,867 | 6,362 | 2,120 | 6,720 | 13,016 | 23,780 | 71,408 |
| Egypt | - | - | 1,063 | 781 | 1,613 | 1,996 | 5,581 | 23,543 |
| Ethiopia | - | - | - | 10 | 28 | 302 | 804 | 2,588 |
| Liberia | - | - | - | 35 | 37 | 289 | 841 | 2,391 |
| Morocco | - | - | - | 73 | 879 | 2,703 | 2,880 | 1,967 |
| South Africa | - | - | - | 312 | 1,022 | 2,278 | 4,360 | 10,002 |
| Other Africa | 6,326 | 8,867 | 5,299 | 909 | 3,141 | 5,448 | 9,314 | 30,917 |
| Oceania | 12,355 | 12,339 | 9,860 | 3,306 | 14,262 | 11,353 | 23,630 | 39,980 |
| Australia | 11,191 | 11,280 | 8,404 | 2,260 | 11,201 | 8,275 | 14,986 | 18,708 |
| New Zealand | - | - | 935 | 790 | 2,351 | 1,799 | 3,775 | 5,018 |
| Other Oceania | 1,164 | 1,059 | 521 | 256 | 710 | 1,279 | 4,869 | 16,254 |
| Not Specified[20, 21] | 33,493 | 488 | 930 | - | 135 | 12,472 | 119 | 326 |

## Immigration by Region and Selected Country of Last Residence: Fiscal Years 1820–2012   (Continued)

| Region and country of last residence[1] | 1980 to 1989 | 1990 to 1999 | 2000 to 2009 | 2010 to 2012 |
|---|---|---|---|---|
| **Total** | **6,244,379** | **9,775,398** | **10,299,430** | **3,136,296** |
| Europe | 668,866 | 1,348,612 | 1,348,904 | 273,097 |
| Austria-Hungary [2, 3, 4] | 20,437 | 27,529 | 33,929 | 12,236 |
| Austria [2, 4] | 15,374 | 18,234 | 21,151 | 9,172 |
| Hungary [2] | 5,063 | 9,295 | 12,778 | 3,064 |
| Belgium | 7,028 | 7,077 | 8,157 | 2,130 |
| Bulgaria [5] | 1,124 | 16,948 | 40,003 | 7,336 |
| Czechoslovakia [6] | 5,678 | 8,970 | 18,691 | 4,200 |
| Denmark | 4,847 | 6,189 | 6,049 | 1,510 |
| Finland | 2,569 | 3,970 | 3,970 | 1,185 |
| France [7] | 32,066 | 35,945 | 44,932 | 12,507 |
| Germany [3, 4] | 85,752 | 92,207 | 122,373 | 21,733 |
| Greece | 37,729 | 25,403 | 16,841 | 3,426 |
| Ireland [8] | 22,210 | 65,384 | 15,642 | 4,837 |
| Italy | 55,562 | 75,992 | 28,329 | 8,572 |
| Netherlands | 11,234 | 13,345 | 17,351 | 4,072 |
| Norway-Sweden [9] | 13,941 | 17,825 | 19,382 | 4,633 |
| Norway [9] | 3,835 | 5,211 | 4,599 | 1,082 |
| Sweden [9] | 10,106 | 12,614 | 14,783 | 3,551 |
| Poland [3] | 63,483 | 172,249 | 117,921 | 20,049 |
| Portugal [10] | 42,685 | 25,497 | 11,479 | 2,474 |
| Romania | 24,753 | 48,136 | 52,154 | 10,891 |
| Russia [3, 11] | 33,311 | 433,427 | 167,152 | 26,164 |
| Spain [12] | 22,783 | 18,443 | 17,695 | 6,675 |
| Switzerland | 8,316 | 11,768 | 12,173 | 2,645 |
| United Kingdom [8,13] | 153,644 | 156,182 | 171,979 | 42,162 |
| Yugoslavia [14] | 16,267 | 57,039 | 131,831 | 13,871 |
| Other Europe | 3,447 | 29,087 | 290,871 | 59,789 |
| Asia | 2,391,356 | 2,859,899 | 3,470,835 | 1,265,277 |
| China | 170,897 | 342,058 | 591,711 | 229,421 |
| Hong Kong | 112,132 | 116,894 | 57,583 | 9,054 |
| India | 231,649 | 352,528 | 590,464 | 195,836 |
| Iran | 98,141 | 76,899 | 76,755 | 27,048 |
| Israel | 43,669 | 41,340 | 54,081 | 14,201 |
| Japan | 44,150 | 66,582 | 84,552 | 20,432 |
| Jordan | 28,928 | 42,755 | 53,550 | 24,552 |
| Korea | 322,708 | 179,770 | 209,758 | 65,572 |
| Philippines | 502,056 | 534,338 | 545,463 | 167,091 |
| Syria | 14,534 | 22,906 | 30,807 | 22,081 |
| Taiwan | 119,051 | 132,647 | 92,657 | 18,286 |
| Turkey | 19,208 | 38,687 | 48,394 | 23,837 |
| Vietnam | 200,632 | 275,379 | 289,616 | 91,129 |
| Other Asia | 483,601 | 637,116 | 745,444 | 356,737 |
| America | 2,695,329 | 5,137,743 | 4,442,226 | 1,259,922 |
| Canada and Newfoundland [15, 16] | 156,313 | 194,788 | 236,349 | 59,135 |
| Mexico [16,17] | 1,009,586 | 2,757,418 | 1,704,166 | 426,866 |
| Caribbean | 790,109 | 1,004,687 | 1,053,969 | 399,016 |
| Cuba | 132,552 | 159,037 | 271,742 | 102,184 |
| Dominican Republic | 221,552 | 359,818 | 291,492 | 141,461 |
| Haiti | 121,406 | 177,446 | 203,827 | 66,584 |
| Jamaica [18] | 193,874 | 177,143 | 172,523 | 59,037 |
| Other Caribbean [18] | 120,725 | 131,243 | 114,385 | 29,750 |

| Region and country of last residence[1] | 1980 to 1989 | 1990 to 1999 | 2000 to 2009 | 2010 to 2012 |
|---|---|---|---|---|
| **Total** | **6,244,379** | **9,775,398** | 10,299,430 | **3,136,296** |
| Central America | 339,376 | 610,189 | 591,130 | 42,228 |
| Belize | 14,964 | 12,600 | 9,682 | 2,805 |
| Costa Rica | 25,017 | 17,054 | 21,571 | 6,688 |
| El Salvador | 137,418 | 273,017 | 251,237 | 52,898 |
| Guatemala | 58,847 | 126,043 | 156,992 | 30,915 |
| Honduras | 39,071 | 72,880 | 63,513 | 19,207 |
| Nicaragua | 31,102 | 80,446 | 70,015 | 9,733 |
| Panama [19] | 32,957 | 28,149 | 18,120 | 4,437 |
| South America | 399,862 | 570,624 | 856,593 | 248,218 |
| Argentina | 23,442 | 30,065 | 47,955 | 12,865 |
| Bolivia | 9,798 | 18,111 | 21,921 | 6,244 |
| Brazil | 22,944 | 50,744 | 115,404 | 34,948 |
| Chile | 19,749 | 18,200 | 19,792 | 5,422 |
| Colombia | 105,494 | 137,985 | 236,570 | 64,263 |
| Ecuador | 48,015 | 81,358 | 107,977 | 31,815 |
| Guyana | 85,886 | 74,407 | 70,373 | 18,011 |
| Paraguay | 3,518 | 6,082 | 4,623 | 1,404 |
| Peru | 49,958 | 110,117 | 137,614 | 40,313 |
| Suriname | 1,357 | 2,285 | 2,363 | 585 |
| Uruguay | 7,235 | 6,062 | 9,827 | 4,155 |
| Venezuela | 22,405 | 35,180 | 82,087 | 28,190 |
| Other South America | 61 | 28 | 87 | 3 |
| Other America [20] | 83 | 37 | 19 | 4 |
| Africa | 141,990 | 346,416 | 759,742 | 299,360 |
| Egypt | 26,744 | 44,604 | 81,564 | 29,090 |
| Ethiopia | 12,927 | 40,097 | 87,207 | 43,238 |
| Liberia | 6,420 | 13,587 | 23,316 | 9,492 |
| Morocco | 3,471 | 15,768 | 40,844 | 12,630 |
| South Africa | 15,505 | 21,964 | 32,221 | 8,419 |
| Other Africa | 76,923 | 210,396 | 494,590 | 196,491 |
| Oceania | 41,432 | 56,800 | 65,793 | 17,344 |
| Australia | 16,901 | 24,288 | 32,728 | 9,285 |
| New Zealand | 6,129 | 8,600 | 12,495 | 3,032 |
| Other Oceania | 18,402 | 23,912 | 20,570 | 5,027 |
| Not Specified [20, 21] | 305,406 | 25,928 | 211,930 | 21,29 |

- Represents zero or not available.

[1] Prior to 1906 refers to country of origin; from 1906 to 2012 refers to country of last residence. Because of changes in country boundaries, data for a particular country may not necessarily refer to the same geographic area over time.

[2] Austria and Hungary not reported separately for all years during 1860 to 1869, 1890 to 1899, and 1900 to 1909.

[3] Poland included in Austria, Germany, Hungary, and Russia from 1899 to 1919.

[4] Bulgaria included Serbia and Montenegro from 1899 to 1919.

[5] Includes Czech Republic, Czechoslovakia (former), and Slovakia.

[6] Finland included in Russia from 1899 to 1919.

[7] Northern Ireland included in Ireland prior to 1925.

[8] Norway and Sweden not reported separately until 1861.

[9] Cape Verde included in Portugal from 1892 to 1952.

[10] Refers to the Russian Empire from 1820 to 1920. Between 1920 and 1990 refers to the Soviet Union. From 1991 to 1999, refers to Russia, Armenia, Azerbaijan, Belarus, Georgia, Kazakhstan, Kyrgyzstan, Moldova, Tajikistan, Turkmenistan, Ukraine, and Uzbekistan. Beginning in 2000, refers to Russia only.

**Immigration by Region and Selected Country of Last Residence: Fiscal Years 1820–2012**  *(Continued)*

[11] United Kingdom refer to England, Scotland, Wales and Northern Ireland since 1925.

[12] Includes Bosnia-Herzegovina, Croatia, Kosovo, Macedonia, Montenegro, Serbia, Serbia and Montenegro, and Slovenia.

[13] Includes both North and South Korea.

[14] Syria included in Turkey from 1886 to 1923.

[15] Includes British North America and Canadian provinces.

[16] Land arrivals not completely enumerated until 1908.

[17] No data available for Canada or Mexico from 1886 to 1893.

[18] Jamaica included in British West Indies From 1892 to 1952.

[19] Panama Canal Zone included in Panama from 1932 to 1972.

[20] New Zealand included in Australia from 1892 to 1924.

[21] Includes 32,897 persons returning in 1906 to their homes in the United States.

Note: Official recording of immigration to the United States began in 1820 after the passage of the Act of March 2, 1819. From 1820 to 1867, figures represent alien passenger arrivals at seaports; from 1868 to 1891 and 1895 to 1897, immigrant alien arrivals; from 1892 to 1894 and 1898 to 2012, immigrant aliens admitted for permanent residence; from 1892 to 1903, aliens entering by cabin class were not counted as immigrants. Land arrivals were not completely enumerated until 1908. For this table, Fiscal Year 1843 covers 9 months ending September 30, 1843; Fiscal Years 1832 and 1850 cover 15 months ending December 31 of the respective years; and Fiscal Year 1868 covers 6 months ending June 30, 1868; and Fiscal Year 1976 covers 15 months ending September 30, 1976.

Source: U.S. Department of Homeland Security.

# NOTES

## CHAPTER 1

1. Aristotle, *Rhetoric* (Whitefish, MT: Kessinger Publishing, 2004), p. 66.

2. See, for example, R. Matthew Montory, Robert S. Horton, and Jeffrey Kircher, "Is Actual Similarity Necessary for Attraction? A Meta-Analysis of Actual and Perceived Similarity," *Journal of Social & Personal Relationships,* 25 (2008): 889–922.

3. See, for example, Ramadhar Singh, Li Jen Ho, Hui Lynn Tan, and Paul A. Bell, "Attitudes, Personal Evaluations, Cognitive Evaluation, and Interpersonal Attraction: On the Direct, Indirect, and Reverse-Causal Effects," *British Journal of Social Psychology,* 46 (2007): 19–42.

4. Emory S. Bogardus, "Comparing Racial Distances in Ethiopia, South Africa, and the United States," *Sociology and Social Research,* 52 (1968): 149–56.

5. Vincent N. Parrillo and Christopher Donoghue, "Updating the Bogardus Social Distance Studies: A New National Survey," *Social Science Journal,* 42:2 (2005): 268.

6. Lyn H. Lofland, *A World of Strangers* (Long Grove, IL: Waveland Press, 1985), p. 16.

7. Georg Simmel, "The Stranger," in Kurt H. Wolff (ed.), *The Sociology of Georg Simmel* (New York: Free Press, 1950).

8. Alfred Schutz, "The Stranger," *American Sociological Review,* 69 (May 1944): 449–507.

9. Ta-Nehisi Paul Coates, "Is Obama Black Enough?" *Time* (February 1, 2007). Retrieved October 5, 2012 (http://www.time.com/time/nation/article/0,8599,1584736,00.html); and Richard Carter, "Once Again, Is Obama Really Black Enough for Black Voters?" *New York Amsterdam News* (May 3, 2007), pp. 10, 41.

10. See Philip V. Ramaga, "Relativity of the Minority Concept," *Human Rights Quarterly,* 14:1 (1992).

11. Lisa M. Osbeck, Fathali M. Moghaddam, and Stephane Perreault, "Similarity and Attraction among Majority and Minority Groups in a Multicultural Context," *International Journal of Intercultural Relations* 21:1 (1997): 113–23.

12. See John Edwards, "Players and Power in Minority-Group Settings," *Journal of Multilingual and Multicultural Development,* 27:1 (2006): 4–21.

13. Charles Wagley and Marvin Harris, *Minorities in the New World* (New York: Columbia University Press, 1967).

14. See Ashley Montagu, *Man's Most Dangerous Myth: The Fallacy of Race,* reprint ed. (New York: Whitley Press, 2008).

15. Michael J. Bamshad and Steve E. Olson, "Does Race Exist?" *Scientific American,* 289 (December 2003): 78–85.

16. See Angela James, "Making Sense of Race and Racial Classification," *Race & Society,* 4:2 (2001): 235–47.

17. See Raphael S. Ezekiel, "An Ethnographer Looks at Neo-Nazi and Klan Groups: The Racist Mind Revisited," *American Behavioral Scientist,* 46:1 (2002): 51–71.

18. Arab American Institute, "Ancestry of Arab Americans by Primary Identification." Retrieved October 5, 2012 (http://www.aaiusa.org/page/file/b8bad613905570ea97_mghwmvb2d.pdf/ancestry.pdf).

19. See C. Loring Brace, *"Race" Is a Four-Letter Word* (New York: Oxford University Press, 2005).

20. Daniel Chirot, *Contentious Identities: Ethnic, Religious, and National Conflicts in Today's World* (New York: Routledge, 2011).

21. William Graham Sumner, *Folkways* (New York: CreateSpace, 2012), p. 13. Originally published in 1906.

22. See Richard Jenkins, *Social Identity,* 3rd ed. (New York: Routledge, 2008).

23. See David L. Rousseau and Rocio Garcia-Retamero, "Identity, Power, and Threat Perception," *Journal of Conflict Resolution,* 51 (2007): 744–71.

24. Brewton Berry, *Race and Ethnic Relations,* 3rd ed. (Boston: Houghton Mifflin, 1965), p. 55.

25. See Molefi Kete Asante, *The Afrocentric Idea,* revised ed. (Philadelphia: Temple University Press, 1998).

26. Martin E. Spencer, "Multiculturalism, 'Political Correctness,' and the Politics of Identity," *Sociological Forum,* 9 (1994): 547–67.

27. Vincent N. Parrillo, "Diversity in America: A Sociohistorical Analysis," *Sociological Forum,* 9 (1994): 523–35.

28. Vincent N. Parrillo, *Diversity in America,* 4th ed. (Boulder, CO: Paradigm Publishers, 2013), pp. 13–14.

29. C. Wright Mills, *The Sociological Imagination,* 40th anniversary ed. (New York: Oxford University Press, 2000), p. 8.

30. Ibid., p. 9.

31. Ibid., p. 146.

32. See, for example, Michele G. Alexander, Marilynn B. Brewer, and Robert W. Livingston, "Putting Stereotype Content in Context: Image Theory and Interethnic Stereotypes, *Personality and Social Psychology Bulletin,* 31 (2005): 781–94.

33. Erving Goffman, *The Presentation of Self in Everyday Life* (Gloucester, MA: Peter Smith Publishing, 1999). Originally published in 1959.

34. See Randall Collins, "Wiley's Contribution to Symbolic Interactionist Theory," *The American Sociologist,* 42 (2011):156–67.

35. Peter L. Berger and Thomas Luckmann, *The Social Construction of Reality* (New York: Penguin Books, 1991). Originally published in 1963.

## CHAPTER 2

1. See, for example, Lynette Spillman, *Cultural Sociology* (New York: Wiley-Blackwell, 2001).

2. The importance of symbols to social interaction has long drawn much attention in sociology. See Joel M. Charon, *Symbolic Interactionism: An Introduction, An Interpretation, An Integration,* 10th ed. (Upper Saddle River, NJ: Prentice Hall, 2009).

3. Institute for Diversity and Ethics in Sport, *The Racial and Gender Report Card.* Retrieved October 1, 2012 (http://www.tidesport.org/racialgenderreportcard.html).

4. Ibid.

5. Bear climbing a tree as seen from other side. Giraffe going past a second-story window. Hotdog on a hamburger roll.

6. This connection between Lippmann's comments, the Droodles, and human response to definitions of stimuli originally was made by Harry C. Bredemeier and Richard M. Stephenson, *The Analysis of Social Systems* (New York: Holt, Rinehart and Winston, 1962), pp. 2–3.

7. Edward O. Wilson, *Sociobiology: The Abridged Edition* (Cambridge, MA: Belknap Press, 2004), p. 280.

8. See Melissa Wagner and Nancy Armstrong, *Field Guide to Gestures: How to Identify and Interpret Virtually Every Gesture Known to Man* (Philadelphia: Quirk Books, 2003).

9. William I. Thomas, "The Relation of Research to the Social Process," in *Essays on Research in the Social Sciences* (Washington, DC: Brookings Institution, 1931), p. 189.

10. Gregory Razran, "Ethnic Dislike and Stereotypes: A Laboratory Study," *Journal of Abnormal and Social Psychology*, 45 (1950): 7–27.

11. Making sandals from tires is common now among certain Africans, Indians, Mexicans, and Vietnamese, and also promoted on eco-friendly websites. See, for example, http://www.hollowtop.com/sandals.htm or http://makezine.com/10/heirloom.

12. See Herbert M. Blalock, *Toward a Theory of Minority Relations* (New York: Wiley, 1967).

13. See Peter Kivisto, "Creating Ethnicity: The Process of Ethnogenesis," *International Migration Review*, 25:2 (1991): 409–10).

14. See, for example, Francis Leo Collins, "Connecting 'Home' with 'Here': Personal Homepages in Everyday Transnational Life," *Journal of Ethnic & Migration Studies*, 35 (2009): 839–59; Vivian Louie, "Growing Up Ethnic in Transnational Worlds: Identities among Second-Generation Chinese and Dominicans," *Identities: Global Studies in Culture and Power*, 13 (2006): 363–94.

15. W. Lloyd Warner and Paul S. Lunt, *The Social Life of a Modern Community*, Yankee City Series, Vol. 1 (New Haven, CT: Yale University Press, 1941).

16. Stephan Thernstrom, "'Yankee City' Revisited: The Perils of Historical Naïveté," *American Sociological Review*, 30 (1965): 234–42.

17. W. Lloyd Warner and Leo Srole, *The Social System of American Ethnic Groups*, reprint ed. (Westport, CT: Greenwood Press, 1976).

18. Matthew Weeks and Michael B. Lupfer, "Complicating Race: The Relationship between Prejudice, Race, and Social Class Categorizations," *Personality and Social Psychology Bulletin*, 30 (2004): 972–84.

19. Stephen Steinberg, *The Ethnic Myth: Race, Ethnicity, and Class in America*, 3rd ed. (Boston: Beacon Press, 2001).

20. Thomas Sowell, *Ethnic America: A History* (New York: Basic Books, 1981).

21. Milton M. Gordon, *Assimilation in American Life* (New York: Oxford University Press, 1964).

22. Ibid., p. 47.

23. See Patricia L. McCall and Karen F. Parker, "A Dynamic Model of Racial Competition, Racial Inequality, and Interracial Violence," *Sociological Inquiry*, 75 (2005): 273–93; Leo Kuper, *Race, Class, and Power: Ideology and Revolutionary Change* (Los Angeles: Aldine Transaction, 2005); and Clair J. Kim, "Imagining Race and Nation in Multiculturalist America," *Ethnic and Racial Studies*, 27:6 (2004): 977–1005.

24. See Cicely R. Hardaway and Vonnie C. MacLoyd, "Escaping Poverty and Securing Middle-Class Status: How Race and Socioeconomic Status Shape Mobility Prospects for African Americans during the Transition to Adulthood," *Journal of Youth and Adolescence*, 38 (2009): 242–56; and Colleen F. Heflin and Mary Pattillo, "Poverty in the Family: Race, Siblings, and Socioeconomic Heterogeneity," *Social Science Research*, 25 (2006): 804–22.

25. E. Franklin Frazier, *The Negro Family in Chicago* (Chicago: University of Chicago Press, 1932); see also *The Negro Family in the United States*, revised ed. (Chicago: University of Chicago Press, 1969).

26. Daniel P. Moynihan, *The Negro Family: The Case for National Action* (Washington, DC: U.S. Department of Labor, 1965).

27. Ibid., p. 5.

28. Ibid., p. 6.

29. Ibid., pp. 30, 47.

30. Daniel P. Moynihan, "Families Falling Apart," *Society* (July–August 1990): 21–22.

31. Originally in Daniel Patrick Moynihan, "A Family Policy for the Nation," *America*, 113 (September 18, 1965): 280–83; see also Moynihan, "Families Falling Apart," p. 21; and David Gergen, "A Few Candles in the Darkness," *U.S. News & World Report* (May 25, 1992): 44.

32. Oscar Lewis, *The Children of Sanchez*, 50th anniversary ed. (New York: Vintage, 2011), originally published in 1961; and *La Vida* (New York: Vintage, 1966), pp. xlii–lii.

33. Ibid., p. xlv.

34. See David L. Harvey and Michael H. Reed, "The Culture of Poverty: An Ideological Analysis," *Sociological Perspectives*, 39 (Winter 1996): 465–95.

35. Edward C. Banfield, *The Unheavenly City: The Nature and Future of Our Urban Crisis* (Boston: Little, Brown, 1970), pp. 210–11.

36. See, for example, William F. Spriggs, "Poverty in America: The Poor *Are* Getting Poorer," *Crisis*, 113 (2006): 14–19.

37. William Ryan, *Blaming the Victim*, revised ed. (New York: Vintage, 1976).

38. Charles A. Valentine, *Culture and Poverty* (Chicago: University of Chicago Press, 1968), p. 129.

39. Harvey and Reed, "The Culture of Poverty."

40. Michael Harrington, *The Other America: Poverty in the United States* (New York: Scribner, 1997), p. 14.

41. Lola M. Irelan, Oliver C. Moles, and Robert M. O'Shea, "Ethnicity, Poverty, and Selected Attitudes: A Test of the 'Culture of Poverty' Hypothesis," *Social Forces*, 47 (1969): 405–13.

42. Eliot Liebow, *Tally's Corner: A Study of Negro Streetcorner Men*, 2nd ed. (Lanham, MD: Rowman & Littlefield, 2003), pp. 222–23.

43. See Manuel Couret Branco, "Family, Religion, and Economic Performance: A Critique of Cultural Determinism," *Review of Social Economy*, 65:4 (2007): 407–24; David Steigerwald, Jemima Pierre, "Black Immigrants in the United States and the 'Cultural Narratives' of Ethnicity," *Identities: Global Studies in Culture and Power*, 11 (2004): 141–70; David Steigerwald, "Our New Cultural Determinism," *Society*, 42 (January/February 2005): 71–75; and Richard C. Bagall, "Lifelong Learning and the Limitations of Economic Determinism," *International Journal of Lifelong Education*, 19 (2000): 20–35.

44. See H. D. Forbes, *Ethnic Conflict: Commerce, Culture, and the Contact Hypothesis* (New Haven, CT: Yale University Press, 1997).

45. Mikael Hjerm and KikukoNagayoshi, "The Composition of the Minority Population as a Threat: Can Real Economic and Cultural Threats Explain Xenophobia?" *International Sociology,* 26: 6(2011): 815–43; Michael A. Zarate, Berenice Garcia, and Azenett A. Garza, "Cultural Threat and Perceived Realistic Group Conflict as Dual Predictors of Prejudice," *Journal of Experimental Social Psychology,* 40 (2004): 99–105.

46. Peter Burns and James G. Gimpel, "Economic Insecurity, Prejudicial Stereotypes, and Public Opinion on Immigration Policy," *Political Science Quarterly,* 115 (2000): 201–25.

47. Thomas F. Pettigrew et al., "Relative Deprivation and Intergroup Prejudice," *Journal of Social Issues,* 64 (2008): 385–401.

48. Ashley W. Doane Jr., "Dominant Group Ethnic Identity in the United States: The Role of 'Hidden' Ethnicity in Intergroup Relations," *The Sociological Quarterly,* 38 (Summer 1997): 375–97.

49. Stanley Lieberson, "A Societal Theory of Race and Ethnic Relations," *American Sociological Review,* 26 (1961): 902–10.

50. William J. Wilson, *Power, Racism, and Privilege* (New York: Free Press, 1976), pp. 52–68.

51. Robert Blauner, "Internal Colonialism and Ghetto Revolt," *Social Problems,* 16 (Spring 1969): 393–406.

52. Ibid., p. 397.

53. See, for example, Fred L. Pincus and Natalie J. Sokoloff, "Does 'Classism' Help Us to Understand Class Oppression?" *Race, Gender, & Class,* 15 (2008): 9–23.

54. See, for example, Cajetan Ngozika Ihewulezi, *The History of Poverty in a Rich & Blessed America* (Bloomington, IN: AuthorHouse, 2008).

55. See Andrew Sum, Ishwar Khatiwada, Joseph McLaughlin, and Sheila Palma, "No Country for Young Men: Deteriorating Labor Market Prospects for Low-Skilled Men in the United States," *Annals of the American Academy of Political and Social Science,* 635:1 (2011): 24–55.

56. Jeff Hitchcock, *Lifting the White Veil* (Roselle, NJ: Crandall, Dustie & Douglass Books, 2003), pp. 115–16.

## CHAPTER 3

1. See Gordon W. Allport, *The Nature of Prejudice,* 25th anniversary ed. (New York: Basic Books, 1979), p. 6.

2. See Christian S. Crandall and Charles Stangor, "Conformity and Prejudice," in *On the Nature of Prejudice; Fifty Years after Allport,* edited by John F. Dovidio, Peter Glick, and Laurie Rudman (New York: Wiley-Blackwell, 2005); Frank R. Westie, "Sociological Analysis of the Phenomenon of Prejudice," *Estudios de Sociologia* (1962):150–60.

3. See, for example, Michael D. Barber, *Equality and Diversity: Phenomenological Investigations of Prejudice and Discrimination* (Amherst, NY: Humanity Books, 2001).

4. Todd D. Nelson, *Handbook of Prejudice, Stereotyping, and Discrimination* (New York: Psychology Press, 2009), pp. 54, 300.

5. L. Perry Curtis Jr., *Apes and Angels: The Irishman in Victorian Caricature,* 2nd ed. (Washington, DC: Smithsonian Press, 1997).

6. T. W. Adorno, Else Frankel-Brunswik, Daniel J. Levinson, and R. Nevitt Sanford, *The Authoritarian Personality* (New York: Harper & Row, 1950).

7. See, for example, Thomas F. Pettigrew, Oliver Crist, Ulrich Wagner, and Jost Stellmacher, "Dirct and Indirect Intergroup Contact Effects on Prejudice: A Normative Interpretation," *International Journal of Intercultural Relations,* 31:4 (2007): 411–25.

8. See Adam D. Galinsky and Gillian Ku, "The Effects of Perspective-Taking on Prejudice: The Moderating Role of Self-Evaluation," *Personality and Social Psychology Bulletin,* 30 (May 2004): 594–604.

9. Brenda Major, Cheryl R. Kaiser, and Shannon K. McCoy, "It's Not My Fault: When and Why Attributions to Prejudice Protect Self-Esteem," *Personality and Social Psychology Bulletin,* 29 (June 2003): 772–81.

10. See Robert A. Baron and Deborah R. Richardson, *Human Aggression,* 2nd ed. (New York: Springer, 2004).

11. Leviticus 16: 5–22.

12. Allport, *The Nature of Prejudice,* p. 244.

13. Stewart E. Tolnay and E. M. Beck, *A Festival of Violence: An Analysis of Southern Lynchings, 1882–1930* (Champaign, IL: University of Illinois Press, 1995.

14. See Leonard Berkowitz, "Frustration-Aggression Hypothesis: Examination and Reformulation," *Psychological Bulletin,* 106 (1989): 59–73.

15. Talcott Parsons, "Certain Primary Sources and Patterns of Aggression in the Social Structure of the Western World," in *Essays in Sociological Theory* (New York: Free Press, 1964), pp. 298–322.

16. For an excellent review of Parsonian theory in this area, see Stanford M. Lyman, *The Black American in Sociological Thought: A Failure of Perspective* (New York: Capricorn Books, 1973), pp. 145–69.

17. Herbert Blumer, "Race Prejudice as a Sense of Group Position," *Pacific Sociological Review,* 1 (1958): 3–7.

18. John Dollard, "Hostility and Fear in Social Life," *Social Forces,* 17 (1938): 15–26.

19. Muzafer Sherif, *The Robbers Cave Experiment: Intergroup Conflict and Cooperation* (Middletown, CT: Wesleyan University Press, 1988).

20. See John Higham, *Strangers in the Land: Patterns of American Nativism, 1850–1925* (New Brunswick, NJ: Rutgers University Press, 2002).

21. Paula D. McClain et al., "Black Americans and Latino Immigrants in a Southern City: Friendly Neighbors or Competitors?" *Du Bois Review: Social Science Research on Race,* 4 (2007): 97–117.

22. See Robert M. Adelman, Cameron Lippard, Charles Jaret, and Lesley Williams Reid, "Jobs, Poverty, and Earnings in American Metropolises: Do Immigrants Really Hurt the Economic Outcomes of Blacks?" *Sociological Focus,* 38:4 (2005): 261–85.

23. See Geoff MacDonald, Paul R. Nail, and David A. Levy, "Expanding the Scope of the Social Response Context," *Basic and Applied Social Psychology,* 26 (2004): 77–92.

24. John Dollard, *Caste and Class in a Southern Town,* 3rd ed. (Garden City, NY: Doubleday Anchor Books, 1957).

25. Thomas Pettigrew, "Regional Differences in Anti-Negro Prejudice," *Journal of Abnormal and Social Psychology,* 59 (1959): 28–36.

26. Jeanne Watson, "Some Social and Psychological Situations Related to Change in Attitude," *Human Relations,* 3 (1950): 15–56.

27. Joanne R. Smith and Winnifred R. Louis, "Do As We Say and As We Do: The Interplay of Descriptive and Injunctive Group Norms in the Attitude-Behaviour Relationship," *British Journal of Social Psychology*, 47 (2008): 647–66.

28. Christian S. Crandall. Amy Eshleman, and Laurie O'Brien, "Social Norms and the Expression and Suppression of Prejudice: The Struggle for Internalization," *Journal of Personality and Social Psychology*, 82 (2002): 359–78.

29. Jenessa R. Shapiro and Steven L. Neuberg, "When Do the Stigmatized Stigmatize? The Ironic Effects of Being Accountable to (Perceived) Majority Group Prejudice-Expression Norms," *Journal of Personality and Social Psychology*, 95 (2008): 877–98.

30. See Charles Stangor, "The Study of Stereotyping, Prejudice, and Discrimination Within Social Psychology," pp. 2–4, in Todd D. Nelson (ed.), *Handbook of Prejudice, Stereotyping, and Discrimination* (New York: Psychology Press, 2009).

31. Eliot Aronson, *The Social Animal*, 11th ed. (San Francisco: Worth, 2011), p. 197.

32. Jason K. Clark, Duane T. Wegener, Pablo Briñol, and Richard E. Petty, "Discovering That the Shoe Fits: The Self-Validating Role of Stereotypes," *Psychological Science*, 20 (2009): 846–52.

33. See Yoshihisa Kashima, Klaus Fiedler, and Peter Freytag (eds.), *Stereotype Dynamics: Language-Based Approaches to the Formation, Maintenance, and Transformation of Stereotypes* (New York: Psychology Press, 2007).

34. David J. Schneider, *The Psychology of Stereotyping* (New York: Guilford Press, 2005).

35. Brian Mullen, Drew Rozell, and Craig Johnson, "Ethnophaulisms for Ethnic Immigrant Groups: Cognitive Representation of 'The Minority' and 'The Foreigner'," *Group Processes and Intergroup Relations*, 3 (2000): 5–24.

36. Brian Mullen, "Ethnophaulisms for Ethnic Immigrant Groups," *Journal of Social Issues*, 57 (2001): 457–75.

37. See Giselinde Kuipers, *Good Humor, Bad Taste: The Sociology of the Joke* (New York: Walter de Gruyter, 2006).

38. Lois Leveen, "Only When I Laugh: Textual Dynamics of Ethnic Humor," *MELUS* 21 (1996): 29–55.

39. U.S. Commission on Civil Rights, *Window Dressing on the Set: Women and Minorities in Television* (Washington, DC: U.S. Government Printing Office, 1977); and *Window Dressing on the Set: An Update*, 1979.

40. Travis L. Dixon, "Crime News and Racialized Beliefs: Understanding the Relationship between Local News Viewing and Perceptions of African Americans and Crime," *Journal of Communication*, 58 (March 2008): 106–25; and Dixon, "Network News and Racial Beliefs: Exploring the Connections between National Television News Exposure and Stereotypical Perceptions of African Americans," *Journal of Communication*, 58 (June 2008): 321–37.

41. Hye-Jin Paek, Michelle R. Nelson, and Alexandra M. Vilela, "Examination of Gender-role Portrayals in Television Advertising across Seven Countries," *Sex Roles: A Journal of Research*, 64 (2011): 192–207; Dennis J. Ganahl, Thomas J. Prinsen, and Sara Baker Netzley, "A Content Analysis of Prime Time Commercials: A Contextual Framework of Gender Representation," *Sex Roles*, 49 (2003): 545–51.

42. Jennifer J. Henderson and Gerald J. Baldasty, "Race, Advertising, and Prime-Time Television," *Howard Journal of Communications*, 14 (2003): 97–112.

43. Melinda Messineo, "Does Advertising on Black Entertainment Television Portray More Positive Gender Representations Compared to Broadcast Networks?" *Sex Roles*, 59 (2008): 752–64.

44. Shannon N. Davis, "Sex Stereotypes in Commercials Targeted toward Children: A Content Analysis," *Sociological Spectrum*, 23 (2003): 407–25.

45. Mark P. Orbe, "Representations of Race in Reality TV: Watch and Discuss," *Critical Studies in Media Communication*, 25 (2008): 345–52.

46. Meera E. Deo et al., "Missing in Action: 'Framing' Race on Prime-Time Television," *Social Justice*, 35 (2008): 145–62.

47. Martha M. Lauzen, David M. Dozier, and Nora Horan, "Constructing Gender Stereotypes through Social Roles in Prime-Time Television," *Journal of Broadcasting & Electronic Media*, 52 (2008): 200–14.

48. Children Now, "Fall Colors: 2003–2004 Prime Time Diversity Report." Retrieved October 1, 2012 (http://www.childrennow.org/uploads/documents/fall_colors_2003.pdf).

49. Matt Sienkiewicz and Nick Marx, "Beyond a Cutout World: Ethnic Humor and Discursive Integration in *South Park*," *Journal of Film and Video*, 61 (2009): 5–18.

50. Scott Coltrane and Melinda Messineo, "The Perpetuation of Subtle Prejudice: Race and Gender Imagery in 1990s Television Advertising," *Sex Roles*, 42 (2000): 363–89.

51. Dana E. Mastro and Susannah R. Stern, "Representations of Race in Television Commercials: A Content Analysis of Prime-Time Advertising," *Journal of Broadcasting & Electronic Media*, 47 (2003): 638–47.

52. Anthony J. Cortese, *Provocateur: Images of Women and Minorities in Advertising*, 3rd ed. (Lanham, MD: Rowman & Littlefield, 2007).

53. Jean Kilbourne, *Can't Buy My Love* (New York: Touchstone Books, 2000).

54. Leslie Baker-Kimmons and Pancho McFarland, "The Rap on Chicano and Black Masculinity: A Content Analysis of Gender Images in Rap Lyrics," *Race, Gender & Class*, 18 (2011): 331–44.

55. Thomas F. Pettigrew and Linda R. Tropp, "A Meta-Analytic Test of Intergroup Contact Theory," *Journal of Personality & Social Psychology*, 90 (2006): 751–83.

56. Gordon Sammut and George Gaskell, "Points of View, Social Positioning and Intercultural Relations," *Journal for the Theory of Social Behaviour*, 40 (2010): 47–64.

57. Elliot Aronson and Neal Osherow, "Cooperation, Prosocial Behavior, and Academic Performance: Experiments in the Desegregated Classroom," *Applied Social Psychology Annual*, 1 (1980): 163–96.

58. Iain Walker and Mary Crogan, "Academic Performance, Prejudice, and the Jigsaw Classroom: New Pieces to the Puzzle," *Journal of Community and Applied Social Psychology*, 8 (1998): 381–93.

59. See, for example, Biren A. Nagda, Linda R. Tropp, and Elizabeth Levy Paluck, "Looking Back as We Look Ahead: Integrating Theory, Research, and Practice on Intergroup Relations," *Journal of Social Issues*, 62 (2006): 439–51; and Ludwin E. Molina and Michele A. Wittig, "Relative Importance of Contact Conditions in Explaining Prejudice Reduction in a Classroom Context: Separate and Equal?" *Journal of Social Issues*, 62 (2006): 489–509.

60. Vincent N. Parrillo, *Diversity in America*, 4th ed. (Boulder, CO: Paradigm Publishers, 2013), pp. 170–72.

61. U.S. Department of Defense, *2010 Demographics: Profile of the Military Community* (Arlington, VA: Military Family Resource Center, 2010), p. iv.

62. See Mark E. Engberg, "Improving Intergroup Relations in Higher Education: A Critical Examination of the Influence of Educational Interventions on Racial Bias," *Review of Educational Research*, 74:4 (2004): 473–524.

63. See Elizabeth L. Paluck and Donald P. Green, "Prejudice Reduction: What Works? A Review and Assessment of Research and Practice," *Annual Review of Psychology*, 60 (2009): 339–67.

64. See Howard J. Ehrlich, *Hate Crimes and Ethnoviolence* (Boulder, CO: Westview Press, 2009).

65. Robert K. Merton, "Discrimination and the American Creed," *Sociological Ambivalence & Other Essays* (New York: Free Press, 1976), pp.1999–2016.

66. Stokely Carmichael, Kwame Ture, and Charles Hamilton, *Black Power: The Politics of Liberation*, reissue ed. (New York: Vintage Books, 1992).

67. See, for example, Juan Manuel Falomir-Pichastor, Daniel Muñoz-Rojas, Federica Invernizzi, and Gabriel Mugny, "Perceived In-Group Threat as a Factor Moderating the Influence of In-Group Norms on Discrimination against Foreigners," *European Journal of Social Psychology*, 34 (2004): 135–53.

68. John Rawls, *A Theory of Justice*, New Edition ed. (Cambridge, MA: Belknap Press, 2005).

69. Joseph Tussman and Jacobus tenBroek, "The Equal Protection of the Laws," *California Law Review*, 37 (September 1949): 341–81.

70. Stanford M. Lyman, "The Race Question and Liberalism: Casuistries in American Constitutional Law," *International Journal of Politics, Culture and Society*, 5 (1991): 183–247.

71. Steven M. Cahn, *The Affirmative Action Debate*, 2nd ed. (New York: Routledge, 2002).

72. Terry H. Anderson, *The Pursuit of Fairness: A History of Affirmative Action* (New York: Oxford University Press, 2005).

73. Quoted in Ian Lopez, *White by Law*, revised ed. (New York: New York University Press, 2006), p. 124.

74. Quoted in Derrick A. Bell, *Silent Covenants: Brown v. Board of Education and the Unfilled Hopes for Racial Reform* (New York: Oxford University Press, 2005), p. 149.

75. "Studies Show Race-Neutral College Admissions Could Work." Retrieved October 5, 2012 (http://www.usatoday.com/story/news/nation/2012/10/03/study-race-neutral-admissions/1609855/).

76. J. Edward Kellough, *Understanding Affirmative Action: Politics, Discrimination, and the Search for Justice* (Washington, DC: Georgetown University Press, 2006), pp. 132–38.

77. Tim J. Wise, *Affirmative Action: Racial Preference in Black and White* (New York: Routledge, 2005), p. 164.

78. Linda Chavez, "No Thanks to Affirmative Action," *The American Prospect*, 13 (2002): 34–35; Chavez, "Court Abandons Colorblind Society," *Human Events*, 59 (June 30, 2003): 1–2; and Thomas Sowell, *Affirmative Action Around the World: An Empirical Study* (New Haven, CT: Yale University Press, 2004).

79. All poll results retrieved October 5, 2012 (http://www.pollingreport.com/race.htm).

80. Brent Berry and Eduardo Bonilla-Silva, "'They Should Hire the One with the Best Score': White Sensitivity to Qualification Differences in Affirmative Action Hiring Decisions," *Ethnic and Racial Studies*, 31 (2008): 215–42.

81. See Brian R. Kowalski and Richard J. Lundman, "Vehicle Stops by Police for Driving While Black: Common Problems and Some Tentative Solutions," *Journal of Criminal Justice, 35*

(2007): 165–81; Stephanie Geiger-Oneto and Scott Phillips, "Driving While Black: The Role of Race, Sex, and Social Status," *Journal of Ethnicity in Criminal Justice*, 1 (2003): 1–25.

82. Human Rights Watch, *Decades of Disparity: Drug Arrests and Race in the United States*. Retrieved October 6, 2012 (http://www.hrw.org/sites/default/files/reports/us0309web_1.pdf).

83. "Transportation." Retrieved October 6, 2010 (http://www.pollingreport.com/transpor.htm).

84. Department of Justice, *Racial Profiling Fact Sheet* (June 17, 2003). Retrieved October 6, 2012 (http://www.usdoj.gov/opa/pr/2003/June/racial_profiling_fact_sheet.pdf).

85. Patricia Y. Warren and Amy Farrell, "The Environmental Context of Racial Profiling," *The ANNALS of the American Academy of Political and Social Science*, 623 (2009): 52–63.

86. American Civil Liberties Union, *The Persistence of Racial and Ethnic Profiling in the United States* (New York: ACLU, 2009).

## CHAPTER 4

1. See Brent Simpson and Michael W. Macy, "Power, Identity, and Collective Action in Social Exchange," *Social Forces*, 82 (2004): 1373–409; Laura S. Billings et al., "Race-Based Social Judgment by Minority Perceivers," *Journal of Applied Social Psychology*, 30 (2000): 221–40.

2. See, for example, Devon Johnson, "Racial Prejudice, Perceived Injustice, and the Black-White Gap in Punitive Attitudes," *Journal of Criminal Justice*, 36 (2008): 198–206; A. E. Taslitz (ed.), "The New Data: Over-Representation of Minorities in the Criminal Justice System," *Law and Contemporary Problems*, 66 (2003): 1–298; Jody Clay-Warner, "Perceiving Procedural Injustice: The Effects of Group Membership and Status," *Social Psychology Quarterly*, 64 (2001): 224–38; and Saundra D. Westervelt and John A. Humphrey (eds.), *Wrongly Convicted: Perspectives on Failed Justice* (New Brunswick, NJ: Rutgers University Press, 2001).

3. Clifford R. Shaw and Henry D. McKay, "Juvenile Delinquency and Urban Areas," *The Chicago School Criminology*, Vol. 6 (New York: Routledge, 2004). Originally published in 1942.

4. Robert Agnew et al., "Socioeconomic Status, Economic Problems, and Delinquency," *Youth & Society*, 40 (2008): 159–81; Per-Olof H. Wikstrom et al., "Do Disadvantaged Neighborhoods Cause Well-Adjusted Children to Become Adolescent Delinquents?" *Criminology*, 38 (2000): 1109–42; and Matthew R. Lee, "Community Cohesion and Violent Predatory Victimization," *Social Forces*, 79 (2000): 683–706.

5. Dana L. Haynie, Harald E. Weiss, and Alex Piquero, "Race, the Economic Maturity Gap, and Criminal Offending in Young Adulthood," *Justice Quarterly*, 25 (2008): 595–622; and Ronald L. Simons and Phyllis A Gray, "Perceived Blocked Opportunity as an Explanation of Delinquency among Lower-Class Black Males: A Research Note," *Journal of Research in Crime and Delinquency*, 26 (1989): 90–101.

6. See Adrienne Frang and Finn-Aage Esbensen, "Race and Gang Affiliation: An Examination of Multiple Marginality," *Justice Quarterly*, 24 (2007): 600–28; Paul R. Vowell and David C. May, "Another Look at Classic Strain Theory: Poverty Status, Perceived Blocked Opportunity, and Gang Membership as Predictors of Adolescent Violent Behavior," *Sociological Inquiry*, 70 (2000): 42–60.

7. John P. Hoffmann and Mikaela J. Dufur, "Family and School Capital Effects on Delinquency: Substitutes or Complements?" *Sociological Perspectives*, 51 (2008): 29–62; and Patricia H.

Jenkins, "School Delinquency and School Commitment," *Sociology of Education,* 68 (1995): 221–39.

8. See Alice Yang-Murray, *Historical Memories of the Japanese American Internment and the Struggle for Redress* (Palo Alto, CA: Stanford University Press, 2008).

9. Tern A. Winnick and Mark Bodkin "Stigma, Secrecy, and Race: An Empirical Examination of Black and White Incarcerated Men," *American Journal of Criminal Justice,* 34 (2009): 131–50; and Tally Moses, "Self-Labeling and Its Effects among Adolescents Diagnosed with Mental Disorders," *Social Science & Medicine,* 68 (2009): 57–78.

10. See Edward W. Taylor and Patricia Cranton, *The Handbook of Transformative Learning* (San Francisco: Jossey-Bass, 2012), pp. 260–73.

11. Gordon W. Allport, *The Nature of Prejudice,* 25th anniversary ed. (New York: Basic Books, 1979), pp. 152–53.

12. Chol Yoo Hyung and Richard M. Lee, "Does Ethnic Identity Buffer or Exacerbate the Effects of Frequent Racial Discrimination on Situational Well-Being of Asian Americans?" *Journal of Counseling Psychology,* 55 (2008): 63–74; and Richard M. Lee, "Resilience against Discrimination: Ethnic Identity and Other-Group Orientation as Protective Factors for Korean Americans," *Journal of Counseling Psychology,* 52 (2005): 36–44.

13. Andrea J. Romero and Robert E. Roberts, "The Impact of Multiple Dimensions of Ethnic Identity on Discrimination and Adolescents' Self-Esteem," *Journal of Applied Social Psychology,* 33 (2003): 2288–305; and J. R. Porter and R. E. Washington, "Minority Identity and Self-Esteem," *Annual Review of Sociology,* 19 (1993): 139–61.

14. Gunnar Myrdal, *An American Dilemma* (New Brunswick, NJ: Transaction Publishers, 1995), pp. 25–28. Originally published by Harper in 1944.

15. Allport, *The Nature of Prejudice,* p. 160.

16. Robert E. Park, "Human Migration and the Marginal Man," *American Journal of Sociology,* 33 (May 1928): 891; see also Everett V. Stonequist, *The Marginal Man* (New York: Scribner, 1937).

17. See Rutledge Dennis (ed.), *Marginality, Power, and Social Structure, Vol. 12: Issues in Race, Class, and Gender Analysis* (Greenwich, CT: JAI Press, 2005).

18. See Adam Weisberger, "Marginality and Its Directions," *Sociological Forum,* 7 (1992): 425–46; also cited in Dennis, *Marginality, Power, and Social Structure,* p. 193.

19. Hubert M. Blalock Jr., *Toward a Theory of Minority Group Relations* (New York: Wiley, 1967), pp. 79–84.

20. Edna Bonacich, "A Theory of Middleman Minorities," *American Sociological Review,* 38 (1973): 583–94.

21. Edna Bonacich and John Modell, *The Economic Basis of Ethnic Solidarity* (Berkeley: University of California Press, 1980), p. 30.

22. Norman Pounds, *The Medieval City* (Santa Barbara, CA: Greenwood Press, 2005); and William E. Deal, *Handbook to Life in Medieval and Early Modern Japan* (New York: Oxford University Press, 2007).

23. See John J. Macionis and Vincent N. Parrillo, *Cities and Urban Life,* 6th ed. (Upper Saddle River, NJ: Prentice Hall, 2013), pp. 40–44.

24. See Allport, *The Nature of Prejudice,* pp. 53–54.

25. Deuteronomy 2:32–35; 3:1, 3–4, 6–7 (King James Version).

26. Dirk Moses, *Colonialism and Genocide* (New York: Routledge, 2008), Chapters 4–5; and Benjamin Madley, "Patterns of Frontier Genocide, 1803–1910: The Aboriginal Tasmanians, the Yuki of California, and the Herero of Namibia," *Journal of Genocide Research,* 6 (2004): 167–92.

27. See F. James Davis, *Who Is Black? One Nation's Definition* (University Park, PA: Penn State University Press, 2001), p. 92; and Winthrop D. Jordan, *White over Black: American Attitudes toward the Negro, 1550–1812,* reissue ed. (Chapel Hill: University of North Carolina Press, 1995).

28. For a discussion of Mexican American lynchings, see William D. Carrigan and Clive Webb, "The Lynching of Persons of Mexican Origin or Descent in the United States, 1848 to 1928," *Journal of Social History,* 37 (2003): 411–38; on black lynchings, see Gregory N. Price, William A. Darity, Jr., and Alvin E. Headen, Jr., "Does the Stigma of Slavery Explain the Maltreatment of Blacks by Whites: The Case of Lynchings," *The Journal of Socio-Economics,* 37 (2008): 167–93.

29. See Colin M. Tatz, *With Intent to Destroy: Reflections on Genocide* (New York: Norton, 2003).

30. Southern Poverty Law Center. Retrieved April 11, 2013 (http://www.splcenter.org/stand-strong-against-hate).

31. Federal Bureau of Investigation, "Hate Crime Statistics 2011," *Uniform Crime Reports.* Retrieved April 11, 2013 (http://www.fbi.gov//about-us/cjis/ucr/hate-crime/2011).

32. Edna Bonacich, "The Past, Present, and Future of Split Labor Market Theory," *Research in Race and Ethnic Relations,* 1 (1979): 17–64.

33. Ibid.

34. Cliff Brown, "The Role of Employers in Split Labor Markets: An Event-Structure Analysis of Racial Conflict and AFL Organizing, 1917–1919," *Social Forces,* 79 (2000): 653–81.

35. Kenneth Hudson, "The New Labor Market Segmentation: Labor Market Dualism in the New Economy," *Social Science Research,* 36 (2007): 286–312.

36. See Manuel Pastor and Vanessa Carter, "Conflict, Consensus, and Coalition: Economic and Workforce Development Strategies for African Americans and Latinos," *Race and Social Problems,* 1 (2009): 143–56; Anani Dzidzienyo and Suzanne Oboler (eds.), *Neither Enemies Nor Friends: Latinos, Blacks, Afro-Latinos* (New York: Palgrave Macmillan, 2005); and Mindiola Tatcho, Jr., Yolanda F. Niemann, and Nestor Rodriguez, *Black-Brown Relations and Stereotypes* (Austin: University of Texas Press, 2003).

37. William M. Newman, *American Pluralism* (New York: Harper & Row, 1973), p. 53.

38. See Ruth H. Bloch, *Gender and Morality in Anglo-American Culture* (Berkeley: University of California Press, 2003); and Joseph W. Scott, *The United States: A Study in Political-Class Racism* (New York: Syracuse University Press, 2002).

39. John Higham, *Strangers in the Land* (New Brunswick, NJ: Rutgers University Press, 2002), p. 247.

40. Milton M. Gordon, *Assimilation in American Life* (New York: Oxford University Press, 1964), pp. 70–71.

41. See Brian Gratton, Myron P. Guttman, and Emily Skop, "Immigrants, Their Children, and Theories of Assimilation: Family Structure in the United States, 1880–1970," *The History of the Family,* 12 (2007): 203–33.

42. See Scott J. South, Kyle Crowder, and Jeremy Pais, "Inter-Neighborhood Migration and Spatial Assimilation in a Multi-Ethnic World: Comparing Latinos, Blacks, and Anglos," *Social Forces,* 87 (2008): 415–43; and Susan K. Brown, "Structural Assimilation Revisited: Mexican-Origin Nativity and Cross-Ethnic Primary Ties," *Social Forces,* 85 (2006): 75–92.

43. Alejandro Portes and Min Zhou, "The New Second Generation: Segmented Assimilation and Its Variants," *The Annals of the American Academy of Political and Social Science,* 530 (1993): 74–96.

44. Newman, *American Pluralism,* p. 63.

45. J. Hector St. John de Crèvecoeur, *Letters from an American Farmer* (Mineola, NY: Dover Publications, 2005), p. 26. Originally published in 1782.

46. Frederick Jackson Turner, The Frontier in American History (North Charleston, SC: CreateSpace, 2011), p. 218. Originally published in 1920.

47. Israel Zangwill, *The Melting-Pot: Drama in Four Acts* (North Charleston, SC: CreateSpace, 2012), p. 145. Originally published in 1921.

48. Actually, any student of Western civilizations would point out that centuries of invasions, conquests, boundary changes, and so on often resulted in cross-breeding and that truly distinct or pure ethnic types were virtually nonexistent long before the 18th century.

49. Samuel P. Huntington, *Who Are We: The Challenges to America's National Identity* (New York: Simon & Schuster, 2005); and "How Anglo Is America?" *Economist,* 373 (2004): 39.

50. See Darren E. Sherkat, "Religious Intermarriage in the United States: Trends, Patterns, and Predictors," *Social Science Research,* 33 (2004): 606–25.

51. Henry Pratt Fairchild, *Immigration: A World Movement and Its Significance* (New York: Forgotten Books, 2012). Originally published in 1913.

52. Will Herberg, *Protestant-Catholic-Jew* (Chicago: University of Chicago Press, 1983), p. 21.

53. Newman, *American Pluralism,* p. 67.

54. Horace M. Kallen, "Democracy versus the Melting Pot," *The Nation* (February 18, 1915), pp. 190–94; and (February 25, 1915), pp. 217–20.

55. Richard D. Alba, "Assimilation's Quiet Tide," *Public Interest* (Spring 1995): 3–4.

# CHAPTER 5

1. Nathan Glazer and Daniel P. Moynihan, *Beyond the Melting Pot,* 2nd ed. (Cambridge, MA: MIT Press, 1970), p. 1.

2. Gary B. Nash, *Class and Society in Early America* (Englewood Cliffs, NJ: Prentice Hall, 1970), p. 19.

3. Lawrence H. Fuchs, *The American Kaleidoscope: Race, Ethnicity, and the Civic Culture* (Hanover, NH: Wesleyan University Press, 1990).

4. Quoted in Thomas E. Woods, Jr., *33 Questions about American History You're Not Supposed to Ask* (New York: Crown Forum, 2007), p. 9.

5. Quoted in Dan Kanstroom, *Deportation Nation: Outsiders in American History* (Cambridge, MA: Harvard University Press, 2007), p. 54.

6. Quoted in Vincent N. Parrillo, *Diversity in America,* 4th ed. (Boulder, CO: Paradigm Publishers, 2013), p. 78.

7. W. S. Shaw to Abigail Adams, May 20, 1798, *Adams Papers,* Vol. 8, No. 48, Massachusetts Historical Society, Cambridge, MA.

8. Quoted in Philip Perlmutter, *Divided We Fall: A History of Ethnic, Religious, and Racial Prejudice in America* (Ames: Iowa State Press, 1992), p. 279.

9. John Higham, *Strangers in the Land* (New Brunswick, NJ: Rutgers University Press, 2002), p. 7.

10. From Harriet Martineau, *Society in America,* 1837, quoted in Parrillo, *Diversity in America,* p. 86.

11. Ralph Waldo Emerson, *Journals of Ralph Waldo Emerson,* Vol. 7 (Charleston, SC: BiblioBazaar, 2008), pp. 115–16.

12. William Bradford, *Of Plymouth Plantation,* edited by Harold Paget (Mineola, NY: Dover Publications, 2006), p. 7.

13. Ibid., p. 14.

14. Ibid., p. 21.

15. Eric Richards, *Britannia's Children: Emigration from England, Scotland, Wales, and Ireland since 1600* (London: Hambledon and London, 2004).

16. See Mark Ellis and Gunnar Almgren, "Local Contexts of Immigrant and Second-Generation Integration in the United States," *Journal of Ethnic & Migration Studies,* 35 (2009): 1059–76.

17. Wilbur S. Shepperson, *Emigration and Disenchantment: Portraits of Englishmen Repatriated from the United States* (Norman: University of Oklahoma Press, 1965), pp. 16–17, 182, 184.

18. A report of the Commissioner of Immigration upon the causes which incite immigration to the United States, 52nd Congress, 1st session (1891–1892), *House Executive Document,* 235, Part I, pp. 260, 282.

19. Rowland Berthoff, *British Immigrants in Industrial America, 1790–1950,* reprint ed. (Kent, England: Russell and Russell, 1968), pp. 103–4.

20. U.S. Office of Immigration Statistics, *2011 Yearbook of Immigration Statistics* (Washington, DC: U.S. Government Printing Office, 2012), Table 2.

21. Katharine W. Jones, *Accent on Privilege: English Identities and Anglophilia in the U.S.* (Philadelphia: Temple University Press, 2002), pp. 217–24.

22. U.S. Office of Immigration Statistics, *2011 Yearbook of Immigration Statistics,* Table 2.

23. See Roger Panetta (ed.), *Dutch New York: The Roots of Hudson Valley Culture* (Yonkers, NJ: Hudson River Museum, 2009), p. 132.

24. Ted Widmer and Arthur M. Schlesinger, Jr., *Martin Van Buren* (New York: Times Books, 2004), p. 7.

25. See Joyce D. Goodfriend, Benjamin Schmidt, and Annette Stott (eds.), *Going Dutch: The Dutch Presence in America, 1609–2009* (Boston: Brill Academic Publishers, 2009); and John Niven and Katherine Speirs, *Martin Van Buren: The Romantic Age of American Politics* (Newtown, CT: American Political Biography Press, 2000).

26. U.S. Census Bureau, *2011 American Community Survey.* Retrieved October 20, 2012 (http://factfinder2.census.gov); see also Terence G. Schoone-Jongen, *The Dutch American Identity: Staging Memory and Ethnicity in Community Celebrations* (Amherst, NY: Cambria Press, 2009).

27. Arthur Henry Hirsch, *The Huguenots of Colonial South Carolina* (Columbia, SC: University of South Carolina Press, 1999), p. 95.

28. John C. Miller, *Crisis in Freedom* (Boston: Little, Brown, 1951), pp. 13, 42–43.

29. Aonghas St-Hilaire, "Louisiana French Immersion Education: Cultural Identity and Grassroots Community Development," *Journal of Multilingual and Multicultural Development,* 26 (2005): 158–72; Jacques M. Henry and Carl L. Bankston III, *Blue Collar Bayou: Louisiana Cajuns in the New Economy of Ethnicity* (Westport, CT: Praeger, 2002).

30. Wayne Curtis, "Cajun Country," *Smithsonian,* 38 (May 2007): 62–65.

31. U.S. Census Bureau, *2011 American Community Survey*; and Rick Bragg, "Reported to Be Vanishing, Cajuns Give a Sharp 'Non'," *New York Times* (August 16, 2001), pp. A1, A20.

32. U.S. Census Bureau, *2011 American Community Survey*, Table S0201.

33. Bruno Ramirez, *Crossing the 49th Parallel: Migration from Canada to the United States, 1900–1930* (Ithaca, NY: Cornell University Press, 2001), pp. 18–20.

34. Benjamin Frankilin, *Autobiography and Other Writings,* edited by Ormond Seavey (New York: Oxford University Press, 2009), p. 259.

35. H. W. Brands, *The First American: The Life and Times of Benjamin Franklin* (New York: Anchor, 2002), p. 218.

36. Don Heinrich Tolzmann, *The German-American Experience* (Amherst, NY: Humanity Books, 2000), p. 405.

37. Douglas Gomery, "German-Language Press in America," p. 197, in *Encyclopedia of American Journalism*, edited by Stephen L. Vaughn (New York: Routledge, 2009).

38. Jay P. Dolan, *The Irish Americans* (New York: Bloomsbury Press, 2009).

39. See James Webb, *Born Fighting: How the Scots-Irish Shaped America* (New York: Broadway Books, 2006).

40. Quoted in James M. Smith, *Freedom's Fetters* (Ithaca, NY: Cornell University Press, 1966), p. 25.

41. Kevin Kenny, *The American Irish: A History* (New York: Longman, 2000).

42. Edward Everett, "Letters on Irish Emigration," in Edith Abbott (ed.), *Historical Aspects of the Immigration Problem, Select Documents*, reprint ed. (New York: Arno Press, 1969), pp. 462–63.

43. Kevin Kenny, "Labor and Labor Organizations," pp. 354–63, in J. J. Lee and Marion Casey (ed.), *Making the Irish American: History and Heritage of the Irish in the United States* (New York: NYU Press, 2007).

44. Margaret Lynch-Brennan, "Ubiquitous Bridget: Irish Immigrant Women in Domestic Service in America, 1840–1930," pp. 332–53, in Lee and Casey, *Making the Irish American*.

45. Kirby A. Miller, *Emigrants and Exiles: Ireland and the Irish Exodus to North America* (New York: Oxford University Press, 1988), pp. 522–26.

46. Ralph Wilcox, "Irish Americans in Sports: The Nineteenth Century," pp. 443–56, in Lee and Casey, *Making the Irish American*.

47. David Noel Doyle, "The Remaking of Irish America, 1840–1880," pp. 213–52, in Lee and Casey, *Making the Irish American*.

48. Patricia J. Fanning, "The Irish American Family," Chapter 3, in Roosevelt Wright, Jr., Charles H. Mindel, Thanh Van Tran, and Robert W. Habenstein (eds.), *Ethnic Families in America: Patterns and Variations,* 5th ed. (New York: Pearson, 2012).

49. Arnold Schrier, *Ireland and the American Emigration 1850–1900* (Chester Springs, PA: Dufour Editions, 1998), p. 34.

50. Kevin Kenny, "Labor and Labor Organizations," p. 360.

51. Cal McCarthy, *Green, Blue, and Gray: The Irish in the American Civil War* (Wilton, Ireland: Collins Press, 2009), pp. 226–28.

52. See Steven P. Erie, *Rainbow's End: Irish-Americans and the Dilemmas of Urban Machine Politics, 1840–1985* (Berkeley: University of California Press, 1990).

53. Judith Waldrop, "Irish Eyes on America," *American Demographics* (March 1989): 6.

54. U.S. Office of Immigration Statistics, *2008 Yearbook of Immigration Statistics*, Table 2, p. 10.

55. Kirk Semple, "As Ireland's Boom Ends, Job Seekers Revive a Well-Worn Path to New York," *New York Times* (July 10, 2009), p. A23.

56. See Nicholas Hope, *German and Scandinavian Protestantism 1700–1918* (New York: Oxford University Press, 1999).

57. Ole E. Rölvaag, *Giants in the Earth*, 9th ed. (New York: Harper, 1999), pp. 9, 485–86.

58. Paul C. Nyholm, *The Americanization of the Danish Lutheran Churches in America* (Minneapolis, MN: Augsburg Publishing, 1963), pp. 249–91.

59. Merle Curti, *The Making of an American Community: A Case Study of Democracy in a Frontier County* (Stanford, CA: Stanford University Press 1969), pp. 84, 96, 101, 104, 112.

60. Carl Chrislock, *Ethnicity Challenged: The Upper Midwest Norwegian American Experience in World War* (Northfield, MN: Norwegian-American Historical Association, 2001), pp. 40, 44.

61. Kendric C. Babcock, *The Scandinavian Element in the United States* (Whitefish, MT: Kessinger Publishing, 2009), pp. 15–16. Originally published in 1914.

62. See Tiffany K. Wayne, *Women's Roles in Nineteenth-Century America* (Santa Barbara, CA: Greenwood Press, 2007).

63. U.S. Census Bureau, *Historical Statistics of the United States, Part II,* Series Z (Washington, DC: U.S. Government Printing Office, 1976), pp. 20–132.

64. Vincent N. Parrillo, *Diversity in America*, 4th ed. (Boulder, CO: Paradigm Publishers, 2013), pp. 170–71.

65. Ibid.

66. J. Hector St. John de Crèvecoeur, *Letters from an American Farmer*, edited by Susan Manning (New York: Oxford University Press, 2009), pp. xxii–xxiii. Originally published in 1782.

## CHAPTER 6

1. Madison Grant, *The Passing of the Great Race* (Whitefish, MT: Kessinger Publishing, 2007), p. 91. Originally published in 1916.

2. Milton M. Gordon, *Assimilation in American Life* (New York: Oxford University Press, 1964), p. 97.

3. Ellwood P. Cubberley, quoted in William J. Reese, *America's Public Schools: From the Common School to "No Child Left Behind"* (Baltimore: Johns Hopkins Press, 2006), p. 125.

4. Ibid., pp. 125–26.

5. *Public Opinion* I (1886): 82–86, quoted in John Higham, *Strangers in the Land: Patterns of American Nativism, 1860–1925* (New Brunswick, NJ: Rutgers University Press, 2002), p. 55.

6. "The Age of Steel," *Public Opinion,* 1 (1886): 355, quoted in John Higham, *Strangers in the Land*, p. 138.

7. Henry Pratt Fairchild, *The Melting Pot Mistake* (1926), quoted in Henry Bischoff, *Immigration Issues* (Santa Barbara, CA: Greenwood Publishing, 2002).

8. Victor R. Greene, *The Slavic Community on Strike* (South Bend, IN: University of Notre Dame Press, 1968), pp. 40–41.

9. Ibid., pp. 49–50.

10. See Charles B. Nam, "Nationality Groups and Social Stratification in America," *Social Forces,* 37 (1959): 328–33.

11. U.S. Department of Homeland Security, *Yearbook of Immigration Statistics: 2011,* Table 3, pp. 12–15. Retrieved October 22, 2012 (http://www.dhs.gov/sites/default/files/publications/

immigration-statistics/yearbook/2011/ois_yb_2011.pdf); U.S. Census Bureau, *2011 American Community Survey.*

12. Henryk Sienkiewicz, *Portrait of America, Letters of Henryk Sienkiewicz,* edited and translated by Charles Morley (New York: Columbia University Press, 1959), pp. 272–73.

13. Ibid., p. 279.

14. William I. Thomas and Florian Znaniecki, *The Polish Peasant in Europe and America* (Whitefish, MT: Kessinger Publishing, 2008). Originally published in 1919.

15. "St. Stanislaus Kostka Church: Who We Are," 2009. Available at http://www.ststansk.com/whoweare.html on September 16, 2009.

16. John J. Bukowczyk, *Polish Americans and Their History: Community, Culture, and Politics* (Pittsburgh: University of Pittsburgh Press, 2006), p. 97.

17. Helena Znaniecki Lopata, *Polish Americans,* 2nd ed. (New Brunswick, NJ: Transaction Publishers, 1994), p. 92.

18. Beverly Duncan and Otis Dudley Duncan, "Minorities and the Process of Stratification," *American Sociological Review,* 33 (June 1968): 356–64; and Stanley Lieberson, *Ethnic Patterns in American Cities* (New York: Free Press, 1963), p. 189.

19. Lopata, *Polish Americans,* p. 95.

20. James S. Pula, "Image, Status, Mobility, and Integration in American Society," *Journal of American Ethnic History,* 16 (1996): 74–94.

21. Department of Homeland Security, *Yearbook of Immigration Statistics: 2011,* Table 5.

22. Based on data from Mark Wischnitzer, *Visas to Freedom,* prepared by Hebrew Immigration Assistance Society (Cleveland, OH: World Publishing, 1956); and U.S. Immigration and Naturalization Service, *Annual Report* (Washington, DC: U.S. Government Printing Office, 1981), Table 13, p. 63.

23. Jerome Davis, *The Russian Immigrant* (Ithaca, NY: Cornell University Library, 2009), p. 98. Originally published in 1922.

24. Edward T. Devine, "Family and Social Work," in Jerome Davis (ed.), *The Russians and Ruthenians in America* (Whitefish, MT: Kessinger Publishing, 2007), p. 32. Originally published in 1922.

25. Davis, *The Russian Immigrant,* pp. 173–74.

26. John Higham, *Strangers in the Land,* pp. 230–31; see also Frederick R. Barkley, "Jailing Radicals in Detroit," *Nation,* 110 (1920): 136.

27. Department of Homeland Security, *Yearbook of Immigration Statistics: 2011,* Table 3.

28. "Russian American Demographics," Amérida Integrated Multicultural Marketing. Retrieved October 22, 2012 (http://www.ameredia.com/resources/demographics/russian.html).

29. Ibid.

30. Alexei Krindatch "Orthodox Christian Churches in the USA," Table 3. Retrieved October 22, 2012 (http://www.hartfordinstitute.org/research/2010-USOrthodox-Census.pdf).

31. "Brain Drain: The Disease Is Not Only Russian," Retrieved October 22, 2012 (http://www.ecolife.ru/jornal/econ/2003-4-1.shtml).

32. "Russian Brain Drain Tops Half a Million," *BBC News World Edition* (June 20, 2002). Retrieved October 22, 2012 (http://news.bbc.co.uk/2/hi/europe/2055571.stm).

33. Wasyl Halich, *Ukrainians in the United States* (New York: Arno Press, 1970), pp. 28–29. Originally published in 1937.

34. Stephen P. Haluszczuk, *Ukrainians of Western Pennsylvania* (Charleston, SC: Arcadia Publishing, 2009), p. 9.

35. Department of Homeland Security, *Yearbook of Immigration Statistics: 2011,* Tables 3, 14.

36. "Ukrainian American Demographics," Amérida Integrated Multicultural Marketing. Retrieved October 22, 2012 (http://www.ameredia.com/resources/demographics/ukrainian.html); U.S. Census Bureau, *2011 American Community Survey.*

37. Department of Homeland Security, *Yearbook of Immigration Statistics: 2011,* Table 2.

38. Emil Lengyel, *Americans from Hungary* (Irvine, CA: Reprint Services Corporation, 1993), p. 128. Originally published in 1948.

39. *New York Tribune* (September 11–12, 1897), pp. 1, 3.

40. Irving Lewis Allen, *Unkind Words* (New York: Bergin & Garvey, 1990), pp. 31, 62.

41. John Korosfoy (ed.), *Hungarians in America* (Cleveland, OH: Szabadsag, 1941), pp. 15–28.

42. Department of Homeland Security, *Yearbook of Immigration Statistics: 2011,* Table 3.

43. U.S. Census Bureau, *2011 American Community Survey.*

44. See Ewa Morawska, "'Diaspora': Diasporas' Representations of Their Homelands: Exploring the Polymorphs," *Ethnic and Racial Studies,* 34 (2011): 1029–48.

45. Quoted in Nicola Sacco and Bartolomeo Vanzetti, *The Letters of Sacco and Vanzetti* (New York: Penguin Classics, 2008), p. 377.

46. Higham reports, for example, that under the heading "Italians" in the 1902 *New York Tribune Index,* 55 of the 74 entries were clear accounts of crime and violence (*Strangers in the Land,* p. 363).

47. For excellent insight into the Italian community of Chicago's West Side, see Gerald D. Suttles, *The Social Order of the Slum* (Chicago: University of Chicago Press, 1971).

48. See Rudolph Vecoli, *The Peoples of New Jersey* (New Brunswick, NJ: Rutgers University Press, 2000), pp. 221–36.

49. Herbert J. Gans, *The Urban Villagers,* rev. ed. (New York: Free Press, 1982), pp. 204–5.

50. William Foote Whyte, *Street Corner Society* (Chicago: University of Chicago Press, 1993), p. 274.

51. Richard D. Alba and Victor Nee, *Remaking the American Mainstream: Assimilation and Contemporary Immigration* (Cambridge, MA: Harvard University Press, 2003).

52. Data extrapolated from U.S. Census Bureau, *2011 American Community Survey,* Table B04006.

53. Department of Homeland Security, *Yearbook of Immigration Statistics,* Table 3; U.S. Census Bureau, *2011 American Community Survey.*

54. U.S. Census Bureau, *Language Use in the United States: 2007* (Washington, DC: U.S. Government Printing Office, 2010), p. 6.

55. See, for example, Charles Hirschman, "Immigration and the American Century," *Demography,* 42 (2005); and Richard D. Alba, "The Twilight of Ethnicity among Americans of European Ancestry: The Case of the Italians," *Ethnic and Racial Studies,* 8 (January 1985): 141.

56. Richard D. Alba, *Italian Americans: Into the Twilight of Ethnicity* (Englewood Cliffs, NJ: Prentice Hall, 1985), p. 159.

57. Order Sons of Italy in America, "Italian American Stereotypes in U.S. Advertising." Retrieved October 24, 2012 (http://www.osia.org/documents/Advertising-Report.pdf).

58. See Virginia Patriarca, "The Crystallized Image of the Italian American on Television and in Hollywood Films," *La Critica Sociologica,* 41 (2007): 119–24; Jonathan J. Cavallero,

"Gangsters, Fessos, Tricksters, and Sopranos," *Journal of Popular Film & Television,* 32 (2004): 50–63.

59. Leonard Dinnerstein and David M. Reimers, *Ethnic Americans,* 5th ed. (New York: Columbia University Press, 2009), p. 65.

60. In 1972, a Boston city survey—the Omnibus Survey—revealed that its sizable Greek immigrant population had a zero unemployment rate, no one on welfare, and a median income $4,000 above the Boston average.

61. Theodore Saloutos, *The Greeks in the United States* (Cambridge, MA: Harvard University Press, 1995), pp. 78–79.

62. Henry Pratt Fairchild, *Greek Immigration in the United States* (Roselle, NJ: Howard Press, 2009), pp. 239, 241–42. Originally published in 1911.

63. U.S. Census Bureau. *2011 American Community Survey,* Table B04006.

64. Department of Homeland Security, *Yearbook of Immigration Statistics: 2011,* Table 3.

65. "Roma in America," U.S. Department of State. Retrieved October 24, 2012 (http://www.america.gov/st/texttrans-english/2009/April/200904071021352ecaganara0.5367657.html).

66. Unión Romaní, "Historical Origins." Retrieved October 24, 2012 (http://www.unionromani.org/pueblo_in.htm).

67. Ian F. Hancock, *We Are the Romani People* (Hatfield, UK: University of Hertfordshire Press, 2003), pp. 26–28.

68. Jan Yoors, *The Heroic Present: Life among the Gypsies* (New York: Monacelli Press, 2005).

69. Anne Sutherland, *Gypsies: The Hidden Americans,* reprint ed. (New York: Waveland, 1986).

70. Ibid.

71. See Lois Ritter and Nancy Hoffman, *Multicultural Health* (Sudbury, MA: Jones & Barlett Publishers, 2010), pp. 317–19.

72. Hancock, *We Are the Romani People,* pp. 102–3.

73. Sutherland, *Gypsies: The Hidden Americans,* pp. 17, 263.

74. Texas State Historical Association, "Roma (Gypsies)." Retrieved October 24, 2012 (http://www.tshaonline.org/handbook/online/articles/RR/pxrfh.html).

75. Vincent N. Parrillo, *Diversity in America,* 4th ed. (Boulder, CO: Paradigm Publishers, 2013), p. 106.

76. See Alice Kestler-Harris, *Out to Work: A History of Wage-Earning Women in the United States,* 20th ed. (New York; Oxford University Press, 2003).

77. Vincent N. Parrillo, *Diversity in America,* p. 107.

78. Ibid.

79. Michael Novak, *Unmeltable Ethnics: Politics and Culture in American Life,* 2nd ed. (New Brunswick, NJ: Transaction Publishers, 1995).

## CHAPTER 7

1. See M. M. Noah, *Discourse on the Evidences of the American Indians Being the Descendants of the Lost Tribes of Israel* (Hong Kong; Forgotten Books, 2012). Originally published in 1837.

2. U.S. Census Bureau, *Facts for Features: American Indian and Alaska Native Heritage Month,* CB11-FF.22 (November 1, 2011).

3. Clements R. Markham, translator, *The Journal of Christopher Columbus* (Boston: Adamant Media Corporation, 2001), pp. 37–38.

4. Quoted in Anthony Benezet, *Some Historic Account of Guinea* (Charleston, SC: BiblioBazaar, 2009), p. 41.

5. See Lawrence A. Clayton, *Bartolome de las Casas* (New York: Cambridge University Press, 2012).

6. Douglas Edward Leach, *Flintlock and Tomahawk, New England in King Philip's War,* reprint ed. (Woodstock, VT: Countryman Press, 2009), pp. 20–22.

7. Ormond Seavey (ed.), *Benjamin Franklin: Autobiography and Other Writings* (New York: Oxford University Press, 2009), pp. 313–14.

8. George Catlin, *Letters and Notes of the Manners, Customs and Conditions of the North American Indians* (Whitefish, MT: Kessinger Publishing, 2005), pp. 102–3. Originally published in 1841.

9. See Timothy J. Shannon, *Indians and Colonists at the Crossroads of Empire: The Albany Congress of 1754* (Ithaca, NY: Cornell University Press, 2003), pp. 6–8.

10. See, for example, James Wilson, *The Earth Shall Weep: A History of Native America* (Boston: Atlantic Monthly Press, 1999), pp. 23–24.

11. See Paula M. Marks, *In a Barren Land: The American Indian Quest for Cultural Survival, 1607 to the Present* (New York: Harper Perennial, 1999).

12. Wilcomb E. Washburn, *The Indian in America* (New York: Harper & Row, 1975), pp. 39–40.

13. See Marilyn G. Bentz, "Child Rearing," pp. 115–18, in Frederick E. Hoxie (ed.), *Encyclopedia of North American Indians* (Boston: Houghton Mifflin Harcourt, 1999).

14. Albert Britt, *Great Indian Chiefs* (Whitefish, MT: Kessinger Publishing, 2008), pp. 8–26.

15. Peter Farb, *Man's Rise to Civilization: The Cultural Ascent of the Indians of North America* (New York: Penguin, 1991), p. 158.

16. See Lawrence W. Gross, "Silence as the Root of American Indian Humor: Further Meditations on the Cosmic Humor of Anishinaabe Culture and Religion," *American Indian Culture and Research Journal,* 31 (2007): 74–8.16; and Donald L. Fixico, *The American Indian Mind in a Linear World: American Indian Studies and Traditional Knowledge* (New York: Routledge, 2004), pp. 1–4.

17. See Jason E. Black, "Native Resistive Rhetoric and the Decolonization of American Indian Removal Discourse," *Quarterly Journal of Speech,* 95 (2009): 66–88.

18. Alvin M. Josephy Jr., *The Indian Heritage of America* (New York: Mariner Books, 1992), p. 324.

19. Janet Klausner, *Sequoyah's Gift: A Portrait of the Cherokee Leader* (New York: HarperCollins, 1993), pp. 97–98.

20. Dale Van Every, *Disinherited: The Lost Birthright of the American Indian* (New York: Discus Avon Books, 1980), p. 163.

21. James Mooney and George Ellison, *James Mooney's History, Myths, and Sacred Formulas of the Cherokees* (Fairview, NC: Bright Mountain Books, 1992), p. 100.

22. Martin Van Buren, *Second Annual Message.* Retrieved October 25, 2012 (http://www.presidency.ucsb.edu/ws/index.php?pid=29480).

23. Farb, *Man's Rise to Civilization,* p. 310.

24. Ibid., p. 309.

25. Ibid.

26. Council of Indian Nations, "Termination Policy 1953–1968." Retrieved October 25, 2012 (http://www.nrcprograms.org/site/PageServer?pagename=cin_hist_terminationpolicy).

27. Josephy, *The Indian Heritage of America,* p. 354.

28. U.S. Census Bureau, *2011 American Community Survey;* Centers for Disease Control and Prevention, *Births: Final Data for 2010,* Vol. 61 (August 2012), Table 1.

29. American Indian Policy Review Committee, "Report on Indian Education" (Washington, DC: U.S. Government Printing Office, 1976), p. 245.

30. American Indian Policy Review Commission, "Report on Urban and Rural Non-Reservation Indians" (Washington, DC: U.S. Government Printing Office, 1976), p. 25.

31. U.S. Census Bureau, *2011 American Community Survey*, Table S0201.

32. U.S. Department of Education, "Tribal Colleges and Universities." Retrieved January 26, 2013 (http://www.ed.gov/edblogs/whiaiane/tribal-colleges-and-universities/tribal-colleges-and-universities-2).

33. Ibid.

34. "Demographics," *Rosebud Sioux Tribe*. Retrieved June 5, 2013 (http://www.bia.gov/WhoWeAre/RegionalOffices/GreatPlains/WeAre/Agencies/Rosebud/index.htm).

35. U.S. Census Bureau, *2011 American Community Survey*, Table S0201.

36. "Businesses," Mississippi Band of Choctaw Indians. Retrieved October 29, 2012 (http://www.choctaw.org/businesses/index.html).

37. "Cherokee Nation Industries," Retrieved October 29, 2010 (http://www.cherokeenationbusinesses.com).

38. Passamaquoddy Indian Nation, "Economy." Retrieved October 29, 2012 (http://www.epa.gov/NE/govt/tribes/passamaquoddyindiantownship.html); and J. M. Hirsch, "Blueberries Equal Big Business in Maine," Associated Press State & Local Wire (August 11, 2006).

39. National Indian Gaming Commission. Retrieved June 5, 2013 (http://www.nigc.gov).

40. Alan Meister, *Indian Gaming Industry Report* (Newton, MA: Casino City Press, 2013); and Tom A. Peter, "As Gaming Grows, Many Tribes Get Left Behind," *Christian Science Monitor* (November 1, 2007), p. 3.

41. Indian Health Service, "HIS Fact Sheets: Indian Health Disparities." Retrieved October 29, 2012 (http://www.ihs.gov//PublicAffairs/IHSBrochure/Disparities.asp).

42. Indian Health Service, op. cit.

43. U.S. Commission on Civil Rights, *Broken Promises: Evaluating the Native American Health Care System* (Washington, DC: U.S. Government Printing Office, 2004), p. 6.

44. National Center for Health Statistics, *Health, United States: 2012* (Washington, DC: U.S. Government Printing Office, 2013), Table 35, pp. 129–30.

45. Faye A. Gary, "Perspectives on Suicide Prevention among American Indian and Alaska Native Children and Adolescents: A Call for Help," *Online Journal of Issues in Nursing*, 10 (2005): 170–211; and Melissa L. Walls, Constance L. Chapple, and Kurt D. Johnson, "Strain, Emotion, and Suicide among American Indian Youth," *Deviant Behavior*, 28 (May/June 2007): 219–46.

46. Steven W. Perry, *American Indians and Crime*, Bureau of Justice Statistics (December 2004). Retrieved June 5, 2012 (http://www.bjs.gov/content/pub/pdf/aic02.pdf).

47. Erik Eckholm, "Gang Violence Grows on an Indian Reservation," *New York Times* (December 14, 2009), p. A14.

48. National Center for Health Statistics, "Deaths: Final Data for 2010," *National Vital Statistics Reports*, 61 (2013): Table 35.

49. Perry, *American Indians and Crime*, p. 10.

50. Philip A. May, "The Epidemiology of Alcohol Abuse among American Indians: The Mythical and Real Properties," *American Indian Culture & Research Journal*, 18 (1994): 124.

51. Michael T. Garrett and Jane J. Carroll, "Mending the Broken Circle: Treatment of Substance Dependence among Native Americans," *Journal of Counseling & Development*, 78 (2000): 380.

52. Jacob E. Cheadle and Les B. Whitbeck, "Alcohol Use Trajectories and Problem Drinking over the Course of Adolescence: A Study of North American Indigenous Youth and Their Caretakers," *Journal of Health and Social Behavior*, 52 (2011): 228–45; and James Moran and Marian Bussey, "Results of an Alcohol Prevention Program with Urban Native American Youth," *Child & Adolescent Social Work Journal*, 24 (2007): 1–21.

53. Renee V. Galliher, Colette M. Evans, and Desmond Weiser, "Social and Individual Predictors of Substance Use for Native Youth," *Journal of Child & Adolescent Substance Abuse*, 16 (2007): 1–16.

54. Stephen Kulis, Maria Napoli, and Flavio F. Marsiglia, "Ethnic Pride, Biculturalism, and Drug Use Norms of Urban American Indian Adolescents," *Social Work Research*, 26 (June 2002): 101–12.

55. See James R. Moran et al., "Measuring Bicultural Ethnic Identity among American Indian Adolescents: A Factor Analytic Study," *Journal of Adolescent Research*, 14 (1999): 405–26.

56. National American Indian Housing Council, "Briefing on Native American Housing," August 3, 2012. Retrieved October 29, 2012 (http://www.naihc.net/index.php/documents/native-housing-update).

57. Robert C. Holman, Aaron T. Curns, James E. Cheek, Joseph S. Bresee, Rosalyn J. Singleton, Karen Carver, and Larry J. Anderson, "Respiratory Syncytial Virus Hospitalizations among American Indian and Alaska Native Infants and the General United States Infant Population," *Pediatrics*, 114 (2004): 437–44.

58. Katherine M. Peters, "Trail of Trouble," *Government Executive*, 33 (April 2001): 95–103; see also Peter Maas, "The Broken Promise," *Parade* (September 9, 2001), pp. 4–6.

59. Friends Committee on National Legislation, "Issues: Native American Trust Fund: Massive Mismanagement." Retrieved November 5, 2012 (http://www.fcnl.org/issues/issue.php?issue_id=112).

60. See The Pluralism Project at Harvard University, "Sweetgrass Hills, MT," 2006. Retrieved November 5, 2012 (http://www.pluralism.org/reports/view/55).

61. Robert Begay, "Doo Dilzin Da: Abuse of the Natural World," *American Indian Quarterly*, 25:1 (2001): 21–27.

62. Navajo Tribal Utility Authority home page. Retrieved November 5, 2012 (http://www.ntua.com).

63. Native American Legal Update, "From Native Lands to Corporate Pockets—Navajo Coal Royalty Claim Rejected," April 17, 2009. Retrieved November 5, 2012 (http://www.nativelegalupdate.com/2009/04).

64. U.S. Environmental Protection Agency, "Addressing Uranium Contamination in the Navajo Nation." Retrieved November 5, 2010 (http://epa.gov/region09/superfund/navajo-nation/index.html).

65. Susan Moran, "The Tribe That Earned a Triple-A Bond Rating," *New York Times* (July 24, 2007), pp. C1, C4.

66. Council of Energy Resource Tribes, "About CERT." Retrieved June 5, 2013 (http://www.certredearth.com/aboutus-member-Tribes.html).

67. "Wastes," Environmental Protection Agency. Retrieved November 5, 2012 (http://www.epa.gov/ebtpages/wastes.html).

68. See "Environmental Justice/Environmental Racism." Retrieved November 5, 2012 (http://www.ejnet.org/ej).

69. Beyond Nuclear, "Radioactivity and Toxic Chemicals Spilled into Soil and Groundwater at Prairie Island." Retrieved November 5, 2012. (http://www.beyondnuclear.org/home/2012/2/7).

70. Serban Negoita et al., "Chronic Diseases Surveillance of St. Regis Mohawk Health Service Patients," *Journal of Public Health Management and Practice,* 7 (2001): 84–90.

71. Tim Higgins, "GM Gets to Dump Polluted Property," *Detroit Free Press* (August 7, 2009), p. A1.

72. "Water Rights Create Legal Disputes," *Utility Business* (July 2001), p. 12.

73. Karl Puckett, "Indian Tribes Exercising Water Rights; Could Mean Less (or Pricier) Water for Others as Drought Lingers," *USA Today* (February 26, 2008), p. 3A.

74. Randal C. Archibold, "Settlement Returns Water to Indians: Giving Hope for a Healthier Way of Life," *New York Times* (August 31, 2008), p. 20.

75. Suzi Parker, "Suburban Sprawl Spurs Fights over Sacred Indian Sites across the U.S.," *Christian Science Monitor* (August 16, 2001), p. 2.

76. See, for example, Granville Ganter, *The Collected Speeches of Sagoyewatha, or Red Jacket* (Syracuse, NY: Syracuse University Press, 2006).

77. Paul Waldie, "North Dakota Votes to Retire Fighting Sioux Nickname," *The Globe and Mail* (June 13, 2012), p. A3; and Kim Murphy, "Oregon Forbids Native American Mascots," *Los Angeles Times* (May 20, 2012), p. A16.

78. See Dee Brown, *Bury My Heart at Wounded Knee* (New York: Holt Paperbacks, 2007).

79. "Wounded Knee: The Media Coup d'État," *Nation,* 216 (June 25, 1973): 807.

80. Daily Yonder, "Settlement Possible in Black Hills Case" (May 12, 2009). Retrieved November 7, 2012 (http://www.dailyyonder.com/settlement-possible-black-hills-case/2009/05/12/2112).

81. Greg Guedel, "Tribes Sue to Improve Fish Habitat," *Native American Legal Update* (October 21, 2009). Retrieved November 7, 2012 (http://www.nativelegalupdate.com/articles/washington-state-law).

82. Elizabeth Cooper, "Oneidas, Counties Might Head Back to Court Again," *Observer-Dispatch* (September 7, 2012); and Ken Belson, "Judge Says Oneida Indians Deserve a Chance for Redress," *New York Times* (May 22, 2007), p. B4.

83. Katherine M. Peters, "Trail of Trouble," pp. 95–96, 103.

84. Associated Press, "Indian-Affairs Plan Aims to Improve Asset Management," *Wall Street Journal* (December 5, 2002), p. A5.

85. "Audit Raises Concerns on Special Education in BIA-Funded Schools," *Education Week* (April 18, 2007), p. 11.

86. U.S. Census Bureau, 2010 Census Summary File 1.

87. U.S. Census Bureau, "State and County Quick Facts," Census 2010.

88. See Donald L. Fixico, *The Urban Indian Experience in America* (Albuquerque: University of New Mexico Press, 2000).

89. See Suhasin Ramisetty-Mikler and Malembe S. Ebama, "Alcohol/Drug Exposure, HIV-Related Sexual Risk among Urban American Indian and Alaska Native Youth: Evidence from a National Survey," *Journal of School Health,* 81 (2011): 671–79; "The Scope of the Problem," *Alchohol Research & Health,* 28 (2004/2005): 111–20; and Paul Spicer, Douglas K. Novins, Christina M. Mitchell, and Janette Beals, "Aboriginal Social Organization, Contemporary Experience and American Indian Adolescent Alcohol Use," *Journal of Studies on Alcohol,* 64 (2003): 450–57.

90. Mei L. Castor, Maile M. Taualii, Alice N. Park, and Ralph A. Forquera, "A Nationwide Population-Based Study Identifying Health Disparities between American Indians/Alaska Natives and the General Populations Living in Select Urban Counties," *American Journal of Public Health,* 96 (August 2006): 1416–22.

91. Fixico, *The Urban Indian Experience in America,* pp. 161–70.

92. Josephy, *The Indian Heritage of America,* p. 32.

93. Ibid.

94. Ibid., p. 34.

95. Ward Churchill, *Kill the Indian, Save the Man* (San Francisco: City Lights Publishers, 2005).

96. See Robert John, "The Native American Family," pp. 361–410, in *Ethnic Families in America,* 5th ed. Edited by Roosevelt Wright, Jr., Charles H. Mindel, Thanh Van Tran, and Robert W. Habenstein (New York: Pearson, 2012).

97. Michael T. Garrett and Eugene F. Pichette, "Red as an Apple: Native American Acculturation and Counseling with or without Reservation," *Journal of Counseling and Development,* 78 (2000): 3–13.

98. Craig D. Freed and Mary Samson, "Native Alaskan Dropouts in Western Alaska: Systemic Failure in Native Alaskan Schools," *Journal of American Indian Education,* 43 (2004): 33–45.

# CHAPTER 8

1. U.S. Department of Homeland Security, Office of Immigration Statistics, *U.S. Legal Permanent Residents: 2012,* March 2013, Table 3.

2. U.S. Census Bureau, *2011 American Community Survey,* Table S0201.

3. "China," *Encyclopaedia Britannica,* 7th ed. (1842), Vol. 6.

4. Otis Gibson, *The Chinese in America* (Charleston, SC: BiblioBazaar, 2009), pp. 51–52. Originally published in 1877.

5. See Stephen E. Ambrose, *Nothing Like It in the World: The Men Who Built the Transcontinental Railroad, 1863–1869* (New York: Simon & Schuster, 2000).

6. Alexander Saxton, *The Indispensable Enemy: Labor and the Anti-Chinese Movement in California* (Berkeley: University of California Press, 1976), p. 63.

7. Hinton Helper, *The Land of Gold: Reality versus Fiction* (Baltimore, 1855), pp. 94–96, quoted in Saxton, *The Indispensable Enemy,* p. 19.

8. "The Growth of the U.S. through Emigration—The Chinese," *New York Times* (September 3, 1865), p. 4.

9. "The Chinese Mission," *New York Times* (June 7, 1868), p. 4.

10. Senator James G. Blaine, *Congressional Record* (February 14, 1879), p. 1301.

11. U.S. Immigration and Naturalization Service, *Annual Report* (Washington, DC: U.S. Government Printing Office, 1926), pp. 170–81.

12. Ibid.

13. American Federation of Labor, *Proceedings,* 1893, p. 73.

14. Albert W. Palmer, *Orientals in American Life* (New York: Friendship Press, 1934), pp. 1–2, 7.

15. Stanford M. Lyman, "Conflict and the Web of Group Affiliation in San Francisco's Chinatown, 1850–1910," *Pacific Historical Review,* 43 (1974): 473–99. This work is an application of ideas developed by Georg Simmel in two theoretical essays, "Conflict" and "The Web of Group Affiliation."

16. S. W. Kung, *Chinese in American Life* (Seattle: University of Washington Press, 1962), p. 89.

17. Stanford M. Lyman, "Marriage and the Family among Chinese Immigrants to America," *Phylon,* 29 (Winter 1968): 32–33.

18. U.S. Immigration and Naturalization Service, *1990 Statistical Yearbook* (Washington, DC: U.S. Government Printing Office, 1991), Table 12, pp. 71–73.

19. Lyman, "Marriage and the Family among Chinese Immigrants to America," p. 327.

20. Ibid., p. 330.

21. Ibid., p. 328.

22. *Congressional Record* (October 21, 1943), p. 8626.

23. See Mark Abrahamson, *Urban Enclaves: Identity and Place in America*, 2nd ed. (New York: Worth, 2006), pp. 67–84.

24. John M. Glionna, "Squalor Amid the Glitter," *Los Angeles Times* (December 28, 2001), p. A1; Asian Community Development Corporation, "Chinatown Community Snapshot 2009" (August 14, 2009), p. 9; and Ko-Lin Chin, *Chinatown Gangs: Extortion, Enterprise, and Ethnicity* (New York: Oxford University Press, 2000).

25. See Miriam Ching Yoon Louie, *Sweatshop Warriors: Immigrant Women Workers Take On the Global Factory* (Cambridge, MA: South End Press, 2001).

26. Ming-Jung Ho, "Migratory Journeys and Tuberculosis Risk," *Medical Anthropology Quarterly,* 17 (2003): 442–58.

27. Ko-Lin Chin, op. cit.

28. See Sheldon Zhang, *Chinese Human Smuggling Organizations: Families, Social Networks, and Cultural Imperatives* (Stanford, CA: Stanford University Press, 2008), pp. 9–10.

29. Jennifer 8 Lee, "A Tour of Chinatown, Manhattan-Style," *New York Times* (September 24, 2009). Retrieved January 26, 2013 (http://www.cityroom.blogs.nytimes.com); see also Peter Kwong, *The New Chinatown,* revised ed. (New York: Hill & Wang, 1996), p. 41.

30. U.S. Department of Labor, "The Asian-American Labor Force in the Recovery." Retrieved November 1, 2012 (http://www.dol.gov/_sec/media/reports/asianlaborforce/#.UJKa0cXAeqY).

31. Stanford M. Lyman, *Color, Culture, Civilization* (Urbana, IL: University of Illinois Press, 1995), p. 283.

32. Morton Grodzins, *Americans Betrayed,* reprint ed. (Chicago: University of Chicago Press, 1974). Originally published in 1949.

33. Lyman, "Generation & Character: The Case of the Japanese-Americans," pp. 279–80.

34. Eugene V. Rostow, "Our Worst Wartime Mistake," *Harper's Magazine* (September 1945): 193–201.

35. See Michi Weglyn, *Years of Infamy: The Untold Story of America's Concentration Camps*, expanded ed. (Seattle: University of Washington Press, 2000).

36. Esther B. Rhoads, "My Experience with the Wartime Relocation of Japanese," in Hilary Conroy and T. Scott Miyakawa (eds.), *East across the Pacific: Historical and Sociological Studies of Japanese Immigration and Acculturation* (Santa Barbara, CA: American Bibliographical Center Clio Press, 1972), pp. 131–32.

37. Ted Nakashima, "Concentration Camp, U.S. Style," *New Republic* (June 15, 1942), pp. 822–23.

38. Justice Robert H. Jackson, dissenting opinion, *Korematsu v. United States of America,* 65, *Supreme Court Reporter* (1944): 206–8.

39. Bill Hosokawa, *Nisei: The Quiet Americans,* revised ed. (Boulder: University Press of Colorado, 2002), pp. 439–46.

40. See Eric K. Yamamoto et al. (eds.), *Rights, Race, and Reparation: Law of the Japanese American Internment* (Sandy, UT: Aspen Press, 2002).

41. See Harry Wray, *Japanese and American Education: Attitudes and Practices* (Charlotte, NC: Information Age Publishing, 2009).

42. U.S. Census Bureau, "Selected Population Profile in the United States," *2011 American Community Survey,* Table S0201; and Arthur Sakamoto, Kimberly A. Goyette, and ChangHwan Kim, "Socioeconomic Attainments of Asian Americans," *Annual Review of Sociology,* 35 (2009): 255–76.

43. C. N. Le. "Interracial Dating and Marriage," *Asian-Nation: The Landscape of Asian America* (2012). Retrieved November 1, 2012 (http://www.asian-nation.org/interracial.shtml).

44. U.S. Office of Immigration Statistics, *2011 Yearbook of Immigration Statistics* (Washington, DC: U.S. Government Printing Office, 2012), Table 2, p. 10.

45. *Morrison et al. v. California* (1934), 291 U.S. Supreme Court Reports (1934), pp. 85–86.

46. Davis McEntire, *The Labor Force in California: A Study of Characteristics and Trends in Labor Force, Employment, and Occupations in California, 1900–1950* (Berkeley: University of California Press, 1952), p. 62.

47. Carey McWilliams, *Brothers under the Skin* (Boston: Little, Brown, 1951), p. 239.

48. Sylvain Lazarus, San Francisco Municipal Court, January 1936, quoted in Manuel Braken, *I Have Lived with the American People* (Caldwell, CA: Caxton, 1948), pp. 136–38.

49. Letter from Sylvester Saturday, in *Time* (May 11, 1936), p. 4.

50. Letter from Ernest D. Ilustre, in *Time* (April 27, 1936), p. 3.

51. McWilliams, *Brothers under the Skin,* p. 244.

52. Bernicio T. Catapusan, "Filipino Intermarriage Problems in the United States," *Sociology and Social Research,* 22 (1938): 265–72.

53. For an excellent sociological study of Filipinos in dance halls, see Paul G. Cressey, *The Taxi-Dance Hall* (New York: Routledge, 2003).

54. R. T. Feria, "War and the Status of the Filipino Immigrants," *Sociology and Social Research,* 31 (1946): 50.

55. U.S. Census Bureau, "Selected Population Profile in the United States," *2011 American Community Survey,* Table S0201; see also Linus Yamane, "Native-Born Filipana/o Americans and Labor Market Discrimination," *Feminist Economics,* 8 (2002): 125–44.

56. U.S. Census Bureau, "Selected Population Profile in the United States," *2011 American Community Survey,* Table S0201; and Yen Le Espiritu, *Home Bound: Filipino Lives Across Cultures, Communities, and Countries* (Berkeley: University of California Press, 2003), pp. 190–92.

57. Pyong Gap Min, *Asian Americans: Contemporary Trends and Issues,* 2nd ed. (Thousand Oaks, CA: Sage, 2005), pp. 180–203.

58. U.S. Office of Immigration Statistics, *2011 Yearbook of Immigration Statistics* (Washington, DC: U.S. Government Printing Office, 2012), Table 2, p. 10; *U.S. Legal Permanent Residents: 2012,* Table 3.

59. Harold H. Sunoo and Sonia S. Sunoo, "The Heritage of the First Korean Women Immigrants in the United States: 1903–1924," *Korean Christian Journal,* 2 (1977): 144, 146, 165; and Bernice H. Kim, "The Koreans in Hawaii," *Social Science,* 9 (1934): 409.

60. Lee Houchins and Chang-su Houchins, "The Korean Experience in America, 1903–1924," *Pacific Historical Review,* 43 (1974): 560.

61. See Jennifer Lee, Esther S. Chang, and Lisa Miller, "Ethnic-Religious Status and Identity Formation: A Qualitative Study of Korean American Christian Youth," *Journal of Youth Ministry,* 5 (2006): 9–40; Young Lee Hertig, *Cultural Tug of War: Korean*

*Immigrant Family and Church in Transition* (Nashville, TN: Abingdon Press, 2002).

62. Kelly H. Chong, "What It Means to Be Christian: The Role of Religion in the Construction of Ethnic Identity and Boundary among Second-Generation Korean Americans," *Sociology of Religion,* 59 (1998): 259–286.

63. U.S. Census Bureau, *2011 American Community Survey*, Table S0201.

64. Miriam Jordan, "In Los Angeles, You Say 'Hola!' I Say, 'Ahn-nyung'," *Wall Street Journal* (June 2–3, 2007), pp. A1, A7; and Dae Young Kim, "Beyond Co-ethnic Solidarity: Mexican and Ecuadorean Employment in Korean-owned Businesses in New York City," *Ethnic and Racial Studies,* 22 (1999): 581–605.

65. Keumjae Park, "I Can Provide for My Children: Korean Immigrant Women's Changing Perspectives on Work Outside the Home," *Gender Issues,* 25 (2008): 26–42.

66. U.S. Census Bureau, "Selected Population Profile in the United States," *2011 American Community Survey*, Table S0201.

67. Emory S. Bogardus, "Comparing Racial Distance in Ethiopia, South Africa, and the United States," *Sociology and Social Research,* 52 (1968): 149–56; Vincent N. Parrillo and Christopher Donoghue, "Updating the Bogardus Social Distance Studies: A New National Survey," *Social Science Journal,* 42:2 (2005): 257–71; Parrillo and Donoghue, "The National Social Distance Study: Ten Years Later," *Sociological Forum,* 28:3 (September 2013).

68. Gurdial Singh, "East Indians in the United States," *Sociology and Social Research,* 30 (1946): 210–11.

69. Joan M. Jensen, "Apartheid: Pacific Coast Style," *Pacific Historical Review,* 38 (1969): 335–40.

70. Gary R. Hess, "The Forgotten Asian Americans: The East Indian Community in the United States," *Pacific Historical Review,* 43 (1974): 580.

71. Singh, "East Indians in the United States," pp. 210–11.

72. "Hindu Invasion," *Collier's,* 45 (March 26, 1910): 15.

73. Hess, "The Forgotten Asian Americans: The East Indian Community in the United States," pp. 583–84.

74. Juan L. Gonzales Jr., "Asian Indian Immigration Patterns: The Origins of the Sikh Community in California," *International Migration Review,* 20 (Spring 1986): 46.

75. Hess, "The Forgotten Asian Americans: The First East Indian Community in the United States," p. 590.

76. Ibid., pp. 593–94.

77. U.S. Office of Immigration Statistics, *2011 Yearbook of Immigration Statistics,* Table 2; *U.S. Legal Permanent Residents: 2012,* Table 3.

78. U.S. Census Bureau, "The Asian Population: 2010," *2010 Census Briefs* (March 2012), pp. 17–18.

79. Susumu Awanohara, "Political Indian Summer," *Far Eastern Economic Review,* 151 (May 23, 1991): 35.

80. Carl Haub and O. P. Sharma, "India's Population Reality: Reconciling Change and Traditions," *Population Bulletin,* 61:3 (2006): 4–5.

81. "India," *CIA World Factbook.* Retrieved November 1, 2012 (https://www.cia.gov/library/publications/the-world-factbook/geos/in.html).

82. See Arpana G. Inman, Erin E. Howard, and Jessica A. Walker, "Cultural Transmission: Influence of Contextual Factors in Asian Indian Immigrant Parents' Experiences," *Journal of Counseling Psychology,* 54:1 (2007): 93–100.

83. U.S. Census Bureau, *The American Community—Asians: 2004,* p. 16.22.

84. Jim Hopkins, "Asian Business Owners Gaining Clout," *USA Today* (February 27, 2002), p. 1.

85. Jonathan Brooks, "American Owned: Gujarati Indians in the Lodging Industry," *Dissertation Abstracts International: The Humanities and Social Sciences,* 64:10 (April 2004): 3855-A.

86. American Community Survey 2009 (ACS09), ACS 2009 (1-Year Estimates), U.S. Census Bureau.

87. Michael Luo, "Study of Taxi Drivers Finds More Immigrants at the Wheel," *New York Times* (July 7, 2004), p. B3.

88. Sarah Kershaw, "The 99 Cent American Dream," *New York Times* (January 23, 1997), p. B1.

89. "Future of Refugees: The Furor and the Facts," *U.S. News & World Report* (May 19, 1975), p. 16.

90. U.S. Office of Immigration Statistics, *2011 Yearbook of Immigration Statistics,* Table 2, p. 10; *U.S. Legal Permanent Residents: 2012,* Table 3.

91. U.S. Census Bureau, "The Asian Population: 2010," *2010 Census Briefs* (March 2012), p. 16.

92. The author wishes to thank Walter H. Slote, Ph.D., and Stephen Young, J.D., for sharing with him their expertise about the Vietnamese and Vietnamese Americans.

93. Walter H. Slote, "Destiny and Determination: Psychocultural Reinforcement in Vietnam," p. 325, in Walter H. Slote and George A. DeVos (eds.), *Confucianism and the Family* (Albany: State University of New York Press, 1998).

94. Ibid., p. 322.

95. Bayard Webster, "Studies Report Refugees Plagued by Persistent Stress," *New York Times* (September 11, 1979), p. C1.

96. Jean S. Phinney and Anthony D. Ong, "Adolescent–Parent Disagreements and Life Satisfaction in Families from Vietnamese- and European-American Backgrounds," *International Journal of Behavioral Development,* 26 (2002): 556–61.

97. U.S. Census Bureau, "The Asian Population: 2010," *2010 Census Briefs* (March 2012), p. 16.

98. David W. Haines, "Ethnicity's Shadows: Race, Religion, and Nationality as Alternative Identities among Recent United States Arrivals," *Identities: Global Studies in Culture and Power,* 14 (2007): 285–312.

99. Betty Rairdan and Zana Roe Higgs, "When Your Patient Is a Hmong Refugee," *American Journal of Nursing,* 92 (1992): 52–55.

100. U.S. Census Bureau, "The Asian Population: 2010," *2010 Census Briefs* (March 2012), p. 19.

101. See, for example, Catherine A. Solheim and PaNhia Yang, "Understanding Generational Differences in Financial Literacy in Hmong Immigrant Families," *Family and Consumer Sciences Research Journal,* 38 (2010): 435–54; Stacey J. Lee, "Learning 'America': Hmong American High School Students," *Education and Urban Society,* 34 (2002): 233–46; Jeanne L. Tsai, "Cultural Orientation of Hmong Young Adults," *Journal of Human Behavior in the Social Environment,* 3 (2001): 99–114.

102. See Stacey J. Lee, *Unraveling the "Model Minority" Stereotype: Listening to Asian American Youth,* 2nd ed. (New York: Teachers College Press, 2009).

103. Federal Bureau of Investigation, "Hate Crime Statistics: 2010." Retrieved April 16, 2013 (http://www.fbi.gov/about-us/cjis/ucr/hate-crime/2011/tables/table-1).

104. Pauline Yoshihashi and Sarah Lubman, "American Dreams," *Wall Street Journal* (June 16, 1992), p. A6.

105. See Nadia Y. Kim, *Imperial Citizens: Koreans and Race from Seoul to LA* (Stanford, CA: Stanford University Press, 2008);

In-Jin Yoon, *On My Own: Korean Businesses and Race Relations in America* (Chicago: University of Chicago Press, 1997).

106. Victor Bascara, *Model-Minority Imperialism* (Minneapolis: University of Minnesota Press, 2006), p. 1.

107. Hye Jin Paek and Hemant Shah, "Racial Ideology, Model Minorities, and the 'Not-So-Silent Partner': Stereotyping of Asian Americans in U.S. Magazine Advertising," *The Howard Journal of Communication*, 14 (2003): 225–43.

108. Miranda Oshige McGowan and James Lingren, "Testing the 'Model Minority Myth'," *Northwestern University Law Review*, 100 (2006): 331–77.

109. David Budge, "Model Minority Tag Hides Dropout Problem," *Times Educational Supplement* (May 7, 2004), p. 16.

110. U.S. Census Bureau, "Income, Poverty, and Health Insurance Coverage in the United States: 2011," *Current Population Reports* (September 2012), PO 60-243, pp. 6, 14.

111. U.S. Census Bureau, *2011 American Community Survey*, Table S0201.

112. U.S. Census Bureau, *The Foreign-Born Population in the United States: 2010* (May 2012), ACS-19.

113. U.S. Census Bureau, "The Asian Population: 2010," *2010 Census Briefs* (March 2012), p. 8.

114. Pyong Gap Lee and Chigon Kim, "Patterns of Intermarriages and Cross-Generational In-Marriages among Native-Born Asian Americans," *International Migration Review*, 43 (2009): 447–70; and Vincent Kang Fu, "Racial Intermarriage Pairings," *Demography*, 38 (May 2001): 147–59.

115. See C. N. Le, *Asian American Assimilation: Ethnicity, Immigration, and Socioeconomic Attainment* (El Paso, TX: LFB Scholarly Publishing, 2007); see also Kyeyoung Park, *The Korean American Dream: Immigrants and Small Business in New York City* (Ithaca, NY: Cornell University Press, 1997).

116. U.S. Census Bureau, *2011 American Community Survey*, Table S0201.

## CHAPTER 9

1. U.S. Census Bureau, "Place of Birth for the Foreign-Born Population in the United States," *2011 American Community Survey*, Table B05006.

2. U.S. Census Bureau, "Total Ancestry Reported," *2011 American Community Survey*, Table B04003; Arab America, "Demographics." Retrieved November 1, 2012 (http://www.arabamerica.com/arabamericans.php).

3. Derived from U.S. Office of Immigration Statistics, *2011 Yearbook of Immigration Statistics*, Table 28, pp. 77–79.

4. Ibid., derived from Table 21, pp. 53–56.

5. Helen Hatab Samhan, "By the Numbers," Allied Media. Retrieved November 1, 2012 (http://www.allied-media.com/Arab-American/AAnumbers.htm).

6. See Chapter 1, pp. x-x.

7. See Nadine Naber, "Ambiguous Insiders: An Investigation of Arab American Invisibility," *Ethnic and Racial Studies*, 23 (2000): 37–61.

8. Andrzej Kulczycki and Arun Peter Lobo, "Patterns, Determinants, and Implications of Intermarriage among Arab Americans," *Journal of Marriage and Family*, 64 (2002): 202–10; Mona H. Faragallah, Walter R. Schumm, and Farrell J. Webb, "Acculturation of Arab-American Immigrants: An Exploratory Study," *Journal of Comparative Family Studies*, 28 (Autumn 1997): 182–203.

9. See Caroline P. Nagel and Lynn A. Staeheli, "'We're Just Like the Irish': Narratives of Assimilation, Belonging, and Citizenship amongst Arab-American Activists," *Citizenship Studies*, 9 (2005): 485–98.

10. Arab American Institute, "Demographics." Retrieved November 2, 2012 (http://www.aaiusa.org/pages/demographics).

11. Vincent N. Parrillo, "Arab American Residential Segregation: Differences in Patterns," *Resources in Education*, ERIC ED 243 991, 1984.

12. U.S. Census Bureau, *2011 American Community Survey*, Table S0201.

13. Ibid.

14. Ibid.

15. Ibid.

16. Ibid.

17. See Jonathan K. Stubbs, "The Bottom Rung of America's Race Ladder: After the September 11th Catastrophe, Are American Muslims Becoming America's New N…s?" *Journal of Law and Religion*, 19 (2003/2004): 115–31; and Matthew Purdy, "For Muslims, Flag-Flying and Fear," *New York Times* (September 14, 2001), p. A9.

18. Philip M. Kayal and Joseph M. Kayal, *The Syrian-Lebanese in America* (New York: Twayne, 1976), pp. 50, 61.

19. Elizabeth Boosahda, *Arab-American Faces and Voices: The Origins of an Immigrant Community* (Austin: University of Texas Press, 2003).

20. Alixa Naff, *The Arab Americans* (New York: Chelsea House, 1998), pp. 59, 72.

21. Cyril Anid, *I Grew with Them* (Jounieh, Lebanon: Paulist Press, 1967), p. 18.

22. See Amaney Jamal and Nadine Naber, *Race and Arab Americans before and after 9/11: From Invisible Citizens to Visible Subjects* (Syracuse, NY: Syracuse University Press, 2008), pp. 147–69.

23. Morris Berger, "America's Syrian Community," *Commentary*, 25(4) (1958): 316.

24. Ibid., p. 311.

25. Kayal and Kayal, *The Syrian-Lebanese in America*, p. 108.

26. U.S. Census Bureau, *2011 American Community Survey*, Table S0201.

27. Ibid.; U.S. Office of Immigration Statistics, *2011 Yearbook of Immigration Statistics*, Table 3.

28. See Michael W. Suleiman (ed.), *Arabs in America: Building a New Future* (Philadelphia: Temple University Press, 2000).

29. U.S. Census Bureau, *2011 American Community Survey*, Table S0201; U.S. Office of Immigration Statistics, *2011 Yearbook of Immigration Statistics*, Table 3.

30. U.S. Office of Immigration Statistics, *2011 Yearbook of Immigration Statistics*, Table 3.

31. Coptic Orthodox Church Network, "Coptic Churches in the United States and Canada." Retrieved November 3, 2012 (http://www.copticchurch.net/topics/directory/churches_all.php); Andrea Elliott, "A Bloody Crime in New Jersey Divides Egyptians Once Again," *New York Times* (January 21, 2005), p. A1.

32. U.S. Census Bureau, *2011 American Community Survey*, Table B04001.

33. Mary C. Sengstock, "Social Change in the Country of Origin as a Factor in Immigrant Conceptions of Nationality," *Ethnicity*, 4 (March 1977): 54–69.

34. Ibid., p. 61.

35. U.S. Census Bureau, *2011 American Community Survey*, Table S0201.

36. U.S. Office of Immigration Statistics, *2011 Yearbook of Immigration Statistics,* Table 2.

37. "State Profiles," Arab American Institute. Retrieved November 3, 2012 (http://www.aaiusa.org/index_ee.php/pages/state-profiles).

38. U.S. Census Bureau, *2011 American Community Survey,* Table S0201.

39. "State Profiles," Arab American Institute. Retrieved November 3, 2012.

40. Louise Cainkar, Ali Abunimah, and Lamia Rael, "Migration as a Method of Coping with Turbulence among Palestinians," *Journal of Comparative Family Studies,* 35 (2004): 2292–40.

41. U.S. Census Bureau, *2011 American Community Survey,* Table S0201.

42. Ibid.

43. Julianne M. Weinzimmer, "The Distant Reach of the Middle East: How Perceptions of Conflict Affect Jewish Israeli American and Palestinian American Identity," *Dissertation Abstracts: The Humanities and Social Sciences,* 69 (2008): 766.

44. Maboud Ansari, *Iranian Americans: An Emerging Ethnic Community* (New York: Edwin Mellen Press, 2013).

45. Ibid.

46. Ibid.; Nilou Mostofi, "Who We Are: The Perplexity of Iranian-American Identity," *The Sociological Quarterly,* 44 (2003): 681–703.

47. Maboud Ansari, *Iranian Americans.*

48. U.S. Office of Immigration Statistics, *2011 Yearbook of Immigration Statistics,* Table 3.

49. Ibid.

50. U.S. Office of Immigration Statistics, *2011 Yearbook of Immigration Statistics,* Tables 28, pp. 7–79.

51. Laura C. Rudolph, "Israeli Americans," *Countries and their Cultures.* Retrieved November 3, 2012 (http://www.everyculture.com/multi/Ha-La/Israeli-Americans.html).

52. Ibid.

53. Ibid.

54. Ibid.

55. Ibid.

56. U.S. Census Bureau, *2011 American Community Survey,* Table S0201; see also Steven J. Gold, "From Nationality to Peoplehood: Adaptation and Identity Formation in the Israeli Diaspora," *Diaspora,* 13 (2004): 331–58.

57. U.S. Census Bureau, loc. cit.

58. John J. Grabowski, "Prospects and Challenges: The Study of Early Turkish Immigration to the United States," *Journal of American Ethnic History,* 25 (Fall 2005): 85–85, 88.

59. Bogardus, "Comparing Racial Distance in Ethiopia, South Africa, and the United States," p. 152.

60. U.S. Census Bureau, *Ancestry 2010.* Available at http://factfinder2.census.gov.

61. Ilhan Kaya, "Identity and Space: The Case of Turkish Americans," *The Geographical Review,* 95 (2005): 431.

62. See Roberta Micallef, "Turkish Americans: Performing Identities in a Transnational Setting," *Journal of Muslim Minority Affairs,* 24 (2004): 233–41.

63. Mona H. Faragallah, Walter R. Schumm, and Farrell J. Webb, "Acculturation of Arab-American Immigrants," *Journal of Comparative Family Studies,* 28 (1997): 182–203.

64. Kristine J. Ajrouch and Amaney Jamal, "Assimilating to a White Identity: The Case of Arab Americans," *International Migration Review,* 41 (2007): 860–79.

# CHAPTER 10

1. U.S. Office of Immigration Statistics, *2011 Yearbook of Immigration Statistics,* Table 2, pp. 10–11.

2. See Audrey Smedley, *Race in North America: Origins and Evolution of a Worldview,* 4th ed. (Boulder, CO: Westview Press, 2011).

3. See Donald B. Redford, *From Slave to Pharaoh: The Black Experience of Ancient Egypt* (Baltimore: The Johns Hopkins University Press, 2007).

4. David M. Goldenberg, *The Curse of Ham: Race and Slavery in Early Judaism, Christianity, and Islam* (Princeton, NJ: Princeton University Press, 2003).

5. Audrey Smedley, *Race in North America,* pp. 161–76.

6. W. E. B. DuBois, *The World and Africa,* rev. ed. (New York: International Publishers, 1979), pp. 19–20.

7. C. Vann Woodward, *The Strange Career of Jim Crow,* 3rd ed. (New York: Oxford University Press, 2002).

8. Gunnar Myrdal, *An American Dilemma,* reprint ed. (New Brunswick, NJ: Transaction Publishers, 1995).

9. Ibid., pp. 75–78.

10. Dewey H. Palmer, "Moving North: Migration of Negroes during World War I," *Phylon,* 27 (Spring 1967): 52–62.

11. W. E. B. DuBois, *Dusk of Dawn* (New York: Schocken Books, 1969), p. 264.

12. Southern Poverty Law Center, "Ku Klux Klan." Retrieved November 7, 2012 (http://www.splcenter.org/get-informed/intelligence-files/ideology/ku-klux-klan).

13. The Supreme Court specifically cited Kenneth B. Clark's study on negative self-image among black schoolchildren. For detailed information on the social scientist's role in the decision, see Kenneth B. Clark, *Prejudice and Your Child,* 2nd revised ed. (Indianapolis: Wesleyan Publishing, 2001).

14. Jerome H. Skolnick, *The Politics of Protest: Violent Aspects of Protest and Confrontation,* 2nd rev. ed. (New York: New York University Press of the Pacific, 2010), pp. 101–2. Originally published in 1969.

15. John F. Kennedy, "Radio and Television Report to the American People on Civil Rights, June 11, 1963." Retrieved November 7, 2012 (http://www.jfklibrary.org).

16. Joint Center for Political and Economic Activities, *National Roster of Black Elected Officials.* Retrieved November 7, 2012 (http://www.jointcenter.org).

17. See Suzanne Staggenborg, *Social Movements* (New York: Oxford University Press, 2010).

18. From the *Report of the National Advisory Commission on Civil Disorders* (Washington, DC: U.S. Government Printing Office, 1968).

19. "Major U.S. Racial Disturbances since 1965," *Facts on File,* 52 (May 7, 1992): 328.

20. Ibid.

21. See Lou Cannon, *Official Negligence: How Rodney King and the Riots Changed Los Angeles and the LAPD* (New York: Basic Books, 2000).

22. See Zulema Valdez, "The Effect of Social Capital on White, Korean, Mexican, and Black Business Owners' Earnings in the US," *Journal of Ethnic and Migration Studies,* 34 (2008): 955–73.

23. Ibid.

24. Richard J. Herrnstein and Charles Murray, *The Bell Curve: The Reshaping of American Life by Differences in Intelligence* (New York: Free Press, 1994).

25. See Steven Fraser (ed.), *The Bell Curve Wars: Race, Intelligence, and the Future of America* (New York: Basic Books, 1995); and Russell Jacoby and Naomi Glauberman, *The Bell Curve Debate* (New York: Three Rivers Press, 1995).

26. See Thomas Sowell, "New Light on Black I.Q.," *New York Times Magazine* (March 27, 1977), p. 57.

27. Audrey Shuey, *The Testing of Negro Intelligence* (Lynchburg, VA: Bell, 1958), p. 318.

28. Arthur R. Jensen, "How Much Can We Boost I.Q. and Scholastic Achievement?" *Harvard Educational Review,* 39 (1969): 1–123. In December 1979, Jensen reexamined this issue, claiming that assumptions about biased tests were inaccurate because mean differences remained despite attempts to raise black test scores; see also Arthur R. Jensen, *Bias in Mental Testing* (New York: Free Press, 1980).

29. Sowell, "New Light on Black I.Q.," p. 57.

30. Ossie Davis, *Life Lit by Some Large Vision: Selected Speeches and Writings* (New York: Simon & Schuster, 2006), pp. 11–12.

31. See "African American Vernacular English," Center for Applied Linguistics. Retrieved November 8, 2010 (http://www.cal.org/topics/dialects/aae.html).

32. Sam Dillon, "Racial Gap in Testing Sees Shift by Region," *New York Times* (July 15, 2009), p. A10.

33. College Entrance Examination Board, *Total Group Profile Report: 2012 College Bound Seniors* (New York: CEEB, 2012), Table 8, p. 3.

34. U.S. Census Bureau, *2011 American Community Survey,* Table S0201; Moshe Semyonov and Noah Lewin-Epstein, "The Declining Racial Earnings' Gap in the United States: Multi-Level Analysis of Males' Earnings, 1960–2000," *Social Science Research,* 38 (2009): 296–311.

35. U.S. Census Bureau, *Income, Poverty, and Health Insurance Coverage in the United States: 2011,* p. 17; *America's Families and Living Arrangements: 2011,* Table C9.

36. U.S. Census Bureau, *2011 American Community Survey,* Table S0201.

37. Ibid.

38. U.S. Census Bureau; *2011 American Community Survey,* Table S0201.

39. See Peter Dreier, "The Future of Community Reinvestment," *Journal of the American Planning Association,* 69 (2003): 341–53.

40. See Dan Immergluck, "Redlining Redux. Black Neighborhoods, Black-Owned Firms, and the Regulatory Cold Shoulder," *Urban Affairs Review,* 38 (2002): 22–41; Gary M. Dymski, "Racial Exclusion and the Political Economy of the Subprime Crisis," *Historical Materialism,* 17 (2009): 149–79.

41. John R. Logan, *The Persistence of Segregation in the Metropolis: New Findings from the 2010 Census.* Retrieved November 9, 2012 (http://www.s4.brown.edu/us2010/Data/Report/report2.pdf).

42. Ibid., pp. 2–3.

43. Ibid., p. 6.

44. See, for example, Roberto M. Fernandez, "Race, Spatial Mismatch, and Job Accessibility: Evidence from a Plant Relocation," *Social Science Research,* 37 (2008): 953–75; and Robert L. Wagmiller, "Male Nonemployment in White, Black, Hispanic, and Multiethnic Urban Neighborhoods, 1970–2000," *Urban Affairs Review,* 44 (2008): 85–125.

45. Richard D. Alba, John R. Logan, and Brian J. Stults, "How Segregated Are Middle-Class African Americans?" *Social Problems,* 27 (2000), 543–58; see also Richard D. Alba and Steven Romalewski, "The End of Segregation? Hardly." Center for Urban Research. Retrieved November 9, 2012 (http://www.urbanresearch.org/projects/hardly-the-end-of-segregation).

46. William J. Wilson, *More Than Just Race: Being Black and Poor in the Inner City* (New York: W.W. Norton, 2009).

47. See, for example, Paul Kivel, *Uprooting Racism: How White People Can Work for Racial Justice,* 3rd ed. (Gabriola Island, British Columbia, CA: New Society Publishers, 2012).

48. Timothy N. Snelly, Jr., "The Psychology of 'Looting.'" Retrieved November 9, 2012 (http://www.useless-knowledge.com/1234/sept/article080.html).

49. Bart Landry, *The New Black Middle Class* (Berkeley: University of California Press, 1987).

50. See James E. Teele (ed.), *E. Franklin Frazier and Black Bourgeoisie* (Columbia: University of Missouri Press, 2002), for a critical analysis of his controversial book.

51. Calculated from U.S. Census Bureau, *2011 American Community Survey,* Tables DP03 and S0201.

52. "The African American Middle Class," *Blueprint of Black America.* Retrieved November 9, 2012 (http://www.blackdemographics.com/middle_class.html); and Ellis Cose, *The Rage of a Privileged Class: Why Do Prosperous Blacks Still Have the Blues?* reprint ed. (New York: Perennial, 1995).

53. Karyn R. Lacy, *Blue-Chip Black: Race, Class, and Status in the New Black Middle Class* (Berkeley: University of California Press, 2008), p. 220.

54. See John R. Logan, *Separate and Unequal: The Neighborhood Gap for Blacks, Hispanics and Asians in Metropolitan America.* Retrieved November 9, 2012 (http://www.s4.brown.edu/us2010/Data/Report/report0727.pdf).

55. Eric D. Knowles, Brian S. Lowery, Caitlin M. Hogan, and Rosalind M. Chow, "On the Malleability of Ideology: Motivated Construals of Color Blindness," *Journal of Personality and Social Psychology,* 96 (2009): 857–96.

56. Stephen Steinberg, *Turning Back,* 3rd ed. (Boston: Beacon Press, 2001).

57. Pew Research Center, "Black-White Conflict Isn't Society's Largest." Retrieved November 9, 2012 (http://pewsocialtrends.org/2009/09/24/black-white-conflict-isnt-societys-largest).

58. U.S. Census Bureau, *2011 American Community Survey,* Table S02010.

59. John R. Logan and Glenn Deane, *Black Diversity in Urban America* (Albany, NY: Lewis Mumford Center for Comparative Urban and Regional Research, 2003).

60. Ibid., Table 6.

61. Suzanne Model and Gene Fisher, "Black–White Unions: West Indians and African Americans Compared," *Demography,* 38 (2001): 177–85.

62. Suzanne Model and Gene Fisher, "Unions between Blacks and Whites: England and the U.S. Compared," *Ethnic & Racial Studies,* 25 (2002): 728–54.

63. U.S. Office of Immigration Statistics, *2011 Yearbook of Immigration Statistics,* Table 2.

64. Central Intelligence Agency, "Haiti," *World Factbook.* Retrieved November 9, 2012 (https://www.cia.gov/library/publications/the-world-factbook/geos/ha.html); Jane Regan, "Forest Land in Haiti Fading Fast; Natural Resource Nudged to the Brink," *Miami Herald* (August 5, 2003), p. A1.

65. Central Intelligence Agency, loc. cit.

66. See Flore Zephir, *The Haitian Americans* (Westport, CN: Greenwood Press, 2004).

67. See Ken Gelder, "Postcolonial Voodoo," *Postcolonial Studies,* 3 (2000): 89–98.

68. Alex Stepick, Guillermo Grenier, Max Castro, and Marvin Dunn, *This Land Is Our Land: Immigrants and Power in Miami* (Berkeley: University of California Press, 2003), pp. 118–22.

69. Melinda Crowley, "Generation X Speaks Out on Civic Engagement and the Decennial Census: An Ethnographic Approach," *Census 2000 Ethnographic Study* (Washington, DC: U.S. Census Bureau, 2003), p. 24.

70. U.S. Census Bureau, *2011 American CommunitySurvey,* Table S0201.

71. Melinda Crowley,"Generation X Speaks Out," pp. 24–25.

72. Philip Kasinitz, *Caribbean New York: Black Immigrants and the Politics of Race* (Ithaca, NY: Cornell University Press, 1992), pp. 77–78; Reuel R. Rogers, *Afro-Caribbean Immigrants and the Politics of Incorporation: Ethnicity, Exception, or Exit* (New York: Cambridge University Press, 2006).

73. See Philip Kasinitz, John H. Mollekopf, and Mary C. Waters, *Inheriting the City: The Children of Immigrants Come of Age* (Cambridge, MA: Harvard University Press, 2009).

74. U.S. Office of Immigration Statistics, *2011 Yearbook of Immigration Statistics,* Table 3; Sam Roberts, "More Africans Enter U.S. than in Days of Slavery," *New York Times* (February 21, 2005), pp. A1, B4.

75. U.S. Census Bureau, *2011 American Community Survey,* Table S0201.

76. Logan and Deane, *Black Diversity in Urban America,* p. 2.

77. Sam Roberts, "More Africans Enter U.S. than in Days of Slavery," p. A1.

78. Marilyn Halter, *Between Race and Ethnicity: Cape Verdean American Immigrants: 1860–1965* (Champaign: University of Illinois Press, 1993), pp. 120–24.

79. Gene A. Fisher and Suzanne Model, "Cape Verdean Identity in a Land of Black and White," *Ethnicities,* 12 (2012): 354–79.

80. Marilyn Halter, *Between Race and Ethnicity,* p. 88.

81. U.S. Office of Immigration Statistics, *2011 Yearbook of Immigration Statistics,* Table 3; U.S. Census Bureau, *Census 2000,* Summary File 3.

82. Jane E. Spear, "Cape Verdean Americans." Retrieved November 10, 2012 (http://www.everyculture.com/multi/Bu-Dr/Cape-Verdean-Americans.html).

83. "Nigeria," *CIA World Factbook.* Retrieved November 10, 2012 (https://www.cia.gov).

84. U.S. Office of Immigration Statistics, *U.S. Legal Permanent Residents: 2012,* Table 3; *2011 Yearbook of Immigration Statistics,* Table 3.

85. U.S. Census Bureau, *2011 American Community Survey,* Table S0201.

86. Kalu Ogbaa, *The Nigerian Americans* (Westport, CT: Greenwood Press, 2003).

87. Vivian Txeng, "Family Interdependence and Academic Adjustment in College: Youth from Immigrant and U.S.-Born Families," *Child Development,* 75 (2004): 966–83.

88. Winston James, "Explaining Afro-Caribbean Social Mobility in the United States: Beyond the Sowell Thesis," *Comparative Studies in Society and History,* 44 (2002): 218–62.

89. Reuel R. Robers, "Race-Based Coalitions among Minority Groups: Afro-Caribbean Immigrants and African-Americans in New York City," *Urban Affairs Review,* 39 (2004): 283–317.

90. Sara Rimer and Karen W. Arenson, "Top Colleges Take More Blacks, but Which Ones?" *New York Times* (June 24, 2004), pp. A1, A18.

91. Mary C. Waters, *Black Identities: West Indian Immigrant Dreams and American Realities* (Cambridge, MA: Harvard University Press, 2002).

92. U.S. Census Bureau, *Interracially Married Couples: 1980 to 2010,* Table 60, p. 54.

93. Richard Delgado and Jean Stefancic, *Critical Race Theory: An Introduction,* 2nd ed. (New York: New York University Press, 2012).

# CHAPTER 11

1. William D. Carrigan and Clive Webb, "The Lynching of Persons of Mexican Origin or Descent in the United States, 1848 to 1928," *Journal of Social History,* 37 (2003): 411–38; and Wayne Moquin, *Documentary History of the Mexican Americans* (New York: Bantam Books, 2000).

2. Population Reference Bureau, *2012 World Population Data Sheet.* Retrieved November 12, 2012 (http://www.prb.org).

3. U.S. Office of Immigration Statistics, *2011 Yearbook of Immigration Statistics* (Washington, DC: U.S. Government Printing Office, 2009), Table 34, pp. 92–93.

4. José Vasconceles, *The Cosmic Race* (Baltimore: Johns Hopkins University Press, 1998).

5. See Julia Preston and Fernanda Santos, "A Record Latino Turnout, Solidly Backing Obama," *New York Times* (November 8, 2012), p. P13.

6. See Matthew C. Gutmann, *The Meanings of Macho: Being a Man in Mexico City,* 10th anniv. ed. (Berkeley: University of California Press, 2006); Rafael L. Ramirez, Rosa E. Casper, and Peter J. Guarnaccia, *What It Means to Be a Man: Reflections of Puerto Rican Masculinity* (New Brunswick, NJ: Rutgers University Press, 2000).

7. U.S. Census Bureau, *2011 American Community Surveys,* Table S0201.

8. See Ismael Garcia, *Dignidad: Ethics through Hispanic Eyes* (Nashville, TN: Abingdon Press, 1998).

9. See, for example, Mark Q. Sawyer and Tianna S. Paschel, "'We Didn't Cross the Color Line, the Color Line Crossed US': Blackness and Immigration in the Dominican Republic, Puerto Rico, and the United States," *Du Bois Review: Social Science Research on Race,* 4 (2007): 303–15.

10. See Lee M. Penyak and Walter J. Petry (eds.), *Religion in Latin America: A Documentary History* (Maryknoll, NY: Orbis Books, 2007).

11. Pew Hispanic Center, "Changing Faiths: Latinos and the Transformation of American Religion." Retrieved November 13, 2012 (http://www.pewhispanic.org/2007/04/25/iv-the-renewalist-movement-and-hispanic-christianity); Pedrito U. Maynard-Reid, *Diverse Worship: African-American, Caribbean, & Hispanic Perspectives* (Downers Grove, IL: Intervarsity Press, 2000), pp. 171–82.

12. See H. B. Cavalcanti and Debra Schleef, "The Case for Secular Assimilation: The Latino Experience in Richmond, Virginia," *Journal for the Scientific Study of Religion,* 44 (2005): 473–83.

13. For some excellent cross-cultural analyses of attitudes regarding distance between people, see Edward T. Hall, *The Hidden Dimension,* reprint ed. (Mangolia, MA: Smith Publishing, 1992); and *The Silent Language,* reprint ed. (Westport, CN: Greenwood Press, 1980).

14. U.S. Census Bureau, *2011 American Community Survey,* Table S0201.

15. U.S. Census Bureau, *The Hispanic Population: 2010,* Census Briefs, Table 5, May 2011.

16. See Alejandro Portes and Rubén G. Rumbaut, *Immigrant America: A Portrait*, 3rd ed. (Berkeley: University of California Press, 2007).

17. U.S. Census Bureau, *2011 American Community Survey*, Table S0201.

18. Ibid.

19. Pew Hispanic Center, "Educational Attainment: Better Than Meets the Eye, but Large Challenges Remain." Retrieved November 12, 2012 (http://pewhispanic.org/files/factsheets/3.pdf).

20. U.S. Census Bureau, *The Hispanic Population: 2010,* Table 4.

21. See Roberto M. De Anda, *Chicanas and Chicanos in Contemporary Society*, 2nd ed. (Lanham, MD: Rowan & Littlefield, 2005), Chapters 5 and 7.

22. See Francisco E. Balderrama and Raymond Rodríguez, *Decade of Betrayal: Mexican Repatriation in the 1930s*, revised ed. (Albuquerque: University of New Mexico Press, 2006).

23. See Avi Astor, "Unauthorized Immigration, Securitization, and the Making of Operation Wetback," *Latino Studies,* 7 (2009): 5–29.

24. Carey McWilliams with an update by Matt S. Meier (ed.), *North from Mexico* (New York: Praeger, 1990), pp. 223–25.

25. See, for example, Jack Schneider, "Escape from Los Angeles," *Journal of Urban History,* 6 (2008): 995–1012.

26. U.S. Census Bureau, *2011 American Community Survey*, Table S0201.

27. Zulema Valdez, "Segmented Assimilation among Mexicans in the Southwest," *The Sociological Quarterly,* 47 (2006): 397–424; and Elaine M. Allensworth, "Earnings Mobility of First and '1.5' Generation Mexican-Origin Women and Men: A Comparison with U.S.-born Mexican Americans and Non-Hispanic Whites," *International Migration Review,* 31 (1997): 386–410.

28. See MALDEF (http://www.maldef.org) and National Council of La Raza (http://www.nclr.org); also Peter Skerry, "Racial Politics in the Administrative State," *Society,* 42 (2005): 36–45.

29. See Robert Bauman, "The Black Power and Chicano Movements in the Poverty Wars in Los Angeles," *Journal of Urban History,* 33 (2007): 277–95; Joseph A. Rodriguez, "Ethnicity and the Horizontal City: Mexican Americans and the Chicano Movement in San Jose," *Journal of Urban History,* 21 (1995), 597–621.

30. National Association of Latino Elected and Appointed Officials, *National Roster of Hispanic Officials.* Retrieved November 12, 2012 (http://www.naleo.org/ataglance.html).

31. U.S. Census Bureau, "Illinois," *2011 American Community Survey.*

32. U.S. Census Bureau, *Current Population Survey, 2011,* Annual Social and Economic Supplement, released November 2012.

33. See, for example, Robert K. Ream and Russell W. Rumberger, "Student Engagement, Peer Social Capital, and School Dropout among Mexican American and Non-Latino White Students," *Sociology of Education,* 81 (2008): 109–39; Mira Mayer, "The Dropout Rates of Mexican American Students in Two California Cities," *Research for Educational Reform,* 9 (2004): 14–24.

34. See Jossianna Arroyo, "'Roots' or the Virtualities of Racial Imaginaries in Puerto Rico and the Diaspora," *Latino Studies,* 8 (2010): 195–219.

35. Mireya Navarro, "For Many Latinos, Racial Identity Is More Culture than Color," *New York Times* (January 13, 2012), p. A11.

36. Joseph P. Fitzpatrick, *Puerto Rican Americans,* 2nd ed. (Englewood Cliffs, NJ: Prentice Hall, 1987), pp. 106–7.

37. U.S. Bureau of Labor Statistics, *Economy at a Glance: Puerto Rico.* Retrieved November 12, 2012 (http://stats.bls.gov/eag/eag.pr.htm).

38. U.S. Census Bureau, *2011 American Community Survey*, Table S0201.

39. See Elizabeth M. Aranda, "Class Backgrounds, Modes of Incorporation, and Puerto Ricans' Pathways into the Transnational Professional Workforce," *American Behavioral Scientist,* 52 (2008): 426–56.

40. Gina M. Prez, *The Near Northwest Side Story: Migration, Displacement, and Puerto Rican Families* (Berkeley: University of California Press, 2004).

41. See Oscar Handlin, *The Uprooted,* 2nd ed. (Philadelphia: University of Pennsylvania Press, 2002), pp. 105–28.

42. Nathan Glazer and Daniel P. Moynihan, *Beyond the Melting Pot,* 2nd ed. (Cambridge, MA: MIT, 1970), pp. 103–4.

43. See Edna Acosta-Belen and Carlos E. Santiago, *Puerto Ricans in the United States: A Contemporary Portrait* (Boulder, CO: Lynne Rienner Publishing, 2006).

44. U.S. Census Bureau, *The Hispanic Population: 2010,* Census Briefs (May 2011), Table 4.

45. See Arlene Dávila, *Barrio Dreams: Puerto Ricans, Latinos, and the Neoliberal City* (Berkeley: University of California Press, 2005).

46. U.S. Census Bureau, *2011 American Community Survey*, Table S0201.

47. Ibid.

48. Ibid.

49. U.S. Census Bureau, *Statistical Abstract: 2012,* Table 37, p. 42.

50. See Cecilia Rodríguez Milanés, *Marielitos, Balseros, and Other Exiles* (Brooklyn, NJ: Ig Publishing, 2009).

51. Robert M. Levine, *Cuban Miami* (New Brunswick, NJ: Rutgers University Press, 2001).

52. See Juan Gonzalez, *Harvest of Empire: A History of Latinos in America,* rev. ed. (New York: Penguin, 2011), Chapter 6; Alejandro Portés and Alex Stepick, *City on the Edge: The Transformation of Miami* (Berkeley: University of California Press, 1994).

53. Marta Diaz Fernandez, "Intergenerational Dynamics in the Cuban Community in Southern Florida: Identity and Politics in the Second Generation," *Cuban Studies,* 31 (2001): 76–101.

54. See C. Alison Newby and Julie A. Dowling, "Black And Hispanic: The Racial Identification of Afro-Cuban Immigrants in the Southwest," *Sociological Perspectives,* 50 (2007): 343–66.

55. U.S. Census Bureau, *2011 American Community Survey*, Table S0201.

56. Ibid.

57. See Louis A. Pérez, Jr. *On Becoming Cuban: Identity, Nationality, and Culture* (Chapel Hill: University of North Carolina Press, 2008); and Alejandro Brice, *An Introduction to Cuban Culture for Rehabilitation Service Providers* (Buffalo, NY: Center for International Rehabilitation Research Information & Exchange, 2002), pp. 8–10.

58. U.S. Office of Immigration Statistics, *20011 Yearbook of Immigration Statistics,* Table 2.

59. Arun P. Lobo, Ronald J. O. Flores, and Joseph J. Salvo, "The Impact of Hispanic Growth on the Racial/Ethnic Composition

of New York City Neighborhoods," *Urban Affairs Review,* 37 (2002): 703–27.

60. U.S. Census Bureau, *2011 American Community Survey,* Table S0201.

61. See Carlos B. Cordova, *The Salvadoran Americans* (Westport, CT: Greenwood Press, 2005).

62. See Susan Bibler Coutin, "Falling Outside: Excavating the History of Central American Asylum Seekers," *Law & Social Inquiry,* 36 (2011): 569–96; Cecilia Mejivar, "Family Reorganization in a Context of Legal Uncertainty: Guatemalan and Salvadoran Immigrants in the United States," *International Journal of Sociology of the Family,* 32 (2006): 223–45.

63. See Claudia Dorrington, "Salvadoran Immigrants and Refugees: Demographic and Socioeconomic Profiles," pp. 393–424, in *Asian and Latino Immigrants in a Restructuring Economy* (Stanford, CA: Stanford University Press, 2001); U.S. Census Bureau, *2011 American Community Survey,* Table S0201.

64. See Jennifer H. Lundquist and Douglas S. Massey, "Politics or Economics? International Migration during the Nicaraguan Contra War," *Journal of Latin American Studies,* 37 (2005): 29–53.

65. See Dorothy Norris-Tirrell, "Immigrant Needs and Local Government Services: Implications for Policymakers," *Policy Studies Journal,* 30 (2002): 58–69.

66. Mireya Navarro, "After Year in Exile in South Florida, Nicaraguans Feel the Tug of 2 Homes," *New York Times* (March 21, 1995).

67. U.S. Census Bureau, *2011 American Community Survey,* Table S0201; U.S. Office of Immigration Statistics, *2011 Yearbook of Immigration Statistics,* Table 2.

68. U.S. Office of Immigration Statistics, loc. cit.

69. U.S. Census Bureau, loc. cit.

70. Ibid.

71. Ibid.; Dylan Conger, "Testing, Time Limits, and English Learners: Does Age of School Entry Affect How Quickly Students Can Learn English?" *Social Science Research,* 38 (2009): 383–96.

72. Charles Hirschman, "The Educational Enrollment of Immigrant Youth: A Test of the Segmented-Assimilation Hypothesis," *Demography,* 38 (August 2001): 317–36.

73. Ramon Grosfoguel and Chloe S. Ramon, "'Coloniality of Power' and Racial Dynamics: Notes toward a Reinterpretation of Latino Caribbeans in New York City," *Identities,* 7 (March 2000): 85–125.

74. See Hyoung-jin Shin, "Intermarriage Patterns among the Children of Hispanic Immigrants," *Journal of Ethnic & Migration Studies,* 37 (2011): 1385–1402.

75. Sharon M. Lee and Barry Edmonston, "Hispanic Intermarriage, Identification, and U.S. Latino Population Change," *Social Science Quarterly,* 87 (2006):1263–79.

76. Daniel T. Lichter, Julie H. Carmalt, and Zhenchao Qian, "Immigration and Intermarriage among Hispanics: Crossing Racial and Generational Boundaries," *Sociological Forum,* 26 (2011): 241–64.

77. Michael J. Rosenfeld, "The Salience of Pan-National Hispanic and Asian Identities in U.S. Marriage Markets," *Demography,* 38 (May 2001): 161–75.

78. Irene Lopez, "'But You Don't Look Puerto Rican': The Moderating Effect of Ethnic Identity on the Relation between Skin Color and Self-Esteem among Puerto Rican Women," *Cultural Diversity & Ethnic Minority Psychology,* 14 (2008): 102–8.

79. See William Kandel, Jamila Henderson, Heather Koball, and Randy Capps, "Moving Up in Rural America: Economic Attainment of Nonmetro Latino Immigrants," *Rural Sociology,* 76 (2011): 101–28.

80. U.S. Census Bureau, *American Factfinder.* Retrieved January 12, 2013 (http://factfinder2.census.gov).

## CHAPTER 12

1. Eileen W. Linder (ed.), *2012 Yearbook of American and Canadian Churches* (Nashville, TN: Abingdon Press, 2012).

2. "U.S. Denominations," Association of Religion Data Archives. Retrieved November 17, 2012 (http://www.thearda.com/Denoms/families/index.asp).

3. See Scott Thumma and Warren Bird, "Not Who You Think They Are: A Profile of the People Who Attend America's Megachurches," Hartford Institute for Religion Research. Retrieved November 17, 2012 (http://hirr.hartsem.edu/megachurch/megachurch_attender_report.htm).

4. The Pew Forum on Religion and Public Life, "'Nones' on the Rise: One-in-Five Adults Have No Religious Affiliation." Retrieved November 21, 2012 (http://www.pewforum.org).

5. See James M. O'Toole, *The Faithful: A History of Catholics in America* (Cambridge, MA: Belknap Press of Harvard University, 2009).

6. Samuel F. B. Morse, *Imminent Dangers to the Free Institutions of the United States through Foreign Immigration and the Present State of the Naturalization Laws.* A Series of Numbers, originally published in the *New York Journal of Commerce,* revised and corrected with additions (New York, 1835).

7. "American Protective Association," *Encyclopedia of Immigration.* Retrieved November 17, 2012 (http://immigration-online.org/17-american-protective-association.html).

8. Thomas J. Curran, *Xenophobia and Immigration, 1820–1930* (Boston: Twayne, 1975), p. 107.

9. Ibid., pp. 130–31.

10. Ibid., pp. 32–35.

11. John Higham, *Strangers in the Land* (New Brunswick, NJ: Rutgers University Press, 2002), p. 59.

12. Curran, *Xenophobia and Immigration, 1820–1930,* p. 78.

13. "Faith on the Hill: The Religious Composition of the 113th Congress," Pew Forum on Religion & Public Life. Retrieved January 26, 2013 (http://www.pewforum.org/Government).

14. Pew Forum on Religion & Public Life, *U.S. Religious Landscape Survey* (Washington, DC: Pew Research Center, 2008), p. 34.

15. James D. Davidson and Tracy Widman, "The Effect of Group Size on Interfaith Marriage among Catholics," *Journal for the Scientific Study of Religion,* 41 (2002): 397–404.

16. Lisa A. Keister, "Upward Wealth Mobility: Exploring the Roman Catholic Advantage," *Social Forces,* 85 (March 2007): 1195–225.

17. Laurie Goodstein, "Catholics Criticize Pope on Abuse Scandal, but See Some Hope," *New York Times* (May 5, 2010), p. A13.

18. Franklin H. Giddings, *Studies in the Theory of Human Society* (Ann Arbor: University of Michigan Library, 2009). Originally published in 1922.

19. See Marc Raphael, *The Columbia History of Jews and Judaism in America* (New York: Teachers College Press, 2009); Oscar Reiss, *The Jews in Colonial America* (Jefferson, NC: McFarland & Company, 2004).

20. Curran, *Xenophobia and Immigration, 1820–1930,* pp. 13, 76–77.

21. Milton L. Barron, "The Incidence of Jewish Intermarriage in Europe and America," *American Sociological Review,* 1 (February 1946): 11.

22. See John Kaufman, *Jew Hatred: Anti-Semitism, Anti-Sexuality, and Mythology in Christianity* (Pomona, CA: Arts Colony Publishers, 2002).

23. Anti-Defamation League, "Audit: 1,080 Anti-Semitic Incidents Reported across U.S. in 2011, a 13 Percent Decrease." Retrieved November 17, 2012 (http://www.adl.org/PresRele/ASUS_12/2011+Audit.htm).

24. Leonard Dinnerstein and David Reimers, *Ethnic Americans: Immigration and American Society,* 5th ed. (New York: Columbia University Press, 2009).

25. See Rebecca Korbin (ed.), *Chosen Capital: The Jewish Encounter with American Capitalism* (New Brunswick, NJ: Rutgers University Press, 2012).

26. Dinnerstein and Reimers, "By 1915, Jews comprised 85 percent of the student body at New York's free but renowned City College, one fifth of those attending New York University and one sixth of the students at Columbia," *Ethnic Americans,* p. 77.

27. Rebecca Korbin, *Chosen Capital,* pp. 15–16.

28. Gerhard Lenski, *The Religious Factor* (New York: Doubleday, 1961), pp. 33–34; John P. Dean, "Patterns of Socialization and Association between Jews and Non-Jews," *Jewish Social Studies,* 17 (July 1955): 252–54; Herbert J. Gans, "The Origin and Growth of a Jewish Community in the Suburbs: A Study of the Jews of Park Forest," in Marshall Sklare (ed.), *The Jews: Social Patterns of an American Group* (Glencoe, IL: Free Press, 1958), p. 227; and Albert I. Gordon, *Jews in Suburbia* (Boston: Beacon Press, 1956).

29. *The National Jewish Population Survey 2000–2001: Strength, Challenge and Diversity in the American Jewish Population* (New York: United Jewish Communities, 2004): 16; Pew Forum on Religion & Public Life, *U.S. Religious Landscape Survey,* p. 34; "Intermarriage Rate among U.S. Jews Increases," *Society,* 40 (2003): 6.

30. Bruce Phillips, "Assimilation, Transformation, and the Long-Range Impact of Intermarriage," *Contemporary Jewry,* 25 (2005): 50–84.

31. Jewish Outreach Institute. Retrieved November 17, 2012 (http://joi.org/about/index.shtml).

32. See Lawrence J. Epstein, *At the Edge of a Dream: The Story of Jewish Immigrants on New York's Lower East Side, 1880–1920* (New York: Jossey-Bass, 2008).

33. See Daniel Friedman, *Jews without Judaism: Conversations with an Unconventional Rabbi* (Amherst, NY: Prometheus Books, 2002).

34. See Uzi Rebhun, "Jewish Identification in Contemporary America: Gans' Symbolic Ethnicity and Religiosity Theory Revisited," *Social Compass,* 51 (2004): 349–66.

35. Jonathan Ament, *Jewish Immigrants in the United States* (New York: United Jewish Committee, 2004), pp. 3–4.

36. See Terryl L. Givens, *People of Paradox: A History of Mormon Culture* (New York: Oxford University Press, 2008).

37. Joseph Smith, *Pearl of Great Price* (Minneapolis: Filiquarian Publishing, 2007), p. 102.

38. See Richard Ostling and Joan K. Ostling, *Mormon America,* rev. ed. (New York: HarperOne, 2008).

39. Sarah Barringer Gordon, *The Mormon Question: Polygamy and Constitutional Conflict in Nineteenth-Century America* (Chapel Hill: University of North Carolina Press, 2002), p. 211.

40. Jack Sullivan, "Mormon Invigorators." Retrieved November 17, 2012 (http://bottlesboozeandbackstories.blogspot.com/2012_04_01_archive.html).

41. See Ray M. Merrill, Jeffrey A. Folsom, and Susan S. Christopherson, "The Influence of Family Religiosity on Adolescent Substance Use according to Religious Preference," *Social Behavior and Personality,* 33 (2005): 821–35; Ray M. Merrill, Richard D. Salazar, and Nicole W. Gardner, "Relationship between Family Religiosity and Drug Use Behavior among Youth," *Social Behavior and Personality,* 29:4 (2001): 347–58.

42. "Bachelor's Degree or Higher, by Percentage, by State." Retrieved November 18, 2012 (http://www.statemaster.com).

43. "Missionary Program," Church of Jesus Christ of Latter-Day Saints. Retrieved November 18, 2012 (http://www.mormon-newsroom.org/topic/missionary-program).

44. U.S. Census Bureau, *Statistical Abstract of the United States 2012,* Table 76.

45. Caroline Winter, "How the Mormons Make Money," *Business Week* (July 10, 2012); Richard Ostling and Joan K. Ostling, *Mormon America,* pp. 124–27.

46. Ibid., pp. 236–38, 361–65, 371–74.

47. See Dorothy Alfred Solomon, *The Sisterhood: Inside the Lives of Mormon Women* (New York: Palgrave Macmillan, 2009).

48. See Sylviane Diouf, *Servants of Allah: African Muslims Enslaved in the Americas* (New York: NYU Press, 1999); Kambiz GhaneaBassiri, *A History of Islam in America: From the New World to the New World Order* (New York: Cambridge University Press, 2010).

49. See Sarah Gualtieri, *Between Arab and White: Race and Ethnicity in the Early Syrian American Diaspora* (Berkeley: University of California Press, 2009).

50. Association of Religion Data Archives, "U.S. Membership Report." Retrieved January 13, 2013 (http://www.thearda.com/rcms2010/r/u/rcms2010_99_US_name_2010.asp); see also "Muslim Life in America," U.S. Department of State. Retrieved January 12, 2013 (http://usinfo.org/enus/education/overview/muslimlife/demograp.htm).

51. Christine Huda Dodge, *The Everything Understanding Islam Book,* 2nd ed. (Avon, MA: Adams Media, 2009), pp. 23–30.

52. See, for example, Stephen Maganini, "Interfaith Leaders Condemn Violence, Anti-Muslim Backlash," *The Sacramento Bee* (November 21, 2009), p. A1; and Oren Yaniv, "We're Appalled Too, So Don't Target Us: Muslim Groups," *New York Daily News* (November 6, 2009), p. 3.

53. "Religion," available at http://www.pollingreport.com/religion.htm on June 8, 2013; "Muslims Widely Seen as Facing Discrimination," Pew Research Center (September 9, 2009). Available at http://people-press.org/report/542/muslims-widely-seen-as-facing-discrimination on June 8, 2013.

54. "Religion," available at http://www.pollingreport.com/religion.htm on June 8, 2013.

55. "Muslims Widely Seen as Facing Discrimination," loc. cit.

56. Joe Mackall, *Plain Secrets: An Outsider among the Amish,* reprint ed. (Boston: Beacon Press, 2009), pp. 143–44.

57. Donald B. Kraybill, *The Riddle of Amish Culture* (Baltimore: Johns Hopkins University Press, 2002), p. xiii.

58. Richard T. Schaefer and William W. Kellner, *Extraordinary Groups: An Examination of Unconventional Lifestyles,* 9th ed. (New York: Worth Publishers, 2011), pp. 50–51.

59. See Charles E. Hurst and David L. McConnell, *An Amish Paradox: Diversity and Change in the World's Largest Amish*

Community (Baltimore: The Johns Hopkins University Press, 2010).

60. Tom Shachtman, *Rumspringa: To Be or Not Be Amish* (New York: North Point Press, 2007), pp. 4–9.

61. Ibid. See also Denise M. Reiling, "The 'Simmie' Side of Life: Old Order Amish Youths' Affective Response to Culturally Prescribed Deviance," *Youth and Society,* 34 (2002): 146–71.

62. Colton Totland, "High Birthrates and Decline in Defections Spur Growth," *Washington Times* (August 10, 2012), p. A1.

63. "An Amish Exception," *Economist* (February 7, 2004), p. 33.

64. Donald B. Kraybill, *The Riddle of Amish Culture,* pp. 41, 283, 290–91.

65. See Charles Price, *Becoming Rasta: Origins of Rastafari Identity in Jamaica* (New York: NYU Press, 2010), pp. 52–53.

66. Barry Chevannes, *Rastafari: Roots and Ideology* (Syracuse, NY: Syracuse University Press, 2001).

67. Ennis B. Edmonds, *Rastafari: From Outcasts to Culture Bearers* (New York: Oxford University Press, 2008), p. 59.

68. Ibid., p. 61.

69. Ibid., p. 141.

70. "Jamaican Americans: Religion," *Countries and Their Cultures.* Retrieved November 18, 2012 (http://www.everyculture.com/multi/Ha-La/Jamaican-Americans.html).

71. The author wishes to thank James Mahon for providing much initial information on Santería.

72. Miquel A. de la Torre, *Santería: The Beliefs and Rituals of a Growing Religion in America* (Grand Rapids, MI: Eerdmans Publishing Company, 2005), p. 15.

73. *What Is Santería?* Retrieved November 18, 2012 (http://www.orishanet.org/santeria.html).

74. Albert J. Raboteau, *Slave Religion: The "Invisible Institution" in the Antebellum South,* 2nd ed. (New York: Oxford University Press, 2005), pp. 89–90.

75. *What Is Santería?* loc. cit.

76. Migene González-Wippler, *Santería: The Religion: Faith, Rites, Magic,* 2nd ed. (Woodbury, MN: Llewellyn Publications, 2003), p. 68.

77. Ibid., pp. 12, 42.

78. "Conflicts Concerning Santeria Sacrifices: Animal and Human; Real and Imaginary." Retrieved November 19, 2012 (http://www.religioustolerance.org/santeri1.htm).

79. "Santeria," Retrieved November 19, 2012 (http://www.adherents.com/Na/Na_581.html).

80. See Johan Wedel, *Santería Healing: A Journey into the Afro-Cuban World of Divinities, Spirits, and Sorcery* (Gainesville: University Press of Florida, 2004).

81. See Nathaniel Samuel Murrell, *Afro-Caribbean Religions: An Introduction to Their Historical, Cultural, and Sacred Traditions* (Philadelphia: Temple University Press, 2010), Chapters 5–6.

82. Mary Vallas, "Animal Sacrifices Spark Religious Fight; Texas Man Wins Court Ruling Upholding Faith-Based Rights," *National Post* (August 14, 2009), p. A3.

83. Because the Western world's use of A.D. (Anno Domini, or "Year of Our Lord") and B.C. (Before Christ) have a Christian orientation, the use of C.E. (Common Era) and B.C.E. (Before the Common Era) often are used instead, particularly when discussing other religions.

84. "Early History of Hinduism." Retrieved November 19, 2012 (http://www.religioustolerance.org/hinduism2.htm).

85. "The Global Religious Landscape," The Pew Forum on Religion & Public Life. Retrieved June 8, 2013 (http://www.pewforum.org/global-religious-landscape-hindu.aspx).

86. "Sacred Texts." Retrieved November 19, 2012 (http://www.religioustolerance.org/hinduism2.htm).

87. See Stephen Knapp, *The Heart of Hinduism: The Eastern Path to Freedom, Empowerment and Enlightenment* (Lincoln, NE: iUniverse Books, 2005).

88. "Hindu Sects and Denominations." Retrieved November 19, 2012 (http://www.religioustolerance.org/hinduism3.htm).

89. "Hinduism: The World's Third Largest Religion." Retrieved November 19, 2012 (http://www.religioustolerance.org/hinduism.htm).

90. Prema A. Kurien, "Multiculturalism and 'American' Religion: The Case of Hindu Indian Americans," *Social Forces,* 85 (2006): 723–41.

91. See Prema A. Kurien, "Being Young, Brown, and Hindu: The Identity Struggles of Second-Generation Indian Americans," *Journal of Contemporary Ethnography,* 34 (2005): 434–69.

92. "Religion." Retrieved November 20, 2012 (www.pollingreport.com/religion.htm); Pew Global Attitudes Project, "U.S. Stands Alone in Its Embrace of Religion among Wealthy Nations (December 19, 2002). Retrieved November 20, 2012 (http://www.pewglobal.org/2002/12/19/among-wealthy-nations).

93. David E. Eagle, "Changing Patterns of Attendance at Religious Services in Canada, 1986–2008," *Journal for the Scientific Study of Religion,* 50 (2011): 187–200; Tearfund, "Churchgoing in the UK." Retrieved November 21, 2012 (http://news.bbc.co.uk/2/shared/bsp/hi/pdfs/03_04_07_tearfundchurch.pdf).

94. Linda M. Chatters, Robert J. Taylor, Kai M. Bullard, and James S. Jackson, "Race and Ethnic Differences in Religious Involvement: African Americans, Caribbean Blacks, and Non-Hispanic Whites," *Ethnic and Racial Studies,* 32 (2009): 1143–63; and George Yancey, "A Comparison of Religiosity between European-Americans, African-Americans, Hispanic-Americans, and Asian-Americans," *Research in the Social Scientific Study of Religion,* 16 (2005): 83–104.

95. See William D'Antonio, "New Survey Offers Portrait of U.S. Catholics." Retrieved November 20, 2012 (http://ncronline.org/news/catholics-america/persistence-and-change#table1); Jay Tolson, "Catholics at a Crossroads," *U.S. News & World Report* (April 7, 2008), pp. 37–43.

96. See, for example, Craig R. Smith, *Daniel Webster and the Oratory of Civil Religion* (Columbia: University of Missouri Press, 2005); and Geiko Muller-Fahrenholz, *America's Battle for God: A European Christian Looks as Civil Religion America* (Grand Rapids, MI: Eerdmans Publishing Company, 2007).

97. See Robert Audi, "Religion and the Politics of Science," *Philosophy & Social Criticism,* 35 (2009): 23–50; and Lenn E. Goodman, "Science and God," *Society,* 45 (2008): 130–42.

98. Lisa Miller, "Islam in America: A Success Story," *Newsweek* (July 30, 2007), p. 26.

99. Ibid.

100. Laurie Goodstein, "Poll Finds U.S. Muslims Thriving, But Not Content," *New York Times* (March 2, 2009), p. A11.

101. Robert Wuthnow, "The *Religious Factor* Revisited," *Sociological Theory,* 22 (2004): 205–18.

## CHAPTER 13

1. See Robert Mayhew, *The Female in Aristotle's Biology: Reason or Rationalization* (Chicago: University of Chicago Press, 2005), p. 71.

2. Gustav LeBon, *Revue d'Anthropologie* (1879), pp. 60–61, quoted in Melissa Hines, *Brain Gender* (New York: Oxford University Press, 2005), p. 186.

3. Gunnar Myrdal, *An American Dilemma: The Negro Problem and Modern Democracy* (New York: Harper, 1944), pp. 1073–78.

4. Helen M. Hacker, "Women as a Minority Group," *Social Forces*, 30 (1951): 60–69.

5. Betty Friedan, *The Feminine Mystique*. (New York: W.W. Norton & Company [1963] 2002), p. 15.

6. See Carol Berkin, *Revolutionary Mothers: Women in the Struggle for America's Independence* (New York: Vintage, 2006), pp. 2–8.

7. Vincent N. Parrillo, *Diversity in America*, 4th ed. (Boulder, CO: Paradigm Publishers, 2012), p. 27.

8. See Mary Kelley, *Private Woman, Public Stage: Literary Domesticity in Nineteenth-Century America* (Chapel Hill: University of North Carolina Press, 2002).

9. Joyce Cowley, "Women Who Won the Right to Vote." Retrieved November 21, 2012 (http://www.marxists.org/history/etol/newspape/fi/vol16/no02/cowley.html).

10. See Alana Jeydel, *Political Women: The Women's Movement, Political Institutions, The Battle for Women's Suffrage, and the ERA* (New York: Routledge, 2005).

11. See Melissa Hines, *Brain Gender* (New York: Oxford University Press, 2005).

12. See Gillian Einstein (ed.), *Sex and the Brain* (Cambridge, MA: MIT Press, 2008).

13. Margaret Mead, *Sex and Temperament in Three Primitive Societies* (New York: Harper Perennial, [1935] 2001).

14. See Judith E. Owen Blakemore and Craig A. Hill, "The Child Gender Socialization Scale: A Measure to Compare Traditional and Feminist Parents," *Sex Roles*, 58 (2008): 192–207; JoNell Strough and Cynthia A. Berg, "Goals as a Mediator of Gender Differences in High-Affiliation Dyadic Conversations," *Developmental Psychology*, 36 (2000): 117–25.

15. See Jaime L. Marks, Chun Bun Lam, and Susan M. McHale, "Family Patterns of Gender Role Attitudes," *Sex Roles*, 61 (2009): 221–34.

16. See A. Michele Lease, Charlotte A. Kennedy, and Jennifer L. Axelrod, "Children's Social Constructions of Popularity," *Social Development*, 11 (2002): 87–109.

17. See, for example, N. Kenneth Sandnabba, Pekka Santtila, Malin Wannas, and Katja Krook, "Age and Gender Specific Behaviors in Children," *Child Abuse & Neglect*, 27 (2003): 579–605.

18. See Estelle Disch, *Reconstructing Gender: A Multicultural Anthology*, 5th ed. (New York: McGraw-Hill, 2008).

19. See Terri D. Conley and Laura R. Ramsey, "Killing Us Softly? Investigating Portrayals of Women and Men in Contemporary Magazine Advertisements," *Psychology of Women Quarterly*, 35 (2011): 469–78; Roy F. Fox, *Harvesting Minds: How TV Commercials Control Kids* (Santa Barbara, CA: Praeger, 2001), pp. 13–16; Scott Coltrane and Melinda Messineo, "The Perpetuation of Subtle Prejudice: Race and Gender Imagery in 1990s Television Advertising," *Sex Roles*, 42 (2000): 363–89.

20. See, for example, Margaret Hunter and Kathleen Soto, "Women of Color in Hip Hop: The Pornographic Gaze," *Race, Gender & Class*, 16 (2009): 170–91.

21. Jean Kilbourne, *Can't Buy My Love: How Advertising Changes the Way We Think and Feel* (New York: Free Press, 2001), pp. 290–91.

22. See, for example, Martha M. Lauzen and David M. Dozier, "Recognition and Respect Revisited: Portrayals of Age and Gender in Prime-Time Television," *Mass Communication and Society*, 8 (2005): 241–56.

23. Erving Goffman, *Gender Advertisements* (New York: Harper Collins, 1988), p. viii.

24. Women's Media Center, "The Status of Women in the U.S. Media: 2012." Retrieved November 23, 2012 (http://wmc.3cdn.net/a6b2dc282c824e903a_arm6b0hk8.pdf); Media Report to Women, *Industry Statistics*. Retrieved January 12, 2013 (http://www.mediareporttowomen.com/statistics.htm).

25. Lillian B. Rubin, *Worlds of Pain: Life in the Working-Class Family*, reprint ed. (New York: Basic Books, 1992).

26. Arlie Hochschild and Anne Machung, *The Second Shift* (New York: Penguin, 2003).

27. Amy Kroska and Cheryl Elman, "Change in Attitudes about Employed Mothers: Exposure, Interests, and Gender Ideology Discrepancies," *Social Science Research*, 38 (2009): 366–82. See also Elisa Kostianen, Tuija Martelin, Laura Kestila, Pekka Matikaijen, and Seppo Koskinen, "Employee, Partner, and Mother," *Journal of Family Issues*, 30 (2009): 1122–50; Amy Kroska, "Exploring the Consequences of Gender Ideology-Work Discrepancies," *Sex Roles*, 60 (2009): 313–28.

28. Elizabeth Miklya Legerski and Marie Cornwall, "Working-Class Job Loss, Gender, and the Negotiation of Household Labor," *Gender & Society*, 24 (2010): 447–74.

29. Yu Shi, "Chinese Immigrant Women Workers' Mediated Negotiations with Constraints on their Cultural Identities," *Feminist Media Studies*, 8 (2008): 143–61.

30. Keumjae Park, "'I Can Provide for My Children': Korean Immigrant Women's Changing Perspectives on Work Outside the Home," *Gender Issues*, 25 (2008): 26–42.

31. See Patricia Dixon, "Marriage among African Americans: What Does the Research Reveal?" *Journal of African American Studies*, 13 (2009): 29–46.

32. See Kimber Springer, "The Trouble between Us: An Uneasy History of White and Black Women in the Feminist Movement," *Signs*, 33 (2008): 732–36.

33. Jen'nan Ghazal Read and Philip N. Cohen, "One Size Fits All? Explaining U.S.-born and Immigrant Women's Employment across 12 Ethnic Groups," *Social Forces*, 85 (2007): 1713–34.

34. R. Claire Snyder, "What Is Third-Wave Feminism? A New Directions Essay," *Signs*, 34 (2008): 175–96; Kimberly Springer, "Third Wave Black Feminism," *Signs*, 27 (2002): 1059–82.

35. April L. Few, "Integrating Black Consciousness and Critical Race Feminism into Families Studies Research," *Journal of Family Issues*, 28 (2007: 452–73.

36. Aretha Faye Marbley, "African-American Women's Feelings on Alienation from Third-Wave Feminism: A Conversation with My Sisters," *Western Journal of Black Studies*, 29 (2005): 605–14.

37. See Valencia Campbell, *Advice from the Top: What Minority Women Say about Their Career Success* (Santa Barbara, CA: Praeger, 2009), pp. 61–78.

38. See Debra Viadero, "AAUW Study Finds Girls Making Some Progress, but Gaps Remain," *Education Week* (October 14, 1998): 9.

39. David M. Sadker, and Karen Zittleman, *Teachers, Schools, and Society*, 3rd ed. (New York: McGraw-Hill, 2011).

40. See Teresa Méndez, "A Bid to Boost Single-Sex Classrooms," *Christian Science Monitor* (May 25, 2004): 11.

41. U.S. Census Bureau, *Statistical Abstract 2012*, Table 588, p. 378.

42. U.S. Department of Labor, *Women in the Labor Force: A Databook* (December 2011), Table 5, p. 13.

43. Rosanna E. Guadagno and Robert B. Cialdini, "Gender Differences in Impression Management: A Qualitative Review," *Sex Roles: A Journal of Research*, 56 (2007): 483–94.

44. Peter T. Kilborn, "For Many in Work Force, 'Glass Ceiling' Still Exists," *New York Times* (March 16, 1995), p. A22.

45. "FORTUNE 500 CEOs: Women on the Rise." Retrieved November 30, 2012 (http://postcards.blogs.fortune.cnn.com/2012/07/18/fortune-500-women-ceos-2).

46. Treasury & Risk, "30 Outstanding Women in Finance." Retrieved November 30, 2012 (http://www.treasuryandrisk.com/2012/05/01/30-outstanding-women-in-finance).

47. See Chris A. Higgins, Linda E. Duxbury, and Sean T. Lyons, "Coping with Overload and Stress: Mean and Women in Dual-Earner Families," *Journal of Marriage and Family*, 72 (2010): 847–59; Heather M. Helms, Jill K. Walls, Ann C. Crouter, and Susan M. McHale, "Provider Role Attitudes, Marital Satisfaction, Role Overload, and Housework: A Dyadic Approach," *Journal of Family Psychology*, 24 (2010): 568–77.

48. Arlie Russell Hochschild, with Anne Machung, *Second Shift: Working Parents and the Revolution at Home*, reissue ed. (New York: Viking Penguin, 2003).

49. Jeanne A. Batalova and Philip N. Cohen, "Premarital Cohabitation and Housework: Couples in Cross-National Perspective," *Journal of Marriage & Family*, 64 (2002): 743–55.

50. U.S. Department of Labor, *Women in the Labor Force: A Databook* (December 2012), Table 16, p. 56.

51. See Hadas Mandel and Michael Shaley, "How Welfare States Shape the Gender Pay Gap: A Theoretical and Comparative Analysis," *Social Forces*, 87 (2009): 1873–1911.

52. Treasury & Risk, loc. cit.

53. Computed from U.S. Census Bureau, "Annual Social and Economic Supplement," *Current Population Survey* (2012), Table PINC-03.

54. See Carol Hymowitz, "While Some Women Choose to Stay Home, Others Gain Flexibility," *Wall Street Journal* (March 30, 2004): p. B1.

55. See Daphne E. Petersen, Krista L. Minnotte, Gary Kiger, and Susan E. Mannon, "Workplace Policy and Environment, Family Role Quality, and Positive Family-to-Work Spillover," *Journal of Family and Economic Issues*, 30 (2009): 80–89; Margaret L. Usdansky and Douglas A. Wolf, "When Child Care Breaks Down: Mothers' Experiences with Child Care Problems and Resulting Missed Work," *Journal of Family Issues*, 29 (2008): 1185–1210.

56. U.S. Census Bureau, *America's Families and Living Arrangements: 2012*, Table C9.

57. U.S. Census Bureau, *2011 American Community Survey*, Table S0201.

58. Quoted in Linda Lemoncheck and James P. Sterba, *Sexual Harassment: Issues and Answers* (New York: Oxford University Press, 2001), pp. 198–99.

59. See Equal Employment Opportunity Commission, "Policy Guidance on Current Issues of Sexual Harassment." Retrieved November 30, 2012 (http://www.eeoc.gov/policy/docs/currentissues.html).

60. See Ashley Parker, "Lawsuit Says Military Is Rife with Sexual Abuse," *New York Times* (February 15, 2011). Retrieved December 1, 2012 (http://www.nytimes.com/2011/02/16/us/16military.html).

61. See Caroline Vaile Wright, and Louise F. Fitzgerald, "Correlates of Joining a Sexual Harassment Class Action, *Law and Human Behavior*, 33 (2009): 265–82; Heather Antecol and Deborah Cobb-Clark, "The Changing Nature of Employment-Related Sexual Harassment," *Industrial and Labor Relations Review*, 57 (2004): 443–61.

62. Justine E. Tinkler, "'People Are Too Quick to Take Offense': The Effects of Legal Information and Beliefs on Definitions of Sexual Harassment," *Law & Social Inquiry*, 33 (2008): 417–45.

63. Robert F. Bales, *Family, Socialization, and Interaction Process* (New York: Routledge, [1955] 2007).

64. Friedrich Engels, *The Origin of the Family, Private Property, and the State* (Honolulu: University Press of the Pacific, 2002), p. 94.

65. See Merry E. Weisner-Hanks, *Gender in History: Global Perspectives*, 2nd ed. (New York: Wiley-Blackwell, 2010), pp. 60–63.

66. Ibid., Chapter 3.

67. See Francine D. Blau, Anne C. Gielen, and Klaus F. Zimmermann, *Gender, Inequality, and Wages* (New York: Oxford University Press, 2012).

68. See, for example, Amy Kroska and Cheryl Elman, "Change in Attitudes about Employed Mothers: Exposure, Interests, and Gender Ideology Discrepancies," *Social Science Research*, 38 (2009): 366–82; Youngjoo Cha and Sarah Thebaud, "Labor Markets, Breadwinning, and Beliefs: How Economic Context Shapes Men's Gender Ideology," *Gender & Society*, 23 (2009): 215–43; Kelly E. Cichy, Eva S. Lefkowitz, and Karen L. Fingerman, "Generational Differences in Gender Attitudes between Parents and Grown Offspring," *Sex Roles*, 57 (2007): 825–36.

## CHAPTER 14

1. Eva Cantarella, *Bisexuality in the Ancient World*, 2nd ed. (New Haven, CT: Yale University Press, 2002).

2. Maurice Godelier and Marilyn Strathern (eds.), *Big Men and Great Men: Personifications of Power in Melanesia* (New York: Cambridge University Press, 2009).

3. See Louis Crompton, *Homosexuality and Civilization* (Cambridge, MA: Belknap Press of Harvard University, 2007), pp. 248, 288, 475.

4. See Jack Drescher, "A History of Homosexuality and Organized Psychoanalysis," *Journal of the American Academy of Psychoanalysis and Dynamic Psychiatry*, 36 (2008): 443–60.

5. See Elizabeth A. Wilson, "Neurological Preference: LeVay's Study of Sexual Orientation," *Substance*, 29 (2000): 23–38; and Simon LeVay, "A Difference in Hypothalamic Structure between Heterosexual and Homosexual Men," *Science*, 253 (1991): 1034–37.

6. Simon LeVay, *Gay, Straight, and the Reason Why: The Science of Sexual Orientation*, reprint ed. (New York: Oxford University Press, 2012), p. 201.

7. See Francesca Iemmola and Andrea Camperio Ciani, "New Evidence of Genetic Factors Influencing Sexual Orientation in Men: Female Fecundity Increase in the Maternal Line," *Archives of Sexual Behavior*, 38 (2009): 393–99.

8. Michael Abrams, "Born Gay?" *Discover*, 28 (2007): 58–83.

9. Barbara L. Frankowski, "Sexual Orientation and Adolescents," *Pediatrics*, 113 (June 2004): 1827–32.

10. George Chauncey, *Gay New York: Gender, Urban Culture, and the Making of the Gay Male World: 1890–1940* (New York: Basic Books, 1995).

11. Ibid., p. 9.

12. Eric Marcus, *Making Gay History: The Half-Century Fight for Lesbian and Gay Equal Rights* (New York: Harper, 2002).

13. David Carter, *Stonewall: The Riots That Sparked the Gay Revolution* (New York: St. Martin's Griffin, 2010).

14. Mary E. Swigonski Robin Mama, and Kelly Ward, *From Hate Crimes to Human Rights: A Tribute to Matthew Shepard* (New York: Routledge, 2002).

15. Steven A. Holmes, "Gay Rights Advocates Brace for Ballot Fights," *New York Times* (January 12, 1994), p. A17.

16. Wilbur J. Scott and Sandra Carson Stanley (eds.), *Gays and Lesbians in the Military: Issues, Concerns, and Contrasts* (New York: Aldine de Gruyter, 1995).

17. Julie Watson, "Don't Ask, Don't Tell Repeal," *Huffington Post* (August 13, 2011); Stephen Benjamin, "Don't Ask, Don't Translate," *New York Times* (June 8, 2007), p. A29.

18. Gary J. Gates and Frank Newport, "Gallup Special Report: The U.S. Adult LGBT Population." Retrieved January 26, 2013 (http://williamsinstitute.law.ucla.edu/research/census-lgbt-demographics-studies/gallup-special-report-18oct-2012); Robert T. Michael, John H. Gagnon, Edward O. Laumann, and Gina Kolata, *Sex in America: A Definitive Survey* (Boston: Little, Brown, 1994); see also Laumann and Michael, *Sex, Love, and Health in America: Private Choices and Public Policies* (Chicago: University of Chicago Press, 2001).

19. Gary R. Hicks and Tien-tsung Lee, "Public Attitudes toward Gays and Lesbians: Trends and Predictors," *Journal of Homosexuality*, 51 (2006): 57–77.

20. Pew Research Center, "In Gay Marriage Debate, Both Supporters and Opponents See Legal Recognition as 'Inevitable'." Retrieved June 9, 2013 (http://www.people-press.org/2013/06/06/in-gay-marriage-debate-both-supporters-and-opponents-see-legal-recognition-as-inevitable).

21. Ibid. See also CBS News, "Poll: With Higher Visibility, Less Disapproval for Gays." Retrieved June 9, 2013 (http://www.cbsnews.com/8301-503544_162-20007144-503544.html).

22. See Thomas F. Pettigrew and Linda R. Tropp, "Allport's Intergroup Contact Hypothesis: Its History and Influence," pp. 262–77, in John F. Davidio, Peter Glick, and Laurie Rudman (eds.), *On the Nature of Prejudice: Fifty Years After Allport* (New York: Wiley-Blackwell, 2005).

23. Pew Research Center, "Majority Continues to Support Civil Unions" (October 9, 2009). Retrieved December 14, 2012 (http://people-press.org/report/553/same-sex-marriage).

24. Ibid.

25. Public Agenda, "Gay Rights: People's Chief Concerns." Retrieved December 13, 2012 (http://www.publicagenda.com/citizen/issueguides/gay-rights).

26. ILGA Europe, "Marriage Equality in Denmark." Retrieved December 14, 2012 (http://www.ilga-europe.org/home/news/latest_news/marriage_equality_in_denmark).

27. "Same-Sex Marriage, Gay Rights." Retrieved December 14, 2012 (http://www.pollingreport.com/civil.htm).

28. Marjorie Connolly, "Support for Gay Marriage Growing, but U.S. Remains Divided," *New York Times* (December 8, 2012).

29. Ibid.; Pew Research Center, "Majority Continues to Support Civil Unions" (October 9, 2009).

30. Gallup, "Religion Big Factor for Americans against Same-Sex Marriage" (December 5, 2012). Retrieved December 14, 2012 (http://www.gallup.com/poll/159089).

31. See J. A. Lavner, J. Waterman, and J. Peplau, "Can Gay and Lesbian Parents Promote Healthy Development in High-Risk Children Adopted from Foster Care?" *American Journal of Orthopsychiatry*, 82 (2012): 465–72; Paige Averett, Blace Nalavany, and Scott Ryan, "An Evaluation of Gay/Lesbian and Heterosexual Adoption," *Adoption Quarterly*, 12 (2009): 129–51.

32. U.S. Census Bureau, *2011 American Community Survey*, Table S02001.

33. Gary Gates, Lee M. V. Badgett, Jennifer Ehrle Macomber, and Kate Chambers, *Adoption and Foster Care by Lesbian and Gay Parents in the United States*, Urban Institute (March 27, 2007). Retrieved December 15, 2012 (http://www.urban.org/url.cfm?ID=411437).

34. World Health Organization, *Disability and Rehabilitation Team*. Retrieved December 15, 2012 (http://www.who.int/disabilities/en).

35. U.S. Census Bureau, "Americans with Disabilities: 2010," *Current Population Reports* (July 2012). Retrieved December 15, 2012 (http://www.census.gov/prod/2012pubs/p70-131.pdf).

36. The Center for an Accessible Society, "Identity, Definitions, and Demographics of Disability." Retrieved December 15, 2012 (http://www.accessiblesociety.org/topics/demographics-identity).

37. "Disability History Timeline," Disability Social History Project. Retrieved December 15, 2012 (http://www.disabilityhistory.org/timeline_new.html).

38. U.S. Census Bureau, "Americans with Disabilities: 2010."

39. George H. W. Bush, "Remarks of President George Bush at the Signing of the Americans with Disabilities Act." Retrieved December 15, 2012 (http://www.eeoc.gov/eeoc/history/35th/videos/ada_signing_text.html).

40. M. V. Castañeto and E. W. Willemsen, "Social Perception of the Development of Disabled Children," *Child: Care, Health, & Development*, 33 (May 2007): 308–18; Dawn Stanton, "Less Than Human," *Psychology Today*, 40 (January/February 2007): 18; and Joan Fleitas, "Sticks, Stones, and the Stigmata of Childhood Illness and Disability," *Reclaiming Children and Youth*, 9 (2000): 146–50.

41. Kessler Foundation and National Organization on Disability, "The ADA: 20 Years Later" (July 2010). Retrieved December 15, 2012 (http://www.2010disabilitysurveys.org/pdfs/surveyresults.pdf).

42. Compiled from EEOC, "EEOC Litigation Statistics, FY 1997 through FY 2011." Retrieved December 15, 2012 (http://www.eeoc.gov/eeoc/statistics/enforcement/litigation.cfm).

43. See Doris Fleischer and Freda Zames, *The Disability Rights Movement: From Charity to Confrontation*, 2nd ed. (Philadelphia: Temple University Press, 2011).

44. See Todd D. Nelson, *Ageism: Stereotyping and Prejudice against Older Persons* (Cambridge, MA: The MIT Press, 2005).

45. U.S. Census Bureau, "2012 National Population Projections." Retrieved June 9 (http://www.census.gov/population//projections/data/national/2012/summarytables.htm).

46. Pew Research Center, "Baby Boomers Retire." Retrieved April 22, 2013 (http://www.pewresearch.org/daily-number/baby-boomers-retire); U.S. Census Bureau, "The Next Four Decades: The Older Population in the United States, 2010 to 2050" (May 2010). Retrieved June 9, 2013 (http://www.census.gov/prod/2010pubs/p25-1138.pdf).

47. Ibid.

48. Wan He, Manisha Sengupta, Victoria A. Velkoff, and Kimberly A. De Barros, *65+ in the United States: 2005*, U.S. Census Bureau, Current Population Reports (Washington, DC: U.S. Government Printing Office, 2005), P23–209, p. 3

49. Ibid., pp. 127–30.

50. National Center for Health Statistics, *Health, United States, 2012,* Table 18, p. 76.

51. He et al., op. cit.

52. William H. Frey, "The Uneven Aging and 'Younging' of America: State and Metropolitan Trends in the 2010 Census," Metropolitan Policy Program (June 2011). Retrieved December 16, 2012 (http://www.brookings.edu).

53. See, for example, Margaret Morganroth Gullette, *Agewise: Fighting the New Ageism in America* (Chicago: University of Chicago Press, 2011).

54. U.S. Census Bureau, "American Householders Are Getting Older, Census Bureau Reports" (November 15, 2012). Retrieved December 16, 2012 (http://www.census.gov/newsroom/releases/archives/families_households/cb12-216.html).

55. National Center for Health Statistics, *Health, United States, 2012,* Table 35, pp. 129–30.

56. See Susan M. Hillier and Georgia M. Barrow, *Aging, the Individual, and Society,* 9th ed. (New York: Wadsworth, 2010), p. 34.

57. S. A. H. van Hooren, A. M. Valentin, H. Bosma, R. W. Ponds, M. P. van Boxtel, and J. Jolles, "Cognitive Functioning in Health Older Adults Aged 64–81: A Cohort Study into the Effects of Age, Sex, and Education," *Aging, Neuropsychology, & Cognition,* 14 (January 2007): 40–54.

58. Karen A. Ertel, Maria Glymour, and Lisa F. Berkman, "Effects of Social Integration on Preserving Memory Function in a Nationally Representative U.S. Elderly Population," *American Journal of Public Health,* 98 (2008): 1215–20.

59. Stacy Tessler Lindau, L. Philip Schumm, Edward O. Laumann, Wendy Levinson, Colm A. O'Muircheartaigh, and Linda J. Waite, "A Study of Sexuality and Health among Older Adults in the United States," *New England Journal of Medicine,* 357 (2007): 762–74.

60. Terrie Beth Ginsberg, Sherry C. Pomerantz, and Veronika Kramer-Feeley, "Sexuality in Older Adults: Behaviours and Preferences," *Age & Ageing,* 34 (September 2005): 475–80; and S. Umidi, M. Pini, M. Ferretti, C. Vergani, and G. Annoni, "Affectivity and Sexuality in the Elderly: Often Neglected Aspects," *Archives of Gerontology & Geriatrics,* 44 (May 2007): 413–17.

61. See, for example, Chetna Narayan, "Is There a Double Standard of Aging? Older Men and Women and Ageism," *Educational Gerontology,* 34 (2008): 782–87.

62. Wan He et al., *65+ in the United States, 2005,* p. 92.

63. Don Lee, "More Older Workers Making Up Labor Force," *Los Angeles Times* (September 4, 2012), p. A1; U.S. Bureau of Labor Statistics, *Older Workers* (July 2008). Retrieved December 27, 2012 (http://www.bls.gov/spotlight/2008/older_workers).

64. See Jacquelyn B. James, Sharon MeKechnie, and Elyssa Besen, "How Age Bias Hurts Business" (May 16, 2012). Retrieved December 27, 2012 (http://agingandwork.bc.edu/blog/how-age-bias-hurts-business).

65. Richard A. Posthuma and Michael A. Campion, "Age Stereotypes in the Workplace: Common Stereotypes, Moderators, and Future Research Directions," *Journal of Management,* 35 (2009): 158–88.

66. Linda Greenhouse, "Justices, in Bias Case, Rule for Older Workers," *New York Times* (June 20, 2008), p. O15.

67. See, for example, "At Chrysler Unit, Buyouts for Older Workers," *New York Times* (February 24, 2007), p. C2.

68. Carmen DeNavas-Walt, Bernadette D. Proctor, and Jessica C. Smith, *Income, Poverty, and Health Insurance Coverage in the United States: 2011,* U.S. Census Bureau, Current Population Reports (Washington, DC: U.S. Government Printing Office, 2012, P60–243, p. 16.

69. Board of Governors of the Federal Reserve System, "Changes in U.S. Family Finances from 2007 to 2010" (June 2012). Retrieved December 27, 2012 (http://www.federalreserve.gov/pubs/bulletin/2012/pdf/scf12.pdf).

70. Wan He et al., *65+ in the United States, 2005,* pp. 105–67.

71. U.S. Census Bureau, *2011 American Community Survey,* Table S0201.

72. U.S. Census Bureau, "America's Families and Living Arrangements: 2012." Table A2. Retrieved January 4, 2013 (http://www.census.gov/hhes/families/data/cps2012.html).

73. Ibid.

74. Wan He et al., *65+ in the United States, 2005,* p. 138.

75. Administration on Aging, U.S. Department of Health and Human Services, "A Profile of Older Americans: 2011." Retrieved January 4, 2013 (http://www.aoa.gov/aoaroot/aging_statistics/Profile/2011/docs/2011profile.pdf).

76. National Center for Health Statistics, *Health, United States, 2008,* Table 107 (Washington DC: U.S. Government Printing Office, 2009), p. 392.

77. See, for example, Dana Goldman, *Health Status and Medical Treatment of the Future Elderly: Final Report* (Washington, DC: RAND Corporation, 2004).

78. Shoshana H. Bardach and Graham D. Rowles, "Geriatric Education in the Health Professions: Are We Making Progress?" *The Gerontologist,* 52 (October 2012): 607–18.

79. Jeanne Batalova, "Senior Immigrants in the United States," *Migration Information Source,* May 2012. Retrieved January 4, 2013 (http://www.migrationinformation.org/usfocus/display.cfm?ID=894); U.S. Census Bureau, American Community Survey.

80. Ron Haskins, "Combating Poverty: Understanding New Challenges for Families," Brookings Institute. Retrieved January 4, 2013 (http://www.brookings.edu/research/testimony/2012/06/05-poverty-families-haskins).

81. See Thanh V. Tran, Tricia Scott, and Anh-Luu T. Huynh-Hohnbaum, "A Measure of English Acculturation Stress and Its Relationship with Psychological and Physical Health Status in a Sample of Elderly Russian Immigrants," *Journal of Gerontological Social Work,* 50 (2008): 37–50; and Ada C. Mui and Suk-Young Kang, "Acculturation Stress and Depression among Asian Immigrant Elders," *Social Work,* 51 (2006): 243–55.

82. For a variation on this concept, see "continuity theory" in Leslie A. Morgan and Suzanne R. Kunkel, *Aging, Society, and the Life Course,* 4th ed. (New York: Springer Publishing Co., 2011), pp. 150–52.

83. John Harris, *Working with Older People* (New York: Routledge, 2008), pp. 30–31.

84. See Jiayin Liang and Baozhen Luo, "Toward a Discourse Shift in Social Gerontology: From Successful Aging to Harmonious Aging," *Journal of Aging Studies,* 26 (2012): 327–34; Chaonan Chen, "Revisiting the Disengagement Theory with Differentials in the Determinations of Life Satisfaction," *Social Indicators Research,* 64 (2003): 209–24.

85. See Naomi M. McCormick, "Preface to Sexual Scripts: Social and Therapeutic Implications," *Sexual and Relationship Therapy,* 25 (2010): 91–95.

86. See, for example, Gregory M. Herek, J. Roy Gillis, and Jeanine C. Cogan, "Internalized Stigma among Sexual Minority

Adults: Insights from a Social Psychological Perspective," *Journal of Counseling Psychology,* 56 (2009): 32–43; and Kimberly F. Balsam and Jonathan J. Mohr, "Adaptation to Sexual Orientation Stigma: A Comparison of Bisexual and Lesbian/Gay Adults," *Journal of Counseling Psychology,* 54 (2007): 306–19.

## CHAPTER 15

1. Vincent N. Parrillo, "Asian Americans in American Politics," in Joseph S. Roucek and Bernard Eisenberg (eds.), *America's Ethnic Politics* (Westport, CT: Greenwood Press, 1982) pp. 89–112.

2. See Marco Martiniello and Jean-Michel Lafleur, "Towards a Transatlantic Dialogue in the Study of Immigrant Political Transnationalism," *Ethnic and Racial Studies,* 31 (2008): 645–63; José Itzigsohn, "Immigration and the Boundaries of Citizenship: The Institutions of Immigrants' Political Transnationalism," *International Migration Review,* 34 (2000): 1126–54.

3. Daisuke Akiba, "Ethnic Retention as a Predictor of Academic Success: Lessons from the Children of Immigrant Families and Black Children," *Clearing House,* 80 (2007): 223–25; Carl L. Bankston, III, "Social Capital, Cultural Values, Immigration, and Academic Achievement: The Host Country Context and Contradictory Consequences," *Sociology of Education,* 77 (2004): 176–79.

4. Cynthia Feliciano, "Education and Ethnic Identity Formation among Children of Latin American and Caribbean Immigrants," *Sociological Perspectives,* 52 (2009): 135–58.

5. Mary C. Sengstock, "Social Change in the Country of Origin as a Factor in Immigrant Conceptions of Nationality," *Ethnicity,* 4 (1977): 61, 64.

6. See Pratyusha Tummala-Narra, "The Immigrant's Real and Imagined Return Home," *Culture & Society,* 14 (2009): 237–52.

7. Marcus L. Hansen, "The Third Generation in America," *Commentary,* 14 (1952): 492–500.

8. Marcus L. Hansen, "The Third Generation," in Oscar Handlin (ed.), *Children of the Uprooted* (New York: Harper & Row, 1966).

9. Peter Skerry, "Do We Really Want Immigrants to Assimilate?" *Society,* 37 (2000): 57–62.

10. Sean Valentine, "Self Esteem, Cultural Identity, and Generation Status as Determinants of Hispanic Acculturation," *Hispanic Journal of Behavioral Sciences,* 23 (2001): 459–68.

11. See Inna Altschul, Daphna Oyserman, and Deborah Bybee, "Racial-Ethnic Self-Schemas and Segmented Assimilation: Identity and the Academic Achievement of Hispanic Youth," *Social Psychology Quarterly,* 71 (2008): 302–20; Alejandro Portes and Dag MacLeod, "What Shall I Call Myself? Hispanic Identity Formation in the Second Generation," *Ethnic and Racial Studies,* 19 (1996): 523–47.

12. Jerry Z. Park, "Second-Generation Asian American Pan-Ethnic Identity: Pluralized Meanings of a Racial Label," *Sociological Perspectives,* 51 (2008): 541–61; Nazli Kibria, "The Construction of 'Asian American': Reflections on Intermarriage and Ethnic Identity among Second-Generation Chinese and Korean Americans," *Ethnic and Racial Studies,* 30 (1997): 523–44.

13. See Paul Spickard, *Japanese Americans: The Formation and Transformations of an Ethnic Group,* rev. ed. (New Brunswick, NJ: Rutgers University Press, 2009).

14. See Lingxin Hao and Han S. Woo, "Distinct Trajectories in the Transition to Adulthood: Are Children of Immigrants Advantaged?" *Child Development,* 83 (2012): 1623–39; Mark Ellis and Jamie Goodwin-White, "1.5 Generation Internal Migration in the U.S.: Dispersion from States of Immigration?" *International Migration Review,* 40 (2006): 899–926.

15. S. Karthick Ramakrishnan, "Second Generation Immigrants? The '2.5 Generation' in the United States," *Social Science Quarterly,* 85 (2004): 380–99.

16. See Jussi Kasperi Ronkainen, "Mononationals, Hyphenationals, and Shadow-Nationals: Multiple Citizenship as Practice," *Citizenship Studies,* 15 (2011): 247–63; Irene Bloemraad, Anna Korteweg, and Gokce Yurdakul, "Citizenship and Immigration: Multiculturalism, Assimilation, and Challenges to the Nation-State," *Annual Review of Sociology,* 34 (2008): 153–79; Rosemary Salomone, "Transnational Schooling and the New Immigrants: Developing Dual Identities in the United States," *Intercultural Education,* 19 (2008): 383–93.

17. See, for example, Mir Hekmatullah Sadat, "Hyphenating Afghaniyat (Afghan-ness) in the Afghan Diaspora," *Journal of Muslim Minority Affairs,* 28 (2008): 329–42.

18. See Mimi Kim, "The Political Economy of Immigration and the Emergence of Transnationalism," *Journal of Human Behavior in the Social Environment,* 19 (2009): 675–89.

19. Thomas Faist, "Towards Transnational Studies: World Theories, Transnationalisation and Changing Institutions," *Journal of Ethnic and Migration Studies,* 36 (2010): 1665–87.

20. See Stephanie J. Nawyn, Linda Giokaj, DeBrenna LaFay Agbenyiga, and Breanne Grace, "Linguistic Isolation, Social Capital, and Immigrant Belonging," *Journal of Contemporary Ethnography,* 41 (2012): 255–82; Humnath Bhandari and Kumi Yasunobu, "What Is Social Capital? A Comprehensive Review of the Concept," *Asian Journal of Social Science,* 37 (2009): 480–510.

21. See Pauline Hope Cheong, Rosalind Edwards, Harry Goulbourne, and John Solomos, "Immigration, Social Cohesion, and Social Capital: A Critical Review," *Criticial Social Policy,* 27 (2007): 24–49.

22. Min Zhou and Susan S. Kim, "Community Forces, Social Capital, and Educational Achievement: The Case of Supplementary Education in the Chinese and Korean Immigrant Communities," *Harvard Educational Review,* 76 (2006): 1–29.

23. William Haller, Alejandro Portes, and Scott M. Lynch, "Dreams Fulfilled, Dreams Shattered: Determinants of Segmented Assimilation in the Second Generation," *Social Forces,* 89 (2011): 733–62.

24. Roger Waldinger and Cynthia Feliciano, "Will the New Second Generation Experience 'Downward Assimilation'? Segmented Assimilation Re-Assessed," *Ethnic & Racial Studies,* 27 (2004): 376–402.

25. Charles Herschman, "The Educational Enrollment of Immigrant Youth: A Test of the Segmented-Assimilation Hypothesis," *Demography,* 38 (2001): 317–36.

26. Reynolds Farley and Richard Alba, "The New Second Generation in the United States," *International Migration Review,* 36 (2002): 669–90.

27. Herschman, "The Educational Enrollment of Immigrant Youth."

28. Kathleen M. Roche, Sharon R. Ghazarian, and Maria Eugenia Fernandez-Esquer, "Unpacking Acculturation: Cultural Orientations and Educational Attainment among

Mexican-Origin Youth," *Journal of Youth and Adolescence,* 41 (2012): 920–31.

29. See Philip Kretsedemas, "Redefining 'Race' in North America," *Current Sociology,* 56 (2008): 826–44.

30. U.S. Department of Homeland Security, *2011 Yearbook of Immigration Statistics,* Table 21, pp. 53–56.

31. Haller et al., op. cit.

32. Jamie Goodwin-White, "Emerging U.S. Immigrant Geographies: Racial Wages and Migration Selectivity," *Social Science Quarterly,* 93 (2012): 779–98; John W. Frazier, *Multicultural Geographies: The Changing Racial/Ethnic Patterns of the United States* (Albany: State University of New York Press, 2010).

33. See John Iceland, *Where We Live Now: Immigration and Race in the United States* (Berkeley: University of California Press, 2009).

34. U.S. Office of Immigration Statistics, *2011 Yearbook of Immigration Statistics,* Table 4.

35. U.S. Census Bureau, "Geographic Mobility: 2011 to 2012." Retrieved June 9, 2013 (http://www.census.gov/hhes/migration/data/cps/cps2012.html); Pew Research Center, "Comings & Goings: Migration Flows in the U.S." Retrieved January 6, 2013 (http://pewsocialtrends.org/maps/migration).

36. Marc J. Perry and Jason P. Schachter, "Migration of Natives and the Foreign Born: 1995 to 2000," *Census 2000 Special Reports* (August 2003), Table 1, p. 3.

37. Robert E. Park, "The Urban Community as a Spatial Pattern and a Moral Order," in Ernest W. Burgess (ed.), *The Urban Community* (Chicago: University of Chicago Press, 1971), pp. 3–18. Originally published in 1926.

38. John Iceland, *Where We Live Now: Immigration and Race in the United States.*

39. See Ming Wen, Diane S. Lauderdale, and Namratha R. Kandula, "Ethnic Neighborhoods in Multi-Ethnic America, 1990–2000: Resurgent Ethnicity in the Ethnoburbs?" *Social Forces,* 88 (2009): 425–60.

40. Richard D. Alba, *Italian Americans: Into the Twilight of Ethnicity* (Englewood Cliffs, NJ: Prentice Hall, 1985), pp. 159–75.

41. See Herbert J. Gans, "Reflections on Symbolic Ethnicity: A Response to Y. Anagnostou," *Ethnicities,* 9 (2009): 123–29; Gans, "Symbolic Ethnicity and Symbolic Religiosity: Towards a Comparison of Ethnic and Religious Acculturation," *Ethnic and Racial Studies,* 17 (1994): 577–92.

42. U.S. Department of Homeland Security, Office of Immigration Statistics, "Estimates of the Unauthorized Immigrant Population Residing in the United States: January 2011," March 2012.

43. Gretchen Livingston and D'Vera Cohn, "U.S. Birth Rate Falls to a Record Low; Decline Is Greatest Among Immigrants," Pew Research Social & Demographic Trends, November 29, 2012.

44. "Immigration." Retrieved January 7, 2013 (http://www.pollingreport.com/immigration.htm).

45. Rakesh Kochhar, C. Soledad Espinoza, and Rebecca Hinze-Pifer, "After the Great Recession: Foreign Born Gain Jobs; Native Born Lose Jobs," Pew Research Hispanic Center, October 29, 2010.

46. George J. Borjas and Leonard F. Katz, "The Evolution of the Mexican-American Workforce in the United States," National Bureau of Economic Research, NBER Working Paper No. 11281 (April 2005).

47. David Card, "Is the New Immigration Really So Bad?" *The Economic Journal,* 115 (2005): 300–23; Tyler Cowen and Daniel M. Rothschild, "Don't Bad-Mouth Unskilled Immigrants," *Reason,* 38:4 (2006): 42–4.

48. James P. Smith, "Immigration Reform," *Rand Review,* Fall 2012.

49. Tamar Jacoby, "Immigration Nation," *Foreign Affairs,* 85:6 (2006): 50–65.

50. Philip Martin and Elizabeth Midgley, "Immigration in America: 2010," Population Bulletin Update (June 2010), p. 2.

51. Tyler Cowen and Daniel M. Rothschild, "Unskilled Doesn't Mean Unnecessary," *Los Angeles Times.* Retrieved January 7, 2013 (http://articles.latimes.com/2006/may/15/opinion/oe-cowen15).

52. "Immigration." Retrieved January 8, 2013 (http://www.publicagenda.com/citizen/issueguides/immigration/publicview/redflags and http://www.pollingreport.com/immigration.htm).

53. "Immigration." Retrieved June 10, 2013 (http://www.pollingreport.com/immigration.htm).

54. U.S. Citizenship and Immigration Services, *About Us.* Retrieved January 7, 2013 (http://www.uscis.gov/portal/site/uscis).

55. Jeffrey S. Passel and D'Vera Cohn, "Unauthorized Immigrant Population: National and State Trends, 2010," Pew Hispanic Center (February 1, 2011); "A Portrait of Unauthorized Immigrants in the United States," (April 14, 2009).

56. Ibid.

57. U.S. Department of Homeland Security, *2011 Yearbook of Immigration Statistics,* Table 34, pp. 92–94.

58. Miriam Jordan, "Migrants' Cash Keeps Flowing Home," *Wall Street Journal* (September 24, 2012), p. A16.

59. U.S. Census Bureau, *2011 American Community Survey* and "Language Use in the United States: 2007," *American Community Survey Reports,* April 2010.

60. U.S. Department of Education, National Center for Education Statistics, *The Condition of Education: 2011* (Washington, DC: U.S. Government Printing Office, 2012), Indicator 6-2011.

61. Migration Policy Institute, "Number and Growth of Students in US Schools in Need of English Instruction." Retrieved January 8, 2013 (http://www.migrationinformation.org/ellinfo/FactSheet_ELL1.pdf).

62. See Kellie Rolstad, Kate S. Mahoney, and Gene V. Glass, "The Big Picture: A Meta-Analysis of Program Effectiveness Research on English Language Learners," *Educational Policy,* 19 (2005): 572–94; and "Weighing the Evidence: A Meta-Analysis of Bilingual Education in Arizona," *Bilingual Research Journal,* 29 (2005): 43–67.

63. See, for example, Carolyn Huie Hofstetter, "Effects of a Transitional Bilingual Education Program: Findings, Issues, and Next Steps," *Bilingual Research Journal,* 28 (2004): 355–77; Linda Jacobson, "Prop. 227 Seen as Focusing on 'Wrong Issue'," *Education Week* (March 1, 2006), pp. 18–20.

64. See, for example, Christine Rossell, "Teaching English through English," *Educational Leadership,* 62 (2005): 32–36.

65. *Horne v. Flores,* No. 08–289 (June 25, 2009), Section 2d(i).

66. See "LULAC History—All for One and One for All." Retrieved January 8, 2013 (http://www.lulac.org/about/history).

67. "Official English," U.S. English. Retrieved January 8, 2013 (http://www.us-english.org/view/8).

68. Rasmussen Reports, "84% Say English Should Be America's Official Language." Available at http://www.rasmussenreports.com/public_content/lifestyle/general_lifestyle/may_2009/

84_say_english_should_be_america_s_official_language [January 24, 2010].

69. Public Agenda, "A Place to Call Home: What Immigrants Say Now about Life in America." Retrieved January 8, 2013 (http://www.publicagenda.com/pages/immigrants-2009-topline).

70. Paul Taylor, Mark Hugo Lopez, Jessica Hamar Martínez, and Gabriel Velasco, "When Labels Don't Fit: Hispanics and Their Views of Identity," Pew Hispanic Center, April 4, 2012.

71. Rubén G. Rumbaut and Alejandro Portes, *Ethnicities: Children of Immigrants in America* (Berkeley: University of California Press, 2002).

72. Rubén G. Rumbaut, Douglas S. Massey, and Frank D. Bean, "Linguistic Life Expectancies: Immigrant Language Retention in Southern California," *Population and Development Review,* 32 (2006): 447–60.

73. U.S. Census Bureau, "Language Use in the United States: 2007."

74. See Barry R. Chiswick and Paul W. Miller, "A Test of the Critical Period Hypothesis for Language Learning," *Journal of Multilingual and Multicultural Development,* 29 (2008): 16–29,

75. Vincent N. Parrillo, *Diversity in America,* 4th ed. (Boulder, CO: Paradigm Publishers, 2013), pp. 183–85.

76. See, for example, Joseph Barndt, *Understanding and Dismantling Racism: The Twenty-First Century Challenge to White America* (Minneapolis: Fortress Press, 2008), pp. 55–65.

77. Anne Phillips, *Multiculturalism without Culture* (Princeton, NJ: Princeton University Press, 2009), p. 6.

78. David A. Hollinger, *Postethnic America: Beyond Multiculturalism,* rev. ed. (New York: Basic Books, 2006).

79. Jeffrey S. Passel and D'Vera Cohn, "U.S. Population Projections: 2005–2050," Pew Research Center (February 11, 2008). Available at http://pewhispanic.org/files/reports/85.pdf [January 24, 2010].

80. U.S. Census Bureau, "2012 National Population Projections." Retrieved January 8, 2013 (http://www.census.gov/population/projections/data/national/2012.html).

81. U.S. Census Bureau, *Statistical Abstract of the United States: 2012,* Table 60, p. 84; David Leonhardt, "Hispanics, the New Italians," *New York Times* (April 21, 2013), p. SR5.

82. Ibid.

83. Michael W. Firmin and Stephanie Firebaugh, "Historical Analysis of College Campus Interracial Dating," *College Student Journal,* 42 (2008): 882–88; Derek A. Kreager, "Guarded Borders: Adolescent Interracial Romance and Peer Trouble at School," *Social Forces,* 87 (2008): 887–910.

84. Christie D. Batson, Zhenchao Qian, and Daniel T. Lichter, "Interracial and Intraracial Patterns of Mate Selection among America's Diverse Black Populations," *Journal of Marriage and Family,* 68 (2006): 658–72.

85. Yuanting Zhang and Jennifer Van Hook, "Marital Dissolution among Interracial Couples," *Journal of Marriage and Family,* 71 (2009): 95–107.

86. George A. Yancey, "Experiencing Racism: Differences in the Experiences of Whites Married to Blacks and Non-Black Racial Minorities," *Journal of Comparative Family Studies,* 38 (2007):197–213.

87. Adam B. Troy, Jamie Lewis-Smith, and Philippe Laurenceau, "Interracial and Intraracial Romantic Relationships: The Search for Differences in Satisfaction, Conflict, and Attachment Style," *Journal of Social and Personal Relationships,* 23 (2006): 665–80.

88. Christie D. Batson, Zhenchao Qian, and Daniel T. Lichter, "Interracial and Intraracial Patterns of Mate Selection Among America's Diverse Black Populations," *Journal of Marriage and Family,* 68 (2006): 658–72; Suzanne Model and Gene Fisher, "Black–White Unions: West Indians and African Americans Compared," *Demography,* 38 (2001): 177–85.

89. George Yancey, "Who Interracially Dates: An Examination of the Characteristics of Those Who Have Interracially Dated," *Journal of Comparative Family Studies,* 33 (2002): 179–90.

90. U.S. Census Bureau, *2011 American Community Survey,* Table S0201.

91. Mireya Navarro, "Beyond Black & White," *New York Times* (May 5, 2008), pp. A22–23.

92. Sonya M. Tafoya, Hans Johnson, and Laura E. Hill, "Who Chooses to Choose Two?" *The American People: Census 2000,* Reynolds Farley and John Haaga (eds.), (New York: Russell Sage Foundation, 2005), pp. 332–51.

93. Julie M. Ahnallen, Karen L. Suyemoto, and Alice S. Carter, "Relationship between Physical Appearance, Sense of Belonging and Exclusion, and Race/Ethnic Self-Identification among Multiracial Japanese European Americans," *Cultural Diversity & Ethnic Minority Psychology,* 12 (2006): 673–86.

94. Jamie Mihoko Doyle and Grace Kao, "Are Racial Identities of Multiracials Stable? Changing Self-Identification and Single and Multiple Race Individuals," *Social Psychological Quarterly,* 70 (2007): 405–23.

95. Haya El Nasser, "Fewer Americans Call Themselves Multiracial," *USA Today* (May 4, 2007), p. 1A.

96. See, for example, Kimberly DaCosta, *Making Multiracials: State, Family, and Market in the Redrawing of the Color Line* (Stanford, CA: Stanford University Press, 2007).

97. Sam Roberts, "Census Figures Challenge Views of Race and Ethnicity," *New York Times* (January 22, 2010), p. A13.

# GLOSSARY

**Acceptance**   A minority response to prejudice and discrimination; based on powerlessness, fear for personal safety, desire for economic security, or split-labor-market theory fatalism.

**Accommodation (pluralistic) theory**   A tendency to accept the situation as it exists, without seeking to change it or make others conform; pluralism.

**Acculturation**   The process by which a group changes its distinctive cultural traits to conform with those of the host society.

**Action-orientation level of prejudice**   A positive or negative predisposition to engage in discriminatory behavior toward members of a particular group.

**Activity theory**   A theoretical perspective that people of all ages require adequate levels of social activity to remain well adjusted.

**Affirmative action**   Deliberate efforts to improve minority representation, as well as their economic and educational opportunities.

**Afrocentrism**   A viewpoint emphasizing African culture and its influence on Western civilization and U.S. black behavior.

**Ageism**   The manifestation of prejudice, aversion, or even hatred toward the old.

**Amalgamation (melting-pot) theory**   The biological and cultural blending of two or more groups of people into a distinct new type; the melting-pot theory. A synonym is marital assimilation.

**Americanization movement**   The effort to have ethnic groups quickly give up their cultural traits and adopt those of the dominant U.S. group.

**Anglo-conformity**   A behavioral adherence to the established white Anglo-Saxon Protestant prototype; what many ethnocentric U.S. residents mean by assimilation.

**Annihilation**   The extermination of a specific group of people.

**Ascribed status**   One's socially defined, unchangeable position in a society based on such arbitrary factors as age, sex, race, or family background.

**Assimilation (majority-conformity) theory**   The process by which members of racial or ethnic minorities are able to function within a society without indicating any marked cultural, social, or personal differences from the people of the majority group.

**Asylee**   An alien found in a country or port of entry who is unable or unwilling to return to his or her country of origin, or to seek the protection of that country, because of persecution or a well-founded fear of persecution.

**Avoidance**   A minority-group response to prejudice and discrimination by migrating or withdrawing to escape further problems; a majority-group attempt to minimize contact with specific minority groups through social or spatial segregation.

**Bilingual education**   Teaching subjects in both English and the student's native language to develop fluency in both.

**Bilingualism**   Fluency in two languages.

**Bipolarization**   Two opposite trends occurring simultaneously.

**Black codes**   Southern state laws enacted during Reconstruction to keep blacks in a condition close to slavery.

**Brain drain**   Emigration of large numbers of skilled workers, professionals, or scientists who are badly needed by their home country.

**Categoric knowing**   A stereotype of others based merely on information obtained visually and perhaps verbally.

**Celibacy**   Refraining from any form of sexual intimacy.

**Chain migration**   A sequential flow of immigrants to a locality previously settled by friends, relatives, or other compatriots.

**Child care**   Supervised, quality care for preschool youngsters while one or both parents work.

**Civil religion**   A shared, nondenominational belief system incorporated into the culture.

**Cognitive level of prejudice**   Beliefs and perceptions about other racial or ethnic groups.

**Conflict theory**   A macrolevel sociological perspective emphasizing conflict as an important influence and permanent feature of life.

**Contact hypothesis**   Friendship with outgroup members corresponds to lower prejudice to that group

**Convenience sample**   A selection of individuals or cases on the basis of feasibility or ease of access, which can be biased and nonrepresentative of the entire population.

**Convergent subculture**   A subgroup gradually becoming completely integrated into the dominant culture.

**Cultural assimilation (acculturation)**   Changing cultural patterns of behavior to those of the host society; acculturation.

**Cultural determinism**   A theory that a group's culture explains its position in society and its achievements or lack thereof.

**Cultural differentiation**   Differences between cultures that make one group distinguishable from another.

**Cultural diffusion**   The spread of ideas, inventions, and practices from one culture to another.

**Cultural drift**   A gradual change in the values, attitudes, customs, and beliefs of the members of a society.

**Cultural pluralism**   Two or more culturally distinct groups coexisting in relative harmony.

**Cultural relativism**   A view of the customs and beliefs of other peoples within the context of their culture rather than one's own.

**Cultural transmission**   The passing of a society's culture from one generation to another.

**Culture**   The values, attitudes, customs, beliefs, and habits shared by members of a society.

**Culture of poverty**   A controversial viewpoint arguing that the disorganization and pathology of lower-class culture are self-perpetuating through cultural transmission.

**Culture shock**   Feelings of disorientation, anxiety, and a sense of being threatened when unpreparedly brought into contact with another culture.

**Cumulative causation**   Gunnar Myrdal's term for the vicious-circle process in which prejudice and discrimination mutually "cause" each other, thereby continuing and intensifying the cycle.

***De facto* segregation**   Physical separation of a group that is entrenched in customs and practices.

**Defiance**   A peaceful or violent action to challenge openly what a group considers a discriminatory practice.

***De jure* segregation**   Physical separation of a group that is established by law.

**Deviance**   Characteristics or behavior violating social norms and therefore negatively valued by many people in that society.

**Dichotomy**   A division into two, possibly contrasting, parts.

*Dignidad*   Hispanic cultural value that the dignity of all humans entitles them to a measure of respect.

**Dillingham Flaw**   Any inaccurate comparison based on simplistic categorizations and anachronistic judgments.

**Discrimination**   Differential and unequal treatment of other groups of people, usually along racial, religious, or ethnic lines.

**Disengagement theory**   A perspective that asserts that people inevitably become more passive and decrease their activity as they reach old age.

**Displaced aggression**   Hostility directed against a powerless group rather than against the more powerful cause of the feelings of hostility.

**Dominant group**   Any culturally or physically distinctive social grouping possessing economic, political, and social power and discriminating against a subordinate minority group.

**Ebonics**   An African American systematic language dialect with its own grammar, pronunciation, and vocabulary.

**Economic determinism**   A theory that a society's economic base establishes its culture and general characteristics.

**Ecumenical movement**   An effort to find universality among all faiths.

**Emigration**   Act of leaving one's country or region to settle in another.

**Emotional level of prejudice**   The feelings aroused in a group by another racial or ethnic group.

**Endogamy**   The tendency for people to marry only within their own social group.

**English-as-a-second-language (ESL) programs**   Teaching children English competence as one would teach English speakers another language.

**English-plus programs**   A dual approach under which foreign-language students learn English and native-born U.S. students develop foreign-language competence.

**Entrepreneurs**   People who set about to carry out any enterprise.

**Environmental justice**   A movement to eliminate environmental harms to all people.

**Environmental racism**   The disproportionate impact of hazardous substances on low-income minority groups, particularly people of color.

**Ethclass**   A social-group classification based on a combination of race, religion, social class, and regional residence.

**Ethnicity**   A cultural concept in which a large number of people who share learned or acquired traits and close social interaction regard themselves and are regarded by others as constituting a single group on that basis.

**Ethnic stratification**   Structured inequality of different groups with different access to social rewards as a result of their status in the social hierarchy.

**Ethnic subcultures**   Ongoing lifestyles and interaction patterns separate from the larger society that are based on religious or other cultural group memberships.

**Ethnocentrism**   A tendency to judge other cultures or subcultures by the standards of one's own culture.

**Ethnogenesis**   A process in which immigrants hold onto some homeland values, adapt others, and adopt some values of the host country.

**Ethnophaulism**   A derogatory word or expression used to describe or refer to a racial or ethnic group.

**Ethnoviolence**   Behavior ranging from verbal harassment and threats to murder against people targeted solely because of their race, religion, ethnicity, or sexual orientation.

**Eurocentrism**   A viewpoint emphasizing Western civilization, history, literature, and other humanities.

**Exploitation**   The selfish use of the labor of others for profit at their expense.

**Expulsion**   The forced removal of a group of people from an area.

**Extended family**   A family unit that includes other kin in addition to parents and children.

**Exurbs**   Newest ring of settlement beyond the old suburbs.

**False consciousness**   Holding attitudes that do not accurately reflect the objective facts of a situation.

**Fast track**   When women delay childbearing or forgo motherhood entirely to give full commitment to management to earn promotions over other candidates.

**Feminization of poverty**   A term describing female-headed households living in poverty.

**First-generation American**   Someone born in another country who immigrated to the United States.

**Flex time**   An arrangement that allows workers, within predetermined limits, to set their own working hours.

**Functionalist theory**   A macrolevel sociological perspective emphasizing societal order and stability, with harmonious interdependent parts.

*Gemeinschaft*   A small, tradition-dominated community characterized by intimate primary relationships and strong feelings of group loyalty.

**Gender-role expectations**   Anticipated behaviors because of one's gender.

**Generation, .5**   immigrant elders who are 65 years and older when they arrive.

**Generation, 1.5**   immigrants under age 10 when they arrive.

**Generation, 2.5**   native-born American with one foreign-born parent.

**Glass ceiling**   A real but unseen discriminatory policy that limits female upward mobility into top management positions.

**Group**   A collectivity of people closely interacting with one another on the basis of shared expectations about behavior.

**Hansen's law**   A theory that what the child of an immigrant wishes to forget, the grandchild wishes to remember; also called the three-generation hypothesis.

**Homophobia**   The fear or hatred of homosexuals and homosexual behavior.

**Ideology**   A generalized set of beliefs that collectively explains and justifies the interests of those who hold them.

**Immigration**   Movement of people into a new country to become permanent residents.

**Indigenous**   Person, plant, or animal in its natural, native habitat.

**Ingroup**   The group to which an individual belongs and feels loyal.

**Institutional discrimination**   Unequal treatment of subordinate groups inherent in the ongoing operations of society's institutions.

**Institutionalized racism**   Unequal treatment of a racial group inherent in the ongoing operations of society's institutions.

**Interactionist theory**   A microlevel sociological perspective emphasizing the shared interpretations and interaction patterns in everyday life.

**Intergenerational mobility**   The change in social status within a family from one generation to the next.

**Intergroup contact hypothesis** A perspective that holds attitudes and behaviors in social interactions depend on the comparative status and affective ties of the participants.

**Internal-colonialism theory** A concept explaining the experiences of blacks, Hispanics, and Native Americans in terms of economic exploitation and rigid stratification.

**Invasion-succession** The ecological process in which one group displaces another group in a residential area or business activity.

**Jigsaw classroom** Use of interdependent, cooperative learning groups as a means to teach as well as reduce prejudice.

**Jim Crow laws** Southern-state segregation laws, passed in the 1890s and early 1900s; covered use of all public facilities, including schools, restaurants, transportation, waiting rooms, rest rooms, drinking fountains, and parks.

**Kye** A rotating credit fund enabling Korean Americans to start or expand their businesses.

**Labeling theory** A perspective addressing how others' categorizations affect one's self-identity and behavior.

**Latent functions** Hidden, unexpected results within a social structure.

**Linguistic relativity** The recognition that different languages dissect and present reality differently.

**Machismo** Value orientation defining masculinity in varying terms of virility, honor, and providing for one's family.

**Macrosocial theories** Any theory that examines the empirical world from the societal level.

**Manifest functions** Obvious and intended results within a social structure.

**Marginality** The situation of individuals who are the product of one culture but are attempting to live within another, and therefore are not fully a part of either one.

**Marianismo** Value orientation defining feminine virtue as accepting male dominance and emphasizing family responsibilities.

**Marital assimilation (amalgamation)** A pattern of intermarriage of minority-group members with dominant-group members. A synonym is melting-pot theory.

**Material culture** All physical objects created by members of a society and the meanings/significance attached to them.

**Matrilineal** When descent and inheritance pass through the female side of the family.

**Matrilocal** The custom of married partners settling in or near the household of the wife's family.

**Medical model** A concept that emphasizes the individual's physical situation and not societal elements that may be affecting it.

**Melting-pot theory** *See* Amalgamation (melting-pot) theory and marital assimilation.

**Microsocial theory** Any theory that looks at the empirical view from a close, individual level.

**Middleman minority** A minority group occupying an intermediate occupational position in trade or commerce between the top and bottom strata.

**Migration** Movement of people into and out of a specified area, either within a country or from one country to another.

**Minority group** A culturally and physically distinctive group that experiences unequal treatment, an ascribed status, and a sense of shared identity and that practices endogamy.

**Minority-minority relations** A focus on interaction patterns between different minority groups.

**Miscegenation** Mixture of races by sexual union.

**Mommy track** When women try to juggle both family and work, which often slows or halts their upward mobility within the company.

**Mortality rate** Number of deaths per 1,000 people in a given year.

**Multiculturalism** Ranges from efforts for an all-inclusive curriculum to an emphasis on separatist pluralism.

**Nativist** One who advocates a policy of protecting the interests of native inhabitants against those of immigrants.

**Negative self-image** The result of social conditioning, differential treatment, or both, causing people or groups to believe themselves inferior.

**Net worth** The difference between assets and liabilities that an individual or household has at any given time.

**Nondenominational** Interchurch; not pertaining to any particular faith.

**Nonmaterial culture** Abstract human creations and their meanings/significance in life.

**Norms** The internalized rules of conduct that embody the fundamental expectations of society.

**Nuclear family** A unit of parents and their children living apart from other relatives.

**Occupational mobility** Ability to change one's job position with regard to status and economic reward.

**Outgroup** Any group to which an individual does not belong or feel loyal.

**Pan-Indianism** Social movement in which tribes not united by kinship join together in a common cause.

**Paralinguistic signals** Use of sounds but not words to convey distinct meanings.

**Parallel social institutions** A subcultural replication of institutions of the larger society, such as churches, schools, and organizations.

**Paternalism** A condescending treatment of adults, managing and regulating their affairs as a father would handle his children's affairs.

**Pentecostal faith** A form of evangelical Christianity that inspires a sense of belonging through worship participation.

**Persistent subculture** A subgroup adhering to its own way of life and resisting absorption into the dominant culture.

**Pluralism** A state in which minorities can maintain their distinctive subcultures and simultaneously interact with relative equality in the larger society.

**Polygyny** A form of marriage joining one male with two or more females.

**Power-differential theory** The theory that intergroup relations depend on the relative power of the migrant group and the indigenous group.

**Prejudice** A system of negative beliefs, feelings, and action orientations regarding a certain group or groups of people.

**Primary structural assimilation** Integration in which dominant- and minority-group members share close, personal interactions in churches, families, social clubs, or gatherings.

**Primogeniture** Inheritance or succession by the eldest son.

**Push-pull factors** A combination of negative elements at home and positive inducements elsewhere that encourage migration from one place to another.

**Race** A categorization in which a large number of people sharing visible physical characteristics regard themselves or are regarded by others as a single group on that basis.

**Racial profiling** Action initiated on the erroneous presumption that individuals of a particular group are more likely to engage in illegal activity than individuals of other groups.

**Racism** False linkage between biology and sociocultural behavior to assert the superiority of one race.

**Random sample** A sample of a population where each member of the population has an equal chance of being in the sample.

**Redlining** Unwillingness of some banks to make loans in lower-income minority neighborhoods.

**Reference group** A group to which people may or may not belong but to which they refer when evaluating themselves and their behavior.

**Refugee** Any person outside his or her country of origin who is unable or unwilling to return because of persecution or a well-founded fear of persecution.

**Relative deprivation** A lack of resources or rewards in one's standard of living in comparison with others in the society.

**Reputational method** A technique for measuring social class by questioning people about others' social standing.

**Role entrapment** The culturally defined need to be "feminine" that prevents many women from doing things that would help them achieve success and self-realization.

**Sanctuary movement** A 1980s religious and political movement of hundreds of Protestant and Catholic congregations that sheltered Central American refugees from immigration authorities.

**Sandwich generation** The generation of people who care for their aging parents while raising their own children.

**Scapegoating** Placing blame on others for something that is not their fault.

**Scientific method** A process involving repeated observation, precise measurement, careful description, theory formulation, and gathering further information based on questions that followed from those theories.

**Secondary group** A collectivity of people who interact on an impersonal or limited emotional basis for some practical or specific purpose.

**Secondary structural assimilation** Integration in which dominant- and minority-group members share the more impersonal public sphere of civic, school, recreational, or work settings.

**Second-generation American** A child born in the United States of immigrant parents; can also refer to a child born elsewhere but raised from a young age in the United States by immigrant parents.

**Segmented assimilation** Refers to a variety of outcomes among or within the contemporary immigrant streams.

**Selective perception** A tendency to see or accept only information that agrees with one's value orientations or that is consistent with one's attitudes about other groups.

**Self-justification** A defense mechanism whereby people denigrate another person or group to justify maltreating them.

**Separatist pluralism** Effort to seek specific, separate group identity rather than a collective U.S. national identity.

**Sexism** Institutionalized prejudice and discrimination based on gender.

**Sexual script** Enactments of complex sets of cultural meanings, the normative cultural contexts that give sex its meaning.

**Shunning** An Amish social-control practice of complete avoidance, including even eye contact.

**Shuttle migration** Large-scale movement back and forth between two countries.

**Slavery reparations** Cash or land compensation to descendants of slaves to rectify past injustices.

**Social capital** Actual or virtual resources available through a network of institutionalized relationships.

**Social class** A categorization designating people's places in the stratification hierarchy on the basis of similarities in income, property, power, status, and lifestyle.

**Social construction of reality** The process by which definitions of reality are socially created, objectified, internalized, and then taken for granted.

**Social discrimination** Exclusion of outgroup members from close relationships with ingroup members.

**Social distance** The degree of closeness or remoteness one desires in interaction with members of a particular group.

**Social identity theory** Holds that ingroup members enhance their self-image by considering their group better than others.

**Socialization process** The process of social interaction by which people acquire personality and learn the culture or subculture of their group.

**Social model** The way in which society adapts to accommodate people with disabilities.

**Social norms** Generally shared rules or expectations of what is and is not proper behavior.

**Social ostracism** Excluding a person or persons from social privileges and interaction.

**Social segregation** A situation in which participation in social, fraternal, service, and other types of activities is confined to members of the ingroup.

**Social stratification** The hierarchy within a society based on the unequal distribution of resources, power, or prestige.

**Social structure** The organized patterns of behavior in a social system governing people's interrelationships.

**Sojourners** Those who stay temporarily.

**Sovereign** Having independent power or authority.

**Spatial assimilation** The process of minority groups integrating into housing markets inhabited by non-Hispanic whites.

**Spatial segregation** The physical separation of a minority group from the rest of society, such as in housing or education.

**Split-labor- or dual-market theory** A concept explaining ethnic antagonism on the basis of conflict between higher-paid and lower-paid labor.

**Status positions** Places a person holds in society as determined by class structure, gender, and occupational roles.

**Stereotype** An oversimplified generalization attributing certain traits or characteristics to any person in a group without regard to individual differences.

**Structural assimilation** Large-scale entrance of minority-group members into primary-group relationships with the host society in its social organizations and institutions.

**Structural differentiation** Status distinctions for different racial and ethnic groups entrenched within the social system.

**Structural pluralism** Coexistence of racial and ethnic groups in separate subsocieties; also may be divided along social class and regional boundaries.

**Subculture** A group that shares in the overall culture of a society while retaining its own distinctive traditions and lifestyle.

**Symbolic ethnicity** Identifying with one's heritage through ethnic foods, holidays, and political and social activities.

**Symbolic interaction** The use of symbols—such as signs, gestures, and language—through which people interact with one another.

**Third-generation American** Someone born in the United States whose grandparents immigrated to the United States.

**Thomas theorem** An observation that if people define situations as real, the situations become real in their consequences.

**Three-generation hypothesis** *See* Hansen's law.

**Total fertility rate** The average number of children born per woman in her lifetime

**Transnationalism** Sustained ties of persons, networks, and organizations across national borders.

**Triple-melting-pot theory** The concept that intermarriage is occurring among various nationalities within the three major religious groupings.

**Underground economy** Individuals or businesses that deal in cash "under the table" and "off the books" so income is not reported and thus not taxed.

**Undocumented alien** Illegal immigrant without a green card or visa authorizing entry.

**Upward mobility** An improvement in one's socioeconomic position.

**Values** Socially shared conceptions of what is good, desirable, and proper or bad, undesirable, and improper.

**Vicious-circle phenomenon** Dynamics of intergroup relations where prejudice and discrimination serve as reciprocal stimuli and responses to reinforce one another.

**Xenophobia** The irrational fear of or contempt for strangers or foreigners.

# PHOTO CREDITS

## CHAPTER 1

**p. 1:** Carlos E. Santa Maria/Shutterstock; **p. 3:** Andresr / Shutterstock; **p. 6:** Michael P. Gadomski/Science Source; John Birdsall/ The Image Works; **p. 9:** Jeff Greenberg/Alamy; **p. 15:** AP Photo/Mark Elias; **p. 16:** The Art Archive at Art Resource, NY; **p. 18:** AP Photo/Tony Dejak; **p. 21:** Andrew Holbrooke/Corbis; **p. 22:** AP Photo/Charles Dharapak

## CHAPTER 2

**p. 25:** The Image Works; **p. 26:** Rebecca J. Moat/US Navy/ZUMA Press/Newscom; **p. 29:** Hyosub Shin/MCT/Newscom; **p. 32:** CREATISTA/Shutterstock; p. 35; David M. Grossman/The Image Works; **p. 36:** The Image Works; **p. 38:** Jim West/Alamy; **p. 40:** Norbert Schwerin/The Image Works; **p. 42:** Mario Tama/Getty Images; **p. 45:** AP Photo/Chris Gardner

## CHAPTER 3

**p. 53:** Mike Fox/ZUMA Press/Newscom; **p. 56:** AP Photo/Steve Spak; **p. 59:** Renay Johnson/ZUMA Press; **p. 62:** Jim West/The Image Works; **p. 66:** Andrei Jackamets/NBC/NBCU Photo Bank/Getty Images;  Michigan State University Museum; **p. 70:** Digital Vision/Getty Images; **p. 72:** Mark Richards/PhotoEdit; **p. 76:** ZUMA Press, Inc./Alamy; **p. 79:** Hill Street Studios/Blend Images/Getty Images

## CHAPTER 4

**p. 83:** Marilyn Humphries/The Image Works; **p. 86:** Walter Bibikow/Danita Delimont/alamy; **p. 88:** Joseph Sohm/Visions of America/Glow Images; **p. 91:** Tony Freeman/PhotoEdit; **p. 92:** Jeff Greenberg/Alamy; **p. 97:** AP Photo/Jerome Delay :**p. 100:** AP Photo/Damian Dovarganes; **p. 102:** Mark Peterson/Corbis; **p. 105:** Vincent Parrillo; **p. 108:** Robert Brenner/PhotoEdit

## CHAPTER 5

**p. 113:** AP Photo/Mary Ann Chastain; **p. 119:** Corbis; **p. 123:** James Schwabel/Alamy; **p. 126:** Cynthia Farmer/Shutterstock; **p. 129:** Bettmann/CORBIS; **p. 133:** David L. Moore - OR10/Alamy; **p. 135:** The Granger Collection, NYC — All rights reserved; **p. 139:** Philip Scalia/Alamy; **p. 141:** Richard Lord/PhotoEdit; **p. 142:** North Wind Picture Archives

## CHAPTER 6

**p. 149:** Piotr Redlinski/Corbis; **p. 153:** Library of Congress Prints and Photographs Division; **p. 157:** The Granger Collection, NYC — All rights reserved; **p. 162:** Vic Bider/PhotoEdit; **p. 167:** Margot Granitsas/The Image Works; **p. 168:** Ukraine Foundation; **p. 169:** American Hungarian Federation; **p. 173:** Gary Crabbe/Alamy; **p. 179:** Raymond Van Tessel; **p. 180:** Bettmann/Corbis

## CHAPTER 7

**p. 187:** LOOK/Robert Harding; **p. 189:** James Montgomery/AGE Fotostock; **p. 192:** Library of Congress Prints and Photographs Division[LC-USZC2-1687]; **p. 196:** Andre Jenny/The Image Works; **p. 201:** Claire Leimbach/Robert Harding; **p. 203:** The Granger Collection, NYC; **p. 212:** Dave G. Houser/Corbis; **p. 214:** Jack Kurtz/The Image Works; **p. 219:** AP Photo/Ben Margot; **p. 222:** Stephen Chernin/Getty Images

## CHAPTER 8

**p. 231:** Ariel Skelley/Blend Images/Corbis; **p. 237:** Library of Congress Prints and Photographs Division[LC-USZC4-4138]; **p. 238:** National Archives and Records Administration; **p. 247:** AP Photo; **p. 251:** Exactostock/SuperStock; **p. 255:** Polaris; **p. 258:** Jim Craigmyle/Corbis; **p. 264:** Jeff Greenberg/Alamy; **p. 268:** Yuri Arcurs/Shutterstock;  269: Ted Pink/Alamy

## CHAPTER 9

**p. 275:** Imtmphoto/Fotolia; **p. 280:** Steven J. Gold; **p. 282:** Syracuse Newspapers/Jim Commentucci/The Image Works; **p. 285:** Najlah Feanny/Corbis; **p. 287:** North Wind Picture Archives; **p. 290:** Danielle Richards; **p. 293:** David McNew/Staff/Getty Images; **p. 296:** Landov Media; **p. 300:** Noel Memorial Library; The Image Works

## CHAPTER 10

**p. 307:** Spotmatikphoto/Fotolia; **p. 313:** Bettmann/Corbis; **p. 316:** Jeff Kowalsky/AFP/Getty Images; **p. 319:** AP Photo; **p. 322:** Landov Media; **p. 327:** David R. Frazier/The Image Works; **p. 334:** Blend Images/Thinkstock; **p. 337:** Marmaduke St. John/Alamy; **p. 338:** Jeff Kravitz/FilmMagic, Inc/Getty Images; **p. 340:** Larry Downing/Reuters/Corbis

## CHAPTER 11

**p. 347:** Michael McCann Photography/Getty Images; **p. 353:** New York City/Alamy; **p. 358:** Barry Austin Photography/Riser/Getty Images; **p. 359:** Paul Conklin/PhotoEdit; **p. 362:** Joe Sohm/The Image Works; **p. 368:** AP Photo/Arizona Daily Star/Chris Richards; **p. 372:** Mario Algaze/The Image Works; **p. 374:** Mariela Lombard/ZUMAPRESS/Newscom; **p. 376:** Mark Ralston/AFP/Getty Images; **p. 380:** AP Photo

## CHAPTER 12

**p. 387:** Timothy Fadek/Corbis; **p. 393:** Monika Graff/UPI/Newscom; **p. 395:** Paul Franklin/Alamy; **p. 398:** Michael J. Doolittle/The Image Works; **p. 403:** AP Photo/Fred Hayes; **p. 406:** Bill Pugliano/Getty Images;  409: Dennis MacDonald/PhotoEdit; **p. 413:** AP Photo/Collin Reid; **p. 417:** Prabhupada's Palace of Gold; **p. 419:** AP Photo/Ron Edmonds

## CHAPTER 13

**p. 427:** Michael Reynolds/Epa/Newscom; **p. 431:** Library of Congress Prints and Photographs Division[LC-USZC2-1189]; **p. 432:** Walter McBride/Corbis; **p. 433:** Elsa/Getty Images; **p. 435:** Rommel Pecson/The Image Works; **p. 440:** Marty Heitner/The Image Works; **p. 444:** Andrew Harrer/Bloomberg/Getty Images; **p. 445:** Ariel Skelley/Corbis; **p. 448:** AP Photo/J. Scott Applewhite; **p. 451:** AP Photo/Matt Dunham

## CHAPTER 14

**p. 457:** The Image Works; **p. 461:** Getty Images; **p. 465:** ©North America Syndicate, Inc.; **p. 466:** Rachel Epstein/The Image Works; **p. 469:** Geoffrey Robinson/Alamy; **p. 472:** AP Photo; **p. 476:** Bob Daemmrich/The Image Works; **p. 481:** PhotoStock-Israel/age fotostock/SuperStock; **p. 485:** Jim West/age fotostock/SuperStock; **p. 487:** AP Photo/Kentucky New Era/Emily Parrino

## CHAPTER 15

**p. 493:** Tom & Dee Ann McCarthy/Corbis; **p. 495:** AP Photo/Ariana Cubillos; **p. 503:** AP Photo/Steve Helber; **p. 505:** Purestock/Alamy; **p. 506:** Library of Congress Prints and Photographs Division[LC-DIG-ppmsca-28687]; **p. 510:** AP Photo/Chris Pizzello; **p. 513:** Aurora Photos/Alamy; **p. 516:** Bob Daemmrich/The Image Works; **p. 520:** Bob Daemmrich/Alamy; **p. 526:** White House Photo/Alamy

# TEXT CREDITS

## CHAPTER 1

**p. 3:** Aristotle; **p. 5:** Springer; **p. 13:** Houghton Mifflin Harcourt Publishing Company; **p. 17:** Pearson Education.

## CHAPTER 2

**p. 32:** of Ralph Linton, Estate ; **p. 34:** Pearson Education ; **p. 40:** U.S.News & World Report ; Vintage Books ; **p. 41:** Little Brown and Co. (New York); **p. 43:** Pearson Education; **p. 49:** Crandall, Dostie & Douglass Books, Inc.

## CHAPTER 3

**p. 54:** Basic Books; **p. 55:** Smithsonian Books; **p. 61:** Oxford University Press (US) ; **p. 63:** Worth Publishers; **p. 63:** Pearson Education; **p. 64:** Giordano, Joseph; **p. 71:** Sage Publication Ltd; **p. 77:** New York University Press; **p. 80:** Pearson Education.

## CHAPTER 4

**p. 90:** Perseus Books Group; **p. 93:** Pearson Education: **p. 108:** University of Chicago Press ; **p. 109:** Public Interest.

## CHAPTER 5

**p. 115:** MIT Press; **p. 118:** Harvard University Press; **p. 119:** Iowa State University Press; **p. 121:** Dover Publications, Inc.; **p. 123:** Russell & Russell; **p. 127:** University of South Carolina Press; Little, Brown and Co. (New York) ;**p. 138:** Parrillo Vincent; **p. 139:** HarperCollins Publishers; **p. 142:** Pine Forge Press; **pp. 145-46:** Pearson Education.

## CHAPTER 6

**pp. 151, 153:** Pearson Education; **p. 155:** Oxford University Press (US); **p. 157:** Greenwood Publishing Group; **p. 158:** Pearson Education; **p.159:** University of Notre Dame Press; **p. 162:** Columbia University Press; **p. 163:** Transaction Publishers; **p. 166:** National Journal Group, Inc.; **p. 167:** Arno Press; **p. 173:** Penguin Putnam, Inc.; **p. 174:** Free Press (Simon and Schuster Inc.); University of Chicago Press; **p. 176:** Columbia University Press; Harvard University Press.

## CHAPTER 7

**p. 191:** Adamant Media Corp.; **p. 194:** Countryman Press; 196: HarperCollins College Publishers (Humanities/Social Sciences); **p. 199:** University of Liége ; 202: Discus Avon Books; **p. 203:** Bright Mountain Books; **p. 204:** Penguin Group; **p. 218:** Pearson Education; **p. 224:** Mariner Books.

## CHAPTER 8

**p. 235:** University of California Press; **p. 239:** Friendship Press; **p. 240:** University of Washington Press; Clark Atlanta University Art Collections; **p. 243:** University of Illinois Press; **p. 245:** American Bibliographical Center Clio Press; **p. 247:** New Republic; **p. 25:** Little, Brown and Co. (New York); Caxton; Time, Inc.; **pp. 256, 259:** University of California Press; **p. 262:** State University of New York Press; Parrillo Vincent.

## CHAPTER 9

**p. 282:** Zogby International; **p. 286:** Paulist Press; **p. 288:** Commentary Magazine; **p. 294:** Associated Faculty Press; **p. 296:** Advameg; **p. 297:** University of Illinois Press; **p. 298:** American Geographical Society; **p. 299:** Parrillo Vincent.

## CHAPTER 10

**p. 311:** International Publishers; **p. 314:** Clark Atlanta University Art Collections; **p. 315:** Schocken Books; **p. 318:** University Press of the Pacific; **p. 325:** Simon & Schuster, Inc..

## CHAPTER 11

**p. 360:** University of New Mexico Press (Rights); **p. 361:** McWilliams, Carey; Praeger Publishers; **p. 366:** Parrillo Vincent; **p. 367:** MIT Press.

## CHAPTER 12

**p. 388:** Pew Forum on Religion & Public Life; **p. 394:** American Sociological Association; **p. 397:** Parrillo Vincent; **p. 409:** Worth Publishers.

## CHAPTER 13

**p. 434:** Vintage Books; **p. 435:** Free Press (Simon and Schuster Inc.); HarperCollins Publishers; **p. 445:** Pearson Education; **p. 446:** Oxford University Press (US); **p. 447:** Springer-Verlag Publishing, Rights & Permissions.

## CHAPTER 14

**p. 462:** The Williams Institute; **p. 464:** Parrillo Vincent; **p. 473:** Pearson Education; **p. 477:** United Nations Population Division.

## CHAPTER 15

**p. 496:** HarperCollins Publisher (Canada); **pp. 497, 498, 511:** Pearson Education; **p. 499:** Parrillo Vincent; **p. 519:** The Population Council.

# INDEX

Democratic Party, Chinese American immigration and, 271
Democratic Republic of Congo, 2
Demographics
  of Arab-American households, 283
  of blacks, 326
  of Greek-American community, 178
  of Hispanic Americans, 355–358
  of older people, 478–480
  in U.S. professional sports, 28
Demonstrations, against status quo, 88–89
Deportation, of Russian immigrants, 166
Derogatory terms, 69
Desegregation, 317–320
  and Civil Rights movement, 318–320
  of schools, 317
Deseret Management Corporation, 402
Deseret Ranch, 402
Detroit
  Arab Americans in, 281
  blacks in, 314
  Iraqi Chaldeans in, 291
  race riot in (1967), 320
"Detroit Syndrome," 476
Deviance
  as minority response, 86–87, 311
  as view of homosexuality, 489
Dichotomy of views, 192
Dignidad, 351
Dillingham, William P., 16
Dillingham Commission, 157
Dillingham Flaw, 16–17, 30, 524, 527
Diné College, 208
Disability. See also People with disabilities
  models of, 470
  status in population, 472
  use of term, 469
Disabled American Veterans, 473
Disabled veterans. See Veterans, disabled
Discrimination, 72–79, 146. See also Bias; Prejudice
  against Aboriginal Australians, 199
  active and passive, 75
  age, 482–483
  against Arab Americans, 300
  avoidance of, 73
  against blacks, 309
  against Catholics, 392
  against Chinese, 232–233
  economic determinism and, 42
  against elderly, 482–483
  ethnic, 2
  against Filipinos, 256, 257
  against Israeli Sephardic Jews, 295
  job, 136
  legislation against, 314, 319
  against Muslims, 407–408
  against people with disabilities, 471, 472
  prejudice and, 72–79
  racial, 320
  sexual harassment as, 448
  social, 75
  against women, 428
Diseases
  of Native Americans, 192
  Old World spread of, 98
Disenfranchisement, 139
Disengagement theory, 488
Displaced aggression, 57
Displaced persons (DPs), after World War II, 164
Displaced Persons Act (1948), 163
Dissimilarity index, 332
Diversity, 2, 5, 260, 276
  of black population, 340–341
  among elderly, 477–478
  ethnic, 388
  in future, 522–524

growth of, 527
  among Hispanic groups, 355
  in Israel, 399
  melting pot and, 106–108
  of Middle Easterners and North Africans, 290
  religious, 399, 419
  of television audience, 68
  in U.S. society, 522–524
Diversity training, 71–72
Dogma, Catholic, 391
Dole, Bob, 473
Dollard, John, 61
Dominant group
  defined, 10
  stereotypes held by, 63–64
Dominant-group responses, 93–103
  annihilation as, 97–98
  exploitation, 101–103
  expulsion as, 95
  hate crimes as, 99–101
  hate groups and, 98–99
  legislative controls as, 93–94
  segregation as, 94–95
  xenophobia as, 96–97
Dominant-group values, Cubans and, 371
Dominant-minority relations, 22, 39
  Hispanic Americans and, 353–354
Dominican Americans, 373–375
  education and, 375
  immigration rate, 373
  social distance ranking (2011), 4
Dowry system, Greek immigrants and, 175
Draft riot, by Irish (1863), 88
"Droodles," 29
Dropouts, 225
  from high school, 329
  race/ethnicity and gender, 357
Drugs. See Medicine
Druze, 399
Dual-career families, married women in, 444
Dual identity, 84, 85
Duality, of remoteness, 458
Dual labor market, 101, 103
DuBois, W. E. B., on racism, 311, 316
Dunkley, Archibald, 412
Durkheim, Émile, 19, 423
Dutch Americans, 125–127
  ancestry of, 130
  population of, 126–127
  social distance ranking (2011), 4
Dutch colonists, 125
Dutch immigrants, 126
Duvalier, François, 336
"DWB" (driving while black), 79
Dylan, Bob, 318
Dysfunctions, functionalists on, 20

East, John Porter, 473
East Asia, undocumented migrants from, 512
Eastern Europe and Eastern Europeans. See also Europeans; specific groups
  before World War I, 171
Eastern Orthodox Church, 177, 286. See also Orthodox Christians; Russian Orthodox Church
  in Greece, 176
Ebonics, 325
Ecological model, of Chicago growth and development, 503
Economic competition, 102
  by Asian Americans, 315
  Chinese sojourners, 60–61
  in Czech Republic, 60
  Japanese American, 243–244
  prejudice and, 63
Economic determinism, 42

Economic globalization. See Globalization, impact on workers and
Economic security, for elderly, 483–485
Economic status
  African-born Americans, 338
  of Asian Americans, 265
  of Hispanic Americans, 356
  Mormons and, 389
  of Native Americans, 224
Economy
  Chinese immigrants and, 235
  as structural condition, 36
  underground, 102
Ecumenical movement, 392
Edmunds-Tucker Act (1887), 401
Education. See also Schools; Universities and colleges
  Afrocentric, 15
  Amish, 410
  of Arab Americans, 283, 290
  of Asian Americans, 271, 272
  assimilation and, 181
  bilingual, 506, 515–517
  of blacks and whites, 323–324
  of Canadian women, 439
  Catholic, 392
  cooperative learning and, 70
  delinquency rates and, 87
  diversity training and, 71–72
  of Egyptian immigrants, 290
  female-earned bachelor's degrees, 441
  of Greek Americans, 175
  of Hispanic Americans, 348, 31, 353, 355–356
  of Jewish Americans, 398
  of Lebanese Americans, 288
  Mormon, 401
  of Native Americans, 207, 209, 211
  of Polish immigrants, 163
  prejudice reduction through, 67, 69
  of second-generation Americans, 497
  for social equality, 440
  of Turkish immigrants, 299–300
Educational Alliance (New York), 398
Educational Amendments Act (1978)
  Native Americans and, 207
EEOC. See Equal Employment Opportunity Commission (EEOC)
Egyptian Americans, 289–291
Egyptians, warfare and, 97
Eisenhower, Dwight D.
  desegregation and, 317
  Indian policy and, 205
Elderly, 475–490
  age discrimination against, 482–483
  demographic changes, 477–480
  economic security for, 483–485
  graying of America and, 476–477
  health care for, 485–486
  as immigrants, 486
  international status of, 477
  lifestyle of, 487
  mental capacities, 481–482
  myths, 480
  poverty of, 486
  sexuality of, 482
  sociological analysis of, 475–476, 486–489
  stereotypes, 480
  suicide rates among, 480
  values, 480
Elders, Asian, 234
Elected officials, black, 320
Elections, of 1852, 1854, and 1856, 120
Elementary Forms of Religious Life, The (Durkheim), 423
Ellis Island, 165, 172

Mohawk Indians, 193, 195, 208
Molly Maguires, 137, 284
Mommy track, 445
Monk, Maria, 390
Mon-Khmer Laotians, 266
Montagu, Ashley, 10
Montgomery, Alabama, bus boycott in, 295
Morality, of Hinduism, 416
Moravians, 159
Moreno, 364
Mores, sexual, of Romani, 179
Morill Act (1962), 400
Mormon Americans, 27, 105, 388, 390,
    400–403
  assimilation and, 400
  contemporary, 402–403
Mormon Genealogical Society, 401
Mormon Tabernacle Choir, 403
Moroccan Americans, 283
Moroni (angel), 400
Morse, Samuel F. B., 390
Mortality rate
  in India, 258
  of Native Americans, 212
Mosques, 404
Movies. *See* Films
Movimiento Estudiantil Chicano de Aztlan, 363
Moynihan, Daniel P., 39, 40, 41, 367
Moynihan Report, 40
Muhammad, 406
Mulattos, 333, 342
Mullen, Brian, 65
Multiculturalism, 108, 494, 506, 520–522
  in France, 522
Multiethnic society, 108
Multi-generational occupational patterning, 45
Multiracial Americans, 525–526
Multiracial warfare, 1992 riot as, 321
Mumps, 98
Mundugamor people, 433
Murguía, Janet, 363
Murphy, Francis, 248
Murray, Charles, 322, 323
Music, influence of, 69
Muslim Americans, 2, 80, 279, 282, 403–408. *See
    also* Arab Americans
  Arab Americans as, 283
  fears of, 508
  from Middle East and North Africa, 276
  settlement by, 423
  social distance ranking (2011), 4
  Turkish American identity and, 297–298
Muslims, 85
  among Christians, 405
  in Crusades, 13, 56
  in France, 521
  Swiss fears of, 407
Mutual-welfare system, for Irish, 136
Myer, Dillon S., 205
My Lai, 56
Myrdal, Gunnar, 314
Myths
  about elderly, 480–482
  about people with disabilities, 472

NAACP. *See* National Association for the
    Advancement of Colored People (NAACP)
Nakashima, Ted, 247
Name calling, 65
Nash, Gary B., 116
Nast, Thomas, on Irish immigrants, 133
Natal Indian Congress (NIC), 259
National Academy of Public Administration
    (NAPA), 222
National Advisory Commission on Civil
    Disorders, 321

National Association for the Advancement of
    Colored People (NAACP), 218, 209, 314
National Association for the Deaf, 473
National Association of Arab Americans, 280
National Black Women's Political Caucus, 69
National Congress of American Indians (NCAI),
    191, 218
National Council of La Raza, 363, 518
National Front Party (France), 521
National Guard, school desegregation and, 317
National Indian Youth Council (NIYC),
    191, 218
Nationalism, cultural, 418
Nationality, 114
  English, 117
Nationality groups, 35
  settlement patterns, politics, and, 143
National Organization for Women (NOW), 432
National Organization on Disability, 473
National Origins Quota Act (1921), 157
National Union for Social Justice, 395
Nation of Islam, 99
Native American Party, 61, 120, 145
Native Americans *See* American Indians
Native peoples. *See* Aborigines, in Australia;
    American Indians
Native population, vs. foreign-born
    population, 502
Nativism, 35, 184, 316
  anti-Catholic, 391
  English language concerns and, 131
  immigrant language retention and, 514
  immigration, bilingual education, and, 506
  IQ tests and, 323
  Japanese and, 244
  against Jewish immigrants, 394
  racism against Italians and Jews and, 153–154
Nativist movement, 120
Natural gas, on Indian lands, 213
Naturalization, 501
  time for, 118
Naturalization Act (1790), 244
Naturalized citizens
  English language and, 516
  by period of entry, 502
Natural resources
  Native Americans and, 213–217
  of Navajo Indians, 214–215
Nature, Native Americans and, 195–196
Navajo Indians, 191, 214–215, 411
  natural resources of, 214
  strip mining and, 214
Nazis, 73
  Roma and, 178
Nearness, 6
Negative self-image, 89–90
Negative stereotyping, 157
"*Negro Family, The: The Case for National Action*"
    (Moynihan), 39
Neighborhoods
  all-white to black, 94
  ethnic, 36
Neo-Confederates, 99
Neo-Nazi organizations, 99
Neshoba, Mississippi, 318
Net worth, 484
New Age movement, 417
New Amsterdam, 109, 125, 146
  English takeover of, 125
  Jewish immigrants to, 393
Newark, race riot in (1967), 320
"New buffalo," Native American casinos as, 210
New England
  foreigners in, 118
  French Canadians in, 129
  religious tolerance in, 116

New feminism, 438
New Guinea, gender variations in, 433
New immigrants
  from Ireland, 138
  Italian and Jewish, 156
  quotas on, 171
New Jersey
  Cuban Americans in, 369
  hate groups in, 99
New Netherland colony, 115
New Orleans, 128
  racism after Katrina, 333
New Sweden, 139
Newton, Huey, 320
New World, Argentinian culture and, 354
New York
  affirmative action and, 77
  Catholic archdiocese of, 391
  children of immigrants in, 523
  Cuban Americans in, 369
  gay community in, 460
  hate groups in, 99
  immigrants in, 137, 295
  Lebanese and Syrian community in, 286
  as New Amsterdam, 146
  Puerto Ricans in, 367
  Russians in, 166–167
Nicaraguan Americans, 375–376
Nicaraguans, 375
Nigeria, 2
  African-born Americans from, 308–309
Nigerian Americans, 339
  immigration rate, 339
  population density, 339
Nineteenth Amendment, 429
Nisei, 248
Nixon, Richard, Indian termination acts
    and, 206
Nizza, Marcos da, 171
Noble Savage concept, 192
Nondenominational megachurches, 388
  unaffiliated groups, 388
Nonimmigrants
  Middle Eastern and North African, 278
Nonintercourse Act (1790), Native Americans
    and, 220
Nonmaterial culture, 26
Nonverbal communication, 30
Non-whites, 85
  citizenship for, 256–257
  in Latin America, 193
  as racial classification, 10
Nooyi, Indra, 444
Norms, 26, 61
North
  Civil Rights movement and, 318–320
  ethnicity in, 312
  lifestyle of black migrant in, 314
  racism in, 312
  segregation in, 312–313
  slavery and, 310
North African immigrants, Middle Easterners
    and, 276–278
North America, Native Americans in, 193
North Carolina
  foreign-born population in, 504
  hate groups in, 99
  sit-ins in, 318
Northern America, immigrants from, 508
Northern Europe and Northern Europeans. *See*
    Europeans; *specific groups*
North Korea, 232. *See also* Korean
    Americans
Norwegian Americans, 141
Novak, Michael, 181
*NowRuz* (Iranian New Year), 294

Japanese in schools and, 244
North Beach neighborhood in, 173
San Jose, 363
San Salvador, Columbus on, 192
Sansei, 248
Santa Fe, New Mexico, Spanish founding
of, 348
Santería, 27
in United States, 415
Santerían Americans, 389, 414–415
animal sacrificing, court rule, 414
Sappho, 458
*Sari*, 257
Sarkozy, Nicolas, 521
Sartre, Jean-Paul, 393
Saturday, Sylvester, 250
SAVAK (Iranian police force), 294
Scalia, Antonin, 215
Scalping, 197
Scandinavian Americans, 118, 139–141
ancestry of (2011), 130
Scapegoating, 58
of Asians in Uganda, 93
of Jews, 92
Scholastic Assessment Test (SAT), 327
School prayer, controversy over, 420
Schools. *See also* Education; Universities and
colleges
Amish attendance in, 411
Catholic parochial, 392
desegregation of, 317
ELL and LEP programs in,
516–518
German language in, 131
Mexican Americans in, 362, 378
segregation in, 240, 313
socialization in, 156
Schutz, Alfred, 7, 458
Scientific method, 15
Scientists, Russian-speaking, 167
Scots, 113
Scots-Irish immigrants, 134
ancestry of (2011), 130
Scots-Irish Presbyterians, 116, 117
Scott, Winfield, 120, 202
Scouting, religion in, 420
Seale, Bobby, 320
Secondary group, 341
Secondary labor market, 102
Secondary structural assimilation, 105
Second-generation Americans, 497
English fluency of, 520
Italian Americans, 175
in New York, 338
Second shift, 437
Secularism, in United States, 389
Secular Jews, 393
Segmented assimilation, 500–501
in second generation, 523
Segregation, 94–95, 331–332
*See also* Desegregation
of Afro-Caribbean Americans, 335
of blacks, 311
of Chinese children, 240
in France, 96
of German immigrants, 129–130
of Hispanic Americans, 382
of Irish immigrants, 136
Jim Crow laws and, 313–314
of Mexican Americans, 362
in North, 314
residential, 269–270, 331–332
of Slavic immigrants, 159
social, 94
in South, 313–314

spatial, 94–95
in states, 313
in television programming, 66
Selection bias, 72
Selective perception, 70
Self-determination, by women, 430
Self-esteem, 57
Self-identification, by race, 526
Self-identity, 424
Self-image, negative, 89
Self-justification, 56–57, 188
Seligman, Joseph, 395
Seminole Indians, 201, 222
Senate, Native Americans in, 255
Senators, descendants of northern and western
Europeans, 143
Seneca Indians, 195, 217
Senility, age and, 481
Senior citizens, 476. *See also* Elderly
myths about, 480–481
state proportions of, 480
"Separate but equal" doctrine, 317
Separatist pluralism, 520
Separation of church and state, 420, 421
Separatist minorities, 423
Separatists, Dutch, 125
Sephardic Jews, 295, 394
September 1, 2001, terrorist attacks,
284–285
Sepulveda, Juan Ginés de, 192
Sequoyah (Cherokee), 202
Serbs, 3, 159
Settlement(s), 420–423
Dutch, 125
early colonial, 122
Hispanic, 378
Irish Catholic, 135
by Israeli Americans in United States, 296
Italian, 173–174
by Lebanese and Syrian immigrants, 286
politics, geography, and, 142
of Turkish immigrants, 298–299
Sexism, 428
law and, 447–448
in print advertising, 435
on television, 68
use of term, 428
Sex objects, women as, 435
Sexual abuse, by Catholic priests, 393
Sexual discrimination, end of, 432, 449
Sexual harassment, 446–447
complaints and actions for, 447
federal guidelines on, 360–361
legal prohibitions against, 362
of women in Japan, 363
*Sexual Harassment of Working Women: A Case of Sex
Discrimination.* (MacKinnon), 446
Sexual identity, as ascribed status, 428
Sexuality. *See also* Gays; Gender;
Homosexuality
of elderly, 482
minority groups and, 250
Mormon, 401
women and, 430
Sexual mores, Romani, 179
Sexual orientation, 458–467
as continuum, 463
use of term, 462
Sexual scripts, 488
Sexual stereotypes, 439
Shalala, Donna, 301
Shari'ah, 406
Shaw, William Smith, 118, 146
Shelters, for homeless, 40
Shepard, Matthew, 464

Shepherd, Margaret Lisle, 390
Shepperson, Wilbur, 122
Sherif, Muzafer, 61
Sherman, William Tecumseh, 310
Shockley, William B., 323
Shop-ins, 89
Shuey, Audrey, 323
Shunning
in Amish society, 408
by Romani, 179
Shuttle migration, 171, 367
Siam. *See* Thailand
Sick role, for individuals with disabilities, 468
Sienkiewicz, Henryk, 162
Sikhs and Sikhism, 42, 85, 255, 257, 389,
417, 527
Silence, among Native Americans, 197–198
Silver Shirts, 395
Similarity-attraction relationship, 3
Simmel, Georg, 6, 458
Simmons, William J., 315
Sinophobia, 236
Sioux Indians, 197, 208, 210
AIM Wounded Knee takeover and, 219
Black Hills seizure and, 219–220
Sit-in demonstrations, 89, 318
*Siyasi* (Iranian political exiles), 294
*Sketchbook* (Irving), 122
Skinheads, 99
Slavery, 310
racial classification system and, 526
Slavery reparations, 310
Slaves
African Muslims as, 403–404
in Hawaii, 189
Romani people as, 178
Slavic Americans, 159–161
*Slavic Community on Strike, The* (Greene), 159
Slavic immigrants, 122, 296
Slovaks, 151, 159
Slovenia, immigration to Italy from, 153
Slovenians, 159
Smallpox, 98
Smith, Al, 391
Smith, Hyrum, 400
Smith, John, 167
Smith, Joseph, 400, 401
Soccer, Hispanic Americans and, 353
Social capital, 499–500
children's of immigrants and, 523
Social class, 37
antagonisms and, 48–49
ethnicity and, 38–39
race and, 333–335
religious clashes and, 116
women and, 437
Social-class differentiation, 37
Social clubs, 105, 246
Social conflict
Amish, 410
between blacks and whites, 335
Social construct
race as, 10
of reality, 21, 28–31
Thomas theorem, 30–31
Social Darwinists, 10–11
Social discrimination, 75
Social disorganization, for elderly, 487
Social distance, 3–6, 57. *See also Specific groups*
Arabs and Muslims, 4–5
Asians, 3
defined, 3
Korean American, 255
non-ethnic whites, 4
of non-Western immigrants, 279